HOLOCAUST

HOLOCAUST

The Nazi Persecution and Murder of the Jews

PETER LONGERICH

OXFORD
UNIVERSITY PRESS

OXFORD
UNIVERSITY PRESS

Great Clarendon Street, Oxford OX2 6DP

Oxford University Press is a department of the University of Oxford.
It furthers the University's objective of excellence in research, scholarship,
and education by publishing worldwide in

Oxford New York

Auckland Cape Town Dar es Salaam Hong Kong Karachi
Kuala Lumpur Madrid Melbourne Mexico City Nairobi
New Delhi Shanghai Taipei Toronto

With offices in

Argentina Austria Brazil Chile Czech Republic France Greece
Guatemala Hungary Italy Japan Poland Portugal Singapore
South Korea Switzerland Thailand Turkey Ukraine Vietnam

Oxford is a registered trade mark of Oxford University Press
in the UK and in certain other countries

Published in the United States
by Oxford University Press Inc., New York

© Peter Longerich 2010

The moral rights of the author have been asserted
Database right Oxford University Press (maker)

First published 2010

British Library Cataloguing in Publication Data

Data available

Library of Congress Cataloging in Publication Data
Library of Congress Control Number: 2010922410

Typeset by SPI Publisher Services, Pondicherry, India
Printed in Great Britain
on acid-free paper by
Clays Ltd., St Ives Plc

ISBN 978-0-19-280436-5

1 3 5 7 9 10 8 6 4 2

Publisher's Acknowledgements

The publishers would like to extend their especial thanks to Professor Jeremy Noakes for his editorial contribution to the preparation of the English edition of this book.

Acknowledgements

It would be impossible to list by name all the friends, colleagues, and other people who in one way or another have contributed to the writing of this book.

I will therefore restrict myself to thanking the many archivists and librarians who have helped me, as well as all my colleagues, both in Germany and abroad, who have given me the opportunity to discuss various sections of the book and some of the arguments to be found within it at various conferences, lectures, and seminars. In fact, I would like to thank everyone with whom I have discussed this subject, in whatever context, over the years.

The whole project would have been impossible without the generous assistance of the German Department of Royal Holloway College, who once again generously gave me leave from my regular academic duties. I would like to thank all my colleagues and students, in particular Maire Davies and Bill Jones. A ten-month research residency at the International Research Centre of the Israeli Centre for Remembrance and Research at Yad Vashem proved particularly enlightening, for which I am very grateful to Israel Gutman, who was at that time the director of the institute. I would also like to thank the Faculty of Social Sciences at the Universität der Bundeswehr in Munich, in particular Michael Wolffsohn and Merith Niehuss, to whom I submitted the original version of this book as my post-doctoral thesis.

The whole project would have been impossible without the generous assistance of the German Department and the School of Modern Languages, Literature, and Culture of Royal Holloway College. I would like to thank all my colleagues and students. In particular I would like to express my deep gratitude to Jeremy Noakes without whom the English edition would not exist.

London and Munich, November 2009

Contents

Contents

Abbreviations

AA	Auswärtiges Amt (Foreign Ministry)
Abt.	Department
ADAP	*Akten zur Deutschen Auswärtigen Politik*
AdV	Alldeutscher Verband
AGK	Archivum Glównej Komisji Badania Zbrodni Hitlerowskich w Polsce
AOK	Army High Command
APL	Archivum Panstwowe w Lublinie
Aufl.	Edition
BAB	Bundesarchiv Berlin
BAM	Bundesarchiv/Militärarchiv
Batl.	Battalion
Bd.	volume
BDC	Berlin Document Centre
BdO	Commander of the Order Police
BdS	Commander of the Security Police
BHSt.A	Bayerisches Hauptstaatsarchiv
Biuletyn	*Biuletyn Glownej Komisji Badania Zbrodni Hitlerowskich w Polsce*
BLI	*Bulletin Leo Baeck Institute*
BT	*Berliner Tageblatt*
CDJC	Centre de Documentation Juive Contemporaine
CdZ	Head of the Civil Administration
CEH	*Central European History*
CV	Centralverein deutscher Staatsbürger jüdischen Glaubens (Central Assocation for Citizens of the Jewish Faith)

DAF	Deutsche Arbeitsfront (German Labour Front)
DAZ	*Deutsche Allgemeine Zeitung*
DG	*Durchgangsstrasse*
DHR	German University Circle
DHV	German National Association of Commercial Employees
DGFP	Documents on German Foreign Policy
DiM	*Dokumenty i Materialy*
DNVP	German National[ist] People's Party
DVFP	German Völkish Freedom Party
EK	Einsatzkommando (Task Force Commando)
EM	Ereignismeldung (Action Report USSR)
EWZ	Einwandererzentrale (Immigration Centre)
FRUS	*Foreign Relations of the United States*
FZ	*Frankfurter Zeitung*
Gestapa	Geheime Staatspolizeiamt (Secret State Police Office)
Gestapo	Geheime Staatspolizei (Secret State Police)
GFP	Geheime Feldpolizei (Secret Military Police)
GG	General Government
GSR	*German Studies Review*
GStaA	Geheime Staatsarchiv Berlin-Dahlem
HGS	*Holocaust and Genocide Studies*
HSSPF	Higher SS and Police Commander
1a	Senior Ranking General Staff Officer
1c	Third Ranking General Staff Officer (Intelligence)
IfZ	Institut für Zeitgeschichte
IKG	Israelitische Kultusgemeinde
IMT	*International Military Tribunal* (Nuremberg)
JA	*Jahrbuch für Antisemitismusforschung*
JDC	Joint Distribution Committee
JR	*Jüdische Rundschau*
KdO	Commander of the Order Police
KdS	Commander of the Security Police
KL	Konzentrationslager (Concentration Camp)
KPD	German Communist Party

Kripo	Criminal Police
KTB	*Kriegstagebuch (War Diary)*
KZ	Concentration Camp
LAF	Lithuanian Activist Front
LBIY	*Leo Baeck Institute Yearbook*
LG	Landgericht (Provincial Court)
LV	Provincial Association
MBliV	*Ministerialblatt fur die innere Verwaltung*
MGM	*Militärgeschichtliche Mitteilungen*
NA	National Archives, Washington DC
NKVD	Soviet People's Commissariat for Internal Affairs
NS, ns	National Socialist
NSDAP	Nationalsozialistische Deutsche Arbeiterpartei (National Socialist German Workers' Party)
NS-Hago	Nationalsozialistische Handels-, Handwerks-und Gewerbeorganisation (National Socialist Association for Commerce, Crafts, and Trade)
NYT	*New York Times*
NZZ	*Neue Züricher Zeitung*
ObdH	Commander-in-Chief of the Army
OKH	Oberkommando des Heeres (Army High Command)
OKW	Oberkommando der Wehrmacht (Armed Forces High Command)
OS	Osabi Archive (Moscow)
OT	Organisation Todt
OUN	Organization of Ukrainian Nationalists
PAA	Politisches Archiv des Auswärtigen Amtes
Pol.Abt.	Political department
RAF	Royal Air Force
Reg.Bez.	Regierungsbezirk (Government District)
RFSS	Reichsführer SS
RGBl	*Reichsgesetzblatt*
RKF	Reichskommisar für die Festigung deutschen Volkstums (Reich Commissioner for Settlement)
RMBliV	*Reichsministerialblatt für die innere Verwaltung*

RSHA	Reichssicherheitshauptamt (Reich Security Head Office)
RVJD	Reichsvereinigung der Juden in Deutschland
RWM	Reichswirtschaftsministerium (Reich Ministry of Economics)
SA	Sturmabteilung (Storm Troop)
SD	Sicherheitsdienst (Security Service)
Sipo	Sicherheitspolizei (Security Police)
SK	Sonderkommando
Sopade	Sozialdemokratische Partei Deutschlands (German Social Democratic Party)
SS	Schutzstaffel (Protection Squads)
SSPF	SS and Police Commander
StA	Staatsarchiv
STA	Staatsanwaltschaft
StdF	Stellvertreter des Führers (Führer's Deputy)
StS	State Secretary
SWCA	*Simon Wiesenthal Center Annual*
TSD	*Theresienstädter Studien und Dokumente*
USHM	United States Holocaust Museum
VB	*Völkischer Beobachter*
VfZ	*Vierteljahrshefte für Zeitgeschichte*
VO	Decree
VOGG	*Verordnungsblatt für das Generalgouvernement*
Vomi	Volksdeutsche Mittelstelle (Ethnic German Agency)
VZ	*Vossische Zeitung*
WL	Wiener Library
WVHA	SS Business and Administration Head Office
YIVO	Yiddischer Vissenschaftlikher Institut
YV	Yad Vashem
YVS	*Yad Vashem Studies*
ZAA	*Zeitschrift für Agrargeschichte und Agrarsoziologie*
ZASM	Zentrum zur Aufbewahrung historisch-dokumentarischer Sammlungen Moskau
z.b.V	zur besonderer Verwendung (for special purposes)
ZfG	*Zeitschrift für Geschichtswissenschaft*

ZGO	*Zeitschrift für die Geschichte des Oberrheins*
ZOB	Zydowsk Organizacja Bojowa (Jewish combat organization)
ZSt	Zentralstelle der Landesjustizverwaltungen zur Aufklärung nationalsozialistischer Verbrechen
ZUV	Zentraler Untersuchungsvorgang
ZZW	Zydowski Zwiazek Wojskowy (Jewish Military Association)

INTRODUCTION

Current State of Research, Methodology

When the German edition of this book appeared twelve years ago in 1998 research on the situation of the murder of the European Jews was in a transitional state because of the opening of the Eastern European archives at the beginning of the 1990s. An intensive phase of research had begun using a large number of documents that had hitherto been inaccessible and asking new questions of more familiar material. Holocaust research had become a steadily developing field and now, at the point when this English edition is being prepared, this process of development has by no means ceased. If it seemed extremely ambitious in the late 1990s to undertake a comprehensive account of the persecution and murder of the European Jews from the perspective of the perpetrators, it is no less so now.

The original aim of this book was to make a contribution to the lively debate amongst Holocaust researchers about when the Nazi leadership took the decision to implement a 'final solution' (*Endlösung*) to what they called the 'Jewish question' (*Judenfrage*). Via an analysis of the processes of decision-making, the book hoped to offer an explanation of the causes of the terrible events that constituted the Holocaust. When I began preparing this book in the mid-1990s, the state of so-called 'perpetrator research' was defined by two opposing schools of thought: on the one side were the 'intentionalists',[1] who made the focus of their analysis the intentions and objectives of Hitler and other leading Nazis, and on the other were the 'structuralists', who emphasized the importance of the bureaucratic apparatus put in place by the Nazis and the ultimately uncontrollable process of what Hans Mommsen termed 'cumulative radicalization'. The debate between the two schools of thought had at that point moved through all the usual phases of academic debates—hypotheses had been developed, the different sides had confronted each other, arguments had been improved and intensified, positions had become entrenched, and the discussion had become increasingly polarized. Research on the decision to implement a 'final solution' had become deeply embedded within this debate and followed the basic pattern that intentionalist scholars assumed the decision had been reached at an early point—in the context of the attack on the Soviet Union or even in the period preceding this[2]—whilst functionalists either assumed, like Christopher Browning, that the decision had been taken in the autumn of 1941,[3] and took the form of a step-by-step process,[4] or took the view that the mass murder of the Jews was the result of developments within the Nazis' apparatus of power that ultimately tended towards a 'final solution' without there being any need for an explicit decision to be taken.[5] Saul Friedländer and Raul Hilberg took a position midway between the two by opting for 'Summer 1941'.[6] In 1997 the debate was revived once more by a suggestion made by Christian Gerlach to the effect that a decision on the 'Final Solution' was made in December 1941 as a direct reaction to the entry of the United States into the war.[7]

The fact that such divergent interpretations were possible is partly explicable by the context of the heated debate between intentionalists and functionalists and their apparently irreconcilable, even mutually antagonistic positions. The style in which this debate was conducted—in the particularly dogmatic manner typical of controversies between German historians—strongly affected the overall character of research on the history of Holocaust perpetrators. Even after the intentionalist-functionalist debate died down, research on the perpetrators in recent years has continued to be dominated by strong dichotomies.

This needs to be explained in more detail. Far from receding, in the last ten years the flood of new work on the Holocaust has swollen. This is particularly true of research into the perpetrators, the so-called *Täterforschung*, a facet of Holocaust research that is overwhelmingly though not exclusively the province of German scholars. Within the field of *Täterforschung* there are clearly three areas in which work has been concentrated: first, the study of the apparatus and membership of the SS and Police, in which the principal focus has been on the Security Police (Sicherheitspolizei) and the SD (Sicherheitsdienst),[8] concentration camps,[9] the bodies responsible for deportations,[10] and the *Einsatzgruppen* or other murder squads;[11] second, regional research so that we now have almost complete coverage of the implementation of the Holocaust in Eastern Europe;[12] third, attempts to find new thematic approaches to the topic of the Holocaust such as ways of establishing a connection between the mass murders and economic planning,[13] vast projects for the deportation of whole ethnic groups,[14] the National Socialists' forced labour programme (*Arbeitseinsatz*),[15] or the expropriation of Jewish property,[16] amongst other areas.

Just as was the case in the debate between structuralists and intentionalists, here too similar attempts can be discerned to try to shape the discussion along the lines of major dichotomies: regional research has initiated a discussion of the role of 'centre and periphery',[17] and the appearance of works emphasizing the 'utilitarian'—which is to say material—interests that were at stake in the murder of the Jews have led to the opposition of 'ideology' and 'rationality'. Within the context of the disagreement between Christopher Browning and Daniel Goldhagen on the motivation of the executions (*Todesschützen*) in the police battalions a debate emerged about whether the perpetrators were mainly driven to carry out these killings by 'situational' factors or whether they were predisposed towards these crimes by the anti-Semitic milieu in which they grew up.[18] The tendency of recent research to emphasize an individual's mindset or *Weltanschauung*, his capacity for independent initiative and the room for manoeuvre available to him is clearly a counter-trend to the older image of a perpetrator at a desk, merely carrying out orders within anonymous structures, behaving like a cog in a great machine.[19]

Whilst such dichotomies and polarized debates can be of use to research, they create the danger that—as was the case with the debate between the intentionalists and structuralists—new polemics are kindled without ever leading to significantly new insights into their subject matter. It seems to me that Holocaust research has now reached a point where the debate has to reach out beyond such oppositions and dichotomies and become accustomed to a mode of discussion that is more complex in structure. It is clear that the battles between one-dimensional explanations can no longer do justice to the complexity of the object of our study—the systematic murder of the European Jews.

The more research develops and is intensified, the more obvious it becomes that oppositional pairings such as intention and function, centre and periphery, rationality and ideology, situation or disposition are not mutually exclusive but illuminate varying aspects of historical reality in complementary, even interdependent ways.[20] However, when one attempts to read the relationship of the antagonisms defined as so irreconcilable by historical research in dialectical terms, it seems virtually pointless to keep on trying to play off one element of the opposition against the other. The contradictions can only be resolved if they are regarded as the starting point for developing historical connections on a higher level.

For example, if one looks back on the debate between structuralists and intentionalists with a degree of hindsight, it becomes clear that both schools have emphasized differing aspects of the same phenomenon that on closer inspection prove to be by no means mutually exclusive. People who pursue their intention to carry out mass murder do so within certain structures; these structures do not act of their own volition, they do so via human beings who combine their actions with intentions. It is the same with centre and periphery: as will be shown as this study progresses, the initiatives of Nazi potentates in the various regions of Germany were an essential component of centrally managed policies, but the leadership role of the centre was itself safeguarded by competitiveness between the various functionaries. Similarly the 'pragmatic' basis for Nazi *Judenpolitik*—Aryanization, the confiscation of living space, the exploitation of the labour force, and so on—was matched up with ideological strategies designed to justify it; and at the same time Nazi ideology was itself validated by the 'successes' of its pragmatic implementation.

In order to set these historical connections into a context, for the 1998 German version of this book I turned to the concept of *Judenpolitik*. This was a contemporary coinage, used by the perpetrators themselves and applied many times before in historical research, particularly in scholarship in German. This presents a difficulty here in that the phrases 'Jewish policy', or better still, 'anti-Jewish policy' are inadequate as translations of *Judenpolitik* since the German word *Politik* combines the senses of 'politics' and 'policy'. This makes it very well suited as a term to describe and analyse the complex process of the persecution of the Jews. In my view, the concept of *Judenpolitik*—which will be used in German throughout this study—comprises the following factors.

First, *Judenpolitik* has the sense of 'policy', the Nazis' long-term intentions and goals in respect of the Jews, their strategy for making real the utopian dream of a racially homogeneous national community via the systematic exclusion, segregation, and elimination of the Jews.

Historical experience shows that even the most radical of political aims, pursued by a determined leadership and implemented by an extensive apparatus of power can seldom be put into practice in a simple and straightforward manner. Political decision-making processes develop their own structures and modalities. What this means for an analysis of the persecution of the Jews and for a study of the Holocaust is that Nazi *Judenpolitik* carved out its own political territory comparable with that of foreign policy, economic policy, and social policy, for example. In this field of politics, whilst the top-level strategies and far-reaching intentions of the major players were undeniably effective, they were subject to the same sorts of friction and distraction as in other political fields or in any large organization. These include rivalry between the protagonists (for which the structures of the Nazi regime were particularly favourable), communication problems between the various levels of the hierarchy, the ponderousness of the mechanisms of power, and so forth.

Above all, however, the field of *Judenpolitik* did not develop autonomously or independently, but functioned within a context determined by the other areas of political activity. It penetrated them and radically transformed them. The National Socialists tended to understand traditional political fields (such as foreign, social, and labour policy) in a racist manner and to redefine them along racist lines. Their starting point was the assumption that there was something akin to an 'international Jewish problem' that foreign policy had to focus on; they assumed that social policy in the Nazi state took the form of welfare provision for 'Aryans' alone and not for the 'racially inferior'; they took it as read that Jewish labour was essentially unproductive and parasitic and therefore, as a matter of principle, only used Jewish people for particularly onerous and humiliating physical work. Similarly they organized their policies on nutrition and housing, the occupation of conquered territory, and other policy areas according to racially determined hierarchies and racially determined conceptual approaches in which anti-Semitism always played a major role.

Finally the overall political context changed with time, and during the war did so with ever-increasing speed. Nazi *Judenpolitik* thus took on quite different forms in different phases of the progress of the 'Third Reich'. For tactical reasons it was modified, retracted, or accelerated; at critical points it developed erratically, disjointedly, and in sequences of action that developed their own internal dynamics. This kind of development cannot be fully grasped by a conventional model of understanding political decision-making (which stresses the formulation of political goals, the process of decision-making itself, and the implementation of those decisions). The implementation of *Judenpolitik* took on its own dynamic such that decision-making and even the formulation of political aims were subsumed within it.

Judenpolitik was subject to sudden shifts; it developed contradictorily, within a complex series of linkages and without any form of precedent. It could not be implemented by people who were merely following orders but required active protagonists who could operate on their own initiative and understand intuitively what the leadership required of them. *Judenpolitik* is characterized by the relatively large scope afforded to the activities of those who put it into practice. This system could only function if the most important aspects of *Judenpolitik* commanded a consensus amongst those involved with it. It would only function if it was actively supported by at least part of the population, the active adherents of National Socialism. It was thus necessary to be able to communicate the aims and mechanisms of *Judenpolitik* to the public at all times and with varying degrees of openness. *Judenpolitik* was thus publicly disseminated, debated, and legitimated—albeit often in a disguised manner.[21]

What seems to me to be crucial to any analysis of this complex phenomenon is the fact that *Judenpolitik* was central to the whole National Socialist movement, indeed that the very aims, the distinctiveness, and the uniqueness of National Socialism as a historical phenomenon were determined by its *Judenpolitik*. This can be clarified in a number of ways.

The basic aim of the Nazi movement was a racially homogeneous national community (*Volksgemeinschaft*) in which the potential for creative energy inherent in the German people could at last come to fruition and where the German people could achieve full self-realization. The Nazi view was that the harmony of the national community to which they aspired would permit the resolution of virtually all the major problems of their age, whether they were aspects of foreign or domestic policy, social, economic, or cultural in nature. It was not possible to establish such a racially homogeneous community because it was based on erroneous beliefs about the division of humanity into different 'races', so Nazi racism could only operate negatively: via negative measures, via discrimination, exclusion, elimination, via the removal of alien elements—in which process, for historical reasons, anti-Jewish measures took on a central role. In the course of this process of exclusion the NSDAP was supposed to succeed in bringing under its control those areas of life that needed to be 'made Jew-free' (*entjudet*). Thus for the Nazis anti-Semitic policies became the key to gaining control first over German society and later over almost the whole of Europe. Their anti-Semitic ideology was not a mere *Weltanschauung*, a hotchpotch of aberrant and perverse ideas, but the very basis of the Nazis' claims for total domination.

This means, I believe, that we should abandon the notion that it is historically meaningful to try to filter the wealth of available historical material and pick out a single decision that led to the 'Final Solution'. This approach is pointless not only because the debate on the 'Final Solution' has evidently reached the limits of what is provable but above all because any attempt to identify a decision taken at a single moment in time runs counter to the extreme complexity of the processes that were in fact taking place. The truth is that those with political responsibility propelled forward, step by step, a highly complicated decision-making process in which a series of points where it was escalated can be identified.

This has a number of consequences for a depiction of the genesis of the 'Final Solution'. First, if we abandon the model that sees a single decision as the trigger for the murder of the European Jews and if we advance beyond the notion of a cumulative process of radicalization that had got out of control and could no longer be steered by anyone, then the various phases in Nazi *Judenpolitik* take on new significance. New perspectives are revealed that show the years 1939 to 1941 as a phase in which the National Socialist regime was already considering genocidal projects against the Jews that appear all the more sinister in the light of the racially motivated programmes of mass murder that were already been carried out against the Polish population and the 'congenitally ill'. It also becomes clearer how in the period from spring 1942 onwards the lives of several million Jewish people depended on how the Nazis' *Judenpolitik* developed. Large Jewish communities could be saved (as they were in France, Italy, Denmark, Old Romania, and Bulgaria) or they were lost (as in Hungary and Greece). Bitter conflicts were also fought over the fate of Jewish forced labour groups. It needs to be made clear that even after the Europe-wide 'Final Solution' had been initiated the continuing development of *Judenpolitik* depended on a chain of decisions and did not merely consist in the 'implementation' of a single decision that had already been taken.

However, when we treat the period 1939 to 1945 as one in which a series of decisions regarding *Judenpolitik* were being taken rather than restricting our analysis to a 'decision-making period' of a few months, then we also need to take the years 1933 to 1939 into consideration as a preparatory period for the phase in which the annihilation of the Jews took place. In the years preceding the war the institutions were created that were to organize the genocide during the war, and this was the period in which *Judenpolitik* was developed and radicalized and in which the regime learned how to deploy this new field of politics in a variety of ways for its own purposes.

The second effect of seeing the emergence of the 'Final Solution' as a complex process rather than as the outcome of a single decision, if we follow the suggestions of Gerlach, Aly, and others and take into consideration new thematic approaches to the analysis of the persecution of the Jews, is that it becomes necessary to see *Judenpolitik* as systematically interlinked with the other central thematic areas, notably in domestic policy but ultimately also with German hegemony on the continent of Europe. For the war years this means that we need to take account of German policies on alliances and inner repression across the whole of Europe, and of the issues of work, food production, and financing the war. It is necessary to show how these areas were redefined in a racist and specifically anti-Semitic sense, and to show how even during the war the Nazi system was attempting to establish the basis for a racist Imperium in which the murder of the Jews was the lowest common denominator in a series of alliances led by Germany. This implies, of course, a very broad programme of research that would exceed the scope of a single monograph. The present study will restrict itself to exploring in outline how such linkages functioned.

Thirdly, if we accept that the decision-making process within Nazi *Judenpolitik* did not come to an end after the 'Final Solution' had been determined upon in principle but that after 1942 decisions were continually being reached that affected the lives of millions of people—in this case it is clear that the implementation of *Judenpolitik* was not only the result of priorities set by the leadership but was increasingly influenced by the behaviour of German allies, by the way that the local administration in occupied territories acted, and not least by the attitude of the local populations and the behaviour of Germany's enemies.

There is a further key factor to be considered, too. The Jewish population that in 1941 faced the plans being made for the 'Final Solution' was defenceless and wholly unprepared, but in the second half of the war it too became an element that influenced the way the perpetrators proceeded. By fleeing, by seeking to escape persecution by living in a hide-away or underground, but also by negotiating with individuals or bribing them, they were attempting to slow down the inexorable process of annihilation and thereby—if only to a limited extent—influencing the behaviour of the perpetrators.

Here research into the perpetrators reaches its limits, or in other words the further into the war is the stage that research concentrates on, the more difficult it becomes to reconstruct the development of the persecution and annihilation of the European Jews by concentrating exclusively on persecutors and their activities. This is not to say that concentrating on the persecutors in the period after 1942 is historiographically impossible or pointless, but that it is important to make precisely clear what the parameters are within which the perpetrators were able to act autonomously.

Fourthly, if the history of the final solution is seen as a chain of ongoing decisions that together come to make up the full context of *Judenpolitik*, then the fate of the other groups persecuted by the Nazis must also be considered, or considered at least in so far as they reveal direct comparisons with or information about the National Socialists' *Judenpolitik*.

These, then, are the fundamental ideas around which this book's depiction of *Judenpolitik* in the years between 1933 and 1945 will be oriented. There is one further significant angle that needs to be considered in more detail, and it concerns the tricky nature of the available sources.

As far as possible this study is based on primary sources. Alongside the documentary holdings of the German administrative departments that are housed in well-known archives in Germany and outside, this study will also consider the holdings of archives in the former Warsaw Pact states that since the 1990s have become accessible to scholars. In practical terms this primarily means Moscow's 'Special Archive' where two collections have been used in some detail: the papers of the Central Association of German Citizens of the Jewish Faith—the Central-verein Deutscher Staatsbürger jüdischen Glaubens (hereafter referred to simply as the Centralverein)—which permits a far more detailed picture of the Nazis' persecution of the Jews in the period from 1933 to 1938 than has hitherto been available; and the papers of the Security Service of the SS (the Sicherheitsdienst, or SD), which cover the period from 1935 to 1940. In addition, papers from various other former Soviet, Polish, and Czech archives are considered, some of which were consulted from copies in Yad Vashem or the US Holocaust Museum in Washington.

For my investigation of the radicalization of Jewish persecution in the occupied Soviet zones in the second half of 1941 I have made extensive use of papers from the Central Office for the Investigation of Nazi Crimes in Ludwigsburg (properly known as the Zentrale Stelle der Landesjustizverwaltungen zur Aufklärung nation-alsozialistischer Verbrechen) via the branch office there of the Bundesarchiv, or Federal Archive of Germany.

Despite what is an almost unmanageably large quantity of documents available for the reconstruction of Nazi *Judenpolitik*, from the point of view of the central decision-making processes for the 'Final Solution' the state of source material can only be described as 'patchy'. This is because the most important decisions that led to the murder of the European Jews were not usually written down; the perpet-rators also systematically attempted to destroy documents that reflected these decisions, and were largely successful in doing so. Documents that have nonetheless survived are scattered between archives in several different countries. In addition, documents relating to the murder of the Jews are written in a language designed to veil their true purpose. And finally, bringing these fragments together is a process that leaves plenty of room for interpretation: in my view the decisive question that such an interpretation has to address is that of the role of *Judenpolitik* within the overall political activity of the regime.

Given these difficulties with source material, a precise reconstruction of the individual complexes of events and actions—including executions, deportations, murders in the concentration camps, and so on—that together constitute the genocide perpetrated against the European Jews is indispensable for any analysis of the decision-making process. The disparate nature of the sources leaves us no alternative but to draw conclusions about decisions from a reconstruction of the individual acts that they gave rise to. Since this study is primarily a reconstruction of the decision-making process the account will necessarily appear somewhat imbalanced or one-sided: whenever the Nazis' *Judenpolitik* enters a new phase the narrative will broaden out, but a policy once implemented will be described relatively briefly. In other words, this book is designed to be an analysis of *Judenpolitik* that goes back to the events themselves in the form of a schematic narrative and where possible only summarizes them when it is necessary to do so in order to reconstruct an aspect of *Judenpolitik*. The account of the gradual radicalization of the persecution of the Jews in the occupied territories of the Soviet Union will, for example, need considerably more space than the depiction of the rapidly executed deportations of the Hungarian Jews in 1944. However, this study is only one-sided in so far as it is chiefly concerned with the perpetrators and only takes account of the reactions of the victims or of third parties when their behaviour permits conclusions to be drawn about the perpetrators.

This book first appeared in Germany in 1998 under the title *Politik der Vernichtung*. For this English edition, the whole of the original text was revised to take account of the latest scholarship in the field of Holocaust studies: the book has been significantly reworked, shortened in some places and extended in others. The cuts that were made chiefly affect Part I on the persecution of the Jews in Germany and Part III on the war against the Soviet Union. The sections that are new to this English version are on anti-Semitism in the Weimar Republic (Introduction), the removal of the Jews (*Entjudung*) from German society (Chapter 1), life in the Polish ghettos (Chapter 7), the Holocaust in Eastern Europe between 1942 and 1944, and the end of the Holocaust (Part V).

HISTORICAL BACKGROUND: ANTI-SEMITISM IN THE WEIMAR REPUBLIC

This study begins with the first anti-Semitic measures taken by the National Socialists immediately after taking over government in 1933. These measures represent the end of the equality of citizenship that the Jews had enjoyed throughout Germany since 1871.

By gradually removing the citizenship rights of German Jews the Nazis were fulfilling one of the principal demands that radical anti-Semites had been making since the 1870s. It is possible to trace a line of development that began with anti-Jewish agitation in the context of the so-called 'Gründerkrach' of 1873 (the stock-market crash that ended the period known as the 'Foundation Years') and continues in the anti-Semites' petition of 1880/1 and in successful political candidatures from anti-Semitic parties from the 1890s onwards. It was also manifested in strongly anti-Semitic agitation on the part of large professional interest groups at that period. The line could be traced further within the right-wing, ethnic nationalist movement known as the 'völkische Bewegung' that formed after the turn of the century and was highly charged with anti-Semitic sentiments, or with the simultaneous breakthrough of a biological-determinist concept of race in various branches of science, which lent spurious respectability to the nonsense talked about the Jewish 'race'.[1] One could argue, too, that this line was continued in the anti-Semitic agitation at the end of the First World War,[2] and in the wave of anti-Semitic hate campaigns and violence in the immediate post-war period, until it culminates in the anti-Semitism of the NSDAP. In this manner a picture could be painted of a virtually constant stream of radical anti-Semitic movements that led inexorably to the anti-Semitic policies of the Nazis.

However, this image of a clear, uninterrupted line of anti-Semitism in Germany is the result only of a superficial examination of history. It is important, too, to consider the political contexts in which such radically anti-Semitic movements developed. Despite its prominence in Imperial Germany, radical anti-Semitism was only a splinter-group and had no decisive influence on the political course of the German state. In comparison with contemporary manifestations of anti-Semitism in other European countries (such as Austria, Hungary, France, or Russia) it by no means represented a vibrant political force. The tide of anti-Semitic action was stemmed by the fact that whilst the political establishment—above all the power base in the Conservative Party—certainly cultivated anti-Semitism, it also resisted the repeal of Jewish emancipation: from a conservative perspective the emancipation of the Jews was a component of the compromise that lay at the foundation of the Empire and could not simply be ignored. Furthermore, the repeal of rights once granted could not easily be reconciled with the claims of the German Empire to be a state founded on the rule of law. Nationalist utopia and populist anti-Semitic agitation were in contradiction to the elitist political conception of many conservatives.[3]

With the end of the First World War, however, the context in which the nationalist radical anti-Semitic movement was to operate changed fundamentally. These new conditions for a breakthrough in radical anti-Semitism in Germany are much more important than the anti-Semitic tradition that can be traced back to the early years of the Second Empire. Two points are decisive with respect to the changed conditions that the end of the First World War brought about.

The first is the completely new status that the radical anti-Semitic movement gained by virtue of a need to renew the basis of nationalism in Germany after its military defeat and the end of the Empire.[4] It was clear that the institutions of the Empire that had collapsed in 1918 (the monarchy, the Imperial government, and the army) could not represent German nationalism any longer and the 'kleindeutsch', Prussian-German interpretation of German history lost conviction with the end of Bismarck's Empire. It was just as obvious that the old hierarchical structures of the Empire, the class society and the nation's religious divide, were obstacles that would have to be comprehensively surmounted if national regeneration were to be possible.[5]

The various attempts to found a new German identity in place of imperial nationalism and create a strong enough sense of nation to overcome the traumatic defeat of 1918 shared one common element: a reversion to the idea of the people as the real source of national energy—or an attempt to found a new nation by regenerating the people and the ideas of nationhood that lay dormant in them.[6] This regeneration could be directly linked to the recent experience of war by suggesting that it was in the trenches of the First World War that class boundaries had been dissolved and the nation reborn.

The fact that this new attempt to found a sense of national identity from within the people was structured in *großdeutsch* or 'greater German' terms (as opposed to stemming from a *kleindeutsch* or 'smaller German' viewpoint) meant that it derived particularly explosive potential from the foreign-policy situation at the end of the war. Policy framed in *großdeutsch* terms effectively gave Germany a stick of dynamite that could blow apart the new Central and Eastern European order that the treaties signed in the suburbs of Paris had created. In concrete terms, consideration was given to the incorporation of German-speaking Austrians and German minorities in Czechoslovakia, Poland, and the Baltic into a 'greater German Reich' which would at the same time take the German minorities in South-Eastern Europe 'under its wing'.

If during the years of the Weimar Republic a concept of nation based on the common ancestry and shared culture of the German people gradually gained acceptance even amongst moderate right-wingers, an attitude such as this was relatively open to the ideas represented by the nationalist *völkisch* movement.[7] The rediscovery of the people via the 'everyday anti-Semitism' of the conservatives or the moderate right was distinct from the *völkisch* position largely because the latter defined the people using racist criteria, raised the idea of the regeneration of the German people to the level of an absolute good, and linked their programme of 'purifying' the German people of alien elements with visions of redemption. However, their point of reference was essentially the same as that of more moderate nationalism: the restitution of the 'body of the people' to full health. Above all a concept of nation that was based on common ancestry and shared culture remained open to the kind of radical anti-Semitism propounded by the *völkisch* movement and especially to the argument that Jews did not form a proper part of the community of the German people because of their distinct culture and alien ancestry. Before 1918 the *völkisch* idea was mostly the province of sectarians, outsiders, and nutcases, but this new context gave it the chance to take centre stage in the process of founding a new German national identity.

The second decisive aspect of the changed conditions in Germany after the First World War was the shift in the relationship of radical anti-Semitic groups to the state. Before 1914 they had in principle been loyal to the system, or in other words they reckoned that the institutions of Imperial Germany would ultimately be amenable to their demands. *If I were Kaiser* was the title of one of the most influential publications from the radical anti-Semitic camp, written in 1912 by Heinrich Class, the President of the Pan-German League.[8] After 1918, however, confronted with the Republic, radical anti-Semitism was uncompromisingly hostile to the new system and linked their demands for amendments to the emancipated status of the Jews with a demand for the removal of the Republic itself, which they claimed was dominated by Jews. Radical anti-Semitic aims were no longer inhibited as they had been before 1914 by such considerations as loyalty to the existing order or respect for a state governed by the rule of law. Radical anti-Semitism became identical with the campaign against the Weimar Republic.

Far-reaching *völkisch* ambitions such as these did seem utopian from the perspective of those emerging from the First World War but their negative corollary, the inner 'cleansing' of a new nation defined along nationalist lines immediately caught on and manifested itself in the form of attacks against a Jewish minority that was clearly visible or had been made visible and had no place in the new nation.

As a direct reaction to the revolution, and then with greater intensity in the second half of 1919, small radical anti-Semitic groups and solo activists began to emerge right across the country. They exploited the general paralysis that the revolution had caused in the larger right-wing organizations, openly indulging in propaganda in favour of the use of force as a means of solving the so-called 'Jewish question' and using such sloganizing to dominate opinion formation in the radical anti-Semitic camp. It was these forces that evidently lay behind the demands for a 'pogrom'; at the same time there was an increase in anti-Semitic acts of violence.[9]

These activities laid the groundwork for the anti-Jewish agitation of the 'German People's Defence and Offence League' (Deutschvölkischer Schutz- und Trutzbund) that can be regarded as the parent organization of many radical anti-Semitic activities in the Weimar Republic. It campaigned for depriving German Jews of their citizenship.[10] In 1922 the League had more than 150,000 members and was developing a raft of anti-Semitic propaganda primarily to attract workers from the Socialist parties.[11] Whilst this strategy was largely unsuccessful the organization's main effect lay in a general radicalization of anti-Semitic attitudes in right-wing associations and parties.[12]

The NSDAP—the German Workers' Party that had been founded in 1919 and changed its name to National Socialist German Workers' Party in 1920—also profited from anti-Semitic agitation such as this. In a series of anti-Semitic points the NSDAP programme for 1920 made provision for the removal of the equal citizenship rights that Jews had enjoyed in the German Empire since 1871.[13] Even if the NSDAP succeeded in becoming the leading force in the Munich radical right wing by 1923, its effectiveness was nonetheless essentially restricted to Bavaria.[14]

Anti-Semitic agitation was also a key element in the activities of the German National People's Party (DNVP) that was formed after the end of the First World War as a successor to Imperial Germany's Conservative Party, and they directed their efforts in particular against 'Eastern Jewish' immigrants.[15] But like the Conservatives in the pre-war period they resisted the demands of their *völkisch* wing for the exclusion of the Jews from German citizenship. After fierce infighting its radical *völkisch*-German wing broke away from the DNVP to form the German Völkisch Freedom Party (DVFP) with similar aims to those of the NSDAP. Its stronghold was in North Germany.[16]

There were many other groups that belonged to the troubled and internally divided *völkisch* camp in the post-war years and also argued for an end to equal citizenship rights for Jews. In its second issue, in 1921, the German Völkisch Yearbook cited nearly seventy 'German national unions, organizations, leagues, and orders' where the adjectives 'German national[ist]', or *deutschvölkisch*, gave an indication of their fundamentally anti-Semitic position.[17]

Amongst these organizations several were fairly substantial. With some 200,000 members in the early 1920s, the 'Young German Order' (Jungdeutscher Orden) represented one of the most important nationalist and radical anti-Semitic organizations of the Weimar years.[18] It rejected the use of anti-Semitic violence and hate campaigns as being 'anti-Semitic rowdyism' but its leadership left no room for doubt that the Young German Order—which naturally had no Jewish members—desired a form of state, known as the 'Young German State', in which 'the Jewish question would be solved in a *völkisch* manner'. Given the nature of the slogans common in such nationalist circles, this could only be interpreted as a call for excluding Jews from German citizenship.[19]

The elitist 'German League' (Deutschbund) formed in 1894 was one of the co-founders of the 'German People's Defence and Offence League' and was characterized by hard-line racist anti-Semitism. In its constitution for 1921 it pledged to 'cultivate pure Germanness in all areas of life' and it saw its principal function as exercising a nationalist influence on other right-wing organizations. In 1925 its membership was greater than 3,000, but in 1930 the entire leadership of the 'German League' joined the NSDAP.[20]

The 'Pan-German League' (Alldeutscher Verband or AdV) had some 50,000 members at its high point in 1922 and its constitution from the same year declared its aims as 'combating all forces that inhibit or harm the *völkisch* development of the German people, in particular the Jewish domination of almost all public, economic, and cultural fields'. In 1924 the AdV excluded Jews from membership.[21] Further such organizations included the 'Tannenberg League', founded in 1925 by General Ludendorff—an umbrella organization for radical right-wing youth and defence associations which together claimed some 30,000–40,000 members[22]— and the 10,000-strong 'Viking League' founded in 1923 by the militia leader Hermann Ehrhardt.[23]

At the beginning of the 1920s a Central Office for Patriotic Associations was founded in order to coordinate the diverse activities of these nationalistic bodies. In 1922 its Secretary, Wilhelm Schultz-Oldendorf, identified 'dealing with the Jewish question' as one of its main tasks,[24] but in 1928 its functions were taken over by the Central German National Office (Deutschvölkische Hauptstelle) which operated as an umbrella organization for a total of twenty-five nationalist groups.[25] Less central, but still associated with the *völkisch* movement, were elements of the Gymnasts' Movement, the Movement for Life Reform, and various occult and theosophical groups. They were all united by the firm conviction that the Jews represented a 'foreign body' within the German people and had to be excluded at all costs—indeed that the nationalist regeneration for which they all strove could only be achieved by 'cleansing' Germany of everything Jewish. Seen as a whole, these various organizations from different areas of public life constituted a substantial socio-cultural movement.[26]

The wave of anti-Semitism that began after the First World War and which was propelled by agitators from these various groups reached its high point in the assassination of the Foreign Minister, Walther Rathenau, in June 1922 and the numerous attacks and violent assaults on Jews that took place in connection with the Hitler Putsch of November 1923. However, both events make it plain that anti-Semitic violence could be restrained using state-sponsored counter-measures: the Rathenau assassination led to the disbandment of the 'German People's Defence and Offence League', and after the forced end of the Hitler Putsch and the dissolution of the NSDAP the overall level of anti-Semitic violence diminished noticeably.

When the NSDAP was refounded in 1925 it maintained its staunchly anti-Semitic stance. The 'Fundamental Guidelines for the Re-establishment of the National Socialist Workers' Party' published in February of that year contain the following statement: 'The energy of the whole movement is to be directed against the worst enemy of the German people: Judaism and Marxism.'[27] By 1928 and the appearance of his 'Second Book', Hitler himself had succeeded in developing out of the vague conglomeration of racial right-wing ideas that most strongly influenced his thinking a more fully developed world-view in which anti-Semitism held a central position: it was the linchpin for all the various ideological clichés that made up his so-called *Weltanschauung*.[28]

A list of such announcements could easily be compiled. The NSDAP group in the Thuringian regional parliament put together a package of seven draft laws in 1926 that to some extent moved beyond the anti-Semitic demands of the NSDAP Party Programme. They included demands for the dismissal of Jewish teachers, the expulsion of Jewish schoolchildren and students from their educational institutions, and the imposition of bans to prevent Jewish doctors, judges, lawyers, and cattle-traders exercising their trades and professions.[29] During the debate on the referendum on the expropriation of former royal houses in April 1926 the NSDAP presented a draft for a law on the 'Expropriation of Banking and Stock-Market Royalty and other Parasites on the People', which included provision for seizing the assets of 'Eastern Jews and other Alien Races who have joined the Reich since 1 August 1914' in their entirety.[30] Two months later the NSDAP group introduced a resolution demanding in addition that the regional government seize, without compensation, the assets of 'those large-scale Jewish concerns (such as Mosse and Ullstein) that have significant public influence'.[31]

In 1928 deputies from the National German Freedom Movement in the Prussian parliament and NSDAP members of the Reichstag submitted requests aiming at the introduction of Alien Law for Jews.[32] In January 1928 the National Socialist member of parliament Wilhelm Frick called for the 'exclusion of Jews from the administration of justice in Germany'.[33] During budget discussions in March 1928 the National Socialist member Count Reventlow invoked the whole NSDAP group in calling for a law that 'would prohibit all further Jewish immigration, expel all Jews who had entered Germany since 1914, and place those remaining under Alien Law, whilst reserving the right to expel them subsequently, and exclude them from all the rights associated with German citizenship'.[34]

In March 1930 the NSDAP group in the Reichstag submitted a draft law according to which anyone 'who contributes towards, or threatens to contribute towards the racial degradation and subversion of the German people by miscegenation with members of the Jewish "blood community" ... should be punished with imprisonment on the grounds of racial treason'. In particularly serious cases the death penalty was proposed.[35]

In the course of budget negotiations Reventlow made two demands in June 1930 that exceeded the provisions already envisaged in the NSDAP Party Programme: he asked for 'all Jews in Germany to be labelled visibly as such' and for 'the names of all Jews to be prefaced by the term "Jew"'. These proposals were to be put into practice by the Nazi regime in 1941 and 1938 respectively, but in 1930 they seemed so absurd that the members of the Reichstag actually laughed at them.[36]

In the summer of 1930 the *Ostdeutscher Beobachter*, the official organ of the National Socialists in East Prussia, demanded that 'children whose racial characteristics suggest a father who was racially negro, oriental, near-Eastern, or Hamitic be killed. National Socialists cannot conceivably permit racially inferior blood and thus poor spiritual conditions to infiltrate the body of the nation once again. The mothers of these bastards must be made infertile.'[37]

The anti-Semitic demands of the NSDAP were thus consistently repeated in public after the refoundation of the Party and were even made more severe. Corresponding activity in parliament shows that the Party would aim single-mindedly at a series of special anti-Semitic laws after seizing power. What we do not know, however, is to what extent anti-Semitic activity characterized the life of the Party before 1933. The subject of anti-Semitism is neglected or even omitted in most regional studies on the rise of the NSDAP.[38] Most historians agree that the Party markedly reduced its anti-Semitic propaganda after the election of 1930, but this thesis is only partially defensible.[39]

It is certainly true to say that by this point the 'Jewish question' was no longer seen as an independent, free-standing issue. A glance at the Party's election posters—one of the National Socialists' most important propaganda vehicles—makes this clear. In 1924 these posters still portrayed the 'puppeteer', the stereotypical caricature of a Jewish capitalist and thus incarnating the very image of the Party's main enemy. But from 1930 anti-Jewish propaganda was linked with other topics, with campaigns against the 'Young Parties' (the forces that were in favour of accepting the Young Plan for reorganizing reparations) in which the relevant posters showed the representatives of these views caricatured as Jews. One of the main posters for the 1930 campaign had the heading 'Battle against Corruption': it not only showed the National Socialist fist smashing a table at which were sitting functionaries caricatured as Jews but also gave the name Sklarek to one of these figures, a man who had been the principal defendant in a major corruption scandal and who featured in right-wing propaganda as the very personification of a fraudulent mentality portrayed as originating with the Eastern Jews.[40]

The NSDAP was adept at deploying anti-Jewish stereotypes in its propaganda with the minimum of overt effort and without always using the word 'Jew'. The most important methods that formed part of this propaganda technique were abbreviation, allusion, symbolism, and personalization. National Socialist propaganda made use of a semantic and visual code that was very easily recognizable to an anti-Semite: it was enough merely to give a Jewish name, to hint at physical characteristics or external traits that were generally associated with Jews, or to use certain words to trigger prejudices about supposedly high levels of wealth controlled by the Jewish population or the omnipresent Jewish conspiracy.[41]

The *CV-Zeitung*, which had seen through this technique, commented in the issue published on 21 September 1928 that Hitler knew very well that he no longer needed to talk about 'Jewish capital' or 'Jewish crimes' and that it was enough to refer to 'international capital' or 'international crime' since years of agitation and propaganda had meant that everyone knew what he wanted to be understood by his words. Hitler deployed this technique after the National Socialists' electoral success in September 1930 with renewed vigour. He was obviously perfectly well aware that the number of those voting for him was greater than the total number of radical anti-Semites in the German population,[42] and a few weeks after the election he gave an interview to *The Times* in which he spoke out against violent anti-Semitism and pogroms, thereby establishing respectable credentials as one of the leading German politicians.[43] 'The movement discountenanced violent anti-Semitism', he was reported as saying. 'Herr Hitler would have nothing to do with pogroms, and that was the first word that had always gone forth from him in turbulent times. Their doctrine was "Germany for the Germans" and their attitude towards Jews was governed by the attitude of Jews towards this doctrine. They had nothing against decent Jews, but if Jews associated themselves with Bolshevism, as many unfortunately did, they must be regarded as enemies. The Party was against all violence, but if attacked was ready to defend itself.' But a more precise analysis of Hitler's speeches shows that he had not altered his basic position. As the NSDAP achieved unprecedented successes in elections in the years from 1930 to 1933, the fundamental elements of Hitler's ideology, 'space' and 'race', were consistently at the forefront of his addresses.[44] On many occasions Hitler stressed how he continued to see the 'Jewish race' as the principal enemy of the German people.

On 29 August 1930, for example, shortly before the National Socialists' huge success in the Reichstag elections, Hitler referred to the Jews in a speech given in Munich: 'The head of another race is on top of the body of our nation, heart and head are no longer one and the same in our people.'[45] In another speech held a few weeks later he depicted the struggle against the Jews—without naming them explicitly—as a divinely appointed task: 'if we appear today as Germans and try to resist the poisonous effect of an alien people, what we are doing is attempting to return into the hands of the almighty Creator the same creature as He has given us.'[46]

There is much here to support the view that the reduction in anti-Jewish attacks was a temporary tactical concession on the part of the National Socialist leadership which, after its electoral success, was trying to enter into a coalition with the

Centre Party. When these plans collapsed, from late 1931 or early 1932 onwards, it seems that more space was made for anti-Semitic tirades.[47]

It is clear from a list of definitive statements compiled and published by the *CV* that in 1931 and 1932 National Socialist speakers made demands that included taking Jews as hostages to ensure that money allegedly taken out of the country be brought back in or to fend off an attack by France. They demanded also that Jews be removed from public office, from the field of journalism, or removed altogether; they insisted that Jews be deprived of citizenship, called for the burning of synagogues, or promised pogroms in the event of an attack on a member of the National Socialist leadership.[48] Speakers indulged themselves in ever more extravagant comparisons of Jews with animals and fantasies of annihilation as they demanded, for example, the 'extirpation' of Jews 'like tapeworm', or insisted that they be made 'harmless . . . like fleas'.[49] The National Socialist Party press seems to have had little occasion to rein in their anti-Semitic propaganda in these years: the *Völkische Beobachter*, the Party's main publication, revelled in violent anti-Semitic tirades;[50] the same was true of Goebbels's newspaper, *Der Angriff*—'attack'— which was tailored for the public of Berlin in particular.

Anti-Semitic activities and attacks by Party followers were just as evident in the years 1930–2 when the Party was officially calling for moderation in the matter of the 'Jewish question' and distanced itself from such actions. After 1930 there was an increase in the number of attacks on cemeteries and desecrations of synagogues, and in the cases where the perpetrators were identified a significant proportion of these actions were committed by NSDAP followers.[51]

NSDAP members repeatedly attacked Jews or 'Jewish-looking' people on the streets,[52] and such activities reached an initial high in the violence organized by the Berlin SA on the Kurfürstendamm on 12 September 1930, the Jewish new year, when more than a thousand SA followers, not in uniform, randomly attacked Jewish passers-by.[53] Immediately after the Reichstag elections of 31 July 1932 NS followers swamped East Prussia and various other regions of Germany with a wave of violent attacks, a number including the use of hand grenades and including the attempted murder of Jewish citizens; the windows of many Jewish businesses were smashed, too.[54] The boycott of Jewish firms and other Jewish institutions, which we shall return to in more detail later, was driven forwards on the authority of the NSDAP. National Socialists even went as far as making accusations of ritual murder in order to fan the flames of anti-Semitism.[55] Women and men received threats because of their alleged 'racial disgrace'.[56] During the election campaign for the poll on 6 November 1932 the Nazi Party made use of massive anti-Semitic propaganda, coining the slogan 'bigwigs and the Lords' Club[57] with the Jew', including a correspondingly large range of examples from their repertoire of anti-Jewish caricatures.[58]

During the period from 1930 to 1933, however, with an eye to a possible coalition with other right-wing forces, the NSDAP officially rejected the rowdy anti-Semitic tendency and stressed its intention of solving the 'Jewish question' in a 'reasonable', or in other words legal, manner.

The *NS Monatshefte*, the Nazi Monthly Journal published an article in its October 1930 volume that explained, on the basis of the Party Programme, how plans for anti-Jewish laws would be put into practice in the 'Third Reich' that was to come. There was a plan, for example, to give Jews a special legal status which would have as a consequence a 'restriction in their simple rights as citizens', including the removal of both active and passive voting rights and of military service. This general restriction imposed on German Jews would 'not exclude further interventions, if they prove necessary'. The author of the article then gave a series of examples that read like a catalogue for the anti-Semitic laws that would be introduced a few years later. In a similar vein, Ernst von Heydebrand von der Lasa, the Deputy Director of the domestic policy office of the NSDAP, published a draft law in 1931 that made provision for the exclusion of Jews from German citizenship.[59]

In contrast to fundamental draft plans such as these, it seems that there were not so many requests for spectacular anti-Jewish laws made by the NSDAP's parliamentary group after 1930 as there had been previously. Nevertheless, in the Prussian parliament there was a demand made that Jews be excluded from theatres and the radio and for a *numerus clausus* to be imposed on Jewish receivers.[60]

Gregor Strasser, who was head of the Nazi Party's national organization, announced in October 1931 that a National Socialist government would ensure that 'the dominance of Jews in Germany would come to an end' and that this meant 'the exclusion of Jews from all areas in which they are in a position to hamper the German economy'.[61] In June 1932 Strasser declared in a radio address that the Party 'did not want to persecute the Jews', but that they did intend a 'German leadership with no trace of Jewish or foreign spirit'.[62]

Possible concerns were assuaged by an explanation given by Goering in May 1932 to an Italian newspaper. He noted the plans for far-reaching special laws to be applied to Jews, but stressed 'that any decent Israelite businessman who wishes to live in Germany as a foreigner under the protection of the law to which all foreigners are subject, will be allowed to pursue his business'.[63] Goebbels defended the anti-Semitic policies of his party again a few weeks before taking power, in an interview with the *Daily Express*.[64]

However, the facts that in Germany in 1933 radical anti-Semitism was elevated to the status of official government policy and that with the help of initial anti-Semitic laws the equality of citizenship of the Jews was destroyed are not attributable solely to the rise of the NSDAP. It was above all crucial that the thought of excluding the Jews from citizenship rights had been becoming an increasingly popular notion in the socio-cultural milieu of the Conservatives, the NSDAP's future partners in government, since the 1920s. This was initially because representatives of a radical anti-Semitic stance *within* conservative-leaning organizations had used demands for expelling Jewish members to trigger a long-lasting debate on the attitude of these organizations to the 'Jewish question'. These discussions often ended with the introduction of an 'Aryan clause', which symbolically expressed the readiness of the whole organization to adopt a radical stance on the 'Jewish question', distance themselves from traditional conservative views, and fall into line behind the National Socialists.

There were two political organizations in particular that paved the way for their move into the National Socialist camp with an 'Aryan clause', the German National[ist] People's Party (DNVP) and the 'Stahlhelm'—the so-called Steel Helmet Veterans' Organization, which would join with the NSDAP in 1931 to form the Harzburg Front and become partners in Hitler's government in 1933.

The DNVP took the decision to exclude Jewish members in 1924 and (for formal reasons) again in 1926.[65] This decision was in line with the ideas of the right wing of the Party that used the Party's cooperation with democratic forces in parliament and coalition governments (in 1925 and 1927) to accuse the leadership of abandoning its fundamental opposition to the Weimar Republic and of bringing it too close to the state that it disliked. With the election of Alfred Hugenberg in 1928 the right wing of the Party prevailed and determined on an alliance with the NSDAP.[66] Hugenberg was himself relatively restrained about making anti-Semitic statements, probably because of his interests as the head of a group of press companies, but it is clear that the exclusion of Jewish members was a precondition for the Nazi-friendly line of development that the Party took. In the Steel Helmet Veterans' Organization the *völkisch* wing under the Deputy Leader, Theodor Duesterberg, gradually succeeded in taking over and bringing about a political alliance with the DNVP and the NSDAP.[67] These forces managed to engineer the exclusion of Jewish members in 1924 and ensured that thereafter the organization routinely took an anti-Semitic stance.

The strong influence of *völkisch* forces on attitudes to the 'Jewish question' was also felt in the 'Reichslandbund' or National Rural League, the successor to the strongly anti-Semitic pre-First World War Farmers' League. The RLB's propaganda shifted in 1924–5 towards the extensive use of anti-Semitic stereotypes under pressure from *völkisch* forces. These were attempting to depict the particular burdens on agriculture, following currency stabilization in 1924, as a conspiracy on the part of international Jewry to force it into subjugation. This way of seeing things was adopted to a large extent by the RLB.[68]

The German National Association of Commercial Employees (DHV) had more than 300,000 members at the end of the 1920s and it undertook a lively programme of anti-Semitic propaganda and education. Under the intellectual leadership of the publicist Wilhelm Stapel, the Association propagated a *völkisch*-cultural brand of anti-Semitism and stressed the essential incompatibility of being both German and Jewish.[69]

Thus the Weimar Republic saw a large number of middle-class associations take steps to exclude their Jewish members, and it is remarkable that the anti-Semitic forces managed to implement this process of exclusion precisely during the most stable period of the Republic, at a time, therefore, when such associations were recovering from the years of inflation and consolidating themselves. For instance, the 'Jewish question'—the demand by *völkisch* members of the association that an 'Aryan clause' be inserted into the constitution—played a major role from the early 1920s onwards at the annual general meetings of the German-Austrian Alpine Club, which was probably the most important of all German leisure and tourist organizations. Important branches such as Berlin and Breslau did in fact succeed in banning Jewish members.[70]

However, discussions about the introduction of an 'Aryan clause' were held in German gymnastic associations (the German League of Gymnasts did not accept Jewish members), in the German Academy, in the Association for Germans Abroad, and other organizations where the anti-Semitic forces did not prevail.[71]

Scattered references to the exclusion of Jews from local associations can be found throughout the literature on regional history, but the question of how far this represented a consistent pattern is an important area that still requires further research—and in the light of the importance of such associations in Germany and their close connections with local politics this omission is all the more scandalous.

Students took a leading role in the spread of radical anti-Semitic ideas in German society. At the beginning of the 1920s almost all the student bodies had ceased to accept Jewish members. The Deutscher Hochschulring, an umbrella organization of student associations (DHR), refounded in 1920, saw itself as particularly *völkisch* and anti-Semitic and quickly became a powerful force in most of the country's universities, the general student councils, and within the German National Student Union. This dominant role found expression above all in the huge influence the DHR had on getting the student body to adopt radical anti-Semitic positions.[72] This occurred for the first time in 1922 when the DHR was able to push through a constitutional amendment according to which the association sanctioned the practice of its members, the German and Austrian student organizations, of not accepting any students of Jewish origin at all.[73]

Five years later the University Circle caused another conflict linked to the 'Jewish question'. It was sparked by the fact that the majority of state-recognized and state-supported student associations accepted Jews into their ranks provided they were German citizens, but did not accept Jews classed as 'Germans from abroad', such as those from Danzig or territories ceded to Poland. When the Prussian Minister of Culture demanded that this practice be changed, in a vote taken in 1927 the majority of the student representatives voted against, which eventually led to the dissolution of the student organizations.[74]

At the end of the 1920s the leading political role amongst student organizations was taken over by the National Socialist League of German Students. After 1929 it ensured that the student associations in a number of universities decided to demand that the number of Jewish students be limited to the proportion of Jewish members of the population in the area of the Reich.[75] Violence against Jewish students and professors was a daily occurrence in German universities towards the end of the Weimar Republic.[76]

Radical anti-Semitic positions also spread within the two principal Christian confessions where they reinforced what were already fairly strong anti-Semitic prejudices that had been formed on confessional or religious grounds.

Within the Protestant Church a group known as the 'German Christians' had formed from the early 1920s onwards, rejecting the Jewish roots of Christianity—most notably the Old Testament and the Jewish ancestry of Jesus himself—and attempting to reconcile Christian theology with Germanic mythology.[77]

Whilst these groups only met with very limited success, from the early 1930s onwards the National Socialists succeeded in mobilizing their supporters on the occasion of church elections, working in particular with the 'Faith Movement of German Christians' who were opposed to 'racial miscegenation' and the 'Jewish mission'. In the church elections of November 1932 the German Christians gathered about a third of all the votes, which roughly corresponded to the proportion of National Socialist supporters in the population at large.[78]

The Church reacted to these forces—which after all challenged the fundamental premises of Christian belief according to prevailing theology—with sympathy and a willingness to dialogue rather than by clearly distancing itself from them. Under the influence of this *völkisch* provocation the spectrum of opinion within the Church moved decisively to the right in the direction of *völkisch* and racist ideas.[79] The indirect influence of the German Christians proved to be much more important than any direct effects they could have by virtue of their position within the Church.

The Königsberg Church Congress of 1927 marked a caesura in the attitude of the Protestant Church to the *völkisch* movement. It witnessed the presentation of the outline for a new political theology in the paradigmatic paper given by the theologian Paul Althaus on 'Church and Nation'. Decisively, his lecture paved the way for recognizing the *völkisch* community as part of the divine order; with this 'theological qualification of the people the principle of the *völkisch* movement received Christian legitimacy'.[80]

Such theological receptiveness for points of view that took account of the people, 'das Volk', meant that whilst in the Weimar Republic anti-Semitism within the Protestant Church was condemned in its overtly violent form, its underlying racist premises were not only not rejected but accepted and even to some extent welcomed. The purely biological concept of race was rejected as irreconcilable with the Christian image of humanity, but the Protestant mainstream's views on race and the racial basis of nationhood (seen as a muddy synthesis of 'blood' and 'spirit') had already been influenced to a high degree by biologistic racial dogma.

After the end of the First World War Catholicism also increasingly came to see 'Volk' and 'nationhood' as components of the divine order of creation. The Catholic concept of nationhood was not for the most part based on ideas of race, however, and it did stress its distance from the *völkisch* camp. Catholic authors did not rely on a material or biological concept of nationhood based one-sidedly on 'blood and soil' ideas but strove to emphasize the 'spiritual' element within their conception of nation. However, they were prepared at the same time to acknowledge biological 'facts' and the Catholic conception of nation thus drew nearer to the related concepts of race used within *völkisch* discourse.[81] The religious anti-Semitism that featured in Catholic circles could therefore be stretched far enough to permit calls for refusing equality of citizenship to Jews from this quarter, too.[82]

The exclusion of Jews from German citizenship was publicly called for at the end of the 1920s and in the early 1930s by a whole series of prominent right-wing intellectuals. What is most remarkable is that a series of leading supporters of the 'conservative revolution'—the intellectual scene that became part of the 'new right' in the early 1930s—had intensified their anti-Jewish attitudes. Whilst they had made unambiguously anti-Semitic comments in the 1920s but had not supported the removal of citizenship from the Jews (indeed had sometimes vociferously opposed it), now they formed part of the growing chorus of proponents of this measure. This group included Wilhelm Stapel, Editor in Chief of the newspaper *German Nation* and organizer of the educational sections of the German National Association of Commercial Employees. Stapel was one of the most influential original thinkers in the *völkisch* camp and represented a 'cultural' concept of nationhood rather than one based one-sidedly on racism. Stapel's close colleague Albrecht Günther similarly joined the group of those proposing that Jews be deprived of citizenship.[83]

Ernst Jünger, the successful author of popular war literature and one of the leading figures in the intellectual right, wrote programmatically in 1930 that a Jew living in Germany would soon 'be faced with his final choice: being a Jew in Germany or not being a Jew', implying that he also believed in the need for a special status for Jews.[84]

The views quoted here were expressed in a series of anthologies or special numbers of periodicals dedicated to the 'Jewish question' and published in the early 1930s. For example, the September 1930 edition of the *Süddeutsche Monatshefte* was devoted to the 'Jewish question'. They were the vehicles for anti-Semites of various hues to give voice to their views, but they also published opponents of anti-Semitism and leading Jewish commentators. These discussions show very clearly how the radical anti-Semites had succeeded in putting the solution to the 'Jewish question' onto the political agenda, in one form or another.

An important stage in the onward march of radical anti-Semitism was the spread of the anti-Jewish boycott movement from the mid-1920s onwards in a variety of different fields of life. There were traces of a systematic boycott of Jewish businesses organized by anti-Semitic circles evident even in Imperial times, especially at Christmas, but it was very substantially intensified during the Weimar Republic, not least in the 'stable' period. Although the Centralverein succeeded in obtaining court judgements against the boycott in a large number of cases, reports in its newspapers show that the boycott movement was growing.[85]

Local National Socialist papers had begun openly encouraging the boycott of Jewish businesses since the end of the 1920s.[86] The boycott became a regular part of National Socialists' local strategies for gaining power in many areas,[87] and from 1931–2 took on a violent form: customers were prevented from entering shops, windows were smashed, and the owners of shops threatened.[88]

The organized boycott of Jewish businesses reached a high point at Christmas 1932. In September of that year the Centralverein identified an office within the National Socialist leadership that was centrally organizing the boycott.[89] The fact that it was already taking on the form of a violent blockade became very clear when the Minister of the Interior from Hesse answered a parliamentary question at the beginning of December by saying that 'the current large-scale campaigns against Jewish business people ... had already led to serious disruptions to public order'. The national government supported this view and in the same month recommended that regional governments deploy the police to restore order 'if for example pickets are set up in front of a shop and grossly offend those attempting to gain entry by making threats, insulting them or in any other way'. The method the National Socialists used to organize the boycott of Jewish businesses in April 1933 thus corresponded to a model that had been tried and tested even before their 'seizure of power'.[90]

From the mid-1920s on, the Centralverein received more and more complaints about discrimination against Jews applying for jobs in large firms. Such discrimination, which the CV mainly attributed to the activities of former army officers working in the personnel departments of these firms, was justified as an attempt to avoid friction with *völkisch*-minded employees. It too grew to the extent of becoming a boycott. According to the CV, the firms principally affected were large banks, the domestic departments of large insurance firms, the chemical industry, heavy industry, mining, shipbuilding, and the firm of Siemens.[91]

As had happened in Imperial times, in the Weimar Republic a large number of hotels, guesthouses, tourist, and spa resorts refused to accommodate Jewish guests and exclusively targeted a *völkisch*-minded public. The most famous example of this form of boycott is the holiday island of Borkum, which was positively proud of banning Jewish visitors. The number of anti-Semitic restaurants and cafés also increased during the 1920s. The CV published blacklists and in 1932 eventually established a tourist office to advise Jewish travellers about the current status of local anti-Semitic activity.[92]

The Director of the CV made the following summary at the end of 1925: it was depressing to note 'that a form of social anti-Semitism that far exceeds what had been the case before the war is now a dominant feature of the reactionary political and social climate; that with many, too many fellow citizens, whilst the atmosphere fostering aggressive anti-Semitic activity has waned, a "passive" anti-Semitism is still present, a tendency to avoid all contact with Jews'.[93]

The boycott movement that originated with the National Socialists and other radical *völkisch* forces was only supported by a minority of the population at large; it was not a truly popular movement, but the openness with which the boycott was propagated proved to be decisive, as did the fact that the boycott, although it was in many instances against current law, was generally tolerated and did not produce a counter-movement to offer resistance. Those who encouraged others to boycott Jewish businesses, heads of personnel who refused to employ Jewish applicants, guesthouse owners who did not accommodate Jews risked no general social disapproval or fatal economic consequences.

It became clear, therefore, that radical anti-Semitism and its central demand for the exclusion of Jews from the rights of citizenship was not limited to the agitation of the NSDAP but gradually took root in the political and social life of the Weimar Republic. The radical anti-Semitic forces had succeeded in forcing the Republic to enter into a debate on the 'Jewish question'.

It was against this backdrop that an informal compromise was worked out in the early 1930s between the National Socialists and their political partners on the right. Whilst the National Socialists indicated that they would give up the overly violent forms of anti-Semitism if they were to take power, their partners in the leadership of the DNVP, the Stahlhelm, and other right-wing organizations were obviously more and more willing to accept the old demand that the Jews be legally driven out of certain areas of public life. This increasing willingness was not evident from public decrees but it was clearly detectable in the public statements of leading right-wing intellectuals and it manifested itself in the policies of organizations discussed above that were prepared to exclude Jews definitively from their membership for fear of criticism from the National Socialist camp.[94]

In 1933 the radical anti-Semites had triumphed in the matter of exclusion after a struggle that had lasted more than fifty years. With the imposition of their radical viewpoint towards the 'Jewish question' they had won a significant symbolic victory that in turn emphasized their leading role amongst the political right.

However, it is not the gradual erosion of conservative reservations about taking on radical anti-Semitic positions that explains how the National Socialists were so easily able to introduce their anti-Semitic policies immediately upon taking power. There is an additional important factor: in the last years of the Weimar Republic there were no significant political or social groupings that might have prevented the success of the radical anti-Semitic movement. The Liberals who had inscribed the emancipation of the Jews on their banners in the nineteenth century (even though they were mainly concerned with founding a German nation state in which non-Christians could also thrive as citizens with equal rights) no longer existed as a political force by the early 1930s.[95] Anti-Semitism was also rife amongst Catholics. For religious reasons, because of the Catholic view of mankind, Catholicism was in essence incompatible with radical racist anti-Semitism. However, this did not cause the Catholic Church to stand up to that form of anti-Semitism; instead it was by no means hostile to a certain weakening of the Jews' position in society so that in the end both variants, religious and racist, were mutually supportive. And the workers' movement, which was relatively clear of anti-Semitism, saw it principally as a diversion from the realities of the class struggle and did not take the anti-Semitic demands of the National Socialists especially seriously. They did not seriously fear their implementation, and in the view of the Socialists these demands ultimately undermined the interests of 'capital' (including the stereotype of the 'Jewish capitalist' that was also prevalent in the workers' movement).[96] This, then, was the political scenario that faced the National Socialists in 1933 when they began to put their anti-Semitic policies into practice.

PART I

RACIAL PERSECUTION, 1933–1939

CHAPTER 1

THE DISPLACEMENT OF THE JEWS FROM PUBLIC LIFE, 1933–1934

Before the war German Jews were the victims of three waves of Nazi anti-Semitism, each of which inaugurated a new stage in their persecution. The unrest of March 1933 was followed by the boycott of 1 April and the first anti-Semitic laws, which initiated the process of driving Jews out of the public sphere. The second wave began in spring 1935 with renewed anti-Jewish attacks, which reached their pinnacle in the summer of the same year. The regime responded by promulgating the Nuremberg Laws, which discriminated against the Jews by assigning them a special status that was defined in increasingly narrow and restrictive terms as time went on. Then, in 1938, after a relatively long preparatory phase that seemed from the outside more like an easing of policy towards the Jews, there followed the third wave of anti-Semitism. After the violent excesses of summer and autumn 1938 had culminated in the November pogrom, the regime decreed the complete disenfranchisement of the German Jews, statutory steps towards their total economic depredation, and their enforced expulsion.

Each of these three waves is marked by a characteristic dialectic between 'campaigns' arising in the 'grass roots' of the Party and measures taken by the Nazi leadership. The anti-Semitic rowdyism of the National Socialist mob was always followed by decrees from the leadership, which in turn instituted a whole series of legal and administrative measures aimed at persecuting the Jews and thereby initiated a new step in the persecution process. These three anti-Semitic waves from the pre-war period must be seen in the context of the racism that was at the heart of National Socialism.

At the heart of National Socialist political thinking was the idea that all the most pressing problems besetting Germany could be solved with the introduction of a fully comprehensive 'new racial order'. What was to be created was a racially homogeneous 'national community' consisting of biologically superior 'Aryan' or 'Germanic' *Übermenschen*. But this racial utopia was based on their absurd and inconsistent concept of race: it was simply not possible to use inherited biological criteria to reduce the populations of Central Europe to their 'racial' components and at the same time maintain the view that the majority of these people represented something approximating to a homogeneous blood-related community. Tellingly, contemporary 'experts' on race solved this problem by qualifying the majority of the population of Central Europe as a racial 'mixture' or blend. This meant that any policy that attempted to define members of the 'Aryan' race according to clearly distinguishable criteria, and to make a positive selection of 'racially valuable' individuals, was doomed to failure from the outset. If the Nazis had actually attempted to implement such policies across the board, either the inhabitants of Central Europe would have been subjected to a form of racial hierarchy defined by the proportion of 'Aryan' blood in their veins, or the definition of 'Aryanism' would have had to be so broad as to apply to a very large proportion of those living on the continent of Europe. In either case, a policy of 'positive' racial discrimination such as this was not workable, and would inevitably founder on its own abstruse premises.

The only practical way to implement racial policy was therefore to use negative criteria. National Socialist racial policy consisted above all in the exclusion of so-called 'alien races' and in the 'racially hygienic filtration' of the weaker members of the native 'Germanic' race. Nazi racial policy thus always consisted of the exclusion or 'eradication' of minorities. For historical reasons, *Judenpolitik* was bound to play a central role within racial policy that operated along 'negative' lines in this manner. The Jewish minority was only superficially integrated into society. There was a traditional image of the Jew as 'enemy', an age-old prejudice, and existing anti-Semitic stereotypes assisted in constructing a scenario in which 'the Jews' represented a serious threat both as 'enemies within' and as the adherents of a worldwide conspiracy. In addition, *Entjudung* or the removal of the Jews, offered considerable advantages to those carrying out anti-Jewish policy since removing the Jews from German society, which was crucial to the idea of racial 'cleansing', was for the National Socialists precisely the same as achieving their goal of total domination. 'Anti-Jewish policy', or 'racial policy' in its broadest sense, was intimately bound up with plans of the NS leadership that reached far beyond the immediate anti-Semitic or racist goals.

Racism and anti-Semitism were not only core components of the National Socialists' ideology but played a key role in the implementation and consolidation of the NSDAP's ambitions for power. By setting about translating their radical aims into anti-Jewish and racial policies after 1933, the NSDAP was quickly creating a new dimension to politics, and one that was wholly dominated by them. At the centre was the intention to rid German society of all forms of 'Jewish influence' and of everything that was in any sense 'racially inferior', and as part of this comprehensive 'cleansing' process the sectors of German society that needed 'cleansing' were also to be subjugated as thoroughly as possible to National Socialist hegemony. This new political dimension had top priority; it cut right across the traditional political spheres such as foreign, economic, or social policy; it dominated, saturated, and transformed them. Almost every conventional political problem could be interpreted as a 'racial problem' or an aspect of the 'Jewish question'.

It was also true, of course, that the goals of foreign, economic, and social policy had implications for the implementation of 'racial' or 'anti-Jewish policy'. As in every conventional sphere of politics, the practical implementation of racial or anti-Semitic goals and the concomitant expansion of the National Socialists' political power was a complicated process. Close attention had to be paid to potentially competing aspirations, to overcoming opposition, making tactical concessions, managing internal rivalries, and establishing a consensus on which direction policy should take.

Within this complex process of implementing new racially dominated power structures, four elements should be highlighted in order to demonstrate clearly what far-reaching implications such a multi-layered transformation had for the entire political system.

First, the 'struggle against the Jews', against racial 'disintegration' and 'alien races' made an important contribution to integrating and mobilizing the National Socialist movement. The Nazis' programmatic approaches within the traditional spheres of politics were contradictory and inadequately thought through, so racism and anti-Semitism functioned as an indispensable surrogate for lack of consistency in these areas.

Second, by implementing a racial model of argument, the means of steering public opinion in the 'Third Reich' were restructured so as to permit the hegemony of racism. What used to be defined as social, economic, domestic, or foreign policy was now subsumed under an all-embracing 'racial problem' or 'Jewish question'. But implementing a racial discourse in a dictatorship was not restricted to the manipulation of the media by the NS propaganda apparatus. In a broader sense it encompassed all the ways in which the public sphere was influenced and manoeuvred, including the day-to-day behaviour of the population, and in particular increases in the control of informal exchanges of information. The gradual segregation of Jewish minorities from mainstream daily activities and the suppression of any criticism of these measures appeared to offer proof that the greater part of the German population was in full agreement with the regime's 'anti-Jewish policy'.

Third, reshaping the public domain was the most important prerequisite for the NSDAP's ability to use the 'racial question' or the 'Jewish problem' for the gradual extension of its own power base, not least at the expense of its conservative coalition partners. Since virtually every political question possessed a 'racial' element, and since every dimension of life was subject to *Entjudung*, the National Socialists had almost unlimited possibilities for intervening in what had hitherto been relatively autonomous areas of existence. In practice, racism made possible the almost complete elimination of a private sphere. Questions such as the choice of a partner and the conception and education of children were no longer the responsibility of the individual but subordinated to racialized concepts of the family. Racism undermined traditional ideas of the equality of the citizenry and led to the creation of radically new criteria for judging personal capacities and capabilities, and therefore also to a redistribution of opportunities for social advancement. Racism established the basis for a new order of financial relationships; articulated, for example, in the 'Aryanization' programme it transformed traditional social policy into notions of 'nurturing the nation'.

Finally, imposing racial and anti-Semitic patterns of thinking onto international and foreign policy appeared to create considerable confusion on the international stage which in part prevented the build-up of a widespread rejection of the Nazi regime from outside Germany.

The First Anti-Semitic Wave during the Nazi 'Seizure of Power'

The very first steps towards the persecution of the Jews taken by the National Socialists clearly demonstrate how National Socialist 'anti-Jewish policy' always remained closely related to aims that had little or nothing to do with the 'Jewish question'. The first wave of anti-Semitism, the attacks on Jewish citizens in March 1933, the boycott that followed on 1 April, and the discriminatory legal measures taken immediately afterwards are all of a piece with the tactics deployed by the National Socialists for the 'seizure of power'.

In the first phase of the National Socialists' 'seizure of power', between 30 January and the Reichstag elections of 5 March 1933, the new government concentrated on its opposition to the Left, the Communist Party (KPD) and the SPD. But even if socialist functionaries of Jewish origin were persecuted with particular intensity,[1] and attacks on Jewish or 'Jewish-looking' people in the street and raids on apartments inhabited by Jews were routine elements in the violence of the SA,[2] this form of attack on Jews was still very much overshadowed by the National Socialists' strategies for the elimination of the workers' movement.

In the second phase of the 'seizure of power', which began after the Reichstag elections of 5 March and lasted until early May, the National Socialists were principally concerned with bringing into line (*Gleichsschaltung*) the *Länder* and local government. Alongside these measures, in March and April, the NSDAP began to take control of the employers' associations, and the organization of the unions and the SPD were paralysed by direct interventions (by this time the KPD had already been crushed). In this phase, and often in direct conjunction with the tumultuous occupation of town halls, union headquarters, and Social Democrat newspaper offices, the National Socialists intensified their attacks on Jewish citizens and Jewish businesses across the whole Reich. Within a few days, two principal targets emerged: lawyers of Jewish origin and businesses in Jewish ownership. At the same time similar campaigns were initiated against department stores, chain stores, and cooperative societies (or in other words against large retailers who were branded by the NSDAP's propaganda aimed at the lower middle class as typical products of the 'Jewish' drive for profit), regardless of whether they were actually owned by Jews or not. This wave of attacks on Jewish businesses, amongst others, was not unexpected: it was the continuation and culmination of the dogged low-level war that the NSDAP had waged against undesirable entrepreneurs since the end of the 1920s. Driving Jewish lawyers out of the judiciary was, as has already been demonstrated, an old keystone of anti-Semitism.[3]

Violence and 'Boycott'

The spread of the first wave of anti-Semitism can be reconstructed precisely.[4] It was begun on 7 March 1933 in the Rhine-Ruhr district, reached central Germany and Berlin on 9 March, hit Hamburg, Mecklenburg, and Frankfurt on 11 March and a series of cities in the south-west on 13 March. Spreading to certain regions in leaps and bounds like this indicates that the violence was organized at district level, from within those Gaus where the functionaries of the Combat League of Small Business (the militant organization of Nazi shopkeepers) and regional SA leaders will have been prominent.

The violence always followed the same pattern: Nazi supporters demonstrated outside the shops, stuck posters on the windows, and prevented customers from entering. There were frequently scuffles, and in most cases the shops were forced to close. These campaigns were often accompanied by violent attacks on Jews, but these did not at this stage take on the shape of a pogrom.[5]

In the very first days the National Socialist leadership had encouraged the attacks on Jewish businesses—the Prussian Minister for the Interior, Goering, for instance, declared on 10 March that he refused to allow 'the police to act as a protection agency for Jewish department stores'.[6] However, the NS leadership very soon began to row against this trend: in a call made on 10 March Hitler warned against any further unauthorized individual campaigns and a decree from the Reich Minister for the Interior issued on 13 March also warned explicitly against 'the closure and intimidation of retail premises'.[7]

In response to these warnings from on high, attacks made by grass-roots Party members on Jewish shops had slackened off by 13 March.[8] In the second half of March, the SA concentrated mainly on measures against unions and the Social Democrats and on preventing all forms of Communist activity. Two events will have caused the NS leadership to present themselves as relatively moderate, sanctioning the use of force only for the complete suppression of 'Marxism'. These were the formal opening of the Reichstag due to take place on 21 March, where the National Socialists wished to portray themselves as partners of the Conservatives on the basis of Prussian traditionalism, and the passing of the Enabling Act slated for two days later, for which the government required the support of the non-socialist parties.

Nonetheless, it was not possible to put a complete end to anti-Jewish violence in this phase. Members of the SA perpetrated what amounted to a pogrom in Creglingen (in the southern German state of Württemberg) on 25 March. They forced their way into the town's synagogue, dragged the male worshippers into the town hall where they humiliated and maltreated them, sometimes very seriously indeed. Two Jewish inhabitants died as a result of their injuries.[9]

During the month of March, alongside the attacks on Jewish shops and businesses, there were many towns in which Jewish lawyers were forcibly removed from the administration of justice. From 9 March on, SA and SS troops occupied court buildings and ejected Jewish members of the legal profession, including judges and public prosecutors.[10] The most famous incident was in Breslau, where the violence forced the regional court to declare a three-day halt to judicial proceedings.[11] Such attacks on court buildings were hugely inflamed by various public declarations and continued throughout the second half of March.[12] Interventions into the area of justice by ordinary members of the Party gave the judicial authorities the excuse to use administrative means to remove Jewish lawyers from their positions,[13] and created the basis on which the subsequent legal exclusion of Jews from the judiciary and the public sector as a whole could quickly be established. For the National Socialists, however, these illegal interventions and their rapid subsequent legalization were also an important step on the way towards control of the entire state apparatus, a first litmus test to establish how resistant or compliant the predominantly conservative civil service actually was, and an opportunity for assessing at the same time the extent to which German nationalist coalition partners would be prepared to tolerate interference in the rule of law at this early stage.

If the Nazi leadership resolved at the end of March to call once more for a boycott of Jewish shops and businesses—centrally coordinated this time—then it did so for a mixture of tactical and fundamentally ideological reasons.[14] The decision to call for a boycott arose from the specific dynamics of the process towards the seizure of power. When the Enabling Act was passed at the end of March the NSDAP had completed an important stage in their plans to ensure a monopoly of power. The next decisive step on the path to total power, the definitive suppression of unions and the SPD and the dissolution of the non-socialist parties, was to take place only after 1 May, the National Labour Day, which they proposed to make into an official public holiday celebrated with great pomp and circumstance. At the end of March, therefore, the NS Party leadership was in a delicate transitional phase in the process towards the seizure of power: grass-roots Party activism could not be allowed to wane, but the activists themselves had to be restrained from being overly brutal towards their political enemies within the unions and the SPD and towards the competition represented by the non-socialist parties. It was moreover important to regain control of the increasingly forceful anti-capitalist drive arising from the Party activists, which was leading to disruptive 'interventions in the economic life of the country' at precisely this point, the second half of March.[15]

Both aims were attainable by means of a controlled resumption of the anti-Jewish boycott. The Party leadership was demonstrating that it was responding to the anti-Semitic demands of the population, and by steering and controlling the whole campaign from the centre, was able to re-establish its authority over the Party membership. The fact that the leadership succeeded in gaining control over the attacks emanating from the activists in certain districts by the middle of March, and that it was to initiate a major propaganda campaign to stoke the flames of the population's anger by the end of March, shows that the leadership was fully in control of the situation and was in no sense propelled into the boycott by the grass-roots membership.

The need to steer this complex internal Party dynamic during the process of the seizure of power was only one of two main motives. By starting a campaign against the German Jews, or in other words by seizing hostages, the NS leadership hoped to be able to stem the rising tide of criticism from abroad. By labelling criticism of this type 'Jewish atrocity stories', which emanated from a relatively small section of foreign Jews, they defined international reaction against the brutalities of the 'seizure of power' in anti-Semitic terms, and at the same time created the pretext for the planned boycott.

Such tactical considerations should not obscure the fact that, only a few months after taking over the reins of government the NSDAP was using the call for a boycott to begin implementing a significant element in its political programme, namely the disenfranchisement of the Jewish minority. This makes it clear that Nazi *Judenpolitik* cannot be understood in merely functional terms, as an instrument designed to mobilize the NS movement; it was one of the central pillars of the NSDAP's ideology, and there was no difference of opinion on this point between the Party leadership and the ordinary Party members.

The campaigns against Jewish businesses undertaken under centralized direction, and pre-empted by the violence of March 1933, were now linked with the continuing attacks on Jewish lawyers to form a comprehensive anti-Jewish crusade underpinned by the authority of the regime. In this way the pressure needed to initiate anti-Semitic legislation—the 'atmospheric' conditions for it— could be created. Under this pressure, the Jews could be removed from public life, and from state institutions in particular, and an appropriate platform could be created for the complete segregation of the Jewish minority that was to follow at a later date.

The successful enforcement of these first anti-Jewish measures allowed the NSDAP to make the 'Jewish question' a dominant factor in domestic policy within only a few months of their coming to power. Problems as distinct as the economic situation of the lower middle class, the seething violence of the SA and the international isolation of the Reich were to be reduced to a single common point of origin, stamped with the slogan 'the Jews are our misfortune'. By unleashing the anti-Jewish campaign the NSDAP succeeded above all in seizing the domestic policy initiative and in maximizing their room for manoeuvre vis-à-vis their conservative coalition partners.

The practical preparations for boycott were begun on 26 March after a conversation between Hitler and Goebbels. They were entrusted to Julius Streicher, district chief or Gauleiter of the area around Nuremberg and one of the most radical anti-Semites in the whole Party, who was made the chair of a 'Central Committee to Combat Jewish Lies about Atrocities and Boycott'.[16] On 28 March the Committee issued a call to prepare the boycott.[17] Responsibility for it was clearly claimed by Hitler in the cabinet meeting held on 28 March 1933, when he informed the cabinet that 'he, the Reich Chancellor himself, had ensured that the appeal would be issued to the National Socialist Party'.[18]

Because acts of violence against Jews were becoming increasingly frequent in the days before the 'boycott' that was to begin on 1 April for an unlimited period,[19] considerable effort was expended to ensure that the whole undertaking would run in a smooth and disciplined manner. To this end Goebbels declared on 31 March that the campaign would be 'suspended on the evening of the first day (this was a Saturday) until the following Wednesday; it would only be relaunched if the 'lies about atrocities' from abroad had not ceased by that point.[20]

Following a tried and tested pattern, on 1 April SA and Hitler Youth guards carrying pre-printed placards were stationed outside Jewish shops and attempted to prevent potential customers from entering. The atmosphere on that day was characterized by crowds of people in the business quarters, gathered round the entrances of the shops being forcibly boycotted. Because their customers were being intimidated, most Jewish shop owners found themselves compelled to shut as the day wore on.[21]

Whilst in the main shopping streets of the cities the impression given was of a carefully regulated Party campaign, in the side streets and in smaller towns attacks on Jewish firms mounted steadily, often with display windows being daubed or smashed. In many towns Jewish citizens were threatened, mistreated, or driven through the streets by squads of SA troops. There were isolated instances of looting. In Kiel a Jewish lawyer who was supposed to have shot and seriously injured an SS man was lynched by the mob whilst in police custody.[22] On the evening of 1 April the boycott was 'suspended' for three days, as planned, and not relaunched thereafter, since the Central Committee announced that the supposed stories from abroad about atrocities in Germany had abated.[23]

The boycott did in fact enable the regime to achieve its intentions. Even if innumerable reports confirm that a proportion of the public deliberately shopped that day in Jewish-owned businesses,[24] the majority of the population evidently acted just as the regime had expected them to. On that day most people avoided going to Jewish shops. The boycott therefore largely achieved its aims.

The regime could also claim as a further aspect of its success the fact that since the end of March, in anticipation of the imminent boycott, a whole series of voices usually heard in opposition to the government had taken a public stance against foreign claims of atrocities being perpetrated in Germany and had mobilized their contacts abroad in like manner.

The National Socialists thus succeeded in presenting foreign responses provoked by their own anti-Jewish campaign as 'anti-German' attacks and in exploiting this skewed picture to send out messages of trustworthiness and images of inoffensiveness to the rest of the world. At this very early point it is apparent how the 'Jewish question', handled with the appropriate political and promotional skill, could be utilized to influence and confuse public opinion not only in Germany but in the rest of the world as well.

It is remarkable that even Jewish organizations and institutions such as the Centralverein deutscher Staatsbürger jüdischen Glaubens (Central Organization of German Citizens of the Jewish Faith) and the Jewish Veterans' Organization, the Boards of the Jewish community in Berlin and elsewhere, as well as many Jewish private individuals and entrepreneurs took part in the attempts to minimize the criticisms of the situation in Germany voiced by those abroad.[25] After a discussion with Goering on 25 March, the Organization of German Zionists and the Centralverein decided on a particularly spectacular course: they sent a joint delegation to London to argue against a boycott of German goods.[26] The fact that on the delegation's return, the Centralverein publicly declared the mission a success,[27] underlines the precarious situation of the German-Jewish officials: the 'success' of their mission could also be seen as confirming the NS argument to the effect that 'the Jews' were responsible for behind-the-scenes propaganda and boycott campaigns against Germany but had supposedly buckled under massive pressure and desisted from their shameful activities.

First Anti-Jewish Laws

In the meantime campaigns by Party activists against Jewish lawyers were being extended. The judicial authorities reacted to these illegal measures by transferring or suspending Jewish judges and public prosecutors, and by imposing quotas for Jewish barristers.[28] These steps were very soon legalized by the Hitler–Papen government, and the official regulation of members of the legal system agreed in cabinet at the beginning of April was quickly extended to the whole of the civil service.

The 'Law for the Re-establishment of a Professional Civil Service' passed on 7 April made provision both for the possible dismissal of civil servants on political grounds and for the compulsory retirement of those civil servants 'who are not of Aryan descent'.[29] In response to an intervention from President Hindenburg, Jewish civil servants who were already in service before 1 August 1914, who had fought at the front, or whose fathers or sons had been killed in the war, were exempted from these regulations. These requirements were also logically to be extended to all workers and employees in the public service. The first decree, issued on 11 April, determined that anyone who had even one Jewish parent or grandparent was to be considered 'non-Aryan'.[30]

The Professional Civil Service Law marked the point at which the legal equality of Jews across the Reich that had been in force since its foundation in 1871 was finally shattered, and it heralded the step-by-step revision of their emancipation. The law also marked a significant infringement of the traditional rights and privileges of the civil service, which were constitutionally protected but, since the Enabling Act, liable to suspension. Whilst the political 'cleansing' of the civil service represented a measure that was not out of line with the kind of personnel changes that usually accompany a change of regime, the dismissal of civil servants 'of non-Aryan descent' was something completely new: a racial criterion was being used to rob part of the civil service of the constitutionally guaranteed status that formed such an important element of the German tradition of the servant of the state. The fact that such a racially motivated political intervention in the existing legal system was accepted by the service meant a significant victory for the NSDAP in its attempt to subjugate the conservative state apparatus that was so wedded to the principle of the constitutional state founded on the rule of law.

The imposition of the 'Aryan principle' in public administration during the next few weeks was perfected using further legal measures. In the months that followed some 50 per cent of a total of about 5,000 Jewish civil servants were deprived of their jobs by the new laws.[31]

The elimination of Jewish civil servants was undertaken by the new government simultaneously with the exclusion of Jewish members of the legal profession from the legal system. Yet more wide-reaching plans to prevent even Jewish doctors from exercising their profession failed initially because of resistance from the Chancellor, Hitler, who did not consider such plans as opportune at that point.[32] Whilst the law concerning admission to the legal profession passed on 7 April[33] did indeed determine that lawyers 'of non-Aryan descent' should lose their right to practise their profession, there were the same exemptions made as in the professional civil service law. As a result of these regulations more than 40 per cent of the Jewish notaries and almost 60 per cent of the Jewish lawyers in the largest German state, Prussia, were initially able to continue to practise. They were, however, subject to innumerable obstacles put in place by the Party, which went as far as forcibly expelling them from court buildings, which happened several times in the spring of 1933.[34]

Jews in other professions regulated by the state, like patent lawyers and accountants, were soon hit by similar measures. Doctors and dentists were excluded from practising in the health insurance system.[35] The 'Law against the Overcrowding of German Schools and Universities' also imposed a quota on the numbers of Jewish pupils and students that could be accepted.[36] Jewish school and university students were subsequently discriminated against in many ways and were excluded from certain activities such as participation in sport.[37]

The National Socialists also took special measures to exclude Jews from the cultural life of the nation. As early as 30 January the former senior functionary of the National Socialist Campaign Group for German Culture, Hans Hinkel, was made 'Commissar without portfolio' in the Prussian Ministry of Culture and given the task of 'removing Jews from cultural life'. In April, Goering directed his attentions to the theatre in particular by making him Head of the Prussian Theatrical Commission.[38] In March and April, as part of the familiar interplay of Party grass-roots 'campaigns' and administrative measures, National Socialist rallies led to theatrical performances and concerts by Jewish artists being disrupted and Jewish musicians and theatre directors being dismissed.[39]

On 6 April 1933 Hitler once more voiced his public support for this policy, at a reception for leading medical officials, where he explained that 'the immediate eradication of the excess of Jewish intellectuals from the cultural and intellectual life of Germany is necessary if justice is to be done to Germany's natural right to an intellectual leadership appropriate to its own kind'.[40]

The middle of April saw the beginning of the 'campaign against un-German thinking' in most universities, where members of the National Socialist Student League systematically combed through the holdings of private lending libraries. On 10 May in many German cities works by left-wing, pacifist, and 'morally corrosive' authors were burned alongside the works of Jewish writers and scientists.[41]

There was a temporary shift in the persecution of the Jews at the beginning of July 1933 when Hitler proclaimed the end of the 'National Socialist Revolution' in a speech to the *Reichstatthalter*, those established by the new regime as the governors of the individual German states.[42] For reasons of foreign, domestic, and economic policy the regime felt compelled to rein in the violence of the SA with the result that attacks on Jews and Jewish property were moderated once more. But the government's intention to find a comprehensive solution to the 'Jewish question' was interrupted after only a few months. Of the three major legislative programmes announced in early July by Hans Pfundtner, Permanent Secretary in the Reich Ministry of the Interior,[43] only one, the sterilization law, was to find its way into cabinet discussions, whilst the two anti-Jewish projects he had listed—a Citizenship Law and a law for the 'Purification and Continuing Purity of German Blood'— were postponed. Nonetheless, the July 1933 law concerning the revocation of naturalization and deprivation of citizenship, did come into force.[44] It was especially important in that it created the legal foundations for removing from the Reich the 'Ostjuden' or Eastern European Jews who had entered since the end of the First World War, by depriving them of their German citizenship.

Hitler explained what had originally been much more extensive planning in the area of racial legislation and the reasons for its temporary postponement in a speech to the *Reichstatthalter* conference on 29 September 1933:

He, the Chancellor, would have preferred to move gradually towards stepping up the rigour with which the Jews in Germany were treated, by creating first of all a nationality law and using this as the basis for ever harsher approaches to the Jews. However, the boycott provoked by the Jews had necessitated immediate counter-measures of the severest kind. People abroad were complaining above all about the legalized treatment of the Jews as second-class citizens.[45]

Thus the regime restricted itself at first to a further series of discrimination measures against Jews in specific areas of life, but not against the Jews as a whole.

On the one hand, therefore, various legal regulations debarred Jews from entering professions that required academic qualifications, such as the law, medicine, dentistry, and pharmacy; those Jews already active in such professions were prevented from continuing to practise them.[46] The foundation of the Reich Chamber of Culture in September 1933 gave the regime the means to exclude Jews definitively from all the cultural professions. The first step was to declare them ineligible to join the new organizations that were compulsory regulators of all activity in the cultural sphere, on the grounds that they did not possess the 'reliability' and 'suitability' that the membership conditions prescribed.[47] The Editorial Law of October 1933 provided the same instrument to prevent Jews from becoming journalists in future.[48]

Legal exclusion conditions ensured that Jews could neither achieve the privileged status of 'Hereditary Peasant' introduced by Nazi agricultural legislation,[49] nor gain access to the newly introduced marriage loans.[50] In July 1933 the army introduced a requirement that soldiers' brides would have to prove their 'Aryan' descent.[51] In February 1934, on their own intiative the Armed Forces introduced the requirements of the Professional Civil Service Act. As a consequence, some seventy soldiers had to leave the army for 'racial' reasons—which represented an important intrusion by the new government into the army's personnel management, previously considered by the military top brass as their autonomous domain, and therefore a symbolically important act of submission by the army to the racist dogmas of the regime.[52]

Deceptive Calm

Because there were no major new persecution measures taken during this period, the second half of 1933 and 1934 are often described as a period of 'relative calm' for the German Jews. However, despite the official end of the 'boycott' the Party grass-roots campaigns against Jews and Jewish businesses were in many cases perpetuated, and Jewish citizens were the victims of petty policies on the part of the state administration that were aimed at displacing or ousting them. The longer this condition obtained, the more profoundly the financial basis of Jewish businesses was affected. Discrimination took various different forms: Jewish tradesmen were driven from marketplaces;[53] Jewish firms were disadvantaged when rationed goods were distributed;[54] farmers were under pressure to break off commercial connections with Jewish traders;[55] Jewish firms were banned from advertising in newspapers and elsewhere;[56] local government ceased all business contacts with Jews[57] and subjected them to arbitrary harassment;[58] again and again the windows of Jewish businesses and apartments were smashed;[59] signs announcing a 'ban on Jews' were displayed; cemeteries were desecrated and synagogues ransacked.[60] 'Racial violators' were physically attacked and mobs organized by the Party prevented the celebration of 'mixed marriages'.[61]

Party activists repeatedly—and successfully—attempted to force people to boycott Jewish shops and required them to be specially marked out as such. Whilst in many villages and small towns Jewish shops were subject to a permanent blockade, in 1934 the militant small-business Party activists who had now formed the National Socialist Trade Organization (NS-Hago) launched measures to boycott Jewish shops within the context of a 'spring campaign' across the whole of the Reich. Similarly comprehensive campaigns were undertaken during the Christmas seasons of December 1933 and 1934.[62] Although both the Party headquarters in Munich and government agencies repeatedly resisted the excesses of boycotts, they were not able to put a truly effective stop to the boycott movement that emanated from the Party activists.[63]

These boycott campaigns and the numerous other discriminatory measures taken against the Jews were always accompanied by violent attacks.[64] These anti-Semitic acts of violence reached a high point on Palm Sunday 1934 in the Upper Bavarian town of Gunzenhausen, when more than a thousand of the inhabitants of this small town marched through the streets, forcibly hauling Jews from their homes and dragging them off to the town prison. One Jewish citizen was later found hanged; another stabbed himself; a few weeks later one of the main perpetrators, who had in the meantime been punished, albeit leniently, shot a Jewish restaurant owner on his own premises. These excesses show how the anti-Semitic hatred of Party activists was liable to explode at any point, even during the phase of 'relative calm' that then supposedly characterized the Nazis' persecution of the Jews.[65]

The Nazi government's unbending severity with regard to the 'Jewish question' was made obvious during an inter-ministerial briefing in November 1934, which at the same time manifested a notable readiness to compromise in the treatment of non-European 'alien races'. During this meeting it was first established that 'adverse consequences of German racial policy over recent months had placed serious strain on relations with various foreign states'. This meant mainly Germany's relations with a series of Asiatic and South American states, who were responding angrily to the discriminatory treatment of their citizens resident in Germany and to the depiction of all *Artfremde* (literally all those 'foreign to the species', i.e. all those of non-European descent) as members of 'inferior' races by the publicity material of the 'Third Reich'. The meeting was agreed that 'the principles underlying the racial politics of the National Socialist world-view must not be compromised even by strong pressure from outside', but also that the 'application of the racial principle in practice should not be permitted to have adverse repercussions in the area of foreign policy, if these were disproportionate to its domestic political benefits'.[66]

Following a suggestion made by Helmut Nicolai, the representative of the Reich Ministry of the Interior, a solution to this problem was found: legislation would in future avoid the term 'non-Aryan' in favour of 'Jewish'.[67] The meeting agreed that in future all decisions about the application of legal requirements against 'foreigners of alien blood' would be exclusively within the purview of the Foreign Office. Any *Artfremder* could be 'exempted from the racial legislation', according to a decree of the Reich Minister for the Interior issued in April 1935, if reasons of foreign policy required this—but only in cases where these 'aliens' were of 'non-Jewish blood'.[68] The aim of the policies formulated in this meeting on 15 November, as expressed more than a year later by the representative of the Foreign Office Bülow-Schwandte, was the 'restriction of racial policy measures to the Jews'.[69]

Jewish Reactions to the First Phase of Persecution

The National Socialists' policy of excluding the Jews from public life affected the members of a minority that was by no means homogeneous.[70] At the beginning of the National Socialist dictatorship some half a million people were living in Germany who professed membership of the Jewish community, and amongst these were about 100,000 who did not have German citizenship (mostly immigrants from Poland and Russia, the so-called *Ostjuden* or Eastern Jews). In addition there were more than 40,000 people who were not Jewish in the confessional sense, but were regarded as Jews by the National Socialists on the grounds of their origins or ancestry.[71]

Whilst the German-Jewish minority was legally and culturally integrated, it is impossible to overlook the particular social structure of this group, which distinguished it clearly from the rest of society. The large majority of Jews lived in large cities, they were mainly members of the middle class, to a large extent of the educated bourgeoisie, they were predominantly active in trade and commerce, and represented a relatively large proportion of the professions. As far as religion was concerned, most classed themselves as liberal Jews, although an ever greater degree of religious indifference was manifest amongst Jews as it was amongst the rest of the population. In sharp contrast to this group was an independent Eastern Jewish proletariat in which orthodox religious conviction was comparatively well represented.[72]

The identity of the overwhelming majority of the German Jews was founded on their being firmly anchored in German culture and in both patriotic and liberal convictions. The very name of the Jewish organization that counted the most members, the Centralverein deutscher Staatsbürger jüdischen Glaubens (literally the Central Organization of German Citizens of the Jewish Faith) was itself an expression of the belief predominant amongst German Jews that the process of acculturation had been successfully completed, for the most part, and that the development of a certain group identity did not represent isolation but was an instrument for making a specific Jewish contribution to the well-being of the German state.

In relation to this main general tendency, the Zionists—who reacted strongly against the idea of a German-Jewish symbiosis—played a comparatively minor role: the Zionist Organization for Germany had only some 20,000 members around 1930.[73]

Even this brief overview suggests clearly that the majority of German Jews were not inclined to abandon their position in Germany over-hastily, and they clung— to the point of self-delusion—to the idea that the 'seizure of power' was a temporary crisis that would blow over. Nonetheless, under the pressures of the boycotts and the National Socialist terror during the phase of seizing power in 1933, an estimated 37,000 Jews left the Reich; politically active, younger, and relatively prosperous Jews were comparatively over-represented amongst these refugees. In 1934, because of the relatively calm situation, only some 23,000 Jews left.[74]

A particular chapter in the history of German-Jewish emigration, in which a clear signal was given for how far the new regime was prepared to work together with the Zionist movement in this area, is the so-called 'Haavara Agreement' concluded in August 1933 by the Reich Finance Ministry, the Zionist Organization for Germany, and the Anglo-Palestine Bank in Tel Aviv. This agreement established special measures for circumventing the restrictive currency legislation that banned the export of foreign currencies and therefore represented a considerable hurdle for those wishing to emigrate. The wealth of Jewish émigrés that remained in Germany was liquidated and an equivalent was transferred to the British Mandate of Palestine in the form of exported German goods. These were then sold, and from the proceeds the German émigrés were provided with the minimum level of capital that enabled them to count as 'capitalists' in the eyes of the British authorities, which in turn guaranteed them fast-track immigration. Of the approximately 50,000 German Jews who emigrated to Palestine before the beginning of the war, several thousand were to profit from this agreement; in this way German goods to the value of more than 100 million Reichsmark were exported to Palestine, as well as to other countries. The regulated emigration of a not inconsiderable proportion of the German Jews was therefore assured by means of a consolidation of the German export market in the Near East, which from the German perspective represented an important breakthrough against the attempts of international Jewish groups, and others, to boycott German goods.[75]

The decision by the majority of German Jews to hang on at first and stay where they were was considerably influenced by the activities of Jewish organizations, which will be investigated in more detail in the course of this overview. In the early days of National Socialist rule, the Centralverein was unable to rid itself of the idea that the continuing existence of the Jews in Germany could be safeguarded after all, if necessary by accepting certain forms of legislative discrimination. It was not until 1935 that the Centralverein (which had to alter its name after the Nuremberg Laws)[76] recognized the illusory nature of such beliefs and began urgently advocating emigration. It is certain, however, that the increasing level of activity on the part of Jewish support organizations contributed to the decision to wait and see.

One consequence of the pressure on the German Jews was that for the first time the heterogeneous Jewish minority in Germany formed a unified representative body to coordinate the various efforts. At the beginning of 1932 the regional organizations of the Jewish communities decided to create a national delegation to safeguard their interests, but in practice it did not become active at that point. Only in September 1933 did the umbrella organizations of the Jewish communities in the individual German states, the Centralverein, the Jewish Veteran Organizations, and the Zionist Organization form a Reichsvertretung or Reich Board of Deputies of German Jews. The President was Rabbi Leo Baeck, universally recognized as a leading figure in the intellectual life of German Jewry.[77]

In addition, on the initiative of the Reich Board, the Central Committee for Support and Development was created on 13 April, as a reaction against the boycott. This Central Committee set itself the task of maintaining and strengthening the position of German Jews by social and economic means, whilst the Reich Association concentrated on political representation and education. The leading Jewish organizations were represented on the Central Committee, which was also chaired by Leo Baeck. In its first appeal, made at the end of April 1933, it opposed what it called 'unimpeded emigration'. The Committee was integrated into the Reich Board in April 1935.[78] As far as its practical activities were concerned, the Central Committee took up the work begun before 1933 by the Jewish support organizations. Economic measures for support were in the hands of the Central Office of Jewish Economic Assistance, founded in March 1933.[79]

A broad range of support measures were coordinated under the umbrella of the Central Committee and the Central Office, including distributing loans, correlating applications for and offers of capital funds, finding jobs for Jews who had been dismissed, and a special support programme for out-of-work academics and artists, to name only the most important measures.[80] An important area in which the Central Committee was active was 'professional restructuring', or the re-education of the predominantly commercially trained Jewish minority for technical, practical, or agricultural professions, which were more likely to be useful for emigrants. It was in the first years of the 'Third Reich' that this work was severely hampered by the authorities.[81]

The Central Welfare Office of the German Jews had been founded in 1917 to coordinate the various socially oriented Jewish organizations, and the main problem that it faced was the severe diminution in resources for the support of people in need that had been caused by the collapse of the small and medium-sized Jewish communities in many towns.[82] Until 1938, even if Jews were discriminated against in many respects, they had the right to support from the social services. Until then, Jewish welfare services were essentially supplementary to this, and embraced many different types of allowances and subsidies.

In 1933 by far the majority of the approximately 60,000 Jewish school-age children attended state-funded schools.[83] At the end of 1933 the newly created Education Committee of the Reich Board passed guidelines for the curriculum in Jewish primary and secondary schools that emphasized the rootedness of the German Jews in Germany. The foundation of new Jewish schools began rather tentatively, but in 1935 there was a significant influx of children into Jewish schools.[84]

In July 1933 the Kulturbund Deutscher Juden (the Cultural Association of German Jews) was formed in Berlin. Its main considerations were to help Jewish artists from the capital who had been dismissed from their positions to find other means of supporting themselves and to spare the Jewish public the need to attend the events organized by the 'Aryanized' culture industry. By 1934 the Kulturbund attracted 20,000 members and was able to offer them a comprehensive programme of culture, in part in its own theatre in Berlin. More Jewish cultural associations were founded in the provinces during the months that followed.[85]

From 1933 Jewish men and women were excluded from sporting clubs and associations, and this strengthened the activities of the existing Jewish sports clubs.[86] In 1934 the Jewish National Committee for Physical Education in Germany was founded as an umbrella organization for the 250 clubs and 35,000 activists.

In 1933 and 1934, therefore, significant initiatives towards the organization of an independent Jewish life were discernable beneath the persecutions, which together formed an impressive picture of Jewish self-determination and which enabled individuals to have a degree of autonomy. From 1935, when the regime imposed the segregation of Jews in all areas of life and increased the restrictions on their economic activity, these early beginnings were to form the basis for a Jewish sector that was independent within Nazi-dominated society, if under attack from all sides.

Racial Persecution of other Groups in the First Years of the Regime

The persecution of the Jews by the National Socialist regime was at the centre of a more widely reaching implementation of racist policy. This approach was determined by two main considerations. First, measures against 'alien peoples' (*Fremdvölkische*) or 'alien half-breeds' (*fremdvölkische Mischlinge*) can be grouped under the heading of 'ethnic racism'—these included measures against Gypsies and the small group of non-Europeans living in Germany, mostly Africans, or the children born of Germans with non-Europeans. The second target of Nazi racial policy— under the slogan of 'racial hygiene'—was the 'eradication' (*Ausmerzung*) of undesirable elements in the 'Aryan' race and was thus directed against those with so-called hereditary diseases, 'social misfits', and homosexuals.

'Racial hygiene' concentrated first above all on those suffering from 'hereditary diseases'. As has already been outlined, the sterilization law of 14 July 1933 provided for the enforced sterilization of men and women in this category, whose offspring would 'most likely' inherit physical or mental deficiencies.[87]

With the establishment of public health departments in the summer of 1934 the regime had at its disposal an important instrument for carrying out 'negative hereditary care'.[88] These health departments evaluated medical and other official documents to identify 'persons with heredity illnesses' and to use these individual cases as the basis for discovering 'inferior hereditary lines' within the German people.

Doctors and other medical personnel were required to notify the authorities of people they believed to be suffering from 'hereditary diseases'. Applications for sterilization could be made by state-registered doctors, the directors of medical institutions, those concerned or their legal representatives, and decisions on such applications were made by the 'hereditary disease courts', made up of a lawyer and two doctors.[89] In by far the majority of cases these courts determined in favour of sterilization; the number of applications refused varied from 1934 to 1936 between 7 and 15 per cent. The total number of those subjected to sterilization will have been about 360,000 in the Altreich (Germany as it was until the end of 1937), although it may have been higher. Both men and women were sterilized, slightly more men than women overall.[90]

There were nine possible diagnoses included under the sterilization law, and of these 'mental deficiency' was the most common, used in more than 50 per cent of cases, followed by 'schizophrenia', 'manic-depression', and 'epilepsy'. These four psychiatric labels—which together accounted for more than 95 per cent of all cases—did not in themselves constitute precise diagnoses of illnesses. Instead mental deficiency and schizophrenia were blanket terms for a wide variety of behaviours that attracted attention or deviated from the norm. 'Mental deficiency', for example, was established using an intelligence test that included general knowledge, facts of the kind taught at school, questions on politics and history, and general moral concepts. Criteria such as thrift, diligence, industriousness, domestic cleanliness, educational success, 'normal' sexual habits, and the like were decisive factors in determining hereditary illness. The supposed 'diagnosis' of such illnesses was in reality a social diagnosis in which the social 'valency' of an individual was determined in the context of a belief in 'racial improvement'. 'Racial hygiene' was not based on anything approaching empirically verifiable evidence about clearly defined inheritable conditions or characteristics; instead it represented a long-term experiment, designed to run over several generations and to eliminate certain 'negative' phenomena felt to be in contradiction to the Nazis' racial ideals using methods for monitoring and controlling human reproduction ('racial enhancement via eradication'). There was a presupposition that illnesses and characteristics can be inherited, which was to be turned into a proof of the possibility of 'racial enhancement' as the results of these experiments became available.

The victims of enforced sterilization came overwhelmingly from the socially disadvantaged groups—pupils at remedial schools, those receiving welfare support, young people in children's homes, people with criminal records, prostitutes, criminals, persons of no fixed abode, families with an 'irresponsibly large' number of children, or unskilled workers who were thought to demonstrate 'mental deficiency' because they were used to carrying out simple repetitive tasks.[91]

There was a 'racial hygiene' component in the exclusion of certain groups from eligibility for loans on marriage that had been legally established in July 1933. Following a decree from the Minister of Finance, spouses who suffered from 'hereditary mental or physical afflictions' that demonstrated that 'their marriage was not in the interests of the community at large' were, with Germans of Jewish origin, ineligible to apply for such loans.[92] The same applied from September 1935 to grants for child support.[93] The logic of this ban was to prevent such 'undesirable' marriages altogether and was taken to its conclusion with the Marriage Health Law of 18 October 1935.[94]

The castration of sex offenders sanctioned by the Law against Dangerous Habitual Criminals passed on 24 November 1935 was also motivated by considerations of 'racial hygiene' (and in June 1935 this law was extended to include homosexuals, provided that the person concerned gave consent). It was not introduced simply to protect the victims but was intended to prevent 'degenerate sexual drives' from being passed on to future generations. On the basis of this law, 2,300 men were compulsorily castrated in the period between 1935 and 1943.[95]

After enforced sterilization, the next step in the logic of racial hygiene was termination of pregnancies, and this was realized in September 1934 when the leader of the Reich doctors' organization, Gerhard Wagner, included in a circular letter Hitler's decision to exempt from punishment abortions carried out to stop babies with 'hereditary illnesses' being born.[96] After much discussion an alteration was made to the Sterilization Law in June 1935 to the effect that women whose sterilization had already been determined upon by the Hereditary Illnesses Tribunal could, with their agreement, have current pregnancies terminated.[97] At the same time, threats of action against those who aborted 'healthy', 'Aryan' children were intensified, and prosecution of this crime was stepped up, which indicates an overwhelmingly racial motivation in this area, too.

The Law for the Protection of the Genetic Health of the German People of 18 October 1935 finally made it necessary for couples who wished to marry to obtain a 'Certificate of Suitability for Marriage' from the local Public Health Department Office.[98] It was originally intended to link this form of 'genetic protection' (*Erbschutz*) with 'racial protection' (*Blutschutz*) in a single law against 'marriages inimical to the welfare of the people', but on Hitler's own initiative at the 1935 Party Conference, these aspects were regulated separately. These 'Certificates of Suitability for Marriage' were not in fact introduced universally. They were only required when the relevant official had 'good reasons' for doubting the appropriateness of a proposed marriage.

The legal measures taken to promote racial hygiene affected one group, 'social misfits' (*Asozialen*), in a particular way. These were groups on the margins of society whose apparently 'deficient' genetic inheritance made the National Socialists feel that they were 'not in a position to fulfil the minimum requirements of the community with respect to their personal, social, and national behaviour'.[99] The sterilization experts were increasingly extending the concept of 'mental deficiency' to include the 'social misfits' such that, although repeated demands for a comprehensive Community Aliens Law to enforce the sterilization of these groups were never officially met, by the end of the 1930s this measure was being enforced in practice. The concept of 'social misfit' was vague, encompassing both prostitutes and their pimps, criminals, persons of no fixed abode, beggars, 'depraved' families or families with too many children, the work-shy, addicts, gamblers, those guilty of any form of perversion, unmarried mothers, fathers who did not support their families financially, those in long-term receipt of state support, Gypsies, and many others.[100]

In the first years of the 'Third Reich' the authorities directed their principal attentions towards various measures for interning 'social misfits' who had nowhere to live, and in doing so greatly increased the population of asylums. In later years, many of these people were to fall victim to the policies of annihilation as 'unnecessary mouths to feed'. On the initiative of the Reich Propaganda Ministry, September 1933 was to see the first 'beggars' week', in which perhaps as many as 100,000 beggars and persons of no fixed abode were arrested. Thereafter many raids like that were carried out. Those arrested would be imprisoned briefly and then sent to workhouses. Between 1934 and 1940 the courts made nearly 8,000 such orders. A few beggars were also sent to concentration camps.[101]

Other official measures were taken to secure the internment of this group of people. From 1934, special camps were designated by some districts for those carrying out the work that was obligatory for those in receipt of welfare support.[102] Those on welfare benefits were increasingly sent to special detention institutions, and in 1934–5 local authorities began to set up their own dedicated 'colonies' for the 'social misfits'.[103]

In the early years, Gypsies were also subjected to increased discrimination and persecution by the authorities, measures which can be interpreted as a radicalization of traditional anti-Gypsy policies. Some states tightened up their regulations on the rights of Gypsies, local authorities discriminated against Gypsies when granting welfare or interpreted the administrative regulations in a restrictive manner. Gypsies were frequently hauled in as part of the operations undertaken against 'social misfits'. From 1935 many municipalities, especially the larger cities, began to accommodate Gypsies in dedicated camps, which were closely guarded and strictly regulated.[104]

However, Gypsies were particularly affected by the new legal requirements governing the control and management of reproduction and were disproportionately the victims of enforced sterilization. Qualified estimates assess that some 2 per cent of all Sinti and Roma aged between 14 and 50 were detailed for sterilization and that about 400 of the 450 people concerned were actually subjected to enforced sterilization.

Gypsies were prevented from marrying those 'of German blood' both by the Blood Protection Law and the Marriage Health Law. (The First Implementation Order of the Blood Protection Law, 14 November 1935, made explicit provision for extending the marriage ban to non-Jewish 'members of alien races', and soon afterwards the Reich Ministry of the Interior confirmed that it was to be applied to 'Gypsies, negroes, and their bastards'.[105]) The racist paradigm thus affected the Gypsies in two different ways, as 'alien races' and as 'inferiors' to be excised from the 'Aryan' race. With the implementation of enforced sterilization and marriage bans on Gypsies the regime was beginning to depart from the traditional paths of Gypsy persecution. The supposedly genetic reasons for 'typically Gypsy' behaviour were now being moved into the heart of Gypsy policy.

Enforced sterilization, exceptions to the regulations on abortion, and the institution of marriage bans gave the National Socialist regime a whole battery of weapons for the social discipline of individuals whose lives—at a more personal level than political opposition—did not conform with National Socialist norms. Those who were in any way inconvenient, conspicuous, non-conformist, or potentially disruptive could be kept in check with the help of these three eugenicist measures. It was precisely the fact that the criteria for making these interventions were indistinct and indefinable that made them a potential threat for all those whose private lives deviated from what was considered to be 'normal'.

Aiming wider even than the control of marginal social groups, and working alongside massive racial 'hygiene' propaganda,[106] the eugenicist measures were designed to form one of the cornerstones of the National Socialist project to establish a new order of values and authority in German society, one determined by the hegemony of 'race'. Sterilization, abortion for reasons of racial hygiene, and bans on marriage represented not only a deep intrusion into people's private lives but were intended to abolish the very notion of a private sphere. Decisions about who to live with, when to start a family, and parenthood were now subject to a state veto.[107] The eugenicist measures helped replace the principle of equality of citizenship with the principle of racial inequality, and did so in a manner that was directly effective at an individual level. In essence there were no limits to the continuing exclusion of citizens from reproduction. Experts juggled with numbers of 'inferior people' that ran into millions.[108] Using racial hygiene arguments it was theoretically possible to use a self-defining position of 'normality' as a basis for declaring everything else, everything different, a 'deviant biological development' and thus open the way to its 'eradication'. It was the very inconsistency and irrationality of the concept of race, which was not scientifically definable, that left it up to the National Socialist state to determine the content of its cherished racial ideals. In reality, a form of 'biologization' subjugated society to the totalizing claims of National Socialist policy.

Another group that should be investigated within the context of racist persecution is homosexuals. Attacks on homosexuality by the NS regime were on the one hand clearly consistent with the long tradition of persecuting homosexuals in Germany, but on the other it is equally clear that such persecution in the 'Third Reich' was radicalized and motivated in a new and distinct manner. The persecution of homosexuals was rooted in population policy and formed a fixed component of the plan for the racial 'enhancement' of German society.

Between the 'seizure of power' and the murder of Ernst Röhm, known to be homosexual, and his followers on 30 June 1934, the NS regime did intensify police measures against visible focal points of the homosexual sub-culture, but the majority of homosexuals were left largely free of persecution.[109] This situation changed when the SA leadership was eliminated and the systematic persecution of homosexuals began. A special section was established in the Gestapo headquarters and in the last months of 1934 large-scale raids on homosexuals were carried out. In the summer of 1935 the relevant paragraph of the penal code (§175) was made significantly more severe, in particular by the introduction of a penalty of imprisonment of up to ten years for certain groups of offenders.[110]

In the course of these racist measures, non-Europeans living in Germany were also affected by policies aimed at the segregation of 'alien peoples'. In 1933 and 1934 the Reich Ministry of the Interior and the Foreign Ministry both had to deal with numerous complaints on the part of non-European states concerning discrimination against foreigners living in Germany and fears that they too might be sterilized.[111] In order to minimize foreign-policy difficulties, as has already been shown, the Reich government was prepared to apply racial policy to foreigners with a degree of flexibility.[112]

Since the spring of 1933 the authorities had been concerned with the special problem of children born of German women and coloured soldiers during the French occupation of the Rhineland.[113] Initially they were identified by the authorities and as early as February 1935 one of the working parties of the Committee of Experts on Population and Racial Policy was to consider the possibility of sterilizing the 'Rhineland bastards'. It was agreed that the decision about whether or not to bring in legislation to deal with this matter should be left to Hitler himself, as will be discussed in Chapter 4.[114]

CHAPTER 2

SEGREGATION AND COMPREHENSIVE DISCRIMINATION, 1935–1937

The second wave of anti-Semitism set in at the beginning of 1935 with renewed violence that went on until late summer 1935. It was for the most part brought to a close by the promulgation of the Nuremberg Laws in September.[1] After Jews had been largely driven out of public and administrative life during 1933 and 1934, the regime was concerned to take one further step towards the complete segregation of the Jewish minority from the German population.

There were three core aims to be realized: the ban on 'racial miscegenation' between Jews and non-Jews; the introduction of a separate citizenship law for Jews; and massive restrictions to the rights of Jews in the areas of finance and the economy. The regime consistently saw segregation as a prerequisite for the ultimate goal of *Judenpolitik*, already in view at this point, namely the complete expulsion of the Jewish minority from Germany.

Realizing these aims meant more to the National Socialists than the intensification of Jewish persecution. They had an important general domestic policy function since they offered significant starting points for improving the Nazi movement's penetration of German society. Demands for a ban on 'racial miscegenation', subjecting people's choice of partner to the control of the National Socialist state, represented a radical break with the concept of the 'private sphere' that had hitherto been a central constitutive element of bourgeois society. Attempts to put these aims into practice questioned the notion that there existed behind a public sphere controlled by the National Socialists an inviolable space into which the individual might withdraw. The regime pursued the same goal of controlling the private sphere whilst simultaneously attempting to prevent eugenically undesirable marriages, and a Marriage Health Law was to follow on immediately after the Nuremberg Laws. Yet again, there are close parallels between anti-Semitic and other racist policies. With the introduction of elite Reich Citizenship Rights (*Reichsbürgerrecht*), not only were Jews given their own special class of limited rights but the very principle of equality of citizenship was abandoned. The Reich Citizen's enjoyment of full legal rights had to be earned—according to plans drawn up and announced publicly—by demonstrating that he fulfilled criteria as yet undefined but which were to be prescribed by the National Socialist state. The measures against Jews planned in the economic sphere (exclusion from certain trades, marking out Jewish businesses, complete expulsion from public office, etc.) not only heralded direct economic advantages for owners of small businesses under the aegis of the NSDAP; they also offered the Nazi movement as a whole the potential to use increased intervention as a means of politicizing the entirety of economic life in a manner that was essentially racially inspired.

The radicalization of the persecution of the Jews in 1935 was closely linked to an intensified attack on the Catholic Church and on conservative circles labelled reactionary by the regime. The main target was the German-nationalist veterans' organization 'Stahlhelm' (Steel Helmet), which was eventually dissolved altogether. After the SA was 'decapitated' in June 1934, the regime began to consolidate its domestic political position on a broad front by eliminating all its opponents. The intensification of anti-Jewish policy was thus only one aspect—if clearly a central one—of the regime's increasing repressiveness.

Preparations for the National Socialists' increasing penetration of the depths of German society were made at the end of 1934 with a comprehensive restructuring of the public sphere. The campaign against 'the Jews', which was conducted alongside attacks against 'the Priests'[2] and 'reactionary forces', was intended to divert Nazi-controlled 'public opinion' from the obvious inadequacies of the 'Third Reich' and focus it instead on new topics, values, and models explaining reality. This restructuring of the public sphere was no mere propaganda campaign; it was a mixture of targeted media deployment, Party-instigated terror and state coercion.

Under the dictatorship, restructuring the public sphere did not just mean using propaganda to lead public opinion in one direction or another, or influencing the public 'mood' in a particular manner. The regime was not primarily concerned with genuinely winning the hearts and minds of the German people. Instead the restructuring of the public sphere was achieved first and foremost as the everyday life of the population began to conform overtly to NS norms and thus give external expression to their acceptance of the regime's politics. The segregation of the Jewish minority, for example, was not only achieved by a series of administrative measures, but above all because the majority of the population demonstrated their distance from the Jews in the conduct of their everyday lives and were thus seen to be bowing to the instructions of the Party. Such behaviour had to occur in full public view, so that the general population's deliberate distancing from the Jewish minority could be presented in the state propaganda as the popular confirmation of the regime's policies. In this way, the 'boycott' of Jewish businesses and the prevention of contact between Jews and non-Jews (which was ensured in a variety of ways, from the numerous residence bans to accusations of 'racial defilement') took on a particular symbolic significance—not only encouraging further discrimination against Jews but demonstrating the apparent endorsement of the regime's racial policies by the people at large.

The innumerable illegal operations undertaken by Party activists against the Jews—boycotts, demonstrations, daubing buildings with paint, smashing windows, and so forth—also played an important role in the process of restructuring the public sphere. These were not merely instances of excessive activism on the part of radical Party supporters but part of a targeted attempt to impose segregation by means of many small-scale trials of strength both against the police, judiciary, and state administration and in the face of an indifferent majority amongst the population. It was a trial run for what was eventually to be the legally sanctioned isolation of the Jews, which would later be adopted by broader sections of the population, with even a degree of relief. The function of the so-called 'individual operations' was as stages in the step-by-step imposition of racial views onto society at large.

If the anti-Jewish campaign of spring and summer 1935 is seen in this broader context, therefore, it is clear that from the point of view of the regime it constituted the key to subordinating the whole of German society to the Nazi regime via the establishment of racial norms.

Anti-Jewish Violence

The hostility to Jewish businesses that had flared up again in the Christmas boycott of 1934 was revived with renewed vigour from early February 1935 in various areas of the Reich, fanned by appeals from regional NS leaders and the Party press. Immediately after the National Socialist triumph in the Saar Plebiscite of 13 January, when 90 per cent of voters opted for reunion with Germany, the foreign-policy considerations that had so far militated against the pursuit of radical anti-Jewish persecution no longer seemed to Party activists to be relevant. As part of the boycott Party activists organized demonstrations, smashing windows and assaulting Jews. These operations were focused in Pomerania, Hesse, the Rhineland, and Franconia. Alongside attacks on Jewish businesses and their proprietors the activists also targeted so-called 'race defilers'. Since the end of

1934 there had been increasing demands from within the Party for legal measures to prevent marriages or sexual relationships between Jews and non-Jews.[3] These unofficial steps were accompanied by measures sponsored by the state. When the Gestapo banned the raising of the swastika by Jews in February 1935, the Reich Minister of the Interior felt obliged to sanction this ruling by issuing a decree, which he did on 27 April.[4] Jews were excluded from the call-up to military service, initiated in May of that year.[5] In addition all émigrés returning to Germany, whether Jews or non-Jews, were sent to internment camps from the beginning of 1935.[6]

At the end of April the instances of anti-Semitic violence began to diminish. There were doubts expressed in various quarters about continuing operations that had not led to changes in how the general public shopped and which had been met with widespread criticism and opposition from the populace at large.[7]

There were evidently also foreign-policy considerations in play. The government was anxious to overcome what was by then its almost complete isolation on the international scene after the formation of the 'Stresa Front', the joint diplomatic reaction of France, Britain, and Italy to the German reintroduction of compulsory military service. Germany was particularly concerned to improve its relations with Great Britain. Hitler's Reichstag speech of 21 May, in which he announced the Reich's wish for peaceful coexistence with other nations and its willingness to seal non-aggression pacts, signalled a phase of détente in questions of foreign affairs. At the same time, negotiations with the British government were taking place, the source of much disquiet amongst the British public, which ended on 18 June with the signing of the Anglo-German Naval Agreement. In the period from the middle of April to the middle of June, therefore, further anti-Jewish violence would have put the foreign policy of the 'Third Reich' at some considerable risk.[8]

Whilst the violence continued to recede in the main areas of unrest from the end of April to the middle of May, by the end of May a second series of anti-Jewish operations was beginning in other areas, intensifying in June and reaching a high point in July 1935. The month of May presents a very uneven picture, therefore, since the first phase of violence was receding in some areas whilst the second was beginning in others.[9]

This unrest came to a climax with serious anti-Semitic violence in Munich at the end of May. There were open confrontations between members of the SA and SS on the one side and the police on the other. The reactions of high-ranking National Socialists demonstrate how inconvenient the government found these spectacular anti-Jewish incidents at this point.[10] The Reichsführer of the SS (Himmler), the Führer's Deputy (Hess), the Gauleiters of Cologne (Grohé) and Hessen-Nassau (Sprenger) all made public declarations of opposition to these 'individual operations'.[11]

In July the Party organization in Berlin made a renewed attempt to radicalize anti-Semitic policies by means of a wave of terror 'from below'.[12] Members of the

Hitler Youth had been organizing demonstrations outside Jewish businesses and restaurants since the beginning of June, and they spread rapidly throughout the city. The anti-Jewish mood had also been stoked up very significantly in a speech by Goebbels, who was also Gauleiter of Berlin, at the 30 June Party rally.

The situation escalated when the Berlin newspaper edited by Goebbels, *Der Angriff*, which was as rabidly aggressive as its name suggests, made an open appeal on 15 July for people to take physical action to prevent disruptions to a Swedish anti-Semitic film supposedly initiated by Jewish cinema-goers. On that evening there were riots on the Kurfürstendamm during which NS activists forced their way into cafés and forcibly drove out Jewish customers, and these ended in confrontations with the police. The events attracted the attention of the international press and led to the dismissal of the Chief of the Berlin Police Force, von Levetzow. Goebbels seized the initiative, issued a ban on the very acts of violence that he had himself been partly responsible for encouraging, and managed to restore at least a superficial level of goodwill between the police, the city authorities, the Gau leadership, and the SA, with a slogan promising the systematic cleansing of Berlin of 'Communists, Reactionaries, and Jews'.[13] The violence in Berlin was the starting gun for a new anti-Semitic propaganda campaign that now extended across the whole of the Reich.

The reports of the Centralverein, the Gestapo, the SPD in exile, and other sources show quite clearly that NS activists were once more carrying out large-scale anti-Jewish operations across the Reich from mid-July onwards. Regional centres for this violence were the Rhineland, Westphalia, Hesse, Pomerania, and East Prussia.[14] The list of the techniques typically employed includes blockading and obstructing Jewish businesses, threatening customers who tried to get past these measures, driving Jews from public swimming pools, smashing windows and daubing shopfronts with paint, desecrating Jewish cemeteries and synagogues, putting up anti-Jewish signs, and preventing the sale of goods to Jews. 'Race defilers' often had to be taken into protective custody by the Gestapo after attacks by Party activists. In many places Jewish economic life was destroyed altogether by the end of the summer as a result of these large-scale hate campaigns.

Radical forces within the Party made an attempt to make a link between the wave of anti-Jewish sentiment and a general reckoning with all 'enemies of the state' still present in Germany. Thus in many cities Party activists organized demonstrations against supposedly anti-social businessmen and senior officials who refused to bow to the demands of local Party bosses.[15] The newspaper *Der Stürmer*, edited by the radical Nuremberg Gauleiter, tried in June to summarize the whole campaign in a nutshell:

Who are the enemies of our state? We group them together under the heading 'reactionaries'. And this reaction is a tangled, many-coloured skein. We can see red flags. We can see coal-black flags. We can see flags of black, red, and gold. We can even see a few black, white, and red flags. The leader of this reactionary rabble is the Jew. The Jew is the general leading the whole reactionary army.[16]

At the end of July, before the anti-Jewish wave of terror and the campaigns of violence had reached their climax, there were already attempts being made by the NS leadership and the Reich government to stem the tide and to address the main anti-Semitic demands of the Party activists with the help of legal measures.

It was quite evident that the wave of terror was not achieving the level of public support that it had intended. It had not succeeded in its original aim of deploying the 'Jewish question' to improve the popular mood, which was still as low as it had been before, and was if anything getting worse during the summer.[17] In a circular to the Party of 9 August Martin Bormann (who ran the office of the Führer's deputy, Hess) informed Party functionaries that Hitler had given the order to all responsible Party offices to cease 'individual operations' against Jews.[18]

The Nuremberg Laws

At the same time as the Party leadership was making efforts to stem the tide of anti-Semitic violence, legal measures were being instituted with the aim of regulating the three key elements behind the campaign of violence: 'racial defilement' and 'mixed marriages'; economic discrimination; and the exclusion of Jews from German citizenship.

Demands for penalties against 'racial miscegenation' were central to the NSDAP's racial policies. In March 1930 the NSDAP group in the Reichstag had introduced a draft bill in this area that made provision for the death penalty in severe cases.[19] Before 1933 the NSDAP leadership had already worked up several draft bills aimed at the 'separation of races'.[20] In 1933, after preliminary work conducted by a group of experts selected from amongst Party functionaries and civil servants, the Prussian Minister of Justice had proposed a draft bill, but it was not taken up by the commission that had been set up to manage the reform of criminal law.[21] After a law had banned 'mixed marriages' for soldiers and reservists in May 1935,[22] and district courts had started to cover for registrars who were refusing to marry Jews and non-Jews,[23] the Reich Minister of the Interior, Wilhelm Frick, publicly announced on 25 July that a law against 'mixed marriages' was in preparation. On the following day he called upon registrars to postpone issuing notices of marriage between Aryans and Jews until further notice, since formal legal regulation of this matter was to follow shortly.[24] The Ministry of Justice had already developed a draft law to combat 'marriages detrimental to the German people', which was intended to prevent marriages with both 'members of alien races' and 'people with hereditary illnesses'.[25] At the Gau Party rally in Essen on 4 August, Frick announced the legal settlement of the 'Jewish question'; at the same event Goebbels had already made an unambiguous demand for an end to marriages between Jews and non-Jews.[26] On 20 August Franz Gürtner, the Minister for Justice, also declared that legal measures would shortly be put in place.[27] What was originally planned was to declare a ban on 'mixed marriages' together with a ban on marriages considered undesirable for eugenic reasons in a law against 'marriages detrimental to the German people'. After the Blood Protection Law (*Blutschutzgesetz*) was passed in September the second issue was left to the Marital Health Law (*Ehegesundheitsgesetz*) in October.[28]

The second major legal anti-Semitic assault demanded by the National Socialists with increasing vigour in the spring and summer of 1935 was the deprivation of citizenship. This was one of the NSDAP's most long-standing demands and had been included in their Party programme of 1920.[29] Following an initiative from the Reich Ministry of the Interior work had begun on a Reich Citizenship Law as early as July 1933, and it was intended to demote 'non-Aryans' to the level of second-class citizens. Preliminary activities were suspended in September 1933, evidently in response to international criticism of these plans.[30]

However, from early 1935 onwards demands from within the Reich Ministry of the Interior were being voiced publicly with increasing urgency. On 26 April Frick announced the new version of the Citizenship Law.[31] The Immigration Law passed in May 1935 had already created room for refusing citizenship to Jews and others who were unwelcome for reasons of race by removing existing immigration rights and transferring responsibilities for decisions to the state authorities.

Under pressure from the continuing boycotts, the third of the National Socialists' key anti-Semitic demands—the judicial restriction of the economic activities of the Jewish minority—took a particular turn in summer 1935.

The way in which the organized street violence was instrumentalized is made clear in a situation report by the section of the SD, the Party intelligence service, responsible for Jewish affairs in August 1935.[32] 'It will not be possible to tackle the Jewish problem thoroughly as long as there are no unambiguous laws in place. This is the situation which gives rise to the individual operations that have so often been condemned.... In order to put a stop in future to these acts of terror, which are committed by National Socialists out of inner conviction, or to be able to identify when operations are undertaken by groups hostile to us, it is desirable, as soon as possible: (1) that a unified policy is developed for all the ministries handling the Jewish question, and (2) that effective laws are passed that will demonstrate to the people that the Jewish question is being dealt with from the top.'

In a speech delivered in Königsberg on 18 August the Reich Minister for Economic Affairs, Schacht, protested against further 'individual operations'.[33] What is more, the speech contained remarkably forthright criticisms of the methods by which Jews were excluded from the economic life of the country. It was, however, in no sense opposed to economic discrimination against Jews, as the interdepartmental meeting held two days later at Schacht's invitation was to show.

At this meeting there was general agreement about the need to put a stop to the violence and the infringements and to pass instead a series of anti-Jewish laws. In line with the discussions that had been held for months, the ban on 'racial defilement', restricted citizenship rights for Jews, and targeted economic measures were at the forefront of the talks.[34]

The anti-Jewish violence only began to recede in September 1935 after Frick had circulated a decree which was dated 20 August but only reached some of the local authorities in early September. In Hitler's name, further 'individual operations against Jews' were forbidden and infringements of this ban would result in the perpetrators being treated as 'agents provocateurs, rebels, and enemies of the state'.[35] In addition, the Party also began to show its clear opposition to the 'individual operations'—Himmler, for example, in an order of 16 August,[36] and the National Socialist Organization of Small Businesses in a statement on 17 August,[37] various of the Gauleiter towards the end of the month,[38] and Streicher in a series of mass meetings[39]—in order to convince the Party activists of the seriousness of the ban on 'individual operations', even though the process of enlightenment took several months.

In August, in the run-up to the Party Conference the campaigns against the Catholic Church and the 'reactionary forces' were scaled down. The decision to step down the campaign against 'political Catholicism' and the Stahlhelm was announced by Hitler on 17 August at a meeting of the official Party speakers in Nuremberg, which was part of the preparations for the Party rally.[40]

Shortly before the start of the rally the Nazi leadership had decided to call a special meeting of the Reichstag in Nuremberg to pass a special 'Flag Law' and have the swastika declared the only legitimate national flag.[41] On 13 September, after the Reich Party Conference had begun, the spontaneous decision was taken to use the session of the Reichstag to pass the long-awaited ban on 'racial defilement', which had already been drafted by civil servants.[42]

On the evening of the same day the 'Jewish expert' of the Reich Ministry of the Interior, Bernhard Lösener, was summoned to Nuremberg where, according to his own report, he was told the following day by Pfundtner and Stuckart, both joint State Secretaries for the Interior, that he had to have ready for proclamation at the Party rally the day after a 'Jewish Law' that would regulate 'mixed marriages' and sexual relations between Jews and non-Jewish Germans.

Lösener portrays graphically how the group of ministerial advisers spent that Saturday producing several drafts of the law that were all sent back by Hitler, who was heavily influenced by Gerhard Wagner, leader of the Reich doctors' organization. The pressure on this group must have increased to an almost intolerable level on the Saturday evening when Hitler suddenly demanded in addition a Reich Citizenship Act or *Reichsbürgergesetz* by the following morning.

Some historians in the past have tended to interpret Lösener's memoirs as a vivid depiction of the largely improvised style of government that characterized the 'Third Reich', but they are quite evidently a document of self-justification. Lösener caricatured the unusual circumstances in which the Nuremberg Laws were finally formulated to distract attention from the fact that their substance corresponded closely with what had been planned for months by the bureaucrats in the ministries, and in a more general form from as early as 1933.[43]

The Reich Citizenship Law eventually passed by the Reichstag put a definitive end to the equality of citizenship enjoyed by Jews in the whole of Germany since 1871, but significantly hollowed out since 1933, by introducing a distinction between 'nationals' (*Staatsangehörige*) and 'citizens of the Reich' (*Reichsbürger*). 'Citizens of the Reich', or in the words of the law 'bearers of full political rights in accordance with law', were 'those nationals of German or related blood who demonstrate by their behaviour that they are willing and suitable to serve the German People and Reich faithfully'. The law did not therefore make access to 'citizenship of the Reich' dependent solely on racial criteria but left room for imposing political conditions for the acquisition of such citizenship. The rights of a 'citizen of the Reich' were to be conferred by a 'Certificate of Reich Citizenship', but more detailed criteria were never formally established.[44]

The 'Law for the Protection of German Blood and German Honour' prohibited marriages and extramarital sexual relations between 'Jews and nationals of German or related blood'. Jews were not permitted to employ female Aryan servants under 45 in their households and were not permitted to raise the Reich flag or the national flag.[45]

Hitler stated at the Party rally that the Blood Protection Law was 'an attempt at the legal settlement of a problem, which, if this proved a failure, would have to be entrusted by law to the National Socialist Party for a definitive solution' and this made it perfectly clear that the street violence of the Party activists had only been suspended and could at any point be resumed so as to continue escalating the persecution of the Jews.[46]

The reports on the public mood that focused on the reception of the two anti-Jewish laws by the population at large offer a mixed picture. They contain enthusiastic approval (especially amongst Party members), acceptance, indifference, and rejection (above all in Catholic and socialist circles). The laws were quietly accepted by the overwhelming majority of the people, but to a varied extent, and this acceptance was noticeably often linked with the expectation that the anti-Jewish 'individual operations' would henceforth cease. At the same time some reservations were voiced about the racist ideology that lay at the root of the laws' conception.[47]

On the other hand, however, the reports also show an increasing distance from the Jewish minority and a lack of interest or indifference towards the fate of the Jews. In particular the reports of the Social Democratic Party in exile make it plain that the anti-Semitic propaganda was aiming for a deeper, more subtle effect: the idea that there might be such a thing as a 'Jewish question' was beginning to gain in resonance amongst the people, the working class included.[48]

The National Socialists' attempts to restructure the public sphere in conformity with racial norms via its campaigns of 1935 was successful in that the policy of segregation initiated by the Nuremberg Laws was evidently gaining in at least passive acceptance by the majority of the people, in one form or another. From the point of view of the regime, it was important that the principle of judicial discrimination against, and the separation of the Jewish minority had been established—without any particular enthusiasm outside Party circles, but also without meeting with notable resistance from the population. Sufficient conditions for continuing the persecution of the Jews had thus been achieved.

An Apparent Lull in Anti-Jewish Policy 1936–1937

Debates about the Definition of Jews

After the promulgation of the anti-Semitic laws of September 1935 two problems occupied centre-stage in further discussions about anti-Jewish policy. These were first the economic measures against German Jews that had long been called for but were not put into law in the Nuremberg Laws, and second—but closely related—the exact and conclusive definition of 'Jewish half-breeds' (*Mischlinge*).[49]

As early as 23 September Ministers Frick and Schacht agreed upon a catalogue of suggestions for further constraining the economic position of the Jewish minority by judicial and administrative means. Schacht was concerned above all to ensure that all planned measures were put into practice as quickly as possible and for the future position of the Jews to be fixed once and for all, in order to minimize superfluous economic unrest. It was important in this context to define clearly and precisely the group known as 'Jewish half-breeds'.[50]

There was disagreement on this question between the stance adopted by the Ministry for the Interior—where the general feeling was that 'half-Jews' should be made citizens of the Reich—and the Führer's Deputy (represented by Gauleiter Wagner)—who wished in general to treat this group as Jews. After lengthy negotiations (Hitler avoided making a decision) there was eventual agreement on a compromise enshrined in the 'First Decree Pursuant to the Reich Citizenship Law' of 14 November 1935.[51]

According to this ordinance a person was defined as a Jew if he was descended from 'at least three racially wholly Jewish grandparents'; a Jew was not permitted to be a citizen of the Reich. However, provisional Reich citizenship (although there were regulations discussed in 1936 and 1937,[52] they were not actually passed) was also to be granted to 'Jewish half-breeds', which is to say those with one or two Jewish grandparents, as long as they were not 'Jews by definition' (*Geltungsjuden*).

People were in future to be treated as 'Jews by definition'—and thus equivalent to Jews—if they were 'half-breeds' with at least two grandparents to whom one or more of the following criteria applied: that they were members of the Jewish religious community, that they were in a marital partnership with a Jew, or that they were descended from a marriage with a Jew that had been joined after the Nuremberg Laws came into force or from a non-marital partnership that had been begun after this point.

On the same day the 'First Decree Pursuant to the Blood Protection Law' was passed, amongst the provisions of which was that 'Jewish half-breeds' with two Jewish grandparents required special permission to marry an 'Aryan'.[53] This permission could be granted by a Reich Commission for Marriage Permits, which was to be established by the Reich Minister for the Interior and the Führer's Deputy. In reality, however, the Party representatives on this body—which immediately changed its title to 'Reich Commission for the Protection of German Blood'—almost always voted against, so its meetings were suspended in 1936 and applications were thenceforth treated as a purely administrative matter.[54]

After the 'Jewish half-breeds' were officially defined, there were further discussions about legislation for anti-Jewish economic measures but they did not result in any concrete action. On the contrary, as the Olympic year of 1936 grew ever closer, a lull in anti-Jewish policy began to set in. Neither more drastic anti-Semitic legislation nor more radical persecution took place. Even the murder of the NSDAP National Group Leader (*Landesgruppenleiter*) in Switzerland, Wilhelm Gustloff, by David Frankfurter in February 1936 did not result in any immediate acts of revenge on the part of the National Socialists.[55]

Nevertheless, even without the more spectacular acts of persecution, continuing attempts to marginalize German Jews in the public sphere still left them in a steadily worsening situation. In particular, the wave of boycotts did not diminish after the Nuremberg Laws, and because Party activists believed that anti-Jewish economic laws were about to be passed they pressed on with the boycotts in the furthest corners of the German Reich.[56]

The Four-Year Plan: Intensifying the Displacement of Jews from Economic Life

Once the Olympic Games were over, and thus once Berlin was no longer in the international spotlight, the regime immediately set about intensifying the persecution of the Jews, and the plans for displacing Jews from the economic life of the country that had been put on hold in the autumn of 1935 were now once more at the heart of planning. Those involved, however, could not get round the fact that in 1936 the Reich was facing a very precarious situation regarding raw materials and a currency crisis, and in these circumstances anti-Jewish measures would certainly damage foreign trade and thus have negative effects on the rapid pace of rearmament. Goering was appointed Commissioner for Raw Materials and Currency in April 1936, and in October of the same year was put in charge of the Four-Year Plan, and this showed that the regime was making attempts both to manage the crisis and somehow to mediate between the desire to displace the Jews economically and forcibly expel them and the need to increase the momentum of rearmament.

It is important not to overlook the close link between the Four-Year Plan (the centralized direction of the regime's rearmament plans) and the anti-Jewish policy. This link was present from very early on, and for Hitler rearmament within the context of the Four-Year Plan was the decisive instrument for waging war on 'international Jewry' supposedly hiding behind the mask of 'Bolshevism'. According to the introduction to the memorandum on the Four-Year Plan that Hitler gave to Goering when he was appointed:

Since the outbreak of the French Revolution the world has been racing ever more quickly towards a new conflict, whose most extreme solution is called Bolshevism but whose content and aims are rather to remove the social strata who currently lead mankind and replace them with a network of Jews spread across the whole world.[57]

The fact that from the outset the Four-Year Plan was conceived as fulfilling an important function in the context of a comprehensive anti-Jewish policy was underlined by those responsible for the Four-Year Plan, at the beginning of 1942, when the 'Final Solution' was fully operational.[58]

The attacks on Jewish wealth were, moreover, one of the original pillars of the Four-Year Plan. Hitler himself had used his memorandum to demand a law 'which would make all Jews liable for whatever damage was sustained by the German economy and the German people as a result of individual instances of such criminality'—an intention that was only to be put into practice after the November 1938 pogroms. The memorandum also contained Hitler's demand that hoarding hard currency should incur the death penalty—something he called 'economic sabotage'—and this too was a demand that future developments would prove was aimed in the first instance at Jewish 'economic saboteurs'.[59]

On 7 July 1936 Goering, in his role as leader of the 'raw materials and currency team' (the group that preceded the Four-Year Plan) had already given Heydrich the task of setting up a 'Currency Investigation Office' (*Devisenfahndungsamt*), which was to be an authority reporting to Goering 'personally and directly'. This office was principally designed to make sure that the customs search and currency investigation authorities applied the complicated currency regulations against Jews with excessive rigour so as to secure pretexts for the financial authorities to 'secure' Jewish money. In taking on his new responsibilities Heydrich thus assumed an important function in the coordination of the efforts of the Security Police, the Four-Year Plan, and the financial management of the expropriation of the German Jews.[60]

It was therefore both an aim and one of the functions of the Four-Year Plan to intensify the persecution of the Jews, which raises the question of whether this does not suggest new grounds for reconsidering the role of Goering in NS anti-Jewish policy development. The letter of appointment that Goering wrote for Heydrich in July 1936 was the first link in a chain of authorizations issued to the Head of the Security Police by the Reichsmarschall. It was followed by Heydrich's appointment as head of the 'Central Office for Jewish Emigration' in January 1939 and ended in the authorization given in July 1941 to make 'preparations for the final solution of the Jewish question'. It is not the case that Goering only took on a central role in Jewish policy after 9 November 1938 in order to clean up the piles of broken glass that resulted from the pogrom; the history of his active engagement in the 'Jewish question' evidently begins more than two years previously.

The civil service resumed its attempts at excluding Jews from the economic sphere immediately after the end of the Olympic Games at a conference of senior government officials that took place on 29 September 1936.[61] Here the representatives of the Reich Ministries of the Interior and of Finance and of the Führer's Deputy initially came to an agreement that the common goal of the 'complete and total emigration' of the Jews should mean the 'emigration of Jews under all possible circumstances'. According to the Permanent Secretary, Stuckart, 'all measures in the area of Jewish policy should be directed at the achievement of this goal. Economic activity on the part of the Jews should only be permitted in so far as it constitutes supporting themselves, but their economic and political situation should not be permitted to suppress their desire to emigrate.' Walter Sommer, a senior official on the staff of the Führer's Deputy, added that 'rich Jews will not generally be keen to emigrate. The Jews should therefore not be given very much room for economic activity. But on the other hand, a Jewish proletariat should also be prevented from forming.'

This premise—the restriction of Jewish economic activity and the prevention of proletarianization—was used as the basis for a series of measures. However, discussion revealed that, because of the general economic situation in Germany, it was necessary to step back from implementing most of the suggested anti-Jewish measures: there was no appetite either for imposing on the public purse a general ban against dealing with Jews or for requiring the enforced dismissal of all Jewish salesmen active in German firms.

On 1 December 1936 two laws were finally passed that put into practice Hitler's demands in the memorandum on the Four-Year Plan. One was a law against economic sabotage assigning the death penalty to anyone transferring their wealth abroad,[62] the other was a modification of the law on currency management that included so-called security measures against anyone suspected of transferring currency abroad.[63] Both laws were subsequently to provide the basis for the largely arbitrary confiscation of large sums of money, mainly from Jews, and for condemning those who had such sums—'economic saboteurs'—to long periods of detention.

In addition to this, as 1936 moved into 1937 the civil service produced three more drafts for anti-Semitic laws. They responded to the plans articulated in the memorandum on the Four-Year Plan for introducing a 'special Jewish tax', for identifying and labelling Jewish businesses, and for formulating a Reich citizenship law.[64] All three drafts were put on hold after further consultation in the spring and summer of 1937. In fact, the exclusion of Jews from the economy that began in earnest at the end of 1936 was at first not achieved by spectacular acts of legislation but via more subtle policies of exclusion and isolation that took many forms.

In the first of these, the boycott of Jewish retail trade took on such proportions that the complete economic annihilation of the few Jews remaining in this sphere could confidently be predicted in the near future. The records of the Centralverein contain many examples of campaigns against Jewish business activity that were implemented with renewed vigour during the Christmas period at the end of 1936.[65] Above all it was on the rural population that pressure was applied to break off business contacts with Jewish cattle dealers. Gestapo reports for 1937 are unanimous, however, in suggesting that despite intensive propaganda many farmers were not prepared to take the initiative in breaking off contact with Jews. In the face of this situation, the Gestapo undertook an operation across the whole area of the Reich in the summer of 1937. With the support of the local authorities, the local police and the Reich Food Estate, farmers who continued to trade with Jews were arrested.[66] Through the continuation and intensification of the 'boycott', conditions were achieved under which many Jews were forced to sell their firms in haste and at less than their true value, only to lose the proceeds in large part or even entirely in the maze of currency regulations.

A second element in the politics of exclusion can be seen in Heydrich's nomination as the head of the Currency Investigation Office in summer 1936 and the introduction of the law authorizing currency management alterations in December of that year, which effectively completed the mechanisms for confiscating the assets of Jews suspected of being about to emigrate ('im Auswanderungsverdacht'). The completely arbitrary nature of this process emerges clearly from the fact that emigration, itself the very goal of NS anti-Jewish policies, was now being used as a pretext to secure assets for the state. The financial authorities and the branches of the Reichsbank had to cooperate actively in the compilation of the documentation necessary to support a suspicion of emigration.[67] By June 1938, according to a communication from the Currency Investigation Office, the Customs Investigation Centres were 'almost exclusively' concerned with 'securing' the assets of Jews who had raised suspicions that they were intending to leave the country.[68]

Via a network of special submissions and regulations for the granting of exemptions, the assets of Jewish businessmen were systematically appropriated by the state. According to paragraph 1 of the Tax Adjustment Law of October 1934, Inland Revenue offices were required to interpret all taxation regulations in accordance with the 'National Socialist world-view', which was in effect equivalent to a blanket instruction to apply the severest imaginable criteria in dealing with Jewish taxpayers.[69] Eventually, as the regulations concerning the tax on leaving the Reich introduced in 1931 were tightened up, and as the premium to be paid on capital transfers was raised ever higher—reaching the level of 90 per cent in June 1938—the assets of emigrating Jews were plundered almost entirely.[70]

Another aspect is demonstrated by the various measures taken to force Jews to hand their business over to 'Aryan' owners or to have them liquidated, often to the advantage of 'Aryan' competitors.[71] The so-called 'Aryanization' of Jewish firms—their transfer to a non-Jewish proprietor usually at a price far below their market-value—was a process that had begun long before it received formal legal sanction in 1938. To all appearances this 'creeping Aryanization' took the form of run-of-the-mill business sales, but in reality such deals were often the enforced result of the threats and obstructions to Jewish economic activity that have been described above. As a direct result of the boycott, from 1933 onwards the number of Jewish businesses being 'Aryanized' grew year on year and the sale prices dropped as increasing pressure was applied to their owners. In addition to the direct sale of some firms, others were 'indirectly Aryanized' as a result of liquidation proceedings that allowed the competition to strip them of their plant and equipment and eventually take over entirely what was left of each firm or the relevant sector of the market.[72] Barkai estimates that by 1935 some 20–5 per cent of all Jewish businesses had been liquidated or transferred to non-Jewish ownership.[73]

The process of 'Aryanization' was such that direct support from the police and the judiciary meant that the buyer was often in a position to force the seller to 'Aryanize' and to tailor the terms of transfer to suit his own best interests. In the very earliest years of the 'Third Reich' accusations of 'racial defilement', or arrests on suspicion of commercial irregularities, or arbitrary intervention on the part of the Gestapo all proved suitable means to ensure that Jewish proprietors became compliant.[74]

According to an analysis of 'Aryanization' reports in the *Jüdische Rundschau* undertaken by the German historian Helmut Genschel, after a temporary lull in 1936 and a reduction in the first half of 1937, there was a slow but significant rise in the instances of 'Aryanization' in the third and fourth quartiles of 1937, which was followed in 1938 by a much more rapid increase in takeovers.[75] Since 1936 the Gestapo had played a regular part in the processes of 'Aryanization'. The Party's Gau economic advisers played a central role and their assent to the transfer of Jewish assets gradually became a necessary part of the process.[76]

Even without legal measures to restrict Jewish commercial activity, and without large-scale anti-Jewish rallies, the process of commercially displacing the German Jews continued 'inexorably in the years 1936 and 1937'.[77] The so-called 'creeping Aryanization' took place according to a logic that was characterized in the 1937 report of the North-Eastern Sector of the SD thus: 'In some areas it has been possible to eliminate Jewish influence immediately using laws and decrees passed by the state, but in the commercial sector it has had to be undermined only gradually.'[78]

Increases in Measures to Expel the Jews

With its efforts in the latter half of 1936 to expel the Jews from the economic sphere, the National Socialist regime was pursuing two main goals: the financing of rearmament and the expulsion of the Jewish minority from Germany. Economic pressure was intended to increase the Jewish population's willingness to emigrate and to improve the incoming flow of capital for the state.

After the first wave of emigration in 1933, when some 37,000 people of Jewish origin left Germany, 1934 saw approximately 23,000 leave; in 1935 there were 21,000 and in 1936 some 25,000.[79] In the latter half of 1937 it became more and more difficult for German Jews to find a place that would take them. On the one hand, after the announcement of British plans to divide Palestine and, after the Arab revolts of April 1936–8, the number of Jews leaving for the British Mandate went down; on the other, there were increasing signs that countries that had so far been willing to accept Jews who wished to emigrate were becoming more restrictive in their immigration policies, as South Africa and Brazil had already shown in 1937. Whilst it is true that some 23,000 Jews left Germany in 1937, the reports of the Jewish Reich National Association indicate that the numbers emigrating began to stagnate in the third quarter of 1937.[80]

During the whole of 1937, representatives of the National Socialist regime were occupied with the question of whether increased emigration to Palestine was desirable from a German perspective if this were to improve chances for the foundation of a Jewish state. The regime had to decide whether it wished to continue its policies intended to drive out the Jews without taking account of the international situation or of their consequences for German foreign policy.

At the beginning of the year the Reich government's policy on the Palestine question seemed clear: on 16 January 1937, the Reich Minister of the Interior informed the German Foreign Office that it was planning to continue to support the policy of Jewish emigration regardless of the destination countries.[81] But after it began to emerge in early 1937 that Britain's Peel Commission might opt for a Jewish state in Palestine, on 1 June the Foreign Minister, Neurath, sent guidelines to the embassies in London and Baghdad and to the Consul General in Jerusalem in which he made it crystal clear that he was against the formation of a Jewish state or 'anything resembling a state'. Such a state would not be sufficient, he said, to receive all the Jews, and like the Vatican for the Catholic Church or Moscow for the Komintern, it would serve as an internationally recognized power base for world Jewry.[82] As formulated in a general order sent to all German consulates by the Foreign Office on 22 June, in contrast to the expected recommendations of the Peel Commission, there was 'significant German interest in making sure that the fragmented condition of the Jews was preserved'.[83]

However, at an inter-ministerial meeting on 29 July the representative from the Reich Ministry of the Interior announced that Hitler was in favour of emigration to Palestine and thus of 'concentrating' the Jews in that area—in direct contradiction of the idea of 'fragmenting' Jewish emigration put forward in the Foreign Office order the previous month. On 21 September, however, this was modified by a representative from the Reich Ministry of the Interior to clarify that the 'Führer' was clearly in favour of the emigration of the Jews, but that he had not made any specific comments on Palestine.[84] Another declaration of principle on Hitler's part has been preserved from January 1938, and from that it is clear that he was positive about emigration to Palestine.[85] This established that the continued expulsion of German Jews, using all available means, took priority over any foreign-policy reservations.

The *Judenpolitik* of the Security Service

In addition to the state administration, the Party, the Four-Year Plan, and the Gestapo, in spring 1937 the division of the Party's Security Service (SD) responsible for Jewish affairs increased its involvement in anti-Semitic persecution. Previously this division—which, as a part of the Party organization, had no claim to any official state executive functions—had concentrated mainly on the collection and analysis of information, but this situation changed when Dieter Wisliceny took over its running in April 1937. At this point a group of relatively young, self-confident activists, including Herbert Hagen, Theodor Dannecker, and Adolf Eichmann, set about reforming the activities of the division.

This group very quickly claimed to be a 'brains trust' endowed with exceptional expertise, and its first task was to develop a consistent conception for future 'Jewish policy'. The self-appointed 'intellectuals' of the Division responsible for Jewish affairs designated the prime goal of 'Jewish policy' as the 'removal' (*Entfernung*) of the Jews from Germany and in this respect they were to all appearances working in line with the various official authorities working on 'Jewish policy'. However, the SD specialists were unusually consistent in their stress on the priority of 'Zionist emigration' and all other main elements of future 'Jewish policy' were subordinated to this main aim, including the 'crushing' of German-Jewish organizations that promoted assimilation, the 'exclusion' of Jews from the economic life of the country, and limited support for (or rather manipulation of) Zionist activities.[86]

In order to assume the leading role they wanted to occupy in the area of 'Jewish policy', this Division's tactics included muscling in on the executive functions of the Gestapo, via which, as Dannecker noted, 'the struggle was being carried out on an exclusively administrative level and [which] for the most part lacked high-level understanding of the subject matter'.[87] These tactics were very much in the spirit of Himmler's 'operational order' of 1 July 1937: all 'matters in principle concerned with the Jews' were thenceforth to be dealt with by the SD, whereas all individual cases or implementation measures were to be the province of the Gestapo.[88] By proceeding skilfully the SD could harness the state apparatus for its own measures concerned with 'principle'.

The Division made a first attempt to break into the direction of Jewish persecution in May 1937 at the point when the international Upper Silesia Accord signed in 1922 was due to expire and when, after a two-month transition period, the German anti-Jewish laws were due to come into force; this had previously been prevented by minority protection measures set out in the Accord. Eichmann, who had been sent to Breslau, now set about seizing all the Jewish civil servants, lawyers, doctors, artists, and others who were to be removed from their positions so that measures against them could be set in train as soon as the transition period had expired.[89]

In the last months of 1937, the position taken by the SD, according to which an increase in economic pressure on the German Jews and limited support for Zionists would force the pace of emigration, in particular to Palestine, underwent something of a crisis. Unrest in the Arab countries meant that emigration to Palestine was decreasing, and at the same time many countries were tightening up their immigration policies, not least because of the impression made abroad by the rigour of German activity in Upper Silesia and because of a widespread fear of mass exodus by German Jews that had been prompted by the intensification of anti-Jewish policy.[90]

The SD reacted to the developing crisis in its deportation policy by sending its specialists Hagen and Eichmann on a—not particularly successful—fact-finding mission to Egypt and Palestine,[91] and by setting up a conference in Berlin in November 1937 for the Jewish specialists of the higher echelons of the SD.[92] The essence of the papers given at this conference was that the persecution of the Jews needed to be intensified and that further measures were needed to enforce Jewish emigration. The SD felt it could resolve the dilemma that support for emigration to Palestine produced—the wholly undesirable emergence of a Jewish state—by calling a halt immediately after the conference to the limited support (or tolerance) it had hitherto shown for Zionist ambitions. This change of direction was not to be declared to Jewish organizations, since, in the words of a working directive issued by the Division, it was 'wholly and exclusively' a question of 'convincing the Jewish population of Germany that its only way out is emigration'.[93] They were to be driven out at all costs, even if it was not certain where they were to go.

CHAPTER 3

INTERIM CONCLUSIONS: THE REMOVAL OF JEWS FROM GERMAN SOCIETY, THE FORMATION OF THE NATIONAL SOCIALIST 'PEOPLE'S COMMUNITY', AND ITS CONSEQUENCES FOR JEWISH LIFE IN GERMANY

At this point I should like to pause to consider the concept of *Judenpolitik* or anti-Jewish policy that is at the heart of this book and to attempt to set the anti-Jewish measures described so far into the context of the policies of the regime as a whole. My central thesis is that the overall effect of the individual measures taken against Jews—but also the measures taken against other groups who were being persecuted for racially motivated reasons—far exceeded the mere exclusion of a group labelled as an enemy by the Nazis. Indeed *Judenpolitik* and in a broader sense racial policy in general was an essential constitutive element in the whole process of extending the National Socialists' grasp on power.

Let us remember that the key aim of the National Socialist movement was to create a racially homogeneous 'Aryan' people's community. This utopian goal was impossible to achieve via 'positive' means, and was hardly even adequately articulated: the concepts of race that underlay it were defined in a wholly arbitrary manner and were unfit for practical politics; it was in no manner clear what the 'Aryan' or 'purely German' character of the utopian ideal was to be.

In practical terms, therefore, the National Socialists approached the formation of the 'people's community' in a negative manner, via measures that discriminated against, excluded, and ultimately 'expunged' those who were supposedly racially inferior or alien. These negative measures were to a large extent substitutes for the unrealizable positive, utopian goals the National Socialists envisaged. The process that was set in train was appalling: the longer it took to fulfil positive promises, the more the negative measures had to be intensified and augmented. Hans Mommsen's description of the process as one of 'cumulative radicalization' is an appropriate description of it. It cannot be emphasized too strongly that anti-Jewish policy occupied an absolutely central role within this process.

As we have seen, in the first years after coming to power the National Socialists systematically segregated the Jewish minority in Germany in pursuit above all of the goal of reorienting the public sphere in Germany. Distancing the general population from the Jews via massive propaganda, acts of terrorism on the part of Party activists, and coercive measures applied by the state was aimed at winning the assent of the population at large to a form of politics that was qualitatively new, based on racist principles. Instituting the hegemony of racism was identical with enforcing the NSDAP's claims to power.

With the stabilization of the regime after 1934 the National Socialists were able to use their racist policies to move beyond the reorientation of public life in order to penetrate and fundamentally restructure individual spheres of people's existences. By the mid-1930s at the latest it is clearly evident that the various racist measures implemented were coming to form a coherent independent field of politics at the heart of the National Socialist dictatorship, a field that can be compared with other more traditional areas such as social policy or economic policy. The emerging 'racial politics' was concerned with excluding certain minorities from individual areas of social life so as to effect a radical alteration of German society as a whole, and anti-Jewish policy was a central part of this undertaking.

Since racial and anti-Jewish policy were key concepts in their aim for the comprehensive and fundamental remodelling of society the Nazis gradually but systematically set about reordering all areas of life. 'Racial policy' and 'anti-Jewish policy' can therefore not only be seen as independent spheres of politics but as their practical implementation progressed there also developed the potential to affect, interfere with, and alter more traditional policy areas.

'Clearing the Jews' from individual areas of life, removing 'Jewish influence' on Germany, meant that these areas themselves fell under the control of National Socialism, the driving force behind the process of change, and were significantly transformed and made more compatible with National Socialist aims and principles. What is true of 'anti-Jewish policy' in the narrow sense is true in the wider sense for 'racial policy' as a whole.

Implementing their anti-Jewish and broader racial policies was central for the National Socialists' exercise of power. This is not meant in a functionalist sense, suggesting that the persecution of Jews and other racially defined groups was merely instrumental or the side effect of a 'pure' form of power politics prioritized by the National Socialists. On the contrary, it is important to understand that the implementation of anti-Jewish and racial policies was the fundamental prerequisite for the National Socialists' exercise of power, that the Nazis used it to put into practice the core of their claims for a new order. 'Racial cleansing' or 'removal of the Jews' were inextricably intertwined with the Nazis' ambitions for total domination.

In what follows I shall use a series of examples to show how anti-Jewish measures went far beyond the persecution of the Jewish minority and transformed whole areas of people's lives by bringing them under the control of the National Socialists. At the same time this provides an opportunity for looking in more detail and more systematically at some aspects of the history of Jewish persecution than has so far been attempted.

I have shown elsewhere how racial politics was used by the National Socialist state as a decisive instrument for penetrating the private spheres of individual citizens and indeed of abolishing these altogether. By the time the Nuremberg Laws had been introduced and 'eugenic' measures had been introduced for certain sectors of the population such policies had become state-sanctioned. Suspending the principle of political equality for all citizens and introducing the certification of Aryan ancestry in various areas of public life makes it clear how far the social status of every individual was affected by the influence of racial politics.

What I intend to explore here is the relationship between the exclusion of Jews and other minorities and the implementation of National Socialist rule on the basis of a number of examples: the transformation of 'social politics', which was mutated into 'National Socialist welfare provision' via the exclusion of Jews and others; the effects of removing Jews from German schools on education policy and its National Socialist remodelling; the consequences of the dominance of racially inspired approaches in the areas of science; and the National Socialists' usurpation of the cultural life of the country, including important areas of everyday culture.

The Exclusion of Jews in Need from Social Policy and its Transformation into National Socialist 'Welfare Provision'

Jewish community welfare services in National Socialist Germany were faced with the problem of having to help an ever-increasing number of impoverished, ageing people, who were progressively being neglected by the state's social services systems.

In summer 1935, many local authorities were beginning to discriminate against the members of the Jewish population who were in need of support in favour of other clienteles. Jews were also excluded from the 'Winter Relief Organization of the German People' that was essentially run on voluntary lines. Here as in other areas of public life, however, the authorities could not proceed arbitrarily: even the Nuremberg Laws did not fundamentally alter the claims of Jewish Germans for social contributions from the state.[1]

After the end of 1935 Jewish welfare agencies were compelled by numerous municipalities to declare the sums they disbursed for support and the public agencies began by deducting these from the state provision. From the same period Jews were increasingly excluded from certain special measures and donations that were not specifically stipulated by law. After 1936 Jews were treated separately from others in need of welfare support, with counters set aside for them in social security offices or accommodation in segregated refuge homes. And social security support was cut.

This all happened not because of any intensification in legal measures for persecution but because the welfare agencies in the local authorities devoted considerable imagination and energy to the development of ever newer and different ways to discriminate against Jews in receipt of support.[2] The German Council of Municipalities (Deutscher Gemeindetag) played an important role in this process of cumulative exclusion; it was used to control and standardize community policies in the 64,000 German municipalities. At a meeting of the Council of Municipalities in June 1937 there was general agreement that such practices be brought into line across the country and, according to one suggestion, Jews should be equated with foreigners when it came to welfare provision.[3] During the following year cities and the Council of Municipalities would come up with a series of new measures for further discriminating against Jews who were in need of support.[4] After the November 1938 pogrom these initiatives were to culminate in an order from the Reich Ministry of the Interior that provided for the complete exclusion of Jews from public welfare provision.[5]

Discrimination against Jews in need, as well as similar measures against Gypsies and 'asocials',[6] contributed significantly to changing the character of social policy as a whole. It was transformed into 'National Socialist Welfare Provision'. Here, unlike in traditional social policy, it was no longer a question of meeting individual needs and supporting the socially disadvantaged; at the centre was the idea that the support of individuals would be made dependent on the assessment of their value for the racially defined 'national community'. The exclusion of the racially 'inferior' was a key constitutive element of this policy.[7]

The Exclusion of Jews from the German Health System and the Implementation of the Racial Hygiene Paradigm in Medicine

During the period of National Socialist dictatorship 'racial hygiene' conceptions that had been represented by a minority of members of the medical professions since the Imperial age became definitive.[8] In close collaboration with jurists, educationalists, social scientists, and members of the social security network, doctors collaborated under the Nazis with population policies that were aimed at preventing the bearers of 'negative' hereditary characteristics from reproducing. This was initially achieved via counselling on hereditary health issues, bans on certain marriages and enforced sterilization; during the war it was pursued via the systematic murder of those defined as 'racially inferior'.[9] The 'elimination' of these 'negative' elements within the German population was regarded as a major contribution towards the convalescence of the 'body of the nation'.

According to the view of racial hygienists, it was important to slow down the 'degeneration' of the population but not only by preventing certain groups from reproducing. The key difference between this and traditional notions of eugenics was that racial hygiene attempted to put an end to 'racial miscegenation', which was seen as particularly damaging, a flashpoint of the first importance for the health of the nation.

In this vein, in a speech to the Reich Party Conference of 1935 the head of the Reich Doctors' Association, Gerhard Wagner, emphasized how 'increasing miscegenation with Jewish blood that is entirely alien to us' would not only have 'the direst consequences, because it ... is against the natural order', but this 'bastardization' with the Jews, 'a people who are already bastardized', might lead to the unhindered spread amongst the German population 'of the hereditary diseases and negative dispositions that are already widespread amongst Jews'.[10]

Racial hygiene not only proclaimed the struggle against 'racial miscegenation' but saw as a significant goal the complete exclusion of Jews from the health system; indeed this was a fundamental condition for the implementation of its ideas. This was not merely a question of excluding Jewish doctors and other medical professionals,[11] or the gradual exclusion[12] of Jewish patients from public health organizations, but above all it was manifested in the battle against so-called 'Jewish medicine', which was a synonym for those tendencies in modern medicine that resisted the triumphal progress of racial hygiene. Above all this meant medicine that was 'mechanical' or 'industrial' or concerned with preventive welfare, allegedly of Jewish origin, and which was concerned with the improvement of the state of the nation's health across the board, without respect to the racial categories of patients. The link between *Entjudung* and the implementation of racial hygiene approaches was expressed programmatically in 1935 by a spokesman for National Socialist medicine: 'All forms of eugenics, every attempt to improve our race will be in vain if we cannot achieve the complete emancipation of questions of medical politics from the influence of Judaism and its spirit.'[13]

Just how closely the demand for the complete *Entjudung* of the health system was linked to the idea of the wholesale improvement of the health of the German nation can be shown particularly clearly in one area of health provision, in natural medicine, which under the National Socialists improved its standing vis-à-vis traditional academic medicine under the banner of 'New German Medicine'.[14] In a 1938 issue of the periodical *Heilpraktiker* we can read that 'the exclusion of Jews from the medical professions' would also 'detoxify the relations between doctors and the practitioners of natural medicine' because 'the Jew...has always been the strongest opponent of natural medicine, which is down-to-earth and socially aware'.[15]

The double process of *Entjudung* and the transformation of medicine along racial hygiene lines was part and parcel of the total occupation of the medical professions and the health system by the National Socialists. Doctors were controlled by Nazi organizations, new institutions were designed along 'popular health' lines, institutes and professorial chairs dedicated to racial hygiene were founded: this all contributed to a fundamental alteration of the structures of the health system and the dominance of National Socialist medicine.

The Anti-Jewish Bias of the German School System and its Nazification

Since 1933, and even more so after the second wave of anti-Semitism in 1935, Jewish pupils at state schools had been exposed to growing discrimination: the goal of these measures was first the exclusion, and finally the expulsion of Jewish pupils from general schools.[16] This occurred in various ways: Jewish pupils were progressively excluded from particular school activities, such as swimming lessons, visits to rural school halls of residence, outings, school parties, and so on. The more everyday school life was made to express National Socialist ideology by rituals (such as the flag ceremony), by symbols (such as the communal Hitler salute at every lesson), and by festivities and memorials, the clearer it became that Jewish pupils could not belong to the 'community' that was to be strengthened by all these measures. On the other hand, they were denied certain benefits such as reductions in school fees[17] or training grants.[18] The introduction of 'Theory of Heredity and Racial Science' as a compulsory, cross-disciplinary subject in all types of schools[19] as early as 1933, the enforcement of political education as well as the increasing pervasion of the various subjects with National Socialist content, particularly in the subjects of Biology, German, and History, but also in Geography, Art, and Music,[20] stamped the Jewish pupils as 'inferior' outsiders. As a rule, Jewish pupils were forbidden to make the transition to higher education; they could sit the school leaving certificate, but did not generally receive the higher education entrance qualification required for enrolment in university studies.

To this was added the fact that the racist and anti-Semitic content was often represented by teachers who victimized and humiliated their Jewish pupils in class, reducing them to exhibits that could be used to 'prove' the correctness of the racial theory that was being taught.

In turn, non-Jewish pupils increasingly kept their distance; the role played in this by the growing presence of the Hitler Youth in schools should not be underestimated. Jewish pupils were humiliated and tormented in a great variety of ways; assaults on Jewish fellow pupils were part of everyday school life, and for many Jewish pupils the daily journey to school became a torture.[21]

The stigmatization, ostracism, and expulsion of Jewish pupils, in spite of the small number of those affected—in 1933 the 45,000 Jewish pupils in public schools constituted less than 1 per cent of the whole pupil body[22]—formed a significant element in the Nazification process of the German school system, and were almost seen, from the NS point of view, as the precondition for it.[23]

From the viewpoint of the National Socialist regime Jewish pupils, as expressed in a statement by the Reich Education Minister published in the press in September 1935, were a 'major obstacle' to the 'united stance of the class community and the untrammelled implementation of the National Socialist education of the young'.[24] Consequently, as the Reich Education Minister announced in the relevant decree from the same month, 'clear separation according to race' was the precondition for the 'creation of National Socialist class communities as the basis for youth education based on the idea of German nationhood'.[25]

A closer analysis of the new educational guidelines demonstrates above all the great difficulties involved in communicating the desired harmonious image of a homogeneous 'Aryan' race and culture in a convincing way. The constant reference to the negative effect of the Jews, who were said to have done their best to prevent the emergence of the genuine German *Volksgemeinschaft* in the past, hence became part of the indispensable repertoire of education as practised on National Socialist terms. National Socialist teachers went so far as to demand the exclusion of Jewish pupils from lessons, since their mere presence irritated them and represented an insuperable obstacle to the communication of National Socialist educational content.[26]

The efforts of the regime to create an entirely 'German' school system were thus essentially based on the propagation of anti-Semitic education content and an educational practice directed against Jewish pupils. The anti-Jewish orientation of school was thus an indispensable part of the implementation of National Socialism in schools.

From the beginning of 1936 Reich Education Minister Rust expressly attempted legally to expel Jewish schoolchildren from general schools; at this time about half of the 45,000 or so Jewish pupils still living in Germany attended general schools. But Rust's plan was initially thwarted by the veto of Hitler, who plainly did not wish to go ahead with this plan in the Olympic Year 1936.[27] In 1937 the Education Minister returned to the plan; once again, in 1937, he suggested the establishment of 'special schools or collective classes for Jewish primary school pupils'.[28]

Accordingly, in 1937 the number of Jewish pupils in general schools fell to about 15,000; the majority of Jewish children now attended Jewish schools or the 'collective classes' mentioned above. But it would not be until 1939 that Jewish pupils were legally forbidden to attend general schools; the process of everyday discrimination and repression continued until that point.[29]

Liberation 'from the Jewish Spirit' and the Construction of a 'German' Science

In almost all academic disciplines after 1933 there is a discernible tendency to give a certain *völkisch*, a genuinely 'German' bias to each subject, by means of a comprehensive expulsion of the 'Jewish spirit'—beginning with the dismissal of Jewish university teachers—and by means of a fundamental removal of the remnants of a superseded 'liberal Jewish era'. The various disciplines were in varying degrees transformed and even partially redefined, in terms of both content and structure. This will be examined rather more closely with reference to a number of examples.

It was not until the era of National Socialism that psychology and psychotherapy first won acceptance as academic disciplines in Germany.[30] The distinction from 'Jewish' psychoanalysis and its destruction as a discipline played an important part in this professionalization process. In psychology this dissociation was attempted in part through the introduction of 'Racial Psychology' and 'Racial Typology',[31] and in psychotherapy by the foundation of a New German Psychotherapy (Neue Deutsche Seelenheilkunde).[32] In both cases what was at stake was not only a theoretical dissociation from psychoanalysis, but a matter of working out the fundamentally different mental make-ups of 'Aryans' and 'Jews'.

The transformation of the discipline of Anthropology (*Volkskunde*) into 'German Anthropology' (*Deutsche Volkskunde*), and its academic establishment on a larger scale, which occurred only during the Nazi period, was linked primarily with the idea of demonstrating the homogeneity and uniqueness of a German national culture beyond all regional differences and European similarities.[33] But the precondition for this, as one of the leading anthropologists stressed, was to make clear, 'how the Jewish spirit deliberately turns against essential foundations of German Anthropology. Jews above all are the first to turn away from the "*Volk as nation*". It is Jews who most strongly emphasize the differences between individual classes and groups within the German *Volk* ... The corroding effects of the Jewish spirit in the German Anthropology of the past can only fully be understood if one takes into account the Jewish influence coming from abroad.'[34] This quotation already makes it clear how the accusation of '*Verjudung*' (Judaization) could be utilized in intradisciplinary disputes.

The advocates of a transformation of sociology into a 'German theory of society' (*deutsche Gesellschaftslehre*) in turn assumed the task of fundamentally renewing the '*völkisches Selbstbewusstsein*'—the '*völkisch* self-awareness' of the Germans. To this end they turned against a 'Western' sociology, meaning one that concentrated on bourgeois, industrial society, and countered it with that of a German *Volkstum* rooted in peasant society; this expressly German-*völkisch* new science was supposed to connect with a traditional lineage represented by names such as Jakob Herder, Ernst Moritz Arndt, and Wilhelm Riehl. Accordingly, refoundation of the subject was concerned with fending off '*volksfeindliche* incursions of Western thought'; particular importance was assigned to the battle against 'Jewish thought, which has sought to talk the German people out of its *völkisch* needs'.[35] 'German sociology' did manage to institutionalize itself in the universities in the mid-1930s, but without developing an 'encompassing theoretical construct'.[36] The place of theory was occupied by practical social research, primarily concerned with 'weeding out' those who were 'inferior' and 'of foreign race' from German society—a task that was to assume growing importance with the conquest of Eastern European territories.

In the discipline of history during the National Socialist era it is possible to identify a powerful shift towards a Germanocentric folk history: along with the *Volkskunde* researchers and social scientists mentioned above, and in cooperation with geographers, archaeologists, and others, an attempt was made to create a new interdisciplinary field of research: *Volkstumsforschung* or ethnicity research.[37]

Volksgeschichte (ethnic history) and *Volkstumsforschung* primarily attempted to record the history and culture of the German people through its differentiation from foreign peoples; the actual roots of the German people could, the *Volkstumsforscher* were convinced, be revealed only when it was successfully freed from being overgrown by alien cultures.

Here—despite the establishment of thematically relevant research institutes[38]—anti-Semitism played a subordinate role. The chief intention was to re-establish German borders in disputes with the country's neighbours. Central to this was the claim to demonstrate the superiority of the character of ethnic Germans in border areas and abroad as against the national character (*Volkstum*) of foreigners, and thus to establish the German claim to hegemony. The fact that *Volkstumsforschung* sought to prove this claim to superiority primarily in a negative way, through the demarcation/separation from 'inferior' peoples, was summed up by one of its leading representatives at the 1934 German Historians' Congress, in a formula that can hardly be beaten for concision: 'Volksgeschichte is at its most elementary level the history of border conflicts.'[39]

Ethnic research was by no means purely based on racial biology: the term völkisch, which became its central concept, expressed the fusion of racist concepts with cultural, historical, and spatial ones.

Ethnicity research (Volkstumsforschung) represented the striking attempt, by overcoming the boundary between scholarship and politics, through close collaboration with political offices and through new institutional structures, to open up career paths to a generation of academics close to the Party via the redefinition of scholarly parameters.

Volkstumsforschung was to achieve practical significance during the war when, as a result of policy advice, cartographic material, statistics, and 'arguments' were made available to justify the displacement of Germany's Eastern borders; within this context it also achieved 'scholarly' preliminary work for the deportation of the Eastern European Jews. Thus Volkstumsforschung, unable to demonstrate the supposed superiority of the German people in a positive way, to a large extent ended up providing anciliary work for genocide. In this way it provided a particularly vivid example of the destructive momentum that lay within National Socialist racial politics in almost all spheres of life.

A further example from the humanities might be mentioned here: the path towards 'völkisch legal renewal' in jurisprudence led towards a consistent countering and denial of pre- and supra-state normative contexts.[40] The new version of the law was to be solely an expression of the 'national community', and that national community was, as one of the leading National Socialist jurists put it, defined by two factors: by 'racial homogeneity' (Artgleichheit) and by the 'common differentiation of friend from enemy'.[41] In fact the new völkisch law—adapted to the 'essence' of the German Volk—was to be reduced to an instrument in the hands of the National Socialist leadership; in this world of ideas there was no room for an autonomous sphere of law. Clearly this 'essential core' of völkisch law was not definable and—if the political leadership was not to be hampered in its actions—was not supposed to be defined more closely. On the other hand it is not difficult to discern, from the given definition, which 'enemy' the 'racially homogeneous' national community united by the new law was supposed to turn against: significantly, the 'völkisch legal renewal' concentrated in its theoretical discussions upon the 'unmasking' of Western and particularly of 'Jewish' jurisprudence.[42]

In legislative practice, significantly, attempts to codify völkisch legal renewal in a comprehensive legal reform did not go beyond the drafting stage, while at the same time an extensive 'special law' for 'ethnic aliens' (Fremdvölkische) was created, one which was to be extraordinarily efficient in the practice of persecution.[43]

In the natural sciences, attempts to establish a 'German physics', a 'German chemistry', or a 'German mathematics' were limited to relatively small groups of researchers, and proved finally to be without consequences. Only the devotees of 'German physics' managed temporarily to secure a series of important posts for themselves. Exactly what the specifically 'German' aspect of the individual subjects was supposed to be remained nebulous. While the representatives of 'German' physics turned against the supposed supremacy of a 'Jewish physics', meaning the theory of relativity in particular, and the devotees of 'German mathematics' also sought to distinguish themselves from a 'Jewish mathematics', German chemistry, as a unified 'theory of matter', resisted a supposedly 'Western' foreign domination of the subject.

The definitive breakthrough of ideas of racial hygiene in medicine and their contribution to a 'weeding-out' population policy (closely bound up with psychiatry, social sciences, educational theory, and jurisprudence) illustrates, on the other hand, the immediate relevance of racist paradigms based on exclusion within academic disciplines for social-political practice.

This survey has made it clear that the 'de-Judaization' (*Entjudung*) of the sciences was not accomplished simply by sacking a few Jewish scientists or removing them from the educational canon. In fact it was a matter of giving the individual subjects an authentically 'German' character via a comprehensive distancing 'from the Jewish spirit' and other 'foreign influences'. The survey has also made it clear that, without permanent reference to the rejected Jewish or foreign 'Other', the paradigm shift to a Germanocentric scholarship could not be achieved, indeed that the planned theoretical reorientation was largely exhausted in that distancing. The *Entjudung* and *völkisch*-racial cleansing of the discipline in question was thus—for want of 'positive rationales'—effectively constitutive; it was not a single action, but a permanent and continuous distancing process which served to conceal the lack of any substantial content in the 'German' renewal.

The intended internal reorientation of the individual subjects succeeded, as we have seen, to various degrees; where its success was modest, it was often limited to rhetorical gestures and remained without significant consequences for practical academic work. However, through the intended Germanocentric conversion of disciplines or partial disciplines—even if this was purely declamatory in character—the theoretical discussions within the individual subjects and thus their identity were also influenced, new structures and career opportunities were created; here lay the starting point for National Socialist academics not only to establish themselves in the individual disciplines, but substantially to change the character of the individual subjects. The keyword *Entjudung* was the starting point for this process of change.

Beyond these theoretical discussions—and the survey has also made that clear—the *Entjudung* and Germanocentric transformation of individual disciplines also had considerable practical consequences: academics who allowed their work to be governed by racist paradigms substantially opened up new areas of work for themselves: the definition and exclusion of those of foreign race.

The *Entjudung* of Cultural Life as the Precondition for a 'German Culture'

The National Socialist project of creating an authentically 'German' culture is inseparably bound up with efforts to achieve a consistent *Entjudung* of cultural life as a whole; indeed, to a considerable extent such negative measures constituted the whole of National Socialist cultural policy.

According to the National Socialist vision, 'culture was the highest expression of the creative powers of a people':[44] every artwork of any distinction could accordingly be interpreted as the expression of primal racial-*völkisch* powers. Every 'clearly distinctive race', as Hitler said in a speech to the Reich Chamber of Culture in 1934, had 'its own signature in the book of art'—citing as an exception 'Jewry', which is 'utterly without its own artistic productive capability'.[45] According to this idea, the liberation of authentically 'German' culture from the Jewish—that is, unproductive, parasitic, alien, corrosive, and finally destructive—influence formed a leitmotif of cultural-political discourse in the National Socialist regime.

However, attempts to define the 'essence' of art rooted in the German or Aryan 'racial soul' remained diffuse:[46] all efforts to free 'German' music or 'German' painting from the context of the European tradition were inevitably destined to fail, while ambitious contemporary attempts to produce 'native' (*arteigene*) artworks appropriate to National Socialism were not as a rule convincingly able to fulfil this claim. The artistic production of the era generally suffered from a lack of originality and ended up predominantly in the production of kitsch.

Consequently, as in many other policy areas, the National Socialist cultural policy makers had no option but to execute the intended homogenization negatively, to produce 'pure' German culture above all by means of the permanent cleansing of 'alien' art. This tendency to define National Socialist art in negative terms became more intense the greater the discrepancy between the bombastic proclamations of a new, National Socialist aesthetic and the actually mediocre products of National Socialist art production grew: the 'cleansing principle' now became an 'absolutely exclusive compulsion to purification'.[47]

In this cleansing policy, the removal of the supposedly dominant Jewish influence in German cultural life was very much in the foreground. This was not only a matter of the exclusion of Jewish artists and the prohibition or destruction of their artworks; the *Entjudung* of German culture also concerned the exclusion of Jews active in the purveyance of culture, since as 'cultural administrators', agents, critics, dealers, and so on, they were made primarily responsible for the distribution and promotion of undesirable modern, 'degenerate' (*entartet*) or simply merely 'foreign' art.[48] The Jews, as 'primarily a business-minded people', according to Hans Severus Ziegler, General Manager of the National Theatre in Weimar and a leading Nazi cultural policy maker, at the opening of the 'Degenerate Music' exhibition in 1938, had turned 'cultural and artistic objects, like the objects of politics, into business commodities'; they had succeeded 'in cutting off the *Volk* from its creative forces, from its gifts and its genius, and thus removing it from the most vivid examples of race and *Volkstum*'; the result was the 'terrible alienation from its better self, from its own essence, from all historic values, from its creative personality'.[49] Hence the 'removal of Jews from cultural life' could not exempt 'art-dealers, cinema owners, publishers and booksellers'.

With the tightening of the conditions of admission into the Reich Chamber of Culture in the spring of 1934, the ground was laid for the definitive *Entjudung* of cultural life as a whole:[50] the Reichsschrifttumskammer (Reich Chamber of Letters) began the process in 1935 with the exclusion of its Jewish members, and other chambers followed this model over the coming months and in the course of 1936.[51] For economic reasons above all, however, a series of exceptional regulations for Jewish artists were put into force. Moreover, Goebbels did not at first manage to exclude Jews completely from the professions of the 'culture business'; the ministerial bureaucracy slowed down this process, so that prohibitions on Jewish cinema-owners, art and antique dealers, and other professions from working came into effect only from 1937.[52] The existing exceptions repeatedly offered National Socialist cultural policy makers, with Propaganda Minister Goebbels at their head, the opportunity finally to demand a 100 per cent 'Jew-free' cultural life;[53] it was the 'Jewish question', still unresolved in spite of all efforts to the contrary, that according to this view stood in the way of a truly homogeneous 'German culture'. In fact it was only after the pogrom of November 1938 that this cleansing process came to an end with the abolition of the last admission regulations for Jewish artists, as well as with the removal of the last Jewish cultural enterprises.[54]

However, that certainly did not mean an end to the efforts to achieve the *Entjudung* of German cultural life. This was because the controlling cultural political institutions—the Propaganda Ministry, the Reich Chamber of Culture, 'The Rosenberg Bureau', the Party Censorship Board, and others—had, following the watchword of *Entjudung* or 'removal of Jewish influence', created an instrument that could be deployed almost at will, to take action against unpopular artistic trends, predominantly against representatives of modern art, and could open up the culture industry to artists close to the Party.[55] This process had still not come to an end with the removal of the Jews: as late as 1942, for example, a National Socialist author recorded the continuing after-effects of 'unworldly and

Jew-lovers lost to their own kind (*artvergessen*)', who had continued the Jewish 'demolition work' even after the assumption of power, and had to be hunted down as 'slaves' and 'comrades' of the Jews.[56] The new 'German' culture could only arise out of a far-reaching cleansing process, permanently dissociating itself from 'foreign' influences that had already penetrated far into the German *Volk*.

The fact that the 'first major German art exhibition' showing Nazi-inspired art, in 1937, was opened at the same time as the propaganda exhibition 'Entartete Kunst' (degenerate art), and in the same place, in Munich,[57] reveals the complementary function that the *Entjudung* of the culture industry and the construction of a 'German' culture had: the new 'German' art was not explicable in its own terms, but needed a constant reference to the negative example of the 'degenerate' trend in art. Although the 'Degenerate Art' exhibition showed primarily non-Jewish artists, in his speech at the Reich Chamber of Culture's annual congress in 1937[58] Goebbels significantly singled out the exhibition as a striking example of 'how deeply the pernicious Jewish spirit has penetrated German cultural life'—a striking example, in fact, of the usefulness of the idea of the *Verjudung* of art as an all-purpose weapon against unpopular trends in art.

The programmatic guidelines for German film, published by a Nazi cultural functionary in 1934, make it clear how 'German character' was to unfold on screen through the removal of actors 'of non-German descent': 'Of particular importance for the education of all Germans into national consciousness will be the depiction of the German character in film. National German film should show the German *Volk* people of its own kind, whose characters and motives it understands, whose words are addressed to it from the soul. Hence the law requires the actors to be of German descent. In future, therefore, actors will appear on the screen in whom the German will see his own race embodied, and who teach him to love and honour his nation. German people, German atmosphere, German disposition, German spirit must make their mark on film. Then it will help to fulfil the great task of German art in holding up to the German *Volk* a mirror of its soul.'[59]

What is particularly interesting about this quotation in our context is the fact that the removal of actors 'of non-German descent' (and other measures for the *Entjudung* of the film industry) should have formed the preconditions for the intended 'German character' of film. But in what concrete way did this 'German character' find expression in the individual film productions?[60] The great mass of films, aimed at the light entertainment of the audience, avoided depicting their protagonists as emphatically 'German', but tried on the contrary—not least by employing a series of non-German stars—to match the international standard of film entertainment.[61] Those films which did risk emphatically 'German' themes generally did so by placing their 'German' or 'Germanic' heroes opposite comically caricatured 'foreigners', whether they were Jews, Slavic 'sub-humans', or Englishmen or Frenchmen identified as Western and decadent (meaning:

Jewish-influenced).[62] The characterization of the 'German' could not occur without a constant reference to the 'non-German'.

The most important change in the repertoires of German theatres after 1933 was due to the fact that Jewish and politically undesirable contemporary dramatists, who had previously written almost 40 per cent of plays performed, now disappeared almost completely, making way for National Socialist and *völkisch* authors, who now dominated repertoires with a share of almost 60 per cent—also to the detriment of foreign dramatists, whose share also fell. The *Entjudung* of theatre repertoires—the banning of plays written by Jewish authors or those reflecting the 'Jewish-liberalist' spirit of the Weimar Republic, was thus the immediate precondition for the conquest of the theatre by authors close to National Socialism.[63]

National Socialist architectural theorists did their best to distance 'German' architecture from a 'degenerate' international or modern architecture described as 'Jewish' or 'culturally Bolshevik'. Jewish speculation had led to the abandonment of 'blood-and-soil-bound' building methods and thus to the deracination of architecture.[64] 'The architectural non-culture, which was propagated under the slogan "New Objectivity", and carried out even in the face of its unanimous rejection by the people, was nothing but an attempt to remove the cultural value of the German *Volk*'s specific homeland and impose Jewish cultural Bolshevism upon it.'[65]

The intended Renaissance of 'German architecture' was linked with the terms *Volk*, organism, homeland, family, blood, and soil, even though no solid architectural programme could have developed from it.[66]

The increasing penetration of everyday life by a Nazi-inspired aesthetic, in areas such as advertising, fashion, and design, for example, was also impossible without a constant polemic against the travesty of a 'Judaized' (*verjudet*) everyday culture. Thus the control of advertising[67] by the Nazi state (via the 'Advertising Council of German Commerce' and the almost complete monopolization of advertising by the Party) went hand in hand with a material and stylistic *Entjudung* and *Verdeutschung* (Germanization) of advertising. Advertising, according to the compulsory guidelines of the Advertising Council, must be German 'in spirit and expression'.[68] What the 'German character' of advertising might have been was never properly explained; attempts to give the guidelines concrete form or even encode them in a law were fruitless. Instead, officials restricted themselves to the contrast between 'respectable' German advertising and supposedly Jewish-dominated 'Anglo-American commercials', although without being able to develop a particularly Nazi style of advertising.

One effort to adapt the everyday look of the 'Third Reich' to National Socialist ideas was the propagation of 'Aryan-style fashion'. Under this slogan the National Socialists throughout the whole of the Reich set up associations and organizations which—supported by strident journalism—were supposed to organize fashion in a uniform manner, encourage export, destroy the exemplary function of Paris, and above all exclude Jewish fashion designers.[69] At the same time, however, it remained entirely unclear what was supposed to be specifically 'German' about the new style: in fact, 'Aryan-style fashion' was more or less exhausted in the struggle against the 'Jewish ready-made', which was represented as the gateway of international, above all French fashion. The complete *Entjudung* of the ready-made industry was depicted as the precondition for the realization of a 'German' fashion, and the polemic against 'alien' fashion did not stop even after successful Aryanization.[70] The slogan of *Entjudung* became a substitute for the lack of creativity of 'Aryan' fashion designers—and in the end it gave National Socialist fashion functionaries crucial controlling functions in the fashion industry.

Even in the design of functional objects and furniture, the regime's attempts—we might think, for example, of the 'Beauty of Work' office of the German Labour Front—to attempt an autonomous design style remained substantially unsuccessful; official declarations distanced themselves from avant-garde visions such as those developed in the 'Jewish' Bauhaus, but design remained to a large extent trapped in the functionalistic design of the Weimar era.[71]

The various examples have demonstrated that the *Entjudung* and racial 'cleansing' of German society was a process that went far beyond the mere removal of the Jews and other unwanted 'foreigners' in the different areas of life. In fact it was a much more comprehensive process: as the homogeneous, entirely German *Volksgemeinschaft* could not be brought about in a positive way, either conceptually or in practice, the National Socialists fell back on imposing it negatively, through permanent differentiation, distancing, and liberation from an apparently omnipresent and omnipotent enemy.

Rhetorical as this process of dissociation remained, the above examples have demonstrated that it affected practically all areas of life and by no means stopped with the actual exclusion of Jews, but remained a lasting theme during the Nazi period. Behind the phase of *Entjudung* there lay a very real claim in terms of political power: the imposition of the Nazis' claim to total power.

The Emergence of a Jewish Sector as a Consequence of the Politics of Repression

The segregation policy promoted on a massive scale in 1935—as a consequence of that year's anti-Semitic campaign—and then again after the end of the Olympic Games from the end of 1936 had profound consequences for the everyday life of the Jewish minority. In so far as such generalizations are possible at all, in the years 1935 and 1936 any private contact still existing between Jews and non-Jews seems largely to have been severed. Numerous reports and memoirs make it clear that the whole range of everyday relationships seems to have been affected by it:

children stopped playing together; the members of youth cliques dispersed; polite gestures such as everyday greetings ceased to be exchanged; neighbours stopped talking to each other; visits to each other's houses and communal visits to pubs became a thing of the past; those friendships and love affairs that still existed fell apart; even the joint participation of Jews and non-Jews in funerals became rarer. Segregation was imposed through an interplay of government departments, the Party apparatus, police, and Gestapo, which was able to rely on the energetic support of the populace.[72] Of course, isolation tended to be more prevalent in smaller towns, where Jews had already become too frightened to go into the streets and had become completely isolated, than it was in the anonymity of the big cities. This strengthened the progress of migration from the countryside to the city and worsened still further the precarious life of those impoverished, isolated Jews in the countryside.[73]

The many consequences of persecution for the life of the Jews themselves cannot be pursued here in every last detail. The consequences for family life and the relations between the sexes, the increased focus upon Jewish culture and a more intense religious life as well as strategies of resistance and survival developed by the various Jewish organizations are themes that have been extensively discussed in the literature.[74] Here we will merely attempt to provide an overview of Jewish self-organization under the immediate pressure of persecution and locate that self-organization within the history of *Judenpolitik*.

The economic consequences of the increasing 'creeping' exclusion of many Jews from the economy, which set in at the end of 1936 after the 'boycott' had already considerably undermined their economic situation, were particularly grave. The considerable reduction of economic possibilities as a consequence of exclusion now led to characteristic relocations of Jewish economic activity, for example to their heightened activity as salespeople (until that profession came under greater pressure from the authorities late in 1937), or the relocation of businesses to homes and thus to typical poverty careers.[75]

Through the discriminatory measures in the economic field something like an autonomous Jewish business cycle came into being: Jews were increasingly forced to fall back on Jews as suppliers and customers, although that Jewish 'internal economy' did not offer sufficient opportunities to make a livelihood; most businesses lived on their capital.[76] A closed Jewish labour market was supported by a Jewish labour exchange until it was closed down late in 1936. It was characteristic of the Jewish commercial sector that the amount of credit provided by loan offices increased steadily until 1936, while the activity of the agency that was supposed to help with the reconstruction of livelihoods declined, since fewer and fewer Jews wanted to engage in businesses.[77]

Under the increasing pressure of exclusion on the one hand, and impelled by Jewish attempts at self-assertion and self-organization on the other, an 'autonomous Jewish sector' came into being, and not only in the commercial world, which facilitated survival for those Jews who had remained in Germany and gave them one last means of support before complete impoverishment. As a result of segregation something like a Jewish 'public service' came into being: Jewish health and education, Jewish welfare, and social security[78] reached a considerable size; a considerable administrative apparatus was maintained in the Jewish communities and in organizations such as the Central Committee and the Reich Board. The establishment of Jewish institutions and the exclusion of Jews from the institutions accessible to the general population occurred as a complementary process.

In 1935–6 the Reich Board of Deputies of the Jews in Germany (originally founded, as an umbrella organization, as the Reich Board of Deputies of German Jews, it had been obliged to assume this new name after the introduction of the Nuremberg Laws in 1935) began to develop more collective places of education.[79] While it transpired that the redistribution of adults did not increase chances of emigration to any significant extent, after 1935–6 these institutions undertook above all the initial training of young Jewish people who were unable find an apprenticeship, or whose training in the commercial professions preferred by Jews seemed pointless.

By 1938 some 30,000 people had been trained in training farms and training centres, two-thirds of them younger than 20. These included a considerable number of young people who were able to train in agricultural professions outside Germany. About 15 per cent of young people between 14 and 25 had thus been covered by the educational measures by 1938.[80]

Finally, the construction of an autonomous Jewish cultural life made further progress.[81] Alongside a sizeable Jewish press[82] this found expression above all in the establishment of Jewish cultural organizations. March 1935 saw the foundation of the Reich Association of Jewish Cultural Societies in Germany, under the supervision of the Propaganda Ministry. With the appointment of Hans Hinkel, the Commissar in the Prussian Ministry of Culture originally commissioned to undertake the 'Entjudung of cultural life', as 'Special Agent for the Cultural Activity of all Non-Aryans' in this ministry in July 1935, and through its simultaneous function as one of the managers of the Reich Chamber of Culture, a close connection was established between the Entjudung of the general cultural industry, and the construction of an autonomous Jewish culture was produced. From August 1935 cultural associations had to become members of the Reich Association, which thus became something resembling a Jewish Chamber of Culture. All programmes of cultural events now needed—after being presented to the Reich Association—permission from the Hinkel Office; organizers, performing artists, and audiences had to be members of the Reich Association. In 1938 there were a total of 76 cultural associations, involving about 50,000 people. The creation of an efficient Jewish cultural organization was—and this connection should not be overlooked—one of the preconditions for the exclusion of the Jews from the general cultural life.

The Jewish school system was considerably expanded under the pressure of persecution. At the start of the Nazi era only around 25 per cent of Jewish primary schoolchildren attended Jewish schools, about half each in private and public schools. During the 1930s the following developments can be observed: the number of Jewish primary schoolchildren declined overall, due to emigration and the falling birth rate, while an ever greater proportion of Jewish schoolchildren left general primary schools. The result of these movements in the Jewish student body for the Jewish public schools was a steady loss of pupils; the number of these establishments, most of which had been barely sustainable one-room schools even before 1933, thus declined from 148 in 1932–3 to 76 in 1937.[83]

The private Jewish primary schools, on the other hand, registered a constant increase in pupil numbers, at least until 1938; later the figures fell again. The number of these schools rose between 1933 and 1937 from twenty-seven to seventy-two.[84] The number of pupils at the public secondary schools—ten schools in all—increased slightly until 1937, while the role of the private Jewish secondary schools remained insignifant.[85]

In 1934 the Reich Board drew up guidelines for education in Jewish primary schools, which were understood as a complement to the state curricula which were also valid for the Jewish schools, and which effectively represented a compromise between German-Jewish, Orthodox, and Zionist educational goals.[86] In 1937 the Reich Board issued new guidelines which took into account the altered outlook for those Jews still living in Germany: unlike 1934, the emphasis was no longer on the rootedness of Jewish culture in the German environment; instead the pupils' orientation towards Jewish tradition and preparation for emigration, especially to Palestine,[87] found expression, for example, in a larger amount of Hebrew education, a greater emphasis on sport and handicraft, as well as in increased efforts to teach 'Palestinian studies'.

Jewish welfare organizations attempted to support the Jews, who were increasingly excluded from official services, in a great variety of ways, through food agencies, services of goods and money, through measures in the field of open social work, health care, and care for the elderly, etc.[88] In 1937 there were only twenty-one Jewish hospitals, fifteen sanatoria, forty-nine children's homes and orphanages, and seventy-six old people's homes and hospices.[89] One of the most successful projects was a Jewish Winter Aid scheme. Once Jews were excluded from the official Winter Aid scheme by the Nuremberg Laws, the Reich Board set up a Winter Aid scheme of its own, under the control of the Reich Commissioner for Winter Aid. It was financed, on the model of the official Winter Aid scheme, by tax-like donations drawn directly from wages or other income, and levied throughout the whole six months of winter.[90] The proportion of the Jewish population who received support from Jewish Winter Aid rose from 20.5 per cent (1935–6) to 24.3 per cent (1938–9).[91]

The creation of autonomous Jewish organizations designed to rescue the Jews excluded from the various social spheres and give them the support they needed to survive also led to the further intensification of the segregation and isolation of the Jewish minority that had been set in motion by the regime. Further to this, the formation of purely Jewish organizations in a later phase of *Juden-politik*, in which they were turned into the organs of a state-controlled enforced community, in many ways made it easier for the NS state to record and control the Jews. It was to prove fatal that Nazi *Judenpolitik* was able to use the extensive attempts to achieve Jewish self-organization for the further intensification of persecution.

CHAPTER 4

THE INTENSIFICATION OF THE RACIAL PERSECUTION OF NON-JEWISH GROUPS BY THE POLICE APPARATUS, 1936–1937

In the first years of the 'Third Reich', National Socialist 'Racial policy' was defined above all by two strategies. By the exclusion and segregation of the Jewish minority, and by the attempt to prevent the reproduction of the so-called *erbkrank*, or hereditarily ill. After the mid-1930s further racial policy measures were added, mainly by the police apparatus and directed specifically against particular groups.

After Himmler took over and reorganized the entire German police force in 1936, over the course of 1937 the Sicherheitspolizei, or 'security police', formed by the merger of the Gestapo and the criminal police (Kripo), intensified the persecution and systematic elimination of marginal groups which were seen as a public danger because of their supposedly 'inferior' hereditary predispositions. In this way the security police acted as an instrument of 'racial general prevention'.[1] This policy, which was closely connected to the continuing segregation of the Jews occurring at the same time, affected four groups in particular: people of non-European origin or children of Germans and non-Europeans, Gypsies, 'asocials', and homosexuals. The exclusion and persecution of groups stigmatized by their different 'racial affiliation' or supposed 'hereditary predispositions' granted the police extensive opportunities for access and control with regard to the population as a whole, whose everyday and social relations were subjected to a dense network of prohibitions and prescriptions.

During the first few years of the 'Third Reich', the criminal police had, under the watchword of 'preventive crime-fighting', attempted through the use of preventive detention, preventive custody, and surveillance measures, systematically to eliminate so-called 'professional criminals'. After the formation of the Reich Criminal Police Office in July 1937 and the centralization of the Kripo as a whole, there was an increasingly apparent tendency to organize crime-fighting on the basis of the findings of 'Criminal Biology'. To this end, after autumn 1937 the Reich Criminal Police Office worked closely with the 'Racial Hygiene Research Institute' in the Reich Health Office, and at the same time the Reich Minister of Justice set up a special 'Criminal Biology Service',[2] and from the beginning of 1938 there was also a 'Headquarters of Criminal Genealogy'[3] within the Reich Criminal Police Office. The findings of 'Criminal Biology' provided the Kripo, within the context of 'preventive crime-fighting', with the strategy of eliminating 'social misfits' as the class actually responsible for criminality. The legal basis for this lay in the unpublished 'Fundamental Decree Concerning Preventive Crime-Fighting by the Police of 14 December 1937' signed by the Reich Interior Minister. This document particularly regulated which group could be taken into the preventive custody of the Criminal Police: 'professional and habitual criminals', people who gave inadequate information about their personal details, as well as 'those who, although not professional and habitual criminals, endanger the generality by their antisocial behaviour'. Preventive custody, fundamentally unlimited, was to be served in 'closed rehabilitation and labour camps... or in some other way'; in fact it was to be served in concentration camps.[4]

In the implementation guidelines for this decree of early April 1938, the Kripo defined 'asocials' (*Asoziale*) on the one hand as 'individuals who through minor but repeated transgressions of the law refuse to fit in with the order taken for granted in a National Socialist state (for example beggars, tramps (Gypsies)), prostitutes, alcoholics, individuals carrying infectious diseases, particularly venereal diseases, who escape the measures of the public health department'; but according to this 'asocial' could also refer to individuals without a previous conviction if they 'evade the duty of work and leave concern for their keep to the generality (e.g. the work-shy, those who refuse to work, alcoholics)'.[5]

Since 'preventive crime-fighting' (as expressly stressed in the fundamental decree of 14 December 1937) was to take its bearings from the findings of 'Criminal Biology', for the use of 'preventive' measures the assessment of the potential perpetrator's family history in terms of 'hereditary biology' was crucial.[6] This form of assessment was of particular importance in the case of 'asocials', since this group could not be defined by any unambiguous criterion (such as previous convictions, for example), but chiefly on the basis of its 'hidden' inferior inherited predispositions: for example, someone not in gainful employment would only become 'work-shy' if other conspicuous 'asocial' qualities could be established. The concept of the 'asocial' was, in its very vagueness, unambiguously racist by nature, since it acted as a negative counter-selection to the striven-for Aryan racial ideal (which also eluded any precise definition).

In January 1938, while the Kripo, who were actually responsible, were still preparing their own measures against the 'work-shy', Himmler ordered an independent Gestapo action against this group. The group in question—individuals capable of gainful employment who had refused jobs offered to them twice without justification, or had taken on the work but then abandoned it without any sound reasons—were to report via the labour offices to the Gestapo stations and be transferred to Buchenwald concentration camp. The operation began on 21 April 1938 and ended officially on 30 April, although it may possibly have extended beyond that date. As a result of the arrests in the context of this operation, by the beginning of June 1938 there were almost 2,000 prisoners in Buchenwald.[7]

The Reich-wide Kripo operation against 'asocials' (operation 'Reich Work-Shy') began in the same month. The fact that this operation was to include all Jews with previous convictions (however minor) clearly reveals the complementary function of racial hygiene and racist anti-Semitism within the National Socialist project of a racially homogeneous social order. (The operation will be examined more closely within the context of the depiction of the third wave of anti-Semitism.)[8]

While the persecution of the Gypsies had proceeded along more or less conventional lines in the first years of the NS dictatorship, between 1936 and 1938 the essential foundations were laid for a systematic persecution of this population group on a racist basis.

After the Reich Ministry of the Interior standardized the stipulations of the laws regarding Gypsies in the *Länder*, in autumn 1936 the Prussian State Criminal Police Office began to centralize the persecution of the Gypsies. In 1937 the office, by now transformed into a Reich Criminal Police Office, took over the 'Gypsy Central Office' that had existed within Munich Police Headquarters since 1899, which now acted as 'Reich Office to Combat the Gypsy Plague'.[9] From the end of 1938 until the middle of 1939, a criminal police apparatus extending all the way down to local police authorities was set up to combat Gypsies.

Since autumn 1937, the Reich Criminal Police Office had worked closely with the Racial Hygiene Research Centre within the Reich Health Authority which, under the direction of Robert Ritter, focused upon the 'Gypsy question'. Since 1937 the Research Centre had undertaken an anthropometrical and genealogical investigation of all Sinti and Roma in the Reich. On the basis of these investigations the Research Centre produced racial hygiene reports in which distinctions were made between 'genuine' Gypsies and 'half-breed Gypsies'. The Criminal Police were able to use this material as a database for the persecution of the

Gypsies. Towards the end of the war, with about 25,000 reports, Ritter's institute claimed to have recorded almost the whole Gypsy population of the Old Reich territory.[10]

After Himmler had taken over the whole of the police in summer 1936, the persecution of homosexuals was also intensified.[11] Even before the end of the year a 'Reich Central Office for Combatting Homosexuality and Abortion' was set up within the Prussian State Criminal Office, which centrally recorded particular categories of male homosexuals. For a time the Gestapo was able to take over control of the Reich Central Office, although with the start of the war this came back within the sphere of responsibility of the Kripo.[12] Himmler indicated the priority given to the suppression of homosexuality with reference to the fact that he had stated in March 1937, at a meeting of Kripo and Gestapo leaders, that he would henceforth measure the effectiveness of the Kripo according to its successes within the sphere of the battle against homosexuality and abortion. Accordingly the number of those sentenced for offences against paragraph 175 of the Reich Penal Code suddenly rose: from 766 (1934) to over 4,000 (1936) and over 8,000 (1938). After 1937, homosexuals with more than three relevant convictions behind them, with sentences each of at least six months' imprisonment, were sent to concentration camps once they had served their regular sentences.[13]

Finally the police apparatus took systematic action against the so-called 'Rhineland Bastards', those young people who were the product of relations between German women and colonial soldiers from the time of the French occupation of the Rhineland. As early as 1935 the Specialist Advisory Board for Population and Race Policy agreed to 'solve' this 'bastard question' by means of sterilization, although they were initially unable to reach agreement upon the procedure.[14] Early in 1937 the decision was redrafted so that Afro-Germans were to be compulsorily sterilized outside the existing legal procedure; a relevant 'special instruction' from Hitler seems to have been produced.[15] Accordingly, in the spring of 1937 a special commission was set up which, over the coming months and with the assistance of three sub-commissions, performed the sterilization of some 600–800 young people.[16]

The practice of German Racial Policy also raised the problem of how the children of German and non-European foreigners, described in Nazi language as 'alien half-breeds' (*artfremde Mischlinge*), were to be treated. For this group, the race legislation was similar. In a document dated February 1937 the Foreign Office indicated that over the previous two years about fifty cases at most had appeared, in which 'the German race legislation was to be applied to non-Jewish alien half-breeds'. It had turned out that the 'domestic political interest in an enforcement of racial legislation was in most cases entirely insignificant, while on the other hand the fear of foreign political disadvantages was always justified and decisive'. Generally, then, the emergency regulation intended for such cases had been applied. The number of those cases in which, because of fundamental 'racial policy' considerations, foreign policy concerns had been set aside and it had been impossible to apply the emergency regulation 'had numbered about 5 over the past 4 years'. In view of this practice, the Foreign Office suggested that the race legislation be fundamentally restricted to Jews and that those race laws already passed be altered, replacing terms such as *artfremd* (alien) or 'non-Aryan' with 'Jewish'.

On 22 April 1937 the Reich Interior Ministry fundamentally adopted a position on the relationship between 'racial policy' and Jewish policy. The Interior Ministry established that the 'final goal of the National Socialist movement... was to eliminate all people of alien blood from the German national body' (*Volkskörper*). Besides, a change in the race laws was inopportune because it would be interpreted abroad as a 'sign of insecurity or even of weakness'.

First, however, 'the most urgent racial problem for the nation, the Jewish question, was to be legally regulated', while the 'question of the legal position of people with other kinds of alien blood must receive consideration only in so far as was unavoidably necessary to the movement's fundamental attitude towards the race question and in view of the basic significance of this question for the continuing existence of the nation'.

If, as a consequence, 'a general restriction of race legislation to the Jews proved impossible in view of both National Socialist principles and general political considerations, this would not rule out the possibility of individual exceptions to stipulations of the race laws, if the foreign political interests of the Reich urgently required it'.

In a response to the Foreign Office's suggestion on 28 April, the director of the Office of Racial Policy of the NSDAP, Walter Gross, also declared his opposition to a change in the race laws 'for educational reasons'. The dogmatism of 'racial policy', these statements reveal, went far beyond the sphere of anti-Jewish policy.[17]

However, there was a significant difference between the persecution of the Jews and other groups considered racially inferior, because although the racial policy measures directed against other groups before 1938 were to some extent more radical than those of anti-Jewish policy (sterilization, compulsory abortion, castration, imprisonment in concentration camps), they were primarily directed, in a 'racially hygienic' sense, towards the elimination of 'inferior' individuals from the 'Aryan race', whereby this negative selection (with the exception of the small group of Afro-Germans) was still preceded by a pseudo-scientific, and yet somewhat elaborate, analysis of individual cases. For National Socialist racial policy, on the other hand, the Jews constituted a minority which, as a closed group, was seen as the enemy.

CHAPTER 5

COMPREHENSIVE DEPRIVATION OF RIGHTS AND FORCED EMIGRATION, LATE 1937–1939

The Third Wave of Anti-Semitism: The Radicalization of Persecution

The Political Context: *Entjudung* and Preparation for War

During 1938 the regime responded to the crisis in which the NS regime's *Judenpolitik* found itself at the end of 1937, when faced with dwindling opportunities for emigration, with a series of radical steps which, taken together, can be described as the third wave of anti-Semitism of the Nazi era.

The impending radicalization of persecution had already been indicated when, after the end of the protection of minorities in the former Upper Silesian voting area, the Reich's anti-Semitic laws were ruthlessly introduced in the summer of 1937. They were accompanied by riots, boycotts, robberies, broken windows, and the like.[1] The more radical course was introduced by Hitler's strongly anti-Semitic speech at the Party rally in 1937, and by the anti-Semitic riots in Danzig (where, because of its status as a 'free city', the German Jewish legislation did not yet apply) in the second half of October 1937.[2] From the end of the year, anti-Semitic propaganda was massively intensified once again.

The clearly more radical course is directly connected with the regime's expansion policy, introduced late in 1937, which Hitler announced to the military leadership and the Foreign Minister on 5 November, and which was then prepared by the comprehensive reshuffle of staff in the armed forces (the dismissal of the War Minister, Werner von Blomberg, and the Commander-in-Chief of the Army, Werner von Fritsch, in February 1938) and in the Reich government (the resignation of Hjalmar Schacht as Reich Minister of Economics in November 1937 and of the Foreign Minister, Konstantin von Neurath, in February 1938). Now all key positions necessary for the waging of war were in the hands of reliable National Socialists. With the transition to a policy of expansion, in the mid-term foreign-policy considerations that had applied until then, and which had hitherto argued against a further intensification of the persecution of the Jews, were dropped.

There was also no longer the fear that the definitive elimination of the Jews from commerce would cause major negative economic repercussions. On the one hand, the general economic situation of the 'Third Reich' had been consolidated, and its dependency on exports had declined. On the other, the economic position of the Jews had already been so undermined by the 'boycott' by Party activists, by the numerous obstacles raised by state authorities, and the more or less compulsory 'Aryanization' or liquidation of businesses, that they no longer represented a major factor in economic life. Finally, by now the network of controlling organizations, taxes, and so on had been perfected to such an extent that the profits achieved by the sale of Jewish businesses went to the state, the Party, and individuals (often linked to the NSDAP) with an interest in Aryanization.

From the regime's perspective there was a further reason to increase pressure on the Jewish minority once again. Following the gradual general propaganda preparation of the population for a major state of emergency in Germany's dealings with foreign powers, the Jewish minority was to be assigned the function of an internal enemy which formed the appropriate object for hatred and aggression.

The transition to the third phase of National Socialist *Judenpolitik*, which had been introduced late in 1937, more intensely since spring 1938, and definitively implemented with the November pogrom, the complete isolation, deprivation of rights, and expulsion of those Jews still living in Germany became the goal.

For a third time after 1933 and 1935 the mood of the population was to be remoulded through a large-scale campaign, a new wave of anti-Semitism; after the exclusion of the Jews from public offices and the separation of the Jewish minority from the non-Jewish population, the final *Entjudung* of German society was placed at the centre of propaganda and of the policy of the regime. Anxieties aroused by the regime's risky foreign policy and its repressive domestic political course were to be deliberately projected upon the image created by the National Socialists of the Jew as enemy.

The renewed radicalization of 'Jewish policy' once again followed the familiar dialectic of 'actions' and administrative or legislative measures, a process lasting about a year, which was to reach its climax in the November pogrom and the subsequent anti-Jewish laws. This third phase of National Socialist 'Jewish policy' also signified a further extension of power in favour of National Socialism: the concluding 'legal' Aryanization gave the NSDAP and its clientele numerous opportunities to extend their influence in the economic sphere: with the passing of diverse special regulations, the Jewish minority was turned into an enforced community that had to lead a life in the shadows and (along with its remaining possessions and its labour potential) was exposed to the arbitrary actions of local potentates. What was crucial, however, was that by virtue of the fact that the open terror of the Party activists, hitherto unknown to such an extent, which culminated on 9 November in lootings, arson, abuse, mass transports, and numerous murders, was sanctioned by the regime, the whole system of government of the 'Third Reich' underwent a qualitative change. If the Party and state leadership had over the past few years, in public declarations at least, repeatedly distanced themselves from the 'individual actions', and with the subsequent legislative measures kept alive the illusion of a degree of legal security, now the regime's street terror was officially legitimized as an understandable expression of 'national rage', and with the subsequent mass internment of Jews in concentration camps was transformed directly into state terror. The laws passed after 9 November amounted to the complete deprivation of the rights of the Jewish minority; they represented a declaration of bankruptcy on the part of the lawyers in the Reich ministries, since what these laws meant in essence was the fact that the Jewish minority would henceforth be subjected to pure terror.

The German Jews had been publicly taken hostage, and the various public threats of extermination voiced by leading representatives of the regime over the coming weeks and months made it clear that the lives of the hostages could be placed at their mercy once again and to a far greater extent than before.

If it had still been possible, up until the November pogrom, to nurture the illusion that the regime gave free rein to terror only in emergencies, before invariably re-establishing order afterwards, and that the state apparatus, bound by norms, could repeatedly put a stop to the illegal 'measures' of the Party base, now the entirely arbitrary, terroristic character of the regime was clearly revealed. The regime no longer only controlled the professional careers of Jewish Germans, their possessions and their everyday behaviour; it had now elevated itself to become master of life and death.

The final capitulation of the conservative elites, and also of the general German population, to National Socialism's total claim to power could not have been more clearly expressed than by this total delivery of a minority defined by racial criteria into the hands of the regime. The total deprivation of the rights of the Jewish minority, the extensive pervasion of German society by National Socialism and the transition to a policy of expansion and heightened preparation for war were three processes which ran in parallel, and not by chance.

New Anti-Jewish Measures

The more intense campaign begun late in 1937 led in early 1938 to a whole series of anti-Jewish laws. Thus, for example, the law concerning changes of surnames and forenames of 5 January 1938 empowered the authorities to revoke name changes that had occurred before 30 January 1933, and to order official changes of forenames. (An implementation order of 17 August 1938 would finally stipulate that Jews might only bear forenames contained in the 'Guidelines for the Bearing of Forenames' passed by the Reich Interior Ministry on the same day, or else had to assume the obligatory additional names Israel or Sara.)

Through the law of 28 March, the Jewish religious associations lost their existing status as public corporations and thus a series of tax privileges. Also in March Jews were definitively excluded from the allocation of public commissions. In February 1938 Jews were excluded from the auction trade and in March from the weapons trade, when a general prohibition against Jews owning weapons was also introduced. In February 1938, through a change in the law concerning income tax, Jews were excluded from child tax benefit. Further discriminatory legal regulations were passed during this period, or else discussed and put on hold.

Early in 1938 Himmler, Reichsführer SS and Chief of the German Police, also opened up a sideline of 'Jewish policy': the systematic expulsion of Eastern European Jews from the Reich. Early in January 1938 he initially ordered that all Soviet Russian Jews be expelled. This meant about 500–1,000 former Russian citizens of Jewish extraction who had fled to the Reich and now, on the basis of existing laws, were being expelled without further explanation. This policy would finally lead to the expulsion of Polish Jews from the Reich in October 1938.[3]

The *Anschluss* and the Austrian Jews

With the *Anschluss* of Austria, in March 1938 about 200,000 more Jews came under immediate German rule. In Austria the persecution of the Jews very rapidly reached a level far more radical than the situation that had built up gradually in the Old Reich over a period of several years. The 'backlog' of anti-Semitic discrimination led, amongst the Austrian National Socialists, amidst the general frenzy of the assumption of power to a spontaneous discharge of hatred and aggression that put the waves of German anti-Semitism in 1933 and 1935 in the shade. Immediately after the German invasion the Austrian National Socialists, in particular in Vienna, launched a hounding (*Hatz*) of Jews, in which men and women were driven together and often forced by a mocking crowd to perform humiliating 'cleaning duties' in public streets and squares and similar places.[4] Over the next few weeks the German anti-Jewish special legislation was introduced in Austria.[5]

But in Austria from the very first, the direct and violent attack on Jewish property was a central component of the persecution measures, while within the Reich at the same time work was still under way on the preparation of the legal foundations for an expropriation of the Jews and the 'individual actions' of Party activists had been successfully contained for more than two years. In Austria, immediately after the *Anschluss* the local Party organs introduced 'Commissars' for Jewish businesses, whereby the transition to open plundering was often fluid. Gradually, however, Josef Bürckel, installed as Reich Governor by the Reich government, managed to bring the commissariats under his control and centralize the *Entjudung* of the economy.[6]

Particularly radical was the action by the National Socialists against the mostly Orthodox Jewish minority in Burgenland, numbering around 3,800 people, some of whom had been driven over the unmanned border, while some had fled to Vienna to disappear. In May, 2,000 Jews were arrested in Vienna and transported to Dachau.[7] In Austria, a few months after the *Anschluss*, not only had the Jews been totally eliminated from the economy, but the first mass deportations had been put into effect. As a result of these measures the pressure upon the Austrian Jews was intensified to the extent that their emigration assumed the character of a mass exodus: in the first five months after the *Anschluss* 46,000 Jews emigrated from Austria.[8]

The Final Exclusion of the Jews from the Economy and the Crisis of Jewish Emigration

The anti-Semitic thrust in 'annexed' Austria was to have a radicalizing effect on the persecution of Jews throughout the whole of the Reich.

If the 'Aryanization' of Jewish assets along legal lines was now introduced in the 'Old Reich' under the influence of the results achieved in Austria, these measures merely ended the factual expropriation of Jewish property, which was already far advanced.

The 'boycott' of Jewish companies, the continued discriminatory state measures against them, manifold pressure on Jewish owners to sell their businesses, were backed up from the end of 1937 by a massive obstruction of access to raw materials in the context of the allocation measures of the Four-Year Plan.[9] The Israeli historian Avraham Barkai estimates that by early 1938, as a result of all these hindrances to Jewish economic activity, around 60–70 per cent of Jewish businesses existing in 1933 were no longer in the hands of their former owners. Of the 50,000 retail businesses in the Old Reich in 1933, by July 1939 only about 9,000 still remained, while the assets in Jewish ownership which, in 1933, were estimated at 10–12 billion Reichmarks (RM), by April 1938 had already fallen to 5 billion.[10] In contrast, between April and November 1938 about 4,500–5,000 Jewish firms of all sizes and business types were 'Aryanized', or no more than 5 per cent of the Jewish businesses existing in 1933.

The recording and earmarking of Jewish businesses now initiated the definitive expulsion of Jews from the economy, 'Aryanization', along legal lines. By the end of 1937 Jewish businesses, following instructions from the Reich Economics Minister, were methodically recorded by the Chambers of Trade and Industry.[11]

The Third Decree of the Reich Citizenship Law of 14 June 1938 finally established that all Jewish businesses were to be included in a special list of enterprises.[12] Work on the recording of the businesses began immediately, and was scheduled for completion by that autumn.[13]

By autumn 1937, many local authorities had begun marking Jewish businesses without waiting for the expected legal regulation. After the passing of the Third Decree, there was an accumulation of cases in which Party activists marked Jewish businesses by daubing them with paint, and local authorities, under pressure from these actions, placed special signs on Jewish shops.[14]

The Commissioner for the Four-Year Plan's 'Decree against Support for the Disguising of Jewish Business Enterprises' of 22 April threatened German nationals with punishment if they helped to camouflage the 'Jewish character' of a business enterprise or carry out hidden transactions on behalf of Jews.[15]

The 'Decree for the Registration of Jewish Assets' of 26 April,[16] as well as the implementing order issued on the same day, obliged all Jews to report all assets over 5,000 marks by 30 June. The implementation order introduced a permit procedure for the sale of Jewish businesses which was to be carried out by the higher government departments.[17] This established the legal condition whereby remaining Jewish businesses could be steered individually towards 'Aryan' owners without resorting to the compulsory expropriation of Jewish assets.

A decree of the Reich Economics Ministry on 5 July 1938 established further particulars for the approval procedure; according to these, among other things, the relevant Gauleiter was to be consulted in the course of the procedure. In a Party order issued two weeks later, Bormann presented the possibilities that this decree created for the Party with unmistakable clarity:[18]

I refer particularly to the fact that the transfer of Jewish businesses to German hands gives the Party the opportunity to proceed with a healthy policy with regard to middle-sized businesses and help national comrades with suitable political and specialist qualities to achieve an independent livelihood even if they lack the requisite financial means. It is the Party's duty of honour to support those Party comrades who because of their membership of the movement have suffered economic disadvantages in the past and help them achieve an independent livelihood, and to support German citizens expelled from abroad who have lost their belongings...It is the Party's duty to ensure that the Jew does not receive an inappropriately high purchase price. In this way Jewry will make reparation for part of the damage that it has done to the German *Volk*.

Bormann further announced: 'Party Comrade Field Marshal Goering plans a fundamental sorting out of the Jewish question. This sorting out will occur in a way that does the greatest justice to the demands of the Party. The Party has accordingly undertaken to avoid all individual actions.'

The intervention of the Party through its Gau and district economic advisers in particular involved a personal and political assessment of interested purchasers and led to massive patronage of Party comrades. In the completion of contracts, 'donations' to the Party were habitual. The Party economic advisers had appropriate channels to use different methods to make the Jewish owner 'happy to sell', for example through repeated official screenings and the imposition of conditions, through arrests or the intervention of the Chambers of Trade and Industry or local authorities who 'suggested the advisability' of the sale.[19]

Between July and October a series of legal regulations was passed, definitively excluding the Jews from a series of further professions.[20] This included in particularly the prohibition on Jews working as real estate brokers or commercial agents; in addition, approval was withdrawn from those Jewish doctors still permitted to practise, and lawyers still working had to abandon their legal practices.

As early as the beginning of 1938, the SD had reached the conclusion that the increasing elimination of Jews from the economy would not necessarily lead to a greater volume of emigration, unless possibilities of reception abroad were also available. In fact, the number of emigrant Jews in the last quarter of 1937 had dropped slightly; within the SD a crisis in 'Jewish policy' was anticipated:

But it must not be forgotten that the possibilities of emigration have declined just as the pressure to emigrate has risen. The mounting exclusion of Jews from German economic life, which had taken a very strong upturn under the pressure of the conditions outlined, is at the same time causing a drop in the income of the Jewish community, and of the political and aid organizations from which to a large extent the emigration funds for less affluent Jews and Jews without means are drawn.

On the other hand, however, 'excessive reliance on foreign aid for the Jews contains the risk that emigration is made dependent on the goodwill of international aid organizations'.[21]

But with the *Anschluss* of Austria, which increased the number of Jews living under the Nazi regime by 200,000, the emigration chances of the 'Old Reich' Jews became even smaller, and from the perspective of the Jewish department of the SD the balance between 'pressure to emigrate' and possibilities of emigration would inevitably be lost. However, if emigration fell again, the massively advancing 'exclusion of Jews from economic life' would lead inevitably to the impoverishment of Jews still living in Germany, and thus to a further decline in emigration. Added to this threatening dilemma was the fact that in March 1938, immediately after the *Anschluss* of Austria, the Jewish Department of the SD learned of a decision by Himmler that called the existing emigration policy into question and clearly made the 'Jewish experts' of the SD deeply insecure. Having received an application to enter Germany from a German Jewish woman living abroad, the Reichsführer SS had ruled that the woman in question had permission to enter the country, 'in so far as she undertook to stay in Germany, as Germany did not want to let go of the Jews, its most valuable collateral'. As this instruction 'fundamentally altered previous "Jewish policy"', the Jewish Department asked, in a document intended for Himmler, for agreement on the following principles of emigration policy:[22]

(a) Those who are to emigrate are
1. The anti-social Jewish proletariat without means...
2. other old and young Jews, frail and without means, to free up the German welfare authorities for more worthwhile tasks and avoid trouble spots

(b) Those who are not to emigrate are
1. all wealthy Jews
2. all Jews who are famous or otherwise suited to acting as collateral.

The draft, the suggestions of which contradicted existing emigration practice, which had had the emigration of affluent Jews as its priority, was passed on to Himmler on 31 March and returned to the SD Department II in early June, signed by both Heydrich and Himmler, without a more detailed statement on the subject from either of them. It was not until the beginning of July that the responsible Gestapo specialist informed the Jewish department that Himmler had said the file was now redundant.[23]

In the spring and early summer of 1938, then, 'Jewish policy' faced a complicated dilemma: in the medium term the forced emigration of the Austrian Jews had to be to the detriment of the chances of emigration of the German Jews, particularly since the mass exodus prompted strong resistance in the potential countries of immigration. But that meant that because of the speedily advancing process of eliminating the Jews from the economy a subproletarian class would come into being, one which was barely capable of emigration and needed somehow to be supported, and yet which was to be expelled as a matter of priority according to the note sent by the Jewish Department in March. In the light of this, a willingness grew within the Party not only to use economic measures, but immediately to heighten 'the pressure to emigrate' through mass anti-Jewish rioting.

The Riots of Spring 1938: Dry Run for the Pogrom

This new wave of riots began in Berlin in May 1938. The Berlin events deserve particular attention, since it was here that the dialectic of agitation and subsequent large-scale state intervention typical of Nazi Jewish persecution occurred in exemplary fashion, and it is possible to observe patterns of action that are already very close to those of the November pogrom.

In May 1938 the Berlin Commissioner of Police, Count Helldorf, in response to a request from Goebbels, presented a 'Memorandum on the treatment of the Jews in the Reich capital in all areas of public life'[24] that contained suggestions for a programme of the almost complete segregation of the Berlin Jews. These were predominantly suggestions that were to be realized over the coming years, including labelling (by special ID cards), exclusion from public schools and cultural and leisure institutions, the marking of Jewish businesses, the concentration of Jews in particular areas of the city, and so on.

When the Jewish Department of the SD was briefly given access to the memorandum, it responded with alarm.[25] It raised the criticism that the memorandum did not embed the planned measures in a Reich-wide concept, and that it contained no references to emigration. Goebbels reacted to these objections, which had been presented to him along with the memorandum,[26] by recommending that the points particularly characteristic of Berlin be turned into general Reich-wide statutory regulations.[27] But he had by no means abandoned the idea of developing, in Berlin, a model for a future 'Jewish policy' throughout the Reich.

During the discussions about the memorandum, early in May 1938 individual local groups of Gau Berlin had begun daubing Jewish shops at night and sticking posters on them.[28] On 31 May, when the Gestapo arrested more than 300 Jews in a major raid on a café on the Kurfürstendamm, presumably in response to the growing 'popular anger', Goebbels criticized this action as 'a complete waste of an opportunity' and demanded more radical measures from the Police Commissioner.[29] On 10 June, a day before he was presented with the memorandum, Goebbels invited the heads of the Berlin police to the Ministry of Propaganda, where he took the opportunity to call for a more radical approach in the 'Jewish question':[30] 'I am really going all the way. Without any sentimentality. The watchword is not law, but harassment. The Jews must leave Berlin. The police will help me to achieve it.'

Over the next few days Goebbels ensured that the anti-Jewish atmosphere that he had systematically stirred up in Berlin was combined with the Reich-wide major action by the criminal police against 'social misfits' to form a campaign against 'Jewish criminals'.

The 'Asocial Operation'[31] was intended to send thousands of tramps, beggars, pimps, and others to concentration camps for the purposes of the 'labour mobilization programme'. In addition, all Jews who had been sentenced to previous convictions of at least one month were to be drawn into this operation. This extension of the operation, as a private remark of Heydrich reveals, goes back to a direct decision by Hitler, to arrest 'anti-social' and criminal Jews across the Reich to carry out important earth-moving works.[32]

In Berlin alone, within the context of the 'Asocial Operation' the police arrested between 1,000 and 2,000 Jews for minor misdemeanours, traffic offences, 'provocative behaviour', and the like. In Buchenwald concentration camp alone there were already more than 1,200 Jewish prisoners in the summer of 1938.[33]

In parallel with this, the anti-Jewish riots that had continued since May in various districts of Berlin were now systematically extended by the Berlin NSDAP to the whole of the city. Not only were Jewish shops and Jewish legal practices 'labelled' with daubings, but many windows were smashed and in the night of 18 June three synagogues and two prayer houses were demolished.[34]

The fierce riots and the mass arrests happening at the same time systematically created a bloodthirsty atmosphere throughout the capital, which Goebbels now plainly wanted to use to enforce the special measures he had demanded against the Jews. On 21 June, however, it was decided at a meeting of the Party and police leadership that the operation should be terminated.[35]

Goebbels noted in his diary entry for 22 June concerning the previous day's events:

Helldorf got my orders completely the wrong way round: I had said, the police acts with a legal face, the Party looks on. The reverse is now the case. I get all the Party agencies together and issue new orders. All illegal actions have to stop. The Jews are to clean their shops up themselves. Funk must get a move on with his measures. And incidentally there is something good about this kind of popular justice. The Jews have been given a shock, and will know better than to see Berlin as their Eldorado.[36]

In fact, however, the operation, as an internal note from the SD reveals, had been terminated after a personal intervention on Hitler's part.[37] In the case of the Berlin June Operation—unlike all other anti-Jewish actions in which the role of the 'Führer' was carefully concealed by the Party—it is possible to reconstruct in detail the central role played by Hitler: not only had the 'Führer' personally authorized the inclusion of Jews in the 'Asocial Operation', and involved himself in details of the propaganda justification of the deployment of police against the Berlin Jews,[38] but now he had personally also declared the end of the operation.

Major riots and broken windows, damage to synagogues, a close collaboration between vandals and police, and finally the attempt to mobilize a supposed popular movement for the enforcement of drastic state measures aimed at the expulsion of the Jews—the essential elements of the Berlin June Operation suggested that this was the dry run, staged to a large extent by Goebbels, for the pogrom that was organized in November. The cause for the termination of the Operation may have been that, in the spring of 1938, the 'Third Reich', in view of the unfolding Sudeten crisis, wanted to avoid anything that might intensify anti-German feeling in the West, and which might increase the chances of a military intervention against the 'Third Reich'—unlike the situation in November, when such foreign policy considerations were no longer relevant.

The SD saw the Berlin Operation as the confirmation of its attitude that the primary goal, the emigration of the Jews, could only be achieved by a systematic policy of expulsion that excluded uncontrolled acts of violence. According to the leader of Division II of the SD, Professor Franz Six, in his message to Higher Command South (Oberabschnitt Süd), the operation in Berlin had shown that in future 'no Party operation' might occur 'without previous authorization from the local police authority', and such operations had to be most keenly overseen by the SD, to channel violent measures against the German Jews.[39] On 5 July SD Headquarters informed the Higher Commands (Oberabschnitte) that the head of the Security Police, Heydrich, had 'because of the events in Berlin, reserved to himself the granting of permission for individual actions against the Jewish population in the Reich'.[40]

The Berlin Operation was followed in June/July by further riots against Jewish businesses, particularly in Frankfurt, Magdeburg, and Hanover, but also in Stuttgart. But by the end of July these attacks, expressed in daubings, boycotts, and so on, had subsided once more.[41]

Forced Expulsion

With the International Conference on Refugees held in July 1938 in Evian on the initiative of President Roosevelt in July 1938, and the formation of the Intergovernmental Committee on Political Refugees, the German side gained the prospect of the expulsion of the Jews from the Reich area being made an internationally soluble 'problem'.[42] First of all, however, according to a report on the conference produced for Heydrich by the Jewish department of the SD, it was 'the most urgent task for the immediate future to cause as many Jews as possible to emigrate under the existing conditions while no decisions have been made by the new Committee'. But foreign currency would have to be raised for the purpose.[43]

With the dissolution on 30 August of the state Zionist organization, already demanded by the Jewish department in February 1938 because of diminishing chances of emigration, the regime finally abandoned the option of encouraging it through apparent support of Zionist efforts to emigrate to Palestine.[44]

Meanwhile in Austria, Eichmann was developing a model that might speed up the expulsion of the Jews, without eating into the Reich's foreign-exchange reserves. Since April Eichmann had been acting as the official responsible for Jewish affairs in the local SD regional headquarters (Oberabschnitt), where he was initially responsible for the control of Jewish organizations. To accelerate the emigration, Eichmann took the initiative and saw to it that Reichskommmissar Bürckel set up a Central Office for Jewish Emigration, formally under the control of SD Oberabschnittsleiter Walther Stahlecker, but actually run by Eichmann himself.[45] In fact, with this office, established by a state official, the Reichskommissar, the SD had for the first time succeeded in exercising executive functions in its own right.[46] Eichmann and the SD's young 'Jewish experts' saw this decision as the opportunity to involve themselves energetically in the persecution of the Jews. The expulsion of the Viennese Jews was to provide the model case.

The Central Office, based in the Palais Rothschild, contained branches of all authorities required to be involved in applications to emigrate. Eichmann was to describe the basic concept of the Central Office in his police interrogation in Jerusalem as 'a conveyor belt. The initial application and all the rest of the required papers are put on at one end and the passport falls off the other end.'[47] By means of this conveyor-belt-like process the applicants could be herded through the building and be stripped almost seamlessly of their remaining assets.

With this money, extorted from Jews who were forced into emigration, Eichmann set up an 'emigration fund'. The Central Office also sent officials from Jewish organizations abroad to negotiate emigration places and obtain foreign currency.[48] By placing the burden of finance for emigration on the expelled individuals themselves, or on foreign-aid organizations, Eichmann had shown in exemplary fashion that one of the chief obstacles to larger-scale emigration, the question of cost, could be solved.

In the balance sheet drawn up by the Central Office for 1938, however, it was apparent that the number of emigrating Austrian Jews had not increased in spite of the introduction of the 'conveyor belt'. Whereas 46,000 Austrian Jews had emigrated in the five months from March to August 1938, the figure for the period between 26 August—the day the Central Office opened—and the end of the year was 34,467—a development that, given the diminishing opportunities for emigration overall, the Jewish department neverthless considered a success.[49]

But the ruthless expulsion of the Jews from Austria was only able to work because of the considerably more radical line taken in that country, particularly through the combination of riots, expulsions, and complete expropriation, and even then only for a limited period of time.

The Sudeten crisis made it very clear to those responsible for Germany's *Judenpolitik* that they constantly had to reckon with the possibility of entering a war before the emigration of the German and Austrian Jews was complete. The previous general plans, on the other hand, had always been based around a longer-term preparation for war, in which the *Entjudung* of Germany was considered an important precondition for the achievement of readiness for war in terms of the economy and morale. Now, though, there was suddenly a real prospect of having in the country, during a war, several hundred thousand people who were seen as enemies of the state.

One initial suggestion as to how this situation might be overcome was made by the head of the SD Jewish Department, Herbert Hagen, early in September under the title 'Activity of the Department in the Event of Mobilization'.[50] Apart from the 'arrest of all Jews of foreign nationality to prevent their making contact with other countries', Hagen suggested (as their deployment in Ersatzreserve II[51] would contradict the 'military ethos of the German army') the 'accommodation of all Jews in special camps and their deployment in munitions production and other work on the home front'; Jewish women who were unfit for war work could 'look after those in need of help'. If mobilization were to occur after the planned census (which was to make the complete record of all Jews possible for the first time, Hagen went on to say, 'the definition of a person's Jewish character should be undertaken according to the stipulations of the Reich Citizenship Law, unless particular reasons relating to the intelligence service or the security police require special treatment'. The document does not reveal whether the term 'special treatment' merely refers euphemistically to an exemption from the stipulations of the Reich Citizenship Law or—which in my view seems more likely—is supposed to refer, according to the usual terminology of the SS, to the liquidation of this group.

Between Sudetenland Crisis and Pogrom: Increasing Attacks on the German Jews

A further brutalization of 'Jewish policy' began in September with the end of the Sudetenland crisis, when Party activists resumed their anti-Jewish operations. As in the summer riots, these activists were still determined to intensify the pressure to emigrate still further. The tension that had built up during September in the face of the expectation of the immediately impending military conflict was now discharged in direct acts of violence by Party activists against Jewish property and Jewish life, which put the activities of the summer in the shade.

This connection between a foreign-policy crisis and increased outbreaks of anti-Semitic hatred was established, for example, in a report by the SD for the month of October,[52] according to which 'the increasing anti-Jewish attitude of the population, which was chiefly caused by the provocative and impertinent behaviour of individual Jews during the period of the foreign policy crisis', found 'its most powerful expression in actions against the Jewish population, which in the south and south-west of the Reich partly assumed the character of a pogrom'.

According to an SD report that would not be dispatched because of the events of 9 November, the operations in late September/October were at first largely concentrated upon the area of the SD regional headquarters South, South-West, West, and Danube, before moving in isolated instances to Danzig and central Germany. The focus of the riots lay without question in Middle Franconia.[53]

In many places synagogues were damaged or destroyed beginning in late September:

+ in Beveringen and Neuenkirchen (Kreis Wiedenbrück) in September;
+ in Neuwedel (Neumark) on the night of 28/9 Sept. 1938;
+ in Mellrichstadt (Lower Franconia) on the night of 30 Sept./1 Oct. 1938;[54]

+ in a small village near Euskirchen on the night of 1/2 Oct. 1938;[55]
+ in Leutershausen on the night of 16/17 Oct.;
+ in Dortmund-Hörde on 27/8 Oct.;[56]
+ in October, in the district of Alzenau (Lower Franconia) two synagogues were damaged by stones;[57]
+ at the end of October a tear-gas grenade was thrown into the synagogue in Ansbach;[58]
+ in October the interior of the synagogue in Langen (Hesse) was destroyed;[59]
+ on 1 November an arson attack was carried out on the synagogue in Konstanz;[60]
+ in Zirndorf near Nuremberg a synagogue was destroyed on the night of 4/5 Nov.[61]

In many places windows were smashed and Jews violently attacked.[62]

The further radicalization of the persecution of the Jews was expressed in the expulsion of Jewish families, some of long standing, from their homes. Particularly in the Gaus of Franconia and Württemberg, according to an SD report for the month of October,[63] 'the Jews of individual towns and villages were forced by the population to leave their homes immediately, taking with them only bare necessities. Most of these actions encouraged by [Party] local branches or district leaders and carried out by the Party formations [SA and SS] were mostly purely local in character.'

The anti-Jewish riots in Vienna were also particularly violent. On the night of 5 October, in various districts of Vienna the Jews living there were forced to clear their homes immediately. It was hoped that this threat, which was later withdrawn, would unleash a panic-stricken flight of the Jews.[64]

Towards the end of October the riots directed against the Jews were concentrated particularly in Franconia, where the Gauleiter Julius Streicher, according to information from the SD, had declared as early as July, with reference to the 'Jewish question', 'that the *Anschluss* has brought the problem to a stage in which fundamental decisions can no longer be ignored. The question could now no longer be addressed by propagandistic means.'[65]

At the end of October, SD regional headquarters South reported that a few days previously all Jews had been registered on file on Streicher's orders: 'The political leaders are expecting a major operation against the Jews within the next few days.' On 24 October 1938, the deputy Gauleiter, Karl Holz, was said to have declared at a local Nazi rally in Nuremberg that it would 'even have been desirable if the exodus of the Jews had been encouraged a little more quickly in Nuremberg as well'.[66]

In response to an enquiry from SD regional headquarters South on 22 October, asking whether the instigators of individual actions 'should still be treated ruthlessly', the Jewish Department of the SD observed on 3 November 'that a general ruling cannot be given, as no decision has yet been received from C (= Heydrich)'.[67]

The Pogrom of 9/10 November 1938: *Reichskristallnacht*

While the Party activists were, with their violent actions, exerting an even stronger 'pressure to emigrate' both on Jews living in Germany and on countries outside Germany, increasingly alarmed by terrifying reports from Germany, the regime decided in the course of October to strengthen its *Judenpolitik* still further.

On the one hand the government considered itself compelled by the international situation—considerably worsened as a result of its own policies—to undertake greater efforts to rearm, for which in turn the remaining assets of the Jews were urgently needed, as Goering made plain at a meeting of the General Council of the Four-Year Plan on 14 October. Goering declared that he was 'under instruction from the Führer to increase armaments to an abnormal degree... He faced unimaginable difficulties. The coffers were empty, manufacturing capacity was full to the brim with contracts for years ahead... He would turn the economy around, with violent means if necessary, to achieve that goal.' Above all the 'Jewish question' must now 'be addressed with all possible means, because they must now leave the economy'.

'Aryanization' was not to be seen, however, as it had been in Austria, 'as a welfare system for inadequate Party members... It was entirely a matter for the state. But he could not make foreign currency available for the evacuation of the Jews. If necessary, ghettos would have to be set up in the individual cities.'[68]

A note by the leader of Main Department IV of the Reich Economics Ministry reveals that Goering had, on 14 October, also ordered the 'Aryanization' of the entire Jewish bank, stock-exchange, and insurance system, and after 1 January prohibited any kind of bank deals by Jews.[69]

In October the regime also found itself confronted by a second problem: it was feared that the Polish government might anticipate the deportation of Polish Jews from the Reich by expatriating that group. It therefore decided on a major deportation of this group. This enterprise was enforced with extraordinary brutality at the end of October, and marks the transition from anti-Jewish actions emanating from the Party base to a centrally directed campaign that was to lead on to the November pogrom.

With its new State Citizenship Law, which came into force on 31 March 1938, the Polish government had created the possibility of withdrawing state citizenship from Polish citizens living abroad for a long period of time. From the point of view of the Nazi regime, this produced the prospect of the 70,000 Polish Jews living in Germany (and many of whom had been born there) becoming stateless people.[70]

Consequently, since May deportations from Poland had been occurring on a larger scale and in August the Decree regarding the Special Police Department for

Foreign Nationals was tightened, unambiguously focusing on Jews. When the Polish Minister of the Interior decreed on 6 October that henceforth admission would be granted only to Poles from abroad who were able to show a special note in their passports, but that this could be withheld by the consulates if there were reasons to deny state citizenship, at the end of October the German police launched the operation to deport all Polish Jews, which had already been in preparation for some time. On the evening of 27 October and the two days that followed, Polish Jews were arrested all over the Reich, brought to collection points and transported under inhuman conditions in sealed and strictly guarded special trains to the border with Poland. The trains stopped just before the Polish border, which had been closed since the run-up to the action and their passengers were driven over the border. After the Polish side had initially turned these people away and thousands of them were wandering back and forth in no-man's-land, internment camps were set up in Polish border towns. The action, which led overall to the expulsion of around 18,000 Polish Jews, ended on 29 October, after Poland had threatened the deportation of German citizens.

Herschel Grynspan's attempt on the life of the Legation Secretary of the German embassy in Paris, Ernst vom Rath, on 7 November, was an act of revenge for the brutal expulsion of Grynspan's Hanover-based parents to Poland that has no historical causal link with the pogrom on 9 November. Grynspan, who had fatally injured vom Rath, merely provided the Nazi regime with an excuse to launch a pogrom which at least parts of the Party base had been urging since the spring of 1938. This pogrom was to form the precondition for a new wave of anti-Semitic laws which had also been prepared since spring 1938 and which, in the view of the Party leadership and in the face of the precarious situation in armaments, urgently had to be put into force. A pogrom would also unleash a new mass exodus among the Jews of the 'Great German Reich' and at the same time exert the necessary pressure upon foreign governments finally to hold the negotiations for an international solution of the 'Jewish question' in Germany.

On the same day of the assassination attempt, 7 November, the Nazi press, following the instructions of the Ministry of Propaganda, announced that Grynspan's crime, an attack by 'world Jewry', would have unforeseeable consequences for the situation of the Jews in Germany.[71] Particularly in Hesse, on 7, 8, and 9 November Party activists organized anti-Jewish riots in which synagogue interiors were destroyed and shops with Jewish owners were smashed.[72]

The actual pogrom was unleashed a few hours after Rath's death on 9 November by an intensely anti-Semitic speech by Goebbels at a meeting of leading Party members in Munich's Old Town Hall, held as it was every year in memory of the National Socialist putsch in 1923. The speculation frequently encountered in the literature that the news of Rath's death arrived during the meeting, and that Hitler immediately informed Goebbels, who immediately seized the initiative and possibly went beyond the goal assigned him by Hitler is, however, an exaggerated account of events.[73] In fact the news of Rath's death arrived before the start of the event in the Rathaussaal in Munich, as Goebbels's diaries reveal: 'In the afternoon the death of the German diplomat vom Rath is announced. That's good... I go to the Party reception in the old Rathaus. Terrific activity. I brief Hitler on the affair. He decides: allow the demonstrations to go on. Withdraw the police. The Jews should feel the people's fury. That's right. I issue appropriate instructions to police and party. Then I give a brief speech on the subject to the Party leadership. Thunderous applause. Everyone dashed to the telephones. Now the people will act.'[74]

After the speech by the Propaganda Minister the senior party officials present at the meeting immediately informed the headquarters of the Gaus and the SA Group staffs that troops of Party members and members of the SA wearing civilian clothes were to destroy synagogues and demolish Jewish shops during the night.[75] The orders that reached the lower echelons were thus inevitably inconsistent.[76]

The most senior Party court of the NSDAP, which, following the November pogrom, had to deal with a whole series of serious crimes such as murder, mistreatment, and rape established the following with regard to the nature of the order on 9 November:

The instructions of the head of Reich Propaganda, issued orally, have probably been understood by all Party leaders present to mean that the Party should not appear as the instigators of demonstrations, but in reality organize and carry them out... The examination of the conditions under which the orders were issued has revealed that in all these cases a misunderstanding has occurred in some link of the chain of command, especially because of the fact that it is obvious to active National Socialists from the *Kampfzeit* that actions which the Party does not want to appear to have organized are not ordered in a clear and detailed manner. Consequently they are accustomed to reading more into such orders than is expressed literally, as it has also in many respects become customary for the person issuing the order, in the interests of the Party—and especially if the order concerns illegal political demonstrations—not to spell out everything and only to suggest what he wishes to achieve with the order.

Because of orders that were 'not always felicitously formulated' many sub-leaders assumed that 'Jewish blood must flow for the blood of Party comrade vom Rath, and that, at any rate according to the will of the leadership, the life of a Jew was of no consequence'.

For these reasons the Higher Party court had also recommended that in the fourteen cases of crimes of killing already heard, proceedings before the state courts be quashed and in most of these cases Party court trials should be abandoned, or only insignificant sentences passed. Only in two cases of rape was the case to be pursued further before the state courts.[77]

This kind of indirect command, to be understood intuitively, was typical of the National Socialists and had the advantage that the issuer of the order assumed no legally demonstrable responsibility, but it did involve the risk that some of the subordinates did not correctly understand the meaning of the instruction in question and either did not act radically enough or in their over-eagerness overshot the mark. This factored-in vagueness in the Party leadership's orders was, as we have seen, typical of the tactic of the 'individual actions' of the Party since 1933, particularly for the anti-Jewish riots in spring and summer 1935 as well as in the spring/early summer of 1938: in the Party base there was always a certain uncertainty as to whether the official Party prohibitions on these individual actions were 'meant seriously' or only intended to mislead the public, so that especially radical activists very often contravened the Party line. But such calamities were an inevitable element of the tactic of indirect command, and they could only have been avoided if the Party leadership had compromised itself with clear orders in writing. But the internal Party contradictions that repeatedly arose as a consequence of hidden orders were primarily shaped by this tactic and not the result of profound contradictions within the NSDAP about the course of the *Judenpolitik* or an expression of the Party's incapacity for goal-oriented action.

The curious aspect of this kind of hidden order was that because of the calculated vagueness, corrective action always had to be taken from above. In the case of the November pogrom this task fell to the Security Police and the SD. The execution of the pogrom was unambiguously a Party matter; the state and Party security apparatus, united in the person of Heydrich, clearly surprised by the action, and yet immediately ready to act, had first of all to perform flanking manoeuvres and adapt to accommodating the large number of prisoners driven together by Party activists.[78]

As they had been ordered to do, in the night of 9/10 November SA and SS troops, mostly in civilian clothes and backed up by Party members, forced their way into synagogues, smashed up the interiors, looted or destroyed the ritual objects, and finally burned down the houses of God. The fire brigades were commanded only to prevent the flames from spreading to the surrounding houses. Likewise, Jewish shops were destroyed, had their windows smashed in, and their storerooms looted or thrown into the street. In many places the Party activists led actual processions, generally accompanied by a curious crowd, roaring anti-Jewish slogans and marching from one object of destruction to the next. The terrorist units forced their way into apartments inhabited by Jews, destroyed the furniture, and made off with valuables. The residents of the apartments were mocked, humiliated, and physically mistreated, in many cases in the most cruel and shocking way; and the 25,000–30,000 Jewish men arrested during the night also had to endure inhuman harassment and torture, which was intensified during their subsequent concentration-camp detention.[79]

The precise number of fatalities who fell victim to these acts of violence is not known; officially the figure was given as ninety-one,[80] but to this there should be added a large number of suicides, as well as the hundreds of Jews who were killed in the following weeks and months in the concentration camps, or died as a result of their detention. In Buchenwald alone 227 of the prisoners delivered died in the first six weeks; 400 Jews involved in the pogrom died in all the camps.[81]

The damage caused between 8 and 10 November, according to Reich Insurance Group in 1939, came to 49.5 million Reichmarks. Of this, over 46.1 million was to Jews of German citizenship, over 1.7 million was to 'Aryans', and more than 1.6 million to foreign Jews.[82] A survey of twenty-four private insurance companies showed that their disbursements for break-in damage caused during the November pogrom were 3.3 million RM higher than the sum that the companies had paid throughout the whole of the rest of the year for that offence.[83]

The individual elements of the pogrom, smashed windows, destruction of synagogues, forced entry to dwellings, looting, mistreatment, even murder, were not new, but they were part of the anti-Semitic repertoire of the Party activists. The pogrom represented a culmination of the anti-Jewish riots that had been going on for years; it was an expression of the fundamental radically anti-Semitic mood at the grass roots of the NSDAP.

Outside the circle of Party activists and supporters of the NSDAP, the pogrom met with little sympathy, but overall the population—doubtless intimidated by this unfamiliar level of violence—responded passively.[84] This acceptance of the pogrom by the majority of the population must have seemed like the crucial success from the perspective of the Nazi regime: it had been possible to treat Jews publicly as non-persons who could be robbed, mistreated, and killed. The pogrom made it clear to everyone that the total exclusion of the Jews from German society had been completed; they had been condemned to a shadowy existence.

This 'social death' of the Jews still living in Germany, decreed by the regime, was the essential element in the organization of the public that the Nazi government associated with the third wave of anti-Semitism in 1938. The 'Jewish question' within Germany, raised repeatedly by the Nazi regime since 1933, was now declared to have been largely 'solved'; after almost six years of radical anti-Semitic policies, the Jews living in Germany had essentially played their part as dangerous aliens to its conclusion. Disregard and contempt for the Jews still living in Germany, indifference to their further fate was now the attitude that propaganda prescribed for the population. With the worsening of the international situation and the approaching war, the 'Jewish question' had to be raised onto the international stage, the Jewish 'enemy' had to be presented as the potential enemy in the capital cities of potential opponents. A *Volksgemeinschaft* under National Socialist rule battling against the 'Jewish global enemy'—that was how one might describe the new arrangement that the Nazi regime, in the phase of transition to war, presented as a leitmotif for the treatment of the 'Jewish question'.

Judenpolitik between the Pogrom and the Start of the War

Discussions of the Party and State Leaderships Concerning Further Anti-Jewish Measures

In the weeks that followed the pogrom, a series of major conferences of leading representatives of the Nazi state were held to discuss further steps in *Judenpolitik*. So far researchers have reconstructed the sessions chaired by Goering on 12 November and 6 December, and the discussion on 16 December, chaired by Frick. At the centre of these debates was the problem, and the solution of that problem: how the planned complete exclusion of the Jews from German society could be harmonized with the goal of forced emigration.

On 12 November, two days after the official announcement of the end of the pogrom, more than a hundred representatives of a great variety of state and Party offices met to discuss further developments in *Judenpolitik*.[85] At this meeting leading representatives of the regime made a series of remarkable declarations on the 'Jewish question', which should be quoted here in some detail.

Goering introduced the session by first referring to the ministerial meeting of 28 April at which the 'Aryanization question' had been discussed, and finally considered the June events in Berlin, the 'dry run' for *Reichskristallnacht*: 'In the meeting at which we first discussed this question and made the decision to Aryanize the German economy, take the Jews out of the economy, put them into the debt register and pension them of, alas we only made very fine plans, which were then only pursued very slowly. Then we had a demonstration here in Berlin. Then the people were told: something decisive is going to happen. But again nothing happened. Now we have had this thing in Paris. After it came more demonstrations, and now something must happen!'

But, Goering went on, 'I have had enough of these demonstrations. They damage not the Jews, but ultimately me, since I am finally responsible for the economy.'

As for 'Aryanization', Goering elaborated, the 'basic idea' was this: 'The Jew is excluded from the economy and signs over his business to the state. He receives compensation for it. This compensation is recorded in the debt register and interest is paid at a particular percentage. That is what he has to live on.'

After Goering had explained further details of the Aryanization process, Heydrich provided a survey of the destruction caused: 101 synagogues were destroyed by fire,[86] 76 demolished; 7,500 shops were demolished. Thirty-five deaths, he later added to the debate, were to be recorded.

In the subsequent discussion, Goebbels made further suggestions: they concerned the prohibition on visiting theatres, cinemas, circuses etc.;[87] the Reich railways were to install special compartments for Jews; Jewish pupils were to be removed from general schools. Goebbels also demanded a decree 'that Jews should be forbidden to visit German swimming pools, beach pools, and German sana-toriums'. They should 'consider whether it might not be necessary to forbid Jews entering German forests. Today Jews are running in packs around the Grunewald [in Berlin]. That's a constant provocation, there are constant incidents... And then that the Jews can't sit around in German parks.'

Finally Heydrich brought the discussion back to the 'basic problem', the question of 'getting the Jews to leave Germany'. Heydrich referred in detail to the experiences they had had with the 'Jewish Emigration Centre' in Vienna, and suggested the creation of a similar institution for the whole of the Reich. Goering agreed with this suggestion.

Next Heydrich suggested an 'Emigration operation for the Jews in the rest of the Reich', which should stretch over 'at least 8–10 years'. In this period one of the chief problems was the 'proletarianization of the remaining Jews', which was already under way; the Jews should be allowed to practise certain occupations.

To be able to keep an eye on the Jews still remaining in Germany, according to Heydrich, they should be identified by a badge. ('A uniform', Goering added.) On the other hand, Heydrich considered unrealistic Goering's suggestion of ghetto-izing the Jews: the 'control of the Jews by the watchful eye of the population as a whole' was the better way.

The fact that the suggestion of large-scale emigration of the German Jews was generally positively received at the meeting was the crucial step for Heydrich and the SD to assume the leading role in future *Judenpolitik*. The development by the 'Jewish department' of a comprehensive plan of expulsion secured in terms of both domestic and foreign policy now had the chance of being declared the official policy of the 'Third Reich'. In contrast it became apparent that Goebbels still clung to the concept of total segregation for the Jewish minority, without his being able to integrate this within an overall plan for a 'solution' of the 'Jewish question'.

Finally Goering made the following fundamental statement about the future of *Judenpolitik*: 'If, in the near future, the German Reich should come into conflict with foreign powers, it goes without saying that we in Germany should first of all let it come to a showdown with the Jews. Besides that, the Führer will now take the initiative with those foreign powers which have brought the Jewish question up, in order to deal with the Madagascar project. He explained it all to me on 9 November. There is no other way. He will say to the other countries, "Why are you always talking about the Jews?—Take them!"'

Just four weeks after this remarkable meeting, on 6 December Goering held a further major discussion with the Gauleiters, Reich Governors, and Oberpräsi-denten, in which he set out the latest guidelines on *Judenpolitik* that 'the Führer' had explained to him in a conversation a few days before.[88]

At the meeting Goering particularly stressed Hitler's decision 'that all decrees to be passed on the "Jewish question" are to be examined by me'. However, Hitler did not want Goering's new role to be publicly revealed, since 'in my present position I would be too compromised both at home and abroad'. Elsewhere he stressed that he actually wanted 'nothing to do with the whole Jewish question. But then of course I don't know how I am to keep my Four-Year Plan, the German economy, in order.'

The most important aspect of the further development of *Judenpolitik* lay in 'vigorously forcing emigration'. Goering discussed the plans pursued by Austrian Economics Minister Fischböck and Schacht to make emigration possible through international loans and a large-scale basic agreement, and analysed individual aspects of the plan, which had already been authorized by Hitler.

The 'Aryanization' of Jewish property was to take place gradually and in a controlled form. Goering expressly warned against a complete expropriation of German Jews, since, in the event of renewed reprisals, the regime would then be forced to go beyond economic measures: 'If—God forbid—any of you or another prominent man were got at by the Jew, the Jew knows that things would come thundering down on him in quite a different way. Then if he has no more goods to lose, he knows how he can be got at.'

Goering went on to reveal a series of concrete decisions made by Hitler with regard to *Judenpolitik*. According to these, Jews were not to be labelled;[89] no prohibitions were to be introduced for selling to Jews; a *Judenbann* (ban on entry by Jews) could be introduced in particular localities. On the ghetto question Goering commented in general terms that 'the Jews would somehow finally be brought together in certain residential districts'.

Goering then revealed his intention of continuing to treat at least some of the German Jews as hostages: 'Of course we will retain a certain category of Jews. Certain Jews, whom I could very easily allow to emigrate, I will not allow to do so because I need them as guarantees that the other tribe outside will also contribute for Jews without means.'

Finally Goering discussed the question of the employment of Jews; it could occur in closed 'worker formations' or, within production facilities, in closed-off areas.

Ten days after this conference, on 16 December 1938, another major discussion of the 'Jewish question' took place, in which several Reich Ministers participated, among them Heydrich and a large number of Gauleiters and heads of the Prussian provincial administration.[90] On this occasion Wilhelm Frick, the Minister of the Interior, clearly distanced himself from the events of 9/10 November, which he described as 'nonsense', 'indeed madness'. The whole action had 'only one positive consequence', namely that the impetus of the Jews to leave Germany had now become so great that 'it is to be hoped that in a few years we will be freed from them'.

Frick went on to discuss Schacht's emigration project, already mentioned by Goering, and made a series of statements concerning the next imminent steps in *Judenpolitik*. In the foreground were the problems that had, at the two Goering conferences, emerged as the chief problems of future *Judenpolitik*: comprehensive emigration, the conclusion of 'Aryanization', the questions of employment, and accommodation.[91]

Legislation after the Pogrom

As early as 12 November 1938, the day when Goering held his first conference on the future of *Judenpolitik*, the first concrete legal and administrative measures had been set in motion. These measures primarily concerned 'Aryanization'. Jews were prohibited from working in retail or business enterprises, and forbidden to offer goods or services at fairs and so on. A Jew could no longer run a business; where Jews occupied posts as managerial employees, they could be summarily dismissed.[92] The Decree to Restore the Appearance of the Streets as affecting Jewish Businesses decreed that Jewish shop- and home-owners were obliged immediately to remove all damage caused in connection with the pogrom. All insurance claims by Jews of German nationality were to be confiscated for the benefit of the Reich.[93] A further act of 12 November imposed an 'atonement payment' of one billion Reichmarks upon Jews with German citizenship.[94] The businesses of domestic and stateless Jews had to be closed immediately, while foreign Jews were granted a deadline of the end of the year.[95]

A decree of 3 December 1938 ordered the compulsory 'Aryanization' of still existing Jewish businesses by officially appointed trustees. Cash, securities, and jewellery could no longer be freely sold, but had to be offered to public purchasing offices; securities were to be put in depositories in foreign exchange licensed banks.[96]

In addition, during the weeks after the pogrom, a whole series of further discriminatory anti-Jewish regulations was introduced:[97] on 15 November 1938 the Reich Education Minister ruled that 'all remaining Jewish pupils in German schools be dismissed immediately';[98] with the law of 8 December Jewish academics were forbidden to do private work in libraries and universities;[99] Jews were prohibited from owning any weapons;[100] they were excluded from any kind of cultural events;[101] they were no longer permitted to drive motor vehicles.[102] A police ordinance of 28 November empowered the authorities to impose spatial and temporal residential restrictions upon the Jews.[103] This provided a major precondition for the implementation of the 'ghettoization' of the German Jews, the details of which were still unclear. This new instrument was immediately applied: the chief of the Security Police determined that Jews were to stay in their homes from midday until 8.00 p.m. on 'days of national solidarity'.[104] A fundamental edict issued by the President of the Reich Labour Exchange introduced a duty of labour for 'all unemployed Jews who are fit for work'.[105]

On 28 December, after a conversation with Hitler, Goering announced the authoritative 'expression of the Führer's will' concerning further measures in *Judenpolitik*.[106] In accordance with this catalogue, which was less severe than the far more radical plans discussed by Heydrich, Goebbels, and Goering after the November pogrom, and which was aimed primarily at the restriction of the mobility of the Jews, a further wave of discriminatory regulations was passed by the ministerial bureaucracy over the ensuing weeks and months: Jews were forbidden to use sleeping and dining cars,[107] rent protection for Jews was largely abolished.[108] Extensive restrictions, as decreed by Hitler, were imposed upon stays by Jews in spas and health resorts.[109]

In the first months of 1939, these were joined by further anti-Jewish measures that had not been contained in Hitler's late-December catalogue. Thus, in January and February 1939 various measures were introduced to force the Jews to hand over to state offices jewellery, precious metals, and other valuable objects.[110] In March 1939 Jews were definitively excluded from military and labour service.[111]

If we consider the anti-Jewish measures passed in the first few months after the November pogrom against the background of the steps discussed in the three great meetings on 12 November, 6 and 12 December, it becomes apparent that the five major problem areas discussed there—emigration, 'Aryanization', labelling, ghettoizing, employment—were addressed at different tempos. While the further intensification of the expulsion of the Jews—which was seen as the decisive beginning of the solution—depended on the international negotiations undertaken by Schacht, 'Aryanization' was pursued with the greatest vigour, spatial concentration began relatively slowly, labelling was rejected or shelved, and the problem of Jewish employment in view of the rapid impoverishment of the Jews was acknowledged relatively late, but then taken up at an accelerated pace. After large-scale 'emigration' proved to be illusory, compulsory employment and spatial restriction (with a tendency towards ghettoization) were combined to form an enforced regime and detention in camps was taken into consideration as the 'interim solution' best suited to a war situation.

Through the legal regulations for 'Aryanization' instituted after the November pogrom, the existing authorization procedure became obligatory for the 'Aryanization' or liquidation of Jewish property.[112] In December 1938 the procedure was straightened out by the relevant ministries and the staff of the Führer's Deputy (StdF), and in February there followed an order from the Führer's Deputy regulating the Party's involvement in the context of the disposal of Jewish property.[113]

A vivid picture of the practice of Aryanization after the pogrom is contained in the special report from the mayor of Berlin on the *Entjudung* of the retail trade in the Reich capital, published in January 1939.[114] According to this, after the pogrom there were 3,700 retailers; of these businesses about two-thirds had been 'eliminated', which had brought considerable relief to the retail trade. In the course of the liquidation procedure, goods 'from Jewish sources' were on offer from Economic Group Retail worth a total of 6 million marks, which typically, after examination by the responsible expert, were assigned an estimated value of only 4.5 million. Where the takeover of Jewish business was concerned, 'immediately after the events of the night of 10 November such a crush began in the various districts that officials, for example from the Mitte district, were kept busy all day doing nothing but providing information to applicants and distributing forms. The first request from applicants normally involved an application for credit for the takeover of a Jewish retail business... For the bulk of applicants, who were entirely uninformed not only about the financial side, but also about the retail sector, this prompted the second question, namely where could they be "sure of finding" a good Jewish business. This too is proof of the fact that elements who have no business experience are interested in acquiring Jewish businesses.' The report went on:

For each individual Jewish retail business there were usually at least 3–4 applicants. Among the retinues [i.e. staffs] various factions then formed, declaring themselves in favour of the various applicants, seeking to support them with numerous visits to more or less responsible officials, while accusing one another of friendship towards the Jews.... The retinues of a medium-sized department store near Görlitzer railway station appeared several times in large numbers at my office even supporting an applicant whom I had already rejected... To introduce a certain order among the countless applicants, with the consent of the Reich Economics Ministry, it was agreed between the Party's Berlin offices and my department to involve the Berlin district leaders heavily in the selection of applicants...

At the front of the queue should be old and outstanding Party members who were injured during the *Kampfzeit*. Next come Party members who want to make themselves independent, but who must have business experience, then those who have suffered loss through demolition work (in the context of the reconstruction of Berlin), and finally long-term employees of Jewish firms, as long as they are not *Judenknechte* ['servants of the Jews'].

In view of the rush of frequently unqualified applicants for Jewish shops, the mayor observed that the 'overall impression' left by 'Aryanization' was 'not pleasant'. He himself had not thought it possible that 'the opportunity as a German to take over Jewish businesses would prompt such an extraordinary rush of applications', or 'that circles of whom it would not have been expected often asked the person reporting whether he didn't have "a good Jewish property available", could provide information about the whereabouts of Jewish furniture etc.'.

To the taxes that had already been introduced, which were specially designed for the economic looting of Jews, further financial burdens were added after the pogrom. The contribution imposed on the German Jews raised a total of 1,127 billion RM.[115] The Jewish Assets Tax, imposed from December 1938, further empowered the authorities to raise taxes for the benefit of the Reich through 'Aryanization'. According to an order of 8 February 1939 issued by the Reich Economics Minister the tax was to constitute 70 per cent of the difference between the official estimated value and the price actually paid.[116] On 10 June 1940, Goering passed an 'Order concerning the Verification of *Entjudung* deals',[117] which was intended as a compensation tax on all those Aryanization sales undertaken since 30 January 1933 in which the buyer had realized a 'disproportionate benefit'.

There was also a special emigration tax, which had been levied since the end of 1938 by police stations or Gestapo offices in various places, and which—to some extent at least—was used for the financing of emigration. One such tax had been levied by the Gestapo in Hamburg since December 1938,[118] while the Chief of Police in Berlin, according to Heydrich, introduced a 'special tax on wealthy Jews', which by February 1939 had already brought in three million RM, which were paid to the Reich Economics Ministry.[119]

These regulations were made standard for the whole Reich area from March 1939. With a decree of 25 February, issued to all Gestapo headquarters,[120] the Chief of the Security Police determined that 'a special tax as a single extraordinary contribution' should be levied on all Jews upon emigration. The tax was to be graded according to the assets of the emigrating individuals, and used to promote the emigration of Jews without assets.[121] By virtue of the fact that the Jews now had to finance their own expulsion, a highly efficient connection between economic robbery and forced 'emigration'—on the model created by Eichmann in Vienna— had been put in place. Altogether the various taxes and levies resulted in the comprehensive financial theft of Jewish property.

Jewish Forced Labour before the Start of the War

Even before *Reichskristallnacht*, bureaucratic efforts had got under way to deploy Jews for forced labour. From the regime's point of view, the tense situation in the labour market suggested, on the one hand, that the Jews excluded from economic life could be used again as a workforce (separated from non-Jewish workers and in subordinate occupations); on the other hand, the regime certainly also hoped that through tough working conditions the pressure towards emigration could be further heightened; an important additional factor for the introduction of forced labour was also the hope of a reduction in state welfare costs.[122] After the pogrom forced labour, alongside forced expropriation, residence prohibition, and detention in camps, became one of the central elements of the forced regime imposed upon the Jews.

Concrete plans for the forced labour deployment of Jews had begun in the summer of 1938. At the meeting held in Goering's office on 14 October, the proposal had been made to establish 'Jewish labour columns';[123] the President of the Reich Labour Exchange had issued instructions to the labour offices to report all Jews registered as unemployed.[124] In Vienna several hundred Jews had been deployed since as early as October in closed columns working apart from other workers; an extension of this 'labour deployment' in Austria—mostly in quarrying and similar heavy labour—was planned. Entirely in the spirit of the forced labour that was to come, in October the Reich Labour Exchange had rejected the suggestion of allowing an autonomous Jewish labour exchange to come into being.[125]

After Goering had stated that he was fundamentally in favour of the establishment of Jewish 'labour formations', at the meeting on 16 December Frick announced that in future all Jews without work and assets were to be deployed in closed labour columns; those who still lived on their remaining assets, on the other hand, represented a 'valuable pawn' and were not to be subjected to the new compulsory measures.[126]

Through a fundamental order of 20 December by the President of the Reich Labour Exchange it was finally determined that 'all unemployed Jews who were fit for work should be employed at a faster rate', and that to this end they should be deployed 'separately' in public and private enterprises.[127]

The German historian Gruner estimates[128] that in May 1939 between 13,500 and 15,000 Jews were employed in the closed labour deployment, primarily for building work and communal work such as garbage removal, street cleaning, and so on. In practice, however, it became apparent that the deployment possibilities for Jewish workers in local government work were limited.[129]

Given these limited possibilities, national deployment in the construction of Autobahns and dams assumed growing importance; in the summer of 1939 more than 20,000 Jews were deployed in such work.[130]

In the face of this tendency to 'erect camps for forced labour' (*Verlagerung*), the obvious idea was to put Jewish workers in barracks in the event of war. On 28 February 1939, under the chairmanship of the Interior Ministry's 'Jewish expert', Bernhard Lösener, representatives of the OKW, the Security Police, and the Order Police, as well as the concentration camp inspectorate, met in the Reich Ministry of the Interior to discuss the question of the 'services to be performed by Jews in the event of war'.[131]

The immediate reason for this discussion was the planned exclusion of the Jews from any form of military service. During the meeting it was agreed in principle that in the event of war the German Jews aged between 18 and 55 should be 'recorded', which would involve the introduction of compulsory registration with the police.

Lösener stated that the Jews should be employed 'in columns, separate from the "German-blooded" workers, primarily in road-building and the supply of the requisite material (quarry work)'. Since 'the work-related deployment' of the Jews was to be seen as 'a substitute for military service', their 'employment and accommodation must also be tackled in a military form'. This was because 'The population would doubtless fail to understand if the Jews were able to pursue their civilian jobs in war without any significant change in their living conditions, while the German-blooded compatriots performed their military duties at the front and at home.'

CHAPTER 6

THE POLITICS OF ORGANIZED EXPULSION

The Extermination Announcements at the Turn of the Year 1938–1939

Still under the immediate effect of the eruption of violence of the November pogrom, towards the end of 1938/beginning of 1939, the declarations of leading National Socialists and the commentaries of the Nazi press began to resonate with threats of the 'extermination' of the Jews.

Thus an article in the SS journal, *Schwarze Korps,* of 24 November 1938 stated: 'Least of all do we want to see these hundreds of thousands of impoverished Jews as a breeding-ground for Bolshevism and a recruiting base for the political and criminal subhumanity that, as a result of the selection process, is disintegrating on the margins of our own nationhood. . . . In the event of such a development, we would face the harsh necessity of wiping out the Jewish underworld just as we are used to wiping out criminals in our orderly state: with fire and sword. The result would be the actual and definitive end of Jewry in Germany, its total extermination.'

After Goering had, at the meeting of 12 November, described 'an important reckoning with the Jews' as 'a foregone conclusion', Hitler was also heard speaking in similar terms on various occasions. When the South African Defence and Economics Minister, Oswald Pirow, visited Hitler at the Berghof on 24 November, to offer him, amongst other things, his services as mediator in an international solution of the German 'Jewish question', he learned from his host that the 'problem of the Jews' would 'be solved in the near future'; this was his 'unshakeable will'. It was not only a 'German, but a European problem'.[1] During the conversation, Hitler moved on to an open threat: 'What do you think, Mr Pirow, if I were to take my protecting hand away from the Jews, what would happen in Germany? The world could not imagine it.'

The minutes of the reception of the Czechoslovak Foreign Minister Chvalkovsky by Hitler on 21 January 1939 recorded the following statement by the 'Führer': 'The Jews would be exterminated here. The Jews did not carry out 9 November 1918 in vain, that day would be avenged.'[2]

In his speech before the Reichstag on the sixth anniversary of the seizure of power on 30 January 1939, Hitler finally expressed himself in a central, lengthy passage on the 'Jewish question'.[3]

And there is one thing that I should like to state on this day, memorable perhaps for others as well as us Germans. In the course of my life I have very often been a prophet and was generally laughed at for it. During my struggle for power it was in the first instance Jewish people who laughed at my prophecies that I would some day assume the leadership of the state and thereby of the entire nation and then, among many other things, achieve a solution of the Jewish problem. Their laughter was uproarious but I think that for some time now the Jews have been laughing on the other side of their faces. Today I will be a prophet again: if international Jewish financiers within Europe and abroad should succeed once more in plunging the nations into a world war, then the consequence will be not the Bolshevization of the world and therewith a victory of Jewry, but on the contrary, the annihilation of the Jewish race in Europe.[4]

These extermination declarations, which strikingly accumulate between November 1938 and January 1939, cannot simply be interpreted as a revelation of the programmatic intention of leading National Socialists, under the effects of the intoxication of violence unleashed in November 1939. But one must consider closely the situation of the regime around the turn of the year 1938/9 to recognize that these declarations were framed in highly ambiguous terms.

The tactical intention of these declarations, particularly Hitler's speech on 30 January, is clear: by means of the threat of annihilation the pressure of expulsion upon the German Jews was to be heightened and the willingness of foreign powers to receive them extorted through a form of blackmail. In this context the contacts that began in November 1938, leading to negotiations between the Reich government and the Intergovernmental Committee created in Evian, are of the greatest importance; the governments of the potential receiving countries and 'international financial Jewry' were to be forced to agree to an extensive solution through emigration by threats, with the help of a loan and the facilitation of German exports (the final abandonment of the boycott against Germany).[5] Secondly, the declaration of the annihilation of the Jews under German rule in the event of a world war was intended to prevent the formation of an anti-German alliance of the Western powers in the event of German military action on the continent. If a war begun by Germany became a world war through the intervention of the Western powers, the Jews in the German sphere of influence would automatically assume the role of hostages under the threat of death. But the threat of extermination contained one further perspective: if it remained ineffective, that is, if emigration made no significant progress and in the event of war the Western powers could not be restrained from intervening, the locus of 'guilt' for a further intensification of the German persecution of the Jews was, in the view of leading National Socialists, already clear.

The Negotiations for an International Solution through Emigration

The international soundings and negotiations which were to be considerably influenced by the 'extermination declarations' had begun in November 1938. While the German government had consistently refused over the previous few months to negotiate with the Intergovernmental Committee formed at the Evian Conference over a financial agreement concerning the promotion of emigration, Goering's instruction of 12 November to encourage emigration 'with all means' created a new situation.

Early in December Schacht had proposed that the emigration of German Jews be financed by an international loan; Schacht was thus picking up the initiative of the Austrian Economics Minister, Hans Fischböck, who had already proposed and concretely pursued a similar plan.[6] According to Schacht's plan, the loan was to be underwritten by foreign Jews and guaranteed by the remaining assets of the German Jews and paid off, like the Haavara Agreement, through additional German exports. Jewish assets not transferred in this way were to be used for the maintenance of Jews unfit for emigration, and would pass to the Reich after their death. In this way Schacht hoped within three to five years to make emigration possible for around 400,000 emigrants who were fit for gainful employment and their families.[7]

After Hitler had agreed to these propositions in principle, at the end of December 1938 Schacht began making the relevant soundings in London.[8] In January he began negotiations with the chairman of the International Committee for Political Refugees, George Rublee.[9] When Schacht was after a short time relieved of his office as President of the Reichsbank, the negotiations were to be concluded by Ministerial Director Wohlthat of the Reich Economics Ministry, by the end of February. However, the plan was not realized as it was only half-heartedly pursued both on the German side (refusal of initialling by the Foreign Ministry) and on the part of the Committee, and rejected both by foreign governments and by Jewish circles.[10]

In the light of these events the question—unanswerable for the time being—arises whether the negotiations with Rublee were really seriously pursued by the regime, or whether they were carried out predominantly for reasons of propaganda. For, however they ended, the German side had grist for its propaganda mill: if agreement was reached, the power of 'international financial Jewry', not leaving its 'racial comrades' in the lurch, was proven; if no solution was reached, this could be seen as proof of a lack of solidarity and 'typical Jewish' egoism and the great influence of the Jews upon governments abroad.

Central Office for Jewish Emigration

In line with the proposals which Heydrich had already made on 12 November, and which had subsequently been given concrete form by the SD, to ensure both the 'final emigration of all Jews' and the 'care of less well-off Jews and those unfit for gainful employment',[11] on 24 January Goering set up a 'Central Office for Jewish Emigration' and parallel with this got under way the subsumption of all Jewish organizations into a single compulsory organization.[12]

The decision to set up the Central Office was made in a series of meetings of government representatives on 18 and 19 January 1939, after the conviction had been reached that the negotiations between Schacht and Rublee would lead to concrete results in terms of emigration.[13]

The Central Office, which was to operate according to the model of the Vienna 'Reichszentrale', employed representatives of the Foreign Office, the Economics and Finance Ministries, and the Ministry of the Interior.[14] The direction of the Reich Central Office was formally undertaken by Heydrich, the manager was the Head of the Gestapo, Heinrich Müller. With the assumption of responsibilities for the emigration of the German Jews which, in the opinion of all the offices involved, was the paramount goal of further persecutory measures, the SS/SD had finally managed to assume a key role in future *Judenpolitik*.

Parallel with this the regime initiated the establishment of a unified organization that would independently secure the minimum level of maintenance and care required for the remaining Jews, and thus make a considerable contribution to the complete isolation of the German Jews from the rest of the population. By February 1939 the structure of this new organization was already in place; called 'the Reich Association of the Jews in Germany', it was subject to the supervision of the Reich Ministry of the Interior, and represented the successor to the 'Reich Board of Deputies of the Jews in Germany', formed in 1933. Compulsory subsumption into this organization was only put into force, however, on 4 July 1939, by the Tenth Decree of the Reich Citizenship Law.[15] The Reich Association was not only to encourage emigration, but also to be responsible for the Jewish school system and Jewish welfare.[16]

Even though no agreement had been reached between the Reich government and the Intergovernmental Committee, after the November pogrom there was once again increased emigration of Jews from the territory of the 'Great German Reich'. Particularly decisive in this was the fact, among other things, that various states, including in particular Great Britain and the United States, took in a larger number of refugees.[17]

Another stream of refugees was destined for the international zone of Shanghai, where there were no restrictions on immigration. In August 1939 there were 14,000 Jewish refugees in Shanghai.[18] By the end of 1939 around 250,000 Jews had emigrated from the Old Reich Territory.[19]

Summary: The State of *Judenpolitik* before the Beginning of the War

Once the third anti-Semitic wave had reached its peak, the National Socialist policy of total segregation of the German Jews had now been realized by extensive measures in all spheres of life. The Jews, excluded from economic life, led a wretched existence in complete social isolation: they lived on savings deposited in blocked accounts, from which sums for their immediate needs could be withdrawn only with permission from the Gestapo, Jewish welfare aid, or the minimal wages from Jewish work deployment. Jews could only be economically active for other Jews, for example as *Rechtskonsulenten* (legal advisers), *Kranken-behandler* (treaters of the sick), or as hairdressers, lodgers etc.[20]

According to the results of the May 1939 census, there were still 213,930 'faith Jews' (i.e. members of synagogues) living in the Old Reich Territory. The concentration of Jews in cities had intensified. There was a disproportionately high level of old people among the Jews living in Germany: 53.6 per cent were over 50, 21.6 per cent over 65. Only 12.7 per cent were children and young people under 20. As a result of emigration there was a considerable surplus of women (57.5 per cent).[21] Only 15.6 per cent of the Jews counted in May were in work, almost 71 per cent of all Jews over 14 came under the category of the 'unemployed self-employed'. There were also 19,716 people who did not belong to the Jewish religious community (more than half were Protestants), but who were graded as 'racial Jews', as well as 52,005 'half-breeds grade I' and 32,669 'half-breeds grade II'.[22]

At the instigation of the NS state the compulsory 'self-administration' of the Jewish minority had been rendered uniform: the religious associations became branches of the Reich Association, the compulsory organization set up in July 1939, which also took over the whole of Jewish care, health, and schooling, as well as all still existing Jewish organizations. The Reich Association with its local and branch offices throughout the country thus became the organization that controlled the isolated Jewish sector. Apart from this, the only remaining autonomous Jewish organization was the Jewish Cultural Association.[23]

If the Reich Deputation of the Jews in Germany, now dissolved, had been a holding organization of independent Jewish organizations and communities, in the new, hierarchical organization autonomy was as good as excluded. The character of the Reich Association as a compulsory organization was also expressed in the fact that it was also responsible for those people who did not belong to the Jewish religious community, but were graded as Jews for 'racial' reasons. On the social level their task now no longer consisted of supporting needy Jews alongside state care; falling back entirely on their own resources, they now also had to undertake the care of the Jews who were completely excluded from the state social system. In this way the regime had not only discharged responsibility and expenses; it had also ensured that the Jewish minority was almost completely isolated from the rest of the population and it had at its disposal a compulsory organization that it made responsible for the execution of official orders.[24]

This set-up, using a Jewish organization to control an isolated Jewish sector and making it responsible for the implementation of the regime's anti-Jewish policies, marked the birth of a new and perfidious form of organization of *Judenpolitik*: the *Judenrat* or Jewish council. After the beginning of the Second World War, the regime was to create institutions with this title in the occupied territories, which were to become the executive organs of German policy. This was despite the vain and desperate hope of their members that they would receive a certain level of autonomy.

At the same time the consequence of the total segregation of the Jewish minority and the total withdrawal of their rights, which the Nazi state had carried out in stages between 1933 and 1939, was that the individual spheres of life affected by *Entjudung*, far beyond the exclusion of the Jews, were subjected to a new system of norms dictated by the National Socialists, the hegemony of racism. As a result of this complex process the engine of this policy, the NSDAP, was able to extend its influence into the most diverse spheres and consolidate its pre-eminent position.

Thus the exclusion of Jews, but also of Gypsies, 'social misfits', and other groups from the circle of those receiving state social services, went hand in hand with a new definition of social policy in terms of *Volksplege* (care for the *Volk*), which would only be available to *gemeinschaftsfähige* (those capable of being part of the community), meaning racially 'valuable' compatriots, while health care was subjected to the criteria of 'racial hygiene'.

In parallel with the exclusion of Jews from the education system, racist paradigms found their way into school education as well as into university teaching and research. The extensive *Entjudung* of the whole of cultural life and journalism was the starting point for the implementation of an aesthetic defined by the National Socialists, which presented itself as uncompromisingly 'German', a dictatorship of taste which also affected such important areas of everyday life as advertising, fashion, and architecture. Anti-Semitic stereotypes were now part of the basic stock of journalism.

The whole process of the exclusion of the Jews from the economy, which—guided by the Four-Year Plan Office—served, on the one hand, to finance rearmament, and, on the other, served the needs of a National Socialist clientele, proved to be a wide gateway for state interventions in the economic sphere, the starting point for the National Socialist command economy established during the war. By excluding the Jews from qualified professions and using the same circle of people for unskilled work in labour columns (like, for example, the detention of the 'work-shy' in concentration camps), the labour market was transformed into 'labour deployment' (*Arbeitseinsatz*), organized not least along racist lines; here important foundations were laid for the slave labour of 'those of alien race' during the war.

The strict prohibitions on everyday contact with Jews could only function with the help of an extensive system of espionage which, in view of the relatively small numbers in the Gestapo and the SD, depended upon the support of the population and in fact functioned so effectively that it inevitably tended towards an abolition of the private sphere. One other consequence of the gradual implementation of anti-Jewish policies was that the open terror of the Party activists was finally acknowledged and legitimized as an appropriate instrument for the implementation of a policy of exclusion.

In the wake of National Socialist *Judenpolitik*, between 1933 and 1939 a widely ramified apparatus of persecution had been constructed. Apart from the special departments of the Gestapo and the SD and the relevant Party offices (such as the Office of Racial Policy or Rosenberg's Institute for Research into the Jewish Question), within the Reich ministries (as for example the Interior Ministry, the Foreign Office or the Propaganda Ministry, special Jewish desks, for the purposes of the 'de-Judaization' (*Entjudung*) of the economy) an extensive apparatus had been set up, and local government had bureaucratically confirmed discrimination against the Jews down to the bottom level of the administration.

The implementation of *Judenpolitik* occurred, as we have seen, in phases, with a certain tension between the NS government, the state bureaucracy, police apparatus, and Party base, and frictions appeared concerning the pace and methods of anti-Jewish policy: the leadership of the regime allowed a great deal of scope for initiative on the part of the various institutions involved in *Judenpolitik*. If these initiatives proved inadequate or if they went too far, the centre intervened correctively. But concerning the bottom line of this policy, the gradual exclusion of the Jews from German society, there was considerable consensus.

With the total exclusion of the Jewish minority from German society *Juden-politik* had, by the start of the war, reached a certain end point. A further intensification of discrimination, a continuation of *Entjudung* was now no longer possible; after six years of active *Judenpolitik* it was hardly the time from a propaganda point of view to treat those Jews who had remained in the country as dangerous adversaries.

The war, however, was to provide entirely new possibilities for a radicalizing 'Jewish and racial policy': in the context of the conquest and penetration of the European continent, new functions within National Socialist policy fell to the 'Jewish race in Europe' and 'world Jewry' (so named by Hitler in his Reichstag speech on 30 January 1939): the National Socialist idea of taking the Jews hostage was now extended across the whole of the continent: the Jewish minorities in the conquered countries became important objects of the German policy of occupation and alliance, and it was at their expense that the 'new order' of the 'new *Lebensraum*' of the German *Volk* was primarily to be achieved. Where *Juden-politik* had until 1939 been one of the most important instruments of the power-political penetration of German society, the extension of persecution to the entire European area and its gradual further radicalization performed in the eyes of the NS regime a key function for the control of the 'new Europe'.

PART II

THE PERSECUTION OF THE JEWS, 1939–1941

The Politics of Annihilation and the War

The beginning of the Second World War saw the inauguration of the National Socialist regime's systematic politics of racial annihilation. The start of the war also marked the start of the physical annihilation of 'alien races' and the 'racially inferior' on a vast scale. In 1939 the National Socialist regime set in train two extensive programmes of mass murder, the so-called 'euthanasia' programme, or the systematic murder of sick and disabled inmates of psychiatric institutions, and the mass murder of members of the Polish elite, including many Jews. The institution of a terrorist regime in Poland, organized on racist lines, established a framework for further murder on a huge scale. This is the context, too, for the extensive deportation programmes that were being developed from the autumn of 1939 onwards and which made provision for the 'resettlement' of all Jews under German rule into a 'reservation' in Poland. In the long term, given the inadequate conditions there, those transported to this 'reservation' were intended eventually to die.

The radicalization of the politics of annihilation at the outset of the war is linked to the key function that the war had within National Socialism: war was synonymous with the opportunity to realize the National Socialist utopia of a comprehensive new social order conceived on racial lines:

Attaining *Lebensraum* (living space) in the East would create the conditions for a 'biological revolution', which could be achieved via a huge increase in the birth rate amongst the 'racially valuable' sections of the population. It would also comprise the permanent extirpation of racially undesirable elements within the National Socialist sphere of influence.

Territorial expansion and the establishment of occupying regimes dominated by the radical elements of the Party and the SS meant a further increase in National Socialist power. By radicalizing policy on the fringes, German society could be converted more rapidly into a racially homogeneous *Volksgemeinschaft* (national community) and the principle of 'selection' (in the form of 'extirpation') could be established as a permanent and all-embracing process.

From the point of view of the National Socialists war represented a means of racial selection, a method for maintaining the 'racially valuable' and thus an important instrument in the establishment of a social order that was able to stand up for itself. The loss of 'racially valuable' individuals in the war also legitimated the violent destruction of large numbers of 'inferior specimens' in order to restore a 'national biological balance'. Such a radical, dehumanizing approach only had a chance of being put into practice in wartime, in a more generally brutalizing atmosphere in which the existence of the individual was already to an extent devalued.

CHAPTER 7

THE PERSECUTION OF JEWS IN THE TERRITORY OF THE REICH, 1939-1940

In the first months of the war there was a characteristic concentration of the jurisdiction of the Security Police (*Sicherheitspolizei*) with respect to the 'Jewish question'. The Gestapo and the Security Police were merged under the Reich Security Head Office (RSHA) in October 1939 and from the beginning of 1940 responsibility for Jewish affairs was concentrated in a new Department, IV D 4 (Emigration and Evacuation), which was altered shortly afterwards to IV B 4 (Jewish Affairs and Evacuation Matters).[1]

Amongst other things, this Department oversaw the Reich Association of Jews in Germany (*Reichsvereinigung der Juden in Deutschland*), founded in July 1939, in respect of which the responsible officials performed their duties in the pettiest, most intransigent, and least cooperative manner possible.[2] The Reich Association of Jews oversaw existing communities and administered them as branch or district associations.[3] The Jewish institutions that still existed (associations, organizations, foundations) were gradually dissolved and their functions incorporated into the responsibilities of the Reich Association.[4]

In autumn 1939 the Jewish schools that were still in existence were also assimilated into the remit of the Reich Association, which was by then heavily overburdened. In October 1939 there were still 9,555 Jewish pupils in a total of 126 schools, including 5 secondary schools, 1 middle school, and a secondary modern.

Two years later, in the autumn of 1941, there were 74 schools remaining for some 7,000 Jewish children of school age, of which only one was a secondary school. By the end of 1941 teaching was impossible in practical terms because of the deportations and numerous other restrictions in the lives of the Jewish population.[5] In 1942 the whole network of Jewish schools was dissolved on the orders of the Gestapo.[6] The existing centres for the education of the Jewish population in agricultural and technical professions, in preparation for their emigration, not only survived but were positively encouraged by the RSHA. However, after the summer of 1941 it pushed for a reduction in their number, and by the end of that year it was aiming to shut them down altogether.[7]

In the first months of the war Jews were almost wholly excluded from German society.[8] The collection of documents edited by Joseph Walk reveals that between the November pogroms and the outbreak of war 229 anti-Jewish regulations were issued, rising to 253 between 1 September 1939 and the beginning of the deportations in October 1941. In September 1939, for example, an (unpublished) general 8 p.m. curfew was imposed on Jews,[9] their radios were confiscated,[10] and their telephones were disconnected in summer 1940.[11] In June 1940 they were excluded from the National Air-Raid Protection League (Reichsluftschutzbund),[12] and an order of the Aviation Ministry of 7 October 1940 assigned them separate air-raid shelters or ensured that they would be kept apart from other inhabitants in the event of an air raid.[13] Jews' ration cards were marked with a 'J',[14] they were only permitted to use certain shops,[15] and the times when they were permitted to shop were strictly regulated by the municipality (and often limited to one hour a day).[16] Jews were systematically discriminated against in the distribution of rations, and by turn refused the right to buy luxury foods[17] and then clothing.[18] These drastic measures had the effect of starving the Jewish population and ensuring that they devoted most of their energies to obtaining food.[19]

In addition, since the summer of 1939 many cities had taken their own measures to stop Jews from moving in.[20] Jews were being driven out of their homes in increasing numbers since the war had begun and were taken into designated 'Jewish houses'.[21] From May 1941 Gestapo units started to erect special 'Jewish camps' on the outskirts of the municipalities.[22]

After the war started the so-called forced-labour deployment of German Jews in segregated work brigades (or *geschlossener Arbeitseinsatz*) was extended. Hitherto, enforced employment had only affected people registered as without an income or in receipt of benefits, but in the spring of 1940 it was extended to include all Jews 'capable of work', which meant above all women. Jews were deployed chiefly in industrial production. In February 1941 41,000 people were involved in this *geschlossener Arbeitseinsatz*, and the regime had thereby effectively exhausted the working potential of the Jewish population.[23]

At the same time the regime continued with its policy of forcing the Jewish minority into exile. In a keynote speech before the Gauleiters held on 29 February

1940 Himmler declared that the continuation of emigration measures was one of his priorities for the rest of that year.[24] According to the reports of the SD, 10,312 Jews emigrated from Germany in the first quarter of 1940.[25] On 24 April the RSHA informed the Gestapo regional offices that they should 'continue to press ahead with Jewish emigration from the territory of the Reich even during the war'.[26] In the process it was important to ensure that 'Jews fit for military service or for work' should if possible not be allowed to emigrate to another European country, and under no circumstances into enemy states.

Euthanasia Programmes

In spring and summer 1939—not coincidentally at a time when intensive preparations for war were under way—the National Socialist regime began to make concrete arrangements for the systematic 'annihilation of lives unfit for further existence'. Such plans had long been the subject of discussion by specialists, with the constant support of the NSDAP.[27] In the field of psychiatry ideas on racial hygiene had been making headway since 1933, and in particular long-term patients thought to be suffering from hereditary deficiencies, resistant to treatment, and otherwise unproductive were not only the preferred targets of enforced sterilization but the day-to-day victims of systematic neglect, since they were considered 'non-contributive mouths to feed'.[28]

A background such as this certainly contributed to the receptiveness among psychiatrists—and the state bureaucracy concerned with psychiatric care—to the idea of systematic 'annihilation' of patients in psychiatric institutions. However, the decision to put this radical idea into practice was intimately linked to the regime's wider orientation towards war. From the perspective of the 'national biological' (*volksbiologisch*) considerations of radical National Socialists, it was not merely legitimate but necessary to compensate for the potential loss of 'healthy' national biological substance (*Volkssubstanz*) due to the war by 'eradicating' the least 'desirable' elements of the population at the same time. Such a drastic intervention could only be contemplated within an atmosphere in which human life was more generally brutalized and devalued, in other words when faced by the vast scale of killing and death that a war represented. Only in the exceptional situation that the war represented was it possible to conceal mass murder behind the façade of supposedly 'war-related' measures, such as the 'freeing up' of the psychiatric institutions for purposes connected with the war, saving the costs of care, and so forth. Justifications with this kind of functionalist rationale were supplied from various branches of the administration, each from its own particular perspective, and were to play a significant role when the 'euthanasia programmes' were eventually carried out. However, historical analysis runs the risk of regarding these apparently 'rational' motives as cumulatively constituting a multi-dimensional context of justification for 'euthanasia' and thus losing sight of the true starting point for the murders—the fact that the National Socialists used the war as a welcome opportunity to put their ideologically founded 'biological revolution' project into practice more radically than had hitherto been possible.

The planning and preparation phase for the 'euthanasia programmes' can only be partially reconstructed, mostly on the basis of statements by those involved made after the end of the war. The mass murder of the disabled and the sick began with a distinct programme of children's 'euthanasia'.[29] It has long been clear that an individual case played an important role in triggering this programme of murders: on the basis of a petition from one set of parents Hitler gave his personal physician, Karl Brandt, the authority to have a severely handicapped child killed. According to more recent research the killing of this child, who had been born in the Leipzig area on 20 February 1939, took place on 25 July 1939.[30] Most probably contemporaneously with this individual case Hitler had charged his personal physician, Karl Brandt, and Philipp Bouhler, the Head of the Chancellery of the Führer of the NSDAP, with devising a process for proceeding in the same manner with similar cases in the future. The Chancellery convened a small group of experts, who established the procedures for the 'euthanasia' of small children. To facilitate their implementation a front organization was formed under the name of the Reich Committee for the Scientific Registration of Severe Illnesses with Hereditary or Predisposed Causes (Reichsausschuss zur wissenschaftlichen Erfassung von erb- und anlagebedingten schweren Leiden).

The deliberations of this group must have taken place in July at the latest, since on 18 August 1939 the Reich Minister of the Interior used an unpublished circular decree to introduce a Requirement to Report Newborn Children with any form of Handicap (*Meldepflicht über misgestaltete usw. Neugeborene*). This constrained medical personnel to report all children who displayed 'severe hereditary illnesses' before the end of their third year to the Health Authorities, who would pass the information forward to the Reich Committee. The Committee submitted the report forms to three experts, who each gave their assessment in turn. If their conclusions were negative, as soon as the parents had given their consent to hospitalization, the children were transferred to one of the approximately thirty so-called 'specialist children's clinics' where they were killed by means of tablets, injections, or by starvation. It is thought that children's 'euthanasia' claimed some 5,000 victims in all.

The fact that the first 'euthanasia' murder took place at the end of July 1939 (and not early in 1939 as has previously been assumed) makes necessary a partial revision of the prehistory of the whole 'euthanasia' programme. Hitler's instruction to carry out adult 'euthanasia' is evidently to be seen in closer chronological connection to the beginning of children's 'euthanasia' than it has been hitherto, and an interpretation of the whole 'euthanasia' complex in the context of direct preparations for the war is therefore much more plausible. From the new dating for the killing of the child in Leipzig it emerges that the decisive discussions during which Hitler, in the presence of Bormann, Lammers, and Leonardo Conti (State Secretary for Health in the Ministry of the Interior and Director of the NSDAP's Main Office for the People's Health), gave instructions for the systematic murder of adult psychiatric institution inmates took place *before* Hitler personally authorized the first individual 'euthanasia' case and not, as has hitherto been supposed, several months afterwards. It now seems highly probable that Hitler's instructions for the 'euthanasia' of children and adults were chronologically in very close proximity, and that they were issued in June or early July 1939. In any case Bouhler and Brandt, who had rapidly conceived a programme for the murder of children on the basis of the Leipzig precedent, succeeded relatively quickly in taking over the task of adult 'euthanasia' from Conti.

It was probably at the end of July that Bouhler arranged a meeting with some fifteen to twenty doctors at which the plans for 'euthanasia' were established on the basis of the supposed necessity of freeing up psychiatric institutions and carers for war-related purposes. With the help of the Technological Institute of the Reich Criminal Investigation Department (Reichskriminalpolizeiamt), which had already developed appropriate poisons for children's 'euthanasia', an apparently suitable method of killing was found: asphyxiation by carbon monoxide.[31] It was significant that during the preparations for 'euthanasia' an instruction for enforced sterilization that had been issued on 31 August (thus immediately before the start of the war) was officially suspended except F-cases, which were seen as particularly serious.[32]

At a meeting of leading 'euthanasia' doctors held on 9 October it was agreed to kill approximately every fifth psychiatric in-patient, or some 65,000–70,000 individuals.[33] Also in October 1939, it seems that Hitler issued a document on his personal notepaper in which he instructed Bouhler and Brandt 'to extend the remit of certain named doctors to grant those who are as far as anyone can humanly judge incurably sick a merciful death (*Gnadentod*) after critical investigation of their state of health'. With this document, which Hitler significantly backdated to 1 September 1939, the activities of those who were responsible for the 'euthanasia' programme and who had so far been acting without any legal basis were legitimized. Terms such as 'critical investigation' and 'merciful death' were intended to obscure the fact that what was being organized was in fact mass murder.[34]

From October 1939 psychiatric institutions were asked to indicate on special forms those patients who were suffering from certain serious psychological conditions and who were 'unemployable or only able to fulfil mechanical tasks'. In addition, without reference to health profile or capacity for work, registration was required for all patients who had been in an institution for more than five years, who had been detained as criminally insane, or who 'do not possess German citizenship or are not of German or similar blood': this formulation referred to patients who were of Jewish, Gypsy, or non-European origin.[35]

However, even before the mass murders of the T4 Programme had begun, patients in institutions for the mentally ill had already been systematically killed, especially in the annexed areas of Poland but also within the Old Reich, in Pomerania. At least 7,700 people fell victim to this programme of mass murder. From the end of September to December members of the Eimann Special Guard Division (Wachsturmbann Eimann)—a unit made up of SS members from Danzig, ethnic German Self-Defence Corps (volksdeutscher Selbstschutz) and members of *Einsatzgruppen* (task forces) in the new Reichsgau of Danzig-West-Prussia—shot thousands of the inmates of psychiatric institutions, most notably patients in the Kocborowo (Conradstein) Mental Hospital. The victims were people incapable of work or those of Polish or Jewish ethnicity.[36]

In October, in the new Reichsgau of Wartheland, patients from the Owinska (Teskau) Mental Hospital were shot if they were not ethnically German.[37] From the end of November patients from two mental hospitals were deported to Poznan, where the Gestapo ran a concentration camp in Fort VI, and there they were suffocated with carbon monoxide in a closed room. This was the first National Socialist mass murder to be carried out using poison gas. In December Nazi top brass including Himmler and Brandt visited Fort VI and were shown the latest killing techniques.[38] From the beginning of 1940 this facility was replaced by mobile units of vans; a special unit under the command of an official of the Criminal Investigation Department, Herbert Lange, deployed these vans to murder patients from the mental hospitals of the Warthegau.[39]

In Pomerania the initiative for murdering the inmates of mental institutions clearly derived from Gauleiter Schwede. In September or October Schwede offered to put the Stralsund Mental Hospital at Himmler's disposal as an SS barracks. In November and December 1939 1,200–1,400 mentally ill patients were ostensibly 'transferred' from Pomeranian institutions to West Prussia; in fact they were shot by the Eimann Special Guard Division. From early 1940 the patients were deported into the Kosten Hospital in the Warthegau, which had already been 'cleared', only to be murdered there in mobile gas chambers by Lange's special unit.[40]

More operations undertaken by Lange's unit to murder the inmates of mental hospitals in the annexed areas can be documented until the middle of 1941, especially in May and June 1940 and June and July 1941.[41] In the autumn of 1941 Lange's unit was detailed to begin carrying out the mass murder of Jews in the Warthegau and at the end of 1941 it was to set up a mobile gas chamber operation in Chelmno in order to be able to perform these murders on a larger scale.[42] Lange's unit therefore represented an important organizational link between the systematic mass murder of the disabled and handicapped and that of the Jews.

The institutions and hospitals 'freed up' in this murderous manner in the annexed areas of Poland and in Pomerania were subsequently occupied by SS units, used as prisons or army quarters, or filled with ethnic German settlers from the Baltic who were in need of accommodation.[43] But it would be wrong to deduce the ultimate motivation for the violent clearance of these buildings from the uses to which they were later put. The murders were committed not for utilitarian reasons but as part of much more broadly conceived policies for biologically revolutionizing the lands under German rule.[44]

In the old area of the Reich the mass murder of the inmates of psychiatric institutions was carried out in a manner that proved to be comparatively expensive and time-consuming. The Chancellery of the Führer of the NSDAP, which had been given the task of putting 'euthanasia' into practice, erected a comprehensive camouflage organization: the whole operation was conducted under the name 'T4', an abbreviation for the address of the 'euthanasia' central office, Tiergartenstraße 4 in Berlin. Cover was provided by a Reich Working Group of Sanatoria and Nursing Homes (Reichsarbeitsgemeinschaft Heil- und Pflegeanstalten); a Public Patient Transport Company (Gemeinnützigen Kranken-Transport GmbH) was created for the transport of victims.[45]

Initially, two killing centres were set up in order to carry out the murders, one in the former Brandenburg prison, the other in the former Grafeneck Mental Hospital in Württemberg. In January 1940 a 'test gassing' of some fifteen to twenty people was performed in Brandenburg; a gas chamber disguised as a shower room was used, in the presence of Brandt, Bouhler, Conti, Viktor Brack, Bouhler's deputy, and other leading 'euthanasia' officials. After this experiment a gas chamber was also installed in Grafeneck. Further 'euthanasia' centres were established in spring 1940 in Sonnenstein in Saxony, Hartheim near Linz, and, in early 1941, Bernburg and Hadamar near Limburg replaced Brandenburg and Grafeneck, which were closed down.

The process for selecting the 'euthanasia' victims had several stages. The report forms filled out by the psychiatric institutions were each sent to three experts by the Berlin Central Office, who gave them only the most cursory treatment and who were explicitly required to decide against the patient in cases of doubt. In this manner not only the mentally ill but also the blind, deaf, and dumb, epileptics, and people with learning disabilities were judged negatively. On the basis of these three votes a senior expert made the final decision, which the Central Office used in order to put together the 'transfer transports'.

Every effort was made to keep those 'transferred' to the 'euthanasia' centres in the dark about their fate until the very last minute. They were first subjected to a kind of reception examination before being taken to the gas chamber that was disguised as a shower room. Death usually followed within a few minutes. After gold teeth had been removed and some corpses selected for autopsy, the mortal remains of the dead were cremated within the perimeter of the institutions.

In the first six months of 1940 the 'euthanasia' killings that formed part of the T4 programme were gradually extended to each of the individual German states and Prussian provinces until almost the whole area of the Reich was covered.

If one attempts to reconstruct in detail the chronological and geographical progress of the mass murder of institutional patients,[46] what emerges is an image of T4 as a completely non-standardized process dependent on a whole range of disparate factors. The number of people killed in the T4 programme rose steadily month by month from January 1940 and in August reached its initial high point with many more than 5,000 victims per month. In the regions affected first (Baden, Württemberg, Berlin, Brandenburg, and Austria) sometimes a much higher proportion of patients was murdered than had originally been intended. This evidently led the organizers of T4 to raise their targets. There is an important document in existence that suggests that by October 1941 the intention was to murder between 130,000 and 150,000 people in total.[47]

On the other hand, the numbers of those actually murdered each month went down after September 1940, clearly because regions were being targeted that did not have their own killing centres. The transportation of patients over large distances proved to be problematic, not least because the population were gradually becoming aware of what was happening. Eventually the numbers of victims reached its nadir between the point when the two killing centres at Brandenburg and Grafeneck were closed in August and the end of the year. There exists a further indication from this period that the 'euthanasia' organizers were reducing their target numbers to 100,000.[48] The construction of gas chambers in Bernburg (Anhalt) and Hadamar (Hessen) early in 1941 made it possible to extend the programme to neighbouring regions that had not hitherto been included, or had been only partially included, especially Hessen and the Prussian province of Saxony. At this point the monthly figures began to increase again sharply and by May were once more well over 5,000 and rising. Now the attention of the 'euthanasia' planners was directed at the richly populated regions of northern and western Germany, which did not have their own killing centres and had so far largely been spared. But before these areas could be fully incorporated into the programme of murders the T4 campaign was stopped, in August 1941, at precisely the moment when the original target of 70,000 victims had been reached. I shall go into the reasons why this came to a halt in more detail later.

Within the context of the T4 programme, therefore, the Chancellery of the Führer of the NSDAP had developed a process through which a large number of people had been murdered in procedures that had been centrally directed, were ostensibly under scientific control, and were bureaucratically managed in the minutest detail. This programme of murder—which was kept secret—had been disguised sufficiently well that, from the outside, the true fates of the patients being 'transferred' only became known very gradually, such that protests and resistance only became effective at a point where the programme had already largely been completed.

With the 'euthanasia' programmes the National Socialist regime had crossed the threshold to a systematic, racially motivated policy of annihilation a little under two years before the mass murder of the Jews began. Important elements of this policy of annihilation that were to play a central role in the murder of the Jews can be identified as early as 1939 and 1940 as part of the planning and execution of the 'euthanasia' campaign. Alongside mass executions and the use of fixed as well as mobile gas chambers, it is particularly important to note that 'euthanasia' involved the development of a complex, work-intensive process that deceived the victims until the last moment and to a large extent also apparently protected the perpetrators from personal responsibility, in that they received the impression of fulfilling only a subordinate role in a scientifically controlled process that obeyed the dictates of reason.

Closer analysis of the T4 programme has shown, however, that carrying out the murders involved considerable variations at different points and in different places, and that these can be attributed to a whole series of factors. The T4 Central Office was decisively reliant on the cooperation of individual psychiatric institutions and that of regional authorities; both were prerequisites for continuity in the deportation of patients to killing centres. Geographical factors, such as the location of the killing centres and the question of which administrative authority (state or province) had responsibility for each individual institution, also played a major role; similarly the conditions operating in individual killing centres affected the extent and speed of the programme of murder to a considerable degree. It is also apparent, however, that the planners were prepared to correct the targets of planned victims upwards or downwards. What looks at first sight like a systematically organized and implemented programme for the murder of 70,000 people is revealed on closer analysis to be a complex network of central planning aims and revisions on the one hand and a many-faceted mode of delivery on the other, which was dependent on several regional and chronological variants. T4 can be seen as a model for the 'Final Solution' in this respect as well.

There is a further parallel between the two: the T4 programme already displays a degree of ambivalence between the attempts on the part of the regime to maintain strict secrecy (but which was impossible, given the sheer extent of the operation)[49] and targeted references on the part of official agencies to the necessity of such radical measures, which must have fed the rumours that were already circulating.[50] This ambivalence can be seen as a phenomenon of the 'open secret': what was happening was already known in outline amongst broad sections of the population, but was not commented on in public in any way at all.

Finally, the fate of the Jewish inmates of the psychiatric institutions within the T4 programme is of particular interest. Since June 1938 they had been separated from the other inmates and were collected together in special institutions from 1940 onwards. From there they were all deported to the killing centres, without regard to medical diagnosis or capacity to work, including the aged and infirm. The systematic murder of some 4,000 to 5,000 Jewish patients thus represents an important 'bridge' between 'euthanasia' and the later annihilation of the whole Jewish population.[51]

CHAPTER 8

GERMAN OCCUPATION AND THE PERSECUTION OF THE JEWS IN POLAND, 1939–1940/1941: THE FIRST VARIANT OF A 'TERRITORIAL SOLUTION'

Mass Shootings of Poles and Jews in Autumn 1939

Alongside the 'euthanasia' programme it was above all with the politics of the occupation of Poland that the National Socialist regime made its decisive step towards a racially motivated policy of annihilation at the beginning of the Second World War.[1]

As early as 23 May Hitler had made a speech to the army top brass in which he spoke of the necessity to achieve 'an extension of our living space in the East' via a war with Poland,[2] and on 22 August, again before members of the army's most senior ranks, he had given the following guidelines: 'Destruction of Poland a priority. Goal is removal of vital forces not reaching a given line. . . . Close hearts to sympathy. Proceed brutally. 80 mill. people must get what is theirs. Their existence must be secured. Right is with the stronger. Greatest rigour.'[3] On 2 October Hitler went on to say how it was vital to ensure that 'there must be no Polish leaders, where Polish leaders exist they must be killed, however harsh that sounds'.[4] At a meeting of departmental heads on 7 September, the Chief of the Security Police and the SD, Reinhard Heydrich, gave instructions to the effect that 'the higher echelons of the Polish population need to be rendered as good as harmless', and on 14 October, to the same body, he made the demand that the 'liquidation of leading Poles' that had already begun be concluded by 1 November at the latest.[5]

In the spirit of these instructions, which could hardly have been expressed more clearly, during the war and the first months of occupation 10,000 Polish citizens were murdered by German units. The pretext for these murders was atrocities that the Poles were said to have perpetrated and which German propaganda claimed had cost the lives of more than 50,000 people. It is true that during the war between 4,500 and 5,500 ethnic Germans lost their lives, partly as members of the Polish army, partly as the civilian victims of acts of war, but some were also transported by order of the Polish authorities, executed by the Polish military, or the victims of violent attack by civilians. The peak was the so-called 'Bloody Sunday of Bromberg', which claimed about a hundred lives and was depicted by Nazi propaganda as a massacre with thousands left dead.[6]

The systematic mass murder of certain sectors of the Polish population, presented as 'retribution' for these attacks, was directed and implemented to a large extent by so-called Einsatzgruppen, 'task forces' or 'death squads'. As in the case of the annexation of Austria, the Sudetenland, and Czechoslovakia, special groups were set up for the war against Poland consisting of members of the SS, the SD, and the police. Initially there were five Einsatzgruppen (two more were added after the start of the war) and they were each assigned to one of the armies; in total, the seven units comprised some 2,700 men.[7] According to an agreement reached with OKH (Army High Command) in July, these Einsatzgruppen officially had the role of dealing with all 'elements hostile to the Reich and to Germany in enemy territory behind the troops engaged in combat'. In addition, as a file note by Heydrich from July 1940 establishes, they received instructions that were 'extraordinarily radical (e.g. the order to liquidate numerous Polish ruling circles, which affected thousands)'. In concrete terms this meant that they had the authority to murder members of the intelligentsia, the clergy, and the nobility, as well as Jews and the mentally ill.[8] Corresponding lists of targets had been drawn up by the Reich Security Head Office (Reichssicherheitshauptamt) as early as May 1939.[9]

When the additional instructions that Heydrich referred to were issued is not clear. Various statements by the Einsatzgruppe leadership suggest that they had already had a meeting with Himmler and Heydrich by August in which they had been told that how they should eliminate the Polish intelligentsia was up to them.[10] This form of highly generalized instruction, giving the junior leadership considerable room for manoeuvre, matches the way the National Socialist leadership proceeded on the Night of Broken Glass (Reichskristallnacht); we shall encounter this tactic of relying on the initiative and intuition of the junior leaderships again when we come to the nature of instructions given to the *Einsatzgruppen* shortly before the beginning of the war against the Soviet Union.

These *Einsatzgruppen* were supported above all by the ethnic German Self-Defence Corps (volksdeutscher Selbstschutz), a militia formed after the start of the war from overwhelmingly National Socialist members of the German minority and integrated into the regular police force (*Ordnungspolizei*).[11] Both *Einsatzgruppen* and the Self-Defence Corps—but also the regular police, the military arm of the SS (Waffen-SS), and army units—shot thousands of Polish civilians during the war, often in the course of retaliation measures against supposed or actual attacks on German troops.[12] In the month of September alone, according to post-war investigations undertaken by the Poles, more than 16,000 people fell victim to such executions.[13] In the course of this massive outbreak of violence against the civilian population hundreds of Polish Jews were arbitrarily murdered by the police, the Self-Defence Corps, and members of the army, and in a series of cases locked into synagogues and burned alive.[14] These murders were part of a wave of anti-Semitic violence that the German occupying forces unleashed on the Jews of Poland from the very beginning of the war and which also manifested itself as looting, mistreatment, rape, public mockery, and more. It should also be emphasized that after September 1939 the *Einsatzgruppen* and the army forcibly drove tens of thousands of Polish Jews across the line of demarcation into the Soviet-occupied areas.[15]

After the end of the war this wave of terror became more systematized. From late October on *Einsatzgruppen* and Selbstschutz carried out the 'intelligentsia campaign' organized by the RSHA,[16] in which groups such as teachers, academics, former officers, and civil servants, the clergy, landowners, and leading members of Polish national organizations, as well as Jews and the inmates of mental institutions became the victims of large-scale mass arrests and executions. Some of the victims were transported to camps, where they either died from the conditions obtaining there or were murdered in mass executions that took place up to the spring of 1940.[17]

There were sometimes other groupings involved in extensive campaigns such as this, just as they were in the murders of civilians during the war. They included the National Socialist Motor Corps,[18] the Paramilitary Police (Schutzpolizei),[19] the Waffen-SS,[20] but above all units from the army itself.[21] In the first four months of German occupation tens of thousands of people were murdered in this way, with a notable focus on the new Reichsgau of Danzig-West-Prussia, where at least ten towns or camps can be identified with certainty, in each of which more than a thousand civilians were shot between autumn 1939 and spring 1940.[22]

In the course of these events in Danzig-West-Prussia in autumn 1939, as well as members of the Polish elites, Jews and the inmates of mental hospitals, in many towns there were smaller groups of 'a-social' individuals killed, including prostitutes, women said to be suffering from sexually transmitted diseases, and Gypsies.

These murders will have been committed for the most part on the authority of lower-ranking policemen, SS, and Selbstschutz functionaries, who had on their own initiative amplified the orders they had received in the spirit of 'racially hygienic cleansing'.[23]

In the newly formed Warthegau, too, Germans were shooting people from the same groups as in Danzig-West-Prussia, beginning in September and continuing throughout October and November, albeit on a smaller scale.[24] More executions occurred in the Polish areas attached to East Prussia, in Upper Silesia and the central and eastern Polish districts.[25] A report made by the commanders of Einsatzgruppe 16 to the Central Office of the SD on 20 October makes it clear just how systematically these murders were being carried out: the planned liquidation of 'radical Polish elements', who the report's author regretted were already largely in detention, could only be continued for a short time, which meant that the number of dead in East Prussia could 'only' reach about 20,000.[26]

The role of the army in these systematic murders was not only restricted to participating in executions or to attacks by individual soldiers. More significant is the fact that the leadership of the army had accepted a 'division of labour' with the SS and the police at the beginning of the campaign. When the Head of Military Intelligence (Abwehr), Canaris, alerted the Head of the OKW, Keitel, on 12 September to the plans for sweeping, comprehensive executions in Poland, Keitel replied that 'this matter has already been decided by the Führer' and that Hitler had made it clear that 'if the army does not want to have anything to do with this, it will have to accept the SS and the Gestapo working visibly alongside them'.[27] After a meeting with Hitler, Brauchitsch, the Commander-in-Chief of the Army (ObdH), informed his senior officers that the Einsatzgruppen in Poland would have 'certain tasks concerning ethnic politics' the fulfilment of which would lie outside the army's areas of responsibility. The army thereby created the parameters for a war that was already being waged in part as an ideological campaign of annihilation, but without itself having to carry out the mass murder of civilians.

Whilst the army tolerated the murder by Einsatzgruppen and during the war against Poland carried out considerable numbers of executions, after the end of the war the resistance of the military (and the civilian administration) to the uncontrollable activities of the Einsatzgruppen and the Selbstschutz began to grow.[28] Again and again there were awkward confrontations between the Self-Defence Corps or Einsatzgruppe units and army officers. In the middle of November the commander of the new military district (Wehrkreis) of Danzig, Lieutenant General von Bock, complained to Gauleiter and Reichstatthalter Forster about the continuation of murders by the Selbstschutz,[29] despite an undertaking to desist given in mid-October.[30] Even though the Self-Defence Corps was supposed to have been dissolved after autumn 1939, in some areas this process was drawn out until spring 1940.[31] In February 1940 Blaskowitz, the Military

Commander (*Militärbefehlshaber*) for the East, protested to the Commander-in-Chief of the Army about the murders of Jewish and non-Jewish Poles.[32]

The racist policies of the National Socialist regime in Poland were also expressed in the separation of Jewish prisoners of war (estimated at some 60,000–65,000) from non-Jewish prisoners, and in the fact that they were treated worse than their Polish comrades, who themselves lived under much more miserable conditions than their Western counterparts. The consequence was a much higher mortality rate amongst Jewish prisoners.[33]

Establishing German Rule in the Occupied Territories

After a short-lived intermediate period of military administration, the fundamental decisions regarding the future governance of Poland were taken in October 1939: extensive areas of Poland were annexed by the Reich; the 'General Government' was established in central Poland and the extent of the eastern Polish areas to be ceded to the Soviet Union was definitively agreed.[34]

In Poland the National Socialists attempted to put into direct practice their utopian dream of a form of rule that was founded on the principle of racial inequality: a relatively narrow section of ethnic Germans and occupying forces from the area of the Reich subjugated the mass of the Polish population, whose Jewish minority was further sharply segregated as a lowest-ranking social group without rights of any kind.[35] After the extension of the General Government to cover eastern Polish areas in the summer of 1941 the Ukrainians and White Russians living there were generally better off than the Polish population.

Within this differentiated system of racist rule the persecution of the Polish Jews must always be seen within the context of 'Poland policy' in general, but also at the same time it should be distinguished from the overall repression of occupied Poland. The gradual intensification of Jewish persecution (expropriation, expulsion, ghettoization, enforced labour, and finally systematic mass murder) was only possible because the mass of the remaining population was extensively terrorized and deprived of its rights. On the other hand, from the perspective of the occupying powers, the persecution of the Jews in Poland represented the decisive starting point for the whole-scale restructuring of Poland along racist lines.

Germany's *Polenpolitik* aimed at the complete annihilation of every form of Polish statehood or national identity. This goal was to be achieved via the systematic mass murder of the Polish elites, by the destruction of Poland's national culture and its education system,[36] by plundering its economy and enslaving its workers,[37] by an arbitrary system of terrorization,[38] and finally via a 'Germanization' of those Poles who appeared appropriately receptive accompanied by the expulsion, displacement, and long-term decimation of the majority of the population.[39]

'Poland policy' inaugurated a radicalization of National Socialist 'race policy'. The fact that in occupied Poland a regime maintained above all by Party and SS functionaries could exercise arbitrary power on the basis of racist precepts made the implementation of further radical measures easier in other areas of National Socialist 'race policy'.

Poland as the Object of German *Judenpolitik*

German 'Jewish policy' in Poland went through four phases between September 1939 and summer 1941. Initially 'Jewish policy' in Poland in September and October 1939 was determined by plans and preparations for a 'Jewish reservation' (*Judenreservat*). A second phase, between autumn 1939 and spring 1940 saw the first deportations of Central European Jews into the 'reservation', whilst fundamental anti-Jewish regulations were put in place by the occupying powers. In a third phase, between the onset of war in the West and autumn 1940, the authorities in the General Government—in the context of the 'Madagascar Project'—made plans for deporting the Jews under German rule to an African colony. From the end of 1940, 'Jewish policy' in the occupied areas was dominated by preparations for the war against the Soviet Union; deportations of Jews 'to the East' seemed therefore to have become a realistic possibility.

Early Plans for a 'Jewish Reservation' in Poland

The basis for Germany's policy regarding the 1.7 million Polish Jews that were now under its rule was evidently only put in place after the start of the war in September and October 1939.[40] From mid-September initial consideration was being given by the German leadership to a huge 'resettlement programme' that was to encompass the Jews of Poland as well as those in the areas of the German Reich.

On 14 September Heydrich reported to a meeting of departmental heads of the Security Police that 'with regard to the Jewish problem in Poland... the Reichsführer [Himmler] was presenting [Hitler] with suggestions that only the Führer could decide upon since they had important foreign-policy ramifications'.[41] A week later, on 21 September, Heydrich told them that 'the deportation of the Jews (*Juden-Deportation*) into the foreign-language Reichsgau' and 'deportation (*Abschiebung*) over the demarcation line' had been authorized by Hitler. However, this process was to be spread over a whole year: 'Jews are to be collected together into ghettos in the cities in order to permit greater control over them and later better opportunities for getting rid of them.' This 'campaign' was to be 'carried out within the next 3 to 4 weeks'. Heydrich summarized his instructions in the following key phrases:

'Jews into the cities as quickly as possible,
Jews out of the Reich into Poland,
the rest of the 30,000 Gypsies also into Poland,
systematic expulsion of the Jews from German areas in goods trains.'[42]

On the same day Heydrich sent an express letter to the chiefs of the Security Police *Einsatzgruppen* headed 'Re: Jewish Question in the occupied areas'.[43] In this, one of the key documents of Germany's *Judenpolitik*, Heydrich first drew the attention of the *Einsatzgruppen* chiefs to the need to distinguish the 'final goal (which will take a long time)' and 'the stages by which this final goal will be reached (which can be undertaken in shorter periods of time)'. The 'overall measures planned (in other words the final goal)' was to be kept 'strictly secret'. The 'instructions and guidelines' that followed in Heydrich's document contain no direct references to the substance of the 'final goal', but instead merely suggestions for the short-term measures to be taken in order to 'encourage the heads of the *Einsatzgruppen* to consider the practicalities'.

Heydrich's 'first prerequisite for the final goal' was the instruction to concentrate 'the Jews from the countryside into the larger towns and cities'. The territories annexed by the Reich would be the first to be 'cleared of Jews'. A 'council of elders' was to be established in all Jewish communities which was to be 'made fully responsible' for the 'precise and punctual implementation of all instructions that have been or will be issued'. The fact that the places in which the Jews were to be concentrated mostly lay near railway lines, and Heydrich's further instruction to the effect that these guidelines should not operate in the district for which Einsatzgruppe 1 was responsible (the area east of Cracow) are important indications of the stage that RSHA planning had reached. Thereafter it was intended to deport the Polish Jews into an area on the eastern border of occupied Poland, where a 'Jewish state under German administration' was planned, as Heydrich confirmed to Brauchitsch a day later.[44] The 'final goal' classed as 'strictly secret' will have involved the more extensive plan that Heydrich had explained to his department heads on 21 September: the deportation of the Jews from the whole of the area of the Greater German Reich into the 'Jewish reservation' and the possibility of their being deported into the eastern Polish area occupied by the Soviet Union, a plan that Hitler was to come back to several times in the days that followed.

After the Soviet Union and Germany had reached agreement on 28 September on the definitive demarcation line separating their zones of influence, and the area between the Vistula and the Bug (later the district of Lublin in the General Government) had been made a German area, the planned 'reservation' was to be situated in this area. This 'nature reserve' or 'Reich ghetto', as Heydrich called it, would not only take Jews but also 'undesirable' Poles from the eastern areas that had been incorporated into the Reich.[45]

On 29 September Hitler told Rosenberg that he wanted the newly conquered Polish territories to be divided into three strips: the area between the Vistula and the Bug was for settling the Jews from the whole of the Reich and 'all other elements that are in any respect unreliable'; there was to be an 'Eastern Wall' erected along the Vistula, and on the old German–Polish border a 'broad belt of Germanization and colonization', and between them a Polish 'statehood' (*Staatlichkeit*).[46] The idea of a 'Jewish reservation' was discussed relatively openly by the National Socialist leadership in the following weeks: Hitler mentioned it to the Swedish manufacturer Dahlerus on 26 September,[47] whilst on 1 October he explained the idea of an 'ethnic cleansing' (*volkliche Flurbereinigung*) in the East to the Italian Foreign Minister.[48] The German press was told of these plans in confidence and immediately speculation on the 'reservation' appeared in the international press.[49] On 6 October Hitler explained in his speech to the Reichstag that the 'most important task' after the 'collapse of the Polish state' was 'a new order of ethnographic relations, which is to say a resettlement of nationalities'; in the course of this 'new order' an attempt would be made 'at ordering and regulating the Jewish problem'.[50]

On the following day, 7 October 1939, Hitler issued the decree for the 'Strengthening of the German Nation' and thereby gave Himmler the double task of, on the one hand, 'collecting and settling' into the Reich 'German people who have had to live abroad, and, on the other, 'arranging the settlement of the ethnic groups within its sphere of interest so as to improve the lines of demarcation between them'. Himmler was specifically to take responsibility: first, for the 'repatriation' (*Rückführung*) of Reich and ethnic Germans, second for the 'exclusion of the detrimental influence of those elements of the population who are ethnically alien and represent a danger to the Reich and the community of Germans' (for which purpose, it went on to say, he would be allowed to assign the elements in question particular areas to live in), and third for the 'formation of new German settlement areas through population transfer and resettlement'. The Reichsführer-SS was instructed to make use of the 'existing authorities and institutions' in order to implement these tasks.[51]

Within the framework of these new responsibilities Himmler concentrated first and foremost on organizing the 'repatriation' (*Heimführung*) of the ethnic Germans from the Soviet Union and the Baltic states into the annexed areas of Poland, which had been agreed on 28 September and over-hastily put into practice, and at the same time set in train the large-scale 'resettlement' of Jews and Poles.

CHAPTER 9

DEPORTATIONS

Deportations Phase I: The Nisko–Lublin Plan of October 1939

The so-called Nisko Project was the first concrete programme for deportation that the SS organized in the context of the authority they had been given to 'eliminate the harmful influence of... elements of the population distinct from the German people' and to place them in 'designated areas of settlement'.

On the day before the Decree for the Strengthening of the German Nation was issued, on 6 October 1939, Heinrich Müller (the Head of the Gestapo) instructed Adolf Eichmann (who was at that time Director of the Central Office for Jewish Emigration (Zentralstelle für jüdische Auswanderung) in Prague) to prepare for the deportation of some 70,000–80,000 Jews from the region of Katowice (Kattowitz), which had recently been formed from the annexed Polish areas. The order also made provision for the deportation of Jews from Ostrava in Moravia (Mährisch-Ostrau).[1] Both expulsion campaigns had already been initiated or planned by either the army or the Gestapo in the Protectorate (German-occupied Czech territory) by the middle of September.[2] It was also on 6 October that Eichmann ordered the compilation in Berlin of a comprehensive list of all Jews, who had hitherto been listed under the particular congregations of which they had been members. This suggests that a much more comprehensive 'resettlement campaign' was being planned.[3]

In the days immediately afterwards Eichmann devoted great energy to the organization of deportations not only from Ostrava and Katowice but from Vienna, too. It is clear from a note sent by Eichmann to the Gauleiter of Silesia that the former's original instructions had in the meantime been extended. Eichmann said that after the first four transports the 'Head of the Security Police, and the RFSS and Head of the German Police had to be presented with a progress report which would then in all probability be passed on to the Führer. They should then wait until the general removal of all Jews was ordered. The Führer has initially directed that 300,000 Jews be transferred out of the Old Reich and the Ostmark.'[4] Eichmann also mentioned this 'order of the Führer's' on his visit to Becker, the Special Representative for Jewish Questions on Bürckel's staff, noting that those Jews still living in Vienna would be driven out in less than nine months.[5]

On 16 October, on a further visit to Vienna, Eichmann envisaged '2 transports per week, each with 1,000 Jews'; on the same day he informed the Director of the Reich Criminal Investigation Department, Artur Nebe, that the deportations from the Old Reich would begin in three to four weeks.[6] Between 12 and 15 October, Dr Franz-Walther Stahlecker, the commander of the Security Police in the Protectorate and Eichmann decided upon Nisko on the San as the target station for these deportations and as the location for a 'transit camp'. This camp, situated right on the border with the district of Lublin, was evidently intended to serve as a kind of filter through which the deportees would be moved to the 'Jewish reservation'. The transportees were promised accommodation in barracks, for which plans were in fact originally made,[7] but these plans were now consciously abandoned.[8]

The deportations were also to include Gypsies. When asked by Nebe as Head of the Reich Criminal Investigation Department 'when he could send the Berlin Gypsies', Eichmann responded that he intended to 'add a few wagons of Gypsies' to the transports from the district of Katowice and the Protectorate. He told Nebe that the deportation of Gypsies from the remainder of the Reich would be initiated some three to four weeks later.[9]

Between 20 and 28 October 4,700 Jews were transported to Nisko from Vienna, Katowice, and Ostrava in a total of six transports.[10] Only a fraction of these people were deployed in the construction of the 'transit camp' on the bank of the San, where they found a meadow churned up by months of rain. By far the greater number of deportees were escorted a few kilometres away from the camp and then driven away by force.

Shortly after the start of the 'resettlement campaign', on 18 October,[11] Müller informed Eichmann that it would be necessary to organize 'the resettlement and removal of Poles and Jews into the area of the future Polish rump state' centrally, via the Reich Security Head Office (RSHA). On 20 October the RSHA issued an order banning the transports;[12] Eichmann was permitted only one train from Ostrava, 'in order to preserve the prestige of the local state police'.[13]

The sudden suspension of the Nisko transports was in all probability due to the fact that these deportations clashed with the large-scale resettlement of ethnic Germans into the incorporated areas that Himmler began on 28 September and with the simultaneous expulsion of Poles and Jews from these same areas. A second reason for the abandonment of the Nisko experiment is probably to be found in reservations on the part of military strategists: Hitler made it clear to Keitel on 17 October that the future General Government 'has military importance for us as a form of advance glacis and can be exploited for the moving of troops'. This perspective could evidently not be reconciled with the idea of a 'Jewish reservation'. However, according to Hitler, in the long term 'the way this area is run ... must make it possible for us also to rid the territory of the Reich of Jews and Polacks'.[14]

Despite the abrupt end of the Nisko campaign, the RSHA steadfastly stuck to its plans for deporting Jews into the district of Lublin. The RSHA informed the SD Main District of Vienna at the end of October that it was quite conceivable that 'individual transports of Jews from Vienna' might still be fitted in.[15] Even the Higher SS and Police Commander in the General Government, Friedrich Wilhelm Krüger, referred on 1 November to plans still in place for a 'particularly dense concentration of Jews'.[16]

Eichmann's short-lived campaign was by no means a personal initiative on his part to compete with Himmler's resettlement project; it was quite clearly a component of the broader resettlement plans that the Reichsführer SS had been trying to introduce since the beginning of October on the basis of his new powers: whilst Himmler was constructing a new organization in the two new Reichsgaus in Poland, supported by the Higher SS and Police Commander, he transferred responsibility for carrying out deportations in the other areas to existing authorities, in other words to the interlocking mechanisms of the Security Police, the SD, and the emigration offices.

As the history of the Nisko campaign shows, the organs of the SS charged with carrying out deportations very clearly did so with the aim of leaving the deported Jews exposed, one way or another, helpless, and without any means of support, in the Lublin 'reservation' and of abandoning them to their own devices or driving them over the demarcation line into the occupied Soviet zone, which was common practice in the district of Lublin at the end of 1939.[17] The Nisko project represented an experiment intended to gain experience as a basis on which to deport all the Jews from the area of the Reich within the pre-war boundaries (and from Upper Silesia, which had been annexed). The somewhat improvised manner in which this campaign was carried out was not merely the result of disorganized incompetence; there was method in its inadequacies. The experiment shows plainly what was envisaged within the SS by the idea of 'resettling' the Jews of the whole area of the Reich in the 'Lublin reservation': it was seen as an illegal campaign of expulsion into an area between the 'Eastern Wall' that was to be constructed and the demarcation line with the Soviet Union. Deportation on such a scale, based on the Nisko model, would have caused the deaths of a great many of those deported; but in the longer term those who initially survived would not have found adequate living conditions or conditions for reproduction and would therefore have been condemned to extinction. The Nisko campaign therefore permits the conclusion that the further-reaching Lublin project was a first version of a 'final solution' policy since its aim was the physical termination of those Jews living within the German sphere of influence.

The radical nature of these aims is confirmed by statements made by leading representatives of the General Government and by other, well-informed National Socialist functionaries. At a meeting of senior Kreis officials and city commissioners from the district of Radom on 25 November, the Head of the General Government, Hans Frank, announced that the majority of the Jews in the area of the Reich would be deported into areas east of the Vistula, adding, 'we should give the Jews short shrift. It's a pleasure finally to be able to get physical with the Jewish race. The more of them that die the better. To smash the Jews is a victory for our Reich. The Jews should be made to feel that we have arrived.'[18] The Propaganda Ministry issued 'confidential information' to the German press on 20 October 1939 which revealed that 'measures have already been taken by the SS to ensure for example that 20,000 Jews from Lodz will be forced this very week to begin their march into the very heart of the country'. The same document makes the lapidary comment that 'no subsistence infrastructure is available for this mass migration'.[19] On the occasion of a visit to the ethnic German village of Cycow on 20 November by a delegation of leading functionaries from the General Government authorities, the District Chief responsible for Lublin explained, 'this extremely marshy area could...serve as a Jewish reservation, which in itself might lead to a sharp reduction in the numbers of Jews'.[20] The Chief of Police from the Upper Silesian industrial areas, Wilhelm Metz, spoke in his December situation report to the District President of the 'battle against the Jews who must be exterminated here most urgently'.[21] Furthermore, Odilo Globocnic, SS and Police Commander in the Lublin District, suggested at a meeting held on 14 February 1940 that the 'evacuated Jews and Poles' in his district 'should feed themselves and obtain support from their people because those Jews have plenty. If this should not succeed, they should be left to starve.'[22] Frank made a similar statement on 23 April at a meeting with the State Secretary, Backe, who was responsible for matters of food and diet: 'I'm not remotely interested in the Jews. Whether they have something to eat or not is the last thing on earth I care about.'[23]

The list of pertinent quotations could be extended. Eduard Könekamp, a speaker at the German Foreign Institute (*Auslandsinstitut*), sent a report to his colleagues from occupied Poland in December 1939 about the situation of the Jews: 'the annihilation of this sub-human group would be in the interests of the whole world. Such a destruction is, however, one of our greatest problems. It can't be done by shooting them. You can't allow people to shoot down women and children either. You can count on losses in the course of evacuation transports here and there, and of the transport of 1,000 Jews that marched out from Lublin 450 are said to have died.'[24] Albrecht Haushofer, who was at this point employed in the information office of the Foreign Office, reported in a letter to his mother on 13 December that he was sitting 'at table with the man whose systematic task it will be to leave a substantial number of the Jews who are to be freighted out into the Lublin ghetto to freeze to death and starve there'.[25]

Deportations Phase II: Autumn 1939 to Spring 1940

Further planning for the deportation of Poles and Jews from the area of the Reich, and in particular from the newly annexed areas, was significantly influenced after October 1939 by the various waves of 'returning settlers', ethnic Germans entering the Reich from the Baltic.[26]

Himmler, who styled himself Reichskommissar for the Strengthening of the German Nation (Reichskommissar für die Festigung deutschen Volkstums) after the authorization issued by Hitler on 7 October—but without any official conferment of this title—announced the first comprehensive programme for the 'resettlement' of Poles and Jews from the annexed territories on 30 October 1939.[27] In the days that followed this plan was modified, as we learn from Bruno Streckenbach, the commander of the Security Police in the General Government who was charged with the 'central planning of settlement or evacuation in the eastern territories'. On 8 November, in Cracow, he informed the Higher SS and Police Leaders responsible for carrying out the deportations that, by the end of February 1940, 'all Jews and Congress Poles from the Reichgaus of Danzig and Posen as well as from Upper Silesia and South-East Prussia will be evacuated' and the remainder of the Polish population there would be categorized either as 'Poles', 'Ethnic Germans', or 'Poles still wanted'. In all it was now planned to 'evacuate approximately 1,000,000 Jews and Poles from the Old Reich'—Germany in the borders of 1937—'or the newly occupied Eastern areas ... in the first instance by the end of February 1940'.[28] In detail this meant '400,000 Poles, including Jews' from West Prussia and 200,000 Poles and 100,000 Jews from the Warthegau,[29] which meant that deportations of the order of some 300,000 people from the area of the Old Reich were envisaged, as they were during the Nisko project.

However, the whole 'resettlement programme' was put under pressure by the streams of ethnic Germans entering the Reich. At the end of October the RSHA had set up a coordination point for the planned resettlement programme jointly with Special Department III ES (immigration and settlement),[30] and by November it was attempting to master the increasingly confused situation with the help of a comprehensive clearance plan. It established a so-called long-range plan (*Fernplan*), according to which all the Jews and any politically undesirable Poles would initially be moved into the General Government, to be followed later, after a 'racial assessment', by the mass of the Polish population. There were no longer plans for a special 'Jewish reservation'. Moreover, the 'long-range plan' was not now aimed at the Jews of the Old Reich area, but for the most part matched considerations of 'ethnicity politics' being worked out simultaneously by the Racial Policy Office of the NSDAP.[31] At the same time a 'short-term plan' was established, according to which 80,000 Jews and Poles were to be removed from the Warthegau in order to house the Baltic Germans who were then in provisional accommodation in camps.[32] And indeed, according to the Higher SS and Police Commander, Wilhelm Koppe's concluding report, between 1 and 17 December there were more than 87,000 people deported from the Warthegau into the General Government,[33] 'politically incriminated Poles, Jews, Polish intelligentsia, criminal and asocial elements'.[34]

Although the original intention of deporting the Jews from the whole of the area of the Reich into occupied Poland was not part of the long-range plan, the RSHA had by no means given up this goal. A note about the 'final solution to the Jewish problem' from the Jewish Affairs Department of the SD dated 19 December 1939 worked on the basis of two possible alternatives:[35] either a 'Jewish reservation' would be created in Poland or the Jews transported from the area of the Reich would 'be accommodated in the future Gouvernement of Poland'. The author of this note also asks the question of whether the 'emigration of the Jews should not still be carried out with a view to creating a reservation', whereby in foreign-policy terms the reservation would constitute a 'good means of bringing pressure to bear on the Western powers': 'perhaps it could be used to raise the question of a worldwide solution at the end of the war'.

On 21 December Heydrich announced that he had appointed Eichmann his 'special expert' for 'dealing with the centralized security police arrangements as the clearance of the Eastern territories was carried out',[36] and made him responsible for all the deportations planned for occupied Poland. These were initially to be put into effect using additional 'short-term plans'.

To start with, a second short-term plan made provision for transporting 600,000 people, all without exception Jews, into the General Government between 15 January and the end of April.[37] (As part of the second short-term plan, it had still been intended in December 1939 to 'resettle' 220,000 Jews and Poles from the annexed Eastern areas into the General Government in January and February.)[38] However, the start of the second short-term plan was put off on several occasions, for the last time on 1 April 1940.[39] In this period those responsible were juggling with different figures for the people to be deported,[40] whilst at the beginning of January Eichmann announced an order from Himmler that once more underlined the intention of deporting the Jews from the annexed territories into the General Government.[41] Amongst other things the Head of the Reichskommissar's Planning Division presented a master plan on 23 January which covered settlement in the incorporated Eastern areas, according to which in the long term 3.4 million Poles were to be deported. The plan also worked on the basis that the approximately 560,000 Jews in this area were also to be deported.[42]

On 30 January 1940 Heydrich announced another decision: some 800,000 to 1 million Poles from the incorporated Eastern territories were to be brought into the area of the Reich as a (provisional) 'workforce'. Only some 40,000 Jews and Poles were to be transported to the General Government from annexed Polish territory, the new 'Ostgaue' (to make room for the Baltic Germans to settle), alongside, from March onwards, 120,000 Poles (to make room for the Volhynian Germans). After this, as a 'last mass movement' it was envisaged that all the Jews from the integrated Polish areas and 30,000 Gypsies from the Reich would be transported to the General Government. In addition, Heydrich announced that 1,000 Jews would be deported at once from the area of the Old Reich, from Stettin. There was no mention here of further deportations of Jews from the Old Reich.[43]

Between 10 February and 15 March it was intended to carry out the deportation of 40,128 Jews and Poles from western Polish cities into the General Government, a campaign referred to as an 'intermediate plan' (the second short-term plan had still not been initiated at that point).[44]

As Heydrich had announced, on 12 and 13 February in addition more than 1,100 Jews were deported from the region of Stettin—almost the whole of the Jewish community of that city—into the area around Lublin. At the same time the RSHA instructed the Gestapo offices to 'concentrate' the German Jews forcibly in certain places across the whole of the Reich, the better to be able to deport them when the time came. This took place before the end of that month in the district of Schneidemühl (in Pomerania), when 544 people—all Jews from that district— were 'collected' in the district capital of Schneidemühl.[45] On 12 March some 160 people were taken from there to Glownew near Poznan.[46] Himmler justified the first deportations from the area of the Old Reich to the Gauleiters on 29 February with the necessity of creating additional space for the Baltic German settlers; he added that they should not 'raise any false hopes' about further deportations from their Gaus.[47] The background to this remark was the fact that on 19 February Goering had put a stop to the deportations from the pre-war area of the Reich into the General Government in order not to endanger the movements of people from the incorporated Polish areas.[48] As a result the measures needed to achieve the further 'concentration' of Jews in certain cities were halted by the RSHA.[49]

The deportations from Stettin and Schneidemühl, and the accommodation of the deportees in ghettos in the Lublin district took place under miserable and sub-human conditions such that in the first six months some 30 per cent of those transported had died.[50]

In his speech to the Gauleiters on 29 February Himmler explained that in the course of the coming year ('provided that the war lasts the whole year') he intended to turn his attention to 'the emigration of the Jews... in so far as this is possible, given the numbers' and in so far as the conditions in the General Government permitted it. 'As far as the 400,000 Jews and half-Jews in the area of the Old Reich or the "Ostmark" and the Sudetengau are concerned', he said, 'despite the war, the emigration of the Jews will continue as normal. We still want to emigrate [*sic*] 6,000–7,000 Jews a month, to Palestine, South America and North America.' Alongside emigration for a maximum possible 80,000 Jews annually, the deportations into the General Government were to start according to the following list of priorities: 'First I have to try to get the Jews out of the eastern provinces, Posen and West Prussia, eastern Upper Silesia and South-East Prussia. Then follows the Old Reich, then the Protectorate. The Gypsies are a separate question.'[51]

However, far-reaching deportation planning met with resistance from Frank. At a leadership meeting on 12 February in Karinhall under the chairmanship of Goering (in his capacity as the most senior figure responsible for dealing with the Jewish question) he had spoken against the 'continuation of resettlement practice so far' and gained Goering and Himmler's agreement to discuss the mechanisms of evacuation with him in more detail.[52]

On 19 February 1940 Goering made it clear in a letter to Heydrich that 'Jews living in the area of the Reich, including the Protectorate of Bohemia and Moravia... —with the exception of special cases—could not be evacuated into the General Government'. In contrast, however, those Jews living in the annexed Polish areas should be 'refused permission to emigrate since they will be transported into the General Government as soon as possible'. 'At this time', he went on, 'a normal evacuation of the 500,000 Jews living in these areas to the overseas countries for which Jewish immigration is possible does not seem feasible.'[53] In the meantime the RSHA had come to the conclusion that an alternative plan—to deport the Jews from the Reich to the Soviet Union—was impossible since it was rejected by the Soviet authorities as most recent research has shown.

After his discussion with Himmler and Goering on 12 February and a further conversation with Hitler on 29 February, Frank agreed that 'at least another 400,000 to 600,000 Jews could come into the country' (the General Government), which he announced at a meeting on 2 March. Two days later he informed the District and City chiefs of Lublin that the area east of the Vistula was still 'intended to be a kind of Jewish reservation'. It was true that they had abandoned the idea of being gradually able to 'transport 7½ million Poles into the Generalgouvernement', but they were still planning 'to remove from the Reich some 100,000–120,000 Poles, some 30,000 Gypsies and a number of Jews to be established at our discretion'. For the 'ultimate goal' was to make the German Reich 'free of Jews'. Frank noted as a positive sign the fact that future transports now depended on his explicit agreement.[54]

On 8 March the German authorities took the decision to postpone the formation of a ghetto in Warsaw, not least because they were assuming that the district
of Lublin would be designated the 'reservation' for the Jewish population of the
General Government and those Jews deported from the Reich.[55]
On 24 March Goering actually banned all deportations into the General
Government until further notice unless they were explicitly authorized by him
and by Frank.[56] This effectively put an end to deportations but was in all
likelihood only a temporary measure in the face of the pressures on the transport
systems caused by the troop movements in the west, since the authorities in the
General Government were expecting the transports to recommence after a few
months.[57] With the cessation of the deportations, however, the project of a special
'Jewish reservation' in Lublin was definitively dropped, while in Warsaw preparations for the construction of a ghetto were immediately resumed.[58]
Between the failure of the Nisko plan in October 1939 and the provisional end of
deportations in March 1940, a total of about 128,000 people had been deported
from the Warthegau into the General Government under the aegis of the first
short-term plan and the intermediate plan, and this figure includes a few tens of
thousands of Jews. As we have seen, the extent and modalities of these 'resettlements' were affected above all by the ethnic German 'returning settlers'. Both the
comprehensive plans for resettlement on the German side (in other words above
all the intention to drive millions of Poles into the General Government) and the
aim of making first the annexed Eastern regions and then the area of the Old
Reich 'free of Jews' had to be postponed for the foreseeable future.
The second short-term plan was to be realized, however, albeit in a modified
version. Between 1 April 1940 and 20 January 1941 130,000 Poles and 3,500 Jews from
the Warthegau were to be transported into the General Government. The second
short-term plan was also the framework for the resettlement of 30,275 ethnic
Germans from the areas around Chelm (German Cholm) and Lublin into the
Warthegau between 2 September and 14 December 1940 (the so-called 'Cholm
campaign') and for the compensatory deportation of 28,365 Poles from that region.[59]
After the deportations into the General Government had more or less stopped, the
Oberpräsident and Gauleiter of Silesia, Josef Wagner, was forced to alter his plans after
having announced in February that 100,000 to 120,000 Poles and 100,000 Jews would
be removed from the annexed area of eastern Upper Silesia into the General Government. The provincial authorities were now concerned with deporting the Jews from
the western part of eastern Upper Silesia (the areas that had been part of the Reich
until 1921/2 and were urgently to be 'Germanized') into the eastern part of eastern
Upper Silesia (a purely Polish area). By the end of June whole districts (*Landkreise*) of
the western areas were 'free of Jews'; about half the whole Jewish population of Upper
Silesia was now living in the three cities of the eastern part of Upper Silesia.[60]
Just as in the other annexed Polish areas, this 'resettling' of Jews was a
component of much more comprehensive resettlement plans. There was therefore

probably in addition an unknown number of Jews amongst the more than 81,000 inhabitants of the province that had to make room for 38,000 ethnic Germans between the autumn of 1941 and the spring of 1942.

Anti-Jewish Measures in the First Months of the Occupation

We have seen how, during the first phase of the German occupation of Poland, not only the *Einsatzgruppen* but also the military administration came to prominence through anti-Semitic measures (the latter albeit only briefly).[61] In the first months of the General Government the ruling authorities set about intensifying and extending these anti-Jewish measures. The core of 'Jewish policy' as exercised in 1939–40 was definition, labelling, forced labour, expropriation, restriction of the freedom of domicile, and the establishment of Jewish-run administrative bodies.

On 23 November 1939 the General Government authorities instituted the compulsory labelling of Jews over 10 years old with a blue Star of David on a white armband.[62] A regulation dated 24 July 1940 established a definition of Jews in accordance with the Nuremberg Laws after Frank had disregarded more far-reaching suggestions.[63] Compulsory labour for all Jews between 14 and 60 had already been introduced in the General Government in October 1939: first labour gangs and then work camps were instituted under the supervision of the SS responsible for putting compulsory labour into practice.[64] In November 1939 Jewish bank accounts were suspended and Jewish businesses were labelled; at the beginning of 1940 instructions were issued for the registration of Jewish capital. The Jews in the General Government were not in fact to be excluded from economic life in general via these regulations but over a longer period they were to be driven out by means of confiscation, 'Aryanization', or the enforced closure of Jewish businesses, amongst other measures.[65] A regulation of 11 November 1939 limited the rights of Jews to live where they pleased: leaving their place of residence required formal permission; a curfew was imposed.[66] From the beginning of 1940 bans were issued on Jews using public transport.[67]

In accordance with the order given in Heydrich's express letter of 21 September 1939 to 'increase the concentration' of Jews in large cities, in many places special Jewish quarters were designated. Closed ghettos were only introduced gradually, however, and on the basis of local initiatives.[68] Preparations for the first large ghetto began in December 1939 in Lodz, but it was only actually established by an order of 8 February 1940.[69] In the rest of the Warthegau further ghettos were set up in the first six months of 1940, Brzeziny in April, Kutno in June, for example. In the district of Zichenau, the annexed area that bordered directly onto East Prussia, the first ghetto was established at the beginning of 1940.[70]

The establishment of ghettos in the General Government seems to have begun in the district of Radom, where the first ghettos appeared at the end of 1939.[71] The first ghetto in Pulawy in the district of Lublin was established in December 1939, and Krasnystaw followed in August 1940.[72] The preparations for a ghetto in Warsaw began in February 1940, but as has already been described, the plan was put back at the beginning of March and work begun only in April.[73]

The 60,000–80,000 Jews living in Cracow, the capital of the General Government in whose deportation Frank was particularly interested, were given permission in spring 1940 to leave the city 'voluntarily' by 15 August 1940; otherwise they would have to count on being expelled by force.[74] After this deadline those Cracow Jews who could not prove they were in work were gradually expelled; in this manner all the Cracow Jews except some 15,000 people were driven out by March 1941; it was only then that a walled ghetto was established for these people in the Podgorze part of the city.[75]

The occupying powers made formal provision for the establishment of Jewish councils in November 1939, and these were made responsible for implementing German regulations,[76] whether they applied to handing over money and goods or organizing gangs of forced labourers. The Jewish councils, which were usually set up by the German authorities, were also responsible in particular for providing accommodation and nourishment for the Jewish population and they organized cultural and educational activities within the ghettos.[77] The Jewish councils had their own 'police force' with which to assert their authority.

The situation of the Polish Jews was characterized by the systematic under-provision of goods necessary for survival[78] and the permanent terror to which the German occupiers subjected them: mistreatment, raids, organized shootings by the gendarmerie, the Gestapo and the SS were commonplace, but so were attacks by members of the German civilian administration and the army. A regime of terror was the norm in the forced labour camps and the death rates were high.[79] Anti-Jewish policies were accompanied by parallel campaigns of systematic anti-Semitic propaganda.[80]

German *Judenpolitik* from Spring 1940 to mid-1941: Comprehensive Resettlement Plans

The Madagascar Plan

In the early summer of 1940 plans for a 'final solution' to the 'Jewish question' via mass deportations were once more making headway within the National Socialist government. Now, after the victory in the West, the French colony of Madagascar began to look like a suitable target destination.[81]

The idea that it would be possible to 'export' large numbers of European Jews to Madagascar of all places had enjoyed a certain resonance in the anti-Semitic circles of various European countries since the end of the nineteenth century. Such 'Madagascar Projects' were combined with various other ambitions and were vigorously revived after 1937/8 not only by leading National Socialist functionaries,[82] but by politicians of other countries, too, and by the speculations of the international press.[83] On the German side these utopian, impracticable notions were to some extent turned into concrete plans in early summer 1940.

An important stimulus evidently derived from Himmler, who presented a memorandum to Hitler on 25 May 1940 in which he set out his intention of 'seeing the concept "Jew" ... completely extinguished by the possibility of a huge emigration of all the Jews to Africa or one of the colonies'.[84] Interestingly, in this memorandum the Reichsführer SS had mentioned a radical alternative to his resettlement plans, namely the 'Bolshevist method of the physical extermination of a people', but for reasons of personal conviction he had rejected this as 'un-Germanic and impossible'.

After Hitler had approved the basic principle underlying this memorandum,[85] the idea of a 'colonial' solution was taken up by the Foreign Ministry, too. On 3 June Franz Rademacher, who had just been named Director of the new 'Department of Jewish Affairs', presented a memorandum to the Director of the Department for German Affairs, Hans Luther, in which he asked for 'a fundamental definition of German war aims in the matter of the Jewish question by the Reich Foreign Minister'. Rademacher saw three possibilities:

(a)   'all Jews out of Europe';
(b)   a 'separation of Eastern and Western Jews', the Eastern Jews, who were considered to be 'the future Jewish intelligentsia, potent and well grounded in the Talmud', would remain 'in German hands (Lublin?) as a bargaining counter (Faustpfand)' in order to 'paralyse the American Jews', whilst the Western Jews would be deported 'out of Europe', possibly to Madagascar;
(c)   a 'Jewish national homeland in Palestine' (where Rademacher immediately committed his doubts to paper with the note 'danger of a second Rome!').[86]

Within a short time Rademacher was given the task of writing a first draft of a comprehensive deportation plan,[87] and began his work at a point where the Madagascar Project enjoyed a high level of support among the National Socialist leadership: Hitler and Ribbentrop explained the plan to Mussolini and Ciano on 17 and 18 June;[88] Hitler mentioned it on 20 June to the Commander-in-Chief of the Navy, Erich Raeder;[89] at the beginning of July Frank informed his colleagues of the Madagascar Plan;[90] at the beginning of August Hitler mentioned the plan to drive all the Jews out of Europe to the German ambassador in Paris, Otto Abetz;[91]and in mid-August he spoke of it to Goebbels.[92] Even representatives of the Jewish communities were semi-officially informed about the Madagascar Plan, including those from the Reich Association, who were told at the end of July 1940, and the Chair of the Warsaw Jewish Council, Adam Czerniakow, who learned of it on 1 July.[93]

By 24 June Heydrich had already intervened in the Foreign Ministry's preparations for the Madagascar Project via a letter to Ribbentrop.[94] The problem of the millions of Jews under German rule (to which Heydrich assigned the figure 3¼ million) could no longer be solved by emigration: 'therefore a territorial final solution is necessary'. Heydrich asked 'to take part...in the discussions that are envisaged on the final solution to the Jewish question'.

A few days later, on 3 July, Rademacher presented a draft for the Madagascar project.[95] His deft formula, 'all Jews out of Europe', showed unambiguously what kind of territorial solution was being sought at this point. He imagined that France would 'place Madagascar at [Germany's] disposal for the solution of the Jewish question', as a mandate: 'the part of the island that has no military importance would be placed under the administration of a German police governor who would report to the office of the Reichsführer SS. The Jews will be able to run their own administration in this territory...' Rademacher's goal was to ensure that the Jews remained 'a bargaining counter in German hands to guarantee the future good behaviour of their racial associates in America'; the Madagascar Project, then, was to function as a form of 'hostage taking', as the 'Jewish reservation' in Poland had been intended to.

Another document by Rademacher, dated 2 July ('Plan for a Solution to the Jewish Question'[96]) contains further information about his intentions. 'From a German perspective, the Madagascar solution means the creation of a huge ghetto. Only the security police have the necessary experience in this field; they have the means to prevent a break-out from the island. In addition, they have experience of carrying out in an appropriate manner such punishment measures as become necessary as a result of hostile actions against Germany by Jews in the USA.'

Whilst Rademacher was obtaining expert opinion on the feasibility of his project,[97] and whilst the Reich Office for Area Planning (Reichsstelle für Raumordnung) was confirming to Goering (who was thereby also involved in the 'planning for the final solution') the existence of sufficient 'settlement possibilities' on the island,[98] the Reich Security Head Office was putting together its own version of the Madagascar Plan, which was ready in booklet form by 15 August.[99] It contained the suggestion that a 'police state' be set up for the four million Jews who would be on the island at that point under German rule. The

RSHA estimated that a period of four years would be necessary to transport these people to Madagascar by ship.

In a later note, dated 30 August, Rademacher explicitly supported a suggestion that had in the meantime been made by Victor Brack,[100] who was based in the Chancellery of the Führer of the NSDAP and responsible for overseeing the 'euthanasia' programme. Brack proposed 'using the wartime transport systems that he had developed for the Führer for the transport of Jews to Madagascar at a later date'. The mention of Brack and the fact that another key figure responsible for the 'euthanasia programme', the Director of the Chancellery of the Führer, Philipp Bouhler, was being considered for the role of Governor in Madagascar, taken together cast the Madagascar Project in a very dark light indeed. Furthermore, Rademacher's document shows that the estimate of the number of Jews that were to be settled on Madagascar had by then reached 6½ million, which suggests that the Jews from the south-east European states and the northern French colonies were now being included in the plans for deportation.

Fantastic though the Madagascar Plan now seems, it cannot simply be dismissed as merely distraction tactics for a *Judenpolitik* that had reached a dead-end.[101] It is precisely the lack of feasibility in this plan that points up the cynical, calculating nature of German *Judenpolitik*: the idea that millions of European Jews would be deported to Madagascar for years and years, and the fact that—without even considering the 'punishment measures' that Rademacher envisaged—a large proportion of the transported Jews would presumably die there relatively quickly as victims of the hostile living conditions they would meet, all this makes it perfectly clear that behind this project lay the intention of bringing about the physical annihilation of the Jews under German rule. However, this was an intention that appropriate 'good behaviour' on the part of the United States might cause to be revised. From the point of view of the RSHA the Madagascar Project was a means of perpetuating the plans for a 'Jewish reservation' in the General Government that were at that time unrealizable, and of extending them to the Jews of Western Europe. When the Madagascar Plan had to be suspended in the autumn of 1940 because of the failure to make peace with Great Britain the preparations for Barbarossa immediately opened up a new perspective for a 'territorial solution' of the 'Jewish question'. For a period of a few months, then, 'Madagascar' stood for 'anywhere' that might permit the execution of a 'final solution', or in other words for the option of initiating a slow and painful end for the Jews of Europe in conditions inimical to life.

Inspired by the intention to annihilate the Jews under German rule, Hitler was to keep coming back to the Madagascar Project time and again until 1942, by which time the idea of 'anywhere' had been replaced by that of 'nowhere'.[102] In the Foreign Ministry the plan was officially shelved in February 1942.[103]

Judenpolitik between the Madagascar Plan and 'Barbarossa'

The German Regime and the Polish Jews

The progress of the war and the overall plans of the National Socialist regime for the fate of the Jews under German rule had direct consequences for *Judenpolitik* in the General Government.

The halt put to deportations of Jews into the General Government in March 1940 was initially seen as a provisional measure.[104] However, in the summer of 1940, after the victory in France, the aim of establishing a 'Jewish reservation' in Poland was definitively abandoned. On 8 July, Frank informed his colleagues a few days later,[105] Hitler had assured him that no further deportations into the General Government would take place, in view of the Madagascar Project. On 9 July Himmler made the definitive end to deportations into Frank's area known internally.[106]

Besides putting an end to the deportations, the war in the West had other consequences for the German occupation of Poland. From September 1939 to April 1940 the occupying power in Poland had carried out mass executions of people who had been held in the context of the so-called 'intelligentsia campaign' or the waves of regional arrests;[107] now, after May 1940, such executions were to be continued on a much greater scale as part of the so-called 'AB campaign' (where AB stands for *Außerordentliche Befriedungsaktion* or 'extraordinary pacification campaign'). As Frank explained to representatives of the police at the end of May, the beginning of the war in the West had presented them with a chance 'of finishing off the mass of seditious resistance politicians and other politically suspect individuals in our area and at the same time of eliminating the inheritance of earlier Polish criminality'. Frank stated quite explicitly that this campaign would 'cost a few thousand Polish lives, above all those from the leading intellectual cadres of Poland' and in this context he cited Hitler when he said, 'the elements of the Polish leadership that we have now identified are to be liquidated'.[108] This is in fact what happened: during the 'AB campaign' some 3,500 members of the intelligentsia and political functionaries, as well as about 3,000 people who had been designated criminals were killed. This policy of the systematic mass murder of the Polish elites was itself bound to have a radicalizing effect on the persecution of the Jews.

After the Department for the Internal Administration of the General Governor had in August 1940 already confirmed the necessity of establishing ghettos that were, however, not to be hermetically sealed,[109] the construction of new ghettos in the General Government evidently gained further impetus in autumn 1940. In

Warsaw[110] and other cities further closed Jewish quarters were set up[111] after the legal basis for such action had been established in September when the Order concerning Domicile Restrictions was issued.[112] However, the formation of ghettos did not follow a unified plan; local authorities' need to gain control was the decisive factor, rather than the failure of the Madagascar Plan. The establishment of ghettos or the designation of certain quarters or areas of a city as Jewish represent only one of the measures that the occupying administration used to deal with the astonishing lack of living accommodation for the Jewish population. Since the occupying power usually tackled its need for space at the expense of the Jews—and moreover undertook several 'deportations' (*Aussiedlungen*) to the 'capital' of the General Government, Cracow, for example, or to recreational resorts—it found itself repeatedly forced to intervene in Jewish living arrangements in a regulatory fashion. This trend increased after spring 1941 when more space was needed to accommodate the eastern army marching into Poland.[113] The original aim for 'concentrating' Jews in larger cities was often not achieved, however; on the contrary, Jews were deported from such places and divided between the surrounding smaller towns.[114]

In the rationing scheme for foodstuffs Jews were in the lowest of ten consumer groups. These rations, which often only existed on paper, were already set at such a low level that they did not permit survival.[115] In order to survive the Jewish population was dependent on smuggling and the black market; the danger of the 'Jewish black market' was a further reason for the occupation administration to intensify their control over the Jewish population and step up their persecution of the Jews.

Until autumn 1941 the authorities generally continued to count on the Jews soon being removed, which is why most anti-Jewish measures were essentially provisional. The situation of the Jews did not worsen as the result of a carefully planned set of policies on the part of the Germans but because of the cumulative effect of inadequate support measures and a regime fundamentally uninterested in their fate. Even the establishment of ghettos was carried out so haphazardly and slowly that it would be wrong to see it as a systematic policy ultimately aimed at the physical annihilation of the Jews. It is quite clear that there was no uniform and unified policy towards the inhabitants of the ghettos. Using the examples of the Lodz and Warsaw ghettos, the historian Christopher Browning has shown that there were two contrasting positions represented simultaneously within the German departments responsible: according to one view, the population of the ghettos should be left to starve, whilst according to the other, opportunities for employment had to be created in order to give the Jews the possibility of sustaining themselves—although in this case the motive was less humanitarian than connected with the fear of disease.[116] In both ghettos the 'productive' line of argument prevailed over the argument for starving the Jews to death. However, it is significant that in the course of this discussion the possibility of gradually annihilating the Jews physically via hunger or disease was openly considered as a serious option that was eventually rejected overwhelmingly on grounds of expediency.

In the summer of 1940 responsibility for enforced labour in the General Government passed from the SS, who had failed in this area, to the civilian administration, which began to regulate the Jewish workers centrally. The main focus of Jewish forced labour in the General Government gradually became the district of Lublin, where Jews (including those from other districts) were assigned by preference to major projects and given rough and ready accommodation and wholly inadequate subsistence.[117] The path of Jewish forced labour took a particular turn in eastern Upper Silesia, where Himmler appointed the Breslau Police Commander Albrecht Schmelt as Director of an office to oversee 'the registration and direction of workforces composed of foreign peoples'. Schmelt systematically set about collecting the Jews 'concentrated' in certain towns in the eastern part of eastern Upper Silesia and deploying them in forced labour groups for road-building and industrial manufacture. In occupied Poland forced labourers' wages were usually either wholly withheld or paid only in very small part; across the camps conditions were appalling, accommodation, food, and medical care were catastrophically bad, and the camp authorities deployed rigid means of repression.[118]

Life in the Ghettos

The situation in the closed ghettos and those areas of towns specially assigned to Jews was characterized by extreme congestion (in the Warsaw ghetto, for example, according to German estimates, using an 'occupancy' figure of 6 to 7 persons per room,[119] there were between 410,000 and 590,000 people living in a little more than 4 square kilometres), by disastrously bad hygiene, wholly inadequate supplies of foodstuffs, by disease, and therefore by a high death rate.[120] For these reasons approximately a quarter of the populations of the two largest Polish ghettos, Warsaw and Lodz, died of 'natural' causes.[121] Raul Hilberg estimates that the total of Polish Jews killed prior to and during the period of ghettoization before the violent ghetto clearances began was approximately 500,000.[122]

The Jewish minority of Poland that was penned into the ghettos in this manner was neither an amorphous mass nor a homogeneous community. The great social differences that existed in the pre-war period, the diverse political trends and the differences in attitudes to religion amongst Jews were maintained under ghetto conditions and even intensified. However, a sociology of ghetto society highlights new phenomena, including the rise of a social class of newly rich and privileged people, the rapid degradation of the intelligentsia, the reduction of the Jewish middle class to an army of slave workers and the tense relationship between the original inhabitants of the ghettos and the newcomers forced to enter them.[123]

The lives of those locked in the ghettos was completely dominated by the daily struggle for survival, which was above all the problem of somehow finding something to eat. Hunger was the leitmotif of ghetto life. Hunger changed both individual and collective behaviour and forced people to cross the boundaries of dignity and to transgress moral norms.

There were various attempts made by the inhabitants of the ghettos to resist the rapid erosion of the standards of civilization. Jewish social self-help organizations were active across a broad range of areas,[124] and religious, educational, and cultural activities offered the possibility of retaining a vestige of human dignity and self-respect. There is evidence of activities such as these, to various degrees, in a series of ghettos; they were partly organized officially by Jewish councils and tolerated by the Germans, but to a large extent they took place 'underground' despite being forbidden by the authorities.[125]

Whatever efforts the Jewish councils and individual inhabitants of the ghettos made to make their lives a little more tolerable, however, they were made within the context of a dyamic of power that consisted of near-omnipotence on the German side and total impotence on the Jewish side. The German authorities nonetheless succeeded to a certain extent both in concealing the reality of this dynamic by forming the Jewish councils as organs of an (in reality non-existent) autonomous administration and in maintaining the illusion of some room for manoeuvre on the Jewish side.

The decisive factor in internal relationships in the ghettos was the omnipotence of the German side, which decided on the extent to which the ghettos were supplied with food and essentials in exchange for goods, objects of value, and money, but which ensured that the conflicts emerging from the inadequate conditions there were resolved by the inhabitants themselves. The German occupying power usually left it to the Jewish councils to distribute the deliveries of foodstuffs, always too small and usually of poor quality. Distribution took place in different ways: ration cards were introduced, free market trade was permitted or meals were served in canteens, the latter often with the support of Jewish self-help organizations. However it was organized, the result was always to privilege those groups that the Jewish councils considered of particular importance for the continuing survival of the ghettos. These included the members of the extensive bureaucratic apparatus created by the Jewish councils but also, and increasingly as time went on, the workforces involved in manufacturing the goods to be supplied to the Germans. In most of the Polish ghettos 1941 marked the point where most of the inhabitants had exchanged virtually all the goods and objects of value they had brought into the ghetto for foodstuffs and other essentials and when more and more people were attempting to survive by working in the ghetto workshops, the so-called 'shops' that produced goods for the Germans.[126] The Jewish councils began to support these plans to make the ghettos 'productive', especially as the shift of emphasis towards work in the ghettos seemed advantageous in comparison with the appalling conditions in the forced labour camps—a contrast sharpened as the occupying power began a new work initiative in spring 1941.[127] It appears that it was not least the initiatives of the Jewish councils that attracted the attention of the Germans to the idea of making the Jews 'productive', in contrast to the Nazi stereotype, according to which Jews were essentially always 'parasitical' and 'unproductive'.

Additional essential supplements to the provisions within the ghettos were obtained via smuggling and the black market, on which the last goods and chattels of the Jews were exchanged for foodstuffs. These methods were officially prosecuted by the Jewish councils, under pressure from the Germans, but in reality were frequently ignored. Despite their merciless persecution of smugglers, the Germans were to some extent forced to accept the existence of the phenomenon in the interests of maintaining the ghetto economy itself. However, smuggling and the black market both eventually contributed to an increased distortion in the equality of distribution for essential goods within the ghettos and thus to sharpening the tensions between ghetto inhabitants themselves.[128]

The diaries and memoirs of ghetto inhabitants[129] show that the decisive factors for survival—access to work, the distribution of living space and of provisions—were part of a complex network of links, contacts, and privileges in which corruption often played a significant role. Lack of transparency in the division of vital resources and the fact that the procedures of the Jewish councils were often seen as arbitrary, unjust, and self-seeking led in many instances to feelings of mistrust, even hatred towards the councils on the part of the ghetto populations.[130] There is no doubt that the often tense relationships between councils and population made the job of the Germans' relatively small administrative apparatus considerably easier.

Initially the Jewish councils attempted to encourage the Germans towards moderation, with the help of petitions, personal meetings, and offers to negotiate—even on occasion using gifts and bribery.[131] Given the extraordinary imbalance in the influence of the occupying power and the Jewish councils there was no alternative to these tactics, but they were bound to remain fruitless in the long run and ultimately only led to the postponement of repressive measures by the Germans. Because they could not resist the demands of the German side the Jewish councils gradually reached the conclusion that it was their task to increase the chances of survival of at least a part of the population of the ghettos by following German orders and acquiescing in the wishes of the occupying powers, and in particular by encouraging the workforce to be as productive as possible. For this reason the councils tended to discipline the population of the ghettos in their own interests—as they believed. The Jewish police therefore often proceeded rigorously in order to preserve the authority of the councils.[132]

It would be too simplistic to derive from this account an image of a Jewish elite that was anxious to conform at all costs. After a detailed examination of the Jewish councils in the General Government and Upper Silesia Aharon Weiss has come to the conclusion that of the 146 Jewish elders originally nominated by the Germans 57 lost their positions because they were not willing to meet the demands that were placed upon them by the Germans: 11 resigned their posts, 26 were replaced, 18 were liquidated and 2 committed suicide. In the light of this it was not so much the individual compliance of those holding these positions that ultimately guaranteed the successful implementation of the Germans' policies as a willingness on the German side to force the institution of the Jewish councils into submission, if necessary using the most brutal of methods. The relatively frequent changes in the occupancy of the council posts had as a further consequence the effect of gradually replacing the members of local elites, who had initially dominated the Jewish councils, with newcomers and outsiders, who had less intimate connections with the local population and therefore tended to reinforce the alienation that was growing between the councils and the population of the ghettos.[133]

If the institution of the Jewish councils tended to bow to the demands of the Germans and was in particular prepared to treat different sectors of the population of the ghettos in a differentiated manner—corresponding to their presumed usefulness to the German occupying power—this was because the Jewish occupants of council posts were guided by the idea that the Germans were pursuing a rationally comprehensible goal and that their behaviour was ultimately calculable or predictable. However, the fact that the policies of the occupying power were based on ideologically racist premises to which all utilitarian perspectives were subordinated was a phenomenon that must have been wholly incomprehensible to the Jewish councils. The reality of a thoroughgoing racist occupation was something without historical precedent.[134]

From the perspective of the persecutors the system established in the ghettos was remarkably efficient. The minimum of effort was needed to facilitate the total exploitation and the near perfect dominance of the ghetto populations. The occupiers could always rely on their instructions being carried out by the Jewish councils, with a different membership if necessary. The 'management' of the ghettos by the Jewish councils guaranteed in almost all cases the resolution of conflict within the ghettos themselves, without bothering the occupying powers with any serious need to intervene.

In the years 1940 and 1941 underground action within the ghettos was restricted to social aid, cultural activities, illegal political meetings, and the production of pamphlets. There was no real basis for any far-reaching organized passive resistance, let alone any active measures.[135] Resistance from the ghettos was not a factor that would cause the German side any serious trouble in 1940–1. On the contrary, the Jewish councils developed a routine of following German instructions, which became fatally habitual: with the intention of preventing the worst, the Jewish councils themselves became the instruments of German anti-Jewish policy.

It would be completely futile to try to analyse the conditions in the ghettos without always remembering and bearing in mind at every stage of the analysis that the ghettos were institutions conceived, realized, and rigorously controlled by the Germans. The slightest degree of insubordination on the part of the Jewish councils was met with the most draconian of punishments.[136] The autonomy of these Jewish councils within the ghettos, which was in any case only vestigial, and the illusions of the inhabitants that derived from the appearance of autonomy, were important components of the perfidious system of control that the Germans employed. From the perspective of the historiography of the perpetrators any judgement of the behaviour of the Jewish councils that does not take into account the true power relations is entirely pointless.

However, turning the ghettos into productive enterprises and increasing the deployment of Jews in forced labour projects within the General Government after spring 1941[137] led to the increased differentiation of the Jewish population according to their 'capacity for work'. This distinction was an important precursor of the concept developed by the SS from autumn 1941: 'annihilation through work'.

Deportations Phase III: The Consequences of the Madagascar Plan

The Madagascar Plan also had a direct effect on 'Jewish policy' in the area of the Reich. In mid-July 1940 the Gauleiter of Berlin, Goebbels, informed leading officials in the Propaganda Ministry that immediately after the end of the war he would have the more than 60,000 remaining Jews of Berlin 'transported to Poland' within no longer than eight weeks. Then the 'other Jew cities (Breslau, etc.)' would have their turn. In early September 1940 the official responsible for 'Jewish affairs', Hans Hinkel, once more confirmed that it was the authorities' intention to deport all the Jews of Berlin immediately after the end of the war.[138] And indeed it was in October 1940 that deportations on the largest scale so far were to take place: the expulsion of the Jewish minorities from Baden and the Saar-Palatinate, who were deported to southern France following the expulsion of Jews and other 'undesirables' from Alsace and Lorraine, which had been earmarked for annexation. By summer 1940 there had been protests in the Gaus of the Palatinate and Baden when the population that had been evacuated from the border zones at the outbreak of war began to return and the Jews also wished to resettle in their former homes; in Breisach and Kehl local Party authorities had on their own initiative driven the returning Jews into the occupied Alsatian zone, although they were allowed to return from there a few weeks later after an intervention from Berlin.[139]

From July onwards, and in especially large numbers in August and September, tens of thousands of 'undesirable persons' (including almost the entire Jewish population of some 3,000) had been transported from Alsace and Lorraine into the unoccupied areas of France.[140] On 28 September Hitler demanded of Gauleiter Josef Bürckel of the Palatinate and Gauleiter Robert Wagner of Baden (who as heads of the civilian administration were simultaneously responsible for Lorraine and Alsace) that in ten years they should be able to report these French areas as 'German, furthermore as purely German'; he said he would not ask 'what methods they had applied'.[141]

The policy of organized deportations also encompassed the regions within the area of the Reich over which these two Gauleiters had authority. On 22 and 23 October all the Jews from Baden and the Saar-Palatinate, approximately 7,000 people, were taken in twelve transports to southern France where the French authorities interned them.[142] It seems that the Gauleiters themselves were responsible for the initiative for these deportations, which were explicitly approved by Hitler.[143]

In parallel to these deportations to southern France preparations were being made in October 1940 for further transports to the General Government. In this context statements made by Hitler in early October on the capacity of the General Government to receive more people are of interest. When Gauleiters Baldur von Schirach and Erich Koch asked General Governor Frank in the course of an informal conversation in Hitler's apartments on 2 October to take 50,000 Jews from Vienna or a larger number of Poles and Jews from the area of Zichenau (now part of East Prussia), Frank refused; Hitler's view, however, was that 'it is irrelevant how large the population in the General Government is', although he did not give a firm opinion on further deportations of Jews.[144]

Frank could also no longer reckon on 'relief' through Jewish emigration: on 25 October 1940 the RSHA placed a ban on Jews leaving the General Government in order not to impair opportunities for Jews to emigrate from the area of the Reich.[145] However, in November Frank succeeded in putting a stop to further movements of Jews from the Warthegau by appealing to the preparations that were already in place for the Eastern military deployment.[146] They were only to be resumed at the beginning of 1941 in the context of the so-called 'third short-term plan'.

At the beginning of November, however, Hitler took the concrete decision to create more space in the annexed Polish territories for more ethnic Germans coming from Romania and the Soviet Union: before the end of the war he wanted some '150,000 to 160,000 Poles and Jews [amongst others] from the recovered areas' to settle in the General Government.[147]

On the same day Gauleiters Erich Koch from East Prussia and Albert Forster from Danzig-West-Prussia began to argue about the quotas for deportations, with the result that Hitler had to 'make peace, laughing' between the two of them, as Goebbels's diaries record. On the same occasion the 'Führer' confirmed that 'we will shove the Jews out of this area, too, when the time is right'.[148]

By the end of the year more than 48,000 former Polish citizens, Jews and non-Jews, were deported into the General Government from the district of Zichenau, which was under the authority of the East Prussian Gauleiter, from Gau Danzig-West-Prussia and from Upper Silesia.[149]

Deportations Phase IV: A Successor to the Madagascar Project

Between November 1940 and January 1941 the German leadership finally abandoned the Madagascar Plan having had to accept that a separate peace with Great Britain was not possible. Within the context of the preparations for 'Barbarossa',[150] they began to develop a new project, a 'Post-Madagascar Plan'.[151]

When the Madagascar Project proved to be pie in the sky at the end of 1940 the deportations into the General Government for which individual Gauleiters had been pressing ever more firmly were resumed. The head of the Reich Chancellery, Hans-Heinrich Lammers, informed Schirach in early December that his request of two months earlier to transport the Jews of Vienna had been approved by Hitler. A first step towards the transportation of a total of 60,000 people that he had in mind was the deportation of 5,000 Jews from Vienna into the General Government in February and March.[152]

Further information about what the RSHA envisaged as a 'solution' for the 'Jewish question' is provided by the elaboration of some ideas that Eichmann prepared for Himmler on 4 December in order to provide him with figures for a speech to Gauleiters and Reichsleiters.[153] Eichmann drew a distinction between two phases, first the 'initial solution to the Jewish question by means of emigration' and then the future 'final solution to the Jewish question', by which he understood 'the resettlement of the Jews from the German people's European economic area into territories yet to be determined'—which was a clear reference to the recent abandonment of the Madagascar Plan. In his notes for Himmler Eichmann wrote that this project would encompass 'a total of some 5.8 million Jews',[154] which is considerably more than the four million that the RSHA reckoned with when preparing the Madagascar Project. Planning had evidently been extended in the meantime to include German allies and satellites in Eastern Europe and the Jews in the French colonies.

In the speech that Himmler made on 10 December he identified 'Jewish emigration' from the General Government as a key future task that would 'create more space for Poles'. The Reichsführer did not identify a destination for this emigration.

Various indications from January 1941 show that 'resettlements' were planned on a huge scale even during the preparation of the third short-term plan. Influenced by the waves of ethnic German 'resettlers' streaming into the area of the Reich from Romania and the Soviet Union, comprehensive plans were being drawn up for expelling more Poles and Jews from the incorporated Eastern territories into the General Government.

At a meeting in the RSHA on 8 January 1941 Heydrich gave the figure of 831,000 to indicate the number of people to be resettled by the end of the year, which included the 60,000 Viennese Jews. Another 200,000 people were to be expelled from the General Government in order to be able to establish huge sites for military exercises.[155] Initially it was proposed to deport 238,000 people in the context of the third short-term plan. But this plan was in fact destined to be suspended as soon as 15 March after about 25,000 people had been transported into the General Government: 19,226 people from the Warthegau who were 'unfit for work' (including 2,140 Jews) and 5,000 Jews from Vienna (instead of the 10,000 that had been planned for the first phase).[156] No preparations had been made for the reception and support of these people who were being transported in the depths of winter, just as had been the case with the Nisko Campaign and with the transports from Schneidemühl and Stettin).[157]

The third short-term plan was, however, not only the first step in the deportation of a million people from the incorporated Eastern territories within the space of a year; it was evidently connected to a much larger programme of deportations that affected the whole area under German control.[158] This all-embracing programme of deportations can be reconstructed from two documents, a note by the Gestapo official responsible for 'Jewish affairs' in Paris, Theodor Dannecker, to Eichmann dated 21 January, and a minute of remarks by Eichmann made on 20 March. Dannecker wrote to Eichmann that it was 'the Führer's will . . . that after the war the Jewish question within the areas ruled or controlled by Germany be brought to a definitive solution'. To this end Heydrich had 'already received a commission to present a plan for the final solution from the Führer via the RFSS [Himmler] and the Reichsmarschall [Goering]'. In response a project had been worked out that was currently with Hitler and Goering. The individual preparations that had to be made would have to 'extend not only to preliminary work aimed at the complete expulsion of the Jews but also to the detailed planning of a resettlement programme in a territory yet to be determined'.[159]

From a statement made by Eichmann on 20 March 1941 at a meeting in the Ministry of Propaganda we learn in addition 'that Party Comrade Heydrich—who has been charged by the Führer with the definitive evacuation of the Jews—made a suggestion to the Führer 8–10 weeks ago that has not been put into practice for the sole reason that the General Government is at the present moment not in a position to accept a single Jew or Pole from the Old Reich'.[160] Regarding the deportation of the Berlin Jews, Eichmann expressed himself extremely carefully, making explicit reference to war production: it might be possible to deport 15,000 people as part of the deportation programme for Viennese Jews already approved by Hitler. This was a perspective that had a sobering effect on Goebbels, who had believed in the imminence of the total deportation of the Jews of Berlin,[161] as emerges from his diaries: 'The Jews can't be evacuated from Berlin, at least not in large numbers, because 30,000 of them are working for armament production.'[162] Despite the resolution to postpone deportations, or at least those of any magnitude, the Gestapo decided officially to inform the Reich Association on 17 March that they should now prepare themselves for deportations.[163]

From this information it emerges that Heydrich had received an instruction from Hitler (via Himmler and Goering) before January 1941 to draw up a first draft of a 'final solution plan' that was to be put into effect after the war and which aimed at the complete deportation of all Jews from Europe. When this project was ready in January 1941, the original aim (as envisaged in the version Heydrich had in December) to direct these deportations to Madagascar had been abandoned without a new 'destination territory' having been identified. But Heydrich had already announced large-scale deportations into the General Government on 8 January, which were in fact begun a short while later, but two months after that Eichmann was talking of how the project could not be realized because of the situation in the General Government, apart from the smaller-scale deportations that were part of the third short-term plan completed on 15 March.

However, the General Government was not the territory for the 'Final Solution' that was 'yet to be determined'; it was only an intermediate station. General Governor Frank said in Cracow on 26 March that Hitler had just agreed that the 'General Government would be the first area to be made free of Jews'. But that was only a long-term aim, as other remarks by Frank on the same day make clear: he spoke of Hitler being determined 'within the next 15 or 20 years to make the General Government a purely German land'. He also stressed the importance of the forced labour groups of Poles and Jews.[164] Moreover, at the start of April, Frank was busy with medium-term planning for the Warsaw ghetto.[165]

But what was the long-term outlook for 'Jewish policy' at this time? Were the deportations into the General Government part of plans for the subsequent physical annihilation of people in this area? The question can be answered by drawing upon a further document first identified by Götz Aly in the Moscow 'special archive'. It is a note made by Heydrich on 26 March 1941 of a conversation with Goering: 'Regarding the solution of the Jewish question, I gave the Reich Marshal [i.e. Goering] a brief report and submitted my proposal to him, which he approved after making a change with respect to Rosenberg's responsibilities and he ordered its resubmission.'[166]

This note evidently refers to the draft of Goering's well-known 'authorization' for Heydrich to 'make organizational, functional and material plans for a complete solution to the Jewish question in the areas of Europe under German rule', dated 31 July.[167] The change made to 'Rosenberg's jurisdiction' in Heydrich's note of 26 March will refer to the passage that in the July document is formulated thus: 'in so far as the jurisdiction of other central authorities is affected, these are to be involved.' The fact that in the draft of this fundamental division of responsibility for preparing the 'Final Solution' Rosenberg's jurisdiction was to be taken into consideration as a 'central authority' allows us to conclude that the area of the Soviet Union was being identified for these 'final solution plans' and that Rosenberg was already being considered as the Director of a 'central authority' (what was later to be the Ministry for the East) for the occupied Eastern territories.

What those involved understood at this point by the 'Final Solution' within the Soviet Union, which was yet to be occupied, is not clear. There were no concrete plans made either for a reservation or for mass murder. Early in 1941 Himmler was temporarily concerned with the possibility of a mass sterilization of Jews and asked Victor Brack, who was based in the Chancellery of the Führer and responsible for overseeing 'euthanasia', to develop an appropriate plan. When this was ready at the end of March 1941 he did not pursue the project any further.[168] It seems that the answer to the question of what was to happen to the people to be deported to the 'East' was being postponed to a time after the planned conquest of the Soviet Union had been achieved. The indifference to the fate of those transported that this suggests was characteristic of the early deportations into the General Government and was commensurate with the leadership style of the National Socialists: at the appropriate time those responsible and actually 'on site' would find some 'solution' or other to the new problems that they were faced with. There are concrete indications from the months before 'Barbarossa' that elements within the National Socialist leadership were arriving at the conclusion that there would be large-scale deportations 'to the East'.

Immediately before the attack on the Soviet Union General Governor Frank explained to Goebbels that he was preparing for the removal of the Jews, as Goebbels noted in his diary, glossing Frank thus: 'in the General Government they are already looking forward to being able to get rid of the Jews. The Jews in Poland are gradually declining. This is a just punishment for having stirred the population up and for provoking the war. The Führer has predicted this to the Jews.'[169] Remarks that he made to his colleagues on 17 July clarify the source of Frank's confidence: according to an assurance given to him by Hitler on 19 June, the Jews would be removed from the General Government in the foreseeable future which would turn into 'transit camps'.[170] Moreover, when the Romanian Head of State, Antonescu, complained to Hitler on 16 August 1941 that German troops had turned back the Bessarabian Jews that Romanian soldiers had just driven into the Ukraine, he reminded Hitler that this practice was in stark contrast to 'the guidelines about the treatment of the Eastern Jews that the Führer had given him in Munich'.[171] This referred to the meeting of the two leaders in Munich on 13 June 1941.

PART III

MASS EXECUTIONS OF JEWS IN
THE OCCUPIED SOVIET ZONES, 1941

CHAPTER 10

LAYING THE GROUND FOR A WAR
OF RACIAL ANNIHILATION

From the outset the war against the Soviet Union was conceived as a campaign of racial domination and annihilation.[1] Victory over the Soviet Union was expected to be rapid, both bringing about a turning point in the progress of the war and at the same time establishing in Eastern Europe an imperium of living space, or *Lebensraum*, for the peoples of the Reich, to be run along lines dictated by racial ideology.

The long-term aims of the war against the Soviet Union may be summarized in the following mutually interdependent clusters. First, for the National Socialist regime, the conquest of the Soviet territories represented the fulfilment of the *Lebensraum* programme that had originally been developed in *Mein Kampf.* It was the realization of a large-scale 'eastern settlement' that had formed part of the programmatic demands of the right for decades previously. The creation of settlement space for millions of people was supposed to establish a 'healthy' relationship between the land at Germany's disposal and the number of people that needed to be accommodated; it was intended to counteract the tendency towards deracination that Germans had suffered since industrialization and thereby inaugurate a higher degree of social harmonization. However, the conquest of *Lebensraum* did not merely serve to alleviate the Germans' alleged urgent need for territory; on the contrary, it was also intended to form the basis for further biological expansion of the 'Aryan race' and in that manner to provide the 'human resources' for future wars of conquest.[2]

The second group of war aims linked the conquest of *Lebensraum* from the outset with a 'policy of unbridled robbery and looting'.[3] It was planned right from the start to feed the troops from the very land they were invading and furthermore to export agricultural produce back into the Reich. Industry in the Soviet Union was to be largely closed down, maintaining production only in a series of areas of interest to Germany, notably in the sphere of raw materials. From the standpoint of the Nazi leadership, both the confiscation of agricultural produce and the seizure of raw materials played an important part in securing Germany against potential blockade and in ensuring that the war against the British Empire could be successfully sustained over a long period.

At the same time, a third set of war aims planned to use the Eastern campaign as a means of annihilating 'Jewish Bolshevism'—that conglomerate, therefore, that only existed in the distorted vision of the National Socialists, which they saw as having been formed out of the cooperation of both of Germany's principal enemies. The image of 'Bolshevism as the domination of the Slavic masses in Soviet Russia by the Jews' had been one of National Socialism's ideological constants since its very earliest days.[4] At the same time, this regime was credited with possessing an almost paradoxical combination of external aggressiveness and internal weakness: whilst 'Russian Bolshevism', in Hitler's words, represented 'the attempt by the Jews to achieve world domination for themselves',[5] the regime allegedly established in Russia by 'the Jews' looked like a house of cards that only needed to be nudged from the outside for it to collapse. It was precisely this ambivalent assessment of 'Jewish Bolshevism'—belligerent on the outside, feeble on the inside—that offered a form of legitimation for a war in the East that bordered on self-delusion: from this angle it appeared both as a legitimate means of self-defence against alleged plans for world domination harboured by the 'Jewish Bolsheviks' and as a historically unique opportunity to conquer a vast empire with relatively little effort.

A fourth cluster of war aims was focused on the radicalization process that would of necessity occur within the 'Third Reich' as a consequence of an ideo-logically motivated conflict conducted with the utmost brutality and thereby far exceeding the bounds of conventional warfare. Such a process would inevitably shift the balance of power once and for all in favour of the National Socialist movement and at the expense of the conservative elites. This process was realized, for example, in the fact that in the preparatory stages before the war began the Wehrmacht appropriated for itself the ideological material of National Socialism and translated it into basic instructions that directly exhorted an army of several million conscripted men to implement radical ideological aims. As this process of radicalization progressed, the Russian campaign offered further possibilities for finding a 'final solution' to the Jewish question in Europe.

It is obvious that long-term aims such as these, linked by the National Socialist leadership with the conquest of the Soviet Union, would by definition entail the death of huge numbers of people. Not only was it planned to liquidate the entire local leadership, the 'Jewish Bolsheviks', but German plans for the ruthless occupation of *Lebensraum* and for the economic exploitation of the countryside would necessarily also deprive the native population of its basis for survival and thereby bring about the deaths of many millions of people. This policy had to be directed primarily, but by no means exclusively, at those who were at the bottom of the Nazis' racial hierarchy—Jews, Gypsies, and other 'racially inferior groups'.

From the beginning of 1941 the Germans' early thoughts on the exploitation of the areas to be conquered for food-supply purposes were developed into a full-scale systematic starvation policy, which would inevitably lead to the deaths of millions of people. This policy formed the basis for economic planning in the eastern territories under attack.[6] The initiative for its formulation lay principally with the State Secretary in the Reich Ministry of Food, Herbert Backe, and its execution was mostly the responsibility of the body concerned with the economic exploitation of the Soviet Union, the Four-Year-Plan Organization, or its close partner the Economic Organization for the East.[7]

The figure of 30 million people—a number corresponding to the increase in population in the areas to be conquered since 1914—was evidently a rough estimate being used for the purposes of orientation. According to the Higher SS and Police Commander, Erich von dem Bach-Zelewski, it was given by Himmler at a meeting with senior SS officers in Wewelsburg Castle in January 1941;[8] the same figure was used by Goering with the Italian Foreign Minister Ciano, in November 1941.[9] One of the outcomes of a meeting of State Secretaries on 2 May 1941 was the assertion that 'without doubt x-million people will starve if we remove what we need from the land they occupy'.[10]

Reducing the population of the areas to be conquered by millions in this way was seen as a necessary measure by the NS leadership—who remembered the blockade imposed during the First World War—in order to secure Germany's 'food autonomy'. It was also seen as a measure designed to create the necessary conditions for controlling the *Lebensraum* they viewed as essential.

In concrete terms what was envisaged was the removal of provisions from the fertile 'Black Earth Zone' in the south of the Soviet Union on a massive scale and the systematic under-provisioning of the nutrition deficiency area in the north with its major industrial centres. In the economic guidelines for the future Economic Organization East (Agricultural Group), issued on 21 May 1941, this plan was formulated thus: 'Many tens of millions of people in this area will become surplus to requirements and will have to die or emigrate to Siberia. Attempts to save the population there from starvation by fetching in surplus provisions from the Black Earth Zone could only occur at the cost of under-provisioning Europe. They will reduce Germany's capacity to hold out during the war and damage the capability of Germany and Europe to resist blockade.'[11] These principles formed part of the guidelines issued by Goering for the conduct of the economy in the newly occupied Eastern zones, the so-called 'Green Folder'.[12]

It is against the background of economic policies such as these, policies that factored in the death of millions of people, that the complex of orders and guidelines issued in the months before 'Barbarossa' must be assessed. These were instructions that were designed to prepare the Wehrmacht for a war of annihilation based on the National Socialists' racial ideology.

The orders that will be cited in the following paragraphs can only be understood if the plans for structuring the regime of German occupation are also clearly grasped. The basic assumption was that the swift advance of German formations would lead to the rapid expansion of the occupied zones. The armies were initially to set up nine Army Rear Areas to the west of the battle zone itself,[13] in order to pacify and control the districts just conquered. As the advance continued these areas were to be handed over to the Rear Areas that were to be set up by the three Army Groups. Gradually, these military authorities would be replaced by political authorities whose precise structure and responsibilities would only be established after the campaign had begun.

Orders and guidelines concerning the preparation of the war of annihilation were then worked out in detail. The first of these, the 'Guidelines for Special Areas relating to Instruction No. 21', contains the following: 'In the operational area of the army the Reichsführer SS is to be given special responsibilities, according to orders from the Führer, for the preparation of the political administration; these responsibilities are a consequence of the struggle between two opposing political systems that is finally to be fought.'[14] What these special duties were hardly remained in doubt after Hitler had given General Jodl the following principle for drawing up the guidelines on 3 March: 'the Jewish-Bolshevist intelligentsia, hitherto the "oppressor" of the people, must be eliminated',[15] and after Jodl himself had given the instruction, 'all Bolshevist chiefs and commissars are to be neutralized immediately'.[16]

As a result of this, the General Quartermaster of the Army, Eduard Wagner, and the Head of the Security Police, Heydrich, were finally able to negotiate the wording of a second agreement, on the 'Regulation for the Deployment of the Security Police and the SD within Army Formations',[17] the content of which had been the subject of discussion between the two organizations since February 1941.[18] According to the decree, 'carrying out certain Security Police tasks in areas outside the force itself necessitates the deployment of special units of the Security Police (SD) within the area of operations'. These special units would be charged with commandeering materials and taking individuals into custody within the Army Rear Areas and with taking steps to 'investigate and combat activities hostile to the Reich' and informing the appropriate commanders within the Rear Areas of the Army Group. They would 'bear responsibility' for carrying out their tasks but take orders from the armies or the commanders of the Rear

Areas of the Army Group 'with respect to mobilization, supplies and accommodation'.[19]

This made it clear that the planned liquidation of ideologically hostile groups
within the army's sphere of operation (commissars, Communist functionaries,
and the 'intelligentsia')—in so far as these groups had not already been arrested
and killed by the Wehrmacht during the battle itself—was the preserve of SS units,
who could count on the logistical support of the army in carrying it out.

It is possible that, in delimiting the authority of the Security Police vis-à-vis the
military in this way, the Army High Command was also aware that the orders of
the SS units were in fact to be couched in more precise terms over a broader area
than the wording of the OKH guidelines actually specified. In the case of the
corresponding order from the High Command with respect to the Regulation of
the Deployment of the Security Police and the SD for the war to be fought in the
Balkans (the 'Marita' and 'Twenty-Five' campaigns), issued on 2 April 1941, the list
of enemies included 'Communists, Jews' in general.[20] But it does not seem
plausible that the relevant instructions for the Balkan war would have been
expressed in tougher terms than those for the war in Russia.

Two programmatic speeches by Hitler to the Wehrmacht generals in March are
important for an analysis of these orders. In these Hitler left no doubt as to what
the nature of the imminent war would be. On 17 March he said that 'the
intelligentsia deployed by Stalin must be annihilated. The leadership machinery
of the Russian empire must be destroyed. It is necessary to use force of the most
brutal kind in the greater Russian area.'[21] From another speech by Hitler on 30
March the Chief of the General Staff, Halder, noted the following key ideas: 'Battle
of two opposing world-views. Devastating judgement of Bolshevism, equivalent to
asocial criminality. Communism monstrous danger for the future. We have to
move away from the standpoint of soldierly camaraderie. Communists are not
comrades, before or after. This is a battle of annihilation. If we do not see it in
those terms then whilst we may beat the enemy, in 30 years we will be faced once
more by the Communist foe. We do not wage war in order to preserve the enemy
intact. Battle against Russia: annihilation of Bolshevist commissars and of the
Communist intelligentsia.'[22]

The 'Decree on the Exercise of the Law and on Special Measures by the Troops'
signed by Hitler on 13 May ordered that criminal offences perpetrated by members
of the Wehrmacht on the civilian population in the East only be pursued by the
Wehrmacht judiciary in exceptional cases. 'Criminal offences perpetrated by
civilian personnel' were not to be investigated by (drumhead) courts martial but
their presumed perpetrators should instead be 'dealt with' or 'expunged' by troops
on the spot. 'Collective violent measures' were to be implemented against towns
where members of the armed forces had been attacked 'insidiously and in an
underhand manner'.[23]

'Guidelines for the Treatment of Political Commissars' signed by the Commander-in-Chief of the Army, General Keitel, on 6 June gave instructions for Soviet commissars to be 'dealt with' by troops as 'the originators of barbarian Asiatic methods of combat'.[24]

Finally, the 'Guidelines for the Conduct of Troops in Russia' of 19 May (which were distributed amongst the troops down to company level) described Bolshevism as 'the mortal enemy of the National Socialist German people' and demanded 'ruthless and energetic measures against Bolshevist agitators, irregulars, saboteurs, Jews and the total elimination of all forms of resistance, active and passive'.[25]

After the Security Police's competences vis-à-vis the Wehrmacht had been firmly delimited, on 21 May Himmler established the command-structure parameters for SS and Police formations in the Eastern zones to be occupied.[26] In this order Himmler determined that the Higher SS and Police Commanders, who were the representatives of the Reichsführer SS on the ground elsewhere, would play a central role in the occupied Eastern zones as well. They were to be assigned to the heads of the planned political administrations, and, during a transitional period, would be responsible for the Rear Area of the Army Group where they would be subordinate to the commanders there 'with respect to mobilization, supplies and accommodation'. Each Higher SS and Police Commander would be assigned 'SS and Police troops and task units of the Security Police to facilitate carrying out the tasks directly assigned to him by me', and, according to Himmler's guidelines for the deployment of such forces: 'The duties of the Security Police (SD) *Einsatzgruppen* and *Einsatzkommandos*' had already been established 'in the letter from the Army High Command (OKH) of 26 March 1941'.[27] The Order Police troops were to complete 'their tasks in accordance with my basic instructions' with the exception of the nine motorized Police Battalions that were under the tactical authority of the Security Divisions. The Waffen-SS formations that had been deployed had 'tasks that are in broad terms similar to those of the Order Police troops and special assignments received directly from me'. If the assignments of the *Einsatzgruppen* had been discussed in detail with the Wehrmacht, then Himmler had succeeded in securing a very much greater degree of autonomy from the Wehrmacht for his Order Police and Waffen-SS formations.[28]

In order to carry out the 'special assignments on behalf of the Führer', therefore, three types of unit (Security Police, Order Police, and Waffen-SS) would be deployed in a total of five different ways: in the Army Rear Areas *Sonderkommandos* of the Security Police and the SD would be deployed; further *Sonderkommandos* (called *Einsatzkommandos*, to distinguish them) would be used in the Rear Areas of the Army Groups; nine battalions of Order Police formations would be tactically subordinated to the Security Divisions in the Rear Areas of the Army Groups, with the Higher SS and Police Commanders authorized to assume direct command for the purposes of 'special assignments';[29] further battalions of Order Police would be deployed in the Rear Areas of the Army Groups; and finally,

Waffen-SS formations would be used in addition, albeit primarily in the areas under political administration and only exceptionally in the Rear Areas of the Army Groups, as later remarks by Himmler made clear.[30] All these formations were under the command of the Higher SS and Police Commanders, who in the first phase of the war were assigned to the commanders of the Army Rear Areas but would later be under the command of the civilian administration leadership.

The deployment of Police and SS formations in the occupied Soviet areas was due to take place in three stages to match the planned structure of the occupation administration: first, the *Sonderkommandos* of the *Einsatzgruppen* in the Army Rear Areas; second, the task *Einsatzkommandos* of the *Einsatzgruppen* in the Rear Areas of the Army Groups and the battalions of the Order Police; third, the SS brigades in the areas under civilian administration. After the war had begun this scheme was treated with some flexibility such that the various formations were also deployed outside the areas they had originally been intended for. The scheme is important above all because it makes clear how plans had been made from the outset for gradually using the formations to combat enemies defined in political and racial terms as the occupied areas became more secure. The massing of formations controlled by the Reichsführer SS in the occupied zones is therefore not to be seen as deriving from decisions taken after 22 June in the light of the way the war was developing; it took place in accordance with plans drawn up before the war had even started.

It is necessary to take a brief look at the way the various formations were put together and at the debated issue of command structures.

From the spring of 1941 onwards the Security Police's NCO School in Pretzsch near Leipzig oversaw the formation of four *Einsatzgruppen* totalling some 3,000 men,[31] based on the experience of the *Einsatzgruppen* deployed in the war against Poland.[32] Einsatzgruppen A, B, and C were due to be assigned to the Army Groups North, Centre, and South; Einsatzgruppe D was destined for the 11th Army, which together with two Romanian armies under its command was to form the south wing of the invasion. The permanent members and the leadership were recruited from the SD, the Gestapo, and the Criminal Police (Kripo), and each unit was reinforced by one reserve battalion of the Order Police and the Waffen-SS, divided amongst the individual commandos, and by further auxiliary personnel (truck drivers, interpreters, radio operators, etc.), who were mostly from the SS and Police.[33] A fifth *Einsatzgruppe* was eventually set up with Eberhard Schöngarth, the commander of the Security Police in Cracow; in early July it was sent to eastern Poland and from August was entitled '*Einsatzgruppe* for Special Purposes'.[34]

The staffs of the *Einsatzgruppen* and *Einsatzkommandos* were divided up into specialist sections in accordance with the Reich Security Head Office model, and these were responsible for SD, Gestapo, and Kripo matters, amongst others.

Within the leadership of the *Einsatzgruppen* one particular type of person dominated: the specialist, a man with some theoretical training (often a degree in law) and practical experience within the police apparatus, committed to National Socialist ideology, a radical agent acting out of conviction.[35] Amongst the seventeen members of the leadership of Einsatzgruppe A—all of whom, without exception, had years of experience in the SS or the police—there were eleven lawyers, nine with doctorates; thirteen had been members of the NSDAP or one of its organizations since before 1933.[36]

Himmler's second-stage formations for the occupied Eastern zones, the Order Police,[37] initially entered the war against the Soviet Union with 23 battalions with a total of 420 officers and 11,640 men; by the end of the year 26 battalions were 'in deployment'.[38] As had originally been intended, nine battalions were under the command of the Security Divisions, one for each of the *Einsatzgruppen* or to reinforce army engineering units (OT); the remainder were assigned to four Police regiments (North, Centre, South, and Special Purposes). Of the twenty-three battalions that began the war, five consisted of experienced professional policemen, a group that made up the bulk of the officer and NCO levels of the other units; seven battalions were made up of older police reservists with no prior service;[39] eleven battalions recruited from young volunteers,[40] who had been signed up during a joint campaign by the SS and the police.[41] 'Suitability for the SS'[42] and 'political reliability'[43] were required of these volunteers, who had hopes of being taken on by the police later. A not inconsiderable number of them came from the 'Ethnic German Militia' that had been involved in numerous massacres in Poland.[44] It was the members of these eleven volunteer battalions with unit numbers in the 300s—obviously highly motivated by this means of selection— who were to 'excel' in many subsequent massacres. Only a minority of the Order Police battalions deployed in the East were populated by 'average' middle-aged Germans, the 'ordinary men' or 'willing executioners' referred to in some of the secondary literature.[45] All these units were led by high-ranking police officers whose experience often extended as far back as the civil conflict and border skirmishes of the post-war period, and a significant proportion of the lower officer ranks had been educated in the SS-Junker schools.[46] The NCOs were largely professional policemen who had been waiting for years for the brutal suppression of an internal enemy that might or might not come to the fore, and after 1938 they had been recruited by choice from the membership of the SS,[47] having already 'proved themselves' in various vicious operations in the war against Poland.[48] The regular ideological indoctrination of these units by educational officers from the SS Race and Settlement Main Office,[49] which had been intensified after the war began,[50] was intended to pave the way for a planned merger with the SS to form a as Himmler called it, 'Corps for the Protection of the State'.[51]

Alongside the Security and the Order Police, using the SS Death's Head Formations unified under a special 'Command staff of the Reichsführung-SS'

Himmler created for himself a special intervention team for those 'special tasks that I will from time to time assign to them', in the words of Himmler's seminal order of 21 May.[52] They were to form the third and largest formation of the SS and Police units deployed in the East. As early as 7 April 1941, Himmler had set up a special task staff under the leadership of Kurt Knoblauch, who had hitherto been mobilization officer at the Party Chancellery, and this body was renamed the 'Command staff of the RFSS' on 6 May.[53] The staff was initially under the command of the SS Leadership Office, but later answered directly to Himmler.

On 1 May two motorized SS brigades were put together from Death's Head regiments and at the same time two SS cavalry regiments in Cracow and Warsaw were brought together; they would later form the SS cavalry brigade. Several of these Death's Head units had already perpetrated a number of acts of violence in Poland since the autumn of 1939 when the 4th Cavalry Squadron had repeatedly shot Polish Jews in the Forest at Lućmierz; in December the 5th Squadron had shot 440 Jews 'escaping' during a forced march from Cholm to Hrubieszów and a few weeks later had murdered all 600 of a transport of Jews being removed from the district of Lublin. Many further murders of Polish Jews and other Polish citizens have been documented.[54] Along with other formations, these units noted for their particular brutality were now—immediately before the start of the war— placed under the command of the Command staff RFSS,[55] which by July 1941 had thus come to have some 19,000 men at its disposal.[56] The Command staff gave Himmler the means of intervening directly in combating politically and racially defined opponents in the occupied Eastern zones and of setting clear priorities for such action.

What were the instructions received by these various formations for their 'deployment' in the East? Historical research has looked at this question in detail with respect to the *Einsatzgruppen*, with controversial results.

Research initially assumed that the leaders of the *Einsatzgruppen* had received an 'order from the Führer' before the start of the attack, an order for the complete annihilation of the Jewish population in the Soviet Union. This view was based on knowledge obtained during the Trial of the Major War Criminals in Nuremberg and in particular from the case against the *Einsatzgruppen* (case 9, the Einsatzgruppen Case) before the American military court. In this trial, Otto Ohlendorf, the former commander of Einsatzgruppe D, managed to convince the court of his version, according to which, a few days before the start of the war, the Director of Department I of the Reich Security Head Office, Bruno Streckenbach, had announced at the *Einsatzgruppe* muster point in Pretzsch that the Führer had given a general order for the murder of all Soviet Jews. Ohlendorf attempted to present this order from the Führer not as a racist programme for the annihilation of all the Jews in the Soviet area but as a general liquidation order primarily aimed at 'securing' the newly won territory, a liquidation that would affect 'the Jews' (he never used the phrase 'all the Jews') but also other population groups.[57]

This version of events was supported by a series of other commando leaders.[58] Only the leader of Einsatzkommando 5, Erwin Schulz, contradicted this account: he testified that the decisive orders had only been communicated to him after the start of the war by Otto Rasch, the leader of Einsatzgruppe C.[59] According to his defence counsel, Rasch himself, who was declared unfit for trial during the proceedings, had said in response to this that he had only received the comprehensive order to murder the Jews in August or September, from Friedrich Jeckeln, Higher SS and Police Commander in Russia-South.[60]

The largely unanimous version of an early comprehensive order for the murder of the Jews was taken up by Helmut Krausnick in his report for the 'Ulm Einsatzgruppe Trial', the highly prominent first major National Socialist trial before a Federal German court.[61] This assessment once more confirmed the model of an early comprehensive order, which had been issued by Hitler in March 1941, in Krausnick's opinion, and had been transmitted to the commando leaders in May. This line of argument was followed in many later trials of Einsatzgruppe members,[62] and was largely accepted by historians after Krausnick had published it in his seminal academic study.[63] It was for a long period one of the main pillars of the 'intentionalist' line of argument.[64] According to this view the leaders of the Einsatzkommandos were henchmen following orders, and put into practice a programme of murders that had been devised at the very highest levels of the National Socialist regime and set in train according to plan in the spring of 1941.

This perspective of earlier research, characteristic of the way the National Socialists' persecution of the Jews was understood in the 1950s and 1960s, can no longer be sustained nowadays. It did not, for example, take account of the fact that in the face of the death sentence handed down by the Military Court, Ohlendorf himself had been forced to recognize the failure of his defence strategy and had resiled from his original version of events, the existence of an early comprehensive order from the Führer.[65] More attention was paid to the fact that Streckenbach, who had unexpectedly returned from internment as a Soviet prisoner of war in 1955, denied ever having transmitted the order in question.[66] On the basis of often intensive interrogations of Einsatzkommando leaders, the Director of the Ludwigsburg Central Investigation Office, Alfred Streim, was able to show convincingly[67] that the alleged early comprehensive order to murder the Jews was in fact constructed for the purposes of Ohlendorf's defence. Ohlendorf put formidable pressure on his co-defendants in order to be able to claim that he had been acting upon orders received, thereby reducing to a minimum the extent to which he had himself been free to act with respect to the atrocities of several Einsatzkommandos. Streim's theses are now broadly accepted by historians.[68]

Streim's argument is supported by a series of statements made by former members of the Einsatzgruppen that expose Ohlendorf's testimony as a defence strategy. Ernst Biberstein, who in 1942–3 was leader of Einsatzkommando 6 and was sentenced to death in Nuremberg, convincingly exposed Ohlendorf's manipulation of historical events as early as 1948 in a detailed note that was to be given to his family if he was executed.[69] There is more testimony that illuminates Ohlendorf's role.[70]

The analysis of statements concerning the deployment of *Einsatzgruppen* made to German lawyers by former leaders of the *Einsatzkommandos* and *Sonderkommandos* between the 1950s and early 1970s also suggest that there was no clear order to murder all the Jews living in the Soviet Union that had been given before the start of the war. These statements differ significantly from each other in respect of place, time, the person transmitting the order, and the content of the order. Whilst one element in the commando leadership clearly stated that far-reaching orders such as this had only been issued weeks after the war had started,[71] the statements of those who mention an early comprehensive order are extremely contradictory, especially when they are traced back over a long period, and are characterized by memory lapses and reservations.[72] Clear evidence in favour of an early comprehensive order is only provided by the statement of commando leader Zapp (Sonderkommando 11a)[73] and—with reservations—by that of Ehler, who had originally been designated leader of Einsatzkommando 8.[74] Some of the former commando leaders instead remember a step-by-step mode of receiving orders, a 'framework order', which was intended to be 'filled in' on the initiative of the commandos and by subsequent orders.[75] The fact that the undifferentiated murder of women and children only began weeks after the campaign started, and the circumstance that the great mass of commando members agree in their claims that they did not receive orders such as this from their leaders until immediately before the massacres themselves both show that briefing the *Einsatzgruppen* was a process that cannot be reduced to the issuing of a single order.

What emerges from all this is the impression of a degree of vagueness in the way orders were issued to *Einsatzgruppen*. A manner of issuing orders in which the subordinate was supposed to recognize the 'meaning' behind the words intuitively is familiar from National Socialist anti-Jewish policy from 1933 onwards, in particular in cases where the orders had something criminal about them. In contrast to the military model of giving and carrying out orders this practice presupposes a certain collusiveness, a strongly developed feeling of consensus amongst those involved about how anti-Jewish policy was going to develop in the future—which is a consensus that we can assume to be present when we remember how the leadership of the *Einsatzgruppen* were recruited from amongst the SS and the police.

On the basis of the existing statements and other evidence we can ascertain what organizational processes were at work in directing the leaders of the *Einsatzgruppen* to carry out their duties. Alongside Streckenbach's visit to Pretzsch in June, a social 'farewell' visit at which there will also have been discussion about upcoming tasks, briefing for the SS leadership took place at a decisive meeting with Himmler in Wewelsburg Castle from 11 to 15 June at which Jeckeln, Pohl, and Heydrich were also present.[76] The commando leaders were briefed at two sessions with Heydrich, first a meeting in the Prince Carl Palace in Berlin (presumably on 17 June), and second an occasion when the *Einsatzgruppe* leadership received instructions from Heydrich in Pretzsch shortly before the outbreak of war, a meeting that took place immediately after the official farewell to the members of the *Einsatzkommandos* who had reported for duty.[77]

Even though the leadership of the *Einsatzgruppen* gave contradictory evidence about their briefings during the war in the East, what emerges unanimously from interrogations is that when such conversations took place the 'firmness' and 'severity' of the deployment about to take place were always stressed, as was the view that the campaign was a conflict between two 'world-views' that had to be carried out completely ruthlessly and that would demand 'sacrifices in blood'. At the same time the central role of the Jews in preserving the Bolshevist system and their 'potential enemy' status were also emphasized.[78]

From the tenor of statements such as these it is clear that the *Einsatzgruppe* leadership was given a line to take in discussions concerning the treatment of Jews and Communists, a line that corresponded to the content of the orders and instructions that pertained to the Wehrmacht (the jurisdiction decree, the commissar order, guidelines for the conduct of the troops). Furthermore it is clear that instructions were given that Heydrich shortly afterwards summarized in writing, making explicit reference, moreover, to the meeting on 17 June: in a letter to the heads of the *Einsatzgruppen* dated 29 June he merely referred to 'attempts at self-purification' that the commandos were to initiate;[79] in a letter to the Higher SS and Police Commanders of 2 July he informed them of the 'most important instructions given by me to the *Einsatzgruppen* and *Einsatzkommandos* of the Security Police and the SD'.[80] In this second letter the point headed 'executions' contains the following list:

> Those to be executed are all
> Functionaries of the Comintern (and all professional Communist
>   politicians of any kind)
> People's Commissars
> Jews in Party and state posts
> other radical elements (saboteurs, propagandists, snipers, assassins,
>   agitators, etc.)

The revealing 'etc.' at the end of that list and the fact that Heydrich wrote in this letter of 'removing all obstacles in the way of attempts at self-purification by anti-Communist or anti-Jewish circles in the areas to be occupied', and of supporting such attempts, 'albeit invisibly',[81] suggest that the range of those to be executed was by no means clearly delimited. One can assume instead that the formulation 'all Jews in Party and state posts' is an understated way of giving the order for annihilating a vaguely defined upper layer of Jews, mostly men, leaving the decision of how exactly to define this layer to the commandos themselves. The instructions given on 2 July do not, for example, expressly forbid the murder of women and children. The significance of the meetings that Heydrich held with the leadership of the *Einsatzgruppen* before the outbreak of war was therefore to make it clear to them that Soviet Jews and Bolshevism represented a closely interlinked collection of enemies, leaving it to them to shoot the Jews under one pretext or another, whether under the heading of state and Party functionaries, or agitators, or propagandists, or merely 'etc.'.

CHAPTER 11

THE MASS MURDER OF JEWISH MEN

In the very first days of the war against the Soviet Union there is evidence to document both the attempts of the *Einsatzgruppen* to initiate 'self-purification processes' and the execution of Jewish men.

Pogroms Organized by the *Einsatzgruppen*

During the early days of the war, in Lithuania, Latvia, Western Ukraine (the eastern Polish area occupied by the Soviet Union), and to a lesser extent also in Belarus,[1] radical nationalist and anti-Semitic forces carried out large-scale pogroms against the local Jewish population. In accordance with the stereotype of 'Jewish Bolshevism' these forces made the Jewish minority responsible for the terror of Soviet occupation and exercised a bloody retribution. This manner of going about things was perfectly in accordance with the German formula of initiating 'attempts at self-purification', 'invisibly' where possible. Despite the disguise, German influence on these pogroms can be demonstrated in a large number of cases, as will be shown in what follows, using the reports made by the *Einsatzgruppen*.[2]

However, even where pogroms were already in progress before German troops arrived, there is evidence that they were not the expression of a spontaneous popular movement. The fact that all the pogroms proceeded in a similar way suggests instead that they were to a very large extent triggered and steered by underground organizations formed under the regime of occupation; there is evidence, too, that in the months before the German attack these underground organizations were cooperating with German agencies and were planning for a radical policy of anti-Semitism after the 'liberation' of their homelands.[3]

It has been proved, for example, that during preparations for the war against the Soviet Union the Germans, and in particular military intelligence and the Reich Security Head Office, were working closely with Lithuanian émigrés who had fled to the German Reich and established their own organization, the LAF (Lithuanian Activist Front), which was in frequent contact with the Lithuanian underground. It is demonstrable, too, that the LAF made use of these channels in order to commit their comrades at home to violent attacks on Jews during the process of 'liberating' their country. It is more than likely that this approach was at least supported by the Germans, given the close cooperation between the LAF and German agencies.[4]

There were similarly close contacts between German agencies and Estonian and Latvian émigré organizations that were also drawn into the preparations for war.[5] The Germans also harnessed both wings of the OUN (Organization of Ukrainian Nationalists) into their plans for attack and will have sustained and strongly encouraged the already radically anti-Semitic OUN in that direction.[6] Whether this also included an appeal to initiate pogroms cannot be demonstrated with sufficient certainty.[7] However, even where it is likely but not provable that local forces were briefed in the run-up to the war the reports of the *Einsatzgruppen* nonetheless show clearly how strong German influence was on the outbreak of pogroms.

In the summary activity report prepared in mid-October by Einsatzgruppe A in the operational area of Army Group A—the so-called Stahlecker Report—there is a detailed account of the 'attempts at self-cleansing' initiated by the Einsatzgruppe itself.[8] 'It was necessarily the responsibility of the *Einsatzgruppe* to set in train the self-purification attempts and guide them into the correct channels in order to achieve the goal of cleansing as quickly as possible. It was no less important to create for a later date the firm and demonstrable fact that the liberated population was of its own accord resorting to the harshest measures against its Bolshevist and Jewish opponents without leaving any trace of instructions from the German side.' It was also 'immediately obvious that only the first days after the occupation would offer opportunities for carrying out pogroms'.

The Stahlecker Report goes on to say that, 'astonishingly', initiating the first pogrom in Kaunas in Lithuania had not proved 'straightforward'; it had only got going after the Lithuanian partisan leaders, who had been brought in to carry it out, had been given 'tips' by the 'small advance commando deployed in Kaunas', again 'without any German instructions or stimulus being discernible from the outside'. During this pogrom, which took place between 25 and 28 July and cost the lives of some 3,800 people, Jewish men were violently dragged from their homes by Lithuanian 'militia', collected together in public squares and killed there or taken to fortresses and shot.[9] By the beginning of July, however, as an incident report makes clear, Einsatzgruppe A had already come to the conclusion that 'no more mass shootings [were] possible' in Kaunas;[10] a stop was therefore put to them.

In Riga the *Einsatzgruppe* succeeded in initiating a pogrom in which 400 Jews were killed, but only after 'appropriate influence [had been exerted] on the Latvian auxiliary police'. Further pogroms in that city were not felt to be 'sustainable' because of the rapid calming of the population in general.[11] At the end of July Einsatzgruppe A reported on pogroms in other Latvian cities: according to these reports 'in Jelgava [Mitau] and the surrounding areas . . . the remaining 1,550 Jews were expunged from the population without trace'.[12]

Pogroms that can be proved to have been initiated by the Germans were above all carried out by Einsatzgruppe C in the Ukraine. In Lvov (Lemberg), where the NKVD (the Soviet People's Commissariat for Internal Affairs) had shot some 3,500 prisoners at the end of June and bloodily suppressed an attempted uprising by the OUN, pogroms were started by the indigenous population on 30 June, the day of the city's occupation by German troops. They were probably initiated by the OUN and its militia. It is likely, however, that a special unit of the Wehrmacht played a key role in triggering this pogrom when it entered the city as an advance guard together with a battalion of Ukrainian nationalists under its command. The pogroms cost at least 4,000 lives and were finally ended by the Wehrmacht on 2 July after it had spent two days observing but not intervening.[13] At that point, however, Einsatzgruppe C took over the organization of murderous activities: over the next few days, by way of 'retribution' for the murders committed by the NKVD, three Einsatzgruppe C commandos that had entered the city murdered 2,500 to 3,000 Jews.[14] At the end of July, Ukrainian groups took back the initiative and were responsible for a further pogrom for which support from the German Special Purposes Commando was probably decisive once again. During the so-called 'Petljura Days' more than 2,000 Jews were murdered in Lviv.[15]

In Zloczow at the beginning of July, under the very eyes of Sonderkommando 4b and tolerated by the city commandant, Ukrainian activists had organized a massacre of the Jewish population in which members of the SS Viking Division took part on a huge scale. The total number of victims is estimated to be at least 2,000.[16] In the district of Tarnopol, too, Ukrainian nationalist murdered Jews under the supervision of Sonderkommando 4b—on 7 July some 70 Jews were 'herded together and finished off with a big salvo'. When it had finished, the commando described its deployment in Tarnopol in an incident report of 11 July, announcing more than 127 executions that it had conducted and a further 600 dead 'as part of the [Ukrainians'] anti-Jewish persecutions inspired by the *Einsatzkommando*'.[17]

There are more 'self-purification attempts' inspired by Einsatzgruppe C that can be documented on the basis of its incident reports. 'In Dobromil the synagogue was torched. In Sambor 50 Jews were murdered by the outraged crowd.'[18] A few days later came the report, 'in Krzemieniec between 100 and 150 Ukrainians were murdered by the Russians.... By way of reprisal the Ukrainians beat 150 Jews to death with clubs.'[19] In Tarnopol and Choroskow they succeeded in 'bringing 600 and 110 Jews to their deaths' in pogroms.[20] What is remarkable, but also characteristic of the attitude of the Germans towards these 'self-purification attempts' is the 'encouragement' (noted by Einsatzgruppe C in an incident report from early July) that the High Command of the 17th Army gave 'for using first the anti-Jewish and anti-Communist Poles living in the newly conquered areas for these self-purification attempts'.[21]

In total, in the areas occupied by the Soviet Union between 1939 and 1941 pogroms have been documented in more than 60 places; estimates place the number of dead at no less than 12,000, possibly as many as 24,000.[22] Despite the large number of victims, however, the Germans were disappointed with the results of the 'self-purification attempts' that they had initiated amongst the Ukrainian population. At the end of July Einsatzgruppe C was forced to admit, 'recent attempts circumspectly to inspire anti-Jewish pogroms have unfortunately not had the desired effect'.[23] The deeper the *Einsatzgruppe* penetrated into the Ukraine, the more it was forced to recognize that the indigenous population was not prepared to carry out pogroms.[24]

Whilst these *Einsatzgruppe* reports create the impression that the initiative for the pogroms had always lain with the commandos themselves—as Heydrich had ordered—there are indications that in many places the pogroms were already under way when the commandos arrived and where the commandos concentrated on escalating the murders and bringing them under their own control. However, a closer analysis of the course of these pogroms shows how—as has already been noted—they were not spontaneous operations by indigenous populations but responses to initiatives from radical nationalist and anti-Semitic forces that had come together in the Organization of Ukrainian Nationalists. Immediately after the withdrawal of the Soviet occupying forces, the OUN had seized the initiative in many places, set up provisional authorities and militias, and in some places, like Lvov, with the imminent end of Soviet domination in sight, had organized uprisings. There is something to be said for seeing the pogroms as components of an OUN strategy to seize power in this transitional phase, and some likelihood that the anti-Semitic components of this strategy were fostered by the German side even before war had broken out.[25]

But even if the pogroms can be attributed in large part to German plans to spark off 'attempts at self-cleansing', it has to be admitted that they would not have been possible if there had not already been a significant potential for anti-Semitic violence in the indigenous population and if they had not been susceptible to mobilization for such murderous campaigns.

This is true of the pogrom that a book by the historian Jan Tomasz Gross has made virtually emblematic of the indigenous population's active participation in and co-responsibility for the murder of Jews, and which has led to a wide-ranging debate on this topic, in Poland especially:[26] the murder of several hundred Jews in the town of Jedwabne on 10 July 1941 by—according to Gross—their Polish neighbours.[27] Some of the victims were killed immediately, others burned alive in a barn. Even if the murders were carried out by local people—or more precisely by a group of forty or so men, distinct from other members of the indigenous population, mostly not from the town itself but from the surrounding area—closer analysis of the crime has now demonstrated that the pogrom was engineered by a unit of the German Security Police. This was probably a commando from the Gestapo office in Zichenau that had been assigned to Einsatzgruppe B as an auxiliary troop and which had organized several pogroms in the western part of the Voivodeship of Bialystok (in which Jedwabne was located); it had recruited local Poles as auxiliary 'pogrom police' for this purpose.[28] This was also in accordance with Heydrich's order of 1 July in which he had described Poles as an 'element...for initiating pogroms'.[29]

Organized Shootings by *Einsatzgruppen* and Police Battalions in the First Weeks of the War

Einsatzgruppe A

Three of the four commandos under Einsatzgruppe A can be shown to have taken part in mass executions of Jewish men in the first days and weeks after the outbreak of war.[30] Einsatzkommando 1a shot 1,150 Jewish men in Daugavpils (Dünaburg) at the beginning of July 1941; the men had first been captured by Latvian auxiliaries after 'they had been supported at the rear by the operations of the *Einsatzkommando*'.[31] After the pogrom in Riga, Einsatzkommando 2 reported the killing of more than 2,000 more Jews by the middle of July, partly 'by Latvian auxiliary police, partly by our own forces'.[32] What this refers to is the infamous commando led by the Latvian Victor Arajas; it played an important role in these shootings, which mostly took place in the Bikernieki Forest.[33] At the end of June and in July the same commando, a company of Police Battalion 13, together with Latvian auxiliaries and members of the army and navy shot what were believed to be several thousand Jews in Liepāja (Libau).[34] In Jelgava (Mitau) a sub-unit of Einsatzkommando 2 shot some 160 Jews, including women and children, apparently in the first half of July.[35]

Einsatzkommando 3 had been organizing mass shootings of Jewish men since early July in the city of Kaunas (Kovno).[36] The leader of this commando, Karl Jäger, reported on 1 December 1941 that the executions that had taken place in Fort VII of the fortress of Kaunas since 4 July had been carried out 'by the Lithuanian partisans but on my orders and arranged by me';[37] according to Jäger's own list, 2,530 Jewish men and 47 women fell victim to these shootings. From 7 July onwards, Jäger went on to report, a group of men in his commando had also begun to carry out mass executions 'in cooperation with the Lithuanian partisans' outside the city of Kaunas, which claimed a total of more than 1,400 people, mostly Jewish men, in the month of July.

Einsatzgruppe A was additionally supported by a commando that was made up of members of the SD and the Gestapo and had been put together in the city of Tilsit near the German border, thus receiving the name Einsatzkommando Tilsit. In the towns of Gargždai (Garsden), Kretinga (Krottingen), and (Palanga) Polangen (in the area immediately over the border with Lithuania), on 24, 25, and 27 June, this unit executed respectively 201, 214, and 111 civilians, mostly Jewish men, by way of 'reprisal' for alleged attacks by civilians on units from the advancing Wehrmacht.[38] In the days that followed, Einsatzkommando Tilsit carried out further 'cleansing operations' in the border zone, including operations on 2 July in Taurage (Tauroggen), on 3 July in Jurbarkas (Georgenburg) and Augustowo, as well as in Marijampole and Wladislawo,[39] during which an incident report, dated 18 July, claims 3,302 people were shot.[40]

More executions by the commando are documented for the whole of July, in many towns and villages, overwhelmingly of Jewish men.[41] The fact that in reports on later shootings carried out in the border zone the data for some towns only includes the numbers of women, older men, and children, and not men of military age, is an indication that the first wave of shootings had already claimed all the Jewish men in that age-group.[42]

These executions were fully in alignment with the intentions of the SS leadership. A telex from the Gestapo office in Tilsit dated 1 July makes it clear that Himmler and Heydrich had visited the border zone at the end of June, had been informed about the 'measures taken' and had 'fully approved' them.[43] A few days later Heydrich expressly confirmed in a written order that the executions carried out by the Einsatzkommando Tilsit were in accordance with his instructions: in Order No. 6 he informed the *Einsatzgruppe* chiefs that he had 'authorized the eastern commanders of the SPSD (Security Police and SD) and the state police offices to undertake cleansing operations in the newly occupied areas opposite their border zones in order to relieve pressure on the *Einsatzgruppen* and *Einsatzkommandos*, and above all to ensure their freedom of movement'.[44]

Einsatzgruppe B

All four of the commandos under Einsatzgruppe B can be shown to have undertaken mass executions of Jewish men during the month of July.[45]

Sonderkommando 7 was responsible for what an incident report calls 'the complete liquidation of male Jewry' in Vilejka by the end of June or early July 1941.[46] The same commando was responsible for shooting 332 Jews in Vitebsk at the end of July or early in August,[47] and for a subsequent 'operation' in Grodek (Gorodok) in which 150–200 Jewish men were shot.[48] Mass shootings of Jewish men by Sonderkommando 7 are documented in Borisov (in July) and in the area around Orsha/Mogilev (late July or early August).[49]

At the beginning of July Einsatzkommando 8 initiated in Bialystok alone two 'operations' in which German courts established that at least 800 and 100 Jewish men were shot dead; thereafter there were two executions in Baranowicze each with at least 100 victims. The commando was involved in mass shootings in Minsk at the end of July and in August during which more than 1,000 Jews were killed.[50] A sub-unit of Einsatzkommando 8 was sent to Slonim in the middle of July where, according to an incident report of 24 July,[51] 'in cooperation with the Order Police a major operation was conducted against Jews and other Communist elements in which c.2,000 persons were arrested for Communist subversion and looting; 1,075 of them were liquidated on the same day'.[52] The leader of Einsatzkommando 8, Otto Bradfisch, testified in respect of this operation that he had already ascertained during the march to Minsk that there was no express order 'to annihilate the Jewish population of a town or area solely on the grounds of their racial identity', but that orders from Einsatzgruppe B were in practice interpreted so broadly that 'every Jew was to be seen as a danger to combat troops and therefore liquidated'.[53] The Commander of Einsatzgruppe B, Artur Nebe, believed in interpreting the orders 'sent from above as if in some places and districts all Jews were to be exterminated irrespective of age or sex'.[54]

A statement made in 1966 by Higher SS and Police Commander for Russia Centre, Erich von dem Bach-Zelewski, indicates that Nebe's attitude is attributable to an instruction from Himmler. According to Bach, Himmler had told Nebe as early as his visit to Bialystok (8 July) that 'every Jew must in principle be regarded as a partisan',[55] and three days later the commander of Police Regiment Centre, whose headquarters were in Bialystok, gave the order for the 'immediate summary shooting of all male Jews aged between 17 and 45 convicted of looting'.[56] These orders therefore opened the way for the annihilation of all those members of the Jewish population who were fit for military service without further conditions.

A report by Einsatzgruppe B from July 1941 contains information about the activities of Einsatzkommando 9 in Vilnius:[57] 'The Einsatzkommando in Vilnius has liquidated 321 Jews there in the period up to 8 July. The Lithuanian order police, who were placed under the command of the *Einsatzkommando* after the disbandment of the Lithuanian political police, were ordered to take part in the liquidation of the Jews. For this purpose 150 Lithuanian officials were assigned to capture the Jews and get them to concentration camps where they were subjected to special treatment on the same day. This work has now begun and more than 500 Jews and other saboteurs are now being liquidated daily.' The total number of Jews killed in Vilnius by Einsatzkommando 9 and Lithuanians during July—mostly men—was at least 4,000–5,000,[58] but is thought to be as many as 10,000.[59]

It is also demonstrable that Himmler intervened directly in the case of Einsatzkommando 9 in order to increase the number of executions. In a report from early July on the activities of a sub-unit of Einsatzkommando 9 that had been sent to the towns of Grodno and Lida the leader of Einsatzgruppe B notes, 'in Grodno and Lida only 96 Jews were liquidated in the first few days. I have given the order for this to be greatly intensified'.[60] The background to this order was the fact that on a visit to Grodno on 30 June Himmler and Heydrich criticized deficiencies in the work of the commando; in a general task order issued on 1 July Heydrich demanded 'greater flexibility in the tactical disposition of the Einsatzkommandos' and deplored the fact that four days after the occupation there were still no members of the Security Police and SD in Grodno.[61] On 9 July Himmler and Heydrich visited Grodno once more,[62] and were evidently reassured that the order for Einsatzgruppe B to intensify liquidations had by then been implemented. According to the incident report: 'The activity of all commandos has developed satisfactorily. Above all, the liquidations have got going properly and now take place in large numbers daily. The implementation of the necessary [!] liquidations is guaranteed under all circumstances.' This passage makes very clear how only a few weeks after the start of the Russian campaign there was a perception that certain liquidation targets had to be systematically attained.

Einsatzgruppe C

All four of the commandos under Einsatzgruppe C can be shown to have undertaken mass executions of Jewish men during the month of July.[63] Even before then, on 30 June in Dobromil, on the orders of the Higher SS and Police Commander Russia South, Friedrich Jeckeln, and the leader of Einsatzgruppe C, Otto Rasch, Einsatzkommando 6 shot at least 80 Jewish men as a 'reprisal' for alleged attacks by departing Soviet troops.[64]

Einsatzkommandos 5 and 6 both participated in the massacre of the Lvov Jews, which was again mainly organized by Jeckeln and the officers of Einsatzgruppe C.[65] The reason given for this massacre in the incident reports was that it was a 'reprisal' for murders of Ukrainian nationalists that had been committed in the city prisons by Soviets immediately before their departure. The reports record:

'approximately 7,000 Jews were rounded up and shot by the Security Police as a reprisal for [these] inhuman atrocities.... Those seized were mostly Jews between 20 and 40; craftsmen and those in specialist trades were exempted where appropriate.'[66] After taking part in the Lvov massacre, Einsatzkommando 5 undertook 'operations' in Berdichev and surrounding districts,[67] including Chmielnik, where 299 people, mostly Jews, were shot in a 'reprisal' operation.[68]

After its deployment in Lvov, Einsatzkommando 6 spent the second half of July in Vinnitsa in the Ukraine, where it carried out further executions, notably one with 146 victims and another that claimed the lives of 600 Jews.[69]

According to its own reports, at the end of June 1941 Sonderkommando 4a had shot more than 300 people in executions carried out in Sokal—people who had first been classified as 'Communists' and then as 'Jewish Communists'.[70] At the beginning of July, again according to its own reports, the commando shot a total of 2,000 Jews in Lutsk 'as a counter-measure for the murder of Ukrainians'.[71] It then moved on to Zhitomir, where it carried out three 'operations' in July, in which more than 600 Jewish men were murdered, and another on 7 August, when 402 Jews were shot.[72] In the second half of July, Sonderkommando 4b shot at least 100 people in Vinnitsa as part of the so-called 'intelligence operation'.[73] The report on this operation makes clear how arbitrarily the *Einsatzkommandos* went about their attacks on the 'Jewish-Bolshevist leadership cadre'. After 'trawling the city for leading Jewish figures produced a less than satisfactory result', the report says, the commando leader 'sent for the city's principal Rabbi and directed him to identify the whole of the Jewish intelligentsia within 24 hours, because this information was needed for registration purposes. When the first batch proved to be numerically insufficient, those members of the Jewish intelligentsia who had presented themselves were sent away with the instruction that they should identify more of their kind themselves and present themselves along with these people the following day. This measure was then used a third time with the result that we were able to seize and liquidate virtually all the Jewish intelligentsia.'[74]

The first summary report on the activities of Einsatzgruppe C in 'the Polish and Russian parts of White Ruthenia [Belarus]' from early July 1941 contains an important indication that the staff of the *Einsatzgruppe* understood the execution orders to mean that they did not only affect Jews 'in Party and state posts'. 'On the basis of the instructions received from the Reich Security Head Office, functionaries of the state and Party apparatus were liquidated in all the towns of Belarus already mentioned. As for the Jews, they were treated in the same way, as the orders directed.'[75]

In the incident report for 20 August Einsatzgruppe C described a 'measure' that reveals just how spurious the term 'reprisal' was as grounds for action. 'In Januszpol, a city with more than 25 per cent Jewish inhabitants, Jewish women have in recent days displayed impertinent and insolent behaviour with respect to the restrictions currently imposed on them. They tore their own and their children's clothes from their bodies. As an interim reprisal measure, the commando that arrived, once order had been re-established, shot 15 male Jews. Further reprisals will follow.'[76] The report ultimately makes it plain that 'reprisal measures against looters and Jews will continue to be carried out as planned [!] as they have already been',[77] and that these 'reprisal measures' were taken systematically and independently of the nature of the situation on the spot.[78]

Einsatzgruppe for Special Purposes

In addition to the four commandos in the *Einsatzgruppe*, there was an additional commando under the leader of the Security Police in Cracow, which had been sent into the eastern Polish area to support Einsatzgruppe C.[79] It too was carrying out mass executions by July, overwhelmingly of male Jews, as the incident report of 3 August documents: 'between 21 and 31 July 1941 3,947 persons were liquidated.'[80] According to an incident report of 9 August, 510 people were killed in Brest-Litovsk and another 296 in Bialystok.[81]

The reports made from early August on by this commando from the eastern Polish area, which was immediately named Einsatzkommando for Special Purposes, show very clearly how excessive the 'reprisals' were at this point and how this was merely a pretext for mass murder: 'in the area around Pinsk one member of the militia was shot in an ambush; 4,500 Jews were liquidated in return.'[82]

Einsatzgruppe D

Einsatzgruppe D was assigned to the 11th Army, which together with two Romanian armies was to form the southernmost spearhead of the invasion. Its activity has to be assessed against the background of Romania's radical anti-Semitic politics: Romania was an ally that had pursued a policy of 'solving' the 'Jewish question since the outbreak of war against the Soviet Union using a mixture of pogroms, massacres, and violent expulsions. The potential for anti-Semitic violence that was thereby released was considerable during the first few weeks of the war; whilst the German *Einsatzgruppen* mostly directed their measures during the first weeks of the war at members of the 'leading' Jewish social groups and only then extended the range of the murders to include men of military age, the Romanian attack was directed at the whole of the Jewish minority from the very beginning.

On 28 July Romanian soldiers and civilians, supported by members of the Wehrmacht, carried out a pogrom in the border city of Jasi that had been prepared by the Romanian secret service. There were countless murders within the city, a mass execution in the courtyard of the police headquarters, and during the subsequent transports in crowded goods trains that shuttled back and forth all day in the scorching heat, without food and water, thousands of people lost their lives—4,000 according to the estimate of the German ambassador.[83]

Whilst reconquering the areas of Bessarabia and the Bukovina that had been ceded to the Soviet Union in 1940 under pressure from Moscow, Romanian police and troops murdered many Jews. They were supported in part by Einsatzgruppe D and members of the Wehrmacht, but largely acted on their own initiative, but also supported by Romanian and Ukrainian peasants and farmers. The Romanian authorities were following a plan dictated by their own government for the systematic 'cleansing' of the country: Jews in rural areas were to be killed on the spot; those living in cities were to be interned in camps.[84] Raoul Hilberg estimates the total number of victims of this campaign at more than 10,000.[85]

These murders left a mixed impression with Einsatzgruppe D, as is shown by one of their reports. 'There would be no objection to the shooting of numerous Jews if the technical aspects of preparation and implementation were not so inadequate.' It was in that sense that the *Einsatzgruppe* wished to influence the activities of the Romanians.[86]

All five commandos from Einsatzgruppe D that were assigned to the German 11th Army attacking from Romanian territory or to the two allied Romanian armies can be shown to have participated in the mass execution of Jewish men in the period up to the beginning of August 1941.[87]

In the city of Belzy, as part of a bloody 'reprisal' by Romanian police and soldiers against the city's Jews in which hundreds were killed, Sonderkommando 10a shot 75 Jewish hostages.[88] A sub-unit of the same Sonderkommando was sent to the town of Kodyma in response to a request from the intelligence officer of the XXX Army Corps because the 'Jews and Bolshevists' there were allegedly intending to sabotage measures being taken by the occupying power. The sub-unit therefore arrested 400 men on 1 August, most of them Jews, subjected them to an 'interrogation' and then shot 98 of them.[89]

On 8 and 9 July Sonderkommando 10b (assigned to the 3rd Romanian Army) took part in a massacre carried out by Romanian troops in Chernivtsi (Czernovitz) in which it killed '100 Jewish Communists' by its own account, ostensibly because advancing German and Romanian formations had been shot at from within the Jewish quarter.[90] At the end of July, Einsatzgruppe D reported that 'of about 1,200 Jews arrested' in the city, '682 had been shot in cooperation with the Romanian police'.[91] Sections of Sonderkommando 10b carried out further executions of Jewish men in other towns over the weeks that followed.[92]

At the beginning of August Sonderkommando 11a reported the liquidation of '551 Jews so far' in Chişinău (Kishinev), citing 'sabotage' and 'reprisal' as the reasons.[93] These executions took place while the leader of Einsatzgruppe D, Ohlendorf's staff was in Chişinău and he witnessed at least one of the shootings.[94] Sonderkommando 11b undertook its first mass executions on 7 August 1941 in Thigina, where an incident report notes that 155 Jews were shot on that date.[95] Einsatzkommando 12 carried out two executions on 20 and 21 July in Babtshinsky, which the 23 August incident report said claimed 94 lives.[96]

Police Battalions

It was not only the *Einsatzgruppen* that were massacring the Jewish civilian population in the occupied Eastern zones in the first weeks of the campaign; various battalions of the German Order Police were also involved.

In Bialystok Police Battalion 309 carried out a massacre as early as 27 June in which at least 2,000 Jews, including women and children, were killed. Members of the battalion drove at least 500 people into the synagogue and put them to an agonizing death by setting fire to the building.[97] The very precise reconstruction of these events undertaken by the Wuppertal District Court in 1973 makes it clear how some fanatical officers in the battalion seized the initiative and transformed the planned arrest of the Jews in the synagogue quarter into a bloodbath; there was looting, and some excesses were perpetrated by policemen under the influence of alcohol. Bialystok was also the scene of a massacre organized by Police Battalions 316 and 322 in the middle of July when a total of about 3,000 Jewish men were killed.[98]

A few days before this mass murder, on 8 July, Himmler appeared in Bialystok together with the head of the Order Police, Daluege.[99] At a meeting with SS and police officers Himmler is said by Bach-Zelewski to have remarked that 'every Jew must in principle be regarded as a partisan'.[100] On the following day Daluege announced to a meeting of members of Police Regiment Centre that 'Bolshevism must now be eradicated once and for all'.[101] Two days later, on 11 July, the commander of Police Regiment Centre issued an order to shoot all Jewish men between the ages of 17 and 45 convicted of looting.[102] The police made the task of 'convicting' Jewish 'looters' very straightforward: three days beforehand, members of Battalion 322 had carried out a search of the Jewish quarter and designated all confiscated goods as 'plunder';[103] Jews were therefore looters by definition.

In the second half of July Police Battalion 316 carried out another massacre in Baranowicze, which probably claimed several hundred victims, and took part in two mass shootings in Mogilev in which 3,700 Jews (including women and children) were killed on 19 September.[104] In Brest-Litovsk, on or around 12 July, Police Battalion 307 shot several thousand Jewish civilians, almost all men between 16 and 60 years old—another alleged 'reprisal'. Immediately before the massacre Daluege, the chief of Police Regiment Centre, Max Montua, Bach-Zelewski, and other Higher SS Commanders had been in Brest.[105]

On 2 August Battalion 322 received a radio message from the Higher SS and Police Commanders to deploy a company 'exclusively for the liquidation of Jews'.[106] In the battalions' war diary for 9 August there is the note: 'comp. arrests all male Jews between 16 and 45 in Bialowicza and carries out the evacuation of all the remaining Jews from Bialowicza'. And the following day has 'the 3rd comp. today carried out the liquidation of all the male Jews in the prisoners' holding camp in Bialowicza. 77 Jews aged between 16 and 45 were shot.'[107]

The same company of the 322nd Battalion shot more Jewish men a few days later in Moravka-Malá near Bialowicza. The battalion's war diary for 15 August notes, '259 women and 162 children were resettled in Kobryn. All male Jews between the ages of 16 and 65 (282 head), as well as one Pole, were shot for looting.'[108] An order must have arrived between 10 and 15 August that increased the upper age-range from 45 to 65.

Conclusions

The following conclusions may be drawn from all these individual cases and examples about the way orders were given to the *Einsatzgruppen* and police battalions. Almost all *Einsatzkommandos* and *Sonderkommandos*, and a number of police battalions, can be shown to have carried out mass shootings of Jewish men of military age at the end of June or in July, a total of thousands of individuals. These shootings were generally carried out under the pretext of 'reprisals', as punishments for 'looting' or as a means of dealing with 'partisans'. This manner of proceeding corresponded to the orders that the *Einsatzgruppen* had received at the beginning of the campaign. Some of the *Einsatzgruppe* commanders even referred explicitly to these orders, as we have seen.

The conduct of the *Einsatzgruppen* followed a single pattern but was not wholly uniform. The upper age limit for the victims differed between *Einsatzgruppen*: whilst in some towns almost the entire male population in the relevant age-range was shot, executions in other places affected varying proportions of the male population. The different unit commanders therefore had a certain amount of room for manoeuvre, which was not completely precise, as has been shown, but left some latitude for initiative.

This manner of 'indirectly' issuing orders that relied on the intuition and initiative of subordinates was highly characteristic of the National Socialist system. It was deployed in cases where procedures were being demanded of subordinates that clearly contravened a valid law. The Party Supreme Court of the NSDAP neatly encapsulated this 'indirect' form of giving orders when it dealt with the question of whether Party members who had participated in the November 1938 pogrom should be punished for committing a serious crime. The Party Supreme Court explained at the time, that 'it was obvious to any active National Socialist from the period of struggle'—i.e. pre-1933—'that operations where the Party does not wish to appear as the instigator will not be regulated with complete clarity and in full detail. As a consequence, therefore, more is to be read into orders of that kind than the words literally state, and on the part of those issuing such orders, in the interests of the Party, the practice of not saying everything but hinting what an order is intended to convey has now become widespread, especially when these orders concern illegal political rallies.'[109] This technique of issuing orders was deployed in 1941 for the mass murder of Soviet Jews. The leaders of individual units had a degree of room for manoeuvre, but only within the framework established by the SS leadership.

CHAPTER 12

THE TRANSITION FROM ANTI-SEMITIC TERROR TO GENOCIDE

Changes in the Parameters for Action in the Area of Deployment and Alterations in the Perception of the Murderers

The original 'security police' model for the way commandos should proceed was to subject Jewish communities to a wave of terror immediately after occupation in order to exclude any possible form of resistance from what was seen as the 'Jewish-Bolshevist complex', whilst simultaneously isolating the Jews from the remainder of the population and stigmatizing them as the real enemies of the occupying power. This model was followed during July and the first half of August by a large proportion of the commandos and police units in an extremely radical manner: they had started to decimate the Jewish male population of military age systematically and indiscriminately. The fact that this expansion of the terror did not happen suddenly at a particular moment but was introduced over a period of time (some commandos did not adopt this policy until September or even later than that) suggests that there was no particular order that decisively brought about this transition. Rather it was a process of increasingly radical interpretations of orders—issued at the start of the campaign and deliberately left vague—to kill everyone who was in some way suspicious. It is most trenchantly summarized in Hitler's crudely brutal formulation from the middle of July: 'shoot dead everyone who so much as blinks at you.'[1]

The more radical approach of the commandos was manifested in a number of ways but especially in the alteration of the procedures for executions and in the invention of more and more reasons for murder. As early as July and August various formations had adopted procedures for execution that maximized the number of people murdered in the shortest possible time.

Executions during the first weeks of the campaign were frequently carried out according to the model of courts martial, which is to say that firing squads were assembled and in order to maintain a veneer of legality sometimes sentences were even read out and salvoes of shots discharged on an officer's order. But commandos very soon found ways to speed up and perfect mass executions: the victims were taken in organized groups at fixed intervals to carefully segregated execution sites, and the executions themselves took place immediately next to, sometimes actually inside, prepared mass graves (in which cases the victims often had to lie on the bodies of those who had been shot moments before). Automatic weapons were used, or victims were killed with a pistol shot to the head or neck.[2]

Where commandos gave any reason at all for their murderous activity, they tended to describe the Jews they killed as 'Bolshevist functionaries', 'Communists', 'Communist sympathizers', or as 'agents'.[3] Later, membership of the 'Jewish intelligentsia' sufficed as a reason for murder, especially in Einsatzgruppe B, whilst Einsatzgruppe C used 'reprisal' as the grounds for all types of actions. During July and August new reasons kept appearing for the liquidation of Jews on the grounds of supposed hostile action against the occupying power. These included arson,[4] dissemination of anti-German propaganda,[5] looting,[6] sabotage,[7] refusal to work,[8] support for partisan groups,[9] or black-market dealing.[10] After September these were supplemented by another 'security police reason', namely 'threat of plague',[11] which was supposed to originate with Jews.

From August the commandos' and battalions' modus operandi began to change fundamentally. The units made a transition from terrorizing and decimating the male population to 'cleansing', targeting individual communities at first but later whole swathes of the country. In other words, they murdered the major part of the local Jewish population, women and children included. Again, this radicalization of the units' mode of operation did not take place all of a sudden; different units changed at different paces and the shift took a while to complete. It was a process that can only be explained by taking a number of factors into account, notably the changing conditions under which the commandos were operating in their area of deployment. From the perspective of the commandos, this cast into doubt the 'security policing' model for the solution to the 'Jewish question' that had prevailed so far. However, this 'crisis' increased their readiness to adapt gradually to a new model that was now being propagated by the leadership of the SS: a policy of systematic ethnic annihilation.

As the war progressed, the commandos found that the further they penetrated into the East the more difficult it became to carry out pogroms. In the Baltic it had only been possible to provoke pogroms in the phase immediately after the occupation and they usually had to be stopped after a few days in order for the occupying force's claim to be 'calming' the situation to remain credible.[12] In the area under Einsatzgruppe C, as we have seen, it had been possible to start pogroms on a large scale in East Galicia and Volhynia. As they moved further into old Soviet territory, however, the Einsatzgruppe was forced to acknowledge the unwillingness of indigenous populations to take part in pogroms.[13] Einsatzgruppe B had a similar experience with their commandos in the Russian or Belarus territories, where indigenous populations were not prepared to take 'self-help measures against the Jews'.[14] The further east into Russian territory the *Einsatzgruppe* went, the fewer Jews they encountered: the proportion of Jews in the population was smaller because of the ban on settlement from Tsarist times and because many Jews had fled.

Because so many Jews had fled, therefore, Einsatzgruppe B found that it was hardly possible 'to maintain liquidation figures at their previous levels simply because the Jewish element is to a large extent not present'.[15] Einsatzkommando 6 noted at about the same time that 'even on the far side of the front' the Jews 'seem to have heard what fate is awaiting them at our hands'. In mid- and eastern Ukraine 70 per cent to 90 per cent of the Jewish population had fled; in some cases it was 100 per cent.[16]

The flight of the Jews also affected Einsatzgruppe C, as can be seen from the incident report of 9 August:[17] 'Since news has obviously spread that, as German troops are marching in the *Einsatzkommandos* are undertaking a systematic trawl of the occupied areas,' the Einsatzgruppe concluded, 'the commandos have now started to avoid operations of any larger size.'

As more and more of the Jewish population started to flee, as German troops made rapid progress, and as the *Sonderkommandos* and *Einsatzkommandos* were anxious to follow as closely behind the spearheads as possible, it became clear that there were often insufficient 'operational forces' at the disposal of the *Einsatzgruppe*.[18] From the end of June to September, in particular, the rapid rate of progress and the lack of manpower meant that huge areas that had been conquered were only superficially combed for Jews.

Einsatzgruppe C noted in October that, 'seen from the perspective of the state police and SD', they were confronted by an huge empty space; 'major successes' could only happen after 10–14 days, which was true 'particularly as regards the Jewish problem'.[19] For Einsatzgruppe B, too, the rapid onward march of German troops means that 'from the perspective of the security police' there was a dangerous 'lacuna' opening up; what was missing was 'so to speak the second wave of security police'.[20]

There was an additional problem for Einsatzgruppen C and D on the southern sector of the front: the influx of tens of thousands of Jews driven out by the Hungarian and Romanian allies. In the case of Romania we know that the head of state, Antonescu, referred to an agreement with Hitler in this regard.[21] Hitler had evidently put his Romanian ally in the picture about the planned large-scale deportations of European Jews to the East even before the war started. However, on their own initiative, Romania and Hungary (which will have been similarly informed) made a premature start with the expulsions that had originally been planned for the period after the Russian campaign had finished. Since on the one hand the Germans did not wish to snub their allies, and on the other did not wish to endanger their supply lines or cause other difficulties because of problems with refugees, they resorted to more radical 'solutions' during the month of August, as will be shown in detail below. Whilst Einsatzgruppe C murdered refugees in what was at that stage a massacre of unparalleled scale and savagery in Kamenetsk-Podolsk, Einsatzgruppe D initially attempted to drive the refugees back using brutal means, which meant that the weakest of them were simply shot. It eventually came to an agreement with the Romanians to intern all the Jews living in the area in question in concentration camps.[22]

Towards the end of the summer, yet another problem arose. Both the German occupation authorities and the central agencies in the Reich gradually began to cast their eyes towards the potential labour that the Jews represented. At first they had made every possible effort to replace the Jewish workforce with non-Jewish labour, but from September 1941 onwards there was a gradual realization that, during the war, it would not be possible to manage without Jewish workers altogether.[23] As we shall see, this problem also emerged in the areas controlled by the *Einsatzgruppen*. During the summer, the victims of mass shootings had principally been Jewish men of military age; but, from the autumn onwards, the selection principle was reversed and Jews capable of work were exempted from the annihilation measures.[24] The occupation authorities adopted a new approach in which the Jewish population was divided into 'useful' and 'superfluous', which had consequences for the way the Jewish minority was fed and housed, particularly in the cities.

Christian Gerlach has developed this line of argument and sees a direct connection between the expansion of the programme of shootings in September and October 1941—the transition to the systematic liquidation of ghettos—and the problems with feeding and housing Jews that were gradually becoming manifest. He has argued that the murder of the Jewish minority can be attributed directly to the failure of the systematic starvation policy that had been in place since the beginning of the war. Because the original plan to starve the general population of cities proved impossible to fulfil, the occupying power concentrated above all on the destruction of the two groups that it had in the meantime isolated from the outside world—the Jews, who represented a considerable proportion of the population of the cities that could no longer be fed, and prisoners of war.[25] In addition, the difficulties with providing food and shelter had a radicalizing effect on the conduct of individual authorities with the respect to the 'Jewish question'.[26]

However, Gerlach has not succeeded in proving this hypothesis about anti-Jewish policy empirically and unambiguously. For, although it seems perfectly plausible that problems with food and shelter did have a certain radicalizing effect on anti-Jewish policy in the occupied zones, his basic proposition—that the expansion of the programme of shootings in summer and autumn 1941 can be attributed above all to the material shortcomings that the occupying power was experiencing—does not seem to me to be an adequate explanation of what took place. Extending the programme of shootings, in my view, represents a process whereby German organizations were gradually steered by their leadership away from a 'security policing' approach and towards a policy of ethnic annihilation. The presupposition for this radical shift was first and foremost a changed perception of the situation by these organizations: during the summer the *Einsatzgruppen* and other SS and police units were forced to conclude that the original security policing approach could not lead to a solution to the 'Jewish question' for reasons suggested above. They therefore became more and more ready to accept a new and more comprehensive approach that the leadership brought in very gradually—with the help of a massive reinforcement of the deadly commandos—the approach that envisaged the blanket ethnic annihilation of the Jewish population.

Extending the campaign of shootings, therefore, had a variety of causes, although a fundamental factor was the racist hierarchy on which the occupying power based its assessment and treatment of the indigenous population and in which the Jews occupied the lowest rung. This way of viewing things, rather than any objective assessment of the difficulties of the situation, was decisive in the occupying power's belief that the annihilation of the Jews would solve a broad range of different problems.

The longer the war lasted, the more completely what was originally a fairly abstract idea of the Jews as the pillars of the Bolshevist regime was replaced by a concept whereby the Jews were endowed with the capacity to present a variety of concrete threats. They were seen as the source of many and various forms of resistance to the occupying power—they spread rumours, sabotaged measures taken by the Germans, started fires, and maintained contact with Soviet partisan groups; they spread plagues, and were active on the black market; by virtue of their mere existence they created problems in the fields of supplies, housing, and labour. Such perceptions make it clear how the racist and radically anti-Semitic attitude of the occupiers created its own distorted image of reality.

The reports of the *Einsatzgruppen* show that Einsatzgruppen B and C, in particular, displayed some considerable perplexity about the 'solution to the Jewish question' in the newly occupied Eastern zones. The staff officers of

Einsatzgruppe B reasoned thus about the situation in Belarus in July 1941: 'The solution to the Jewish question during the war seems impossible in this area and given the extra-large numbers of Jews it can only be reached via evacuation and resettlement.' They described the Jews' 'accommodation in ghettos', which was in train across the board, as 'a matter of high priority and, in the light of the large number of Jews, a particularly difficult one'.[27]

After August the matter of the labour deployment of the Jewish population also began to emerge in the reports from the *Einsatzgruppen*. Einsatzgruppe C, for example, reported on the developments in the Ukraine in the first half of August and suggested that the Jews should be exhausted in cultivating the extensive Pripet Marshes and those on the north bank of the Dnieper or on the Volga.

In an incident report for September 1941,[28] on the basis of their previous observations Einsatzgruppe C came to the following conclusion: 'The work of the Bolshevists depends on Jews, Russians, Georgians, Armenians, Poles, Latvians, and Ukrainians: the Bolshevist apparatus is not by any means identical with that of the Jewish population.... If we entirely dispense with the Jewish labour-force, then the economic rebuilding of Ukrainian industry or the expansion of urban administrative centres is virtually impossible. There is only one possibility, which the German administration in the General Government has neglected for a long time: the solution of the Jewish question via the full-scale deployment of the Jewish labour-force. That would bring with it the gradual liquidation of Jewry, a development that corresponds perfectly with the economic conditions of the country.'

Einsatzkommando 6 of Einsatzgruppe C, which according to an incident report of 12 September had drawn attention to the fact that 70–90 per cent of the Jewish population of many central and eastern Ukrainian towns had fled—rising to 100 per cent in some cases—drew the following striking conclusion from this phenomenon: 'this can be seen as a success deriving indirectly from the work of the Security Police, since the cost-free deportation of hundreds of thousands of Jews—mostly over the Urals, to judge by the results of interrogations—makes a substantial contribution to the solution to the Jewish question in Europe.'[29]

This problem had been brewing since July and had produced a situation that was very difficult grasp as a whole. Pogrom activity was declining, more and more Jews were fleeing, although there were refugees turning up in the areas that the commandos were leaving behind, it was impossible to control the vast areas of territory with such small units, there was an ever-increasing need for a larger labour-force, and the food supply was increasingly precarious. The original 'security policing' approach had been designed for the duration of a short war and had essentially consisted of overwhelming Jewish communities with a sudden wave of terror immediately upon occupation; as the war dragged on, this policy was clearly reaching its limits.

Mass executions in August had killed tens of thousands of people and in the light of this the units that were carrying them out began to question the mid- and longer-term perspectives for continued Jewish persecution in the occupied Eastern zones. How broadly should the range of victims be drawn? And where would the human resources for carrying out further murders be found? How were they to prevent Jews escaping murder by fleeing? How could the mass murder of Jewish skilled workers be justified in the face of the growing need for labour?

This degree of uncertainty on the part of the commandos explains their readiness to adjust to the new and far more radical approach to Jewish persecution in the East that had been pursued by the SS leadership since July. Indeed, it explains how their commitment towards the success of this new approach, involving a high degree of initiative on their own account, tentatively in July, but thereafter massively, especially in August and September, contributed towards its breakthrough. The *Einsatzkommandos*, now considerably strengthened in terms of personnel, started to expand the range of the executions by murdering women and children, whilst at the same time collaborating with the military and civil authorities to confine the survivors of these massacres in ghettos. In this manner rural districts in particular were rendered 'free of Jews'. Because the survivors were often absorbed into the labour force by the German authorities, the goal of the complete annihilation of the Jewish minority was initially postponed, but only until 1942.

The step-by-step implementation of the annihilation policies included a complementary role for Jewish ghettos.[30] These began to be set up from the second half of July onwards, initially primarily in order to keep the Jewish population under control, to free up living space (principally in devastated cities), and to gain the capacity to set up Jewish labour gangs for clearing operations and the like. At the same time Jews could thereby also be excluded from participation in the economic life of their communities. Just as with the occupation of Poland, the formation of ghettos was by no means a standardized procedure.

At first ghettos were set up in response to pressure from the Wehrmacht. The economic staff of the Wehrmacht was demanding the immediate ghettoization of the Jews in the occupied Eastern territories as early as 14 July.[31] A meeting between the head of the Military High Command's armaments section, Georg Thomas, and the state secretary for the Four-Year Plan, Paul Körner, on 31 July came to a similar conclusion: 'quarter the Jews in barracks and use them in units as labour gangs'.[32] Nevertheless, the Army High Command did not issue the order that recommended the establishment of ghettos until 19 August, and then under certain conditions. The commanders of the Rear Army Areas North, Central, and South gave differing instructions in this respect.[33]

Alfred Rosenberg, the Reich Minister for the Eastern Territories, had described the 'establishment of ghettos and labour gangs' as the 'key solution' to the 'Jewish problem' in a directive for the Reichskommissar for the Ukraine, who had yet to be appointed,[34] and the civilian administration was similarly demanding the formation of ghettos in many towns.[35] The *Einsatzgruppen* were just as strongly in favour, too. A plan for the establishment of ghettos in Kaunas and Minsk[36] by Einsatzgruppen A and B can be found in the incident reports for mid-July. The Minsk ghetto was in fact set up on the orders of the Field Commandant dated 19 July, and that in Kaunas was sealed on 15 August.[37]

It was also in mid-July that Einsatzgruppe B—which had described the 'solution to the Jewish question during the war' as 'impossible' in the old Soviet areas—suggested the establishment of Jewish councils in all cities, in order to identify Jews and deploy them for the purposes of forced labour, but above all to set up ghettos across the whole area: in fact, the 'implementation of this task' was 'ongoing'.[38] The same group reported further success at the end of July:[39] 'where it was necessary and possible, and with the agreement of the responsible local and field command posts, ghettos were being set up, councils of Jewish elders formed, the visible identification of Jews implemented and work gangs established, etc.'

Einsatzgruppe D evidently also did not see the 'solution to the Jewish question' at the end of August 1941 in the immediate and total annihilation of the Jews, as can be seen in an incident report from the 25th of that month:[40] 'the solution to one of the most important problems, the Jewish question, has also been tackled, even if tentatively. In Kishinev there were 60,000–80,000 Jews before the war. . . . On the initiative of the *Einsatzkommando* the Romanian town commandant set up a Jewish ghetto in the old town. This currently comprises some 9,000 Jews. They have been formed into work gangs and set to work for various German and Romanian agencies on clearing and other operations.'

The same *Einsatzgruppe* reported at the beginning of October that 'the first part of the Jewish question has been solved'. The nature of this 'solution' emerges from the remainder of the report, and consisted in the registration and marking-out of Jews, the formation of Jewish councils, ghettoization, and enforced labour.[41]

The establishment of ghettos, the 'first part' of the 'solution to the Jewish question', was thus a provisional measure in the eyes of the *Einsatzgruppen*, which was initially planned only for the duration of the war. This explains why the *Einsatzgruppen* both extended the range of the murders during the summer to include women and children, making whole districts 'free of Jews' and, at the same time, took measures that were aimed at preserving part of the Jewish population. It was still the case that, from their perspective, the 'Final Solution' to the 'Jewish question'—the complete annihilation of the Jews—had been postponed until after the war. They were still mainly concerned with murdering as many of those Jews who were not capable of work as possible. Ghettos played an important part in this approach because they achieved the necessary degree of control over the Jewish workforce, which for the moment the authorities were unwilling to dispense with. This view gradually prevailed during the summer of 1941 in place of the previous approach, which favoured selective terrorization of the Jewish leadership, and was still predominant during the autumn and winter of 1941 to 1942.

At that point, and with massive acceleration from spring 1942, there followed a third phase in which the population of the ghettos was selectively screened and murdered, and in which whatever remained of the Jewish population living outside the ghettos was traced and killed in so-called 'cleansing campaigns' that were generally described as anti-partisan measures. This third phase will be described in a later chapter.[42]

Himmler's 'Mission' and the Deployment of the SS Brigades

As the original 'security policing' approach to the 'Jewish question'—a selective campaign of terror—was replaced by policies aiming at total ethnic annihilation, the SS Brigades under the command of the Higher SS and Police Commanders for Russia South and Russia Centre played a decisive role at the end of July and in early August. The mass murders perpetrated by these formations attained new dimensions of horror and made the whole process of annihilation considerably more radical. These massacres enabled the Higher SS and Police Commanders once and for all to seize the initiative and take over the leading role in the process of annihilation.

The deployment of the SS Brigades in the East had been planned since spring, and it was clear that the brigades were to be used as a third team after the *Einsatzgruppen* and police battalions. The starting signal for their deployment was given at a meeting with Goering, Lammers, Rosenberg, and Keitel on 16 July in which Hitler had set out some of the principles for the future occupation of the Eastern territories and revealed his far-reaching plans for annexation and the brutality with which he intended to deal with the indigenous population.[43] According to Hitler, 'the fundamental need is to divide up the huge cake manageably so that we can, first, control it, second, administer it, and third, exploit it'. The partisan war that the enemy had launched had its advantages, he said: 'it gives us the chance to exterminate what stands in our way.' He went on: 'this huge area must be returned to peace as soon as possible, of course, and this can best happen if you shoot dead anyone who so much as blinks at you.'

The Führer's decree on the Administration of the Newly Occupied Eastern Areas established that, after the end of the military campaign, the administration would be transferred into civilian hands. The basic structure of the occupation administration was also set out, with Reichskommissars at its head under the command of a newly appointed Reich Minister for the Occupied Eastern Territories, Alfred Rosenberg.[44] Rosenberg, however, had to take account of the special competences of other agencies, and these included, in particular, Himmler's special responsibilities, which Hitler had set out in his second decree, also signed on 17 July, on Securing and Policing the Newly Occupied Eastern Areas.[45] This decree determined that 'securing and policing the newly occupied Eastern areas is the responsibility of the Reichsführer SS and the Head of the German Police'. He was authorized to give the Reichskommissars instructions for carrying out these tasks, and, in the case of 'instructions of a general nature or of fundamental political importance', Rosenberg was to be involved. In order to ensure that these areas were 'effectively secured by police measures' each Reichskommissar was assigned a Higher SS and Police Commander, who was to be under his 'direct and personal' command; similarly, the other commissars were also assigned SS and Police Commanders. This decree conferred responsibility for the 'police' solution of the 'Jewish question' in the occupied Eastern areas on Himmler.[46]

The 'major campaigns' that were to be undertaken by the Higher SS and Police Commanders in the weeks that followed (which will be described later in this chapter) show how Himmler understood his responsibility to 'secure through police measures' these areas. He saw his mission as gradually making large areas 'free of Jews', or in other words as extending the shootings on the one hand and concentrating the surviving Jewish population in ghettos on the other. The conduct of the SS and Police formations in the following weeks and months does not allow us to infer without doubt that an order to murder all the Soviet Jews was given to the Reichsführer SS in mid-July. Given the expectation of the National Socialist leadership to end the war in a short time, and in any case not later than the start of the winter, fulfilling such an order would hardly have been possible with the forces they had at their disposal. Instead, we have to assume that mass shootings and ghettoization were seen at that point as measures anticipating the 'Final Solution' planned for after the end of the war—the deportation of the Jews into a single area that would not be able to support them.

Settling the spheres of competence and responsibility in Himmler's favour on 16–17 July corresponded to what had for months been the direction of planning for the administration of the occupied Eastern territories. Hitler had by no means been carried away by victory-induced euphoria to make the decision during the discussions of 16 July for Himmler to be given far-reaching instructions to deploy large-scale murder squads;[47] this deployment had long been planned and was merely set in motion on 16–17 July. Himmler's decree of 21 May had already mentioned the Higher SS and Police Commanders earmarked 'to carry out the special orders given to me by the Führer in respect of the area under political administration',[48] and a discussion amongst the Reichsführer SS's Command Staff on 8 July suggests that the units under the Command Staff would mainly be deployed in the area under political administration.[49] Only after the basic structural principles of the political administration had been determined by Hitler, after the first Reichskommissars had been named and the priority of 'securing and policing the occupied Eastern areas' had been established could the time come for Himmler to deploy the third of his teams of police and SS forces, the SS Brigades.

Himmler had one very significant political motive in making his mission to 'secure through police measures' the Eastern areas as radical as possible and in extending it in the direction of a war of ethnic annihilation: intensifying the mass murder of the Jews in the East was a key component of his attempts to extend his competence as Reichskommissar for the Strengthening of the German Nation as soon as possible to the Eastern areas in order to bring them under the control of the SS via a violent ethnic 'reordering' of the newly conquered 'living space'.[50]

Already in June, before the war had begun, Himmler had suggested to Lammers that he should be entrusted with '*politically* securing and policing' the occupied East European areas and given the responsibility for 'pacifying and consolidating the political situation', whereby he should 'take into particular account the need to fight Bolshevism and his task as the Reichskommissar for the Strengthening of the German Nation'.[51] But these desires on Himmler's part had met with resistance from Rosenberg and had not been taken into account by Hitler when areas of responsibility were settled on 16 and 17 July: Hitler had specifically restricted Himmler's powers to 'securing through police measures', albeit after a long debate. However, Himmler had not been distracted by this setback to his leadership ambitions in the East, but had simply begun to take practical measures to 'reorder' the Eastern areas even before the war had ended. To this end, only two days after the outbreak of war he told his head of planning, Konrad Meyer, to present a draft of an extended version of the 'Overall Eastern Plan' (*Generalplan Ost*) within three weeks and ensure that it covered the areas that were to be conquered.[52] This draft was completed by 15 July before Himmler had to accept the division of responsibility in the East with Rosenberg, Goering, and the Reichskommissars after the decisions taken by Hitler on 16 and 17 of that month. But Himmler continued to work on the basis that the responsibility he had been given in October 1939 for 'the strengthening of the German nation' was valid in the occupied zones, too.

On 11 July Himmler had told the 'Ethnic Germans' Office', which answered to him, to gather details of 'ethnic Germans' in the occupied Soviet Union, an activity that was to run hand in hand with the work of the *Einsatzgruppen*.[53] On 17 July, the same day that he was formally charged with 'securing through police measures' these areas, he ordered the SS and Police Commander in the district of Lublin, Odilo Globocnik, to establish a network of police and SS bases in the newly occupied areas centred on Lublin. In other words, under the banner of 'Police/SS' Himmler was already beginning to take concrete settlement measures.

On 16 August Himmler informed SS Colonel Guntram Pflaum, the manager of the 'Lebensborn' organization (the 'Fount of Life'), which dealt with those illegitimate babies conceived by SS men with 'good' and 'unmixed' blood, that his future operational territory would include 'the whole of the occupied European areas of the USSR',[54] even though at this point Hitler had not made any firm decisions on the 'Germanization' of former Soviet areas.[55] In August, the main office of the

Reich Commissariat for the Strengthening of the German Nation opened a branch office in Riga.[56] And at the beginning of September Himmler finally triumphed over Rosenberg[57] and Hitler announced that the competences of the Reichskommissar for the Strengthening of the German Nation would now be extended to the occupied Eastern areas.[58]

Himmler's stubborn attempts to use his policing responsibilities as the basis for an ethnic 'reordering' of the Eastern areas were not limited to settlement and Germanization measures. The mission that Hitler had given Himmler in October 1939 had not only encompassed the 'formation of new German settlement areas via relocation' but, as a necessary prerequisite for the planned 'ethnic consolidation', also entailed 'excluding the noxious influence of. . . sections of the population alien to the *Volk*'. Himmler had attempted to put this section of his remit into practice in Poland by initiating mass deportations, but, when measured against his ambitious overall plan, had more or less failed. The conclusion that Himmler must have drawn from his experiences here was not to wait until the end of the war for the 'ethnic consolidation' but to start the 'exclusion' of 'sections of the population alien to the *Volk*' before then by making whole areas 'free of Jews'. Removing the Jews almost altogether was the first step on the way to a huge programme of deportation, resettlement, and extermination—one need only think of the figure of 30 million that the population of the Soviet Union was to be reduced by, according to the plans for Barbarossa. The Jews were seen by the Nazi leadership as the pillars of the Communist regime, and thus the one to be tackled first; by tackling the Jews (rather than those sections of the population classed as Slavic) Himmler was able to put his policies of ethnic annihilation into practice as part of his mission to 'secure [the occupied areas] through police measures'. He could be certain that any campaign of annihilation targeted directly at the Jews would receive the assent of the Nazi leadership, since it merely anticipated what had been planned in any case for the period after the war was over. Himmler could cite at least three orders from the Führer in support of his programme: his mission for the strengthening of the German nation, the 'special orders from the Führer for the area under political administration' that he mentioned in his instructions of 21 May, and the mission received from Hitler on 17 July. It was also evident, as will be explained in Chapter 14, that the general radicalization of German *Judenpolitik* in August and September 1941, when the regime concentrated its propaganda efforts against an international 'Jewish conspiracy', started to mark German Jews with the yellow star and prepared deportation from the Reich, had a further radicalizing effect on the mass killings in the East. Himmler must have perceived anti-Jewish measures as a confirmation of his brutal approach.

What has previously been described as an inconsistent transition over the period between July and September/October 1941 from policies of selective terrorization of the Jews towards policies of ethnic annihilation can therefore be equated with the systematic implementation of the first stage of Himmler's 'living space conception'. He was acting in this matter as an exponent of the most radical forces within National Socialism, who wished to implement qualitatively new policies in the occupied areas even whilst the war itself was continuing.

It is against these general observations that the deployment of the SS Brigades in July 1941 and the expansion of the killing in the following months should be seen. According to the initial invasion plans, the SS Brigades were to be deployed no earlier than ten days after the start of the attack.[59] However, after the war had started, the command staff troops were immediately thrown into a gap in the front, on Hitler's orders, and assigned to an army corps of the Wehrmacht evidently for the purpose of securing territory.[60] When this task had been declared complete after a few days, the command staff units began preparing for their future tasks by carrying out simulations and combat exercises.[61]

On 10 July Himmler decided that all SS squads deployed in the areas under Higher SS and Police Commanders would not only be economically responsible to them, as before, but also tactically: 'it has to be stressed to the Wehrmacht that in the Rear Area the Higher SS and Police Commander will make decisions on all matters that are the responsibility of the Reichsführer SS. . . . This also applies to the SD.'[62] On the same day, during his visit to Bialystok, Himmler discussed with Bach-Zelewski the planned deployment of the SS Cavalry Squads.[63] On 19 and 22 July, immediately after Hitler had given Himmler responsibility for 'securing the newly occupied Eastern areas through police measures' and had enhanced the position of the Higher SS and Police Commanders, the two SS Cavalry Regiments that had been merged into a single SS Cavalry Brigade at the beginning of August were subordinated to Bach-Zelewski, while the 1st Brigade was placed under the command of Jeckeln, the Higher SS and Police Commander for Russia South.[64] On 21 July Himmler met the chief of the Army Rear Area South, Karl von Roques, presumably in order to discuss the deployment of the 1st SS Brigade under Jeckeln in von Roques's area of authority.[65]

A few days later, after a long journey through Lithuania and Latvia, the officer in the command staff responsible for intelligence matters, Hauptsturmführer Rudolf May, who had come from the Home SD,[66] composed a report that contains an important reference to the fact that the attitude to the 'Jewish question' prevalent amongst the Security Police and Wehrmacht forces there was open to much more radical measures: 'Lithuanians and Latvians are taking the law into their own hands against the large number of Jews in the Baltic states. Their measures are tolerated by the offices of the Wehrmacht and the Security Police there. Whether the Jewish problem can be solved once and for all only by shooting male Jews in large numbers is doubted by those involved.'[67] A few days later still, two[68] of the three SS Brigades under the command staff were to demonstrate how Himmler and his command staff envisaged 'solving the Jewish problem once and for all'.

CHAPTER 13

ENFORCING THE ANNIHILATION POLICY: EXTENDING THE SHOOTINGS TO THE WHOLE JEWISH POPULATION

Himmler's decision to subordinate two of the three SS Brigades under his command staff to Higher SS and Police Commanders Jeckeln and Bach-Zelewski and deploy them directly for the execution of Jews in the occupied Eastern areas meant that the murder of the Jewish civilian population acquired a new dimension after the end of July 1941. All police and SS units were now extending the range of those shot to include women and children. This escalation was again inconsistent and did not occur in parallel in all areas, but was introduced gradually. Nonetheless, in all cases it followed a fundamental underlying pattern.

Higher SS and Police Commander Russia Centre and Einsatzgruppe B

In the area behind the mid-section of the front the SS Cavalry Brigade was responsible for bringing the murder campaign to a completely new level.[1] This brigade, composed of two former cavalry regiments, carried out an initial 'cleansing operation' in the Pripet Marshes between 29 July and 12 August under the leadership of Higher SS and Police Commander Russia Centre, Erich von dem Bach-Zelewski. For this operation the brigade received special 'guidelines for combing marsh areas using mounted units' that had been signed by Himmler himself: 'If the population as a whole is hostile, sub-standard in racial and human terms, or even, as is very often the case in marsh areas, made up of criminals who have settled there, then all those who are suspected of supporting partisans are to be shot, women and children are to be transported, cattle and provisions confiscated and secured. The villages are then to be burned to the ground.'[2]

Shortly afterwards, on a visit to Baranowicze on 30 July at which he briefed Bach-Zelewski, Himmler toughened that order still further. He now ordered the shooting of all Jewish men and in addition demanded that violent measures were to be taken against women. He deliberately avoided making explicit a requirement to shoot women, as is indicated by a radio message from the 2nd Cavalry Regiment on 1 August: 'Explicit order from the Reichsführer SS. All Jews must be shot. Drive Jewish women into the marshes.'[3] There was a similarly brutal order given by the commander of the mounted unit of the 1st Cavalry Regiment on 1 August to his men, albeit one that was not wholly clear with regard to the treatment of women: 'No male Jews are to be left alive, no families left over in the towns and villages.'[4]

Further developments show that Himmler's order was understood in various different ways. The 1st Cavalry Regiment assumed that it had been ordered to murder all Jews without distinction and, from 3 August onwards, the SS Cavalry (and in particular members of the mounted unit) therefore shot thousands of Jews in Chomsk, Motol, Telechany, Svyataya Volya, Hancewicze, and other places— men, women, and children. The net in these 'operations' was usually cast so wide that they were effectively aiming at the total annihilation of the Jewish inhabitants of each place.[5] On 11 August the mounted unit reported that it had shot 6,504 people, although the full total can be estimated at about 11,000 victims.[6]

Between 5 and 11 August the mounted unit of the 2nd SS Cavalry Regiment also shot thousands of Jewish civilians, 6,526 people according to the regiment's own reports, but in total probably nearer 14,000.[7] The murder of at least 4,500 (in fact probably 6,500) in Pinsk was the 'high point' of this 'operation'.[8] The victims in Pinsk were almost all Jewish men, as they were in all the other massacres carried out by the 2nd Regiment. The Regiment reported that 'Jewish looters' had been shot, some urgently needed craftsmen excepted; the report goes on to say that 'driving the women and children into the marshes was not as successful as it ought to have been because the marshes were not deep enough for them to sink all the way in'.[9] The final report made by the Brigade on 18 September 1941, covering both phases of their 'cleansing operation', lists altogether '14,178 looters shot, 1,001 partisans shot and 699 Red Army supporters shot'.[10] In fact the total number of Jews murdered in August by the Brigade will have exceeded 25,000.[11]

In the following weeks the Cavalry Brigade pursued their 'cleansing operation' almost uninterruptedly and shot thousands more Jews, chiefly under the pretext of combating 'partisans'. From the beginning of September on members of the 2nd Regiment also shot women and children.[12] The mass murder of Jewish civilians that the Cavalry Brigade began so terribly in the first half of August, and which claimed the lives of thousands of women and children, had a radicalizing effect on all the units that were under the command of the Higher SS and Police Commander Russia Centre, Bach-Zelewski. It is true that the total of those murdered by Einsatzgruppe B in those weeks was lower than in July, but the decisive shift was that shooting women and children was now the norm across the whole *Einsatzgruppe*.[13]

In the first half of August members of Einsatzkommando 9 in Vileyka shot at least 320 Jews in various 'operations', including women and children;[14] a few weeks previously Sonderkommando 7a had already 'liquidated all the male Jews' in that area.[15] The leader of Einsatzkommando 9, Alfred Filbert, indicated whilst being interrogated that the command to shoot women and children had been given to him by Nebe, the leader of Einsatzgruppe B, at the beginning of August.[16] After the murders in the area around Vileyka, Einsatzkommando 9 marched to Vitebsk in August and murdered thousands more people in a series of 'operations' carried out from then until October.[17]

According to his testimony after the war,[18] the leader of Einsatzkommando 8, Otto Bradfisch, also heard from Nebe in the first half of August that 'there is an order from the Führer in place according to which all the Jews, women and children included, are to be destroyed'. Bradfisch further testified that a short while later, when Himmler was in Minsk on 15 August[19] viewing a shooting by Bradfisch's commando, he also told him that 'there is an order from the Führer in place for the shooting of all Jews. This order must be followed, however difficult that may be for us.'[20]

The indiscriminate shooting of women and children can be proved to have been the practice of Einsatzkommando 8 from August onwards, but in an intensified form in September and October. One section of Einsatzkommando 8 stationed in Bobruisk carried out at least seven shootings and in a single one of the 'operations' that must have taken place in the first half of September at least 400 men, women, and children were killed.[21] Another section of Einsatzkommando 8 (this one stationed in Borisov) murdered all 700 inhabitants of the Sembin ghetto in August,[22] and thereafter, probably in the first half of September, a further 'major operation' was carried out in Lahoisk in which, according to an incident report of 23 September, 920 Jews were killed with the support of a commando of the SS Division 'Das Reich'.[23] This 'operation' also involved the murder of all the Jewish women and children in the town since it was thenceforth described as 'free of Jews'. At about the same time, this commando murdered another 640 Jews in Nevel and 1,025 in Yanovichi, and in both cases the reason given was the need to prevent the spread of contagious diseases.[24] Further massacres, each with several hundred victims, were carried out by the same commando in various places before the end of September.[25]

According to incident reports,[26] at around the end of September the section of Einsatzkommando 8 stationed in Borisov and parts of the commando that had remained behind in Minsk together shot '1,401 Jews in a major operation in Smolowicze [Smolevichi]', men, women, and children. The relevant report goes on to say, 'now that this cleansing operation has been carried out there are no Jews remaining in the north, south, or west of Borisov'. Police Battalion 322 shot a total of 257 Jews on 28 August in Antopol—this was part of a major 'special operation' in which the Higher SS and Police Commander Russia Centre reported 1,170 Jews murdered in the areas around Antopol and Bereza-Kartuska.[27]

On 1 September Police Battalion 322 had shot '914 Jews, including 64 women' in Minsk after a discussion between Bach-Zelewski and Daluege on 29 August.[28] The reason given in the battalion's war diary for shooting so large a number of Jewish women was that they were 'picked up during a raid for not wearing the Star of David'.[29] This execution was in fact part of a series of raids and shootings that claimed approximately 5,000 victims in the Minsk ghetto between 14 August and 1 September.[30]

On 25 September Battalion 322 performed the 'lock-down' and search of a village as part of a 'demonstration exercise' for representatives of the Wehrmacht (including divisional and regimental commanders), the police, and the SD. The unit's war diary reports that during this 'exercise' it had not been possible to arrest any partisans but that 'a check performed on the population showed the presence of 13 Jews and 27 Jewesses as well as 11 Jewish children. Of these, 13 Jews and 19 Jewesses were executed in cooperation with the SD.'[31] Only when this bloody demonstration had been completed did Einsatzgruppe B set about the indiscriminate murder of members of the Jewish population within its sphere of operations. This involved the massacre of thousands of Jews on each occasion, including women and children.

On 2 October a company of Police Battalion 322 in Mogilev (which is where Bach-Zelewski had his headquarters) undertook a 'special operation on the orders of the Higher SS and Police Commander' and picked up '2,208 Jews of both sexes' (a formulation that implies the inclusion of children). These people were all shot in an operation also involving members of the Ukrainian militia.[32] On 19 October, four days before Himmler arrived for an inspection of Bach's new headquarters in Mogilev, the incident reports confirm that 'a large-scale anti-Jewish operation was carried out in which 3,726 Jews of both sexes and all ages were liquidated', which is a clear indication that children were once more amongst the victims.[33] This operation involved Einsatzkommando 8 and Police Battalion 316. These two massacres in Mogilev heralded a whole series of similar 'major operations' in the east of Belarus under Bach-Zelewski's command.

From then on, city by city, town by town, district by district the whole of the Jewish population, except a few remaining members of the workforce, was shot. These 'operations' involved *Einsatzkommandos*, the Order Police, the civilian administration, and indigenous auxiliary police officers. The focus lay on major cities with large Jewish populations in the eastern portion of the occupation zone. Thus, to name only the most significant places, the Vitebsk ghetto was cleared between 8 and 10 October and 4,090 Jews were shot (according to reports by Einsatzkommando 9);[34] when the Borisov ghetto was cleared on 20 and 21 October, at least 6,500 Jews were shot after 1,500 people with specialist training had been filtered out;[35] in Gomel Einsatzkommando 8 shot 2,500 inhabitants of the ghetto on 3 and 4 November;[36] in Bobruisk November saw the deaths of 5,281 Jews at the hands of Einsatzkommando 8 and Police Battalion 316 during their 'special operation' to make the city 'free of Jews'.[37] Other cities saw further mass executions, although exact dating and precise figures are not always easy to establish.[38]

Executions evidently progressed without let or hindrance during the winter of 1941–2. Einsatzgruppe B had already reported 45,467 liquidations by the end of October, in which Einsatzkommandos 8 and 9 were able to demonstrate particularly high figures (28,218 and 11,452 respectively).[39] By the end of February 1942, that *Einsatzgruppe* had reported a total of 91,012 victims.[40]

Higher SS and Police Commander Russia South and Einsatzgruppe C

Higher SS and Police Commander Jeckeln and the 1st SS Brigade played key roles in extending the range of murders in the southern section of the front. The 1st Brigade, which was under Jeckeln's command, was already including Jewish women in the murders by the end of July 1941, which was the point at which (at the request of the 6th Army) it conducted a 'cleansing operation' in the area around Zwiahel between 27 and 30 July.[41] Jeckeln's deployment order to the Brigade includes the instruction that, besides the commissars, suspicious 'female agents or Jews...are to be treated accordingly'.[42] The Brigade reported that as a result of this 'operation' it had arrested 1,658 Jews (allegedly people 'who have significantly aided and abetted the Bolshevist system'); 800 people, 'Jews and Jewesses between the ages of 16 and 60', had been shot.[43] Following this, units from the Brigade carried out further 'operations' in August and shot 1,385 people on the same pretext, including 275 Jewish women and 1,109 Jewish men.[44]

In the following weeks Jeckeln gave further 'cleansing assignments' to the 1st SS Brigade. Members of the Brigade shot 232 Jews in Tschernjachov (Chernyachov) on 7 August; after Himmler had expressed his disquiet to Jeckeln about the inactivity of the 1st Brigade and had summoned him to a meeting,[45] it shot 300 Jewish men and 139 women on or around 20 August in Starokonstantinov; between 2 and 7 September it murdered '1,009 Jews and Red Army supporters'.[46] In fact the Brigade almost certainly murdered more people between the end of July and the middle of August than their own reports suggest. The total is probably around 7,000 Jewish men, women, and children.[47] The activity reports of the 1st SS Brigade for August and September and Jeckeln's radio messages confirm that in this period the Brigade was continuously shooting Jews.[48]

At the end of August Jeckeln carried out a massacre in Kamenetsk-Podolsk that far exceeded all the Brigade's previous 'operations': according to the incident report of 22 August, 'a commando under orders from the Higher SS and Police Commander [shot] 23,600 Jews in three days', men, women, and children.[49] The victims in Kamenetsk-Podolsk were mostly Jews who had been deported as 'burdensome foreigners' by the Hungarian authorities in July and August into the recently occupied Galician areas. These were largely people who had come under Hungarian rule when Karpato-Ukraine (formerly Slovakian) was annexed in 1939. It is evident from the minutes of a meeting held on 25 August with the Quartermaster General of the Army that this massacre was planned in advance. At that meeting an officer of the Quartermaster General's staff referred to Jeckeln's commitment to complete the liquidation of the Jews deported into Kamenetsk-Podolsk by 1 September.[50] Of the 18,000 Jews deported from Hungary some 14,000–16,000 were shot at the end of August about 15 km from Kamenetsk-Podolsk by Jeckeln's staff company and Police Battalion 320 along with further thousands of Jews from the local area; the Ukrainian militia and Hungarian soldiers helped seal off the area.[51]

After 'a total of 44,125 persons, mostly Jews' had been shot by 'formations under the Higher SS and Police Commander' in the month of August alone, according to incident reports,[52] Jeckeln went on with his massacres. In the early days of September a commando under the Higher SS and Police Commander Russia South executed '1,303 Jews, including 876 women over the age of 12', again according to incident reports.[53] The murder of more than 3,000 Jews still living in the Zhitomir ghetto that took place on 19 September with the participation of Sonderkommando 4a is also in all likelihood to be laid at Jeckeln's door.[54] Jeckeln certainly played a leading role in the massacre of the Kiev Jews in Babi Yar, which involved Sonderkommando 4a, Police Regiment South, Battalions 45 and 303 and a company of Waffen-SS. This mass execution, which incident reports indicate claimed the lives of 33,771 Jews,[55] was planned on 26 September in a meeting attended by Jeckeln, the head of Einsatzgruppe C, Otto Rasch, the leader of Sonderkommando 4a, Paul Blobel, and the City Commandant of the Wehrmacht. This massacre was 'justified' as a reprisal for a huge fire in the city that had allegedly been started by Jews.

Jeckeln was also responsible for the massacre of the Jews in Dnepropetrovsk on 13 October, where, according to the incident reports, of some 30,000 Jews remaining in the city, 'approximately 10,000 were shot by a commando of the Higher SS and Police Leader on 13 October 1941'. In this series of massacres, personally supervised by Jeckeln up to October, 1941, more than 100,000 people were murdered. This wave of mass murders provides the background for the activities of Einsatzgruppe C and the Police Battalion deployed in the southern parts of the occupied Soviet Union during the late summer and autumn. Some of these units had already been directly involved in the major 'operations' initiated by Jeckeln. Jeckeln was responsible for giving the decisive impetus that prompted the commandos and police battalions to move towards the comprehensive annihilation of the Jewish population.[56]

Erwin Schulz, the leader of Einsatzkommando 5, testified that during his stay in Berdichev (between 24 July and 17 August) Rasch, Commander of the Einsatzgruppe C, had summoned him to Zhitomir to explain that not only those Jews who were not being used as labour but also their wives and children were to be shot. Rasch claimed that this order came from Jeckeln. Schultz testified further to the effect that, as a result, he went at once to Berlin to have this order confirmed by Streckenbach, head of personnel at the Reich Security Head Office. Streckenbach, he said, had spoken with Heydrich and then confirmed that this order came directly from Hitler. Streckenbach corroborated this version of the sequence of events in his testimony after the war. Schulz's response was to ask to be replaced, a request that was granted.[57]

The murder by Einsatzkommando 5 of every single inhabitant of a town, including women and children, can be documented for the first time for the middle of September 1941 (in other words probably following the departure of Schulz). On 15 September, as an incident report explains, the town of Boguslav was made 'free of Jews' 'via the execution of 322 Jews and 13 Communist functionaries'.[58] On 22 and 23 September Einsatzkommando 5 carried out a 'major operation' in Uman in which, according to their own report, 1,412 Jews were shot.[59] In Cybulov, on 25 September, 70 Jews were shot; 537 Jews (men, women, and young people) were shot on 4 October in Pereyaslav; and shortly thereafter in Koshchevatoye 'all the Jews in the town' were executed.[60]

On the basis of the generalized order to murder issued in August, the number of the people killed by Einsatzkommando 5 increased considerably. For the period between 7 September and 5 October, the commando reported that '207 political functionaries, 112 saboteurs and looters, as well as 8,800 Jews had been liquidated'.[61] A few weeks later, the Commando reported that 'as of 20 October 1941, the number of those executed by Einsatzkommando 5 came to 15,110'.[62]

Einsatzkommando 6 (sub-unit Kronberger) began shooting Jewish women in October in Krivoi-Rog after Himmler had inspected it on 3 October.[63] On 20 October, Krivoi-Rog was declared 'free of Jews'. In the incident report of 19 November Einsatzkommando 6 stated that '1,000 further Jews had been shot'.[64]

From the beginning of August onwards, Sonderkommando 4a shot women in large numbers in the area around Zhitomir, and shortly thereafter also children.[65] In Bila Zerkva, too, 500 men and women were shot on 8 or 9 August by the vanguard of Sonderkommando 4a designated for Kiev. The Jewish children who had initially been abandoned in a school building to fend for themselves were shot on 19 and 22 August by the members of Sonderkommando 4a. The second round of shootings could only take place after the Commander in Chief of the 6th Army, von Reichenau, had intervened and lifted a ban on shooting children that had been imposed by the staff of an infantry division.[66] According to commando reports, before the end of August in Fastov 'the entire Jewish population aged between 12 and 60, 252 in all, were shot'.[67] In Radomyshl on 6 September, a further 1,668 Jewish men, women and children were executed.[68] In Zhitomir, where they were based and where a ghetto had been established, Sonderkommando 4a proceeded to murder all Jewish inhabitants regardless of age or sex. After multiple mass executions in the second half of August that claimed several thousand lives, 3,145 Jews were shot in the course of liquidating the ghetto on 19 September 1941, according to the commando's own report.[69] By 24 August Sonderkommando 4a had shot 7,152 people in all, again according to its own reports.[70]

Police Battalion 45, which was part of Police Regiment South, began to murder Jews regardless of their age or sex at the end of July and at the beginning of August. The first victims were the entire Jewish population of the town of Shepetovka, where the Battalion had been based between 26 July and 1 August 1941. According to the account of Battalion Commander Besser made after the war, this meant some 40 to 50 men and women, but in reality this figure was probably significantly higher.[71] Besser claimed to have been acting on orders from the Commander of the Police Regiment South, who in turn had referred to a general order for liquidation issued by Himmler.[72]

In the following weeks the Battalion repeated this pattern in other Ukrainian villages. It murdered Jewish men and women in Slavuta (according to the declaration of Higher SS and Police Commander for Russia South this came to 522 people),[73] in Sudylkov (471 dead) and in Berdichev (where there were 1,000 victims).[74] When Besser's successor, Rosenbauer, was being briefed on his tasks as Battalion Commander by the Higher SS and Police Commander for Russia South, Jeckeln, according to his own testimony he was given very clear instructions: 'Jeckeln said that there was an order from Reichsführer SS Himmler that would be the basis for solving the Jewish question. The Ukrainians would become a slave population working only for us. We had no interest, however, in letting the Jews multiply, so the Jewish population had to be exterminated.'[75]

Police Battalion 314, which was likewise part of Police Regiment South, was also shooting women and children as early as July. This can be documented for the first time in the case of a company of the Battalion on 22 July in a town near Kovel: the private diary of a member of the Battalion states that on that day 217 people, among them entire families, had been shot.[76]

In December 1941 the Higher SS and Police Commander for Russia South organized the murder of the Jews of Kharkov—Jeckeln's successor, Prützmann, was represented by Korsemann who had been chosen to become Higher SS and Police Commander for the Caucasus. Sonderkommando 4a and Police Battalion 314 shot between 12,000 and 15,000 Jews.[77] Further massacres followed in Stalino (on 9 January), Kramatorsk (on 26 January), Artemovsk (also in January), and Zaporozhe (in March 1942).[78]

Einsatzgruppe D

The way Einsatzgruppe D acted continued to be determined by the *Judenpolitik* of Germany's Romanian allies. From the end of July on, Romanian troops were expelling tens of thousands of Jews from the reconquered areas of Bessarabia and the Bukovina over the Dniester and into Soviet territory under German occupation. Einsatzgruppe D had been assigned to drive the Jews back again. In this context it also began to include women and children in the shootings.[79] The fact that the Jews expelled from Hungary had been murdered on a hitherto unprecedented scale by Jeckeln at the end of August in Kamenetsk-Podolsk, leaving some 23,600 dead, will also have had repercussions for the manner in which Einsatzgruppe D acted.

The shooting of women and children in the area of Einsatzgruppe D is documented for the first time for the period at the end of August. On or around 29 August, in the region of Yampol, Einsatzkommando 12 shot several hundred women and children from a convoy of more than 11,000 people, which the commando was driving over the Dniester bridge into Romanian-occupied territory.[80]

Shortly thereafter, at least three, but probably all four of the commandos of Einsatzgruppe D began the systematic murder of the entire Jewish population of a number of villages. The decisive order for the transition to this new stage of mass murder came at the end of August or the beginning of September from Otto Ohlendorf. Gustav Nosske, who was leader of Einsatzkommando 12, stated on this point in 1969 that around the beginning of September, Ohlendorf, together with Rasch, the Leader of Einsatzgruppe C, visited him and revealed 'that there is now an order from the Führer according to which all Jews are to be killed indiscriminately'. Until that point, he said, murders of Jews had been carried out 'only in the context of a general order for the security and pacification of the area behind the lines'.[81]

A report of Einsatzgruppe D for September 1941 reflects this new modus operandi. It states that 'the majority of our forces have been employed for the purposes of political pacification in places that showed evidence of incipient Jewish and communist terrorist groups, especially in the area of Ananyev and

Dubăsari. In this area pacification was carried out extremely thoroughly.'[82] The German 'pacification operations'[83] were predicated on the way the Romanian occupying powers were operating: they had begun using camps and ghettos to imprison the 150,000 to 200,000 Jews who had remained in Transnistria and the approximately 135,000 Jews who had been systematically deported from Bessarabia and the Bukovina into this area. Moreover, Jeckeln's massacre of 23,600 Jews deported from Hungary in Kamenetsk-Podolsk took place relatively close to Einsatzgruppe D's area of operation and will have had a radicalizing effect on its attitude.

In fact, by 'extremely thorough' pacification Einsatzgruppe D meant the murder of the entire population of both villages. On 28 August in Ananyev, Sonderkommando 10b 'shot about 300 Jewish men and women',[84] or in other words all the Jews who had arrived in the town.[85] It then split into smaller sub-units that carried out murders in other places.[86] A sub-unit of Einsatzkommando 12 that had halted in Dubăsari at the end of August or early September killed small groups of Jews there virtually every day.[87] In mid-September on the other hand, the sub-unit first murdered all of the approximately 1,500 Jewish inhabitants of the town and then a few days later a further 1,000 Jews from the nearby areas. Drexel, the sub-unit leader, testified on this point that he had received orders from a member of the staff of Ohlendorf's group 'to shoot the Jews living in Dubăsari'.[88]

Sonderkommando 10a carried out an execution in Berezovka, also probably in September, in which 200 Jewish men, women, and children were killed. The presence at this 'operation' of the commander of Einsatzgruppe D, Ohlendorf, is documented.[89] The deputy leader of the commando, Otto-Ernst Prast, stated under interrogation in 1965 that shortly before these executions his unit, which was already in Berezovka, had been told of an 'order from the Führer' for the comprehensive shooting of all Jews. A second lieutenant from the same unit testified that Ohlendorf and Seetzen, the leader of Sonderkommando 10a, had announced in Berezovka that 'from now on the Jewish question is going to be solved and that means liquidation'.[90]

In September 1941 the main body of Einsatzgruppe D crossed the River Bug and thus left the Romanian zone of influence, the area called 'Transnistria' between the Dniester and the Bug. At the end of September, Sonderkommando 11a, together with a sub-unit of the Einsatzkommando 12 and probably with support from Sonderkommando 11b, shot all the inhabitants of the ghetto in Nikolayev, where the headquarters of the staff of Einsatzgruppe D was now located. This involved some 5,000 women, men, and children.[91] At around the same time, probably a few days later, the entire Jewish population of Kherson was murdered by Sonderkommando 11a.[92]

The mass executions of Ananyev, Dubăsari, Nikolayev, and Kherson that took place between the end of August and the end of September marked the transition to the undifferentiated murder of the Jewish civilian population in the area under

Einsatzgruppe D. In this instance, too, Himmler personally inspected the mass murders: for the period from 30 September until 6 October, we have evidence that Himmler carried out an inspection tour in the Ukraine in which he also visited Nikolayev and Kherson, so that it is clear that he was present in both places either during or directly after the mass executions.[93]

In the conclusion to its incident report for 26 September Einsatzgruppe D reported: 'Commando's sphere of operations made free of Jews: from 19 August to 15 October, 8,890 Jews and Communists executed. Total number: 13,315. Currently the Jewish question in Nikolayev and Kherson is being solved. About 5,000 Jews were dealt with.'[94] About a week later, the report states: 'the commandos have continued to clear the area of Jews and Communist elements. In particular, the cities of Nikolayev and Kherson have been freed of Jews and functionaries still present were dealt with accordingly.'[95]

At this point, October 1941, Sonderkommando 11b was still in the Romanian zone of occupation west of the Bug to take part in the conquest of Odessa that was eventually achieved on 16 October. When a Soviet commando that had remained behind in the city blew up the headquarters set up by the Romanian army a week later, the Romanians reacted by carrying out a massacre of the Jews of Odessa that probably claimed 40,000 victims. The Sonderkommando played its part in this massacre by carrying out the mass execution of hostages.[96]

Einsatzgruppe D continued its mass murders in the months that followed. In the first half of October it reported that 'the areas newly occupied by the commandos have been rendered free of Jews'.[97] In the Einsatzgruppe's October report it claimed: 'the solution of the Jewish question has been energetically undertaken by the Security Police *Einsatzgruppen* and the SD, in particular in the area east of the Dnieper. The areas newly occupied by the commandos have been made free of Jews. In the process 4,891 Jews were liquidated. In other places the Jews have been marked out and registered. This made it possible to put labour gangs of up to 1,000 strong at the disposal of the Wehrmacht offices.'[98]

Various massacres by Sonderkommando 10a can also be documented in detail. This unit shot the whole of the Jewish population of the city of Melitopol in mid-October; a few days later, on 18 and 19, it murdered all 8,000 Jewish inhabitants of Mariupol and a week after that the Jewish population of Taganrog, some 1,800 people.[99] In December Sonderkommando 11b murdered the Jewish population of Karasubasar, Alushta, and Eupatoria.[100] In November and December Sonderkommando 10b murdered the Jewish inhabitants of Skadovsk, Feodosia, Kertsh, and Dzhankoy.[101]

In November, Ohlendorf moved his staff to Simferopol in the Crimea. On 9 December it and Sonderkommando 11b murdered the 1,500 Krymchaks living in the city (these were a Muslim group that the SS categorized as 'Jewish'), and between 11 and 15 December, assisted by members of two police reserve battalions, they murdered the entire Jewish population of the city.[102]

However, it was not only the SS and Police units that had been dispatched from the Reich into the Soviet Union that had begun the systematic murder of the major part of the Jewish population across a wide area in the autumn of 1941. Romanians and ethnic Germans in the Romanian area of influence, Transnistria, also pursued the same goals. Between December 1941 and February 1942 the Romanians murdered at least 70,000 Jews in ghettos as part of the bloody 'clearance' of the county of Golta.[103] A militia composed of ethnic Germans also played a considerable role in the murders in Transnistria: it was guided in its activities by a Sonderkommando of the SS Ethnic Germans' Office that had been sent to Transnistria to protect ethnic Germans. The Germans in Transnistria murdered more than 28,000 Jews in the winter of 1941–2 alone.[104]

The Reich Commissariat Eastland (Einsatzgruppe A)

Transition to Shooting Women and Children

Einsatzkommando 3 and Einsatzkommando Tilsit both began to shoot women and children at the end of July and the beginning of August. For Einsatzkommando 2 this seems to have taken place during the month of August.

The comprehensive report of the leader of Einsatzkommando 3, Jäger, shows that from the very beginning women were also being shot in the executions carried out by this Einsatzkommando in Lithuania, although in far fewer numbers than men.[105] At this point the shooting of women was regarded as justified when there was even a vague suspicion that they were involved in Communist activity or connected with the partisans. A fundamental change can be observed, however, as in the case of other commandos, in the month of August. According to the Jäger report, 'in cooperation with Lithuanian partisans', Einsatzkommando 3 shot 213 Jewish men and 66 Jewish women in Rassainiai on 5 August. A few days later, between 9 August and 16 August, it shot '294 Jewish women, 4 Jewish children' in the same place. It is also noteworthy that for 15 and 16 August the shooting of a total of '3,200 Jewish men, Jewish women, and Jewish children' in Rokiskis is reported. Not only is this number far higher than for previous executions, but also the summary form of the report (without the distinction hitherto made between women, men, and children) indicates a new procedure. It thus seems likely that between 5 August and 16 August at the latest, the commando charged with carrying out these murders received a new order: now it was on principle no longer necessary to discriminate between men and women and the murder of children was permitted.

In the following days, too, the number of women shot by Einsatzkommando 3 sometimes reached the same level as the number of men, in some cases even significantly higher. The large number of children murdered points to the likelihood that the transition had now taken place to the indiscriminate shooting of Jews of any age and both sexes. Accounts in the Jäger report include, among other items, 'Panevėžys, 23 August: 1,312 Jewish men, 4,602 Jewish women, 1,609 Jewish children; Zarasai, 26 August: 767 Jewish men, 1,113 Jewish women, 687 Jewish children; Utena and Molėtai, 29 August 1941: 582 Jewish men, 1,731 Jewish women, 1,469 Jewish children; Mariampolė, 1 September 1941: 1,763 Jewish men, 1,812 Jewish women, 1,404 Jewish children.' On 2 September, Einsatzkommando 3 also reported the shooting of women and children from Vilna: 'Apart from 864 Jewish men, 2,019 women and 817 children were shot.'[106] In Daugavpils in Latvia, a sub-unit of Einsatzkommando 3 shot more than 9,000 Jews, among them a large number of women and children in several 'operations' between 13 July and 21 August, with the support of Latvian forces.[107]

Einsatzkommando 2, which was stationed in Latvia, had liquidated almost 18,000 Jews by September or had had them shot by Latvian auxiliaries.[108] The high number of victims points to the possibility that this commando had also begun shooting women and children.

By the end of July and the beginning of August, Einsatzkommando Tilsit, which was operating in the border areas, had begun systematically extending the shootings beyond the group of men of military age. Members of the commandos returned to places that had already been ravaged but where surviving Jewish family members had been imprisoned by the Lithuanian 'order patrol'. Thus, with the support of Lithuanians, at least 100 to 200 Jews (women, old men, and children) were shot in Jurbarkas (Georgenburg) and Virbalis at the end of July and the beginning of August; in Gargždai (Garsden) in August and September at least 100 women, children, and elderly men were shot. The District Court of Ulm that was later charged with examining these activities found more such executions had taken place continuing into September.[109]

In contrast to Einsatzgruppen B and C this huge increase in the number of murder victims in the area under Einsatzgruppe A was not attributable to the deployment of a brigade of the Waffen-SS. Higher SS and Police Commander Hans-Adolf Prützmann evidently did not deploy the 2nd SS Brigade that had been put at his disposal for a short time in September for the shooting of Jews. He had sufficient indigenous auxiliary units available, in addition to the *Einsatzgruppen*, who were more than prepared to undertake these murders.

In the same period in which the murders were extended to include women and children and the numbers of those killed rose in leaps and bounds a remarkable controversy sprang up between the civilian authority that had just taken over and Einsatzgruppe A. It concerned the future of 'anti-Jewish policy' and because of the deeply entrenched positions that were taken it merits further attention here.

The August 1941 Controversy in the Reich Commissariat Ostland about Future 'Guidelines for the Treatment of Jews'

On 2 August 1941 the Reichskommissar for the Ostland (the Baltic States and White Russia), Hinrich Lohse, sent the administration of the Higher SS and Police Commander for Riga a draft of provisional guidelines for the treatment of Jews in his area of responsibility that he planned to issue a few days later. This draft corresponded in substance to the oral instructions Lohse had already issued to his staff in the speech he made on taking over the post on 27 July in Kaunas.[110] Amongst other things, it made provision for the seizure of the Jews within the Reich Commissariat, for marking them out with the Star of David, for implementing bans on their exercising any profession, for bans on their use of certain facilities, and for regulations concerning registration and handing over accumulated Jewish wealth. The 'flat land', that is, the countryside, was to be 'cleansed of Jews', ghettos were to be formed, and forced labour gangs were to be set up.[111]

Higher SS and Police Commander Prützmann, the leader of Einsatzgruppe A and the head of the Security Police, Stahlecker, both responded to these suggestions with great alarm,[112] since from their perspective they represented a challenge to their division of responsibilities and were not in accordance with the situation as they saw it.

Stahlecker drew up a paper on Lohse's draft in which he explained his position thus: 'The measures proposed in the draft for dealing with the Jewish problem do not conform with the orders given by Einsatzgruppe A of the Security Police and the SD for the treatment of Jews in the Eastland. Nor have the new possibilities that exist in the Eastland for clearing up the Jewish problem been taken into account. The Reichskommissar is evidently seeking a temporary solution to the Jewish problem in the Eastland that corresponds to the situation that has been established in the General Government. On the one hand, he fails to take account of the changes in the situation brought about by the effects of the Eastern campaign, and on the other, he avoids confronting the radical possibilities for dealing with the Jewish problem, which have emerged for the first time in the Eastland.'[113] One difference between the Eastland and the General Government, he said, was the need there to use the Jews as part of the labour force. 'These necessities have not been manifest in the area under the Reichskommissar for the Eastland with the exception of the question of skilled craftsmen in a very few towns and are hardly likely to present themselves in the future.... Perspectives derived from the need to use the Jews for labour will simply not be relevant for the most part in the Eastland.' And in addition, the Jews in the Eastland, in contrast to the General Government, are 'mostly supporters of Bolshevism' and would contribute in no small measure to creating agitation.

After making further criticisms of the measures proposed in the provisional guidelines, Stahlecker explained how he saw the solution to the 'Jewish problem' in the Reich Commissariat Eastland. If it was 'already' necessary to proceed with 'resettlement from the flat lands into the cities', Stahlecker claimed, this had to be implemented 'across the board and in the following manner': 'Across the broad areas of the Eastland certain districts will be set aside for Jewish reservations as required.... In the Jewish reservations male and female Jews will be housed separately. Boys will remain with their mothers until they reach puberty. The Jews can immediately be set to perform gainful work within the Jewish reservations.... If there is a workforce available over and above this, the Jews can be deployed in chain-gangs for road-building even outside the reservations. If the cleansing of Europe of all the Jews has not by then become official policy other possibilities for work can be created at a later date by setting up technical and industrial enterprises within the Jewish reservations. Housing and food will only be approved in the Jewish reservations to the extent that it is absolutely necessary to maintain their ability to work.'[114] All Jews who were needed outside the sealed 'reservation' would have to be housed in closed camps. All Jews would also have to be visibly identified as such.

At the end of his response Stahlecker summarized the 'advantages' of his approach: 'an almost 100 per cent immediate cleansing of the whole of the Eastland of Jews, preventing Jews from multiplying, possibilities for the most ruthless exploitation of Jewish labour, a significant easing of the later transportation of Jews into a Jewish reservation outside Europe'. Finally, he suggested that 'before a fundamental set of instructions is published, we need to discuss all these questions in detail face to face, especially as the draft directly affects fundamental orders to the Security Police received from higher up which cannot be discussed in writing'.[115]

How is this document to be assessed? There is an obvious contradiction between the mass executions that were taking place at the same time in Lithuania and the 'solution' suggested here. At first sight a conjecture proposed by Christopher Browning looks plausible, namely that this is a 'cover story' put together for the civilian administration by the *Einsatzgruppe* in order to disguise the decision to murder all the Jews in the 'Eastland' that had already been taken.[116] Two days before writing this document on 6 August 1941, but after making an application to the Reich Security Head Office on 21 July for the approval of a concentration camp in Riga under the auspices of the Security Police, Stahlecker had received permission to set up a detainee camp as an 'extended police prison'.[117] The plan for a large camp in the Riga area was pursued by the Security Police over the coming months despite the fact that the shootings were being extended. These constant efforts, and the fact that in Riga (as in Minsk) preparations for setting up a ghetto had already been begun in July,[118] can be read as an indication that at the end of July or early in August even Einsatzgruppe A was not assuming that they would be able to murder the entire Jewish population of Latvia in a series of mass executions, despite the fact that liquidations had at that point just been extended to women and children. Instead they were focusing on an intermediate solution for the survivors of the first wave of murders, having been informed at first hand of the latest status of the 'Jewish question' by Himmler's visit to Riga on 30 July.[119]

The explanations given to Lohse by Stahlecker are in accordance with the 'guidelines' issued by the Reich Security Head Office in the summer of 1941 (the exact date is not certain).[120] These instructions assumed that 'the Jewish question would be solved for the whole of Europe by the end of the war at the latest'. 'Preparatory part-measures' that were to be carried out included 'moving [the Jews] to ghettos and separating the sexes' and in particular the 'complete and unrelenting utilization of Jewish labour'. 'Reprisal measures' against local populations were to be tolerated, but in contrast mass executions by *Einsatzkommandos* under the Reich Security Head Office were not mentioned in the guidelines—they were regulated by orders transmitted only orally.

The contradiction between the reality of mass executions and the image created by the 'guidelines' issued by the Reich Security Head Office and the explanations given by Stahlecker at the beginning of August can be explained if one assumes that in the latter two documents what is being described is only the fate planned for the Jews of the Baltic states who had not fallen victim to the first wave of mass executions and who were initially intended to live under the German occupation administration until the end of the war and the ultimate decision on the 'Final Solution'. The *Einsatzgruppe* staff reacted with such alarm to Lohse's initiative not because they feared that Lohse wanted to hold back the mass murder of the Jews in the Baltic states that was taking place literally before his very eyes—the Reichs-kommissar did not intend this, and could not have achieved it—but quite simply because they thought it raised issues about who would be responsible for the treatment of the surviving Jews. The debate between the *Einsatzgruppen* and the Security Police on the one hand and the civilian administration on the other is therefore comprehensible only if one remembers that those involved all assumed that by the time Lohse's planned 'guidelines' were implemented the majority of the Jews in the Baltic states would already have been murdered.

The extension of the shootings in Einsatzgruppe A's area to women and children cannot therefore be seen as proof that a decision had already been taken to murder all the Jews in the area under the control of the *Einsatzgruppe*. Given the vast number of those already murdered in August, the *Einsatzgruppe* would easily have been in a position to carry out such a far-reaching programme of murders within a few months, but in fact it did not seem to wish to pursue such a line. The final decision to annihilate each and every one of the Jews living in the Baltic states had, in the view of those concerned, not yet been taken. The controversy between Stahlecker and Lohse of summer 1941 demonstrates that the murder of the Jews in the occupied Eastern areas cannot be understood as the implementation of a single order issued by the National Socialist hierarchy. It was a process that went through a series of different phases and in which the mid-level protagonists possessed considerable room for manoeuvre.

When Reichskommissar Lohse sent the draft for his planned 'Provisional Guidelines for the Treatment of Jews in the Reich Commissariat' to the Reich Ministry for the East on 13 August he had added an introduction to the text, which was otherwise unaltered. This addition was a safeguard against accusations that he was infringing upon areas for which the Security Police was responsible: 'With reference to the definitive solution to the Jewish question in the area of Reich Commissariat Eastland, the instructions given in my speech on 27 July 1941 in Kaunas will apply.[121] Where further measures have been taken in carrying out these oral instructions of mine, especially those taken by the Security Police, they are not covered by the following guidelines. These provisional guidelines are only intended to ensure minimum measures to be taken by Commissars General or Area Commissars if, and only if, further measures with respect to a definitive solution to the Jewish question are not possible.' On 18 August Lohse sent a signed copy of these guidelines to the Commissars General.[122]

Continuation of the Mass Executions in the Autumn of 1941

As Einsatzkommando 3 continued its series of murders in Lithuania in the flat land in September 1941, it was single-handedly responsible for the deaths of some 25,000 Jews. After one swathe of country after another had thereby been rendered 'free of Jews',[123] the commando turned to the step-by-step murder of the people who had been corralled in the ghettos set up in the main cities. These murder operations were primarily directed at those who were assessed as incapable of work; the surviving specialist workforce and their dependents were repeatedly scrutinized for their 'capacity for work' and gradually murdered in 'operation' after 'operation'.

In the autumn of 1941 a new phase of Jewish persecution began in Lithuania and the other areas of the Reich Commissariat, the second wave of murders that aimed ultimately at the systematic annihilation of all the Jews (with the exception of a limited and continually reduced number of those able to work). The Germans no longer assumed, as they had in August, that the 'Final Solution' to the Jewish question would be postponed until after the war, and in consequence they did not focus on medium-term solutions such as housing Jewish men and women separately. Instead, in autumn 1941 the total destruction of the Jews was, from the perspective of those responsible, a goal that could be achieved according to plan within a very short time.

In Kaunas, where a ghetto had been set up in the middle of August, more than 1,608 men, women, and children ('ill or suspected of being infectious') were murdered on 26 September; on 4 October another 1,845 people were murdered on the pretext of a 'punishment operation'; on 29 October after a large-scale filtration operation 9,200 people were shot ('cleansing the ghetto of superfluous Jews').[124]

The methodical nature of the activities of the Germans can also be demonstrated using the example of the annihilation of the Jews in Vilnius, where all the inhabitants of the ghetto except a tiny core of specialist workers were systematically killed over a period of a few months. At the beginning of September, a major series of arrests was made and 3,700 men, women, and children were shot in the woods at Ponary; the surviving Jewish population was resettled into two new ghettos. During September further shootings took place and thousands more were killed. On 1 October, the day of Yom Kippur, several thousand men were taken out of the ghetto and shot, mostly those who were not registered as specialist workers. In the middle of October the so-called Small Ghetto was dissolved and some 15,000 people murdered. Towards the end of the month the occupants of the Large Ghetto who were fit for work were transferred into the Small Ghetto and those who remained were shot in two 'operations' by the beginning of November, which cost 8,000 and 3,000 lives respectively. On 20 and 21 December those without identity papers to confirm that they were skilled workers or their dependents were shot—a total of 15,000 people.[125]

In Jäger's report for 1 December the situation in Lithuania is described thus: 'I can confirm today that the goal of solving the Jewish problem in Lithuania has been achieved by Einsatzkommando 3. There are no more Jews in Lithuania except worker Jews and their families. That makes: in Šiauliai c.4,500, in Kaunas, c.15,000, in Vilnius, c.15,000.'[126] Jäger added, as if by way of apology, 'I also wished to bump off these worker Jews and their families but this was strongly resisted by the civilian administration (the Reichskommissar) and the Wehrmacht and provoked the following ban: these Jews and their families must not be shot.' By the end of November Jäger gave a total figure for those murdered in the General Region of Lithuania of 125,000 people, overwhelmingly Jews.

At the end of October the rural areas of Latvia were also 'wholly cleansed' of Jews. The survivors were imprisoned in the ghettos of Liepāja (Libau), Daugavpils (Dünaburg), and Riga, where the enforced resettlement was only completed at the end of that month. In November and December the Latvian Jews were also almost wholly annihilated in a series of large-scale 'ghetto operations'. First of all, between 7 and 9 November, at least 3,000 Jews were murdered in the Daugavpils ghetto, where similar 'operations' had already taken place in August and September.[127] Friedrich Jeckeln, who had just been made Higher SS and Police Commander for Russia North and who, when he had held the same office in Russia South, had been responsible for the death of an estimated 100,000 Jews, claimed to have received an explicit order directly from Himmler on or around 10 November to liquidate the ghetto in Riga. On Jeckeln's orders, during Riga's Bloody Sunday on 29–30 November, more than 10,000 people were shot outside Riga near the railway station at Rumbuli. Previously, Jeckeln had had 4,500 working Jews separated from the rest and put into a separate area of the ghetto, the 'Small Ghetto'. In a second major 'operation' on 8 and 9 December—also at Rumbuli—the total of Jewish victims from Riga rose to 27,800, on Jeckeln's own admission.[128] In Liepāja between 15 and 17 December a further 2,350 Jews were murdered, which meant the whole population of the ghetto except for 350 craftsmen.[129]

Of only 4,500 Jews living in Estonia the invading army had merely encountered some 2,000. The male Jews above the age of 16 and the female Jews fit for work and between 16 and 60 were imprisoned in provisional camps and most of the men were shot. Einsatzgruppe A reported from Estonia as early as October that 'the rural communities are now already free of Jews'.[130] In February the women and children in a camp near Pskov (Pleskau) who had not been detailed for forced labour were also murdered on the instructions of Higher SS and Police Commander Jeckeln.[131]

In the areas of Belarus under civilian administration the 'major operations' aimed at women, men, and children began in October. They were carried out by a sub-unit of Einsatzkommando 6, the Commando of the Security Police Minsk (formerly Einsatzkommando 1b), the Order Police and the Wehrmacht.[132] They began initially with the 'cleansing' of the 'flat land'. For this purpose, according to a report by the division commander, Reserve Police Battalion 11, which was part of the 707th Security Division, was deployed for a 'major operation' between 8 and 15 October 1941 'under the command of the Intelligence Office at Minsk'. This involved shooting more than 2,000 people in Smilovichi in Rudensk and other Belarusian towns—people who had been labelled 'partisans, Communists, Jews and other suspicious rabble'. The battalion was supported by two companies of Lithuanian auxiliary police, the Secret Field Police and the Engineers' Company of the 707th Division. The reports and orders signed off at the same time by the divisional commander are very clear with respect to the treatment of Jews in the 'area to be secured': they talk of 'annihilation' and 'extermination'. The statement made by the battalion leader in 1960 that he received the order for the 'operation' from the staff of the 707th Division therefore seems perfectly credible.[133] At the same time that this series of mass murders was being carried out, a sub-unit of Einsatzkommando 3 murdered more than 3,000 Jews in the areas around Minsk and Borisov.[134]

Following the 'major operation' in the area of Smilovichi, members of the battalion shot '1,000 Jews and Communists' in the city of Koydanava (now Dzerzhinsk) on 21 October (again with the support of the Lithuanians). There exists a report by the Regional Commissioner, Heinrich Carl, concerning the deployment of the battalion on 27 October in Slutsk, which the Commissar General in Minsk, Kube, was to use as the occasion to petition the Reichskommissar Eastland for disciplinary proceedings to be initiated against all the officers of the battalion.[135] In his report Carl describes how, on the morning of the 27th, an officer of Reserve Police Battalion 11 announced to him the order to liquidate of all the Jews in the city. The battalion command had disregarded his energetic protest that the vast majority of the Jews there were irreplaceable skilled workers. The deputy commander of the unit had explained, he said, that 'he had received the order from the commander to free the whole city from Jews, making no exceptions, as they had in other towns. This cleansing was to happen for political reasons, and economic factors had never played any part at all.'

The order was implemented despite Carl's protest and his report describes it as being carried out with 'what amounted to sadism.... During the operation the city itself presented a terrifying picture. With indescribable brutality on the part of the German police and in particular of the Lithuanian partisans, the Jewish people and some Belarusians were fetched out of their houses and herded together. There were gunshots ringing out across the whole city and the bodies of murdered Jews were piled up in the streets.... Many times I had to force the German police and Lithuanian partisans out of workshops literally at gunpoint, using my revolver.' Furthermore, 'the police battalion engaged in looting during the operation in an outrageous manner...not only in Jewish houses but in the houses of the Belarusians too. They took with them everything usable, such as boots, leather, textiles, gold and other valuables.' Carl concluded his report, 'Please grant me only one wish: "Protect me from this police battalion in future!".'[136]

On 30 October Police Battalion 11 undertook a further 'operation' in Kletsk. The situation report by the Commandant in Belarus for the first half of October concludes its comments on this 'cleansing operation in the area of Slutsk-Kletsk' by saying that '5,900 Jews were shot'.[137] At the beginning of November the battalion was removed from the formation of the 707th Division and assigned again to Police Regiment Centre.[138]

The massacres in the General Commissariat of Belarus reached a temporary apogee in the major 'operation' in Minsk in which, between 7 and 11 November, the Commando of the Minsk Security Police shot on its own reckoning 6,624 Jews from the ghetto there.[139] On 20 November and 10 and 11 December, the same group committed two further massacres in which 5,000 and 2,000 people were killed respectively.[140] In the period around 13 November, of the 16,000 Jews in the city and the district of Slonim all but 7,000 previously selected skilled workers were murdered by the Security Police and the SD. The District Commissar responsible for this mass murder, Gert Erren, reported that 'the operation...freed me from unnecessary mouths to feed and the 7,000 or so Jews that are still present in the city of Slonim are all bound into the labour process, are working willingly because they are under constant threat of death and will be checked over and sorted for further reduction in the spring'.[141]

These examples show that the police battalions could be deployed for mass shootings of Jewish civilians under very different command structures. The battalions were either deployed in the context of a police regiment, sent in as support for *Einsatzkommandos*, or used for 'special operations' or 'major operations' by the Higher SS and Police Commander in which case for the duration of the relevant 'operation' their subordination to a security division was suspended. It sometimes happened, however, that police battalions undertook such 'operations' precisely within the context of a security division, as the example of Reserve Police Battalion 11 makes clear.

In the activity report of Einsatzgruppe A for November 1941 the situation in the whole of Reich Commissariat Eastland is described thus: 'The Jewish question in the Eastland should be regarded as solved. Large-scale executions have decimated the Jewish population and the remaining Jews have been ghettoized. Special measures have so far been necessary only for individual Jews who have been able to escape the grasp of the Security Police.'[142]

The Role of the Local Voluntary Troops (*Schutzmannschaften*)

The murder of hundreds of thousands of civilians in the newly occupied territories during the first months of the war was only possible because the Germans succeeded in recruiting willing executioners for their policies of racial annihilation from the indigenous populations of the areas that had been conquered.

After German agencies had begun to set up auxiliary police formations in the occupied zones during the first few weeks of the war,[143] Himmler gave an order on 25 July 1941 to set up 'voluntary troop formations'.[144] These units were to be made up of Ukrainians, Balts, and Belarusians, but only men who had not been conscripted into the Red Army or non-Communist prisoners of war.[145] At the end of July 1941 the head of the Order Police, Kurt Daluege, decreed that these new formations would be called 'local voluntary troops' or *Schutzmannschaften*, and be run by reliable officers or sergeants from the German police.[146]

In Lithuania and Latvia, such voluntary troop units were formed from the local partisan units and auxiliary formations that had come together in the first phase of the occupation as early as August. Ukrainian voluntary troops can be documented from October 1941; Belarusian and Estonian from the beginning of 1942.[147] According to the head of the Order Police, Daluege, at the end of 1941 there were in the Reich Commissariat Eastland 31,652 local volunteers and 14,452 in the Ukraine. In the course of 1942 these forces would grow to a strength of more than 300,000. Such troops therefore became one of the most important organs of containment and repression within the German occupying forces and played an indispensable role in the persecution of the Jews.[148] Whilst these bodies were initially recruited exclusively from volunteers, during 1942 more and more pressure was put on the male members of local populations to join these units.[149]

Usually a distinction was made between local volunteer troops on individual duties (in other words attached as auxiliaries to the local German police authorities) and battalions of volunteer troops,[150] which were mobile reserves that were often deployed outside their local areas.[151] In addition to guard and containment duties volunteer troops were mainly deployed in mass executions of Jews and Communists, or for 'cleansing' and partisan 'operations' whose victims were usually Jews who were under general suspicion as 'supporters of armed gangs'. There is detailed documentation for the participation of Lithuanian Volunteer Battalion no. 12, which was under the immediate command of the German Reserve Police Battalion 11, in the mass murders perpetrated by this unit in Belarus—and in particular for its participation in the massacres of Smilovichi, Rudensk, Koydanava, and Slutsk in October and November 1941.[152]

Murders of the Mentally Ill, Gypsies, and 'Asians'

The mass murder of the Jews in the newly occupied areas is at the heart of policies of racial annihilation, but other groups also fell victim to them, notably the mentally ill, the Gypsies, and so-called 'Asians'.

As had been the case in Poland in 1939 and 1940, the inmates of medical and care institutions in the newly occupied areas were also murdered in huge numbers.[153] Murders of this type can be documented for all four *Einsatzgruppen*. Einsatzgruppe A, for example, murdered patients in a Lithuanian asylum in Aglona on 22 August 1941 (claiming 544 victims),[154] in asylums in Mariampole (also in Lithuania) and Mogutovo, near Luga (with 204 victims in total),[155] and in mental homes in Riga and Jelgava (Mitau), where 237 mentally ill Jews were murdered.[156] Einsatzgruppe B also participated in such murders, as the incident report of 9 October 1941 indicates: 'in Chernigov the mad will be treated in the usual way. In Minsk 632 mentally ill patients were given special treatment, and in Mogilev 836.'[157]

After September 1941, Einsatzgruppe B, under the command of the head of the Reich Criminal Bureau Artur Nebe, began to look for alternative methods for murdering the inhabitants of the asylums. In Minsk there was an attempt made by the Institute for Criminological Technology in September to use explosives to murder the inmates; shortly afterwards in Mogilev asylum inmates were murdered using vehicle exhaust fumes. On the basis of such experiments those responsible made a decision to use gas as the method of choice, which, as part of the 'euthanasia' programme, had already been responsible for the deaths of tens of thousands of people. Gas vans such as those that had been deployed by Sonderkommando Lange in the Warthegau since the beginning of 1940 were now commissioned for use in the occupied Eastern areas. The murder of the mentally ill in Mogilev using gas in October 1941 is an important step in the transfer of killing techniques that had been developed in the context of the 'euthanasia' programme to the systematic murder of the Jews.[158]

All the commandos of Einsatzgruppe C can also be shown to have murdered the sick. In September 1941, at the request of the local commander's office in Vasilkov, Sonderkommando 4a shot 200 Jews but also a number of mentally ill women; a sub-commando of the same unit shot 270 mentally ill patients on 24 October in Chernigov,[159] Sonderkommando 4b shot 599 inmates from the Poltava asylum at the beginning of November,[160] and Einsatzkommando 5 murdered 300 mentally ill Jews on 18 October in Kiev.[161] The incident reports say of Einsatzkommando 6 that 'by 12 November 1941' it had shot '800 of a total of 1,160 mentally disordered inmates of the asylum of Igrin near Dnepropetrovsk.[162] Murders of asylum inmates by Einsatzgruppe D during 1942 are widely documented.[163]

Prisoners of war and civilians who in the eyes of the *Einsatzgruppe* troops had an 'Asiatic' appearance also fell victim to the policies of annihilation.[164] The Soviet Commissars had already been described in the 'Guidelines for the Treatment of Political Commissars' as 'the originators of barbarian Asiatic methods of combat',[165] and the 'Guidelines for the Conduct of troops in Russia' had read, 'the Asiatic soldiers of the Red Army in particular are inscrutable, incalculable, guileful, and unfeeling'.[166] Behind the National Socialist stereotype of the 'Asiatic' enemy was the image that large sections of the originally Slavic peasant population had been extirpated by the Soviet regime whilst, as a result of 'intermingling' with Asiatic or Mongolian races, the remainder of the population represented a worthless but latently dangerous 'sub-humanity' that 'the Jews' dominated with the help of Bolshevist ideology. The danger supposedly emanating from this conglomerate was elucidated by Himmler speaking in July 1941 to soldiers from the Waffen-SS. According to Himmler, in the East 'the same struggle against the same sub-human peoples, the same inferior races' that have sometimes gone 'under the name of the Huns, at others ... under the name of Magyars, or under the name of Tartars, or under the names of Ghenghis Khan and the Mongols'.[167]

The murder of 'Asiatic' people in the Soviet Union is one of the chapters in the history of the Nazi regime's policies of racial annihilation that have yet to be written. Only a few isolated examples are currently available. The systematic murder of 'Asiatic'-looking people by the *Einsatzkommandos* can be documented from the civilian prisoner camp in Minsk that had been set up by the Wehrmacht in 1941, in which almost the entire non-Jewish male population of military age had been imprisoned.[168] The 'Asiatics' were viewed there with the same suspicion and treated in the same undiscriminating manner as 'Bolshevist functionaries, agents, criminals'.[169] They were shot because their external appearance made them appear to be 'elements of inferior value with a predominantly Asiatic look'.[170] The same blanket justification was given by Einsatzgruppe B, for example, when they shot 83 men from the civilian camp in Mogilev on 15 October 1941. These were said to be 'racially inferior elements with an Asiatic look' that 'it would not be responsible to allow to remain behind the lines any further'.[171]

Gypsies living in the Soviet Union also fell victim to the Nazis' policies of racial annihilation, although they were not pursued with anything like the same merciless determination as the Jews. This was the case in 1941 and also for later periods. *Einsatzkommandos* were shooting small groups of Gypsies on their advance in summer and autumn 1941: Einsatzkommando 3 did so on 22 August, and Einsatzkommando 8 in the second half of September.[172] The group staff of Einsatzgruppe C reported in September that during the previous days '6 asocial elements (Gypsies) and 55 Jews had been dealt with', amongst others, and Sonderkommando 6 reported in October that it had apprehended a 'band of Gypsies' and executed 32 people.[173] The next evidence of the murder of Gypsies is for spring 1942, when large numbers were killed.[174]

The Participation of the Wehrmacht in the Murders

It has already become clear as this part has progressed that the Wehrmacht actively supported many of the 'operations' of the *Einsatzgruppen* and other SS and police units. This prompts the question of how far the Wehrmacht itself played an active and material role in the annihilation of the Jewish population of the Soviet Union.[175] Numerous appeals from officers in the higher echelons of the Wehrmacht show quite distinctly that the ideological war of annihilation against the 'Jewish-Bolshevist complex' was waged with the same intensity within the ranks of the Wehrmacht itself as in the guidelines and orders issued by the leadership at the beginning of the war.

According to an order for Panzer Group 4 of 2 May, the war that was by then imminent was to be 'the age-old battle of the Teutons versus the Slavs, the defence of European culture in the face of a Muscovite-Asiatic deluge, resistance to the onslaught of Jewish Bolshevism'. Every act in battle was to be 'motivated by an iron will to achieve the total, merciless annihilation of the enemy', and there should be in particular 'no quarter given to the proponents of today's Russian Bolshevist system'.[176] The Commander of the 6th Army, Walther von Reichenau, spoke in an order dated 10 August of the 'necessary execution of criminal, Bolshevist, and mainly Jewish elements' that would have to be carried out by the organs of the Reichsführer SS.[177] The Commander of the 11th Army, Erich von Manstein, described 'Jewry' in an order of 20 November as 'the middle-man between the enemy at our backs and the remains of the Red Army that are still fighting on and the red leaders'.[178] The Commander of the 17th Army, Karl-Heinrich von Stülpnagel, gave an order on 30 July not to take indiscriminate reprisal measures against the civilian population but—if the deed could not be pinned on to the Ukrainians—to concentrate on 'Jewish and Communist inhabitants', amongst whom the 'Jewish Komsomol members' in particular were to be 'regarded as perpetrators of sabotage and responsible for forming young people into gangs'.[179]

What effect did orders and guidelines such as these have on the conduct of the troops? This part has already demonstrated a high degree of cooperation between the Wehrmacht on the one hand and the Police and the SS on the other. It was not merely the case that the Wehrmacht was informed in full detail about the shootings perpetrated by the SS and Police formations, as can be shown from the reports reaching intelligence officers.[180] In addition, units of the Wehrmacht supported mass shootings by the Police and the SS in a variety of ways, such as providing transport and munitions, for example.[181] Members of the Wehrmacht took part directly in these 'operations', either sealing off the areas in which they took place or joining the firing squads themselves.[182] Christian Gerlach has provided a number of examples that prove how, during the conquest of Belarus in the summer of 1941, front-line troops made attacks on Jews that sometimes involved carrying out shootings.[183]

Troop leaders sometimes evidently had some difficulty in keeping their soldiers' participation in such executions within the bounds of 'due order'. The fact that the willing participation of soldiers in executions was repeatedly forbidden is an indication of how volunteering in this manner was not merely confined to isolated instances.[184] The same analysis can be made of the numerous orders that were issued by various Wehrmacht formations in the early months of the Russian campaign that forbade the participation of soldiers in pogroms, looting, arbitrary shootings, and other attacks on the Jewish civilian population.[185] That such attacks were part of the everyday reality of war can be demonstrated with a large number of individual examples.[186]

The role of the Wehrmacht in the annihilation of the Jewish civilian population was by no means exhausted by instances of excess such as those, or by isolated examples of support for the SS and Police during executions. Agencies and units of the Wehrmacht, and in particular military intelligence, the security divisions, the Secret Field Police, and the military police as well as local or field command posts, did in fact cooperate so closely with the SS and the Police that one can legitimately speak in this context of a systematic cooperation and division of labour. 'Suspect' civilians—mostly Jews—were routinely handed over to the SD;[187] as the next section will show, the Wehrmacht delivered Jewish prisoners of war and others defined by racist or political criteria, to the SS; *Einsatzkommandos* and police units were requested by offices of the Wehrmacht for 'cleansing' or 'pacification operations', or for 'collective reprisal measures';[188] intelligence officers, the military police and the Secret Field Police made themselves available for 'operations'.[189] In putting anti-Jewish measures such as registration, marking out, and ghettoization into place, local command posts created the structural conditions for the murder of the Jews. In particular, it can be proved that large-scale murder 'operations' in the military zone of occupation were set up and carried out by the relevant local or field command posts of the Wehrmacht in close consultation with SS and Police units.[190] There is some evidence that the military occupation authorities showed a similar degree of cooperation in this respect as the civilian authorities in the areas further to the west.[191]

The role of the Wehrmacht in the annihilation of the Jewish civilian population of the Soviet Union was not limited to the ideological indoctrination of the troops and direct support for 'operations' carried out by the SD and the Police. Substantial formations from the Eastern Army took part directly in the mass murder of Jews within the broader context of large-scale operations. We have already seen that Police Battalion 11 under the 707th Division carried out a 'cleansing operation' in Belarus with the support of the Secret Field Police and the Division's Company of Engineers that claimed several thousand Jews as its victims. The orders of the 707th Division, which are preserved in the State Archive in Minsk, demonstrate that this was not an operation initiated by the SS or Police in which the Wehrmacht merely played a supporting role. This 'operation' was part of a comprehensive approach to annihilation in which the Division played a decisive role.

On 16 October, thus immediately after the end of the 'major campaign' in the area around Smilovichi in Rudensk, the Divisional Commander ordered an increased deployment of patrols by his formation and noted, 'as far as these patrols are concerned, we have to ensure that the Jews are well and truly removed from the villages. We are continually finding that they are the only support that the partisans have for surviving now and over the winter. Their annihilation must therefore be carried out uncompromisingly.'[192]

In his report for the period between 11 October and 10 November, the Divisional Commander (who also had the title 'Commandant in Belarus') noted, 'it has been observed that the Jews often leave their homes and move out into the countryside, probably southwards, in an attempt to escape the operations targeted at them. Because they persist in making common cause with the Communists and partisans, this alien element will be completely eradicated. The operations that have been carried out so far took place in the east of the district rather than in the old Soviet border areas and on the stretch of railway between Minsk and Brest-Litovsk. And in addition, in the area under the Commandant in Belarus the Jews in the countryside will be assembled in ghettos in the larger towns.'[193]

An officer of the War Economy and Armaments Department, who was in Minsk on 25 October 1941 for a meeting, passed on in his report the following suggestion from the First Officer of the General Staff of the Division to his office: 'All Jews and other disruptive elements should be replaced by specialist workers from amongst the prisoners of war.' For the 'security formations' deployed in Belarus 'the only appropriate instructions are those associated with the worlds of Karl May and Edgar Wallace' is how the First Officer [Ia] of the Division characterized the mood prevailing in his unit.[194]

An order to the 707th Division from 24 November is quite unambiguous in this respect: 'As previous orders have already indicated, the Jews must disappear from the flat lands and the Gypsies must also be destroyed. The implementation of large-scale anti-Jewish operations is not the task of units from this Division. These will be carried out by civilian or police authorities, where appropriate on the instructions of the Commandant in Belarus if he has the necessary units at his disposal, or if there are reasons of security or collective measures at issue. Where small or moderate-sized groups of Jews are encountered in the countryside they can either be dealt with at once or brought together in ghettos in the larger towns that have been identified for this purpose where they will then be handed over to the civilian authorities or the SD. Whenever operations of any size are carried out the civilian authorities are to be informed in advance.'[195]

In his report for November, the First Officer of the Division wrote, 'The measures instigated against the Jews as supporters of Bolshevism and leaders of the partisan movement have had noticeable success. We will continue to gather them together in ghettos and liquidate Jews found guilty of partisan activity and rabble-rousing and thereby best promote the pacification of the countryside.'[196] This meant therefore that the 'cleansing' of the 'flat lands' that Reichskommissar Lohse had already ordered in his 'guidelines' for handling the Jewish question on 18 August was a task apportioned between the civilian administration, the Police and SS, and the Wehrmacht.[197] The Wehrmacht combed the 'flat lands' and 'cleansed' them of Jews and Gypsies, which is to say that it liquidated them or transferred them to ghettos. Larger-scale 'operations' were not the responsibility of the Division but fell to the Police; more substantial 'operations' like this could also be carried out by the Division if it had appropriate units at its disposal or if there were particular military grounds for doing so, such as 'reasons of security' or 'collective measures'.

The unit commanders of the 707th Division therefore had fairly broad room for manoeuvre within the scope of these orders. If they encountered Jews in a given town they had three possibilities if they decided not to leave the whole matter to the Police: they could take action against the Jews they encountered either 'for reasons of security', or using the pretext of collective reprisal measures, or within the context of general instructions for 'cleansing' the territory. In the matter of whether the Jews thus encountered should be 'dealt with' by the Division itself or handed over for imprisonment in a ghetto the unit leaders of the 707th Division also had plenty of freedom for manoeuvre.

Whether the operations of the 707th Division aimed at 'cleansing the flat lands' were one component in a programme of annihilation carried out by the other security divisions of the army cannot be stated with complete confidence on the basis of documentary material currently available. There is, however, an indication that the procedures of the 707th Division were by no means to be attributed to an isolated initiative on the part of a single Divisional Commander. As early as August 1941, a Regimental Commander in the 221st Security Division had made his assessment of the situation known to his superiors and it conforms to the pattern of the activities of the 707th: 'The Jewish question must be solved in a radical manner. I suggest the confinement of all the Jews living in the countryside in assembly camps and work camps under guard. Suspect elements must be removed.'[198] The 354th Infantry Regiment also took part in the massacres carried out by Einsatzkommando 8 that ensured that the area around Krupka in Belarus was rendered 'free of Jews'.[199]

There is in addition much evidence that units from the Wehrmacht were taking measures against the Jewish civilian population as part of anti-partisan or reprisal 'operations' in accordance with the distorted image they had been fed of the 'Jewish-Bolshevist complex'. How widespread this practice was—whether it is true that the Wehrmacht was generally a participant in the genocide and acting on the pretext of a war against partisans or of collective reprisals—cannot be established with certainty on the basis of research carried out so far.[200] There is significant evidence that, as the conduct of the war by the military became increasingly brutal overall, there was less and less differentiation between different sections of the population.[201]

Although there is considerable evidence to suggest that the Eastern Army was implicated in the annihilation of the Jewish civilian population—right down to large-scale 'cleansing operations'—it would in my view be inaccurate and inappropriate simply to align the Wehrmacht with the death squads of the Police and the SS without further differentiation. It is much more important to stress precisely the distinctive functions of the Police and the SS on the one hand as bodies inflicting terror and aiming at the annihilation of the Jews and the Wehrmacht on the other as a military organization. At the same time, however, it is vital not to lose sight of the functional interplay of these different remits within the context of the war of annihilation. The basis for the division of functions between the Wehrmacht and the SS/Police is of particular importance here: as a matter of principle the military left the mass murder of Communists and Jews to Himmler's forces. This distinction in principle still pertained even if it was treated very flexibly in practice. Thus, just as formations of the SS and Police could be used for front-line duties, Wehrmacht units and military agencies frequently participated in, and even helped organize, the 'cleansing operations' behind the front line.

In any discussion of how to assess the role of the Wehrmacht in the murder of the European Jews it is important not to underestimate the fact that the division of responsibilities in principle was much more significant than the participation of individual Wehrmacht units in specific 'operations' whose extent is sometimes difficult to ascertain. However, because the Wehrmacht leadership declared itself satisfied with the basic principles of the ideological war and permitted a second war against the civilian population behind its front line, it too, bears the responsibility for implementing the Holocaust.

The Fate of Jewish and Non-Jewish Prisoners of War

From the very earliest stages, the policies for annihilating the Jewish population of the Soviet Union particularly affected the Jewish soldiers of the Red Army. They were amongst those groups of prisoners who were separated out in the camps and liquidated as a matter of course. The relevant orders from the Reichsführer SS have been preserved. In Deployment Order no. 8 from 17 July 1941 Heydrich instructed the commanders of the Security Police in the General Government and the Gestapo in East Prussia to detach special *Einsatzkommandos* to comb the prisoner-of-war camps in those areas.[202] These commandos were to conduct a 'political monitoring of all inmates' and separate out certain groups of prisoners, including state and Party functionaries, Red Army commissars, leading economic figures, 'members of the intelligentsia', 'agitators', and, quite specifically, 'all Jews'.

Heydrich had already come to an agreement with the Prisoner of War Department of the Armed Forces High Command about separating out the different groups of prisoners that were mentioned in the annex to Deployment Order no. 8. The whole tenor of these guidelines is marked by the conception of an ideological war of annihilation; they oblige the commandants of the prisoner-of-war camps to work closely with the *Einsatzkommandos*. The commandants are enjoined in these guidelines to overcome any doubts they might have about international or criminal law or any human considerations: the campaign in the East, they claim, demands 'special measures that must be carried out free of bureaucratic and administrative influence by those willing to accept responsibility'.[203] Neither here nor in any other order from the Armed Forces or Army High Commands is it specifically laid down that the Jewish prisoners were to be handed over to the *Einsatzkommandos*; however, the guidelines were formulated such that the camp commandants were to leave the choice to the commandos.[204]

This order was supplemented by Deployment Orders no. 9, dated 21 July, and no. 14, of 29 October 1941, which instructed the rest of the State Police headquarters in the Reich and the *Einsatzgruppen* in the occupied Eastern areas to detach Sonderkommandos to search the prisoner-of-war camps.[205] Even before such explicit permission had been given, the *Einsatzgruppen* in the occupied Eastern areas had already filtered prisoners out of the camps in large numbers, which would not have been possible without the cooperation of the camp commandants.[206]

The commandos reported the prisoners selected in this way by name to the Reich Security Head Office, which usually ordered their execution 'as inconspicuously as possible'.[207] The prisoners screened out within the Reich were executed in concentration camps, by far the majority in a so-called 'Genickschussanlage', an apparatus for shooting people in the back of the neck disguised as a height-measurement stadiometer. Within the occupied Eastern areas the *Einsatzgruppen* had the right to decide which prisoners would be killed, and the executions were performed by members of the *Einsatzgruppen* or police battalions.[208] There were many occasions, however, on which a prisoner who had already been selected was killed by the guard detail itself.[209] On the other hand, however, there is a whole series of examples that demonstrates how the camp commandants attempted to limit or even prevent the activities of the *Einsatzkommandos*.[210]

The total number of prisoners 'screened' and liquidated in this manner is unknown. Alfred Streim suggests 140,000 victims as a minimum, but estimates that the true total is 'considerably higher'.[211] According to the reports of individual screening operations that have been preserved, amongst what were probably hundreds of thousands of victims of these 'operations'[212] there was a large proportion of Jews. The chronological 'high point' for these operations was the second half of 1941, when the number of captured Red Army members was at its highest and when the policy of 'labour deployment' had not yet been conceived.

From September 1941 onwards, there were also special 'prisoner of war assessment commissions' from the Ministry for the East that screened the camps alongside the commandos from the Security Police. These commissions did not merely attempt to find those amongst the members of certain racial groups whom they might win over as collaborators, they also practised 'negative' selection in that they looked for 'seditious Soviet functionaries, Commissars, Politruks, etc., long-serving professional soldiers in the Soviet Army, Jews, [and] criminal elements'. The prisoners of war seized in this manner had to be reported to the camp commandant for 'appropriate treatment', which meant execution.[213]

However, prisoners of war who had not been identified as Jews, Communists, or members of the intelligentsia and who therefore remained in the Wehrmacht's camps also fell victim in large numbers to the policies of annihilation. Soviet soldiers who had surrendered to German troops were often killed on the spot.[214] There is much documentary evidence to show that this practice was widespread. Numerous orders to Wehrmacht units have been preserved that explicitly demand the taking of 'no prisoners', although there are also orders that appealed to the troops to refrain from indiscriminate shootings.[215] Army Group Centre described the situation in a report from August 1941 which mentions 'the corpses of soldiers lying all over the place after military action, without weapons, with their hands raised and with injuries inflicted from close range'.[216] How widespread this practice was cannot now be reconstructed: soldiers who were shot by German troops after being taken prisoner do not appear in any statistics relating to prisoners of war.

This practice can be attributed to the gradual brutalization of the war, but closer analysis of how prisoners were fed and treated generally shows that the systematic destruction of Soviet prisoners of war was an integral component of German policy towards the Soviet Union. Congruently with the hunger strategy that the German leadership proposed from the very beginning of the war, the mass of Red Army members captured by the Wehrmacht were never provided with adequate foodstuffs.[217]

Christian Gerlach has reconstructed the decision-making process that led to those responsible on the German side (Goering, Backe, Quartermaster General Wagner, and others) taking the conscious decision, as part of the means of addressing the general food shortages in October 1941, to lower the already meagre rations for non-working prisoners such that their death by starvation was foreseeable.[218] At a meeting on 16 September 1941 at which problems with food supplies were being discussed, Goering said that a reduction in the rations for the German population was out of the question given the 'mood at home during the war', and that, on the contrary, rations should be increased. As a consequence of these priorities, it was unavoidable, he said, that in the occupied areas the level of nutrition would inevitably decline: 'on principle, in the occupied areas only those who are working for us should be fed'. Provisions for 'Bolshevist prisoners' could only be determined 'in relation to their work performance for us'. Put more plainly, this meant that those prisoners who were not working would in future not be fed.[219]

Correspondingly, the rations for prisoners of war were massively reduced by the Quartermaster General in an order dated 21 October 1941.[220] The conclusions implied by this approach were drawn by Quartermaster General Wagner at a heads of department meeting on 13 November 1941: 'prisoners of war in the camps who are not working will have to starve.'[221] On the day after that far-reaching order from Wagner, 22 October, Backe informed Goebbels personally that the levels of sustenance had now reached critical levels; Goebbels's view was that they would have to 'take more rigorous measures in respect of prisoners of war'.[222]

Nutrition levels, living conditions in what were mostly very primitive camps (often they were only fenced-in areas of land where the prisoners had to fend for themselves in holes in the ground or tents), and the long distances travelled on foot or in transports in open goods wagons even in winter—all these factors meant that in the autumn and winter of 1941 the Soviet prisoners of war began to die in huge numbers.[223] Many were killed as a result of indiscriminate use of arms by camp guards, since the Wehrmacht leadership had practically given those detailed to guard the Soviet prisoners carte blanche to use their weapons at will. This is made clear in a quotation from the instruction for the treatment of Soviet prisoners of war of 8 September 1941:

Thus ruthless and forceful intervention is required given the slightest sign of any form of obstructiveness, especially towards Bolshevist rabble-rousers. Obstructive behaviour and active or passive resistance must be thoroughly eliminated via the use of the weapon (bayonet, rifle butt and firearm). . . . With Soviet prisoners of war it is necessary for purely disciplinary reasons to use weapons with particular severity. Anyone who fails to use his weapon in carrying out an order, or who uses it with insufficient force, is liable to punishment.[224]

After the German leadership had taken the decision in October 1941 to use prisoners of war as forced labour, this did not initially have any direct effects on the situation of most prisoners. Only a minority of prisoners of war were deployed for work[225] (in March 1942 there were only 167,000; this figure rose to reach 488,000 in October). Improvements in nutrition and accommodation for the prisoners only filtered through very gradually. The change of direction therefore came too late for most prisoners: on 1 February 1942 almost 60 per cent of the 3.35 million Soviet prisoners of war who had been captured by then had died.[226] By the end of the war the situation had not improved significantly, even though more efforts were being made from summer 1943 onwards to use Soviet prisoners for work details. Of the 5.7 million Red Army members taken prisoner by the Germans during the war, approximately 3.3 million died.[227]

Conclusion

This part has described the inconsistent process taking place over several months during 1941 whereby a transition occurred from a restricted mode of terrorism aimed mainly at Jewish men of military age to a strategy of ethnic annihilation. The decisive turning point that initiated this transition was the mass shooting of women and children by units and formations of various types; this began as early as July and August. It should be remembered, too, that, even in the period before this point, when operations were mostly directed against men, there was no ban in principle on shooting women and children, too. Jewish women were shot by SS and Police formations from the very earliest days, singly or in small groups, if they were seen as in any way 'suspect' (i.e. likely to be 'agents' or 'active Communists'). There is a large quantity of evidence to show that the shooting of women increased in the second half of July and that, alongside this shift in practice, some children were also being shot.

It was not the *Einsatzkommandos*, however, but other SS and Police units that moved over in late July to the systematic shooting of Jewish women and children not suspected of any misdeeds but targeted merely because they were Jews. The two SS Brigades played a precursor role in this. The 1st SS Brigade reported at the end of July that 800 'Jews, male and female, aged between 16 and 60' had been shot, and a few days later, that 275 Jewish women had been shot between 3 and 6 August. In total the Brigade is thought to have murdered 7,000 Jewish people by the middle of August. It can also be established that two Police battalions, Battalions 45 and 314, carried out the execution of a larger number of women and children before then, in July. All these units were under the command of Higher SS and Police Commander for Russia South, Friedrich Jeckeln, under whom the massacre of 23,600 Jews in Kamenetsk-Podolsk took place at the end of August. This mass murder can be described as the initial spark for igniting systematic genocide in the area under the Higher SS and Police Commander for Russia South. It primarily affected commandos in Einsatzgruppe C, but those in Einsatzgruppe D were also affected.

The 1st Regiment of the SS Cavalry Brigade, which was under the Higher SS and Police Commander for Russia Centre, reacted to Himmler's brutal orders by shooting women and children from early August on, indeed in some places the entire Jewish population of a town. The 2nd Regiment initially restricted executions to Jewish men, but from early September women and children were also amongst their victims. But it was not only the inclusion of women and children amongst those shot but the extraordinary number of the victims of the Brigade— some 25,000 people by the middle of August—that led to the general radicalization of the process of murder amongst the units in the area under the Higher SS and Police Commander for Russia Centre, in the course of which police battalions and *Einsatzkommandos* also significantly extended their murderous activity.

In a series of cases it can be proved that the *Einsatzkommandos* that had been instructed by group staff to increase their rate of murder started shooting women and children in places where earlier 'cleansing operations' had already claimed the men as their victims or had caused the men to flee. In the case of Einsatzkommando 9 in Vileyka, for example, it can be shown that the commando leader first cleared it with the *Einsatzgruppe*'s rearguard support before he shot women and children, and Sonderkommando 4a took a few days before deciding to shoot the children who had survived in Bila Zerkva, again with the backing of the Army Commander. Both instances show that there was no clear order to shoot women and children in existence from the very beginning, but that the commandos were confronted with situations by their group staffs, probably quite deliberately, in which they had to decide for themselves what the nature of the task they had been charged with actually was. Einsatzkommando Tilsit also shot women, old men, and children at the end of July and in early August on the Lithuanian border after it had earlier executed the men of military age in the same towns. Einsatzkommando 3 can be shown to have started to shoot women and children in the first half of August. These murders, too, took place in towns where members of the same commando had already shot the men shortly before.

The situation of the sub-unit of Einsatzkommando 3 stationed in the citadel in Daugavpils (Dünaburg) was somewhat different. Between the end of July and the middle of August it executed large numbers of men unfit for work, women, and children and thus proceeded in the same way that would be typical in the months to come for the selection of victims within the ghettos.

There was a different context again for the shooting of women and children in the area covered by Einsatzgruppe D, when members of Einsatzkommando 12 shot several hundred Jewish refugees from a large group who were being driven back over the Dniester into Romanian-controlled territory because they could not keep pace with the marching tempo.

The murderous practice of including women and children in shootings therefore spread amongst the commandos only gradually and not in a uniform manner. One of the two sub-units of Einsatzkommando 8 was already shooting women and children in August, but the other seems only to have taken this step in September. Einsatzkommando 5 also only started to do this in September: by his own admission, commando leader Schulz could not make up his mind to put into practice the order he had received in August. And Sonderkommandos 7a and 7b cannot be shown to have carried out large-scale operations in this period at all.

We can reconstruct the manner in which the order to murder women and children was passed on from the testimonies of various commando leaders. These show that they were orally instructed to include women and children in the murders in August and September by their commanding officers (Filbert and Bradfisch by Nebe; Schulz by Rasch; Nosske and Drexel by Ohlendorf).

With the mass shooting of women and children, the decisive step on the way towards a policy of racial annihilation had been taken. After the various units had crossed this threshold they moved on to 'major operations' (again each at a different pace) that affected the great mass of the Jewish civilian population. These were the comprehensive 'cleansing operations' designed to make whole swathes of the country 'free of Jews', and the mass executions of thousands in the ghettos that had been established in the meantime.

The first such comprehensive 'cleansing operations' are documented for early August in Lithuania, where a few days after it had begun systematically shooting women and children Einsatzkommando 3 dramatically increased its total number of victims. The same can be shown to have happened in Latvia from August (Einsatzkommandos 2 and 3). Similar 'cleansing operations' took place in Belarus, the work divided between Police Battalion 11 and the 707th Division of the Wehrmacht. Einsatzgruppe D followed a similar strategy from the end of August on with Einsatzkommando 12 and Sonderkommando 10b in Transnistria, Einsatzkommando 8 in September in the area around the Belarusian city of Borisov, and Einsatzkommando 5 from September in the Ukraine.

The series of shootings in Daugavpils (Dünaburg) in Latvia at the end of July was followed by further massacres in the Baltic ghettos from September onwards, which claimed thousands of victims. In the area covered by Einsatzgruppe B, after the 1st Cavalry Regiment had already murdered the entire Jewish population of certain places at the beginning of August, early October saw the exhaustive 'major operations' in which all Jews were indiscriminately murdered. In the area under Einsatzgruppe C these 'major operations' began as early as the end of August (Kamenetsk-Podolsk); Einsatzgruppe D started them in mid- to late September (Dubăsari and Nikolayev).

What can be concluded from this is that the range of executions was not extended as a result of a uniform series of orders but within a broad context for the issuing of orders that gave individual units considerable leeway over a certain period and room for manoeuvre that was used by the commandos according to the situations they encountered and based on their own assessments of the position. Factors such as the number of Jews present in the relevant district, the density with which commandos were deployed, collaboration with local forces, the attitude of allies, the degree of ghettoization, labour needs, the occupying forces' need for accommodation, the nutritional situation, and others all played a significant role in the development of the commandos' activities. These factors influenced the decision as to how, in what way and at what speed the two complementary annihilation strategies of 'cleansing' the 'flat lands' and 'major operations' in the ghettos would be implemented. The relatively large leeway that the units enjoyed, however, was reduced from the end of summer 1941: individual instructions, inspections, and such like by the SS leadership began to impose a degree of uniformity on the conduct of commandos to produce a strategy for 'spaces free of Jews'.

The Higher SS and Police Commanders evidently played a decisive role in the transition to a comprehensive racial cleansing, not least because the terrible wave of mass murders that they initiated in August and which reached hitherto unimagined magnitudes effectively meant that they seized the initiative from the *Einsatzgruppe* leadership. The role of the Higher SS and Police Commanders, Himmler's plenipotentiaries, but also Himmler's own indefatigable inspections during this period both point towards the central role that the Reichsführer SS fulfilled in the implementation of this process. A starting point can even be identified: the moment when the 'securing of [the Eastern areas] by policing measures' was made Himmler's responsibility on 17 July. Himmler's political motivation must have been his belief that the radicalization of ethnic 'cleansing' in the East would provide him with his way in to taking on the complete 'reordering' of *Lebensraum* in the East. The long-term utopian plans for a 'new order' in the Eastern areas to be conquered foresaw the need to reduce the indigenous population there by 30 million, and it was intended that they should be implemented, at least in part, during the war. This anticipation of the future was bound to end in the destructive measures that constituted a politics of annihilation.

This all suggests that it is doubtful whether the extension of executions in the occupied Eastern areas in summer and autumn 1941 can be adequately understood using the paradigm of 'coming to a decision, giving an order, carrying the order out' that has its origins in the military. It casts into doubt, too, whether the search for a decisive 'order' which triggered the radicalization of the persecution of the Jews in the occupied areas can constitute an adequate research strategy.

Hitler's fundamental decision of 16–17 July about where responsibility was to lie in the occupied Eastern areas, and Himmler's appearance in Minsk on 14–15 of that month merely represent certain situations in a much more complex process in which decisions and their implementation were intimately linked. The starting point is characterized by a degree of consensus between the decision makers that the persecution of the Jews would indeed be intensified and radicalized as the war progressed. This consensus situation was the basis for instructions formulated in a very general manner and reckoning with the need for subordinates to use their initiative, instructions that were then transmitted via a series of different channels, and which created not a clear-cut command structure but a 'climate of command'. In the first instance, this gave individual initiative considerable room for manoeuvre; later on the whole process was steered and made more uniform at senior leadership level. This is a dialectical process, then, in which the top levels of leadership and the organs implementing decisions radicalized each other. However, each element in this process is essential for putting the whole process into practice, and the process cannot be distilled into a single 'order from the Führer' or one instruction authorized by Hitler.

The reports made by the *Einsatzgruppen* allow us to construct at least an approximate estimate of the number of people murdered in the occupied Eastern areas during the first months of the war. Einsatzgruppe A reported that it had killed 118,000 Jews by mid-October and more than 229,000 by the end of January 1942.[228] Of these 80,000 had been killed in Lithuania alone by mid-October, and by the end of January this figure had reached 145,000; in Latvia the totals were 30,000 by mid-October and 35,000 by January; in Estonia some 1,000 indigenous Jews had been killed by the end of January; in Belarus the figure was 41,000 and in the old Soviet areas within the area covered by the Einsatzgruppe some 3,600 had been killed. Einsatzgruppe B reported 45,467 shootings by 31 October 1941 and in its situation report of 1 March 1942 it noted a total of 91,012 who had received 'special treatment' since the start of the war. The figures for Einsatzkommandos 8 and 9—60,811 and 23,509 respectively—are particularly horrific.[229] The total number of Jews murdered by Einsatzgruppe C was 75,000 by 20 October.[230] Einsatzgruppe D reported on 12 December 1941 that it had shot 54,696 people to date, and on 8 April 1942 the total was 91,678 of which at least 90 per cent were Jews.[231]

These monstrous figures indicate the huge extent of the mass murders but they do not represent precise statistics for the numbers of victims. It is not out of the question that, in order to underline their assiduousness, some commandos reported exaggerated totals or reported the same figures twice. On the other hand, whilst the *Einsatzgruppe* reports contain data on the Jewish victims who had been killed by other units, this information is neither reliable nor complete, especially when one considers the numbers of civilians murdered by units of the Wehrmacht or by the local militias.

Nevertheless, the total number of Jewish civilians killed by the end of 1941 during the first two phases of the persecution of the Jews in the occupied Eastern areas must be of the order of at least 500,000.

PART IV

GENESIS OF THE FINAL SOLUTION ON A EUROPEAN SCALE, 1941

CHAPTER 14

PLANS FOR A EUROPE-WIDE DEPORTATION PROGRAMME AFTER THE START OF BARBAROSSA

Decision on the Final Solution in the Summer of 1941? The Interpretation of Some 'Key Documents'

In parallel with the preparation and escalation of the racist war of extermination against the Soviet Union, from the spring of 1941 onwards a general, gradual radicalization of *Judenpolitik* can be observed within the whole German sphere of influence. Historians dispute whether a key decision to murder all European Jews lies behind this radicalization, and when the decision occurred. Thus the first months[1] of 1941, the summer,[2] the autumn,[3] or even December[4] of the same year are given as possible dates for a 'Führerentscheidung' (decision by the Führer) in the 'Jewish question'; on the other hand there is a tendency to stress more strongly the idea that decisions were made as part of an ongoing process, that no concrete individual decision by Hitler can be assumed,[5] and that there was a series of individual decisions by the dictator that led to an escalation of the persecution of the Jews.[6]

Having already rejected the thesis of a decision to implement the 'Final Solution' early in 1941 or in the spring of that year,[7] we should like now to deal primarily with arguments that may be introduced to support the theory that a decision to murder all European Jews was made some time in the summer of 1941. This thesis still seemed plausible even into the 1970s and 1980s; until that point there were good reasons for holding the view that Hitler had ordered the murder of Jews living in the Soviet Union in the spring or summer of 1941. Both decisions—the one to murder the Soviet Jews and the other to murder the European Jews—seemed inseparably connected or at least closely related in temporal sequence. As we have already seen in the previous chapter, however, the thesis of an early order from the Führer to murder the Soviet Jews is no longer tenable, but must make way for the idea of a gradual and progressive radicalization process that lasted from spring until autumn 1941.

From this sophisticated perspective, Christopher Browning above all has developed a theory based on the idea that the fate of the European Jews was only decided as part of a lengthier decision-making process: Browning proceeds on the assumption that in mid-July 1941, in a state of euphoria about his imminent victory, along with the decision to escalate the extermination policy in the Soviet Union, Hitler set in motion the decision-making process that led to the extension of the 'Final Solution' to the Jews in the rest of Europe. Then, in mid-September 1941, along with the decision in principle to deport the German Jews, but still with reservations, he had agreed to the murder of the deportees, and in October, once again filled with the euphoria of victory, a start had been made on putting this decision into action. Thus, for Browning, the events of the summer and the late summer are of the greatest importance.[8]

In my view, however, there is no convincing documentary evidence for the thesis of one or indeed of several decisions by the Führer in the spring and/or summer of 1941. Thus Heydrich's 'authorization' issued by Goering on 31 July 1941 is certainly not, as some authors assume,[9] the crucial authorization of the head of the RSHA to carry out an order already issued by Hitler to murder the European Jews. In the letter Heydrich was not given the task of implementing the 'Final Solution'; in fact, Heydrich asked Goering, who had had formal responsibility for the 'Jewish question' since 1938, and had put Heydrich in charge of emigration in January 1939, to sign a declaration drafted by him.[10] This authorized him 'to make all necessary preparations from an organizational, functional, and material point of view for a total solution of the Jewish question within the German sphere of influence in Europe' and he received the task of presenting an 'overall draft' for the corresponding 'preparatory measures'.[11]

The formulation contained in this authorization, that where 'the competencies of other central authorities are affected by these matters, they are to be involved', must have referred in particular to Rosenberg's Eastern Ministry. For, once before, in late March 1941, it had proved impossible to implement Goering's authorization because the competencies of Rosenberg, already designated as Eastern Minister, had not been clarified.[12] But now a formula had been found that took Rosenberg's responsibilities into consideration.

This makes it clear that the preparations for the 'total solution' entrusted to Heydrich were to take in the occupied Soviet territories, and hence at first the planned mass deportation of the European Jews to the East.[13]

In fact Heydrich was not to make use of his authorization until November 1941, when he issued invitations to the Wannsee Conference and included a copy of the letter signed by Goering in the invitation. Heydrich's 'empowerment' was thus primarily a formal 'legitimation designed for third parties'[14] and not the commission to implement the 'Final Solution'.

Neither is there any evidence to sustain Richard Breitman's thesis that in late August, a few weeks after Heydrich's 'authorization' by Goering, a fully elaborated 'plan' by Heydrich to murder the European Jews with gas had been authorized by Himmler. The entry for 26 August 1941 in the diary kept by Himmler's adviser, on which Breitman relies, actually refers to the authorization of a 'travel schedule' for Heydrich. The head of the Security Police intended to fly to Norway.[15] Likewise, Tobias Jersak's thesis that Hitler had made a decision in mid-August to murder all European Jews in direct response to the Atlantic Charter can be seen as speculative and relatively easy to refute.[16]

The statements of two major perpetrators, Adolf Eichmann and Rudolf Höß, referring to a 'decision by the Führer' concerning the murder of the European Jews in the summer of 1941, are also highly questionable. Höß made the following statement on the subject in a memorandum he wrote in Cracow prison in November 1946:[17] 'In the summer of 1941, I cannot at present give the precise moment, I suddenly received an order to see the Reichsführer-SS in Berlin, issued by his adjutant's office. Contrary to his usual custom, he revealed to me, without the presence of an adjutant, in broad terms the following: the Führer had ordered the Final Solution of the Jewish question, we—the SS—were to implement this order. The existing extermination sites in the East are not capable of carrying out the intended major actions. I have therefore selected Auschwitz for this purpose, firstly because of its favourable location in terms of transport requirements, secondly the area selected there is easy to close off and disguise. I had at first sought a senior SS-Führer for this task; but in order to avoid difficulties of competence from the outset, this won't happen, and you will perform this task' In fact the time mentioned, 'summer 1941' cannot be accurate, because the 'existing extermination sites in the East' did not yet exist at that point.[18]

Höß's further statements, that 'shortly afterwards' or, as he stated in April in Nuremberg, 'around 4 weeks later'[19] Eichmann visited him in Auschwitz, are plainly false. Some further particulars of that visit as described by Höß indicate the spring of 1942; possibly Höß is also conflating memories of various visits by Eichmann to Auschwitz. There are also indications that Höß is confusing the summer of 1941 with events in the summer of the following year.[20] But if we must assume such confusion in Höß's memory, he ceases to be a reliable witness for a 'Führerbefehl' issued in summer or autumn 1941.[21]

Eichmann in turn said under questioning in Jerusalem: 'In June, I think, it was the start of the war, June or July, let's say July, the start of the war. And it might well have been two months later, it could also have been three months later. At any rate it was late summer. I'll tell you why I know it was late summer when Heydrich summoned me to him. Called me, and he said to me: the Führer, all those things about emigration and so on and so on, with a little speech before-hand: "The Führer has ordered the physical extermination of the Jews."... And then he said to me, Eichmann, go and see Globocnik, Lublin... The Reichsführer has already given Globocnik the relevant instructions, and take a look at how far he has got with his plans. I think he's using the Russian tank trenches here for the extermination of the Jews.'[22]

He had then, Eichmann continued, gone to Lublin and travelled on from there with Globocnik's Jewish expert, Hans Höfle, to look at the construction of an extermination camp in wooded grounds, the name of which he was unable to remember. The construction was explained to him by a captain in the Schutzpo-lizei, who can be unambiguously identified as Christian Wirth, the first camp commandant of Belzec and later inspector of 'Aktion Reinhard': they visited two to three wooden cottages still under construction, and Wirth explained that the plan was to kill people with exhaust fumes from a submarine engine. Eichmann told this story over the course of the years in various and slightly differing versions.[23]

Christopher Browning above all has relied on this statement, which he sees as confirmation that in mid-September 1941, along with the decision to deport the German Jews, Hitler had given the order to murder the deportees in principle, but still with reservations.

But for two reasons Eichmann's statement does not usefully support the thesis of an order from the Führer for the murder of the European Jews in the summer of 1941. For one thing, his chronology of events is incorrect. He reports that he had seen the extermination camp under construction at a time when the trees 'were still in the full glory of their leaves', which indicates a time no later than October;[24] we know, however, that the construction of the first extermination camp at Belzec (in the district of Lublin) did not begin until 1 November, and most importantly Wirth was only transferred to Globocnik in December.[25] The minutes of the interrogation show that Eichmann himself was unsure about the date and place of the meeting. In the course of his questioning he concedes that it might have been Treblinka, and later he is even certain of it. That would mean that the journey did not take place until the spring of 1942 or, which is more likely, that he was transferring impressions of a later journey to Treblinka to his visit to Lublin.[26] His description of the places in dense woodland also seems rather to indicate

Treblinka. While in his interrogation he described the construction of wooden barracks, he later remembered 'cottages' like the ones used in Auschwitz for the first gas chambers.[27] He always described—also on another occasion—his meeting with Wirth in the context of other visits to other concentration camps and murder centres, but was uncertain about the dating and sequence of those journeys. Thus he remembered visiting Chelmno after his meeting with Wirth, saying it had been cold but no longer winter. As the first murders in Chelmno took place in December 1941, that visit cannot have been in 1941, but must have taken place in the spring of 1942 at the earliest, as Eichmann himself concedes.[28] His subsequent visit to Minsk, where he witnessed a shooting, would then have occurred in the spring of 1942, as Christian Gerlach has suggested.[29] His account of being sent to Auschwitz by Heydrich around four weeks after the issuing of the Führer command, where he visited the gas chambers in the so-called 'bunkers' (converted farmhouses),[30] also shows how confused his memory of the chronology was. These gas chambers were similarly only finished in the spring of 1942. His memories of these journeys are thus not only unclear, but it is possible that he has conflated various different journeys.

There is also a second argument for mistrusting Eichmann's statements. Eichmann had a fundamental reason for providing the earliest possible date for the journey, and representing it as the consequence of an unambiguous decision on the part of the Führer to murder all European Jews, but at the same time making it appear purely a matter of information.

There is in fact much to suggest that Eichmann was sent to the extermination sites, the destinations of the deportations that he had organized, in order to assess the murder capacity of the camps and then to establish the pace and extent of the deportation. It is also conceivable that the result of his inspection trips was itself the precondition for the decision to begin the deportations on a European scale. At any rate, after the war one would have been able to draw the conclusion from his travels that he played a far more active part in the 'Final Solution' than he, always presenting himself as a subordinate receiver of orders, was prepared to admit. Thus, Eichmann placed great emphasis on representing his journeys as the consequence of an order from the Führer that had already been made. He had to make them appear to have taken place in 1941 and he had to stress that they were not connected to any concrete commissions. But there is much to suggest that he made these journeys predominantly at a later point in time, in the spring of 1942, when the deportations were initiated on a larger scale.[31]

Eichmann's statements are in my view completely unsuited as evidence of a *Führerbefehl* for the murder of the European Jews in the summer or late summer of 1942.

In a critical reading, then, three of the main sources on which research into the reconstruction of the genesis of the 'Final Solution' relied until a few years ago— Goering's empowerment of 31 July 1941 and the statements of Eichmann and

Höß—can no longer be seen as key documents. But in the sections below we will see that entirely different sources, neglected or even unknown in earlier research, can be used to reconstruct the decision-making process that led to the 'Final Solution'.

Reflections on the Fate of the Polish Jews in the Summer of 1941

Various indications suggest that—with the beginnings of the mass murder of the Soviet Jews fresh in their minds—during the summer of 1941 the German occupying authorities in Poland were working on more radical 'solutions' for the 'Jewish question'.

On 16 July the director of SD-Section Posen, Rolf Höppner, sent Eichmann a note in which he had summed up 'various meetings in the Reichsstatthalterei here' (in the immediate entourage of Gauleiter Greiser).[32] In this a series of suggestions for the 'solution of the Jewish question in the Reichsgau' had been made, which in Höppner's view sounded 'to some extent fantastical', but which were feasible nonetheless.

These suggestions included on the one hand the idea of building a camp for 300,000 Jews in the Warthegau. There those Jews who were fit for work were to be put into work gangs; all Jewish women still capable of childbearing were to be sterilized. But Höppner made one other suggestion: 'This winter there is a danger that it will no longer be possible to feed all the Jews. It should seriously be considered whether it would not be the most humane solution to finish off those Jews not fit for work by some quick-acting means. At any rate this would be more pleasant than letting them starve to death.'

Four days later, on 20 July 1941, Himmler commissioned Globocnik, alongside construction and settlement projects, to build a concentration camp for 20,000–25,000 prisoners as well as the expansion of SS and police bases in the district;[33] a few days previously, on 17 July, he had made him responsible for the construction of SS and police bases throughout the whole of the new Eastern sphere.[34]

In the district of Lublin, the territory originally planned as a 'Jewish reservation', Globocnik already maintained a considerable number of labour camps, and in the spring of 1941 was busy having Jewish forced labourers carry out extensive earthworks.

Both of Himmler's commissions to Globocnik were clearly directly connected with the Führer's decree of 17 July, in which Hitler transferred the 'police security of the newly occupied Eastern territories' to Himmler.[35] Globocnik was accordingly the man chosen to establish the district of Lublin as a basis for the future Eastern empire of the SS. Globocnik now had much more room to play with, and he was to use it for the organizational preparations for mass murder.

After the start of the Russian campaign, Governor General Frank saw the deportation of the Jews in his territory as imminent. Hitler had granted him permission for this, on 19 June, even before the start of the war. Frank, therefore, forbade the further formation of ghettos in his territory, which would in future 'be more or less nothing but a transit camp'.[36]

After Galicia had been allocated to the General Government by a decree from the Führer, the following day Frank applied—unsuccessfully—to Lammers for the annexation of the Pripet Marshes as well as the area around Bialystok. By way of justification he said that the 'Pripet Marshes offered the possibility of involving workers usefully in cultivation work on a large scale. As a model for this, Frank must have been thinking about the improvement work in the district of Lublin, for which a large number of Jewish forced labourers had been used.[37] Quite plainly Frank was thinking of realizing the old idea of a 'Jewish reservation', in a territory in which from July onwards thousands of indigenous Jews would be murdered in large 'cleansing actions'. On 22 July 1941 Frank once again referred to Hitler's approval and announced that the 'clearance' of the Warsaw ghetto would be ordered in the next few days.[38]

At this point the planned 'deportation' of the Jews to the 'East' was not—as it was to become only a few months later—a metaphor for the planned mass murder within the General Government; in October, Frank tried to win Rosenberg's agreement for the deportation of the Jews from the General Government.

The Deportation of the German Jews: Preparations and Decisions

On 22 July, in a discussion with the Croatian head of state, Slavko Kwaternik, Hitler reiterated his intention to deport the Jews from the German sphere of influence:[39] 'If there were no Jews left in Europe the unity of the European states would no longer be disturbed. Where the Jews are to be sent, whether to Siberia or to Madagascar, is irrelevant. He would approach every state with this demand.'

However, because of the military situation the Nazi leadership was forced to postpone its original intention of implementing large-scale deportations to the newly occupied territories after the expected victory in the East. On 15 August, at a meeting in the Ministry of Propaganda, which was actually supposed to concern the introduction of a special marking for Jews, Eichmann announced the current state of the deportation plans that he had already talked about in the same place in March.[40] According to this, Hitler had rejected Heydrich's suggestion to carry out evacuations from the Reich during the war; as an alternative, Heydrich now initiated a proposal 'aimed at the partial evacuations of the larger cities'.[41]

On 18 August, Hitler confirmed this information in conversation with Goebbels. The 'Führer' had agreed, Goebbels recorded in his diaries, that the Jews of Berlin should be deported to the East as quickly as possible, as soon as the first transport opportunity presented itself. 'There, in the harsher climate, they will be worked over.' This would happen 'immediately after the ending of the Eastern campaign', so that Berlin will become a 'city free of Jews [*judenfrei*]'.[42] Thus the general prohibition on deportation for the duration of the war—or at least for the duration of the war in the East—was maintained. At the same meeting, however, Hitler had agreed to the introduction of a 'Jewish badge' in the Reich, and with the idea that non-working Jews would henceforth receive reduced rations, because, as Goebbels put it, 'he who does not work, shall not eat'.[43]

Immediately after his conversation with Hitler, Goebbels once more began an anti-Semitic propaganda campaign, in which he pursued the goal above all of preparing Party activists for a further radicalization of the persecution of the Jews, and demonstrating to the general population that they were in a global conflict with 'the Jews'. Thus, a circular from the Reich Ring for National Socialist Propaganda (an internal instruction for Party propagandists) of 21 August 1941 stated: 'Since the start of the Eastern campaign it has been plainly apparent that a large proportion of the population has once more become more interested in and aware of the significance of the Jewish question than in the previous months. None the less it is important that we should draw the attention of the German people still more to the guilt of the Jews.'[44]

The 'weekly slogan' of the Reich propaganda headquarters of the NSDAP for 7 September 1939, a poster that was hung in many Party display cases, contained Hitler's prophecy of 30 January 1939 that the result of a new world war would 'not be the Bolshevization of the earth and thus the victory of Jewry' but 'the extermination of the Jewish race in Europe'.[45]

One central point in this campaign was the polemic against a brochure printed privately in the United States,[46] in which an author by the name of Kaufman had, amongst other things, demanded the sterilization of the German people. Kaufman was now presented as a close adviser of Roosevelt (which was pure invention); the brochure, it was argued, showed the true plans of the American Jews, who had forced Roosevelt to sign the Atlantic Charter. At the same time as its anti-Jewish propaganda campaign, the German propaganda apparatus heightened its polemic against Roosevelt, who was portrayed as a stooge of the Jews and the Freemasons.[47] Hitler's decision to mark out the German Jews in the middle of August 1941, vigorously demanded by Goebbels and other senior Nazis, must also be seen in the context of this intensified anti-Jewish propaganda. The Jews, thus branded as an internal enemy, should, as Goebbels wrote, 'be forced out of the public sphere' and demonstratively excluded from certain goods and services.[48] During these days the general tenor of anti-Semitic propaganda consisted in portraying the radicalization of the persecution of the Jews within the German sphere of influence as a precautionary defensive measure against an omnipresent enemy.

When the anti-Jewish propaganda campaign reached its first climax in September, Hitler revised his decision, only one month old, to veto the deportation of the German Jews while the war was still going on. The explanation for this dramatic step the sources suggest in the first instance is the decision by the Soviet leadership on 28 August 1941 to deport the Volga Germans to Siberia, which had been announced early in September.[49]

Goebbels's diary entry for 9 September makes it clear that the Nazi leadership saw this decision as legitimizing the further radicalization of its policy: 'For the Reich to win, so many countless people must make the severest sacrifices that it should lead us to remain harsh and ruthless, take things to the extreme, and finally erase the word "compliance" from our vocabulary.'

The idea that the long-planned deportation of the Central European Jews was now to be undertaken as 'retaliation' for the Soviet step was demonstrably put about by Rosenberg, who had a suggestion to this effect passed to Hitler on 14 September.[50]

At the same time, presumably on 16 September, the German ambassador in Paris, Otts Abetz, suggested to Himmler that the Jews living in France and the rest of occupied Europe be deported to the occupied Eastern territories. Himmler, who was very intensely preoccupied with the plans for the 'Jewish question' and 'Eastern settlement', responded positively.[51] On 17 September Hitler seems to have talked to Ribbentrop about Rosenberg's suggestion,[52] and on 18 September Himmler informed the Gauleiter in the Warthegau, Greiser: 'The Führer wants the Old Reich and the Protectorate to be emptied and liberated of Jews from west to east as soon as possible. As a first stage I am therefore anxious to transport the Jews of the Old Reich and the Protectorate, if possible this year, to the Eastern territories that have recently come into the Reich, before deporting them further eastwards next spring. I intend to put around 60,000 Jews from the Old Reich and the Protectorate into the Litzmannstadt ghetto—which, as I have heard, has sufficient capacity—for the winter.'[53] Heydrich, who was responsible for this 'Jewish emigration' would approach him at the right time.

However, this letter was preceded by enquiries on Himmler's part concerning possible deportation destinations, which can be traced back to the beginning of September 1941. On the evening of 2 September, following a midday conversation with Hitler, Himmler had talked to the Higher SS and Police Commander (HSSPF) of the General Government, Friedrich Wilhelm Krüger, about 'the Jewish question—resettlements from the Reich'. After it turned out that the General Government was not suitable for this purpose, Himmler had approached Wihelm Koppe, the HSSPF in the Warthegau, who sent him a letter on 10 September dealing with the deportation of 60,000 Jews to Lodz.[54] Hitler's decision to start the deportations even before the victory in the East may in the final analysis have been influenced by interventions by Rosenberg, Ribbentrop, and others. However, he must have become attracted by the idea at the beginning of September, a time when he knew nothing of the imminent deportation of the Volga Germans. It was the military successes which began in September 1941 that made the deportations possible in the first place. To that extent there really was a connection between the course of the war and the radicalization of the persecution of the Jews, even if, in the light of closer analysis of the complex decision-making process, Browning's assertion that in the 'euphoria of war' a major preliminary decision had been made about the 'Final Solution' appears to over-dramatize developments.[55]

After the decision had finally been made to deport the German Jews, , following a meeting with Heydrich, in his diary entry for 24 September Goebbels confirmed his intention to 'evacuate the Jews from Berlin as soon as possible. That will happen as soon as we have sorted out the military situation in the East. They are all finally to be transported [to the] camps set up by the Bolsheviks. These camps were built by the Jews; so what could be more appropriate than that they should now be populated by the Jews.'[56]

In fact the reasons for Hitler's decision to begin the deportation of the German Jews were complex ones. The fate of the Volga Germans only served as a pretext to carry out the plan of a deportation of the Jews living within the German sphere of influence, which had been pursued for two years and had become definitely envisaged for the end of the Eastern campaign.

The first set of reasons is identified in a note by the Eastern Ministry's liaison in Hitler's headquarters, Werner Koeppen,[57] dated 21 September: 'The Führer has so far made no decision as regards reprisals against the German Jews because of the treatment of the Volga Germans. As Ambassador von Steengracht told me, the Führer is considering suspending this measure pending the possibility of America joining the war.' It is not impossible that Koeppen's note reflects the state of the information available to Steengracht, the representative of the Foreign Ministry in the Führer's headquarters, before he learned of the deportation order on 18 September. In that case, Hitler would have decided at short notice to implement the 'reprisal', the deportation, before the USA entered the war. But if we assume that, on 20 September, Steengracht was already aware of the deportation order, then the 'reprisal' could be taken to mean more than the deportation itself.

At any rate, Koeppen's note is a very important indication that the attitude of the United States played an important part in the decision to deport the German Jews. The increasing rapprochement between the United States and Great Britain had reached a crucial stage with the passing of the Land-Lease Act by Congress on 11 March 1941, and in the summer of 1941 signs were accumulating that the USA would soon enter the war: the landing of American troops in Iceland on 7 July, the announcement of the Atlantic Charter by Roosevelt and Churchill during their conference in Placentia Bay (Newfoundland) between 9 and 12 August, followed very attentively by the Germans, and, finally, Roosevelt's declaration, delivered after a further contretemps on the high seas, that the American navy would henceforth fight any warship belonging to the Axis powers that entered waters essential for American defence ('Shoot on sight order').[58]

The tenor of the anti-Jewish propaganda campaign, in which Roosevelt was depicted as a stooge of 'world Jewry', which planned to exterminate the German people, suggests that the Nazi regime established a connection between America's threatened entry into the war and the fate of the Jews under its control. From the very first the regime had seen the Jews within its sphere of influence as potential hostages for the good conduct of the Western powers, an attitude that Hitler had summed up in the 'prophecy' of 30 January 1939 with his threat of extermination. It is also clear that in the summer of 1940 they contemplated the idea of using the Jews, due for deportation to Madagascar, as hostages in order to guarantee the good conduct of the United States.[59]

The argument that the deportations which were now beginning on a larger scale also represented a threatening gesture towards the Western Allies is also supported by the fact that not only was no effort made to keep the deportations secret, but that in fact they were generally implemented in the public eye. Goebbels, who was unhappy with this procedure,[60] issued a directive that foreign correspondents seeking information should be told that the Jews were being sent to the East for 'work deployment'; in internal propaganda, on the other hand, no further information was to be provided about the deportations.[61] The coverage in the international press, which had been reporting these procedures in detail since the start of the deportations, corresponded to Hitler's intention to exert pressure on the United States.[62]

The second set of reasons behind the decision to start the deportations concerned the internal political situation. As a result of the deportations of the Jews from the largest cities of the Reich, which was accompanied by a further intensified anti-Jewish propaganda campaign[63], 'the Jews' were to be named and shamed to the general population as the 'wire-pullers' behind the bombing raids on the German cities. They were to be demonstratively punished for that, while at the same time the inhabitants of those cities immediately benefited from that punishment through the 'liberation' of Jewish apartments.[64] Admittedly the bombing raids in the autumn of 1941 were still—compared with later raids—on a relatively small scale,[65] but in view of the lack of military success in the East they were a major source of unease; and that unease was to to be discharged in anti-Jewish emotions as a form of psychological unburdening. As a result of this, a particular situation came about, whereby, on the one hand, the perception of the public was to be specially directed by anti-Semitic propaganda to the openly implemented deportations, while, on the other hand the propaganda concerning the deportations themselves, their goal, and the fate of the deportees was kept completely silent.

The aerial war gave the regime the excuse to speed up the process of evicting the Jews from their apartments, which had already been intensified in the summer of 1941.[66] It is quite possible that this local policy of displacement had an additional influence on the central decision-making process.[67] But it was only through the specifically National Socialist linking of a housing shortage with 'Jewish policy' (and not, for example, the absence of housing itself), that an 'inherent necessity' (*Sachzwang*) had been created which triggered the displacement policy in the cities.

The linking of deportation and housing must also be seen as an attempt on the part of the regime to popularize the evictions from which many people immediately profited or hoped to profit by means of a certain complicity. The situation was similar with regard to the utilization of household goods from the former Jewish households to the advantage of those who had been bombed out of their houses.

The third collection of motives has to do with the difficulties with which the German occupying authorities in various European countries found themselves confronted in the late summer of 1941. Three months after the start of the war against the Soviet Union the primarily Communist resistance movement began to form and become active against the occupying power. The occupying authorities generally reacted by shooting hostages.

The military commander in Serbia had already begun shooting hostages on a large scale since July.[68] Shootings as reprisals for attacks by the resistance first occurred in France on 6 September, in Belgium on 15 and 26 September, and in Norway also in mid-September.[69] Heydrich, who had been deputy Reich Protector in Prague since late September, even declared a civil state of emergency after taking office, and set up summary courts martial. During the emergency, between 27 September and 29 November, 404 people (men and women) were shot.[70] In Greece the resistance movement also carried out a series of attacks at the end of August and in September.[71]

The escalation of the German hostage policy was expressed in the order issued by the OKW on 16 September concerning the 'Communist resistance movement in the occupied territories'. This decreed that as atonement for one German soldier killed the death penalty for 50–100 Communists must be seen 'as appropriate'.[72]

However, since the National Socialist leadership largely assumed an identity between Communism and Jewry, from their point of view in an increasingly brutal war it was entirely consistent to act more harshly against the Jewish minorities even outside Eastern Europe, if it was assumed that they were primarily the ones offering support to the resistance movement. That the Nazi leadership proved so determined to start the deportations of European Jews in late summer 1941 must, therefore, also be due to the phantom of a Europe-wide Jewish-Communist resistance movement. As we shall see, in the autumn of 1941 various occupying authorities were independently to concentrate the policy of reprisals for attacks by the resistance movement on the Jewish minority: in October 1941 in Serbia, the Wehrmacht began systematically shooting the male Jewish population in 'retaliation' for attacks, and in November in France the military authorities began primarily arresting Jews and Communists rather than shooting hostages.

If the various motives behind the decision to start the deportations are so extraordinarily complex, one thing connected them: in autumn 1941 the Nazi leadership began to fight the war on all levels as a war 'against the Jews'. Above all the leadership proved determined not to be diverted by the course of the war from their original intention, pursued since autumn 1939, to deport the Jews in their sphere of influence to the East and leave them there to their fate.

The implementation of the deportations at first encountered great difficulties. Early in October, the plan to send 60,000 people to the Lodz ghetto met with massive resistance from the head of the Wehrmacht Armaments Office, Georg Thomas[73] and the responsible District President Friedrich Uebelhör, an attitude that was to provoke Himmler's anger.[74] The Lodz ghetto, according to Uebelhör, was not a 'decimation ghetto' into which more people could be crammed, but a 'work ghetto'.[75]

The office of the Reich governor in the Warthegau, Artur Greiser, after negotiations with Eichmann, managed to limit the originally planned number of 60,000 deportees to Lodz to 25,000 Jews and Gypsies. Early in October 1941, the RSHA agreed to deport a further 50,000 people to the ghettos of Riga and Minsk.[76]

On 6 October Hitler announced over lunch that all Jews were to be 'removed' from the Protectorate, not only to the General Government, but 'immediately further eastwards'. At the time, however, this was not possible because of the lack of transport space. At the same time as the 'Protectorate Jews', the Jews were to 'disappear' from Vienna and Berlin.[77]

In Prague four days later, on 10 October, Heydrich announced—in Eichmann's presence—the deportation of the first 5,000 Jews from Prague, and spoke in general terms about the deportations:[78] 'SS Brigadeführer Nebe and Rasch could also take Jews into the camps for Communist prisoners within the area of military operations.[79] This has already been introduced according to SS-Stubaf. [Sturmbannführer] Eichmann.... The Gypsies due for evacuation could be brought to Stahlecker in Riga, whose camp is set up on the pattern of Sachsenhausen.' Hitler wanted 'the Jews to be removed from German space if possible by the end of the year'.

Preparations for Deportations from France and Other Territories under German Control

The example of occupied France makes it clear that the deportation measures resumed in September 1941 very quickly acquired a Europe-wide dimension, that in the wake of these preparations the initiative of the occupying authorities was awakened, and the entire *Judenpolitik* was radicalized in this way.[80]

The number of Jews living in France had increased, particularly through the immigration from Eastern Europe of 80,000 at the end of the nineteenth century, to around 260,000 in 1939.[81] Because of the various war-related movements of refugees, and the forced deportations from Alsace-Lorraine and the German Gaus of Baden and Saar-Palatinate there were—according to German information—in 1941 some 165,000 Jews in the militarily occupied northern zone (around 90 per cent of them in Paris) and around 145,000 in the unoccupied southern zone.[82]

More than half of the Jews living in France were not French citizens, and many who did have French citizenship had acquired it only in the period after the First World War; the liberal naturalization law of 1927 was significant here.[83]

In September 1940 the military government in the occupied zone introduced a (religion-oriented) definition of Jews, had Jewish passports and shops specially marked, and ordered a special registration of the Jews. In particular, this was to serve as the basis for the 'file on the Jews' at the Paris Préfecture, on the basis of which the large-scale arrests in the French capital were carried out. In November 1940 the military government introduced the 'Aryanization' of Jewish property, which was also implemented from July 1941 by the Vichy government.

However, since the summer of 1940, the Vichy government had also passed anti-Semitic legislation which applied to both zones. After July, when people not descended from a 'French father' were dismissed from the civil service, with the introduction of the Statut des Juifs in October the term 'Jew' was defined according to the model of the Nuremberg Laws, and employment bans and restrictions were passed.

In March 1941, at the prompting of the Germans, the Vichy government formed a special Commissariat for the Jews, led by Xavier Vallat, a notorious anti-Semite. In June 1941 the Vichy government introduced a second Statut des Juifs that tightened the definition of Jews and extended the employment restrictions. In November 1941 the Vichy government forced the formation of a single Jewish organization, a national Jewish council, the Union Générale des Israélites de France, which was to serve over the next few years as a transmission belt for the *Judenpolitik* and an umbrella organization for the total welfare of the Jews. As a result of the internment of deportees from Germany, as well as other foreign or 'stateless' Jews, by 1941 there were already over 20,000 Jews in camps in the southern zone.[84]

As early as August 1940, the German embassy in Paris had applied to the military administration to 'prepare for the removal of all Jews from the occupied territory,'[85] and since January 1941 the representative of the Security Police in France had pursued the project of building concentration camps for German, Austrian, and Czechoslovakian Jews.[86]

In April 1941, far-reaching demands were formulated within the military administration, addressed to Vallat, the Commissioner for the Jews in the Vichy government: Jews of non-French nationality were to be expelled, 3,000–5,000 Jews who were particularly 'undesirable' for political, criminal, or social reasons, regardless of their nationality, were to be interned, further anti-Jewish laws were to be passed, and preparations for the emigration of Jews of French nationality were to begin.[87]

On 14 May the first stage in this plan was initiated: on that day, at the instigation of the occupation authorities, the French police arrested more than 3,700 German, Polish, Czech, and Austrian Jews in Paris and interned them in the camps of Pithiviers and Beaune La Rolande. Three months later, between 20 and 23 August 1941, the German occupation authorities, supported by the French police, organized further raids in Paris, in the course of which more than 4,000 foreign and French Jews were arrested and transported to a third camp, Drancy.[88]

During these raids, on 21 August, the resistance movement began to carry out a series of attacks on members of the Wehrmacht. The occupation authorities reacted initially with reprisals against arrested Communists, some of whom were condemned to death by French courts, and some shot by the military authorities, who had declared all the French prisoners in their custody to be hostages. After further attacks in October these retaliatory measures, which had hitherto taken ten lives, were considerably extended at Hitler's prompting. In October the occupation authorities carried out their first mass executions: ninety-eight hostages were executed in retaliation for two further fatal attacks.[89]

The military administration, which thought further mass shootings of French citizens were counter-productive, as they were likely to fan the flames of the resistance, now hit on the idea of connecting the reprisals with the measures it had already begun against the Jews: it deliberately extended the reprisals to Jews and varied the methods used: apart from the shootings, collective fines were to be imposed on the Jews, and a larger number of Communists and Jews transported 'to the East' for forced labour. Thus, from December onwards, Jews and Communists were selected en masse for deportations which, after being initially postponed because of the poor transport situation, were to begin in March 1942.[90]

Two considerations in particular must have had a considerable influence on this decision by the military administration to direct the reprisals deliberately at the Jewish part of the population. On the one hand, even the military saw 'the Jews' at the centre of the Resistance, and thus equated Jews with all forms of anti-German activity, as had occurred on a much larger scale in the East. On the other hand, the military must have speculated that a reprisal directed against Jews, in their eyes a foreign body in French society, would be more easily accepted. In addition, thousands of Jews had already been interned in overcrowded camps, and it was known that their deportation to the East was in any case envisaged in the long term. Bringing these deportations forward and declaring them a 'reprisal' was, from the perspective of the military administration, merely anticipating the 'emigration' of the French Jews, which had been planned in any case.

On the other hand, however, through this linking of reprisals and deportations the military administration provided the RSHA with an excellent legitimation for the start of the deportations, which could now be described as a deportation of particularly dangerous elements who had been imprisoned a long time previously. It thereby joined the many institutions which had, in the second half of 1941, urged an acceleration of the deportations and thus contributed to a radicalization of the persecution of the Jews. It also appears remarkable that, by concentrating reprisals against Jews, the German military in France was assuming precisely the attitude adopted by the military administration in Serbia at the same time.[91] If we also take into account the indiscriminate murder of the Jewish population in the occupied Soviet territories in the autumn of 1941 (word of which spread quickly in Wehrmacht circles, through personnel transfers etc.), the attitude of the military in Paris does not seem coincidental.[92]

However, in August 1941—at the time of the large-scale anti-Jewish raids in Paris—the expert on Jewish affairs at the German embassy and its contact with the SD, Carltheo Zeitschel, had begun to present his ambassador with increasingly radical suggestions for the 'solution of the Jewish question'. After a suggestion that all Jews under German rule be sterilized,[93] on 22 August he requested that Jews from the whole of Europe be deported to the occupied Eastern lands, as 'it was anticipated that a special territory was being created for indigenous Jews'. Zeitschel asked the ambassador, Otto Abetz, to present this idea to Ribbentrop and ask him to discuss this project with Rosenberg and Himmler. Zeitschel knew that the latter was 'at the moment very receptive about the Jewish problem', and, 'given his current attitude and in the light of his experience of the Eastern campaign, could provide extraordinarily strong support for the implementation of the idea that has just been developed'.[94]

On 16 September, Abetz met Himmler and the latter agreed, as Zeitschel had suggested, to the eastward deportation of the Jews interned in occupied France as soon as the necessary means of transport were available.[95]

Zeitschel's request reached Himmler when the decision to deport the Central European Jews was immediately imminent. The same day, according to his diary, Himmler discussed the subjects 'Jewish question. Resettlement to the East' with Ulrich Greifelt, the chief of staff of his agency for the Strengthening of the German Nation, and with Konrad Meyer, his Chief of Planning for Eastern Settlement. Also, on the same day, Abetz met Hitler, who on this occasion held forth in extravagant and extraordinarily brutal fantasies about the configuration of his future empire in the East.[96] At the same time, as we have already said, Hitler had been presented with Rosenberg's suggestion for the 'deportation of all the Jews of Central Europe', which he presumably discussed with Ribbentrop on 17 September. Also, on 18 September, at Hitler's request, Himmler informed Greiser about the imminent deportation of 60,000 Jews to Lodz.[97]

Apart from Himmler's ready undertaking to Abetz to deport the Jews in France as well, various indications suggest that, in the eyes of the Nazi leadership, the beginning of the deportation to Lodz actually represented the starting point for the launch of the long-planned deportation of all Jews within the German sphere of influence to Eastern Europe.

On 20 October 1941 Himmler made an offer to the Slovakian head of state to deport the Slovakian Jews to Poland.[98] Heydrich, in turn, explained in a letter to the army Quartermaster General on 6 November 1941, that a series of bombings of Paris synagogues on the night of 2 to 3 October was carried out by a French anti-Semitic group with the consent of his Paris office. Permission had only been granted for this after he had heard 'from the top as well—expressed in the strongest terms—that Jewry was identified as the responsible arsonist in Europe, who must vanish from Europe once and for all'.[99] On 4 October, at a meeting in the Eastern Ministry, Heydrich warned that Jews would continue to be claimed to be indispensable workers. This, according to Heydrich, 'would scupper the plan for a total resettlement of the Jews from our occupied territories'.[100] The Foreign Ministry's Jewish expert, Franz Rademacher, still assumed in a letter of October 1941 that those Serbian Jews who survived the reprisals of the Wehrmacht 'would be deported along the waterways to the reception camps in the East', as soon as 'the technical possibility' for this existed 'within the context of the total solution of the Jewish question'.[101]

A further reference to the planned extension of the deportation programme is contained in a note from Hitler's army adjutant, Major Engel, concerning a meeting in the Führer's headquarters on 2 November 1941, in which, amongst others, Hitler, Himmler, and General Jodl took part. According to this note, Himmler spoke of the 'displacement of those of other races (Jews)', in this context mentioning Riga, Reval (Tallinn), and Minsk as 'main points' and stressed the Jewish population of Thessaloniki as a particular source of danger; a series of assassinations had in fact occurred in the Thessaloniki area. Hitler had agreed with him and demanded 'that the Jewish element be removed from T' and went on to issue the special powers Himmler had demanded. In fact, however, the deportation of the Jews from Thessaloniki would not occur until 1943.[102] Finally, Christopher Browning has drawn attention to reports by a Dutch SS informant, according to which he was already aware early in December 1941 that the deportation of the German Jews, also to Eastern Poland, which 'meant a partial extermination of Jewry', would occur the following spring.[103]

Overall, this chapter presents us with the following picture: in September and October 1941 Hitler made the decision that there should be extensive deport-ations from the German-dominated sphere, particularly from Central and Western Europe. On the other hand, there are no unambiguous indications that at this point—beyond general ideas of a physical 'Final Solution'—there was already a concrete plan in existence for the systematic murder of these people in the immediate future. The combination of the deportation machinery with the killing technology already familiar from the 'euthanasia' programme to form a programme of systematic extermination would not occur until the spring of 1942. The construction of gas killing chambers in Chelmno, Belzec, Auschwitz, and other places did also begin, like the major deportations, in the autumn of 1941, but all of these projects originally had a regional connection.

CHAPTER 15

AUTUMN 1941: THE BEGINNING OF THE DEPORTATIONS AND REGIONAL MASS MURDERS

The Preconditions are Created: The End of 'Euthanasia' and the Transfer of Gas Killing Technology to Eastern Europe

The transfer to Eastern Europe of the gas killing technology developed in the context of the euthanasia programme since 1939 occurred in parallel with the start of the deportations. The crucial precondition for this was that on 24 August 1941 Hitler ordered the ending of the 'Euthanasia' programme.[1] Moreover, this decision was not made abruptly or spontaneously, but was generally expected by the Nazi leadership.

The suspension of the euthanasia action plainly occurred because the Nazi regime wished to avoid provoking further agitation among the population by murdering sick people, but it tellingly occurred at a moment when the original quota of 70,000 murdered patients had been reached. While in the first months of the T4 programme, a higher percentage of patients from institutions had been murdered than originally planned, and in the autumn of 1940 the planned figure had risen from 70,000 victims to between 130,000 and 150,000, in 1941, in the face of mounting protests and growing agitation about the murders among the population, the planned goals of the programme had to be lowered again, to 100,000 patients initially.[2]

When the euthanasia action spread to the three provinces of Hanover, the Rhineland, and Westphalia in the summer of 1941, and church protests increased, the programme was further restricted until it was finally suspended.[3]

The governor of Westphalia, Kolbow, mentioned as early as July 1941 that the action would end in two to three weeks.[4] On 22 August Goebbels noted, about a discussion with the Westphalian Gauleiter Alfred Meyer, in which they had both talked about the 'Church situation':[5] 'Whether it was right to get involved in the euthanasia question on such a scale as has happened in the past few months must remain a moot point.' At this juncture Goebbels assumed that the mass murder of patients was to cease: 'At least we can be glad that the action connected with it is coming to an end. It was necessary.'

However, in the summer of 1941 the T4 organization had initiated a follow-up programme: the systematic killing of concentration camp prisoners who had been selected by medical commissions in the camps. As early as the spring of 1941, in response to a query from Himmler,[6] the T4 organization had begun to deploy medical commissions in four concentration camps. By the autumn they had selected 2,500 prisoners and handed them over to the 'euthanasia' killing centres.[7] Immediately after the end of the T4 action in August 1941, the second, much more extensive phase of the action, carried out under the abbreviation 14f13, began in September: by November the medical commissions had selected a total of 11,000–15,000 people, who were murdered in the killing institutions of the T4 organization.[8] In the same period part of the T4 organization was deployed for a 'special task'—which cannot be more precisely reconstructed—in the occupied Soviet territories,[9] and it was only after this second part of Action 14f13 was concluded that the T4 staff were used on a larger scale from March 1942 within the context of the 'Final Solution' in Poland.

What is remarkable in our context is the close temporal link between the end of the first euthanasia action in August in the context of T4 and the decision to deport the German Jews in September, as well as the concrete preparations for other mass murders of Jews in other territories under German occupation, or their start in October 1941. While in view of the fact that the euthanasia programme had become public knowledge, the regime did not want to hazard any further agitation among the population and stopped the T4 programme, they would respond to certain expressions of displeasure prompted by the introduction of the Jewish star in September 1941 with increased repression and intimidation.[10]

The starting point for the deployment in Eastern Europe of the killing technology already used in the context of the euthanasia programme must also have occurred in August 1941. On a visit to Minsk Himmler is believed to have issued the order to seek killing methods that would put less of a strain on the perpetrators, SS men and Police than the mass executions.[11] Shortly after this visit Bach-Zelewski, the HSSPF for Russia Centre, tried—presumably in vain—to call Herbert Lange, the leader of the Sonderkommando that had for a long time been murdering patients in gas vans, to a 'presentation' in Minsk.[12] Nebe, the leader of Einsatz-gruppe B and at the same time Chief of the Reich Criminal Police Office, who was also likely to have been present at the meeting with Himmler, turned to the Criminal Technical Institute with a request for appropriate support. Experts from the institute then came to Belarus. After a further attempt to kill mentally ill people near Minsk with explosives had led to terrible results,[13] patients were killed in walled-up rooms with car exhaust fumes introduced from outside in a mental institution in Mogilev as well as in Novinki and Minsk (Himmler had visited the latter on 15 August).[14]

On the basis of these experiences, amongst other things, the decision was made to create transportable gas chambers for the *Einsatzgruppen*. The model for this was one already used by Lange's Sonderkammando to murder Polish mental patients in the winter of 1939/40, except that now, instead of using carbon monoxide from gas canisters the exhaust from the vehicle was introduced directly into the closed vehicle body itself. The requisite conversion of the vehicles was undertaken by the Criminal Technical Institute.[15] Early in November 1941, during an experiment in Sachsenhausen concentration camp, around thirty prisoners were killed in one of these vehicles.[16]

In the occupied Soviet territories the gas vans were first used to murder people around November, early December. By the end of 1941 an estimated total of six of these original-series gas vans was deployed by all four *Einsatzgruppen*.[17]

At around the same time, from October/November 1941, gas vans were also deployed in the murder of Jews in the Warthegau by Sonderkommando Lange. For 8 December there is evidence of the use of gas vans in Chelmno, a gas-van station that had been built in the meantime.[18] In this territory, as already described in detail, they were familiar with this killing technology, since as early as 1940 and again in the summer of 1941 mental institution inmates had been murdered using gas vans.[19]

In parallel with the development of gas vans, however, steps were taken to set up stationary gas chambers in the occupied Eastern territories. There exists a letter, dated 25 October 1941, from the Adviser on Racial Issues in the Eastern Ministry, Wetzel, to Reichskommissar Lohse concerning these preparations. Wetzel was responding to a report from Lohse on 4 October 'concerning the solution of the Jewish question':[20]

With reference to my letter of 18 October I wish to inform you that Oberdienstleiter Brack of the Führer's Chancellery has already declared himself willing to work on the production of the required accommodation as well as the gassing apparatus. At present, the apparatus in question is not available in sufficient numbers. It must first be manufactured. Since in Brack's view the manufacture of the apparatus in the Reich presents far greater difficulties than on the spot, Brack considers it most expedient to send his people, especially his chemist Dr Kallmeyer, to Riga forthwith, and take charge of everything else.

Lohse was to request this staff from Brack. Eichmann had agreed to the procedure: 'According to Sturmbannführer Eichmann, camps for Jews are to be set up in Riga and Minsk to which Jews from the Old Reich may also be sent. At present, Jews are being evacuated from the Old Reich, to Litzmannstadt but also to other camps, before later being sent to the East, if fit for work, for work deployment.' According to 'circumstances ... there is no objection to those Jews who are not fit for work being removed with Brack's aids'. Those 'fit for work, on the other hand, will be transported East for work deployment. It should be taken as read that among the Jews who are fit for work men and women are to be kept separate.'

In fact, however, in Riga it was not gas chambers (described as 'accommodation') that were used but, as mentioned above, gas vans.

The decision to build a first extermination camp in Belzec in the district of Lublin, where murder was to be carried out with exhaust fumes from a solidly mounted engine, may be assumed to have been made in mid-October, and building work began in early November. At the end of 1941, the construction of a second extermination camp in the district of Lublin, Sobibor, may have been prepared.[21] It is possible that in November/December 1941 the installation of a further extermination camp in Lemberg (district of Galicia) was being considered.[22] In fact Brack made staff from the T4 Action available for Belzec, Sobibor, and the camp at Treblinka which was built later—the extermination camps of what would later be known as 'Aktion Reinhardt'. There were around ninety-two people whom Brack sent to the General Government in stages. The basic agreement that this work should go ahead appears to have been made with Himmler on 14 December 1941. In December 1941 Christian Wirth arrived in Lublin, further groups in March 1942, and in June 1942, a time when the systematic murder of the Jews in the districts of Lublin and Galicia had already begun, or was being extended to the remaining districts of the General Government.[23]

While in Belzec, the Warthegau, and the occupied Eastern territories mass murders were in preparation or had already been carried out using engine exhausts, the leadership of Auschwitz concentration camp chose a different path.

Various categories of prisoners were systematically murdered in Auschwitz in the autumn of 1941: Soviet prisoners of war who had already been shot or beaten by guards since first arriving in the summer, also, from the summer of 1941, sick prisoners (as part of Action 14f13), Jewish forced labourers from Upper Silesia who were regularly handed over as 'unfit for work' by 'Organisation Schmelt', and Poles handed over for execution by the Kattowitz Gestapo.[24] The plan to expand

Auschwitz concentration camp to a capacity of 30,000 prisoners was followed, at the end of September 1941, by the order to construct another camp for prisoners of war in Auschwitz and, early in October, its capacity was raised from an initial 50,000 to 100,000 prisoners.[25] In the wake of these measures the camp leadership decided to undertake a far larger number of executions.

To this end, alongside experiments with fatal injections,[26] tests were begun with the poison gas Zyklon B, which had been used in Auschwitz for disinfection since July 1941.[27] It appears that in early September 600 Soviet prisoners of war who had been deemed by a Gestapo commission to be 'fanatical Communists', as well as 250 sick prisoners, were murdered with Zyklon B in a cellar in block 11. Later, presumably in the middle of September 1941, a further 900 Soviet prisoners of war were murdered with the gas after the 'morgue' ('Leichenkammer') in the crematorium had been provisionally converted for this purpose.[28] There is a series of indications that even before the end of the year several smaller groups of Jews were also murdered in Auschwitz with Zyklon B; presumably they were the ones who had been selected from the Schmelt camps as no longer fit for work.[29]

The commandant of Auschwitz, Rudolf Höß, states in his memoir written in Cracow prison that the question of a suitable poison gas was discussed during a visit by Eichmann. However, the dating of this visit is uncertain. Some statements by Höß suggest the autumn of 1941, others suggest a later time, such as the spring of 1942.[30] While he himself was not in Auschwitz, Höß wrote, his deputy used Zyklon B on his own initiative to murder Soviet prisoners of war; later he agreed with Eichmann to use this gas in future.[31] This plainly self-exculpatory account, which, for understandable reasons, was in fact disputed by Eichmann during his hearing in Jerusalem,[32] makes it clear once again that Höß is hardly an ideal witness for the history of Auschwitz concentration and extermination.

In the course of the planned expansion of the camp complex and with regard to the high number of prisoners killed and those who lost their lives in other ways as a result of the disastrous conditions of imprisonment, on 21 and 22 October the construction of a new and considerably larger crematorium facility, consisting of a total of fifteen cremation chambers, was discussed with representatives of the specialist firm Topf & Söhne.[33] The American historian Michael Thad Allen has indicated that there were already plans at this time to incorporate a ventilation system along with the aeration system that was already a standard part of such a facility. He takes this as proof that there were already plans at this point to use the room as a gas chamber because the introduction of warm air—which fundamentally contradicts the task of a 'morgue'—was plainly intended to distribute the Zyklon B more quickly. Aside from this, the plans indicate that the pipes in question were to be cemented in; Allen presumes that they were thus to be protected against damage from victims struggling against death. Robert Jan van Pelt and Deborah Dwork, on the other hand, date the conversion of the 'morgue' into a gas chamber only to September 1942, when the building was already under construction.[34] If we accept Allen's dating—the current state of research does not allow the question to be definitively resolved—one cannot conclude that a decision was made a short time previously (in October 1941) to murder the European Jews. The installation of a gas chamber in the new crematorium corresponded to what had already been done provisionally in the old crematorium; it was nothing really new, and it was primarily used on non-Jewish victims who were being murdered at this time. There was also the fact that time was being taken over the construction of the crematorium: it was not started until August 1942, not in the old camp, but in Birkenau, and the crematorium was finally completed in March 1943. Similarly, it was only in August 1942 that the decision was taken considerably to extend the capacity of the crematorium. It was decided, on the basis of the same plans, to build a second crematorium in Birkenau, which was finally completed in June 1943. Auschwitz played no part in the planning for the murder of the European Jews in 1941; the advocates of a radical *Judenpolitik* seem to have become aware of its potential only in January 1942, in connection with Himmler's order to confine Jews from Germany in concentration camps.[35] Hence, it would be wrong to assume that the conversion of Birkenau camp complex would have gone ahead at full speed immediately after a decision by the Führer in the summer or autumn of 1941 to murder the European Jews.

In November 1941 the same firm, Topf & Söhne, also received a commission to construct a gigantic incineration facility with thirty-two chambers in Mogilev (Belarus). The reason given to the firm was that such a facility was needed for the hygienic removal of corpses because of the great danger of epidemics in the East. As the construction was not completed, the superfluous ovens came to Auschwitz.[36] It is not inconceivable that this planned crematorium facility was actually intended for the construction of an extermination camp in Mogilev, whose function was assumed in the course of the coming months by Auschwitz and the extermination camps in Poland.[37]

Thus, in Auschwitz, in the autumn of 1941—still independent of the plans for the 'Final Solution' that were going on at the same time—various developments were under way which would only a few months later make the camp seem practically predestined to assume a central role in the murder of the European Jews: the expansion of the camp, for which a new purpose had to be found when it proved after a few months that because of the mass deaths among Soviet prisoners of war the original numbers of prisoners would not be reached; the hitherto unparalleled expansion of the capacity of the crematoria; and finally the experiments with poison gas.

Accordingly, late in 1941, preparations were made to construct extermination camps in Riga, in the area around Lodz (Chelmno), in Belzec, and in Auschwitz, presumably in Mogilev near Minsk, and possibly in Lemberg (Lvov).[38] Hence, facilities for mass murder with gas were prepared near all the ghettos that had been selected as destinations for the first three waves of deportation from the

Reich. In Auschwitz they were intended for a large number of predominantly non-Jewish prisoners, and possibly in the district of Galicia to cover the area that was to become an important link to the future colonial territories further to the east. The temporal parallels between the start of the deportations and the preparation and installation of these murder facilities in the autumn of 1941 reflect the planning of the Nazi regime to extend the strategy of *judenfrei* areas, already applied in the Soviet Union, to the Polish territories. In certain regions that were of central importance for the further population displacements planned as part of the racist 'New Order', at least those members of the local Jewish population who were 'unfit for work' were to be exterminated. Parallel efforts by various parties during these months to develop technologies for the mass killing of people with gas are clear indications that preparations were generally under way to carry out mass murders on a large scale in the near future. (In the case of Auschwitz these preparations did not primarily affect Jewish prisoners, but Soviet prisoners of war and sick prisoners.[39]) However, the plans for systematic mass murder among the Jewish population had so far affected only certain regions, and the intention to deport the remaining Jews to the occupied Soviet territories after the end of the war was also a plan for the 'Final Solution', the physical destruction of the European Jews. However, it was a plan that was to be realized in the long term and not primarily through actions of direct murder. At this point, the plans to murder people with gas concerned hundreds of thousands, not millions of people.

The fact that the agents in question had still not received an order by late summer and autumn 1941 to kill all European Jews with gas as quickly as possible, but that this plan only took shape over the course of the next few months, clarifies, amongst other things, the complicated story of the transfer of the murder technology. From 1940 onwards, in the context of the 'Euthanasia' programme, a 'tried and tested' technology and a complex organization for the implementation of mass murder had been developed, which, from August 1941, was available for other purposes. Instead of transferring this well-practised and available apparatus to Eastern Europe in one piece, and deploying it for the systematic murder of the Jews, only part of the staff of the T4 organization was gradually deployed, or even—as in the case of Riga—offered in vain, while with the gas vans an essentially already familiar technology was redeveloped and in Auschwitz completely new purposes were found for the use of Zyklon B. This was a complicated process in which the various agents, SSPF Globocnik, Gauleiter Greiser in the Warthegau, the camp leadership of Auschwitz, as well as the Security and Criminal Police were all clearly working independently and in a largely uncoordinated fashion. All of this shows that in the autumn of 1941 no overall plan for the murder of the European Jews had been set in motion step by step, but that subordinate organizations—albeit within the context of a centrally controlled policy—were largely developing their own initiatives.

At the start of this part we closely examined Eichmann's statements about the journeys he made between the autumn of 1941 and the spring of 1942 to the extermination sites. Even if we have reached the conclusion that these statements cannot be a key source for the dating of the 'Führer's decision' to implement the 'Final Solution', it does seem remarkable that at this crucial time Eichmann, who was responsible for the deportations, visited the places in which extermination camps were built: Belzec, Chelmno, Treblinka, and Minsk. For Lemberg (Lvov), which he also visited, there is also, as we have already described, an indication of the planned construction of an extermination camp. Three of these extermination camps—Belzec, Chelmno, and Minsk—were directly linked with the deportations from the German Reich.[40] Presumably Eichmann's journeys were part of the efforts of the RSHA to coordinate the various initiatives for the implementation of the mass murder programmes in the various regions with the plans of head office.

Administrative Preparations for the Deportations

The RSHA deportation programme for the Jews of the German Reich and the continuing plans for the deportation of Jews from the whole area under German control were safeguarded from late summer 1941 by a series of administrative measures.

One major precondition for the implementation of the deportations was the visible identification of Jews. But the introduction of the yellow 'Jewish star' on 19 September 1941, which German Jews had to wear visibly on pain of punishment, was primarily motivated by the wish more easily to exclude the Jews from certain locations, from the purchase of certain goods, and from the acceptance of certain services.[41] This form of identification had already been carried out for a long time by various offices within the Third Reich.[42] In August 1941 Goebbels took up this project, which was also pursued at the same time by other senior Nazis,[43] with renewed vigour. By marking out the Jews as an 'internal enemy' he hoped to lend additional weight to a propaganda campaign designed to inculcate in the population an understanding that Germany was in a global conflict with 'the Jews'.[44] After agreement had been reached concerning the identification of the Jews at an inter-ministerial meeting in the Propaganda Ministry on 15 August,[45] on 17 August Hitler granted Goebbels permission for this identification,[46] which was ordered on 5 September by police decree.[47]

The decree of 3 October 1941 concerning the employment of Jews[48] as well as the Implementation Order of the Reich Minister of Labour on 31 October[49] followed the trend of withdrawing almost all kinds of employment protection from those Jews still in work. On 23 October, at a meeting with Eichmann and Lösener, representatives of the Economy and Armament Office of the OKW won the agreement that the Jews still in 'closed work deployment' would not be deported for the time being.[50]

Early in November 1941 the Reich Finance Ministry passed regulations about the removal of the property of 'Jews who are due for deportation to a town in the Eastern territories within the next few months'.[51] The relatively complicated procedure for property removal set out in this decree was considerably simplified by the Eleventh Implementation Decree of the Reich Citizenship Law passed on 25 November:[52] a Jew 'whose normal residence is abroad' (that is, 'who resides there under circumstances which show that he is not only temporary staying there') would lose German citizenship. His property 'falls to the Reich with the loss of his citizenship'. According to a supplementary ruling by the Reich Ministry of the Interior in December, 'abroad' referred to all occupied territories, particularly the General Government and the Reichskommissariats of Ostland and Ukraine.[53]

On 18 October Himmler discussed the planned emigration ban in a telephone conversation with Heydrich.[54] Finally, on 23 October a decree from the RSHA in Himmler's name generally prohibited the emigration of Jews from the German sphere of influence; exceptions from this general prohibition were, however, allowed.[55]

While these administrative measures affected the Jews in the Reich, the ban on the emigration of Jews issued in October 1941 already affected all Jews within the German sphere of influence.[56] Two memoranda from the head of the German department in the Foreign Ministry, Martin Luther, mark the period in which a basic decision against further emigration must have been made. On 13 October Luther noted that the suggestion of deporting Spanish Jews residing in France to Spanish Morocco was 'a suitable contribution to the solution of the Jewish question in France'. Four days later, however, on 17 October, Luther maintained that the RSHA had opposed this deportation 'because of the measures to be taken after the end of the war for the fundamental solution of the Jewish question'.[57] The decision to ban emigration was thus made at precisely the same time as the deportation of the Jews from the Reich began. It was a crucial precondition for the existing plan of the total deportation of all Jews under German rule to the occupied Eastern territories *after the end of the war.*

Immediately after the emigration ban the Germans began to put in place the necessary preconditions to involve the allied nationals living in the Reich in the deportations: in November the Foreign Ministry officially asked the governments of Slovakia, Croatia, and Romania whether they had any objections to the deportation of their Jewish nationals living in Germany. The governments of all three countries replied positively; but the Slovakian government agreed only after lengthy hesitation, and made it an express condition that its claims to the property of its deported nationals were entirely secured.[58]

The First and Second Waves of Deportation from the 'Greater German Reich'

In fact the deportations from the Reich began in mid-October.[59] In a first wave, between 15 October and 9 November, some 25,000 people were taken to Lodz in twenty-five transports, 10,000 Jews from the Old Reich, 5,000 each from the Protectorate and Vienna and 5,000 Gypsies from the Burgenland. Between 8 November and 6 February a total of thirty-four transports went to Riga,[60] Kovno (Kaunas),[61] and Minsk.[62] Originally this wave of deportations was supposed to have ended by the beginning of December, and to have involved 50,000 people.[63] The deportations to Minsk had to be interrupted at the end of November because of transport problems; by this time some 8,000 people had been deported to the ghetto there. The deportations to Riga and Kovno (Kaunas) were suspended in early February, when the planned figure of 25,000 people had almost been reached.

However, as early as November 1941, the RSHA assumed that the deportations which could not be completed, as originally planned, in the course of that year would be continued the following spring with a third wave of deportations. This appears in a note from Goebbels concerning a discussion with Heydrich on 17 November:[64] 'Heydrich tells me about his intentions regarding the deportation of the Jews from the Reich . . . In the third instalment, which becomes due at the beginning of next year, it should follow the procedure that I have suggested, clearing city by city, so that when the evacuation begins in one city it is also brought to an end as quickly as possible and the disturbance of public opinion caused by it does not have too long and damaging an effect. Heydrich is also acting very consistently with regard to this issue.' In his entry for 22 November 1941 Goebbels noted in his diary that Hitler had agreed to 'city-by-city' deportation.

The deportations were organized by Eichmann's 'special department' in the RSHA, which was now responsible for 'Jewish matters and Evacuation Affairs'; by the spring of 1941 it already had a staff of 107.[65]

Responsibility for the implementation of the deportations lay with the regional Gestapo offices, or with the Central Offices for Jewish Emigration in Austria and in the Protectorate, which were controlled by the Gestapo. In larger cities the Gestapo themselves organized the deportations, while in smaller towns and in the countryside, where the Gestapo did not have offices of its own, it was the duty of the local authorities, mayors, and district administrators, to implement the deportations. Generally speaking, the administrative apparatus of the Jewish communities was used to assemble the deportation lists and information about the victims.[66]

The deportations required considerable bureaucratic effort, and many offices were involved.[67] Arrangements had to be made with the Reich railways concerning the provision of special trains, the fixing of timetables, and the calculation of travel costs.[68] The deportation trains, most of which consisted of goods wagons, at first generally carried 1,000 people; later, attempts were made to increase the number of passengers. In accordance with an agreement reached in September, the uniformed Order Police were assigned to guard the trains.[69]

Special efforts were made to seize any remaining property from the victims of the deportations; this called for close collaboration with the financial authorities. The people selected for deportation had to make a complete declaration of their property before the beginning of the deportation; with the final notification of the transport date the victims were then informed that their property had been retrospectively confiscated. Here too efforts had been made to close any legal loopholes. Thus, for example, transfers of property were expressly forbidden. According to the 11th decree implementing the Reich Citizenship Law, this confiscated property was assigned to the Reich as soon as the transport crossed the German border.[70]

The prospective deportees had to turn up a few days before the departure of the train at collection points, where a meticulous check occurred. It was painstakingly established what the deportees were allowed to take with them; their luggage—they were allowed 50 kg per person—was searched, and many items were often confiscated at random. Body searches were also performed. The property lists were examined, and the victims had to hand over any valuable objects or personal papers. Finally a bailiff from the local court arrived to issue stateless Jews, who were not covered by the 11th ordinance, an order for the confiscation of their property. In this way the legal appearance of these expropriations was preserved.[71]

The collection points were rooms belonging to the Jewish communities, market or exhibition halls, gastronomic enterprises, abandoned factories, and so on, often building complexes in the centre of town. The way from the collection point to the station was often covered on foot in closed columns, or on open trucks.[72] This often occurred in broad daylight, as many surviving photographs confirm.[73] The first part of the deportations thus occurred 'in full view'; it was often the subject of lively debates.[74]

The victims had to pay a special fee for the transport; only a fragment was actually used for the costs arising, most of it disappearing on arrival. On the pretext of covering the costs for indigent fellow travellers, in the run-up to the deportation the Jews who still had property had been obliged to hand over a quarter of their property as a 'donation' to a special RSHA account. This transfer had nothing to do with the actual costs of the transport either, but merely served, from the perspective of the RSHA, to keep part of the Jewish property out of the clutches of the financial administration and use it for their own ends.[75] The carefully examined luggage that was loaded separately onto goods wagons before the start of the journey generally disappeared, never to be seen again.[76]

The property left behind was exploited by the financial administration. Thus household goods were given away to the poor, sold, or auctioned.[77] The apartments were taken over by the local administrations and rented out; these 'Jewish apartments' were in great demand.[78] In many places there was a regular run on these desirable properties.

So the whole process was geared towards the careful erasure of the complete social existence of the deportees, while at the same time maintaining the appearance of legality and making sure not only that the victims themselves paid for their own deportation, but that the RSHA, the state administration, and many private citizens profited from Jewish property.

Although the deportations occurred in public, and the population paid close attention to them, state propaganda was silent about these mass deportations, about their destinations and the fate that awaited the deportees. The negative reception from parts of the population, particularly in Berlin, to the compulsory identification of the Jews, which was noted with irritation by the Propaganda Ministry, may have been responsible for this silence. A police decree, the full text of which was not published but the content of which was announced via the media, forbade the population—under threat of imprisonment in a concentration camp—to have any public contact with Jews. Repression had to stand in for propaganda, which was plainly ineffective. Against the background of these experiences, on 23 October Goebbels ordered that the deportations were no longer to be mentioned in home propaganda. Anti-Semitic propaganda was now intensified once more, but concrete details were no longer to be revealed.[79]

We have already referred to the deportation of 5,000 Burgenland Gypsies to Lodz early in November 1941, a procedure that makes it especially clear that the story of the Holocaust cannot be written without an eye for other groups who were persecuted for racist reasons, since important parallels exist with the persecution of the Jews. As regards the deportation from Burgenland, which had been planned since April 1940, this was not the first deportation of Gypsies. As early as May 1940 2,370 Gypsies had been deported from the Reich to various parts of the General Government. Plainly the occupying authorities had no idea what to do with the Gypsies: some gave them private accommodation, some used them as forced labourers, some left them to their own devices. The majority of the Gypsies perished as a result of poor conditions, others were executed, some managed to return illegally to the Reich, some somehow survived in the General Government.[80]

The Gypsies deported to Lodz in November 1941 were confined to a special, separate section of the Lodz ghetto. The ones who survived the appalling conditions in this camp were murdered in Chelmno in January 1942.

The deportation to Lodz was followed early in 1942 by a further mass deportation of Gypsies: in February 1942, 2,000 East Prussian Gypsies were deported to Bialystok. Some members of the group, deemed to be 'assimilated', were sent back to East Prussia in the course of 1942, on condition that they agreed to be sterilized. The rest were deported in the autumn of 1942 to the Brest-Litovsk ghetto, whose inhabitants had been murdered a short time previously. In the spring of 1944 these people were deported to Auschwitz.[81]

Announcements of Extermination

In the autumn of 1941, many statements were issued by leading National Socialists or well-informed functionaries deliberately addressing the imminent 'extermination' of the Jews. Thus, for example, the foreign political editor of *Der Stürmer*, Paul Wurm, wrote on 23 October to his old acquaintance Rademacher, the Jewish expert at the Foreign Ministry:[82] 'On my way back from Berlin, I met an old Party member who is working on the settlement of the Jewish question in the East. Soon some of the Jewish vermin will be exterminated by special measures.'

In his table-talk on 25 October Hitler once again recalled the 'prophecy' he had made on 30 January 1939, adding the following train of thought: 'This race of criminals has the two million dead from the World War on its conscience and now hundreds of thousands more. Let nobody say to me: we can't send them into the swamps [in Russia]! Who's worrying about our people? It's good if the fear that we are exterminating the Jews goes before us.'[83] On 16 November 1941, under the heading 'The Jews are to blame', Goebbels published a leading article in which he also returned to Hitler's prophecy of 30 January 1939: 'At present we are experiencing the realisation of this prophecy, and in the process Jewry is suffering a fate, which may be harsh but is more than deserved. Pity or regret is entirely inappropriate in this case.'[84] With his formulation that 'world Jewry' was now suffering 'a gradual process of extermination', Geobbels made clear which fate finally awaited the Jews whose deportation from the German cities had been under way for some weeks. Two days later Rosenberg spoke at a press conference about the imminent 'eradication' (*Ausmerzung*) of the Jews of Europe: 'Some six million Jews still live in the East, and this question can only be solved by a biological extermination of the whole of Jewry in Europe. The Jewish question will only be solved for Germany when the last Jew has left German territory, and for Europe when not a single Jew stands on the European continent as far as the Urals ... And to this end it is necessary to force them beyond the Urals or otherwise bring about their eradication.'[85]

On 18 November 1941, at a meeting with the Great Mufti of Jerusalem, who had fled to the camp of the Axis powers, Hitler had announced that Germany was 'resolved to urge one European nation after the other, step by step, to contribute to the solution of the Jewish problem, and when the time comes to turn to non-European peoples with a similar appeal'. He would 'carry on the fight until the total destruction of the Jewish-Communist European empire', and in the 'not too distant future' reach the southern tip of the Caucasus. Germany was not, however, pursuing imperial goals in the Arabian world, but was working for the liberation of the Arabs. 'The German objective would be solely the destruction of Jews residing in the Arab sphere under the protection of British power.'[86] While this statement must admittedly be interpreted from a tactical perspective, it also shows that Hitler's fantasies of extermination already reached beyond the European sphere.

These quotations may of course be interpreted in different ways. If we consider them in connection with the expansion of the mass murders in certain regions which had already begun at the same time, or were under preparation, in my opinion they represent components of a process of radicalization that had been set in motion. The quotations make it clear that the Nazi leadership was in the process of further escalating the original intention to deport the Jews under German rule to the East where they were to die out under unbearable conditions. In view of the comprehensive mass murders in the occupied Eastern territories, which were also extended to Galicia in October, and with the first preparations for the systematic murder of the Jews by gas in certain regions of Poland, the organizers of the *Judenpolitik* developed increasingly terrible ideas of how the 'extermination' or 'Final Solution' of the European Jews, envisaged since the beginning of the war, was to be understood in concrete terms. A programme or a plan for the systematic murder of all European Jews is admittedly not yet discernible at this point, but the atmosphere for turning such a monstrous intention into action was unambiguously present.

A Regional 'Final Solution' in the Warthegau, Late 1941

From mid-October onwards, a total of 25,000 Jews and Gypsies from across the Reich were transported to the already overcrowded Lodz ghetto.

At around the same time, presumably still in October 1941, the mass murder of indigenous Jews began in the district of Konim in the southern Warthegau.[87] In late November, in an 'action' lasting several days, 700 Jews were murdered in gas vans in the Bornhagen (Kozminek) camp in the district of Kalisch.[88] The unit deployed was the 'Sonderkommando' Lange under HSSPF Warthegau Koppe, which had already murdered thousands of inmates of institutions for the mentally ill in the annexed Polish territories in 1939/40 and again in June/July 1941.[89] In October 1941 Lange's unit had been summoned to Novgorod by Himmler to murder patients in mental institutions there.[90] His driver confirmed that in autumn 1941 Lange had himself driven through the Warthegau to find a suitable location for a stationary killing installation. Once an appropriate building had been found in Chelmno, on 8 December Lange's unit started using gas vans to murder Jews there. At first most of the victims were indigenous Jews deported to Chelmno from various ghettos in the Warthegau.

From January 1942, those murdered in Chelmno were primarily inhabitants of the Lodz ghetto.[91] In a first wave of deportations, between 16 and 29 January, the first 10,000 inhabitants of the ghetto were deported to Chelmno. Chaim Rumkowski, who performed his office as Jewish Elder in an autocratic fashion, had managed to halve the figure of 20,000 people demanded by the Germans, and to keep the selection of this group—'undesirable elements', Polish Jews who had recently arrived in the ghetto from the provinces, and others—under his own control.[92] Over the months that followed, however, it would prove that these 'successes' were mercilessly exploited by the Germans to involve the apparatus of the Lodz Jewish council more and more closely in the machinery of deportation.

A letter dated 1 May 1942 to Himmler from Artur Greiser, the Gauleiter for the Warthegau,[93] provides a major clue for the reconstruction of the decision to wreak mass murder among the Jews of the Warthegau. In this letter Greiser informed the Reichsführer SS that the 'action concerning the special treatment of some 100,000 Jews in my Gau territory, authorized by you in agreement with the head of the Reich Security Head Office, SS Obergruppenführer Heydrich [could be] concluded in the next 2–3 months'. If Himmler and Heydrich had to 'authorize' this mass murder, we can assume that the suggestion must substantially have come from Greiser.[94] The planned number of 100,000 Jews 'unfit for work' and thus abandoned to murder can also be identified in another document from January 1942.[95] Presumably, then, the murder of the 100,000 people (Polish Jews 'unfit for work') was the 'service in return' that Greiser had demanded from Himmler if he was to receive 25,000 Jews and Gypsies (rather than the 60,000 people originally stated by Himmler) into the Lodz ghetto. Some months later—some time in summer or autumn 1942—Hitler gave Greiser, when he again addressed the 'Jewish question' in his Gau, a free hand—special authorization was no longer required to murder a certain number of people.

Eastern Upper Silesia: Forced Labour and Murder of Jews 'Unfit for Work'

As in the Warthegau, in eastern Upper Silesia the extensive resettlement plans that Himmler had introduced in 1939 in his capacity as Reichskommisar for the Strengthening of the German Nation, had been suspended in the spring of 1941 because of the concentration of troops in the East. Until then, some 38,000 ethnic Germans had been settled in this area and more than 81,000 indigenous people, including an unknown number of Jews, had been expelled to the General Government. After the suspension of the resettlement, in the eastern part of the annexed territory, predominantly settled by Poles, we have the following picture: while, since 1940, the Jewish population from the whole of eastern Upper Silesia had been concentrated in certain towns in this 'eastern strip' of the province, thousands of Poles who had been driven from their homes were stuck in 'Polish camps', and there were also thousands of ethnic Germans who could not be accommodated in 'transit camps'.

The idea of work deployment was very much a central pillar of *Judenpolitik* in eastern Upper Silesia at this time. In October 1940 Albrecht Schmelt, the Police President of Breslau (also president of the district (*Regierungspräsident*) since May 1941) had received a special commission from Himmler to organize the work deployment of the 'ethnic aliens' (meaning Jews) in eastern Upper Silesia. A priority of this was work on the Silesian section of the Berlin–Cracow autobahn as well as deployment in the munitions industry and in Wehrmacht manufacturing plants. In autumn 1941 Schmelt had 17,000 Jewish forced labourers under him, most of them in camps.[96]

The priority given to work deployment had an ambivalent effect on *Judenpolitik* in eastern Upper Silesia: the aim of intensively exploiting the prisoners did initially protect those Jews who were 'fit for work'—but only until their remaining energy had been exhausted by disastrous accommodation, undernourishment, overexertion, and so on. The fact that only Jews who were 'fit for work' were needed gave those responsible a 'rational' reason for the removal of those who were not. From mid-November 1941 the Schmelt Organization proceeded to separate out those prisoners in the camps who could not be used for work, sporadically at first but then systematically, to transport them to Auschwitz, and have them killed there in Krematorium I. So these murders began in that crucial part of the history of the camp, when mass murders with Zyklon B were beginning there.[97] The 'work deployment' of the Jews thus created the reason for the selection of those 'fit for work' and those 'unfit for work', and that distinction was an important step in the transition to the policy of systematic extermination. At the same time, however, it is completely unclear whether the murder of prisoners who were no longer fit for work derived from an initiative from the Schmelt Organization, whether those responsible were acting on instructions from above, or whether those at the centre of the decision-making process and those at the periphery encouraged one another. At any rate, the exploitation of the Jewish workforce was not the opposite pole of extermination policy, but an integral component of it.

The General Government: Escalation of the Murders in Galicia and Preparation of 'Aktion Reinhard' in the District of Lublin

From the spring of 1941 the government of the General Government had worked on the basis that the Jews living there would be expelled to the conquered Soviet territories. On 13 October, in a personal conversation, Frank once again suggested to Rosenberg that the 'Jewish population of the General Government be [deported] to the occupied Eastern territories'. Rosenberg replied that at that time there was no possibility 'for the implementation of resettlement plans of this kind'. However Rosenberg did declare himself willing in future 'to encourage Jewish emigration to the East, particularly since the intention existed to send asocial elements within the Reich to the thinly inhabited Eastern regions'.[98] From that point onwards the government of the General Government began to think about a 'final solution' of the 'Jewish question' in their own territory.

One important factor in the general radicalization of *Judenpolitik* in the General Government was a series of sessions of the region's administration which Frank held in the district capitals after his return from the Reich (14–16 October in Warsaw, 17 October in Globocnik's district of Lublin, 18 October in Radom, 20 October in Cracow and in Lvov (Lemberg) for the first time on 21 October). The session in Lublin on 17 October discussed the 'third decree' on residence restrictions in the General Government, which was issued a few days later and introduced the death penalty for those who left the ghetto.[99] This effectively launched a manhunt for those Jews living outside the ghetto. The impending 'evacuation' of the Jews from the city of Lublin was also discussed; initially '1,000 Jews [were to be] moved across the Bug'.[100] On 20 October, at the government meeting in Cracow, Governor Wächter indicated 'that an ultimately radical solution to the Jewish Question was unavoidable, and that no allowances of any kind—such as special exemptions for craftsmen—could be made'.[101] At the meeting on 12 October in Lvov, Eberhard Westerkamp, the Head of the Department for the Interior of the General Government, announced that 'the isolation of the Jews from the rest of the population' should be enforced as soon and as thoroughly as possible. On the other hand, however, Westerkamp pointed out that 'a government order has prohibited the establishment of new ghettos, since there was hope that the Jews would be deported from the General Government in the near future', even though a few days previously Rosenberg had declared that 'hope' to be an illusion.[102]

The attitude prevailing amongst the German ruling class in occupied Poland may be fairly represented by statements made by the head of the office of health of the government of the General Government, Jost Walbaum, at a doctors' conference held between 13 and 16 October: 'There are only two ways: we condemn the Jews in the ghetto to death by starvation or we shoot them.'[103]

While the treatment of the 'Jewish question' at these meetings suggests that the government of the General Government pursued a uniform anti-Jewish policy throughout the whole of the territory under its control, two districts played a pioneering part in the implementation of the 'Final Solution' in the General Government.

An important factor in the preparations for the 'Final Solution' in the General Government was the incorporation of Galicia, a territory where large-scale executions had already been carried out and continued to take place, into the General Government on 1 August 1941. Until September, the Special Purpose Einsatzkommando operating in this territory was exclusively directed against a vaguely defined Jewish upper class. This unit was to form the office of the Commander of the Security Police in the district of Galicia, after its incorporation into the General Government on 1 August 1941.[104] From early October, however, the Security Police in Galicia began murdering members of the Jewish population indiscriminately. In Nadworna on 6 October, for example, 2,000 women, men, and children were murdered by members of the Stanislau branch of the Security Police.[105] According to the head of the Security Police in Stanislau, Krüger, this 'action' had been previously planned down to the smallest details at a meeting with the commander of the Security Police in Lvov, Fritz Katzmann.[106] From early October such massacres occurred almost every week. The massacre among the Jews of Stanislau on 12 October 1941 (the so-called 'Bloody Sunday', in which around 10,000–12,000 people were murdered) is particularly noteworthy.[107] The Security Police in Galicia were thus, independent of their political status, following the same pattern of radicalization as the units in the occupied Eastern territories. These mass executions would inevitably further radicalize the 'Jewish policy' throughout the whole of the General Government.

Concrete preparations for mass murder of the Jews in the General Government had also been undertaken since October in the neighbouring district of Lublin, the territory which had been set aside in 1939 as a 'Jewish reservation', and which was to serve in the spring of 1942 as a reception zone for the third wave of deportations from the Reich, as well as for deportations from Slovakia.

The SS Police Commander of the district of Lublin, Odilo Globocnik, played a key role in the preparations for the murder of the Jews of the district. On 13 October, the same day as Rosenberg disappointed Frank's hopes of quick deportations to the occupied Eastern territories, Globocnik[108] met Himmler, to speak to him about the proposal he had made two weeks earlier, to limit the 'influence of the Jews' against whom it was necessary to take steps 'of a security policy nature'.[109] It was probably at this meeting that Globocnik received the assignment to build Belzec extermination camp.[110]

A personal letter sent by a colleague of Globocnik's, Hauptsturmführer Hellmuth Müller, on 15 October 1941 to the head of the Main Office for Race and Settlement, Otto Hofmann, makes it clear that decisions concerning Globocnik's radical plans for the future of *Judenpolitik* in his district were actually made in mid-October. Müller wrote that Globocnik saw 'the political conditions in the GG basically as a transitional stage'. Globocnik, who was strongly opposed to the governor of the district in this respect, considered the 'gradual cleansing of the entire GG of Jews and also of Poles for the purpose of securing the Eastern territories etc. to be necessary. He is, in this connection, full of good and far-reaching plans the implementation of which is hampered only by the, in this respect, limited influence of his current office. For, before he can act he needs the support of the civil offices and authorities of the GG, which will only cooperate on the basis of existing laws and decrees.'[111]

Müller's letter, which corresponds to the state of information before Globocnik's trip to Berlin, thus shows that Globocnik had at this point not yet been given any extensive authorization to implement the destruction of the Jews. That changed fundamentally, however, after Globocnik had returned from his trip to the Reich, and Frank had been informed by Rosenberg that a deportation of the Jews from the General Government to the occupied Soviet territories was illusory. Müller's letter also makes it clear that, as far as Globocnik was concerned, the mass murder of Jews in his district was only the first step to a far more comprehensive 'new order' in terms of population policy in the district of Lublin, aimed at the settlement of ethnic Germans and the expulsion of the Polish population.[112] In the short term, however, the plans for the mass murder of indigenous Jews were to be used primarily to free up accommodation in the overcrowded ghettos of the district, which was to be filled with Jews from the Reich and Slovakia.

Subsequent events make it plain that the meeting between Himmler and Globocnik on 13 October 1941 was actually of considerable importance in terms of the transition to mass murder. At the beginning of November and two to three weeks after the meeting, after the 'Jewish question' had been discussed several times at the meetings of the government of the General Government, work began on the construction of the first extermination camp, Belzec, a relatively small collection of barracks.[113] From December 1941 onwards, the euthanasia staff assigned to the T4 organization began arriving in Lublin.[114]

As has already been outlined, according to Eichmann's own statements he visited the camp while it was still under construction in late summer or autumn. Given the advanced state of the building work that he describes, a date in the winter would seem more likely. However, it is also possible that in his recollections he was confusing this visit with a later visit to Treblinka, which was also under construction at the time.[115] Some weeks after work began in Belzec. On 27 and 28 November 1941 a meeting of T4 specialists was held in Pirna (Saxony). There, as one of the participants wrote beforehand to his wife, 'future developments' would be discussed.[116]

However, there was another reason why mid-October was a particularly critical phase in *Judenpolitik* in the the district of Lublin. On 20 October 1941, accompanied by Ribbentrop, Himmler met the Slovakian President, Joseph Tiso, his Prime Minister and Foreign Minister, Vojtech Tuka and the Slovak-ian Interior Minister, Sano Mach, and made the head of the Slovakian state the offer of deporting the Slovakian Jews to a particularly remote area of the General Government.[117] There is much to suggest that this offer formed the starting point for the construction of a second extermination camp in the district of Lublin, Sobibor.[118] There are—unconfirmed—indications that the building of Sobibor was already being prepared in late 1941, but that the beginning of construction was postponed until the spring of 1942.[119] When the deportation of the Slovakian Jews, first mooted in October 1941, began in May 1942 it was in fact Jews from the district of Lublin who were first murdered in Sobibor. But, from June onwards, the Slovakian Jews were included as well.

There are also indications that in November 1941 the district physician in the district of Galicia, Dorpheide, tried to have staff from the T4 organization made available to him in Lvov, the district capital, to murder mentally ill people. This might, however, have to do with the construction of another extermination camp in the district of Galicia which was never realized.[120]

The fact that Belzec's capacity for murder was initially limited (the camp was to be considerably extended in the spring), and that the construction of the other extermination camps in the General Government began only in the spring of 1942, indicates that, in the autumn of 1941, Globocnik had still received no orders to make preparations for the murder of all the Jews in the General Government, but that his assignment covered the district of Lublin, and perhaps already the district of Galicia as well.[121]

The further radicalization of the persecutory measures in the General Government, particularly in the districts of Lublin and Galicia, had already been heralded since the beginning of 1942. On 20 January 1942 the Department of Population and Welfare of the government of the General Government called upon the relevant district governors' offices to provide detailed information about the existing ghettos and their Jewish inhabitants.[122]

In the district of Lublin compulsory identity cards were introduced for Jews in early February, and in March the papers of those still required as workers were marked accordingly.[123] From January 1942 the civil administration in the district of Galicia had planned the 'resettlement' of Jews unfit for work from Lvov to the surrounding communities (*Gemeinden*) in the district. Early in January the district (*Kreis*) leaders were ordered to have the Jewish councils arrest any Jews who had immigrated illegally and 'hand them over to the relevant security office to be transported to camps for intensified, long-term forced labour service'.[124] In practice, this meant 'extermination through work' in the SS forced labour camps.[125] The 'action' itself, which was originally to take place on 1 March, was then postponed to the period after 1 April.[126] It is unclear whether the planned 'resettlement' to the rural communities was a euphemism for deportation to Belzec, or whether the plans were further radicalized in the first months of 1942.[127] At any rate the Jewish council was 'instructed to provide a list all those Jews and Jewish families who were not engaged in productive labour'.[128]

General Commissariat Ostland: The Mass Murders in Kovno (Kaunas), Riga, and Minsk

From the beginning of October 1941 the Security Police in the territory of the German-installed General Commissariat Ostland (incorporating the Baltic states and Belarus) once again pursued the plan already set out in August 1941 for the construction of a large concentration camp near Riga. The reason it now gave was the need to accommodate the expected 25,000 Jews transported from the Reich.[129] This wish was authorized by the RSHA. In the further negotiations with the civil administration Franz Stahlecker, the BdS Eastland, referred expressly to a 'wish' of Hitler's to set up a large concentration camp for Jews from the Reich and the Protectorate in the area around Riga and Mitau.[130]

However, Reichskommissar Hinrich Lohse, the head of the civil administration, tried to prevent this project. As we have already seen, while Lohse was trying to find an alternative, Wetzel, the Jewish expert of the Eastern Ministry, in his notorious memorandumn of 25 October, offered to send him euthanasia staff to build a gas chamber in Riga.[131]

On 8 November, ignoring the Reich Commissar's protests, Lange informed Lohse about the imminent arrival of 50,000 Jews, 25,000 each for Riga and Minsk. The first transport would arrive in Riga on 19 November. As the construction of the planned concentration camp had not advanced in the meantime, the first five Riga transports could be redirected to the ghetto in Kovno (Kaunas). There was also, Lange wrote, a temporary possibility of accommodation in Jungfernhof (Jumpravmuiza), in the grounds of a former airport.[132] The following day, Lohse's political adviser, Friedrich Trampedach, wrote to the Eastern Ministry with a request to stop these transports as 'Jewish camps must be moved considerably further to the East'.[133] The Eastern Ministry replied immediately that the camps in Riga and Minsk were only temporary measures: 'Jews are going further East...Hence no concerns.'[134]

A short time before, another message from the Eastern Ministry had reached Lohse's office, in which the Reich Commissar had been asked to respond to accusations from the RSHA that he had 'prohibited the executions of Jews in Libau'. On 7 November Lohse's adviser Trampedach had also, in response to complaints from Wehrmacht authorities, instructed the District Commissar of Vilnius to prevent further shootings of Jewish skilled workers; in a file note he had demanded 'fundamental instructions' on this matter. Moreover, early in November a complaint from District Commissar Kube concerning murder actions carried out by the SS in Belarus had reached Lohse.[135] Thus, there were reasons enough for Lohse to request fundamental clarification about further action in the 'Jewish question'.

Lohse reacted to these objections on 15 November. He made it clear to the Eastern Ministry that he had banned the 'arbitrary executions of Jews in Libau' because 'the manner of their execution had been unacceptable'. Lohse now requested the Eastern Ministry for clarification about whether its position could be understood as being 'that all the Jews in the Ostland are to be liquidated', and whether this was to occur 'without concern for age and sex and economic interests' (e.g the Wehrmacht's interest in 'skilled workers in munitions factories').[136]

The reply from the Eastern Ministry reached Riga on 22 December: referring to 'oral discussions' that had taken place in the meantime, it was stated that 'economic concerns...should be fundamentally disregarded in dealing with the problem'. All doubtful cases were to be resolved directly with the HSSPF. Thereupon Lohse abandoned his protest.[137]

This clear answer from the Eastern Ministry had come after Rosenberg had had a conversation with Himmler lasting several hours, concerning *Judenpolitik* amongst other things.[138] Three days later, at a press conference in the Eastern Ministry, Rosenberg had delivered his confidential declaration, already mentioned above, in which he had spoken openly of the 'biological extermination of the whole of Jewry in Europe', and stated that 'they were to be forced over the Urals or otherwise exterminated'.[139]

The first transport to the Minsk ghetto left Hamburg on 8 November.[140] The previous day the German Security Police and auxiliaries had murdered some 12,000 inhabitants of the Minsk ghetto in a 'large action'. The Jews from the Reich were now placed in their accommodation. Protests against the deportations came from various sources: the commanders of the Army Group Centre, Field-Marshall von Bock, and the Wehrmacht Commander Ostland raised objections, in particular because of the overstretched transport situation.[141] On 16 December, the Commissar General for White Russia, Wihelm Kube, advised Lohse against further transports of Jews from the Reich, since he wanted to see 'people who come from our cultural background' treated differently from the 'indigenous, animalistic hordes'.[142] The Minsk deportations were actually suspended after eight transports (the last one left Vienna on 28 November).

However, when the deportations to Riga began on 19 November, the construction of the concentration camp planned for the German Jews in the area of Riga had not even begun.[143] The Jews transported from Germany were to build the camp themselves, in unimaginably primitive conditions in the middle of winter.[144] As in Lodz and in Minsk, the relevant offices in Riga were placed in an impossible situation in November 1941 when they were called upon to accommodate 25,000 Jews in the shortest possible time; the officials on the ground responded to the challenge with a radical, murderous solution.

The first five transports meant for Riga, from Frankfurt am Main, Munich, Vienna, Breslau, and Berlin, with around 5,000 people, were redirected via Kaunas. All the transportees were shot there immediately on arrival at Fort IX by the murder units of Einsatzkommando 3.[145] And as in Minsk, in Riga the inhabitants of the ghetto fell victim to mass murder: between 29 November and 1 December around 4,000 Latvian Jews and between 8 and 9 December an estimated over 20,000 further ghetto-dwellers were shot.[146] In his Soviet prison, HSSPF Friedrich Jeckeln, the man responsible for the murders, stated that he had received the order to liquidate the ghetto directly from Himmler in November. Himmler had also ordered him to kill 'all Jews in the Ostland down to the last man'.[147] During the first massacre, 1,000 Jews deported from Berlin were also shot in the early morning of 30 November, immediately on arrival.

After this mass murder, however, the shooting of Jews from the Reich was temporarily suspended. This is borne out by an entry in Himmler's telephone diary for 30 November 1941 about a conversation with Heydrich: 'Transport of Jews from Berlin. No liquidation.'[148] However, by this time, the Berlin Jews had already been murdered. On 1 December Himmler sent a radio telegram to Jeckeln, stating that 'unauthorized acts and contraventions' of the 'guidelines issued by myself or by the Reich Security Main Office on my behalf' for how the 'Jews resettled to the Ostland territory' were to be 'treated' would be 'punished'. At the same time he summoned Jeckeln to discuss the 'Jewish question' on 4 December.[149]

From the way Himmler had phrased his 1 December telegram it becomes clear that the murder of the 6,000 people from the Reich had neither been expressly ordered nor explicitly forbidden; 'guidelines' were in place, but no precise instructions or orders. No general policy for the immediate murder of those deported to the Eastern European ghettos existed, as is demonstrated by the fate of the deportees to Lodz and Minsk, who were initially put in ghettos there. If we assume that the RSHA or Himmler had issued such an explicit order to murder deportees in Riga, and the Reichsführer SS had revoked it on 30 November, Jeckeln's rebuke fom Himmler would make no sense; in that case he would only have been acting on orders. However, no express prohibition seems to have existed either; had it done so, Himmler would have referred to such a prohibition in his telegram to Jeckeln, and not referred in general terms to 'guidelines'. It appears that it was not envisaged from the start that the Jews deported from Central Europe would be murdered on arrival. Instead, it seems that Jeckeln acted on his own initiative, on the assumption that the RSHA's 'guidelines', which were drafted in general terms and of which we are inadequately informed, permitted such action in view of the extremely difficult situation in Latvia, where there was no available accommodation for the deportees who were arriving in quick succession.

There is some reason to believe that the rapid deportations to Riga, like those to Lodz and Minsk, were deliberately used to create 'intolerable situations' as a way of effectively forcing the local authorities to find more radical 'solutions'. Greiser in Lodz had responded with his proposal to murder 100,000 indigenous Jews and the HSSPF for Russia-Centre had organized a mass murder in the Minsk ghetto.

However, while Jeckeln had reacted in the desired way with the liquidation of the Riga ghetto, by executing the Central European Jews he had gone beyond the desired goal (at this point). There was, though, a tension characteristic of the process of putting the murder machinery in motion between general orders that were to be understood intuitively, and independent initiatives on the part of the local authorities, and on this occasion there had to be intervention from the top to control matters. Himmler intervened, for once, in order to de-escalate the situation rather than—as with his other interventions—to radicalize it still further.

Himmler's intervention had at first led to a complete halt to the systematic murder of those deported to Latvia: the Jews of the next twenty-two transports that arrived in Riga were confined in the Riga ghetto or the two camps of Salaspils and Jungfernhof. There do seem, however, to have been two exceptions. Significant indications suggest that, on 19 January 1942, most of the passengers of a transport from Theresienstadt, more than 900 people, were shot immediately on arrival, and that at the end of January around 500 Jews, from a transport either from Berlin or Vienna, were also shot.[150] At the end of March and the beginning of April 1942, selections of Jews no longer fit for work also took place in the Riga ghetto and Jungfernhof: the victims were mainly Jews from Vienna and Berlin. In the ghetto we may assume that 3,000 died, and in the Jungfernhof, in an 'action' on 26 March, around 1,800 people.[151]

'Final Solution' in Serbia, Autumn 1941

After the German military administration had ruled in May that Jews and Gypsies were to be marked, dismissed from public service, deployed in forced labour, and have their property confiscated,[152] the anti-Jewish policy was further intensified with the start of the attack on the Soviet Union. The Jewish community of Belgrade now had to supply forty hostages a day. From the beginning of July onwards, hostages from this community, Communists and Jews, were shot almost daily as 'retaliation' for acts of resistance.[153] In August, the arrests were extended to all Jewish men. In Serbia too, then, the 'retaliatory measures' were directed against the hostile image of 'Jewish Bolshevism'. In spite of these shootings the Serbian resistance against the occupying power grew steadily. When twenty-two German soldiers were killed in a further attack, on 4 October the Plenipotentiary Commanding General in Serbia, Franz Böhme, ordered,[154] as 'reprisal and atonement . . . that 100 Serbian prisoners be shot for every murdered German soldier'. Those to be executed were prisoners from the concentration camps in Sabac and Belgrade, 'predominantly Jews and Communists'.[155] In fact, between 9 and 13 October some 2,000 Jews and 200 Gypsies from these camps were shot.[156] Böhme had received express support for his policy of directing his retaliatory measures primarily against Jews from Martin Luther, the head of the

German department of the Foreign Ministry, and from Eichmann, the Jewish specialist of the RSHA. In his memorandum to the AA representative in Belgrade, dated 16 September, Luther had recommended that the arrested Jewish men be treated as hostages across the board,[157] and in a phone call to the Jewish expert of the Foreign Ministry on 13 September 1941 Eichmann had suggested that this group be shot.[158]

On 10 October Böhme issued a general order to shoot 100 prisoners or hostages 'for every German soldier or ethnic German (men, women or children) killed or murdered', 'for every wounded German soldier or ethnic German 50 prisoners or hostages'. The following were to be 'immediately' arrested as hostages: 'all Communists, male inhabitants suspected of being so, all Jews, a certain number of nationalist and democratically minded inhabitants'.[159]

In accordance with this scheme, a few days later an additional 2,200 men, Jews and Gypsies once again among them, were shot for 10 members of the Wehrmacht killed in battle and 24 wounded.[160] In the two weeks following the order of 10 October, Wehrmacht units killed over 9,000 Jews, Gypsies, and other civilians.[161] At the beginning of November, 8,000 Jewish men, or almost all the Jewish men that the occupying forces had been able to round up, were executed by the firing squads.[162] The families of the victims were interned in a concentration camp during the winter and murdered the following spring, in gas vans.

During the 'retaliatory actions' Wehrmacht firing squads had also shot around 1,000 Roma. Unlike the Jewish minority, however, the Gypsies living in Serbia, whose numbers far exceeded 100,000, were spared mass murders on this scale; this clearly demonstrates the differences in the intensity of the persecution of the two population groups.[163]

Interim Conclusion: The Transition to Regional Murder Actions

Taken as a whole, the decisions described above provide the following picture: from the end of July the shootings in the Soviet Union were gradually extended to include women and children, from August onwards certain places were made *judenfrei*, and in October, in practically all parts of the occupied territory, the policy of murdering the entire Jewish population apart from a small number of people 'fit for work' was implemented. Late in August 1941 the 'euthanasia murders' in the Reich came to an end in their existing form, which meant that the staff were freed up and initially deployed on a short-term basis in the context of action 14f13. Mid-September saw the gas experiments in Mogilev in which the murderous technology of euthanasia was tried out in the Eastern territories for the first time. Presumably towards the end of September the decision was made to murder around 100,000 people from the Warthegau. At the beginning of October the Security Police began large-scale mass shootings in the district of Galicia in the territory of the General Government, in which murder was carried out just as indiscriminately as in occupied Soviet territory. In parallel with this, the Wehrmacht began systematically shooting Jewish men and Gypsies in Serbia. In mid-October Globocnik received the assignment to build an extermination camp (Belzec), and in the days that followed the government of the General Government began organizational preparations for the mass murder of the Polish Jews. The middle of October, however, was a particularly critical phase in *Juden-politik* in the district of Lublin for a different reason. On 20 October Himmler proposed to the Slovakian head of state that the Slovakian Jews be deported to a particularly remote area within the General Government this may have been the starting point for the construction of the second extermination camp at Sobibor.[164] In November the T4 murder specialists were assigned to Globocnik. In October preparations began for the construction of extermination camps in Riga and presumably also in the area around Minsk (Mogilev); there are indications of similar plans for Lvov in November. Non-Jewish prisoners were first murdered in Auschwitz with Zyklon B in September 1941. In the course of the enlargement of the camp in October, a larger crematorium was ordered for Auschwitz. In 1942 the cremation ovens originally intended for Mogilev were diverted to Auschwitz. In November Reich German Jews were also shot during the massacres of Lithuanian Jews by Security Police in Riga and Kaunas. However, Himmler put a stop to this murderous practice, which was not in line with RSHA policy at this point.

These events are so closely connected that they permit the following conclusions to be drawn. In autumn 1941 the Nazi regime clearly decided to murder several hundred thousand Jews deemed unfit for work in areas that seemed particularly important from a strategic point of view. This decision followed on directly from Hitler's order, issued in mid-September, to deport the German Jews. This swift radicalization of the decision-making process is connected with the change in the original plan to deport 60,000 Jews to Lodz ghetto. This led to two interrelated decisions: first, the gradual modification and extension of the deport-ation programme. This was first directed to the ghettos of Minsk and Riga. However, after October there are increasing signs that it was to be extended to the district of Lublin and also to include Jews from outside the Reich. Secondly, there was the bloody decimation of the reception areas (Lodz, Riga, Minsk, Lublin) affected by the deportations. Conceivably, the decision made in autumn 1941—largely reconstructed from the course of events—may also have included the district of Galicia. This is suggested by references to the planned construction of an extermination camp in Lvov, but also by the particular role that Galicia was to play in 1942 (alongside Lublin) in the implementation of the 'Final Solution' within the General Government. With this decision to carry out a mass murder of the Jews in particular regions of Poland, the policy introduced shortly before in the Soviet Union to create *judenfrei* areas, in which only a minority of forced labourers confined in ghettos was left alive, was now extended to territories in occupied Poland. The parallels with what was happening during October in Serbia, where the Wehrmacht extended their reprisals to a comprehensive anni-hilation campaign against the Jewish population, are quite plain. Moreover, it can be no coincidence that, a short time later, the military administration in France began directing its retaliatory programme against Jews who were to be transported to the East as hostages. However, the reconstruction of these regional mass murders, which were now being implemented or were in preparation, does not allow us to conclude that a decision to murder immediately all European Jews had been made in autumn 1941.[165] At that point the murder of hundreds of thousands of people was being prepared, but not of millions.

However, the politics of extermination had by now attained such a dynamic momentum that the further extension of the murders to the whole of Europe was the logical next step for those responsible. The further move to the mass murder of all European Jews could only have been halted if the leadership of the regime had now introduced a radical change of course—and that would have been precisely the opposite of what Hitler intended at this point.

Thus, it would be a mistake to see the preparations for the regional mass murders which began in autumn 1941 solely as a spontaneous reaction to the obvious failure of a deportation programme to the Soviet Union, a territory which had not yet, contrary to expectations, been conquered.[166] It was rather that events represented a logical continuation of the *Judenpolitik* that had been pursued so far. For the comprehensive deportation programme for the European Jews, planned since the beginning of 1941 and now under way, had been a 'final solution' policy from the outset, that is to say it was the fixed aim to destroy those people who had been deported to the occupied Soviet territories once the war was over. Thus, the regional mass murders of those Jews who were 'unfit for work' represent a radicalization and acceleration of that 'final solution' policy. In the wake of the mass shootings in Eastern Europe, the idea of a 'final solution', still vague at first, began to assume sharper outlines, while the original post-war prospect for this 'final solution' increasingly became a feasible project that was implemented on a growing scale already during the course of the war. With the decision in Septem-ber to carry out mass deportations from the Reich to ghettos that were already appallingly overcrowded, this radicalization and acceleration were deliberately introduced by the Nazi leadership: the authorities in the reception areas were quite intentionally presented with 'impossible situations'. More radical solutions were demanded of them, while at the same time various institutions (the Institute of Criminal Technology, the T4 organization, the Lange gas-van unit and Auschwitz camp leadership) offered different variants of one such radical solution; the mass murder of people with poison gas.

What were the crucial impulses behind this process of radicalization? Was it primarily the policy from the centre—in other words from Hitler's manic obsession, increased in various ways by the course of the war, to create a Europe free of Jews—or was it above all independent initiatives on the part of the various power holders that advanced the radicalization process, as a series of major studies of the Holocaust in various Eastern European regions suggest?[167]

The independent initiatives on the part of figures on the periphery—Greiser in the Warthegau, Globocnik in Lublin, Jeckeln and Lange in the Ostland, the Security Police in Galicia, the Wehrmacht in Serbia and others—should not be underestimated. However, if we see the simultaneous activities of these various agents in context, it becomes clear that they were acting within the framework of an overall policy that was always directed from the centre. The initiatives emanating from them, which led either to shootings or to the provision of gas vans or the construction of extermination camps to murder a large number of Jews, were responses to a policy dictated by the centre, and the centre was always in a position to prevent too great an escalation of this policy, as the suspension of the murders of Reich German Jews in the Ostland by Himmler at the end of November 1941 demonstrates.

Thus, it would seem pointless to try to debate whether the policies of the centre and the initiatives of the periphery were crucial for the unleashing of the Holocaust. It would be more true to say that they stood in a dialectical relationship to one another, that is, that the centre could only act because it knew that its impulses would fall on fertile ground at the periphery, and the decision makers at the periphery based their own actions on the assumption that they were in harmony with the policy pursued by the centre.

In other words: just as the extension of the shootings to women and children in the Soviet Union from the summer of 1941 onwards could not simply have been ordered, the extension of mass murders to particular regions of occupied Europe in the autumn of 1941 required a very complicated interaction between headquarters and the executive organizations, a *mélange* of orders and intentions on the part of the central authorities and independent initiatives and intuition on the part of the regional powerholders, which could finally be channelled and rendered uniform by the centre, albeit at a far higher level of radicalization. However, we have been familiar with the essential elements of this radicalization process, particularly the interaction between the centre and the executive organizations, since the beginning of National Socialist policy towards the Jews in the 1930s.

In late 1941, once again, it was the centre that began to combine the various approaches into an extension of the murders and draw up a unified programme for the destruction of all European Jews which was to assume form in the spring and summer of 1942.

CHAPTER 16

THE WANNSEE CONFERENCE

On 29 November, when Heydrich invited a number of state secretaries, senior officials, and SS officers to a meeting on 9 December,[1] at which he wished to discuss the planned 'overall solution of the Jewish question in Europe', the original intention of the Nazi leadership to undertake the 'Final Solution' of the 'Jewish question' after the end of the war had already been superseded: the Nazi regime had by then killed several hundred thousand people, although in official parlance *Judenpolitik* had not reached the stage of the 'Final Solution'.

With the conference Heydrich plainly intended to outline the mass murders in the various occupied territories to a number of senior officials of the Party and the SS as well as leading civil servants as part of a 'solution to the European Jewish question' ordered by Hitler and directed by the RSHA, and to ensure that they, and especially the ministerial bureaucracy, would share both knowledge of and responsibility for this policy.

The fact that on 8 December Heydrich was forced by the events of the war to postpone the conference at short notice to 20 January 1942 gave him six weeks to rethink his strategy for this major meeting. The change in the entire war situation that followed the declaration of war on the USA may also have contributed to the further radicalization of his attitude in the meantime.

A day after the declaration of war on the United States, on 12 December 1942, Hitler made a speech to the Gauleiters and Reich leaders of the Party, in which he once again returned to his 'prophecy' of 30 January 1939, as Goebbels's diaries reveal:[2]

As regards the Jewish question, the Führer is resolved to make a clean sweep. He prophesied to the Jews that if they were to bring about another world war, they would bring about their own destruction as a result. This was not empty talk. The world war is here, the destruction of the Jews must be the necessary consequence. The question must be seen without sentimentality. We are not here to show sympathy with the Jews, we must sympathize with our own German people. If the German people has once again sacrificed around 160,000 fallen in the Eastern campaign, the authors of this bloody conflict will have to pay with their lives.

The fact that the world war was now 'here' gave particular emphasis to Hitler's prophecy, delivered repeatedly since early 1939, that the Jews of Europe would be destroyed in the event of a world war. But it seems excessive to see Hitler's speech on 12 December as the announcement of a fundamental decision on Hitler's part to murder the European Jews.[3] It was more like a further appeal to accelerate and radicalize the extermination policy that had already been set in motion with the mass executions in the Soviet Union, in Poland, and Serbia and the deportations from Central Europe. In its radical rhetoric, this appeal corresponds (sometimes literally) to Hitler's statements of 25 October, but also to Goebbels's article on 16 November and Rosenberg's press conference on 18 November. From the period around mid-December there are further indications that Hitler wanted to radicalize the persecution of the Jews still further after the USA joined the war, although one could not conclusively deduce a 'fundamental decision' on Hitler's part to murder the European Jews from all of these documents.[4] Neither can Himmler's brief note in his office diary about a conversation with Hitler on 18 December be seen as additional evidence for Hitler's 'fundamental decision' made a few days previously.[5] The words: 'Jewish question/to be extirpated as partisans' represent a renewed confirmation on Hitler's part that the mass murders of the Soviet Jews were to be continued and intensified, albeit with the reservations already given.[6]

The minutes of the Wannsee Conference provide very little information about what Heydrich actually said in the SS villa on the Wannsee.[7] Its author, Eichmann, noted only the results, not the exact course of the conference. According to his own recollections, the participants used far more drastic language; on Heydrich's instructions, he had used euphemistic language in the minutes.[8]

As we do not know the exact words used in the conference, and since Eichmann's statements incriminating third parties can only be trusted with certain reservations, the minutes should not be used as a basis for speculations about what was 'actually' said at the conference. Instead it should be read as a guideline authorized by Heydrich and revealed to representatives of a number of authorities by the RSHA, which had been commissioned to deal with the final solution of the Jewish question. The starting point for an interpretation of the

RSHA's *Judenpolitik* at the beginning of 1942 should not be the conference as such, but rather Heydrich's subsequent distillation of it, which he then used for external purposes.

The central passage of Heydrich's address concerning the general aims of the future 'Jewish policy' is as follows:[9] 'After appropriate prior approval by the Führer, emigration as a possible solution has been superseded by a policy of evacuating the Jews to the East.' These 'actions' (the deportations that had already been begun) were to be regarded merely as 'temporary solutions' (*Ausweichmöglichkeiten*), nonetheless 'practical experience would be accumulated' which would be 'of great importance for the impending final solution of the Jewish Question'. The impending 'final solution' was envisaged as involving 11 million Jews, a figure which was broken down by country in a statistical addendum to the minutes. This list not only includes Jews living in areas under German control, but also those of Great Britain, Ireland, Portugal, Sweden, Switzerland, Spain, and Turkey. Included in the 700,000 Jews for unoccupied France are those of the North African colonies. Heydrich thus clearly distinguished the programme of deportations that had already been set in motion from a far more comprehensive plan, whose execution he said was 'dependent on military developments', and could therefore only be fully realized after a German victory. According to the minutes, Heydrich made the following remarks about the 'Final Solution' that he envisaged: 'As part of the development of the final solution the Jews are now to be put to work in a suitable manner under the appropriate leadership. Organized into large work gangs and segregated according to sex, those Jews fit for work will be led into these areas as road-builders, in the course of which, no doubt, a large number will be lost by natural wastage.' The 'remainder who will inevitably survive' will, 'since they are the ones with the greatest powers of endurance', 'have to be dealt with accordingly' to prevent their becoming 'the germ cell of a new Jewish regeneration'. Initially the Jews were to be taken to 'transit-ghettos', from which they were to be 'transported further towards the East'.

Heydrich thus developed the conception of a gigantic deportation programme which would only be fully realizable in the post-war period. Those Jews who were deported 'to the East' were to be worked to death through forced labour or, if they should survive these tribulations, they would be murdered. The fate of those 'unfit for work', children and mothers in particular, was not further elucidated by Heydrich. In the context of the speech as a whole, however, and of the murderous practice that had predominated for months in the occupied Soviet territories, and since the beginning of December in Chelmno, it is clear that they too were to be killed, because Heydrich wanted to prevent the survival of the 'germ cell of a new Jewish regeneration' at all costs.

Heydrich's statement indicates that the RSHA was at this time still proceeding according to the plan, followed since the beginning of 1941, of implementing the

'Final Solution' of the Jewish question after the end of the war in the occupied Eastern territories. Heydrich also made it clear what was understood by the phrase 'Final Solution': the Jews were to be annihilated by a combination of forced labour and mass murder. The fact that it was Jewish forced labour that gained importance early in 1942 suggests that Heydrich's remarks should be taken literally.[10] Tellingly, only a few days before the Wannsee Conference, on 12 January 1942, the HSSPF Ukraine instructed the Commissars General in Brest-Litovsk, Zhitomir, Nikolayev, Dnepropetrovsk, and Kiev to start immediately preparing for the establishment of ghettos so that 'Jews from the Old Reich could be accommodated in the course of 1942'.[11] By contrast, there is no evidence that there was any plan at this point to deport the Jews from Central and Western Europe directly to extermination camps on Polish soil. On the contrary, the first deportations from countries outside Germany, those from Slovakia and France, which began in the spring of 1942, as well as the 'third-wave' deportations from the Reich, which were taking place at the same time, did not lead directly to the gas chambers of the extermination camps. It was not immediately before or after the Wannsee Conference, but in the spring of 1942 that the capacity of the extermination camps was hastily extended at very short notice.

The minutes of the Wannsee Conference do, however, make it clear that, on the one hand, the idea of a post-war solution was being firmly adhered to, while at the same time there was a debate over the proposal to exempt the Jews in the General Government and the occupied Soviet territories from this general plan and kill them in the short term.

Five weeks before the Wannsee Conference, Governor General Frank had already learned that the deportation of the Jews from the General Government could not be counted on even in the medium-to-long term.[12] He drew the conclusions from this knowledge at a meeting on 16 December:[13]

In Berlin they said to us, 'Why are people making such a fuss? We can't do anything with them in the Ostland or in the Reichsommissariat either; liquidate them yourselves!' Gentlemen, I must ask you to resist any sense of compassion. We must annihilate the Jews wherever we find them and whenever this is at all possible, in order to maintain here the whole structure of the Reich.

However, the method and time-frame for this mass murder were still undecided in mid-December 1941, as we can see from Frank's further remarks:

We can't shoot these 3.5 million Jews, we can't poison them, but we will be able to intervene in a way that will somehow lead to their successful extermination—in the context of the greater measures that are to be discussed in relation to the Reich. The General Government must become just as free of Jews [judenfrei] as the Reich. Where and how that happens is a matter for the official bodies that we must set up and deploy here, and in due course I shall let you know how effective they are being.

The determination of the leadership of the General Government to achieve this 'successful extermination' in the short term provides the context for the remarks made by the State Secretary, Bühler,the representative of the government of the General Government, towards the end of the Wannsee Conference. Bühler stated that the General Government would 'welcome it if the final solution to this question could begin in the General Government, because, in the first place, the problem of transportation does not play a decisive role here and because these measures will not be obstructed by issues involving labour deployment'. Moreover, the approximately 2.5 million Jews who were to be removed from the General Government 'as soon as possible' were overwhelmingly 'unfit for work'. Thus Bühler was clearly proposing that the majority of the Jews in the General Government should be murdered within the General Government itself, and that they should no longer be used, as Heydrich had suggested, 'to build roads' in the occupied Eastern territories.

Then the conference participants went a step further, and discussed the question of how the Jews in the General Government and the occupied Soviet territories were actually to be 'removed'—in other words they talked in concrete terms about the method for murder: 'In the concluding stages different possible solutions were discussed. Both Gauleiter Dr Meyer [the representative of the Eastern Ministry] and State Secretary Dr Bühler argued that certain preliminary measures for the final solution should immediately be taken in the relevant area itself, although in such a way as to avoid causing disquiet among the local population.'

These 'preliminary measures', however, can only have meant one thing: the construction of extermination camps in the district of Lublin: Belzec was already under construction, while Sobibor may have been at the planning stage. However, the minutes do not provide any evidence that any decision was taken on the proposals of Meyer and Bühler at the conference itself.

In fact the Wannsee Conference took place at a watershed. The original plan, for which concrete steps had already been taken, for the comprehensive deportation and annihilation of the Jews in camps in the occupied Soviet territories ('road-building' as a synonym for forced labour in inadequate conditions) was still being adhered to. However, at the same time it had become clear that the precondition for this, an impending victory, could not be expected at least in the short term, while in the meantime hundreds of thousands of people had been killed in the occupied Polish territories, in Serbia, and the Soviet Union, and there were plans to extend these massacres.

Thus, the Wannsee minutes that have survived provide a snapshot of a stage reached in a process in the course of which the SS leadership had shifted its perspective away from the idea of a post-war 'final solution' to the new aim of implementing ever more stages of the 'Final Solution' during the war, in other words to 'anticipate' it, while at the same time this new perspective still included the post-war period. During this critical period, the deportation to the occupied Soviet territories increasingly became a fiction, while mass murder in the General Government increasingly became reality. During the greatest crisis of the war so far, the 'Final Solution' of the 'Jewish question' that had originally been intended, namely the mass deportations to the occupied Soviet territories, was becoming increasingly illusory. In this context Heydrich wished to convey the impression to those responsible for the persecution of the Jews that the RSHA had a plan whereby the mass murders which had begun in different ways in various occupied territories, which represented a hitherto unimaginable realization of state terror, could lead to a 'total solution' that could be implemented in the long term.

While Heydrich adhered to the scheme of deportations to the occupied Eastern territories and allowed no doubts that the deportees would be violently killed there, the minutes of the discussion make it clear that other solutions had already been considered, namely the possibility of murdering all the Jews in the General Government *in situ*. This idea was plainly accepted after the Wannsee Conference, and it also became gradually accepted that the deportations from the rest of Europe, originally planned for the occupied Soviet territories, were to be diverted to the extermination sites under construction in the General Government. On 20 January 1942, Heydrich had two chief concerns: the deportations had to be accepted (everything that happened after the deportations was an internal SS matter, and no longer had to be agreed with other institutions). Secondly, the category of those to be deported had to be established: the status of *Mischlinge* and those married to non-Jews had to be clarified.

This latter issue was dealt with in the second part of the conference. Heydrich suggested that '*Mischlinge* of the first degree' who were married to 'Aryans' were as a rule to be deported or dispatched to a 'ghetto for the aged'. Heydrich pointed out that the complicated classification of *Mischlinge* by the Nazi racial laws would have required numerous individual decisions. The State Secretary in the Reich Ministry of the Interior, Wilhelm Stuckart, objected to the 'endless administrative work' that this would inevitably produce, and suggested 'a move to compulsory sterilization'. This disagreement could not be settled at the conference, and was thus to be addressed in several subsequent meetings, albeit without any conclusive results.[14]

However, by being included in the detailed discussion of the problems surrounding *Mischlinge* and 'mixed marriages', the representatives of the ministerial bureaucracy came to share both knowledge of and responsibility for the 'Final Solution'. For, with the concerns they raised against the inclusion of marginal groups in the deportations, the representatives of the ministerial bureaucracy had made it plain that they had no concerns about the principle of deportation per se. This was indeed the crucial result of the meeting and the main reason why Heydrich had detailed minutes prepared and widely circulated.

PART V

THE EXTERMINATION OF THE EUROPEAN JEW, 1942–1945

CHAPTER 17

THE BEGINNING OF THE EXTERMINATION POLICY ON A EUROPEAN SCALE IN 1942

By the middle of 1942, the Nazi regime was to consolidate and unify the mass murders that it had begun in the occupied Soviet territories in the summer of 1941, and in certain other regions of Eastern and South-Eastern Europe, into a comprehensive programme for the systematic murder of the Jews under German rule. The authorities gradually moved away from the idea that the mass murders were anticipations of the 'Final Solution' that was to be carried out to its full extent only after the end of the war; instead, in the middle of 1942, the conviction had become established that the 'Final Solution' could be achieved by an intensification and expansion of these murders during the war itself.

This transition to the systematic and comprehensive extermination of all Jews under German rule contained a radical change in the idea of the temporal sequence of the 'Final Solution', but at the same time it meant a change in the context of justification into which the murders were placed. If the mass murder of the Soviet Jews had originally been justified with reference to the extermination of the Jewish-Bolshevik complex, as the war progressed the idea became increasingly established that the systematic 'cleansing' of the country of all Jews was a first step in the construction of an empire of *Lebensraum* built on a foundation of racism. The deportation of the Jews of Central and Western Europe since autumn 1941 had in turn created 'factual constraints' in the deportation zones where there were no possibilities of accommodation and these, as we have seen, were used to justify the murder of indigenous Jews.

Even during these first waves of murder in Eastern Europe a distinction had been introduced between those elements who were 'capable of work' and those who were not, and thus had begun in this way to erect a further context of justification for the mass murders which was, from the spring of 1942, transferred to the overall European extermination programme that was under way. The idea—ignoring realities—of a gigantic Jewish 'workforce' provided a seemingly rational justification for mass murder in two respects: Jews who were 'capable of work' were ruthlessly deployed in forced labour in camps and ghettos until they were fatally exhausted, while those Jews who were 'incapable of work' or 'not deployable' were immediately killed as 'useless mouths'.

The launch of the systematic Europe-wide murder of the Jews was a complex process. In order to make it more comprehensible, in this chapter we will first give an account of two interlinking processes that led to the extension of the murders to the whole of Europe in the first months of 1942: first of all the intention pursued by the SS since the beginning of 1942 to deploy Jews in large numbers as forced labourers, and thus to kill them ('extermination through labour'); secondly, the intention closely connected with this, to murder Jews in Poland who were 'incapable of work', an intention that had been realized in the districts of Lublin and Galicia since March 1942 with the help of stationary gas chambers; thirdly, the beginning of the deportations of the Jews from Central and Western Europe from the spring of 1942 onwards, to the district of Lublin, the zone which was at this time the centre of the extermination of the Polish Jews and—where individuals 'capable of work' were concerned—to Majdanek and Auschwitz concentration camps.

As we shall see in the course of this chapter, from May and June 1942 a series of further developments began which made a crucial contribution to the further intensification of the mass murders that had already begun, and to their extension into the whole of Europe: first of all, the systematic murder of Jews from Central and Eastern Europe who were not capable of work; secondly, the extension of systematic mass murder to the whole of Poland and the renewal of major murder actions in the occupied Soviet territories; thirdly, the spread of the deportations to the extermination camps to the rest of Europe.

'Extermination through Labour'

The SS had already developed the basis for a policy of 'extermination through work'[1] in the late summer of 1941 in the occupied Soviet territories. The concept had been explicitly formulated by Einsatzgruppe C in September 1941, when they suggested the 'solution of the Jewish question by a large-scale work deployment of the Jews', which would lead to 'a gradual liquidation of Jewry', and corresponded to the 'economic conditions of the country'.[2] In fact the *Einsatzgruppen* in the occupied Eastern territories had proceeded, to some extent since July and more intensively since August and September 1941, to confine some of the Jewish population in ghettos as part of the now systematic extermination policy, and to use them as a labour pool.

This policy did not follow a fixed and detailed plan, but was a modification of the extermination policy under the conditions of the protracted war; the removal of the greatest possible number of Jews was to be harmonized with the rising demand for labour. In this way a variant on the extermination policy came into being: part of the Jewish population was progressively decimated by 'work details' that exceeded their physical capacities, by minimal food and care, and by constant selection of those who were no longer 'capable of work' or no longer 'needed'.

From autumn 1941, more intensively from spring 1942, the SS transferred this system to other areas of their empire, namely the prisoners within the concentration camp system and the Jews in occupied Poland. With the beginning of the 'Final Solution'—alongside the mass executions in the East, the progressive plans for deportations from Central and Western Europe, and the ongoing construction of extermination camps in Poland—a fourth complementary element was formed: the murderous Jewish *Arbeitseinatz* (work programme), which became a pillar of the extermination policy.

In autumn 1941 Himmler began to toy with the idea of mobilizing the potential labour-force in the concentration camps with a view to the SS's gigantic building projects in the 'Ostraum'.[3] On the one hand, he introduced measures to make forced labour in the concentration camps, which had hitherto constituted above all a repressive measure, effective in economic terms.[4] On the other hand, in September 1941 Himmler received the Wehrmacht's agreement that a large number of Soviet prisoners of war would be handed over to the SS; accordingly, he ordered the expansion of the Auschwitz-Birkenau and Lublin-Majdanek concentration camps to receive prisoners of war.[5] These prisoners were to be used for forced labour.

However, because of the mass deaths of the exhausted prisoners (a considerable number of whom had also been executed in the wake of the camp selections described above[6]) these plans collapsed. From late 1941 Himmler received no more prisoners of war from the Wehrmacht.[7] After Hitler's corresponding decision of general principle in October 1941, Soviet prisoners of war were indeed to be deployed on a large scale in the German arms industry, but not within the concentration camps.[8]

But at the same time the SS saw an ever greater need for manpower, first in connection with their peacetime construction programme, which will be described below, and from the spring of 1942 increasingly also for the construction of their own armaments production—a project that would finally fail in the face of resistance from industry.[9] Accordingly, the SS pressed ahead with revision of the whole work programme of concentration camp inmates towards a more efficient exploitation of the inmate workforce. The organizational foundations for this project were laid between January and March 1942, through the incorporation of the two Main Offices, Budget and Buildings Main Office and Administration and Business Main Office, and the Concentration Camp Inspectorate into the newly formed SS Business and Administration Main office (WVHA) under Oswald Pohl.[10]

Around the New Year in 1942, the plans of the Budget and Buildings Main Office were gradually taking shape for the peacetime building programme of the SS and the police. Prompted by Himmler to plan as generously as possible, the SS Main Office chief, Hans Kammler, submitted a building programme costing in the region of 20 to 30 billion Reichsmarks, containing, in particular, the planned settlements in the 'Ostraum'. To be able to realize this programme, Kammler planned to set up SS construction brigades consisting of 'prisoners, prisoners of war, Jews etc.' totalling 175,000 men.[11]

Himmler set out his ideas for an 'economization' of the concentration camp in a note written in late March 1942, responding to statements by Kammler, now director of construction in the WVHA. Here Himmler criticized the fact, for example, that Kammler had set the work performance of a prisoner at only 50 per cent of that of a German worker. It was precisely in the raising of the individual performance rates of the prisoner workers, Himmler stressed, that 'the greatest pool of labour resides. The chance to extract it is given to the head of the 'Business and Administration Main Office'.[12] The WVHA's director, Pohl, stressed this change in the concentration camp system, by now under way, in a report for Himmler on 30 April: according to this report, the 'preservation of prisoners only for reasons of security, education, or prevention is no longer the priority'; it was rather that the 'emphasis [had] shifted to the economic side'.[13] In an order issued the same day[14] Pohl made the concentration camp commandants 'responsible for the deployment of the workforce. This deployment must be exhausting in the true sense of the word in order to achieve the greatest possible performance.'

It is quite plain that the 'exhausting' work programme of the prisoners was an obstacle to their economically effective use in the armaments industry, which also proceeded correspondingly slowly in the spring of 1942. Because of under-nourishment, the disastrous living conditions in the camps, and constant excessive physical demands as well as the security provisions that obstructed the running of the work programme, the prisoners were comparatively unproductive; despite low wages (which were to be paid to the SS), the deployment of prisoners was relatively unprofitable from the point of view of the armaments industry.[15] The SS did not take the route of encouraging greater output from prisoners by offering incentives, as had been successfully attempted with Soviet prisoners in 1942.[16] The prevalent idea was to terrorize the prisoners into achieving higher performance rates before replacing the soon exhausted slave labourers by new workers.

This unproductive, lethal deployment of forced labourers in a time of mounting labour shortages is often seen as confirmation of the unconditional precedence of ideological motives over economic considerations within the Nazi system, and is singled out for its profoundly irrational and self-destructive character. But identifying such an evident 'discrepancy between the physical extermination of the ideological adversary and the exploitation of his workforce to develop the armaments industry'[17] assumes a bipolarity between 'world-view' and 'rationality' that was alien to the world of the SS. If instead we start with the idea prevalent among the SS leadership around the end of 1941 and beginning of 1942 that the occupation and reordering of the 'Ostraum' was imminent, then the interconnection of terror and total exploitation to death, the system of 'extermination through work' appears as a horribly consistent anticipation of the barbaric methods of rule intended for the East. Just as the planned conquest in the East, which was to ensure the rule of the 'Aryan race' for centuries to come, destroyed any economic calculations, concerning the work of the prisoners too, the SS went far beyond any considerations of profitability. This was made easier by the fact that the initial plan was to deploy the prisoners for SS projects above all; at first the idea was construction, then later SS armaments production.[18]

From the point of view of the SS, mass murder and mass production were easily linked with the system of 'extermination through work'. The concentration camp system could also be extended, and the proof for its adaptability to the conditions of war demonstrated. Above all, 'extermination through work' could be used to defuse the argument repeatedly levelled against the SS during their murder campaigns in the Soviet Union: the 'pointlessness' of the extermination of urgently required manpower. This was because with 'extermination through work' a context was established that provided an 'objective' justification for the extermination of people 'unfit for work'.

When the plans for the deployment of prisoners as forced labourers became gradually more concrete around the end of 1941 and the beginning of 1942,[19] Himmler showed himself determined to deploy a large number of Jewish prisoners above all, especially in order to find a quick replacement for the Soviet prisoners of war who were by now exhausted. In preparation for the planned major construction and armaments tasks, on 26 January 1942 Himmler briefed the head of Department D of the WVHA on its new tasks: 'Since no more Russian prisoners of war may be expected in the near future, I will send a large number of Jews who have been emigrated [sic!] from Germany to the camps. Prepare to receive 100,000 male and up to 50,000 female Jews in the concentration camps within the next four weeks. Major economic tasks will confront the concentration camps in the weeks to come.'[20] Over the next few months, in fact, the deportations from the Reich were to go to the district of Lublin, where some of those Jews 'capable of work' had to perform forced labour in Majdanek and other camps. On the other hand, several thousand Slovakian Jews were to be deported chiefly to Auschwitz, where they were also to be deployed in forced labour projects.[21] Both camps had originally been intended to receive a large number of Soviet prisoners of war. But it was to become apparent that apart from the goal of the economic exploitation of the Jewish prisoners, Himmler achieved one thing above all with this new policy: he created a pretext for the murder of the prisoners who were now 'superfluous', who were not used for the 'work programme'.

We have access to a key document that reveals especially clearly the close connection between 'extermination through work' and the murder of those 'unfit for work'. It is a letter from the chief of the Gestapo, Müller, to the commander of the Security Police in Riga, Karl Jäger, written on 18 May 1942. In it he says that because of a 'general (!) decree by the Reichsführer SS and head of the German police', 'Jews between the ages of 16 and 32 are to be excluded from the implementation of special measures until further instructions. These Jews are to be added to the closed work programme. Concentration camp or labour camp.' This exemption implicitly contains a reference to the fundamental guidelines that existed for the treatment of older prisoners, younger prisoners unfit for work, and children within the concentration camp system at this point in time: they were subject to the 'special measures'. We do not know whether Himmler's order, which Müller quotes here, the original of which has not yet been found, is more precise with regard to the group of people to whom the exemption did not apply. We will return to this subject elsewhere.[22]

This order by Himmler came at a time when pressure on Jews still working in German industry was constantly mounting. In March 1942, Goering had forbidden the deportation of this group,[23] but his prohibition had had very little effect, since the Reich Security Head Office (RSHA) interpreted the exemptions for those Jews in the 'closed strategic work programme vital to the war effort' in an increasingly restrictive way.[24] Goebbels's diary entry for 29 May reveals that Hitler responded to the Propaganda Minister's urging to commission Speer 'to ensure as quickly as possible that Jews employed in the German armaments business be replaced by foreign workers'.[25] In view of the transport moratorium imposed in mid-June, the RSHA initially deported mainly elderly Jews to Theresienstadt, but in September 1942 Hitler was to stress once again, at a conference on armaments, that 'withdrawing the Jews from the armaments factories in the Reich' was of prime importance.[26]

But it was not only the concentration camp system that was restructured through the policy of 'extermination through work' between autumn 1941 and spring 1942. The impact of the new policy may also be observed in occupied Poland, both in annexed Upper Silesia and in the General Government.

We have already described how in the camps of the Schmelt Organization in Upper Silesia, which held 30,000 to 40,000 Jewish forced labourers in spring 1942, selections had been carried out since November 1941, sporadically at first, but soon systematically, and those no longer fit for work were brought to Auschwitz, where they were murdered.[27]

In the ghettos and labour camps of the General Government there had also been high mortality rates before, but that had been part of the German policy of general decimation of the Jewish population, in which the 'Final Solution' had been deferred until the post-war period. Initially from autumn 1941, but more intensively from spring 1942, the system of 'extermination through work', alongside the gas chambers, executions, and deportations, became a leading element in the systematic murder of the Jews of the General Government.

In autumn 1941 in the district of Galicia, the SS launched what was probably the largest forced labour project in which a Jewish labour-force was deployed: the expansion of the strategically important road connection from Lemberg (Lvov) towards the Donets basin, known as *Durchgangsstrasse* (transit road) IV (DG IV).[28] In October 1941 Fritz Katzmann, the SSPF of the district of Galicia, had thousands of Jews put in concentration camps to work on road construction under the most severe conditions. Katzmann's verbal instruction to the director of the camp was to shoot any Jews who were unfit for work or who tried to escape, and to kill hostages for any escapees who were not caught; the number of victims was a matter of indifference. Early in 1942 Himmler transferred to a series of SSPFs responsibility for the extension of further sections of DG IV in the Ukraine, and on 7 February he transferred the overall running of the project to the HSSPF of Ukraine and southern Russia, Prützmann. An order issued by the Führer on 19 February placed extremely high priority on the expansion of major communications, including the DG IV.

Using key German workers, members of the OT, about 50,000 Ukrainian forced labourers, as many prisoners of war, and some 10,000 Jews were deployed on DG IV in 1942. The existence of some thirty camps for Jewish workers in the construction sector has been demonstrated, and some twenty more on the Ukrainian part of the road.[29] The running of the extremely primitive camps, in which disastrous conditions prevailed, was placed in the hands of members of the SS and the police; in some cases it was also exercised by OT staff, and the camps were guarded by police and local guard units. After all those new prisoners who arrived in the camp who were 'not fit for work' (old people, children, the sick) had been singled out and murdered, camp inmates were constantly being shot for inadequate levels of work, minor infringements of camp regulations, or purely on a whim. When the work came to an end late in 1943/early in 1944, other large-scale shootings occurred. Eighty-four shootings have been identified, in which some 25,000 Jews were murdered.[30]

The forced labour project for the expansion of DG IV can be seen as a pilot project for the takeover of all the forced labour in the General Government by the SS and police leaders in spring/summer 1942. As we will show,[31] the 'deployment' of Jewish workers did not, from the point of view of the SS leadership, contradict the extermination policy, but formed an integral part of it.

Deportations from Central and Western Europe

The deportations which resumed on a large scale in 1942 were preceded in January and February 1942 by a series of public declarations by Hitler, in which he unambiguously recalled his 'prophecy' of January 1939, that in the event of a new 'world war' the Jews would be 'exterminated'. Pertinent passages appear both in his New Year proclamation,[32] his speech in the Sportpalast on the anniversary of the 'seizure of power',[33] and in his declaration on the occasion of the celebration of the twenty-second anniversary of the Party's Foundation on 24 February 1942.[34] The fact that with America's entry into the war National Socialist Germany was actually waging a world war, Hitler's constant habit of dating his prophecy to the day of the outbreak of war, and the fact that he now no longer spoke of 'destroying' (vernichten), but of 'exterminating' (ausrotten), gave his threat a particular emphasis.

The Third and Fourth Wave of Deportation from the Greater German Reich

The further deportations from the Reich, which began in substantial numbers in the spring of 1942, were announced in a dispatch from Eichmann to the Gestapo regional and district headquarters dated 31 January 1942.[35] In it he wrote that the 'recent evacuation of Jews to the East carried out in individual areas' represented 'the beginning of the final solution of the Jewish question in the Old Reich, the Ostmark, and the Protectorate of Bohemia and Moravia'. However, at that point, 'only some state police [Gestapo] headquarters could be involved in view of limited reception possibilities in the East and difficulties with transport'. But 'new reception possibilities [would be] worked on with the aim of deporting further contingents of Jews'.

The dispatch also identified those groups of people who were not yet to be deported: Jews living in 'mixed marriages', Jews of foreign citizenship (excluding stateless Jews as well as those of former Polish and Luxembourg citizenship); 'Jews in closed strategic work programmes' as well as the elderly and the frail. The separation of married couples as well as the separation from their families of children up to the age of 14 years was to be avoided.

On 6 March 1942 Eichmann held a meeting with the representatives of the Gestapo headquarters or Gestapo offices which were entrusted with the task of carrying out the deportations. Here it became clear that by this time a further Reich-wide deportation programme had been established.[36] Eichmann announced that at first 55,000 Jews would be deported from the Reich territory including the 'Ostmark' and the Protectorate: 20,000 Jews were to be evacuated from Prague, 18,000 from Vienna. 'The size of the other transports conforms proportionally to the numbers of Jews still present in each State Police office/headquarters precinct.' Individually, the transports could not be assigned a precise time. All that was available were 'empty "Russian trains"/worker transports to the Old Reich, which were going back empty to the General Government and will now be used by the RSHA with the agreement of the OKH'.

Eichmann also announced that it was intended that most of the Jews left in the Old Reich would in all likelihood be deported to Theresienstadt in the course of the summer or the autumn. Theresienstadt was being cleared at the time, and '15–20,000 Jews from the Protectorate could move there temporarily'. This would be done, Eichmann added, in order to 'preserve outward appearances'—a reference to the fact that the RSHA had internally reached the conclusion that the pretext for the deportations, the supposed 'work programme' in the East, could be easily seen through if, as had happened previously, old people were also deported to the East European ghettos.

The third wave of deportations from the Reich was in the end to last from mid-March to mid-June, and there are at least forty-three transports that are individually known about; it may, however, have been over sixty, so that, if we assume an average of 1,000 people per transport, a figure on the scale cited by Eichmann of 55,000 deportees would probably have been reached.[37]

The identifiable transports came primarily from the areas of the Old Reich that were considered to be in danger from air raids (twenty-three trains) and from the Protectorate (fourteen trains from Theresienstadt as well as one from Prague). They were destined for a series of ghettos in the district of Lublin (particularly Izbica, Piaski, Zamozc), whose inhabitants had been murdered in Belzec a short time previously. Four transports ended in the Warsaw ghetto.[38] As a rule the deportation trains from the Reich stopped in Lublin, where men who were assessed as 'fit for work' were taken from the trains and brought to the Majdanek camp.[39]

Hence the pattern of deportations of the Central European Jews and the murder of the Jews of Eastern Europe corresponded to events already described that took place in Lodz, Riga, and Minsk. The living conditions in the ghettos of the General Government led to the miserable death of by far the majority of deportees within a few months. Those who did not die in the ghettos were generally deported to the extermination camps in the General Government.

The surviving documents of the German administration in the district of Lublin indicate that here—under the designation 'Judenaustausch' (exchange of Jews)—the indigenous Jews were 'taken out' of the individual communities (i.e. sent to Belzec), and replaced by 'Reich Jews'.⁴⁰

The 'Judenreferent' (expert on Jewish affairs) of the SSPF Lublin and coordinator of the deportation and extermination programme in the district, Hans Höfle, asked the district administration on 16 March, in other words immediately before the arrival of the first transports, 'whether 60,000 Jews could be unloaded on the stretch between Lublin and Trawniki'.⁴¹ As surprising as this announcement was, over the next few months the district administration was only informed at short notice about the arriving trains, whose inmates it then distributed summarily, and in agreement with the SSPF (Höfle), to the Jewish residential quarters, which he had recently 'cleared'.⁴² Through this improvised procedure and the chaotic conditions that prevailed as a result of it, the district administration was placed under the pressure of artificially created 'factual constraints'; the deportations of the indigenous Jews, who had to make way for the impending arrival of the 'Reich Jews', thus appeared as the inevitable consequence of a decision that had been made outside their own sphere of responsibility.

Towards the end of the third wave of deportations, in June 1942, some transports had been assembled that deviated from the previous pattern: on 10 June 1942, in 'retaliation' for the death of Heydrich, 1,000 Jews were deported from Prague to Majdanek and placed both there and in the camps in the surrounding area.⁴³ Finally, from mid-June the last transports of the third wave were directed towards Sobibor extermination camp, where the majority of deportees were murdered in the gas chambers, after even smaller groups of people had been taken off the trains during a stop in Lublin. This is attested with certainty for a transport from Theresienstadt, one from Berlin and one from Vienna, which arrived in Sobibor between 15 and 19 June. It is possible that exactly the same fate befell the people on two further Theresienstadt transports which reached the district of Lublin on 15 and 16 June.⁴⁴ As early as 18 May, however, half of a group of around 800 people who had been deported from Theresienstadt to Siedliszcze, had been brought to Sobibor along with the indigenous Jews and murdered there.⁴⁵

But the actual turning point in the deportation practice occurred only in the middle of June 1942: only from that point onwards were Jews on the trains from the Reich, after the selection of those 'fit for work' in Lublin, generally sent directly to the extermination camps.

While the third wave continued, in May 1942 a fourth wave of deportations arrived from the Reich, destined for the occupied Eastern regions. As already described, the deportations to Minsk planned during the second wave were interrupted in November 1941, and only continued until February 1942 in the case of Riga. The transports to Minsk now resumed; between May and September, in at least seventeen transports,⁴⁶ some 16,000 people were deported from the territory of the 'Greater German Reich', interrupted only from mid-June to mid-July by a military transport moratorium: now those deported to Minsk were no longer confined to the ghetto, and instead the trains were moved on to a stop near the estate of Maly Trostinets, where from 11 May 1942 almost all deportees were shot on the spot or murdered in gas vans.[47] In April 1942 Heydrich is supposed to have announced the resumption of deportations and the impending murders during a visit to Minsk.[48]

Thus, with the deportations to Minsk in May and the transports to Sobibor in mid-June, a new phase of the extermination policy began. Now the deportees were no longer accommodated temporarily in ghettos or labour camps, before perishing as a result of the disastrous living conditions, or being murdered in an extermination camp on the grounds that they were no longer 'fit for work'; now the great majority of deportees were shot directly at the end of the journey or suffocated in gas vans. The previous pattern, according to which the indigenous Jews were deported to the extermination camps to 'make room' for the Jews arriving from the Reich had thus been abandoned. The murder machinery was thus completely freed from the context of 'resettlement', 'expulsion', and 'work programme'; the goal, the death of the deportees, thus emerged with even greater clarity.

As long as the murder machinery was contained within the old pattern, it was at least possible to maintain the fiction that the murders were the result of 'factual constraints' produced by 'resettlement' and the 'work programme': the 'clearing' of the ghettos for the suddenly arriving deportees; execution of deportees from the Reich because there were no adequate reception facilities (as in Riga and Kovno (Kaunas) in late 1941); the selection of those no longer fit for work, as 'room was needed' again, and 'no food was available'; ruthless deployment for forced labour in the service of the war economy; renewed selection. Because of the systematically excessive demands made upon them the local offices of the civil administration and the security police were placed in situations that spasmodically required more and more radical solutions, or which offered them a framework of action in which such radical solutions could be presented as 'factually justified'.

The transport moratorium introduced for the West–East railway in June saw the start of the deportations of those people from the Reich who, as Eichmann had announced in January, had for various reason been exempted from the 'Eastern transports'; these were elderly and frail people, decorated veterans with their wives and children under the age of 14, and Jewish spouses from a 'mixed marriage' that no longer existed, who were freed from labelling regulations, as well as single 'half-breeds' who were 'deemed' to be Jews under the Nuremberg Laws. These deportations went to Theresienstadt,[49] which served not only as the 'old people's ghetto' for German Jews, but also above all as a transit camp for those deported from the Protectorate, who numbered around 74,000.[50]

In June and July 1942 a total of sixteen special trains each carrying about 1,000 elderly people from the Reich set off for Theresienstadt; after a further timetable programme decided in early August, twenty-one further special trains followed between mid-August and early October. On top of this, because of the transport moratorium that prevailed between June and July, the German authorities had fallen back on coupling one or two passenger wagons, each carrying fifty passengers to already scheduled trains; between June and October 1942, more than 100 such 'small' transports were organized. Overall during this period some 45,000 German and Austrian Jews were deported to the 'old people's ghetto' of Theresienstadt.[51] But even after this wave of deportations many smaller transports to Theresienstadt occurred throughout the winter of 1942–3.[52]

In the second half of 1942 there were further deportations from the Reich which went to Eastern European ghettos or directly to extermination camps. Various references indicate that in July three smaller transports from the Reich with a total of 700 passengers reached the Warsaw ghetto. Between August and October 1942 five deportations from Berlin and Theresienstadt went to Riga, as well as a further deportation from these two places to Raasiku near Reval (Tallinn).[53]

In September and October ten deportation trains travelled from Theresienstadt, mostly with an average of 2,000 passengers, to Treblinka extermination camp, as well as one train from Darmstadt.[54] Another three trains from Berlin, two from Vienna, and one from Theresienstadt, all of which travelled directly to Auschwitz in the first half of 1942, can be confirmed with certainty.[55]

In the last quarter of 1942 the regime intensified the pressure on those Jews still present in the Reich. During the armaments discussion from 20 until 22 September 1942 Hitler spoke of the 'importance of removing the Jews from the armaments factories in the Reich'.[56] Some days later he told Goebbels of his resolution 'to remove the Jews from Berlin at all cost'; Jewish workers were to be replaced by foreigners.[57] At the same time Himmler agreed with Justice Minister Thierack to assume responsibility for all 'asocial elements', including all Jews, Gypsies, Russians, and Poles, and their 'extermination through work'.[58]

On 5 November the RSHA announced an order from Himmler in which all concentration camps in the Reich were to be made 'Jew-free', and all Jewish prisoners were to be transferred to Auschwitz and Lublin.[59] However, it was only with the intensified recruitment of foreigners and prisoners of war for armaments production after the beginning of 1943 and the general toughening of domestic policy after Stalingrad that the preconditions for this new phase in deportations were in place.

Slovakia

In February 1942, in response to a request from Himmler, the Foreign Office sent a request to the Slovakian government for 20,000 Jewish workers to be sent to the Reich for deployment 'in the East'.[60] This request, as we have seen, was preceded by an offer that Himmler made to the Slovakian head of state on 20 October 1941 during a visit to the Führer's headquarters, to the effect that the Slovakian Jews be deported to a special territory in the General Government; in addition, the Slovakian government had already declared its agreement that Slovakian nationals be included in the deportations.[61] When the Slovakian government responded to the German request of February 1942, it was thus knowingly taking the first step towards the deportation of all Slovakian Jews.

The Slovakian Jews who had been subjected to a special law and increasingly excluded from public and business life since April 1939, in other words immediately after the foundation of the state,[62] were now recorded on police files; all people deemed to be 'fit for work' between the ages of 16 and 45 were registered separately and gradually rounded up and put in special camps.[63] On 25 March the first 1,000 girls and young women were deported to Auschwitz to work as forced labourers. The original deportation plan had allowed for the deportation of some 13,000 men to the Majdanek camp and 7,000 women to Auschwitz.[64] In fact, between 26 March and 7 April four transports of young women (about 3,800 in all) arrived in Auschwitz and four transports with a total of 4,500 young men in Majdanek.[65] On the basis of a request, issued by Himmler through the Foreign Office, the Slovakian government finally declared itself ready to deport all the Slovakian Jews (another 70,000 people).[66]

On 10 April Heydrich explained the deportation programme in Bratislava.[67] The following day the deportations of whole families began. Now the deportation plan was changed: seven transports are known to have arrived in Auschwitz, where the deportees were deployed in forced labour; another thirty-four transports set off for the district of Lublin at around the same time.[68] The subsequent fate of the people deported to this area is comparable with those who were deported to the same area at the same time from the Reich. The Slovakian Jews were mostly transported to places from which the indigenous Jewish population had been taken to the extermination camps of Belzec and Sobibor. Accommodation in these places—for which in general no preparations whatsoever had been made—was in some cases only a brief stop before further deportation to the extermination camps, in others it became an imprisonment under wretched conditions that lasted for months and even years. Again, those men who were fit for work were taken out of the transports that came via Lublin and imprisoned in Majdanek camp; in all there may have been 8,500 men, of whom 883 were still living in the camp in July 1943.[69]

Since the beginning of June the inmates of a total of ten transports that were not deemed 'fit for work' at the selection in Lublin and were not locked up in Majdanek camp, women and children above all, had no longer been placed in a ghetto, but rather taken directly to Sobibor extermination camp where they were murdered. This meant that the Slovakian Jews too were now caught up in that escalation of extermination to which the Jews deported to Minsk from the 'Greater German Reich' had fallen victim since mid-May. The last Sobibor transport set off from Slovakia on 14 June, a day before the deportations from the Reich to the district of Lublin were stopped.[70]

After this all Slovakian transports came to Auschwitz where, beginning with the train that arrived on 4 July 1942, a selection now regularly occurred on the ramp: Jews who were 'fit for work' were sent to the camp, while those deemed 'unfit for work', meaning in particular all children, their mothers, and elderly people, were murdered in the gas chambers immediately after their arrival. By 21 October we are able to identify eight transports from Slovakia whose inmates suffered this fate.[71]

But information and rumours about the fate of the deportees trickled in to Slovakia and led to growing resistance against the continuation of the existing Slovakian policy. The Catholic Church in Slovakia and the Vatican intervened, leading politicians spoke out against a continuation of the deportations and tried to sabotage any persecutory measures; dissent was also voiced by leading representatives of business. The general contextual conditions in domestic politics were favourable to this attitude of opposition: after Prime Minister Tuka, the most important representative of a radical and unconditionally pro-German policy, had been to a large extent deprived of power in the spring of 1942, within the Slovakian government there was a gradual transition to a more moderate policy.[72]

We should not ignore the fact that a significant role in the formation of this increasing opposition to the continuation of a radical anti-Jewish policy was played by a Jewish resistance group that had formed within Ustredna Zidov (the central Jewish council), the official compulsory organization for the Slovakian Jews: the so-called 'subsidiary government' around the Zionist youth leader Gisi Fleischmann and the rabbi Michael Dor Weissmandel.[73] They systematically collected information concerning the fate of the deportees, used a great variety of methods to stir up resistance to the deportations within influential Slovakian circles, and made contact with Jewish and non-Jewish organizations abroad. The 'subsidiary government' went so far as to bribe the German 'Jewish adviser', Dieter Wisliceny, with a considerable sum of dollars to bring the deportations to a standstill; but the question of whether this method really played any part in the decision to stop the deportations remains unresolved.

At the end of June—some 50,000 Slovakian Jews had been deported—it became apparent that there were hardly any people left for further deportations. Of the 89,000-strong Jewish minority, a considerable proportion—more than 25,000—had letters of protection from various offices or fell under particular exceptional categories.[74] In July another four transports went off, two in September and one in October, then they were stopped by the Slovakian authorities. Altogether, almost 58,000 people had been deported in fifty-seven transports.[75]

France and the First Outlines of a Deportation Programme
for Western Europe

In the face of continuing attacks by the French resistance, at the end of 1941 the military administration in France continued its policy of reprisals: on 15 December 95 hostages, including 58 Jews, were shot, a high monetary penalty to be paid by the Jewish population of the occupied zone had been established, and 1,000 Jews and 500 Communists designated for a transport 'to the East'. In order to fill this quota, the occupying forces, again with the support of the French police, had arrested 743 Jewish men, who were held along with 300 men previously arrested at the Compiègne camp: the actual deportation, however, was at first delayed for lack of means of transportation.[76]

After Eichmann had approved the deportation of these 1,000 people on 1 March,[77] according to information from Theodor Dannecker, the expert for Jewish affairs of the Gestapo, it was agreed at a meeting in the RSHA on 4 March to suggest that the French government deport 'some 5,000 Jews to the East'. These were 'initially to be male Jews who were fit for work, no older than 55', who were also French citizens.[78] Also according to Dannecker, Heydrich is supposed to have agreed at this discussion that after the first 1,000 people 'another 5,000 Jews were to be transported from Paris in the course of 1942'; for 1943 he had announced 'further major transports'.[79]

The first 'hostage transport', totalling 1,112 people, of whom half were French Jews and half Jews of other nationality, arrived in Auschwitz on 30 March.[80] For the deportation of a further 5,000 people, Eichmann had given more detailed instructions to the commander of the Security Police in France, Helmut Knochen, on 12 March: only Jews of German, French, formerly Polish, and Luxembourg nationality were to be deported, of whom no more than 5 per cent were to be women.[81] In March responsibility for all police matters and expressly all sanctions had been transferred to the newly created office of a Higher SS and Police Commander in France; the position was occupied by Karl Oberg, the former SSPF in the district of Radom.[82]

By the end of May—as a response to further attacks by the resistance movement—a further 471 people, Jews and Communists, had been shot in the occupied zone; the military administration had also designated so many people for deportation as a reaction to individual assassination attempts that the quota of 5,000 Jews set out in the March deportation plans of the RSHA had already been reached.[83] On 13 May, Dannecker established at a meeting with the head of the railway transport department, Lieutenant General Kohl, on 13 May, that he was an 'uncompromising adversary of the Jews' who 'agrees 100 % to a final solution of the Jewish question with the goal of the total extermination of the adversary'.[84] The next five transports, each with 1,000 people, left Compiègne between 5 June and 17 July, destined for Auschwitz.

During a visit to Paris at the beginning of May, Heydrich is supposed to have announced that 'greater, more perfect, more numerically fruitful' solutions were in preparation to kill the Jews of Europe.[85] At the same time Heydrich objected to further hostage shootings in France, welcome news for the military, who assumed that deportations from France would be less provocative to the Resistance than executions in the country itself.[86]

On 11 June 1942 a meeting was held in the RSHA attended by the 'Jewish experts' in Paris, The Hague, and Brussels. Dannecker recorded that the meeting concluded that 'for military reasons' 'an evacuation of Jews from Germany to the Eastern deportation zone' could not be carried out during the summer. 'RFSS has therefore ordered that large numbers of Jews should be transferred either from the South East (Serbia) or from the occupied Western territories to Auschwitz concentration camp for the purposes of work. The fundamental condition is that the Jews (of both sexes) are between the ages of 16 and 40. 10 % of Jews unfit for work can be sent with them.' At the meeting an agreement was reached about the quotas from the occupied Western territories: according to this, 15,000 Jews were to be deported from the Netherlands, 10,000 from Belgium, and 100,000 from France, including from the unoccupied zone. 'The transports are to start moving from 13 July, about 3 per week.'[87]

The original plans of early March, in which the RSHA had planned the deportation of a total of 6,000 Jews from France for 1942, had thus been considerably extended. The determining factor here was not only the 'military grounds', the transport moratorium caused by the German summer offensive; it was rather that in March/early April the RSHA's plans had consolidated to such an extent that the outlines of an initial Europe-wide deportation programme became visible, in the context of which not only the Reich and Slovakia were to be made 'Jew-free', but a considerable proportion of the Jews living in the occupied Western territories were to be deported and murdered.

One important clue to the existence of such a programme is a minute[88] from the office of the Slovakian Prime Minister, Tuka, dated 10 April, concerning a visit from Heydrich on the same day. On this occasion Heydrich explained to Tuka that the planned deportation of the Slovakian Jews was 'only part of the programme'. At that point a 'resettlement' of a total of 'half a million' Jews was occurring 'from Europe to the East'. Apart from Slovakia, the Reich, the Protectorate, the Netherlands, Belgium, and France were affected.

Now (at the meeting in the RSHA on 11 June) this programme was modified and accelerated in view of the impending transport stoppage in June: now, within a few weeks, the deportation of a total of 125,00 Jews from the occupied Western territories was to begin within a few weeks, and at the same time it was made clear that this first big wave of deportations—like the agreements with Slovakia—was to encompass the Jews (aged between 16 and 40) meant for the 'work programme' in particular.

But the quota of 100,000 Jews to be deported from France, cited on 11 June, could not be reached, as Dannecker wrote to the RSHA, saying that there was no 'definitive clarity about the number of Jews to be taken on from the unoccupied zone, and he was now only in a position' 'of being able to name departure stations for c.40,000 Jews'.[89] Eichmann informed Rademacher about the new changes in the deportation plans on 22 June 1942. According to these, from mid-July or early August, in daily transports of 1,000 people each, 'first of all 40,000 Jews from the French occupied zone, 40,000 Jews from the Netherlands and 10,000 Jews from Belgium are to be transported for the work programme to Auschwitz camp'.[90] According to this plan, these transports were estimated to take three months.

However, the next day, 23 June, the RSHA Jewish desk received a new instruction from Himmler, as Dannecker learned in Paris from Eichmann at the beginning of July. This stated: 'all Jews resident in France are to be deported as soon as possible.' The 'previously planned rate (3 transports each of 1,000 Jews every week)' must 'be significantly raised within a short time ... with the goal of freeing France entirely of Jews as soon as possible'.[91] This order from Himmler to implement the 'Final Solution' in France completely and as quickly as possible must be seen as part of the escalation of the extermination policy directed against the Jews throughout the whole of Europe; we have already examined the measures that applied to the German Reich and Slovakia, and in the following sections we shall describe the corresponding radicalization in Eastern Europe.

On 27 June, Carltheo Zeitschel, the fanatical 'Jewish expert' within the German embassy and liaison with the SD, noted of a conversation with Dannecker that the latter required '50,000 Jews to be transported from the unoccupied territory to the East as soon as possible'.[92] In negotiations with HSSPF Carl Oberg, the chief of police of the Vichy government, René Bousquet, declared himself willing, at the beginning of July, to arrest stateless or foreign Jews in the unoccupied zone as well as to make the police under his command available for the arrest of Jews in the occupied zone; this collaboration, however, would also be limited to foreign or stateless Jews.[93] ('Stateless' referred in particular to those Jews who had lost their citizenship as a result of German race legislation or the events of the war.) The Vichy government acceded to this outcome of the negotions.[94] But at this point Dannecker, Eichmann's Jewish expert in France, was working on the assumption, as he reported to Berlin, that in a '2nd phase' those Jews naturalized as a result of the French immigration legislation of 1919 and 1927 'could be tackled'.[95]

The 'Final Solution' in Eastern Europe 1942

Poland

The Deportations from the Districts of Lublin and Galicia to the
Extermination Camps of Belzec and Sobibor

On 20 January 1942 the population and welfare department of the General Government demanded that its offices attached to the district governors 'send a list of ghettos in their district as soon as possible', and forward their population figures.[96] These statistics had already been used in the preparation for the deportations in the districts of Lublin and Galicia.

They could start on this since Belzec extermination camp, the construction of which had begun the previous November, was completed in March 1942. Belzec, in the south-eastern part of the district of Lublin, directly on the railway line to Lemberg (Lvov) was to be the prototype of the extermination camps built in the General Government. It covered a relatively small area, a rectangle with sides about 270 m long, and initially consisted of a barrack with three gas chambers. The staff consisted of 20 to 30 Germans, and 90 to 120 so called 'Trawnikis': Soviet prisoners of war, Ukrainians, and ethnic Germans who had passed through the Trawniki SS training camp in the district of Lublin, run by Globocnik. Apart from that, there was a Jewish work unit in Belzec whose members were repeatedly replaced by newly arrived prisoners and murdered.

A spur line made it possible to move railway wagons directly into the camp. Here the victims were led to believe that they were in a transit camp. Men, woman, and children were separated; they had to undress, hand over their valuable objects, women had their hair cut off. The people were then driven naked along a narrow, fenced path, known as the '*Schlauch*', or 'tube', to the gas chambers, which were disguised as shower rooms. An engine produced the deadly exhaust fumes which would generally kill the victims in an agonizing way within 20 to 30 minutes.[97] Jewish forced labourers then had to take the corpses of the murdered people out of the gas chambers and transport them to the large graves in the camp grounds, which had been dug by Jewish forced labourers in 1940.

In the district of Lublin the deportations began in mid-March: between 16 March and 20 April the ghetto in the district capital, Lublin, was almost completely cleared in two phases.[98] This enterprise was run by SS and police chief Odilo Globocnik and by units of the Security Police, the Order Police, and Trawniki men, while the civil administration provided essential support.[99] Himmler had stayed there immediately before the beginning of the clearance of the Lublin ghetto, which marks the beginning of the systematic murder of the Jews in the General Government and became the model for many similar 'campaigns'. He had met HSSPF Friedrich Krüger in Lublin on 13 March, and Globocnik the following day.[100]

During the clearance of the Lublin ghetto, many people had already been shot within the ghetto; a few thousand people were retained *in situ* as a workforce, and some 30,000 were deported to Belzec, where they were murdered. The fiction of a 'resettlement' to the occupied Eastern territories was outwardly maintained, but within a short time information about the fate of the deportees within the whole of the General Government filtered out into the Reich.[101] Thus, for example, the propaganda minister, Goebbels, was informed about the murders in the district of Lublin as early as 27 March, as his diary reveals: 'Starting with Lublin, the Jews are now being deported from the General Government to the East. A rather barbaric procedure is being applied, one which should not be described in greater detail, and little remains of the Jews themselves.' Goebbels's remark that '60% of them must be liquidated, while only another 40% can be deployed in work' provides a significant indication of current German plans. The ghettos in the General Government that were being 'vacated', Goebbels went on, would 'now be filled with Jews deported from the Reich, and the procedure is to be repeated there after a certain time'.[102]

A statement by Eichmann to the Israeli police also reveals that Globocnik had been given the task of murdering the majority of the Jews in the district, namely those 'incapable of work'. According to Eichmann's information, once the mass murder had already begun, Globocnik had acquired Heydrich's authorization to kill a further 150,000, probably 250,000 people.[103] The statement by Christian Wirth's adjutant, Joset Oberhauser, according to which initially only 'Jews from various ghettos who are unfit for work should be liquidated', points in the same direction, and it was only in April or May that Globocnik was given the order 'systematically to exterminate the Jews'.[104]

In parallel with the start of the clearance of the ghetto of Lublin came the deportation of Jews from the Reich and Slovakia to the district of Lublin, which had already been set aside for the planned 'Jewish reservation' since autumn 1939. As we have already described, the people deported to the district were accommo-dated in places from which the local Jews deemed 'unfit for work' were deported to Belzec. These deportations from the rural areas of the district began on 24 March. By mid-April some 14,000 Jews had been deported from these small communities to Belzec; then the extermination camp was temporarily closed. The reasons for this are not entirely clear. It is possible that Wirth, who had built the camp and run it during its first phase, saw his task as over; he had at first only been delegated to Globocnik by the T4 programme.[105]

In mid-March, in the district of Galicia, too, a new wave of mass murders began and, for the first time, deportations to extermination camps. From mid-March until early April 1942 about 15,000 people, inhabitants of the ghetto of Lemberg (Lvov) who were deemed 'incapable of work', were deported to Belzec. Further thousands of inhabitants from the smaller ghettos of the district took the same journey between mid-March and around 8/9 April, while thousands more from these ghettos were murdered on the spot.[106] These deportations were also directed by Globocnik's staff.

The systematic clearance of the *Kreise* (counties) began in the district of Lublin, independently of the arrival of Jews from other countries and even before the civil administration could begin to record all Jews capable of work. The victims—apart from about 2,000 forced labourers who were deported to Majdanek—were sent to Sobibor, the second extermination camp in the General Government, which had been built in the meantime and the construction and operation of which was based on Belzec.[107] Belzec, on the other hand, as mentioned above, had initially been shut down in the middle of April. More than 55,000 people fell victim to this wave of deportations, which was interrupted on 10 June. The deportations from the district of Lublin would not be resumed until August/September.[108]

Extension of the Murders to the Other Districts

The temporary stop to the deportations from the district of Lublin in early June is likely to have been due to the decision to extend the mass murder of the Jews to the whole of the General Government. The deportations now encompassed the district of Cracow, while Globocnik's specialists will probably already have been engaged with the preparations for the deportations from other districts, namely Warsaw. This decision quickly to extend mass murder to the other districts can only be reconstructed on the basis of the course of the deportations. It must have happened between the attack on Heydrich on 27 May and his death on 4 June. Himmler's address to SS and police leaders at Heydrich's funeral in Berlin on 9 June contains an important indication of such a momentous decision: 'Within a year we will definitely have completed the mass migration of the Jews; then no more will migrate.' [109]

With the appointment of HSSPF Krüger as state secretary for security issues in the General Government in May 1942 the weight of the SS had decisively grown compared to that of the civil administration. In particular, Krüger was assigned responsibility for all 'Jewish affairs' by the implementation order of 3 June, which concerned his new position as state secretary.[110] In this way, the SS had created the organizational preconditions for the murder of all the Jews in the General Government by means of a combination of executions, deportations to particular extermination camps, and forced labour.

The murder of the Jews throughout the General Government—like the mass murders in the districts of Lublin and Galicia—was to be organized by Globocnik's staff. The whole campaign was run under the heading 'Aktion Reinhardt' or 'Aktion Reinhard', a posthumous tribute to Reinhard Heydrich, who had died on 4 June 1942 as the result of an assassination attempt some days previously.[111] Individually, the 'Reinhardt Actions' encompassed the extermination of the Jews of the General Government and the district of Bialystok in the three extermination camps of Belzec, Sobibor, and Treblinka as well as in Majdanek; it also included the murder of other Jews in these camps as well as the utilization of the goods and chattels of those who had been murdered, as well as the deployment of the Jews for forced labour.[112]

On 3 June 1942, the day when Krüger's authority was decisively extended, Globocnik sent Himmler several memos concerning 'ethnic policy' in the district of Lublin. The content of these memos is not known in detail, but two of these papers concerned the fate of the Jews,[113] another the issue of 'German-ness' (*Deutschtum*). Himmler only returned to these proposals during a further meeting with Globocnik on 9 July. In the meantime—from about 19 June until 7 July— because of the imminent offensives in the East a general transport moratorium had been imposed, and Himmler was also preoccupied with other issues because of the death of Heydrich.[114]

On 18 June a police meeting in Cracow agreed, as Krüger put it, that the 'problem of Jewish resettlement urgently requires a decision'. Once the transport moratorium was over, 'the Jewish campaign must be stepped up'.[115] At this meeting, representatives of the civil administration, the district chiefs Ludwig Losacker (Galicia), Herbert Hummel (Warsaw), and Michael Oswald (Radom) pressed for an acceleration of the deportations, particularly, as the arguments presented had it, in order to tackle 'smuggling' more effectively, and avoid in advance any problems with the imminent 'harvesting'; Hummel wanted to remove those Jews who were 'unfit for work' from the Warsaw ghetto 'within a reasonable time', in order to increase the profits of the ghetto industry still further. On 22 June, at a meeting of heads of the main departments, Krüger again urged those in charge of the General Government to intensify measures against 'the Jews'; he encountered resistance from the head of the Main Labour Department, Dr Max Frauendorfer, who warned that a 'resettlement of the Jews' will 'have profound effects on all sectors of public life'; in his plea for the preservation of Jewish workers, Frauenhofer referred expressly to Himmler, Speer, and Sauckel.[116] The civil administration thus wanted to speed up the deportations for reasons of food and 'security', but to keep the workers in the ghettos and camps. A few weeks later Krüger was to take over the issue of Jewish forced labour in the General Government and ignore such considerations.

A few days previously, on 12 June, Himmler had ordered that the measures for the 'Germanization' of large areas in the East, including the General Government, be implemented at a faster rate, within twenty years. Early in July Krüger suggested that the General Government be designated for settlement by Germans.[117]

Meanwhile, since the end of May, and increasingly since the temporary suspension of the deportations in Lublin district on 10 June, more than 16,000 Jews had been deported from the district of Crakow to Belzec and murdered, until these deportations were suspended because of the transport moratorium on 19 June.[118] In Belzec the murders had been resumed, after Wirth, who had left the camp in April 1942, had returned to Belzec at the end of May; his return was clearly connected with the assignment of additional T4 staff to the General Government as agreed by Himmler and Brack with the Chancellery of the Führer of the NSDAP.[119] In May, or by the beginning of June at the latest, work had begun on the third extermination camp, Treblinka in the district of Warsaw.[120] In the district of Radom by mid-June all the preparations had been made for a deportation of the Jews living there.[121]

The murder of the Jews in the General Government had not by any means been interrupted by the transport moratorium. In the district of Lublin, for example, numerous small 'actions' took place, but also mass executions, as for example— between June and September—in Tyszowcew, Josefow, Lomazy, Serokomla, and Biala Podlaska with a total of 3,500 victims.[122] In the district of Galicia, too, the mass executions were continued.[123]

The transport moratorium also meant the end of the deportations from the Reich and Slovakia to the district of Lublin. All the transports from Slovakia now went directly to Auschwitz, where the greater proportion of deportees, beginning with the transport of 4 July, was directly murdered in the gas chambers without even being admitted to the camp. After the lifting of the transport moratorium the deportations from the Reich went above all to Minsk and, over the months that followed, to Riga, Treblinka, and Auschwitz.

After the lifting of the transport moratorium the overall situation within the General Government emerged as follows: in the second week of July, the transports from the district of Cracow to Belzec were resumed, after the transport moratorium had been used to extend the capacity of the gas chambers there by a considerable amount. On the other hand, Sobibor became inoperative because of repairs on the railway tracks until the beginning of October, and here too the pause was used to build additional gas chambers.[124] The transports from the district of Cracow lasted until November, with the bulk of the deportations concentrated in August and September.[125]

Meanwhile the decisive preconditions for the initiation of the deportations had also been created in the other districts. Himmler played a central part in this. After heralding, on 9 June, the end of the Jewish 'mass migration' within a year, he now seemed to have staked everything on accelerating the murder of the Jews of the General Government as far as possible.

On 9 July Himmler discussed with Krüger and Globocnik the latter's suggestions (which have not survived) of 3 June, which we know focused on *Judenpolitik* in the district.[126] After Himmler had met Hitler several times on 11, 12, and 14 July, he pressed for greater transport capacities. In response to a request from Karl Wolff, the chief of his personal staff, the state secretary in the ministry of transport, Albert Ganzenmüller, assured him at the end of July that, since

22 July, a 'train carrying 5,000 Jews has been travelling from Warsaw to Treblinka every day, and twice a week a train from Przemysl (district of Lublin) to Belzec'.[127] On 17 and 18 July Himmler visited Auschwitz, where he was shown people being murdered in a gas chamber.[128] Statements that he made with visible satisfaction on the evening of 17 July at a reception given by the Gauleiter of Upper Silesia led one of his listeners to conclude that the Nazi leadership had now decided to murder the European Jews, information that was passed on to Switzerland and from there reached the West through the telegram from Gerhart Riegner, the representative of the World Jewish Congress in Geneva.[129] After his stay in Auschwitz on 18 July Himmler visited Globocnik in Lublin and on 19 July, from Lublin, he gave HSSPF Krüger the crucial order that the 'resettlement of the entire Jewish population of the General Government should have been implemented and completed by 31 December 1942'. After this date, no Jews were to be able to stay in the General Government, apart from the 'assembly camps' of Warsaw, Tschenstochau (Czestochowa), Cracow, and Lublin.[130] This meant that he had set a time limit for the extermination of the great majority of the Polish Jews.

Warsaw

After the completion of Treblinka extermination camp, 50 km from Warsaw, near the railway line to Bialystok,[131] from 22 July deportations began from the Warsaw ghetto to what was the biggest death factory in the General Government. There were more than 350,000 people in the Warsaw ghetto at this point, more than in any other ghetto in Eastern Europe. By 12 September the Germans had managed to deport more than 250,000 from Warsaw to Treblinka, to murder them in the gas chambers there—an average of 5,000 people every day. How was it possible to murder a quarter of a million people in only seven weeks without encountering any notable resistance? Israel Gutman, who as a survivor of the Warsaw ghetto has made research into the subject his life's work, has tried to answer this question by describing the events of the summer of 1942 as a process set in motion with diabolical skill by the Germans and then continuously radicalized.[132]

    The original order for the deportation that the Jewish council announced with a billposting campaign in response to German demands, provided for numerous exceptions: these applied in particular to those working for the extensive administration of the Jewish council, who were in employment or even only fit for work, and they were supposed to apply both to the immediate members of these people's families and to people in poor health who were unable to travel. This gave the majority of ghetto-dwellers the illusion that they could escape deportation. This illusion must have been fed by the fact that in the previous few months the German ghetto administration had made considerable efforts to make the ghetto economy more productive, thus giving the impression that it was banking on the continuing existence of the ghetto in the medium term.[133] That such considerations had by now been replaced by a strategy of the systematic extermination of Jews living in Europe was not apparent to the inhabitants of the ghetto.

The first actions were carried out by the Jewish ghetto police. The German forces remained in the background, while the Polish police began the outward cordoning-off of the ghetto. Gradually individual blocks and streets within the ghetto were cordoned off, the people from the houses were driven to a central collecting point, the 'Umschlagplatz', where the selection took place. People with work permits were generally not designated for deportation; the rest were transported to Treblinka on goods trains. In this way the Germans had managed to set the deportation process in motion with the help of the authority of the Jewish council and the Jewish police.

From the beginning of August the method used by the Germans began to change: German police and their Ukrainian and Latvian auxiliary troops intervened increasingly in events, they became more brutal in their approach, the selection was performed more and more indiscriminately, identification papers were ignored more and more often. The only thing that mattered now was to fill the daily deportation quota. The Jewish council—the chairman, Czerniakow, had committed suicide on the second day of the deportations—was completely marginalized, indeed it was forced in August to draw up deportation lists of its members and their relatives; the Jewish 'police' were forced to join in by means of very severe punitive measures.

It seems that the great majority of ghetto inhabitants, in the face of the plainly irresistible events and the power of their tormentors, either fell into resignation and apathy or yielded to mostly illusory hopes of survival. They clung to the hope that they would not be caught up in the actions or would survive the selection. Information about the mass murder in Treblinka that was circulating in the ghetto was overlaid with different-sounding, more optimistic rumours, according to which the 'resettlement' led only to a camp where one could go on living.[34] The generally disastrous living conditions—during the actions no food entered the ghetto—clearly reinforced the tendency to succumb to an unavoidable fate. Exhortations from the Germans, to the effect that those who reported voluntarily for deportation would be rewarded with extra rations, proved successful in this situation.

Finally, in early September, an extensive selection took place lasting several days of all those people remaining in the ghetto, in which 35,000 people—10 per cent of the original population of the ghetto—were selected out as a usable workforce. They were now, along with 20,000 to 25,000 people who stayed hidden in the ghetto, to form the population of the Warsaw ghetto. The rest were deported. Among the last to be deported were the great majority of the approximately 2,000 members of the Jewish police. Apart from the 250,000 people murdered in Treblinka, 11,000 more were deported to labour camps, and about 10,000 were murdered during the actions in the ghetto.

After the halt to the deportations from Warsaw, the bulk of deportations within the district of Warsaw shifted to the smaller communities from which tens of thousands of people had also been deported to Treblinka by the beginning of October.[135]

The Deportations from the Other Districts
in Summer and Autumn 1942

In August the deportations in the district of Lublin were resumed. The purpose now was the complete murder by the end of the year of those Jews in the district who were 'not fit for work'.[136] In August the death transports went above all to Treblinka, in September they were largely interrupted, and in October/November (after the halt to the deportations from the district of Warsaw) they were brought to their conclusion with the utmost energy, with the trains travelling to Treblinka, to Sobibor (which could be reached by rail again after 8 October), and to Belzec (which was closed in December).

At the beginning of August the deportations to Treblinka began in the district of Radom as well: first of all there were two actions in the town of Radom itself on 4 and 5 August, and on 16 and 17 August; from 20 August the ghettos in the administrative district were cleared. These actions reached their climax with the clearance of the biggest ghetto in the district, Tschenstochau, between 22 September and 7 October, in which 33,000 people were deported to Treblinka. At the end of October some transports from this district were also sent to Belzec. At the beginning of November the clearances in the district of Radom were concluded. *In toto*, more than 300,000 people from this district were murdered in less than three months.[137]

After systematic preparations in the second half of July, at the instigation of SSPF Katzmann, in late July the mass murder of the Jewish population of Galicia was resumed with the deportations from Przemysl to Belzec. In Lemberg (Lvov) alone, in the big 'August action' between 10 and 25 August we may assume that more than 40,000 Jews, about half of the then Jewish population of the city, were arrested and deported to Belzec in goods trains, into each of which about 5,000 people were crammed, and murdered there.[138] During this action, in which hundreds of people were murdered on the spot, including the patients in the hospitals and the children in the Jewish orphanage, Himmler and Globocnik stayed in the city on 17 August.[139] Initially those spared from deportation involved many fit for work, mostly men and women under the age of 35. They were now locked up in a ghetto in which there were 36,000 Jews in September. The 'selections', however, had been carried out under such chaotic conditions that we cannot speak of a systematic separation of Jews who were 'fit for work' from those who were not.

The deportations from the counties (*Kreise*) of the district of Galicia were also resumed at the end of July and—interrupted by a fourteen-day pause during the

Lvov campaign—systematically continued.[140] Again, thousands of people were shot on the spot, but the largest part of the Jewish population was deported to Belzec. In most county towns ghettos were now set up for the surviving Jews, where they had not existed before. Between the end of July and the beginning of September 140,000 Jews had been murdered in the district of Lublin. At the beginning of October 1942, however, the regular deportations to Belzec extermination camp came to a standstill, as the murder machinery could no longer keep pace with the large number of deportees. The gas chambers had been extended, but the area of the camp proved too small and threatened to collapse under the large number of murder victims.

In October a second wave of murders began in the district of Lublin, in which the Jewish communities were almost entirely wiped out.[141] It would seem that Krüger and Katzmann made considerable efforts, precisely because of the growing difficulties—the halt in deportations to Belzec, the constant arguments with army headquarters and the civil administration over the question of preserving Jewish workers, the increasing number of Jews escaping as knowledge about the mass murder spread—to achieve by any means the goal set by Himmler of finishing the murder campaigns by the end of the year, not least by intensifying the mass executions. In December Belzec extermination camp had to be closed because of the difficulties that had been becoming apparent for some time, and between 15 December and 15 January a transport moratorium was imposed. In 1942 a total of 300,000 Jews must have been murdered in eastern Galicia, since according to German data 161,000 Jews were still alive.[142]

Seen overall, we have the following picture: while after the lifting of the transport moratorium in July and Himmler's order of 19 July the deportations were first channelled from the district of Warsaw to Treblinka and from the district of Cracow to Belzec, the focus of the mass murders was shifted from late summer and in autumn 1942 to the districts of Galicia, Radom, and Lublin.

The actions in which the majority of the Jewish population of the General Government were murdered between the spring and autumn of 1942 followed a consistent pattern that had first been applied in the clearance of the ghetto of Lublin and had been constantly refined since then. These operations were run by a special 'resettlement staff' and carried out by the Security Police and the Order Police, with the Trawniki generally deployed to cordon off the actions. The civil administration performed indispensable services in the preparation of the actions: it produced the statistics of the Jewish population, moved the rural population to certain collecting ghettos, and issued identification papers for those Jewish workers who were still required. Equally indispensable was the close collaboration with the Reich railways, which had to ensure the regular availability of the deportation trains.

The effectiveness of the campaigns themselves was based on the element of surprise and calculated terror, designed to throw the population of the ghetto into a panic and prevent any resistance. The Jewish councils were informed a short time before the imminent 'resettlement', and the Jewish police were forced to help drag the people from the houses, usually in the early hours of the morning. If the clearing of a ghetto lasted days or even weeks, an attempt was made to conceal the planned extent of the overall operation and cover the ghetto with a series of shock operations. The people driven to collection points were always subjected to a selection: it decided who was to be sent in packed goods trains to the extermination camps. The selection process was often quite capricious, and those who had been selected for work were often designated for transport to the extermination camps. If those responsible for the mass murder had initially used the slogan that those 'unfit for work' were to be removed, in order to create the impression that the murder was based on a rational calculation, this claim was now in practice rendered absurd.

Throughout the entire process people who hid or failed to follow instructions were shot, but also often murdered on an utter whim. After the execution of the 'actions' the streets of the ghettos were often scattered with corpses.

A Jewish work troop immediately had to start clearing up; at the same time any valuable objects or other property that were found were collected and sorted. The exploitation of the personal belongings of the victims was an integral component of 'Aktion Reinhardt'.[143]

Treblinka

In the second half of 1942 the Treblinka camp was to assume a central role in the extermination process in comparison with the two other extermination camps, Belzec and Sobibor.

The camp complex covered an area of around 20 hectares and, in a densely forested setting, was screened off from the eyes of the outside world.[144] Having its own spur line made it possible to drive the deportation trains, each crammed with 6,000 or 7,000 people, directly into the camp. At first Treblinka held a building with three gas chambers into which the deadly exhaust fumes were fed from a tank engine. In autumn 1942 the murder capacity of Treblinka, like that of the two other Aktion Reinhardt camps, was extended: a larger building was built, containing an estimated ten chambers. The staff of the camp consisted of about 30 to 40 SS men, mostly staff from Aktion T4 as well as between 90 and 120 Trawniki men. There was also a work unit of Jewish prisoners who were within a very short space of time 'selected', murdered, and replaced by new companions in misery.

In the first phase of the camp, dating from 23 July to 28 August 1942, the murder of thousands of people every day had the qualities of a crazed massacre. Many people who attempted to escape the trains as they approached the camp were shot by the guards outside the camp. Often the shootings were continued within the camp itself; if the gas chambers were not working or were overburdened, actual mass executions were carried out, and there were also numerous random murders. Often people arriving in the camp were faced with indescribable images. The arrival area was scattered with corpses. The guards reacted to the panic that arose with further shootings.[145]

These circumstances, but also the inability of the camp administration to collect the valuable items stolen from the Jews and pass them on to Aktion Reinhardt headquarters, led to an inspection of the camp and its temporary closure.

The camp was now reorganized and rebuilt under the auspices of Christian Wirth, the Inspector of the Sonderkommando Action Reinhardt; the previous commander, Irmfried Eberl, was dismissed and replaced by Franz Stangl, the commander of Sobibor extermination camp.[146] On 4 September the murder in Treblinka was resumed. To make it easier for people to leave the wagons a ramp had been built, and with the corresponding erection of buildings the impression was created of being in a railway station. Frail people who might have suffered from the tempo of the murder process were now selected immediately after their arrival and brought to the camp hospital, where they were shot. The remaining crowd were told that they were now in a transit camp; after they had undressed and handed over their valuables, they were driven down the fenced-off and concealed 'tube' (*Schlauch*) to the gas chambers, where they were murdered.

By the end of 1942 precisely 713,555 people had been murdered in Treblinka. This figure appears in a telegram from Höfle that was found some years ago in the decoding reports of the radio reconnaissance department of the British Secret Service.[147] This document provides us with the figures of the victims who had been murdered in the other Aktion Reinhardt camps. According to this report, 434,598 persons had been murdered in Belzec by the end of 1942. Since Belzec was already closed at this point, this represents the total number of murders for this extermination camp. The corresponding figures for Sobibor and Lublin-Majdanek are 101,370 and 24,733 respectively. This brings the total number of people killed in the Aktion Reinhardt camps at this point to 1,274,166.[148]

By the end of 1942, according to official German figures, only 298,000 of originally 2.3 million Jews were still living in the General Government.[149] If we assume that 300,000 Jews might have managed to escape from the German to the Soviet sector after the occupation of the country, and if we also take into consideration the figure of 100,000 Jews who were murdered in Galicia in the summer and autumn of 1941 and the winter of 1941/2[150] as well as the increased mortality rates[151] in the ghettos before the start of the liquidations, we reach the conclusion that almost 1.5 million Polish Jews fell victim to the ghetto clearances of 1942. It thus represents the largest single murder campaign within the Holocaust.

It is hardly comprehensible that this series of gigantic mass murders could have been played out almost entirely according to plan, without its terrible course being impeded by any external factors. Thus the 'actions' could be carried out in the closed-off ghettos without any disturbances being feared from the Polish population living in the immediate vicinity.

On the Jewish side there was practically no resistance. As we have seen, the wave of ghetto liquidations caught the Jewish councils entirely unawares, they had no chance of stopping the murder machinery or even obstructing its efficiency. Since the start of the German occupation the Jewish councils had set about ensuring as far as possible the survival of the population of the ghettos through a policy of submissiveness to the German occupying forces. This attitude basically ruled out any response of resistance.

But beyond this, apart from desperate individual acts of resistance, there were clearly no organized groups or spontaneous initiatives within the Polish ghettos that might even have attempted to resist the bloody actions. It was only in the spring of 1942, in the wake of the first clearances, that the first resistance groups came into existence, although they only resisted the definitive liquidation of the ghettos the following year in Warsaw and a number of other places. By this time, however, only a small minority of Polish Jews remained alive.[152]

The Takeover of Jewish Forced Labour by the SS

In parallel with the expansion of systematic mass murder to the whole territory of the General Government, Himmler's organization took on the entire responsibility for Jewish forced labour, the sphere that had for a long time constituted the only barrier against the complete murder of the Jewish population. In the hands of the SS, forced labour—in the sense of 'extermination through work'— now became an integral component of the murder programme in the General Government.[153]

In May and June it had still looked as if Jewish workers would continue to be deployed on a large scale in the General Government, and as if the extension of murder to the whole territory of the General Government would continue to involve primarily those members of the Jewish population who were 'unfit for work'. The Senior Quartermaster of the military commander,[154] State Secretary Dr Josef Bühler,[155] and the director of the Labour Division of the General Government, Frauendorfer,[156] the latter as late as 22 June, had insisted on receiving Jewish workers, and on 9 May HSSPF Krüger had issued a regulation intended to replace Polish, Ukrainian, and other 'Aryan non-German workers' with Jewish specialists. On 20 May HSSPF Krüger had promised the Wehrmacht Armaments Inspection to replace Polish workforces deported to the Reich with 100,000 Jews.[157]

After HSSPF Krüger had become responsible for all 'Jewish affairs' at the beginning of June, the Labour Administration informed the Labour Offices on 25 June that Jews could only be procured by agreement with the security and police commanders. On 17 July Krüger informed the Armaments Inspection that the previous agreements about workforce deployment were invalid, because armaments factories would henceforth be supplied with Jewish forced labourers who had been brought together in camps controlled by the Higher SS and Police Commanders.[158] Also in July, at the time when the deportations had been resumed, particularly from Warsaw, Krüger ordered that only Jews between the ages of 16 and 35 could be used. This crucial restriction, which corresponded to an instruction from Himmler probably issued in May 1942, amounted to a death sentence for all people outside that age-group.[159]

After the incident in Przemysl (the local Wehrmacht commandant had prevented the removal of the local Jewish workforce by closing a bridge[160]), Krüger ordered all Jewish forced labour camps to be closed. On 5 September, the head of OKW, Keitel, gave the order for all Jewish workforces in the General Government to be replaced by Poles.[161] The director of armaments inspection in the General Government, Curt Ludwig Freiherr von Gienanth, was dismissed for protesting against this measure.[162]

However, during the armaments conferences that took place between 20 and 22 September 1942, in view of the dramatic labour shortage, Hitler declared himself in agreement with Sauckel's suggestion that, for the time being, qualified Jewish specialist workers should continue to be employed in the General Government.[163] Himmler, who clearly discussed the consequences of this decision with Hitler on 22 September 1942,[164] now revised the intention he had expressed in July 1942 to murder all the Jews in the General Government by the end of 1942. Instead, on 9 October 1942, he ordered the 'so-called armaments workers' in textile factories etc. in Warsaw and Lublin to be consigned to concentration camps. The Jews working in the 'real armaments factories' were to be gradually removed from these factories, so that in the end there would be 'if possible only a few large Jewish concentration camp concerns in the East of the General Government'. 'However, there too, according to the Führer's wishes the Jews are eventually to disappear.'[165]

Police regulations issued in October and November 1942 ordained that (apart from the forced labour camps), 'Jewish residential districts' might only continue to exist in a total of fifty-four places.[166] The Jews held there and in the camps were declared 'labour prisoners' of the Higher SS and Police Commanders.[167] Apart from these, there still existed the so-called 'Jewish camps' in the various armaments factories; the forced labourers imprisoned there, according to an agreement between HSSPF Krüger and the commander of the military district, were subject to the Wehrmacht armaments inspection.[168] With these regulations the SS had created the crucial precondition for henceforth keeping alive only those Jews working in armaments production. For all others, including the family members of the slave labourers, this amounted to a death sentence.

The Annexed Polish Territories: Upper Silesia and the Warthegau

In the Polish territory directly annexed by the Reich, in Upper Silesia and the Warthegau, the systematic murder of the Jewish population began in 1942.

It appears important for the overall development of the Holocaust that it was in May, the point in time when the murders in the district of Lublin were extended, that the SS set in motion a further 'regional final solution' on Polish territory: on 12 May 1942 Heydrich ordered the abolition of the police border which had until then separated the western strip of Upper Silesia (the territory with a relatively sizeable German population) from the eastern part (predominantly inhabited by Poles) and offered a guarantee that the Jews forcibly 'resettled' from west to east would not be able to return. With this decision on Heydrich's part it was clear that the 'deportation territory' would in future no longer be required. The same day thousands of Jews unfit for work from Sosnowitz and Bendzin as well as a number of other places were deported to Auschwitz and murdered there.[169] On 12 August a selection of the Jews living in Sosnowitz and Bendzin began, and lasted several days; some 11,000 people, the old and the sick and mothers with children, were finally killed in Auschwitz, around 9,000 people were deported to the labour camps of the Schmelt Organization . Between May and August 1942 a total of around 38,000 Jews were deported from the 'Eastern Strip', about 20,000 to Auschwitz, the rest to the Schmelt camps, in which a total of over 50,000 Jewish slave labourers were deployed in January 1943, including several thousand Jewish men, most of whom were taken from transports arriving from France in Kosel, Silesia, in August, September, and October 1942. The deportations to Auschwitz were organized by the Kattowitz (Katowice) Gestapo. It was not until October 1942 that, on the initiative of the city authorities, the Jewish residential districts in eastern Upper Silesia were turned into closed ghettos. Up until summer 1943, however, the forced labour programme was maintained to its fullest extent.[170]

In the Warthegau, where 10,000 people had been deported from the Lodz ghetto to Chelmno in January 1942,[171] the mass murders had been continued in the first months of 1942. In February 7,025, in March another 24,687, and in early April 2,349 people were deported to Chelmno and murdered in gas vans, and then the deportations were at first suspended. The Security Police spread the rumour that the resettled people had been lodged in a large camp in Kolo (Warthbrücken).[172]

At the end of April, in response to demands from the German authorities, Chaim Rumkowski, the head of the Jewish council in Lodz, announced the 'resettlement' of those Jews who had been deported to Lodz in the autumn of the previous year. The recent deportations were to include, in particular, those who 'didn't work'—and that was the great majority of this group of originally 20,000 people, more than 2,000 of whom had already succumbed to the terrible living conditions in the ghetto.[173] In fact, between 4 and 13 May, 10,914 of these 'Reich Jews' had been deported to Chelmno and murdered there.[174] The dating indicates that this mass murder should be seen in a larger context. Since 11 May 1942, Jews had been systematically murdered in Maly Trostinets after their arrival in Minsk. The first direct deportations to the Sobibor extermination camp began in mid-June. All of this indicates that the systematic murder of the deported German Jews, still forbidden by Himmler in November 1941, had received the go-ahead by the central authorities around April 1942.

In Lodz the deportations were continued in September 1942 after a lengthy pause. The first victims were the patients of the ghetto hospitals, which were cleared by the Jewish police on the night of 31 August/1 September on German instructions. On 4 September, Rumkowski announced that, at the request of the German authorities, 25,000 ghetto-dwellers under the age of 10 and over the age of 65 as well as all the sick had been evacuated from the ghetto. To make the action possible, an 'exit ban', a prohibition on all travel, was imposed from 5 to 9 September. The Jewish police now searched the ghetto systematically block by block and arrested children, the old, and the sick. By 12 September these people—according to the statistics of the Council of Elders they numbered 15,685—were taken to collection points and deported to Chelmno, where they were murdered.[175]

The official Ghetto Chronicle kept by the Jewish Council of Elders notes that after the end of the action there were practically no children under 10 or old people left in the ghetto.[176] The number of inhabitants of the ghetto was now just 90,000—more than 70,000 fewer than at the beginning of the year.[177]

Auschwitz

We have already described how the SS set about extending Auschwitz concentration camp complex into a centre for systematic mass murder, independent of the construction of the extermination camps in the context of Aktion Reinhardt.

In Auschwitz, from September 1941, thousands of prisoners, including Jewish prisoners from Upper Silesia, had been murdered with Zyklon B. Since October 1941, in the wake of the expansion of the camp complex, which was intended to receive large numbers of Soviet prisoners, a new crematorium was planned, which was to receive a considerably larger gas chamber than the ones subsequently built into the old crematorium in Auschwitz 'Stammlager', the original camp. Finally, in January 1942, Himmler had ordered that Auschwitz should take large numbers of Jewish forced labourers from the Reich, to replace the absent Soviet prisoners of war.

But the Jewish prisoners from the Reich failed to materialize. As we have seen, from March onwards they had been deported to the district of Lublin, where those who seemed to be 'fit for work' were held for forced labour in Majdanek camp. Instead, in the spring of 1942 three groups of Jewish prisoners came to Auschwitz: the first mass transports of Jews to Auschwitz were made up of Slovakian Jews, of whom four transports of young women, some 3,800 in total, arrived between 26 March and 7 April.[178] They were followed by Jewish hostages from France who had been deported 'to the East' in reprisal for attacks by the French Resistance. The first transport of 1,112 persons arrived in Auschwitz on 30 March and was followed by five more between 7 June and 18 July.[179] A third group of Jewish prisoners who came to Auschwitz were the Jews from the ghettos of annexed eastern Upper Silesia, from Sosnowitz, Bendzin, and other places; these deportations began, as we have seen, in mid-1942.[180]

Even before these transports from Slovakia, Upper Silesia, and France reached Auschwitz, those in charge of Auschwitz concentration camp had set about installing additional gas chambers, one after the other, in two farmhouses that lay outside the camp itself, as the building work on the new crematorium had not even begun. The first farmhouse, the 'Red house', or Bunker I, was used for the first time on 20 March 1942 to kill people with Zyklon B: the victims were a further transport of Jews 'unfit for work' from the Schmelt camps in Upper Silesia. Afterwards, this building was used above all to murder the Jews of Upper Silesia.[181] The second farmhouse, the 'White house' or Bunker II, was first used on 4 July 1942 to murder, in the same way, 628 people selected from a transport recently arrived from Slovakia. From that day on, the selection of Jews 'unfit for work'— particularly children and their mothers—and their subsequent murder in the gas chambers became standard practice in Auschwitz.

The Second Wave of Extermination in the Soviet Union

In the rear area of Army Group Centre, which essentially encompassed White Russian and Russian territory, the great majority of Jews had already been murdered in 1941. According to an official census, 22,267 Jews still lived in the territory at the beginning of 1942, mostly in labour camps and remote towns. In this military administrative area the murders were continued throughout the whole of the winter and during the spring. By around the middle of the year almost all the ghettos had been liquidated; the last ghetto to be exterminated in this way was probably the one in Smolensk, where around 2,000 people were killed on 15 July 1942. After this date, in the military administrative area Centre, there were only a few thousand Jews who lived in camps or were hiding in the woods. These murders were carried out in particular by Einsatzkommandos 8 and 9, supported by the Order Police and Wehrmacht units. Thus in February alone, according to a report, Wehrmacht troops killed 2,200 'Jews (Bolsheviks)'. The sequence of actions was generally agreed with the leaders of the army rear area and the local garrisons.[182]

In the rear area of Army Group South, that is eastern Ukraine, there was a similar picture. Here too the mass murders continued throughout the winter of

1941/2, in Charkov, for example, where on 16 December the liquidation of 12,000–15,000 Jews began, in Stalino (now Donetsk) on 9 January, or in Zaporozhe at the end of March. Early in the spring the majority of the Jews living in this territory had been shot. The murders were substantially carried out by Sonderkommandos 4 and 5 of Einsatzgruppe C, again supported by the Order Police. In the Ukraine, too, the mass executions were generally carried out in agreement with the local Wehrmacht authorities, and in this territory too Wehrmacht units, particularly the Secret Field Police, engaged independently in the shooting of Jews.[183] Little is known about the murder of Jews in the rear area of Army Group North, Russian territory south of Leningrad. Here, the Security Police were present in relatively low numbers (sub-units of Commandos 1a and 1b).[184]

To the west, in the General Commissariat of White Ruthenia, abutting the military administrative area Centre, the murder actions proceeded in a different manner. Here the murder campaigns almost came to a standstill around the turn of 1941/2. This had variously to do with the frozen ground that made it impossible to dig pits to bury the victims—an explanation that is plainly not sound, as the continuation of the shootings in the military administrative area during the winter shows: either the ground was blown up, or already existing pits were used. A second reason repeatedly given for the decline in shooting actions appears more plausible; the civil administration did not want to lose the specialist workers, who were urgently needed.

In spite of these difficulties, the KdS (Commander of the Security Police) for Minsk stressed at a meeting of the administrative heads of the General Commissariat of White Ruthenia on 23 January 1942 that the goal of the 'complete liquidation' of the Jews was still being pursued. He thus promised, in the following spring, to 'relaunch the large-scale executions'.[185] At this point the KdS of White Ruthenia believed there was a realistic prospect of 'liquidating' the 'Jewish question' within his area of responsibility within two months.[186]

For the months of January and February there are only—somewhat dubious—references to two actions in Minsk in which up to 3,000 people may have been shot.[187] In March there were mass executions above all in the area of Vileyka, namely in Vileyka itself, in Ilya, Krasne, Rakov, and Radoschkowicze (Radoszyce), and also—outside this area—in Lida, Baranowicze, and Slutzk as well as in Kopyl. In this way more than 8,000 people were murdered in March.[188]

In the large ghettos that had been set up after the murder of the majority of the Jewish population in the General Commissariats of Lithuania and Latvia, the situation remained relatively quiet in 1942. There were few large massacres. This did not apply, however, to the area around Riga. Between February and April 1942, in the Riga ghetto and the Jungfernhof camp, some 5,000 people were selected in a number of actions as 'unfit for work' and transported out in motor vehicles—supposedly to a new camp near Dünamünde, actually to the Bikernieki Forest, where they were shot.[189]

At a meeting of the General Commissars held by Reichskommissar Ostland (Baltic states) on 26 March, a certain perplexity was expressed about the future course of the anti-Jewish policy. There was general agreement that 'the Jewish question must be resolved clearly and urgently'. However, the following sentence in the minutes suggests that in the meantime mass executions were no longer seen as the solution: 'It is felt to be regrettable that the method employed hitherto, however much it might represent a political liability for us, has for the time being been abandoned.' However, Generalkommissar Kube's following suggestion that the liquidation should be effected 'in accordance with correct procedures [korrekter]' shows that they did not generally wish to abandon this means. It was agreed that the solution did not lie in ceasing to distribute food to the Jews, as was happening at the time.[190]

In April the occupying forces in the area of Vileyka carried out two further mass executions in Dohyno with 800 and 1,200 victims respectively, another in Krzywicze (Krzeszowice) (400 fatalities), and on 1 April 1,200 Jews were murdered in Kopyl,[191] as well as various murders in Minsk with at least 500 fatalities.[192] The KdS Minsk reported that his department had killed 1,894 Jews in April alone.[193] In spite of these mass murders, however, in April 1942 the number of massacres and murder victims in White Ruthenia declined in comparison with the previous months.

In May 1942, however, the murders resumed systematically and on a large scale; plainly the intensified murderous activities coincided with a visit by Heydrich to Minsk, which appears to have occurred in April.[194] While, on 11 May, the KdS Minsk demanded that the Gendarmerie throughout the whole of the General Commissariat supply summary statistical data about the Jewish communities, under the heading 'Selection of Jewish specialist workers', the murder of the great majority of the Jews still living there, organized according to a plan by the Security Police and the civil administration, had already begun on 8 May. Over the following five days more than 16,000 Jews were shot in all the ghettos in the area.[195]

This action was the starting point for the extension of the murder actions to all areas of the occupied territory of White Russia. In the district of Glebokie an EK 9 unit and other agencies murdered at least 12,000 Jews between 29 May and 20 June.[196] From May onwards, the branch of the SD in Vileyka, which took part in numerous mass murders even outside its area of responsibility, intensified the programme of mass murders that had resumed in March, and had murdered more than 5,000 people there by the end of September.[197] At the beginning of 1943 only 3,000 Jewish artisans were still living in the area of Vileyka.[198]

In the district of Slutzk, where two actions had been carried out in Slutzk and Kopyl as early as the end of March, further massacres took place between May and August.[199] In Slonim the ghetto was liquidated on 29 June, and 7,000 people were murdered. In the weeks that followed there were also further massacres in the area of Slonim with thousands of fatalities. In September the district commissar,

Gerhard Erren, stated that of 25,000 Jews originally living in his area only around 500 remained.[200] In the district of Novogrodek, at least 2,900 Jews were shot in various places between April and June, and more than 8,000 in early August in Novogrodek and other localities.[201] In the district of Hansewitschi (Hancewicze) almost 2,000 people were shot in Lenin on 14 August.[202]

In the district of Baranowicze—after a first major 'action' in Mir in March or April—mass executions were carried out in July and August in the towns of Kletzk, Lachowicze, Gorodeya, Moltschad, in Mir again, and in various other places, killing at least 7,000 people. Further executions occurred in September and October in Baranowicze, Gorodicze, Polonka, and Stolpce. According to the district commissar, in 1942 a total of 23,000 people were murdered in this region.[203] In Minsk, between 28 and 31 July about 10,000 people were killed, apart from White Russian Jews also 3,500 ghetto inhabitants who had been transported from Central Europe.[204] In the last few weeks of the year further mass murders took place in the district of Glebokie, leading to over 7,000 victims, in Baranawicze, Dvorzec, Slonim (where the last surviving 500 Jews were murdered), and in Novogrodek.[205]

At the end of July, Commissar General Wilhelm Kube drew up an initial record of the massacres, when he reported to Reichskommissar Hinrich Lohse, 'in the last 10 weeks we have liquidated about 55,000 Jews'.[206] The 'we' makes clear the extent to which the civil administration had also shouldered the task of the mass murders.

Between December 1941 and mid-May 1942, unlike the murders that continued uninterrupted in the military administrative area of Army Group South, which abutted the Commissariat on the east, only relatively few massacres are documented within the sphere of the Ukraine Reich Commissariat and most of those may be attributed to local initiatives. One exception to this was the area of Vinnitsa in the General District of Zhitomir, where it was planned to locate Hitler's field headquarters. All the Jews were gradually murdered in a designated high-security area. By 10 January, 227 Jews from Strishavka had been shot, and on 10 April, according to the report of the Reich Security Service, which was responsible for cordoning off the new headquarters, '4,800 Jews were killed in Vinnitsa'. In July the remaining 1,000 unskilled workers were murdered.[207] The massacre of the Jews of Chmelnik, 120 km from Vinnitsa, to which we may assume that 8,000 people fell victim, may be connected to this development.[208]

In February and March 1942, the last surviving Jews in the General Commissariat of Nikolayev were murdered. The Commissar General reported on 1 April that there were 'no Jews or half-Jews left' in the district.[209] In April 1942, in the District Commissariat of Dunayevzny (General Commissariat of Volhynien-Podolien), according to a Soviet Commission report, 2,000 Jews are alleged to have been driven into a phosphorus mine that was then blown up. According to these documents, mass shootings are also supposed to have taken place there in the spring of 1942.[210]

In the other areas of the Reich Commissariat Ukraine, however, the focus of *Judenpolitik*, as pursued by the civil administration between December and April, was on the formation of ghettos. At a meeting of the Reich East Ministry on 10 March 1942 the temporary continuing engagement of Jewish artisans and skilled workers was confirmed.[211]

However, as in the General Commissariat of White Ruthenia, the Reich Commissariat of the Ukraine began a new wave of murders which led in the summer to the total extermination of the Jewish population in the Reich Commissariat. This wave of murders began around 20 May in the General Commissariat of Wolhynien-Podolien (Volhynia-Podolia), where massacres occurred in, among other places, Dubno (27 May, with at least 4,000 fatalities) Korec (21 May).[212] On 27 May, in the General Commissariat of Zhitomir, there were simultaneous massacres in several places in the district of Gaissin, namely in Teplick (769 victims), Ternovka (2,300), and Sobolevka (several hundred victims). The local garrison of Gaissin, the local police, the Vinnitsa branch of the KdS, and Hungarian soldiers were all involved in these massacres.[213] In Monastyrishch, also in the General Commissariat of Zhitomir, some 3,000 Jews were shot towards the end of May.[214]

At the beginning of June, in the General Commissariat of Volhynia-Podolia there followed massacres in Kovel (Kowel) with some 5,000 victims,[215] as well as, immediately afterwards, in Luck.[216] The murders were also extended to the General Commissariats of Kiev and Nikolayev. However, information for these two regions is sparse.

We have the following information for the General Commissariat of Kiev: in June 1942 1,500 Jewish residents of Zvenigorodka (Swenigorodka) were murdered.[217] There are also reports from Schuma Batl. 117 about 'a major "Jewish action" in Shpola (Schpola)', also in the District Commissariat of Zvenigorodka, which lasted from 13 until 17 May 1942. This was evidently the liquidation of the ghetto.[218]

In the General Commissariat of Nikolyev (Nikolajew), in the village of Stalindorf (district of Kherson), the elderly Jewish men and women who had survived the first wave of murders were killed.[219] In Ingulec in the General Commissariat of Dnepropetrovsk, according to a Soviet Commission report, on the night of 10 June some 1,800 people, mostly Jews, were shot.[220]

As in White Ruthenia the murders were intensified again in July. On 13 and 14 July, the KdS of Rovno, who was responsible for Volhynia-Podolia, along with other units, murdered all the 5,000 Jews still living in the city. On 27 and 28 July, 5,673 Jews from Olyka and the surrounding areas, the entire Jewish population, were shot. In Berdichev in the General Commissariat of Zhitomir the members of the KdS outstation murdered the last Jews living there, at least

300, on 15/16 July 1942.[221] The escalation of the murders since July corresponded to developments in the General Government. On 19 July, Himmler had ordered the extermination of the Jewish population there by the end of the year, and after 22 July the deportations began from the Warsaw ghetto—5,000 people per day—to Treblinka extermination camp.

From the end of August 1942 the murders in the Ukraine became even more widespread and systematized; the goal was now the complete extermination of the Jewish population.

At the meeting of the district commissars in Luck, held between 28 and 31 August, the representatives of the civil administration agreed with the KdS that, during the coming five weeks, they would kill all the Jews in the General Commissariat of Volhynia-Podolia with the exception of 500 skilled workers. During this meeting, Reichskommisar Koch's deputy gave an assurance that these 'hundred per cent cleansings' were 'also the emphatic wish of the Reichs-kommissar'.[222] This 'wish' on Koch's part may also have had something to do with the fact that he had just had higher delivery quotas imposed upon him by Berlin.[223] Shortly before the conference, between 19 and 23 August, about 15,000 Jews had been murdered in the city.

After this massacre the occupying power systematically set to work on the General Commissariats of Volhynia-Podolia and Zhitomir murdering county by county almost all the Jews still living there.

The murders in Volhynia-Podolia are comparatively well documented. The Pinsk out-station 9 of the SD played a considerable role in the destruction of the ghettos in the District Commissariats of Pinsk and Stolin, most of which had been set up in the spring of 1942. The shootings themselves were carried out by the SD.[224] They were supported by the district commissars, the Gendarmerie, local auxiliary police, as well as several police battalions. The biggest of these massacres took place in Pinsk in late October/early November and cost far more than 15,000 people their lives, perhaps even more than 26,000. The destruction of the ghetto had been ordered by Himmler at short notice.[225]

After this the first ghetto to be destroyed in August was the one in Mokrov, in which 280–300 people were shot. On 3 September 1942 the ghettos in Kozan-grodek and Lakhva were destroyed. During the night of 2/3 September the 500 inhabitants of the ghetto in Kozangrodek were shot. Then the execution com-mando squad of Pinsk SD travelled to the neighbouring town of Lakhva and murdered 500, possibly 2,000 people there.

On 18 September, during the liquidation of the Luniniec ghetto between 1,000 and 2,800 people were murdered. In the period between 9 and 12 September 1942, the ghettos in the department of Stolin were destroyed, with 8,000 to 10,000 people murdered.[226] After that the murder detachment returned its attention once more to the District Commissariat of Pinsk. On 24 and 25 September, during the liquidation of the ghetto of Yanov, between 1,500 and 2,000 people were murdered. At around the same time in Drohotshin (in the neighbouring District Commissariat of Kobrin) between 1,500 and 2,000 people were also killed. Then the members of the Pinsk SD station set about wiping out the ghetto in Pinsk itself with the help of units of the Order Police. This mass murder lasted from 29 October until 1 November and involved at least 16,200 victims.

There is a written order from Himmler to HSSPF Prützmann about this massacre, dated 27 October 1942: 'On the basis of the reports I have received, the ghetto in Pinsk should be seen as the headquarters of the entire bandit movement in the Pripet Marshes. I therefore recommend, despite the existence of economic concerns, that the ghetto in Pinsk be immediately dealt with and destroyed. A thousand male workers should, if the action allows it, be handed over to the Wehrmacht to make wooden huts. But the work of these 1,000 workers may only take place in a closed and heavily guarded camp. If this guard cannot be guaranteed, these 1,000 are also to be exterminated.'[227]

In the district of Antoniny (also in the General Commissariat of Volhynia-Podolia), the German civil administration had interned the population that was fit for work, over 300 people, in forced labour camps in Orlincy and Antoniny in October 1941. At the beginning of 1942, in three places, small ghettos for Jews who were not fit for work were set up. These people were murdered in July 1942 by members of the KdS post Staro-Konstantinov, as were those Jews fit for work who were still alive in autumn 1942.[228] For the district of Kamentsk-Podolsk there is a report from the SD out-station there, issued at the beginning of August, which stated that 1,204 victims had been recently killed during two actions in three villages in Rayon Dunayevtse.[229]

In August, in the District Commissariat of Kremenec (Kreminanec), members of the KdS out-station, with the help of the District Commissariat, the Gendarmerie, Ukrainian volunteers, and the police battalion 102 murdered the Jews still living in the ghettos. Between 10 August and early September 1942 the ghetto in Kremenec, which was set up early in 1942, was liquidated, with 8,000–12,000 people murdered. Over the next few months 1,500 'work-Jews' who were excluded from the action were also shot.[230] This was followed on 13 August by the murders of 238 Jews from Berezhy as well as 1,000–2,000 people from the ghetto of Potschajew (Pochayev). During the three days that followed, 5,000 Jews from the ghetto of Wischnewez (Wisnowiec) were murdered, and on 14 August and the days that followed the Jews of Schumsk (Szumsk) were massacred leaving around 2,000–3,000 people dead.[231]

The ghetto of Sarny, built in April 1942, into which the Jews from the towns of the surrounding district had been driven, was cleared on 25 August, and the Jews put in a camp. On 28 August all the Jews from the camp along with about 200 Gypsies were shot next to prepared pits. Figures for the victims vary between 10,000 and 17,000. On 20 August, the ghetto of Rafalovka was encircled by Ukrainian militias, who took some 3,000 Jews out of the ghetto on 29 August and had them shot by the same firing squad that had previously been active in Sarny.[232]

In the district of Kobryn, at a date that can no longer be precisely established, between 11,000 and 14,500 Jews from Kobryn Bereza-Kartuska, Antopol, Drogitschin (Drogichin), and other towns were shot. Some of the people were deported in railway trains to the vicinity of the town of Bronnaja (Bronnaya) Gora, where a shooting facility had been set up.[233] In Ljudvipol (Sosnovoye) in the District Commissariat of Kostopol 1,500 Jews from the ghetto there, which had been set up in April 1942, were shot in August or September (possibly on 14 September).[234] In Vladimir-Volynsky 13,500 people were murdered at the beginning of September, and with the dissolution of the ghetto of Dubno on 5 October about 3,000.[235] In the liquidation of the ghetto of Lubomil in October 1942 about 8,000 people died.[236]

In the massacre in Brest-Litovsk on 15 October 1942, in which the local SD outstation, the gendarmerie, a police unit, and various other police agencies took part, at least 10,000–15,000 people were killed.[237] In September, in the District Commissariat of Brest at least 5,000 people had already been killed in several ghettos and camps.[238] In the liquidation of the ghettos of Sdolbunov, Misocz, and Ostrog, all immediately to the south of Rovno, over 2,000 people in all were murdered on 13, 14, and 15 October.[239] In the District Commissariat of Dunajewzy (Dunayevtsy), according to a Soviet Commission report, a total of 5,000 Jews are supposed to have been shot in the spring and autumn of 1942.[240]

In November the SS and the occupying administration extended the murder actions to the north, into White Russian Polesia, and again to the south. After the last Jewish forced labourers had been murdered in Luck on 12 December, the workers in Podolia suffered the same fate: 4,000 people fell victim to the murders in Kamenetsk-Podolsk in November 1942, and a similar number in Starokonstantinov on 29 December 1942. Not only did the civil administration provide the crucial impulse for total extermination at short notice, but the District Commissars also played a considerable part in the organization of the individual massacres.[241]

For the Ukraine, therefore, we have the following overall picture: altogether, between May and December 1942, some 150,000 Jews fell victim to the massacres carried out by the police and the civil administration in Volhynia between May and December 1942, and in Podolia just to the south at least 35,000. There were also several thousand victims in the General Commissariat of Shitomir (Zhitomir). At the end of 1942, only a few thousand Jewish skilled workers remained alive.[242]

By mid-October 1942 the district of Bialystok, which was not part of the General Government, but was under the control of the Governor of the Province of East Prussia and Reichskommissar of the Ukraine, Erich Koch, and formed a bridge between the two territories, had been caught up in the systematic extermination.

After an initial deportation of 3,300 people from the ghetto of Ciechanowiec to Treblinka on 15 October, the majority of the Jews of the district had been rounded up into five large collection camps at the beginning of November (Kielbasin, Volkovysk, Zambrov, Boguze, and one more near Bialystok), while ghettos continued to exist only in Bialystok, Grodno, Pruzany, Sokolka, and Krynki. In the months of November, December, and January (interrupted by a transport moratorium from mid-December until mid-January) more than 80,000 people were transported mainly to Treblinka, some also to Auschwitz, and murdered there. Finally, at the beginning of February, some 10,000 people from the Bialystok ghetto, which had hitherto been spared, were deported to Treblinka, after more far-reaching plans for the deportation of 30,000 people which Himmler had already approved in December, had proved to be impracticable. In mid-February, a similar 'action' occurred in Grodno, with more than 4,000 victims who were deported to Treblinka.[243]

The HSSPF Russia South, Hans-Adolf Prützmann, reported to Himmler on 26 December 1942 that following the 'anti-Partisan campaign' between 1 September and 1 December 1942 a total of 363,211 'Jews had been executed' within his area of responsibility, which included Ukraine and Bialystok. On 29 December Himmler passed on the report to Hitler, who took note of it.[244]

Unlike the situation in Poland, where the inhabitants of the ghettos in 1942 reacted in a largely 'passive' way to the 'actions', the second wave of massacres in the occupied Soviet territories encountered considerable organized and largely armed resistance. In many places resistance groups formed against the occupying forces, even though the chances of success were extremely poor. They had hardly any firearms, so that the resistance fighters often only had home-made incendiary materials, knives, and tools that had been converted into weapons. It was also extraordinarily difficult for the resistance groups in the individual ghettos, isolated from one another, to receive information about the overall picture, and it was impossible to develop a unified resistance strategy. It also proved extraordinarily difficult for the resistance fighters to win support within the ghetto population. It was not just the fact that the extraordinarily bad living conditions meant that any remaining energy was absorbed by the daily fight for survival, but above all the fear that any acts of resistance would be avenged with collective reprisal against the general population of the ghetto. There was also the often hostile attitude of the non-Jewish indigenous population and the difficulties involved in making contact with non-Jewish resistance groups, let alone receiving support from such groups. In other words, the resisters knew from the outset that their rebellion had little prospect of success. But the fact that resistance could exist on a considerable scale in spite of this can be explained above all by the fact that few illusions about the brutality of the German occupying forces could still exist among those who had survived the first wave of murders in the summer and autumn of 1941.[245]

The pattern of these resistance activities was, in spite of the isolation of the ghettos, always the same: small resistance groups organized a few weapons and prepared to confront a new German 'action'. In part, these preparations were also backed by the Jewish council and the Jewish police, in part they occurred without their support or even against their will.

In fact this resistance tactic was applied in a large number of ghettos: resistance groups attacked the German police and native auxiliary forces as they made their way into the ghetto, and set the ghetto itself on fire. Shielded by the flames, the inhabitants of the ghetto attempted a mass break-out; this always cost a large number of Jewish people their lives. Apart from such mass break-outs, fleeing secretly into the forests, individually or in groups, presented the most significant opportunity to escape mass murder; as such it also represented a form of resistance against the German policy of extermination. Overall, only a small minority managed to escape into the forests, where few in turn survived.

Apart from such organized, violent acts of resistance, and flight, there were many other forms of individual resistance: ghetto-dwellers refused to follow instructions from the Germans, tried to hide in their houses or to barricade them up; in many cases spontaneous attacks by individuals on policemen have also been demonstrated.[246] Shalom Cholawsky and Shmuel Spector have reconstructed individual acts of resistance for White Russia and Volhynia. Spector has assembled figures for twenty-seven towns in Volhynia for which, in the period between May and September 1942, the mass flight of several hundred or several thousand people is documented in each place, particularly in the towns of Dubrovitsa, Rokitno, Tuchin, and Luck as well as in the camps of Poleska and Kostopol. In Tuchin the resistance group set up by the head of the Jewish council set fire to the ghetto and carried out an armed resistance for several days; there were similar revolts in several other places.[247] Spector estimates that mass escapes were successful in another twenty places, and gives the overall figure for people who sought to escape being murdered through flight or by building hiding-places (so-called 'bunkers') as 47,500, or a quarter of the total Jewish population of Volhynia at the start of 1942. In spite of this considerable degree of resistance and flight, the forests gave the fleeing Jews little protection; by far the majority of escapees died as a consequence of the completely inadequate living conditions, or were tracked down and killed by the occupiers or by indigenous forces.

Cholawsky's findings for western Belarus, a territory that had belonged to Poland until 1939 and was occupied by the Soviet Union from 1939 until 1941, are as follows: in Neswiecz (Nesvizh) on 21 July 1942 a Jewish resistance group responded with organized armed resistance to an attempt by German occupying forces to carry out a selection; the ghetto was set on fire and some fighters managed to escape into the forests.[248] The following day another resistance group in Kletsk managed to resist a German 'action' along similar lines.[249] In Lakhva, at the beginning of September, a similar act of resistance against the planned liquidation of the ghetto was followed by a successful mass break-out.[250] Cholawsky also assembled information on over a dozen Belarus towns which show that underground groups there were attempting in a similar way to respond to the German 'actions' with organized resistance and mass break-outs, which were in many cases successful, and in other cases failed for various reasons.[251] Finally, in a series of other Belarus towns groups of ghetto-dwellers managed to escape to the forests.[252]

A resistance group had also formed in the town of Slonim, Polish until 1939, then occupied by the Soviets, and incorporated since August 1941 into the German General District of Belarus. In June 1942 it opened fire on the marching SS and police and killed five Germans. Other Jewish resistance fighters from the territory of Slonim, who had joined the partisans to form an autonomous fighting group, took part in an attack on the occupying troops in Kosovo near Slonim, which prevented the planned liquidation of the ghetto there.[253]

The resistance group which had formed in Baranowicze, also in western Belarus, was on the other hand taken by surprise by the German 'action' at the end of September/beginning of October 1942, and was unable to launch the planned revolt; several dozen resistance fighters managed to escape into the forests.[254]

In Minsk, on former Soviet territory, a resistance group was already forming in August 1941, which concentrated on getting the greatest possible number of ghetto-dwellers suitable for partisan warfare into the forests. Over the years up to 10,000 people were taken out of the ghetto in small groups; about 5,000 survived. This was only made possible by the close collaboration with the resistance movement in the city of Minsk as well as with Soviet partisan units operating in the area of Minsk, and because of general support by the indigenous population, in which anti-Semitism was not very widespread.[255]

The number of Jews who escaped into the forests throughout the whole territory of Belarus is estimated at between 30,000 and 50,000 people, or between 6 and 10 per cent of the whole Jewish population that had remained in place.[256]

The resistance actions were unable to prevent the mass murders, but they did contribute to the fact that thousands of Jewish people survived, albeit mostly in terrible conditions, and they did serve a significant symbolic purpose: a considerable proportion of the Jewish population resisted their murderers or avoided mass murder through flight. The fact that at least some of the victims were capable of reacting actively to the German policy of extermination was not only of great significance for the self-perception of the victims, but also had consequences for the perpetrators: they had to acknowledge that they could not massacre defenceless people without encountering resistance and putting themselves in danger. Dozens of German policemen and their indigenous helpers lost their lives as a result of acts of resistance, and tracking down escaped Jews absorbed considerable resources of the occupying forces. In reality, then, it became apparent that the omnipotent delusion of the calculable total extermination of an entire population group could not be carried out without consequences. It became spasmodically apparent that the reaction of the victims was able to set limits on the actions of the perpetrators.

So the pattern of 'major actions' running according to plan and almost entirely smoothly, which characterized the liquidations of the Polish ghettos in 1942, would not be repeated in the occupied Soviet territories. Just as resistance on a large scale was only possible here because of the experiences of the first wave of murders that happened in 1941, in Poland the experiences of 1942 resulted during the following year in the final 'liquidations' of the ghettos also encountering massive resistance in some cases. Thus, the crucial precondition for the emergence of an armed resistance movement was always the particular concrete experience of the German policy of extermination.

Interim Summary: The Escalation of the Extermination Policy in Spring/Summer 1942

In describing events in Eastern Europe we have already cast our eye over the whole of 1942, as the wave of murders that began in the spring, was intensified throughout the rest of the year, and finally encompassed almost the whole of German-occupied Polish and Soviet territory, had to be seen in context. In this context we should like to return once more to the first months of 1942 and analyse the way in which this wave of killing was set in motion and attempt to reconstruct the decision-making process underlying these events.

For spring and summer 1942 a chain of events and developments may be reconstructed which, seen in context, represent a crucial escalation of anti-Semitic policy: the mass murders already under way or definitely planned in the Soviet Union and in certain other regions (Warthegau, the districts of Lublin and Galicia, Serbia), and the deportations that had been started or prepared since autumn 1941 were now linked together and extended into a Europe-wide programme of the systematic murder of all Jewish people living in that space.

Since autumn 1941, a general rethink had begun among those involved in *Judenpolitik* in a process that can no longer be fathomed in all its details: reacting to the mass murders in Eastern Europe, the main players reached the conviction that the 'Final Solution', which had originally been envisaged as the European Jews slowly dying out in an inhospitable territory somewhere in the 'East', could be at least partially carried out during the war, that it could be anticipated by killing as many Jews as possible through a combination of inhuman living and working conditions and direct murder actions. During the winter of 1941/2 and the spring of 1942 the comprehensive plan emerged, presumably in stages, to kill all the Jews in Europe if possible during the war. In parallel with this establishment of the temporal horizon, ideas crystallized about where and how this genocide was to occur: in occupied Poland, with the aid of poison gas.

We can reconstruct three stages in the process by which the genocidal ideas assumed concrete form: between December 1941 and January 1942 Hitler gave clear signals that after the war had expanded into a world war *Judenpolitik* should be further radicalized to include the 'extermination' of the Jews on a large scale. During the Wannsee Conference, Heydrich still assumed a gigantic deportation programme towards the occupied Eastern terrritories, which could only be realized to its full extent after the end of the war. But his address also reveals that the leadership's ideas of how the deportees would die had in the meantime assumed concrete form: from now on the plan included a combination of 'extermination through work' and mass murder of those who survived the exertions and clearly also those who were 'unfit for work'. Apart from this, there had already been talk at the Wannsee Conference of taking the Polish Jews out of the planned deportation programme and murdering them on the spot, and the murder methods had also been discussed.

The second stage of this radicalization process can be dated to March. Now the policy of systematic extermination that had also been introduced in Poland in autumn 1941 was extended to the district of Lublin and to Galicia, while at the same time the deportations, which had also begun in autumn 1941, were extended to other territories in Central and Western Europe.

In the middle of March 1942 the murder of the majority of the Jews in the districts of Lublin and Galicia was set in motion. Here the murder quota of 60 per cent cited by Goebbels is particularly important. Globocnik had already begun the corresponding preparatory work—the construction of Belzec extermination camp—in October 1941. The mass murder of the Jews of the Warthegau had also been initiated in October 1941, the murders in Chelmno began at the beginning of December. In both cases the mass murders occurred in connection with the deportations from the Reich. In the meantime, at the latest by the beginning of March, the RSHA had established an initial plan for a third wave of deportations for the Jews of the Reich (including the Protectorate), to occur in early March; in the course of this a total of 55,000 people were to be deported to the General Government, particularly the district of Lublin. This programme began in March.

In parallel with this, in February, Germany developed a programme together with Slovakia that was initially to cover the deportation of 20,000 Jews, but which was extended at the end of March, at Himmler's urging, to all the Jews living in that country. The destinations of the deportations were the district of Lublin and Auschwitz concentration camp. The Jewish hostages from France were also deported to Auschwitz from March onwards.

Clearly the mass murders in the district of Lublin and the deportations from the Reich and Slovakia to that area were linked. The old 'reservation plan' had been revived, according to which 'room was made' in the ghettos of the district through mass murders. A decision to link deportations and mass murder in this way must at any rate have been made before the beginning of March.

From Heydrich's statements during his visit to Tuka in early April we know that the deportations from the Reich and Slovakia were already part of an overall plan, presumably developed in March, for the deportation of around 500,000 people from Central and Western Europe, for which, however, no concrete time frame can be demonstrated at this point.

Even more serious, however, is the third stage of this process of radicalization, which was prepared at the end of April and came into full effect in May and June. Only now were the regional murders linked into a programme of systematic murder of the European Jews covering the whole of Europe.

In early May the deportations from the district of Lublin were expanded with the systematic clearance of the counties (*Kreise*). At the end of May, with the deportations from the district of Krakau (Gracow), there began the extension of the murders to the other territories within the General Government, until in July and August the districts of Warsaw and Radom were also included. The significant preparatory measures for this extension of the murders to the whole of the General Government included the extension of Krüger's powers in May/early June and the start of the construction of Treblinka in May or June at the latest. So the corresponding decisions must have been made before May. At about the same time the decision must have been made to carry out a mass murder among the Jews of annexed Upper Silesia, to which tens of thousands of people fell victim between May and August. However, because of the transport moratorium, the mass murder of the Jews of the General Government could not begin to its full extent until July. Finally, the transport moratorium had a radicalizing effect on the development of mass murder. It accelerated the deportations from the western territories and the planners of the mass murder entered something like a phase of consolidation after which the whole programme was resumed with much greater impetus in July.

At around the same time as this fundamental decision concerning the Jews in the General Government, at least before mid-May, a further momentous decision must have been made: the deportations of Jews from Central Europe were increased beyond the quota cited in March, and most or all of these people were murdered when the transports arrived at their destinations. This was the fate suffered by the Jews arriving from the Reich to Minsk from mid-May onwards, and the deportees from Slovakia from the beginning of June in Sobibor. And the great majority of those Jews who had been deported to Lodz from the Reich in autumn 1941 were now, in the first half of May, deported to Chelmno in a series of transports and murdered there.

In parallel with these events, the mass murder of the Soviet Jews which had begun in the summer of 1941 was given a fresh impulse in May 1942: now the murders began on a large scale again, before leading in the summer to the total extermination of the indigenous Jewish population.

The decision-making process underlying the systematic genocide remains largely obscure and must be reconstructed from the course of events. The entries in Himmler's office diary for late April provide an initial clue: Himmler met Heydrich a total of seven times over only eight days between late April and early May 1942 in three different places (Berlin, Munich, and Prague). This unusually intensive series of discussions is framed by two lengthy meetings that Himmler had with Hitler on 23 April and 3 May 1942 in the Führer's headquarters.[257] The attempt on Heydrich's life and his subsequent death (27 May and 4 June) must have had a further radicalizing effect on this decision-making process; we need only recall Himmler's announcement at Heydrich's funeral on 4 June that he would end the Jewish 'migration' within a year.

At the beginning of June the RSHA established a concrete deportation programme for the West which was to be realized within three months from mid-July. With this Western programme the plans which first became apparent in early April were realized and adapted to the conditions introduced by the transport moratorium in the East in June/July. But, as early as June 1942 Himmler demanded the speedy and complete deportation of all the Jews in France.

The people in these transports from the West, the Slovakian Jews, who from early July onwards were transported to Auschwitz in the wake of the transport moratorium and those Jews from the Reich who, starting with the first transport from Vienna on 17 July, arrived in Auschwitz, met with the same fate: from 4 July onwards most of them were, in so far as they were 'unfit for work', murdered in the two hastily erected makeshift gas chambers, Bunkers I and II.

In the middle of July, after the end of the transport moratorium, the deportation and murder programme had been set fully in motion. Now, during a visit to Globocnik on 19 July, Himmler established a concrete timetable for the major part of this programme, the extermination of the Jews of the General Government. This was a day after he had visited Auschwitz and three days after he had, at the Führer's headquarters, demanded increased transport opportunities from the Reich railways. By the end of the year, the Jews of the General Government would have been murdered, apart from a few people who were fit for work and were to be placed under the control of the SS.

At about the same time, the decision must have been made to send almost all further transports from the Reich directly to the extermination camps and no longer to ghettos.

Finally, as will be outlined in the next section, already in the summer of 1942 the Germans had introduced the crucial steps to extend the deportation programme beyond Eastern Europe. While the occupation authorities in Western Europe set about undertaking deportations beyond the quota of 125,000 people for 1942 decided in June, in July the German government approached its allies, Romania, Bulgaria, Croatia, Hungary, and Finland, to secure the deportation of the Jews living in those countries.

Deportations from the Occupied Western Territories in the Second Half of 1942

Continuation of the Deportations from France

After six deportation trains carrying some 6,000 Jews had already set off from France to Auschwitz between March and early July 1942, and with the SS having established plans for the deportation of a total of 125,000 people from France, Belgium, and the Netherlands in June, between 19 July and 7 August a further ten transports carrying a total of around 10,000 people set off for Auschwitz. These deportees, 'stateless Jews', had been arrested in Paris during a major raid on 16 and 17 July.[258] The age limit for the deportation had now been raised to 55 for women and 60 for men. The inmates of these transports were now, as the Jews from Slovakia had been, subjected to a selection in Auschwitz; after that those people deemed 'unfit for work' were murdered in the gas chambers immediately upon their arrival.

In August, as agreed with the Vichy government in July, the deportations of the stateless Jews from the unoccupied zone began (Transports 17–19). After Himmler had agreed to a suggestion from the French Prime Minister, Pierre Laval, in early July that children under the age of 16 should also be included in the deportations, between 17 and 26 August over 2,000 children whose parents had already been taken to Auschwitz in the previous transports were also deported with the following five transports. Transports 24–39 (their departure dates were between 26 August and 30 September 1942) were stopped at Kosel in Silesia, where men who were fit for work had to leave the trains to be deployed as forced labourers with the 'Schmelt Organization'.[259]

At a meeting held in his office on 28 August Eichmann demanded that all stateless Jews be removed from France by the end of October 1942 (after that the deportations had to be postponed until February); along with the 25,000 people deported already that meant a further 50,000 people. 'The end of June '43', Eichmann continued, was envisaged as a 'final deadline for the evacuation of the remaining foreign Jews'.[260]

In order to guarantee this quota of deportations, at the end of August more than 6,500 stateless Jews had been arrested in the unoccupied zone, who were deported during the following months, along with around 3,000 Jews of foreign origin who had been kept in internment camps in the south of France for a long time. These included a large number of children who had been separated from their mothers.[261] As these deportations met with strong hostility from the French population and led to the open opposition of the Church, at the beginning of September 1942 the Vichy government made it clear to the Germans that further arrests and deportations could no longer be carried out in the unoccupied zone. Since HSSPF Oberg, in view of the general political situation in France, and with regard for President Laval's domestic prestige, had secured a decision from Himmler that no French citizens were to be deported from the occupied zone for the time being,[262] the occupation authorities now arrested foreign Jews in the occupied zone (Greeks and Romanians above all), who were deported in November in four further transports. After this came the expected halt in deportations until February 1943. The total figure of deportees from France for 1942 was approximately 42,000.[263]

Extension of the Deportations to the Netherlands and Belgium

Since the summer of 1940 the occupation administration had begun to introduce the anti-Jewish measures customary in German-occupied territory into the Netherlands as well: a definition of Jews on the model of the Nuremberg Laws was introduced; Jewish officials were dismissed from public service, a Jewish council (Joodse Rat) responsible for the execution of German orders was formed, Jewish property was expropriated.[264] In March 1941 the German Security Police established the Central Office for Jewish emigration, which dealt at first with those Jews living in the Netherlands. In May 1942 Jews were ordered to wear the yellow star and, at the beginning of 1942, labour camps for Jews were set up, in which ultimately some 15,000 people were held.[265]

At the beginning of 1941, the first deportations of Dutch Jews had already begun, at first (comparable to the situation in France at the end of the year) as 'a reprisal' for Dutch acts of resistance. By the end of the year 850 Dutch Jews had been deported to Mauthausen concentration camp, where they had been subjected to the most extreme hard labour; none was to survive to the end of the war.[266]

Immediately after the RSHA's decision in June 1942 to deport 40,000 Jews from the Netherlands, preparations got under way. The representative of the Foreign Ministry in the occupied Netherlands, Otto Bene, reported to Berlin early in July 1942 that the deportation of around 25,000 stateless Jews from the Netherlands would begin in mid-July and take about four months; after that the deportation of Jews with Dutch citizenship would begin.[267]

As early as June 1942 the Central Office for Jewish emigration had informed the chairman of the Dutch Jewish council of an imminent 'police labour deployment' of the Dutch Jews in Germany.[268] After the freedom of movement of the Jews had been greatly restricted by a series of regulations at the end of June, on 5 July 4,000

Jews, most of them living in Amsterdam, were summoned to report to Westerbork transit camp to join the 'labour deployment'. Only some of those summoned actually appeared, but the occupation authorities managed to exert so much pressure that enough Jews arrived in Westerbork to assemble the first two transports to Auschwitz carrying over 2,000 Jewish men.

By 12 December, another forty transports were dispatched from Westerbork to Auschwitz, so that by the end of the year about 38,000 people had been deported and the quota announced by Eichmann in June had hence almost been reached. As with the French transports, from the end of August many of the trains were halted at Kosel in Silesia, where men who were 'fit for work' were separated from the rest.

In no other country under German occupation did the Security Police manage to carry out the arrests and deportations so smoothly as in the Netherlands. Tellingly, the deportation victims were not generally captured in raids or 'actions', but arrested in their homes. The relatively calm progression of the arrests and the continuous course of the deportations may be explained by a series of factors that played into the hands of the Germans: the relatively strong position of the SS and radical Party forces in the occupation authorities, the comprehensive registration of Jews living in the Netherlands and their relatively pronounced trust in the measures of the authorities, the cooperative stance of the Dutch authorities and parts of the police apparatus, an ingenious system of 'exemptions' from the deportations that left the majority of Jews in relative safety at first, the fact that a relatively large number of people had always been put in camps, the weakness of the Dutch resistance, and other factors.[269]

There were still about 52,000 Jews in Belgium at the end of 1940, only about 10 per cent of whom were Belgian citizens.[270] From October 1940, and more intensively in the spring of 1941, the German military administration introduced the measures against the Jews that were customary in German occupied territory: definition, registration, dismissal from state employment, and 'Aryanization'; the formation of a 'Jewish council', the Association des Juifs en Belgique.[271]

In comparison with similar steps in the Netherlands, these measures were carried out much more slowly and inefficiently, not least because the German Security Police in Belgium was given comparatively little room to manoeuvre by the military administration, and the Belgian administrative apparatus was not so associated with the anti-Jewish measures. There was also the fact that the Jews living in Belgium, precisely because of their relatively low level of integration, mistrusted the measures of the authorities and tried to elude them, and the fact that in Belgium both the national resistance organization, which had come into being relatively early, and specifically Jewish resistance groups could provide greater support than in the Netherlands.[272]

After the RSHA's decision in June 1942 to deport 10,000 Jews from Belgium to the extermination camps, the initial focus was upon Jews who had become stateless.[273] In July 1942 Jews who were unemployed and who did not have Belgian citizenship were summoned to report to the collection camp of Malines for 'labour deployment in the East'. When this did not occur on the desired scale, raids were carried out.[274]

The first transport left Malines on 4 August 1942, heading for Auschwitz. By the end of October 1942, a total of sixteen further transports had followed, so that the quota of 10,000 people specified by the RSHA was already reached by 15 September and the Security Police set themselves a goal of 20,000 deportees by the end of 1942.[275] By the end of 1942, 16,882 Jews had been deported from Belgium, all the foreign or stateless Jews. As in the case of the deportations from France and the Netherlands, in a series of transports workers were taken off the trains at Kosel in Silesia.

After the first deportations of 6,000 hostages from France the deportations in the second half of 1942 were extended to the whole of the occupied Western territories and set in motion on a large scale. The following overview may further clarify this development:

After Heydrich's statement in April 1942 that a deportation of a total of 'half a million' Jews from the Protectorate, Slovakia, Belgium, France, and the Netherlands was taking place, in June the RSHA had established concrete deportation quotas until the end of the year for France (100,000), the Netherlands (15,000), and Belgium (10,000). In July these numbers had been altered, because of difficulties arising in France, to 40,000 each for France and the Netherlands and 10,000 for Belgium.

In July the order was issued that in the next four months 25,000 stateless Jews were to be deported from the Netherlands. In mid-December 38,000 people overall were to be deported. In Belgium the originally specified quota of 10,000 people had already been filled in September, and towards the end of the year considerably exceeded with far more than 16,000 victims. At the end of August Eichmann pursued the intention of deporting a total of 75,000 people from France by the end of October, and all 'foreign' Jews by the end of June 1943. In fact, by the end of the year 42,000 people had been deported from France.

Efforts to Involve Germany's Allies in the Deportation Programme (Summer 1942)

After the deportations from Central and Western Europe to the extermination camps had begun in July 1942, the RSHA immediately set about involving other German allies in the murder programme above all in South-Eastern Europe, apart from Slovakia, which had agreed to the deportation of Jews living in the country. The Foreign Ministry was heavily involved in this policy.

As a general rule the Germans initially—as a first step to the involvement of the allies in the extermination programme—tried to win the consent of the countries in question to the deportation of their Jewish citizens living in the Reich or in the occupied territories. The governments of Romania, Croatia, and Slovakia had already declared their agreement with this process at the end of 1941.[276]

A second batch of such requests followed in the summer of 1942. In July, the Foreign Ministry managed to win the consent of the Bulgarian government to the deportation of its Jews living in the Reich by responding to a suggestion from the Bulgarian Foreign Minister Popoff in 1941 that henceforth all Jews with European citizenship should be treated the same.[277] The deportation of Bulgarian Jews was quickly extended to the occupied Western territories.[278] In August 1942 the Romanian government again expressly declared its agreement with the inclusion of the country's Jews in the German deportation measures. The Romanian government had in fact already given such a declaration in November 1941, but in the meantime it had become concerned about the possible worse treatment of Romanian Jews in comparison with Hungarian Jews in a similar position. However, the German Foreign Ministry had been able to allay these concerns.[279] In contrast, in August 1942 the Hungarian government resisted the German deportation plan. In response, the Germans asked Hungary to withdraw Jews of Hungarian citizenship from the whole of the German sphere of influence by the end of the year; this deadline was later extended a number of times.[280]

Also, in August 1942, the Foreign Ministry approached the Italian government with a request either to agree to include the Italian Jews in Germany's Jewish persecution measures, or to withdraw this group of people from the occupied Western territories by the end of the year.[281] In their reply, on 10 October 1942, the Italians made it clear that they had to protect Jews with Italian citizenship in the Mediterranean area because of their important economic role for reasons of national interest. Involvement in the German deportation programme in the occupied Western territories would weaken this position and must therefore be rejected.[282]

The willingness on the part of the allies to consent to the inclusion of their Jews living in Germany or in the occupied territories in the German deportation programme was to smooth the way to bringing about a general agreement on the part of the allies to hand over their Jews. As early as the end of 1941, in the 'wishes and suggestions' that he had noted as part of the preparations for the Wannsee Conference, the desk officer for Jewish affairs in the Foreign Ministry had stressed to the RSHA that they should 'express their willingness to the Romanian, Slovakian, Croatian, Bulgarian and Hungarian governments to evacuate to the East the Jews living in those countries as well.'[283]

While the deportation of the Slovakian Jews had already begun in the spring of 1942, the Germans did not develop any initiatives towards the other four countries named (Romania, Bulgaria, Hungary, and Croatia) during the next six months. On the contrary, a suggestion by the Foreign Ministry's Jewish desk officer, Rademacher, in May 1942, concerning the 'Abtransport' (transporting away) of the Croatian Jews received a negative response from the RSHA[284] and in June 1942 the German embassy in Sofia received the instruction to give a basically positive response to any wishes by the Bulgarians concerning the deportation of their Jews, but to point out that this could not occur in the course of the current year.[285] In July 1942, however, this picture would fundamentally change.

In July 1942 the German police attaché in Zagreb was commissioned by the RSHA to prepare the 'resettlement' of the Croatian Jews to the 'German Eastern territories'. At this point over half of the more than 30,000 Jews living in the country had been interned in camps by the Ustasha regime.[286]

The Croatian government formed after the occupation of the country, which was based on the Fascist Ustasha movement, had already passed its first anti-Jewish law on 30 April 1941 according to which the approximately 30,000 Jews in the country were defined on the model of the Nuremberg Laws. A wave of anti-Jewish legislation followed on the German model: 'mixed marriages' were forbidden, the Jews were to be labelled, their property confiscated. This policy must be seen in the context of the policy of the Ustasha regime to create a homogeneous Croatian nation and systematically exclude Serbs (who constituted 30 per cent of the population), Jews, and Gypsies from citizens' rights.

This mass murder of the Jews must in turn be seen in the context of the mass murders of Serbs and Gypsies. A few weeks after the foundation of the Ustasha state, the displacement of Serbs resident in Croatia to German-occupied Serbia began, while the Ustasha were already organizing various massacres. After Hitler had encouraged the new Croatian head of state, Ante Pavelic, in his policy of 'ethnic corridor cleansing' on his visit to Berlin,[287] and in a German-Croatian treaty an exchange of 170,000 Slovenians from Serbia had been agreed against the corresponding number of Serbs from Croatia, a massive wave of displacement and flight began, in the course of which possibly as many as 200,000 Serbs reached Croatia. Around 200,000 Serbs were forced to convert to Catholicism. In addition to this, however, Ustasha units began large-scale massacres of Serbs and interned Serbs in concentration camps built on the German model, in which a large number were murdered. Most of the prisoners were interned in the notorious camp complex at Jasenovac. The number of victims in this camp alone is estimated as 60,000–80,000; we may assume a total number of far more than 200,000 victims.[288]

In parallel with the anti-Serbian policy, the persecution of the 30,000 to 40,000 Jews in Croatia also escalated. From May 1941 onwards more than half of the Jewish population was interned in such camps; the majority of the Jewish prisoners lost their lives in these camps. A large number of the Jewish prisoners were executed immediately after entering the camp; the survivors were exposed to constant 'murder actions' by the guards or lost their lives because of the terrible conditions or as the result of epidemics.[289]

On 31 July 1942 all Croatian Jews were summoned for registration. In those parts of Croatia occupied by German troops (there was also an Italian zone of occupation) further Jews were arrested in addition to the large number already interned. On 13 August the first deportation train left Zagreb for Auschwitz containing 1,200 Croatian Jews.[290] Seven railway transports to Auschwitz had already been specified for the month of August;[291] in fact four trains can be shown to have arrived in Auschwitz that month.[292] Thus, in the summer of 1942, 4,927 Jews were deported from Croatia and murdered in Auschwitz almost without exception.[293]

In July 1942, German efforts to extend the deportations were also directed towards Romania. Romania had taken an active part in the German extermination policy towards the Jews in the newly conquered Eastern territories. In the newly conquered territories of Bessarabia and Bukovina an estimated 50,000 people lost their lives in massacres; the surviving Jewish population of that territory, around 150,000 Jews, had been deported to the area between Dnjestr and Bug, where at least 65,000 more people perished through hunger, epidemics, and shootings; in the Ukraine Romanian forces had also taken an active part in the German extermination policy, particularly in the massacre in Odessa.[294]

The approximately 320,000 Jews living in Romania itself had been subject to constantly tightened anti-Semitic special legislation since 1938. From early 1942 onwards they were registered by a newly created compulsory body, the Centrala Evreilor din Romania.[295] The deportation of 60,000 Jewish men to Bessarabia in August 1941 as forced labourers had only failed because of a German intervention that sought at all costs to prevent further mass deportations to German-occupied Ukraine while the war was going on.[296]

In July 1942 the adviser on 'Jewish questions' at the German embassy in Bucharest, Gustav Richter, and the deputy Prime Minister, Mihai Antonescu, agreed to the deportation of the Romanian Jews authorized by Marshal Antonescu, which was to begin around 10 September 1942. The transports were to go to the district of Lublin where, as the German plenipotentiary Manfred Killinger reported to the Foreign Ministry 'the part that was fit for work will be deployed in a work programme, and the rest subjected to special treatment'.[297] The immediately imminent deportations were already being publicly announced.[298]

However, the fact that this agreement was reached behind the back of the Foreign Ministry greatly annoyed Foreign Minister Ribbentrop. He demanded that the director of the German department, Martin Luther, explain his previous measures in the area of *Judenpolitik*[299] and, on 25 August, issued a directive that the measures agreed with the Romanians were to be continued, but that no further initiatives were to be developed with regard to Hungary, Bulgaria, and the Italian-occupied zone of Croatia.[300]

In issuing this directive Ribbentrop, concerned about his authority, found himself in complete agreement with the RSHA. For it too did not consider that, in summer 1942, the preconditions yet existed for deportations from Hungary, Bulgaria, and the Italian-occupied zone of Croatia.

Thus, on 21 August, Luther had already recorded in a note that the Hungarian government had not yet been approached because 'the Hungarian legislation concerning the Jews does not yet promise sufficient success'.[301] In fact the people of Jewish descent living in Hungary (including the annexed former Czechoslovak, Romanian, and Yugoslavian territories), over 800,000 in number, were at this point subject to anti-Semitic laws that corresponded more or less to the Nuremberg Laws.[302] In August 1941, admittedly, 16,000–18,000 'foreign' Jews (Jews who had lost their Hungarian citizenship because of the anti-Semitic legislation) had been deported to the newly occupied Eastern territories, the great majority of them being killed in the massacre of Kamenetsk-Podolsk.[303] In January 1942, in the wake of a 'cleansing action', Hungarian troops had shot thousands of civilians, including hundreds of Jews. But the Hungarian government made no arrangements to extend this policy to Jews with Hungarian citizenship.[304]

In July 1942, when the Hungarian military attaché in Berlin submitted his government's proposal that all Jews living in Hungary 'illegally' be resettled to Transnistria,[305] Himmler decided that the evacuation from Hungary of Jews of non-Hungarian citizenship who had fled to the country should be delayed until Hungary declared itself willing to include its own Jews in the planned measures.[306]

Along very similar lines, Eichmann too declared on 25 September 1942 his lack of interest in the deportation of foreign Jews from Hungary, as this would have been only a 'partial' action that 'according to experience' required the same expenditure of effort as the comprehensive deportation of all Jews living in a country. One should therefore wait until Hungary was ready to include the Hungarian Jews in the deportations as well.[307]

At the beginning of 1941, the Bulgarian government had passed special laws against the Jews living in the country (removal from public service, confiscation of property) which, after the Balkan campaign in the spring of 1941, were extended to the occupied Greek (Thracian and eastern Macedonian) or Yugo-slavian (Macedonian) territories with their native Jews numbering between 4,000 and 7,000.[308] If these measures were, from the German point of view, far from adequate preconditions for the deportation of Jews living in Bulgaria, this situation changed very quickly in the course of the summer of 1942, plainly still influenced by the preparations for the deportations from Croatia and Romania.

On 26 August a Commissariat for Jewish Affairs was set up and the same decree extended the term 'Jew' in a racist sense and laid the legal foundation for deportations.[309] After these measures had been introduced, at the beginning of September the RSHA immediately urged the deportations from Bulgaria.

In September even Ribbentrop allowed himself to be persuaded to withdraw his opposition to the inclusion of Bulgaria in the deportation programme.[310]

Since the start of the preparations for the deportations in Croatia, the Foreign Ministry and the RSHA had assumed that the deportation of the Jews from the German-occupied zone would be followed at the end of August by the deportation of the Jews from the Italian-occupied zone to Auschwitz.[311] The Croatian government had declared its agreement with this procedure, but Luther expected 'certain difficulties' on the part of the Italians.[312] However, in response to a request that came via the German Embassy in Rome Mussolini initially decided, or so Luther informed Ribbentrop on 11 September, 'to treat the Jews in the Italian-occupied parts of Croatia in the same way...as in the rest of Croatia'.[313]

But since Ribbentrop, as we have shown, had instructed Luther on 25 August to develop no further initiatives with regard to the Jews in the Italian-occupied zone for the time being out of concern for the German-Italian alliance, he now proved extremely displeased about the request made to the Italian government; they had 'interfered in a Croatian-Italian question...which contradicted the principle of not making ourselves spokesmen for Croatian interests where the Italians were concerned, but giving Italy precedence in Croatia in every respect'.[314]

With regard to Greece, too, the RSHA became active in July 1942, the time when the initiative was being taken to set in motion the first wave of deportations from South-Eastern Europe. But preparations for immediate deportation were not at first made, as it was hoped above all that they would reach a uniform procedure in both occupied zones. (In the Italian zone of occupation there were at this point about 13,000 Jews, in the German zone of occupation about 55,000; there were also around 4,000 Jews living in the north-east of the country, which was allocated to Bulgaria.)[315] As in Croatia the policy initially pursued here was to avoid a conflict with Rome at all costs.

In July 1942 the RSHA informed the Foreign Ministry of its desire to introduce anti-Jewish measures, namely universal labelling and internment of Jews who had fled Germany. But the Italians, who had been approached with this in mind, did not approve of the labelling of the Jews in their zone of occupation.[316]

Also in July 1942 the German military administration introduced forced labour for Jewish men. Thousands were deployed on hard physical labour in very severe working conditions; hundreds died and a mass flight to the Italian zone began. The emphatic demand by the Germans that Jews throughout the whole of Greece be compulsorily labelled could not be enforced because of the dilatory treatment of the requests by the Italian government.[317]

The German efforts to organize deportations in the summer of 1942 also focused on another country. After the war, former Prime Minister Rangell reported that in July 1942, on a visit to Finland, Himmler had addressed the topic of 'Finnish Jews'; he, Rangell, however, had brought the discussion to a close by pointing out that in Finland (where some 2,000 Jews lived) there was no 'Jewish question'.[318]

These initiatives and negotiations on the part of the Germans with their allies allow us to draw the conclusion that a fundamental decision had been made in July in favour of a deportation from the allied states. At the same time, priorities had been set, in which the state of anti-Semitic measures taken in the individual countries was crucial. First of all, the Jews were to be deported from Croatia and Romania; in Croatia, the Jewish population had already been largely interned, while in Romania registration had been introduced and because of the massacres in the newly conquered territories there could be no doubt about the radically anti-Semitic stance of this ally. The deportations from Hungary and Bulgaria had, on the other hand, been postponed to a later time because of the unsatisfactory state—from the German point of view—of *Judenpolitik* in those countries, while the issue of the deportation of the Jews from the Italian-occupied territories in Croatia and Greece remained shelved because of the fundamental attitude of the Italian government towards the 'Jewish question'. Himmler's unsuccessful foray into Finland in July 1942 produced the same result.

Intensified Efforts to Extend the Deportations in Autumn 1942

On 23 September 1942 Mihai Antonescu, on a visit to Hitler's headquarters, again confirmed to Ribbentrop his intention to deport the Romanian Jews.[319] During or immediately after this visit a fundamental decision must have been made by the German leadership to intensify the deportations across the whole of Europe. For the next day, 24 September, Ribbentrop instructed Luther by telephone to 'accelerate the evacuation of the Jews from the most diverse of countries in Europe'. Ribbentrop had ordered that 'we should now approach the Bulgarian, the Hungarian, and Danish governments with the intention of setting in motion the evacuation of the Jews from these countries as soon as possible'. Where Italy was concerned, Ribbentrop had reserved further action to himself: either he would clarify the issue with Ciano or it would be discussed between Hitler and Mussolini.[320] The fact that Ribbentrop was thus abruptly revoking his instruction of 25 August to stay out of the deportation question indicates that he was obeying a decision from Hitler. Immediately prior to this, at the armaments discussion held between 20 and 22 September, Hitler had called for the removal of those Jews still working in armaments production within the Reich and their deportation.[321]

On 25 September—the previous day the Croatian Prime Minister Ante Pavelic had been received in the Führer's headquarters, where he had talked to Hitler and Ribbentrop about the 'Jewish problem' in Croatia[322]—Ribbentrop issued a directive concerning the deportation of Jews in the Italian zone of Croatia, to which Mussolini had already agreed in principle. The question should tentatively be raised in Rome about 'how matters stood', although one should not strive for 'an actual demarche demanding, for example, that the Duce's decision concerning the instructions should be quickly passed on to the military authorities in Croatia'.[323]

In fact, however, apart from Croatia, all the allies who had come to be included in the German deportation plans in the course of 1942 would thwart German intentions in autumn 1942. This applied to Slovakia, where the deportations came to a complete stop,[324] to Romania, which withdrew from the deportation agreement that it had given in July, to Bulgaria and Hungary, which had been newly included in the deportation programme in September, and to Italy, which prevented further deportations from its occupied zone in Croatia. In the last quarter of 1942, the RSHA only managed to organize deportations from one other country, Norway, possibly in place of Denmark, which had been brought into play in September.

As regards Romania, in the last quarter of 1942 the Germans were forced to acknowledge that the deportation agreed there in July was being delayed.[325] Towards the end of the year, the RSHA decided to postpone the deportations from Romania to the following spring. On 14 December, Luther described this postponement to the German embassy in Sofia as not very serious, as the 'deportation' (*Abtransport*) was 'not in any case desirable during the main winter months'. Things should be kept 'in flux' so that at the beginning of spring 'one could expect the measures to continue'.[326] In January 1943, however, Himmler reached the conclusion that further attempts to move the Romanian government to hand over their Jews were pointless. He, therefore, proposed that the 'Jewish adviser' be withdrawn from the German embassy in Bucharest.[327]

On 16 October Luther ordered the German ambassador in Sofia to 'discuss the question of a transport to the East of the Jews due for resettlement according to the new Bulgarian regulations' with the Bulgarian government. Luther was starting from the premise that these plans could be connected with the forthcoming deportations from Romania. But Ambassador Adolf Beckerle learned from the Bulgarian Prime Minister that the German offer was basically welcome, but the Bulgarians wanted first to 'concentrate (the Jewish workers) and deploy them for road-building'.[328] After further discussions in mid-November, Beckerle still believed that the transport of the 'the majority of the Bulgarian Jews' was possible in the near future.[329] In parallel with this, Richter, the 'Jewish adviser' at the German embassy in Bucharest, approached Protisch, the press attaché at the Bulgarian embassy there, who had been specially commissioned by his government to investigate Romania's 'Jewish policy'. Richter suggested that perhaps 'the resettlement of the Jews of Bulgaria in collaboration with the Reich, which has already been decided upon', could be undertaken. He indicated that the 'Reich office responsible for the solution of the Jewish question was very interested in such a collaboration.'[330] As early as November, however, a detailed report from the SD foreign department reached the conclusion that further intensification of the persecution of the Jews would encounter indifference and resistance.[331] The deportations that had originally been planned were thus, as in the case of Romania, postponed to the following year.

In late September 1942 Luther also took the initiative with the Hungarian government.[332] On 5 October, unofficially at first, he put the German demands about the 'Jewish question' to the Hungarian Ambassador in Berlin, Dominik Sztojay. The Hungarian government was to declare itself in agreement with the deportation of the Hungarian Jews from Germany and the occupied countries, or fetch them back to Hungary by 31 December 1942. At the same time, Luther drew up a comprehensive programme for the 'treatment of the Jewish question in Hungary', including the deportation of the Hungarian Jews.[333]

At this meeting Sztojay pointed out amongst other things that the Hungarian Prime Minister, Miklos Kállay, was particularly interested to learn 'whether the Jews would be able to go on living after their evacuation to the East'. In this context certain rumours were circulating, which he himself, of course, considered unbelievable, but which concerned Kállay. He did not want 'to be accused of handing over the Hungarian Jews after their evacuation to misery or worse'. Sztojay seemed content with Luther's answer that all evacuated Jews would 'initially find employment in road-building', and would later be 'accommodated in a Jewish reservation'.

On 17 October, the German ambassador in Budapest handed over the German demands in an official form.[334] Within the Foreign Ministry, however, it soon became clear that the Hungarian government was far from willing to start the deportation of the Hungarian Jews.[335] However, towards the end of November, Himmler assumed that the deportations could soon be set in motion. To this end, he suggested to Ribbentrop that he send an experienced adviser, Wisliceny perhaps, to the German embassay in Budapest as a 'consultant on Jewish questions'.[336] As a 'first instalment' one could deport 100,000 Jews from the annexed Slovakian and Romanian territories, a suggestion already made to Wisliceny by a Hungarian contact when he was staying in Budapest in October.[337]

But this suggestion contradicted the official Hungarian position, which was hardening at this time. In a note of 2 December 1942, the Hungarian ambassador in Berlin summed up his government's attitude to the German proposals of 17 October.[338] According to this, the Hungarian government was only prepared to withdraw its Jews from the German sphere of influence if all foreign Jews also living there were forced to take the same step. The labelling of Jews living in Hungary, or indeed their deportation, was for various reasons impossible at the present time.

Luther's attempts, beginning in October 1942, to clarify the further stance of the Italians with regard to the deportation of Croatian Jews from Italy's occupied zone, also did not lead to the desired outcome.[339] Although Mussolini had, in August 1942, agreed with the German demand to hand over the Jews living in the Italian occupied zone, senior Italian officers and officials were determined to prevent this from happening.[340]

While these initiatives were still fully under way, on 22 October Luther presented Ribbentrop with a lengthy paper containing the suggestion that Italy be addressed about the 'Jewish question' at the level of Foreign Ministers or the Heads of State. The Italians should be exhorted to agree to the deportation of all Italian Jews from the whole of the German sphere of influence; to draw up Jewish legislation on the German model and coordinate their position vis-à-vis other states with Germany.[341]

In fact, however, the Italian occupation authorities would not hand over the Jews living in their zone; instead, from October 1942 they began interning them, more than 2,600 people according to official Italian figures. Jews who had or who could claim Italian citizenship were brought to Italian territory, and the others were accommodated on the Croatian coast, away from the hands of the Germans.[342]

Ribbentrop's directive of September 1942, to demand of the Danish government the deportation of Jews living there, is probably directly traceable to the extraordinary displeasure with which Hitler reacted to developments in that country in September 1942. For a time, Hitler expressed the view that the particularly restrained form of German occupation in that country should be radically changed, and it should henceforth be ruled with an iron fist as a 'hostile country'. The first consequence was that SS Gruppenführer Werner Best was appointed Reich Plenipotentiary in Denmark. However, Best also represented a relatively elastic policy in Denmark, one irreconcilable with the demand for the handover of the Jews living in the country.[343]

It seems possible that the deportation of the Norwegian Jews in the autumn of 1942, which had plainly been prepared in a rush, and the history of which cannot be reconstructed in detail, formed a kind of second-best solution given that the deportation of the Danish Jews was undesirable for general political reasons to do with the occupation of the country. Some 2,000 Jews were living in Norway at the end of 1942. By that point they had been subjected to the usual measures, such as removal from public service, confiscation of property, stamping of passports, and other things besides. From autumn 1942 a statistical office set up by Quisling's party began drawing up a list of Norwegian Jews.[344] Thus the technical preconditions for deportation were in place, and in October 1942 the RSHA, clearly on the spur of the moment (the lack of preparations concerning the preparation of transport capacity indicates as much) decided to go ahead with it. On 23 October the Norwegian police received the order to prepare for the detention of all Jews.

On 26 October the arrest of all Jewish men between the ages of 15 and 54 began, on 25 November that of the women and children. The next day a German transport ship containing 532 Jews set sail for Stettin (Sczeczin).[345] Further deportations occurred in November 1942, in February 1943 and 1944, bringing the total numbers of deportees to 770. Ninehundred and thirty Norwegian Jews had fled to Sweden.[346]

CHAPTER 18

THE FURTHER DEVELOPMENT OF THE POLICY OF EXTERMINATION AFTER THE TURNING OF THE WAR IN 1942–1943: CONTINUATION OF THE MURDERS AND GEOGRAPHICAL EXPANSION OF THE DEPORTATIONS

In the second half of the war—apart from the efforts to secure the space controlled by Germany in a political, military, and police sense, and alongside the complex of economic and food policy—*Judenpolitik* was a main axis of Germany's occupation and alliance policies. In the view of the National Socialist leadership the more the war advanced the greater the significance of the systematic murder of the Jews for the solidarity of the German power bloc. This increasingly important alteration in the function of *Judenpolitik* provides a significant explanation for the fact that the murder of millions in the second half of the war was not only continued, but even expanded.

Under military pressure, Nazi Germany was less and less in a position to draft even sketchily the main features of a 'New Europe' in accordance with racial principles. If it had seriously made such an attempt, the issue of the racial 'inequality' of the peoples living on the continent, the core element of National Socialism, would inevitably have been raised, and the numerous unresolved questions of borders and minorities would have come onto the agenda. If, on the one hand, the National Socialists did not want to abandon their claim to open the door to a completely new kind of order for the European continent, but, on the other, did not want to abandon the way in which this project was to be realized, they had no other option but concretely to anticipate their racist utopia in a negative way. From this point of view the *Entjudung* of the German sphere of influence represented the claim to be the start of a comprehensive racist new order, but was actually—because of the inconsistency and impracticability of a 'positive' racial policy—the substitute for the unfeasible 'new order' on a racial basis.

In the second half of the war, the continuation and radicalization of *Judenpolitik*, the only practicable element of the racist utopia of the National Socialists, became the iron band with which the 'Third Reich' held together the power bloc that it dominated. For with the implementation of the murder of the Jews within the German power bloc, the executive organizations—German occupying administrations, local auxiliary organizations, collaborative governments or allies—were turned into lackeys and accomplices of the extermination policy and, given the unprecedented nature of this crime, irretrievably bound to the engine of this policy, the leadership of National Socialist Germany.

In addition to this, there was the fact that any further radicalization of persecution was bound to strengthen the power of the SS and radical Party forces within the occupying administrations or the German diplomatic apparatus and, via the periphery of the German sphere of rule, alter the overall character of the regime in favour of those forces. The implementation of *Judenpolitik* within the German sphere of influence thus amounted to the definitive realization of National Socialism's total claim to power. But this was, from the perspective of National Socialism, the sole key to success in this war.

If we see *Judenpolitik* at the intersection of these considerations, it becomes clear that from the perverted perspective of the Nazi leadership, it had effectively become a guarantee for the complete victory of the National Socialist Revolution.

Continuation of the Policy of Extermination in Eastern Europe

Poland

In October and November 1942, HSSPF Krüger had, through police decree, defined a total of fifty-four 'Jewish residential districts'[1] in the General Government, most of them parts of earlier ghettos. Alongside these, there was a large number of camps for Jewish forced labourers. At this point, the deportations to the extermination camps were temporarily shelved.

At the beginning of 1943, however, the mass murders and deportations in the General Government began again on a large scale. By deciding to reorganize the 'labour deployment' the Nazi leadership believed that they would be able largely to do without the Jewish workforce. Those ghettos that still existed were liquidated in the course of 1943 (apart from Lodz), the people still living there were shot on the spot or deported to the extermination camps; a minority were sent to forced labour camps. The SS also took control of Jewish forced labour, thus ensuring that the only Jews who would remain temporarily alive were those who were absolutely required for war production.

In the district of Galicia the mass murders resumed at the beginning of 1943, after a decision by HSSPF Krüger, which he must have made at the end of 1942.[2] In January, SSPF Katzmann had some 10,000 people shot in an 'action'. They were from the Lemberg ghetto, in which around 24,000 people had lived up to that point. Subsequently the reduced ghetto was run as a 'Jewish camp'; further shootings occurred regularly. After the Lemberg massacre the office of the KdS Lemberg ravaged the smaller ghettos and labour camps in the district, where massacres leading to thousands of fatalities were carried out. From March 1943 onwards an increasingly large number of 'actions' took place in the smaller ghettos of the district. These mass murders were accelerated still further from the end of March.[3]

In the district of Radom the last deportations occurred in January 1943. They affected the town of Radom as well as Szydlowiec, Sandomierz Radomsko, and Ujazd; the victims were deported to Treblinka.[4] All that existed now in the district of Radom was labour camps under the control of the SS and police commanders, as well as so-called 'Jewish camps' directly attached to armaments factories, for which the armaments inspection department of the Wehrmacht was responsible. In the district of Krakau (Cracow), in March 1943, the ghetto in the city of Cracow was the last ghetto to be definitively cleared. Those 'fit for work' ended up in Plaszow labour camp (ZAL Plaszow).[5] Also in January the deportations from Warsaw to Treblinka resumed after their interruption in November.[6]

In January 1943, after a visit to Warsaw, Himmler ordered that the ghetto there be destroyed. Some of those factories that still existed were to be dissolved, and the 16,000 workers there were to be deported 'to a KL [Konzentrationslager = concentration camp] ideally to Lublin'. The factories actually working for armaments production were to be 'centralized somewhere in the General Government'.[7]

When the relocation of production to Lublin at short notice proved impossible, on 15 February Himmler ordered a concentration camp to be built inside the Warsaw ghetto, so that control could be exerted directly over those ghetto inhabitants who had been claimed as workers by the armaments factories.[8] In the meantime, the SS had once again begun to deport Jews 'unfit for work' from the Warsaw ghetto: between 18 and 22 January around 5,000 to 6,000 people were deported from the Warsaw ghetto to Treblinka and murdered there.[9]

In the months that followed concrete preparations were made within the SS empire to bring about the planned transfer of the Jewish forced labourers. To this end Globocnik negotiated with the WVHA to establish the 'Ostindustrie', which was officially founded in March 1943. This holding company was an attempt to create an armaments company run by the SS itself, which was to work with Jewish forced labourers and Jewish property. In fact, over the next few months, the Ostindustrie was to maintain various factories in the districts of Lublin and Radom, and deploy around 10,000 Jewish workers who were interned in labour camps. But they produced no armaments, only for the most part simple items of everyday use.[10]

In the spring of 1943, however, a development occurred which led the Nazi leadership to the decision to conclude the 'Final Solution' in the General Government as quickly as possible, and no longer to take Jewish workers into consideration. This last escalation of *Judenpolitik* in the General Government was prompted by the Warsaw ghetto uprising of April and May 1943.

Resistance organizations had formed in the Warsaw ghetto after the start of the major deportations of summer 1942: the Zydowska Organizacja Bojowa (ZOB, Jewish combat organization), originally formed from three Zionist youth organizations, later joined by other groups, some of them non-Zionist. At the same time the revisionist wing of the Zionists formed an autonomous organization, the Zydowski Zwiazek Wojskowy (ZZW, Jewish Military Association).

After the temporary halt to the deportations in October 1942 there were still between 55,000 and 60,000 people in the ghetto. In view of the attitude of the majority of ghetto-dwellers who could hardly have any illusions about their fate any longer, the resistance had a good prospect of receiving wide support for a revolt from the ghetto population.

When the Germans began a partial deportation of the ghetto-dwellers on 18 January, they encountered armed resistance by ZOB fighters, who were able to disrupt the execution of the arrests to such an extent that with 5,000 to 6,000 deportees the Germans were able to deport fewer people than they had originally intended.

Over the next few months the resistance fighters got ready for the final engagement with the Germans: they got hold of more weapons and prepared for a guerrilla war on the urban terrain by setting up fortified positions and escape routes. The rest of the ghetto population, whose will to resist had been intensified by the events of January, began to set up hiding-places, known as 'bunkers' in the cellars of the houses.

When the Germans began the definitive clearance of the ghetto on 19 April, they found themselves facing several hundred armed fighters, while most of the ghetto population sought refuge in the bunkers.

It took the far superior and heavily armed troops, led by SS Brigadeführer Jürgen Stroop, four weeks, until 16 May 1943, to put down the revolt. They only succeeded by using explosives and incendiary devices moving from house to house, hiding-place to hiding-place. Despite putting up tremendous resistance, the resistance groups were wiped out, apart from a small number who were able to escape. Apart from this thousands of ghetto-dwellers were killed during the fighting; the survivors were deported either to the gas chambers of Treblinka or to labour camps. Their attackers suffered several dozen fatalities.

There is good reason to identify the revolt as a popular uprising: in the ruins of the ghetto the fighters found support from the ghetto-dwellers, many of whom shared the fate of the resistance fighters and perished under miserable circumstances.[11]

There was also armed resistance against the planned liquidation of ghettos in other places. Thus in Czenstochowa a small group of Jewish fighters resisted the attempted clearance of the ghetto on 25 June 1943 and went down fighting. In Cracow, in the winter of 1942–3, a Jewish resistance group launched attacks on German installations outside the ghetto; the group left the ghetto the following spring as it was about to be liquidated. In a number of smaller ghettos armed resistance groups formed, escaping into the surrounding forests in the face of the imminent liquidation of the ghettos. In other places it can be shown that preparations for armed resistance existed, but either came to nothing or is only inadequately documented.[12]

The Nazi leadership's resolution, sparked by the Warsaw ghetto uprising, to murder all the Jews in the General Government, is reflected in a series of sources from between April and May 1943. Thus, for example, Goebbels's diary entry for 25 April reads: it is high time 'for us to remove the Jews as quickly as possible from the General Government'. Himmler stressed in May, to Greifelt, the head of his Central Office for Nationality Questions (Hauptamt für Volkstumsfragen), that it was an 'urgent task in the General Government ... to remove the remaining 300,000–400,000 Jews there'.[13]

HSSPF Krüger, who was responsible for the General Government, declared on 31 May that he had 'only recently received the order to carry out the "Entjudung"'; according to Krüger, Himmler wanted the employment of Jews deployed in the armaments industry to cease; a desire that Krüger did not think he was able to fulfil because of irreplaceable skilled workers.[14]

With the Warsaw ghetto uprising still fresh in the minds of the Germans, from April 1943 the liquidation of the still existing ghettos and small labour camps in the district of Lublin was intensified. The inmates were either shot on the spot or deported to the larger labour camps, Majdanek above all. Most of these 'resettlements' occurred in May.

Also in May 1943 Katzmann ordered the dissolution of all still existing ghettos in the district of Galicia and had a 'general liquidation plan' prepared to this end.[15] These mass murders were carried out with the utmost brutality between the end of May and the end of June 1943; some 80,000 people fell victim to them. Apart from the mass executions, from the end of 1942 until June 1943 some 15,000–25,000 people were deported to Sobibor. At the end of June 1943 Katzmann reported that 'all Jewish residential districts have been dissolved with effect from 23.6.43'. This meant that the district of Galicia was 'Jew-free apart from the Jews in camps controlled by the SS and police commanders'. There were still twenty-one 'Jewish camps' with a total of 21,156 inmates; the camps were, however, 'still being continually reduced'. In his concluding report Katzmann gave the figure of 434,329 Jews who had been 'resettled' between the spring of 1942 and 27 June 1943.[16]

Accordingly, in June 1943 there were only a few tens of thousands of Jews in labour camps in the General Government, which were largely controlled by the SS.

On 19 June, however, given the increase in resistance in the General Government, Himmler received the order from Hitler 'that the evacuation of the Jews was to be radically enforced and seen through in spite of any unrest arising over the next 3 to 4 months'. In addition, Hitler extended Himmler's authority in the field of partisan control, particularly by declaring the General Government to be a 'Partisan Combat Zone' (*Bandenkampfgebiet*). To rule out any possible resistance from employers who still had Jews working for them, Himmler now deliberately pursued the policy of declaring those ghettos and camps still in existence to be concentration camps. This applied not only in the General Government, but also in the Reichskommissariat Ostland, the other territory under German occupation in which Jews lived in any significant numbers.[17]

In the district of Lublin the Jewish labour deployment was massively reduced between June and October 1943, and was now employed in principle only for the needs of the Wehrmacht. The workers were barracked in SSPF labour camps which were to be brought under the control of the WVHA and run as sub-camps of Majdanek concentration camp.[18] This regulation, it was agreed early in September 1943 between Pohl, Krüger, and Globocnik, was to be applied to all labour camps in the General Government. This was done in January 1944: now the still existing labour camps in Plaszow (near Cracow) and the labour camps in Lemberg, Lublin, and Radom were turned into concentration camps.[19] After the Warsaw ghetto, declared to be a concentration camp in January 1943, was finally dissolved on an order from Himmler in June 1943, and all traces of its existence were removed,[20] there were concentration camps specially set up for Jewish forced labourers in each of the four remaining district capitals of the General Government.

In the district of Galicia, in June and July 1943 SSPF Katzmann had almost all the labour camps liquidated and their inmates murdered.[21] In July 1943 Himmler also ordered that Sobibor extermination camp be transformed into a concentration camp and that prisoners be used to sort captured ammunition.[22]

The radicalization of German *Judenpolitik* after the Warsaw ghetto uprising, and Hitler's instruction to Himmler on 19 June also meant the end for by far the majority of those Polish Jews who had so far managed to survive in the Polish territories directly administered by the Reich—eastern Upper Silesia, Warthegau, and the district of Bialystok.

In eastern Upper Silesia—paradoxically, in spite of its proximity to Auschwitz extermination camp—a relatively large proportion of the Jewish population had remained alive up until early summer 1943; the systematic forced labour deployment in the context of the 'Schmelt Organization' granted them the chance of survival until that point. In early summer 1943, however, the civil administration in Upper Silesia, which had always worked on the assumption that the Jewish forced labour deployment was only a transitory phenomenon, prepared to replace Jewish workers with non-Jews. The definitive decision to liquidate the ghetto was also presumably made with the Warsaw ghetto uprising still in mind; it was prompted by Himmler's order on 21 May 1943 according to which all Jews in the Reich, including the Protectorate, were to be deported 'to the East' or to Theresienstadt by 30 June. This order contained a supplement according to which Eichmann was to discuss the 'Abbeförderung' (transportation) of the Eastern Silesian Jews on the spot with Schmelt. Between 22 and 24 June 1943, 5,000 Jews from Sosnowitz and Bendzin were deported to Auschwitz. On 1 August the liquidation of the two ghettos began: a total of over 30,000 Jews were transported from Sosnowitz and Bendzin in around fourteen transports to Auschwitz, where some 6,000 were deployed as forced labourers and the rest were murdered. On 16 August these two large ghettos were completely cleared. Ten days later the last ghetto in Warthenau, holding a total of 5,000 people, was liquidated. Of the 100,000–120,000 Jews who had lived in Upper Silesia at the time of the German invasion, at least 85,000 had been murdered by the end of the war.

On 11 June, Himmler ordered the Lodz ghetto to be turned into a concentration camp; however, this order never came into effect.[23] The alternative attempts by Himmler and Pohl to achieve the transfer of the production capacity available in the ghetto to Lublin were also defeated by Greiser's resistance. In February 1944 the Gauleiter in the Warthegau, Artur Greiser, agreed with Himmler that the ghetto should be retained as a 'Gau-ghetto'; only as many Jews should be allowed to live there as was 'absolutely necessary for the interests of the armaments economy'.[24]

In August 1943 Himmler had ordered that the forced labour camps in the Warthegau, of which there were still more than 100, be liquidated. This had been done by October 1943: the forced labourers either ended up in Lodz ghetto or were deported to Auschwitz and murdered there.[25] In June 1944, on the basis of an agreement that Himmler and Greiser had made in February 1944, those inhabitants of the Lodz ghetto who were either unfit for work or no longer needed from the viewpoint of the ghetto administration were murdered with gas vans in the specially reactivated extermination camp at Chelmno. By mid-July 1944 more than 7,000 people died this way. However, Himmler had presumably already issued the order to dissolve the ghetto completely in May 1944. In August the great majority of the ghetto-dwellers, still more than 68,000, were deported to Auschwitz, where all of them were murdered, apart from some 2,000 people who were deployed as forced labourers. Around 1,300 ghetto-dwellers stayed behind in Lodz for clearing-up work.[26]

Between 16 and 23 August 1943 the Bialystok ghetto was finally liquidated. The various Jewish resistance groups that had formed a united front only in July 1943, fiercely resisted the 'action' and involved the German police in battles that lasted five days. After the uprising was put down, 150 fighters managed to escape the ghetto and join the partisans.[27]

In August 1943 more than 25,000 people were deported from Bialystok either to Treblinka, where they were murdered, or, if they were deemed to be 'fit for work', deported to Majdanek, where they were deployed in forced labour. The complete liquidation of the ghetto was run by Globocnik. Plans originally in place to transfer the factories in the ghetto to Lublin had in the meantime been abandoned by Globocnik; instead a unit of the Ostindustrie plundered the factories that still existed in Bialystok. The over 1,000 Jews who had stayed in Bialystok after the 'action' were also deported to Lublin.[28]

In 1942–3 tens of thousands, possibly as many as 100,000 Jews living in Poland had managed to escape the ghetto liquidations and get away. Thus, in an extensive study of escape from the Warsaw ghetto, Gunnar Paulsson reached the conclusion that a total of some 28,000 Jews went into hiding outside the ghetto and of those around 40 per cent, or 11,500, survived. The mass of escapes occurred after the big deportations of 1942: of 55,000 to 60,000 remaining ghetto-dwellers more than 13,000 escaped. These people survived on the 'Aryan' side of Warsaw, either in hiding-places or under false identities; as many Poles were living illegally in Warsaw, a certain infrastructure of illegality had been created that made access to fake papers relatively easy.[29]

In the district of Galicia, particularly after 1943, thousands of Jews managed to find refuge in hiding-places, mostly in the homes of non-Jewish acquaintances, far more than 1,000 in Lemberg alone.[30] Other Jews used fake papers to find jobs as 'Ostarbeiter' in the Reich or at one of the building sites run by the Todt Organisation in occupied Europe.[31]

Other escapees tried to survive in forest camps that they had built themselves.[32] The Israeli historian Shmuel Krakowski estimates the number of Jews who escaped into the forests in the four districts of the 'old' General Government (i.e. without Galicia) in 1942–3 at 50,000 and in his seminal study of the Jewish resistance in Poland he presents figures which suggest that the great majority of these escapees were killed by German Jagdkommandos (Hunting Commandos).[33]

After the liquidation of the ghettos, from the summer of 1943 the focus of the persecution of the Jews in the General Government shifted clearly to the tracing of these people who had fled into the forests or otherwise gone into hiding, often in the wake of the anti-partisan campaigns that were now being intensified.[34]

In the district of Lublin these raids began in May 1943. The monthly surveys by the district Commander of the Order Police indicate a total of 1,657 victims for the period between May and October 1943, under the heading 'Jews exterminated'.[35] In the district of Galicia, from July 1943 onwards, the police intensified their raids in the forests and killed thousands of Jews.[36]

Poles who offered Jews hiding-places were generally shot, in many cases the whole family was murdered, in extreme cases the entire population of the village in question. Conversely, denunciations of hidden Jews were rewarded with bounties; the SSPF in the district of Lublin, for example, ordered that such informants be given up to a third of the property of the Jewish victim who had been hunted down.[37]

Armed resistance in the ghetto clearances in Bialystok and Vilna, the mass escape from Treblinka in August 1943, and particularly the prisoner revolt in Sobibor on 14 October, in which eleven SS members had been killed,[38] all of this in the face of the threatened Soviet invasion, must have been what led Himmler to give Krüger the order, in October 1943, to liquidate the most important camps still in existence in the district in Lublin. Early in November the prisoners in the Lublin camp complex were shot during a two-day massacre, under the code name 'Harvest Festival', and the same fate awaited the prisoners in the camps of Trawniki and Poniatowa. The total number of victims reached around 42,000.[39] Sobibor extermination camp had also been dissolved after the attempted uprising on 14 October. After this, in the district of Lublin there were only a few smaller forced labour camps with several thousand Jewish prisoners, which were cleared from February 1944; most of the prisoners were deported to the west.[40]

During the Harvest Festival murders in the district of Lublin, at the beginning of November 1943 the German police also murdered the Jewish inmates of the Szenie labour camp in the district of Cracow (Krakau), and a few days later the inmates of ZAL (labour camp) Plaszow in Cracow. On 19 November the Jewish forced labourers in the Janowska camp in Lemberg (Lvov) were murdered.[41]

In his notorious speech to the Reichs- and Gauleiters in Posen (Poznan) on 4 October 1943, Himmler gave an assurance that the 'Jewish question in the countries occupied by us ... will be resolved by the end of the year'.[42]

Occupied Soviet Territories

After the big wave of murders in Ukraine in 1942 Jews only lived in any numbers in the occupied Soviet territories in Reichskommissariat Ostland. In summer 1943, 72,000 Jews still lived in this territory. According to the State Secretary, Alfred Meyer, Rosenberg's deputy in the Ministry of the East, 22,000 of these had already been selected for 'resettlement', meaning murder.[43] Of the 30,000 or so Jews still living in the General Commissariat of White Ruthenia in 1943, the occupying forces killed around half.[44]

Thus, on 8 February, the KdS station in Minsk murdered all the Jews in Slutsk in the wake of an anti-partisan action; in view of the resistance of the ghetto-dwellers, District Commissar Heinrich Carl ordered that the ghetto be burned down along with its entrenched inhabitants—this was the same Carl who had complained to his superiors about the cruel behaviour of Lithuanian auxiliary police against the Jews of Slutsk.[45] About 3,000 people lost their lives in this action. In the district of Vileyka, between February and April 1943, the members of the local KdS station murdered almost all the Jews living there, around 5,000 people. There was also a large number of Jewish people who tried to hide outside ghettos and camps, and were hunted down and murdered by German units and their local auxiliaries; according to the figures of the SSPF of White Ruthenia, Curt von Gottberg, 11,000 were killed between November 1942 and March 1943 alone.[46]

The remaining three ghettos in the General District of White Ruthenia were destroyed between August and October 1943. On 13 August Himmler issued an order to restrict the labour deployment of the Jews, which was adopted by the OKH on 29 September as 'binding for the whole of the field army in the East'. As a result, interventions by Wehrmacht posts in favour of Jewish work commandos were effectively scotched.[47]

The ghetto of Glebokie near Vilna was liquidated on 20 August following a further anti-partisan action. In August 1943 the inhabitants of the ghetto resisted their planned deportation to Majdanek; the majority of the ghetto-dwellers, between 2,000 and 3,000 people, lost their lives in the ghetto, which was set on fire by German forces.[48] The ghetto of Lida was dissolved in September, and some 4,000 inhabitants were deported to the concentration camps of Sobibor and Majdanek.[49]

Finally, the Minsk ghetto was cleared in September in a number of stages. Some of the 10,000 or so ghetto-dwellers still living there were sent to Auschwitz and Sobibor extermination camps, others murdered on the spot, and yet others deported to the district of Lublin for forced labour. In October 1943 the surviving ghetto-dwellers were murdered in the extermination centre of Trostinets near Minsk.[50]

In Lithuania and Latvia, where there were still large numbers of Jews, Himmler acted in 1943 as he had in occupied Poland: he endeavoured to turn those Jews who were still 'fit for work' into concentration camp inmates, so that he would have total control over their future fate.

On 2 April 1943, Himmler issued the order to build a concentration camp in Riga, dated retrospectively to 13 March.[51] On 21 June, after a meeting with leading SS functionaries, Himmler ordered that 'all remaining Jews in the territory of Ostland be brought together in concentration camps'. At the same time, with effect from 1 August 1943, he prohibited 'the removal of Jews from concentration camps for work' and again issued the order for the construction of a concentration camp near Riga. Those 'members of the Jewish ghettos not required', Himmler finally specified, were to be 'evacuated to the East', meaning murdered.[52] With this order Himmler gained total control over the Jewish forced labourers in the Reichskommissariat of Ostland. This decision of Himmler's was closely connected with the order to conclude the 'Final Solution', which Hitler had given him two days previously. It is also significant that, on 21 June, Himmler appointed Bach-Zelewski as head of the anti-partisan units (*Bandenkampfverbände*), after Hitler had extended his authority in this sphere. The internment of the surviving Jews in concentration camps, constant selection of the Jewish forced labourers in the concentration camps, and the hunting down of Jews in hiding under the cloak of 'anti-partisan combat'—these, then, were the instruments with which Himmler planned to bring the 'Final Solution' to its conclusion in the General Government and in the Reichskommissariat Ostland. Moreover, immediately after the issuing of the order on 21 June, the Security Police in Latvia began to withdraw the workers who were, in their view, not important to the war effort, from individual firms.

The Kaiserwald concentration camp, which had been built near Riga on Himmler's instructions, was to achieve a capacity of 2,000 inmates at the most; in fact it was to act as a transit camp. Here labour columns were assembled which were marched to the individual firms where they were lodged in primitive accommodation, known as 'barracks', near the production facilities.[53] In these camps and in Kaiserwald continual selections of those unfit for work took place; on 28 April 1944 the children were removed from all the camps and murdered.[54]

The Riga ghetto was, by contrast, dissolved. As in the Kaiserwald camp and in the 'barracks' only Jews who were actually in the 'work programme' were supposed to live there. On 2 November the Security Police drove together the children and the sick in the ghetto and deported them to Auschwitz.[55] After that the ghetto was gradually cleared once and for all. The two other large ghettos remaining in the Baltic, the ghettos of Kaunas and Vilnius (Vilna), were removed in September 1943.

The Kaunas (Kovno) ghetto was turned into a concentration camp ('KZ Kauen') on 15 September. By this point many of the ghetto-dwellers were already living in work camps outside the ghetto, which were now subordinated to the concentration camp. A total of 2,800 Jews were deported to Estonia and deployed as forced labourers; those 'unfit for work' were murdered. On 27 March 1944 prisoners who were not used as slave labour, 1,800 children, and elderly people were murdered.[56]

In the spring of 1943 the smaller ghettos in the district of Vilnius were dissolved, and the bulk of the inhabitants murdered, the smaller part interned in the Vilnius ghetto, and in June and July the same thing happened to the labour camps in this area.[57] In August and September the remaining 20,000 or so inhabitants of the ghetto were herded together; most of them were dispatched to Estonian and Latvian concentration camps, while around 4,000 people were deported to

Sobibor or murdered in the mass execution centre at Ponary. After the final liquidation of the ghetto at the end of September 2,500 Jews were left in labour camps in Vilna.[58] The Vaivara concentration camp in Estonia was set up on 15 September 1943 in direct connection with the action against the ghettos of Vilnius and Kaunas. It served as a transit camp for the Jews deported from the ghettos of Vilnius and Kaunas as well as from the Reich, Theresienstadt, Poland, and Hungary. Some 20,000 people passed through this camp and were distributed around smaller labour camps.[59]

While the examples of Slutsk and Glebokie make it clear that in 1943 the Jewish population of White Russia continued its resistance against the policy of extermination, conditions in the Baltic were rather different. Here, after the major ghetto actions in 1941, in which the majority of the Jewish population had already been murdered, resistance groups formed in various ghettos beginning in early 1942. However, the fact that a long phase of relative calm began, one which was to last until 1943 during which as a rule no 'actions' occurred, in the final analysis produced a negative effect on resistance activities. The high percentage of Jews employed 'productively' fed the illusion that the Germans were at least leaving those Jews 'fit for work' and their relatives alive.

In Kaunas a Communist and a Zionist underground group combined forces in the summer of 1943; the underground activities were covered up by the chairman of the Jewish council, Elkes. The focus of the work of the underground lay in reinforcing the resistance of the ghetto-dwellers through cultural and educational activities. Several hundred resistance fighters finally managed to flee the ghetto in small groups and join the partisans in the forests. No attempt at an uprising in the ghetto was undertaken.[60]

In Vilnius the FPO resistance group founded early in 1942 prepared for an armed uprising. However, their activities were considerably frustrated by the chairman of the Jewish council, Jacob Gens, for fear of reprisals against the ghetto-dwellers. When the ghetto was cleared in several 'actions' in August and September 1943, the FPO did not, as planned, manage to light the initial spark for a general uprising through armed resistance. The surviving resistance fighters continued the struggle in the forests.[61] There were also underground movements in the ghettos of the Lithuanian towns of Schaulen and Svencian, but they did not attempt an uprising.[62]

In Lithuania in 1943–4 a total of around 1,150 ghetto-dwellers fled to the forests as participants in resistance groups and a further 650 did so independently. This meant that a total of 4.5 per cent of the ghetto population managed to escape extermination through flight.[63]

In the Latvian capital of Riga, an underground organization with several hundred members formed early in 1942. In October 1942 the attempt to bring a group of resistance fighters out of the ghetto failed; the secret organization was eliminated by the occupying forces.[64]

Continuation of the Deportations

German Reich

After Hitler's decision in September 1942 to replace those Jews still working in armaments production, the preparations for a sudden (*schlagartig*) deportation of this group began in late 1942. In view of the large-scale recruitment of foreign workers planned for early 1943, the replacement of Jewish skilled workers did not seem to pose an insuperable problem.[65]

The 'withdrawal of all Jews still engaged in the work process' began on 27 February 1943. In Berlin alone, the SS Bodyguard units (Leibstandarte) arrested some 7,000 people in their workplaces or homes; a few days later they were deported to Auschwitz.[66] At this point there were no plans to deport Jews living in 'mixed marriages'; they were also arrested, but they were released to go home. In Berlin, however, hundreds of men from this group were held in two buildings belonging to the Jewish community, presumably to have staff available to replace the deported employees. Remarkably, there was a spontaneous public protest by the families of these men, who stood for days outside the building on Rosenstrasse. But the fact that the Gestapo finally released the men held in Rosenstrasse was not the result of this protest; at this point there had been no plans to deport them in any case.[67]

After this surge in deportations (between early January and mid-March 1943 a total of sixteen transport trains, most of them carrying 1,000 people each, had gone to Auschwitz[68]), 31,897 people of Jewish origin still lived in the Reich, more than 18,515 of them in Berlin. Of the Jews living in the Reich 17,517 were free of the obligation to wear the yellow star.[69] From then on the deportations continued only on a smaller scale.[70]

The major deportations to Theresienstadt in the summer of 1942 were followed by numerous smaller transports. From November 1942 until mid-1943 there were almost 100 of these, each one usually carrying 50 or 100 people. The only special train to Theresienstadt, involving more than 1,200 people, left Berlin on 17 March 1943.[71]

In December 1943 the RSHA ordered the 'change of residence' to Theresienstadt of certain groups hitherto spared deportation. This was to start at the beginning of the year and particularly affected were the Jewish spouses of mixed marriages that no longer existed, and who—because of the existence of children who were not deemed to be Jewish—had been free of the obligation to wear the yellow star.[72] In 1943, ten transports had gone from Theresienstadt to Auschwitz, each carrying more than 1,000, but in some cases far more than 2,000 people.[73]

During the whole of 1944 further smaller deportations left the Reich for Auschwitz. In particular, during that year further large transports left

Theresienstadt for Auschwitz: three carrying 2,500 people in May, and a further eleven in September and October, with between 1,500 and 2,500 people.[74]

In January 1945, in one last action, the RSHA planned to deport those Jews still 'on work deployment' to Theresienstadt, but also the elderly, the sick, and children hitherto excluded from the deportations. But because of military developments this plan could not be carried out across the whole of the Reich.[75]

Netherlands

In the Netherlands,[76] from which 38,000 people had been deported by the end of 1942, the deportations resumed in January 1943, after a one-month 'Christmas break'. As a rule, one train per week travelled to Auschwitz from the collection camp of Westerbork. In the middle of January a second camp was opened at Vught. In March, when the murder of the Jews from Thessaloniki began in Auschwitz, the Dutch transports went to Sobibor extermination camp, where almost all deportees were murdered immediately on their arrival. In May, presumably in connection with the general radicalization of *Judenpolitik* after the Warsaw ghetto uprising, the RSHA ordered that the number of those to be deported from the Netherlands be raised forthwith: between 18 May and 20 July, almost 18,000 people were deported to Sobibor, including children from the Vught labour camp, accompanied by their mothers. Of the 34,313 people who came to Sobibor from the Netherlands by 20 July, only 19 would survive. After a five-week break the deportations resumed on 24 August at weekly intervals—with interruptions in September/October and between November and January—primarily to Auschwitz. From September 1944 some transports also went to Theresienstadt and some to the 'delivery camp' (*Auslieferungslager*) of Bergen-Belsen. It was only in the spring of 1944 that the pace of the deportations slowed. However, on 3 September 1944, another 1,019 people were deported to Auschwitz; the last deportation from the Netherlands, to Bergen-Belsen, was carried out on 13 September.[77] Overall, 107,000 Jews living in the Netherlands were deported; around 102,000 of those died.

Belgium

From the end of 1942 the RSHA and the German department of the Foreign Ministry urged that Jews of Belgian citizenship, who had so far been spared, should now be deported. In December 1942 Luther requested that the Brussels office of the Foreign Ministry, 'in association with the military commander, consider the possibility of extending the measures already taken to all the Jews in Belgium, and round them up in the collection camps until they could be transported... A thorough cleansing of Belgium of the Jews must occur sooner or later at all costs.' The deportation of Belgian Jews should begin as soon as possible.[78]

The director of the Foreign Ministry office in Brussels, Werner von Bargen, confirmed in January 1943 that after the deportation of all foreign Jews it was also planned to 'get rid of' some 4,000 Jews with Belgian citizenship 'at the same time'; however, because of a shortage of rolling stock no deportations were possible. And the capacity of the single camp, Mechelen, was not enough to intern all the country's Jews there.[79] It was not until 29 June that the Gestapo office in Brussels informed Mechelen camp that because of an order from Himmler, 'Jews of Belgian citizenship must now be included in the deportation actions without delay'.[80]

On 3 and 4 September large numbers of Belgian Jews were arrested in a raid in Brussels and Antwerp. On 20 September 1943 the first transport train carrying only Belgian Jews left the country.[81] In 1943 a total of six deportations occurred, involving almost 6,000 people. In 1944 there were four further transports with over 2,300 people.[82] All trains went to Auschwitz.

However, these deportations did not go completely smoothly. One of the trains, the twentieth RSHA transport from Belgium, was the target of a unique rescue action. On 19 April 1943, the day the ghetto uprising in Warsaw began, three members of the Belgian resistance stopped the train and freed seventeen prisoners from a wagon. More than 200 other deportees managed to jump off the train as it continued on its journey, and found refuge with Belgian citizens.[83]

The number of Jews deported from Belgium and murdered is estimated at around 28,500, which is to say that about 32 per cent of the pre-war Jewish population had been killed.[84] Around 1,000 of these were Belgian nationals.[85]

In spite of this shockingly high death toll, the Jews in Belgium had better chances of survival than those in the neighbouring Netherlands, where about 102,000, or 73 per cent of the entire Jewish population of around 140,000 people were murdered. In Belgium as many as 25,000 Jews, or almost 50 per cent of the Jews resident in Belgium, managed to survive in the underground. There are a variety of reasons for their superior chances of survival. On the one hand, in Belgium the SS played a relatively small part in the military administration; the military was primarily concerned with the security situation, and set in motion the anti-Jewish measures preceding the deportations at a relatively slow pace. In Belgium—unlike the Netherlands—the government apparatus was not actively involved in the persecution of the Jews, and the subordinate administrative organizations carried out the German instructions relatively carelessly. Not least for that reason, it proved impossible to construct a system of arrest and deportation in Belgium similar to that in the Netherlands. Instead, attempts were made to arrest the Jews in raids, a process that prompted panic and encouraged flight into illegality. One final significant factor in the survival of the Jews was that, by virtue of the fact that the large majority of them were not integrated into Belgian society, they had maintained a healthy suspicion of the adminsitrative measures preceding the deportations. Last of all, the Jews in Belgium benefited from the fact that there was a stronger national resistance movement than there was in the Netherlands, and that there were more specifically Jewish resistance organizations working closely with the general resistance movement.[86]

Croatia

The deportations also continued in the zone of Croatia occupied by the Wehrmacht: in May 1943, some 2,000 people were deported to Auschwitz in two further transports.[87] If the deportations of August 1943 are included, more than 7,000 Jews were deported from the German-occupied zone of Croatia to Auschwitz.

In the spring of 1944 Himmler ordered Hans Helm, the police attaché in Belgrade, to 'sort out the Jewish question in Croatia as quickly as possible'. Himmler's order documents the determination on the part of the Germans to track down small groups of Jews, even in the most remote corner of their occupied territory and in what was a very critical phase of the war, and murder them. However, Helm had to report that a few hundred Jews still lived in Croatia, but they were claimed for urgent work by the Ustasha state, or shielded against persecution by Ustasha functionaries.[88] Thousands of Jews had escaped to the Italian-occupied zone, and most of them were able to escape the German occupation there even after the collapse of Italy—we will explore this in greater detail below.[89] Many Croatian Jews had also escaped the German occupation zone to join Tito's Partisans. Overall, however, only around 7,000 of the originally 30,000–40,000-strong Jewish minority were to survive the Holocaust in Croatia.[90]

Intensified Efforts to Deport Jews from Third-Party States within the German Sphere of Influence in 1943

In 1943 the Foreign Ministry continued its efforts to include in the deportations the Jews from occupied, allied but also neutral states, who lived outside their native lands, but within the German sphere of influence. While the Swiss had agreed early in 1943 to the German proposal that Jews of Swiss citizenship be requested to return to Switzerland,[91] on 22 January the Foreign Ministry also turned to the governments of Spain, Portugal, Denmark, Finland, and Sweden, and requested them to fetch their Jewish nationals back from occupied Western Europe by the end of March.[92] The deportation of those 2,400 Turkish Jews who had not been expressly protected by the government in Ankara, for which reminders had been issued since early 1943 by the Security Police, was postponed several times by the Foreign Ministry until September 1943, when the Turkish government finally declared itself willing to request these people to return to Turkey.[93]

With its decree of 24 February 1943 the Foreign Ministry established that Jews from a total of fifteen countries as well as stateless Jews were 'to be included in any measures generally made against Jews in that sphere or in such measures yet to be made'. This included Jews from Poland, Luxembourg, Slovakia, Croatia, Serbia, Romania, Bulgaria, Greece, the Netherlands, Belgium, France, Estonia, Latvia, Lithuania, and Norway. Jews of Italian, Finnish, Swiss, Spanish, Portuguese, Danish, and Swedish citizenship were to be 'given the opportunity to "return" to their so-called "home-lands"' by 31 March 1943, while Jews from other states were to be left unharmed.[94] These deadlines, however, were postponed in varying degrees. Thus the deadline set for the Italians, 31 March 1943, was extended several times, and the date fixed for Hungary during 1942 (31 December 1942) was also extended several times.

In July 1943 the RSHA turned to the Foreign Ministry with the request that a total of ten states 'be given a definitive final date of 31 July, and thus declare their agreement that after that deadline the general anti-Jewish measures be also applied to all foreign Jews remaining within the German sphere of influence, with the exception of Jews from hostile states and Argentina'.[95] After the Foreign Ministry had declared its agreement and informed the states in question,[96] on 23 September 1943—after Italy seceded from the Axis alliance—the RSHA instructed the offices of the Security Police and the Higher SS and Police Commanders to deport Jews from Italy, Switzerland, Spain, Portugal, Denmark, Sweden, Finland, Hungary, Romania, and Turkey—divided by sex—to Buchenwald and Ravensbrück concentration camps.[97]

The German Policy of Extending the Deportations after the Allied Landing in North Africa (Late 1942 until Summer 1943)

Even after the turn of the war in winter 1942/3, the RSHA tried to extend deportations to a series of other countries or regions: Greece, Bulgaria, and the Italian-occupied zones in Greece, Yugoslavia, and the southern zone of France (where deportations had occurred temporarily in the summer of 1942). In these areas the 'Jewish question' was plainly to be radically solved early in 1943. With the ceasefire between Italy and the Allies in September 1943, new conditions were to be set once again for *Judenpolitik* within the block under German rule.

The direct consequence of the geographical extension of the war after the Allied landings in Morocco and Algeria in October 1942 was that a further large Jewish group was exposed to German attack: the Jews of French North Africa, who had already been included among the victims of the coming 'Final Solution' envisaged at the Wannsee Conference.[98] With the occupation of Tunisia in November 1942 some 85,000 Jews came under German control. The German occupiers introduced forced labour for Jews; some 5,000 Jews were affected by these measures, but most of them managed to escape the camps set up for this purpose. The German occupying forces had also sent around twenty arrested Jewish activists to the extermination camps. In addition, there were large-scale confiscations of Jewish property, and large sums of money were extorted.

In the spring of 1943, the concrete deportation preparations under discussion reveal that in Fortress Europe the RSHA was clearly planning a radical 'solution' of the 'Jewish question' in Greece, Bulgaria, and France.

Greece

After all efforts to reach a common approach towards the 'Jewish question' with the Italian occupying forces had collapsed the previous year, towards the end of 1942/beginning of 1943 the Foreign Ministry and the RSHA resolved to act independently in the German-occupied zone.[99]

On 7 January Luther informed the ambassador in Athens, Günther Altenburg, that the Foreign Ministry was interested in the quickest possible introduction of anti-Jewish measures in Greece.[100] At the beginning of February 1943 Alois Brunner of the RSHA's Jewish desk joined Dieter Wisliceny (who had been temporarily removed from his post as Jewish adviser in Pressburg (Bratislava)) at the head of a *Sonderkommando* sent to Thessaloniki to prepare the deportation. Already in February, the marking and ghettoizing of the Jews of Thessaloniki had been introduced together with further restrictions.

Between mid-March and mid-May 1943, the Jews of Thessaloniki and the surrounding Macedonian communities were deported, in some sixteen transports, and two more followed in mid-August. Almost all of these 45,000 people were murdered in Auschwitz. In August a small transport of a total of 441 Jews went to the 'exchange camp' of Bergen-Belsen: these were either Jews with Spanish citizenship, high-ranking representatives of the Jewish community of Thessaloniki, or collaborators who had assisted the SD.[101] When the Germans once again requested an extension of the deportations to the Italian-occupied zone, the Foreign Ministry in Rome suggested in March that the Italian Jews in Greece be excluded from the persecutory measures, and the Greek Jews be interned. But both the Jewish desk of the Foreign Ministry and Eichmann, the individual within the RSHA responsible for the deportations, considered these suggestions inadequate.[102]

Bulgaria

Shortly before Brunner and Wisliceny arrived in Greece, in January 1943 Theodor Dannecker had taken up his role as 'Jewish adviser' at the German embassy in Sofia.[103] On 22 February 1943, the Bulgarian Commissar for the Jews and Dannecker had reached an agreement for the deportation of 20,000 Jews by May 1943.[104] Those affected were all the Jews from the Bulgarian-occupied zones of Thrace (Greece) and Macedonia (Yugoslavia), as well as around 6,000–8,000 Jews from Old Bulgaria. In fact, in March 1943, the Jews living in Thrace—over 4,000—and those living in Macedonia—over 7,000—were arrested by the Bulgarians and deported to the General Government, where most of them were murdered in Treblinka.[105]

However, the preparatory measures for the deportation of the Jews of Old Bulgaria, for which work had begun in March, had to be interrupted and postponed because of massive protests, especially by a group of deputies around the parliamentary vice president, Dimiter Peshev.[106] In April 1943, Tsar Boris stressed to Ribbentrop that only 'Communist elements' among the Jews of Old Bulgaria should be deported. In contrast, the German Foreign Minister insisted on a radical solution.[107]

In May 1943 the Jews of Sofia were resettled, amidst high levels of protest in the capital, to surrounding provincial towns.[108] But the Bulgarians were not ready for the next step, expected by the Germans, the deportation of the Jews to Poland.[109]

France

After the occupation of southern France by German and Italian troops on 11 November 1942, the Jews in this area were also exposed to direct German action.[110] The Vichy government had already agreed to the deportation of foreign and stateless Jews in the summer of 1942, but had interrupted this in September 1942 in the face of strong public protest.[111]

In January and February 1943, at the instigation of the German Security Police in Paris, predominantly foreign and stateless Jews, but also those of French citizenship living in Marseilles (where the old harbour district was completely destroyed) and in other places across France were arrested and placed in the camps of Drancy and Compiègne along with the Jews already interned there.[112] On 9 February the deportations resumed: by early March four transports had gone from Drancy collection camp to Auschwitz, and four more to Sobibor.[113]

On 10 or 11 February 1943 in Paris, Eichmann presented a maximum programme for the deportation of all Jews living in France, including French nationals. This plainly coincided with the concrete preparations for deportation in Greece and Bulgaria.

But the commander of the Security Police in France, Helmut Knochen, resisted Eichmann's suggestion in a letter to Heinrich Müller, head of the Gestapo, on 12 February 1943: if 'large-scale measures were to be taken against all Jews with French citizenship at this time' they could 'expect political setbacks'. In France an imminent Allied victory was generally expected, and they were trying to ensure that 'no further measures be taken against the Jews in order to show the Americans that they were unwilling to obey the instructions of the German government'. However, Laval would approve measures against the Jews if he 'received some political concession for it from Germany towards the French people'. In a discussion on the same day Laval had declared 'that the Americans had already [stated] to France that France would receive all the previous Italian colonies and would get all the French colonies back and France would receive more than the Rhine border in Europe. The Germans had made him no promises for the post-war period. In my view Laval will swallow the Jewish measures if he receives a political assurance of some form.'[114]

This statement illustrates clearly the centrality of *Judenpolitik* for Germany in the second half of the war. With the deportation of French citizens the Vichy government had been made an accomplice of the German extermination policy to a much greater extent than had already occurred with the deportations from the unoccupied zone in the summer of 1942: but this meant that their prospects of reaching an agreement with the Western powers must dramatically fade. However, in view of the military situation, which had changed since the previous summer, a political price had to be paid to the French.

In this letter Knochen referred to a further significant limitation on the possibility of intensifying German Jewish policy throughout the whole of France: as long as the Italian occupying forces opposed the persecution measures of the Vichy authorities, through their own behaviour they were providing the French government with arguments against anti-Jewish measures.

Since 1942, the Italian occupation authorities had in fact refused several times to implement anti-Jewish measures by the Vichy authorities;[115] in a large renewed arrest action in the southern zone in which, in mid-February, Jewish men of foreign citizenship were arrested by the Vichy police and finally 2,000 people were handed over to the Germans for deportation to Sobibor, the Italian occupying authorities had compelled the liberation of the Jews arrested by the French police.[116]

Efforts by the Germans to compel the Italians to take a more severe attitude towards the Jews living in their zone were to remain unsuccessful. After Ribbentrop addressed this question when talking to Mussolini on a visit to Rome on 25 February[117] and instructed the German ambassador, Eberhard von Mackensen, to pursue the matter further, the 'Duce' assured Mackensen on 17 March that he would instruct the Italian military not to get involved in the matters of the French police.[118] However, he changed his mind a short time later.

Influenced by the ideas of Italian diplomats and military officers, he transferred the solution of the 'Jewish question' in the Italian zone of occupation to the Italian police, and appointed a 'general inspector of the racial police', whom he entrusted with the task of evacuating the Jews from the coastal zone to the hinterland. By doing this he had removed the supposed security risk that the Germans had always presented as the reason for their demand to hand over the Jews.[119] Over the months that followed the Italians were to continue their obstructive policy towards German *Judenpolitik* in a similarly effective way.[120]

Unlike the commander of the Security Police, Knochen, who took into account the overall political context, Heinz Röthke, the Gestapo Jewish expert in Paris, took the hard line represented by Eichmann. On 6 March he wrote in a memorandum: 'The transport of the Jews from France must not be allowed to stop before the last Jew has left French soil, and that must happen before the end of the war.'[121] To achieve this goal within a few months,[122] the Italians had 'categorically to be led to abandon their hitherto adverse attitude', while on the other hand the circle of people due for deportation (a total of 49,000 Jews had been deported from France so far, 12,000 of them from the southern zone) had to be widened. To this end all Jews from the old occupied zone must be assembled in Paris; the French government must hand over all foreign Jews who were 'capable of deportation' (i.e. no longer under the protection of their home countries); and a law must be passed revoking French citizenship for Jews naturalized after 1927 or after 1933. In this way, Röthke thought, he could implement the 'mass transportation from April 1943 (8,000–10,000 Jews each week)'.

These suggestions by Röthke reveal the continuity in the RSHA's deportation planning. After Eichmann had set out his plan, at the end of August 1942, to deport all foreign Jews from France 'by the end of June 1943',[123] Röthke intended to achieve this goal by a radical acceleration of the deportations between April and June; between 90,000 and 100,000 people were involved. Afterwards, he wanted to begin the intended deportation of Jews of French citizenship.

But Röthke's suggestions, which he renewed at the end of the month,[124] encountered resistance from BdS Knochen. In a letter to Eichmann[125] dated 29 March 1943, Knochen made it clear that no deportations were to occur in the near future, as 'measures against Jews of French citizenship can hardly be implemented for political reasons because of the attitude of the Marshall [Petain]' and, because of the Italian position, no unified approach towards the 'Jewish question' in France was assured. On the other hand, Knochen did adopt one of Röthke's suggestions: the French citizenship laws, shortly to be introduced, meant that some 100,000 Jews would lose their citizenship and be deported, a figure that Knochen deliberately set too high in order to obtain Eichmann's consent.[126]

The positions of Eichmann and Röthke, on the one hand, and Knochen, on the other, clearly represent the two fundamentally different approaches towards *Judenpolitik* which became clear within the leadership of the German occupation:

while Eichmann and Röthke wanted to speed up the deportations precisely because of the military setbacks, and bring them to their conclusion before the end of the war, and were ready to put the French government under pressure to achieve this, Knochen argued that the deportations should be implemented only on a limited scale and with French consent, and that they should thus be treated as a significant element in collaboration policy.

In fact the Vichy government seemed prepared to revoke the citizenship of Jews with French citizenship as demanded by the German security police. In April, the chief of police, Reneé Bousquet, produced a draft law to denaturalize those Jews who had entered the country since 1932. On the prompting of the Germans, the entry date was altered to 1927, as already provided for in a draft presented by Jewish Commissioner, Louis Darquier de Pellepoix, in December 1942, but taken no further.[127]

Since the German Security Police now assumed that within a relatively short space of time they would be able to deport a large number of Jews who had had their citizenship revoked, in spring they reduced the number of arrests and the deportations were suspended between 25 March and 23 June.[128]

On 8 June 1943, however, Himmler urged the HSSPF in France, Carl-Albrecht Oberg, to secure publication of the denaturalization law, which had already been signed by Laval.[129] In Himmler's view, the deportations to the Reich were to be concluded by 15 July 1943 since, as Himmler put it, referring to the military situation, they had to 'guard against all possible events'.

Immediately after this conversation the RSHA's deportation specialist, Alois Brunner, arrived in Paris at the head of a command unit and, along with Röthke and Hagen, drew up a plan for the deportation of the Jews who were to be denaturalized. The plan was to deport the families of this group as well, both Jews and non-Jews. A raid was scheduled for 24 June; but the date was repeatedly postponed, as the legal precondition, the denaturalization law, did not exist.[130] In June, when Röthke requested 250 members of the Security Police from Gestapo chief Müller for the implementation of the raid, Müller refused; given the shortage of available manpower on the German side, the planned action could only be executed with the support of the French police.

On 20 July 1943, however, Laval resolved to sign a new, harsher version of the denaturalization law, which had been produced in the meantime by the head of the French Office of Jewish Affairs, Darquier, and, in line with Brunner's plans, to revoke French citizenship from the family members of those denaturalized since 1927, thus creating the precondition for deportation.[131] However, on 25 July, the day of the fall of Mussolini, Laval decided to suspend publication of the denaturalization law.[132] On 7 August Laval told Oberg and Knochen that he planned to revert the law to the state of Bousquet's draft.[133] On further prompting by the Germans Laval gave formal reasons for the decision: Pétain himself had to sign the law.[134] But on 24 August the French head of state declared himself unwilling to provide this signature.[135]

By now, however, the Gestapo Jewish desk in Paris had developed an alternative plan: in case the planned action against the French Jews who were to be denaturalized, as Röthke had said in July, brought in 'only a meagre result', 'all traceable Jews' were to be rounded up 'in a large-scale operation involving the forces of the Security Police (SD) commando and Einsatzkommandos with the assistance of German troops'. All Jews 'were to be transported to the East out of the area occupied by us in 1943, or taken back by the states still resisting this'.[136]

Reservations Concerning Italy, Germany's Chief Ally

Before September 1943, the Germans made no serious attempt to persuade the Italian government to hand over the 40,000 or so Jews living in the country who had been subjected to special racial legislation since 1938.[137] When Himmler discussed the persecution of the Jews of Eastern Europe with Mussolini in October 1942, his interlocutor avoided any further discussion of the subject with an evasive turn of phrase.[138]

The Italian policy of protecting the Jews against the German persecutory measures in their occupied zones in Greece, France, and Croatia irritated the Germans not least because their Italian ally was thus endangering the unified nature of *Judenpolitik* throughout the whole of the German sphere of influence, and thus encouraging other governments to deviate from their radical line.[139] Italy's policy was, as Himmler pointed out to Ribbentrop in January 1943[140] 'for many circles in France and throughout Europe the pretext for holding fire on the Jewish question, because they point out that not even Italy, our Axis partner, goes along with us on the Jewish question'.

In February Ribbentrop 'urgently' requested the Italians to be informed 'that the anti-Jewish measures of the Reich Security Head Office ... must not be sabotaged any further. Our efforts with regard to the governments of Croatia, Romania, Bulgaria and Slovakia to deport the Jews resident in those countries have also encountered great difficulties with those governments because of the attitude of the Italian government.'[141]

During his visit to Salzburg, at the beginning of April 1943, Mussolini may have voiced the prospect of interning the Jews in his country; that at least was what Ribbentrop assured the Hungarian Ambassador, Sztojay, when he tried to convince him a short time later that Hungary should tighten up its Jewish policy.[142]

Visiting Rome in the spring of 1943, the 'Jewish expert' at the German embassy in Paris, Carltheo Zeitschel, concluded that the German embassy in Rome would never 'be able to crack such a hard nut as the Jewish question in Italy in the interest of the Axis alliance'. The SD in turn was not able to act autonomously in Italy.[143]

The German Policy for the Further Extension of the Deportations after the Collapse of Italy

After Italy's departure from the Axis alliance and the occupation of much of the former ally's territory and its zones of occupation by the Wehrmacht, the policy of the systematic murder of the Jews was once again extended to a number of territories. The application of the extermination policy to the former Italian-occupied zone of southern France also led to the radicalization of the persecution in the rest of France, where no distinction was now made between French nationals and non-French people. The decision to deport the Danish Jews is also closely related to the radicalization of German policy after the secession of the Italian ally even if its history lies before these events. The German interventions in Slovakia and above all in Hungary in 1944 were finally exploited by the Nazi regime into a ruthless further intensification of mass murder, even in the face of military defeat.

Former 'allies' now made way for merciless regimes of terror that were completely dependent on the 'Third Reich', and which were bound to their German masters to the bitter end.

The 'De-Judaization' of Denmark as the Turning Point in German Extermination Policy

Werner Best, appointed Reich Plenipotentiary in Denmark in November 1942, continued the relatively restrained policy towards the Danish Jews. In a note of January 1943, Best made it clear that an intensified *Judenpolitik* would inevitably destroy the basis of the previous occupation policy, namely collaboration with the Danish constitutional monarchy. No Danish government would pass anti-Semitic legislation, and in the end the Germans would be forced to set up their own occupying administration.[144] Best once again confirmed this position in April.[145] As the scenario outlined by Best was highly undesirable for the Germans at this point, Luther, Ribbentrop, and even Himmler agreed with Best's stance.[146]

However, the acts of sabotage, strikes, and unrest that increased during the summer of 1943 brought an end to the restrained occupation policy that they recommended. Best now advocated a radical change of direction: he suggested that the position of the Reich Plenipotentiary be strengthened. He should govern the country in a kind of 'personal rule', based on the Danish administration (with an 'administrative committee' or a cabinet of specialists at its head) as well as with the help of increased powers in the sphere of internal security, namely his own police units. This solution, which Best had presented as a negative scenario in

January, now clearly struck him as a realistic alternative to the German policy of occupation, which was by now losing its way.[147]

For a time, Best's plans were thwarted by Hitler's decision, at the end of August, to declare a military emergency in Denmark. A few days later, however, Hitler once again gave Best full political responsibility for the German occupation in Denmark.[148] Ribbentrop gave this mandate further concrete form by ordering the installation of a non-political cabinet of specialists.[149]

However, this mandate proved barely possible to implement, as Best learned from leading Danish figures a few days after his return to Copenhagen on 6 September. Danish politicians were no longer willing to compromise themselves by collaborating further with the Germans at government level. However, the head of the Danish administration was prepared to make himself available to the Reich Plenipotentiary. This purely administrative solution did not correspond to the mandate that he had received from Ribbentrop, but in the given situation it struck Best as the only possible solution.[150]

To be able to explain the failure of the formation of a government to Berlin, and to provide a motive for a transition to a police regime under his leadership, Best had to be interested in intensifying the existing crisis. Such a controlled radicalization, however, could be achieved most simply by activating the 'Jewish question' in Denmark. The deportation of the Danish Jews was precisely the means with which the change of policy from a policy of collaboration to a police regime could be secured; on the other hand, the Germans assumed that such a measure would affect a relatively small minority in Danish society, so that it might later be possible to calm the situation.

On 8 September 1943, Best suggested to the Foreign Ministry that it use the state of emergency to attempt a 'solution of the Jewish question' in the country. If one waited until the lifting of the state of emergency, one would have far greater difficulties with the hostile reaction on the part of the Danish population, which was to be expected at any event. 'If the measures were taken during the present state of emergency,' Best argued, 'the possibility remains that a constitutional government can no longer be formed, so that an administrative committee under my direction would have to be formed and I would have to legislate by decree.' By this time, in fact, Best already knew that there was no longer any chance of forming a constitutional government, and that he would be forced to take over power in Denmark himself, with the help of the administrative committee. Best also stressed that in order to implement the deportations he would need the police units he had already requested. Thus the deportation of the Jews would also open up the way for a transition to a police regime, and it would immediately provide Best with the troops he needed.[151]

Best's proposal for the deportation of the Danish Jews—presented on the day of the announcement of the Italian-Allied ceasefire—was approved by the German leadership. Hitler's decision that the Danish and Italian Jews be deported, conceived as a warning to two insubordinate nations, thus occurred more or less simultaneously. However, it transpired relatively quickly that the preparations for the deportation of the Danish Jews had not been kept secret, and that failure was likely. Best thus decided, after unsuccessfully presenting his concerns to the German leadership,[152] to let the date for the wave of arrests leak out. If this happened, a week-long 'head-hunt'[153] would be obviated by the escape of the Jews, and further complications for the already difficult situation in Denmark would be avoided. In the meantime, Best's plans for the future form of occupation rule (a strong Reichkommissar utilizing the Danish administration) had assumed concrete form, leading him to envisage an imminent end to the state of emergency.[154] In other words, if the 'Final Solution' in Denmark had seemed like the ideal instrument for the accomplishment of a radical change of course in occupation policy, it had now become counter-productive to the further operation of the system of occupation. The will to accomplish the policy of extermination reached its limits where *Judenpolitik* threatened to lose its function within the system of occupation.

Thus, in the interest of the general occupation policy, Best was able to allow the great majority of Jews living in Denmark to escape to Sweden as the result of an unprecedented rescue action.[155] If we consider *Judenpolitik* in Denmark within this larger context, it can come as no surprise that early in October Best, pre-emptively represented the flight of the Jews to the Foreign Ministry as a success: 'Since the objective goal of the Jewish action in Denmark was the de-Judaization of the country and not the most successful head-hunt, it must be recognized that the Jewish action achieved its goal. Denmark is free of Jews, as no Jew who falls under the relevant regulations can legally live and work here any longer.'[156]

Compared with the situation in other countries with a greater collaborative potential, in Denmark, a country largely free of anti-Semitism and one with very little sympathy for the Nazi regime, the implementation of *Judenpolitik* did not serve to integrate native forces into the German policy, but rather the opposite. It had the function of excluding the Danish parties from the system of 'supervised administration', and of consolidating its transformation into a police state.

Within the *Judenpolitik* that the Nazi regime pursued within its sphere of influence, the action in Denmark in autumn 1943 represented a turning point. Until now *Judenpolitik* had fulfilled an important integral function within the German collaboration and alliance policy, by involving the respective 'partner' in the German policy of a racist reorganization of the continent and making it an accomplice in a crime on a massive scale. But this policy did not go entirely smoothly. When the deportations were set in motion, the attitude of the allied or collaborating government had to be taken into account, which meant that the deportations happened slowly or not on the desired scale (Slovakia, France) or not at all (Old Romania, Italian occupied territories).

After the turning point of the war in the winter of 1942/3 it became more and more difficult to implement deportations in cooperation with allied or collaborating governments (to a limited extent this ocurred in Bulgaria and France; efforts with regard to Hungary and the Italian-occupied territories remained ineffective at first). However, the Germans did not abandon their policy, since precisely in view of the worsening military situation they saw the intensification of the persecution of the Jews and the associated compromising of their 'partners' as an important safeguard for the cohesion of the block under their rule. Attitudes towards the 'Jewish question' became an important gauge for the German side, on which they could read the loyalty of their partners.

Goebbels's diaries document this way of thinking on the part of the German leadership with regard to the allies Romania[157], Italy,[158] and Bulgaria[159]: too 'lax' a treatment of the persecution of the Jews was seen as an indication of the weakness and lack of loyalty of the allies. But that meant, according to the logic of German *Judenpolitik*, that a radicalization of the persecution on the German model bound the allies irreversibly to the German Reich.

'Most of our contemporaries', Goebbels wrote in March 1943, recording remarks made to him by Hitler, 'failed to realize that the wars of the twentieth century were racial wars, and that in racial wars there has only ever been survival or extermination, and that we must therefore understand that this war too will end with just such a result.'[160]

Three weeks previously he had noted of a conversation with Goering, 'Goering is completely clear about everything that would threaten us all if we were to weaken in this war. He has no illusions about it. Particularly in the Jewish question we are so locked in that there is no escape left for us. And that is as it should be. From experience, a movement and a people that have broken the bridges behind them, fight much more relentlessly than those who still have the possibility of retreat.'[161]

It should not be overlooked that it was the three states that successfully resisted German *Judenpolitik*—Italy, Romania, and Bulgaria[162]—that succeeded in leaving their alliances with Germany with separate ceasefires between September 1943 and 1944. This stepping out of line on the part of—from the German perspective—the 'pro-Jewish' allies must have served as a confirmation of their policy that any kind of compromise on *Judenpolitik* was to be avoided at all costs.

In other words: if *Judenpolitik* had originally (along with economic policy and military security and cooperation) been one of the main axes of German occupation and alliance policy, it now threatened to undermine earlier forms of collaboration and alliance. In future, deportations, where they were not organized by the German occupation apparatus itself, were only possible with the help of terror regimes which were entirely under the control of the Nazi regime, had little support from the local population, and were prepared to act with extreme brutality against it.

The Allied landing in North Africa, with the shift of power that it brought to the whole of the Mediterranean area still under Axis control, had constituted the starting point for an expansion of persecution: the Jews of Tunisia and southern France had now fallen into the immediate clutches of their German persecutors, while in early 1943 the RSHA was organizing mass deportations from Greece and Bulgaria. The further military successes of the Western Allies, the rising prospect of an Allied landing on the continent, and the advance of the Red Army, but above all the Warsaw ghetto uprising in April/May 1943 led to a further burst of radicalization in the spring/early summer, which we have already examined with reference to the Holocaust in Poland and the occupied Soviet territories. But this new radicalization was also evident in Western and South-Eastern Europe. It was apparent in the deportation of thousands of children from the Netherlands, it was seen in the demands of the RSHA to start the deportation of Jews with Belgian citizenship, and it lay behind Himmler's call on 8 June to deport French Jews who were due to be denaturalized by 15 July. But the radicalization can also be observed in German *Judenpolitik* in Croatia in May 1943, when the Germans were urging that the deportations be taken to their conclusion; and it was also apparent in Slovakia, where a new initiative was introduced in the spring of 1943, to spur the government there to resume deportations.

A further burst of radicalization began in September 1943, after Italy's secession. On the one hand, *Judenpolitik* now had the new function just referred to, on the other hand, as was seen in Denmark, the German deportation machinery lacked the power to implement further deportations on its own; it was forced more than ever to rely on the collaboration of local forces. Where that collaboration worked, the murder machine was horribly effective.

Italy

After the ceasefire in September 1943, the invasion of the Wehrmacht, and the formation of a new Fascist government in the northern half of the country, the RSHA was resolved ruthlessly to deport the Jews living in that part of the country, numbering between around 33,000 and 34,000.[163]

In October, Dannecker was sent to Rome as leader of a small *Einsatzkommando*.[164] Two days after a large-scale raid on 16 October, more than 1,000 Jews were deported from the Italian capital to Auschwitz. Dannecker's commando went on to organize further raids in other Italian cities, so that by the end of the year almost 1,400 people had been deported to Auschwitz in four transports. But the RSHA reached the view that this approach had not produced 'any noteworthy result', as the great majority of Jews living in Italy had by now gone into hiding.[165]

At the beginning of December, representatives of the Foreign Ministry and the RSHA therefore agreed to involve the Italian authorities in the persecution.[166] To achieve this, they exploited the fact that the government of the 'Social Italian

Republic' had independently ordered the internment of all Jews in late November, without at first officially informing the Italians about the final goal of the persecution, deportation, and mass murder. The Fascist state was thus to be enmeshed in a murderous complicity with the 'Third Reich'.

In accordance with this new persecution strategy Dannecker's mobile commando was replaced early in 1944 by a special Jewish department attached to the commander of the Security Police, led by Friedrich Bosshammer, also a colleague of Eichmann. With the help of the apparatus of the BdS, Bosshammer had the chance to deploy the Italian police as an auxiliary organization for systematic persecution. Beginning in January, the office of the BdS demanded that the Italian police hand over the interned Jews. Bosshammer ignored Italian laws forbidding the arrest of certain groups (the elderly, those married to non-Jews, etc.). In mid-March Bosshammer took over the Fossoli camp from the Italian authorities and made it the central collection camp for the Jews arrested by the Italian police and the branch commandos of the BdS. In August 1944, given the approaching front, the central collection camp was transferred to Bolzano.

Overall, throughout 1944 at least fifteen transports carrying more than 3,800 Jews left Italy for Auschwitz, where the great majority were murdered. Meanwhile over 80 per cent of the Jews living in Italy managed—thanks to the solidarity of the Italian population—to escape the clutches of their persecutors.[167]

Since September 1943, Odilo Globocnik, himself originally from Trieste, and one of the men chiefly responsible for the extermination of the Polish Jews, had been appointed HSSPF to the 'Operation Zone of the Adriatic Coastal Region', along with part of the Einsatzkommando Reinhard. This was the area around Trieste which had been directly incorporated into the territory of the Greater German Reich. The Risiera di San Sabba, a former rice mill, served as a collection camp for the Jews arrested in this area. From December 1943 until February 1943, twenty-two transports carrying more than 1,100 Jews left Trieste for Auschwitz, the last one reaching Bergen-Belsen. Over 90 per cent of the deportees were murdered.[168]

Former Italian Zones of Occupation in Greece and Croatia

After the Wehrmacht had taken over the Italian zones of occupation in Greece as well as Albania, Montenegro, and the Dodecanese (the eastern Aegean group of islands, Italian since 1912), in response to Italy's departure from the war, a further (approximately) 16,000 Jews came under German control.[169]

After an 'action' in March 1944 against the Jews living in the former Italian zone of occupation on the Greek mainland, on 2 April a transport carrying a total of 5,000 people left Athens for Auschwitz, reaching the camp nine days later after unimaginable hardships.[170] Between May and August 1944 the members of the Jewish communities on the Greek islands (Corfu, Rhodes, Crete) were arrested by the Wehrmacht, transported to the mainland, and deported to Auschwitz in two transports.[171]

When the Italian occupation of Croatia ended in September, the majority of the Jews who had by now been rounded up in an internment camp on the island of Rab were able to escape to a zone controlled by the People's Liberation Army; around 200 Jews were captured by the Gestapo and deported to Auschwitz in the second half of March. The same fate awaited several hundred Jews in other parts of the formerly Italian-occupied zone.[172]

Further Radicalization of the Persecution in France

Immediately after the German troops marched into the Italian-occupied zone of southern France on 8 September, following the ceasefire between Italy and the Allies, Brunner's *Sonderkommando* began to hunt down those Jews who had so far been left unmolested.[173]

Brunner concentrated particularly on Nice, where about 20,000–25,000 Jews, mostly refugees, were living. Without French support, however, he managed only to deport 1,800 people to Drancy within three months.[174]

The security police had always seen the Italian resistance to the German persecution of the Jews as a significant hindrance to a radical 'solution' of the Jewish question across the whole of France. From the point of view of the Security Police, the removal of this factor opened up the possibility of radicalizing the persecution of the Jews across France on the massive scale sketched out by Eichmann and Röthke in the summer of 1943,[175] and deporting, where possible, all Jews living in France regardless of their nationality.

Since as early as August 1943, the Gestapo had stepped up their arrests of French Jews across the whole of France for alleged infringements of the French anti-Jewish laws.[176] After the head of the militia, Darmand, had replaced Bousquet as general secretary of the police, on the orders of the Security Police the French police increasingly participated in the arrest of French Jews in the provinces.[177]

But after the French government had been reshuffled to the right in March 1944,[178] there was no further reason for the Germans to take into consideration French objections and reservations about the deportations. For the French government's support among the population was in any case so weak that the country could only be kept under control by means of a rule of terror.

On 14 April 1944, Brunner and Knochen ordered all Jews, regardless of their nationality, to be arrested, with the exception of people living in 'mixed marriages'. Rewards were offered for denunciations. In the four months leading to the cessation of the deportations in August 1944 more than 6,000 people were deported.[179] By then a total of almost 76,000 Jews had been deported from France, a further 4,000 had died in camps or been murdered in the country. This meant that, as a whole, a quarter of the Jews living in France had become victims of the

Holocaust. Among the deportees were around 24,000 French nationals, including 8,000 children of foreign parents who were born in France, and 8,000 naturalized Jews.[180] Around two-thirds of the deportees were deported from occupied France, and about a third from southern France, unoccupied until 1942.[181]

Slovakia

By the time of the temporary cessation of the deportations from Slovakia in October 1942, around 58,000 people had been deported from the country to occupied Poland.[182] Around 24,000 Jews had been excluded from the deportions by so-called 'writs of protection' issued by the Slovakian authorities. The Germans repeatedly stressed their demand for the resumption of the deportations, but could not impose their will on Slovakia.

After a German initiative in early summer 1943—clearly in the context of the general radicalization after the Warsaw ghetto uprising (the parallel with the German initiatives in France and Croatia is plain)—in June, the ambassador, Hans Ludin, had to report to the Foreign Ministry that the 'implementation of the evacuation of the Jews from Slovakia' had 'presently reached a dead end'. The Prime Minister, Vojtech Tuka, wanted to continue the 'resettlement' and was requesting 'the diplomatic support of the Reich'. The Secretary of State, Weizsäcker, advised him to inform President Tiso that the halt to the deportations was causing surprise in Germany.[183]

At this point there were more than 18,000, possibly up to 25,000 Jews, living in Slovakia.[184] More than 15,000 of these were claimed to be indispensable by the Slovakian authorities; a few thousand were imprisoned as forced labourers in concentration camps within Slovakia.

In July 1943, the head of department Inland II of the Foreign Ministry, Horst Wagner, informed the ambassador, Ludin, on Ribbentrop's instructions, that 'there were not at present any plans to approach the Slovakian government concerning the final stage of the cleaning up of the Slovakian Jewish question'. However, the Foreign Ministry's South-Eastern Europe expert, Edmund Veesenmayer, would soon informally tell President Tiso, in the course of a visit to Pressburg, of 'the continuing interest in the cleaning up of the Jewish question in Slovakia'.[185]

After an initial visit in July, in December 1943 Veesenmayer began negotiations with Tiso, and won his agreement that the remaining Jews still living in Slovakia, whose numbers were estimated as between 16,000 and 18,000, were to be 'taken to Jewish camps' by 1 April 1944 at the latest.[186] In fact the Slovaks did not keep their part of the agreement. Efforts by Veesenmayer, by now the German ambassador in Hungary, to organize the deportation of the Slovakian Jews in the wake of the deportation of the Hungarian Jews, were unsuccessful.[187]

The refusal of the Slovakian government to comply with German demands has much to do with the change of political climate that had occurred in Slovakia since early in 1942, but increasingly since early 1943, with the defeat at Stalingrad. The deportations had encountered opposition among influential circles of the Slovakian population, and that attitude of opposition became more marked after details of the fate of the deportees leaked out and, with the Red Army's advance towards the national border, it became increasingly likely that this blatant crime would be punished.[188]

Given the delaying response of the Slovakian government towards its German ally, the last phase of the persecution of the Jews in the country only started after the beginning of the popular uprising in Slovakia in August 1944 and the occupation of the country by German troops. Himmler appointed his close confidant Gottlob Berger, head of the SS Main Office, 'commander of German troops in Slovakia' and Hermann Höfle, who had played a central part in 'Aktion Reinhardt', as HSSPF. He also appointed a commander of the Security Police (BdS) for the territory, which was not treated as an occupied country, but as an ally. However, the BdS was also assigned its own *Einsatzgruppe*, H, assembled from five *Einsatzkommandos*. These commandos erected a system of bases around the country, and began hunting Jews living in Slovakia, most of whom were imprisoned in the camp at Sered. In the face of opposition from the Slovakian government, the SS imposed the resumption of the deportations: between September 1944 and March 1943 eleven transports left Slovakia. Almost 8,000 people were deported to Auschwitz, more than 2,700 to Sachsenhausen, and over 1,600 to Theresienstadt.[189] An unknown number of these deportees lost their lives during the transports, as a result of their conditions of imprisonment and the death marches implemented after the dissolution of the concentration camps.

Hungary

During 1943 the Nazi regime continued its policy of exerting pressure on the Hungarian government to persuade it to deport its Jews. In January Luther attempted to influence the Hungarian ambassador to this end,[190] while in March 1943 the Foreign Ministry asked Bormann[191] once again to inform his guest, a Hungarian minister, about German requests: the exclusion of the Jews from the cultural and economic life of Hungary.

At what became known as the first Kleßheim Conference on 17 and 18 April 1943, Ribbentrop responded to Horthy's question about 'what he should do with the Jews' ('he couldn't kill them, after all') quite unequivocally that they must 'either be exterminated or taken to concentration camps'. Hitler interjected that Jews were 'to be treated like tuberculosis bacilli, which could affect healthy bodies'.[192] At the end of April, Ribbentrop told the Hungarian ambassador, Döme Sztojay, that Germany planned to deport all Jews from the area under

German control, and that it expected its allies to participate in these measures.[193] Hitler's strong personal interest in this matter is also revealed by a passage in Geobbels's diaries from early May. According to this, Hitler had told the Reichsleiters and Gauleiters that the 'Jewish question' was being resolved 'worst of all by the Hungarians'; Horthy, who was 'extraordinarily strongly enmeshed with the Jews through his family', would fight tooth and nail against really tackling the Jewish problem.[194]

In his report of 30 April Veesenmayer, who had been sent to Hungary to investigate the situation in the country, established a close connection between the Hungarian reticence concerning *Judenpolitik* and the expectations prevailing in the post-war era. He wrote that the government and wide sections of the bourgeoisie expected 'clemency and benevolent treatment' from the British and the Americans 'because of their hospitable attitude towards Jewry. They see Jewry as a guarantee of "Hungarian concerns" and believe that through the Jews they can demonstrate that it was only under duress that they waged this war alongside the Axis powers, but through latent sabotage indirectly provided a contribution to the opponents of the Axis powers.'[195] Thus it had to be German policy—this is the logical conclusion to be drawn from these trains of thought—to strive to tear up that 'guarantee', if they wanted to keep Hungary on their side.

In late May 1943, however, Prime Minister Kállay demonstrated in a speech that he did consider the 'complete resettlement of Jewry' as the 'definitive solution' of the 'Jewish question', but that he would only address this once he had had 'an answer to the question of where the Jews are to be resettled to'. So the Germans could not expect speedy consent to the deportations from the Hungarians.[196]

The Germans gradually set about undertaking the solution of the 'Jewish question' in Hungary without Kállay. In a further report about the situation in Hungary, which he wrote after a further fact-finding trip to Budapest in December 1943,[197] Veesenmayer stressed that the solution of the 'Jewish question' in Hungary represented 'a rewarding and compelling task for Reich policy . . . grappling with it and cleaning it up'. In writing that the 'cleaning up' of the 'Jewish question' was 'the precondition for the engagement of Hungary in the Reich's battle for defence and existence', Veesenmayer once again made it clear that the intensification of the persecution of the Jews in Hungary was the ideal instrument to render their 'ally' compliant.

The Hungarian government's stubborn refusal to hand over the Jews resident in the country was, from the point of view of the Nazi regime, the decisive gauge with which the progressive erosion of Hungarian loyalty to the Reich since Stalingrad could be measured. The German insistence on the issue proved crucial in keeping the 'ally' under control. If the Hungarian government, so the German calculation ran, could be forced to hand over the Jews domiciled in the country, the Hungarians would lose their 'guarantee' vis-à-vis the Western Allies, and would thus be bound for good or ill to their German 'partner'.

At the beginning of 1944, the German–Hungarian relationship increasingly deteriorated. In February 1944 Hungarian troops retreated from the Ukraine; their secret negotiations with the Western Allies were just as well known to the Germans as the war-weariness and the growing anti-German attitude in the country. With the occupation of the country by German troops in March 1944, the formation of the new Hungarian government under Sztojay, previously the mission head in Berlin, the appointment of Veesenmayer as the new ambassador and Plenipotentiary of the Greater German Reich in Hungary (effectively the German governor), and the establishment of an SS apparatus in the country, the political and technical preconditions for the deportations were in place.[198]

At Veesenmayer's instigation, in April the Sztojay government offered 50,000 Jewish workers for armaments projects; a further 50,000, it was agreed, would follow in May.[199] According to a familiar pattern, 'labour deployment' provided the pretext on the basis of which the SS prepared the complete deportation and extermination of the Hungarian Jews. The perfidious system of concentration and deportation tested in German-occupied Europe for years was to be installed in Hungary, with the active support of the Hungarian authorities and without encountering any notable resistance among the non-Jewish population—in a form that had been more or less perfected.[200]

In March and April the new Hungarian government was induced to introduce comprehensive anti-Jewish legislation that created preconditions for the deportations. On 23 April the Hungarian trade ministry had all Jewish shops closed and expropriated, and on 26 April the Hungarian cabinet undertook to send 50,000 Jewish forced labourers ('with their families') to Germany, and put the compulsory organization of Hungarian Jews, already established by Eichmann, under Hungarian control.[201]

The Germans were not only exceedingly well informed about the legislative and administrative measures of the Hungarian government, but also exercised, 'in constant personal contact' and 'in an advisory capacity in the drafting and implementation of ordinances', a 'control' over the 'operation of Hungarian Jewish laws'.[202]

On the orders of the *Sonderkommando* of the RSHA, which had been sent to Budapest, and of which Eichmann had personally assumed leadership, a Jewish council was set up, initially for the capital, later for the whole country.[203]

On 27 April Goebbels recorded statements by Hitler about Horthy, which reveal that the Hungarian Reich administrator had become so involved in German *Judenpolitik* that he could now to some extent be seen as a relatively reliable ally: 'At any rate, he now no longer obstructs the cleansers of public life in Hungary; on the contrary, he is now murderously angry with the Jews and has no objections to us using them as hostages. He even suggested the same thing himself... At any rate the Hungarians will not escape the rhythm of the Jewish question. Whoever says A must say B, and the Hungarians, having started with

Judenpolitik, can for that reason not halt it. From a certain point onwards *Judenpolitik* propels itself.' After further anti-Semitic tirades the dictator continued: 'By and large one can say that a long-term policy is only possible in this war if one starts out with the Jewish question.'[204]

To simplify the deportations, the country was divided into zones. In each zone the Jews were first brought by the Hungarian police from smaller villages to the larger towns, where ghettos or camps were set up. After this, zone by zone, the deportations to Auschwitz occurred, in only a few days in each case.[205] First the territories annexed by Hungary from 1938 onwards, the Carpatho-Ukraine (Zone I) as well as Northern Transylvania (Nordsiebenbürgen) (Zone II). The 'concentration' began in the Carpatho-Ukraine on 16 April, in Northern Transylvania on 3 May, the deportations to Auschwitz from these two zones on 15 May. They were gradually followed by the Old Hungarian Provinces (Zones III–V), where the concentration process was completed on 3 July and the deportations on 6 July. The final zone was to be Budapest, and the deportation of the 200,000 or so Jews living there.[206]

The first two trains carrying almost 4,000 people, officially presented as the first contingent in the context of the agreed allocation of Jewish workers to the Reich, had already left Hungary at the end of April for Auschwitz, where 2,700 deportees were murdered in the gas chambers immediately on arrival.[207]

In early May, the pace of the deportations was considerably accelerated: at a timetable conference on 4/5 May, aiming for a target set no later than the start of the conference,[208] it was established that 12,000 Jews should be deported per day rather than the 3,000 originally agreed.[209] From 14 May, four transports a day left Hungary, each carrying 3,000 Jews. By the time the deportations were halted in early July, a total of 437,000 people had been deported from the five zones, almost exclusively to Auschwitz. There were two exceptions: at the end of June around 15,000 people were brought to Strasshof near Vienna and deployed in forced labour so that, as Eichmann put it, they could be 'put on ice'.[210] This statement of Eichmann's is connected with the negotiations that had begun in the spring between the SS and the Jewish rescue committee, Vaada, about buying the freedom of Jews. We shall examine this more closely in the next section. As a concrete result of these negotiations 1,684 people were deported to the exchange camp of Bergen-Belsen, also in June, from where they were able to travel to Switzerland over the next few months. The remaining Hungarian Jews, 433,000 in all, were deported to Auschwitz in transports lasting three to four days;[211] of these some 10 per cent were deemed to be fit for work, the rest, far more than 10,000 people per day, were murdered immediately on arrival.[212]

At the beginning of July, preparations were already under way to deport the Jews living in Budapest, who had already been forced to move into houses marked with yellow stars.[213] In the face of the worldwide protests against the imminent deportations,[214] Sztojay informed Veesenmayer on 6 July that Horthy had ordered a halt to the deportations.[215]

In response, the Germans tried to enforce the resumption of the deportations. On 8 July, when Sztojay asked Veesenmayer whether they could accept offers from various states to grant a certain number of Jews permission to enter or to pass through, Hitler, when asked about this, replied that they could accept these offers, as long as 'the transport of Jews to the Reich, temporarily stopped by the Reich governor, be brought quickly and immediately to an end'.[216] On Ribbentrop's instructions, in mid-July Veesenmeyer gave Horthy an ultimatum to resume the deportations.[217]

After Eichmann, on his own responsibility, had more than 2,700 Jews deported to Auschwitz from two Hungarian internment camps[218] in the second half of July, the Hungarian government, under severe pressure from the Germans, agreed to the resumption of the deportations from the end of the month.[219] A few days later, however, Horthy declared himself in agreement only with the imprisonment of the Jews in special camps, but not with their deportation.[220] What was decisive for this step was that on 23 August Romania had declared its secession from the Axis alliance, and joined the anti-Hitler coalition. On 29 August Horthy gave the newly formed Hungarian government under Prime Minister Lakatos express instructions—kept secret from the Germans—to end the persecution of the Jews. Surprisingly, however, Himmler had already issued the order for all further deportations from Hungary to be suspended,[221] and in September the *Sonderkommando*, Eichmann, also left Hungary.[222]

At first glance, Himmler's attitude seems surprising in view of the stubborn German efforts over the previous few months to set the deportations in motion.[223] But if we adopt the perspective of the Nazi regime, for whom the deportations represented an important political instrument to bind the Hungarian allies to the Reich, for good or ill, as accomplices of an unparalleled crime, it becomes clear that at the end of August the Germans must finally have become aware that further insistence on a continuation of the deportations threatened to become counter-productive, as it must inevitably lead to the end of the Horthy regime and possibly to the loss of their Hungarian ally.

However, the situation changed fundamentally in mid-October, after Horthy had declared Hungary's withdrawal from the war as the result of secret ceasefire negotiations with the Soviet Union, and the Arrow Cross Party under Ferec Szàlasy seized power with German support.[224] Now the Germans tried once again to set the deportations in motion: their new Hungarian partners were to be irresistibly bound to their allies as accomplices of mass murder. But, as the complete deportation of the Budapest Jews to Auschwitz could no longer be carried out because of the transport situation and the destruction of the gas chambers in Birkenau undertaken in the autumn of 1944,[225] Eichmann, who had returned to Budapest immediately after the putsch, now once again demanded that Hungary put 50,000 workers at the disposal of the Reich, although he in fact intended to double this figure at a later date.[226] In negotiations with the Hungarians, an agreement was reached for 25,000 Jewish 'loan workers', then revised to 50,000, and, at the end of October, the people in question were marched to the Austrian border in the most cruel and extreme conditions.[227] However, because of the high death rate, Szàlasy had the marches suspended on 21 November. On the same day Ribbentrop instructed Veesenmayer, at his next meeting with the Hungarian prime minister, to urge him to 'press ahead energetically with the evacuation of the Budapest Jews'.[228] In December the Jews who had remained in Budapest were confined in a ghetto. There, along with the inhuman living conditions, they were exposed to the terror of the Arrow Cross supporters, until Budapest capitulated in February.[229]

The End of the Holocaust

Removal of Traces

In 1942 the SS initiated the strictly secret 'Action 1005'. The goal of this enterprise was to destroy the traces of the mass murders, in particular to remove the human remains of the victims in the mass graves.[230] The man appointed to lead the action was Standartenführer Paul Blobel. As a pioneer officer in the First World War, as well as a former Einsatzkommando leader, he no doubt appeared well qualified for the task. The *Sonderkommandos* under him consisted of members of the Security Police and the SD as well as the Order Police. The removal of the corpses themselves had to be undertaken by prisoners, who were in turn murdered after a certain amount of time and replaced by new prisoners. In June 1942 the first attempts were made to burn the remains in Chelmno extermination camp, and this activity was then extended to the other extermination camps as well. In Sobibor this had been happening since the summer of 1942, and in Auschwitz-Birkenau, where the first crematoria had not been built until July 1942, in the autumn of 1942, in Belzec, which had been closed in December 1942, between the end of 1942 and the spring of 1943, and in Treblinka since the spring of 1943.[231]

In June 1943 the commandos began to open the mass graves in the occupied Soviet territories, first in the Ukraine, then in White Russia, and finally in the Baltic states. To remove the traces of the murders in occupied Poland, in 1944 *Sonderkommandos* were established under the five commanders of the Security police and the SD in the General Government, and under the HSSPF responsible for the annexed Polish territories. Aktion 1005 Sonderkommandos can also be identified in Yugoslavia.[232]

The *Sonderkommandos* were extraordinarily thorough in the removal of the corpses: the mass graves were opened up, the corpses were burned on piles of wood or steel grilles, then the ashes were examined for valuable objects, gold teeth above all, before the bones were ground and the ashes scattered or buried. Then all other traces that could have indicated the places of execution were removed, and the murder scene dug over and planted.

According to the wishes of the perpetrators, no traces of the extermination camps themselves were to remain either. The so-called palace, in which the installations of Chelmno extermination centre were housed, was blown up in the spring of 1943.[233] On the grounds of Belzec and Treblinka, all buildings were removed after the end of the mass murders, the grounds were planted, and a farm was built. The same was done in Treblinka, where the murders in the gas chambers continued until August 1943. In summer 1943, after the mass murders there were ended, Sobibor was temporarily turned into a concentration camp, where the prisoners were deployed in the sorting of captured ammunition. After the uprising of October 1943 this camp too was closed, and here too the grounds were planted and an agricultural establishment constructed.[234]

During the German retreat in July 1944, Majdanek was set on fire, but the gas chambers and other traces of the mass murders remained, so that as early as the summer of 1944 the Soviets could begin to document the procedures in this extermination camp, the first to be seized by Allied troops. In Auschwitz in November and December technical installations were removed from the gas chambers and crematoria; the crematoria were blown up and the remains covered with soil and planted.[235]

The fundamental intention of the SS was to clear not only the mass murder sites but the concentration camps, and where possible to destroy them; all proof of the crimes was to be destroyed, no witnesses were to fall into the hands of the Allies. That meant that the prisoners were either to be murdered or 'evacuated' from one camp to the other. The SS saw the prisoners who were 'fit for work' as living capital that would be exploited to the bitter end.

Himmler reserved a special policy for the Jewish prisoners: beginning in mid-1944 he offered them to the Western Allies as barter, presumably to open up channels of negotiation which might be used in peace feelers. The extent to which the SS would really have been prepared to release large numbers of Jewish prisoners on a quid pro quo basis, which would have meant returning to the pre-war policy of expulsion, or whether they only appeared to offer such negotiations in order to construct a dialogue with the Western Allies is impossible to establish beyond doubt. It is also unclear whether Himmler was acting in accord with Hitler in these complicated manoeuvres, or whether he was from the outset pursuing a policy of his own to secure his position against the threatening collapse of the Third Reich, and it is equally unclear whether the negotiations undertaken by Eichmann and Wisliceny were fully in accord with Himmler's plans. But it is also entirely imaginable that these efforts to establish contacts with the West were part of a double game: if the Western Allies agreed to enter negotiations with the Nazi regime over the surviving Jews, either one could extend such negotiations to other 'humanitarian' issues and use them as peace feelers, or one could abandon the negotiations and effectively compromise the other side, sowing suspicion between the Western Allies and the Soviet Union or revealing the USA and Great Britain as stooges of Jewish interests, thus bolstering the claim of German military propaganda that Germany was waging a war against world Jewry.[236]

Thus, Himmler saw the Jewish prisoners as hostages with whom one could, in one way or another, exert an influence on the Western Allies. This attitude was not new: it can already be demonstrated in connection with *Kristallnacht*; the reason for taking Jews as hostages to prevent the Americans from entering the war seems to have played a part in starting the deportations of the German Jews in the autumn of 1941, and from 1942 the SS leadership repeatedly allowed individual Jews to travel to neutral countries abroad in return for high payments in foreign currency.[237] Himmler had received express permission from Hitler for this in December 1942, and in that context pursued the project of holding around 10,000 Jews back in a special camp as 'valuable hostages'.[238] It was in accordance with this idea that the 'holding camp' at Bergen-Belsen was set up, which Himmler placed under the control of the Business and Administration Head Office, to rule out the possibility of agencies outside the SS having access to the camp.[239] Finally, the German Jewish adviser in Slovakia, Wisliceny, had in 1942 accepted a large sum in dollars from the Jews. It remains unresolved whether this payment had any causal connection with the suspension of deportations from Slovakia. Thus, treating Jewish prisoners as negotiating counters was not a new procedure.[240]

In March 1944, representatives of the Vaada Aid and Rescue Committee, supported by Zionist organizations, contacted Wisliceny, who had by now begun preparations for the deportations in Budapest as a member of *Sonderkommando* Eichmann. Negotiations were carried out concerning the departure from the country of a large number of Hungarian Jews in return for foreign currency or goods; the SS's desire for 10,000 lorries proved to be at the core of this. The Jewish negotiators made several large advance payments in dollars. In compliance with an agreement made with Eichmann, Vaada representatives went to Istanbul to make contact with the Allies, since the possibility of as many as several hundred thousand people leaving the country and the receipt of material benefits in return was only imaginable with Allied support. But the mission failed: the two Vaada emissaries were arrested by the British in Syria, and the British steadfastly refused to get involved in bartering of this kind.[241]

Meanwhile Vaada, represented by Rudolf Kastner, continued to negotiate with the SS in Budapest. Two operations emerged out of this. On the one hand, at the end of June 15,000 Jews, rather than being sent to Auschwitz, were deported as forced labourers to Austria where, as Kastner said, quoting Eichmann, they were to be 'put on ice', to be kept ready for further barter negotiations. It seems probable that this step was not a substantial concession on Eichmann's part, but that he was only responding to an urgent request from Kaltenbrunner to send forced labourers to the area around Vienna. Also, at the end of June, in accordance with an agreement made between Kastner and Eichmann, 1,684 Hungarian Jews were taken to Bergen-Belsen on a special transport. From there they travelled to Switzerland in two groups, in August and December. In the meantime, Kurt Becher, the head of the equipment staff of the HSSPF in Hungary, the man responsible for the exploitation of stolen Jewish property, took over the negotiation of the benefits to be expected in return from the Jews, first with the representatives of Vaada, then, from August 1944, also with the representative of the JDC in Switzerland, Saly Mayer. Until January 1945 further discussions were held in Switzerland between representatives of the SS and Jewish organizations, covering large-scale barter deals of people for money or goods. Becher succeeded in securing the attendance of a representative of the War Refugee Board, an American government body, at one of these meetings early in November in Zurich; he had thus achieved the goal that Himmler linked with these negotiations, namely contact with official American agencies. But these discussions produced no results whatsoever, either in terms of further rescue projects or of possible peace feelers.[242]

But in the meantime negotiations on another plane had achieved a concrete success: as a result of direct discussions between former Swiss President Jean-Marie Musy and Himmler—they were held in Vienna in October 1944 and in Wildbad (Black Forest) in January 1945—in February 1,200 Jews were released from Theresienstadt to Switzerland.[243] In the last phase of the war, Himmler would once again try to use the fate of the Jewish concentration camp inmates as a starting point for making contact with the Allied side.

The negotiations concerning the release of Jewish prisoners show once again how flexibly *Judenpolitik* could be administered. Even if the goal of the systematic murder of the European Jews was of prime importance to the SS, at the same time Himmler was prepared to make tactical concessions in the form of the release of smaller contingents of prisoners, if other targets—the shortage of foreign currency, the SS's need of equipment, the possibility of establishing negotiating channels with the Western Allies—were temporarily of prime importance. Himmler also seems to have been prepared to negotiate seriously over the release of larger groups of Jews, if it meant that the collapse of the Third Reich could be delayed or even prevented as a result. Hitler did not agree with this approach as Himmler was forced to recognize: the Führer reacted with great indignation when he subsequently learned of the release of the Jews to Switzerland, and forbade similar steps in the future.[244]

The Clearing of the Concentration Camps and the Death Marches

As early as 17 June 1944 Himmler transferred to the Higher SS and Police Commanders the right of command over the concentration camps in the event of 'A Case' (initially an uprising by inmates, but then above all the approach of enemy troops).[245] Accordingly, the HSSPF established precisely when the clearance was to take place and organized it in collaboration with Department D of the WVHA. As to the further fate of the inmates, organizational measures taken at an intermediate level were to prove crucial. Thus, right into the final phase of the war the perpetrators had a great deal of room for manoeuvre as far as the murder of Jews and other prisoners was concerned.

The clearance and evacuation led to a new selection of the prisoners. While in some concentration camps German prisoners were released, weak and sick prisoners—mainly Jewish—were generally murdered in the camps before the order to evacuate was given. The evacuation marches then ordered by the camp authorities—in some cases there were also railway transports—generally occurred in winter conditions, with inadequate provisions or none at all. There were inadequate breaks and accommodation and the escorting troops, often with local help, murdered the prisoners who were left behind. In these columns, generally composed of members of all categories of prisoners, the chances of survival of the Jewish prisoners were worst because of their generally advanced exhaustion.

As a rule the sub-camps were cleared first and the prisoners brought to the main camp. The goal of the so-called 'evacuations' of the main camps was in turn the concentration camps in the centre of the German Reich. Bringing together a large number of prisoners in fewer and fewer camps generally led to an almost total breakdown of supplies for the prisoners in the camps and a further worsening of already almost unbearable conditions. Instead of the imminent liberation that many prisoners expected from the Allied advance, for most prisoners the occupation of Germany meant a further intensification of their torment, which often continued for months.[246]

The former ghettos and camps for Jewish forced labourers in the Baltic, which had been turned into concentration camps on Himmler's instructions, were cleared in the summer of 1944. The clearance of the camp complex around the Kaiserwald concentration camp in Riga began in June 1944. At first the sub-camps were gradually closed, and the prisoners brought to Kaiserwald; the prisoners who were no longer fit for forced labour, as well as all children, were separated from the rest and murdered. From August until October the prisoners were brought by ship to Danzig, where they were confined in the concentration camp.[247]

From Kaunas concentration camp the surviving 8,000 Jews were deported to the west by rail and on barges, the women to Stutthof, the men to sub-camps of

Dachau. Prisoners who were 'unfit for work' were separated out and taken to Auschwitz.[248] Also in August 1944 all camps of the Vaivara complex were dissolved and most of the prisoners shipped to Tallinn and from there to Stutthof.[249]

In the summer of 1944 the camp commandant of Stutthof, Günther Hoppe, received the order from the Department D inspector of the WVHA with responsibility for the concentration camps, that all Jewish prisoners in Stutthof were to be murdered by the end of the year. To this end, in autumn 1944 a clothes delousing installation was turned into a gas chamber. Here, from September 1944 onwards, groups of between twenty-five and thirty-five people—mostly female Jewish prisoners from the Baltic and Hungary—were murdered with Zyklon B. A second gas chamber was set up in an abandoned railway wagon.[250] At the end of 1944, when the clearance of Stutthof camp began, to avoid the approaching front, there were still 47,000 prisoners there, two-thirds of them Jewish.[251]

In mid-January at least 6,000 prisoners, predominantly Jewish women, were driven out of the sub-camps of Stutthof concentration camp, situated in East Prussia, towards the Baltic. Around 50 per cent of the prisoners lost their lives. In the coastal town of Pamnicken the escort troops—supported by local Nazis and members of the Gestapo from Königsberg—carried out a massacre among the surviving prisoners, in which around 200 people were killed. As far as one can tell, this murder was carried out on the initiative of the leader of the escort troops, who wanted to get rid of the prisoners so that they could get away more quickly from the advancing Red Army.[252]

At the end of the year the first railway transports carrying prisoners left Stutthof main camp, until Hoppe finally ordered the partial clearance of the camp on 25 January. Eleven columns, each of 1,000 prisoners, were formed, who marched on foot towards Lauenburg, 140 km away. Only around a third of the prisoners reached the town; when the Red Army reached Lauenburg in mid-March they found around 15,000 survivors of the death march from Stutthof.[253]

In the summer of 1944 the SS began moving about half of the prisoners from Auschwitz concentration camp—there were about 130,000 people there at the time—to other concentration camps.[254] The 'evacuation' of Auschwitz concentration camp, in which by then there were still 67,000 prisoners, began in mid-January 1945. Over 56,000 prisoners were driven westwards in marching columns of whom an estimated two-thirds were Jews. In accordance with an order from HSSPF Breslau, Heinrich Schmauser, that no prisoners were to fall into the hands of the enemy, the guards shot all prisoners who could not keep up with the marching pace. Given the terrible conditions on the marches, an estimated quarter of the prisoners fell victim to this practice. Some of the marching columns reached Groß-Rosen concentration camp in Lower Silesia, which became the transit camp for the camps and prisons cleared in the East.[255]

The Groß-Rosen concentration camp complex, which had numerous sub-camps, was cleared from January 1945 onwards, and the clearance of the completely overcrowded main camp began in February: it is demonstrable that 44,000 prisoners were moved on rail transports to concentration camps further to the west, an unknown figure dying on the way.[256]

As a result of the clearance of the camps in the East, there was now a large number of Jewish prisoners in the camps in the Reich. In Ravensbrück concentration camp the camp authorities had been preparing for the evacuation since January 1943—at this point 48,000 prisoners were crammed together in the camp—and systematically murdered the weak prisoners by leaving them to die in special death zones, giving prisoners injections of poison, shooting them, and finally, in January 1945, converting a wooden barrack into a provisional gas chamber, in which a total of several thousand prisoners were murdered.[257]

In March 1945 Himmler once again returned to the idea of using Jewish prisoners as hostages. In the middle of that month, during a visit to Germany by his personal doctor Felix Kersten, who had by now moved to Sweden and had contact with the Swedish foreign minister, he told Kersten—or so Kersten claimed—that the concentration camps would not be blown up as the Allies approached, further killing of the prisoners was forbidden, and the prisoners were instead to be handed over to the Allies.[258]

For a short time Himmler ordered the camp commandants not to kill any more Jewish prisoners, saying that they must combat death rates among the prisoners. The order was personally passed on to concentration camp commandants by Pohl.[259]

During his meeting with Himmler in March, Kersten informed his contact at the World Jewish Congress, Hillel Storch, that Himmler had also agreed to release 10,000 Jewish prisoners to Sweden or Switzerland.[260] And in fact large numbers of Jewish prisoners were able to reach Sweden. Since February Himmler had been in direct contact with the vice-president of the Swedish Red Cross, Count Folke Bernadotte, who was responsible for trying to secure the release of the Scandinavian concentration camp prisoners on behalf of the Swedish government. They were first brought together in Neuengamme concentration camp near Hamburg and finally Bernadotte managed to ensure that they were brought to Sweden by columns of Red Cross medical orderlies—the legendary 'white buses'—via Denmark to Sweden. Above all because of the sustained pressure from the Swedish government, but also possibly as the result of efforts by other parties,[261] far more than the 8,000 Scandinavian prisoners were saved in the end, namely more than 20,000 people, including several thousand Jews.[262]

However, contrary to Himmler's pledge, the camps of Dora-Mittelbau and Buchenwald—on the express orders of the Reichsführer SS—were not handed over to the Allies, but also cleared at the beginning of April. The SS managed to bring around 28,000 from a total of 48,000 prisoners in Buchenwald out of the camp, at least a third of whom had lost their lives by the end of the war.[263]

The camp of Bergen-Belsen with its 60,000 prisoners, around 90 per cent of them Jewish, was handed over to the British army by the SS on 15 April 1945. Food supplies in the camp had completely collapsed, and there had been an outbreak of typhus. Between January and the liberation of the camp, 35,000 prisoners had lost their lives, and a further 14,000 died in the first five days after the liberation.[264]

Also in mid-April, the department responsible for the concentration camps held one last conference in which—in accordance with Himmler's order—the evacuation of the last concentration camps not liberated by the Allies must have been discussed: these were Sachsenhausen, Dachau, Neuengamme, Flossenbürg, and Ravensbrück. In mid-April there is evidence that Himmler directly instructed Flossenbürg camp that no prisoners could fall alive into the hands of the enemy, an order that must also have applied to other camps. Over the next few days the SS leadership refused to comply with the requests from the International Red Cross and hand over the last camps.[265]

The last death marches went in two directions: the prisoners from the camps of Flossenbürg and Dachau marched southwards, those from Ravensbrück, Sachsenhausen, and Neuengamme northwards, according to the division of the still unoccupied Reich territory into two parts, which was still under way. The motives for these last violent marches are unclear: perhaps the objective was to deploy the prisoners as slave labourers in the construction of fortresses (for example, for a planned alpine fortress that was never realized), and another factor must have been the SS's intention to hand over as few prisoners as possible, but instead to take them along on the retreat for as long as possible, to be able to use them as hostages in last-minute negotiations.

On 19 April 25,000–30,000 prisoners set off on a march towards Dachau, which only some of the prisoners reached, while the remaining columns remained stuck in the chaos prevailing in Upper Bavaria.[266] Of the 32,000 Dachau prisoners more than 8,500 were driven towards Austria, and at least 1,000 died. On 2 May the guards left and the camp was liberated by American troops.[267]

In the overcrowded Mauthausen camp and its sub-camps, which held many Jewish prisoners, some 41,000 prisoners died in the first months of 1945 leading up to the camp's liberation in early May. In addition, around 2,000 people were murdered in the gas chambers of Mauthausen camp.[268]

The Sachsenhausen prisoners, 33,000 of them, were forced to march towards Schleswig-Holstein on 20 April, and from Ravensbrück 20,000 prisoners were also sent northwards towards Schleswig-Holstein on 18 and 24 April. In the chaos of collapse, however, the marching columns gradually dissolved, the guards disappeared, and the hour of the prisoners' liberation had arrived.[269]

The clearance of Neuengamme began on 19 April: 9,000 prisoners also had to march to Schleswig-Holstein. Prisoners deemed 'unfit to march' and 'sick' were murdered in the camp itself.[270]

Finally, on 25 April, the seaborne transport of the surviving 4,500 prisoners from Stutthof began. The ships travelled to Neustadt in the Bay of Lübeck, where the prisoners from Neuengamme had already been shipped in on three passenger boats, possibly a measure that had something to do with the release of prisoners to Sweden. Two of these ships were, however, set on fire by a British air attack, and most of the prisoners were killed, while those who were able to escape were killed on the beach, as were the Stutthof prisoners who were camped there, completely exhausted.

Estimates suggest that between a third and a half of the 714,000 and more people who were in the concentration camp system at the beginning of 1945 fell victim to the clearances.[271] Of the 714,000 prisoners at the beginning of 1945, some 200,000 were Jews; the number of Jewish victims in the final phase of the 'Third Reich' is estimated to be somewhere between 70,000 and 100,000. In that last phase there was no comprehensive and deliberate policy to murder all Jewish prisoners still held, and Himmler's negotiations did not lead to a consistent policy of sparing Jewish hostages. Rather, the last phase of the Holocaust, marked by the clearance of the concentration camps and the death marches, but also by the efforts—successful on a smaller scale—to release prisoners, shows that until the very last days of the war the fate of the European Jews under the SS terror regime depended on very contradictory decisions made at various levels of the SS hierarchy. This, once again, makes it clear that the murder of the European Jews was not an automatic programme of murder set in motion by a single order issued from behind a desk, but rather that the implementation of the general decision to practice systematic murder was repeatedly frustrated by different intentions and thus distracted and delayed. Accordingly, it becomes apparent that it took a vast amount of initiative and energy at all levels of the SS hierarchy actually to implement the systematic murder of the European Jews—and that the desire to destroy was still present through to the last days of the war.

The Nazi Regime's Policy Towards the Gypsies in the Second Half of the War: Parallels with and Differences from the 'Final Solution'

At the end of 1942 the Nazi regime proceeded to step up the persecution of the Gypsies in a decisive fashion. Up until this point the *Zigeunerpolitik* (policy towards the gypsies) had been marked by 'unsimultaneities and contradictions'.[272] The overview below should make this clear.

In the Netherlands the Gypsies, a group comprising only a few hundred people, had at first been subjected to certain residence restrictions and intensified police checks, and finally, in 1943, as part of the measures directed against the entire 'travelling' population, held at collection points. The measures against the equally small group of Gypsies in Belgium and northern France were limited to certain prohibitions and intensified control.[273]

As in the Netherlands and Belgium, in France the Gypsies, along with the rest of the non-sedentary population, had been driven out of the security zone by the Atlantic coast or the Channel. In October 1940 the military administration had ordered the construction of collection camps for Gypsies in the occupied northern zone. Several thousand people not following a settled way of life, Gypsies and others, ended up in these camps. In the unoccupied southern zone the prohibition on wandering, passed in April 1940, continued to be applied in principle.

In the occupied Soviet Union, in Poland and Serbia, Gypsies had already been murdered in their thousands in 1942. But the comparison with the persecution of the Jews shows the different degrees of intensity of the extermination policy: Gypsies tended to be killed in the wake of the 'actions' against the Jews, a policy of systematic and total murder of the Gypsies cannot be demonstrated in these three Eastern or South-Eastern European countries.

The regimes in the South-East European satellite states pursued their own 'Gypsy policy'. In May 1942 the Croatian Security Police ordered the arrest of all Gypsies, except those of the Muslim religion. The Gypsies were concentrated in the camp of Jasenovac; there those 'unfit for work' were literally slaughtered, while those 'fit for work', where they did not fall victim to the unimaginably terrible conditions of imprisonment, were also murdered in large numbers. The precise figure of victims is unknown, as are the numbers for the Gypsy population; the estimates for Jasenovac vary between 10,000 and 40,000, for the whole of Croatia between 25,000 and 50,000 dead.[274]

In Romania, where a Gypsy minority of around 300,000 people existed, in 1942 on the orders of the Romanian government between 20,000 and 26,000 Gypsies were deported to Transnistria. By far the greatest number of them died as a result of the devastating conditions there.[275]

In Slovakia Gypsies, like Jews, were excluded from citizenship in 1939 if they behaved in a socially maladjusted way, that is, if they did not belong to families following a settled way of life or in regular work. Measures introduced as early as 1941 for the arrest of Gypsies seem to have been pursued seriously only after the German intervention in the summer of 1944. After that point the German Einsatzgruppe H murdered Gypsies in larger numbers, possibly as many as 1,000 people.[276]

Under the rule of the Arrow Cross Party, many Roma were arrested in Hungary at the end of 1944 and deported to concentration camps in the Reich, where they were used as forced labourers.[277]

At the end of 1942, the SS and police apparatus came to the conclusion that, as far as the Gypsies living in Germany were concerned, henceforth distinctions were to be made between, on the one hand, the 'racially pure' Sinti and Lalleri (including the 'half-breeds' (*Mischlinge*) in those groups capable of assimilation) and, on the other, the Roma and other 'half-breeds', and that this second group was to be systematically murdered. The 'racially pure' Gypsies were to be taken to a 'reservation' in the General Government after the end of the war and there, pursuing their 'racially specific' way of life in isolation, be returned to their allegedly 'Aryan' roots. The remaining Gypsies, on the other hand, were to be deported to camps. On 16 December 1942, Himmler, after rebutting initial concerns on the part of Hitler and the Party Chancellery, issued the order that 'Gypsy half-breeds, Roma Gypsies, and members of Gypsy clans of Balkan origin not of German blood' be sent to concentration camps. This decision coincided directly with the preparation of the last major wave of Jewish deportation from the Reich, which the Nazi regime had plainly been preparing since December 1942, and the deportation of even non-Jewish prisoners in concentration camps also ordered by Himmler in December. In view of the mass recruitment of new foreign workers these intensified deportations did not seem to represent a notable risk for armaments production. Added to this was the fact that after the turning point in the war introduced by the Allied landing in North Africa, the Germans intensified *Judenpolitik* in various countries on the new 'southern front' (in France, Greece, and Bulgaria). This may have contributed to a general radicalization of the decision-making process and the accelerated implementation of further deportations.[278] 'Socially adjusted' Gypsies were not to be deported, although the criteria for this selection remain unclear.[279]

The deportation of the Gypsies involved the 'Greater German Reich', including the Protectorate and the district of Bialystok, Belgium, and the Netherlands. The first Gypsy transport from the Reich arrived in Auschwitz-Birkenau on 26 February 1943; by July 1944 around 23,000 people had been deported to the Gypsy camp (which was not segregated according to sex).[280]

From April 1944 those Gypsies still 'fit for work' were moved from Birkenau to concentration camps in the Reich, some 1,600 people in all. Of the other Gypsies deported to Birkenau around 6,000 were still alive in the spring of 1944. In May 1944 the camp authorities decided to liquidate the Gypsy camp in view of the immediately impending extermination action against the Hungarian Jews. After a first attempt in May had been defeated by the resistance of the camp inmates, on 2 and 3 August almost 300 Gypsies were murdered in the gas chambers in Auschwitz; only around 1,600 people, former soldiers and the relatives of soldiers, were spared.[281] Of the 22,600 people originally confined in the Gypsy camp 19,300 perished.

The sterilization of 'maladjusted' Gypsy half-breeds in the Reich was systematically undertaken by the Criminal Police in 1944. The written agreement of the victims was often forced with threats of deportation. Overall an estimated 2,000–2,500 Gypsies were sterilized.[282]

The figure for Gypsies murdered on racial grounds under German rule can no longer be established with any kind of precision. In Germany an estimated 15,000 people were killed as Gypsies or Gypsy half-breeds, in Austria around 8,000, and in Czechoslovakia around 35,000. In Belgium/northern France and the Netherlands it must have been several hundred people; in the occupied Soviet territories at least 10,000, possibly very many more, and in Poland around 8,000.[283]

These figures themselves show that the Roma were not persecuted with anything like the same intensity as the Jews. Neither did the persecution of the Gypsies include all the countries under German rule; after 1942 there were no deportations whose goal was the immediate murder of the deportees in extermination camps. On the other hand the persecution of the Gypsies reveals numerous parallels with the persecution of the Jews; the fate of the Gypsies makes it plain that *Judenpolitik* was part of a more widely based *Rassenpolitik*.

CONCLUSION

In this study we have made an attempt to interpret the decision-making process leading to the systematic murder of the Jews of Europe within the wider context of German *Judenpolitik*. As a result we have identified four distinct stages of escalation between the start of the war and the summer of 1942, in the course of which the Nazi leadership developed and set in motion a programme for the systematic murder of the European Jews. We have argued that the decisive turning point leading to the 'Final Solution' occurred as early as autumn 1939 and we have shown that the radicalization of *Judenpolitik* occurred within the context of a *Rassenpolitik*, but that no other group was persecuted with the same relentlessness and the same disastrous consequences as the Jews of Europe.

In the years between 1933 and 1939 *Judenpolitik* within the German Reich remained closely associated with the National Socialist seizure and maintenance of power. The 'de-jewification' (*Entjudung*) of German society, in the broader sense the implementation of a racist policy, provided the Nazis with the instrument for gradually penetrating the individual spheres of life in German society and subjecting them to their total claim to power. In the years between 1933 and 1939, not only did this key function of *Judenpolitik* become apparent, but it also became evident that a particular tactic for the phased implementation of the policy was being developed: the regime leadership set general goals and the subordinate organizations utilized the broad scope they were given for the exercise of considerable individual initiative and did so to a degree in competition with one another. But the frictions and tensions that arose could not disguise the fact that the goal of the expulsion of the Jews from German society was based on a broad consensus within the National Socialist movement. The initiation and radicalization of the persecution of the Jews cannot simply be traced back to a chain of decisions taken at the top of the Nazi regime; it would be more accurate to say that a new political field was constituted and developed, in which complex structures and autonomous dynamics then developed, without the leaders of the regime losing control of the overall process of *Judenpolitik*.

This policy was clearly exhausted with the November pogrom and the subsequent legal measures. After the German Jews had been reduced to the status of a plundered minority, completely stripped of its rights, even Nazi propaganda had difficulty evoking dangers that this completely powerless minority could have represented; it was barely possible to supply motives for further anti-Semitic 'actions'.

On the other hand, however, the Nazi regime had not managed to expel all the German Jews. Now it became apparent that, as a result of the plundering of the Jewish minority, a relatively large group of people had been left behind, which was no longer in a position to emigrate. With war on the horizon, the regime set about subjecting this group to total tyranny.

After the November pogrom the Nazi regime proceeded to declare the Jews to be hostages menaced by 'destruction' (*Vernichtung*). Remarkably, Hitler himself, in referring to extermination in his speech of 30 January 1939, did not speak of the German Jews but prophesied—expressly in the instance of a 'global war'—the 'destruction of the Jewish race in Europe'.

However, from the perspective of the National Socialists, the idea of extermination was not a tactically motivated threat but the logical consequence of the notion that dominated the whole of National Socialist policy, that the German people were engaged in a struggle against 'international Jewry' in which their very existence was at stake. The National Socialists saw war as the chance to realize their utopian ideas of an empire ordered along racist lines. From their point of view, war served to legitimate the idea of compensating for the loss of the 'racially valuable' by extirpating the racially 'inferior' in the interests of maintaining 'ethnic biological' equilibrium. It was the emergency of war that produced the opportunity for such an unparalleled break with the humanitarian tradition.

Even during the war against Poland, in mid-September 1939, the German leadership began seriously to address their plans for *Lebensraum* by developing a gigantic resettlement programme for the newly conquered territories. This programme involved the deportation of all Jews living in territory under German control to a 'Jewish reservation' in conquered Poland. These plans were actually set in motion with the so-called 'Nisko Action' in October 1939, but had to be suspended after a short time. In fact, however, the Nazi regime kept to the plan of a 'Jewish reservation' in the district of Lublin and repeated fitful attempts were made to achieve such a mass programme through small-scale deportations.

In fact the plan for a 'Jewish reservation' was aimed at concentrating the Jews from the whole of the German sphere of influence in an area which lacked adequate living conditions, and to cause the death of these more than two million people through undernourishment, epidemics, low birth rates, and so on, possibly over a period of several generations. Plainly such a long-term plan contained the potential to blackmail the Western powers that the leadership of the 'Third Reich' needed in order to construct a *Lebensraum* empire without being disturbed by outside intervention.

The plan for a reservation was thus an initial project for the 'final solution of the Jewish question', a long-term plan involving the deaths of the great majority of Jews living under the control of the Nazi regime. The radical nature of this project becomes fully clear when one views it within the context of the mass murders that the Nazi regime unleashed after the start of the war: the shootings of tens of thousands of Polish civilians (including thousands of Jews), as well as the 'euthanasia' programme, the murder of the sick and the disabled.

Over the next two years, the 'Jewish reservation' project was maintained (in modified form). After the victory over France, the regime concentrated on Madagascar, and early in 1941, as part of the preparations for 'Barbarossa', a plan was developed to deport the Jews under German rule to the territories in the East, which the Germans thought they were about to conquer. Common to all these plans was the prospect of the physical 'Final Solution', even if this was to extend over a long period of time.

Many historians have assumed that a fundamental decision to murder the Jews was taken sometime during the course of 1941 and that therefore one can clearly distinguish an early phase during which 'territorial' solutions were conceived from a later 'final solution phase'. However, this view fails to perceive what was at the core of the plans of National Socialist *Judenpolitik*: the 'territorial solution' was also always conceived as a 'final solution', because in the final analysis its goal was the annihilation of the vast majority of the Jews.

By autumn 1939, then, the point had already been reached at which those involved in *Judenpolitik* began to gear themselves up for the extermination of the European Jews. The measures taken by the regime from 1941 onwards were merely the concrete realization of the extermination already envisaged in 1939. There were only vague ideas of how and over what period of time this extermination was to occur in practice. The 'destruction of the Jewish race in Europe', threatened by Hitler on 30 January 1939, was initially an option, the realization of which was still dependent on certain conditions. From 1941 onwards, when the systematic destruction of the European Jews was actually realized, the idea of what was meant by 'Final Solution' was to be radicalized. General notions of annihilating the Jews within the German sphere of influence over the long term were now developed by the National Socialist leadership into a comprehensive programme of mass murder which was essentially to be implemented even before the end of the war. The abstract concept of 'destruction' (*Vernichtung*) or 'Final Solution' used by the perpetrators allowed them to develop their plans, which since 1939 had been geared towards the death of the European Jews, in stages towards this systematic murder programme. However, since 1939 extermination and 'Final Solution' had equated to millions of deaths.

This radicalization of the process leading to systematic mass murder occurred in the context of the expanding war. For the National Socialists, the racial war for *Lebensraum* included from the outset the prospect of exterminating what they had defined as the Jewish enemy, particularly when the war grew into a world war and the dream of a *Lebensraum* empire was thus endangered.

This link between war and extermination policy does not represent an inevitable automatism, and it would be wrong to imagine that a 'decision' to murder the European Jews was taken around the start of the war. The link was, in fact, the result of National Socialist policy. For the extermination process to be actually set in motion crucial preconditions had first to exist: the 'reservation' had to be definitely determined and established. So long as this had not occurred, extermination remained an intention that could also under certain circumstances be revoked.

In the summer of 1941 the extermination policy reached the second stage of its escalation with the murder of the Soviet Jews. While tens of thousands of Jewish men eligible for military service had been shot during the first few weeks of the war in Russia (and earlier in the mass executions in Poland), from the end of July, but more intensively from August, September, and October 1941, hundreds of thousands of men, women, and children were murdered. This transition from a terroristic modus operandi to a murderous 'ethnic cleansing' cannot be adequately explained by the elation of victory, nor by a change of mood provoked by the failure of the blitzkrieg strategy in autumn/winter 1941.

In fact, in the summer of 1941, the Germans began the 'New Order' (*Neuordnung*) of the conquered *Lebensraum*, precisely as originally planned without waiting for military victory. However, while the war continued the planned reordering of the 'Ostraum' had to be restricted to purely negative measures. The mass murder of the Soviet civilian population, that is those who stood at the lowest level of the Nazis' racist hierarchy, and in their distorted perception formed the chief supports of the Bolshevik system, was from the perspective of the National Socialist leadership an anticipation of the plans discussed before the start of the war, according to which millions of people on Soviet territory were to fall victim to the 'New Order' of the *Lebensraum*.

One factor that may have been crucial to the initiation of genocide in Soviet territory in late summer 1941, which had been planned since the beginning of the same year, was an initiative by Himmler, who wished, through his brutal treatment of the Jewish civilian population, to transfer his competencies as Reichskommissar for the Strengthening of the German Nation to the newly conquered territories, as was also finally sanctioned by Hitler. By ordering in July 1941 the inclusion of elderly men, women, and children in the campaign of extermination through shooting, Himmler was preparing the ground for the 'ethnic cleansing' that was intended to be carried out by the SS and was doing so even while the war was still going on and before the apparatus of the occupying administration could be consolidated. It is plain that in doing this Himmler was anticipating Hitler's intentions; Hitler himself had done everything he could to make sure even before the beginning of the invasion that this war would have the character of a campaign of racist extermination, and he was fully informed about the actions of the *Einsatzgruppen*.

This is not to say, however, that the gradual extension of the murders to the general Jewish civilian population can simply be seen as the result of an order from the Führer or an independent initiative on the part of Himmler which had been authorized by Hitler. The crucial point is that there was from the outset a consensus among the decision makers that the persecution of the Jews should be further and further radicalized in the further course of the war. On the basis of this consensus, general instructions in line with the intuition of the subordinates were issued in certain situations; in this way wider scope was given to independent initiatives. In the end the entire process was coordinated and standardized at the top. The leadership at the centre and the executive organizations on the periphery radicalized one another through a reciprocal process.

The third stage of escalation in the transition to the systematic extermination of the Jews occurred in the autumn of 1941. It consisted of two crucial decisions: on the one hand Hitler's decision made in mid-September 1941 to deport the Jews from the whole of the Reich including the Protectorate of Bohemia and Moravia, if possible that same year, to the incorporated Polish territories, and further eastwards the following spring. If the first step was originally seen as being the deportation of 60,000 Jews to the Lodz ghetto, this intention was soon modified and extended: now 25,000 Jews and Gypsies were to be deported to the ghettos of Riga and Minsk. We know that at this point a third wave of deportations was already planned for the start of the following year. Between September and November, with the marking of the German Jews, the general prohibition on emigration imposed upon Jews throughout the whole of the area under German control, and the withdrawal of citizenship and the remaining property of those deported from Germany, major administrative preparations for the deportation had also been made.

Thus, in September 1941, Hitler set in motion the plan, made early in 1941, to deport the European Jews to the territories of the Soviet Union that were soon to be conquered, although without waiting for the victory over the Red Army. The fact that, although the war was not going to plan, Hitler insisted on the implementation of the final variant of the reservation plan that had been pursued since 1939—with its genocidal consequences—seems to be more significant for the analysis of the decision-making process than any additional factors (the issue of accommodation, repression because of the deportations of the Volga Germans, etc.), which, from the point of view of the Nazi leadership, argued in favour of the instigation of the deportations in autumn 1941. As with the Nisko and Madagascar plans, the Nazi leadership clearly associated the idea of 'hostage-taking' with the first deportations. The United States were to be dissuaded from entering the war through the more or less open threat to liquidate the deported Jews, entirely in the spirit of Hitler's prophecy of 30 January 1939.

The decision that Hitler made in autumn 1941 gradually to deport the Jews under German rule to the East was linked to a second momentous decision (but one which cannot be reconstructed in detail), namely to carry out the mass murder of the indigenous Jews in the provisional reception areas. Now areas 'free of Jews' were also to be created in the occupied Polish territories, as they had been in the Soviet Union since the end of the summer. With the prospect of sending tens of thousands of Central European Jews to the already completely overcrowded ghettos, more radical solutions were demanded of the local authorities.

Reichsstathalter Greiser himself had proposed that the indigenous Jewish population in the Warthegau should be 'reduced' by 100,000 'in compensation for' the reception of Jews from the Reich in Lodz, that is these people were to be killed with gas vans. Further large-scale massacres were carried out until the end of 1941 among the local Jewish population in the other sites destined to receive Jews from the Reich, namely the ghettos of Minsk and Riga. When Einsatzkommando 2 began shooting thousands of Jews deported from the Reich immediately after their arrival in Riga or Kovno (Kaunas), the murder of the Reich German Jews was suspended by a direct intervention from Himmler. Thus, a distinction was still being made between the Eastern European and Central European Jews.

In the General Government too, particularly in the district of Lublin, preparations for a mass murder of the local Jewish population began in October 1941. Previously, the government of the General Government had been informed that they could not expect to deport any more Jews eastwards from that territory for the foreseeable future. In October preparations began for the construction of the first extermination camp at Belzec, and at, the same time, with the so-called 'Schiessbefehl' (order to shoot on sight) the death penalty was introduced for leaving the ghetto. The goal of these measures was to murder the Jewish population that were 'unfit to work', initially in the district of Lublin. These plans may also have applied to the district of Galicia, which had only been part of the General Government since 1 August and where, like the *Einsatzgruppen* in the other occupied territories, the Security Police had been carrying out similar massacres among the Jewish civilian population since October. References to the construction of an extermination camp in Lemberg (Lvov) are significant in this context. However, the construction of an extermination camp in Belzec (and possible plans for Lemberg) cannot be seen as specifically intended for the murder of the entire Jewish population of the General Government. The occupying forces initially concentrated on making preparations for those Jews who were 'unfit for work' in the district of Lublin, where a third wave of deportations was expected the following spring. Thus, in autumn 1941 the murder of hundreds of thousands of people had been planned, but not yet of millions. As far as the fate of the remaining Polish and other European Jews was concerned, the older plan of a mass deportation to the Soviet Union (with ultimately genocidal consequences) had not yet been abandoned. At any rate a dynamic of mass murder had now been set in motion, which could only have been halted by a radical change of direction in the regime's *Judenpolitik*.

In the autumn/winter of 1941 facilities for killing with gas were established not only in Belzec (and possibly in Lemberg) as they had been in Chelmno. Further possible locations have been identified through plans for the installation of such facilities in Riga, and corresponding references to Mogilev (not far from Minsk). There is also the offer that Himmler made to the Slovakian head of state on 20 October, to deport Slovakian Jews to a particularly remote area of the General Government, possibly the basis for the construction of the second extermination camp at Sobibor. The use of gas as a means of killing had thus initially begun in the planned deportation zones. Parallel with this we should consider the events in Serbia, where the Wehrmacht began systematically shooting Jewish men and Gypsies in October. In November the military administration in France also began deliberately to direct their retaliatory measures against Jews, who were to be transported to the East as hostages. In October, November, and December threatening statements by National Socialists also accumulated concerning the deadly fate that awaited the Jews.

As confusing as the overall picture may seem at first sight, it does become clear that, within the space of a few weeks in autumn 1941, German organizations in various occupied territories began to react with remarkable similarity to the new situation in *Judenpolitik* created by Hitler's September decision to deport the German and Czech Jews, by organizing mass shootings (Galicia, Serbia), deploying gas vans (Warthegau) or preparing the construction of extermination camps (district of Lublin, Auschwitz, Riga, possibly Mogilev-Belarus).

If we see these activities in context, it becomes irrefutably clear that the German power holders on the 'periphery' were always acting in the context of an overall policy guided by the 'centre', meaning Hitler and the SS leadership. The centre was always in a position to prevent an escalation of a policy which it found undesirable, as is demonstrated for example by Himmler putting a halt to the murders of Reich German Jews in the Ostland in late November 1941.

However, the centre was only able to guide this process and set it in motion because it knew that impulses issuing from the centre were picked up with great independent initiative by the authorities in the 'periphery'. Just as the extension of the shootings to women and children in the Soviet Union from the summer of 1941 onwards was not simply ordered, the extension of the mass murders to particular regions of occupied Europe in autumn 1941 also required a very complicated interaction between the centre and the executive organizations, involving orders and guidelines from the centre, as well as independent initiatives and intuition on the part of the regional power holders, which were finally channelled and coordinated by the centre, albeit at a much higher level of radicalization.

The Wannsee Conference of 20 January 1942 provides an important insight into the RSHA's policy of consolidating the various approaches for an extension of the murders and thereby designing a comprehensive programme for the impending 'Final Solution'. While, on the one hand, the Germans continued to adhere to the old programme of deporting all Jews to the occupied Eastern territories after the end of the war, they were already engaging with the new prospect of implementing ever larger stages of the 'Final Solution' even during the war, although the murder method was not yet entirely clear. The idea of a gigantic forced labour programme developed by Heydrich, with deadly consequences for those affected, may well in fact have reflected ideas actually held within the RSHA.

From the autumn of 1941 the SS had also developed the perfidious system of 'extermination through work'. Within this system, not only were many people worked to death in a very short time, but it also meant that a hurdle had been erected that those people who were no longer fit for work, or who were not capable of being deployed, were unable to surmount. The perfidious nature of the system of 'extermination through work' was also particularly apparent where there were only a few forced labour projects for Jews, or none at all, as it provided a pretext for marking out those Jews who were 'non-deployable' as 'superfluous'. Jewish 'work deployment' formed an important complementary element in the early phase of the 'Final Solution'.

In the first months of 1942, the deportations were extended in accordance with the declarations of intent made at the Wannsee Conference. In March 1942 Eichmann announced a third wave of deportations involving a total of 55,000 people from the territory of the 'Greater German Reich'. This third wave actually began on 20 March 1942 and lasted until the end of June. Its destination was ghettos in the district of Lublin, the original 'Jewish reservation'.

Now, at the beginning of March 1942, a decision must again have been made to practice mass murder in the reception zone, in the district of Lublin. This decision also applied to the adjacent district of Galicia. In the eyes of the Nazi leadership Galicia represented something like an advance base for the planned New Order of *Lebensraum* in the East and, since the autumn of the previous year, had been already the scene of large-scale mass shootings.

The statement in Goebbels's diaries that the intention was to murder 60 per cent of the Jews living in the two districts is particularly important here. The decision to implement mass murder in the two districts, made early in March, had been prepared since October 1941 by SSPF Globocnik, who was responsible for this mass murder in both districts. The measures taken in the district of Lublin demonstrate important parallels with the mass murder of the Jews in the Warthe-gau, which was also introduced in autumn 1941, although unlike Greiser Globoc-nik used stationary gas chambers. As in the Warthegau, and as in Riga and Minsk, the mass murder of the indigenous Jews in the district of Lublin was directly linked to the deportations from the Reich.

With the start of the third wave of deportations to the district of Lublin and the completion of the first extermination camp in the General Government the option of a later resettlement to the East had been definitively abandoned. Most of the people deported to the district of Lublin died miserably in the ghettos after a short time, or were also deported to extermination camps. However the façade of a programme of resettlement and work deployment was maintained. During this third wave of deportations, which occurred between March and June, the RSHA prepared a Europe-wide deportation programme conceived on a much larger scale.

Between 25 March 1942 and the end of June, 50,000 Jews were deported from Slovakia to Auschwitz concentration camp on the basis of the agreements with the Slovakian government. The deportation of hostages from France to Auschwitz also began in March 1942.

It is clear from a remark by Heydrich to Tuka on 10 April that these first deportations from territories outside the 'Greater German Reich' were already part of a Europe-wide programme. According to this, it was planned initially to deport to the East half a million Jews from Slovakia, the Reich, the Protectorate, The Netherlands, Belgium, and France.

This introduced the fourth stage of escalation in the transition to the 'Final Solution'. Now, in spring 1942, the previous scheme for the deportation of Central European Jews to particular areas in which the indigenous Jews had first been murdered was abandoned. In late April/early May the decision must evidently have been made henceforth to murder Jews indiscriminately.

It can be assumed that in late April or May the Nazi regime made the decision to extend the mass murder of the Jews, which was already in progress in the districts of Lublin and Galicia, to the whole of the General Government. At the same time, the decision must have been made to implement a mass murder among the Jews of annexed Upper Silesia. The systematic mass murder of the Jews in the General Government began in June, but was then interrupted for a few weeks because of the transport ban. The transport ban, introduced because of the offensive in the East, finally had a radicalizing effect on the extermination policy: it accelerated the deportations from the Western territories, and, during this period, the planners of the mass murder clearly had an opportunity to rethink and consolidate their ideas so that the overall programme could resume in July with much more devastating effect. It was during this phase that the SS took over Jewish forced labour in the General Government and thus maintained control over those prisoners who were 'fit for work' and so initially excluded from extermination.

At around the same time as this fundamental decision regarding the Jews in the General Government, at any rate before mid-May, significant decisions must have been made as a result of which the operation of the extermination machinery was further extended. On the one hand, it was decided that the deportations from the territory of the 'Greater German Reich' should be intensified beyond the quota set in March, and on the other the regime now set about murdering either all or almost all of the Jews deported from Central Europe when the transports arrived at their destinations in Eastern Europe. This happened to Jews deported from the Reich in Minsk from mid-May, and from early June in Sobibor to the Jews deported from Slovakia.

It can be assumed that on 17 April 1942 Himmler had already ordered the murder of over 10,000 Central European Jews still living in the Lodz ghetto, who had been deported there in October 1941 and survived the inhuman conditions in the ghetto.

With these decisions, probably made in the second half of April or early May, which came into effect in May/June, the Nazi regime definitively abandoned the idea of a 'reservation' in the eastern area of the General Government or the occupied Eastern territories which had increasingly become a fiction given the mass murder that was already under way. The link between this renewed escalation of the extermination policy and military developments, in other words the preparations for the summer offensive in the East, is just as apparent as the fact that, in view of the mass recruitment of workers from the occupied Soviet Union, in the spring of 1942 the Nazis believed they would soon be able to do without Jewish forced labourers.

At the beginning of June a concrete programme of deportations was established for the West, which according to the plan was to be realized within three months beginning in mid-July. This meant that the 'European' plans first discernible in early April were to be continued and adapted to the conditions set by the transport ban in June/July. In June 1942, however, Himmler went a step further and called for the rapid and complete deportation of all Jews from France.

The transports from Western Europe and—because of the transport ban—also those from Slovakia were now directed to Auschwitz. There, from early June, the great majority of deportees (as before in Minsk and Sobibor) fell victim to the new and more radical variation of the extermination policy: immediately after their arrival they were killed with poison gas, after a 'selection' had taken place on the railway ramp.

In May 1942 the mass murder of the Soviet Jews, which had begun in the summer of 1941, received a new impulse: the murders now resumed on a large scale, before ending in the summer of 1942 in the complete extermination of the indigenous Jewish population.

After the lifting of the transport ban in July 1942, the deportation and murder programme was fully operational, and we know that Himmler insisted on convincing himself of the functioning of the extermination programme by paying an inspection visit. At the end of that inspection, on 19 July he issued the order that the 'resettlement' of the entire Jewish population of the General Government was to finish at the end of 1942.

During the summer of 1942 the first preparations were made to organize larger numbers of deportations from the West and the South-East of those parts of Europe under the control of the 'Third Reich'.

This acceleration and radicalization of the extermination programme in spring and summer 1942 clearly reflected the decision of the Nazi leadership essentially to implement the intended 'Final Solution' during the war. After the USA entered the war the 'Third Reich' faced the necessity of waging a long-term war on several fronts, and this new situation also necessarily altered the status of the systematic mass murder of the Jews. With the extension of this last and most radical stage of *Judenpolitik* to all the territories under German control, the entire German sphere of influence was subjected to the hegemony of racism. The occupied and allied states were drawn into the 'New Order policy' and, for better or worse bound to the German leadership by their participation in an unparalleled crime. The extermination policy thus came to underpin the German policy of occupation and alliance. This central function of the mass murder of the Jews for the maintenance of German rule on the continent also serves to explain the great efforts made by the Nazi leadership to involve more and more countries in the extermination programme by the end of the war.

During the second half of the war *Judenpolitik*—along with efforts to provide political military and police security for the territory under German rule, and alongside the issues of economic and food policy—became a major axis of German occupation and alliance policy. The more the war advanced, the greater the significance that the systematic murder of the Jews assumed, from the point of view of the National Socialist leadership, for the cohesion of the German power block. Because the executive organizations of the mass murders—whether they were German occupying administrations, local auxiliaries, governments willing to collaborate, or allies—were made henchmen and accomplices of the extermination policy, and bound to the engine of that policy, the leadership of Nazi Germany. The altered and more important role given to *Judenpolitik* provides a significant explanation for the fact that the murder of millions in the second half of the war was not only continued but even extended.

During the war something that we have already been able to observe in Germany during the 1930s was repeated on a European scale. Just as it had been impossible to implement a racist policy in a 'positive' way within the German Reich, during the war the Nazi regime was in no position to introduce its planned racist 'reorganization' of Europe through constructive measures. All the measures taken in this direction either failed pitifully or laid bare the absurdity of National Socialist ideas of race.

If the National Socialists did not wish to abandon their aspiration to start the racist reorganization of the European continent even during the war, they were obliged to undertake concrete measures in anticipation of their racist utopia in a negative way. The *Entjudung* of the German sphere of influence—because of the inconsistency and lack of feasibility of a 'positive' racial policy—became the substitute for the unrealizable racial 'New Order'.

There was an additional effect that we have also been able to observe since 1933 with regard to *Judenpolitik* in Germany: the further radicalization of the persecution reinforced the power of the SS and the radical Party forces within the occupying administrations and finally led to an overall gain in importance for these forces within the Nazi system of rule. The total implementation of the *Judenpolitik* within the entire German territory was thus tantamount to the definitive realization of National Socialism's total claim to power. However, from the perspective of the National Socialists, *Judenpolitik* was far more than a mere instrument for the extension of their power: they saw its radical implementation as a matter of their own survival.

Even though all the major decisions concerning the National Socialist Europe-wide 'Final Solution' programme had been made by mid-1942, in the time remaining until the end of the war it turned out that the implementation of the mass murders, because of the central role occupied by the *Judenpolitik* within Germany's occupation and alliance policy, made great additional demands on the Nazi leadership. *Judenpolitik* was not a programme that ran automatically, but a series of systematically organized mass murders that could only be implemented if the National Socialist regime created the appropriate preconditions.

It is possible to identify three further periods during the second half of the war in which the Nazi regime further escalated its *Judenpolitik*: the phase between the Allied landing in North Africa and the Warsaw ghetto uprising, hence the months November 1942 to May 1943, that is the period during which the Axis powers lost the military initiative; autumn 1943, when Italy left the alliance and the German Reich occupied further territories previously controlled by Fascist Italy; finally, the period from spring to summer 1944, during which the German Reich occupied Hungary and Slovakia.

As a consequence of the Allied landing in North Africa which, from the point of view of the German leadership, threatened the whole southern flank of Europe, the Jews of Tunisia and France had found themselves directly in the clutches of the German persecutors, while at the beginning of 1943 the RSHA organized mass deportations in Greece and Bulgaria. The further military successes of the Western Allies, but above all the Warsaw ghetto uprising in April/May 1943, led to a further burst of radicalization of *Judenpolitik*, which can be demonstrated by the intensification of the persecution in Poland, in the occupied Soviet territories, in the Netherlands, in Belgium, in France, in Croatia, and in Slovakia.

After Italy's departure from the Axis alliance *Judenpolitik* was extended to Italian territory under German control as well as to the former Italian zones of occupation in Croatia, Greece, and France. That same period coincides with the attempt to deport the Danish Jews, which can be seen as Germany's reaction to growing resistance in that country.

With the occupation of Hungary and Slovakia and the deportation of the Jews living in those countries, in 1944 the Third Reich attempted to prevent both states leaving their alliance with Germany.

It became apparent, however, that, after the turning point of the war in the winter of 1942/3, it became increasingly difficult to implement the deportations in participation with governments allied or collaborating with Germany. They succeeded in Croatia, to a limited extent in Bulgaria and France; efforts with regard to Hungary and the Italian-occupied territories remained initially ineffective; Romania and Slovakia, which had originally been enthusiastic participants in German *Judenpolitik*, now changed their attitude. However, the Germans did not abandon their policy, since precisely in view of the deteriorating military situation they saw the intensification of the persecution of the Jews and the related compromising of their 'partners' as an important means of securing the German-ruled block.

It was particularly important here that the three states which successfully resisted German *Judenpolitik* during this phase—Italy, Romania, and Bulgaria—managed to leave the alliance with Germany between September 1943 and September 1944 through separate ceasefires. This departure of what Germany saw as its 'philo-Semitic' allies must have looked like confirmation of their policy not to compromise in any way on *Judenpolitik*.

If *Judenpolitik* had originally been one of the chief axes of German occupation and alliance policy, it now entered a phase in which it began to destroy Germany's policy of collaboration and alliance. *Judenpolitik* could only be implemented if a regime of terror was installed in countries where it was completely under the control of the Nazis, and it could only be implemented with the support of indigenous forces.

This policy was to prove horribly efficient in Hungary and Slovakia. It was initially adopted in France and northern Italy, but finally foundered on a lack of support from local forces. All regimes that became collaborators with German *Judenpolitik* in the second half of the war collapsed with the Third Reich: the Vichy regime, the Republic of Salò, the Arrow-Cross regime in Hungary, and the clerical-fascist Slovakian Republic.

The example of Denmark shows that *Judenpolitik* was not feasible without the conditions described: a regime dependent on Germany and support from local forces. The alternative, implementing the deportations with the help of German forces, foundered on a lack of staff resources and the fact that such an action would have destroyed the political basis of the German occupation policy in Denmark.

As far as the mass murders in territories directly under German control were concerned, it has become clear that *Judenpolitik* produced a particularly high percentage of victims in those areas in which a civilian administration was preparing the construction of a 'Greater German Reich' with the support of the

SS. This applies to the Reich, including the annexed territories, the Protectorate, Bohemia and Moravia, Poland and the occupied Soviet territories, but particularly also to the Netherlands. The Jews living there only had a chance of survival if they managed to escape before the start of the murders; there were also limited possibilities of surviving by going into hiding, which increased towards the end of the war. But the numbers of victims were also very high in two territories which were controlled by a military administration and were not the target of a Germanization policy: in Greece and Serbia. In Belgium there was a German military administration and the country was also the target of German ideas of Germanization; but the percentage of Jewish victims was—if compared with the Netherlands—considerably lower, which may be down to the lower pressure of persecution, the sluggish Belgian authorities, the more cautious behaviour of the victims, and the helpfulness of the Belgian population. Norway was also considered a 'Germanic' country, and ruled by a civilian administration, but more than half of the small Jewish minority managed to escape the deportations in the autumn of 1942.

This brief survey of the fate of the Jews in the countries occupied by and allied with Germany shows once again that the German persecution of the Jews proceeded in very different ways in the individual territories within the German sphere of influence in the second half of the war. A large number of factors affected *Judenpolitik*, which for these reasons could be accelerated, slowed down, modified, and suspended. It was, among other things, because of this flexibility, the ability to adapt to rapidly changing conditions, that the persecution of the European Jews by the Nazi regime produced such terrible results.

Notes

Introduction

1. Among the most important contributions to Holocaust research by the intentionalists were: Helmut Krausnick, 'The Persecution of the Jews', in Hans Buchheim et al., *Anatomy of the SS-State* (London, 1968), 1–124; Gerald Fleming, *Hitler and the Final Solution* (London 1984); and Andreas Hillgruber, 'Die ideologisch-dogmatische Grundlage der nationalsozialistische Politik der Ausrottung der Juden in den besetzten Gebieten der Sowjetunion und ihre Durchführung, 1941–1944', *German Studies Review* 2 (1979), 263–96. See also Lucy Dawidowicz, *The War against the Jews 1933–1945* (London, 1975). For brief discussions of the intentionalist/functionalist debate as it related to the Holocaust see the chapter on the Holocaust in Ian Kershaw, *The Nazi Dictatorship: Problems and Perspectives of Interpretation*, 4th edn (London, 2000); and the chapters 'Hitler and the Third Reich' and 'The Decision-Making Process', in Dan Stone, ed., *The Historiography of the Holocaust* (London, 2004).

2. Helmut Krausnick, the leading representative of the intentionalists, worked on the assumption that a decision by Hitler on the 'Final Solution' had been made in conjunction with the decision to commit genocide on the European Jews, which he placed in spring 1941. See Krausnick, 'The Persecution of the Jews', 59 ff. A similar position is taken by Hermann Graml, who assumes that Himmler and Heydrich had learned of Hitler's intention to murder the European Jews in the first half of June 1941. See Hermann Graml, *Reichskristallnacht. Antisemitismus und Judenverfolgung im Dritten Reich* (Munich, 1988), 222–3. In *Der Holocaust* (Munich, 1995), 50 ff., Wolfgang Benz sees the 'genesis of the final solution' as early as the time of the Madagascar Plan. More recently the idea of an early decision has been revisited by Richard Breitman who, working against the tide of current research, dates a decision by Hitler and Himmler at the beginning of 1941. See Richard Breitman, *The Architect of Genocide: Himmler and the Final Solution* (London, 1991), 146 ff.

3. Uwe Adam, *Die Judenpolitik im Dritten Reich* (Düsseldorf, 1972), 312, places the timing of the decision between September and November 1941 as a 'way out' of a 'dead-end situation' for everyone since, although the German leadership had begun deporting the Jews from Germany, the original intention of 'moving the deportees into the conquered areas of Russia' could not be realized because of the stage the war was at. Philippe Burrin favoured dating the decision to murder the European Jews between the middle of September and October: he emphasized its link to the critical military

situation. See Philippe Burrin, *Hitler and the Jews: The Genesis of the Holocaust* (London, 1994), 115 ff. Christopher Browning had also placed the decision in the same period, although in contrast to Burrin he regarded the victory over Russia that the Nazis felt was imminent as a decisive factor. Browning has always stressed the close connection between the decision to murder the European Jews and the decision to murder all the Soviet Jews in July 1941, as in his latest contribution to the topic in *The Origins of the Final Solution: The Evolution of Nazi Jewish Policy 1939–1942* (London, 2004), 426–7. In this excellent work he has differentiated his position still further and here argues that in mid-September (in connection with the start of deportations) Hitler decided in principle to murder the deportees and that by the end of October the course had been set. In arguing in this manner, Browning is closer to the idea of a process of decision-making seen as a fluid continuum (see pp. 532 ff.). Götz Aly has also indicated a preference for seeing the early part of October as the critical period in which 'an official decision may have been made'. See Götz Aly, *'Final Solution': Nazi Population Policy and the Murder of the European Jews* (London, 1999), 231.

4. See Wolfgang Scheffler, *Judenverfolgung im Dritten Reich, 1933–1945* (Berlin, 1960).

5. See Martin Broszat, 'Hitler and the Genesis of the "Final Solution": An Assessment of David Irving's Theses', in H. W. Koch, ed., *Aspects of the Third Reich* (Basingstoke, 1985), 390–429, 405. This develops the hypothesis that the annihilation of the Jews developed 'not only as a prior will to destruction but also as a "way out" of a cul-de-sac that they had manoeuvred themselves into'. He goes on to argue that 'once it had been begun and institutionalized, the practice of liquidation nonetheless took over and in the end de facto turned into an all-encompassing "programme" '. Hans Mommsen makes a similar point in 'The Realization of the Unthinkable: The "Final Solution of the Jewish Question" in the Third Reich', in Hans Mommsen, ed., *From Weimar to Auschwitz: Essays in German History* (Cambridge, 1991), 224–53, 251. He establishes beyond dispute that 'it could be categorically denied that Hitler initiated the policy of genocide in the form of a direct "order from the Führer" (*Führerweisung*)' (p. 417). In his polemic against the intentionalist school of thought Mommsen advocated the view 'that Hitler virtually hid behind the annihilation process that was already underway', in Eberhard Jäckel and Jürgen Rohwer, eds, *Der Mord an den Juden im Zweiten Weltkrieg. Entschlußbildung und Verwirklichung* (Stuttgart, 1985), 66.

6. See Saul Friedländer, 'Vom Antisemitismus zur Judenvernichtung: Eine historiographische Studie zur nationalsozialistischen Judenpolitik und Versuch einer Interpretation', in Jäckel and Rohwer, *Der Mord*, 18–62 (p. 47); and Raul Hilberg, 'Die Aktion Reinhard', ibid. 125–36.

7. Christian Gerlach, 'The Wannsee Conference, the Fate of the German Jews, and Hitler's Decision in Principle to Exterminate All European Jews', *Journal of Modern History* 70 (1998), 759–812. A similar view had already been taken by the Dutch historian L. H. Hartog, *Der Befehl zum Judenmord. Hitler, Amerika und die Juden* (Bodenheim, 1997).

8. Robert Gellately, *The Gestapo and German Society: Enforcing Racial Policy 1933–1945* (Oxford, 1990); Michael Wildt, ed., *Die Judenpolitik des SD, 1935 bis 1938. Eine Dokumentation* (Munich, 1995); Gerhard Paul and Klaus Michael Mallmann, eds, *Die Gestapo. Mythos und Realität* (Darmstadt, 1995); Jens Banach, *Heydrichs Elite. Das Führerkorps der Sicherheitspolizei und des SD, 1936–1945* (Paderborn, 1998); Gerhard Paul and Klaus

Michael Mallmann, eds, *Die Gestapo im Zweiten Weltkrieg* (Darmstadt, 2000); Holger Berschel, *Bürokratie und Terror. Das Judenreferat der Gestapo Düsseldorf, 1935–1945* (Essen, 2001); Erik Arthur Johnson, *The Nazi Terror: Gestapo, Jews and Ordinary Germans* (London, 1999); Michael Wildt, *Generation des Unbedingten. Das Führungskorps des Reichssicherheitshauptamtes* (Hamburg, 2002); Michael Wildt, ed., *Nachrichtendienst, politische Elite und Mordeinheit. Der Sicherheitsdienst des Reichsführers SS* (Hamburg, 2003).

9. Ulrich Herbert, Karin Orth, and Christoph Dieckmann, eds, *Die nationalsozialistischen Konzentrationslager. Entwicklung und Struktur*, 2 vols (Göttingen, 1998); Robert Jan van Pelt and Deborah Dwork, *Auschwitz: 1270 to the Present* (New Haven, 1996); Karin Orth, *Das System der nationalsozialistischen Konzentrationslager. Eine politische Organisationsgeschichte* (Hamburg, 1999); Michael Thad Allen, *The Business of Genocide: The SS, Slave Labor and the Concentration Camps* (Chapel Hill, NC, 2002).

10. Hans Safrian, *Die Eichmann-Männer* (Vienna, 1993), in paperback as *Eichmann und seine Gehilfen* (Frankfurt a. M., 1995); Wolfgang Scheffler and Diana Schulle, eds, *Buch der Erinnerung. Die ins Baltikum deportierten deutschen, österreichischen und tschechoslowakischen Juden*, 2 vols (Munich, 2003); essays in Birthe Kundrus and Beate Meyer, eds, *Die Deportation der Juden aus Deutschland. Pläne—Praxis—Reaktionen 1938–1945* (Göttingen, 2004); Alfred Ottwaldt and Diana Schulle, *Die 'Judendeportationen' aus dem Deutschen Reich 1941–1945. Eine kommentierte Chronologie* (Wiesbaden, 2005).

11. Ralf Ogorreck, *Die Einsatzgruppen und die 'Genesis der Endlösung'* (Berlin, 1996); Peter Klein, ed., *Die Einsatzgruppen in der besetzten Sowjetunion 1941/42. Die Tätigkeits- und Lageberichte des Chefs der Sicherheitspolizei und des SD* (Berlin, 1997); Martin Cüppers, *Wegbereiter der Shoah. Die Waffen-SS, der Kommandostab Reichsführer-SS und die Judenvernichtung 1939–1945* (Darmstadt, 2005).

12. Christian Gerlach, *Kalkulierte Morde. Die deutsche Wirtschafts- und Vernichtungspolitik in Weißrußland, 1941 bis 1944* (Hamburg, 1999); Christian Gerlach, *Krieg, Ernährung, Völkermord. Forschungen zur deutschen Vernichtungspolitik im Zweiten Weltkrieg* (Hamburg, 1998); Bernhard Chiari, *Alltag hinter der Front. Besatzung, Kollaboration und Widerstand in Weißrußland, 1941–1944* (Düsseldorf, 1998); Dieter Pohl, 'Schauplatz Ukraine. Der Massenmord an den Juden im Militärverwaltungsgebiet und im Reichskommissariat 1941–1943', in Norbert Frei, Sybille Steinbacher, and Bernd C. Wagner, eds, *Ausbeutung, Vernichtung, Öffentlichkeit. Neue Studien zur nationalsozialistischen Lagerpolitik* (Munich, 2000); Wendy Lower, *Nazi Empire Building and the Holocaust in Ukraine* (Chapel Hill, NC, 2005); Andrej Angrick, *Besatzungspolitik und Massenmord. Die Einsatzgruppen in der südlichen Sowjetunion 1941–1943* (Hamburg, 2003); Andrew Ezergailis, *The Holocaust in Latvia, 1941–1944: The Missing Center* (Riga and Washington, 1996); Andrej Angrick and Peter Klein, *Die 'Endlösung' in Riga. Ausbeutung und Vernichtung, 1941–1944* (Darmstadt, 2006); Thomas Sandkühler, *Die 'Endlösung' in Galizien. Der Judenmord in Ostpolen und die Rettungsinitiative von Berthold Beitz, 1941–1944* (Bonn, 1996); Dieter Pohl, *Nationalsozialistische Judenverfolgung in Ostgalizien, 1941–1944. Organisation und Durchführung eines staatlichen Massenverbrechens* (Munich, 1997); Dieter Pohl, *Von der 'Judenpolitik' zum 'Judenmord'. Der Distrikt Lublin des Generalgouvernements 1939–1944* (Frankfurt a. M., 1993); Bogdan Musial,

Deutsche Zivilverwaltung und Judenverfolgung im Generalgouvernement. Eine Fallstudie zum Distrikt Lublin, 1939–1944 (Wiesbaden, 1999); Michael Mallmann and Bogdan Musial, eds, *Genesis des Genozids. Polen 1939–1941* (Darmstadt, 2004); Bogdan Musial, ed., *'Aktion Reinhardt'. Der Völkermord an den Juden im Generalgouvernement, 1941–1944* (Osnabrück, 2004); Sybille Steinbacher, *'Musterstadt' Auschwitz. Germanisierungspolitik und Judenmord in Oberschlesien* (Munich, 2000); Michael Alberti, *Die Verfolgung und Vernichtung der Juden im Reichsgau Wartheland, 1939–1945* (Wiesbaden, 2006); Götz Aly and Christian Gerlach, *Realpolitik, Ideologie und der Mord an den ungarischen Juden 1944/1945* (Stuttgart and Munich, 2002). Vincas Bartusevicius, Joachim Tauber, and Wolfram Wette, eds, *Holocaust in Litauen. Krieg, Judenmorde, und Kollaboration* (Cologne, 2003); Peter Klein, *Die Ghettoverwaltung Litzmannstadt 1940 bis 1944. Eine Dienstelle in Spannungsfeld von Kommunalburokratia und staatlicher Verfolgungspolitik* (Hamburg, 2009). Christoph Dieckmann is preparing to publish his Ph.D. on the Holocaust in Lithuania; he is also the author of 'Der Krieg und die Ermordung der litauischen Juden', in Ulrich Herbert, ed., *Nationalsozialistische Vernichtungspolitik 1939–1945. Neue Forschungen und Kontroversen* (Frankfurt a. M., 1998), 293–329.

13. See especially vols v and ix of the *Beiträge zur nationalsozialistischen Gesundheits- und Sozialpolitik: Sozialpolitik und Judenvernichtung. Gibt es eine Ökonomie der Endlösung?* (Berlin, 1987); *Bevölkerungsstruktur und Massenmord. Neue Dokumente zur deutschen Politik der Jahre 1938–1945* (Berlin, 1991); Götz Aly and Susanne Heim, *Architects of Annihilation: Auschwitz and the Logic of Destruction* (London, 2002).

14. Aly, *'Final Solution'*.

15. Jan Erik Schulte, *Zwangsarbeit und Vernichtung: Das Wirtschaftsimperium der SS. Oswald Pohl und das SS-Wirtschafts-Verwaltungshauptamt, 1933–1945* (Paderborn, 2001).

16. See essays by Aly and Gerlach in Wolfgang Dressen, ed., *Betrifft: 'Aktion 3'. Deutsche verwerten jüdische Nachbarn. Dokumente zur Arisierung* (Berlin, 1998); Frank Bajohr, *'Arisierung' in Hamburg. Die Verdrängung der jüdischen Unternehmer 1933–45* (Hamburg, 1997), 331 ff. See Gerhard Botz's earlier study *Wohnungspolitik und Judendeportation in Wien 1938 bis 1945. Zur Funktion des Antisemitismus als Ersatz nationalsozialistischer Sozialpolitik* (Vienna and Salzburg, 1975).

17. Wendy Lower, ' "Anticipational Obedience" and the Nazi Implementation of the Holocaust in the Ukraine: A Case Study of Central and Peripheral Forces in the Generalbezirk Zhytomyr, 1941–1944', *HGS* 16 (2002), 1–22.

18. See Browning, *Ordinary Men: Reserve Police Battalion 101 and the Final Solution in Poland* (New York, 1992); and Daniel J. Goldhagen, *Hitler's Willing Executioners: Ordinary Germans and the Holocaust* (London, 1996). On the debate between these two authors see in particular their contributions to the volume edited by Michael Berenbaum and Abraham J. Peck, *The Holocaust and History: The Known, the Unknown, the Disputed, and the Reexamined* (Bloomington and Indianapolis, 1998). On the Goldhagen debate in Germany and the USA, see Franklin H. Littell, ed., *Hyping the Holocaust: Scholars Answer Goldhagen* (Merion Station, 1997); Johannes Heil and Rainer Erb, eds, *Geschichtswissenschaft und Öffentlichkeit. Der Streit um Daniel J. Goldhagen* (Frankfurt a. M., 1998); Robert R. Shandley, ed., *Unwilling Germans?*

The Goldhagen Debate (Minneapolis, 1998); Geoff Ely, ed., *The 'Goldhagen Effect': History, Memory, Nazism—Facing the German Past* (Ann Arbor, 2000).

19. In this context see Gerhard Paul's highly polemical work, which focuses on the deficits of the structuralist school in particular using the most recent research on perpetrators: 'Von Psychopathen, Technokraten des Terrors und "ganz gewöhnlichen Deutschen". Die Täter der Shoah im Spiegel der Forschung', in Gerhard Paul, ed., *Die Täter der Shoah. Fanatische Nationalsozialisten oder ganz gewöhnliche Deutsche* (Göttingen, 2002), 13–80.

20. That this movement to advance beyond one-dimensional explanations has in fact long been in train can be shown using three straightforward examples: Ulrich Herbert showed in his Best biography of 1996 that when implementing racist policy there was no contradiction for the perpetrators between their overall world-view and the logic of a given individual situation (see Ulrich Herbert, *Best. Biographische Studien über Radikalismus, Weltanschauung und Vernunft, 1903-1989* (Bonn, 1996)). Gerhard Paul rightly renounces any attempt to try to create a homogeneous image of the perpetrators and shows that Nazi perpetrators came from a range of different social milieus, had highly diverse educational backgrounds, and belonged to several different generations (see Paul, 'Psychopathen'). The social psychologist Harald Welzer has demonstrated that when analysing the behaviour of mass murderers historians have hitherto only very sporadically made use of explanations available in the work of sociologists (see Harald Welzer, *Täter. Wie aus ganz normalen Menschen Massenmörder wurden* (Frankfurt a. M., 2005)).

21. This is the subject of my book *'Davon haben wir nichts gewusst'. Die Deutschen und die Judenverfolgung, 1933-1945* (Munich, 2006).

Historical Background: Anti-Semitism in the Weimar Republic

1. On anti-Semitism in Imperial Germany, see for example: Richard S. Levy, *The Downfall of the Anti-Semitic Political Parties in Imperial Germany* (New Haven and London, 1975); Werner Mosse and Arnold Paucker, eds, *Juden im Wilhelminischen Deutschland, 1890-1914* (Tübingen, 1976); Werner Jochmann, *Gesellschaftskrise und Judenfeindschaft in Deutschland, 1870-1945* (Hamburg, 1988); Peter Pulzer, *Jews and the German State* (Oxford, 1992); Michael A. Meyer, ed., with Michael Brenner, *German-Jewish History in Modern Times*, 4 vols (New York and Chichester, 1996–8), vol. iii: Steven M. Löwenstein et al., *Integration in Dispute, 1871-1918*; Peter Alter, Claus-Ekkehard Bärsch, Peter Berghoff, et al., *Die Konstruktion der Nation gegen die Juden* (Munich, 1999); Shulamit Volkov, *Antisemitismus als kultureller Code. Zehn Essays*, 2nd edn (Munich, 2000).

2. On anti-Semitism in the First World War, see Jochmann, *Gesellschaftskrise*, and Werner Angress, 'The German Army's "Judenzaehlung" of 1916: Genesis—Consequences—Significance', in *LBIY* 23 (1978), 117–37.

3. See James N. Retallack, *Notables of the Right: The Conservative Party and Political Mobilisation in Germany 1876-1918* (London, 1988).

4. On anti-Semitism in the Weimar Republic, see Arnold Paucker, *Der jüdische Abwehrkampf gegen Antisemitismus und Nationalsozialismus in den letzten Jahren der Weimarer*

Republik (Hamburg, 1968); Dirk Walter, *Antisemitische Kriminalität und Gewalt. Judenfeindschaft in der Weimarer Republik* (Bonn, 1999); Michael Wildt, *Volksgemeinschaft als Selbstermächtigung. Gewalt gegen Juden in der deutschen Provinz 1919 bis 1939* (Hamburg, 2007), 69 ff.

5. On nationalism in the Weimar Republic, see: Ernst von Salomon, *Der Fragebogen* (Hamburg, 1951); Kurt Sontheimer, *Antidemokratisches Denken in der Weimarer Republik* (Munich, 1962); Klemens von Klemperer, *Germany's New Conservatism: Its History and Dilemma in the Twentieth Century* (Princeton, 1968); Heide Gerstenberger, *Der revolutionäre Konservatismus. Ein Beitrag zur Analyse des Liberalismus* (Berlin, 1969); Marjrjatta Hietala, *Der neue Nationalismus in der Publizistik Ernst Jüngers und des Kreises um ihn* (Helsinki, 1975); Klaus Fritzsche, *Politische Romantik und Gegenrevolution. Fluchtweg in der Krise der bürgerlichen Gesellschaft: Das Beispiel des 'Tat'-Kreises* (Frankafurt a. M., 1976); Joachim Petzold, *Wegbereiter des deutschen Faschismus. Die Jungkonservativen in der Weimarer Republik* (Cologne, 1983); Yuji Ishida, *Jungkonservative in der Weimarer Republik. Der Ring-Kreis 1928–1933* (Frankfurt, 1988); Jost Hermand, *Old Dreams of a New Reich: Volkish Utopias and National Socialism* (Bloomington, 1992). In *Ordnungen der Ungleichheit—die deutsche Rechte im Widerstreit ihrer Idee 1871–1945* (Darmstadt, 2001), 79 ff., Stefan Breuer shows how after 1848 liberal and conservative camps came to an agreement over the concept of state nationalism (*Staatsnation*) and distanced themselves from ethnically based concepts of the state.

6. On the German notion of the people (*das Volk*) see above all Reinhard Koselleck, 'Volk, Nation', in Otto Brunner, Werner Conze, Reinhard Koselleck, eds, *Geschichliche Grundbegriffe. Historisches Lexikon zur politischen und sozialen Sprache in Deutschland*, vol. vii (Stuttgart, 1992), 141–431. See also Peter Fritzsche, *Germans into Nazis* (Cambridge, Mass., 1998).

7. On the pre-1918 *völkisch* movement see Uwe Puschner, *Die völkische Bewegung im wilhelminischen Kaiserreich. Sprache, Rasse, Religion* (Darmstadt, 2001).

8. Daniel Frymann [Heinrich Class], *Wenn ich der Kaiser wär—Politische Wahrheiten und Notwendigkeiten* (Leipzig, 1912).

9. See Walter, *Antisemitische Kriminalität*, 27 ff. and Wildt, *Volksgemeinschaft*.

10. On the history of the League's foundation, see Uwe Lohalm, *Völkischer Radikalismus. Die Geschichte des Deutschvölkischen Schutz- und Trutz-Bundes, 1919–1923* (Hamburg, 1970), 19 ff.

11. On its structure and mode of operation, see Lohalm, *Völkischer Radikalismus*, 78 ff.

12. See ibid. 194 ff.

13. Exclusion from state citizenship (nos. 4,5), exclusion from public office (no. 8) and from the press (no. 23). Cited from J. Noakes and G. Pridham, eds, *Nazism 1919–1945*, vol. i: *The Rise to Power 1919–1934* (Exeter, 1998), 14–16.

14. See also the collection of Hitler's speeches in Eberhard Jäckel, ed., *Adolf Hitler, Sämtliche Aufzeichnungen, 1905–1924* (Stuttgart, 1980).

15. See Walter, *Antisemitische Kriminalität*, 41 ff. and Werner Liebe, *Die Deutschnationale Volkspartei 1918–1924* (Düsseldorf, 1956).

16. See Jan Striesow, *Die Deutschnationale Volkspartei und die Völkisch-Radikalen, 1918–1922*, 2 vols (Frankfurt a. M., 1981), ii. 282 ff.

17. *Deutschvölkisches Jahrbuch* 2 (1921), 125 ff. (compiled by Alfred Roth).

18. On the Jungdeutscher Orden see Klaus Hornung, *Der Jungdeutsche Orden* (Düsseldorf, 1958).

19. On this see the official organ of the Order, *Der Jungdeutsche*, in particular the issues of 5 Apr. 1924 (Mahraun on Young Germans and Jews); 27 Jan. 1926 (a speech given by Mahraun on 25 Jan.) and 12 June 1926 (an editorial on the 'Jewish question').

20. See the article 'Deutschvölkischer Schutz- und Trutzbund', in Dieter Fricke, ed., *Lexikon zur Parteiengeschichte. Die bürgerlichen und kleinbürgerlichen Parteien und Verbände in Deutschland (1789–1945)* (Cologne, 1983–6), ii. 562 ff.

21. See the article 'Alldeutscher Verband' in the *Lexikon zur Parteiengeschichte*, i. 13 ff.

22. See the article 'Tannenbergbund' in the *Lexikon zur Parteiengeschichte*, iv. 180 ff.

23. See the article 'Bund Wiking' in the *Lexikon zur Parteiengeschichte*, i. 368 ff.

24. See the article 'Deutscher Wehrverein' in the *Lexikon zur Parteiengeschichte*, ii. 330 ff.

25. See the article 'Deutschbund' in the *Lexikon zur Parteiengeschichte*, i. 517 ff.

26. See the *völkisch* organizations listed in n. 17 and M. R. Gerstenhauer, *Der völkische Gedanke in Vergangenheit und Zukunft. Aus der Geschichte der völkischen Bewegung* (Leipzig, 1933).

27. *Völkischer Beobachter* (*VB*), 26 Feb. 1925.

28. Eberhard Jäckel, *Hitlers Weltanschauung: A Blueprint for Power* (Middletown, Conn., 1992), continues to be the major study of this subject.

29. *Abwehrblätter* 36/11–12 (1926), 67.

30. *Verhandlungen des Deutschen Reichstags*, vol. 408, doc. 2232 (28 Apr. 1926).

31. *Verhandlungen des Deutschen Reichstags*, vol. 409, doc. 2486.

32. *CV-Zeitung*, 20 Mar. 1928; *Abwehrblätter* 38/7–8 (1928), 54.

33. *Verhandlungen des Deutschen Reichstags*, vol. 394, doc. 12462 (27 Jan. 1928).

34. *Verhandlungen des Deutschen Reichstags*, vol. 395, docs 13717–18 f. (24 Mar. 1928).

35. *Verhandlungen des Deutschen Reichstags*, vol. 440, doc. 1741, Law for the Protection of the Geman Nation (12 Mar. 1930).

36. *Verhandlungen des Deutschen Reichstags*, vol. 425, doc. 2978 (26 June 1930).

37. *Abwehrblätter*, 40/1–2 (1930), 16, citing the *Ostdeutscher Beobachter*, 2/2.

38. See Oded Heilbronner, 'The Role of Antisemitism in the Nazi Party's Activity and Propaganda: A Regional Historiographical Study', in *LBYB* 35 (1999), 397–439.

39. See e.g. Richard Bessel, *Political Violence and the Rise of Nazism: The Stormtroopers of Eastern Germany 1925–1934* (New Haven, 1984), 89.

40. Gerhard Paul, *Aufstand der Bilder. Die NS-Propaganda vor 1933* (Bonn, 1990), ill. 47.

41. This technique has been analysed by Dietz Bering, *Kampf um Namen. Bernhard Weiss gegen Joseph Goebbels* (Stuttgart, 1991) using the example of National Socialist propaganda against the Deputy President of the Berlin Police, Bernhard Weiss: in order to brand him as Jewish the Nazis gave him the first name 'Isidor'.

42. Paul, *Aufstand*, 236 ff.

43. Constantin Goschler, ed., *Hitler. Reden, Schriften, Anordnungen. Februar 1925 bis Januar 1933*, vol. iv: *Von der Reichstagswahl bis zur Reichspräsidentenwahl Oktober 1930—März 1932. Teil 1. Oktober 1930—Juni 1931* (Munich, 1994), doc. 8, p. 22.

44. Hitler, *Reden*, iv/1, doc. 29, p. 110 (speech in Bielefeld, 16 Nov. 1930), 106 ff.; ibid., doc. 96 (speech in Kaiserslautern 26 Apr. 1931), 305 ff.; Christian Hartmann, ed., *Hitler*

Reden, iv/2, doc. 67 (speech in Gießen, 9 Nov. 1931), 185 ff.; ibid., doc. 70 (speech in Darmstadt, 13 Nov. 1931), 193 ff.; Christian Hartmann, ed., *Hitler. Reden*, iv/3, doc. 4 (speech in Lemgo, 8 Jan. 1932), 18 ff.

45. Ibid. iv/1, doc. 97, p. 371 (speech at the National Socialist rally in Munich, 29 Aug. 1930).
46. Ibid. iv/1, doc. 14, p. 31 (speech in Munich, 25 Oct. 1930).
47. *CV-Zeitung*, 20 Feb. 1931.
48. *Die Stellung der Nationalsozialistischen Deutschen Arbeiterpartei (NSDAP) zur Judenfrage. Eine Materialsammlung vorgelegt vom Centralverein deutscher Staatsbürger jüdischen Glaubens E.V* (Berlin, 1932).
49. Collection of relevant quotations in the *CV-Zeitung*, 11 Dec. 1931.
50. See e.g. the article 'German Frankfurt supports Adolf Hitler. 70,000 at the third Meeting of the Day', in *VB*, no. 212, 30 July 1932.
51. Documented in *Friedhofsschändungen in Deutschland, 1930–1932. Dokumente der politischen und kulturellen Verwilderung unserer Zeit*, compiled by the Central-Verein, 6th edn (Berlin, 1932). The *CV-Zeitung* continually documented the destruction of Jewish cemeteries.
52. There is a large body of documentation on this in the CV archive.
53. *CV-Zeitung* 18 Sept. and 25 Sept. 1930.
54. *CV-Zeitung*, 5 Aug. and 12 Aug. 1932.
55. *VB*, 1 Apr. 1932, 'Two Jews violate and slaughter a young German girl'.
56. *CV-Zeitung*, 12 Dec. 1930.
57. The Herrenclub was an elite Berlin club for nobles and leading industrialists and officials.
58. *CV-Zeitung*, 4 Nov. 1932; Paul, *Aufstand*, ill. 78.
59. *Deutsches Recht*, I (1933), 53–63 and 96–105; cf. Adam, *Judenpolitik*, 30.
60. Alfred Wiener, 'Programmerfüllung oder Agitation. Was würde eine Hitler Mehrheit tun?', *CV-Zeitung*, 24 June 1932.
61. *CV-Zeitung*, 11 Dec. 1931.
62. *CV-Zeitung*, 24 June 1932.
63. Ibid.
64. *CV-Zeitung*, 9 Dec. 1932.
65. See Lewis Hertzman, *DNVP: Right-Wing Opposition in the Weimar Republic 1918–1924* (Lincoln, Nebr., 1963), 162–3.
66. See John A. Leopold, *Alfred Hugenberg: The Radical Nationalist Campaign against the Weimar Republic* (New Haven, 1977); Heidrun Holzbach, *Das 'System Hugenberg'. Die Organisation bürgerlicher Sammlungspolitk vor dem Aufstieg der NSDAP* (Stuttgart, 1981); and Friedrich Freiherr von Gaertringen, 'Die Deutschnationale Volkspartei', in Erich Matthias and Rudolf Morsey, eds, *Das Ende der Parteien: 1933* (Düsseldorf, 1960), 544 ff.
67. See Volker Berghahn, *Der Stahlhelm. Bund der Frontsoldaten 1918–1933* (Düsseldorf, 1966).
68. Hans Reif, 'Antisemitismus in den Agrarverbänden Ostelbiens in der Weimarer Republik', in idem, ed., *Ostelbische Agrargesellschaft im Kaiserreich und in der Weimarer Republik. Agrarkrise-junkerliche Interessenpolitik-Modernisierungsstrategien* (Berlin, 1994).

69. Iris Hamel, *Völkischer Verband und nationale Gewerkschaft. Der Deutschnationale Handlungsgehilfenverband 1893–1933* (Frankfurt a. M., 1967) and the article 'Deutschnationaler Handlungsgehilfenverband', in *Lexikon zur Parteiengeschichte*, ii. 457–75.

70. See Helmuth Zebhauser, *Alpinismus im Hitlerstaat. Gedanken, Erinnerungen, Dokumente* (Munich, 1998), 70 ff.; Alfred M. Müller, 'Geschichte des Deutschen und Österreichischen Alpenvereins. Ein Beitrag zur Sozialgeschichte des Verbandswesens', Ph.D. thesis (Münster, 1979). See also *Abwehrblätter*, vol. 35 (1925), part 1/2, pp. 2–3; part 4/6, p. 22; part 7/8; part 11/12, pp. 51–2 and vol. 38 (1928), part 1/2, pp. 8–9.

71. *Abwehrblätter*, 35/11–12 (1925), 51–2; 36/1–2 (1926), p. 1.

72. See Jürgen Schwarz, *Studenten in der Weimarer Republik; Die deutsche Studentenschaft in der Zeit von 1918–1923 und ihre Stellung zur Politik* (Berlin, 1971); Helma Brunck, *Die Deutsche Burschenschaft in der Weimarer Republik und im Nationalsozialismus* (Munich, 2000); Ulrich Herbert, ' "Generation der Sachlichkeit". Die völkische Studentenbewegung der frühen zwanziger Jahre in Deutschland in Frank Bajohr', in Werner Johe and Uwe Lohalm, eds, *Zivilisation und Barbarei. Die Widersprüchlichen Potentiale der Moderne* (Hamburg, 1991), 115–44; Michael H. Kater, *Studentenschaft und Rechtsradikalismus in Deutschland* (Hamburg, 1975) and the articles entitled 'Deutscher Hochschulring' and 'Deutsche Studentenschaft' in the *Lexikon zur bürgerlicher Parteien*, ii. 116–27 and i. 367 ff.

73. Schwarz, *Studenten*, p. 260.

74. Ibid.

75. Kater, *Studentenschaft*, 146–7.

76. On this see ibid. 153 ff.; Brunck, *Burschenschaft*, pp. 212 ff.

77. Kurt Nowak, *Evangelische Kirche und Weimarer Republik. Zum politischen Weg des deutschen Protestantismus zwischen 1918 und 1932* (Göttingen, 1981), 247 ff. Founder members of this group had published a programmatic pamphlet entitled 'German Christianity on a purely evangelical basis' in Leipzig in 1917.

78. Ibid. 253 ff.; Klaus Scholder, *Die Kirchen und das Dritte Reich*, i: *Vorgeschichte und Zeit der Illusionen 1918–1934* (Frankfurt a. M., 1977), 239 ff.

79. See Scholder, *Kirchen*, 124 ff; Manfred Gailus, *Protestantismus und Nationalsozialismus. Studien zur nationalsozialistischen Durchdringung des protestantischen Sozialmileus in Berlin* (Cologne, 2001); Marikja Smid, *Deutscher Protestantismus und Judentum 1932/1933* (Munich, 1990); and Jonathan R. C. Wright, '*Above Parties': The Political Attitudes of the German Protestant Church Leadership 1918–1933* (Oxford, 1974).

80. Scholder, *Kirchen*, 142.

81. Hermann Greive, *Theologie und Ideologie. Katholizismus und Judentum in Deutschland und Österreich, 1918–1935* (Heidelberg, 1969), 43 ff., 100 ff., and 127 ff.; Olaf Blaschke, *Katholizismus und Antisemitismus im Deutschen Kaiserreich* (Göttingen, 1997).

82. Greive, *Theologie*, 129 ff.

83. On Stapel see Heinrich Kessler, *Wilhelm Stapel als politische Publizist* (Nuremberg, 1967); Gerstenberger, *Der revolutionäre Konservatismus*, pp. 79–95; and Hamel, 'Völkischer Verband'.

84. On Jünger, see Hans-Peter Schwartz, *Der konservative Anarchist. Politik und Zeitkritik Ernst Jüngers* (Freiburg, 1962); Hietala, *Der neue Nationalismus*; and Ernst Jünger,

'Über Nationalismus und Judenfrage', *Süddeutsche Monatshefte* (Sept. 1930), 843–5 (here p. 845).

85. See e.g. 7 Feb. 1930, 9 May 1930, 19 Dec. 1930, 2 Dec. 1930, 16 Jan. 1931, 29 May 1931, 25 Dec. 1931, 11 Mar. 1932, 8 July 1932, 9 Sept. 1932, 28 Oct. 1932, 4 Nov. 1932, 2 Dec. 1932, 16 Dec. 1932, 14 Jan. 1933.

86. Examples for boycott calls in the National Socialist Party press can be seen in the pamphlet published by the Centralverein on the attitude of the NSDAP to the 'Jewish question' and in the CV's archives: OS, 721-1-2548 and 2549.

87. On this see Heinrich Uhlig, *Die Warenhäuser im Dritten Reich* (Cologne, 1956), 31 ff. On the technique of the boycott campaign before 1933 see e.g. the well-documented case of Osnabrück, where National Socialists and another radical right-wing group used this means from 1928 onwards: Peter Junk and Martina Sellmeyer, *Stationen auf dem Weg nach Auschwitz. Entrechtung, Vertreibung, Vernichtung. Juden in Osnabrück 1900–1945* (Osnabrück, 1988), 35 ff. Other local examples can be found in Ingrid Buchloh, *Die nationalsozialistische Machtergreifung in Duisburg. Eine Fallstudie* (Duisburg, 1980), 137; and Helmut Genschel, *Die Verdrängung der Juden aus der Wirtschaft in Dritten Reiches* (Berlin 1966), 97 (Hanover) and for Karlsruhe in Manfred Koch, 'Die Weimarer Republik: Juden zwischen Integration und Ausgrenzung', in Heinz Schmitt, ed., *Juden in Karlsruhe. Beiträge zu ihrer Geschichte bis zur nationalsozialistischen Machtergreifung* (Karlsruhe, 1990), 155–88 (p. 161).

88. There is a collection of materials in Bundesarchiv Berlin (BAB, 15.01, 13859); see also Uhlig, *Warenhäuser*, 67 ff.

89. *CV-Zeitung*, 2 Sept. 1932, refers to the report of the *Völkischer Beobachter*, 195, p. 3. The *CV-Zeitung* also cited the Nazi Thuringian Minister Marschler, who announced at a conference for small businesses that a government decree was being prepared that would ban civil servants from using Jewish shops and department stores: *CV-Zeitung*, 2 Dec. 1932.

90. OS, 721-1-2474.

91. *CV-Zeitung*, 30 July 1926, 9 Mar. 1928, 29 June 1928.

92. For details see Jacob Borut, 'Antisemitism in Tourist Facilities in Weimar Germany', *YVS*, 28 (2000), 7–50; Michael Wildt, ' "Der muß hinaus! Der muß hinaus!" Antisemitismus in deutschen Nord- und Ostseebädern 1920–1935', *Mittelweg 36*, 10/4 (2001–2), 3–25; Frank Bajohr, *'Unser Hotel ist judenfrei'. Bäder-Antisemitismus im 19. und 20. Jahrhundert* (Frankfurt a. M., 2003).

93. *Abwehrblätter*, 36/1–2 (1926), 1 ff.

94. In 1932 the DNVP imposed the 'Aryan clause' with particular rigour and also excluded 'half-Jews'. The Party leader justified this attitude as necessary in order not to give the National Socialists cause for 'violent agitation'; these policies were in any case not religiously motivated but derived from 'national political' concerns (BAB, R 8005, Nagel to the Landesverband Pommern, 23 Mar. 1932 and to A.R., 17 Dec. 1932). The national headquarters of the Stahlhelm informed the local organizations on 2 January 1931 that they should not accept any 'comrades linked with the Jewish tribe' (i.e. those married to Jewish women). The memo was triggered by a query from a local Stahlhelm committee which feared that NSDAP members in the organization might take offence at the presence of such people (BAB, R 72/273).

95. On the collapse of the Liberal parties see, above all, Larry E. Jones, *German Liberalism and the Dissolution of the Weimar Party System 1918–1933* (Chapel Hill, NC, 1988).
96. On the SPD and anti-Semitism see Lars Fischer, *The Socialist Response to Antisemitism in Imperial Germany* (Cambridge, 2007); and Andrew G. Bonnell, 'Was German Social Democracy before 1914 Antisemitic?', *German History* 27/2 (2009), 259–69.

1. The Displacement of the Jews from Public Life, 1933–1934

1. Examples in Heinrich August Winkler, *Der lange Weg nach Westen. Deutsche Geschichte vom Ende des alten Reichs bis zum Untergang der Weimarer Republik* (Munich, 2000), 878–9; Edgar Mais, ed., *Die Verfolgung der Juden in den Landkreisen Bad Kreuznach und Birkenfeld, 1933–1945* (Bad Kreuznach, 1988), 168; Ulrich Föhse, 'Erst Mensch dann Untermensch. Der Weg der jüdischen Wuppertaler in den Holocaust', in Klaus Goebel, ed., *Wuppertal in der Zeit des nationalsozialismus* (Wuppertal, 1984), 65–80; Marion A. Caplan, *Between Dignity and Despair: Jewish Life in Nazi Germany*, (New York, 1998), 18 ff.
2. These acts of violence were picked up by press reports in the weeks after 30 Jan. 1933: *CV-Zeitung*, 16 Feb. 1933; *Vossiche Zeitung (VZ)*, 2 Mar. 1933. Violence towards Jews in this phase has been demonstrated with impressive force by Buchloh in her detailed study of events in Duisburg (*Machergreifung*). See n. 5 below.
3. On the National Socialists' seizure of power, see Karl Dietrich Bracher, Wolfgang Sauer, and Gerhard Schulz, *Die nationalsozialistische Machtergreifung. Studien zur Errichtung des totalitären Herrschaftsystems in Deutschland* (Cologne and Opladen, 1960); Winkler, *Der lange Weg*; Gotthard Jasper, *Die gescheiterte Zähmung. Wege zur Machtergreifung Hitlers 1930–1934* (Frankfurt a. M., 1986).
4. On the first wave of anti-Semitism, see Uwe Adam, *Judenpolitik im Dritten Reich* (Düsseldorf, 1972), 46 ff.; Avraham Barkai, *Vom Boykott zu 'Entjudung'. Der wirtschaftliche Existenzkampf der Juden im Dritten Reich 1933–1943* (Frankfurt a. M., 1988), 23 ff.; Saul Friedländer, *Nazi Germany and the Jews: The Years of Persecution 1933–39* (New York and London, 1997), 9 ff.; Helmut Genschel, *Die Verdrängung der Juden aus der Wirtschaft im Dritten Reich* (Göttingen, 1966), 43 ff.; Kurt Pätzold, *Faschismus, Rassenwahn, Judenverfolgung. Eine Studie zur politischen Strategie und Taktik des faschistischen deutschen Imperialismus, 1933–1935* (Berlin, 1975), 13 ff.; Günther Plum, 'Wirtschaft und Erwerbsleben', in Wolfgang Benz, ed., *Die Juden in Deutschland. 1933–1945. Leben unter nationalistischer Herrschaft* (Munich, 1988), 268 ff.; Heinrich Uhlig, *Die Warenhäuser im Dritten Reich* (Cologne, 1966), 71 ff.; Leni Yahil, *Die Shoah. Überlebenskampf und Vernichtung der europäischen Juden* (Munich, 1998), 101 ff.
5. See the reports of the *VZ* and the *Frankfurter Zeitung (FZ)* from 7 to 14 Mar. 1933 and *The Times*, 11 to 18 Mar. 1933. On the beginning of this wave of anti-Semitism in the Ruhr district, see *Jüdischer Rundschau*, 10 Mar; Ingrid Buchloh, *Die nationalsozialistische Machtergreifung in Duisburg. Eine Fallstudie* (Duisburg, 1980), 136; Bundesarchiv Berlin (BAB), 15.01, 13859, Report of the Chamber of Industry and Trade for Essen, Mühlheim and Oberhausen to Reich Ministry of Economics (RWM) for 8 March, and telegrams from the German Industry and Trade Meeting of 10 March. Further details are available in regional studies.

6. *VZ*, 11 Mar. 1933.

7. BAB, 15.01, 13859, published in the *VZ* on 13 March and the *VB* on 14 March.

8. Uhlig, *Warenhäuser*, 209; *Documents on German Foreign Policy*, 2nd series, V, 14 ff., telegrams from Rumbold to Vansittart, 26 March and 2 April; *Foreign Relations of the United States, Diplomatic Papers* 1933, II, pp. 323 ff., Report by the General Consulate in Berlin, 21 Mar. 1933.

9. Stephan Schurr, 'Die "Judenaktion" in Creglingen on 25 March 1933', in Gerhard Naser, ed., *Lebenswege Creglinger Juden. Das Pogrom von 1933. Der schwierige Umgang mit der Vergangenheit* (Eppe, 2000).

10. See Lothar Gruchmann, *Justiz im Dritten Reich 1933–1940. Anpassung und Unterwerfung in der Ära Gürtner* (Munich, 1988), 124 ff.

11. *VZ* and *FZ*, 12 and 13 Mar. 1933. On 10 March *The Times* began to devote a daily article to events in Germany, in which attention was drawn to violent acts. See in particular the issues of 11–18 March. See also Horst Göppinger, *Die Verfolgung der Juristen jüdischer Abstammung durch den Nationalsozialismus* (Villingen and Schwarzwald, 1963), 21–2; Tillmann Krach, *Jüdische Rechtsanwälte in Preußen. Über die Bedeutung der freien Advokatur und ihre Zerstörung durch den Nationalsozialismus* (Munich, 1991), 172 ff.

12. Krach, *Rechtsanwälte*, 181 ff.

13. Gruchmann, *Justiz*, 126 ff.

14. On the boycott see Michael Wildt, *Volksgemeinschaft als Selbstermächtigung. Gewalt gegen Juden in der deutschen Provinz 1919 bis 1939* (Hamburg, 2007), 115 ff.

15. See Pätzold, *Faschismus*, 66; for complaints about these interventions, see BAB, R 43II/397 and 1195, and 01, 15514.

16. Elke Fröhlich, ed., *Die Tagebücher von Joseph Goebbels Teil I: Aufzeichnungen 1923–1941*. Band 2/III *Oktober 1932–März 1934*, ed. Angela Hermann, 27 to 31 March 1933 (Munich, 1987–2005), 156 ff. On the preparations for the boycott, see Barkai, *Boykott*, 26 ff.

17. *VB*, 29 Mar. 1933.

18. Karl-Heinz Minuth, ed., *Akten der Reichskanzlei. Die Regierung Hitler*, i/1 (Boppard a.Rh., 1983), 272.

19. *VZ*, 28, 29, and 30 Mar. 1933; further details in Peter Longerich, *Politik der Vernichtung. Eine Gesamtdarstellung der nationalsozialistischen Judenverfolgung* (Munich, 1998), 36.

20. *FZ*, 1 Apr. 1933.

21. *VZ* and *FZ* for 1 and 2 Apr. 1933. On the course of the boycott and the reaction of the population, see Pätzold, *Faschismus*, 74 ff.; Ian Kershaw, *Popular Opinion and Political Dissent in the Third Reich, Bavaria 1933–1945* (Oxford, 1983; 2nd edn, 2008), 231–2; David Bankier, *Die öffentliche Meinung im NS-Staat. Die 'Endlösung' und die Deutschen. Eine Berichtigung* (Berlin, 1995), 85 ff.; Longerich, *Politik*, 34 ff.; FRUS 1933, II, 344 ff. (telephone call to the US State Department, 1 April); *The Times*, 3 Apr. 1933; Hannes Ziegler, 'Der 1. April 1933 im Spiegel der Berichterstattung und Kommentierung der katholischen Presse in der Pfalz', in Alfred Hans Kuby, ed. *Juden in der Provinz. Beiträge zur Geschichte der Juden in der Pfalz zwischen Emanzipation und Vernichtung* (Neustadt a.d.W., 1989), 103–26.

22. Dietrich Hauschildt, 'Vom Judenboykott zum Judenmord', in Erich Hoffmann and Peter Wulf, eds, *'Wir bauen das Reich'. Aufstieg und erste Herrschaftsjahre des Nationalsozialismus in Schleswig-Holstein* (Neumünster, 1983), 335–60.

23. *VB* 4 Apr. 1933 (announcement made by the Committee on 3 April).

24. This is a topos in the memoirs of German Jews and is emphasized in many local studies: Walter Tausk, *Breslauer Tagebuch 1933–1940* (Frankfurt a. M., 1974), 31 Jan. and 1 Apr. 1933; Kurt Ball and Jakob Kaduri, *Das Leben der Juden in Deutschland. Ein Zeitbericht* (Frankfurt a. M., 1963), 88; Monika Richarz, ed., *Jüdisches Leben in Deutschland*, vol. iii: *Selbstzeugnisse zur Sozialgeschichte 1918–1945* (Stuttgart, 1982), 231 ff.; Joseph Werner, *Hakenkreuz und Judenstern. Das Schicksal der Karlsruhe Juden im Dritten Reich* (Karlsruhe, 1988), 34 ff.; Benigna Schönhagen, *Tübingen im Dritten Reich* (Tübingen, 1991), 122; Joachim Meynert, (*Was vor der Endlösung geschah. Antisemitische Ausgrenzung in Minden-Ravensberg 1933–1945* (Münster, 1988), 78 ff.) is right to object, however, that such cases of solidarity on the part of the non-Jewish population are probably exaggerated in retrospect.

25. On the activities both of Jews and non-Jews, see Pätzold, *Faschismus*, 71–2 and Genschel, *Verdrängung*, 47–8. See also *CV-Zeitung* of 30 Mar. 1933 with a range of explanations from various organizations, and *CV-Zeitung* of 6 Apr 1933 with documentation of the Centralverein activities of recent days 'against stories about atrocities disseminated abroad'. On the activities of the Centralverein in this regard, see the following documents: OS, 721-1-2567; 721-1-2291; 721-1-2485. See also corresponding material in: BAB, R 43II/600.

26. Minuth, *Regierung Hitler*, i/1. 272. The evaluation of this journey is debated: see Avraham Barkai, '*Wehr Dich!*'. *Der Centralverein deutscher Staatsbürger jüdischen Glaubens 1893–1938* (Munich, 2002), 280 ff., which has further details on the partly contradictory reactions of the Centralverein to the first measures taken by the NS regime, which according to Barkai should be seen against a background of 'general Jewish confusion' during these months (ibid. 284 ff., here 293–4).

27. *CV-Zeitung*, 13 Apr. 1933.

28. Gruchmann, *Justiz*, 126 ff.; Krach, *Rechtsanwälte*, 188 ff.

29. *Reichsgesetzblatt* (*RGBl*), 1933, I, p. 175, On the background to the law for the professionalization of the civil service, see Gruchmann, *Justiz*, 132 ff.; Hans Mommsen, *Beamtentum im Dritten Reich. Mit ausgewählten Quellen zur nationalsozialistischen Beamtenpolitik* (Stuttgart, 1968), 39 ff.; Adam, *Judenpolitik*, 51 ff.; Dietmut Majer, '*Fremdvölkische' im Dritten Reich. Ein Beitrag zur nationalsozialistischen Rechtsetzung und Rechtspraxis in Verwaltung und Justiz unter besonderer Berücksichtigung der eingegliederten Ostgebiete und des Generalgouvernements* (Boppard a.Rh, 1981), 39 ff., 157 ff.

30. *RGBl*, 1933, I, p. 195.

31. According to Barkai, *Boykott*, 36.

32. Minuth, *Regierung Hitler*, i/1. 323.

33. *RGBl*, 1933, I, p. 188. See Krach, *Rechtsanwälte*, 202 ff.

34. Krach, *Rechtsanwälte*, 241 ff.

35. Adam, *Judenpolitik*, 72–3; Majer, *Fremdvölkische*, 238–9; Michel Köhn, *Zahnärzte 1933–1945. Berufsverbot—Emigration—Verfolgung* (Berlin, 1994), 42.

36. *RGBl*, 1933, I, p. 225. The first implementation orders issued on the same day imposed a 5 per cent maximum of Jewish students on schools and university faculties (ibid. 226).

37. Albrecht Götz von Olenhusen, 'Die "nicht arischen" Studenten an den deutschen Hochschulen. Zur nationalsozialistischen Rassenpollitik, 1933–1945', *Vierteljahrshefte für Zeitgeschichte (VfZ)* 14 (1966), 180 ff.; Josef Walk, *Jüdische Schule und Erziehung im Dritten Reich* (Frankfurt a. M., 1991), 49 ff.
38. Majer, *Fremdvölkische*, 262 ff.; Alan Steinweis, 'Hans Hinkel and German Jewry 1933–1941', in *LBIY* 37 (1993), 209–19.
39. Examples in OS, 721-1-2557 US; and Ulrich Knipping, *Die Geschichte der Juden in Dortmund während der Zeit des Dritten Reiches* (Dortmund, 1977) (for Dortmund), 24–5. In an interview with the *VB* on 5 May 1933, asked about the enforced cancellations of concerts by Bruno Walter and Otto Klemperer, Hinkel said it was 'not possible' to deploy SA or SS troops to protect concert halls.
40. *VB*, 7 Apr. 1933.
41. Anselm Faust, 'Die Hochschulen und der "undeustche Geist". Die Bücheverbrennung am 10. Mai 1933 und ihre Vorgeschichte', in *'Das war ein Vorspiel nur'. Bücherverbrennung in Deutschland 1933: Voraussetzungen und Folgen* (Berlin, 1983), 31–50. Translator's note: 'appropriate to its own kind' is a translation of 'arteigen', a biological term literally meaning 'species-specific'.
42. Speech to the *Reichstatthalter*, 6 July 1933, published in Minuth, *Regierung Hitler*, i/1. 629 ff.
43. The speech was printed as a pamphlet: Hans Pfundtner, *Die neue Stellung des Reiches* (Berlin, 1932), 32 ff. Before the initiative was passed to the Reich Ministry of the Interior, a group of Party functionaries and civil servants had been working on a comprehensive law to regulate the position of Jews in Germany since the beginning of April. Details in Cornelia Essner, *Die 'Nürnberger Gesetze' oder die Verwaltung des Rassenwahns* (Paderborn, 2002), 76 ff.
44. *RGBl*, 1933, I, p. 480, 14 July 1933. Cf. Majer, *Fremdvölkische*, 195 ff.
45. Minuth, *Regierung Hitler*, i/1. 865 (*Reichsstatthalter* conference of 28 Sept. 1933).
46. Details in Adam, *Judenpolitik*, 75 ff. and Longerich, *Politik*, 50–1.
47. Adam, *Judenpolitik*, 78–9; Alan Steinweis, *Art, Ideology, and Economics in Nazi Germany: The Reich Chambers of Music, Theater and the Visual Arts* (Chapel Hill, NC, 1993), 104 ff.; *Reichskulturkammergesetz* of 22 Sept. 1933, *RGBl*, 1933, I, pp. 661–2; first implementation order, ibid. 797 ff.
48. Adam, *Judenpolitik*, 79; *Schriftleitergesetz*, *RGBl*, 1933, I, p. 713.
49. Reich Entailed Farm Law (*Erbhofgesetz*), 29 Sept. 1933; *RGBl*, 1933, I, p. 685.
50. Implementation Order on the Granting of Marriage Loans of 20 June 1933, *RGBl*, 1933, I, p. 377.
51. *Heeres-Verordnungsblatt 1933* (Army Regulations), 20 July 1933.
52. Decree of the Armed Forces Minister, 26 Feb. 1934, published in Klaus-Jürgen Müller, *Das Heer und Hitler. Armee und nationalsozialistisches Regime 1933–1940* (Stuttgart, 1969). See also Müller, *Armee und Drittes Reich 1933–1939* (Paderborn, 1987).
53. Documentation in OS, 721-1-3168 and 721-1-3140.
54. OS, 721-1-3160.
55. OS, 721-1-3160.
56. OS, 721-1-3131.
57. OS, 721-1-3148.

58. Wolfram Selig has collected examples in *Das Leben unter Rassenwahn. Vom Antisemitismus in der 'Hauptstadt der Bewegung'* (Berlin, 2002), 66 ff. The authorities removed trade licences for flimsy reasons, imposed arbitrary fees for providing official information, and fines for no justification.

59. See for example BAB, 15.01, 26059, Half-monthly reports of the Hesse State Police Office for March 1934 and the Report of the Kassel Gestapo Office for the first quarter of 1934, 16 Apr. 1934, published in *Die Lageberichte der Geheimen Staatspolizei über die Provinz Hessen-Nassau 1933–1936*, ed. Thomas Klein (Cologne, 1986), i. 80–1.

60. Examples of this may be found in OS, 721-1-3182 (Altengronau Cemetery), 2675 (Oberseemen Synagogue), 2335 (Synagogues in East Prussia); Kassel Gestapo Office Report for the first quarter of 1934, 16 Apr. 1934, published in *Der Regierungsbezirk Kassel 1933–1936. Die Berichte der Regierungspräsidenten und der Landräte*, ed. Thomas Klein (Darmstadt, 1985), i. 80–1 (Synagogues in Baumbach, Tann, and Korbach); Knipping, *Geschichte*, 52 (Dortmund Cemetery), Meynert, *Endlösung*, 83 (Herford Synagogue).

61. BAB, 15.01, 2659, half-monthly report of the Hesse State Police Office for March 1934; 26060, monthly report of the Köslin Gestapo Office for February 1934.

62. On these measures see Barkai, *Boykott*, 73–4; Longerich, *Politik*, 39 ff. and 50 ff.; Pätzold, *Faschismus*, 145 ff.

63. See e.g. *VB*, 14 Mar. 1934 and 18/19 Dec. 1934 and the opinions of the Reich Finance Minister of 16 Dec. 1933 (cf. *Jüdische Rundschau (JR)* 29 Dec. 1933).

64. For examples see the Report of the Gestapo Office in Kassel for the 1st quarter of 1934, 16 Apr. 1934, published in Klein, ed., *Die Lageberichte*, pp. 80–1.

65. Ian Kershaw, 'Antisemitismus und Volksmeinung. Reaktionen auf die Judenverfolgung', in Martin Broszat and Elke Fröhlich, eds, *Bayern in der NS-Zeit*, ii (Munich, 1979), 295–6.

66. BAB, R 43II/720a, note of 9 Feb. 1935.

67. *Akten zur deutschen Auswärtigen Politik (ADAP)* 1918–1945 series C, vol. 3/2 (Göttingen, 1978), no. 331, minutes of the meeting of 15 Nov. 1934.

68. BAB, R 43II/720a, decree of 18 Apr. 1935.

69. *ADAP*, series C, vol. 3/2, no. 458, 25 Jan. 1936.

70. For the situation of the German Jews at the beginning of the Nazis' rule, see the contributions in Meyer, ed., *German-Jewish History in Modern Times*, vol. iv, and Wolfgang Benz, ed., *Die Juden in Deutschland, 1933–1945. Leben unter nationalsozialistischer Herrschaft* (Munich, 1988).

71. Oscar Schmelz, 'Die Demographische Entwicklung der Juden in Deutschland von der Mitte des 19. Jahrhunderts bis 1933', *Zeitschrift für Bevölkerungswissenschaft* 1 (1982), 70 ff.

72. Esra Benathan, 'Die demographische und wirtschaftliche Struktur der Juden', in Werner Mosse, ed., *Entscheidungsjahr 1932. Zur Judenfrage in der Endphase der Weimarer Republik* (Tübingen, 1965), 87–131; Avraham Barkai, 'Die Juden als sozio-ökonomische Minderheitsgruppe in der Weimarer Republik', in Walter Grab and Julius H. Schoeps, eds, *Juden in der Weimarer Republik. Skizzen und Portraits* (Stuttgart, 1986), 330–46; Paul Mendes-Flohr, 'Jewish Cultural Life under National Socialism', in Meyer, ed., *German-Jewish History*, iv. 125–53, esp. 149 ff.

73. Avraham Barkai, 'The Organized Jewish Community', in Meyer, ed., *German-Jewish History in Modern Times*, iv. 72–101, esp. 90 ff. on the Zionists.

74. Herbert A. Strauß, 'Jewish Emigration from Germany: Nazi Policies and Jewish Response', *LBIY* 25 (1980), 326. The exact number of émigrés cannot be established. Differing estimates can be found in Salomon Adler-Rudel, *Jüdische Selbsthilfe unter dem Nazi Regime 1933–1939. Im Spiegel der Berichte der Reichsvertretung der Juden in Deutschland* (Tübingen, 1974), 216; Documents of the Reich Association, 11 and 459; and in Susanne Heim, ' "Deutschland muss ein Land ohne Zukunft sein". Die Zwangsemigration der Juden 1933 bis 1938', in Eberhard Jungfer et al., *Arbeitsmigration und Flucht. Vertreibung und Arbeitskräfteregulierung im Zwischenkriegseuropa. Beiträge zur nationalsozialistischen Gesundheits- und Sozialpolitik*, vol. xi (Berlin, 1993).

75. Francis Nicosia, *The Third Reich and the Palestine Question* (Austin, 1985), 41 ff.; Werner Feilchenfeld, Wolf Michaelis, and Ludwig Pinner, *Haavara-Transfer nach Palästina und Einwanderung deutscher Juden 1933–1939* (Tübingen, 1972).

76. The Centralverein had to replace the word 'state citizens' in its name with the name 'nationals'. For the Centralverein in the years 1933–5 see Barkai, *'Wehr Dich'*, 300 ff.

77. Adler-Rudel, *Selbsthilfe*, 9 ff.; Günter Plum, 'Deutsche Juden oder Juden in Deutschland' in Benz, ed., *Juden in Deutschland*, 35–74, esp. 49 ff.

78. Adler-Rudel, *Selbsthilfe*, 10–11. On the foundation of the National Delegation, see Esriel Hildesheimer, *Jüdische Selbstverwaltung unter dem NS-Regime. Der Existenzkampf der Reichsvertretung und Reichsvereinigung der Juden in Deutschland* (Tübingen, 1994), 11–12. On the whole issue, see also Clemens Vollnhals, 'Selbsthilfe bis 1938', in Benz, ed., *Juden in Deutschland*, 314–412.

79. Vollnhals, *'Selbsthilfe'*, 363 ff.

80. Adler-Rudel, *Selbsthilfe*, 124 ff.

81. Ibid. 347 ff.

82. Ibid. 150 ff.

83. According to Joseph Walk, *Jüdische Schule und Erziehung im Dritten Reich* (Frankfurt a. M., 1991), 80 ff. and 105 ff., in 1933 less than 10,000 Jewish schoolchildren attended the 117 public and private Jewish primary and secondary schools, and some 3,500 attended the 10 private institutions of higher education. On the Jewish school system see Ruth Röcher, *Die jüdische Schule im nationalsozialistischen Deutschland 1938–1942* (Frankfurt a. M., 1992); Adler-Rudel, *Selbsthilfe*, 19 ff. and Vollnhals, *'Selbsthilfe'*, 330 ff.

84. Adler-Rudel, *Selbsthilfe*, 25–6. According to the figures compiled here and taken from the reports of the National Delegation, which may be somewhat exaggerated, in 1935 some 16,000 of the 30,000 Jewish primary and secondary school pupils and about 4,000 of the 13,800 pupils in institutions of higher education attended Jewish schools.

85. Volker Dahm, 'Kulturelles und geistiges Leben', in Benz, ed., *Juden in Deutschland*. See also Elke Geisel and Henry M. Broder, *Premiere und Pogrom. Der jüdische Kulturbund 1933–1941. Texte und Bilder* (Berlin, 1992).

86. Hajo Bernett, *Der jüdische Sport im nationalsozialistischen Deutschland* (Schorndorf, 1978). The most important sports associations that existed before 1933 were the Makkabi movement and the *Sportbund Schild des Reichsbundes jüdischer Frontsoldaten* (the

Sporting Association Shield of the National Association of Jewish Front-Line Soldiers). First of all, in 1933, sports arenas and clubs were closed to Jewish associations across the board. In the run-up to the Olympic Games these restrictions were reversed in 1934, but from 1937 they were stepped up again (ibid. 85 ff.).

87. *RGBl*, 1933, I, p. 529.

88. Law for the Standardization of the Health Service, 3 July 1934: *RGBl*, 1933, I, p. 531. On its activity, see Gisela Bock, *Zwangssterilisation im Nationalsozialismus. Studien zur Rassenpolitik und Frauenpolitik* (Opladen, 1986), 187 ff.

89. Ibid. 195 ff.

90. Ibid. 230 ff.; Christian Ganssmüller, *Die Erbgesundheitspolitik des Dritten Reiches. Planung, Durchführung, und Durchsetzung* (Cologne, 1987), 45.

91. Bock, *Zwangssterilisation*, 301 ff.

92. Second Implementing Decree of the Reich Minister of Finance on the Granting of Loans on Marriage of 26 July 1933, *RGBl*, 1933, *I*, p. 540.

93. Ganssmüller, *Erbgesundheitspolitik*, 134–5.

94. Marriage Health Law, *RGBl*, 1935, I, p. 773.

95. *RGBl*, 1933, I, p. 995. Cf. Bock, *Zwangssterilisation*, 95 ff. In addition there was an unknown number of 'voluntary' castrations.

96. Bock, *Zwangssterilisation*, 97 ff.; Ganssmüller, *Erbgesundheitspolitik*, 116 ff.

97. *RGBl*, 1935, I, p. 773.

98. *RGBl*, 1935, I, p. 1246.

99. Leaflet from the Racial Politics Office of the Danube Gau, reprinted in Klaus Scherer, *'Asozial' im Dritten Reich. Die vergessenen Verfolgten* (Münster, 1990), 51.

100. Bock, *Zwangssterilisation*, 365–6.

101. Wolfgang Ayaß, *'Asoziale' im Nationalsozialismus* (Stuttgart, 1995), 20 ff.

102. Ibid. 57 ff.

103. Ibid. 123 ff.

104. Michael Zimmermann, *Rassenutopie und Genozid. Die nationalsozialistische 'Lösung der Zigeunerfrage'* (Hamburg, 1996), 81 ff.; see also Guenter Lewy, *The Nazi Persecution of the Gypsies* (New York, 2001), 15 ff.

105. First Implementation Decree of the Law for the Protection of German Blood and German Honour 14 November 1935, *RGBl*, 1935, I, pp. 1134–6; *Ministerialblatt für die Innere Verwaltung* (1935), p. 49.

106. Bock, *Zwangssterilisaation*, 90 ff.

107. Cf. ibid. 104 ff. The author is right to describe this as 'the state's conquest of the private sphere'.

108. Ibid. 85.

109. Burkhard Jellonek, *Homosexuelle unter dem Hakenkreuz. Die Verfolgung von Homosexuellen im Dritten Reich* (Paderborn, 1990), 80 ff.

110. *RGBl*, 1935, I, pp. 839 ff., Law for Amendments to the Penal Code of 28 June 1935.

111. Bock, *Zwangssterilisation*, 353.

112. For details, see above, p. 49.

113. Reiner Pommerin, *'Sterilisierung der Rheinlandbastarde'. Das Schicksal einer farbigen deutschen Minderheit, 1918–1937* (Düsseldorf, 1970), 44 ff.

114. Ibid. 71 ff.

2. Segregation and Comprehensive Discrimination, 1935–1937

1. Literature on the second wave of Jewish persecution and its reception amongst the populace includes: Kurt Pätzold, *Faschismus, Rassenwahn, Judenverfolgung. Eine Studie zur politischen Strategie und Taktik des faschistischen deutschen Imperialismus (1933–1935)* (Berlin, 1975), 197 ff.; Kershaw, *Opinion*, 232 ff.; Kershaw, 'The Persecution of the Jews and German Popular Opinion in the Third Reich', *LBIY* 26 (1981), 261–89 (264 ff.); Hans Mommsen and Hans Obst, 'Die Reaktion der deutschen Bevölkerung auf die Verfolgung der Juden 1933–1943', in Hans Mommsen and Susanne Willems, eds, *Herrschaftsalltag im Dritten Reich. Studien und Texte* (Düsseldorf, 1988), 377 ff.; Werner T. Angress, 'Die "Judenfrage" im Spiegel amtlicher Berichte 1935', in Ursula Büttner, ed., *Das Unrechtsregime*, vol. ii: *Verfolgung, Exil, Belasteter Neubeginn* (Hamburg, 1986), ii. 19–38; David Bankier, *Die öffentliche Meinung im NS-Staat. Die 'Endlösung' und die Deutschen. Eine Berichtigung* (Berlin, 1995), 56 ff. and 98 ff. The following summary is based on a more detailed exposition in Peter Longerich, *Politik der Vernichtung* (Munich, 1998), 65 ff., which is itself based on a detailed examination of reports by the Gestapo and the *Regierungsbezirk* presidents, published and unpublished (Geheime Staatsarchiv Dahlem (GStaA), Rep 90 P and Bundesarchiv Berlin (BAB), R 18, R 58 and 15.01), reporting by the Social Democratic Party in exile (Sopade), Centralverein documents and the literature on regional history. Much of this material has now been published in *Die Juden in den geheimen Stimmungsberichten 1933–1945* with CD-ROM, ed. Otto Dov Kulka and Eberhard Jaeckel (Düsseldorf, 2004).
2. The Nazis used the derogatory term 'Pfaffen'.
3. For details see Longerich, *Politik*, 78 ff. There are also many examples in the submission of the Centralverein to the RWM of 15 Feb. 1935 (OS, 721–1–2300).
4. See Uwe Adam, *Die Judenpolitik im Dritten Reich* (Düsseldorf, 1972), 118. The Gestapo ban took effect on 12 Feb. 1935: BAB, R 58/276.
5. Military Law (*Wehrgesetz*) of 21 May 1935. *RGBl*, 1935, pp. 609 ff.
6. Gestapo Decree, probably of 28 Jan. 1935, quoted in Verfügung Landrat Eschwege, 14 Mar. 1936, published in Thomas Klein, ed., *Der Regierungsbezirk Kassel 1933–1936. Die Berichte der Regierungspräsidenten und der Landräte* (Darmstadt and Marburg, 1985), i. 712.
7. Details in Longerich, *Politik*, 82 ff. Those who opposed a continuation of the violence included the Führer's Deputy in an order of 11 Apr. 1935 in Institut für Zeitgeschichte (IfZ) VAB, A 63/35 and the Reich Minister for Economic Affairs, Schacht in his memorandum on 'The Imponderables of Export' of 3 May 1935 in *Akten zur deutschen auswärtigen Politik* (*ADAP*), Series C, vol. iv. 120 ff.
8. See Norbert T. Wiggershaus, *Der deutsch-englische Flottenvertrag vom 18. Juni 1935* (Bonn, 1972). According to his own account, in the course of the negotiations between Britain and Germany the leader of the British delegation, Lord Lothian, had indicated to Ribbentrop that an improvement in the treatment of Jews in Germany was a prerequisite for a successful outcome. By doing so, Lothian was responding to a request made by Chaim Weitzmann, the President of the World Zionist Organization.

See the Weizmann–Lothian correspondence in *Deutsches Judentum unter dem Natio-nalsozialismus. Dokumente zur Geschichte der Reichsvertretung der deutschen Juden 1933–1939*, ed. Otto Dov Kulka (Tübingen, 1997), i. 214 ff.

9. Details in Longerich, *Politik*, 83 ff.

10. There is detailed material on this point in BAB, 15.01, 27079/35. See also Pätzold, *Faschismus*, 216 ff., including material on the aftermath.

11. National Archives Washington DC (NA), T 175 R 180, Himmler's order of 7 June 1935; IfZ, Decree of the Führer's Deputy V 123/35 or 14 June 1935; *Westdeutscher Beobachter*, 29 May 1935; *Frankfurter Zeitung (FZ)*, 3 June 1935.

12. Details in Longerich, *Politik*, 85 ff.

13. This was the headline in *Der Angriff* for 16 July 1935.

14. Cf. Longerich, *Politik*, 88 ff.

15. Ibid. 89 ff.

16. Edition 25 (1935). *Der Stürmer* is referring here to the colours of socialists, Catholics, the Weimar Republic, and Imperial Germany respectively.

17. This is evident from the relevant 'reports on the popular mood', above all those prepared by the Gestapo and the Sopade. See *Deutschland-Berichte der Sozialdemokra-tischen Partei Deutschlands (Sopade) 1934–1940* (Frankfurt a. M., 1980) (Sopade, August 1935, A 42-A46, and Longerich, *Politik*, 90 ff.).

18. IfZ, circular from the Führer's Deputy, R 164/35 of 9 Aug. 1935.

19. *Verhandlungen des Reichstages*, vol. 440, Appendices, Document 1741. In an earlier speech Hitler had already demanded the death penalty for 'every Jew caught with a blond woman'. See *Hitler, Sämtliche Aufzeichnungen 1905–1924*, ed. Eberhard Jäckel (Stuttgart, 1980), no. 355, 2 Feb. 1922.

20. Cornelia Essner, *Die 'Nürnberger Gesetze' oder die Verwaltung des Rassenwahns 1933–1945* (Paderborn, 2002), 77 ff., which has the most detailed survey of the genesis of the Nuremberg Laws.

21. 37th meeting of the Criminal Law Commission of 5 June 1934, published in Jürgen Regge and Werner Schubert, eds, *Protokolle der Strafrechtskommission des Reichsjus-tizministeriums* (Berlin and New York, 1988), part II, vol. ii, 223 ff. Further details in Essner, 'Nürnberger Gesetze', 96 ff.

22. Military Law of 21 May 1935, *RGBl*, 1935, I, pp. 609 ff.

23. Lothar Gruchmann, *Justiz im Dritten Reich. Anpassung und Unterwerfung in der Ära Gürtner 1933–1940* (Munich, 1980), 871–2.

24. *Ministerialblatt für die innere Verwaltung (MbliV)*, 1935, p. 980.

25. Essner, 'Nürnberger Gesetze', 106 ff.

26. *VB*, 7 Aug. 1935; Goebbels's speech is reproduced in the issue for 5 Aug. 1935.

27. See below, p. 59.

28. According to Arthur Gütt (from the Reich Ministry of the Interior) at a meeting on 25 Sept. 1935 (R 2/12042, cited in Gisela Bock, *Zwangssterilisation im Nationalsozialis-mus. Studien zur Rassenpolitik und Frauenpolitik* (Opladen, 1986), p. 101).

29. English trans. in J. Noakes and G. Pridham, *Nazism 1919–1945* (Exeter, 1983), i. 14.

30. See above, p. 40.

31. *Berliner Illustrierte Nachtausgabe*, 27 Apr. 1935.

32. OS, 500-3-316, Situation Report for the first Half-Year 1935, 17 Aug. 1935.

33. NG 4067, *International Military Tribunal* (*IMT*) (Nuremberg) xiii. 698. Unusually this speech was reproduced in the daily press and distributed by the Reichsbank as a special pamphlet. The draft for the speech, which is in the Bank's archives, is more detailed and more critical in its approach to the 'individual operations' than the printed version (BAB 25–01, 6992). Cf. Albert Fischer, *Hjalmar Schacht und Deutschlands 'Judenfrage'. Der 'Wirtschaftsdiktator' und die Vertreibung der Juden aus der Wirtschaft* (Cologne, 1995), 161 ff.; and Pätzold, *Faschismus*, 234 ff.

34. There are three versions of the minutes of this meeting, one from the Reich Ministry of the Interior (BAB, R 18/5513, 27 Aug. 1935), with in addition manuscript notes by Bernhard Lösener, the head of the Jewish desk in the Reich Ministry of the Interior (IfZ, Fb 71/2); one from the Foreign Ministry (PA, Inland II A/B, 34/3 II, published in *ADAP*, series C, vol. 4, 559 ff., 21 Aug. 1935); and one from the Gestapo (OS, 500-1-379 US, II 1 B 2, 20 Aug. 1935).

35. BAB, R 43II/602.

36. BAB, MF 3572; cf. Pätzold, *Faschismus*, 241.

37. BAM, RW 19/9, Report on a Weapons Inspection, VI (Münster), appendix.

38. For example, Gauleiter Bürckel on 26 August 1935 on the occasion of the 'Saar Liberation Festival' (*FZ*, 27 Aug. 1935) and the Deputy Gauleiter of Westphalia South at a workers' meeting on 23 August (*VB*, 24 Aug. 1935). See also the leading article of the SS newspaper, *Das Schwarze Korps*, 21 Aug. 1935.

39. In Berlin (*FZ*, 16 Aug. 1935 and GStaA, Rep 90 P 2,1, Situation report for August), Magdeburg (GStaA, Rep 90 P, 10,3) and Hamburg (*Hamburger Fremdenblatt*, 31 Aug. 1935.

40. Elke Fröhlich, ed. *Die Tagebücher von Joseph Goebbels, Teil I: Aufzeichnungen 1923–1941* Band 3/I April 1934–Februar 1936. Bearbeitet von Angela Hermann, Hartmut Mehringer, Anne Munding und Jana Richter (Munich, 2005). Entry for 19 Aug. 1935, pp. 278–9.

41. The impetus for this decision was the so-called New York swastika incident: a judge in New York had ordered the release from prison of workers who had ripped the swastika flag from a German ship and in doing so had attacked the 'Third Reich'. Cf. Bankier, *Meinung*, 65–6.

42. Fröhlich, *Goebbels Tagebücher*, Entry for 15 Sept. 1935, p. 294.

43. Karl Schleunes, *The Twisted Road to Auschwitz: Nazi Policy towards German Jews 1933–39*, (Urbana, Ill., 1970), 122 ff. For critiques of this document and its treatment by historians, see in particular Essner, 'Nürnberger Gesetze', 113 ff. The crucial elements of the Blood Protection Law (*Blutschutzgesetz*) were already present in the draft bill prepared in the Reich Ministry of Justice in summer 1933 for the prevention of 'marriages detrimental to the German people'.

44. *RGBl*, 1935, I, p. 1146. English trans. in *Nazism 1919–1945*, ii: *State, Economy and Society 1933–1939*, ed. J. Noakes and G. Pridham (Exeter, 2000), 342–3.

45. *RGBl*, 1935, I, pp. 1146–7. *Nazism 1919–1945*, ii. 341–2.

46. *Parteitag der Freiheit. Reden des Führers und ausgewählte Kongreßreden am Reichsparteitag der NSDAP* (Munich, 1935), 110 ff. (here 113–14).

47. On the reaction of the people to the Nuremberg Laws see Bankier, *Meinung*, 105 ff.; Kershaw, 'Persecution', 270 ff.; Otto Dov Kulka, 'Die Nürnberger Rassengesetze und die

deutsche Bevölkerung im Lichte geheimer NS-Lage- und Stimmungsberichte', *Viertel-jahrshefte für Zeitgeschichte (VfZ)* 32 (1984), 582–624; Longerich, *Davon*, 96 ff.

48. Sopade, September 1935, A 10 ff., pp. 1019 ff.; for more details see Longerich, *Politik*, 107–8.

49. On 'anti-Jewish policy' following the Nuremberg Laws see Adam, *Judenpolitik*, 145 ff.; Avraham Barkai, *Vom Boykott zu 'Entjudung'. Der wirtschaftliche Existenzkampf der Juden im Dritten Reich 1933–1939* (Frankfurt a. M., 1988), 67 ff.; Helmut Genschel, *Die Verdrängung der Juden aus der Wirtschaft im Dritten Reich* (Berlin, 1966), 116 ff.; Pätzold, *Faschismus*, 272 ff.; Longerich, *Politik*, 112 ff.

50. BAB, R 18/5513; cf. Fischer, *Schacht*, 184–5. The purpose of the discussion was to clarify problems raised at the ministerial meeting on 20 Aug. 1935 (see above, p. 59).

51. *RGBl*, 1935, I, pp. 1333–4. English version in *Nazism 1919–1945*, ii. 344–5. On the pre-history of this ordinance see Adam, *Judenpolitik*, 134 ff. and Essner, 'Nürnberger Gesetze', 155 ff.

52. See below, p. 65.

53. *RGBl*, 1935, I, pp. 1934–5; cf. Adam, *Judenpolitik*, 141.

54. Adam, *Judenpolitik*, 145–6.

55. Bankier, *Meinung*, 111; Adam, *Judenpolitik*, 153.

56. Sopade, August 1936, A 12, pp. 973 ff. and December, A 111 ff., pp. 1648 ff.; Situation Reports and Complaints by the CV in OS, 721-1-243, 244, 1344, 2317; cf. Barkai, *Boykott*, 73 ff. on the 'creeping displacement' ('schleichende Verdrängung').

57. Wilhelm Treue, 'Hitlers Denkschrift zum Vierjahresplan 1936', *VfZ* 3 (1955), 184–203. English translation in *Nazism*, ed. Noakes and Pridham (Exeter, 1984).

58. See below, p. 314 ff.

59. Treue, 'Denkschrift', 93.

60. BAB, R 58/23a; Adam, *Judenpolitik*, 184, wrongly dates the foundation of the office to February 1938.

61. BAB, R 18/5514, 29 Sept. 1938; cf. Barkai, *Boykott*, 127.

62. *RGBl*, 1936, I, p. 999.

63. *RGBl*, 1936, I, pp. 1000–1.

64. See below, pp. 119–20.

65. Material can be found OS, 721-1-755, 2335, 2555, 2723, 3164 (details in Longerich, *Politik*, 122 ff.).

66. Falk Wiesemann, ' "Juden auf dem Lande": Die wirtschaftliche Ausgrenzung der jüdischen Viehhändler in Bayern', in Detlev Peukert and Jürgen Reulecke, eds, *Die Reihen fast geschlossen: Beiträge zur Geschichte des Alltags unterm Nationalsozialismus* (Wuppertal, 1981), 384 ff.

67. On this, see e.g. the special investigation reports of the Currency Investigation Office in Berlin, in which the supposed intentions of business owners suspected of wishing to emigrate were outlined: OS, 1461-1-66, 67, 68, 70, 103 includes numerous reports of that kind from the period 1936–41. On the support of the Reichsbank, see Fischer, *Schacht*, 201; further details in Longerich, *Politik*, 24–5.

68. Currency Investigation Office, Berlin, Prinz AlbrechtStr. 8, 14 July 1938 to RFSS-Chief RSHA (OS, 500-1-600).

69. *RGBl* 1934, I, p. 923; cf. Stefan Mehl, *Das Reichsfinanzministerium und die Verfolgung der deutschen Juden* (Berlin, 1990), 36.

70. See Dorothee Mußgnung, *Die Reichsfluchtsteuer 1931–1953* (Berlin, 1993); Barkai, *Boykott*, 111–12; Mehl, *Reichsfinanzministerium*, 41 ff.

71. On 'Aryanization', see Frank Bajohr, *Arianization in Hamburg: The Economic Exclusion of Jews and the Confiscation of their Property in Nazi Germany* (New York, 2002); Barkai, *Boykott*; Franz Fichtl, Stephan Link, Herbert May, et al., *'Bambergs Wirtschaft judenfrei'. Die Verdrängung der jüdischen Geschäftsleute in den Jahren 1933 bis 1939* (Bamberg, 1998); Genschel, *Verdrängung*; Barbara Händler-Lachmann and Thomas Werther, *Vergessene Geschäfte, verlorene Geschichte. Jüdisches Wirtschaftsleben in Marburg und seine Vernichtung im Nationalsozialismus* (Marburg 1992); Gerhard Kratzsch, *Der Gauwirtschaftsapparat der NSDAP. Menschenführung-Arisierung-Wehrwirtschaft im Gau Westfalen-Süd* (Münster, 1989); Dirk Laak, 'Die Mitwirkenden bei der "Arisierung". Dargestellt am Beispiel der rheinisch-westfälischen Industrieregion, 1933–1940', in Ursula Büttner, ed., *Die Deutschen und die Judenverfolgung im Dritten Reich* (Hamburg, 1992), 231–57; Uwe Westphal, *Berliner Konfektion und Mode. Die Zerstörung einer Tradition 1936–1939* (Berlin, 1986); Katharina Stengel, ed., *Vor der Vernichtung. Die staatliche Enteignung der Juden im Nationalsozialismus* (Frankfurt a. M., 2007).

72. Kratzsch, *Gauwirtschaftsapparat*, 173 ff., notes the relatively small number of firms 'Aryanized' in the district of South Westphalia: 'putting an end to the economic activities of the Jews took the form of liquidation rather than Arianization'.

73. Barkai, *Boykott*, 80 ff.

74. For individual examples from 1935 to 1937, see Barkai, *Boykott*, pp. 85–6; see also Laak, 'Die Mitwirkenden', 239–40 and 244.

75. Genschel, *Verdrängung*, 135 ff.

76. See Kratzsch, *Gauwirtschaftsapparat*, 146 ff. Party members, for example, were required by a Party regulation to obtain the consent of its Gau economic advisers when assuming control of a Jewish business. Without proof of this consent the firms were not free of the ban on advertising in the public press, etc.

77. Barkai, *Boykott*, 65.

78. OS, 500-3-316.

79. Herbert A. Strauß, 'Jewish Emigration from Germany: Nazi Policies and Jewish Response', in *LBIY*, 25 (1980), 174.

80. IfZ, MA 727/3.

81. Politisches Archiv des Auswärtigen Amtes (PAA), Inland II A/B 83–21a, vol. 1a; cf. Francis R. Nicosia, *The Third Reich and the Palestine Question* (Austin, 1985), 114 ff.

82. *ADAP*, series D, vol. 4, no. 561; cf. Nicosia, *Third Reich*, 121.

83. *ADAP*, series D, vol. 4, no. 463; cf. Nicosia, *Third Reich*, 122.

84. Ibid. 134.

85. See below, p. 105.

86. See *Die Judenpolitik des SD 1935–1938*, ed. Michael Wildt (Munich, 1995), 15–16.

87. OS, 500-1; 7 Apr. 1937.

88. BAB, R 58/239, in Wildt, *Judenpolitik*, 118 ff.

89. See Wildt, *Judenpolitik*, 34–5, and Eichmann's 'Disposition for Handling the Jews in the SD South-Eastern Sector', 10 May. 1937, OS, 500-1-403.

90. On the problems for emigration see Nicosia, *Third Reich*, 136; Strauß, 'Emigration'; the report of the National Delegation of Jews in Germany for 1937 (IfZ, Ma 727/3). The crisis was reflected in situational reports made by the Jewish Division of the SD for October and November 1937 (OS, 500-3-316).
91. See the report in BAB, R 58/954.
92. Texts of the papers and additional material related to preparations are in OS, 500-3-322 and 500-3-424. The programme and the papers are published in Wildt, *Judenpolitik*, 123 ff. (and see Wildt's detailed commentaries, 45 ff.).
93. OS, 500-1-506, published in Wildt, *Judenpolitik*, 156 ff.

3. Interim Conclusions: The Removal of Jews from German Society, the Formation of the National Socialist 'People's Community', and its Consequences for Jewish Life in Germany

1. Wolf Gruner, *Öffentliche Wohlfahrt und Judenverfolgung. Wechselwirkung lokaler und zentraler Politik im NS-Staat 1933–1942* (Munich, 2002), 69 ff.
2. Ibid. 89 ff.
3. Ibid. 105 ff.
4. Ibid. 114 ff.
5. Ibid. 157 ff.
6. Ibid. 101 ff. and 116 ff.
7. See Hans-Uwe Otto, Heinz Sünker, 'Volksgemeinschaft als Formierungsideologie des Nationalsozialismus. Zur Genesis und Geltung von "Volkspflege" ', in Hans-Uwe Otto and Heinz Sünker, eds, *Politische Formierung und soziale Erziehung im Nationalsozialismus* (Frankfurt a. M., 1991), 50–77.
8. This process is outlined in Paul Weindling, *Health, Race and German Politics between National Unification and Nazism, 1870–1945* (New York, 1989): Robert Proctor, *Racial Hygiene: Medicine under the Nazis* (Cambridge, Mass., and London, 1988); Peter Weingart, Jürgen Kroll, and Kurt Bayertz, *Rasse, Blut und Gene. Geschichte der Eugenik und Rassenhygiene in Deutschland* (Frankfurt a. M., 1988); Christian Ganssmüller, *Die Erbgesundheitspolitik des Dritten Reiches* (Cologne, 1987); Hans-Walter Schmuhl, *Rassenhygiene, Nationalsozialismus, Euthanasie* (Göttingen, 1987).
9. See below Parts II-V.
10. *VB*, 14 Sept. 1935. On the role of anti-Semitism in 'racial hygiene' see above all Lars Renssmanns, 'Antisemitismus und "Volksgesundheit". Zu ideologiehistorischen Verbindungslinien im politischen Imaginären und in der Politik', in Christoph Kopke, ed., *Medizin und Verbrechen. Festschrift zum 60. Geburtstag von Walter Wuttke* (Ulm, 2001), 44–82.
11. Proctor, *Racial Hygiene*, 147 ff.
12. See the measures outlined in Joseph Walk, ed., *Das Sonderrecht für die Juden im NS-Staat. Eine Sammlung der gesetzlichen Massnahmen und Richtlinien—Inhalt und Bedeutung* (Heidelberg, 1981), ii. 178, 491; and iv. 393.
13. Wilhelm Michael, 'Der Jüdische Fabrikmediziner', in *Der Weltkampf. Monatsschrift für Weltpolitik, völkische Kultur und die Judenfrage aller Länder*, 3 (1935), 65–8 (here 66–7);

facsimile in *Medizin im Nationalsozialismus. Ein Arbeitsbuch* (Rottenburg, 1982), 171–4 (172–3).

14. Walter Wuttke, ' "Deutsche Heilkunde" und "Jüdische Fabrikmedizin" ', in Hendrik van den Bussche, ed., *Anfälligkeit und Resistenz. Zur medizinischen Wissenschaft und politischen Opposition im 'Dritten Reich'*, (Berlin and Hamburg, 1990), 23–54.

15. Cf. Rensmann, *Medizin*, 63–4, and Wuttke, *Heilkunde*, 31.

16. See Vollnhals, 'Selbsthilfe', 32 ff.; Walk, *Jüdische Schule*, 77 ff.; Peter W. Schmidt, ed., *Judenfeindschaft und Schule in Deutschland 1933–1945. Materialien zur Ausstellung der Forschungsstelle für Sozialgeschichte an der Pädagogischen Hochschule Weingart* (Weingart, 1988); Benjamin Ortmeyer, *Schicksale jüdischer Schülerinnen und Schüler in der NS-Zeit—Leerstelle deutscher Erziehungswissenschaften. Bundesrepublikanische Erziehungswissenschaften (1945/49–1955) und die Erforschung der nazistischen Schule* (Witterschlick and Bonn, 1998).

17. Corresponding regulations for Berlin (1933, No. I 241) and Prussia (1934, No. I 394) are identified in Walk, ed., *Das Sonderrecht*.

18. Guidelines for the award of training grants, 20 Mar. 1938 in Hans J. Apel and Michael Klöcker, *Volksschule im NS-Staat* (Bonn, 2000), 92 ff.

19. Decree by the Prussian Minister of Science, Art, and National Education, 13 Sept. 1933, in Renate Fricke-Finkelnburg, ed., *Nationalsozialismus und Schule Amtliche Erlasse und Richtlinien* (Opladen, 1989), 214; as a stimulus for the distribution of subjects over all eight years of elementary school: Alfred Endt, *Rassenpolitische Erziehung in der Volksschule. Betrachtungen und unterrichtspraktische Handreichungen für eine artgemäße Erziehung* (Leipzig, 1936); anti-Semitism recommended as a cross-disciplinary subject in all school types and at all ages: Fritz Fink, *Die Judenfrage im Unterricht* (Nuremberg, 1937).

20. On the individual school subjects see the essays in Reinhard Diethmar, ed., *Schule und Unterricht im Dritten Reich* (Neuwied, 1989) and Horst Gies, *Geschichtsunterricht unter der Diktatur Hitlers* (Cologne, 1992); Henning Heske, *'und morgen die ganze Welt ...' Erdkundeunterricht im Nationalsozialismus* (Gießen, 1988).

21. The experience of increasing discrimination and mistreatment is a regular component of the memories of Jewish pupils, see e.g. the account 'Marta Appel' in Monica Richarz, ed., *Jewish Life in Germany: Memoirs from Three Centuries* (Bloomington, Ind., 1991), 351–60; the examples in the anthology Margarete Limberg and Hubert Rübsaat, eds, *Sie durften nicht mehr Deutsche sein. Jüdisches Alltagsleben in Selbstzeugnissen 1933–1938* (Berlin, 2003), 208 ff. and in Röcher, *Jüdische Schule*, 68 ff. Marion Kaplan, *Between Dignity and Despair; Jewish Life in Nazi Germany* (Oxford, 1998), 94 ff. Rita Meyhöfer, *Gäste in Berlin? Jüdisches Schülerleben in der Weimarer Republik und im Nationalsozialismus* (Hamburg, 1996), 132 ff.; Ortmeyer, *Schicksale*, 163 ff.; also the examples in local history, e.g. Peter Junk and Martina Sellmeyer, *Stationen auf dem Weg nach Auschwitz. Entrechtung, Vertreibung, Vernichtung. Juden in Osnabrück 1900–1945* (Osnabrück, 1988), 54 ff.; Dieter Goerts, *Juden in Oldenburg 1930–1938* (Oldenburg, 1988), 105 ff.; Stefanie Schüler-Springorum, *Die jüdische Minderheit in Königsberg/Preussen* (Göttingen, 1996), 338 ff.

22. Figures on the development of the Jewish school student body at general schools according to Röcher, *Schule*, 71.

23. On the Nazification of schools see—apart from the literature mentioned in n. 19—in particular: Ottwilm Ottweiler, *Die Volksschule im Nationalsozialismus* (Weinheim and Basle, 1979); Margarete Götz, *Die Grundschule in der Zeit des Nationalsozialismus. Eine Untersuchung der inneren Ausgestaltung der vier unteren Jahrgänge der Volksschule auf der Grundlage amtlicher Maßnahmen* (Bad Heilbrunn, 1997); Barbara Schneider, *Die Höhere Schule im Nationalsozialismus. Zur Ideologisierung von Bildung und Erziehung* (Cologne, Weimar, and Vienna, 2000); Harald Scholtz, *Erziehung und Unterricht unterm Hakenkreuz* (Göttingen, 1985).

24. 10 Sept. 1935, quoted from Meyhöfer, *Gäste in Berlin*, 98.

25. Published in Röcher, *Jüdische Schule*, 279.

26. See the examples ibid. 71–2.

27. Walk, *Jüdische Schule*, 54 ff.

28. Decree of 2 July 1937, published in Fricke-Finkelnburg, ed., *Nationalsozialismus und Schule*, 267 ff.

29. See below p. 117.

30. Mitchell Ash, 'Psychologie', in Frank-Rutger Hausmann, ed., *Die Rolle der Geisteswissenschaften im Dritten Reich 1933–1945* (Munich, 2002), 229–64; Ulfried Greuter, *Die Professionalisierung der deutschen Psychologie im Nationalsozialismus* (Frankfurt a. M., 1984); Geoffrey Cocks, *Psychotherapy in the Third Reich: The Göring Institute* (Oxford, 1985); James E. Goggin and Eileen Brockman Goggin, *Death of a 'Jewish Science': Psychoanalysis in the Third Reich* (Lafayette, Ind., 2001); Regine Lockot, *Erinnern und Durcharbeiten. Zur Geschichte der Psychoanalyse und Psychotherapie im Nationalsozialismus* (Frankfurt a. M., 1986).

31. Greuter, *Professionalisierung*, 205 ff.; admittedly these new partial disciplines were unusable for psychological practice, but as demonstrated they did prove important for the legitimization of the subject.

32. See the programmatic article by Matthias Heinrich Goering, the most important representative of this trend and founder of the Institute for Psychological Research and Psychotherapy, in *VB* 3 Dec. 1938: 'Deutsche Seelheilkunde—Ein deutsches Wissenschaftsgebiet, das fast ausschließlich in jüdischen Händen lag'. Mentor of the group around Goering was the Swiss psychotherapist Carl Gustav Jung, who, in an article for the *Zentralblatt für Psychotherapie und ihre Grenzgebiete* (1934, issue 1/2), compared the fundamentally different psychological constitution of Jews and 'Aryans' (Lockot, *Erinnern*, 87 ff.).

33. Hannsjost Lixfeld, *Folklore and Fascism: The Reich Institute for German Volkskunde* (Bloomington, Ind., 1994). James R. Dow and Hannsjost Lixfeld, eds, *The Nazification of an Academic Discipline: Folklore in the Third Reich* (Bloomington, Ind., 1994); Helge Gerndt, ed., *Volkskunde und Nationalsozialismus. Referate und Diskussionen einer Tagung der Deutschen Gesellschaft für Volkskunde, München 23 bis 25 Oktober 1986* (Munich, 1987); Wolfgang Jacobeit, Hannsjost Lixfeld, Olaf Blochhorn, eds, *Völkische Wissenschaft. Gestalten und Tendenzen der deutschen und österreichischen Volkskunde in der ersten Hälfte des 20. Jahrhunderts.* (Vienna, Cologne, and Weimar, 1994); Gretchen E. Schafft, *From Racism to Genocide: Anthropology in the Third Reich* (Urbana and Chicago, 2004). Contemporary work: Adolf Spamer, ed., *Die deutsche Volkskunde*, 2 vols, 2nd edn (Leipzig and Berlin, 1934/5) provides a very good survey of

the efforts of the various divisions of *Volkskunde* to demonstrate the homogeneity and exclusiveness of German national culture in spite of all empirical findings to the contrary.

34. Karl Kaiser, *Lesebuch zur Geschichte der deutschen Volkskunde* (Munich, 1939), 214; cf. Christoph Daxelmüller, 'Nationalsozialistisches Kulturverständnis und das Ende der jüdischen Volkskunde', in Gerndt, *Volkskunde und Nationalsozialismus*, 149–68.

35. See in particular the programmatic text by Karl Heinz Pfeffer: *Die deutsche Schule der Soziologie* (Leipzig, 1939) (quotation p. 3). As a further example one might quote Max Hildebert Boehm, *Volkskunde* (Berlin, 1937), 3: 'By being associated with the revolutionary trends of the age, which Riehl fought passionately against, sociology inevitably acquired a highly international character. It had an equally subversive effect on state and *Volk* through its abstract way of thinking about society, so it is no coincidence that Jewry in particular took it on board. Its chief area of interest was the life-forms of the urbanized masses.' For another programmatically important contribution see Gunther Ipsen, *Programm einer Soziologie des Deutschen Volkstums* (Berlin, 1933). Research literature: Ottheim Rammstedt, *Deutsche Soziologie 1933–1945. Die Normalität einer Anpassung* (Frankfurt a. M., 1986); Joachim S. Hohmann, ' "Instrument von Kontrolle und Lenkung" Ländliche Soziologie unterm Hakenkreuz', *ZAA* 45 (1997), 227–35; Carsten Klingemann, *Soziologie im Dritten Reich* (Baden-Baden, 1996).

36. Rammstedt, *Soziologie*, 165.

37. Alan Steinweis, 'Nazi Historical Scholarship and the "Jewish Question" ', in Wolfgang Bialas and Anselm Rabinbach, eds, *Nazism and the Humanities* (Oxford, 2007); Michael Fahlbusch, *Wissenschaft im Dienst der nationalsozialistischen Politik? Die Volksdeutschen 'Forschungsgemeinschaften' von 1931–1945* (Baden-Baden, 1999), 887; Ingo Haar, *Historiker im Nationalsozialismus. Deutsche Geschichtswissenschaft und der 'Volkstumskampf' im Osten* (Göttingen, 2000); Willi Oberkrome, *Volksgeschichte: Methodische Innovation und völkische Ideologisierung in der deutschen Geschichtswissenschaft 1918–1945* (Göttingen, 1993).

38. See Patricia von Papen, 'Schützenhilfe nationalsozialistischer Judenpolitik. Die "Judenforschung" des "Reichsinstituts für Geschichte des neuen Deutschland", 1933–1945', in Fritz Bauer Institut, ed., *'Beseitigung des jüdischen Einflusses ... '. Antisemitische Forschung, Eliten und Karrieren im Nationalsozialismus* (Frankfurt and New York, 1999), 17–43; and Dieter Schiefelbein, 'Das "Institut zur Erforschung der Judenfrage in Frankfurt am Main". Antisemitismus als Karrieresprungbrett im NS-Staat', ibid. 43–72.

39. Oberkrome, *Volksgeschichte*, 191 (the man in question is Kleophas Pleyer). See also Michael Burleigh, *Germany Turns Eastwards: A Study of Ostforschung in the Third Reich* (Cambridge, 1988).

40. Lutz Raphael, 'Radikales Ordnungsdenken und die Organisation totalitärer Herrschaft: Weltanschauungseliten und Humanwissenschaftler im NS-Regime', *Geschichte und Gesellschaft* 27 (2001), 5–40, 15 ff.; Bernd Rüthers, *Entartetes Recht. Rechtslehren und Kronjuristen im Dritten Reich*, 2nd edn (Munich, 1989); Michael Stolleis, *Recht im Unrecht. Studien zur Rechtsgeschichte des Nationalsozialiszmus* (Frankfurt, 1994); Arno Buschmann, *Nationalsozialistische Weltanschauung und Gesetzgebung: 1933–1945*, 2 vols (Vienna, 2000).

41. 'Die immanente, gemeinschaftsverbindliche Rechtsauffassung kann sich nur bilden aus der Gemeinschaft; sie hat darum eine wirkliche, das heißt durch Artgleichheit und gemeinsame Unterscheidung von Freund und Feind gebildete Gemeinschaft zur Voraussetzung' (Ernst Forsthoff, 'Recht, Richter und nationalsozialistische Revolution', *Deutsches Adelsblatt* (1933), 714–15); cf. Diemut Majer, *Grundlagen des nationalsozialistischen Rechtssystems* (Stuttgart 1987), 122.

42. Revealed with particular vividness in the contributions to the congress held in 1936: Die deutsche Rechtswissenschaft im Kampf gegen den jüdischen Geist. An account of the congress is given in *Das Judentum in der Rechtswissenschaft*, 8 vols (Berlin, 1936). See Christian Busse, ' "Eine Maske ist gefallen". Die Berliner Tagung "Das Judentum und die Rechtswissenschaft" 3./4. Oktober 1936', *Kritische Justiz* 33 (2000), 580–93.

43. Diemut Majer, *'Fremdvölkische' im Dritten Reich. Beitrag zur nationalsozialistichen Rechtssetzung und Rechspraxis in Verwaltung und Justiz unter besonderer Berücksichtigung der eingegliederten Ostgebiete und des Generalgouvernements* (Boppard, 1981).

44. Goebbels in his speech at the opening of the Reichskulturkammer (Reich Chamber of Culture) on 15 Nov. 1933, 'Die deutsche Kultur vor neuen Aufgaben', printed in Joseph Goebbels, *Signale der neuen Zeit* (Munich, 1934), 323–36, 328.

45. 'Der deutschen Kultur Zukunftsaufgabe', printed in Ernst Adolf Dreyer, ed., *Deutsche Kultur im neuen Reich. Wesen, Aufgabe und Ziel der Reichskulturkammer* (Berlin, 1934), 9–22.

46. This is apparent, for example, in Hitler's attempt, in his speech at the launch of the Große Deutsche Kunstausstellung (Great German Art Exhibition) in Munich in 1937, to define the concept of 'German' in art: according to this, 'being German' in art meant 'being clear', 'logical and above all also true'. In, Peter-Klaus Schustered, *Die 'Kunststadt' Munich 1937. Nationalsozialismus und 'Entartete Kunst'* (Munich, 1987), 242–52, 246.

47. Franz Dröge and Michael Müller, *Die Macht der Schönheit. Avantgarde und Faschismus oder die Geburt der Massenkultur* (Hamburg, 1995), esp. 231; Christian Ehalt, *Inszenierung der Gewalt: Kunst und Alltagskultur im Nationalsozialismus* (Frankfurt a. M., 1996); Alan E. Steinweis, *Art, Ideology, and Economics in Nazi Germany: The Reich Chambers of Music, Theater, and the Visual Arts* (Chapel Hill, NC, and London, 1993). On the fruitless efforts to define 'Deutschtum' in music, see especially Pamela M. Potter, *Die deutscheste der Künste. Musikwissenschaft und Gesellschaft von der Weimarer Republik bis zum Ende des Dritten Reiches* (Stuttgart, 2000), 251 ff.; and Michael Meyer, *The Politics of Music in the Third Reich*, 2nd edn (New York, 1993), 253 ff.; on the comparison between 'German' and 'Jewish' music see Michael H. Kater, *Die mißbrauchte Muse. Musiker im Dritten Reich* (Vienna and Munich, 1998), 147 ff.; on the 'Aryanization' of musical life, Erik Levi, *Music in the Third Reich* (Basingstoke, 1994), 41 ff.

48. Thus, for example, in Hitler's opening speech at the launch of the Great German Art Exhibition in 1937, quoted in Schustered, *Kunststadt*, 243: Jewry had 'taken over those methods and institutions that form public opinion and finally govern it. Jewry was particularly able to use its position in the press, with the help of so-called art criticism, not only gradually to confuse views of the essence and duties of art and its purpose, but to dissipate the general healthy response in this field.'

49. Hans Severus Ziegler, *Entartete Musik* (Düsseldorf, 1938), 5, 8, 10.
50. Steinweis, *Art*, 108 ff.
51. Dahm, 'Leben', 115, 197–8, 219–20, 237–8; Steinweis, *Art*, 110 ff.; Walk, *Sonderrecht*, ii. 31, ii. 95, and ii. 142.
52. The Reichskulturkammer's policy of excluding Jews from professions in the cultural sphere had been interrupted in January 1936 at the insistence of the Reichswirtschaftskammer (Reich Chamber of Commerce); this attitude was initially confirmed at the important inter-ministerial session of 29 Sept. 1936 (cf. above p. 64). BAB, R 18/5514, 29, Sept. 1936.
53. Thus in Goebbels's diaries from between 1935 and 1938 one repeatedly comes across the Propaganda Minister's demand for the complete *Entjudung* of the Reich Chamber of Culture, for example in the entries for 4 Sept. 1935 and 5 Oct. 1935 in Elke Fröhlich, ed., *Die Tagebücher von Joseph Goebbels*, Teil I: *Aufzeichnungen 1923–1941*, vol. iii/I *April 1934–Februar 1936*, Bearbeitet von Angela Hermann et al. (Munich, 2005), 286, 305, as well as 2 July 1936, 11 Dec. 1936, ibid., vol. iii/II *März 1936–Februar 1937*, Bearbeitet von Jana Richter (Munich, 2001), 122, 286: 5 June 1937, 21 Sept. 1937, 9 Oct. 1937, 24 Nov. 1937, ibid., vol. iv *März–November 1937*. Bearbeitet von Elke Fröhlich (Munich, 2000), 168, 320, 350, 419; 13 Jan. 1938, 9 Feb. 1938, 18 May 1938, 27 July 1938, ibid., vol. v: *December 1937–Juli 1938*. Bearbeitet von Elke Fröhlich (Munich, 2000), 95, 144, 306, 396; or for the 'Aryanization' of all cultural enterprises in 7 Dec. 1937, 9 Dec. 1937, 15 Dec. 1937, 16 Dec. 1937, ibid., vol. v, pp. 38, 42, 53, 55; cf. Steinweis, *Art*, 112.
54. On 31 Jan. 1939 the Reich Economics Minister ordered that enterprises of a cultural nature be expropriated (Walk, *Sonderrecht*, iii. 126, 31 Jan. 1939). On 3 Jan. 1939 Goebbels published guidelines for the Reich Chamber of Culture, according to which all 'full Jews' were to be excluded; certain exceptions were still allowed for so-called *Mischlinge* and *Versippte* ('half-breeds' or those related to Aryans). Cf. Steinweis, *Art*, 116 ff.
55. This is demonstrated in exemplary fashion in Eva Weissweiler, *Ausgemerzt! Das Lexikon der Juden in der Musik und seine mörderischen Folgen* (Cologne, 1999), with reference to the work of the assessors in the Central Music Office within the Rosenberg Office.
56. Walter Hansen, *Judenkunst in Deutschland. Quellen und Studien zur Judenfrage auf dem Gebiet der bildenden Kunst. Ein Handbuch zur Geschichte der Verjudung und Entartung deutscher Kunst 1900–1933* (Berlin, 1942), 12.
57. Dröge and Müller, *Macht*, 232, point this out. Significantly, the exhibition of 'Degenerate Music', in Düsseldorf in 1938, was held in immediate connection with the Reich Music Week in the same city, at which the 'new' musical culture was preached cf. Levi, *Music*, 41 ff.
58. Goebbels, 'Rede zur Jahrestagung der Reichskulturkammer', 26 Nov. 1937, in Hans Volz, ed., *Von der Großmacht zur Weltmacht* (Berlin, 1938), 416–26.
59. Walther Plugge (member of the governing council of the Reich Film Chamber), 'Wesen und Aufgaben des Films und der Reichsfilmkammer', in Ernst Adolf Dreyer, ed., *Deutsche Kultur im Neuen Reich. Wesen, Aufgabe und Ziel der Reichskulturkammer* (Berlin, 1934), 114–28, 116.
60. On film in National Socialism see amongst others: Yizhak Ahren, Stig Hoernshoej-Moller, and Christoph B. Melchers, *'Der ewige Jude'. Wie Goebbels hetzte. Untersuchungen zum*

nationalsozialistischen Propagandafilm (Aachen, 1990); Gerd Albrecht, *Nationalsozialistische Filmpolitik. Eine soziologische Untersuchung über die Spielfilme des Dritten Reiches* (Stuttgart, 1969); Boguslaw Drewniak, *Der deutsche Film 1938–1945. Ein Gesamtüberblick* (Düsseldorf, 1987); Dorothea Hollstein, *Antisemitische Filmpropaganda. Die Darstellung der Juden im nationalsozialistischen Spielfilm* (Munich, 1971); Felix Moeller, *Der Filmminister. Goebbels und der Film im Dritten Reich* (Berlin, 1998); Eric Rentschler, *The Ministry of Illusion: Nazi Cinema and its Afterlife* (Cambridge, Mass., and London, 1996).

61. In this context Ernst Offermannst, *Internationalität und europäischer Hegemonialanspruch des Spielfilms der NS-Zeit* (Hamburg, 2001); Karsten Witte, *Lachende Erben, Toller Tag. Filmkomödie im Dritten Reich* (Berlin, 1995), speaks of 'Germanised Americanism' (pp. 102 ff.)

62. For example, to mention only the most familiar productions, in the films *Jud Süß, Kolberg, Bismarck, GPU,* or *Ohm Krüger.*

63. Thomas Eichler, 'Spielplanstrukturen 1929–1944', in Thomas Eichler, Barbara Panse, and Henning Rischbieter, eds, *Theater im 'Dritten Reich': Theaterpolitik, Spielplanstruktur, NS-Dramatik* (Leipzig, 2000), 279–486. On theatre in the NS Regime, see also Hans Daiber, *Schaufenster der Diktatur. Theater im Machtbereich Hitlers* (Stuttgart, 1995); Boguslaw Drewniak, *Das Theater im NS-Staat. Szenarium deutscher Zeitgeschichte 1933–1945* (Düsseldorf, 1983); Konrad Dussel, *Ein neues, ein heroisches Theater? Nationalsozialistische Theaterpolitik und ihre Auswirkungen in der Provinz* (Bonn, 1988).

64. Thus, for example, the leading NS architectural historian Schultze-Naumburg in a very programmatic statement (introduction to Karl Willi Straub, *Architektur im Dritten Reich* (Stuttgart, 1932), in Anna Teut, *Architektur im Dritten Reich 1933–1945* (Frankfurt a. M., 1967). 62 ff.).

65. Gerdy Troost, *Das Bauen im Neuen Reich,* 2nd edn (Bayreuth, 1939), 9.

66. Joachim Petsch, *Baukunst und Stadtplanung im Dritten Reich. Herleitung, Bestandsaufnahme, Entwicklung, Nachfolge* (Munich and Vienna, 1976); Dieter Münk, *Die Organisation des Raumes im Nationalsozialismus. Eine soziologische Untersuchung ideologisch fundierter Leitbilder in Architektur, Städtebau und Raumplanung im Dritten Reich* (Bonn, 1993).

67. Uwe Westphal, *Werbung im Dritten Reich* (Berlin, 1989); Matthias Rücker, *Wirtschaftswerbung unter dem Nationalsozialismus: rechtliche Ausgestaltung der Werbung und Tätigkeit des Werberats derDeutschen Wirtschaft* (Frankfurt a. M., 2000); Hartmut Berghoff, 'Von der "Reklame" zur Verbrauchslenkung. Werbung im nationalsozialistischen Deutschland', in Hartmut Berghoff, ed., *Konsumpolitik. Die Regulierung des privaten Verbrauchs im 20. Jahrhundert* (Göttingen, 1999), 77–112.

68. 14th /15th proclamation by the Advertising Council, 28 September or 30 December 1935, published in Rücker, *Wirtschaftswerbung,* 367 ff.

69. On the *Entjudung* of fashion, see: Uwe Westphal, *Berliner Konfektion und Mode, 1836–1939. Die Zerstörung einer Tradition* (Berlin, 1986); Golria Sultano, *Wie geistiges Kokain ... Mode im Dritten Reich* (Vienna, 1994); Almut Junker, *Frankfurt Macht Mode: 1933–1945* (Frankfurt a. M., 1999).

70. Thus, even in September 1938, the central organ of the SS, the *Schwarze Korps,* accused the fashion magazine *Die Dame* (this 'confessional front of the fashion fools') of being 'alien in spite of Aryanization' 29 Sept. 1938, cf. Westphal, *Konfektion,* 137.

71. Sabine Weißler, ed., *Design in Deutschland 1933–45. Ästhetik und Organisation des Deutschen Werkbundes im 'Dritten Reich'* (Giessen, 1990); Joachim Petsch, *Eigenheim und gute Stube. Zur Geschichte des bürgerlichen Wohnen* (Cologne, 1989), 183 ff., Hans Scheerer, 'Gestaltung im Dritten Reich. Der Versuch einer Dokumentation zur Sozialutopie des Design im Nationalsozialismus 1933–1945', *form* 69, 70, 71 (1975), 21–8, 27–34, 25–32; Chup Friemert, *Schönheit der Arbeit. Produktionsästhetik im Faschismus. Das Amt 'Schönheit der Arbeit' von 1933 bis 1939* (Munich, 1980).

72. Robert Gellately, *Hingeschaut und Weggesehen. Hitler und sein Volk* (Munich, 2002), 189 ff., reveals, through a random sample of files from the Würzburg Gestapo that of 210 cases of racial defilement, 'behaviour friendly to the Jews' or criticism of Germany's *Judenpolitik* investigated by the Gestapo, almost 60 per cent were persecuted on the basis of denunciations from the population and 13 per cent on the basis of denunciations by Party or Party members. This makes it clear that the persecution of the Jews by the Gestapo depended to a large extent upon the cooperation of the population, i.e. on denunciations. Johnson, *Nazi Terror*, 150 ff., revealed through a random sample that 41 per cent of 66 investigations against Jews pursued by the Gestapo between 1933 and 1939 in Krefeld were based on denunciations; the author attributes much less importance to informers from the population than does Gellately.

73. See esp. Kaplan, *Dignity*, 56 ff. There are many examples of the increasing isolation of the German Jews in the essay collections and in the local histories, e.g, Meynert, *Endlösung*, 130–1. The documents in Edgar Mais, ed., *Die Verfolgung der Juden in den Landkreisen Bad Kreuznach und Birkenfeld 1933–1945* (Bad Kreuznach, 1988) illustrate the complete isolation of Jews in Kreuznach and the surrounding district.

74. Barkai, *Wehr dich*; Kaplan, *Dignity*; Hildesheimer, *Jüdische Selbstverwaltung*;

75. Barkai, *Boykott*, 88 ff.

76. Ibid. 91 ff.

77. Adler-Rudel, *Selbsthilfe*, 131 ff.

78. Ibid. 47 ff.

79. Ibid.; Vollnhals, 'Selbsthilfe', 383 ff.

80. Barkai, *Boykott*, 96 ff.; Adler-Rudel, *Selbsthilfe*, 70–1.

81. Dahm, 'Leben', 107 ff.

82. Katrin Diehl, *Die jüdische Presse im Dritten Reich zwischen Selbstbehauptung und Fremdbestimmung* (Tübingen, 1997), 123 ff. lists a total of 146 Jewish newspapers and magazines, including 56 local newspapers. On the Jewish press see also Herbert Freeden, *Die jüdische Presse im Dritten Reich. Eine Veröffentlichung des Leo Baeck Instituts* (Frankfurt a. M., 1987).

83. Walk, *Jüdische Schule*, 80 ff.; Vollnhals, 'Selbsthilfe', 341 ff.

84. Walk, *Jüdische Schule*, 96 ff.

85. Ibid. 105 ff. and 111 ff.

86. Ibid. 122 ff.

87. Ibid. 149 ff.; published in 265 ff.; for a comparison of the guidelines see also Röcher, *Jüdische Schule*, 132 ff.

88. See also, in greater detail, Adler-Rudel, *Selbsthilfe*, 165 ff.; Barkai, *Boykott*, 103 ff.; Vollnhals, 'Selbsthilfe', 163–4.

89. Barkai, *Boykott*, 107.

90. Adler-Rudel, *Selbsthilfe*, 161 ff.; Barkai, *Boykott*, 107–8; Vollnhals, 'Selbsthilfe', 400 ff.

91. Adler-Rudel, *Selbsthilfe*, 163–4.

4. The Intensification of the Racial Persecution of Non-Jewish Groups by the Police Apparatus, 1936–1937

1. Herbert, *Best*, 170 ff.; Patrick Wagner, *Volksgemeinschaft ohne Verbrecher. Konzeptionen und Praxis der Kriminalpolizei in der Zeit der Weimarer Republik und des Nationalsozialismus* (Hamburg, 1996).

2. Michael Zimmermann, *Rassenutopie und Genozid. Die nationalsozialistische 'Lösung der Zigeunerfrage'* (Hamburg, 1996), 126.

3. Wagner, *Volksgemeinschaft*, 271.

4. Referred to in Wolfgang ' "Ayaß, Ein Gebot der nationalen Arbeitsdisziplin." Die Aktion "Arbeitsscheu Reich" 1938', in *Feindererklärung und Prävention. Kriminalbiologie, Zigeunerforschung und Asozialpolitik* (Berlin, 1988), 43 ff.

5. Quoted and commented upon in Ayaß, 'Gebot', 54. On this issue in greater detail, see Karl-Leo Terhorst, *Polizeiliche planmäßige Überwachung und polizeiliche Vorbeugehaft im Dritten Reich. Ein Beitrag zur Rechtsgeschichte und vorbeugender Verbrechensbekämpfung* (Heidelberg, 1985).

6. See e.g. the article by the deputy head of the Reich Criminal Police Office, Paul Werner: 'Die vorbeugende Verbrechensbekämpfung durch die Polizei', *Kriminalistik*, Issue 12 (1938), 59–61.

7. Ayaß, 'Gebot', 47 ff.

8. See below, pp. 103–4.

9. Zimmermann, *Rassenutopie*, 106 ff.

10. Ibid. 125 ff.; see also. Guenter Lewy, *The Nazi Persecution of the Gypsies* (New York, 2000), 43 ff.

11. Burkhard Jellonek, *Homosexuelle unter dem Hakenkreuz. Die Verfolgung von Homosexuellen im Dritten Reich* (Paderborn, 1990), 285.

12. Ibid. 122 ff.

13. Ibid. 139.

14. See above, p. 51.

15. Bock, *Zwangssterilisation*, 354, refers to the calculation of the costs of the operation on 17 June 1937 in BAB, R 2/12042.

16. Rainer Pommerin, *'Sterilisierung der Rheinlandbastarde'. Das Schicksal einer farbigen deutschen Minderheit, 1918–1937* (Düsseldorf, 1979), 77 ff.

17. All documents in PAA, Inland I, Partei 87/2.

5. Comprehensive Deprivation of Rights and Forced Emigration, late 1937–1939

1. *Jahresbericht SD-OA Südost für 1937* (OS 500-1-316), Sopade, Nov. 1937, A 53 ff. and July 1937, A 30–1.

2. Erwin Lichtenstein, *Die Juden der Freien Stadt Danzig unter der Herrschaft des Nationalsozialismus* (Tübingen, 1973), 56 ff.; see also Samuel Echt, *Die Geschichte der Juden in Danzig* (Leer, 1972), 172–3. OS, 500-3-316 Lagebericht 15 Oct.–31 Oct. 1937.

3. Details in Longerich, *Politik*, 161 ff., Additional material in OS, 501-3-583 (69).

4. Herbert Rosenkrantz, *Verfolgung und Selbstbehauptung. Die Juden in Österreich 1938–1945* (Munich, 1978), 22–3; Gerhard Botz, *Nationalsozialismus in Wien. Machtübernahme und Herrschaftssicherung 1938/39*, 3rd edn (Buchloe, 1988), 93 ff. on pogroms in March.

5. Rosenkrantz, *Verfolgung*, 31 ff.

6. Ibid. 26 ff. and 60 ff.

7. Rosenkrantz, *Verfolgung*, 45 ff.; Wolfgang Neugebauer, ed., *Widerstand und Verfolgung im Burgenland 1933–1945. Eine Dokumentation* (Vienna, 1979).

8. OS, 500-1-625, note, 16 May 1939.

9. Adam, *Judenpolitik*, 176; Letter from the Reich Minister of Economics to the Supervisory Offices concerning the curtailment of the distribution of raw materials, OS, 500-1-343, 27 Nov. 1937.

10. Barkai, *Boykott*, 141–2.

11. Gerhard Kratzsch, Der *Gauwirtschaftsapparat der NSDAP. Menschenführung, 'Arisierung', Wehrwirtschaft in Gau Westfalen-Süd* (Münster, 1989), 185.

12. *RGBl*, 1938, I, p. 627.

13. Kratzsch, *Gauwirtschaftsapparat*, 185 ff.

14. Ibid. 131.

15. *RGBl*, 1938, I, p. 414.

16. *RGBl*, 1938, I, pp. 414–15. See further details in Genschel, *Die Verdrängung*, pp. 151–2.

17. *RGBl*, 1938, I, pp. 415–16.

18. IfZ Anordnung Nr. 89/38, 2 Aug. 1938.

19. Kratzsch, *Gauwirtschaftsapparat*, 218 ff. On 'donations' to the Party see also the examples in Bajohr, *'Arisierung'*, 307–8 and Franz Fichtl et al., *Bambergs Wirtschaft judenfrei. Die Verdrängung der jüdischen Geschäftsleute in den Jahren 1933 bis 1939* (Bamberg, 1998), 142–3.

20. Barkai, *Boykott*, 133–4; Adam, *Judenpolitik*, 188 ff.

21. Lagebericht 1 Jan.–31 Mar. 1938, OS, 500-1-316.

22. OS, 500-1-549.

23. This is apparent from the marginal notes, ibid.

24. OS, 500-1-603, edited and introduced by Wolf Gruner: '"Lesen brauchen sie nicht zu können: …" Die Denkschrift über die Behandlung der Juden in der Reichshauptstadt auf allen Gebieten des öffentlichen Lebens vom Mai 1938', *Jahrbuch für Antisemitismusforschung* 4 (1995), 305–41.

25. OS, 500-1-603, Statement by Hagen, 17 May 1938.

26. Meldung II 112 an II 1, 28 June 1938, concerning the Memorandum Concerning the Treatment of the Jews in the Reich Capital; cf. Gruner, 'Denkschrift', 310 ff.

27. OS, 500-1-603, Meldung II 112 v. 28 June.

28. OS, 500-1-645 US. Bericht UA Berlin v. 29 June 1938 and Bericht II 112, 24 June 1938.

29. Goebbels's Diary, entry of 4 June 1938. See Fröhlich, *Die Tagebücher* Teil I, vol. v, p. 333.

30. Entry for 11 June 1938. Ibid. 340.

31. On the 'Asocial Action', Ayaß, 'Gebot'.

32. OS, 500-1-261 (88).

33. Harry Stein, *Konzentrationslager Buchenwald 1937–1945* (Göttingen, 1999), 23.

34. OS, 500-1-645, Berichte v. 24 June and 29 June. For further details see also the extracts from the reports of the SD-OA Ost of 16 June, 17 June, 18 June. The reports in the *Völkischer Beobachter* on the events (esp. 19 June and 21 June) provide an exemplary demonstration of the attempt to connect the 'asocial question' with the 'Jewish question'.

35. OS, 500-1-645 Bericht I 112, 5 July 1938.

36. Elke Fröhlich, ed., *Die Tagebücher von Joseph Goebbels*, Teil I: *Aufzeichnungen 1923–1941*, vol. v: *Dezember 1937–Juli 1938* (Munich, 2000), 355.

37. OS, 500-1-261, letter to SD-Führer OA Süd.

38. When Hagen, on Heydrich's instructions, complained to Under Secretary Berndt in the Ministry of Propaganda of false figures that the *VB* had given concerning the supposed migration of Jews to Berlin on 21 June, Berndt informed him that the quotation of these—wrong—numbers had occurred 'with the permission of the Führer on the order of the Reich Minister of National Enlightenment and Propaganda as arguments for the defence of the Operation against the Jews' (OS, 500-1-645, note from Hagen, 30 June 1938).

39. OS, 500-1-645.

40. OS, 500-1-645, signed Six.

41. OS, 500-1-380, Report SD-OA Südwest; OS, 500-1-645, radio broadcast SD-OA Elbe; 500-1-261, report SD-OA Hanover.

42. Ralph Weingarten, *Die Hilfeleistung der westlichen Welt bei der Endlösung der deutschen Judenfrage. Das 'Intergovernmental Committee on Political Refugees' IGC 1938–1939* (Bern, Frankfurt a. M., Las Vegas, 1981).

43. OS, 500-1-649, 29 July 1938.

44. OS, 500-1-610, Auflösungs-Erlass des RFFS v. 23 July 1938 and additional material.

45. BAB, R 58/486: quoted in Rosenkrantz, *Verfolgung*, 122–3.

46. On the history and foundation of the Central Office, Safrian, *Eichmann-Männer*, 23 ff.; Rosenkrantz, *Verfolgung*, 120 ff.

47. *The Trial of Adolf Eichmann*, 9 vols (Jerusalem, 1992–5), vii. 101.

48. OS, 500-1-625, Minute, 16 May 1939.

49. Ibid.

50. OS, 500-3-318, 3 Sept. 1938, Schreiben II 112 für II 1.

51. A military reserve consisting of unfit and limited-service men under 35 who had not been trained.

52. OS, 500-1-316 Zentral-Abteilung II/1 v. 1 Oct. 1938–31 Oct. 1938.

53. OS, 500-1-630 US.

54. Details from SD report, ibid.

55. OS, 721-1-2555, Report LV Rheinland of the CV, 3 Oct. 1938.

56. Report in OS, 500-1-630.

57. Kershaw, *Opinion*, 258.

58. Ibid. 259.

59. Wolf-Arno Kropat, *Kristallnacht in Hessen. Der Judenpogrom vom November 1938. Eine Dokumentation* (Wiesbaden, 1988), 23.

60. Ernst Bloch, *Geschichte der Juden von Konstanz im 19. und 20. Jahrhundert. Eine Dokumentation* (Konstanz, 1971), 138–9.
61. OS, 721-1-2555, Report LV Rheinland of the CV v. 3 Oct. 1938.
62. OS, 721-1-630 US and 721-1-2555.
63. OS, 500-1-316. Situation Report of the Central Department II/1, 1 Oct. 1938–31 Oct. 1938.
64. Ibid.; cf Rosenkrantz, *Verfolgung*.
65. OS, 500-1-549 US, extract from the daily news bulletin—I 12—6 July 1938.
66. OS, 500-1-630 SD-OA Süd 28 Oct. 1938 (according to a communication from the Stabskanzlei to II 112, 28 Oct. 1938).
67. OS, 500-1-630. The matter was put off until 1 December and then overtaken by the events of 9 November.
68. Session on 14 Oct. 1938, PS 1301 in IMT XXVII, 160 ff.
69. OS, 1458-1-454, note, 18 Oct. 1938.
70. On the Polish deportation see Trude Maurer, 'Abschiebung und Attentat. Die Ausweisung der polnischen Juden und der Vorwand für die "Kristallnacht"', in Walter Pehle, ed., *Der Judenpogrom 1938. Von der Kristallnacht bis zum Völkermord* (Frankfurt a. M., 1988), 52–72. Sybil Milton, 'The Expulsion of Polish Jews from Germany October 1938 to July 1939: A Documentation', *LBIY* 29 (1984), 169–99; Longerich, *Politik der Vernichtung*, 195 ff.; Bettina Goldberg, 'Die Zwangsausweisung der polnischen Juden aus dem Deutschen Reich im Oktober 1938 und die Folgen', *Zeitschrift für die Geschichtswissenschaft* 46 (1988), 52–72; Michael G. Esch, 'Die Politik der polnischen Vertretungen im Deutschen Reich 1935 bis 1939 und der Novemberpogrom 1938', *Jahrbuch für Antisemitismusforschung*, 8 (1999), pp. 131–54; extensive material on this subject in OS, 500-1-88.
71. The press conferences and newspaper reports are quoted in Dieter Obst, '*Reichskristallnacht*'. *Ursachen und Verlauf des antisemitischen Pogroms vom November 1938* (Frankfurt a. M., 1991), 65 ff.; and Benz, 'Der Rückfall in die Barbarei. Bericht über den Pogrom', in Pehle, *Der Judenpogrom*, 14 ff. On the pogrom, see also Wildt, *Volksgemeinschaft*, 301 and *passum*.
72. On the events in Kurhessen, see Obst, *Reichskristallnacht*, 67 ff.; Kropat, *Kristallnacht*, 21 ff.
73. This is the view of Obst, *Reichskristallnacht*, 79–80; the central role of Goebbels is also stressed in Philippe Burrin, *Hitler and the Jews: The Genesis of the Holocaust* (London, 1994), 59–60.
74. Diary entry for 10 Nov. 1938 in Elke Fröhlich, ed., *Die Tagebücher von Joseph Goebbels*, Teil I: *Aufzeichnungen 1923–1941*, vol. vi. Bearbeitet von Jana Richter (Munich, 1998), 180. Vom Rath, attended to by Hitler's personal doctor Brandt with the express task of 'consultation and immediate report', had died at about 4 p.m. (*VB*, 9 Nov. 1938); the arrival of the news of his death in Munich in the course of the afternoon is also confirmed by Reich Chief of Press Otto Dietrich (*12 Jahre mit Hitler* (Munich, 1955), 56) and the Gauleiter of Magdeburg-Anhalt, (Rudolf Jordan, *Erlebt und Erlitten. Weg eines Gauleiters von Munich bis Moskau* (Leoni am Starnberger See, 1971), 180).
75. Cf. Peter Longerich, *Die braunen Bataillone. Geschichte der SA* (Munich, 1989), 232–3.

76. See Goering in his speech to the Gauleiters etc. on 6 Dec. 1938 (cf. note 88), in which he attempted to represent the murders committed on 9 November as the result of misunderstandings.

77. BAB, NS 36/13; also 3063-PS *IMT* xxxii. 20 ff.

78. This was the purpose of the telegrams that Müller and Heydrich dispatched to the Gestapo offices during the night. BAB, R 58/276; also 33051-PS, *IMT* xxxi. 515 ff. and 74-PS, *IMT* xxv. 376 ff.

79. Detailed account in Obst, *Reichskristallnacht*. Barbara Distel, ' "Die letzte ernste Warnung vor der Vernichtung". Zur Verschleppung der "Aktionsjuden" in die Konzentrationslager', *Zeitschrift für die Geschichtswissenschaft* 46 11(1998), 985–91; and Heiko Pollmeier, 'Inhaftierung und Lagerführung deutscher Juden im November 1938', *Jahrbuch für die Antisemitismusforschung* 8 (1999), 107–30. Distel and Pollmeier refer to more than 26,000 prisoners, Stein, *Konzentrationslager*, to 30,000. See also Ben Barkow, ed., *November Pogrom 1938. Die Augenzeugeberichte der Wiener Library London* (Frankfurt a. M., 2008).

80. BAB, NS 36/13; quoted in Peter Longerich, *Die Ermordung der Europäischen Juden* (Munich, 1989), 43 ff.

81. See Stein, *Konzentrationslager*, about conditions in Buchenwald concentration camp, where a 'special camp' was set up for the arrested Jews. The camp staff mistreated these Jews particularly badly; the days between 10 and 14 November turned into a week of murder. This violent 'welcome ritual' was also performed in the other concentration camps; but the mistreatment continued long after. The prisoners' everyday existence in the camp was characterized by hunger, overcrowded huts, indescribable conditions of hygiene and theft by the staff. See also Distel, 'Warnung', and Pollmeier, 'Inhaftierung'.

82. OS, 1458-1-98, Annex to the Reich Economic Minister's minutes of the departmental meeting of 26 Jan., 28 Jan. 1939; this figure, which has made it possible to correct earlier estimates in the research literature, was first published in Longerich, *Politik*, 203. These figures have been confirmed in the thorough investigation of this complex by Gerald Feldman, *Allianz and the German Insurance Business 1933–1945* (New York, 2001), 269.

83. OS, 1458-1-98, Aufstellung Fachgruppe Feuerversicherugen und Nebenzweige, 21 Dec. 1938.

84. On the atmosphere; see Bankier, *Meinung*, 118 ff.; Longerich, *Politik*, 204–5.

85. 1816 PS, *IMT* xxviii. On this meeting see also the description in Walter Strauss, 'Das Reichsministerium des Innern und die Judengesetzgebung. Aufzeichnungen von Doktor Bernhard Lösener', *Vierteljahrshefte für Zeitgeschichte* 9/3 (1961) (note from Lösener), 286 ff.

86. According to Adolf Diamant, *Zerstörte Synagogen vom November 1938. Eine Bestandsaufnahme* (Frankfurt a. M., 1978), during the whole Nazi era some 1,200 synagogues and prayer rooms within the Reich in its 1938 borders were destroyed, most of them during the November pogrom, the rest mostly as a result of war damage.

87. These prohibitions had already been passed by the Reich Chamber of Culture on the day of the meeting, 12 Nov. See Walk, *Sonderrecht*, iii. 12.

88. OS, 1458-3-2216. On this meeting see also the circular of the Baden Gau headquarters, quoted in: *Dokumente über die Verfolgung*, Nr. 339, commented upon in Adam, *Judenpolitik*, 218.

89. As early as 14 November Department II of SD Headquarters, on the instructions of Heydrich, presented five drafts for a badge for the identification of the Jews: OS, 500-1-659.

90. Published by Götz Aly and Susanne Heim in *Beiträge zur nationalsozialistischen Gesundheits- und Sozialpolitik*, 9 (1991), Dokument 1, 15–21.

91. Amongst other things, Frick made the following statements on the issue: Jews were to leave the retail trade by January 1939; profits made through 'Aryanization' were to be skimmed off; rent control for Jews would be abolished within the next few days; Jews were to be concentrated in certain buildings. Otherwise, for the employment of the Jews there were ideas for 'labour columns' and for the existence of certain Jewish businesses.

92. First Decree for the Elimination of the Jews from Economic Life, *RGBl*, 1938, I, p. 1580. The first implementation provision of 23 Nov. 1938 regulated further details, *RGBl*, 1938, I, p. 1642.

93. *RGBl*, 1938, I, p. 1581.

94. *RGBl*, 1938, I, p. 1579; the implementation order by the Reich Minister of Finance of 21 Nov. 1938 governed taxation. Walk, *Sonderrecht*, iii. 21 and 24; cf. Barkai, *Boykott*, 151.

95. According to Kratzsch, *Gauwirtschaftsapparat*, 203.

96. Decree for the deployment of Jewish assets, *RGBl*, 1938, I, pp. 1709 ff.

97. Listed in Adam, *Judenpolitik*, 212 ff.

98. Fricke-Finkelnburg, *Nationalsozialismus und Schule*, 271.

99. Walk, *Sonderrecht*, iii. 56.

100. Decree against the Ownership of Weapons by Jews, 11 Nov. 1938, *RGBl*, I, p. 1573.

101. Decree of the President of the Reich Chamber of Culture, 12 Nov. 1938; see Walk, *Sonderrecht*, iii. 12.

102. Order of the Reichsführer SS and Chief of German Police, revealed in the press on 8 Dec. 1938. See *VB* 8 Dec. 1938.

103. *RGBl*, 1938, I, pp. 1676, 1704.

104. Walk, *Sonderrecht*, iii. 37.

105. Dieter Maier, *Arbeitseinsatz und Deportation. Die Mitwirkung der Arbeitsverwaltung bei der nationalsozialistischen Judenverfolgung in den Jahren 1939–1945* (Berlin, 1994), 26 ff.; Wolf Gruner, *Der geschlossener Arbeitseinsatz deutscher Juden. Zur Zwangsarbeit als Element der Verfolgung 1938–1943* (Berlin, 1997), 66 ff.

106. 069-PS, IMT xxv. 131 ff.

107. Walk, *Sonderrecht*, iii. 154.

108. Law concerning Rental Relationships with Jews, 30 Apr. 1939 (*RGBl*, 1939, I, p. 864).

109. Circular of the Reich Minister of the Interior, *RMBliV*, p. 1291, 16 June 1939.

110. Instruction by the Reich Minister of Economics of 16 Jan. 1939. Walk, *Sonderrecht*, iii. 106 and Third Decree to implement the Decree concerning the Reporting of Jewish Property of 21 Feb. 1939, *RGBl*, I, p. 282.

111. Decree to Alter the Decree concerning Medical Examination and Recruitment of 7 Mar. 1939, *RGBl*, 1939, I, p. 425.

112. On 'Compulsory *Entjudung*', see Kratzsch, *Gauwirtschaftsapparat*, 202 ff.

113. Cf. ibid. 204–5; circular of 25 Feb. 1939.

114. BAM, RW 19/2374, 5 Jan. 1939. On the practice of Aryanization see also the case study of Marburg: Barbara Händler-Lachmann and Thomas Werther, *Vergessene Geschäfte*,

verlorene Geschichte. Jüdisches Wirtschaftsleben in Marburg und seine Vernichtung im Nationalsozialismus (Marburg, 1992), 116 ff.

115. Barkai, *Boykott*, 151.

116. Bajohr, '*Arisierung*', 279.

117. *RGBl*, 1940, I, pp. 891–2.

118. Leo Lippmann, '...Dass ich wie ein guter Deutscher empfinde und handele'. *Zur Geschichte der Deutsch-Israelitischen Gemeinde in Hamburg in der Zeit von Herbst 1935 bis zum Ende 1942* (Hamburg, 1994), 71–2.

119. Minutes of the first meeting of the Reich Central Agency, 11 Feb. 1939 (*ADAP*), series D, vol. 5, no. 665.

120. OS, 500-1-550.

121. For assets of 1 million RM the grading was 10 per cent, larger assets were to be assessed at even higher rates in individual cases.

122. See Maier, *Arbeitseinsatz*, 22 ff. (especially on history and motivation) and Wolf Gruner, *Arbeitseinsatz*, 40 ff.

123. See above.

124. Maier, *Arbeitseinsatz*, 23–4.

125. Gruner, *Arbeitseinsatz*, 50–1.

126. BAB, R 18/5519, 'Entwurf für die Ansprache Fricks auf der Konferenz'; cf. Gruner, *Arbeitseinsatz*, 62.

127. Maier, *Arbeitseinsatz*, 26 ff.; Gruner, *Arbeitseinsatz*, 66 ff.

128. Ibid. 92.

129. Further details in Gruner, *Arbeitseinsatz*, 84 ff. See, for example, the survey carried out in Berlin municipal business operations about whose results the Mayor was informed early in March 1939: STA Berlin, Rep 01-02 GB 1281 (YV, JM 10660), the Councillor in Charge of Municipal Business Operations, 7 Mar. 1939 to the Mayor; cf. Gruner, *Arbeitseinsatz*, 90.

130. Ibid. 106.

131. OS, 504-2-2 (20), minute by the Chief of Security Police, 1 Mar. 1939, quoted in Konrad Kwiet, 'Forced Labour of German Jews in Nazi Germany', *LBIY* 36 (1991), 389–410. Cf. also Gruner, *Arbeitseinsatz*, 83–4.

6. The Politics of Organized Expulsion

1. *ADAP*, series D, vol. 4, no. 273.

2. *ADAP*, series D, vol. 4, no. 158, 167 ff.

3. Speech of 30 January, quoted in Max Domarus, *Hitler. Reden und Proklamationen* (Wiesbaden, 1973), ii. 1047 ff., for the passage in question 1055–8.

4. Domarus, *Hitler. Reden*, ii. 1057. Stefan Kley, 'Intention. Verkündung, Implementierung. Hitlers Reichstagsrede vom 30 Januar 1939', *Zeitschrift für die Geschichtswissenschaft* 48 (2000), sees this statement from Hitler as the announcement of the firm intention of the dictator, who was at this time already resolved to murder the European Jews. Kley deduced this from his view that in January 1939 Hitler had firmly decided upon a world war, and had thus sought himself to bring about the precondition that he had introduced for the murder of the Jews, the 'world war'. (See Kley,

Hitler, Ribbentrop und die Entfesselung des Zweiten Weltkriegs (Paderborn, 1996), 201 ff.) The author himself concedes that 'no direct path leads...from Hitler's intentions to the events' since, as we know, the systematic murder of the Jews of Europe did not start until 1941/2; the forced emigration still being practised in 1939 is even in diametrical opposition to the supposed genocidal intention. For these reasons alone the reconstruction of a firm 'intention' on Hitler's part to murder the European Jews in early 1939 is problematic if not nonsensical.

5. For greater detail see the following section.

6. On the Fischböck plan: Aufzeichnung des Leiters der Politischen Abteilung des AA, 14 Nov. 1938, *ADAP*, series C, vol. 5, no. 650. The passing of the negotiation contract on to Schacht is the background for the remark made by Goering in the conference on 6 December: 'I therefore request the gentleman—the man in question will know what I mean—that he will carry out no further negotiations here.'

7. On the Schacht–Rublee negotiations see Ralph Weingarten, *Die Hilfeleistung der westlichen Welt bei der Endlösung der deutschen Judenfrage. Das 'Intergovernmental Committee on Political Refugees' IGC 1938–1939* (Bern, Frankfurt a. M., Las Vegas, 1981), 127 ff.; Fischer, *Schacht*, 216 ff.

8. BAB, 25-01, 6641, letter from Rublee to Schacht, 23 Dec. 1938 with the outline for the project.

9. Details about the plan and the negotiations in note from Schacht, 16 Jan. 1939, BAB, 25-01, 5541, *ADAP*, series C, vol. 5, no. 661.

10. Weingarten, *Hilfeleistung*, 135 ff.

11. OS, 500-1-506, undated note ('Secret! Jewry) from the Jewish Department.

12. BAB, R 58/276.

13. On 10 January Schacht had informed Stuckart in broad terms about the agreement he hoped to reach with Rublee. Subsequently, on 18 January a discussion was held with senior SS and police officials in Heydrich's office, followed by another discussion with Stuckart and, on the following day, a meeting with Schacht. In these discussions there was general agreement that Schacht's ideas should be made the basis of further emigration policy (minutes of 19 Jan. 1939); both documents in OS, 500-1-638.

14. Report on the first working discussion of the Committee of the Reich Central Office for Jewish Emigration on 11 Feb. 1939, *ADAP*, series D, vol. 5, no. 665, pp. 786 ff. At the meeting the establishment of Central Offices in Berlin, Breslau, Frankfurt., and Hamburg was announced.

15. *RGBl*, 1939, I, p. 1097. Details of the history in Wolf Gruner, 'Poverty and Persecution: The Reichsvereinigung, the Jewish Population and Anti-Jewish Policy in the Nazi State 1933–1945', *YVS* 27 (1999) 28 ff.; and Esriel Hildesheimer, *Jüdischer Selbstverwaltung unter dem NS-Regime. Der Existenzkampf der Reichsvertretung und Reichsvereinigung der Juden in Deutschland* (Tübingen, 1994), 79 ff.

16. Further details see below, pp. 134–5.

17. See Herbert A. Strauß, 'Jewish Emigration from Germany: Nazi Policies and Jewish Response', *LBIY* 25 (1980), 313–61 (I) and 26 (1981), 343–409.

18. Ibid. 383 ff.

19. Ibid. 326.

20. Barkai, *Boykott*, 169 ff.

21. Bruno Blau, 'Die Juden in Deutschland von 1939 bis 1945', *Judaica* 7 (1951), 270–84, 278.
22. Ibid. 273.
23. Barkai, *Boykott*, 171–2. On the continuation of Jewish cultural life after the November pogrom see Volker Dahm, 'Kulturelles und geistiges Leben', in Benz, ed., *Die Juden in Deutschland*, 223 ff.
24. Barkai, *Boykott*, 171–2; Hildesheimer, *Selbstverwaltung*, 80 ff.

7. The Persecution of Jews in the Territory of the Reich, 1939–1940

1. Michael Wildt, *Generation des Unbedingten. Das Führungskorps des Reichssicherheitshauptamtes* (Hamburg, 2002), 358 ff.
2. Esriel Hildesheimer, *Jüdische Selbstverwaltung unter dem NS-Regime. Der Existenzkampf der Reichsvertretung und der Reichsvereinigung der Juden in Deutschland* (Tübingen, 1994), 116 ff.
3. Ibid. 132 ff.
4. Ibid. 153 ff.
5. Ruth Röcher, *Die Jüdische Schule im nationalsozialistischen Deutschland 1933–1942* (Frankfurt a. M., 1992), 86 ff.; Joseph Walk, *Jüdische Schule und Erziehung im Dritten Reich* (Frankfurt a. M., 1991), 217 ff.
6. Hildesheimer, *Selbstverwaltung*, 163–4.
7. Ibid. 165 ff.
8. See Uwe Adam, *Die Judenpolitik im Dritten Reich* (Düsseldorf, 1972), 258 ff. and Avraham Barkai, *Vom Boykott zu 'Entjudung'. Der wirtschaftliche Existenzkampf der Juden im Dritten Reich 1933–1943* (Frankfurt a. M., 1988), 183 ff.
9. Special Measure, Joseph Walk, *Das Sonderrecht für die Juden im NS-Staat. Eine Sammlung der gesetzlichen Massnahmen und Richtlinien—Inhalt und Bedeutung* (Heidelberg, 1981), iv. 2; Adam, *Judenpolitik*, 259. The news reached Victor Klemperer, for example, on 13 September 1939 (three days after it had been decreed) via a messenger from the local office of the Protestant Church to which Klemperer belonged (Viktor Klemperer, *I Shall Bear Witness: The Diaries of Viktor Klemperer 1941–1945* (London, 1999), i. 378).
10. *Dokumente zur Geschichte der Frankfurter Juden 1933–1945* (Frankfurt a. M., 1963), no. 433.
11. Special Measure, Walk, *Sonderrecht*, iv. 115 (Decree of the Reich Postal Ministry, 19 July 1940).
12. Statutes of the 'Reichsluftschutzbund', 28 June 1940, *RGBl*, I, p. 992; Adam, *Judenpolitik*, 258–9.
13. Special Measure, Walk, *Sonderrecht*, iv. 127.
14. Adam, *Judenpolitik*, 260 ff.
15. Special Measure, Walk, *Sonderrecht*, iv. 10 (Decree of the Chief of the Security Police concerning Special Food Shops for Jews, 12 Sept. 1939).
16. Konrad Kwiet, 'Nach dem Pogrom. Stufen der Ausgrenzung', in Wolfgang Benz, ed., *Die Juden in Deutschland. 1933–1945. Leben unter nationalsozialistischer Herrschaft* (Munich, 1988), 605 ff.

17. Kwiet, *Pogrom*, 606 ff. and in more detail Regina Bruss, *Die Bremer Juden unter dem Nationalsozialismus* (Bremen, 1983), 151 ff.

18. Special Measure, Walk, *Sonderrecht*, iv. 67 (Decree of the Reich Minister of Economics, 23 Jan. 1940). This measure meant that Jews did not receive clothing coupons, tokens for knitting or sewing, or shoes. They were provided with second-hand clothing by the municipality (see Hildesheimer, *Selbstverwaltung*, 168).

19. This emerges particularly clearly from Victor Klemperer's diaries.

20. For examples see Joseph Werner, *Hakenkreuz und Judenstern. Das Schicksal der Karlsruher Juden im Dritten Reich* (Karlsruhe, 1988), 281 (Karlsruhe); Horst Matzerath, 'Der Weg der Kölner Juden in den Holocaust. Versuch einer Rekonstruktion', in Gabriele Rogmann and Horst Matzerath, eds, *Die jüdischen Opfer des Nationalsozialismus aus Köln. Gedenkbuch* (Cologne, 1995), 534 (Cologne). The *Oberpräsident* (provincial governor) responsible for the Rhine Province issued a general ban on moves into cities on 15 Feb. 1940 (Herbert Lepper, *Von der Emanzipation zum Holocaust. Die israelitischen Synagogengemeinde zu Aachen 1801–1942; geschichtliche Darstellung Bilder, Dokumente, Tabellen, Listen* (Aachen, 1994), ii, doc. 1109).

21. Vienna was in the forefront of such developments. Partly because of direct pressure from the NSDAP the majority of Jews had been driven out of their homes by the end of 1938. In September and October 1939 plans were drawn up for the settlement of Vienna's Jews in closed camps, but they were dropped as the Nisko Programme began (see Gerhard Botz, *Wohnungspolitik und Judendeportation in Wien 1938 bis 1945. Zur Funktion des Antisemitismus als Ersatz nationalsozialistischer Sozialpolitik* (Vienna, 1975), 57 ff. and 94). In September 1938 in Berlin Speer had masterminded the confiscation of Jewish homes in his capacity as General Building Inspector for the Reich Capital, and in January 1939 he began to systematize the utilization of homes that Jews had been forced to leave as a result of a relaxation in the regulations governing notices to quit (see Susanne Willems, *Der entsiedelte Jude. Albert Speers Wohnungspolitik für den Berliner Hauptstadtbau* (Berlin, 2000), 105 ff.). In summer 1939 Speer began to create 'Jew-free districts' in the city and after January 1941 the Jews were driven out of their homes in organized 'clearance operations' (ibid. 134 ff. and 186 ff.). In Karlsruhe the majority of Jews still living in the city were accommodated in the 'Jewish houses' by the end of April 1939 (Werner, *Hakenkreuz*, 280). On 1 April 1940 the decision was taken in Aachen to bring together the remaining Jews in 'Jewish houses' (Lepper, *Emanzipation*, ii. 134). Between October and November 1939 a total of 47 'Jewish houses' were established in Leipzig, which initially received Jewish tenants from municipal housing (Klemperer, *Zeugnis*, i. 503). In Minden/Ravensberg 'Jewish houses' were set up in the larger districts from 1939 but filling them took until autumn 1940 (Joachim Meynert, *Was vor der 'Endlösung' geschah. Antisemitische Ausgrenzung in Minden-Ravensberg 1933–1945* (Münster, 1988), 227–8). On 'Jewish houses' see Wolf Gruner, *Der geschlossene Arbeitseinsatz deutscher Juden. Zur Zwangsarbeit als Element der Verfolgung, 1938–1943* (Berlin, 1997), 249 ff.

22. Wolf Gruner has identified 38 such camps: *Arbeitseinsatz*, 250.

23. For more detail on this see ibid. 107 ff.

24. Heinrich Himmler, *Geheimreden 1933 bis 1945 und andere Ansprachen*, ed. Bradley F. Smith and Agnes F. Peterson (Frankfurt a. M., 1974), 115 ff.

25. OS, 500-1-597.
26. OS, 503-1-324.
27. On euthanasia see Michael Burleigh, *Death and Deliverance: Euthanasia in Germany 1900–1945* (Cambridge, 1994); Ernst Klee, *'Euthanasie' im NS-Staat. Die 'Vernichtung lebensunwerten Lebens'* (Frankfurt a. M., 1983); Henry Friedlander, *The Origins of Nazi Genocide: From Euthanasia to the Final Solution* (Chapel Hill, NC, 1995); Hans-Walther Schmuhl, *Rassenhygiene, Nationalsozialismus, Euthanasie. Von der Verhütung zur Vernichtung 'lebensunwerten Lebens', 1890–1945* (Göttingen, 1987).
28. On the 'misery of psychiatry' before the outbreak of the Second World War, see in particular Dirk Blasius, *'Einfache Seelenstörung'. Geschichte der deutschen Psychiatrie 1800–1945* (Frankfurt a. M., 1994), esp. 145 ff.; Burleigh, *Death*, 43 ff.; Ludwig Siemen, *Menschen blieben auf der Strecke. Psychiatrie zwischen Reform und Nationalsozialismus* (Gütersloh, 1987); Hans Walter Schmuhl, 'Kontinuität oder Diskontinuität? Zum epochalen Charakter der Psychiatrie im Nationalsozialismus', in Franz-Werner Kersting, Karl Teppe, and Bernd Walter, eds, *Nach Hadamar. Zum Verhältnis von Psychiatrie und Gesellschaft im 20. Jahrhundert* (Paderborn, 1993), 112–36.
29. On children's 'euthanasia', see Friedlander, *Origins*, 84 ff.; Klee, *'Euthanasie'*, 77 ff.; Burleigh, *Death*, 93 ff.; Schmuhl, *Rassenhygiene*, 182.
30. Ulf Schmidt, 'Reassessing the Beginning of the "Euthanasia" Programme', *German History* 17 (1999), 543–50, and Udo Benzendörfer, 'Bemerkungen zur Planung bei der NS-"Euthanasie"', in Boris Böhm and Thomas Oelschläger, eds, *Der sächsische Sonderweg bei der NS-'Euthanasie'* (Ulm, 2001), 21–54.
31. On the organizational preparations for the T4 programme see Friedlander, *Origins*, 77 ff.; Burleigh, *Death*, 93 ff.; Schmuhl, *Rassenhygiene*, 182.
32. Klee, *'Euthanasie'*, 85–6; Instruction for Implementation of the Law concerning Prevention of Children with Hereditary Illnesses and of the Marriage Health Law, 31 Aug. 1939 (*RGBl*, I, p. 1560). Sterilizations did nevertheless take place until the end of the war, albeit in limited numbers. 'F-cases' were those where the threat of 'reproductive activity' was great (*fortpflanzungsgefahr*).
33. Götz Aly, 'Medizin gegen Unbrauchbare', in Götz Aly et. al., *Aussonderung und Tod. Die klinische Hinrichtung der Unbrauchbaren* (Berlin, 1985), 20 ff.
34. Nuremberg Document (ND) PS-630.
35. According to Rieß's estimate, Volker Rieß, *Die Anfänge der 'lebensunwerten Lebens' in den Reichsgauen Danzig-Westpreußen und Wartheland 1939/40* (Frankfurt a. M., 1995), 355.
36. See esp. ibid. 23 ff.
37. Ibid. 243 ff.
38. Ibid. 290 ff.
39. Ibid. 321 ff.; Matthias Beer, 'Die Entwicklung der Gaswagen beim Mord an den Juden', *VfZ* 35 (1987), 404 ff.; Eugen Kogon et al., eds, *Massentötungen durch Giftgas. Eine Dokumentation* (Frankfurt a. M., 1986), 62 ff.; Klee, *'Euthanasie'*, 105 ff.
40. Ibid. 222 ff. See also esp. Heike Bernhardt, *Anstaltspsychiatrie und 'Euthanasie' in Pommern 1933 bis 1945. Die Krankenmorde an Kindern und Erwachsenen am Beispiel der Landesheilanstalt Ueckermünde* (Frankfurt a. M., 1994).
41. Ibid. 188 and 288 ff.

42. See below pp. 290–1.
43. Rieß, *Anfänge*, 104 ff., 131, 135–6, 168, 256, and 334.
44. Götz Aly's assertion that the murder of more than 10,000 mentally ill patients in the East was 'causally linked to the "Heim-ins-Reich" [home into the Reich] movement of 60,000 Baltic Germans' is therefore unconvincing (Aly, *Final Solution: Nazi Population Policy and the Murder of the European Jews* (London, 1999), 70 ff.). Aly himself notes (p. 116) that the murder of the inmates of the Kocborowo Mental Hospital began on 22 September, and thus before the Soviet–German Resettlement Agreement. Even the request made on 23 October 1939 by Sandberger, Head of the Central Immigration Office, for 5,000 beds to be cleared for ethnic German migrants came too late to explain the murders that had already begun earlier in October in Neustadt, Schwetz, and Owinska (pp. 70–1). It is also important to note the other purposes that psychiatric institutions were put to, as detailed by Rieß; Schwede explicitly justified the deportations from his Gau in this manner (citing the construction of an SS barracks in the hospital at Stralsund). The most important factor that argues against Aly's interpretation is the fact that mass murders in the occupied zones were only an anticipatory measure in advance of the 'euthanasia' programmes being planned at the same time across the whole of the Reich and were directly linked to the eruption of violence against other civilian groups in the newly conquered areas. In this context the links to the resettlement of ethnic Germans are of secondary importance, one factor only in the acceleration of the mass murder of the inmates of psychiatric institutions. In the same way Aly's examples of South German institutions being filled with ethnic German emigrants in the second half of 1940 (pp. 120–2) do not constitute sufficient evidence for his thesis that 'the self-created pressure to accommodate ethnic German settlers in camps now also began to accelerate the murder of German psychiatric patients in the southern part of the Reich as well' (p. 120). Aly again distorts his argument when he identifies a secondary phenomenon (the use of 'freed-up' institutions) as the main cause of the murder of the sick and debilitated. Statistics published by Klee (*'Euthanasie'*, 340–1) suggest that of the 93,521 institutional beds 'freed up' by the end of 1941 (a figure which includes both the more than 70,000 people murdered in the gas chambers and those who died or were killed in the institutions themselves), only 8,577 were used for ethnic German settlers, whilst more than half served army or SS purposes, especially as reserve military hospitals.
45. On the organization of T4 see Klee, *'Euthanasie'*, 109 ff.; Friedlander, *Origins*, 68 ff.; Burleigh, *Death*, 133 ff.
46. See in particular the information in Heinz Faulstich, *Hungersterben in der Psychiatrie, 1914–1949* (Freiburg, 1998), 260 ff., which is complemented by detailed studies on individual institutions and regions as follows: Hermann J. Pretsch, ed., *'Euthanasie'. Krankenmorde in Südwestdeutschland. Die nationalsozialistische 'Aktion T4' in Württemberg 1940 bis 1945* (Zwiefalten, 1996); Christina Vanja and Martin Vogt, eds, *Euthanasie in Hadamar. Die nationalsozialistische Vernichtungspolitik in hessischen Anstalten* (Kassel, 1991); Heinz Faulstich, *Von der Irrenfürsorge zur 'Euthanasie'. Geschichte der badischen Psychiatrie bis 1945* (Freiburg, 1993); Ludwig Hermeler, *Die Euthanasie und die späte Unschuld der Psychiater. Massenmord, Bedburg-Hau und das Geheimnis rheinischer Widerstandslegenden* (Essen, 2002); Uwe Kaminsky, *Zwangs-*

sterilisation und 'Euthanasie' im Rheinland. Evangelische Erziehungsanstalten sowie Heil- und Pflegeanstalten 1933–1945 (Cologne, 1995); Boris Böhm and Thomas Oelschläger, eds, *Der sächsische Sonderweg bei der NS-'Euthanasie'* (Ulm, 2001); Thomas Schilter, *Unmenschliches Ermessen. Die nationalsozialistische 'Euthanasie'-Tötungsanstalt Pirna-Sonnenstein 1940/41* (Leipzig, 1999); Dietmar Schulze, *'Euthanasie' in Bernburg. Die Landes-Heil- und Pflegeanstalt Bernburg/Anhaltinische Nervenklinik in der Zeit des Nationalsozialismus* (Essen, 1999); Thomas Stöckle, *Grafeneck 1940. Die Euthanasie-Verbrechen in Südwestdeutschland* (Tübingen, 2002); Thorsten Sueße and Heinrich Meyer, *Abtransport der 'Lebensunwerten'. Die Konfrontation niedersächsischer Anstalten mit der NS-'Euthanasie'* (Hanover, 1998); Bernd Walter, *Psychiatrie und Gesellschaft in der Moderne. Geisteskrankenfürsorge in der Provinz Westfalen zwischen Kaiserreich und NS-Regime* (Paderborn, 1996); Michael von Cranach and Hans-Ludwig Siemen eds, *Psychiatrie im Nationalsozialismus. Die Bayerischen Heil- und Pflegeanstalten zwischen 1933 und 1945* (Munich, 1999).

47. *International Military Tribunal (IMT)*, xxxv. 681 ff., 906-D, a note from Sellmer (from the staff of the Führer's Deputy) on a visit by Werner Blankenburg from the Chancellery of the Führer of the NSDAP (Brack's deputy), 1 Oct. 1940: '30,000 done, a further 100,000–120,000 waiting'.

48. Elke Fröhlich, ed., *Die Tagebücher von Joseph Goebbels*, Teil I: *Aufzeichnungen 1923–1941* Dezember 1940–Juli 1941, bearbeitet von Elke Fröhlich (Munich, 1998). Entry for 31 Jan. 1941, p. 119 (on a conversation with Bouhler): '40,000 are gone, 60,000 still have to go.'

49. In the planning stages, for example, Brack considered that secrecy could not be taken as read if there were to be, as was proposed at that point, some 60,000 victims (according to a witness statement by his colleague Hefelmann, quoted in Aly, *Final Solution*, 28). On the imperfect secrecy surrounding euthanasia, see Winfried Süß, *Der Volkskörper im Krieg. Gesundheitspolitik, Gesundheitsverhältnisse und Krankenmord im nationalsozialistischen Deutschland 1939–1945* (Munich, 2003), 129–30.

50. For examples of 'Euthanasia' propaganda see Klee, *'Euthanasie'*, 76–7 and 176–7.

51. Friedlander, *Origins*, 263 ff.

8. German Occupation and the Persecution of the Jews in Poland, 1939–1940/1941: The First Variant of a 'Territorial Solution'

1. On the war against Poland and the first phase of occupation, see Dieter Pohl, *Von der 'Judenpolitik' zum 'Judenmord'. Der Distrikt Lublin des Generalgouvernments 1939–1944* (Frankfurt a. M., 1993); Christian Jansen and Arno Weckbecker, *Der 'Volksdeutsche Selbstschutz' in Polen 1939–40* (Munich, 1992); Horst Rohde, 'Hitlers erste "Blitzkrieg" und seine Auswirkung auf nordostEuropa', in Klaus A. Maier et al., *Die Errichtung der Hegemonie auf dem europäischen Kontinent* (Stuttgart, 1979), 79–156; Czeslaw Madajczkyk, *Die Okkupationspolitik Nazideutschlands in Polen 1939–1945* (Cologne, 1988); Helmut Krausnick, 'Die Einsatzgruppen vom Anschluss Österreichs bis zum Feldzug gegen die Sowjetunion. Entwicklung und Verhältnis zur Wehrmacht', in Helmut Krausnick and Hans-Heinrich Wilhelm, *Die Truppe des Weltanschauungskrieges. Die Einsatzgruppen der Sicherheitspolizei und des SD, 1938–1942* (Stuttgart, 1982), 32 ff.

2. *IMT*, xxxvii. 546 ff., O79–L.

3. *ADAP*, series D, vol. 7, no. 193; Winfried Baumgart, 'Zur Ansprache Hitlers vor den Führern der Wehrmacht am 22. August 1939. Eine quellenkritische Untersuchung', *VfZ* 2 (1968), 120–49.

4. *IMT*, xxxix. 425 ff., 172-USSR, statement by Hitler, 2 Oct. 1939.

5. BAB, R 58/825, 8 Sept. 1941 and 16 Oct. 1941.

6. Jansen and Weckbecker, *Selbstschutz*, 27 ff.; Wlodzimierz Jastrzebski, *Der Bromberger Blutsonntag. Legende und Wirklichkeit* (Poznan, 1990).

7. Krausnick, 'Einsatzgruppen', 33 ff. A detailed account of the leadership can be found in Alexander B. Rossino, *Hitler Strikes Poland: Blitzkrieg, Ideology, and Atrocity* (Lawrence, Kan., 2003), 29 ff.

8. Krausnick, 'Einsatzgruppen', 107.

9. Dorothee Weitbrecht, 'Die Ermächtigung zur Vernichtung. Die Einsatzgruppen in Polen im Herbst 1939', in Klaus-Michael Mallmann and Bogdan Musial, eds, *Genesis des Genozids. Polen 1939–1941* (Darmstadt, 2004), 57; Dan Michman, 'Why did Heydrich write the *Schnellbrief*? A Remark on the Reason and on its Significance', *YVS* 32 (2004), 439–40.

10. Weitbrecht, 'Ermächtigung', 59 ff.

11. Jansen and Weckbecker, 'Selbstschutz', 82 ff.

12. The role of the *Selbstschutz* has been exhaustively examined in Jansen and Weckbecker, ibid. 111 ff. On the participation of the army in the murders see Joachim Böhler, '*Auftakt zum Vernichtungskrieg. Die Wehrmacht in Polen 1939*' (Frankfurt a. M., 2006). On the *Einsatzgruppen* see Rossino, *Hitler*, 88 ff. and his 'Nazi Anti-Jewish Policy during the Polish Campaign: The Case of the Einsatzgruppe von Woyrisch', *GSR* 24 (2001), 35–54 and Klaus-Michael Mallmann, Joachim Böhler, and Jürgen Matthäus, eds, *Einsatzgruppen in Polen. Darstellung und Dokumentation* (Darmstadt, 2008).

13. Madajczyk, *Okkupationspolitik*, 12.

14. For examples, see Rossino, *Hitler*, 90–1 and 99.

15. Christopher Browning, *The Origins of the Final Solution: The Evolution of Nazi Jewish Policy September 1939 to March 1942* (London, 2004), 25 ff., 56–7; Böhler, ' "Tragische Verstrickung" ', 45 ff.

16. Jansen and Weckbecker, 'Selbstschutz', 154 ff.

17. Ibid. 96 ff. and 154.

18. Ibid. 96 ff.

19. On the role of uniformed police in these murders see Klaus-Michael Mallmann, ' " . . . Mißgeburten, die nicht auf diese Welt gehören". Die deutsche Ordnungspolizei in Polen 1939–1941', in Mallmann and Musial, eds, *Genesis*, 71–89.

20. Martin Cüppers, ' " . . . auf eine so saubere und anständige SS-mäßige Art". Die Waffen-SS in Polen 1939–1941', in Mallmann and Musial, eds, *Genesis*, 90–110.

21. Jansen and Weckbecker, 'Selbstschutz', 168 ff.; Pohl, *Judenpolitik*, 22 ff.; Szymon Datner, 'Crimes Committed by the Wehrmacht during the September Campaign and the Period of Military Government', *Polish Western Affairs* 3 (1962), esp. 322 ff.

22. Jansen and Weckbecker, 'Selbstschutz', 154 ff. and 212 ff.

23. Rieß, *Anfänge*, 173 ff.

24. Jansen and Weckbecker, 'Selbstschutz', 156 and 224 ff.

25. Ibid. 156–7 and 228–9.

26. IfZ, Fb 52.

27. File note by Oberstleutnant Lahousen, published in Helmuth Groscurth, *Tagebücher eines Abwehroffiziers 1938–1940. Mit weiteren Dokumente zur Militäropposition gegen Hitler* (Stuttgart, 1970), 357 ff. According to Lahousen's (unverifiable) testimony in Nuremberg (*IMT*, ii. 492 ff. and iii. 30), at this meeting Keitel told Canaris to 'raise a rebellion' in Galician Ukraine 'with the extirpation of the Jews as its goal'; only when Canaris refused was this remark about the *Einsatzgruppen* made (cf. Eberhard Jäckel, *Hitlers Herrschaft. Vollzug einer Weltanschauung* (Stuttgart, 1986), 95 and 172).

28. On this resistance see Krausnick, 'Einsatzgruppen', 80 ff.

29. Quoted in Groscurth, *Tagebücher*, 409 ff.

30. Meeting of the Chief of the General Staff of the Army High Command in the new Military District of Danzig with HSSPF Hildebrand and the *Selbstschutz* commander responsible for the area of West Prussia von Alvensleben, 13 Oct. 1939, in Jansen and Weckbecker, 'Selbstschutz', 175.

31. Ibid. 193 ff.

32. Note made by Blaskowitz for a presentation to the ObdH, 6 Feb. 1940, in Ernst Klee, Willi Dressen, and Volker Riess, eds, *'Schöne Zeiten'. Judenmord aus der Sicht der Täter und Gaffer* (Frankfurt a. M., 1988), 14 ff.

33. Schmuel Krakowski, 'The Fate of Jewish Prisoners of War in the September 1939 Campaign', *YVS*, 12 (1977), 297–323.

34. On the establishment and replacement of the military administration see Hans Umbreit, *Deutsche Militärverwaltungen 1938/39. Die militärische Besetzung der Tschechoslowakei und Polens* (Stuttgart, 1977), 85 ff., and Madajczyk, *Okkupationspolitik*, 18 ff. On the dismemberment of Poland, see Rohde, 'Blitzkrieg', 136 ff.

35. On the system of 'ethnic inequality' in Poland see especially Diemut Majer, *'Fremdvölkische' in Dritten Reich. Ein Beitrag zur nationalsozialistischen Rechtsetzung und Rechtspraxis in Verwaltung und Justiz unter besonderer Berücksichtigung der eingegliederten Ostgebiete und des Generalgouvernements* (Boppard, 1981). From the extensive literature on the German politics of occupation, the following deserve special mention: Martin Broszat, *Nationalsozialistische Polenpolitik* (Stuttgart, 1961); Gerhard Eisenblätter, 'Grundlinien der Politik des Reichs gegenüber der Generalgouvernement', diss. (Frankfurt a. M., 1969); Madajczyk, *Okkupationspolitik*; Werner Röhr, ed., *Die faschistische Okkupationspolitik in Polen (1939–1945)* (Bonn, 1969).

36. Hans-Christian Harten, *De-Kulturation und Germanisierung. Die nationalsozialistische Rassen- und Erziehungspolitik in Polen 1939–1945* (Frankfurt a. M., 1996).

37. Madajczyk, *Okkupationspolitik*, 541 ff.

38. Wlodzimierz Borodziej, *Terror und Politik. Die deutsche Polizei und die polnische Widerstandsbewegung im Generalgouvernement 1939–1944* (Mainz, 1999). See also Majer, *Fremdvölkische*, 864 ff. on the arbitrary penal system in the General Government.

39. Ibid. 387 ff.

40. Christopher Browning, 'Nazi Resettlement Policy and the Search for a Solution to the Jewish Question', *GSR* 9/3 (1986), 8; reprinted in Browning, *The Path to Genocide*; and Pohl, *Lublin*, 22.

41. BAB, R 58/825, 15 Sept. 1939.

42. BAB, R 58/825, Departmental Heads meeting, minute of 27 Sept. 1939. The 'German areas' referred to in point 1 of the summary remarks clearly indicated the annexed Polish territories, whilst 'Jews out of the Reich' (point 2) meant those in the rest of the Reich area, as is clear from the parallel intention (in point 3) to deport 30,000 Gypsies (i.e. almost all those living in the area of the Reich).

43. *Faschismus—Ghetto—Massenmord. Dokumentation über Ausrottung und Widerstand der Juden in Polen während des zweiten Weltkriegs*, ed. Tatiana Berenstein et al. (Frankfurt a. M., 1962), 37 ff.; ND 3363-PS.

44. Note of the conversation between Heydrich and Brauchitsch, published in Groscurth, *Tagebücher*, 361–2.

45. BAB, R 58/825, Departmental Heads meeting of 29 September, minute of 1 Oct. 1939. Correspondingly the exceptional regulation for the area under Einsatzgruppe I mentioned in the express letter of 21 September was lifted: YV, 053/87, Eichmann's note dated 29 Sept. 1939.

46. Hans-Günther Seraphim, ed., *Das Politische Tagebuch Alfred Rosenbergs aus den Jahren 1933/35 und 1939/40* (Göttingen, 1956), 81.

47. Andreas Hillgruber, ed., *Staatsmänner und Diplomaten bei Hitler. Vertrauliche Aufzeichnungen über Unterredungen mit Vertretern des Auslands*, vol. i (Frankfurt a. M., 1967), 29–30 (26 Sept. 1939).

48. *ADAP*, series D, vol. 7, no. 176, minute of 2 Oct. 1939.

49. Confidential Information (Communications of the Ministry for Propaganda), 9 Oct. 1941, in Jürgen Hagemann, *Die Presselenkung im Dritten Reich* (Bonn, 1970), 145; Jonny Moser, 'Nisko: The First Experiment in Deportation', Simon Wiesenthal Center Annual (*SWCA*) 2 (1985), 3, observes that the Belgrade paper *Vreme* had already reported on the reservation plans on 19 Sept. 1941.

50. *Verhandlungen des deutschen Reichstages*, vol. 460, pp. 51 ff.

51. *IMT* xxvi. 255–6, 686-PS.

9. Deportations

1. The note Eichmann made on 6 Oct. 1939 goes on to say that 'this activity should serve in the first instance as a way of building up experience such that on this basis the evacuation of larger masses of people could be facilitated' (YV, 053/87, Gestapo Documents from Ostrava). On the autumn 1939 deportations see: Miroslav Kárny, 'Nisko in der Geschichte der Endlösung', *Judaica Bohemiae* 23 (1987), 69–84; Seev Goshem, 'Eichmann und die Nisko-Aktion im Oktober 1939. Eine Fallstudie zur NS-Judenpolitik in der letzten Etappe vor der "Endlösung" ', *VfZ* 27 (1981), 74–96; Moser, *Nisko*; Seev Goshem, 'Nisko—ein Ausnahmefall unter den Judenlagern der SS', *VfZ* 40 (1992), 95–106; Hans-Günther Adler, *Der verwaltete Mensch. Studien zur deportation der Juden aus Deutschland* (Tübingen, 1974), 125 ff.; Browning, *Resettlement*; Hans Safrian, *Die Eichmann-Männer* (Vienna, 1993), 68 ff. There is more information in the volume of

conference proceedings edited by Ludmila Cermáková-Nesládková, *The Case of Nisko in the History of the 'Final Solution of the Jewish Problem' in Commemoration of the 55th Anniversary of the First Deportation of Jews in Europe* (Ostrava, 1994).

2. On 13 September the Quartermaster General of the OKH had given the order for all Jews in the eastern part of Upper Silesia to be deported eastwards over the San and thus into the area that agreements with the Soviet Union had designated as the Soviet sphere of influence. This occurred on a huge scale. See Alfred Konieczny, 'Die Zwangsarbeit der Juden in Schlesien im Rahmen der "Organisation Schmelt" ', *Beiträge zur Nationalsozialistische Gesundheitspolitik und Sozialpolitik: Sozialpolitik und Judenvernichtung. Gab es seine Ökonomie der Endlösung?*, 5 (1983), 94. In addition, on 18 September a discussion led by Stahlecker, the Commander of the Security Police (BdS) in the Protectorate had envisaged the deportation of 8,000 Jews from the area of Ostrava immediately bordering on Silesia into Galicia: YV, 053/87, telex from the Stapostelle Brünn from 19 Sept. 1939.

3. Ibid., note dated 6 Oct. 1939.

4. Ibid., note by Günter dated 11 Oct. 1939.

5. Note by the Special Representative dated 10 Oct. 1939 (original not preserved; excerpt made later), quoted by Gerhard Botz, *Wohnungspolitik und Judendeportation in Wien 1938 bis 1945. Zur Funktion des Antisemitismus als Ersatz nationalsozialistischer Sozialpolitik* (Vienna, 1975), 105 (from the Austrian State Archive).

6. YV, 053/93, telegram from SD Danube to the SD Headquarters, 16 Oct. 1939.

7. At the meeting held in the Stapo Branch Office in Ostrava on 9 October, there was some discussion of the details for the construction of these barracks (ibid., note by Dannecker, 11 Oct. 1939).

8. Ibid., note from the Central Office in Vienna, 17 Oct. 1939. According to this note, Gauleiter Bürckel, who had been informed of the latest discussions with Eichmann by one of his colleagues, was 'more than happy…that the planned resettlement of the Jews into barracks did not need to take place, since the costs per head of the construction of the barracks alone would have amounted to 330 RM'.

9. Ibid., telegram from the SD Headquarters to the Stapo Branch Office in Ostrava, 13 Oct. 1939 and response from SD Danube, 16 Oct. 1939.

10. See Safrian, *Eichmann-Männer*, 77 ff. On the execution of these deportations, see Goshen, 'Eichmann', 86; Herbert Rosenkranz, *Verfolgung und Selbstbehauptung. Die Juden in Österreich 1938 bis 1945* (Munich and Vienna, 1978) (on Vienna); on the deportation from Ostrava, see Karny, 'Nisko', 96 ff. and Lukas Pribyl, 'Das Schicksal des dritten Transports aus dem Protektorat nach Nisko', *Theresienstädter Studien* (2000), 297–342; there is detailed material on this in YV, 053/86.

11. Ibid., note on the contents of a telex and Eichmann's views on it. Eichmann did not receive this until 21 October in Nisko.

12. Ibid., note from the Gestapo Branch Office in Ostrava dated 21 Oct. 1939. In a letter to Bürckel from 9 Nov. 1939, Himmler made it clear once more that he had 'put a stop to the transportation of Jews until further notice because of the technical difficulties'. See Botz, *Wohnungspolitik*, 196, and *IMT* xxxii. 255 ff., 3398-PS.

13. Ibid., note from the Gestapo Branch Office in Ostrava dated 24 Oct. 1939.

14. *IMT* xxvi. 378–9, 864-PS, minute of 20 Oct. 1939. On military reservations about the further concentration of Jews in the area around Lublin see also the remark made by

Krüger on 1 Nov. 1939 in *Das Diensttagebuch des deutschen Generalgouverneurs in Polen 1939–1945*, ed. Werner Präg and Wolfgang Jacobmeyer (Stuttgart, 1975), 56. The negative attitude of the OKW with regard to a 'massing (*Zusammenballung*) of Jews' near the demarcation line is also mentioned in the so-called 'long-term plan' of the RHSA (*c.* November 1941, BAB, R 69/1146).

15. Ibid., SD Danube to the Stapo Branch Office in Ostrava, 28 Oct. 1939.
16. *Diensttagebuch*, ed. Präg and Jacobmeyer, 56.
17. Bogdan Musial, *Deutsche Zivilverwaltung und Judenverfolgung im Generalgouvernemnt. Eine Fallstudie zum Distrikt Lublin 1939–1944* (Wiesbaden, 1999), 127–8.
18. *Faschismus*, ed. Berenstein et al., 46.
19. Hagemann, *Presselenkung*, 146.
20. *IMT* xxx. 84 ff. (95), 2278-PS.
21. Quoted from Sybille Steinbacher, *'Musterstadt' Auschwitz. Germanisierungspolitik und Judenmord in Ostoberschlesien* (Munich, 2000), 120.
22. Pohl, *Judenpolitik*, 52.
23. *Diensttagebuch*, ed. Präg and Jacobmeyer, 186.
24. Quoted from Götz Aly and Susanne Heim, *Vordenker der Vernichtung. Auschwitz und die deutschen Pläne für eine europäische Ordnung* (Hamburg, 1991), 204.
25. *Karl Haushofer: Leben und Werk*, vol. ii: *Ausgewählter Schriftwechsel, 1917–1946*, ed. Hans-Adolf Jacobsen (Boppard am Rhein, 1979), no. 226.
26. Longerich, *Politik*, 262. On the deportations and plans for deportations after autumn 1939, especially those relating to Jews in the annexed Polish areas after autumn 1939, see in particular Adler, *Verwaltete Mensch*, 106 ff.; Aly, 'Final Solution', 33 ff., and Browning, *Origins*, 43 ff.
27. BAB, R 75/3b, published in *Faschismus*, ed. Berenstein et al., 42–3.
28. Minute in *Biuletyn Glowncj Komisji Badania Zbrodni Hitlerowskich W Polsce (Biuletyn)*, XII, document 3. On this see also Krüger's report made at a workshop for the district administrators (*Landräte*) of Cracow held on the same day (*Diensttagebuch*, ed. Präg and Jacobmeyer, 60–1): 'the most urgent matter is the return of 25,000 ethnic Germans from the Bug–Vistula area. By spring 1,000,000 Poles and Jews must be removed from East and West Posen, Danzig, Poland and Upper Silesia and taken into the General Government. The return of the ethnic Germans and the reception of the Poles and Jews (10,000 per day) must be achieved according to plan.'
29. Minute of the meeting of 8 Nov. 1939 (see previous note); circular from the HSSPF Warthegau, Koppe, 12 Nov. 1939, AGK, *Bühler-Prozess*, 8.
30. BAB, R 58/240, note by Best dated 31 Oct. 1939; cf. Karl-Heinz Roth, 'Erster "Generalplan Ost April/May 1940" von Konrad Meyer', in *Dokumentationsstelle zur NS-Sozialpolitik Mitteilungen*, vol. 1 (1985), 34.
31. See the memorandum by two of the members of the Racial Policy Office, G. Hecht and E. Wetzel, on 'The Question of How to Treat the Population of the Former Polish Areas seen from a Racial Political Perspective' (BAR, R 49/75, 25 Nov. 1939, published in *Documente Occupationis Teutonicae* (Doc. Occ.) (Poznan, 1949), v. 2 ff.
32. Letter from Heydrich to the HSSPF in Cracow, Breslau, Poznan, and Danzig and telex on the details of the short-term plan dated 28 Nov. 1939: *Biuletyn Glownej Komisji Badania Zbrodni Hitlerowskich W Polsce*, vol. XII, documents 4 and 5. A copy of the

completed 'long-range plan' has not so far been discovered, but there is a draft in existence, undated and unsigned, which was presumably made by Department III of the RSHA: BAB, R 69/1146, in *1999* 11 (1997), 50–71.

33. BAB, R 75/3b, letter from HSSPF Koppe to the RSHA, dated Poznan, 18 Dec. 1939 (*Biuletyn*, XII, document 8).

34. BAB, R 75/3b: concluding report by Koppe, dated 26 Jan. 1940 (published in *Faschismus*, ed. Berenstein et al., 48).

35. BAB, R 58/544, II-112. The SD headquarters was at precisely this point being transformed into Department III of the RSHA.

36. BAB, R 58/276 (also published in *Biuletyn*, XII, document 9); the letter referred to the in-house meeting of 19 Dec. 1939.

37. Götz Aly, *'Final Solution': Nazi Population Policy and the Murder of the European Jews* (London, 1999), 41–2, quoted from AGK, UWZ, P 197. On these plans see also Frank's statements on 19 Jan. 1940 (*Diensttagebuch*, 93 ff.).

38. According to Aly, *'Final Solution'*, 41 (based on AGK, UWZ, P 197).

39. Aly, *'Final Solution'*, 43–4, 46–7, 80.

40. For details see Longerich, *Politik*, 266–7.

41. Note dated 8 Jan. 1940 on an interministerial meeting held on 4 Jan. 1940; see Kurt Pätzold, *Verfolgung, Vertreibung, Vernichtung. Dokumente des faschistischen Antisemitismus 1933 bis 1942* (Leipzig, 1984), 256–7.

42. BAB, R 113/10 (published with an introduction by Karl-Heinz Roth and supplementary documents in *Mitteilungen*), 45 ff. There is a suggestion for the dating of the document in the marginal note 'zum Vermerk vom 24.1.40'.

43. BAB, R 58/1032, meeting of 30 Jan. 1940 in the RSHA; published in *Faschismus*, ed. Berenstein et al., 50 ff. On the limitations placed on the plans for deportation, see Browning, *Origins*, 54 ff.

44. Frank Golczewski, 'Polen' in Wolfgang Benz, ed., *Dimensionen des Völkermords. Die Zahl der jüdischen Opfer des Nationalsozialismus* (Munich, 1991), 429. On the intermediate plan see Browning, *Origins*, 63 ff.

45. OS, 503-1-385, express letter dated 12 Feb. 1940. This document was first drawn to historians' attention by Wolf Gruner, 'Von der Kollektivausweisung zur Deportation der Juden aus Deutschland', in Christoph Dieckmann et al., eds, *Beiträge zur Geschichte des Nationalsozialismus*, vol. xx: *Die Deportation der Juden aus Deutschland, Pläne, Praxis, Reaktionen 1938–1945* (Göttingen, 2004), 39.

46. BAB, R 43II/1412; see Adler, *Verwalteter Mensch*, 140 ff.

47. Speech to the Gauleiters, 29 Feb. 1940, Himmler, *Geheimreden*, 139. This thesis was adopted by Aly, *'Final Solution'*, 60–1, but the deportations were evidently a component of a plan that encompassed the whole of the Reich, as Gruner was the first to demonstrate. Those affected, however, saw the transportations as an act of revenge on the part of the Gauleiter and the Mayor after the 'resettlement' of Jews in the district of Stettin had been thwarted in January after an intervention from the RVJD (WL, 02/425, report by Arthur Abrahamson dated 1 Sept. 1941). Cf. Jakob Toury, 'Die Entstehungsgeschichte des Austreibungsbefehls gegen die Juden der Saarpfalz und Badens (22/23. Oktober 1940—Camp de Gurs)', *Jahrbuch des Instituts für Deutsche Geschichte* 15 (1986), 432–3, who finds this thesis plausible.

48. See p. 159.

49. OS, 500-1-385, 15 Mar. 1940; cf. Gruner, 'Von der Kollektivausweisung', 40.

50. Jakob Peiser, *Die Geschichte der Synagogengemeinde zu Stettin* (Würzburg, 1965), 133–4 and report WL 02/425. See also Else Rosenfeld and Getrud Luckner, eds, *Lebenszeichen aus Piaski Briefe Deportierter aus dem Distrikt Lublin 1940–1943* (Munich, 1968), e.g. report of Frau G.M., 27 ff.

51. Himmler, *Geheimreden*, 138–9.

52. *IMT* xxxvi. 299 ff., 305 EC.

53. Discussed in Aly, '*Final Solution*', 49. The text is cited in a letter from Goering dated 4 Apr. 1940 to the Trustee Offices (*Treuhandstellen*) in the eastern areas (original in the State Archive, Posen). That the Zentralstellen Für Jüdische Auswanderung in Berlin und Wien, in fact agencies of the RSHA, had asked Soviet authorities for a resettlement of the German Jews at the beginning of 1940, is the astonishing revelation of the most recent research in Russian archives. See Parel Polian, 'Hätte der Holocaust beinahe nicht stattgefunden? Überlegungen zu einem Schriftwechsel im Wert von zwei Millionen Menschenleben' in: Johannes Hürter and Türgen Zarusky, eds, *Besatzung, Kollaboration, Holocaust. Neue Studien zur Verfolgung und Ermordung der europäischen Juden*, 1–20.

54. *Diensttagebuch*, ed. Präg and Jakobmeyer, 2 and 4 Apr. 1940, 127 ff., 143 ff.

55. Report of the Director of the Resettlement Department of the Governor of the district of Warsaw, Waldemar Schön, dated 20 Jan. 1941 in *Faschismus*, ed. Berenstein et al., 108 ff.

56. Paul Sauer, ed., *Dokumente über die Verfolgung der jüdischen Bürger in Baden-Württemberg durch das NS-Regime* (Stuttgart, 1965), ii, no. 409.

57. See below, 165.

58. See n. 157.

59. Aly, '*Final Solution*', 51 and 98.

60. Steinbacher, '*Musterstadt' Auschwitz*, 118 ff.

61. The *Einsatzgruppen* had already begun to register Jews, establish councils of Jews, deploy forced labour, confiscate property, and organize emigration (Pohl, *Lublin*, 27; Krausnick, 'Einsatzgruppen', 71–2). In the phase of military administration the heads of the civilian authorities, who were subordinate to the high command of the army, had instituted the labelling of Jews, the expropriation of Jewish businesses and the confiscation of raw materials (Pohl, *Lublin*, 28).

62. Regulation on the labelling of Jews, male and female, in the General Government, 23 Nov. 1939, *Verordnungsblatt für das Generalgouvernement* (*VOGG*), 61; Adam, *Judenpolitik*, 255.

63. Regulation on the determination of the concept 'Jew' in the General Government, *VOGG*, 231; see *Diensttagebuch*, ed. Präg and Jakobmeyer, 6 May 1940, 193.

64. Regulation on the introduction of enforced labour for the Jewish population of the General Government, dated 26 Oct. 1939 (*VOGG*, 5 ff.).

65. Pohl, *Lublin*, 72 ff.

66. *VOGG*, 231–2.

67. Regulation on the use of railways by Jews in the General Government, dated 26 Jan. 1940 (*VOGG*, p. 45); see also Pohl, *Lublin*, 66–7.

68. Pohl, *Lublin*, 66.

69. Published in English translation in Alan Adelson and Robert Lapides, *Lodz Ghetto: Inside a Community under Siege* (New York, 1989), 31–2.

70. Golczewski, 'Polen', 436.

71. Ibid. (Piotrków in October 1939, Radomsko in December 1939).

72. Pohl, *Lublin*, 68.

73. On this see AGK, *Bühler-Prozess*, 66 (published in *Faschismus*, Berenstein et al., 108 ff.), report by Schön dated 20 Jan. 1941, district workshop in Warsaw, *Bühler-Prozess*, 35 (published in Berenstein et al., *Faschismus*, 86), report by Schön dated 8 Apr. 1940.

74. AGK, *Bühler-Prozess*, 94, General Governor to the district heads, 25 May 1940. On Cracow see also ed. *Diensttagebuch*, eds, Präg and Jakobmayer, entries for 12 Apr. 1940, 22 May 1940, 10 June 1940, 15 July 1940, and 2 Aug. 1940, and Golczewski, 'Polen', 433 ff.

75. Regulation of the Governor of the district of Cracow, Otto Wächter, on the establishment of a ghetto in Cracow, 3 Mar. 1941 (*Faschismus*, ed. Berenstein et al., 118 ff.).

76. Regulation on the establishment of Jewish Councils, 28 Nov. 1939 (*VOGG*, 72).

77. The role of the Jewish councils as the agents of the German occupying powers, especially in the context of managing the ghettos, is the subject of intense historiographical debate, which cannot be explored in detail here. For an introduction to this topic see Gustavo Corni, *Hitlers Ghettos: Voices from a Beleaguered Society 1939–1944* (New York, 2002), 62 ff. and for further secondary literature on the ghettos see below, n. 129.

78. See Browning, *Origins*, 151 ff.

79. See Pohl, 'Lublin', 55 ff.

80. Majer, *Fremdvölkische*, 507; Pohl, 'Lublin', 65–6.

81. On the Madagascar Project see Adler, *Verwaltete Mensch*, 69 ff.; Magnus Brechtken, '*Madagaskar für die Juden': Antisemitische Idee und politische Praxis* (Munich, 1997) (which also has a comprehensive summary of the older literature); Christopher Browning, *The Final Solution and the German Foreign Office* (New York and London, 1978), 35–43; Hans Jansen, *Madagaskar-Plan. Die beabsichtigte Deportation der europäische Juden nach Madagaskar* (Munich 1997), esp. 320 ff.; Leoni Yahil, 'Madascar- Phantom of a Solution for the Jewish Question', in Bela Vago and George Mosse, eds, *Jews and Non-Jews in Eastern Europe 1918–1945* (New York, 1974).

82. By Streicher, Goering, and Rosenberg, for example; cf. the references in Brechtken, '*Madagaskar*', 61.

83. Brechtken, '*Madagaskar*', 81 ff.

84. Published in *VfZ* 5 (1957), 194–8 (with a short introduction by Krausnick). English translation in J. Noakes and G. Pridham, *Nazism 1919–1945*, vol. iii (Exeter, 1988), 324–6. In this memorandum Himmler went on to suggest that 'racially valuable' children should be taken away from their Polish parents; true, this was 'cruel' and 'tragic', but preferable to 'extermination'; the note on Hitler's reaction was made on 28 May 1940.

85. According to Himmler's handwritten note (28 May 1940) on the memorandum, Hitler had judged it 'very good and correct'; he was to 'deal with it ... in complete secrecy' and show it to Frank, 'to tell him that the Führer thinks this is right'.

86. PAA, Inland IIg 177, a short overview of the new and most urgent tasks, Dept. D III. The long version of the same day's document that is preserved in Inland A/B 347/3 has the title 'Thoughts on the Tasks and Duties of Dept. D III'.

87. PAA, Inland IIg 177, Überblick, handschriftlich Notiz Rademachers v. 2 Aug. 1940.

88. *Ciano's Diary 1939–1943*, ed. Malcolm Muggeridge (London, 1947), 267; Paul Schmidt, *Statist auf diplomatischer Bühne, 1923–1945. Erlebnisse des Chefdolmetchers im Auswärtigen Amt mit den Staatsmännern Europas* (Bonn, 1953), 494–5.

89. Gerhard Wagner, ed., *Lagevorträge des Oberbefehlshabers der Kriegsmarine vor Hitler 1939–1945* (Munich, 1972), 106 ff.

90. See below p. 165.

91. PAA, Inland IIg/177, note by Luther dated 15 Aug. 1940; published in *ADAP*, series D, vol. 10, no. 345.

92. Elke Fröhlich, ed. *Die Tagebücher von Joseph Goebbels. Teil I. Aufzeichnungen 1923–1941* Band 8. April–November 1940, bearbeitet von Jana Richter, 17 Aug. 1940, p. 276. (On a conversation with Hitler on the previous day): 'Some time in the future we want to ship the Jews out to Madagascar. There they too can set up their own state.' What is important here is that the sentence is part of a paragraph from a monologue in which Hitler pursues his vision of a large-scale 'cleansing' after the end of the war: criminals would have to be 'deported to an island', whilst 'asocial elements' would have to be 'extirpated'.

93. *Akten der Reichsvereinigung*, YV M 51/45, meeting on 25 June 1940; Adam Czerniaków, *Im Warschauer Ghetto. Das Tagebuch von Adam Czerniaków 1939–1942* (Munich, 1986), 88.

94. PAA, Inland IIg 177.

95. 'The Jewish Question in the Peace Treaties' (PAA, Inland II g 177, published in *ADAP*, series D, vol. 10, 92 ff.).

96. PAA, Inland IIg 177.

97. Material in PAA, Inland IIg 177.

98. BAB, R 113/1645, Results of the space planning survey of Madagascar, 21 Aug. 1940; see Brechtken, '*Madagaskar*', 254 ff.

99. In PAA, Inland IIg 177.

100. Incorrectly referred to as 'Oberbefehlsleiter Brake'.

101. Which is Reitlinger's 'smoke-screen' thesis. See Gerald Reitlinger, *The Final Solution: The Attempt to Exterminate the Jews of Europe* (London and New York, 1961), 77 ff., according to which the Foreign Ministry was concerned above all with finding arguments against emigration from the axis powers; Richard Breitman in *The Architect of Genocide: Himmler and the Final Solution* (London, 1991), 138 f. argues that the RSHA saw the Madagascar Plan as a more or less fantastic means of achieving their aim of gaining planning responsibility for a comprehensive deportation of all the Jews under German rule. Adam (*Judenpolitik*, 307 ff.), Browning (*Resettlement*, 19), Brechtken, and Jansen take the plan more or less seriously. Leni Yahil (*Madagascar*, 696) identifies the key problems of the Madagascar Plan when she calls it a 'phantom': it was a project that the National Socialists persisted with but without regard to the non-existent settlement possibilities on the island of Madagascar.

102. See Peter Longerich, *The Unwritten Order: Hitler's Role in the Final Solution* (Brunscombe Port, 2003), 185.

103. See Brechtken, '*Madagaskar*', 270 ff., which has full details and references; Henry Picker *Hitlers Tischgespräche im Führerhauptquartier* (Stuttgart, 1976), 29 May 1942, p. 340 and 24 July 1942, p. 456; PAA, Inland IIg 177, Rademacher to Bielfeld, 10 Feb. 1942 (on the end of the Project).

104. It was originally planned to resume large-scale deportations on 5 May or 1 August; the officer responsible for Jewish matters in the Department of Interior Administration in the General Government, Heinrich Gottong, informed the District Governors on 6

Apr. 1940 that a plan was being worked on according to which 400,000 Jews would be taken to the General Government after 1 May 1940, with 'the whole of the Jewish population [being] collected in one area' later (Sign. 891, published in *Faschismus*, ed. Berenstein et al., 55). On 5 Apr. 1940 (*Diensttagebuch*, ed. Präg and Jakobmeyer, 158) Frank referred his colleagues to the need 'to receive 120,000 Poles from the Reich and 35,000 Gypsies immediately and after 1 August 1940 about 450,000 Jews...and in addition there will be another 60,000 Poles from Soviet Russia'.

105. *Diensttagebuch*, ed. Präg and Jakobmeyer, 12 July 1940, p. 252.

106. Note on a meeting at IV D 4, 9 July 1940 (Biuletyn, XII (1960), doc. 38). On 12 July Heydrich and Frank came to an agreement whereby the mass resettlement campaigns planned in December 1939 would no longer be carried out, with the 'ongoing Volhynian campaign' and the 'Jewish evacuation campaign that will probably start this August' (i.e. the deportation of the Jews from the integrated eastern territories) going ahead. Telex from Günther (RSHA) to Höppner (UWZ Poznan), 1 July 1940 (Biuletyn, XII, doc. 37).

107. Madajczkyk, *Okkupationspolitik*, 186 ff.

108. *Diensttagebuch*, ed. Präg and Jakobmeyer, 30 May 1940, 209 ff.

109. Report by the Director of the Resettlement Department to the Governor of the District of Warsaw, Waldemar Schön on the Warsaw Ghetto, 20 Jan. 1941; published in *Faschismus*, ed. Berenstein et al., 110 ff.; cf. Pohl, 'Lublin', 67.

110. By order of the District Governor, Ludwig Fischer, on 2 October, after Frank had sent a reminder *Faschismus*, ed. Berenstein et al., 102 ff.; and *Diensttagebuch*, ed. Präg and Jakobmeyer, 12 Sept. 1940, p. 281.

111. In October 1940 a ghetto was established in Minsk Marzowiecki near Warsaw, and another in Chelm in the district of Lublin; at the beginning of 1941 an order for resettlement was given within Otwock (in the district of Warsaw; cf. Golczewski, 'Polen', 436–7). On the (often fruitless) attempts at forming ghettos in the district of Lublin, see Pohl, 'Lublin', 67.

112. Order of 13 Sept. 1940; *Faschismus*, ed. Berenstein et al., 98 ff.

113. In Czestochowa (District of Radom) in April 1941 a closed Ghetto was set up; the same happened in the city of Lublin in March and April 1941: Golczewski, 'Polen', 433 ff.; Pohl, 'Lublin', 85 ff.; *Faschismus*, ed. Berenstein et al., 124 ff. (Order for the Establishment of a Ghetto in Kielce, 31 Mar. 1941).

114. Musial, *Zivilverwaltung*, 133 ff.; Pohl, 'Lublin', 87 (for the city of Lublin).

115. Musial, *Zivilverwaltung*, 159 ff.

116. See Christopher Browning, 'Nazi Ghettoization: Policy in Poland 1939–1941', in Browning, *The Path to Genocide: Essays on Launching the Final Solution* (Cambridge, 1992), 28–56.

117. Musial, *Zivilverwaltung*, 164 ff.

118. Steinbacher, *Auschwitz*, 147 ff.

119. Schön report (see n. 109). For further examples from other ghettos, see Corni, *Hitler's Ghettos*, 119 ff.

120. For general studies of the ghettos and the role of the Jewish councils see later footnotes and the following: Corni, *Hitler's Ghettos*; L. Trunk, *Judenrat: The Jewish Councils in Eastern Europe under Nazi Occupation* (New York, 1972); Doron Kiesel et al., eds, '*Wer*

zum Leben,wer zum Tod': Strategien jüdischen Überlebens im Ghetto (Frankfurt a. M. and New York, 1962). Of importance for the continuation of scholarly dialogue on the Jewish councils are above all the published proceedings of two conferences: the YIVO Colloquium of 1967 (*Improvised Jewish Governing Bodies under Nazi Rule* (New York, 1972)) and the International Historical Conference in Yad Vashem of 1977 (Yisrael Gutman and Cynthia Haft, eds, *Patterns of Jewish Leadership in Nazi Europe, 1933–1945* (Jerusalem, 1979)). Further literature on the complex issue of the Jewish councils includes: Werner Bergmann, 'The Jewish Council as an Intermediary System: Socio-logical Analysis of the Role of the Jewish Councils in Eastern Europe', in Yehuda Bauer et al., eds, *Remembering for the Future: Working Papers and Addenda* (Oxford and New York, 1989), iii. 2830–50; Dan Michmann, 'Judenräte und Judenvereinigungen unter nationalsozialistischer Herrschaft', *ZfG* 46 (1998), 293–304. The most copious literature is on the two largest ghettos, Lodz and Warsaw, although these both represent exceptions in many respects. Most relevant for the period 1939 to 1941 are: Israel Gutman, *The Jews of Warsaw, 1939–1943: Ghetto, Underground, Revolt*, trans. Ina Friedman (Jerusalem and Bloomington, Ind., 1982); Ruta Sakowska, *Menschen im Ghetto. Die jüdische Bevölkerung im besetzten Warschau 1939–1943* (Münster, 1999); Hanno Loewy and Gerhard Schoenberner, eds, *Unser einziger Weg ist Arbeit. Das Getto in Lodz 1940–1944* (Frankfurt a. M. and Vienna, 1990). There is detailed documentation available for Warsaw (see n. 129) and Lodz: Alan Adelson and Robert Lapides, *Lodz Ghetto: Inside a Community under Siege* (New York, 1989); Lucjan Dobroszycki, ed., *The Chronicle of the Lodz Ghetto 1941–1944* (New Haven and London, 1984); Peter Klein, *Die Ghettoverwaltung Litzmannstadt 1940 his 1944: eine Dienststelle im Span-nungsfeld von Kommunalburokratie und staatlicher Verfolgungspolitik* (Hamburg, 2009). On diaries and journals see n. 129. Studies of the smaller and medium-sized ghettos are still a desideratum for research.

121. On illness, disease and death in the ghettos see Corni, *Ghettos*, 194 ff.; on Warsaw see Charles G. Roland, *Courage under Siege: Starvation, Disease and Death in the Warsaw Ghetto* (New York, 1992).

122. Hilberg, *Destruction*, 269.

123. On ghetto society and everyday life, see Corni, *Ghettos*, pp. 168 ff.; and Trunk, *Judenrat*, 368 ff.

124. See esp. Trunk, *Judenrat*, 115 ff. (public welfare) and 143 ff. (medical aid). On social self-help in the Warsaw ghetto, see Sakowska, *Menschen im Ghetto*, pp. 81 ff.; on medical care see Roland, *Courage*.

125. On cultural and religious life, see Corni, *Ghettos*, 146 ff.; Trunk, *Judenrat*, 186 ff.; Sakowska, *Menschen im Ghetto*, 129 ff. (on Warsaw); Gila Flan, 'Das kulturelle Leben im Getto Lodz', in Kiesel et. al., eds, '*Wer zum Leben*', 77–96.

126. On the topic of work see Corni, *Ghettos*, 227 ff. In Lodz the Chair of the Jewish council, Rumkowski, pursued a plan to make the ghettos productive from spring 1940 onwards, which bore fruit during 1941 (ibid. 238–9). In Warsaw ghetto inhabitants began to work in large numbers (both inside and in German firms outside the ghetto). Ghettos in autumn 1941 (ibid. 242–3; Gutman, *The Jews of Warsaw*, 74 ff.). Trunk (*Judenrat*, 78) adduces various examples from 1940 in which Jewish councils took the initiative in founding so-called 'shops'.

127. Pohl, 'Lublin', 88; Trunk, *Judenrat*, 400 ff., describes the shift to a work-survival strategy.
128. On smuggling see Corni, *Ghettos*, 139 ff. In Warsaw in particular smuggling included the illegal 'export' of those goods produced in the ghetto that significantly exceeded the production quotas permitted by the Germans (Gutman, *Jews of Warsaw*, 75; see also Carol Battick, 'Smuggling as a Form of Resistance in the Warsaw Ghetto', *Journal of Holocaust Education* 4/2 (1995), 199–204).
129. For the Polish ghettos we now have a large number of published diaries and letters as well as contemporary records and transcripts that are based on contemporary records. For Lodz see Oskar Rosenfeld, *Wozu noch Welt. Aufzeichnungen aus dem Ghetto Lodz*, ed. Hanno Loewy (Frankfurt a. M., 1994); Hanno Loewy and Andrzej Bodek, *'Les Vrais Riches'. Notizen am Rand: Ein Tagebuch aus dem Ghetto Lodz (Mai bis August 1944)* (Leipzig, 1997); David Sierakowiak, *The Diary of David Sierakowiak: Five Notebooks from the Lodz Ghetto*, ed. Alan Adelson (New York and Oxford, 1996); Yosef Zelkovitsh, *In those Terrible Days: Writings from the Lodz Ghetto*, ed. Michal Unger, trans. Naftali Greenwood (Jerusalem, 2002). For Warsaw see: *To Live with Honor and Die with Honor!... Selected Documents from the Warsaw Ghetto Underground Archives 'O. S.' ('Oneg Shabbath')*, ed. and annotated Joseph Kermish (Jerusalem, 1986); Emmanuel Ringelblum, *Polish-Jewish Relations during the Second World War*, ed. Joseph Kermish and Shmuel Cracowski (New York and Jerusalem, 1976), an essay on the Warsaw ghetto written in 1943; Emmanuel Ringelblum, *Notes from the Warsaw Ghetto: The Journal of Emmanuel Ringelblum*, ed. and trans. Jacob Sloan (New York, Toronto, and London, 1958); Mary Berg, *Warsaw Ghetto: A Diary*, ed. S. L. Schneiderman (New York, 1945); 'Daily Entries of Hersh Wasser', intro. and notes Joseph Kermish, *YVS* 15 (1983), 201–81; Abraham Lewin, *A Cup of Tears: A Diary of the Warsaw Ghetto* (Oxford, 1988). See also Janina Baumann, *Winter in the Morning: A Young Girl's Life in the Warsaw Ghetto and Beyond 1939–1945* (London, 1986); Adam Czerniakow, *The Warsaw Diary of Adam Czerniakow: Prelude to Doom*, ed. Raul Hilberg, Stanislaw Staron, and Josef Kermish (Chicago, 1999); Chaim Kaplan, *Scroll of Agony: The Warsaw Diary of Chaim A. Kaplan*, ed. A. I. Katsch (New York, 1973); Janusz Korczak, *Ghetto Diary* (New Haven and London, 2003); Konrad Plieninger, *'Ach, es ist alles ohne Ufer...'. Briefe aus dem Warschauer Ghetto* (Göttingen, 1996), which are letters by Josef Gelbart; Eugenia Szajn-Lewin, *Aufzeichnungen aus dem Warschauer Ghetto. Juli 1942 bis April 1943* (Leipzig, 1994); Michal Zylberberg, *A Warsaw Diary* (London, 1969); Stanislaw Adler, *In the Warsaw Ghetto. An Account of a Witness: The Memoirs of Stanislaw Adler* (Jerusalem, 1982). For Cracow, see Halina Nelken, *Freiheit will ich noch erleben. Krakauer Tagebuch* (Gerlingen, 1996). On the critical assessment of these contemporary records, see Robert Moses Shapiro, ed., *Holocaust Chronicles: Individualizing the Holocaust through Diaries and Other Contemporaneous Personal Accounts* (Hoboken, 1999).
130. On the relationship of councils and ghetto inhabitants see Trunk, *Judenrat*, 379 ff. Corni (*Ghettos*) stresses the respect that these councils also enjoyed alongside widespread criticism.
131. On the attitude of the Jewish councils to the Germans see Corni, *Ghettos*, 77 ff. and Trunk, *Judenrat*, 388 ff.

132. On methods of keeping order in the Jewish community, see Corni, *Ghettos*, 106 ff. and Trunk, *Judenrat*, 475 ff.

133. Aharon Weiss, 'Jewish Leadership in Occupied Poland: Postures and Attitudes', *YVS* 12 (1977), 335–65.

134. This problem has been examined by Dan Diner: 'Die Perspektive des "Judenrats". Zur universellen Bedeutung einer partikularen Erfahrung', in Kiesel et al., eds, '*Wer zum Leben*', 11–36.

135. Gutman, *Jews*, 119 ff. The same conclusion about underground action by the Socialist League in this period is reached by Daniel Blatman, *For our Freedom and yours: The Jewish Labour Bund in Poland 1939–1949* (London, 2003), 44 ff. In Corni's account of resistance in the ghettos (*Ghettos*, 293 ff.) there are virtually no data for the period before the onset of the deportations, and the same is true of Trunk, *Judenrat*, 451 ff.

136. See Corni, *Ghettos*, 70–1.

137. Pohl, 'Lublin', 88.

138. Willi A. Boelke, ed., *Kriegspropaganda 1939–1941. Geheime Ministerkonferenzen im Reichspropagandaministerium* (Stuttgart, 1966), 492 (6 September). By the end of the war it was envisaged that *c.*500 Jews per month would be 'sent to the South-East'.

139. Toury, 'Austreibungsbefehls', 436–7.

140. Ibid.

141. BAB, R 43 II/1334a; Toury, 'Austreibungsbefehls', 446.

142. Anonymous report from Karlsruhe dated 30 Oct. 1940, published in Sauer, *Dokumente der Verfolgung*, no. 441 (= NG 4933; see also other relevant documents here), which may have come from groups associated with the Confessing Church (*Bekennende Kirche*); cf. Toury, 'Austreibungsbefehls', 453. The report assumes that it was originally the intention to deport to France all the other Jews from the Reich area, including the Protectorate.

143. Toury ('Austreibungsbefehls', 443) notes that in a draft for a letter made on 7 December Rademacher initially used the formulation 'deportation ordered by the Führer' which he corrected to 'deportation approved by the Führer': Toury assumes that the initiative for these deportations (which are often referred to as the 'Bürckel campaign') was Gauleiter Wagner's.

144. Minute taken by Bormann: *IMT*, xxxix. 425 ff.

145. *Faschismus*, ed. Berenstein et al., 59, circular of 23 Nov. 1940 from the government of the GG to the governors of the districts informing them of the ban dated 25 Nov. 1940.

146. Telex from Frank to Greiser, 2 Nov. 1940, reproduced in express telex from the Inspector of the Sipo and the SD in Poznan to the RSHA, 5 Nov. 1940 (Biuletyn, XII (1960), doc. 50); Aly, '*Final Solution*', 126–7.

147. Franz Halder, *Kriegstagebuch. Tägliche Aufzeichnungen des Chefs des Generalstabs des Heeres 1939–1942*, ed. Hans-Adolf Jacobsen (Stuttgart, 1962), vol. ii, 4 Nov. 1940.

148. Elke Fröhlich, ed., *Die Tagebücher von Joseph Goebbels*, Teil I: *Aufzeichnungen 1923–1941*, Band 8, bearbeitet von Jana Richter (Munich, 1998), 5 Nov. 1940, ('yesterday'), p. 406.

149. These totals are derived from Polish sources and research in Werner Röhr, ed., *Die faschistische Okkupationspolitik in Polen (1939–1945)* (Bonn, 1989), 356–7.

150. Hitler's directives no. 18 (Russia) from 12 Nov. 1940 and no. 21 from 18 Dec. 1940 (Operation Barbarossa), Wolfgang Hubatsch, *Hitlers Weisungen für die Kriegführung 1939–1945. Dokumente des OKW* (Frankfurt a. M., 1962), 71 and 84 ff. are central to this point.

151. On the deportation plans after the failure of Madagascar, see Browning, *Origins*, 213 ff.

152. Adler, *Verwaltete Mensch*, 147 ff.; Gruner, *Kollektivausweisung*; Alfred Gottwaldt and Diana Schulle, *Judendeportationen aus dem Deutschen Reich 1941–1945. Eine kommentierte Chronologie* (Wiesbaden, 2005), 46 ff.

153. BAB, NS 19/3979.

154. This figure is certainly not a 'first reference' to the later total of the victims of the systematic murder of the European Jews, as Wolfgang Benz suggests in *Dimension des Völkermords*, 2; it does not include the Soviet Jews, for example. Cf. Aly, '*Final Solution*', 126. On the day before, 3 December 1940, Eichmann had informed the Reich Interior Ministry official responsible for 'Jewish affairs', Bernhard Lösener, about the 'plans that the Reich Security Office had for the conclusive solution of the Jewish question in the German Reich'. They included the intention 'to transport the Jews from the whole area of Europe under German rule to Madagascar after the war, within the context of a four- or five-year plan'. This plan embraced six million people. (Note by Lösener with Eichmann: BAB, R 18/3746, quoted by Bernhard Lösener, 'Als Rassereferent im Reichsministerium des Innern', *VfZ* 9/3 (1961), 296–7.)

155. According to Krüger's report on 15 January in Cracow: *Diensttagebuch*, ed. Präg and Jacobmeyer, 327 ff. On 11 January Frank had told Krüger that Hitler had described accepting 800,000 Jews and Poles into the General Government as unavoidable (ibid., 11 Jan. 1941, pp. 318 ff.).

156. For details see Aly, '*Final Solution*', 141. On the deportations from Vienna, see Safrian, *Eichmann-Männer*, 97–8 and Adler, *Verwaltete Mensch*, 147 ff.

157. Relevant documents in YV, JM 10454 (= Lublin Archive, Gouvern. Distr. Lubl., Sign. 892), and various reports in Else R. Behrend-Rosenfeld, ed., *Lebenszeichen Piaski. Briefe deportierte aus dem Distrikt Lublin 1940–1943* (Munich, 1968), 165 ff.

158. Cf. Aly, '*Final Solution*', 127–8.

159. CDJC, V-59, published in Serge Klarsfeld, *Vichy-Auschwitz. Die Zusammenarbeit der deutschen und französischen Behörden bei der 'Endlösung der Judenfrage' in Frankreich* (Nördlingen, 1989), 361 ff.

160. Published in Adler, *Verwaltete Mensch*, 152.

161. Goebbels had left lunch with Hitler on 17 March under the impression that Vienna would very soon be 'free of Jews' and Berlin would soon 'have its turn' but had 'evidently made a wrong estimation of the timescale'. 'I will discuss that with the Führer and Dr Franck [*sic*]. He will set the Jews to work and they are pretty compliant. Later they will have to get out of Europe completely'; Elke Fröhlich, ed., *Die Tagebücher von Joseph Goebbels*, Teil I, *Aufzeichnungen 1923–1941*, Band 9: *Dezember 1940–März 1941*, bearbeitet von Elke Fröhlich (Munich, 1998), 18 Mar. 1941, p. 193.

162. Ibid. Entry for 22 Mar. 1940, p. 199. This matches a remark of the former League of Nations High Commissioner for Danzig, Carl J. Burkhardt, found by Breitmann (*Architekt*, 152) to the effect that two absolutely trustworthy civil servants from the

Ministry of War and the Foreign Ministry had seen a written order by Hitler giving instructions for the area of the Reich to be made 'free of Jews' by the end of 1942.

163. BAB, 75 C Re 1, no. 45, summons of 17 Mar. 1941.

164. *Diensttagebuch*, ed. Präg and Jacobmeyer, 26 Mar. 1941, pp. 338–9.

165. Ibid., 3 Apr. 1941, pp. 343 ff.

166. Aly, *'Final Solution'*, 172, citing ZASM 500-3-795.

167. 710-PS in *IMT* xxvi. 266.

168. ND NO-203, Brack to Himmler, 28 Mar. 1941. According to a statement made by Brack in May 1947, Himmler had given him this task in January 1941 because he feared the miscegenation of Polish and Western European Jews (*Trial of the War Criminals before the International Military Tribunal* (Washington, DC, 1947–9), i. 732).

169. Elke Fröhlich, ed., *Die Tagebücher von Joseph Goebbels*, Teil I: *Aufzeichnungen 1923–1941*, Band 9, bearbeitet von Elke Fröhlich (Munich, 1998), entry for 20 June 1941, p. 390.

170. *Diensttagebuch*, ed. Präg and Jacobmeyer, 17 July 1941, p. 386.

171. *ADAP*, series D, vol. 13, no. 207.

10. Laying the Ground for a War of Racial Annihilation

1. Studies of the attack on the Soviet Union include Horst Boog et al., *Germany and the Second World War*, vol. iv: *The Attack on the Soviet Union* (Oxford, 1999); Peter Jahn and Reinhard Rürup, eds, *Erobern und Vernichten. Der Krieg gegen die Sowjetunion* (Berlin, 1991); Andreas Hillgruber, *Hitlers Strategie. Politik und Kriegführung 1940–1941* (Frankfurt a. M., 1965); Gerd R. Ueberschär and Wolfram Wette, eds, *'Unternehmen Barbarossa'. Der deutsche Überfall auf die Sowjetunion 1941* (Paderborn, 1984); Christian Hartmann, Johannes Hürter, and Ulrike Jureit, eds, *Verbrechen der Wehrmacht. Bilanz einer Debatte* (Munich, 2005); Bernd Wegner, ed., *Zwei Wege nach Moskau. Vom Hitler-Stalin-Pakt zum 'Unternehmen Barbarossa'* (Munich, 1991).

2. Gerd Ueberschär, ' "Russland ist unser Indien". Das "Unternehmen Barbarossa" als Lebensraumkrieg', in Hans Heinrich Nolte, ed., *Der Mensch gegen den Menschen. Überlegungen und Forschungen. Zum deutschen Überfall auf die Sowjetunion 1941* (Hanover, 1992), 66–77.

3. Rolf-Dieter Müller, 'Von der Wirtschaftsallianz zum kolonialen Ausbeutungskrieg', in Boog et al., *Attack* 98–189 (here p. 157). On the economic aspects of the war see in particular Christian Gerlach, *Kalkulierte Morde. Die deutsche Wirtschafts- und Vernichtungspolitik in Weissrussland 1941 bis 1944* (Hamburg, 1999), 59 ff.

4. Andreas Hillgruber, 'Der Ostkrieg und die Judenvernichtung', in Ueberschär and Wette, eds, *'Unternehmen Barbarossa'*, 219–36.

5. Adolf Hitler, *Mein Kampf* (London, 1969), 604–5.

6. Gerlach, *Kalkulierte Morde*, 66 ff. On planning for food-supply policies, see Gerlach, 'German Economic Interests, Occupation Policy, and the Murder of the Jews in Belorussia 1941–1943', in Ulrich Herbert, ed., *National Socialist Extermination Policies: Contemporary German Perspectives and Controversies* (New York, 2000); Götz Aly and Susanne Heim, *Vordenker der Vernichtung. Auschwitz und die deutschen Pläne für eine neue europäische Ordnung* (Hamburg, 1991), 366–7, and Rolf-Dieter Müller,

'From Economic Alliance to a War of Colonial Exploitation', in Boog et al., eds, *Germany and the Second World War*, vol. iv: *Attack*, 118–224.

7. The Economic Organization for the East was directed by the Head of the War Economy and Armaments Department, General Georg Thomas, who received comprehensive authority for the economic exploitation of the Soviet Union from Goering, who was formally responsible for this.

8. *IMT* iv. 535–6. Bach-Zelewski dates the meeting in Nuremberg at January 1941 but it must have taken place between 12 and 15 June of that year (see note 76); Peter Witte et al., *Der Dienstkalender Heinrich Himmlers 1941/42* (Hamburg, 1999), 172.

9. Goering to Ciano on 15 Nov. 1941: '20–30 million people will starve in Russia this year. Perhaps that is for the best, since there are peoples that need to be decimated.' Czeslaw Madajczyk, *Die Okkupationspolitik Nazideutschlands in Polen 1939–1945* (Cologne, 1988), 92.

10. 2718-PS, *IMT* xxxi. 84 ff.

11. EC 126, *IMT* xxxvi. 135 ff., 145.

12. NG 1409.

13. By March 1942 there were thirteen Army Rear Areas.

14. Hans-Adolf Jacobsen, 'Kommissarbefehl und Massenexekutionen sowjetischer Kriegsgefangener', in Hans Buchheim et al., *Anatomie des SS-Staates* (Munich, 1979) doc. 1.

15. Percy Ernst Schramm, ed., *Kriegstagebuch des Oberkommandos der Wehrmacht 1940–1945 (KTB)*, i. 341.

16. Bundesarchiv/Militärarchiv (BAM), RW 4/v, 522 (= *IMT* xxvi. 53 ff., 447-PS).

17. On 26 March Wagner was able to present a first draft of the order, drawn up after discusssions with Heydrich: Bundesarchiv Berlin (BAB), RW 4v/575, published in Jacobsen, 'Kommissarbefehl', doc. 2. On 16 April Wagner met Himmler, Heydrich, the Head of the Order Police, Kurt Daluege, and Hans Jüttner (Chief of Staff in the SS Main Leadership Office) in a hotel in Graz, clearly in order to discuss the draft (Himmler, *Dienstkalender*, ed. Witte, 150). The negotiations are presented in detail by Andrej Angrick, *Besatzungspolitik und Massenmord. Die Einsatzgruppe D in der südlichen Sowjetunion 1941–1943* (Hamburg 2003), 41 ff.

18. Gerlach, *Kalkulierte Morde*, 81.

19. RH 22/155. Jacobsen, 'Kommissarbefehl', doc. 3.

20. RH 31-Iv.23; cf. Jürgen Förster, 'Operation Barbarossa as a War of Conquest and Annihilation', in Boog et al., ed., *Germany and the Second World War*, iv. 481–521; and Walter Manoscheck, '*Serbien ist Judenfrei'. Militärbesatzungspolitik und Judenvernichtung in Serbien 1941/42* (Munich, 1993), 41–2.

21. Halder, *KTB* ii. 317 ff., 320.

22. Ibid. 335 ff., 336–7.

23. BAM, RH 22/155, published in Reinhard Rürup, *Der Krieg gegen die Sowjetunion 1941–1945. Eine Dokumentation* (Berlin, 1991), 45; for details of the genesis of this measure see Förster, 'Operation Barbarossa'; and Ralf Ogorreck, *Die Einsatzgruppen und die Genesis der 'Endlösung'* (Berlin, 1996), 19 ff. The accompanying letter by the Commander-in-Chief of the army of 24 June (Disciplinary Decree; Jacobsen, 'Kommissarbefehl', doc. 10) pursues the line of the need to prevent the excessive implementation of this order from the Führer by the troops on the ground. The activity report made by the

intelligence officer of the Third Tank Group for the period between January and July 1941 (BAB, RH 21-3/v, 423) shows how the intelligence officers and military judges of the Group were informed of the order on 11 June by Special Purpose General Müller: 'One of the two enemies must fall by the wayside, those who hold hostile view are to be finished off, not preserved.... The severity of the war demands severe punishments (remember the First War: the Russians in Gumbinnen: shooting dead all the inhabitants of villages on the route between Tilsit and Insterburg in case the route was damaged). Where there is any doubt about who the perpetrators are, suspicion will often have to suffice. It is often not possible to provide unambiguous proof.'

24. BAM, RH 2/2082, published in Rürup, *Der Krieg gegen die Sowjetunion*, 46. On the Commissar Order in general see Felix Römer, *Der Kommissarbefehl Wehrmacht und NS-Verbrechen an der Ostfront 1941/42* (Paderborn, 2008) .

25. BAM, RH 22/12. There are similarities in the tenor of the instructions drawn up by the Army Propaganda Department for the Implementation of Propaganda in the case of Barbarossa (BAM, RW 4/v, 578) and the June edition of the journal *Troop Information*.

26. NOKW 2079, published in Jacobsen, 'Kommissarbefehl', 184–5.

27. Meaning the OKH order of 28 April, which corresponded to the Wagner–Heydrich draft made on 26 March (see above, pp. 182–3).

28. Angrick, *Besatzungspolitik*, 56 ff.

29. Originally the Wehrmacht had obviously tried to accommodate all the Order Police battalions in permanent tactical subordination to its own security formations, but had not succeeded in doing so (Halder, *KTB* ii. 371).

30. At a meeting on 8 July 1941 Himmler made it unambiguously clear that the units under the command of the command staff would be deployed in the areas under political administration. 'It is possible to deploy the larger formations in the Army Rear Areas. Members of the command staff and of the units under its command have in principle no business in the operational area or the Army Rear Area': Command staff, note Ia, meeting of 8 July 1941 (YV, M 36/3).

31. On the formation of *Einsatzgruppen* see Angrick, *Besatzungspolitik*, 74 ff.; Helmut Krausnick, 'Die Einsatzgruppen vom Anschluss Österreichs bis zum Feldzug gegen die Sowjetunion. Entwicklung und Verhältnis zur Wehrmacht', in Helmut Krausnick and Hans-Heinrich Wilhelm, *DieTruppe des Weltanschauungskrieges. Die Einsatzgruppen den Sicherheitspolizei und des SD 1938–1942* (Stuttgart, 1981), 19 ff.; Peter Klein, ed., *Die Einsatzgruppen in der besetzten Sowjetunion 1941/42. Die Tätigkeits- und Lageberichte des Chefs der Sicherheitspolizei und des SD* (Berlin, 1997); Hans-Heinrich Wilhelm, 'Die Einsatzgruppe A der Sicherheitspolizei und des SD 1941/42. Eine exemplarische Studie', in Krausnick and Wilhelm, *Truppe*, 281 ff.; Hans-Heinrich Wilhelm, *Die Einsatzgruppe A der Sicherheitspolizei und des SD 1941/42* (Frankfurt a. M., 1996), 11 ff.

32. In the cases of the campaigns against Denmark and Norway and of the war in the West the Wehrmacht had largely succeeded in preventing the formation of such units. See Krausnick, 'Einsatzgruppen', 107 ff., and Krausnick, 'Hitler und die Befehle an die Einsatzgruppen in Sommer 1941', in Eberhard Jäckel and Jürgen Rohwer, eds, *Der Mord an den Juden in Zweiten Weltkrieg: Entschlussbildung und Verwirklichung* (Stuttgart, 1985) (the publication of a note by Heydrich of 2 July 1940).

33. The 909 members of Einsatzgruppe A in February 1941 were made up as follows: 37 SD members, 55 Kripo employees, 85 Stapo workers, 134 Order Police, 257 Waffen-SS men, 185 truck drivers, 53 emergency services personnel (who had for the most part not been part of the SS or Police), 9 telex operators, 23 radio-operators, 22 female employees, 26 administrators, 3 special representatives.

34. Krausnick, 'Einsatzgruppen', 180–1.

35. Ulrich Herbert, Best. Biographische Studien über Radikalismus, Weltanschauung und Vernunft 1903–1989 (Bonn, 1996), gives further details of this type.

36. Wilhelm, 'Einsatzgruppe A', in Krausnich and Wilhelm, Truppe, 281 ff.

37. On the Order Police see Andrej Angrick et al., eds, 'Da hätte man schon ein Tagebuch führen müssen'. Das Polizeibataillon 322 und die Judenmorde im Bereich der Heeresgruppe Mitte während des Sommers und Herbstes 1941', in Helga Grabitz et al., Die Normalität des Verbrechens (Berlin, 1994), 325–85; Christopher Browning, Ordinary Men: Reserve Police Battalion 101 and the Final Solution in Poland (New York, 1992); Daniel J. Goldhagen, Hitler's Willing Executioners: Ordinary Germans and the Holocaust (New York, 1996); Konrad Kwiet, 'Auftakt zum Holocaust: Ein Polizeibataillon im Osteinsatz', in Wolfgang Benz, ed., Der Nationalsozialismus: Studien zur Ideologie und Herrschaft (Frankfurt a. M., 1993), 92–110; Jürgen Matthäus, 'What about the "Ordinary Men"? The German Order Police and the Holocaust in the Occupied Soviet Union', (HGS) 10 (1996), 134–50; Klaus-Michael Mallmann, 'Vom Fussvolk der "Endlösung". Ordnungspolizei, Ostkrieg und Judenmord', Tel Aviver Jahrbuch 25 (1997), 355–91; Edward B. Westermann, Hitler's Police Battalions. Enforcing Racial War in the East (Lawrence, 2005). The work of Hans-Joachim Neufeldt, Jürgen Huck, and Georg Tessin, Zur Geschichte der Ordnungspolizei, i and ii (Koblenz, 1957) omits the whole complex of the role of the police in the murder of the European Jews, but is indispensable for an understanding of the organizational history of the Order Police; see in particular Part II: Georg Tessin, Die Stäbe und Truppeneinheiten der Ordnungspolizei, 5–19, to which the current section of the present study is heavily indebted.

38. See BAB, R 19/97, a lecture by Kurt Daluege at the meeting of the commanders and inspectors of the Order Police, 1 to 4 Feb. 1942, and the unused manuscript by Daluege, 'Der Winterkampf der Ordnungspolizei im Osten' (BAB, R 19/382). On individual units, see Longerich, Politik, 308–9.

39. Ibid.

40. This was the 'increased police protection', made up of men born between 1901 and 1909, authorized at a level of 95,000 at the start of the war (BAB, R 19/382, address by Daluege, 16 Jan. 1941). At the beginning of 1940, of the 64,872 police reservists called up, there were only 8,513 in the battalions (OS, 500-5-26a, address by Daluege, 19 Jan. 1940). At the start of 1942 this figure was only 7,325 from a total of 117,525 reservists called up (BAB, NS 19/335, lecture by Daluege at the meeting, 1–4 Feb. 1942). The overall strength of all the battalions was just over 60,000 (BAB, NS 19/335, memo from the Chief of the Order Police, 20 Aug. 1940).

41. The volunteers from the so-called '26,000-man-campaign' were taken from those born between 1918 and 1920 (applicants to join the police) or 1905 and 1912 (employment as patrolmen) (Bayerisches Hauptstaatsarchiv (BHSt.A), Reichsstatthalter Epp, decrees of the RFSS of 11 Oct. 1939 and 31 Oct. 1939; decree of the Reich Minister of the Interior of 25 Oct. 1939). Volunteers were deployed in a total of 31 battalions, which means (not

counting the officers and NCOs) some 400–50 volunteers per battalion, or only half of the 26,000 recruited (cf. NS 19/395, memo from the Chief of the Order Police of 20 Aug. 1940).

42. See Tessin, *Stäbe*, 14. According to the Chief of the Order Police, Daluege, only one in four of the applicants fulfilled the police criteria: of the 160,000 applications made in the context of the '26,000-man-campaign' at the beginning of 1940, 51,000 had been enrolled to date, of whom '7,100 born between 1905 and 1912 and roughly 6,000 from between 1918 and 1920 were enrolled as fit for police duty' (OS, 500-5-26a, address by Daluege, 19 Jan. 1940).

43. BAB, NS 6/821, decree of the Party Chancellery, A 28/41 from 4 June 1941 concerning the political assessment of recruits to the SS Police Division and the Police Battalions. As a result, the commanders of the Police Training Battalion sought political assessment of their recruits from the NSDAP district leaders.

44. See above, pp. 44 ff.

45. See Browning, *Ordinary Men*; Goldhagen, *Executioners*. On the Goldhagen debate, see Introduction, n. 18.

46. Bernd Wegner, *Hitlers Politische Soldaten: Die Waffen SS 1933–1945 Leitbild, Struktur und Funktion einer nationalsozialistischen Elite*, 4th edn (Paderborn, 1982), 142 and 49 ff.

47. Leaflet signed by Himmler, September 1938: StA Munich, PolDir. 8466.

48. See above, p. 45.

49. National Archives Washington DC (NA), T 175 R 6, 15 Apr. 1937 and decree of 5 June 1937.

50. BHSt.A, Reichsstatthalter Epp, 366, Richtlinien für die Durchführung der weltanschaulichen Schulung der Ordnungspolizei während der Kriegszeit.

51. Wegner, *Soldaten*, 110 ff. On the ideological indoctrination of the Order Police, see also Jürgen Matthäus, 'Antisemitism as an Offer: The Ideological Indoctrination of the SS and Police Corps during the Holocaust, Lessons and Legacies' in Dagmar Herzog ed., *Lessons and Legacies, vii: The Holocaust in International Perspective* (Evanston, 2006), 116–28.

52. See Yehoshua Büchler, 'Kommandostab Reichsführer SS: Himmlers Personal Murder Brigades in 1941', *HGS* 1/1 (1986), 13–14; Martin Cüppers, *Wegbereiter der Shoah. Die Waffen SS, der Kommandostab Reichsführer SS und die Judenvernichtung 1939–1945* (Darmstadt, 2005), 64 ff.

53. BAB, NS 19/3508, SS-Leadership Office, 24 Apr. 1941 and 6 May 1941.

54. For details, see Cüppers, *Wegbereiter*, 33 ff.

55. BAB, NS 19/3508, order by Himmler of 17 June, effective from 21 June 1941.

56. BAM, M 806 (copies from the Military Archive in Prague), actual strength at the end of July 1941.

57. Ohlendorf spoke in his testimony at the main trial (Case 9, IfZ, MB 19, German transcript, roll 13, pp. 484 ff., esp. p. 525) of a 'special order' that read, 'that over and above the general tasks of the Security Police and the SD, the *Einsatzgruppen* and *Einsatzkommandos* had the additional responsibility of keeping the rearguard clear by killing Jews, Roma, Communist functionaries, active Communists and all persons who might endanger the troops'. At his interrogation on 24 April 1947 (NOU2890) and in his testimony at the Trial of the Major War Criminals he also always spoke of 'Jews' and

'Communists' and other groups in one breath when describing the designated victims. Cf. Ogorreck, *Einsatzgruppen*, 49 ff.

58. Paul Blobel, Sk 4a. IfZ MB 19, roll 14, pp. 746 ff. (esp. 752); Walter Blume, Sk 7a, (ibid., roll 15, pp. 208 ff. (esp. 218); see also NO 4145, interrogation on 29 June 1947); Gustav Nosske, Einsatzkommando 12, and Martin Sandberger, Sk 1a. IfZ MB 19, roll 15, pp. 596 ff. (esp. pp. 610 ff.).

59. IfZ, MB 19, roll 14, pp. 139 ff. (esp. pp. 168–9, 170, 177 ff., 191 ff.).

60. IfZ, MB 19, roll 13, pp. 314 ff.

61. Judgement of the District Court in Ulm of 29 Aug. 1958 See Irene Sagel-Grande et al., *Justiz und NS-Verbrechen. Sammlung deutscher Strafurteile wegen nationalsozialistischer Tötungsverbrechen*, 22 vols (Amsterdam, 1968–81), xv, no. 465. See also Krausnick's report for the Auschwitz Trial (published as Krausnick, 'The Persecution of the Jews', in Buchheim et al., *Anatomy*, 1–74 and his expert witness statement in the trial against Kroeger (Zentralstelle der Landesjustizverwaltungen zur Aufklärung nationalsozialistischer Verbrechen (ZSt), 204 AR 1258/66, p. 23, transcript of the main proceedings, pp. 97–8); the second expert witness, Seraphim, challenged this version, however. There was a similar confrontation between the two expert witnesses in the Darmstadt trial of Sonderkommando 4a (Judgement of the District Court in Darmstadt, 19 Nov. 1968, ZSt, 204 AR-Z 269/60); the court took Krausnick's line, as did the Hanover District Court in the trial of Einsatzgruppe 2 (ZSt, II 207 ARZ 18/58, judgement of 14 Oct. 1971), and rejected Seraphim's view 'that an order to annihilate the Jews had not been given to the *Einsatzgruppen* or *Einsatzkommandos* before the start of the Russian campaign but only in the second half of July 1941 after it had transpired that the pogroms had not had their desired effect'. Some courts were not convinced by the thesis of an early comprehensive order: see the judgement of the District Court in Düsseldorf of 5 Aug. 1966 (ZSt, II 204 ARZ 266/59), which took Seraphim's view, or the judgement of the same court of 9 Jan. 1973 (where the expert witness was Wolfgang Scheffler).

62. The version of an early comprehensive order was accepted by the following cases (in addition to those listed in n. 61): Judgement of District Court I in Munich of 21 July 1961 (Einsatzkommando 8) (= Sagel-Grande et al., *Justiz und NS-Verbrechen Die deutschen Strafverfahren wegen nationalsozialistischen Tötungsverbrechen*. Zusammengestellt im Institut für Strafrecht der Universität von Amsterdam von Prof. C. F. Ritter and Dr W. de Mildt (*Justiz und NS-Verbrechen*), xvii, no. 519); ZSt, 204 AR-Z 269/60, Judgement of the District Court in Darmstadt of 29 Nov. 1968 (Sonderkommando 4a); II 202 ARZ 81/59, Judgement of the District Court in Cologne of 12 May 1964 (Einsatzkommando 8); II 202 AR 72a/60, Judgement of the District Court in Berlin of 6 May 1966 (Einsatzkommando 9); Judgement of the District Court in Essen of 29 Mar. 1965 (Sonderkommando 7a) (= Sagel-Grande et al., *Justiz und NS-Verbrechen*, xx, no. 588). The Judgement of the District Court in Cologne of 12 May. 1964 (Einsatzkommando 8) (= Sagel-Grande et al., *Justiz und NS-Verbrechen*, xx, no. 573) represents an exception in that the Court worked on the basis of a comprehensive order to annihilate the Jews but did not indicate when it believed this order was given. The view that orders were given step by step, with only the commando leaders informed at first, as taken by the Darmstadt District Court (ZSt, 204 AR-Z 269/60, 19 Nov. 1968),

was the basis of the judgement of the Munich District Court of 15 Nov. 1974 (II 213 AR 1902/66). The District Court in Tübingen took a similar view on 10 May 1961 (EK Tilsit) (= Sagel-Grande et al., *Justiz und NS-Verbrechen*, xvii, no. 509).

63. Krausnick, 'Einsatzgruppen', 150 ff.

64. For references see the Introduction, p. 2, nn. 1,2.

65. On 9 November 1948 Ohlendorf testified to the effect that in the areas where they had been stationed, 'alongside the regular tasks of defence and reporting the *Einsatzgruppen* and *Einsatzkommandos* received the additional order that for security reasons they were to kill political commissars, Communist activists, Jews and Gypsies and all other persons who are a danger to our security'. He then stated unambiguously that 'as far as the killing of the Jews was concerned, the activities of the *Einsatzgruppen* had nothing to do with the so-called final solution for the Jewish question' (AR-Z 269/60, supplementary vol. viii; see also IfZ, Gd 01.54). In his appeal for clemency made to Military Court II in July 1950, he also stated that the order from the Führer transmitted in the areas where the troops had been stationed was 'not a criminal programme of racial annihilation' (quoted from Ogorreck, *Einsatzgruppen*, 49–50).

66. His presence in Pretzsch can be explained relatively easily by the fact that Streckenbach had the additional responsibility of being the Inspector for the Security Police School.

67. After Streim's critique of Krausnick in Alfred Streim, *Die Behandlung sowjetischer Kriegsgefangener im 'Fall Barbarossa': Eine Dokumentation* (Heidelberg, 1981), 74 ff., the two sides clashed in 1985 at the Stuttgart conference on the 'Final Solution' (see the debate in Eberhard Jäckel and Jürgen Rohwer, eds, *Der Mord an den Juden im Zweiten Weltkrieg. Entschlußbildung und Verwirklichung* (Stuttgart 1985), 88–106). The controversy was continued in the *SWCA* 4 (1987), 309–28, 6 (1989), 311–29 and 331–47. Longerich, 'Vom Massenmord zur "Endlösung". Die Erschießungen von jüdischen Zivilisten in den ersten Monaten des Ostfeldzuges im Kontext des nationalsozialistischen Judenmordes', in Wegner, *Zwei Wege*, 251–74, has further information on this controversy.

68. Angrick, *Besatzungspolitik*, 98 ff.; Browning, 'Beyond "Intentionalism" and "Functionalism". The Decision for the "Final Solution" Reconsidered', in Browning, *The Path to Genocide: Essays on Launching the Final Solution* (Cambridge, 1992), 101; Phillipe Burrin, *Hitler and the Jews: The Genesis of the Holocaust* (London, 1994), 93 ff.; Konrad Kwiet, ' "Juden und Banditen". SS Ereignismeldungen aus Litauen 1943/1944', *Jahrbuch für Antisemitismusforschung* 2 (1983), 406; Ogorreck, *Einsatzgruppen*, 47 ff.; Michael Wildt, *Generation der Unbedingten. Das Führungskorps des Reichssicherheitshauptamtes* (Hamburg, 2002), 553 ff. On the other hand, Breitman, *Architect*, 290, regards Krausnick's position, which confirms his own view of an early plan for annihilation, as more convincing.

69. Biberstein was not executed and the document he passed to his lawyer is available at ZSt, 415 AR 1310/63, 45, 8128 ff. Biberstein made it clear that no order from the Führer to murder the Jews was ever issued to the *Einsatzgruppen* in the occupied Eastern areas. He suggested that the comprehensive shootings in the first phase of the war, which far exceeded the bounds of the original liquidation orders, had been initiated by Higher SS and Police Commander Jeckeln and a few 'ambitious and fanatical *Einsatzgruppe* leaders such as Stahlecker, Nebe, Rasch and Ohlendorf'. The 'Final Solution', he

claimed, only began when the *Einsatzgruppen* and *Einsatzkommandos* had been transformed into offices of the Security Police, in other words after the autumn of 1941. The *Einsatzgruppen* were therefore not the instrument of a 'final solution' that had already been determined upon, but an important tool in its accomplishment that only became possible after the mass murders of Jews by the *Einsatzgruppen*—however motivated—seemed to have confirmed the distorted picture of the Jewish-Bolshevist arch-enemy.

70. e.g. Nosske, ZSt, 76/59, 2, 315 ff., 30 July 1964 and II 213 AR 1902/66 main document XI, 13 Mar. 1969, 2610 ff., and in similar vein the testimony of defence counsel Rudolf Aschenauer who had been involved in the Nuremberg trials, published in Hans-Heinrich Wilhelm, *Rassenpolitik und Kriegführung. Sicherheitspolizei und Wehrmacht in Polen und der Sowjetunion* (Passau, 1991), 227 ff.; cf. Angrick, *Besatzungspolitik*, 102 ff.

71. Erwin Schulz: ZSt, 207 AR-Z 76/59, vol. 6, pp. 58 ff., 22 Mar. 1971; cf. Ogorreck, *Einsatzgruppen*, 82–3, with references to further interrogations; Gustav Nosske: ZSt, II 213 AR 1902/66, correspondence file 2, pp. 597 ff., 24 May 1971; similarly ZSt, 76/59, 2, pp. 315 ff., 30 July 1964; Ogorreck, *Einsatzgruppen*, 91–2; Karl Tschierschky, ZSt, 207 AR-Z 76/59, vol. 8, pp. 34–41, 14 May 1971; ZSt, 201 AR-Z 14/58, vol. 7, pp. 3327 ff., 14 Aug. 1959; cf. Ogorreck, *Einsatzgruppen*, 59; Otto Bradfisch, ZSt, 202 AR-Z 76/59, vol. 11, p. 7605, 8 Oct. 1971; ZSt, 202 AR-Z 81/59, vol. 2, pp. 531 ff. (cf. Ogorreck, *Einsatzgruppen*, 73); Erhard Kroeger, ZSt, 76/59, vol. 9, pp. 14 ff., 28 Aug. 1967; cf. Ogorreck, *Einsatzgruppen*, 83 ff. Two leaders, Günther Herrmann (ZSt, 4 AR-Z 11/61, 5, pp. 24 ff., 11 Oct. 1962 and pp. 108 ff., 1 Feb. 1963; cf. Ogorreck, *Einsatzgruppen*, 80–1) and Erich Ehrlinger (ZSt, 204 AR-Z 21/58, 4, pp. 2421 ff., 5 May 1959) only admitted that they had been ordered to shoot Jewish men by the heads of their *Einsatzgruppen* after the invasion of the Soviet Union. Ehrlinger later drew back from this statement and claimed that Jews had not expressly been mentioned in the relevant orders but had been involved 'in so far as they were seen as carriers of Bolshevism' (ZSt, 201 AR-Z 76/59, vol. 9, pp. 100 ff., 23 June 1971; cf. Ogorreck, *Einsatzgruppen*, 62 ff.).

72. Walther Blume: ZSt, 201 AR-Z 76/59, 39, pp. 9 ff. (bzw 7118 ff.), 11 May 1971; thus also already in ZSt, 202 AR-Z 96/60, 9, pp. 3104 ff., 19 Dec. 1962; cf. Ogorreck, *Einsatzgruppen*, 68 ff. Woldemar Klingelhöfer: ZSt, 202 AR-Z 287/60, 1, pp. 207 ff., interrogation of 2 Nov. 1961; ZSt, 201 AR-Z 76/59, 9, pp. 122 ff., interrogation of 30 June 1971. Martin Sandberger, ZSt, 201 AR-Z 76/59, 2, pp. 34 ff., 30 Sept. 1957; also in ZSt, AR-Z 246/59, 2, pp. 209 ff., 18 Feb. 1960 and ZSt, 201 AR-Z 76/59, 2, pp. 351 ff., 30 Nov. 1964 and 1 Dec. 1964; ZSt, II 207 AR-Z 18/58, 11, pp. 2313 ff., 3 Nov. 1965; on Sandberger's statements cf. Ogorreck, *Einsatzgruppen*, 59 ff. Rudolf Batz, ZSt, 207 AR-Z 7/59, 11, pp. 1255 ff., 26 Jan. 1961 and pp. 1279 ff., 27 Jan. 1961; cf. Ogorreck, *Einsatzgruppen*, 65f. Karl Jäger, ZSt, 207 AR-Z 14/58 pp. 1883 ff., 15 June 1959; cf. Ogorreck, *Einsatzgruppen*, 67–8. Alfred Filbert, ZSt, 207 AR-Z 14/58, 54, pp. 171 ff., 11 May 1959; ZSt, 201 AR-Z 76/59, 11 (= supplementary volume II, vol. xii of the Hamburg files), pp. 7563 ff., 23 Sept. 1971; cf. Ogorreck, *Einsatzgruppen*, 74–5.

73. ZSt, 201 AR-Z 76/59, 12, pp. 7766 ff., 9 Dec. 1971; ibid. 4, application for pre-investigation, 29 Dec. 1969, quoting from an earlier interrogation (pp. 5324–5 of the Hamburg files); STA Munich, 114 Ks 8/71, pp. 3980 ff., 3 Jan. 1968. Cf. Ogorreck, *Einsatzgruppen*, 88–9, with references to further interrogations.

74. ZSt, 204 AR 1258/66, 23.
75. Quoting Blume literally and Filbert in summary: see n. 72.
76. BAB, NS 19/3957, 11–15 June 1941. This will have been the meeting at which Bach-Zelewski says Himmler spoke about the imminent decimation of the Russian population by 30 million (cf. n. 8)—which Bach-Zelewski dated at January 1941.
77. This emerges clearly from statements about this meeting.
78. See for example: ZSt, 201 AR-Z 76/59 2, 315–325 30 July 1964, Gustav Adolf Nosske; ibid. 6, pp. 58 ff, 22 Mar. 1971, Erwin Schulz; 207 AR-Z 7/59, Red Files, 8, pp. 1523 ff., 14 Aug. 1966, Erhard Grauel, Deputy Commando Leader, Einsatzkommando 3; 204 ZSt, AR 1258/66, 17, pp. 5 ff. 1 Aug. 1967, Friedrich Buchardt, speaker for the staff of the Einsatzgruppe B, 1 Aug. 1964.
79. BAB, R 70 SU/32.
80. BAB, R 70 SU/31, published in Peter Longerich, ed., *Die Ermordung der europäischen Juden. Eine umfassende Dokumentation des Holocaust 1941–1945* (Munich, 1989), 116 ff. English translation in J. Noakes and G. Pridham, eds. *Nazism 1919–1045*, vol iii: *Foreign Policy, War, and Racial Extermination* (Exeter, 1988), 489.
81. This is the text of the letter of 29 June.

11. The Mass Murder of Jewish Men

1. Gerlach, *Kalkulierte Morde*, 536.
2. Bogdan Musial, however, assumes that Soviet crimes in the summer of 1941 'had as a consequence the brutalization of the German-Soviet war' and led to a corresponding radicalization of the persecution of the Jews by Germans (cf. summary in *Deutsche Zivilverwaltung und Judenverfolgung im Generalgouvernement*, 291–2). He fundamentally underestimates the influence the Germans had in triggering the pogroms and the high level of potential violence against Jews that was expressed in the orders given by the German side before the start of the war.
3. See Karlis Kangeris, 'Kollaboration vor der Kollaboration? Die baltischen Emigranten und ihre "Befreiungskomitees" in Deutschland 1940/41', in Werner Röhr, ed., *Europa unterm Hakenkreuz. Okkupation und Kollaboration (1938–1945). Beiträge zu Konzeption und Praxis der Kollaboration in der deutschen Okkupationspolitik* (Berlin and Heidelberg, 1994), 165–90.
4. Siegfried Gasparaitris, '"Verrätern wird nur dann vergeben, wenn sie wirklich beweisen können, dass sie mindestens einen Juden liquidiert haben." Die Front Litauischer Aktisten (LAF) und die antisowjetischen Aufstände 1941', in ZfG 49 (2001), 886–904. The quotation in the title of this article means 'traitors are only forgiven when they can genuinely prove that they have liquidated at least one Jew', and is from an appeal circulated by the LAF in Lithuania in March 1941. See also Michael MacQueen, 'The Context of Mass Destruction: Agents and Prerequisites of the Holocaust in Lithuania', HGS 12 (1998), 27–48.
5. For Latvia see Hans-Heinrich Wilhelm, 'Offene Fragen der Holocaust-Forschung. Das Beispiel des Baltikums', in Uwe Backes, Eckhard Jesse, and Rainer Zitelmann, eds, *Die Schatten der Vergangenheit. Impulse zur Historisierung des Nationalsozialismus* (Frankfurt a. M., 1990), 403–25, n. 22.

6. See Rsyzard Torzecki, 'Die Rolle der Zusammenarbeit mit der deutschen Besatzungs-macht in der Ukraine für deren Okkupationspolitik 1941 bis 1944', in Röhr, ed., *Europa unterm Hakenkreuz*, 239–72.

7. Dieter Pohl, *Nationalistische Judenverfolgung in Ostgalizien 1941–1944* (Munich, 1996), 56–7, has a relevant reference, albeit a somewhat vague one.

8. Bericht v. 15 Oct., 180-L, *IMT* xxxvii. 670 ff.

9. On the pogrom in Kaunas (Kowno), see: ZSt, 207 AR-Z 14/58, 297 ff., report by retired Colonel von Bischoffshausen of 19 Apr. 1959, published in Ernst Klee et al., eds, '*Schöne Zeiten*'. *Judenmord aus der Sicht der Täter und Gaffer* (Frankfurt a. M., 1988), 35–6 (where there are also other witness statements concerning what happened there from trials 207 AR-Z 14/58 and 201 AR-Z 21/58). See also Ereignis Meldung (EM) 8 and the collection of documents by Avraham Tory, *Surviving the Holocaust: The Kovno Ghetto Diary* (Cambridge, Mass., 1990), 7 ff.

10. EM 19.

11. On Riga see also EM 15 and ZSt, II 207 AR-Z 7/59, judgement of the District Court in Hamburg.

12. EM 40. Details on events in Jelgava (Mitau) may be found in Andrew Ezergailis, *The Holocaust in Latvia* (Washington, 1996), 156 ff.

13. EM 24; Pohl, *Ostgalizien*, 60 ff.; Hannes Heer, 'Einübung in den Holocaust: Lemberg Juni/Juli 1941', *ZfG* 40 (2001), 389–408, sees in this pogrom an 'enactment' of something carefully prepared by the Germans.

14. Pohl, *Ostgalizien*, 69.

15. Ibid. 64–5. The 'reason' for the pogrom was the 15th anniversary (delayed by two months) of the murder of Ukraine's former (anti-Semitic) prime minister, Simon Petljura.

16. EM 24, and Bernd Boll, 'Zloczow, Juli 1941: Die Wehrmacht und der Beginn des Holocaust in Galizien', *ZfG* 50 (2002), 901–16.

17. EM 14 and EM 19. On Sonderkommando 4b see Ogorreck, *Einsatzgruppen*, 135 ff.

18. EM 14 from 6 July 1941.

19. Ibid.

20. EM 47.

21. EM 10.

22. Andrzey Zbikowski, 'Local Anti-Jewish Pogroms in the Occupied Territories of Eastern Poland, June–July 1941', in Lucjan Doboszycki and Jeffrey S. Gurock, eds, *The Holocaust in the Soviet Union: Studies and Sources on the Destruction of the Jews in the Nazi Occupied Territories of the USSR, 1941–1945* (New York and London, 1993), 173–9— where 35 places are named for eastern Galicia alone. Zbi Aharon Weiss, 'The Holocaust and the Ukrainian Victims', in Michael Berenbaum, ed., *A Mosaic of Victims: Non-Jews Persecuted and Murdered by the Nazis* (New York, 1990), 109–15 refers to 58 pogroms in West Ukraine, including Volhynia. On the number of victims, see Pohl, *Ostgalizien*, 67. Bogdan Musial, '*Konterrevolutionäre Elemente sind zu erschiessen*'. *Die Brutalisierung des deutsch-sowjetischen Krieges im Sommer 1941* (Berlin and Munich, 2000), 172, makes reference to numerous other places in which pogroms occurred.

23. EM 47.

24. EM 81 and EM 112.

25. Pohl, *Ostgalizien*, 54 ff.

26. Documented in (amongst others) Jacek Borkowicz et al., eds, *Thou Shalt not Kill: Poles on Jedwabne* (Warsaw, 2001); Antony Polonsky and Joanna B. Michlic, eds, *The Neighbors Respond: The Controversy over the Jedwabne Massacre in Poland* (Princeton and Oxford, 2004) and the contributions to *YVS* 30 (2002).

27. Jan T. Gross, *Neighbors: The Destruction of the Jewish Community in Jedwabne, Poland* (Princeton and Oxford, 2001).

28. See in particular the contribution by Edmunt Dimitrów in the volume edited by him with Pawel Machcewicz and Tomasz Szarota, *Der Beginn der Vernichtung. Zum Mord an den Juden in Jedwabne und Umgebung im Sommer 1941. Neue Forschungsergebnisse polnischer Historiker* (Osnabrück, 2004); see also Dariusz Stola, 'Jedwabne: Revisting the Evidence and Nature of the Crime', *HGS* 17 (2003), 139–52; and Radoslaw J. Ignatiew, 'Findings of Investigations 1/00/Zn into the Murder of Polish Citizens of Jewish Origin in the Town of Jedwabne on 10 July 1941', in Polonsky and Michlic, eds, *The Neighbors Respond*, 133–6, and Marek Jan Chodakiewicz, *The Massacre in Jedwabne July 10, 1941: Before, During, and After* (New York, 2005).

29. BAB, R 70/32, published in Peter Klein, ed., *Die Einsatzgruppen in der besetzten Sowjetunion 1941/42. Die Tätigkeits- und Lageberichte des Chefs der Sicherheitspolizei und des SD* (Berlin, 1997), 320–1.

30. On the early executions by Einsatzgruppe A see Hans-Heinrich, Wilhelm, *Einsatzgruppe A der Sicherheitspolizei und des SD 1941/42* (Frankfurt a. M., 1996) and the overview by Wolfgang Scheffler in Klein, ed., *Die Einsatzgruppen*.

31. EM 24; Ezergailis, *Holocaust*, 272 ff.

32. EM 24.

33. Judgement of the Hamburg District Court of 21 Dec. 1979. ZSt, 207 AR-Z 7/59. On the Arajas commando, see Ezergailis, *Holocaust*, 173 ff.; on the murders in the Bikernieki Forest, ibid. 222 ff.

34. Klee, ed., *'Schöne Zeiten'*, 122 ff.; Max Kaufman, *Churbn, Lettland: The Destruction of the Jews of Latvia* (Munich, 1947), 305; Margers Vestermanis, 'Ortskommandantur Libau. Zwei Monate deutscher Besatzung im Sommer 1941', in Hannes Heer und Klaus Naumann, eds, *Vernichtungskrieg. Verbrechen der Wehrmacht 1941–1945* (Hamburg, 1995), 219–26. On the shootings in Liepāja (Libau) see also the statements by Werner Schäfer, naval officer, from 16 July 1959 (ZSt, 207 AR-Z 7/59, Red Files, 8, pp. 1557 ff.), Georg Rosenstock, leader of the 2nd commando of Police Battalion 13, 2 Nov. 1959 (ibid.) and Kawelmacher, marine commandant of Liepāja (207 AR-Z 18/58, pp. 22 ff.).

35. ZSt, II 207 AR 1779/66.

36. The so-called Jäger Report (OS, 500-1-25 and USSR Central Document Office 108).

37. Ibid.

38. OS, 500-1-758, telex from the Gestapo office in Tilsit of 1 July 1941 and EM 14. In the trial of former members of the Tilsit Einsatzkommando, which took place in 1958 in Ulm, the historian Helmuth Krausnick, employed as an expert witness, took the view that the commando leader, Böhme, had been told on 23 June by the leader of Einsategruppe A, Franz Stahlecker, that in this border area all the Jews including women and children were to be shot. This view formed part of the judgement of the court and this fact was cited again and again by Krausnick as a confirmation of his thesis in favour of an

early comprehensive order for the murder of the Jews in the occupied Eastern zones. A closer analysis of the witness statements, however, and of newly discovered documents shows that this thesis is not tenable (see Longerich, *Politik*, 326 ff.). The executions perpetrated by the Tilsit Commando were not the first steps in carrying out a general order for the murder of all Jews that had only recently been transmitted to the commando, as Krausnick assumed, but part of a series of 'reprisal operations' originally initiated by the Wehrmacht.

39. EM 19.
40. EM 26.
41. EM 19 and the judgement of the Ulm District Court of 29 Aug. 1958, (= Sagel-Grande, *Justiz und NS-Verbrechen*, no. 465); Streim, *SWCA* 6 (1989), 333 ff.
42. See below, p. 31.
43. Also in EM 26. For Himmler's journey see also the diary of his personal assistant, Brandt, for 30 June 1941 (BAB, NS 19/3957).
44. OS, 500-1-25 (also ZSt, Dok. SU 401). See also EM 11.
45. On the first murders committed by Einsatzgruppe B in Belarus, see Gerlach, *Kalkulierte Morde*, 540 ff., and the overview of Einsatzgruppe B by Gerlach in Klein, ed., *Einsatz-gruppen*, 52–70.
46. EM 50, 12 Aug. 1941. On Sonderkommando 7a see also the judgement of the Essen District Court of 29 Mar. 1965 (= Sagel-Grande, *Justiz und NS-Verbrechen*, xx, no. 588), and Ogorreck, *Einsatzgruppen*, 114 ff.
47. EM 50 and judgement of the Essen District Court of 29 Mar. 1965 (= Sagel-Grande, *Justiz und NS-Verbrechen*, xx, no. 588).
48. Ibid.
49. Ogorreck, *Einsatzgruppen*, 116 ff., esp. p. 120.
50. Judgement of the Munich I District Court of 21 July 1961 (= Sagel-Grande, *Justiz und NS-Verbrechen*, xvii, no. 519, pp. 672 ff.); judgement of the Kiel District Court of 8 Apr. 1964 (= Sagel-Grande, *Justiz und NS-Verbrechen*, xix, no. 567, pp. 790 ff.); ZSt, 202 AR-Z 81/59, vol. 1, charge of 19 Apr. 1960.
51. EM 32 (24 July 1941).
52. On the reconstruction of this event, see the judgement of the Cologne District Court of 12 May 1964 (= Sagel-Grande, *Justiz und NS-Verbrechen*, xx, no. 573, pp. 171 ff.).
53. ZSt, 208 AR-Z 203/59, C-vol. I, testimony of Bradfisch, 9 June 1958, pp. 2 ff.
54. Ibid.
55. For example in his interrogation on 20 Apr. 1966 (ZSt, 73/61, 6, pp. 1510 ff.). Bach-Zelewski erroneously dated the meeting as 12 July 1941.
56. See *KTB*, chapter 3, 13.7 (YV, 053/88): 'Appeal by Company Chief Lieutenant Colonel of the Protection Police Riebel (special jurisdiction, conduct towards Jews)'.
57. EM 21. See also the judgement of the Berlin District Court of 22 June 1962 (= Sagel-Grande, *Justiz und NS-Verbrechen*, xviii, no. 540a) and the judgement of the Essen District Court of 29 Mar. 1964 (= Sagel Grande, *Justiz und NS-Verbrechen*, xx, no. 588); on the activities of Einsatzkommando 9 in Vilnius cf. Ogorreck, *Einsatzgruppen*, 125 ff.; and Yitzhak Arad, *Ghetto in Flames: The Destruction of the Jews in Vilna in the Holocaust* (Jerusalem, 1980), 66 ff.

58. Judgement of the Berlin District Court of 22 June 1962 (= Sagel-Grande, *Justiz und NS-Verbrechen*, xviii, no. 540a); ZSt, II 202 AR 72a/60, judgement of the Berlin District Court of 6 May 1966.

59. 207 AR-Z 14/58, note on Einsatzkommando 3, 27 Sept. 1961, Correspondence File 6, pp. 1151 ff.

60. EM 21 for 13 July 1941; ZSt, II 202 AR 72a/60, judgement of the Berlin District Court of 6 May 1966.

61. BAB, R 70 SU/32.

62. For the visits on 30 June and 9 July, see Brandt's diary (BAB, NS 19/3957) and Bach-Zelewski's diary (BAB, R 20/45b).

63. On the early executions carried out by Einsatzgruppe C, see the contribution by Dieter Pohl in Klein, ed., *Einsatzgruppen*, 71–87 and his 'Schauplatz Ukraine. Der Massenmord an den Juden im Militärverwaltungsgebiet und im Reichskommissariat 1941–1943', in Norbert Frei, Sybille Steinbacher, and Bernd C. Wagner, eds, *Ausbeutung, Vernichtung, Öffentlichkeit. Neue Studien zur nationalsozialistischen Lagerpolitik* (Munich, 2000), 135–73.

64. Testimony of Kroeger, 28 Aug. 1967 (ZSt, 76/59, 9, pp. 14 ff.). For further information on Dobromil: ZSt, 204 AR 1258/66, charge of 30 Jan. 1968, and judgement of the Tübingen District Court of 31 July 1969. According to incident report 24 there were 132 victims.

65. Ogorreck, *Einsatzgruppen*, 142 ff. Cf. Pohl, *Ostgalizien*, 60 ff., and Thomas Held, 'Vom Pogrom zum Massenmord. Die Vernichtung der jüdischen Bevölkerung Lembergs im Zweiten Weltkrieg', in Peter Fässler et al., *Lemberg—Lwów—Lviv* (Cologne, 1993), 113–66. See also ZSt, 204 AR 1258/66, charge of 30 Jan. 1958.

66. EM 24 (16 July 1941).

67. EM 47 (9 Sept. 1941).

68. EM 86 (17 Sept. 1941).

69. EM 38, EM 47, and EM 86.

70. EM 24; ZSt, 114 AR-Z 269/60, final report, Sonderkommando 4a, 30 Dec. 1964, 150, and the judgement of 29 Nov. 1968; see also the testimony of Ostermann, 3 Nov. 1965 (12, 2459) and Pfarrkicher, 4 Apr. 1962 (3, pp. 539 ff.). For this and the following operations by Sonderkommando 4a see especially Ogorreck, *Einsatzgruppen*, 130 ff.

71. EM 14.

72. ZSt, 114 AR-Z 269/60, final report, Sonderkommando 4a, 30 Dec. 1964; Georg Pfarr-kircher, 4 Apr. 1962 (3, 539 ff.); Johannes Erich August Fischer, 30 Oct. 1963 (7, pp. 1374 ff.); judgement of 29 Nov. 1968.

73. Ibid., final report of 28 Aug. 1962; vol. 2, 387 ff., interrogation of Paul Walter, 24 Oct. 1961; vol. 21, pp. 140 ff., testimony of Heinrich Schlimme, 19 Nov. 1963.

74. EM 47 (9 Aug. 1941).

75. EM 17 (9 July 1941).

76. EM 58 (20 Aug. 1941).

77. EM 47 (8 Aug. 1941).

78. On further 'reprisal operations' in the area of Einsatzgruppe C see EM 20 (17 July 1941) and EM 24 (16 July 1941, Dobromil and Zloczow).

79. EM 17 (9 July 1941).

80. EM 43 (5 Aug. 1941).

81. EM 47 (9 Sept. 1941).
82. EM 58 (20 Aug. 1941). It was not the commando that was responsible for this massacre, however, but the SS Cavalry Brigade. See below, p. 220.
83. Angrick, *Besatzungspolitik*, 140 ff.; Radu Florian, 'The Jassy Massacre of June 29–30, 1941: An Early Act of Genocide against the Jews', in Randolph L. Braham, ed., *The Destruction of Romanian and Ukrainian Jews during the Antonescu Era* (New York, 1997), 63–86; Radu Ioanid, *The Holocaust in Romania: The Destruction of Jews and Gypsies under the Antonescu Regime 1940–1944* (Chicago, 1999), 63 ff. The total number of victims is disputed (ibid. 85–6).
84. Ioanid, *Holocaust*, 90 ff.; Jean Ancel, 'The German-Romanian Relationship and the Final Solution', *HGS* 19/2 (2005), 256–7.
85. Raul Hilberg, *The Destruction of the European Jews* (New York, 1985) 771.
86. Activity and Situation report no. 1, NO 2651, published in Peter Klein, ed., *Die Einsatzgruppen*, 112 ff. and 121.
87. On the early executions carried out by Einsatzgruppe D, see Angrick, *Besatzungspolitik*, 131 ff., and the overview by the same author in Klein, *Einsatzgruppen*, 88–110. There is an English version: 'The Escalation of German-Romanian Anti-Jewish Policy after the Attack on the Soviet Union', *YVS* 26 (1998), 203–38.
88. EM 25; Angrick, *Besatzungspolitik*, 165 ff.
89. EM 37 and RH 20/11–488, report Ic/XXX AK of 2 Aug. 1941 (= NOKW 650) and further documents in the same folder; cf. also the account in Angrick, *Besatzungspolitik*, 166–7, Ogorreck, *Einsatzgruppen*, 153–4, and Krausnick, 'Einsatzgruppen', 238–9.
90. BAM, RH 20-11/488, report by Sonderkommando 10b to Army Group South, 9 July 1941 (= NOKW 587 and 3453); cf. Angrick, *Besatzungspolitik*, 148 ff.; Ogorreck, *Einsatzgruppen*, 154–5.
91. EM 40.
92. Ibid. Chotin, for example, was 'gone through', and '150 Jews and Communists were liquidated'. Cf. Angrick, *Besatzungspolitik*, 159 ff.
93. EM 45; see also Angrick, *Besatzungspolitik*, 177 ff.
94. Ibid., testimony of Zöllner, 26 Apr. 1962.
95. EM 45; State Archive Munich, Case against Sonderkommando 11b, charge of 19 Aug. 1971; see also the testimony of the accused, Johannes Paul Schlupper, 18 May 1962 (5, pp. 1008–9) and the interrogations of Johannes Nentwig, 25 Apr. 1962 (5, pp. 1070 ff.), and August Rosenbauer, 23 Sept. 1969 (18, p. 3823). See also EM 45; Angrick, *Besatzungspolitik*, 186 ff.
96. EM 61; State Archive Munich, 119 c Js 1/69, charge of 28 Oct. 1972. There are important details in the testimonies by Hermann Siebert, 13 Nov. 1951 (vol. 5, pp. 630 ff.), Karl Becker, 4 Aug. 1970 (vol. 3, pp. 300 ff.), Erich Rohde, 3 June 1970 (vol. 5, pp. 584 ff.), and Erich Hanne, 17 Dec. 1969 (vol. 3, pp. 362 ff.).
97. Judgement by the Wuppertal District Court of 24 May. 1973 (ZSt, V 205 ArZ 20/60).
98. Andrei Angerick et al., ' "Da hätte man Tagebuch führen müssen". Das Polizeibataillon 322 und die Judenmorde im Bereich der Heeresgruppe Mitte während des Sommers und Herbstes 1941', in Helge Grabitz et al., eds, *Die Normalität des Verbrechens. Bilanz und Perspektiven der Forschung zu den nationalsozialistischen Gewaltverbrechen* (Berlin, 1994); *Unsere Ehre heist Treue: Kriegstagebuch des Kommandostabes*

Reichsführer SS. Tätigkeitsberichte der 1. und 2. SS-Inf.-Brigade, der 1.SS Kav.-Brigade und von der Sonderkommandos der SS (Vienna, 1965), 334 ff.; judgement of the District Court of Bochum against members of Police Battalion 316 who were also involved in the massacre (Bochum District Court, 6 June 1968, ZSt, II 202 AR-Z 168/59).

99. YV 053/12, *Kriegstagebuch (KTB), Unsere Ehre*, 322 (8 July 1941).
100. In his interrogation of 20 Apr. 1966, for example (ZSt, 73/61, 6, pp. 1510 ff.).
101. Ibid., YV 053/127, *KTB* 322 (9 July 1941).
102. Ibid (12 July 1941)
103. Ibid. (8 July 1941).
104. ZSt, II 202 AR-Z 168/59, order of the state prosecutor of Dortmund, 8 Nov. 1968. On these shootings see also the judgement of the District Court of Freiburg on 12 July 1963 (= Sagel-Grande, *Justiz and NS-Verbrechen*, xix, no. 555).
105. Note by the public prosecution department, Lübeck, 9 Sept. 1965 (ZSt, AR-Z 82/61). See also the testimonies of Wilhelm Niehoff, 27 Feb. 1962 (1, pp. 12 ff.), Richard Pelz, undated (1, pp. 354 ff.), Friedrich Niehoff, 18 Aug. 1966 (11, pp. 2723 ff.). Cf. Gerlach, *Kalkulierte Morde*, 546 ff.
106. YV 053/127, *KTB* 322 (2 Aug. 1941).
107. YV 053/127.
108. YV 053/127 (15 Aug. 1941).
109. BAB, NS 36/13, published in Longerich, *Ermordung*, 43–4.

12.   The Transition from Anti-Semitic Terror to Genocide

1. *IMT* xxxviii. 86 ff. (221-L).
2. Angrick, *Besatzungspolitik*, 152, reconstitutes an execution that was conducted like a court martial on 8 July in Czernowitz (Sonderkommando 10b); the first shootings of Einsatzkommando Tilsit took place in a similar manner (Matthäus, in Christopher Browning, *The Origins of the Final Solution: The Evolution of Nazi Jewish Policy 1939–1942* (London, 2004), 254). On the change in practice for executions, see pp. 260–1. The new, more effective procedures are explained in the so-called Jäger Report of Einsatzkommando 2 of 1 Dec. 1941 (OS, 500-1-25). See also the judgement of the District Court of Kiel of 8 Apr. 1964, which stresses the differences in execution procedures using the example of Einsatzkommando 8 (= Sagel-Grande, *Justiz and NS-Verbrechen*, xix. 773).
3. EM 19, EM 24, and EM 32.
4. EM 24, EM 73.
5. EM 73, EM 80.
6. EM 32, EM 47.
7. EM 46, EM 47.
8. EM 50, EM 67.
9. EM 58, EM 68.
10. EM 59.
11. EM 88, EM 90, and EM 94.
12. See above, p. 194.
13. See above, p. 195.

14. EM 67.
15. EM 73.
16. EM 81.
17. EM 47.
18. For details see Krausnick, *Truppe*, 209 ff. The commandos sometimes urged that they be deployed not only in the Army Rear Area or the Rear Area of the Army Group but also in the combat area (see for example the Stahlecker report, 180-L, *IMT* xxxvi. 670. ff., or Activity and Situation Report no. 1, NO 2651, published in Klein, ed., *Einsatzgruppen*, 112 ff. and 113).
19. EM 111.
20. EM 27.
21. *ADAP*, series D, vol. 12, no. 207.
22. For details, see below, pp. 227 ff.
23. Gerlach, *Kalkulierte Morde*, 574 ff., which has various examples. Gerlach notes amongst other things that for the attitude of the central authorities the meeting of the General Council of the Four-Year Plan on 19 Sept. 1941 meant a change of direction towards the use of Jews for work details (ibid. 582; the invitation to this meeting and its agenda are in NG 1853).
24. Gerlach, *Kalkulierte Morde*, 583.
25. Ibid. 628 ff.
26. Ibid. 645 (in summary).
27. EM 31.
28. EM 111.
29. EM 94.
30. On the formation of ghettos, see above all Gerlach, *Kalkulierte Morde*, 521 ff. and 574 ff.
31. BAM, RW 31/11, cf. Aly, *'Final Solution'*, 190.
32. BAB, RW 12/189; cf. Aly, *'Final Solution'*, 192.
33. At the end of August or the beginning of September, the formation of ghettos in the larger cities was specifically encouraged by the commander of Rear Army Area South (BAM, RH 22–6, 28 Aug. 1941 and NOKW 1584). The commander of Rear Army Area North described the formation of ghettos in an order dated 3 Sept. 1941 as not a priority (BAM, RH 26–285/45 and NOKW 2204). The commander of Rear Army Area Centre had been issuing orders for the formation of ghettos since July (cf. Gerlach, *Kalkulierte Morde*, 524–5).
34. 1028-PS, *IMT* xxvi. 567 ff.
35. Gerlach, *Kalkulierte Morde*, 530 ff.
36. EM 19 and EM 21.
37. Published in Paul Kohl, *'Ich wundere mich, dass ich noch lebe'. Sowjetische Augenzeugenberichte* (Gütersloh, 1990), 218.
38. EM 31.
39. EM 43.
40. EM 63.
41. EM 106.
42. See below, Chapter 17.
43. 221-L, *IMT* xxxviii. 86 ff.

44. BAB, R 43II/683a. Rosenberg had already been assigned the task of establishing an 'Office for Eastern Questions' by Hitler at the beginning of April. On Rosenberg's preparations for the war against the Soviet Union, see Yitzhak Arad, 'Alfred Rosenberg and the "Final Solution" in the Occupied Soviet Territories', *YVS* 113 (1979), 265 ff.

45. NG 1688; published in, *Führer-Erlasse 1939–1945*, ed. Martin Moll (Stuttgart, 1997), no. 99.

46. Cf. the letter from Stahlecker (leader of Einsatzgruppe A) to Heydrich dated 10 Aug. 1941 (Staatsarchiv (StA) Riga, 1026-1-3) in which he draws attention to the fact that 'the handling of the Jewish Question is part of the police's role in securing the newly occupied Eastern territories so that, according to points I and II of the Führer's decree on the securing of the occupied Eastern areas by the police of 18 July 1941, the Reichsführer SS is entitled to issue instructions to the Reichskommissar'.

47. In the view of Christopher Browning, most recently in *Origins*, 309 ff.

48. See above, p. 184.

49. YV, M 36/3 (copies from the Military Archive in Prague), Meeting Minute Ia: 'The units subordinated to the Command Staff are to be deployed in the area of political administration. A commitment of larger units in the Rear Army Area is possible. Members of the Command Staff and the units assigned to it have no business either in the operational areas or in the Rear Army Areas.'

50. Cf. Rolf-Dieter Müller, *Hitlers Ostkrieg und die deutsche Siedlungspolitik. Die Zusammenarbeit von Wehrmacht, Wirtschaft und SS* (Frankfurt a. M., 1991), 94 ff.

51. According to a communication from Lammers of 10 June 1941 (BAB, R 6/21). On this see Rosenberg's opinion, 14 June 1941 and the 'Denkschrift über Aufgaben und Befugnisse des Reichsministers für die besetzten Ostgebiete bzw. Die Reichskommissare und über Befugnisse des Reichsführers SS, Chef der Deutschen Polizei sowie des Reichskommissars für die Festigung deutschen Volkstums', which Rosenberg sent to Lammers on 27 Aug. 1943 (no. 3726).

52. NS 19/1739.

53. NO 4724, Reichsführer SS to Lorenz and Heydrich (11 July 1941).

54. Addendum to communication of 11 July 1941, ibid. The original order to Pflaum had also been issued on 11 July.

55. BAB, NS 22/971, file note by Bormann dated 16 Aug. 1941: 'There is no clarity about which areas should most quickly be Germanized after the end of the war, and it cannot for the moment be obtained, since the Führer will only take the necessary decisions after the end of the war.'

56. BAB, R 6/23, Himmler to Rosenberg, 19 Aug. 1941, and Rosenberg to Lammers, 23 Aug. 1941.

57. BAB, R 6/23 (cf. Müller, *Ostkrieg*, 98). In a file note on a conversation with Goering on 9 Aug. 1941 Rosenberg mentioned that Goering too was assuming 'that the task assigned to the Reichsführer SS with respect to the strengthening of the German nation was limited exclusively to the area of the German Reich' (ibid.).

58. OS, 1323-1-53 and BAB, R 43 II/684a, letter of 6 Sept. 1941 from Lammers to Rosenberg concerning Himmler's competences.

59. Meeting between Knoblauch and Jüttner on 2 July 1941 (BAM, Film WF800, copies from the Military Archive in Prague).

60. *KTB* Commando Staff RFSS, 27 July 1941, published in *Unsere Ehre*.
61. Ibid. (9 July 1941 and 17 July 1941).
62. Ibid. (10 July 1941).
63. Witte et al., eds, *Dienstkalender*, 183.
64. *KTB* Commando Staff RFSS. The Cavalry Brigade was formed on 2 Aug. 1941.
65. Witte et al., eds, *Dienstkalender*, 21 July 1941, p. 186.
66. On May see Cüppers, *Wegbereiter*, 68.
67. BAM, Film M 806 (copies in the Military Archive in Prague), Activity Report for 20–7 July 1941 dated 28 July 1941.
68. In contrast to the two other Command Staff Brigades, the 2nd SS Brigade was not deployed for the murder of Jews in summer and autumn 1941. Whilst it was subordinated to the Higher SS and Police Commander Russia North, Hans Prützmann, in September 1941, it was evidently used most frequently for military purposes. Prützmann did not need a large SS formation in his area, since for the mass murder of Jews in the Reich Commissariat Ostland he had local militias at his disposition (see KTB Command Staff for September and October, published in *Unsere Ehre*).

13. Enforcing the Annihilation Policy: Extending the Shootings to the Whole Jewish Population

1. The most detailed account is in Cüppers, *Wegbereiter*, 151 ff.; see also Büchler, 'Kommandostab' and Gerlach, *Kalkulierte Morde*, 555 ff.
2. *KTB* Commando Staff RFSS, 28 July 1941, published in *Unsere Ehre*, 220 ff.
3. BAM, RS 3–8/36; on the meeting with Himmler see also BAB, R 20/45b, Bach-Zelewski's diary, 31 July 1941.
4. BAM, RS 4/441, Divisional Order no. 28.
5. Cüppers, *Wegbereiter*, 142 ff., shows at several points mass shootings of women and children by the 1st Cavalry Regiment from the first half of August, which are not mentioned in the regimental reports. By the beginning of September the 1st Regiment was avoiding all mention of the murder of women and children in its reports, although this is contained in the reports of the Regiment's individual squadrons (ibid. 194).
6. BAM, RS 4/441; Cüppers, *Wegbereiter*, 151.
7. Ibid.
8. The District Court in Braunschweig notes 4,500 victims in its verdict (= Sagel-Grande, *Justiz und NS-Verbrechen*, xx, no. 570, 20 Apr. 1964), which is based on EM 58. Higher (and probably more realistic) figures are to be found in Cüppers, *Wegbereiter*, 155 ff. The mass murder was described as a 'reprisal' for two alleged assaults on members of the town militia (EM 58).
9. 2nd Cavalry Regiment, Mounted Unit, report of 12 Aug. 1941, USHM, RG-48.004, Reel 2, Box 24 (copies in the Military Archive in Prague), published in *Unsere Ehre*, 227 ff.
10. USHM, RG-48.004, Reel 2, Box 24.
11. Cüppers, *Wegbereiter*, 203.
12. Ibid. 194 ff.
13. According to Gerlach's account of the events of August 1941 (*Kalkulierte Morde*, 566 ff.).

14. Judgement of the Berlin District Court of 22 June 1962 (= Sagel-Grande, *Justiz und NS-Verbrechen*, xviii, no. 540); ZSt, II 202 AR 72a/60, judgement of the Berlin District Court of 6 May 1966. On EK 9, see Ogorreck, *Einsatzgruppen*, 186 ff.

15. EM 50.

16. 202 AR-Z 73/61, vol. 6, pp. 1580 ff., 22 Feb. 1966; see also the interrogation of Filbert of 23 Sept. 1971 (ZSt, 201 AR-Z 76/59, vol. 11, pp. 7563 ff.).

17. ZSt, II 202 AR 72a/60, Judgement of the Berlin District Court of 6 May 1966; judgement of the Berlin District Court of 22 June 1962 (= Sagel-Grande, *Justiz und NS-Verbrechen*, xviii, no. 540).

18. ZSt, 201 AR-Z 76/59, 8 Oct. 1971 (11, pp. 7605 ff.).

19. Bradfisch (ZSt, 201 AR-Z 76/59, 8 Oct. 1971, vol. 11, pp. 7605 ff.).

20. On another occasion Bradfisch said that the same information had been given to him by Himmler in Mogilev: StA Munich, 22 Ks 1/1961, 1, pp. 136 ff., 22 Apr. 1958. On this visit by Himmler to Minsk, see Gerlach, *Kalkulierte Morde*, 571 ff.

21. EM 90 and EM 92 v. 21 Sept. and 23 Sept. 1941; judgement of the 1st Munich District Court of 21 July 1961 (= Sagel-Grande, *Justiz und NS-Verbrechen*, xvii, no. 519); ZSt, 202 AR-Z 81/59, indictment of 19 Apr. 1960.

22. Gerlach, *Kalkulierte Morde*, 570.

23. EM 92 for 23 Sept. 1941; judgement of the Cologne District Court of 12 May 1964 (= Sagel-Grande, *Justiz und NS-Verbrechen*, xx, no. 573). Gerlach, *Kalkulierte Morde*, 585–6, dates these 'actions' to 9 Sept. 1941.

24. EM 92; Gerlach, *Kalkulierte Morde*, 586.

25. Ibid. 586.

26. EM 108 for 9 Oct. 1941; judgement of the Cologne District Court of 12 May 1964 (= Sagel-Grande, *Justiz und NS-Verbrechen*, xx, no. 573).

27. BA, NS 33/22, telex of 1 Sept. 1942; Angrick et al., *Tagebuch*, 342; YV 053/128, *KTB* attachments, report of 30 Aug. 1941. According to the attached statistics for the executions this affected only men.

28. YV 053/127, 29 Aug. 1941.

29. Ibid., 1 Sept. 1941. On these shootings see also the witness statements by Alois Fischer, 27 Oct. 1965 (ZSt, AR-Z 6/65, 2, pp. 484 ff.) and Friedrich Soier, 19 Oct. 1965 (ibid., pp. 383 ff.).

30. Gerlach, *Kalkulierte Morde*, 568. EM 90 reported a total of 2,278 victims.

31. Ibid.; StA Minsk 655-1-1 (copy USHM, Roll 4), file note on the progress of 'combat against partisans' from 25 and 26 Sept. 1941. See also witness statement by Nagel, Battalion commander, ZSt AR-Z 52/59, supplementary vol. 2, 318–19. Cf. Angerick et al., *Tagebuch*, 345–6.

32. Angrick et. al., *Tagebuch*, 346 ff.; YV053/27, Kriegstagebuch of Police Battalion 322, 2/3 Oct. 1941. On the mass murder in Mogilev as the 'starting point for total annihilation', see Gerlach, *Kalkulierte Morde*, 587 ff.

33. EM 133; Judgement of the 1st Munich District Court of 21 July 1961 (= Sagel-Grande, *Justiz und NS-Verbrechen*, xvii, no. 519); ZSt, 202 AR-Z 81/59, indictment of 19 Apr. 1960; Judgement of the Kiel District Court of 8 Apr. 1964 (= Sagel-Grande, *Justiz und NS-Verbrechen*, xix, no. 567).

34. Like those of Bobruisk and Gomel, this mass murder only appears in Activity and Situational Report no. 8, which covers the first half of December (NO 2659, in Klein ed., *Einsatzgruppen*, 263 ff.); see Gerlach, *Kalkulierte Morde*, 596–7.

35. Wilhelm, 'Einsatzgruppe A', 576 ff.; Gerlach, *Kalkulierte Morde*, 597 ff.

36. Activity and Situational Report no. 8, NO 2659, mentions '2,365 Jews'; cf. Gerlach, *Kalkulierte Morde*, 599.

37. Activity and Situational Report no. 8, NO 2659; ZSt, 202 AR-Z 81/59, indictment of 19 Apr. 1960 and judgement of the Munich District Court of 21 July 1961. Gerlach, *Kalkulierte Morde*, 599–600 dates this mass murder to 7 and 8 Nov. 1941.

38. Gerlach, *Kalkulierte Morde*, 599 ff.

39. EM 133.

40. Einsatzgruppe B, Activity and Situational Report of 1 Mar. 1942, ZUV 9 quoted from Gerlach, 'Einsatzgruppe B' in Klein, ed., *Einsatzgruppen*, 62.

41. NOKW 1165, report by the Higher SS and Police Commander South to AOK 6, 1 Aug. 1941 on 'cleansing action' carried out from 28 July to 30 Aug. 1941.

42. BAM, RH 22/5, 25 July 1941. On the murders carried out by the 1st Brigade in July and August, see Cüppers, *Wegbereiter*, 165 ff., and Bernd Boll, 'Aktionen nach Kriegsbrauch. Wehrmacht und 1. SS-Infanteriebrigade 1941', *ZfG* 48 (2000), 775–88.

43. Activity Report by the 1st SS Brigade, 30 July 1941 for 27 July–30 July (*Unsere Ehre*, 197 ff.). See also BAB, NS 33/39 and NS 33/22, Activity Report of the Command Staff RFSS, 6 Aug. 1941 for the period from 28 July to 3 Aug. 1941.

44. Activity Report by the 1st SS Brigade for the period from 3 Aug. to 6 Aug. (*Unsere Ehre*, 898–9). See also Schmuel Spector, *The Holocaust of the Volhynian Jews, 1941–1944* (Jerusalem, 1990), 76–7, for more details.

45. *Dienstkalender*, ed. Witte, 12 Aug. 1941, p. 191; BAB, NS 33/320, Adj. RFSS, 11 Aug. 1941 and NS 33/312, Command Staff, 12 Aug. 1941. At the same time the Cavalry Brigade had already shot a large number of Jews.

46. 1st Brigade's Activity Report for 6 Aug.–10 Aug. dated 10 Aug. 1941 (*Unsere Ehre*, 111 ff.); EM 59 from 21 Aug.; BAB, NS 33/22, Command Staff report on activity between 1 Sept. and 7 Sept. dated 10 Sept. 1941. On the involvement of Police Battalion 320, see ibid., report by the Higher SS and Police Commander South of 20 Aug. 1941.

47. Cüppers, *Wegbereiter*, 174. Cüppers identifies inaccuracies in the reporting that can be attributed to technical and calculation errors; his own estimates are based on a more comprehensive assessment of further sources.

48. KTB Command Staff, in *Unsere Ehre*, 110 ff. Further details in Cüppers, *Wegbereiter*, 203 ff.

49. EM 60; see also Jeckeln's reports to the Command Staff (BAB, NS 33/22), 27–30 Aug. 1941).

50. ND 197-PS, minute of 27 Aug. 1941.

51. Randolph Braham, 'The Kamenets-Podolsk and Délvidék Massacres: Prelude to the Holocaust in Hungary', *YVS* 9 (1973), 133–56; Klaus-Michael Mallmann, 'Der qualitative Sprung im Vernichtungsprozess. Das Massaker von Kamenez-Poldolsk Ende August 1941', *Jahrbuch für Antisemitismusforschung (JA)* 10 (2001), 237–64.

52. EM 94.

53. EM 88; see also BAB, NS 33/22, telex Higher SS and Police Commander South (5 Sept. 1941).

54. See below, p. 220.

55. EM 106. On the massacre in Babi Yar see Krausnick, *Einsatzgruppen*, 189–90; Hartmut Rüß, 'Wer war verantwortlich für das Massaker von Babi Jar?', *Militärgeschichtliche Mitteilungen* (*MGM*) 57 (1998), 483–508; Klaus Jochen Arnold attempts, with arguments I do not find entirely convincing, to play down the involvement of the army in the massacre ('Die Eroberung und Behandlung der Stadt Kiew durch die Wehrmacht im September 1941: Zur Radikalisierung der Besatzungspolitik', *MGM* 58 (1999), 23–63).

56. On Einsatzgruppe C, see Dieter Pohl, 'Schauplatz Ukraine. Der Massenmord an den Juden im Militärverwaltungsgebiet und in Reichskommissariat 1941–1943', in Norbert Frei et al., eds, *Ausbeutung, Vernichtung, Öffentlichkeit. Neue Studien zur nationalsozialistischen Lagerpolitik* (Munich, 2000), 135–73; and 'Einsatzgruppe C', in Klein, ed., *Einsatzgruppen*, 71–87.

57. ZSt, 201 AR-Z 76/59, vol. 6, 58 ff., 22 Mar. 1971. See also ibid., vol. 2, 375–6, 7 Feb. 1957: ibid., vol. 4, application for prior investigation, 29 Dec. 1969. See also 204 AR-Z 266/59, indictment of 30 Dec. 1964. On the interrogation of Schulz und Streckenbach, see Ogorreck, *Einsatzgruppen*, 190 ff. and Wildt, *Generation*, 561 ff.

58. EM 119 (20 Oct. 1941).

59. EM 119.

60. EM 119.

61. EM 111.

62. EM 132.

63. *Dienstkalender*, ed. Witte et al., 3 Oct. 1941, p. 224.

64. EM 135.

65. Judgement of the Darmstadt District Court of 29 Nov. 1968.

66. Ibid. On the shootings see also the testimony of airman Friedrich Wilhelm Liebe, 14 June 1965 (IfZ, Gd 01.54, 49). The whole process is documented in detail in chapter 7 of Klee et al., 'Schöne Zeiten'.

67. EM 80, 11 Sept. 1941. See also ZSt, 114 AR-Z 269/60, final report, 30 Dec. 1968.

68. Judgement of the Darmstadt District Court of 29 Nov. 1968 and EM 88. Further executions with more than 100 victims each are verifiable for Berditschew, Winniza, Iwankow, and Taraschtscha (ZSt, 114 Ar-Z 269/60, final report, 30 Dec. 1968).

69. EM 106.

70. EM 80.

71. ZSt, II 204 AR-Z 1251/65, Besser indictment and judgement.

72. Ibid., charge sheet.

73. Ibid., charge sheet of Besser, NS 33/22, telex of the Higher SS and Police Commander Russia South, 19 August.

74. ZSt, 204 AR-Z 1251/65, indictment.

75. Interrogation on 11 Mar. 1969 (ibid., 7, pp. 1320 ff.).

76. ZSt, 204 AR-Z 1251/65 D, final note of the Bavarian State Criminal Office, 19 Dec. 1977. See also reports in BAB, NS 33/22, telex of the Higher SS and Police Commander South of 21 Aug. 24 Aug. and 27 Aug. with reports on shootings by Battalion 314.

77. Pohl, 'Schauplatz', 148; NO 2662, Activity and Situation Report no. 11 for March 1942.

78. Pohl, 'Schauplatz', p. 149; NO 2662, Activity and Situational Report no. 11 (for Artemovsk).

79. Angrick, *Besatzungspolitik*, 193 ff.

80. Testimony of Nosske, 9 Apr. 1962 (StA Munich, 119 c Js 1/69, vol. 4, pp. 482 ff.); testimony of Max Drexel, 17 Apr. 1962 (vol. 2, pp. 132 ff.), Karl Becker, 22 Sept. 1961 (vol. 3, pp. 274 ff.), and that of Erwin Harsch, 1 Dec. 1947 (vol. 7, pp. 1604 ff.). See also Angrick, *Besatzungspolitik*, 200 ff.; Ogorreck, *Einsatzgruppen*, 157 ff.

81. II 213 AR 1902/66, Main Document XI, interrogation of Nosske, 13 Mar. 1969, pp. 2610 ff.; similarly also in ZSt, II 213 AR 1902/66, Correspondence File, vol. 2, pp. 5, 97 ff., 24 May 1971; on Nosske's testimony, see Ogorreck, *Einsatzgruppen*, 207 ff.

82. BAM, RH 20-11-488, report by the representative of the Head of the Sipo and the SD to the commander in the Rear Army Area South, 11 Sept. 1941.

83. Ioanid, *Holocaust*, 176 ff.

84. NOKW 1702, report from the local command post at Ananjev of 3 Sept. 1941; Angrick, *Besatzungspolitik*, 232 ff.

85. NO 4992, testimony of Robert Barth, 12 Sept. 1947.

86. Angrick, *Besatzungspolitik*, 234.

87. StA Munich 119 c Js 1/69, indictment of 28 Oct. 1970 and judgement; testimony of inhabitant Iwan Andrejewitsch Jordanow, 23 July 1969 (vol. 6, 705 ff.); testimony of Erich Rohde, 3 June 1970 (vol. 5, pp. 584 ff.).

88. Ibid., testimony of Max Drexel, 17 Apr. 1962 (vol. 2, pp. 132 ff.); interrogation of Erich Rohde, 3 June 1970 (vol. 5, 584 ff.); Angrick, *Besatzungspolitik*, 239 ff.

89. Angrick, *Besatzungspolitik*, 235.

90. ZSt, 213 AR 1898/66, 12, 2777 ff., testimony of Erich Bock from 17 Mar. 1965, and 13, pp. 2800 ff., testimony of Otto-Ernst Prast from 16 Mar. 1965.

91. Ibid., indictment of 8 Mar. 1966; testimony of Zöllner, 28 Apr. 1962, 3 May. 1962 (vol. 4, pp. 934 ff.), Karl Heinrich Noa, 18 Aug. 1965 (vol. 11, pp. 2292 ff.), and Otto Eichelbaum, 25 June 1964 (vol. 8, pp. 1888 ff.). On the participation of members of EK 12: StA Munich, 119 c Js 1/69, testimony of Karl Becker, 22 Sept. 1961 (vol. 3, pp. 274 ff.). See also NOKW 3233, report on the activity of SK XI a in Nikolayev between 18 Aug. and 31 Aug. 1941; cf. Angrick, *Besatzungspolitik*, 241 ff.

92. StA Munich, 118 Ks 268, indictment of 8 Mar. 1966; testimony of Günther Kosanke, 12 Apr. 1962 (vol. 4, pp. 888 ff.); BAM, RH 20-11/488, report on the activity of SK 11a in Cherson between 22 Aug. and 10 Sept. 1941. Cf. Angrick, *Besatzungspolitik*, 251 ff.

93. Breitman, *Architect*, 211 ff.; BAB, NS 19/3957.

94. EM 95. The figure of 8,890 is already mentioned in EM 89 (20 Sept. 1941).

95. EM 101 (2 Oct. 1941).

96. Ioanid, *Holocaust*, 177 ff.; Dora Litani, 'The Destruction of the Jews of Odessa in the Light of Rumanian Documents', *YVS* 6 (1967), 135–54. On the involvement of SK 11 see in particular Angrick, *Besatzungspolitik*, 294 ff.

97. EM 116 (17 Oct. 1941).

98. Activity and Situation Report no. 6, NO 2656 (in Klein, ed., *Einsatzgruppen*, 222 ff., 232).

99. Angrick, *Besatzungspolitik*, 309–10, 311 ff., and 315–16.

100. Ibid. 345 ff.
101. Ibid. 350 ff.
102. Ibid. 338 ff.
103. Jean Ancel, 'The Romanian Campaign of Mass Murder in Trans-Nistria, 1941–1942', in Randolf Braham, ed., *The Destruction of Hungarian Jewry: A Documentary Account* (New York, 1963), 87–134; Ioanid, *Holocaust*, 182 ff.
104. Angrick, *Besatzungspolitik*, 284 ff.; Ioanid, *Holocaust*, 187 ff.
105. Jäger Bericht, OS, 500-1-25.
106. Ibid.
107. Ibid. On this see the study compiled from witness testimony by Jakub Z. I.Wtjedni, *Iz istorie Daugawpilskojo Geto*, in: *Daugawpilskaja jewrejsuaja obschina* (Daugavpils, 1993), 287–394; testimony of Fritz Lesch, 8 July 1959 (ZSt, 204 AR-Z 21/58, pp. 2747 ff.).
108. EM 96; for the calculation see Wilhelm, *Einsatzgruppe A*, 113.
109. Judgement of the District Court in Ulm of 29 Aug. 1958 (= Sagel-Grande, *Justiz und NS-Verbrechen* xv, no. 465).
110. See below, p. 235.
111. StA Riga, 1026-1-3, published as 1138-PS, *IMT* xxvii. 18 ff.
112. See correspondence from Tschiersky, aide in the staff of EG A to Jäger and Stahlecker, 5 Aug. 1941, and Stahlecker's query to Heydrich of 5 Aug. 1941, both in StA Riga, 1026-1-3.
113. Draft document on the establishment of provisional guidelines for the treatment of the Jews in the area of the Reich Commissariat Ostland (MS corrections), 6 Aug. 1941, StA Riga 1026-1-3, published in Hans Mommsen, *Herrschaftsalltag im Dritten Reich. Studien und Texte* (Düsseldorf, 1988), 476.
114. This sentence was added in manuscript and replaces the original: 'The following solution to the Jewish problem takes account of all the angles so far explained.'
115. This last sentence was also added in manuscript.
116. Christopher Browning, 'Beyond "Intentionalism" and "Functionalism": The Decision for the Final Solution Reconsidered', in Browning, *The Path to Genocide: Essays on Launching the Final Solution* (Cambridge, 1992), 110.
117. OS, 504-2-8, correspondence of 21 July and 4 August. The permission granted in correspondence from 4 August was on 2 Aug. 1942 (according to a telex from the RSHA to BdS Riga from 22 June 1942: ibid.; the process is also in ZSt, Documentation USSR, no. 401). On the authorization see Wilhelm, *Einsatzgruppe A*, 129.
118. EM 19 and EM 21. The ghetto in Minsk was set up following an order issued on 19 July 1941.
119. EM 48.
120. *IMT* xxv. 302 ff., 212 PS v; dated to July or August by Uwe Adam, *Die Judenpolitik im Dritten Reich* (Düsseldorf, 1972), 306. English trans. in *Nazism*, ed. Noakes and Pridham, iii. 507–9.
121. Lohse's address is mentioned in his manuscript 'Ostland baut auf': YIVO, Occ E 3-3.
122. StA Riga, 1026-1-3.
123. EM 88.
124. Jäger report, OS, 500-1-25; ZSt, 207 AR-Z 14/58, 6, pp. 1151 ff., note from 27 Sept. 1961.
125. ZSt, 207 AR-Z 14/58, 6, pp. 1151 ff, note of 27 Sept. 1961; see also Arad, *Ghetto*, 102 ff.

126. OS, 500-1-25.

127. ZSt, II 207 AR-Z 104/67, indictment of 9 Jan. 1976.

128. ZSt, 207 AR-Z 7/59, judgement of the Hamburg District Court on 23 Feb. 1973; Ezergailis, *Holocaust*, 239 ff.; minutes of the interrogation of Jeckeln by the NKVD, 14/15 Dec. 1945 and testimony before the Riga Military Court as part of the proceedings of 26 Jan. to 3 Feb. 1946; published in Wilhelm, 'Einsatzgruppe A', 566 ff.

129. War diary of the SS and Police Garrison Commander Liepāja (Libau), BAB, R 70 SU 12 (published in Wilhlem, 'Einsatzgruppe A', 571 ff.).

130. EM 111.

131. Cf. Wilhelm, 'Einsatzgruppe A', 203 ff.; ZSt, 207 AR-Z 246/59, 2, pp. 303 ff., final report of 7 Apr. 1960.

132. State Archive, Minsk, 378-1-698 (copy in USHM, Minsk-films, roll 2), Commandant in Belarus, 10 Oct. 1941. See also the situation repory by the Commandant in Belarus, 1 Oct. 1941–15 Oct. 1941 (State Archive, Minsk, Impulevicius case); Res.Pol.Btl.11, situation report on the special deployment in Minsk, 21 Oct. 1941 (ibid.). See also Christopher Browning, *Ordinary Men: Reserve Police Battalion 101 and the Final Solution in Poland* (New York, 1992), 18–19; and Gerlach, *Kalkulierte Morde*, 609 ff.

133. Interrogation of Lechthaler, 4 July 1960 (ZSt, 202 AR-Z 262/59, pp. 51 ff.).

134. OS, 500-1-25; Jäger, *Bericht*; English version in Ernst Klee et al., *'The Good Old Days'* (New York, 1992), 46–58.

135. In letter of 1 Nov. 1941, NO 2456.

136. *IMT*, xxvii. 1 ff., 1104 PS, 30 Oct. 1941. The authenticity of these details is confirmed by the interrogation of Carl on 15 Dec. 1959 (ZSt, 202 5 AR-Z 262/59, pp. 51 ff.).

137. Situation report by the Commandant in Belarus, 1 Oct. 1941–15 Oct. 1941 (State Archive, Minsk, Impulevicius case).

138. State Archive, Minsk, 378-1-698 (copy in USHM, Minsk-films, roll 2), Daily Orders of the Commandant in Belarus.

139. EM 140.

140. Gerlach, *Kalkulierte Morde*, 625.

141. Situation report by Area Commissar Gert Erren, 24 Jan. 1942, Centre de Documentation Juive Cointemporaine (CDJC), CXLVa-8 (IfZ, FB 104), published in Schoenberger, ed., *Wir haben es gesehen*, 131 ff. The shooting of 9,400 Jews from the ghetto on 13 November is confirmed by Nachum Alpert, *The Destruction of Slonim Jewry: The Story of the Jews of Slonim during the Holocaust* (New York, 1989), 84. On Slonim, cf. Gerlach, *Kalkulierte Morde*, 621 ff.

142. NO 2658.

143. See e.g. BAM, RH-18/91, Order from the Army High Command, 18, of 9 July 1941, concerning the establishment of an auxiliary police.

144. For 1941 see Richard Breitman, 'Police Auxiliaries in the Occupied Soviet Territories', *SWCA* 7 (1990), 23–39.

145. BAB, R 19/326, 25 July 1941.

146. Ibid., 31 July 1941.

147. Breitman, 'Police Auxiliaries', 24–5.

148. Martin C. Dean, *Collaboration in the Holocaust: Crimes of the Local Police in Belorussia and Ukraine 1941–1944* (New York, 2000), 60.

149. Dean, *Collaboration*, 65 ff.

150. BAB, R 19/326, 6 Nov. 1941. In addition there were fire-service teams and auxiliary teams for work details and for guarding prisoners of war.

151. Latvian and Lithuanian battalions were deployed in this manner in Belarus, the Ukraine, and the General Government. See the appendix in Tessin, *Stäbe*.

152. On the deployment of these volunteer battalions see cf. Breitmann, 'Police Auxiliaries', 26–7.

153. See the collection of documents edited by Angelika Ebbinghaus and Gerd Preissler 'Die Ermordung psychisch kranker Menschen in der Sowjetunion. Dokumentation', in Götz Aly, Angelika Ebbinghaus, Matthias Hamann, et al., eds, *Aussonderung und Tod. Die klinische Hinrichtung der Unbrauchbaren* (Berlin, 1985).

154. EM 88.

155. Report of 15 October, 180-L, *IMT* xxxvii. 670 ff.

156. EM 96.

157. EM 108.

158. For details, see below, p. 241.

159. EM 135.

160. EM 135.

161. EM 132.

162. EM 156 (16 Jan. 1942); cf. also the judgement of the Wuppertal District Court of 30 Dec. 1965, published in *Justiz and NS-Verbrechen* xxii, no. 606.

163. Ebbinghaus and Preissler, eds, 'Ermordung', 101 ff.

164. Breitman, *Architect*, 246. See also Breitman's details (pp. 178 ff.) of the systematic extirpation of the Turkmenians interned in German camps.

165. See Ch. 10, n. 24.

166. BAM, RH 22/12. There is a similar tenor to the instructions compiled by the Department of Wehrmacht Propaganda for dealing with propaganda in the case of Barbarossa (BAM, RW 4/of 578) and the June issue of the paper, *Information for the Troops*. On the nature of the propaganda in general, see Jürgen Förster, 'Operation Barbarossa as a War of Conquest and Annihilation', in Horst Boog et al., eds, *Germany and the Second World War*, vol. iv: *The Attack on the Soviet Union* (Oxford, 1996), 525 ff, and Pohl, *Herrschaft*, 254 ff.

167. George H. Stein, *Geschichte der Waffen-SS* (Düsseldorf, 1978), 113–14; cf. Breitman, *Architekt*, 235.

168. EM 21.

169. EM 36.

170. EM 73.

171. EM 133, EG B.

172. Jäger's report and EM 92; cf. Michael Zimmermann, *Rassenutopie und Genozid. Die nationalsozialistische 'Lösung der Zigeunerfrage'* (Hamburg, 1996), 260.

173. EM 94 (25 Sept. 1941) and EM 119 (20 Oct. 1941).

174. For this reason Zimmermann's claim (*Rassenutopie*, 262) that in the middle of August 1941, in parallel with the extension of the range of murders to include the entire Jewish population of the Soviet Union, 'the order to murder [the Jews] had obviously been extended to include the Gypsies' is not plausible.

175. See Hannes Heer and Klaus Naumann, *War of Extermination: The German Military in World War II 1941–1944* (New York, 2004). This question has been widely debated in Germany over past years, in particular in connection with the two exhibitions 'Crimes of the Wehrmacht', designed by the Hamburg Institute for Social Research: Hannes Heer and Klaus Naumann, *Vernichtungskrieg. Verbrechen der Wehrmacht. Bilanz einer Debatte* (Hamburg, 1995) (English translation 2004); *Verbrechen der Wehrmacht. Dimensionen des Vernichtungskrieges 1941–1944* (Hamburg, 2002); Christian Hartmann, Johannes Hürter, and Ulrike Jüreit, eds, *Verbrechen der Wehrmacht. Bilanz einer Debatte* (Munich, 2005); Karl-Heinrich Pohl, ed., *Wehrmacht und Vernichtungspolitik. Militär im nationalsozialistischen System* (Göttingen, 1999); Christian Hartmann, 'Verbrecherischer Krieg—verbrecherishe Wehrmacht? Überlegungen zur Struktur des deutschen Ostheeres 1941–1944' in *VfZ* 52 (2004), 1–75, demonstrates that it is impossible to calculate the percentage of soldiers who were involved in crimes. See most recently Dieter Pohl, *Die Herrschaft der Wehrmacht. Deutsche Militärbesatzung und einheimische Bevölkerung in der Sowjetunion 1941–1943* (Munich, 2008).

176. NOKW 2510.

177. NOKW 1654.

178. *IMT* xxxiv. 129 ff., 4064-PS.

179. NOKW 1693.

180. Krausnick, 'Einsatzgruppen', 223 ff.

181. See ibid. 235. At the mass murder of the Kiev Jews in September 1941, for example, the leaflets that summoned the Jews to the collection points were printed by a Wehrmacht propaganda company (ZSt, 204 AR-Z 269/60, judgement of 29 Nov. 1968). A loudspeaker van from a propaganda company was sent for the executions in Zhitomir (see above, p. 200). See also NO 4234, interrogation of Braune, leader of Commando 11b: 'The 11th Army had given an order that the executions in Sinfernopol should be completed before Christmas. We therefore received trucks, petrol and personnel from the army for this purpose.'

182. Lutsk (see above, p. 200); Kodyma (p. 202); Liepāja (Libau, p. 196). Members of the Military Police took part in the shooting of the Jews of Feodosia in December 1941 (N. Kunz, 'Feld- und Ortskommandanturen auf der Krim und der Judenmord', in W. Kaiser, ed., *Täter im Vernichtungskrieg: der Überfall auf die Sowjetunion und der Völkermord an den Juden* (Berlin, 2002), 68–9).

183. Gerlach, *Kalkulierte Morde*, 537–8.

184. Thus the order from Reichenau of 10 August forbade Wehrmacht members to take part in shootings that had not been ordered by the military; however, it permitted the deployment of teams of men to seal off certain areas if the SD approached the local commandant (NOKW 1654). The commanding general of the xxx corps also banned voluntary participation in executions on 2 August 1941; these had to be under the command of army officers (NOKW 2963). Cf. Krausnick, 'Einsatzgrupppen', 240–1, who has further details on this issue.

185. Compilation in Krausnick, 'Einsatzgruppen', 228 ff.

186. Including Lvov and Tarnopol: details in Longerich, *Politik*, 338 and 340. In Uman on 21 October members of the Wehrmacht took part in excesses committed by the Ukrainian militia against the Jewish population (EM 119).

187. For example from the civilian camps set up by the Wehrmacht, including Minsk and Zwiahel: (details in Longerich, *Politik*, 336 and 674). For further examples see Krausnick, 'Einsatzgruppen', 236.

188. For example by the intelligence officer of the 17th Army on 22 September 1941, who asked Sonderkommando 4b for reprisals against the Jews in Kremenchuk because of sabotage attacks (NOKW 2272); other examples include Zhitomir, Chmielnik, and Zwiahel (details in Longerich, *Politik*, 383, 343f, 338 and 368).

189. See for example EM 32 (EG B): 'With the assistance of the Secret Field Police, intelligence troops, and the Military Police the series of operations against Bolshevist agents, political Commissars, members of the NKVD, etc. was continued. In Barano-wicze a further 381 people were liquidated. They were Jewish activists, functionaries and looters.' In EM 128 Einsatzgruppe C complains that despite excellent cooperation with the Wehrmacht in general terms, when it came to the 'Jewish question', there was 'no complete understanding demonstrated by the lower Wehrmacht agencies, with the exception of the Secret Field Police, the intelligence service, and intelligence officers. For further examples see Krausnick, 'Einsatzgruppen', 242–3; Theo Schulte, *The German Army and Nazi Policies in Occupied Russia* (Oxford, 1989), 203; Hannes Heer, 'The Logic of the War of Extermination: The Wehrmacht and the Anti-Partisan War of Extermination', in Hannes Heer and Klaus Naumann, eds, *War of Extermination: The German Military in World War II 1941–1944* (New York, 2004), 92–126, Gerlach, *Kalkulierte Morde*, 538–9.

190. Bila Zerkva (see above, p. 226), Einsatzkommando Tilsit (p. 197). The massacre at Babi Yar was planned on 26 September in the presence of the city commandant; the one in Zhitomir was planned in conjunction with the field commandant's office (see above, pp. 224 and 226). Field and city commandants were also involved in preparations for the major 'operations' against the Jews in Kharkov in which 20,000 people were killed in December 1941 and January 1942 (Bernd Boll and Hans Safrian, 'On the Way to Stalingrad: The 6th Army 1941/42', in Heer and Naumann, eds, *War of Extermination*, 237–71). Similar cooperation has been shown to have taken place in the Crimea; see Kunz, 'Feld- and Ortskommandanturen'. Pohl, *Wehrmacht*, 248ff. continous these research findings

191. Reference should be made here once more to the situation in Belarus as described by Gerlach: in the autumn and winter of 1941 the large-scale 'ghetto operations' were taking place precisely in the eastern area that was under military occupation (Genlach, *Kalkulierte Morde*, 585 ff.). The Commandant responsible for the Rear Army Area in the southern segment of the front, 553, reported that more than 20,000 Jews were killed between August 1941 and summer 1942 (Schulte, *Army*, 231). There has not yet been a systematic, comprehensive investigation of annihilation policies in the occupied Soviet Union that draws a comparison between military areas and those under civilian administration. It would only be able to come to valid conclusions with the help of a comprehensive assessment of the materials in East European archives.

192. State Archive. Minsk, 378-1-698 (copy in USHM, Minsk-films, roll 2), Commandant in Belarus, 10 Oct. 1941.

193. BAM, RH 26-707/2, 10 Nov. 1941.

194. NA, T 77, R 1179.

195. State Archive, Minsk, 378-1-698 (copy in USHM, Minsk-films, roll 2), Commandant in Belarus, 24 Nov. 1941.

196. BAM, RH 26-707/5, 8 Dec. 1941.

197. See above, p. 232 ff. On this 'cleansing operation' by the Wehrmacht, see in particular Hannes Heer, 'Killing Fields: The Wehrmacht and the Holocaust in Belorussia 1941–1942', in Heer and Naumann, eds, *War of Extermination*, pp. 55–79.

198. BAM, RH 26–221/21, Commander of the 350th Infantry Regiment, 19 Aug. 1941; cf. Heer, 'Killing Fields', 66–7.

199. Christian Gerlach, 'German Economic Interests, Occupation Policy and the Murder of the Jews in Belorussia, 1941/43' in Ulrich Herbert, ed., *National Socialist Extermination Policies: Contemporary German Perspectives and Controversies* (New York, 2000), 210–39, 231.

200. See the examples in Boll and Safrian, 'Way', 267–8 (for the 6th Army).

201. See in particular Omer Bartov, *The Eastern Front 1941–1945: German Troops and the Barbarization of Warfare* (Houndmills, 1985); Truman Anderson, 'Die 62. Infanterie-Division. Repressalien im Heeresgebiet Süd, Oktober bis Dezember 1941', in Heer and Naumann, *Vernichtungskrieg*, 297–323, proves that for this formation and the Army Rear Area there were isolated 'reprisal operations' against Jews carried out in autumn 1941, but that from 1942 it was increasingly Ukrainians who were targeted. See Boll and Safrian, 'Way', 286 ff., on the 'indiscriminate terror inflicted on the whole of the civilian population' (p. 289) from the end of 1941.

202. NO 3414, published in Jacobsen, 'Kommissarbefehl', 200 ff. For details on the issue of orders with respect to Soviet prisoners of war, see Alfred Streim, *Die Behandlung sowjetischer Kriegsgefangener im 'Fall Barbarossa'* (Kaarlsruhe, 1981), 52 ff.; and Christian Streit, *Keine Kameraden: Die Wehrmacht und die sowjetischen Kriegsgefangenen 1941–1945* (Stuttgart, 1978), 87 ff.

203. Ibid. The original of the order has not been preserved. Its content corresponds to section III of the Instructions for the Treatment of Soviet Prisoners of War issued on 8 Sept. 1941.

204. Streit, *Keine Kameraden*, 109.

205. BAB, R 58/272 and NO 3422, published in Jacobsen, 'Kommmissarbefehl', 205 ff. and 220–1.

206. Streim, *Behandlung*, 127–8; Streit, *Keine Kameraden*, 100 ff.

207. Streim, *Behandlung*, 97 ff.; Streit, *Keine Kameraden*, 94.

208. Streim, *Behandlung*, 127.

209. Ibid., 129 ff.; Streit, *Keine Kameraden*, 94 ff.

210. Ibid., 96 ff.

211. Streim, *Behandlung*, 244.

212. Streit, *Keine Kameraden*, 105, also does not give a definite figure. On the basis of deployment orders 8 and 9 Reinhard Otto, *Wehrmacht, Gestapo and sowjetische Kriegsgefangene im deutschen Reichsgebiet 1941/42* (Munich, 1998), estimates the total number of prisoners murdered in concentration camps in the area of the Reich at 38,000; those who were murdered in the occupied Soviet areas and the General Government need to be added.

213. State Archive, Moscow, 7021-148-101 (also Central Office, Documentation 301, General Order of 23 Sept. 1941).

214. Streit, *Keine Kameraden*, 106 ff.

215. Gerlach, *Kalkulierte Morde*, 774 ff., gives various examples of this.

216. Ortwin Buchbender, *Das tönende Erz. Die Propaganda gegen die Rote Armee im Zweiten Weltkrieg* (Stuttgart, 1978), 104.

217. Streit, *Keine Kameraden*, 137 ff.

218. Gerlach, *Kalkulierte Morde*, 796 ff.

219. *IMT* xxxvi. 107–8.

220. Gerlach, *Kalkulierte Morde*, 799.

221. NOKW 1535.

222. Elke Fröhlich, ed. *Die Tagebücher von Joseph Goebbels*, Teil II: Band 2: *Oktober-Dezember 1941*. Bearbeitet von Elke Fröhlich (Munich, 1996), 23 Oct. 1941, 161–2.

223. On the transportation and accommodation of prisoners, see Streit, *Keine Kameraden*, 162 ff. and Streim, *Die Behandlung*.

224. Instructions for the Treatment of Soviet Prisoners of 8 Sept. 1941 (NO 3417, published in Jacobsen, 'Kommissarbefehl', 217 ff.).

225. Streit, *Keine Kameraden*, 211.

226. Ibid. 136.

227. Ibid. 244 ff.

228. Einsatzgruppe A, overall report up to 15 Oct. 1941, report of 15 Oct. 1941, 180-L, *IMT* xxxvii. 670 ff.; in addition there were 5,500 Jews murdered by Einsatzkommando Tilsit and Jews murdered in 'pogroms': overall report by Einsatzgruppe A from 10 Oct. 1941 to 31 Jan. 1942, Ifz, Fb 101/35.

229. EM 133 and OS, 500-1-770, activity and situation report by Einsatzgruppe B for the period between 16 and 28 Feb. 1942. The numbers of the victims of this *Einsatzgruppe* are calculated in Christian Gerlach, 'Einsatzgruppe B', in Peter V. Lein, ed., *Die Einsatzgruppen in der besetzten Sowjet unions 194/42. Die Tätigkeits- und Lageberichte des Chefs der Sicherheitspolizei und des SD* (Berlin, 1997), 62.

230. EM 128 (3 Nov. 1941).

231. EM 145 and EM 190.

14. Plans for a Europe-Wide Deportation Programme after the Start of Barbarossa

1. According to Richard Breitman, *The Architect of Genocide: Himmler and the Final Solution* (London, 1991) 145, a fundamental decision had already been made in the first months of 1941; Himmler had then made the decisions for its execution in the summer of 1941 (ibid. 167 ff.). An early decision by Hitler, which he only imparted gradually to his subordinates, is also accepted by Helmut Krausnick, 'The Persecution of the Jews', in Hans Buchheim et al., *Anatomy of the SS State* (London, 1968), 17–139; Hermann Graml, *Reichskristallnacht. Antisemitismus und Judenverfolgung im Dritten Reich* (Munich, 1988), 207; Wolfgang Benz, *The Holocaust: A German Historian Examines the Holocaust* (New York, 1999), 61 ff.

2. Raul Hilberg, 'Die Aktion Reinhard', in Eberhard Jäckel and Jürgen Rohwer, eds, *Der Mord an den Juden im Zweiten Weltkrieg* (Stuttgart, 1985), 125–36.

3. Philippe Burrin, *Hitler and the Jews: The Genesis of the Holocaust* (London, 1989), 154 ff.; Uwe Dietrich Adam, *Judenpolitik im Dritten Reich* (Düsseldorf, 1972), 312; on Browning's position see below, p. 522, n. 8.

4. Christian Gerlach, 'The Wannsee Conference, the Fate of the German Jews, and Hitler's Decision in Principle to Exterminate All European Jews', *Journal of Modern History* 70 (1998), 759–812; L. J. Hartog, *Der Befehl zum Judenmord. Hitler, Amerika und die Juden* (Bodenheim, 1997).

5. This is the position represented by Martin Broszat in 'Hitler und die Genesis der "Endlösung". Aus Anlass der Thesen von David Irving', *VfZ* 25/4 (1977),

739–75; and Hans Mommsen, 'The Realization of the Unthinkable: The "Final Solution of the Jewish Question" in the Third Reich' in Gerhard Hirschfeld, ed., *The Politics of Genocide: Jews and Soviet Prisoners of War in Nazi Germany* (London, 1986), 93–144.

6. Peter Longerich, *Politik der Vernichtung. Eine Gesamtdarstellung der nationalsozialistischen Judenverfolgung* (Munich, 1998); Dieter Pohl, *Nationalsozialistische Judenverfolgung in Ostgalizien 1941–1944. Durchführung eines staatlichen Massenverbrechen* (Munich, 1996), 139 ff.

7. See pp. 173–6.

8. Thus most recently in Christopher Browning, *The Origins of the Final Solution: The Evolution of Nazi Jewish Policy 1939–1942*, 309 ff., recapitulated pp. 424 ff. On the development of his position cf. particularly the accounts in 'The Decision Concerning the Final Solution', in Christopher R. Browning, *Fateful Months: Essays on the Emergence of the Final Solution* (New York, 1985), 8–38; and 'Beyond "Intentionalism" and "Functionalism": The Decision for the Final Solution Reconsidered', in Christopher R. Browning, *The Path to Genocide Reconsidered: Essays on the Final Solution* (Cambridge, 1992) 86–124.

9. Graml, *Reichskristallnacht*, 222 ff.; Krausnick, in Jäckel and Rohwer, *Mord*, 201; Breitman, *Architekt*, 192–3; Leni Yahil, *The Holocaust: The Fate of European Jewry 1932–1945* (New York, 1990), 254–5. Browning, who initially interpreted the document as an authorization for mass murder ('Decision', 22), now holds the view (*Origins*, 353) that it was an assignment to prepare a 'feasibility study' for the extension of the systematic murder begun in the Soviet Union to the rest of occupied Europe. In my view Browning's refutation of Aly's reinterpretation of the document (ibid. 517, n. 36) is not appropriate: Browning wrongly assumes that in March 1941 Heydrich had already received Goering's acceptance of his draft, which—and this is the crucial point in Aly's convincing interpretation—was *not* the case. In fact Goering ordered 're-submission', which Heydrich did in July.

10. Rudolf Aschenhauer, ed., *Ich, Adolf Eichmann. Ein historischer Zeugenbericht* (Leoni am Starnberger See, 1980), 479) confirms that the memo was drafted in the RSHA; Goering's official diary records a meeting with Heydrich on 31 July, 6.15 p.m. (IfZ, ED 180/5).

11. *IMT* xxvi. 710-PS.

12. See pp. 175–6.

13. See Götz Aly, *'Final Solution': Nazi Population Policy and the murder of the European Jews* (London, 1999), 172–3. (Frankfurt a. M., 1995). The discovery of this document confirms the view that has long been represented by authors like Adam (*Judenpolitik*, 308–9), Burrin (*Hitler*, 134), and Broszat, ('Genesis', 747).

14. See Jäckel, Introduction to *Mord*, 15.

15. Breitman, *Architect*, 198; *Der Dienstkalender Heinrich Himmlers 1941/42*, ed. Peter Witte et al. (Hamburg, 1999), 26 Aug. 1941, p. 198.

16. Tobias Jersak, 'Die Interaktion von Kriegsverlauf und Judenvernichtung. Ein Blick auf Hitlers Strategie im Spätsommer 1941', *Historische Zeitschrift* 268 (1999), 311–74. Jersak puts forward the view that Hitler had seen the Atlantic declaration of 14 August 1941 as the definitive entry of the US into the anti-German alliance, and with this event in mind he had resolved in mid-August 1941 to suspend his policy aimed at world domination and introduce the murder of all European Jews, as he held 'the Jews' largely responsible

for Germany's encirclement. Goebbels's diaries clearly reveal, however, that Hitler agreed with Goebbels that the Atlantic Charter was a 'propaganda bluff'. If Churchill, both men agreed, had actually pursued the intention of drawing the United States into the war, this tactic had totally failed. So it is not convincing to see the Atlantic Charter as the cause of a 'change of strategy' on Hitler's part, and a related decision to implement the 'Final Solution', or even as the origin of the decision to implement the 'Final Solution' (Elke Frölich, ed., *Die Tagebücher von Joseph Goebbels*, Teil II (Munich, 1966), 15.–21 Aug. 1941, especially 19 Aug. 1941 concerning the conversation with Hitler), 263.

17. Rudolf Höß, *Commandant of Auschwitz: The Autobiography of Rudolf Hoess* (London, 1959), 206 ff.; in agreement with this the statement made on 14 Apr. 1946, *IMT* xi. 438–66.

18. Breitman's attempt, to date the meeting of Höß and Himmler in Auschwitz to 13–15 July 1941 (Breitman, *Architekt*, 250), is unconvincing for this and other reasons. See Longerich, *Politik*, 696 ff.

19. *IMT* xi. 441.

20. Burrin, *Hitler*, 197, on the other hand suggests that Höß might have been a year out in his calculations; likewise Jean-Claude Pressac, *Die Krematorien von Auschwitz* (Munich, 1994), 136, who dates the meeting as early June 1942; equally sceptical about the dating to summer 1941 are Hans Safrian, *Die Eichmann-Männer* (Vienna, 1993), 106, and Karin Orth, 'Rudolf Höß und die "Endlösung der Judenfrage". Drei Argumente gegen deren Datierung auf den Sommer 1941', *Werkstatt Geschichte* 18 (1997), 45–57. There is one other statement that suggests that when Höß said 1941 he meant 1942 (*IMT* xxxiii. 275 ff., 3968-PS); but even if we impute this error to him, the chronology proposed by Höß cannot be made consistent with the known facts (Longerich, *Politik*, 697).

21. Thus in his latest work, *Origins*, Browning no longer uses Höß's statement to support his thesis, as he still did in 'Decision,' 22–3, albeit with major reservations.

22. *The Trial of Eichmann*, vii. 169–70; also the statement in the main trial, ibid. iv. 1559.

23. In the so-called 'Sassen interviews', given before his abduction from Argentina, he stated that Heydrich had already informed him about the Führer's order after the Wehrmacht's first great military successes in Russia in the battles of Bialystok and Minsk (that was at the end of June). In his memoirs (Götzen, September 1961), Eichmann identifies Wirth as the police captain in question (p. 174). On the various versions of his statements on this subject see Christian Gerlach, 'The Eichmann Interrogations in Holocaust Historiography', *HGS* 15/3 (2001), 428–52; and David Cesarani, *Eichmann: His Life and Crimes* (New York, 2004), 143 ff.

24. *Trial of Eichmann*, vii. 174. Eichmann gives this as his reason for giving the date as late summer or autumn. But he does not speak expressly of autumn. (Götzen: Note about foliage.)

25. See p. 280.

26. *Trial of Eichmann*, vii. 171 and 179. When describing a second trip to the Treblinka camp, which was by now completed, he becomes increasingly certain that this was the camp he saw under construction (ibid. 229); later he admits that it might have been Sobibor (ibid. 400).

27. In the Götzen manuscript, p. 175, also under questioning, *Trial of Eichmann*, vii. 372–3.

28. Ibid. vii. 174. In his statement to the court, after further acquainting himself with the subject from Reitlinger's book on the history of Chelmno, he admitted that the visit

might have taken place at the end of December 1941 or shortly afterwards (ibid. iv. 1560).

29. Ibid. vii. 210 ff.; Gerlach, 'Eichmann Interrogations', 436.

30. *Trial of Eichmann* vii. 378, 384.

31. Browning, *Origins*, 523–4, now assumes that Eichmann met Wirth in September 1941, and not in Belzec but in a kind of experimental facility that Wirth had built before the construction of Belzec. Wirth could, Browning suggests, already have supervised the construction of this facility even before being definitively moved to Lublin. Apart from the fact that this claim is purely speculative, Browning's proposed chronology seems too crowded. According to Browning, Hitler made the main decision concerning the murder of the Jews in mid-September and charged his Führer Chancellery with its implementation, whereupon Brack and Bouhler went to see Globocnik and Wirth went to Lublin to undertake his experiments and then present them to Eichmann—all in less than fourteen days. It seems much more plausible that the plans for Belzec extermination camp only began in October 1941, just as Wetzel only offered Brack's support to Hinrich Lohse, the Reichskommissar in Ostland (Baltic States), on 25 October. See p. 279. Browning's assertion that Wirth had already spoken of an impending transfer to a euthanasia institution in the district of Lublin, is based solely on a post-war witness statement (NO 3010, Bodo Gorgaß); and Brack and Bouhler's trip to Lublin, which Brack dates in his trial as 'early September', cannot yet have taken place at this time, as Burrin, *Hitler*, 199, has already shown. In early September Globocnik had not yet been informed about impending deportations from the Reich, which, according to Brack's statement, he spoke about when the two men met (*Trials of War Criminals*, Case 1, trial transcript, 7502-3, 14 May 1947). But we know from Himmler's official diary that Brack and Bouhler met Himmler on 14 December 1941, and that this was the only meeting throughout that whole period. The subject for discussion at the meeting with Brack is given as 'euthanasia', and in a later memo Brack reminds Himmler that in the context of the 'Judenaktion' he (Himmler) had 'expressed the opinion to him that, for reasons of camouflage, work should get under way as soon as possible' (BAB, NS 19/1583). In contrast to Browning's account, this meeting matches the other dates that we have for the transfer of T4 staff to Poland (see p. 280).

32. BAB, R 58/954; in Peter Longerich, ed., *Die Ermordung der europäischen Juden* (Munich, 1989), 74–5.

33. Two notes from the RFSS, 21 July 1941 (Berlin Document Centre (BDC)-Akte Globocnik).

34. On this complex, material in BDC files Globocnik.

35. See above pp. 214–15.

36. *Das Diensttagebuch des deutscher Generalgouverneurs in Polen 1939–1945*, ed. Werner Präg and Wolfgang Jacobmeyer (Stuttgart, 1975), 17 July 1941, p. 386.

37. BAB, R 6/21, in a memo to Lammers on 19 July 1941 Frank explained the planned extension by saying that 'elements of the population (Jewish ones above all) were to be provided with a productive occupation that was useful to the Reich'. Frank returned to the subject of the planned annexation at a meeting on 22 July (IfZ, MA 120).

38. IfZ, MA 120; in the published edition of the official diary only as a paraphrase. On 21 July Frank had told Senior Medical Officer (*Obermedizinalrat*) Dr Jost Walbaum, the

'Health leader' of the General Government, of his decision that in the impending removal of the Jews from the General Government 'the dissolution of the Warsaw ghetto was the first thing to be got under way' (ibid.).

39. *ADAP*, series D, vol. 12, 2, 835 ff.
40. See p. 174.
41. Bernhard Lösener, 'Als Rassereferent in Reichsministerium des Innern', *VfZ* 9/3 (1961), 303, reproduction of a note for Frick.
42. Fröhlich, ed., *Tagebücher Goebbels*, II, i, 19 August 1941, pp. 265–6.
43. Ibid. 265.
44. Plettenberg City Archive (=YV, 051/202). See also Goebbels's instruction which he submitted on the same day at his Ministry's internal propaganda meeting: Special Archive, Moscow, 1363–3.
45. Gerald Fleming, *Hitler and the Final Solution* (London, 1984), 79.
46. Theodore N. Kaufman, *Germany Must Perish* (Newark, NJ, 1941), 104, published early 1941. See also Wolfgang Benz, 'Judenvernichtung aus Notwehr? Die Legende um Theodore N. Kaufman', *VfZ* 29 (1981), 615–30. The polemic against the Kaufman pamphlet had been going for around four weeks, but was now intensified; *Tagesparole der RPL*, N. 732, 23 July 1941 (BAB, ZSg. 100/21); VB 24 July; Fröhlich, *Tagebücher*, Teil II, vol. i, 24 July 1941, pp. 116–17; Goebbels in *VB*, 17 August; Wolfgang Diewerge, a staff member of the Propaganda Ministry, published a pamphlet against Kaufman's text, under the title 'Das Kriegsziel der Weltplutokratie', which was distributed on a large scale: Dokumentarische Veröffentlichung zu dem Buch des Präsidenten der amerikanischen Friedensgesellschaft Theodor Nathan Kaufman 'Deutschland muss sterben', September 1941
47. Jürgen Hagemann, *Die Presselenkung im Dritten Reich* (Bonn, 1970), 155.
48. Fröhlich, ed., *Die Tagebücher*, Teil II, vol. i, 20 Aug. 1941, p. 278.
49. Decree of the Supreme Soviet, 28 August 1941, in Alfred Eisfeld and Victor Herdt, eds, *Deportation, Sondersiedlung, Arbeitsarmee. Deutsche in der Sowjetunion 1941–1956* (Cologne, 1996), 54–5.
50. According to the notebooks of his contact man in the OKH, Otto Bräutigam; see H. D. Heilmann, 'Aus dem Kriegstagebuch des Diplomaten Otto Bräutigam', in Götz Aly et al., eds, *Biedermann und Schreibtischtäter. Materialien zur deutschen Täter-Biographie. Institut für Sozialforschung Hamburg. Beiträge zur nationalsozialistischen Gesundheits- und Sozialpolitik* 4 (1987), 144.
51. Details see below p. 274.
52. Peter Witte, 'Two Decisions Concerning the "Final Solution to the Jewish Question". Deportations to Lodz and Mass Murder in Chemno', *HGS* 9 (1995), 330. According to Himmler's official diary he telephoned the Foreign Office that evening. Further evidence for the date of the decision can be drawn from a marginal note by the Foreign Office's Jewish expert, Rademacher, dated 13 September 1941, on a memo from Benzler (the Foreign Office's Plenipotentiary in Belgrade) dated 12 September 1941, which reveals that Eichmann had not at this point been informed about the decision to resume the deportations ('Eichmann schlägt Erschießen vor', facsimile in Robert M. W. Kempner, *Eichmann und Komplizen* (Zurich, 1961), 291).
53. BAB, NS 19/2655, published in *Ermordung*, ed. Longerich 157.

54. Wolf Gruner, points this out in 'Von der Kollektivausweisung zur Deportation der Juden aus Deutschland 1938–1945', in Birthe Kundrus and Beate Meyer, eds, *Die Deportation der Juden aus Deutschland. Pläne—Praxis—Reaktionen* (Gottinger, 2004), 48. Individual documents: *Dienstkalender*, 2 and 4 Sept. 1941; some days later Eichmann informed Rademacher of the German Department of the Foreign Office that it was currently impossible to accommodate Jews from Serbia or the Reich in the General Government (handwritten note from Rademacher on telegram from Belgrade Embassy, 13 September 1941, printed as facsimile in Kempner, *Eichmann und Komplizen*, (291). Koppe's memo of 10 Sept. 1941 has been lost, but it can be reconstructed from the Brieftagebuch (epistolary diary) of the personal staff of the RFSS (cf. commentary, *Dienstkalender*, ed, Witte et al., entry for 4 Sept. 1941, p. 205).

55. Browning, *Origins*, 426.

56. Fröhlich, ed., *Die Tagebücher*, Teil II, vol. i. 480–1.

57. BAB, R 6/34, Koeppen-Aufzeichnungen, 21 Sept. 1941.

58. For the context see David Reynolds, *The Creation of the Anglo-American Alliance 1937–41: A Study in Competitive Co-operation* (Chapel Hill, NC, 1981), 213 ff.

59. See p. 164.

60. Fröhlich, *Die Tagebücher*, Teil II, vol. ii: *Oktober-Dezember 1941* (Munich, 1996), 24 Oct. 1941, p. 169.

61. Minutes of the propaganda conference, 23 Oct. 1941, NS 18 alt/622. Details in Peter Longerich, *'Davon haben wir nichts gewusst'! Die Deutschen und die Judenverfolgung 1933–1945* (Munich, 2006), 182–3.

62. See e.g. *Neue Zürcher Zeitung* (*NZZ*) of 20 Oct. 1941 (UPI-Meldung 18 October) concerning deportations from the Rhineland and from Berlin to Poland: 'In the evening a large number of Jews from the Rhineland arrived in Berlin, before being transported along with a number of Berlin Jews to Poland or other Eastern European countries. According to reports, the number of these Jews is approaching 20,000. It has been reported that around 1,500 Jews left the capital yesterday. They are to be transported to Litzmannstadt (formerly Lodz) and later possibly brought to the General Government.' The *New York Times* carried this report as early as 18 October 1941 with further details concerning the situation of the Berlin Jews: on 22 October the *NZZ* reported, on the basis of a United Press International report of 20 October, that the deportations would continue, involving a total of 20,000 people.

63. Longerich, *'Davon haben wir nichts gewusst'*! 183–4.

64. It was not only the Jewish apartments that were in great demand; in many cities auctions of Jewish household goods took place from 1941 onwards. For details see pp. 287–8.

65. Of the five cities affected by the first wave of deportations, only for Hamburg can a simultaneous intensification of air attacks be demonstrated: between 15 and 30 September 1941 a series of attacks left a total of 138 dead: Hans Brunswig, *Feuersturm über Hamburg* (Stuttgart, 1978), 452. In August and September Berlin had again suffered a series of attacks without—in comparison with the previous year—the situation becoming a great deal more dramatic. In August 1941 only 537 dwellings had been left uninhabitable (Speer-Chronik, IfZ, ED 99, vol. 1). No bombs fell on Munich in 1941 see Hans-Günter Richardi, *Bomber über München. Der Luftkrieg von 1939 bis 1945,*

dargestellt am Beispiel der 'Hauptstadt der Bewegung', (Munich, 1992), 67 ff.; in Frankfurt a. M., Cologne, and Düsseldorf bombing raids were recorded, but little damage was done; see *Die geheimen Tagesberichte der Deutschen Wehrmachtführung im Zweiten Weltkrieg, 1939–1945*, ed. Kurt Mehner, vol. iii (Osnabrück, 1992).

66. The records of the office of the Inspector General for the Reich capital reveal that in August 1941 Speer had 'started a further action to clear some 5,000 Jewish dwellings', after a first action had been launched early in 1941 and another in May 1941 to liberate 'Jewish dwellings'. See Susanne Willems, *Der entsiedelte Jude. Albert Speers Wohnungsmarktpolitik für den Berliner Haupstadtbau* (Berlin, 2002), 27 ff., 195 ff., and 258 ff. In September 1941 the Jews in Hanover were forced at short notice to move into sixteen houses on the basis of an initiative from the Gau headquarters, which had been pursuing this plan since March; it was planned to resettle them in barrack accommodation; see Marlis Buchholz, *Die hannoverschen Judenhäuser. Zur Situation der Juden in der Zeit der Ghettoisierung und Verfolgung 1941 bis 1945* (Hildesheim, 1987), 28 ff.; see also report in the *New York Times*, 9 Sept. 1941. In May 1941 the Jews of Cologne were ordered at short notice to leave a row of 'Jewish' houses in the desirable neighbourhoods, although the plan to accommodate them in barracks did not come about; see Horst Matzerath, 'Der Weg der Kölner Juden in den Holocaust. Versuch einer Rekonstruktion', in Gabriele Rogmann and Horst Matzerath, eds, *Die jüdischen Opfer des Nationalsozialismus aus Köln. Gedenkbuch* (Cologne, 1995), 534. On the deportation of the Jews of Breslau to Tomersdorf near Görlitz see Willy Cohn, *Als Jude in Breslau, 1941. Aus den Tagebüchern von Studienrat a. D. Dr. Willy Cohn* (Jerusalem, 1975), 8, 9, 15, 23 August, 11 September 1941.

67. See for example Witte, 'Decisions', 323–4, who provides evidence of the considerable initiative on the part of the Hamburg Gauleiter in getting the deportations from Hamburg under way. Browning, *Origins*, 386, quotes a statement from a post-war trial before Cologne district court, according to which the Gauleiter of Cologne sent a delegation to Hitler to demand the deportation of the Cologne Jews.

68. Walter Manoschek, *'Serbien ist judenfrei'. Militärische Besatzungspolitik und Judenvernichtung in Serbien 1941/42* (Munich, 1993), 43 ff.

69. Ahlrich Meyer, ' " ... dass französische Verhältnisse anders sind als polnische". Die Bekämpfung des Widerstands durch die deutsche Militärverwaltung in Frankreich 1941', in Guus Meershoeck et al., eds, *Repression und Kriegsverbrechen. Die Bekämpfung von Widerstands- und Partisanenbewegungen gegen die deutsche Besatzung in West- und Südosteuropa* (Berlin, 1997), 43–91; Wolfram Weber, *Die Innere Sicherheit im besetzten Belgien und Nordfrankreich, 1940–1944. Ein Beitrag zur Geschichte der Besatzungsverwaltungen* (Düsseldorf, 1978), 59 ff.; Fritz Petrick, ed., *Die Okkupationspolitik des deutschen Faschismus in Dänemark und Norwegen (1940–1945). Dokumentenauswahl* (Berlin and Heidelberg, 1992), 33.

70. Detlev Brandes, *Die Tschechen unter deutschem Protektorat. Besatzungspolitik, Kollaboration und Widerstand im Protektorat Böhmen und Mähren bis Heydrichs Tod*, vol. i (Munich, 1969), 207 ff.

71. Peter Klein, 'Die Rolle der Vernichtungslager Kulmhof (Chelmno), Belzec und Auschwitz-Birkenau in den frühen Deportationsvorbereitungen', in Dittmar Dahlmann and Gerhard

Hirschfeld, eds, *Lager, Zwangsarbeit, Vertreibung und Deportation. Dimensionenen der Massenvebrechen in der Sowjetunion und in Deutschland 1933–1945* (Essen, 1999), 473.

72. On 28 September Keitel modified the order to the effect that, depending on the situation, hostages from nationalist and democratic bourgeois circles were also to be shot. See *Kriegstagebuch des Oberkommandos der Wehrmacht (Wehrmachtführungsstab)*, ed. Percy Ernst Schramm, led by Helmuth Greiner and Percy Ernst Schramm, vol. i: *1940/41*, document no. 101, 16 Sept. 1941 (Frankfurt a. M., 1961) and *IMT* xxvii. PS-1590, S.373–4).

73. Ibid., 11 Oct. 1941 and Himmler's negative reply, 22 Oct. 1941

74. BAB, NS 19/2655, Uebelhör to Himmler, 4 Oct. 1941 and 9 Oct. 1941, Heydrich to Himmler, 8 Oct. 1941, Himmler to Uebelhör and Greiser, 10 and 11 Oct. 1941; further material in the same dossier.

75. Ibid., 4 Oct. 1941.

76. BAB, 19/2655, Heydrich to Himmler, 8 Oct. 1941.

77. BAB, R 6/34 a, reports of Werner Koeppen, Rosenberg's permanent representative to Hitler; See Martin Vogt, 'Selbstbespiegelungen in Erwartung des Sieges. Bemerkungen zu den Tagesgespräche Hitlers im Herbst 1941', in Wolfgang Michalka, ed., *Der Zweite Weltkrieg. Analysen, Grundzüge, Forschungsbilanz* (Munich, 1989), 649.

78. SUA, 114-2-56 (also YVA, M 58/23).

79. Heydrich may have meant camps for civilian prisoners, like the ones that existed in Minsk and Mogilev. See Christian Gerlach, 'Plans for an SS Extermination Camp in Mogilev Belorussia', *HGS* 7/1 (1997), 62.

80. For literature concerning the preliminary phase of the deportations from France, see: Serge Klarsfeld, *Die Endlösung der Judenfrage in Frankreich. Deutsche Dokumete 1941–1944* (Paris, 1977); Klarsfeld, *Vichy-Auschwitz. Die Zusammenarbeit der deutschen und französischen Bechörden bei der 'Endlösung der Judenfrage' in Frankreich*, vol. i (Nordlingen, 1989), 17 ff.; Ulrich Herbert, 'The German Military Command in Paris and the Deportation of the French Jews', in Herbert, *National Socialist Extermination Policies: Contemporary German Perspectives and Controversies* (New York, 2000) 148 ff.; Susan Zuccotti, *The Holocaust, the French and the Jews* (Lincoln, Nebr., 1999), 641 ff.

81. On the persecution of the Jews, on the history of the Jews in France and their situation in 1940/1 see in particular Zuccotti, *Holocaust*, 7 ff. and Renée Poznanski, *Jews in France during World War II* (Hanover and London, 2001).

82. Dannecker to Zeitschel, 20 Oct. 1941, NG 3261. There were also several thousand Jewish prisoners of war.

83. Zuccotti, *Holocaust*, 53–4.

84. On their situation see, in particular, ibid. 65 ff.

85. CDJC, XXIV-1, Note, from Best, 19 Aug. 1940, in Klarsfeld, *Vichy*, 356.

86. CDJC, V 63, Note, 28 Jan. 1941, in Klarsfeld, *Vichy*, 363–4.

87. This is revealed by a 'plan drawn up for a meeting' that the leader of the administrative staff of the military administration, Werner Best, previously a department head in the Reich Security Head Office, drew up in early April in preparation for a meeting of the military commander with the Vichy Commissioner for the Jews, Vallat: CDJC, XXIV-15a, in Klarsfeld, *Vichy*, 366–7.

88. Klarsfeld, *Vichy*, 25 und 28 ff.

89. Herbert, 'German Military Command', 140.

90. Ibid. 150.

91. For the deportation of the French Jews, the same cynical 'argument' was used as had previously been deployed by the head of the administrative staff of the military commander in Serbia, Harald Turner, in a letter to SS-Gruppenführer Hildebrandt: it was 'actually wrong' to shoot Jews for Germans killed by Serbs, but 'we happened to have them in the camp' (see below, p. 300).

92. On these reflections see Herbert, 'German Military Command', 153 ff.

93. CDJC, V-8, 21 Aug. 1941, in Klarsfeld, *Vichy*, 367. Zeitschel was prompted to draw up this plan by Theodor N. Kaufman's book, which suggested the sterilization of all Germans (see above, p. 266).

94. CDJC, V-15, in Klarsfeld, *Vichy*, 367–8. Zeitschel was absolutely certain, as a further note on 14 September about the internment of Spanish Jews reveals (CDJC, VI 126), that 'in the end after the war all Jews are to be expelled from all European states', and hence no consideration was to be given 'to any Jews of so-called other nationality'.

95. *Dienstkalender* ed. Witte et al., 211–12. Zeitschel informed Dannecker, the Gestapo's Jewish expert in Paris, about the content of the meeting on 8 October, CDJC, V-16.

96. *ADAP*, series D, vol. 13,2. No. 327, 16 Sept. 1941.

97. See p. 269.

98. *Dienstkalender*, ed. Witte et al., 20 Oct. 1941, p. 241. For details see pp. 295 f.

99. CDJC, I-28, previously published in: Klarsfeld, *Vichy*, 369–70. Burrin, *Hitler and the Jews*, 145, interprets this memo as an authentic reflection of the 'Führer's order' to implement the final solution; the 'deportation order' was 'also an annihilation order'. In the interpretation of this memo, however, we must bear in mind that the reason that Heydrich assumed responsibility for the attack and at the same time invoked Hitler's authority was because he wanted above all to protect the organizer of the attack, the commander of the Security Police in France, Knochen, against serious accusations from the military commander. On the synagogue attacks see also Claudia Steuer, *Theodor Dannecker. Ein Funktionär der Endlösung* (Essen, 1997), 59 ff.

100. BAB, NS 19/1734; this statement was connected to Heydrich's demand that there should in future be no experts on Jewish questions working within the Eastern Ministry.

101. PAA, Inland II g/194, 28 Oct. 1941, in: *ADAP*, series D, vol. 13, 570 ff.

102. IfZ, ED 53, the so called 'Engel diary', actually handwritten notes by Engel from the post-war period, presumably on the basis of contemporary notes, 2 Nov. 1941. In the Engel edition, Hildegard von Kotze, ed., *Heeresadjutant bei Hitler 1938–1943. Aufzeichnungen des Majors Engel* (Stuttgart, 1974), 111, wrongly dated (2 Oct. 1941). A meeting between Himmler and Hitler on 2 November 1941 is confirmed by the entry in Himmler's official diary. On the attacks in Salonica see Klein, 'Rolle der Vernichtungslager', 473.

103. Browning, *Origins*, 579. The original is in the Rijksinstitut voor Oorlogsdocumentatie in The Hague.

15. Autumn 1941: The Beginning of the Deportations and Regional Mass Murders

1. There are various indications that the euthanasia action in summer 1941 occurred under pressure of protests *and* according to plan, after the originally cited quota of around 70,000 patients to be killed had been reached. The planned number, by now raised to 130,000–150,000, then lowered again to around 100,000 victims (*IMT* xxxv. 906-D, pp. 681 ff., note from Sellmer about Blankenburg visit, 1 Oct. 1940) would probably have been reached in quantitative terms if a similarly high percentage of patients from mental institutions had been murdered throughout the whole of the T4 action as had occurred in the first few months of the systematic murders of patients in south-west Germany, around Berlin, or in Austria. In fact, however, the number of murdered patients fell the more the action spread into the regions. This was particularly true of the provinces of Hanover, Rhineland, and Westphalia, which were only involved in summer 1941. See Heinz Faulstich, *Hungersterben in der Psychiatrie. 1914– 1949; mit einer Topographie der NS-Psychiatrie* (Freiburg im Breisgau, 1998), 260 ff. There is evidence to suggest that protests on the part of church circles increasingly served to curb the euthanasia programme in 1941, and led the organizers to bring their planned numbers back down to the original figure of 70,000 victims. Thus, for example the governor (*Landeshauptmann*) of Westphalia, Karl Kolbow, in a note dated 31 July 1941, remarked that 'the action in Westphalia is progressing briskly, and will be over in 2 to 3 weeks' (facsimile in Karl Teppe, *Massenmord auf dem Dienstweg. Hitlers 'Euthansie'. Erlass und seine Durchführung in den Westfälischen Provinizalanstalten* (Münster, 1989), 21). (I am grateful to Peter Witte for important references in this field.)

2. On the development of the euthanasia programme pp. 136–42; on the planned figures, see *IMT* xxxv. 906-D, 681 ff., note from Sellmer about Blankenburg visit, 1 Oct. 1940; Fröhlich, ed., *Tagebücher Goebbels*, I, x, 30 Jan. 1941. On the suspension of the euthanasia programme see Michael Burleigh, *Death and Deliverance: 'Euthanasia' in Germany 1900–1945* (Cambridge, 1994), 176 ff.; Henry Friedländer, *The Origins of Nazi Genucide: From Euthanasia to the Final Solution* (Chapel Hill, NC, 1995) 111 ff.

3. Faulstich, *Hungersterben*, 260 ff., gives a clear picture of how the murder quotas rose in the individual regions and then fell again.

4. Note from 31 July 1941; facsimile in Teppe, *Massenmord* 21.

5. Fröhlich, *Die Tagebücher*, Teil II, *Diktate 1941–1945*, vol. i (Munich, 1996), 23 Aug. 1941, p. 299.

6. Walter Grode, *Die 'Sonderbehandlung 14f13' in den Konzentrationslagern des Dritten Reichs* (Frankfurt a. M., 1997), 82–3; Ernst Klee, *'Euthanasie' im NS-Staat. Die Vernichtung lebensunwerten Lebens* (Frankfurt a. M., 1985), 345.

7. Grode, *'Sonderbehandlung'*, 84 ff.

8. Ibid. 113 ff., also Friedlander, *Origins*, 143 ff.

9. Patricia Heberer, 'Eine Kontinuität der Tötungsoperationen. T4-Täter und die "Aktion Reinhard" ', in Bogdan Musial, ed., *'Aktion Reinhard'. Der Völkermord an den Juden un Generalgouvernement 1941–1944* (Osnubrück, 2004), 285–308, 292, suggests that this may

have concerned the killing of German soldiers who had suffered very serious and irreversible injuries.

10. See Longerich, *Davon*, 159 ff.

11. This process was reconstructed from eyewitness accounts: Matthias Beer, 'Die Entwicklung der Gaswagen beim Mord an den Juden', *VfZ* 35 (1987), 407; Staatsanwaltschaft Munich, case against Karl Wolff (ZSt, ASA 137), 140 ff.; *Dienstkalender*, ed. Witte et al., 15 Aug. 1941, p. 195. Christian Gerlach, *Kalkulierte Morde. Die deutsche Wirtschafts- und Vernichtungspolitik in Weissrussland 1941 bis 1944* (Hamburg, 1999), 647–8, presents some admittedly rather weak evidence to suggest that preparations for the construction of the gas vans had already begun at the end of July 1941.

12. Gerlach, *Kalkulierte Morde*, 648; PRO HW 16/32, 16 August and 18 August 1941.

13. Beer, 'Entwicklung', 408: A. Ebbinghaus and G. Preisler, 'Die Ermordung psychisch kranker Menschen in der Sowjetunion. Dokumentation', in Götz Aly et al., eds, *Aussonderung und Tod. Die klinische Hinrichtung der Unbrauchbaren* (Berlin, 1985), 83 ff. Gerlach, *Kalkulierte Morde*, 648, points out that the assignment given to Nebe may not have come directly from Himmler, as Bach-Zelewski had claimed in a post-war statement, but from himself.

14. Beer, 'Entwicklung', 408; Ebbinghaus and Preissler, 'Die Ermordung', 88 ff.; statement from Widmann, 11 Jan. 1960, ZSt, 202 ARZ 152/159, 33 ff. Also statement from Georg Frentzel, 27 Aug. 1970, and Alexander N. Stepanow (chief doctor at the psychiatric institution in Mogilev), 20 July 1944, both in StA Munich, Zentraler Untersuchungsvorgang 9 (Ermittlungsakten des Ministeriums für Staatssicherheit der DDR).

15. Beer, 'Entwicklung', 409 ff.; Aussage Widmann in ZSt, 202 AR-Z 152/59, pp. 33 ff., 11 Jan. 1960.

16. Beer, 'Entwicklung', 411.

17. Even before Christmas 1941 further vehicles were driven from Berlin to Einsatzgruppe A in Riga: Beer, 'Entwickling', 413. For SK 4a (Einsatzgruppe C) Beer, 'Entwickling', 412. For EK 8 (Einsatzgruppe B): statement from Otto Matonoga, 8 June/9 June 1945 to Soviet investigators (StA Munich, Zentraler Untersuchungsvorgang 9). In Einsatzgruppe D, according to a witness, a gas van was used at the end of 1941. Beer, 'Entwickling', 413; LG Munich, 119 c Js 1/69, Urteil; statement by Jeckeln of 21 Dec. 1945 in Hans-Heinrich Wilhelm, 'Die Einsatzgruppe A der Sicherheitspolizei und des SD—Eine exemplarische Studie', in Helmut Krausnick and Hans-Heinrich Wilhelm, eds, *Die Truppe des Weltanschauungskrieges. Die Einsatzgruppen der Sicherheitspolizei und des SD 1938–1942* (Stuttgart, 1981), 548.

18. Eugen Kogon et al., eds, *Nationalsozialistische-Massentötungen durch Giftgas* (Frankfurt, 1983), 110 ff.

19. For details see Ch. 7, p. 139.

20. ND NO 365, also published in Helmut Krausnick, 'The Persecution of the Jews', in Hans Buchheim et al., eds, *Anatomy of the SS-State* (London, 1968), 114–15.

21. See p. 280.

22. Ibid.

23. Heberer, 'Eine Kontinuität der Tötungsoperationen', 295. The meeting between Himmler and Brack has been substantiated in the official diary entry for 14 December 1941 with the note 'Euthanasia'; see, *Dienstkalender*, ed. Witte et. al., 290. On the allocation

of Brack's staff see also in particular the memo from Brack to Himmler dated 23 June 1942, in which he declared himself willing to make further staff available and recalls the earlier agreement with Himmler (BAB, NS 19/1583).

24. Cf. and Robert-Jan van Pelt and Deborah Dwork, *Auschwitz 1270 to the Present* (New Haven, 1996), 280 ff.; Franciszek Piper, *Vernichtung in Auschwitz 1940–1945. Studien zur Geschichte des Konzentrations- und Vernichtungslagers Auschwitz*, vol. iii (Oswiecim, 1999), 88 ff.; On the murders of Jewish forced labourers see Sybille Steinbacher, '*Musterstadt' Auschwitz. Germanisierungspolitik und Judenmord in Ostoberschlesien* (Munich, 2000), 276–7.

25. Jan Erik Schulte, *Zwangsarbeit und Vernichtung. Das Wirtschaftsimperium der SS. Oswald Pohl und das SS Wirtschafts- und Verwaltungshauptamt 1933–1945* (Paderborn, 2001), 50 ff.

26. Stanislaw Klodzinski, 'Phenol', in *Die Auschwitz Hefte*, vol. i (1994), 277–81; see also Danuta Czech, *Kalendarium der Ereignisse im Konzentrationslager Auschwitz-Birkeanau 1939–1945* (Reinbek b. Hamburg, 1969), 108 and 151.

27. Jean C. Pressac, *Die Krematorien von Auschwitz. Die Technik des Massenmordes* (Munich, 1984), 19.

28. On the other hand the date of December 1941, suggested by Pressac, *Krematorien*, 41–2, does not seem convincing. That the murder of these prisoners occurred in early September 1941 can be reliably assumed thanks to Klodinski's investigation based on interviews with around 200 former inmates. According to Franciszek Piper, *Die Zahl der Opfer von Auschwitz* (Oswiecim, 1993), 23, this mass murder was already preceded by experiments with poison gas in August 1941; see also Czech, *Kalendarium*, 115 ff., and Jerzy Brandhuber, 'Die sowjetischen Kriegsgefangenen im Konzentrationslager Auschwitz', *Hefte von Auschwitz* 4 (1961), 5–46, and Wojciech Barcz, 'Die erste Vergasung in Auschwitz', in H. G. Adler et al., eds, *Auschwitz: Zeugnisse und Berichte* (Cologne and Frankfurt a. M., 1983), 17–18.

29. Cf. Browning, *Origins*, 398, 421; Steinbacher, '*Musterstadt' Auschwitz*, 276–7, demonstrates the murder of Jews from the Schmelt camps since November 1941 but leaves the question of the killing method open.

30. Rudolf Hoess, *Commandant in Auschwitz* (London, 1959), 207 ff.

31. Ibid. 208–9.

32. *Trial of Eichmann*, vii. 376 ff.

33. OS, 502-1-312, Topf Company to building management, 31 Oct. 1941; See Pressac, *Krematorien*, 31 ff.

34. Michael Thad Allen, 'The Devil in the Details: The Gas Chambers of Birkenau, October 1941', *HGS* 16/2 (2002), 189–216; van Pelt and Dwork, *Auschwitz*, 322; Browning, *Origins*, 358, has spoken out in favour of Allen's dating

35. See pp. 317 f.

36. Pressac, *Krematorien*, 38 ff.

37. See Götz Aly, '*Final Solution': Nazi Population Policy and the Murder of the European Jews* (London, 1999), 223–4; Christian Gerlach, 'Failure of Plans for an SS Extermination Camp in Mogilew, Belorussia', *HGS* 7 (1997), 60–78.

38. Evidence for this may be found in Sandkühler's work on Galicia, see Thomas Sandkühler, '*Endlösung' in Galizien: Der Judenmord in Ostpolen und die Rettungsinitiativen von Berthold Beitz, 1941–1944* (Bonn, 1996), 156 ff.

39. See Hitler's statements in the discussion about 'Eastern questions' on 16 July; *IMT* xxxviii. 86 ff., 221-L.

40. For Lemberg, however, there is only one reference to plans for the construction of an extermination camp. In the area of Minsk thousands of Jews deported from the Reich were murdered in Maly Trostinets from the spring of 1942 onwards.

41. This is evident in a presentation by the Propaganda department of Goebbels's ministry dated 17 August 1941, which—clearly in connection with Hitler's speech the same day— lists the arguments for a marking of the Jews (MA 423, in H. G. Adler, *Der Verwaltete Mensch. Studien zur Deportation der Juden aus Deutschland* (Tübingen, 1974), 50–1).

42. On the history of this: on 21 April Goebbels had commissioned his Secretary of State, Leopold Gutterer, to prepare for the marking of the Berlin Jews: *Kriegspropaganda* (Boelcke) and *Akten der Parteikanzlei*, 2 parts, ed. Helmuth Heiber et al. (Munich 1983 and 1991), Mikrofiches, vol. 4, 76074, memo Tießler, 21 Apr. 1941. It was subsequently established in the Propaganda Ministry that a proposal for cross-Reich identification of the Jews had already been proposed by Himmler or Heydrich (IfZ, MA 423, Taubert to Tießler 22 Apr. 1941 and memo of Tießler, 25 Apr. 1941). Goering had received such a proposal from the Führer's Deputy (StdF) and the SD the previous year, when Heydrich had first suggested the marking of Jews after *Kristallnacht* (ibid., 76069, from BAB, NS 18alt/842, memo from Reischauer to Tießler, 24 May 1941).

43. On 14 August the State Secretary in the Ministry of the Interior, Wilhelm Stuckart, in a memo to Lammers, had supported Karl Hermann Frank's suggestion that marking should be introduced in the Protectorate (ND NG 1111). Heydrich too had asked Bormann—after consulting Goering—in a memo of 17 August 1941 to urge Hitler to agree to the marking of the Jews, as the draft from the Propaganda Department for Goebbels of 17 August 1941 makes plain (IfZ, MA 423). With his initiative Goebbels thus came just ahead of other offices.

44. See p. 266 on the propaganda campaign.

45. In Walter Strauß, ed., 'Bernhard Lösener, "Als Rassenreferent im Reichsministerium des Innern"', *VfZ* 9 (1961), 262–313, 302 ff.

46. Fröhlich, ed., *Die Tagebücher*, Teil II, vol. ii, 19 Aug. 1941, p. 265. Goebbels had already recorded his intention to mark the Jews in his diary entry for 12 Aug. 1941, p. 218.

47. *Reichsgesetzblatt* (*RGBl*) 1941, I, p. 547; See express letter from the Reich Interior Ministry, 15 Sept. 1941, with guidelines for the implementation of the police regulation of 1 Sept. 1941. See Paul Sauer, ed., *Dokumente über die Verfolgung der Judischen Bürger in Baden-Württemberg durch das nationalsozialistische Regime*, vol. ii (Stuttgart, 1966), 207 ff. Cf. Adler, *Verwaltete Mensch*, 47 ff.

48. *RGBl*, 1941, I, p. 675.

49. *RGBl* 1941, I, pp. 681–2.

50. See Longerich, *Vernichtung*, 446.

51. Decree, 4 November 1941; see Joseph Walk, ed., *Das Sonderrecht für die Juden im NS-Staat. Eine Sammlung der gesetzlichen Massnahmen und Richtlinien—Inhalt und Bedeutung* (Heidelberg, 1981), iv. 261.

52. *RGBl*, 1941, I, pp. 722 ff.

53. Order from the Reich Minister of the Interior of 3 December, ND NO 5336, in Adler, *Verwaltete Mensch*, 503–4, and commentary, ibid. 491 ff.

54. BAB, NS 19/1438.

55. CDJC, XXVb-7.

56. Cf. in general Adler, *Verwaltete Mensch*, 29 ff.

57. PAA, Pol Abt. III 245; See Christopher Browning, *The Final Solution and the German Foreign Office* (New York, 1978), 66.

58. Cf. PAA Inland II g 174: Luther's request via the German embassies in the three countries, 10 November. Agreement from the Romanian, Croatian, and Slovakian governments was conveyed by telegram from the German embassy heads in Bucharest, Agram, and Pressburg on 13 November 1941, 20 November 1941, and 4 December 1941; Luther informed Eichmann about the result of his efforts on 10 January 1942. Cf. Browning, *Final Solution*, 67–8.

59. Heydrich to Himmler, 19 October, *Eichmann Trial*, Doc. 1544. The best overview of the first two deportation waves is now contained in the book by Alfred Gottwaldt and Diana Schulle, *Die 'Judendeportationen' aus dem Deutschen Reich, 1941–1945. Eine kommentierte Chronologie* (Wiesbaden, 2005). Less recent literature includes, alongside the groundbreaking work by H. G. Adler, *Verwaltete Mensch*, the essays by Ino Arndt and Heinz Boberach on the German Reich, Ino Arndt on Luxembourg, Jonny Moser on Austria, and Eva Schmidt-Hartmann on Czechoslovakia, all in the collected volume Wolfgang Benz, ed., *Dimension des Völkermords. Die Zahl der jüdischen Opfer des Nationalsozialismus* (Munich, 1991). On the deportation of the Burgenland Gypsies, see Michael Zimmermann, *Rassenutopie und Genozid. Die nationalsoialsozialistische Lösung der 'Zigeuerfrage'* (Hamburg, 1996), 223 ff.

60. On the deportations to Riga, see Wolfgang Scheffler, 'Das Schicksal der in die baltischen Staaten deportierten deutschen, österreichischen und tschechoslowakischen Juden 1941–1945', in Wolfgang Scheffler and Diana Schulle, eds, *Buch der Erinnerung. Die ins Baltikum deportierten deutschen, österreichischen und tschechoslowakischen Juden*, vol. i (Munich, 2003), 1–43; Gottwaldt and Schulle, '*Judendeportationen*', 110 ff. A total of 19,283 people were deported to Riga in twenty transports between 27 November 1941 and 6 February 1942.

61. The transports originally meant for Riga had been diverted to Kovno. Without exception, the 5,006 people deported there in those five trains between 17 and 25 November 1941 were shot, as were the inmates of the first Riga transport: Wolfgang Scheffler, 'Massenmord in Kowno', in Scheffler and Schulle, eds, *Buch der Erinnerung*, i. 83–7; Gottwaldt and Schulle, '*Judendeportationen*', *98 ff.*

62. On the seven deportations to Minsk that took place between 11 November and 5 December 1941, see Gottwaldt and Schulle, '*Judendeportationen*', 84 ff.

63. IfZ, Fb 95, 27, note from Gotenhafen, 24 Oct. 1941, summary of a discussion with Eichmann.

64. Fröhlich, *Die Tagebücher*, Teil II, vol. ii, 18 November 1941, p. 309.

65. Browning, *Origins*, 378. At the time Eichmann's office was still called the 'Special Department for Jewish matters and Evacuation Affairs'.

66. Adler, *Verwaltete Mensch*, 354 ff. Adler still provides the most detailed overview of the deportations.

67. Details ibid. *passim.*

68. This collaboration is described in Raul Hilberg, *Sonderzüge nach Auschwitz* (Mainz, 1981).
69. Adler, *Verwaltete Mensch*, 450 ff.
70. Ibid. 499 ff.
71. Ibid. 380 ff.
72. That the deportations occurred openly in many places and were observed by the population is documented in many local studies; see e.g. Michael Zimmermann, 'Die Deportation der Juden aus Essen und dem Regierungsbezirk Düsseldorf', in Ulrich Borsdorf und Mathilde Jamin, eds, *Über Leben im Krieg. Kriegserfahrungen in einer Industrieregion, 1939–1945* (Reinbek b. Hamburg, 1989), 126–42, on the deportation of the Jews of Essen, as well as Zimmermann, 'Die Gestapo und die regionale Organisation der Judendeportation. Das Beispiel der Stapo-Leitstelle Düsseldorf', in Gerhard Paul und Klaus-Michael Mallmann, eds, *Die Gestapo. Mythos und Realität* (Darmstadt, 1995), 357–72; Frank Bajohr, '"damit bitte keine Gefühlsduseleien". Die Hamburger und die Deportationen', in Die Forschungsstelle für Zeitgeschichte und das Institut für die Geschichte der deutschen Juden, eds, *Die Deportation der Hamburger Juden 1941–1945*, 2nd edn (Hamburg, 2002), 13–29. Scheller and Schulla, *Buch der Erinnerung* provides numerous other examples to show that the first stage of the deportations (as a closed march from a collection point to the station) took place publicly in many places at the end of 1941, including the cities of Berlin, Würzburg and Nuremberg, Hamburg, Kassel, Bielefeld, and Hanover (contributions from Klaus Dettmer, Eckehard Hübschmann, Jürgen Sielemann, Monica Kingreen, Monika Minninger, and Peter Schulze).
73. Summarized in the volume of photographs by Klaus Hesse and Philipp Springer, *Vor aller Augen. Fotodokumente des nationalsozialistischen Terrors in der Provinz* (Essen, 2002), 135 ff.
74. This is apparent in official surveys, some of which included critical voices: Stapostelle Bremen, 11 Nov. 1941, Stadt Münster, Bericht aus der Kriegschronik, 1 Dec. 1941; SD Außenstelle Minden, reports on 6 Dec. 1941 and 12 Dec. 1941, and SD Hauptaußenstelle Bielefeld, 16 Dec. 1941. These reports can be found in the publication compiled by Otto Dov Kulka and Eberhard Jäckel, *Die Juden in den geheimen NS-Stimmungsberichten, 1933–1945* (Düsseldorf, 2004), Nos. 3371, 3401, 3387, 3388, 3386. That the deportations did not meet with indifference on the part of the public is also apparent from diaries, letters, and reports from foreigners who were staying in the Reich at the time.
75. Adler, *Verwaltete Mensch*, 562 ff.
76. Ibid. 414.
77. Ibid. 491 ff. and 589 ff. and Wolfgang Dressen, *Betrifft: 'Aktion 3'. Deutsche verwerten jüdische Nachbarn* (Cologne and Berlin, 1998). The topic of the auctions and the putting to other uses of Jewish household goods for the benefit of German citizens is, in recent years, increasingly being covered in local studies; for example: Jehuda Barlev, *Juden und jüdische Gemeinde in Gütersloh, 1671–1943*, 2nd edn (Gütersloh, 1988), 113; Matthias Krispin et al., *Ein offenes Geheimnis. 'Arisierung' in Alltag und Wirtschaft in Oldenburg zwischen 1933 und 1945* (Oldenburg, 2001), 119 ff.; Christiane Kuller, '"Erster Grundsatz: Horten für die Reichsfinanzverwaltung". Die Verwertung des Eigentums der deportierten Nürnberger Juden', in Christoph Dieckmann et al., *Die Deportation der Juden*

aus Deutschland. Pläne—Praxis—Reaktionen, 1938–1945 (Göttingen, 2004), 160–79; Regina Bruss, *Die Bremer Juden unter dem Nationalsozialismus* (Bremen, 1983), 217–18; M. Buchholz, 'Die hannoverschen Judenhäuser. Zur Situation der Juden zur Zeit der Ghettoisierung und Verfolgung. 1941 bis 1945', *Quellen und Darstellungen zur Geschichte Niedersachsens* 101 (1987); Bernd-Lutz Lange, *Davidstern und Weihnachts- baum. Erinnerungen von überlebenden* (Leipzig, 1992); in his study of Hamburg, Frank Bajoh estimates around 100,000 beneficiaries of Jewish property in Hamburg and the immediate area (*'Arisierung' in Hamburg. Die Verdrängung der jüdischen Unternehmer 1933–1945* (Hamburg, 1997), 331 ff.).

78. Adler, *Verwaltete Mensch*, 606 ff.; Susanne Willems, *Der entsiedelte Jude. Albert Speers Wohnungspolitik für den Berliner Hauptstadtbau* (Berlin, 2000). The NSDAP district headquarters in Göttingen reported in December 1941 that 'the intention to transport the Jews out of Göttingen in the near future' had become 'generally known among the populace'; in consequence, the headquarters was 'overrun' with applications for allo- cations of the abandoned dwellings (Kulka and Jäckel, *Juden*, No. 3400, NSDAP Kreisleiter Göttingen, report 19 Dec. 1941).

79. Details in Longerich, *'Davon haben wir nichts gewusst'*, 171 ff. The police regulation of 24 Oct. 1941 was reproduced in Goebbels's article 'Die Juden sind schuld' (The Jews are to blame) on 16 Nov. 1941 in the weekly journal *Das Reich* in the form of ten commandments on the treatment of Jews. On the avoidance of the subject of the deportations in German propaganda see Goebbels's instruction at the internal propa- ganda conference on 23 Oct. 1941 (BA, NS 18alt/622).

80. Zimmermann, *Rassenutopie*, 176 ff.

81. Guenter Lewy, *The Nazi Persecution of the Gypsies* (New York, 1999), 112 ff.; Zimmer- mann, *Rassenutopie*, 228 ff.

82. PAA, Inland II AB, 59/3; Cf. Browning, 'Decision', 27.

83. Werner Jochmann, ed., *Adolf Hitler: Monologe im Führer-Hauptquartier 1941–1944. Die Aufzeichnungen Heinrich Heins* (Hamburg 1980), 25 Oct. 1941, p. 106.

84. *Das Reich*, no. 46, 1941. English translation in J. Noakes and G. Pridham, eds, *Nazism 1919–1945*, vol. iii: *Foreign Policy, War and Racial Extermination*, rev. edn (Exeter, 2001), 515 ff.

85. Minutes of the speech; quoted in Hans-Heinrich Wilhelm, *Rassenpolitik und Kriegfüh- rung. Sicherheitspolizei und Wehrmacht in Polen und der Sowjetunion* (Passau, 1991), 131–2, following PAA, Pol XIII, 25, VAA-Berichte; Cf. the note from a reporter, published in Jürgen Hagemann, *Die Presselenkung im Dritten Reich* (Bonn, 1970), 146.

86. *ADAP* D XIII/2, no. 415, record of meeting between Hitler and the Great Mufti in the presence of the Reich Foreign Minister on 28 November 1941 and 30 November 1941. Arguably, Hitler's statement to a visitor who was not a close and trustworthy ally cannot be seen as a revelation of the dictator's last and most secret intentions, but primarily as an attempt to use the striking idea of the 'destruction' of the Jews of Palestine as a common interest of German and Arab policy to distract the Great Mufti from his desire to receive a public declaration from Hitler that the German government supported the liberation of all Arabs. For, at that point, Hitler did not want to make such a declaration, fearing that the French Protectorate government in Syria would react to such a signal by switching to the Allied camp.

87. Ian Kershaw, ' "Improvised Genocide"? The Emergence of the "Final Solution" in the Warthegau', *Transactions of the Royal Historical* Society, 6th ser., 2 (1992), 65: in 1942 information reached the United States that in October 1941 the Jews of the district of Konin, 3,000 people in all, had been systematically murdered. These figures were confirmed by a German investigation (see ZSt, 206 AR-Z 228/73).

88. Ruling of Stuttgart district court, 15 Aug. 1950, in Irene Sagel-Grande et al., *Justiz und NS-Verbrechen. Sammlung deutscher Strafurteile wegen nationalsozialistischer Tötungsverbrechen, 1945–1966*, vol. vii (Amsterdam, 1972), 231a.

89. Aly, *'Final Solution'*, 70 ff.

90. PRO, HW 16/32, 4 Oct. 1941.

91. Statement by Lange's driver, *Justiz und NS-Verbrechen* xxi, no. 594, LG Bonn, ruling of 23 July 1965; see Kogon et al., eds, *NS-Massentötungen*, 110 ff.

92. Lucjan Dobroszycki, ed., *The Chronicle of the Lodz Ghetto 1941–1944* (New Haven and London, 1984), 96–7 and 124–5.

93. *Faschismus-Ghetto-Massenmord. Dokumentation über Ausrottung und Widerstand der Juden in Polen während des zweiten Weltkrieges*, ed. Tatiana Berenstein et al. (Frankfurt a. M., 1962), 278.

94. The Lodz Gestapo report for 9 June 1942 also refers to the central role of Greiser ('Judentum'); *Faschismus*, Berenstein et al., eds, 285.

95. Monitoring report by the Forschungsamt, 16 Jan. 1942, YVA, 051/13b; See Klein, 'Rolle der Vernichtungslager', 474.

96. Steinbacher, *'Musterstadt' Auschwitz*, 135 ff.

97. Ibid. 273 ff. The author was unable to clarify whether the Jewish workers were also suffocated with gas or executed. On the start of murders with Zyklon B in Auschwitz cf. pp. 281 ff.

98. *Diensttagebuch*, ed. Präg and Jakobmeyer, 14 Oct. 1941, p. 413.

99. Ibid., esp. 427–8. The decree was back-dated to 15 October; see , *Faschismus*, Berenstein et al., 128–9.

100. IfZ, MA 120. This was the result of a meeting that Frank held with a small group, plainly following on from the government meeting. Bogdan Musial (*Deutsche Zivilverwaltung und Judenverfolgung im Generalgouvernement. Eine Fallstudie* (Wiesbaden, 1999), 196 ff.) on the other hand, sees the statement as already containing the plan to kill these people in the district itself. This, he writes, should be seen as the 'prelude to state-organized mass murder'. At the meeting on 17 October 1941, Musial states, Frank had already been commissioned by Hitler to take part in the systematic murder of the Jews of the General Government, which Hitler had already decided upon. (In fact, on 17 October, Frank mentioned that he would soon be appearing frequently in Lublin 'because of a special commission from the Führer', but he does not identify that commission more closely.) Musial's argument is unconvincing. The transcripts of the meetings do record that the representatives of the civil administration attempted to persuade one another, using radical rhetoric, of the need to set *Judenpolitik* on the road to mass murder; but they do not show that the measures for the implementation of a genocide that had already been decided upon and which were to cover the whole of the General Government, were discussed here. The planned 'transfer' of the 1,000 Jews from Lublin (possibly to the district

of Galicia, where the mass shootings had begun) precisely shows that at this point there were no plans yet to murder millions. The Nazis were still talking about crossing the threshold to genocide, but were not yet at a stage at which mass murder was being organized and executed. In fact the murderous plans at this point were likely to have been restricted to Jews unfit for work in the districts of Lublin and Galicia, a commission that Globocnik hid from the civil administration. See also Dieter Pohl, *Von den 'Judenpolitik' zum 'Judenmord'. Der Distrikt Lublin des Generalgouvernements 1939–1944* (Frankfurt a. M., 1993), 108, who states that these plans were 'precisely at the threshold between plans for expulsion and for mass murder'.

101. IfZ, MA 120, in abbreviated form in *Diensttagebuch*, ed. Präg and Jacobmeyer, 436.
102. Ibid.
103. Tagungsbericht, ZStL Polen 98, 1-213.
104. Dieter Pohl, *Nationalsozialistische Judenverfolgung in Ostgalizien 1941–1944. Die Organisierung und Durchführung eines staatlichen Massenverbrechens* (Munich, 1996), 140 ff. Typical of this phase, for example, is the 'intelligence action' in Stanislau on 3 August, in which 600 men were shot (Urteil LG Münster v. 31 May 1968, 5 Ks 4/65, IfZ Gm 08.08). On these first murders see also Sandkühler, *'Endlösung'*, 148 ff.
105. Pohl, *Ostgalizien*, 138.
106. IfZ, Gm 08.08, Münster district court. 31 May 1968, 5 Ks 4/65, statement from the director of the field office, Krüger, vol. xxx. 96-7.
107. On Stanislau, see Pohl, *Ostgalizien*, 144 ff.
108. *Dienstkalender*, ed. Witte et al., 233
109. BAB, BDC-Akte Globocnik, memo to Himmler, 1 Oct. 1941. Cf. Pohl, *Lublin*, 101.
110. This is also the view of the editors of the *Dienstkalender*, p. 233, n. 35.
111. BDC-Akte Globocnik. The letter refers to having 'fundamentally agreed with' Globocnik's ideas concerning the 'German settlement' of the district of Lublin and the 'gradual expulsion of the indigenous population', but this agreement on Himmler's part does not, as Breitman, *Architect*, 186, claims, refer to the 'cleansing' of the district of Jews.
112. Musial sees a direct connection between the decision to build Belzec and plans for the settlement of ethnic Germans. See Musial, *Zivilverwaltung*, 201 ff., and Musial, 'The Origins of "Operation Reinhard". The Decision-Making Process for the Mass Murder of the Jews in the Generalgouvernement', *YVS* 28 (2000), 113-53. The author himself does admit, however, that the ambitious plans for the German settlement of the district would still not have been feasible even with the murder of the 300,000 inhabitants ('Origins', 151-2). Musial's assertion that Belzec was intended for the murder of the Jews across the whole of the General Government within a timeframe of around ten years is pure speculation (*Zivilverwaltung*, 207-8).
113. 208 AR-Z 252/59, 6 Nov. 1979, statement by Stanislav Kozal. Building start on 1 November, published in *Nationalsozialistische Massentungen*, ed. Kogon et al. (Frankfurt a. M., 1985), 152-3. This date is confirmed by the study of Michael Tregenza, 'Belzec Death Camp', *Wiener Library Bulletin* 30 (1977), 8-25.
114. See pp. 280 ff.
115. See pp. 262 ff.

116. Peter Chroust, 'Selected Letters of Doctor Friedrich Mennecke', in Götz Aly, *Cleansing the Fatherland: Nazi Medicine and Racial Hygiene* (Baltimore, 1994), 242–3, 25 Nov. 1941.

117. *Dienstkalender*, ed. Witte et al., 20 Oct. 1941, p. 241. The editors quote from a declaration by Mach on 26 Mar. 1942 to the Slovakian council of state, which mentions the German offer (see n. 167, below).

118. Klein, 'Rolle der Vernichtungslager', 478, has already referred to this.

119. Jules Schelvis, *Vernichtungslager Sobibor* (Amsterdam, 2003), 37; on the preparations for its construction there is a statement by the Polish railway worker Piwonski, from 1975: ZSt Dok. 643, 71-4-442; cf. Browning, *Origins*, 365. It cannot, however, be clearly established whether these building preparations in autumn 1941 actually refer to an extermination camp; it could equally be another planned building that was later converted.

120. Sandkühler, *'Endlösung'* 159 ff.

121. Pohl, *Lublin*, 101 and 105–6.

122. APL, Governor, district of Lublin, Judenangelegenheiten, Sygn. 270.

123. Pohl, *Lublin*, 109 ff.

124. StA Lwów, R 35 (Governor, district of Galicia), 12–97, Rundverfügung des Distrikt-gouverneuers.

125. Sandkühler, *'Endlösung'*, 141 ff.

126. StA Lwów, R 37 (Stadthauptmann Lemberg), 4–140, File note re meeting of district administration, concerning meeting on 9 January 1940.

127. Sandkühler, *'Endlösung'*, 148 ff., and Pohl, *Ostgalizien*, 180 ff., have different view on this.

128. Minute of 10 Jan. 1942, as in n. 126.

129. Lange to Stahlecker, 1 Oct. 1941, OS, 504-2-8. As early as August, Einsatzgruppe A had received permission to set up an 'enlarged police prison'. The further suggestion, already submitted by Stahlecker on 21 July and renewed on 25 August, that the planned camp should be described as a 'concentration camp' had been rejected by the RSHA: OS, 504-2-8, RSHA II C 3 an Ek 2, 17 Sept. 1941. On the deportations to Riga, the murders that took place there, and the conditions in which the deportees lived, see the overview by Wolfgang Scheffler, 'Das Schicksal der in die baltischen Staaten deportierten deustchen, österreichischen und tschechoslovakischen Juden 1941–1945', in Schefffler and Schulle, eds, *Buch der Erinnerung*, i. 1–45.

130. YIVO, Occ E 3–29, File note Drechsler, 20 Oct. 1941.

131. YIVO, Occ E 30, Minute RK Ostland, 27 Oct. 1941. On the gas chamber letter see above, pp. 279–80.

132. YIVO, Occ E 3–30.

133. YIVO, Occ E 32, RK Ostland, II a 4, 9 Nov. 1941.

134. YIVO, Occ E 26, telegram from Leibbrandt to RK Lohse, 13 Nov. 1941.

135. *IMT* xxvii. 2–3, 1104-PS. Kube sent Lohse the report from the District Commissioner of Sluzk, in which he had complained about the massacre by Police Batallion 11 in the district capital on 27 October 1941.

136. YIVO, Occ. E 3–28; also 3363-PS, *IMT* xxxii. 436.

137. 18 December 1941, YIVO, Occ E 3–28. The phrase 'fundamentally disregarded' and the reference to any 'dubious cases' that might arise, show that the Eastern Ministry did

not wish to confirm in this way Lohse's question as to whether 'all Jews' in the Ostland were to be liquidated.

138. Breitman, *Architect*, 218; BAB, R 43 II/684a, Brandt to Lammers, transmission of Himmler's file note concerning the conversation.

139. See p. 289.

140. For literature on the deportations to Minsk and the events that took place there, the following provide important information about Minsk: Safrian, *Eichmann-Männer*, 150 ff; Karl Löwenstein's notebooks, idem, *Minsk. im Lager der deutschen Juden* (Bonn, 1961); and the memoirs of Heinz Rosenberg, *Jahre des Schreckens...und ich blieb übrig, dass ich Dir's ansage* (Göttingen, 1985).

141. Hans-Heinrich Wilhelm, *Die Einsatzgruppe A der Sicherheitspolizei und des SD 1941/42* (Frankfurt a. M., 1986), 124–5, refers to personal notes by Bock, a copy of which is in the possession of the author; YIVO, Occ E 3–34.

142. YIVO, Occ E 3–36.

143. This is apparent from Leibrandt's communication to Lohse on 4 December 1941: this suggests Heydrich now wanted to set up the camp near Pleskau: YIVO, Occ E 3–35; published in Gertrude Schneider, *Journey into Terror: The Story of the Riga Ghetto* (New York, 1979), 184.

144. On this see Scheffler 'Schicksal', 13 ff.

145. Jäger-Bericht, IfZ, Fb 101/29. See Wolfgang Scheffler, 'Massenmord in Kowno', in Scheffler and Schulle, eds, *Buch der Erinnerung*, 83–92.

146. Gerald Fleming, *Hitler and the Final Solution* (London, 1985), 76 ff; EM 151, 5 Jan. 1942.

147. Statement, 15 Dec. 1945 to Soviet investigators, in Wilhelm, 'Einsatzgruppe A', 566–7.

148. Published in *Dienstkalender*, ed Witte et al., 278. The time was 13.30.

149. Ibid., 30 Nov., 4 Dec. 1941, p. 284; PRO, HW 16/32, telegrams from Himmler to Jeckeln, 1 Dec. 1941 and 4 Dec. 1941.

150. Andrej Angrick and Peter Klein, *Die 'Endlösung' in Riga: Ausbeutung und Vernichtung, 1941–1944* (Berlin, 2006), 239 ff; on the first shootings see H. G. Adler, *Theresienstadt 1941–1945: Das Antlitz einer Zwangsgemeinschaft* (Tübingen, 1960), 799.

151. Angrick and Klien, *Riga*, 338 ff.

152. Walter Manoschek, *'Serbien ist judenfrei'. Militärbesatzungspolitik und Judenvernichtung in Serbien 1941/42* (Munich, 1993), 35 ff.

153. Ibid. 43–4.

154. Ibid. 49 ff.

155. Ibid. 79 ff. The order initially spoke of 2,100 victims, but the number was raised by 100 after another German soldier was killed.

156. Manoschek, *Serbien*, 86 ff.

157. NG 3354; Manoschek, *'Serbien'*, 104.

158. NG 3354; Manoschek, *'Serbien'*, 102.

159. Ibid. 84–5.

160. Ibid. 96–7.

161. Ibid. 86.

162. PAA, Inland IIg 104, Rademacher report, 7 November; Manoschek, *'Serbien'*, 102 ff.

163. Zimmermann, *Rassenutopie*, 248 ff.

164. *Dienstkalender*, ed. Witte et al., 20 Oct. 1941, p. 241. The editors quote from an explanation by Mach, dated 26 Mar. 1942, to the Slovakian council of state, which mentions the German proposal.

165. The position represented here differs particularly from the versions given by Burrin and Browning.

166. This view is held by Mommsen and Broszat.

167. I am thinking primarily of the works of Pohl, Sandkühler, Musial, and Gerlach.

16. The Wannsee Conference

1. PAA, Inland II g 177, memo from Heydrich to Luther. On 1 December HSSPF Krüger und State Secretary Bühler of the General Government were invited to clarify the question of competencies concerning the 'Jewish problem' (note from Eichmann and invitation letter of 1 December; it was already included in the Eichmann trial as Dokument T 182, published in *Tagesordnung Judenmord. Die Wannsee-Konferenz am 20. Januar 1942. Eine Dokumentation zur Organisation der 'Endlösung'*, (Berlin, 1992), ed. Kurt Pätzold and Erika Schwarz; facsimile in Yehoshua Büchler and Yehuda Bauer, 'A Preparatory Document for the Wannsee "Conference" ', *HGS* 9 (1995), 121–9. For literature on the Wannsee Conference see: Mark Roseman, *The Villa, the Lake, the Meeting: Wannsee and the Final Solution* (London, 2002); Christian Gerlach, 'Die Wannsee-Konferenz, das Schicksal der deutschen Juden und Hitlers politische Grundsatzentscheidung alle Juden Europas zu ermorden', *Werkstattgeschichte*, 18 (1997), 7–44; Eberhard Jäckel, 'The Purpose of the Wannsee Conference', in James S. Pacy and Alan P. Wertheimer, eds, *Perspectives on the Holocaust: Essays in Honor of Raul Hilberg* (Boulder, Colo., 1995); Peter Klein, *Die Wannsee-Konferenz vom 20. Januar 1942. Analyse und Dokumentation* (Berlin, 1995); Pätzold and Schwarz, *Tagesordnung*; Safrian, *Eichmann-Männer*, 171 ff.; Wolfgang Scheffler, 'Die Wannsee-Konferenz und ihre historische Bedeutung', in *Erinnern für die Zukunft* (Berlin, 1995).

2. Elke Fröhlich, ed., *Die Tagebücher*, Teil II, vol. ii, 13 Dec. 41, pp. 498–9.

3. This is the argument put forward by Gerlach, 'Wannsee-Konferenz'.

4. This is what Rosenberg recorded in his diary concerning a discussion with Hitler on 14 December, at which he presented him with the manuscript of a planned speech at the Sportpalast (Rosenberg, *Tagebuch*, PS-1517, *IMT* xxvii. 270 ff., 16 Dec. 41, also published in Wilhelm, *Rassenpolitik*, 132): 'Where the Jewish question is concerned, I would say that, following the decision, the remarks about the New York Jews should perhaps be changed somewhat. I would take the view that one should not speak of the extermination of the Jews. The Führer agreed with this stance and said they had burdened us with the war and brought destruction; no wonder they were the first to feel the consequences.' In Gerlach's view, the 'decision' mentioned by Rosenberg is Hitler's 'fundamental decision', which must in that case have been made between 7 and 14 December ('Wannsee-Konferenz', 24). In my view, however, the 'decision' plainly refers to Germany's declaration of war upon the United States, as a result of which the German policy pursued hitherto of keeping the USA out of the war with 'reprisals' against the German Jews and with propaganda deliberately directed at the 'Jewish warmongers' around Roosevelt, had been superseded. Any further anti-Semitic threats

directed against the USA would now even be counter-productive, because they only demonstrated the lack of effectiveness of German propaganda hitherto; on the other hand the German leadership could not bring itself to expose the terrible realization of the 'prophecy' with an offensive propaganda campaign going beyond general hints.

5. *Dienstkalender*, ed. Witte et al., 294. According to Gerlach ('Wannsee-Konferenz', 22 and 27), the term 'partisan' should be taken to mean that in view of the now imminent war on two fronts Hitler had fallen into a 'kind of fortress-continental-Europe mentality', and saw the European Jews in general as dangerous enemies in his own hinterland. As far as one can tell, however, there is no evidence for the use of the term 'partisan' to describe the European Jews in Hitler's otherwise stereotypical anti-Semitic diatribes. On the other hand the idea that the Jews in the occupied Soviet territories were generally partisans or helpers of partisans and must therefore be removed was so widespread among the Germans even by the end of 1941 that Hitler's statement seems quite clear.

6. See Gerlach, 'Wannsee-Konferenz'. However, Gerlach does not explain why Himmler, whom he takes to have been present during Hitler's address on 12 December, himself left no notes about the 'fundamental decision', but—as one of those chiefly responsible for the murder of the Jews—was only informed by Hitler about that decision six days later. Similarly it seems questionable whether one can really, with Gerlach, draw such extensive conclusions from the fact that during these days a series of discussions was held by people who played a leading role in the 'Final Solution', but about the contents of which we have no detailed information (pp. 23–4).

7. PAA, Inland IIg 177, conference minutes. Published in Longerich, *Ermordung*, 83 ff. For an English translation see Noakes and Pridham, eds, *Nazism*, iii. 535–41.

8. *Trial of Eichmann*, vii. 879 (text written by Heydrich and Müller); IfZ G 01 (trial transcript, German version), session of 24 July: in fact the terms used at the conference were 'killing', 'elimination', and 'annihilation'

9. See n. 7.

10. On the issue of forced labour at this point see Longerich, *Politik*, 476 ff. The details will be examined in the following chapter.

11. Zhitomir City Archive, P 1151-1-137. I am most grateful to Wendy Lower for allowing me to have a copy of this document.

12. *Diensttagebuch*, ed. Präg and Jacobmeyer, 457–8.

13. Ibid., 16 Dec. 1941.

14. Cf. especially Cornelia Essner, *Die 'Nürnberger Gesetze' oder die Verwaltung des Rassenwahns* (Paderborn, 2002), 410 ff.; Jeremy Noakes, 'The Development of Nazi Policy towards the German-Jewish Mischlinge 1933–1945', *LBIY* 34 (1989), 291–354; John A. S. Grenville, 'Die "Endlösung" und die "Judenmischlinge" in Dritten Reich', in Ursula Büttner, ed., *Das Unrechtsregime*, vol. ii: *Verfolgung—Exil—Belasteter Neubeginn* (Hamburg, 1996), 91–122.

17. The Beginning of the Extermination Policy on a European Scale in 1942

1. In a narrow sense the expression 'extermination through work' refers to the delivery, agreed between Justice Minister Thierack and Himmler, of judicial prisoners to the SS. (See Goebbels's note about conversation with Thierack, 15 Sept. 1942 (Nuremberg

Document (ND) 682-PS) and Thierack's file note about his conversation with Himmler, 18 Sept. 1942 (ND 654-PS); cf. Hermann Kaienburg, 'Zwangsarbeiter an der "Straße der SS"', *1999*, 11 (1996), 13–39, 14.) Here the term is used in a broader sense.

2. EM 86.

3. Cf. Karl-Heinz Roth, '"Generalplan Ost"—"Gesamtplan Ost"', in Mechthild Rössler and Sabine Schleiermacher, eds, *Der 'Generalplan Ost'. Hauptlinien der nationalsozialistischen Planung und Vernichtungspolitik* (Berlin, 1995), 73 ff.; BAB, NS 19/2065.

4. Cf. Hermann Kaienburg, *Vernichtung durch Arbeit. Der Fall Neuengamme* (Bonn, 1990), 144 ff.

5. Jan Erik Schulte, *Zwangsarbeit und Vernichtung. Das Wirtschaftsimperium der SS. Oswald Pohl und das SS-Wirtschafts- und Verwaltungshauptamt, 1933–1945* (Paderborn, 2001), 334 ff.

6. See pp. 247 f.

7. Schulte, *Zwangsarbeit*, 351 ff.; Christian Streit, *Keine Kameraden. Die Wehrmacht und die sowjetischen Kriegsgefangenen 1941–1945* (Stuttgart, 1978), 212–13.

8. Ibid. 204.

9. Individual cases in Walter Naasner, *Neue Machtzentren in der deutschen Kriegswirtschaft, 1942–1945* (Boppard, 1994), 300 ff.

10. Himler's decision on amalgamation presumably coincided with a meeting on 10 Jan. 1942. See *Der Dienstkalender Heinrich Himmlers 1941/42*, ed. Peter Witte et al. (Hamburg, 1999), 105; the corresponding order from Pohl was passed on 19 Jan. 1942 (NO 495); further details in Schulte, *Zwangsarbeit*, 357.

11. Schulte, *Zwangsarbeit*, 343 ff.

12. BAB, NS 19/2065; cf. Roth, 'Generalplan Ost', 74–5.

13. 129-R, *IMT* xxxviii. 362 ff.; cf. Naasner, *Machtzentren*, 269.

14. 129-R, *IMT* xxxviii. 365 ff.; Naasner, *Machtzentren*, 269; Roth, 'Generalplan Ost', 77.

15. Hermann Kaienburg, 'Zwangsarbeit: KZ und Wirtschaft im Zweiten Weltkrieg', in W. Benz et al., *Die Ort des Terrors. Gechichte der nationalsozialistischen Konzentrationslager*, vol. i: *Die Organisation des Terrors* (Munich, 2005), 229 ff.; and Mark Spoerer, *Zwangsarbeit unter dem Hakenkreuz. Ausländische Zivilarbeiter, Kriegsgefangene und Häftlinge im Deutschen Reich und im besetzten Europa, 1939–1945* (Stuttgart and Munich, 2001), 183 ff. Spoerer refers to the fact that it was also advantageous from the point of view of industry to deploy forced labourers, as companies were dependent on armaments commissions for capital preservation or growth.

16. Kaienburg, *Vernichtung*, 145, 314 ff.; Naasner, *Machtzentren*, 274 ff.

17. Falk Pingel, *Häftlinge unter NS-Herrschaft* (Hamburg, 1978), 118. Naasner similarly establishes the 'irreconcilability of the SS economy with the fundamental requirements of economic planning' (*Machtzentren*, 274).

18. On the forced labour of concentration camp inmates see, apart from the literature already mentioned, Reiner Fröbe, 'Der Arbeitseinsatz von KZ-Häftlingen und die Perspektive der Industrie', in *'Deutsche Wirtschaft'. Zwangsarbeit von KZ-Häftlingen für Industrie und Behörden* (Hamburg, 1991), 33–78, also in Ulrich Herbert, ed., *Europa und der 'Reichseinsatz'. Ausländische Zivilarbeiter, Kriegsgefangene und KZ-Häftlinge in Deutschland 1938–1945* (Essen, 1991), 351–74; the essays in the collection Hermann Kaienburg, ed., *Konzentrationslager und deutsche Wirtschaft* (Opladen, 1996); Bernd

C. Wagner, *IG Auschwitz. Zwangsarbeit und Vernichtung von Häftlingen des Lagers Monowitz 1941–1945* (Munich, 2000).

19. Naasner, *Machtzentren*, 300–1. Fröbe, 'Arbeiteinsatz', 34, indicates that concentration camp inmates were used predominantly for building work throughout the whole of 1942, some in the erection of industrial plant, but not generally in production.

20. Berenstein et al., eds, *Faschismus-Ghetto-Massenmord. Dokumentation über Ausrottung und Widerstand der Juden in Polen während des zweiten Weltkrieges* (Frankfurt a. M., 1962), 268. On this decision and its effects see in particular Michael Thad Allan, *The Business of Genocide: The SS, Slave Labor and the Concentration Camps* (Chapel Hill, NC, 2002), 148 ff.; and Schulte, *Zwangsarbeit*, 361. A day before, Himmler had already telephoned Heydrich to give him the task of putting 'Jews in the Kl.s'. See *Dienstkalender* ed. Witte et al., 25 Jan. 1942, p. 326. The decision to deport Jews to the concentration camps and use them as slave labourers may have been made in the course of a meeting that Himmler held on 14/15 January with the heads of the SS-Hauptämter. A few days after that conference Pohl issued an order in Himmler's name to set up the Wirtschafts- und Verwaltungshauptamt (ND NO 495). On 17 Jan. 1942 the following telegram was sent by the Reich Minister for the Occupied Eastern Territories (Rosenberg) to Reichskommissar Lohse, which clearly indicates a fundamental change in the question of the preservation of Jewish workers: 'The Economic Leadership Staff East have issued instructions that Jewish skilled industrial and craft workers are to be retained for work, since they are of great value to the war economy in individual instances. Their retention must be ensured through negotiation with the local offices of the Reichsführer SS' (BAB, R 92/1157). See Wolfgang Scheffler, 'Das Schicksal der in die baltischen Staaten deportierten deutschen, österreichischen und tschechoslovakischen Juden 1941–1945. Ein historischer Überblick', in Wolfgang Scheffler and Diana Schulle, *Buch der Erinnerung. Die ins Baltikum deportierten deutschen, österreichischen und tschechoslovakischen Juden 1941–1945* (Munich, 2003), i. 6. Finally, we should bear in mind that only a few days after this meeting, on 20 Jan. 1942, at the Wannsee Conference, Heydrich made his remarks about the columns of Jewish slave labourers who were to be taken to the East for 'road-building'.

21. See p. 325.

22. ZSt, Doc. USSR 401, quoted in Peter Klein, *Die Einsatzgruppen in der besetzten Sowjetunion 1941/42* (Berlin, 1997), 410–11. This might be the letter that Wislicency mentioned in an interrogation: according to this, in the summer of 1942 he had seen an instruction from Himmler to Heydrich. In this letter the complete extermination of the Jews on Hitler's orders was ordered; only those Jews who were fit for work were to be excluded from the extermination and placed in concentration camps (*Trial of Eichmann*, Doc. 856).

23. Reference to this in dispatch from the Reich Labour Minister, 27 March: *IMT* xxxvii. 493, L-061.

24. Wolf Gruner, *Der geschlossene Arbeitseinsatz deutscher Juden. Zur Zwangsarbeit als Element der Verfolgung 1938–1943* (Berlin, 1997), 291 ff.; H. G. Adler, *Der verwaltete Mensch. Studien zur Deportation der Juden aus Deutschland* (Tübingen, 1974), 216 ff.

25. Elke Fröhlich, ed., *Die Tagebücher von Joseph Goebbels*, Teil II: *Diktate 1941–1945*, vol. iv, bearbeitet von Elke Fröhlich (Munich, 1995), entry 30 May 1942, p. 405; cf. Gruner, *Arbeitseinsatz*, 298 ff.

26. See p. 324.

27. Sybille Steinbacher, *'Musterstadt' Auschwitz. Germanisierungspolitik und Judenmord in Ostoberschlesien* (Munich, 2000), 276–7.

28. Cf. Kaienburg, 'Jüdischer Arbeitslager an der "Strasse der SS" ', *Zeitschrift für Sozialgeschichte des 20. und 21. Jahrhunderts* 11 (1996), 13–39. On the Galician section of DG IV: Thomas Sandkühler, *Die 'Endlösung' in Galizien. Der Judenmord in Ostpolen* (Bonn, 1996), 141 ff.; Dieter Pohl, *Nationalsozialistische Judenvefolgung in Ostgalizien* (Munich, 1996), 167 ff., 338 ff.

29. Kaienburg, 'Jüdische Arbeitslager', 26; Pohl, *Ostgalizien*, 338 ff.

30. Kaienburg, Jüdische Arbeitslager', 37.

31. See below, p. 341.

32. 'But the Jew will not exterminate the European nations, but will be the victim of his own attack' (Max Domarus, *Hitler. Reden 1932 bis 1945*, vol. iv (Wiesbaden, 1973), 1821).

33. 'We are clear about the fact that the war can only end either with the extermination of the Aryan peoples, or with the disappearance of Jewry from Europe' (Domarus, *Hitler. Reden*, iv. 1828–9).

34. 'my prophecy will be fulfilled not with the destruction of Aryan humanity through this war but rather with the extermination of the Jews'. See *VB*, 26 Feb. 1942 and Domarus, *Hitler. Reden*, iv. 1844.

35. ND PS 1063, printed in Peter Longerich, *Die Ermordung der europäischen Juden* (Munich, 1989), 165–6. See also guidelines on the technical implementation of the evacuation of Jews to the General Government (undated, presumably January 1942), IfZ, Erlass-Sammlung Gestapo Würzburg, printed in Adler, *Verwaltete Mensch*, 191–2. On the deportations from the Reich see ibid. for Germany Ino Arndt and Heinz Boberach, in W. Benz, ed., *Dimension des Völkermords. Die Zahl der jüdischen Opfer des Nationalsozialismus* (Munich, 1996), 23–65; for Austria Jonny Moser, pp. 67–94, for Czechoslovakia, Eva Schmidt-Harman, pp. 353–80; Henry Friedländer: 'The Deportation of the German Jews: Post-War German trials of Nazi Criminals', *LBYB* 29 (1984), 201–26.

36. Besprechungsprotokoll of 9 Mar. 1943, Eichmann, Doc. 119, printed in Longerich. *Ermordung*, 167–8.

37. See the schedule in Peter Longerich, *Die Politik der Vernichtung. Eine Gesamtdarstellung der nationalsozialistischen Judenverfolgung* (Munich, 1998), 485–6, based on the information of the International Tracing Service in Arolsen and various individual sources; Alfred Gottwaldt and Diana Schulle, *Die 'Judendeportationen' aus dem deutschen Reich 1941–1945. Eine kommentierte Chronologie* (Wiesbaden, 2005), 182 ff. An activity report by the agent for the Four-Year Plan, traffic group, mentions 37 special trains of Jews, or only 16 more than can be individually identified (R 26 IV/v., 47; see Christian Gerlach, 'The Wannsee Conference, the Fate of the German Jews, and Hitler's Decision in Principle to Exterminate all European Jews', *Journal of Modern History* 70 (1998), 40).

38. Gottwaldt and Schulle, *Judendeportationen*, 167 ff.

39. On the separation of transports in Lublin: note from Reuter, Abteilung Bevölkerungs-wesen und Fürsorge, 17 Mar. 1942 about communication from Höfle the previous day, quoted in Hans-Günther Adler, *Theresienstadt 1941–1945. Das Antlitz einer Zwangsge-meinschaft, Geschichte, Soziologie, Psychologie,* 2nd edn (Tübingen, 1960), 50–1.

40. Archivum Panstwowe w Lublinie (APL), Gouverneur Distrikt Lublin, Judenangelegen-heiten, Sygn. 273, Vermerke Distriktsverwaltung Lublin, Unterabteilung Bevölkerungs-wesen und Fürsorge, 20 and 23 Mar. 1942, with individual information concerning arriving Central European and deported local Jews. Details in Longerich, *Politik,* 487.

41. Note from Reuter, Abteilung Bevölkerungswesen und Fürsorge, 17 Mar. 1942 concern-ing message from Höfle the previous day (quoted from Adler, *Theresienstadt,* 50–1).

42. Example in Peter Witte, 'Letzte Nachrichten aus Siedliszcze. Der Transport Ax aus Theresienstadt in den Distrikt Lublin', *Theresienstädter Studien und Dokumente* (1996), 98–113.

43. Gottwaldt and Schulle, *Judendeportationen,* 213.

44. Ibid. 211 ff. The authors produce a certain amount of admittedly weak evidence to suggest that the first deportation trains went straight to Sobibor after 3 June, or that the passengers of those trains were brought to Sobibor after a stopover lasting only a few days.

45. Hans Safrian, *Die Eichmann-Männer* (Vienna, 1993), 179.

46. Two transports from the old Reich, nine from Vienna, six from Theresienstadt; one transport from Theresienstadt only got as far as Baranowicze (a large 'ghetto action' was taking place in Minsk), where the deportees were shot immediately after their arrival on 31 July 1942. Details in Longerich, *Politik,* 48 ff., assembled from the docu-ments of the International Tracing Service (YV, JM 10.73), from the files of the main railway station administration [Mitte] in Minsk (StA Minsk, 378-1-784) and the find-ings of the Heuser trial (Judgement LG Koblenz, 21 May 1963, published in *Justiz* xix, no. 552); Gottwaldt and Schulle, *Judendeportationen,* 237 ff.; on the transport to Bar-anowicze (see above): Jakov Tsur, 'Der verhängnisvolle Weg des Transportes AAy', *Terezin Studies and Documents* 2 (1995), 107–20.

47. On this subject we have the reports of Sonderkommando set up by the Waffen-SS Battalion z.b.V. See *Unsere Ehre heist Treue. Kriegstagebuch des Kommandostabes Reichsführer SS. Tätigkeitsberichte der 1. and 2. SS-Inf. Brigade, der 1. SS Kav.-Brigade und von der Sonderkommandos der SS* (Vienna, 1965), 236 ff

48. Judgement LG Koblenz of 21 May 1963, printed in *Justiz* xix, no. 552 (Heuser-Verfahren), p. 192.

49. Adler, *Verwaltete Mensch,* 193 ff. and Moser, 'Österreich' in Benz, ed., *Dimensionen,* 80–1; see also Victor Klemperer, *To the Bitter End: The Diaries of Victor Klemperer 1942–45* (London, 1999), 8 July 1942, p. 91.

50. Hartmann, 'Tschechoslowakei', in Benz, ed., *Dimension,* 365–6.

51. On the course of the deportations in detail, Gottwaldt and Schulle, *Judendeportationen,* 260 ff.

52. Ibid. 337 ff.

53. Ibid. 250 ff.

54. Ibid. 226 ff.

55. Ibid. 393 ff.

56. W. Boelke, *Deutschlands Rüstung im Zweiten Weltkrieg. Hitlers Konferenzen mit Albert Speer 1942–1944* (Frankfurt a. M., 1969), 189.

57. Fröhlich, *Die Tagebücher* Teil II, vol. v. Entry for 30 Sept. 1942, p. 606.

58. BAB, R 22/5029, Report of the Justice Minister, 18 Sept. 1942; also *IMT* xxvi. 654 PS.

59. ND NO 5522.

60. On this subject, and on the implementation of the deportations see Ladislav Lipscher, *Die Juden im slowakischen Staat 1939–1945* (Munich, 1980), 99 ff.; Raul Hilberg, *The Destruction of the European Jews* (New Haven, 2003), ii. 766 ff.; Christopher Browning, *The Find Solution and the German Foreign Office: A Study of Referat D III of Abteilung Deutschland 1940–43* (New York and London, 1978), 94 ff.; Yehoshua Büchler, 'The Deportation of Slovakian Jews to the Lublin District of Poland in 1942', *HGS* 6 (1991) 151–66.

61. *Dienstkalender*, ed. Witte et al., 20 Oct. 1941, p. 241. The editors quote from a declaration by the Slovakian Interior minister, Mach, on 26 Mar. 1942 to the Slovakian State Council, from which the German offer comes.

62. Lipscher, *Juden*, 31 ff.

63. Ibid. 102 ff.

64. Büchler, 'Deportation', 152.

65. Ibid. 153.

66. PAA, Büro StSekr, Bd. 2, published in *ADAP*, E II, 161–2.

67. See p. 328.

68. Büchler, 'Deportation', 153, 166; and Danuta Czech, ed., *Kalendarium der Ereignisse im Konzentrationslager Auschwitz-Birkenau 1939–1945* (Reinbek b. Hamburg, 1989).

69. Büchler, 'Deportation', 160.

70. Ibid. 166.

71. Czech, *Kalendarium*.

72. Cf. Lipscher, *Juden*, 129 ff.; on interventions by the Church, see Livia Rothkirchen, 'Vatican Policy and the "Jewish Problem" in Independent Slovakia (1939–1945)', *YVS* 6 (1967), 27–53.

73. Livia Rothkirchen, 'The Dual Role of the "Jewish Center" in Slovakia', in Yisrael Gutman and Cynthia J. Haft, eds, *Patterns of Jewish Leadership in Nazi Europe, 1933–1945. Proceedings of the Third Yad Vashem International Historical Conference, Jerusalem, April 4–7, 1977* (Jerusalem, 1979), 219–27; Yahuda Bauer, *Freikauf von Juden?* (Frankfurt a. M., 1996).

74. Lipscher, *Juden*, 114–15.

75. According to Büchler, 'Deportation', 8, transports went to the district of Lublin and 19 to Auschwitz.

76. Serge Klarsfeld, *Vichy-Auschwitz. Die Zusammenarbeit der deutschen und französischen Behörden bei der 'Endlösung der Judenfrage' in Frankreich* (Nördlingen, 1989), 34 ff.; Ulrich Herbert, 'Die deutsche Militärverwaltung in Paris und die Deportation der französischen Juden', in Christian Jansen et al., eds, *Von der Aufgabe der Freiheit. Politische Verantwortung und bürgerliche Gesellschaft im 19. u. 20. Jahrhundert* (Frankfurt a. M., 1995), 439; details of the start of the 'Final Solution' in France are examined in the article by Ahlrich Meyer, 'Der Beginn der "Endlösung" in Frankreich—offene Fragen', *Sozialgeschichte* 18 (2003), 35–82.

77. Klarsfeld, *Vichy*, 43.

78. 1216-RF, Minute by Dannecker, 10 Mar. 1943 published in Klarsfeld, *Vichy*, 374–5.

79. Note by Zeitschel, 11 Mar. 1942 published in Klarsfeld, *Vichy*, 375.

80. Klarsfeld, *Vichy*, 376–7.

81. CDJC, XXVb-29, published in Klarsfeld, *Vichy*, 375–6.

82. R. B. Birn, *Die Höhere SS- und Polizeiführer. Himmlers Vertreter im Reich und in den besetzten Gebieten* (Düsseldorf, 1986), 446–7.

83. Herbert, 'Militärverwaltung', 440.

84. CDJC, XXVb-29, published in Klarsfeld, *Vichy*, 379.

85. This is according to the report of Walter Bargatzky, working as a lawyer in the military administration, Hotel Majestic; Walter Bargatzky, *Hotel Majestic* (Freiburg, 1987), 103, on the basis of information from an auricular witness; cf. Herbert, 'Militärverwaltung', 448.

86. Bargatzky, *Hotel Majestic*, 94. See also identical information from the former chief judge attached to the military commander, 29 Oct. 1949, quoted from Hans Luther, *Der französische Widerstand gegen die deutsche Besatzungsmacht und seine Bekämpfung* (Tübingen, 1957), 214. See Ulrich Herbert, *Best. Biographische Studien über Radikalismus, Weltanschauung und Vernunft 1903–1989* (Bonn, 1996), 320.

87. 1217-RF, note from Dannecker, 15 June 1942; published in Klarsfeld, *Vichy*, 379–80; see also ibid. 66–7.

88. Moreshet-Archive, Givat Haviva, Israel (copy from Prague city Archive); already published in *Tragédia slovenských Židov. Fotografie a Dokumenty* (Bratisalava, 1949) and quoted in in Gerald Reitlinger, *The Final Solution: The Attempt to Exterminate the Jews of Europe, 1939–1945* (New York, 1961).

89. CDJC, XXVb-38, note concerning telephone conversation with Novak, 18 June 1942 published in Klarsfeld, *Vichy*, 383.

90. ND NG 183 published in Klarsfeld, *Vichy*, 384–5.

91. 1223-RF, Dannecker note of 1 July 1942 published in Klarsfeld, *Vichy*, 390–1.

92. 1220-RF, in Klarsfeld, *Vichy*, 388.

93. Cf. Klarsfeld, *Vichy*, 68 ff. and 90 ff.

94. CDJC, XXVI-40, Hagen note of 4 July 1942 and 1225-RF, Minute by Dannecker, 6 July 1942, published in Klarsfeld, *Vichy*, 393 ff. and 398–9.

95. CDJC, XLIX-35, Dannecker to Eichmann, July 1942, in Klarsfeld, *Vichy*, 399–400.

96. APL, Gouverneur Distrikt Lublin, Sygn. 270.

97. Yitzhak Arad, *Belzec, Sobibor, Treblinka: The Operation Reinhard Death Camps* (Bloomington, Ind., 1986), 23 ff. and 68 ff.

98. Cf. in particular Dieter Pohl, *Von der 'Judenpolitik' zum 'Judenmord'. Der Distrikt Lublin des Generalgouvernements 1939–1944* (Frankfurt a. M., 1993), 113 ff. and also David Silberklang, 'Die Juden und die ersten Deportationen aus dem Distrikt Lublin', in Bogdan Musial, ed., *'Aktion Reinhardt'. Der Völkermord an den Juden im Generalgouvernement 1941–1944* (Osnabrück, 2004), 141–64.

99. See in particular Bogdan Musial, *Deutsche Zivilverwaltung und Judenverfolgung im Generalgouvernement. Eine Fallstudie zum Distrikt Lublin 1939–1944* (Wiesbaden, 1999), 229 ff.

100. BAB, NS 19/3959; see Pohl, *Lublin*, 110.

101. Pohl, *Lublin*, 116–7.
102. Elke Fröhlich, ed., *Die Tagebücher von Joseph Goebbels*. Teil II. Band 3. *Januar-März 1942* (Munich, 1994), 561.
103. *Trial of Eichmann*, vii. 240.
104. Statement, 10 Nov. 1964, StA München I 110 Ks 3/64, 14, 2918 ff.; see Pohl, *Lublin*, 125–6.
105. Pohl, *Lublin*, 118 ff.; Silberklang, 'Juden', 150 ff.; Musial, *Zivilverwaltung*, 254 ff.
106. Dieter Pohl, *Nationalsozialistische Judenverfolgung in Ostgalizien 1941–1944. Die Organisation und Durchführung eines staatlichen Massenerbrechens* (Munich, 1996), 179 ff.
107. On Sobibor see Arad, *Belzec*, 30 ff.
108. Pohl, *Lublin*, 120 ff.
109. Bradley F. Smith et al., eds, *Himmler Geheimreden 1933 bis 1945* (Frankfurt a. M., 1974), 159.
110. *VOGG*, 1942, 321 ff., 'Erlass über die Überweisung von Dienstgeschäften auf den Staatssekretär für das Sicherheitswesen'; cf. Pohl, *Lublin*, 125.
111. Both spellings occur in the files, but also 'Reinhart'. Heydrich himself is known to have allowed his first name to be used in the variant 'Reinhardt'. Individual evidence in Peter Black, 'Die Trawniki-Männer und die Aktion Reinhard', in Musial, ed., *'Aktion Reinhardt'*, 309–52, 308–9.
112. See Globocnik's 'Meldung über die wirtschaftliche Abwicklung der Aktion Reinhardt' of 5 Jan. 1944, 402-PS, *IMT* xxxiv. 70 ff., 72.
113. BAB, NS 19/1755, the content of the papers not only emerges from the covering letter; this was a memo, 'The State of Jewish Labour' in which the 'shortcomings and questions are revealed that require an order to deal with them', and a piece entitled, 'The Jews in the district of Lublin', along with the third paper dealing with 'Germanness' (*Deutschtum*). This was passed on by Himmler's personal staff to the Staff Headquarters of the Reichskommissar for the Strengthening of the German Nation.
114. Pohl, *Lublin*, 126–7.
115. *Das Diensttagebuch des deutschen Generalgouverneurs in Polen 1939–1945*, ed. Werner Präg and Wolfgang Jacobmeyer (Stuttgart, 1975), 506 ff. See also the interpretation in Christian Gerlach, 'Die Bedeutung der deutschen Ernährungspolitik für die Beschleunigung des Mordes an den Juden 1942. Das Generalgouvernment und die Westukraine', in Christian Gerlach, *Krieg, Ernährung, Völkermord. Forschungen zur deutschen Vernichtungspolitik im Zweiten Weltkrieg* (Hamburg, 1998), 197 ff., who stresses the role of nutritional policy in the 'acceleration' of the murder of the Jews.
116. *Diensttagebuch*, ed. Präg and Jacobmeyer, 515 ff.
117. Pohl, *Lublin*, 127.
118. Ibid. 122; Pohl, *Ostgalizien*, 197.
119. Arad, *Belzec*, 73.
120. Arad, *Belzec*, 37 ff.
121. Police meeting, 18 June 1942, Report by Deputy Department Head, Alfons Oswald; in *Diensttagebuch*, ed. Präg and Jacobmeyer, 511.
122. Pohl, *Lublin*, 131–2 and Christopher Browning, *Ordinary Men. Reserve Battalion 101 and the Final Solution in Poland* (New York and London, 1992), 55 ff.

123. Pohl, *Ostgalizien*, 196–7.

124. Arad, *Belzec*, 80–1; BAB, NS 19/2655, Ganzenmüller to Wolff, 28 July 1942.

125. On the deportations from the individual districts see the lists in Arad, *Belzec*, 383 ff.

126. On this and the following see Pohl, *Lublin*, 127–8.

127. BAB, NS 19/2655, 29 July 1941, here also Himmler's letter of thanks of 13 August.

128. *Dienstkalender*, ed. Witte et al., 491 ff.; Rudolf Höß, *Commandant in Auschwitz* (London, 1959), 210, 223 ff.

129. Walter Laqueur and Richard Breitman, *Breaking the Silence* (New York, 1986); Hoess, *Commandant*, 236–7.

130. BAB, NS 19/1757, printed in Longerich, *Ermordung*, 201. See also Pohl, *Lublin*, 128.

131. See the overview by Jace Andrzej Mlynarczyk, 'Treblinka—ein Todeslager der "Aktion Reinhard"', in Musial, ed., *'Aktion Reinhardt'*, 257–81. On the building phase also Arad, *Belzec*, 37 ff.

132. Israel Gutman, *The Jews of Warsaw 1939–1943: Ghetto, Underground, Revolt* (Bloomington, Ind., 1982), 197 ff.

133. Christopher Browning, 'Nazi Ghettoization Policy in Poland 1939–1941' in Browning, *Path to Genocide*, 28–56, 47 ff.

134. Gutman, *Jews*, 219 ff.

135. Arad, *Belzec*, 392–3.

136. Pohl, *Lublin*, 132 ff.; Arad, *Belzec*, 387 provides a different date for the start of the deportation.

137. Arad, *Belzec*, 393 ff.; Jacek Mlynarczyk, 'Organisation und Durchführung der "Aktion Reinhardt" im Distrikt Radom', in Musial, ed., *'Aktion Reinhardt'*, and Mlynarczyk, *Judenmord in Zentralpolen. Der Distrikt Radom im Generalgouvernement 1939–1945* (Darmstadt, 2007). Robert Seidel, *Deutsche Besatzungspolitik in Polen. Der Distrikt Radom 1939–1940* (Paderborn 2006), 310 ff.

138. Pohl, *Ostgalizien*, 216 ff.

139. BAB, NS 19/3959, Office diary of the personal secretary.

140. Pohl, *Ostgalizien*, 223 ff.

141. Ibid. 238 ff.

142. Ibid. 245.

143. On the methods employed in ghetto clearances see Mlynarczyk, *'Judenmord'*, 251 ff.

144. On Treblinka see the overview by Mlynarczyk, 'Treblinka', 257–81. On the building phase, see Arad, *Belzec*, 37 ff.

145. Arad, *Belzec*, 81 ff.

146. Ibid. 89 ff.

147. PRO, HW 16/23, messages 12 and 13/15, transmitted 11 Jan. 1943, in Peter Witte and Stephen Tyas, eds, 'A New Document on the Deportation and Murder of Jews during "Einsatz Reinhardt" 1942', *HGS* 15 (2001), 468–86. In the original document the figure for Treblinka is 71,355; this should, however, be 713,555, as the addition of the remaining numbers reveals. The number of victims for Belzec is confirmed by calculations produced by the German Holocaust historian Wolfgang Scheffler in a report of 1973. He calculated the number of victims in this extermination camp as 441,442, and had thus been only 7,000 away from the true figure. See Wolfgang Scheffler, ' Die Zahl der in den Vernichtungslagern der "Aktion Reinhard" ermordeten Juden', in Helge Grabitz

and the Judicial Authority Hamburg, eds, *Täter und Gehilfen des Endlösungswahns. Hamburger Verfahren wegen NS-Gewaltverrechen 1946–1996* (Hamburg, 1998), 215–41.

148. This figure is also quoted in the Korherr-Bericht, the report by the SS chief statistician on the state of the 'Final Solution' at the end of 1942 (ND NO 5194).

149. Korherr-Bericht, ND NO 5194.

150. Thomas Sandkühler, *'Endlösung' in Galizien. Der Judenmord in Ostpolen und die Rettungsinitiative von Berthold Beitz, 1941–1944* (Bonn, 1996), 461.

151. Korherr estimated the surplus deaths and the number of emigrations in the General Government up to 31 Dec. 1942 as 427,920 in Korherr-Bericht, Kurzfassung, ND NO 5193.

152. Cf. the overview in Gustavo Corni, *Hitlers Ghettos: Voices from a Beleaguered Society 1939–1944* (London and New York, 2002), 300 ff.

153. Pohl, *Ostgalizien*, 215; Pohl, *Lublin*, 157 ff.; Sandkühler, *'Endlösung'*, 181 ff.

154. IfZ, MA 679/9, 9 May 1942; see also MA 679/8, *KTB* Oberquartiermeister, 8 May 1942, discussion at armaments inspection.

155. *Diensttagebuch*, ed. Präg and Jacobmayer, 11 May 1942, p. 495.

156. Ibid. Hauptabteilungsleitersitzung, 22 June 1942, pp. 516–17.

157. Sandkühler, *'Endlösung'*, 182.

158. Pohl, *Ostgalizien*, 15.

159. BAB, NS 19/1765, Minute of the chief of staff of the SSPF Cracow, 27 July 1942, printed in Longerich, *Ermordung*, 202 ff. This concerns a 'new order' by Krüger. On Himmler's order of 18 May 1942.

160. Pohl, *Ostgalizien*, 235.

161. BAB, NS 19/2462.

162. BAB, NS 19/352, Letter from Gienanth to OKW, 18 Sept. 1942; letter from Himmler to head of WVHA etc., 9 Oct. 1942 (ibid.); cf. Naasner, *Machtzentren*, 362.

163. Boelcke, ed., *Deutschlands Rüstung*, 189.

164. See *Dienstkalender*, ed. Präg and Jacobmayer, 22 Sept. 1942, p. 566. Presentation to Führer: 'Jewish emigration—what is to be done next?' Himmler's next point for discussion, as noted in his presentation draft, is: 'Settlement of Lublin—Lorrainers, Germans from Bosnia, Bessarabia etc' and 'conditions Gen. Gouv.—Globus' (Globocnik's nickname). The fact that the 'emigration', i.e. murder of the Jews from the district of Lublin could not be implemented at the rate notified by Himmler clearly had repercussions on Globocnik's settlement projects.

165. ND NO 1611, printed as a facsimile in Helge Grabitz and Wolfgang Scheffler, *Letzte Spuren: Ghetto Warschau, SS-Arbeitslager Trawniki, Aktion 'Erntefest': Fotos und Dokumente über Opfer des Endlösungswahns im Spiegel der historischen Ereignisse*, 2nd edn (Berlin, 1993), 179.

166. *VOGG* 665–6, 1 Nov. 1942, Polizei VO 28 Oct. 1942 and 683 ff., 14 Nov. 1942, Polizei VO 10 Nov. 1942.

167. This was how the SSPF for Galicia, Katzmann, put it in his report to HSSPF Krüger on 30 June 1943 See Berenstein et al., *Faschismus*, 358 ff., 361. In this context Katzmann mentioned another 'instruction' issued in autumn 1942 by the Higher SS and Police Commander to implement 'the accelerated total resettlement of the Jews'.

168. Mlynarczyk, 'Organisation', 191–2, based on BAM, RH-53-23/700.

169. It is generally accepted by scholars even today that the deportations from Upper Silesia had already begun on 15 February 1942 (see Czech, *Kalendarium*, or Steinbacher,

'*Musterstadt' Auschwitz*,' 277). This mistaken view is based on information from Martin Broszat, who referred to a letter to him from the International Tracing Service in Arolsen dated 27 Mar. 1958. A glance at the original of this letter shows, however, that in Arolsen at the time 'deportations of Jews from Beuthen could only be established from 15.5.1942 [*sic!*]'. I should like to thank Klaus Lankheit of the Archive of the Institut für Zeitgeschichte in Munich for letting me have a copy of the original of this letter.

170. Steinbacher, '*Musterstadt' Auschwitz*, 278 ff.

171. See p. 291.

172. Lucjan Dobroszycki, ed., *The Chronicle of the Lodz Ghetto 1941–1944* (New Haven and London, 1984), 128, 131–2, 136 ff., 140 ff., 145, 157.

173. Dobroszycki, ibid. (p. 139) states that there had already been around 3,000 fatalities by the end of March.

174. Ibid. 153–4, 156–7, 159 ff., and 194.

175. Ibid. 248 ff.

176. Ibid. 261.

177. Ibid. 266 and 127.

178. Longerich, *Politik*, 492.

179. Individual evidence can be found in Czech, *Kalendarium*.

180. Steinbacher, '*Musterstadt' Auschwitz*, 285–6.

181. Czech, *Kalendarium*, 20 March; for 12 May 1942 Czech shows that in Bunker I 1,500 Jewish men, women, and children from Sosnowitz were murdered.

182. According to Christian Gerlach, *Kalkulierte Morde. Die deutsche Wirtschafts und Vernichtungspolitik in Weissrussland 1941 bis 1944* (Hamburg, 1999), 683 ff., the number of 2,200 murdered Jews is quoted from the activity report for the month of February of Abwehrkommando III (B), 12 Mar. 1942, BADH FW 490, A. 28.

183. Dieter Pohl, 'Schauplatz Ukraine: Der Massenmord an den Juden im Militärverwaltungsgebiet und im Reichskommissariat 1941–1943', in Frei et al., eds, *Ausbeutung, Vernichtung, Öffentlichkeit. Neue Studien zur nationalsozialistschen Lagerpolitik* (Munich, 2000), 148 ff.

184. Helmut Krausnick and Hans-Heinrich Wilhelm, *Die Truppe des Weltanschauungskrieges. Die Einsatzgruppen der Sicherheitspolizei und SD, 1938–1942* (Stuttgart, 1981), 177–8.

185. StA Minsk, 370-1-53; Gerlach, *Kalkulierte Morde*, 689. The explanation for the drop in executions given here is also found in IfZ, Fb 101/35, Lagebericht der EG A für den Zeitraum 16 Oct. 1941–31 Jan. 1942 and in Fb 104/2, Aufzeichnung der Abt. II des KdS, early 1942.

186. IfZ Fb 101/35, EG A report for the period 16 Oct. 1941–31 Jan. 1942.

187. Gerlach, *Kalkulierte Morde*, 690; ZSt, II 202 AR-Z 184/67; Final Report of 28 July 1967.

188. Gerlach, *Kalkulierte Morde*, 690–1, 700 (Slutsk); ZSt, II 202 AR 629/73, Instruction of 14 Jan. 1982.

189. Andrej Angrick and Peter Klein, *Die 'Endlösung' in Riga: Ausbeutung und Vernichtung 1941–1944* (Berlin, 2006), 338 ff. Scheffler and Schulle, eds, *Buch der Erinnerung*, 11 ff. and 26–7.

190. IfZ Fb 104/2.

191. ZSt, II 202 AR 629/73, Instruction of 14 Jan. 1982; cf. Gerlach, *Kalkulierte Morde*, 695 and 700; according to Gerlach, Djatlowo (district of Slonim) may possibly be added to this, with 400 victims

192. Wassili Grossmann et al., eds, *Das Schwarzbuch. Der Genozid an den sowjetischen Juden* (Reinbek, 1995), 251–2. Gerlach, Kalkulierte Morde, 690.

193. ZSt, UdSSR 401, 412, Reports from the occupied Eastern territories, no. 10, 3 July 1942, Annex 10.

194. The court reconstructed this visit in the course of the Heuser trial: Irene Sagel-Grande et al., *Justiz und NS-Verbrechen. Sammlung deutscher Strafurteile wegen nationalsozialistischer Tötungsverbrechen 1945–1966* (Amsterdam, 1968–81), xix, no. 552, Judgement of 21 May 1963, 192.

195. Gerlach, *Kalkulierte Morde*, 695–6; ZSt, II 202 AR 629/73, Instruction 14 Jan. 1982; II 202 AR-Z 94d/59, Indictment of 15 May 1966. See also Judgement Landgericht of 17 July 1969 in Sagel-Grande et. al., eds, *Justiz und NS-Verbrechen*, xxxii, no. 712, and IfZ, Fb 85/I, Gebietskommissar Lida, 8 Apr. 1943: 'The district of Lida had a figure of 20,000 Jews. In a single action of five days in May last year they were finished off [erledigt] down to 4,500.'

196. Gerlach, *Kalkulierte Morde*, 697; Martin Dean, *Collaboration in the Holocaust: Crimes of the Local Police in Belorussia and Ukraine, 1941–1944* (New York, 2000), 84–5.

197. Activities Report of the outstation, 27 May 1942, in *Unsere Ehre*, 247–8, Gerlach, *Kalkulierte Morde*, 698–9; ZSt, 202 AR-Z 5/60, Judgement LG Bochum v. 11 Apr. 1979.

198. ZSt, 202 AR-Z 37/60, 5, 1850 ff., Gebietskommissar Haase at the conference of Gebietskommissare, 8 Apr. 1943.

199. Gerlach, *Kalkulierte Morde*, 700.

200. Ibid. 700–1, 202; ZSt, SA 477, Judgement LG HH v. 25 June 1974; Dean, *Collaboration*, 87.

201. Gerlach, *Kalkulierte Morde*, 701.

202. Ibid. 702.

203. Ibid. 702–3; ZSt, AR-Z 16/67, Vermerk Staatsanwaltschaft Oldenburg, 19 Dec. 1969.

204. Gerlach, *Kalkulierte Morde*, 704; Tätigkeitsbericht Gruppe Arlt, in *Unsere Ehre*, 252–3.

205. Gerlach, *Kalkulierte Morde*, 705.

206. ND 3428-PS, *IMT* xxxii. 279 ff., Report of Kube to RK Ostland, 31 July 1942.

207. Pohl, 'Ukraine', 158; ZSt, AR-Z 122/68, Staatsanwaltschaft München I, Einstellungsverfügung v. 11 Oct. 1972 and volume of documents with copies of correspondence of the Reich Security Service from Kiev City Archive; ZSt, 04 a AR 1632/68, Verdict of the Superior Penal Division of the Land court in Duisburg, 6 Sept. 1968.

208. Pohl, 'Ukraine', 158; there is an account of this massacre in Grossmann et al., eds, *Das Schwarzbuch*, 81.

209. CDJC, CXLIV-474, Situation Report for April 1942, quoted in Pohl, 'Ukraine', 158–9.

210. Zst, II 204 AR-Z 437/67 Final Report, 15 Apr. 1970

211. BAB, R 6/69.

212. Schmuel Spector, *The Holocaust of the Volhynian Jews: 1941–1944* (Jerusalem, 1990), 184.

213. Ibid.

214. ZSt, II 204 AR-Z 139/67, Instruction Leiter Zentralstelle NRW v. 5 Apr. 1977.

215. ZSt, AR-Z 26/61, Judgement LG Oldenburg v. 28 Sept. 1966.

216. Pohl, 'Ukraine', 159.

217. ZSt, AR-Z 76/70, 160 ff., Instruction Zentralstelle Staatsanwaltschaft Dortmund, 20 Dec. 1977.

218. ZSt, AR-Z 76/70, 1f, Instruction Zentralestelle v. 27 July 1970, Lagebericht des Aufsichtsoffiziers des SchumaBtl. 117 v. 15 June 1942 (78d-f) and Activity Report of the Schuma Btl. 117 an KdG Kiew v. 27 July 1942 (78s-u); ferner II AR-Z 131/67, Investigations of the District Commissar of Tschudnow Final Report, 29 Aug. 1975, 2, 360 ff.

219. Dean, *Collaboration*, 83.

220. ZSt, AR-Z 67/67.

221. Judgement LG Berlin v. 9 Mar. 1960, in *Justiz und NS-Verbrechen* 16, no. 490; Pohl, 'Ukraine', 160.

222. Dean, *Collaboration*, 93. The minutes of the session are to be found in in BAB R 6/243; Report of the KdS on the result of the meeting, 31 Aug. 1942, quoted in Gerlach, *Kalkulierte Morde*, 714.

223. Gerlach, *Kalkulierte Morde*, 711 ff.

224. ZSt, 204 AR-Z 393/59, Indictment Frankfurt a. M., 28 Mar. 1966; Judgement LG Frankfurt a. M. 6 Feb. 1973 (SA 447).

225. Gerlach, *Kalkulierte Morde*, 719 ff.; Himmler's order on 27 Oct. 1942 was recorded in writing and is quoted in Helmut Heiber, *Reichsführer! Briefe an und von Himmler* (Stuttgart, 1968), 165.

226. These are the ghettos of David Gorodok, Gorodiscze, Wysock, and Stolin.

227. Quoted in the Frankfurt indictment of 27 Mar. 1966.

228. ZSt, 204 AR-Z 442/67, Zentralestelle, Final Report, 18 Mar. 1971.

229. Dean, *Collaboration*, 93, based on Case ZSt, AR-Z 393/59. This also includes further information about the murders in Kremenec and Schumsk.

230. ZSt, II 204 AR-Z 163/67, Instruction Zentralstelle Staatsanwaltschaft Dortmund, 22 Nov. 1976; Instruction Zentralestelle, 31 Mar. 1970.

231. See also the interim report by the Israeli police, 22 Sept. 1968, in the files of the same trial.

232. ZSt, AR-Z 113/67, Final Report, 18 Mar. 1970 and Instruction Zentralstelle Staatsanwaltschaft Dortmund, 10 June 1976.

233. Gerlach, *Kalkultierte Morde*, 710 and 718.

234. ZSt, II 204 AR-Z 111/67, 159 ff., Interim Report, Zentrale Stelle 23 May 1967 and 182 ff., Final Report of the Zentrale Stelle, 10 Apr. 1968.

235. Pohl, *Ukraine*, 161.

236. ZSt, AR 225/60, Final Report, 29 Aug. 1962.

237. ZSt, 204 AR-Z 334/59, 1134 ff., Instruction Leiter Zentralstelle v. 8 Dec. 1965. Gerlach, *Kalkulierte Morde*, 717, gives the figure of 16,000–19,000 dead.

238. Gerlach, *Kalkulierte Morde*, 716–17. This includes, among other things, the towns of Domatschewo (Domatshchevo) und Tmaaschowka (Tmashchovka).

239. ZSt, Landgericht Nürnberg-Fürth, Judgement (SA 368), 27 May 1963; on Sdolbunow also II 204 AR 251/59 G Judgement, Landgericht Stade, 3 Feb. 1960.

240. ZSt, II 204 AR-Z 437/67, Final Report, 15 Apr. 1970.

241. Pohl, 'Ukraine', 161, refers to civilian officials carrying out murders on their own account.

242. Pohl, 'Ukraine', 162; Spector, *Holocaust*, 186. On the murders of the Generalkommissariat of Zhitomir see Wendy Lower, *Nazi Empire Building and the Holocaust in Ukraine* (Chapel Hill, NC, 2005), 132 ff., who examines them in the context of German occupation and settlement policy.

243. Arad, *Belzec*, 131 ff., 396–7; Sara Bender, *The Jews of Bialystok during World War II and the Holocaust* (Waltham, 2008), 185 ff. 1967 (Bielefeld, 2003), 186–208; Gerlach, *Kalkulierte Morde*, 723 ff.

244. NO 3392, printed as a facsimile in the illustrations to Gerald Fleming, *Hitler and the Final Solution* (London, 1984).

245. On the Jewish resistance in the Soviet Union in 1942 and the conditions under which it began, see Spector, *Holocaust*, 188 ff.; Shalom Cholawsky, *The Jews of Bielorussia during World War II* (Amsterdam, 1998). Shmuel Spector provides an overview in 'Jewish Resistance in Small Towns of Eastern Poland', in Norman Davies and Antony Polonsky, eds, *Jews in Eastern Poland and the USSR 1939–46* (New York, 1991), 138–44; Isaiah Trunk, *Judenrat: The Jewish Councils in Eastern Europe under Nazi Occupation* (New York, 1972), 451, contains a typology of the attitude of the Jewish councils towards the resistance, which covers the whole period of the Holocaust in Eastern Europe.

246. Examples in Spector, *Holocaust*, 206 ff. and Cholawsky, *Jews*, 203.

247. Spector, *Holocaust*, 189 ff.; see esp. tables and figures, pp. 198–9.

248. Cholawsky, *Jews*, 185 ff.

249. Ibid. 192.

250. Ibid. 193.

251. Ibid. 159 ff. There is further literature on some of these locations. See Yehuda Bauer, 'Jewish Baranowicze in the Holocaust', *YVS* 31 (2003), 95–151; Hans Heinrich Nolte, 'Destruction and Resistance: The Jewish Shtetl of Slonim 1941–44', in Robert W. Thurston and Bernd Bonwetsch, eds, *The People's War: Responses to World War II in the Soviet Union* (Urbana and Chicago, 2000), 19–53; Nachum Alpert, *The Destruction of Slonim Jewry: The Story of the Jews of Slonim during the Holocaust* (New York, 1989); Jakow Suchowolskij, 'Es gab weder Schutz noch Erlösung, weder Sicherheit noch Rettung. Jüdischer Widerstand und die Untergang des Ghettos Glubokoje', *Dachauer Hefte* (2004), 11–38; on Glebokie also Gerlach, *Kalkulierte Morde*, 739.

252. Cholowasky, *Jews*, 209 ff.

253. Nolte, 'Destruction'.

254. Bauer, 'Jewish Baranowicze'.

255. Reuben Ainsztein, *Jüdischer Widerstand im deutschbesetzten Osteuropa während des zweiten Weltkrieges* (Oldenburg, 1993), 221 ff. This account is largely based on the memoirs of one of the leaders of the resistance in the Minsk Ghetto: Hersch Smoliar, *Resistance in Minsk* (Oakland, Calif., 1966).

256. Gerlach, *Kalkulierte Morde*, 744.

257. Himmler's diary does not reveal what was discussed at these meetings. The only exception is his presentation to Hitler on 3 May: Himmler's surviving diary reveals that issues of the Waffen-SS were discussed; but further, non-military themes were also discussed, which Himmler did not record (*Dienstkalender*, ed. Witte et al., 415, n. 6).

258. Klarsfeld, *Vichy*, 122. On the raids and deportations of summer 1943 see also Poznanski, *Jews*, 251 ff.

259. The deportations are individually documented in Czech, *Kalendarium*, and in Klarsfeld, *Vichy*.

260. CDJC, XXVb-147, Protokoll, 1 Sept. 1942, published in Klarsfeld, *Vichy*, 447–8.

261. Ibid. 168.

262. CDJC, XXVc-177, letter from BdS Knochen to RSHA, 23 Sept. 1942, in Klarsfeld, *Vichy*, 469.

263. Ibid. 474.

264. Bob Moore, *Victims and Survivors: The Nazi Persecution of the Jews in the Netherlands 1940–1945* (London, 1997), 54 ff.

265. Ibid. 79 ff.

266. Ibid. 66 ff.

267. PAA, Inland II g 189, 3 July 1942; cf. Browning, *Final Solution*, 101.

268. On the beginning and course of the deportations, see Jacob Presser, *The Destruction of the Dutch Jews* (New York, 1969), 146 ff.; Moore, *Victims*, 91 ff.; Gerhard Hirschfeld, *Fremdherrschaft und Kollaboration. Die Niederlande unter deutsche Besatzung, 1940–1945* (Stuttgart, 1984), 145 ff.

269. For individual details see Moore, *Victims*, and Ron Zeller and Pim Griffioen, 'Judenverfolgung in den Niederlanden und in Belgien während des Zweiten Weltkrieges. Eine vergleichende Analyse', 1999. *Zeitschrift für Sozialgeschichte des 20. und 21. Jahrhunderts*, part 1 (1996), 30–54. On the problem of Dutch collaboration, see Hirschfeld, *Nazi Rule*.

270. PAA, Inland II g 182, Dienststelle Brüssel to the AA, 11 Nov. 1942. On the German persecution of the Jews in Belgium, see Maxime Steinberg, *L'Etoile et le Fusil. La Question Juive 1940–1942* (Brussels, 1983); Hilberg, *Destruction*, 635 ff., and the essays in the collection, Dan Michman, ed., *Belgium and the Holocaust: Jews, Belgians, Germans* (Jerusalem, 1998).

271. Hilberg, *Destruction*, 641 ff.

272. Some significant results of the comparison by Zeller and Griffioen in 'Judenverfolgung'.

273. Telegram from Dienststelle AA Brüssel to AA, 9 July 1942, published in S. Klarsfeld and M. Steinberg, *Die Endlösung der Judenfrage in Belgien. Dokumente* (Paris, 1980), 32–3. According to this, there were concerns on the part of the military administration about the deportation of Jews of Belgian nationality.

274. Juliane Wetzel, 'Frankreich und Belgien', in Benz, *Dimension* 129.

275. Report Dienststelle AA Brüssel, 24 Sept. 1942 as well as Militärbefehlshaber to Feld- und Oberfeldkommandanturen, 25 Sept. 1942, published in Klarsfeld and Steinberg, *Endlösung*, 45 ff.

276. See p. 285.

277. PAA, Inland II g 177, note from Luther, 21 Aug. 1942; Inland II g 183, German Embassy to AA, 6 July 1942; cf. Frederick Barry Chary, 'Bulgaria and the Jews: "The Final Solution", 1940 to 1944', Ph.D. University of Pittsburgh, 1968, 77. On the events at the end of 1941 see PAA, Inland II g 183, Note of 27 Nov. 1942 (also published in *Akten zur Deutschen Auswärtigen Politik* (*ADAP*) E I 132–3) and [presentation note] Luther, 4 Dec. 1941, in the same file.

278. Browning, *Final Solution*, 103.

279. The procedure is shown in PAA, Inland II g 200; cf. Browning, *Final Solution*, 103–4.

280. See PAA, Inland II g 208, note from Luther, 11 Aug. 1942 and letter from Luther to German Embassy, 17 Aug. 1942, ibid. See Randolph L. Braham, *The Politics of Genocide: The Holocaust in Hungary*, rev. edn, 2 vols (New York, 1994), 261 ff.

281. PAA, Inland II g 208, [presentation note] from Luther for Ribbentrop, 19 Sept. 1942, cf. Meir Michaelis, *Mussolini and the Jews: German-Italian Relations and the Jewish Question in Italy, 1922–1945* (Oxford, 1978), 317 ff.

282. PAA, Inland II g 192, cf. Browning, *Final Solution*, 107.

283. PAA, Inland II g 177.

284. Browning, *Final Solution* 93.

285. PAA, Inland II g 183, instruction from Luther, 19 June 1942.

286. PAA, Inland II g 194. See Hilberg, *Destruction*, 756 ff.; Holm Sundhausen, 'Jugoslawien', in Benz, ed., *Dimension*, 323. Sundhausen quotes the report by the German ambassador, Kasche, of 24 July 1942 in Inland II g 78/2, H 300390 ff.

287. Andreas Hillgruber, ed., *Staatsmänner und Diplomaten bei Hitler. Vertrauliche Aufzeichnungen über Unterredungen mit Vertretern des Auslandes 1939–1941* (Frankfurt a. M., 1961), i. 575 ff., Note of 9 June 1941 concerning the conversation of 6 June 1941. The expression 'ethnic cleansing' (*Flurbereinigung*) was used by Hitler.

288. Jozo Tomasevich, *War and Revolution in Yugoslavia: Occupation and Collaboration*, (Stanford, 2001), 392 ff.

289. Hilberg, *Destruction*, 756 ff.; Tomasevich, *War*, 592 ff.

290. Hilberg, *Destruction*, 714 f.

291. PAA, Inland II g/86, 300363.

292. Czech, *Kalendarium*, 18, 22, 26 and 30 Aug. 1942.

293. ND NO 5193, Bericht des Inspektors für Statistik (Korherr-Bericht), 19 Apr. 1943.

294. See p. 229.

295. On the Romanian *Judenpolitik* see Jean Ancel, 'German-Romanian Relations during the Second World War', in Randolph L. Braham, ed., *The Tragedy of Romanian Jews* (New York, 1994), 57–76; Braham, 'Antonescu and the Jews', *YVS* 23 (1993), 213–80; Hilberg, *Destruction*, 808 ff.; Krista Zach, 'Rumänien', in Benz, *Dimension*, 31 ff. Radu Ioanid, *The Holocaust in Romania: The Destruction of Jews and Gypsies under the Antonescu Regime 1940–1944* (Chicago, 1999).

296. PAA, Inland II g 203, Killinger to D III, 6 Aug. 1941.

297. PAA, Inland II g 200, Message from Killinger to AA v. 12 Aug. 1942; Browning, *Final Solution*, 115 ff.

298. The Romanian Commissar for the Jews, Lecca, announced to members of the German press on 7 August that the Jews would be 'resettled' from Romania 'within a short time'; in PAA, Inland II g 200, Report by Richter. The *Bukarester Tageblatt* reported the following day under the heading 'Romania cleansed of Jews', that 25,000 Jews had already been deported 'to the East, via Transnistria' in September and October. Further contingents were to follow in the spring of 1943; by the autumn of 1943 all Jews were to have left Romania.

299. PAA, Inland II g 177, note by Luther, 21 Aug. 1942.

300. PAA, Inland II g 177.

301. PAA, Inland II g 177, note by Luther, 21 Aug. 1942.

302. Details of the Hungarian *Judenpolitik* in Braham, *Politics*.

303. See p. 224.

304. Braham, *Politics*, 214 ff.

305. PAA, Inland II g 208, letter from OKW, Wehrwirtschaftsamt to AA, 21 July 1942; cf. also Braham, *Politics*, 284 ff.

306. PAA, Inland II g 208, Himmler to Ribbentrop, 30 Nov. 1942.

307. In the same file.

308. Frederik Chary, *The Bulgarian Jews and the Final Solution 1940–1944* (Pittsburgh, 1981), 44 ff. and 80 ff.

309. Ibid. 80 ff.

310. PAA, Inland II g 183, Presentation note by Luther of 10 September; Note by Sonn-leithner, 15 Sept. 1942. On these deportation preparations See Chary, *Bulgarian Jews*, 113 ff.; Browning, *Final Solution*, 123; Hans-Joachim Hoppe, 'Bulgarien', in Benz, *Dimension*, 285–6.

311. PAA, Inland II g 194, Presentation note by Luther for Ribbentrop, 24 July 1942 and AA to Envoy Kasche, 10 Aug. 1942; cf. Browning, *Final Solution*, 115.

312. PAA, Inland II g 177, Presentation note by Luther for Ribbentrop, 11 Sept. 1942; see Daniel Carpi, 'The Rescue of Jews in the Italian Zone of Occupied Croatia', in Daniel Cesarani and Sarah Kavanaugh, eds, *Nazi Holocaust: Critical Concepts in Historical Studies* (London, 2004), v. 670–730.

313. Ibid.

314. PAA, Inland II g 194, note for Luther, 17 Sept. 1942; cf. Browning, *Final Solution*, 122–3.

315. Details in Hagen Fleischer, 'Griechenland', in Benz, *Dimension*, 241 ff. and Mark Mazower, *Inside Hitler's Greece: The Experience of Occupation, 1941–1944* (New Haven and London, 1993), 235 ff.

316. PAA, Inland II g 190, Suhr to Rademacher, 11 July 1942. On the Italian attitude see also Daniel Carpi, 'Notes on the History of the Jews in Greece during the Holocaust Period: The Attitude of the Italians (1941–1943)', in Cesarani and Kavanaugh, eds, *Nazi Holocaust*, v. 731–68, 738 ff.

317. See PAA, Inland II g 190; dealt with in detail in Browning, *Final Solution*, 136–7, 140–1.

318. Hannu Rautkallio, *Finland and the Holocaust: The Rescue of Finland's Jews* (New York, 1987), 163 ff. See critical comments on this in William B. Cohen and Jörgen Svensson, 'Finland and the Holocaust', *HGS* 9 (1995), 94–120, esp. 82–3.

319. See Hillgruber, *Staatsmänner*, ii. 106 ff. about the Hitler–Antonescu discussion and PAA, Inland II g 200, report from Richter, 26 Nov. 1942 about Antonescu's statements concerning his special discussion with Ribbentrop. See also Browning, *Final Solution*, 124–5.

320. PAA, Inland II g 208, note from Luther to Weizsäcker of 24 Sept. 1942.

321. See p. 324.

322. See Hillgruber, *Staatsmänner*, ii. 111 ff. report, 25 Sept. 1942, about the meeting of 24 Sept.

323. PAA, Inland II g 194, Büro RAM to Luther, 25 Sept. 1942.

324. See pp. 326, 404.

325. See various documents by Richter and Luther in PAA, Inland II g 200.

326. PAA, Inland II g 177.

327. See Hilberg, *Destruction*, 845 f.

328. PAA, Inland II g 183, Deutsche Gesandtschaft an AA, 2.11.

329. PAA, Inland II g 183, report of 16 Nov. 1942, attached Bulgarian verbal note of 12 Nov. Cf. on this subject Chary, *Bulgarian Jews*, 118 ff.

330. IfZ, MA 1538/2 (NA, T 175/658), vol. 9, note about discussion on 23 Oct. 1942, in which the Romanian Judenkommissar, Lecca also took part, 24 Oct. 1942.

331. PAA, Inland II g 183, sent by Schellenberg, 21 Nov. 1942.

332. Cf. Braham, *Politics*, 287 ff. and Browning, *Final Solution*, 128 ff.

333. PAA, Inland II g 208, report from Luther about this to Ribbentrop, 6 Oct. 1942.

334. Instruction from Luther to Jagow, 14 October; report from Jagow, 17 Oct. 1942, both in PAA, Inland II g 208.

335. See PAA, Inland II g 208, report from Jagow of 27 October and 13 Nov. 1942 about conversations with Kállay.

336. Ibid., letter from Himmler to Ribbentrop, 30 Nov. 1942.

337. ND NG 4586, report from Wisliceny, 8 Oct. 1942; cf. Braham, *Politics*, 288 ff.

338. PAA, Inland II g, message from Luther to Rademacher, 14 Dec. 1942.

339. See the extensive correspondence between the missions and Luther in October and November 1942, in PAA, Inland II g 194. On this process, in greater detail, Browning, *Final Solution*, 137 ff.

340. See in particular Carpi, 'The Rescue of Jews', 670–720, 465 ff.

341. PAA, Inland II g 192.

342. PAA, Inland II g 194, Report from the legation in Zagreb.

343. Hans Thomsen, *Deutsche Besatzungspolitik in Dänemark 1940–1945* (Düsseldorf, 1971); See Herbert, *Best*, 330 ff.

344. Samuel Abrahamsen, *Norway's Response to the Holocaust* (New York, 1991), 83 ff.

345. Ibid. 104 ff. On the deportation of the Norwegian Jews see also Hilberg, *Destruction*, 584 ff.

346. Abrahamsen, *Norway's Response*, 130 ff.

18. The Further Development of the Policy of Extermination after the Turning of the War in 1942–1943: Continuation of the Murders and Geographical Expansion of the Deportations

1. Decrees of 28 Oct. and 14 Nov. 1942; *VOBlGG*, 665–6 and 683 ff.

2. See Katzmann Report (018-L, *IMT* xxxvii. 391 ff.) of 30 June 1943: 'With the further instruction of the Higher SS and Police Leader the accelerated total resettlement of the Jews to be carried out.' This decision, must, as the context of the report reveals, have been made after the decree of 10 Nov. 1942 and before the erection of the large camp in Lemberg for 8,000 Jews.

3. Pohl, *Ostgalizien*, 248 ff.

4. Arad, *Belzec*, 393 ff.; Mlynarczyk, *Judenmord*, 277; Seidel, *Besatzungspolitik*, 339 ff.

5. Frank Golczewski, 'Polen', in Benz, ed., *Dimension*, 476.

6. Ibid. 392–3.

7. ND NO 1882, Himmler to Krüger, 11 Jan. 1943.

8. NS 19/1740; see also Himmler's order to Krüger, 16 Feb. 1943. On 23 July 1943 Pohl informs Himmler that the concentration camp in the Warsaw ghetto has been constructed (ibid.).

9. Arad, *Belzec*, 392; Gutman, *Jews*, 307 ff.

10. Jan Erik Schulte, 'Zwangsarbeit für die SS: Juden in der Ostindustrie Gmbh', in Norbert Frei et al., *Ausbeutung, Vernichtung, Öffentlichkeit: Darstellungen und Quellen zur Geschichte von Auschwitz* (Munich, 2000), 43–74.

11. Literature on the Warsaw Ghetto Uprising: Gutman, *Jews*; Daniel Blatman, *For Our Freedom and Yours: Jewish Labour Bund in Poland 1939–1949* (Jerusalem, 1998); Reuben Ainsztein, *The Warsaw Ghetto Revolt* (New York, 1979).

12. Shmuel Krakowski, *War of the Doomed* (New York, 1984).

13. BAB, NS 19/2648, 12 May 1943; see also the file note from Himmler, 10 May 1943, in which he stated that the 'evacuation of the remaining 300,000 Jews in the General Government was to be carriedout...at the greatest speed' (original published in *Faschismus*, ed. Berenstein et al., no. 278, S.354–5); cf. Sandkühler, *Endlösung*, 197

14. *Diensttagebuch*, ed. Präg and Jacobmeyer, 31 May 1943, p. 682; see also Himmler's telephone notes, 20 May 1943: 'Judenevakuierung' (BAB, NS 19/1440).

15. Pohl, *Ostgalizien*, 246 ff.; Sandkühler, *Endlösung*, 194 ff.

16. Report from Katzmann to Krüger, 30 June 1943; published in *Faschismus*, ed. Berenstein et al., no., 284, pp. 358 ff. It is, however, unlikely that Katzmann was actually in a position to name the number of victims with such great precision; the figure he gives must therefore refer only to the extent of the mass murder for which he was responsible.

17. BAB, NS 19/1432, file memorandum Himmler, 19 June 1943, resolution Bandenbekämpfung.

18. Pohl, *Lublin*, 160. Pohl, Krüger, und Globocnik agreed to take over the camps in a discussion held on 7 Sept. 1943 (note from Pohl on the same day, ND NO 599, published in *Faschismus*, ed. Berenstein et al., no. 370, pp. 459–60).

19. ND NO 1036, Minute of 19 Jan. 1944 betr. die Umwandlung der Zwangsarbeitslager der SSPF in KZ.

20. BAB, NS 19/1740, 11 June 1943., Himmler to Pohl and Kaltenbrunner. Himmler specified that 'a large park be laid out' on the area of the former ghetto.

21. Pohl, *Ostgalizien*, 348 ff.; Schulte, 'Zwangsarbert', 59.

22. BAB, NS 19/1571, Himmler's, order of 5 July 1943; after objections from Pohl and Globobnik Himmler withdrew his order on 20 July 1943 (letter from Brandt, 20 July 1943, ibid.), but on 24 July 1943 he renewed his instruction.

23. By September 1943 he distanced himself from this order again, but in December he renewed it.

24. *Faschismus*, ed. Berenstein et al., no. 290, pp. 369–70, letter from Greiser to Pohl, 14 Feb. 1944. Reference is also made there to Himmler's order of 11 June 1942, the original of which has disappeared. In greater detail, see Michael Alberti, *Die Verfolgung und Vernichtung der Juden im Reichsgau Wartheland, 1939–1945* (Wiesbaden, 2006), 472 ff.

25. Alberti, *Verfolgung*, 473–4.

26. Ibid. 481 ff.

27. Encyclopedia of the Holocaust, article on Bialystok. On the history of this see Sara Bender, 'From Underground to Armed Struggle—The Resistance Movement in the Bialystok Ghetto', YVS 23 (1993), 145–71; Bender, *Jews*, 243 ff.

28. Arad, *Belzec*, 396; Sara Bender, 'The "Reinhardt Action" in the Bialystok District', in Freia Anders et al., *Bialystok in Bielefeld. Nationalsozialistische Verbrechen vor dem Landgericht Bielefeld, 1958 bis 1967* (Bielefeld, 2003), 204 ff.

29. Gunnar S. Paulsson, *Secret City: The Hidden Jews of Warsaw, 1940–1945* (New Haven and London, 2002), esp. table, p. 57 and summary of the results, pp. 231 ff.

30. Pohl, *Ostgalizien*, 363 ff.

31. Ibid. 362; a few such cases are described in memoirs: thus, for example, Helene Kaplan managed to reach Oberammergau (Helene Kaplan, *I never left Janowska* (New York, 1991)); Stefan Szende reached Norway with Organisation Todt and escaped from there to Sweden (Stefan Sender, *Der letzte Jude aus Polen* (Zurich, 1945)). Binca Rosenberg, who lived in the ghetto of Kolomyja, assumed a false identity in 1943 and survived the end of the war as a waitress in Heidelberg (Binca Rosenberg, *Versuch zu überleben... Polen 1941–1945* (Frankfurt a. M., 1996)).

32. Pohl, *Ostgalizien*, 368 ff.

33. Krakowski, *War*, 11.

34. Christopher Browning, ' "Judenjagd": Die Schlussphase der "Endlösung" in Polen', in Jürgen Matthäus and Klaus-Michael Mallmann, eds, *Deutsche, Juden, Völkermord. Der Holocaust in Geschichte und Gegenwart* (Darmstadt, 2006), 177–89, points out, on the basis of contemporary reports, that the police in the General Government routinely killed a large number of people who had escaped the ghettos. But it was only from summer 1943 onwards that these 'Jew-hunts' became the focus of police work.

35. Pohl, *Lublin*, 168 ff.

36. Pohl, *Ostgalizien*, 371 ff.

37. Order by the SSPF, 13 Mar. 1943, published in *Faschismus*, ed. Berenson et al., no. 275, p. 352. On the practice in the district of Lublin see also: Pohl, *Lublin*, 168 ff., Musial, *Zivilverwaltung*, 308 ff. The procedure was similar in the district of Galicia: Pohl, *Ostgalizien*, 366.

38. On Treblinka und Sobibor see Ainsztein, *Widerstand*, 396 ff.

39. Helge Grabitz and Wolfgang Scheffler, *Letzte Spuren: Ghetto Warschau, SS-Arbeitslager Trawniki, Aktion 'Erntefest'*, 2nd edn (Berlin, 1993), 328 ff.

40. Pohl, *Lublin*, 168–9.

41. Schulte, 'Zwangsarbeit', 69.

42. ND PS-1919.

43. ND NO 1831, Minute of the meeting of 20 Aug. 1943 concerning Reich labour deployment issues with special reference to the conditions in the occupied territories, which took place on 13 July 1943.

44. On the following see Gerlach, *Kalkulierte Morde*, 733 ff.

45. Cf. pp. 237 f.

46. Gerlach, *Kalkulierte Morde*, 733 ff.

47. BAB, NS 2/83, 13 Aug. 1943, RFSS concerning Jewish labour deployment in the occupied East; NOKW 2386, *Kriegstagebuch* Oberkommando 3. Panzer-Armee, Quartiermeister 2, 4 Nov. 1943; cf. Gerlach, *Kalkulierte Morde*, 739.

48. Gerlach, *Kalkulierte Morde*, 739; Jakow Suchowolskij, 'Es gab weder Schutz noch Erlösung, weder Sicherheit noch Rettung. Jüdischer Widerstand und de Untergang des Ghettos Glubokoje', *Dachauer Hefte* (2004), 11–38; on Glebokie see also Gerlach, *Kalkulierte Morde*, 739.

49. Gerlach, *Kalkulierte Morde*, 739–40.

50. Ibid. 741 ff.

51. OS, 504-2-8. On this in detail see Angrick and Klein, *Endlösung*, 382 ff.

52. ND NO 2403. Participants in this meeting, apart from Bach-Zelewski, included the HSSPF Russia North, Prützmann, the HSSPF East, Krüger, the head of the RSHA, Kaltenbrunner, the director of the WVHA, Pohl, and the head of the Command Staff of the RFSS, Knoblauch.

53. Angrick and Klein, *Endlösung*, 381 ff.

54. Scheffler, 'Schicksal', 39.

55. Angrick and Klein, *Endlösung*, 401.

56. Avraham Tory, *Surviving the Holocaust: The Kovno Ghetto Diary*, ed. Martin Gilbert, (Cambridge, Mass., and London, 1990), 468 ff.; Alfred Streim, 'Konzentrationslager auf dem Gebiet der Sojetunion', *Dachauer Hefte* 5 (1989), 176; *Enzyklopädie des Holocausts*, Article 'Kowno'.

57. Yitzhak Arad, *Ghetto in Flames: The Struggle and Destruction of the Jews in Vilna in the Holocaust* (New York, 1981), 355 ff.

58. Ibid. 401 ff.

59. Streim, 'Konzentrationslager', 177–8; *Enzyklopädie des Holocaust*, article 'Vaivara'.

60. Corni, *Hitlers Ghettos*, 308–9; Tory, *Surviving the Holocaust*.

61. Ainszstein, *Widerstand*, 236 ff.; Arad, *Ghetto in Flames*, 373 ff.

62. Dov Levin examines these ghettos in his study *Fighting Back: Lithuanian Jewrys's Armed Resistance to the Nazis 1941–1945* (New York and London, 1997). He also deals with the ghettos of Vilnius (Wilna) and Kaunas (Kovno).

63. Ibid. 174–5.

64. *Enzyklopädie des Holocaust*, article on Riga.

65. Gruner, *Arbeitseinsatz*, 311 ff.

66. Adler, *Verwaltete Mensch*, 224 ff. The Berlin action was linked with the resettlement of ethnic Germans from the region of Lodz to Zamosz in the district of Lublin; some of the Poles resident there were to have been deported to the Reich to replace the Jewish workers deported from there. See Bruno Wasser, *Himmlers Raumplanung im Osten; der Generalplan Ost in Polen 1940–1944* (Basle, 1993), 135 ff.

67. See Wolf Gruner, *Widerstand in der Rosenstrasse. Die Fabrik-Aktion und die Verfolgung der 'Mischehen' 1943* (Frankfurt a. M., 2005) which corrects Nathan Stolzfuß, *Resistance of the Heart: Intermarriage and the Rosenstraße Protest in Nazi Germany* (New Brunswick, NJ, 2001). Significantly, in his diary entry for 11 Mar. 1943 Goebbels regretted the arrest of 'Jews, male and female, from privileged marriages', which had led to 'fear and confusion'. See Elke Fröhlich, ed., *Die Tagebücher von Joseph Goebbels*. Teil II: *Diktate 1941–1945*. Band 7: *Januar–März 1943* (Munich, 1993), 528.

68. Frederik Gottwaldt and Diana Schulle, *Die 'Judendeportationen' aus dem deutschen Reich 1941–1945* (Wiesbaden, 2005), 400 ff.

69. Adler, *Verwaltete Mensch*, 201.

70. Gottwaldt and Schulle, *Judendeportationen*, 419 ff.

71. Ibid. 337 ff.

72. ND 3363-PS, 18 Dec. 1943; Adler, *Verwaltete Mensch*, 202. See the significantly elevated figures of the deportees to Theresienstadt for Hamburg (Transport 19 Jan. 1944) and Berlin (10 Jan. 1944): *Hamburger jüdische Opfer des Nationalsozialismus. Gedenkbuch* (Hamburg, 1995), xix and *Gedenkbuch Berlins der jüdischen Opfer des Nationalsozialismus* (Berlin, 1995), 1422.

73. Gottwaldt and Schulle, *Judendeportationen*, 400 ff.

74. Ibid. 427 ff.

75. Ibid. 204.

76. On the deportations from the Netherlands see Hirschfeld, 'Niederlande', in Benz et al., *Dimension*, 137–66 Presser, *Destruction*; Moore, *Victims*, 100 ff.; Hilberg, *Destruction*, 624 ff.

77. Figures concerning the deportations and the number of victims in Hirschfeld, 'Niederlande', 162 ff.

78. PAA, Inland II g 182, 4 Dec. 1942. On the Jewish persecution in Belgium from 1942 onwards see Wetzel, 'Frankreich und Belgien', 130; Hilberg, *Destruction*, 642 ff.; S. Klarsfeld and M. Steinberg, *Die Endlösung der Judenfrage in Belgien. Dokumente* (Paris, 1980).

79. PAA, Inland IIg, 5 Jan. 1943.

80. Published in Klarsfeld and Steinberg, *Endlösung*, 70.

81. Wetzel, 'Frankreich und Belgien', 130.

82. Ibid. 135.

83. Marion Schreiber, *Silent Rebels: The True Story of the Raid on the Twentieth Train to Auschwitz* (London, 2003).

84. Wetzel, 'Frankreich und Belgien', 130. This figure includes 5,000 victims who fled to France and were deported from there to Auschwitz. The pre-war Jewish population is estimated at 90,000, of whom 42,000 were registered as Jews in autumn 1942. The Germans calculated additional unrecorded children (ibid. 109–10).

85. Zeller and Griffioen, 'Judenverfolgung', pt. I, 41.

86. This is a summary of the significant findings of Zeller and Griffioen, 'Judenverfolgung'.

87. PAA, Inland II g 194, correspondence between the Foreign Ministry and the embassy March/April; according to Czech's *Kalendarium*, the trains arrived in Auschwitz on 7 and 13 May.

88. PAA, Inland IIg 194, Helm's report from 18 Apr. 1944.

89. See below, pp. 402 f.

90. Hilberg, *Destruction*, 718.

91. See the telegram from the embassy in Berne to Luther, 4 Jan. 1943, Inland II g 204; see. Browning, *Final Solution*, 155.

92. Klingenfuß to Eichmann, PAA, Inland II g 203 a; on this complex, see Browning, *Final Solution*, 154 ff.

93. Ibid. 155.

94. PAA, Inland II g 177.

95. PAA, Inland II g 177, Presentation note by Wagner, 12 July 1943.

96. See the telegram from the embassy in Berne to Luther, 4 Jan. 1943, Inland II g 204; cf. Browning, *Final Solution*, 155.

97. ND NG 2652.

98. They were contained in Heydrich's figure of 700,000 French Jews living in the 'unoccupied zone'.

99. On the deportation of the Greek Jews, See Hilberg, *Destruction*, 740 ff.; Fleischer, 'Griechenland', in Benz, ed., *Dimension*, 241 ff.; Danuta Czech, 'Deportation und Vernichtung der griechischen Juden im KL Auschwitz', in *Hefte von Auschwitz* 11 (1970), 5–37.

100. PAA, Inland II g 190.

101. On the transports see the schedule in Fleischer, 'Griechenland', 273; on the Bergen-Belsen Transport, ibid. 255 ff.

102. See PAA, Inland II g 190; Browning, *Final Solution*, 161–2; Jonathan Steinberg, *All or Nothing: The Axis and the Holocaust 1941–1943* (London, 1990), 94 ff.; and Meir Michaelis, *Mussolini and the Jews: German-Italian Relations and the Jewish Question in Italy, 1922–1945* (Oxford, 1978), 313 ff.

103. Chary, 'Bulgaria', 124 ff.; on the persecution of the Jews in Bulgaria in 1943 see in particular also Hoppe, 'Bulgarien', 285 ff.; Nir Baruch, *Der Freikauf. Zar Boris und das Schicksal der bulgarishen Juden* (Sofia, 1996); Michael Bar-Zohar, *Beyond Hitler's Grasp: The Heroic Rescue of Bulgaria's Jews* (Holbrook, 1998); on Dannecker see Claudia Steur, *Theodor Dannecker. Ein Funktionär der 'Endlösung'* (Essen, 1997), 92 ff.

104. Chary, 'Bulgaria', 129 ff.; see also Baruch, *Freikauf*, 103 ff. Translation of the preserved original in Dieter Ruckhaberle and Christiane Ziesecke, eds, *Rettung der bulgarischen Juden—1943. Eine Dokumentation* (Berlin, 1984). This exhibition catalogue also contains other major documents in facsimile.

105. Chary, 'Bulgaria', 178 ff., 197 ff., 224 ff.

106. Ibid. 178 ff.; Baruch, *Freikauf*, 120 ff.

107. Ribbentrop to Beckerle, 4 Apr. 1943, PA, Büro Staatssekretär Bulgarien, 5; cf. Chary, 'Bulgaria', 269–70.

108. Chary, 'Bulgaria', 275 ff.

109. Ibid. 295 ff.

110. On the Jewish question in France after the occupation of the southern zone see Klarsfeld, *Vichy*, 193 ff.; Susan Zuccotti, *The Holocaust, the French and the Jews* (London, 1993), 166 ff.; Renee Poznanski, *Jews in France during World War II* (London, 2001), 356 ff.

111. Klarsfeld, *Vichy*, 194 ff.

112. Ibid. 200 ff.

113. Transport nos. 46–53, 9 Feb.–25 Mar. 1943; details in Klarsfeld, *Vichy*, document section.

114. CDJC, XXVI-71, published in Klarsfeld, *Vichy*, 489 ff.; on this see also ibid. 208.

115. This involved the marking of identity cards and food cards and the internment of Jews without French nationality in the border and coastal regions: Klarsfeld, *Vichy*, 198 ff.

116. Klarsfeld, *Vichy*, 205, 210 ff.; Daniel Carpi, *Between Hitler and Mussolini: The Jews and the Italian Authorities in France and Tunisia* (London, 1994), 113–14.

117. Klarsfeld, *Vichy*, 198, 206, 214 ff.; Carpi, *Between*, 105 ff.

118. Klarsfeld, *Vichy*, 220; Carpi, *Between*, 125 ff.; Letter from Mackensen to the Foreign Ministry, 18 Mar. published in Klarsfeld, *Vichy*, 510–11.

119. Klarsfeld, *Vichy*, 220 ff.; Carpi, *Between*, 129 ff.
120. Details in Klarsfeld, *Vichy*, 226 ff.; Carpi, *Between*, 136 ff.
121. Current state of the Jewish question in France, CDJC, XXVc 214, published in Klarsfeld, *Vichy*, 501–2.
122. He later spoke in terms of three months: Note for Knochen of 27 Mar. 1943, CDJC, XLVI–V, 27 Mar. 1943, published in Klarsfeld, *Vichy*, 516 ff.
123. See p. 363.
124. Note for Knochen of 27 Mar. 1943, CDJC, XLVI–V, 27 Mar. 1943, published in Klarsfeld, *Vichy*, 516 ff.; see ibid., 224–5.
125. CDJC, XXVc-235, published in Klarsfeld, *Vichy*, 519.
126. Klarsfeld, *Vichy*, 224.
127. Ibid. *Vichy*, 230 ff.
128. Ibid. 232.
129. Hagen to Röthke, 16 June 1943, CDJC, XXVII-17, published in Klarsfeld, *Vichy*, 535.
130. Klarsfeld, *Vichy*, 242 ff., 255–6.
131. Ibid. 239 ff.
132. Ibid. 256.
133. Note by Hagen, 11 Aug. 1943, CDJC, XXVI 35, Klarsfeld, *Vichy*, 550–1.
134. Note by Röthke, 15 August about discussion with Laval the previous day, CDJC, XXVI-36; Klarsfeld, *Vichy*, 551 ff.; see the account ibid. 262 ff.
135. Note from the head of state to Ambassador Brinon, 24 Aug. 1943, CDJC, XXVII-33; Klarsfeld, *Vichy*, 557; see the account ibid. 270.
136. Current state of the Jewish question in France, 21 July 1943; Klarsfeld, *Vichy*, 545 ff.
137. On the history of the Italian Jews under Fascism see Susan Zuccotti, *The Italians and the Holocaust: Persecution, Rescue and Survival* (New York, 1987); Michaelis, *Mussolini*.
138. Himmler's note about his visit to Mussolini on 11–14 Oct. 1942, published in Helmut Krausnick, 'Himmler über seinen Besuch bei Mussolini', *VfZ* 4 (1956), 423–6.
139. The different attitudes towards the 'Jewish question' are examined in detail in Steinberg, *All or Nothing*.
140. Müller to Bergmann AA, 25 Feb. 1943 with a quotation from Himmler's letter to Ribbentrop, 29 Jan. 1943, published in Klarsfeld, *Vichy*, 495 ff.
141. ND NG 4956, Teleprinter message from the special train Westphalia to Wolf; Reply from Abteilung Deutschland, 24 Feb. 1943.
142. Sztojay to Horthy, 28 Apr. 1943, published in *Eichmann in Ungarn. Dokumente*, ed. Jenó Levai, (Budapest, 1961), 61 ff.
143. Message to Knochen, 24 May 1943 CDJC, XLVIIIa-24, Klarsfeld, *Vichy*, 528.
144. Best's letters to AA, 13 Jan. 1943, PAA, Inland II g 184 (*ADAP* E V, 39). Shortly before, Best had discussed the situation with Luther and Rademacher in Berlin after Luther had decided to postpone further measures for the time being. PAA, Inland II g 184, note by Rademacher of 23 Dec. 1942. On these events see Herbert, *Best*, 361–2; Browning, *Final Solution*, 160–1.
145. Report by Best of 24 Apr. 1942, ibid., *ADAP* E V, no. 344.
146. Luther to Ribbentrop, 28 Jan. 1943 and Ribbentrop's marginal notes on this document of 1 Feb. 1943 (PAA, Inland II g 184). Himmler decided in June that 'provisional Jewish

measures in Denmark should be suspended until he issues a new order on this question'; ibid., Wagner to Kaltenbrunner, 30 June 1943.

147. Best to Himmler, 22 Aug. 1943, BAB, NS 19/3302; cf. Herbert, *Best*, 351; further Telegram to AA, 30 Aug. 1943, *ADAP* E VI, 259.

148. Telegram from Ribbentrop (Führerhauptquartier) to Best, 31 Aug./1 Sept. 1943, PAA, Inland II g 184, *ADAP* E VI, 268.

149. PAA, Inland II g 184, Telegram of 31 Aug. 1943, *ADAP* E VI, 259, note 4.

150. Report by Best, 6 September, PAA, Inland II g 184, *ADAP* E VI, 282; Herbert, *Best*, 358.

151. PAA, Inland II g 184 (*ADAP* E VI, 287). On the interpretation of the telegram see esp. Herbert, *Best*, 362 ff. Best aimed for the right of command over all police troops in Denmark, and wanted to set up a special court with himself at its head. See telegram to AA, 1 Sept. 1943, *ADAP* E VI, 271.

152. Ribbentrop's 'note for the Führer', 23 Sept. 1943, *ADAP* E VI, 344.

153. As Best put it in his telegram of v. 5 Oct. 1942.

154. Telegram to AA, 20 Sept. 1943, *ADAP* E VI, 332.

155. For greater details see Leni Yahil, *The Rescue of Danish Jewry* (Philadelphia, 1983), 223 ff. Gunnar S. Paulsson, ' "The Bridge over Oeresund". The Historiography on the Expulsion of the Jews from Nazi-Occupied Denmark' in *Journal of Contemporary History* 30 (1995), 431–64, and (ibid., 465–79) the reply by Hans Kirchhoff, 'Denmark: A Light in the Darkness of the Holocaust? A Reply to Gunnars S. Paulsson'. See also Hans Kirchhoff, 'The Rescue of the Danish Jews in October 1943' in David Bankier and Israel Gutman eds, *Nazi Europe and the Final Solution* (Jerusalem, 2003), 539–55.

156. PAA, Inland II g 184, telegram 5 Oct. 1942.

157. Fröhlich, *Die Tagebücher*, Teil II, Band 4, 4 June 1942, p. 444; ibid., Band 12, 11 May 1944, p. 270.

158. Ibid., Band 6, 13 Dec. 1942, p. 439; ibid., Band 9, 7 Aug. 1943, pp. 231–2; ibid., Band 11, 14 Jan. 1944, pp. 87–8.

159. Ibid., Band 8, 30 May 1943, p. 22; ibid., Band 13, 23 Aug. 1944, pp. 295–6.

160. Ibid., Band 8, 21 Mar. 1943.

161. Ibid., Band 7, 2 Mar. 1943, p. 454.

162. In the case of Bulgaria, the Western powers expressly made the signing of the ceasefire with Bulgaria in September 1944 dependent on the repeal of the Bulgarian anti-Semitic laws. Baruch, *Freikauf*, 159 ff. See also pp. 148–9, according to which there were indications that the American side, in their first probings concerning the withdrawal of Bulgaria from the Axis, raised the issue of Bulgaria's policy towards the Jews

163. On the persecution of the Jews in Italy after September 1943 see Lliana Picciotto Fargion, 'Italien', in Benz, ed., *Dimension*, 199–227; Michaelis, *Mussolini*, 342 ff.; Lutz Klinkhammer, *Zwischen Bündnis und Besetzung. Das nationalsozialistische Deutschland und die Republik von Salò* (Tübingen, 1993), 530 ff.

164. On Dannecker's work in Italy see Steuer, *Dannecker*, 113 ff.

165. Presentation note by Wagner, 4 Dec. 1943, PAA, Inland II g 192, in *ADAP* E VII, 111.

166. Ibid.

167. Michaelis, *Mussolini*, 388–9.

168. Fargion, 'Italien', 206 and 222–3.

169. On this see Fleischer, 'Griechenland', 260 ff.

170. See the memoirs of Errikos Sevillias, *Athens-Auschwitz* (Athens, 1983). In April there was also a corresponding 'action' in Albania, in which around 300 Jews were arrested and deported via Belgrade to Bergen-Belsen. See Gerhard Grimm, 'Albanien', in Benz, ed., *Dimension* 227.

171. Fleischer, 'Griechenland', 265 ff.

172. Sundhausen, 'Jugoslawien', 325.

173. On German *Judenpolitik* in France after the collapse of Italy see Klarsfeld, *Vichy*, 276 ff.; Steinberg, *All or Nothing*, 163; Zuccotti, *Holocaust*, 180 ff.; Poznanski, *Jews*, 390 ff.

174. Klarsfeld, *Vichy*, 278 ff.; Zuccotti, *Holocaust*, 181 ff.

175. See pp. 392 ff.

176. Klarsfeld, *Vichy*, 289.

177. Ibid. 298 ff.; Zuccotti, *Holocaust*, 190 ff.

178. On the government reshuffle see Eberhard Jäckel, *Frankreich in Hitlers Europa. Die deutsche Frankreichpolitik im Zweiten Weltkrieg* (Stuttgart, 1966), 293–4.

179. CDJC, CXXXII-56, Klarsfeld, *Vichy*, 574 ff.; Zuccotti, *Holocaust*, 197 ff.

180. Klarsfeld, *Vichy*, 320. Slightly different figures quoted in the literature may be found in Juliane Wetzel, 'Frankreich und Belgien', in Benz, ed., *Dimension*, 132–3.

181. Hilberg, *Destruction*, 699 f.

182. Ladislav Lipscher, *Die Juden im slowakischen Staat 1939–1945* (Munich, 1979), 114.

183. NG 4407, 29 June 1943.

184. Lipscher, *Juden*, 137 ff.; Gilda Fatran, 'Die Deportation der Juden aus der Slowakei', *Bohemia* 37 (1996), 98–119, 98–9; Tatjana Tönsmeyer, 'Die Einsatzgruppe H in der Slowakei in Finis Mundi—Endzeiten und Weltenden im östlichen Europa', in Joachim Hösler and Wolfgang Hösler, eds, *Festschrift für Hans Lemberg zum 65. Geburtstag* (Stuttgart, 1998), 167–88.

185. 21 July 1943, ND NG 4749.

186. Report by Veesenmayer, 22 Dec. 1943, ND NG 4651; see also Statement by Wisliceny, ND NG 1823.

187. Hilberg, *Destruction*, 789 f.

188. Lipscher, *Juden*, 144 ff.; Ivan Kamenec, 'Die erfolglosen Versuche zur Wiederaufnahme der Deportationen der slowakischen Juden', *TSD* (2002), 318–37.

189. Lipscher, *Juden*, 178–9; Fatran, 'Deportation', 116 ff.

190. PAA, Inland II g 208, Luther to Ribbentrop, 16 Jan. 1942; cf. Browning, *Final Solution*, 132.

191. PAA, Inland II g 208, Bergmann to Bormann. 9 Mar. 1943.

192. *IMT* xxxv. 428, D-736.

193. Sztojay to Horthy, 28 Apr. 1943, in *Eichmann in Ungarn*, ed. Lévai, 61 ff. On German activities with regard to Hungary in the spring and summer of 1943 see Braham, *Politics*, 250 ff.

194. Diary entry 8 May 1943, See Fröhlich, *Die Tagebücher*, Teil II, Band 8, p. 236 on statements by Hitler the previous day.

195. *ADAP* E VI, no. 43.

196. *Donauzeitung*, 1 June 1943, cf. Hilberg, *Destruction*, 876.

197. Report of 10 Dec. 1943, NG 5560, in Randolph L. Braham, *The Destruction of Hungarian Jewry: A Documentary Account* (New York, 1968), no. 110.

198. Braham, *Politics*, 381 ff.; on the organization of the occupying administration, ibid. 406 ff.

199. Ibid. 396 ff.

200. In Götz Aly and Christian Gerlach, *Der letzte Kapitel Realpolitik, Ideologie und der Mord an den ungarischen Juden* (Stuttgart, 2002) the authors argue in contrast that four stages of escalation can be perceived within the decision-making process concerning the deportation of the Hungarian Jews (Aly and Gerlach, *Kapitel*, 249 ff.). Thus, according to them, there had been no 'long planned preparation of the deportations', no deportation plan existing from the beginning; the decision for ghettoization and deportation was to be seen not as a 'unique act' but as an 'interactive process' (ibid. 252, 266, 416). In their view many factors must be taken into account to explain this process: the redistribution of resources (finance, labour, food supplies, military and economic potential), the disposing of social burdens, internal political mobilization in Hungary, relations with the German ally, etc. In their view, 'Hungarian pressure' played a large part in the acceleration of the deportations (ibid., summary on p. 265). This interpretation is the result of an analysis of situational factors and in my view takes too little account of the intention of the Germans, demonstrable as early as the end of 1941, and pursued continuously from then onwards, to set the deportations in motion with the help of the Hungarians. It was the German occupation that created the crucial preconditions for radicalizing the anti-Semitic policy of the Hungarian government to such an extent that the deportations could begin. The events of 1944 must be seen in this perspective. Moreover, in my view, Aly and Gerlach overstress rational motives (*Zweck-rational*) in their analysis of the decision-making process. Thus, for example, the Germans plainly had no genuine interest in an effective exploitation of the workforce of the Jewish prisoners, as Aly and Gerlach themselves show in their account of the treatment of the deported workers: only a very few of the 200,000 Jewish forced labourers were in fact deployed in the context of the Fighter Programme for which they had originally been requested. Instead, they worked mostly in functions that had little to do with the war and with no regard for their qualifications. Because of their bad treatment, the productivity of the forced labourers, who had been robbed of all material and emotional support by separation from their families, was poor and mortality rates were extremely high so that a third of the forced labourers had died by the end of the war (ibid. 409).

201. Ibid. 259.

202. Veesenmayer to the AA, 22 Apr. 1944, BD no. 144.

203. Braham, *Politics*, 510 ff. and 446 ff.

204. Diary entry 27 Apr. 1944 in Fröhlich, *Die Tagebücher*, Teil II, Band 12, p. 199.

205. Braham, *Politics*, 573 ff.

206. Ibid. 674 ff.

207. Ibid. 662 ff.

208. Veesenmayer was already working on the basis of four transports each carrying 3,000 Jews on 4 May 1944: telegram to the AA (BD, No. 153).

209. BD, no. 157, Thadden to German Mission in Bratislava, 6 May 1944.

210. See Braham, *Politics*, 733 ff.

211. The figure of 433,000 also contains several thousand Jews who were deported to Auschwitz after the official halt to deportations.

212. Braham, *Politics*, 780 ff.

213. Ibid. 850 ff.

214. Ibid. 1205 ff.

215. Telegram from Veesenmayer to Ribbentrop, 6 July 1944, *ADAP* E VIII, 101.

216. PAA, Inland II g 210; Braham, *Destruction*, 700–1. Ribbentrop to Veesenmayer, 10 July 1944. Veesenmayer to the AA, 24 Aug. 1944. On this complex, Braham, *Politics*, 884–5.

217. PAA, Inland II g 209; Braham, *Politics*, 887–8.

218. Braham, *Politics*, 890 ff.

219. PAA, Inland II g 210, Gesandtschaft Budapest to the AA, 19 Aug. 1944, in *ADAP* E VIII, 167. On the events in August see Braham, *Politics*, 911 ff.

220. PAA, Inland II g 210, Veesenmayer to AA, 24 Aug. 1944.

221. PAA, Inland IIg 209, Veesenmayer to Ribbentrop in Braham, *Destruction*, no. 214.

222. Braham, *Politics*, 916.

223. Bauer's view, (*Jews for Sale? Nazi Jewish Negotiations, 1933–1945* (New Haven and London, 1994), 221), that Himmler's order to halt the deportations of 24 August has to do with the beginning of negotiations between Kurt Becher and Saly Mayer in Switzerland, concerning the possible release of Jews for foreign currency or the delivery of goods, cannot be verified. In order to influence these negotiations effectively, it would have made more sense, as had already happened in Strasshof in June, to keep certain contingents of deportees within the territory of the German Reich in camps as hostages.

224. Braham, *Politics*, 947 ff.

225. At this point the the decision to dismantle the extermination facilities in Auschwitz had either already been taken or was about to happen. See Czech, *Kalendarium*, 31 Dec. 1944 (last murder with gas) and 25 Nov. 1944 (start of the destruction of the crematoria).

226. Veesenmayer's report to the AA, 18 Oct. 1944, *ADAP* E VIII, 275. Eichmann kept to this intention until at least mid-November (Veesenmayer, report 13 Nov. 1944, PAA, Inland II g 209).

227. Braham, *Politics*, 957 ff.

228. PAA, Inland IIg 209.

229. Braham, *Politics*, 976 ff.

230. Shmuel Spector, '"Action 1005": Effacing the Murder of Millions', *HGS* 1 (1990), 157–73.

231. Ibid. 159 ff.

232. Ibid. 161 ff.

233. Adalbert Rückerl, *NS Vernichtungslager in Spiegel deutscher Strafprozesse. Belzec, Sobibor, Treblinka, Chelmno* (Munich, 1977), 280–1.

234. Arad, *Belzec*, 165 ff., 370 ff.

235. Sybille Steinbacher, *Auschwitz: A History* (London, 2005), 123 ff.

236. On this see Bauer, *Sale*; Richard Breitman and Shlomo Aronson, 'The End of the "Final Solution"?: Nazi Plans to Ransom Jews in 1944', *Central European History* (*CEH*) 25 (1992), 177–203.

237. Alexandra-Eileen Wenck, *Zwischen Menschenhandel und Endlösung. Das Konzentrationslager Bergen-Belsen* (Paderborn, 2000), 78 ff.

238. *Dienstkalender*, ed. Witte et al., Agenda, 10 Dec. 1942, pp. 637 ff. Himmler's entry read: '4. special camp for Jews with relatives in America'. '5 Resettlement of the Jews—release

in return for foreign currency—not in favour—more important as hostages.' To the phrase 'release in return for foreign currency' Himmler, plainly as a result of the discussion, later added the words 'from abroad'. In a note made the same day, Himmler recorded that Hitler had given him permission for the 'release of Jews in return for foreign currency' if they 'bring in notable amounts of foreign currency from abroad', quoted ibid. 639. On the building of the special camp: BAB, NS 19/2159, RFSS to Müller, December 1942.

239. Wenck, *Menschenhandel*, 102 ff.

240. See p. 326.

241. Wenck, *Menschenhandel*, 289 ff.; Bauer, *Sale*, 145 ff.; Braham, *Politics*, 1069 ff.

242. Wenck, *Menschenhandel*, 294; Braham, *Politics*, 733 ff., 1088 ff.; Bauer, *Sale*, 196 ff. Braham gives a figure of 18,000–20,000 people for the Austrian transports.

243. Bauer, *Sale*, 225 f.

244. Breitman and Aronson, 'The End of the Final Solution?', 202

245. Ibid.

246. On the clearance of the concentration camps and the death marches see Karin Orth, *Das System der nationalsozialistischen Konzentrationslager. Eine politische Organisationsgeschichte* (Hamburg, 1999), 270 ff.; Daniel Blatman, 'Die Todes-märsche—Entscheidungsträger, Mörder und Opfer', in Ulrich Herbert et al., eds, *Die nationalsozialistischen Konzentrationslager. Entwicklung und Struktur* (Göttingen, 1998), ii. 1063–92; Yehuda Bauer, 'The Death Marches, January—May 1945', in Michael Marrus, ed., *The Nazi Holocaust* (Westport, Conn., 1989), ii. 491–511.

247. Angrick and Klein, *Endlösung*, 419 ff.

248. Christoph Dieckmann, 'Das Ghetto und das Konzentrationslager in Kaunas 1941–1944', in Herbert et al., eds, *Konzentrationslager*, 458.

249. Streim, 'Konzentrationslager', p. 184.

250. Angrick and Klein, *Endlösung*, 436 ff.

251. Blatman, 'Todesmärsche', 1071.

252. Orth, *System*, 282–3; Reinhard Henkys, 'Ein Todesmarsch in Ostpreußen', *Dachauer Hefte* 20 (2004), 3–21; Blatman, 'Todesmärsche', 1079 ff.

253. Orth, *System*, 282 ff.; Angrick and Klein, *Endlösung*, 442 ff.

254. Orth, *System*, 271 ff.; Andrzej Strzelecki, 'Der Todesmarsch der Häftlinge aus dem KL Auschwitz', in Herbert et al., eds, *Konzentrationslager*, ii. 1093–112.

255. Orth, *System*, 276 ff.; Strzelecki, 'Der Todesmarsch', 1093–112; Blatman, 'Todes-märsche', 1073, on the proportion of Jewish prisoners.

256. Orth, *System*, 279 ff.

257. Ibid. 282 ff.; Bernhard Strebel, *Das KZ Ravensbrück. Geschichte eines Lagerkomplexes* (Paderborn, 2003), 459 ff.

258. The original document has been lost; this is only passed on in Felix Kersten, *Totenkopf und Treue. Himmler ohne Uniform* (Hamburg, n.d), 343.

259. NO 1210, statement from Höß, 14 Mar. 1946; Orth, *System*, 303.

260. According to the British Embassy's report to the Foreign Office, letter dated 27 Mar. 1945, PRO FO 188/526.

261. This also includes the journey by Norbert Masur, a Jew of Swedish nationality, who visited Himmler on behalf of the World Jewish Congress in April 1945, and won

from him, amongst other things, the agreement that 1,000 Jewish women would be freed from Ravensbrück: PRO, FO 188/526, Masur's report; in 1945 Masur published a longer version of his meeting with Himmler (Norbert Masur, *En Jude Talar Med Himmler* (A Jew Speaks with Himmler), (Stockholm, 1945)). In mid-March the President of the International Red Cross, Carl Jacob Burkhardt, met Kaltenbrunner and discussed, amongst other things, the transfer of Jewish prisoners to Switzerland, See Jean-Claude Favez, *The Red Cross and the Holocaust* (Cambridge, 1999), 258 ff., esp. 265.

262. Bauer, *Sale*, 242 ff.; on the problem of the different figures for Jews who were rescued see Steven Koblik, *Stones Cry Out: Sweden's Response to the Persecution of the Jews, 1933–1945* (New York, 1988), 138–9.

263. Orth, *System*, 305 ff.; Harry Stein, 'Buchenwald—Stammlager', in Wolfgang Benz and Barbara Distel, eds, *Der Ort des Terrors. Geschichte der nationalsozialistischen Konzentrationslager*, vol. iii: *Sachsenhausen, Buchenwald* (Munich, 2006), 301–56, 345. Katrin Greiser, *Thüringen 1945. Todesmärsche aus Buchenwald. Überblick, Namen, Orte* (Weimar, 2001), 5–16; Christine Schäfer, *Die Evakuierungstransporte des KZ Buchenwald und seiner Außenkommandos* (Weimar-Buchenwald, 1983); Katrin Greiser, 'Die Auflösung des Lagerkomplexes Buchenwald und die Todesmärsche aus den Aussenlagern in Rheinland und in Westfalen in März und April 1945', in Jan Erik Schulte, ed., *Konzentrationslager in Rheinland und Westfalen 1933–1945: Zentrale Stenerung und regionale Initiative* (Paderborn, 2005), 281 ff.

264. Wenck *Menschenhandel*, 374 ff.; from the extensive British literature on the liberation of Belsen cf. Joanne Reilly, *Belsen: The Liberation of a Concentration Camp* (London, 1998).

265. Orth, *System*, 310 ff.; Stanislav Zámečnik, 'Kein Häftling darf lebend in die Hände des Feindes fallen. Zur Existenz des Himmler-Befehls vom 14./18.April 1945', *Dachauer Hefte* 1 (1985), 219–31.

266. Orth, *System*, 315–16.

267. Ibid. 317 ff; Stanislav Zámečnik, 'Dachau-Stammlager', in Wolfgang Benz and Barbara Distel, eds, *Der Ort des Terrors. Geschichte der nationalsozialistischen Konzentrationslager*, vol. ii: *Frühe Lager: Dachau-Emslandlager* (Munich, 2005), 233–74, 29–30.

268. Orth, *System*, 319 ff.; Hans Maršálek, *Die Geschichte des Konzentrationslagers Mauthausen. Dokumentation* (Mauthausen, 1974), 130

269. Orth, *System*, 321 ff.; Hermann Kaienburg, 'Sachsenhausen-Stammlager', in Benz and Distel, eds, *Der Ort des Terrors*, iii. 17–72, 66; Strebel, *Das KZ Ravensbrück*, 501.

270. Orth, *System*, 325 ff.

271. Blatman, 'Todesmärsche', 1067.

272. Michael Zimmermann, *Rassenutopie und Genozid. Die nationalsozialistische 'Lösung der Zigeunerfrage'* (Hamburg, 1996), 233.

273. Ibid. 235 ff., on the Gypsy policy in Western Europe.

274. Ibid. 284 ff.

275. Ibid. 286.

276. Ibid. 289 ff.

277. Ibid. 292.

278. Ibid. 297.
279. Ibid. 305 ff.
280. Ibid. 326 ff.
281. Ibid. 339 ff.
282. Ibid. 359 ff.
283. Ibid. 381 ff.

Bibliography

Archival Sources

The documents marked with* were viewed as copies in Yad Vashem, those with ** in the US Holocaust Museum in Washington

Bundesarchiv Berlin

MF	Microfilm-Collection
NS 19	Reichsführer SS
NS 22	Reichsleitung der NSDAP
NS 33	SS-Führungshauptamt
NS 36	Oberstes Parteigericht der NSDAP
R 18	Reichsinnenministerium
R 2	Reichsfinanzministerium
R 19	Ordnungspolizei
R 20	Ordnungspolizei
R 22	Reichsjustizministerium
R 36	Deutscher Gemeindetag
R 43 II	Reichskanzlei
R 49	Reichskommissar für die Festigung Deutschen Volkstums
R 55	Reichspropagandaministerium
R 58	Reichssicherheitshauptamt
R 69	Einwandererzentralstelle Litzmannstadt
R 70	Polizeidienststellen in den eingegliederten und besetzten Gebieten
R 75	Umwandererzentralstelle Litzmannstadt
R 113	Reichsstelle für Raumordnung
15.01	Reichsinnenministerium (formerly in Potsdam)
25.01	Reichsbank (formerly in Potsdam)
49.01	Reichserziehungsministerium (formerly in Potsdam)
BDC-Files	

Bundesarchiv/Militärarchiv, Freiburg

M   Microfilms of the Institut für Militärgeschichte der DDR
RH 2   OKH
RH 20   Armeen
RH 31   Deutsche Heeresmission Rumänien
RW 4   Wehrmachtführungsstab
RW 19   Wirtschafts- und Rüstungsamt

Zentrale Stelle der Landesjustizverwaltungen (ZSt)

Documentation
Investigatory and trial documents
Indictments and Sentences

Politisches Archiv des Auswärtigen Amtes, Bonn (PAA)

Abteilung Deutschland
Büro Staatssekretär
Politische Abteilung

Staatsanwaltschaft München

Prozeßakten
ZUV-Akten

Bayerisches Hauptstaatsarchiv München

Reichsstatthalter Epp

Staatsarchiv München

Polizeidirektion München

Stadtarchiv Plettenberg*

Akten Bürgermeister Plettenberg

Staatsarchiv Ludwigsburg

EL 332   Trial documents
K 110 SD   UA Württemberg

Geheimes Preußisches Staatsarchiv, Berlin (GStA)

Rep 90 P   Preußisches Innenministerium

Landesarchiv Berlin, Stadtarchiv

Rep. 01   Oberbürgermeister

Institut für Zeitgeschichte, München (IfZ)

ED 180
Gruppe Fa
Gruppe Fb
Gruppe G Court Documents
MA Microfilms
MB Subsequent Trials
Nuremberg Documents from the Series NG, NO, NOKW, PS
Anordnungen, Rundschreiben, Verfügungen des Stellvertreter des Führers bzw. der
Partei-Kanzlei

Russian State Archive Moscow

Fonds 7021   Außerordentliche staatliche Kommission zur Ermittlung von
                    Verbrechen der Besatzungszeit

Osobi Archive, Moscow**

Fonds 500   RSHA
Fonds 501   SD/Gestapo
Fonds 721   Centralverein
Fonds 1458
Fonds 1461

State Archive Minsk

Fonds 378   German Occupation Agencies**
Fonds 655   German Occupation Agencies**
Impulevicius-Trial

State Archive Riga

Fonds 1026

State Archive Vilnius

Fonds 1444

Archivum Głównej Komisji Badania Zbrodni Hitlerowskich w Polsce (AGK)*
Bühler Trial

Archivum Panstwowe w Lublinie (APL)*
Governor of Lublin District

State Archive Lwów**

R 35   Governor of Galicia District
R 37   Stadthauptmann Lemberg

Prague Archive of Military History*

Kdostab Reichsführer SS

Prague State Archive (SUA)*

Bestand 124   Reich Protector

Yad Vashem

051	Miscellaneous files
053	Gestapo files Mährisch-Ostrau
JM	Microfilms
M 36	Prague Archive of Military History
M 51	Reichsvereinigung der Juden in Deutschland

Witness Documentation
International Tracing Service Ahlen

National Archives Washington DC

T 175	Himmler Files
RG 457	British wireless intercepts

YIVO-Institute, New York

Berlin Collection

Wiener Library London

Witness Documentation
Manuscripts

Centre de Documentation Juive Contemporaine*

Files of German Occupation Authorities

Printed Original Sources

Akten zur Deutschen Auswärtigen Politik 1918–1945, Series C (1933–1937), 6 vols (Göttingen 1971–1981), Series D (1937–1941), 13 vols (Baden-Baden and Göttingen 1950–70), Series E (1941–5), 8 vols (Göttingen, 1969–79).

Akten der Reichskanzlei. Die Regierung Hitler, Teil I 1933/34, ed. Karl-Heinz Minuth, 2 vols (Boppard a. Rh., 1983).

Aly, Götz, and Heim, Susanne, 'Staatliche Ordnung und organische Lösung. Die Rede Hermann Görings "über die Judenfrage" vom 6. Dezember 1938', *Jahrbuch für Anti-semitismusforschung* 2 (1993), 378–404.

Auschwitz. Zeugnisse und Berichte, ed. H. G. Adler, Hermann Langbein, and Ella Lingens-Reiner, 2nd edn (Cologne, 1979).

Baumgart, Wilfried, 'Zur Ansprache Hitlers vor den Führern der Wehrmacht am 22. August 1939. Eine quellenkritische Untersuchung', *VfZ* 16 (1968), 120–49.

Bevölkerungsstruktur und Massenmord. Neue Dokumente zur deutschen Politik der Jahre 1938–1945, ed. Susanne Heim und Götz Aly (Berlin, 1991).

Boelke, W., *Deutschlands Rüstung im Zweiten Weltkrieg. Hitlers Konferenzen mit Speer 1942–1944* (Frankfurt a. M., 1969).

Büchler, Yehoshua, and Bauer, Yehuda, 'A Preparatory Document for the Wannsee "Conference"', *HGS* 9 (1995), 121–9.

Czech, Danuta, *Kalendarium der Ereignisse im Konzentrationslager Auschwitz-Birkenau 1939–1945* (Reinbek b. Hamburg, 1989).

Deportation, Sondersiedlung, Arbeitsarmee. Deutsche in der Sowjetunion 1941 bis 1945, ed. Alfred Eisfeld and Victor Herdt (Cologne, 1996).

The Destruction of Hungarian Jewry: A Documentary Account, ed. Randolph L. Braham, 2 vols (New York, 1981).

Deutsches Judentum unter dem Nationalsozialismus, vol. i: *Dokumente zur Geschichte der Reichsvertretung der deutschen Juden 1933–1939*, ed. Otto Dov Kulka (Tübingen, 1997).

Deutschland-Berichte der Sozialdemokratischen Partei Deutschlands (Sopade), Prague/Paris 1934–1940, new edn (Frankfurt a. M., 1980).

Diamant, Adolf, *Chronik der Juden in Dresden. Von den ersten Juden bis zur Blüte der Gemeinde und deren Ausrottung* (Darmstadt, 1973).

——— *Chronik der Juden in Leipzig. Aufstieg, Vernichtung und Neuanfang* (Chemnitz and Leipzig, 1993).

Der Dienstkalender Heinrich Himmlers 1941/42, ed. Peter Witte et al. (Hamburg, 1999).

Das Diensttagebuch des deutschen Generalgouverneurs in Polen 1939–1945, ed. Werner Präg and Wolfgang Jacobmeyer (Stuttgart, 1975).

Documents on British Foreign Policy, 1919–1939, 2nd ser., 21 vols, 3rd ser., 9 vols (London, 1947–84, 1949–55).

Dokumente über die Verfolgung der jüdischen Bürger in Baden-Württemberg durch das nationalsozialistische Regime, ed. Paul Sauer, 2 vols (Stuttgart, 1965).

Dokumente zur Geschichte der Frankfurter Juden 1933–1945, ed. Kommission zur Erforschung der Geschichte der Frankfurter Juden (Frankfurt a. M., 1963).

Dokumenty i Materialy do Dziejów okupacji niemieckiej w Polsce, 3 vols, Warszawa, Lodz (Kraków, 1946).

Düsseldorf, Donnerstag, den 10. November 1938. Texte, Berichte, Dokumente, ed. Barbara Suchy (Düsseldorf, 1989).

Eichmann in Ungarn. Dokumente, ed. Jenó Levai (Budapest, 1961).

Die Einsatzgruppen in der besetzen Sowjetunion 1941/42. Die Tätigkeits- und Lageberichte des Chefs der Sicherheitspolizei und des SD, ed. and intro. Peter Klein (Berlin, 1997).

Einsatz im 'Reichskommissariat Ostland'. Dokumente zum Völkermord im Baltikum und im Weissrussland 1941–1944, ed. Wolfgang Benz et al. (Berlin, 1998).

Die Endlösung der Judenfrage. Deutsche Dokumente 1941–1944, ed. Serge Klarsfeld (Cologne, 1977).

Die Endlösung der Judenfrage in Belgien. Dokumente, ed. Serge Klarsfeld and M. Steinberg (Paris, 1980).

Die Ermordung der Europäischen Juden. Eine umfassende Dokumentation des Holocaust 1941–1945, ed. Peter Longerich (Munich, 1989).

'Die Ermordung psychisch kranker Menschen in der Sowjetunion. Dokumentation', ed. Angelika Ebbinghaus and Gerd Preissler, in Götz Aly, Angelika Ebbinghaus, and Matthias Hamann et al., eds, *Aussonderung und Tod. Die klinische Hinrichtung der Unbrauchbaren* (Berlin, 1985), 9–74.

Die Erste Republik. Dokumente zur Geschichte des Weimarer Staates ed. Peter Longerich (Munich and Zurich, 1992).

Faschismus—Ghetto—Massenmord. Dokumentation über Ausrottung und Widerstand der Juden in Polen während des zweiten Weltkrieges, ed. Tatiana Berenstein, Bernhard Mark, and Adam Rutkowski (Frankfurt a. M., 1962).

Die faschistische Okkupationspolitik in Polen (1939–1945), ed. and intro. Werner Röhr (Cologne, 1988).

Feuchert, Sacha, ed., *Die Chronik des Gettos Lodz/Litzmannstadt*, 5 vols (Göttingen, 2007).

Foreign Relations of the United States: Diplomatic Papers 1933, 5 vols (Washington, 1949–52).

Friedhofsschändungen in Deutschland 1923–1932. Dokumente der politischen und kulturellen Verwilderung unserer Zeit, ed. Central-Verein, 6th edn (Berlin, 1932).

Führer-Erlasse 1939–1945, ed. Martin Moll (Stuttgart, 1997).

Gedenkbuch Berlins der jüdischen Opfer des Nationalsozialismus. 'Ihre Namen mögen nie vergessen werden!' (Berlin, 1995).

Die geheimen Tagesberichte der Deutschen Wehrmachtführung im Zweiten Weltkrieg, 1939–1945, ed Kurt Mehner, vol. iii (Osnabrück, 1992).

Gestapo Hannover meldet ... Polizei und Regierungsberichte für das mittlere und südliche Niedersachsen zwischen 1933 und 1937, ed. and intro. Klaus Mlynek (Hildesheim, 1986).

Grabitz, Helge, and Scheffler, Wolfgang, *Letzte Spuren: Ghetto Warschau, SS-Arbeitslager Trawniki, Aktion 'Erntefest'. Fotos und Dokumente über Opfer des Endlösungswahns im Spiegel der historischen Ereignisse*, 2nd edn (Berlin, 1993).

Gruner, Wolf, '"Lesen brauchen sie nicht zu können...". Die Denkschrift über die Behandlung der Juden in der Reichshauptstadt auf allen Gebieten des öffentlichen Lebens vom Mai 1938', *Jahrbuch für Antisemitismusforschung* 4 (1995), 305–41.

Halder, Franz, *Kriegstagebuch. Tägliche Aufzeichnungen des Chefs des Generalstabs des Heeres 1939–1942*, ed. Hans-Adolf Jacobsen and Alfred Philippi, 3 vols (Stuttgart, 1962–4).

Hamburger jüdische Opfer des Nationalsozialismus. Gedenkbuch (Hamburg, 1995).

Adolf Hitler. Monologe im Führerhauptquartier. Die Aufzeichnungen Heinrich Heims, ed. Werner Jochmann (Hamburg, 1980).

'Hitlers Denkschrift zum Vierjahresplan 1936', *VfZ* 3 (1955), 184–203.

Hitler. Reden, Schriften, Anordnungen. Februar 1925 bis Januar 1933, ed. Bärbel Düsik et al., vols i–vi (in part volumes), Supplementary volume (Munich, 1992–8).

Hitlers Tischgespräche im Führerhauptquartier, ed. Henry Picker (Stuttgart, 1976).

Adolf Hitler, Sämtliche Aufzeichnungen, 1905–1924, ed. Eberhard Jäckel (Stuttgart, 1980).

Hitlers Weisungen für die Kriegführung 1939–1945. Dokumente des Oberkommandos der Wehrmacht, ed. Walther Hubatsch, 2 edn (Frankfurt a. M., 1962).

Ich, Adolf Eichmann. Ein historischer Zeugenbericht, ed. Rudolf Aschenhauer (Leoni am Starnberger See, 1980).

International Military Tribunal: Der Prozeß gegen die Hauptkriegsverbrecher vor dem Internationalen Militärgerichtschof, 14.10. 45–1. 10. 46, 42 vols (Nuremberg, 1947–9).

Die Juden in den geheimen NS-Stimmungsberichten 1933–1945 with CD Rom, ed. Otto Dov Kulka and Eberhard Jaeckel (Düsseldorf, 2004).

Juden vor Gericht. 1933–1945. Dokumente aus hessischen Justizakten, ed. Ernst Noam and Arno Kropat (Wiesbaden, 1975).

Die Judenpolitik des SD 1935 bis 1938. Eine Dokumentation, ed. Michael Wildt (Munich, 1995).

Die jüdischen Opfer des Nationalsozialismus in Hamburg (Hamburg, 1965).

Judenfeindschaft und Schule in Deutschland 1933–1945. Materialien zur Ausstellung der Forschungsstelle für Schulgeschichte an der Pädagogischen Hochschule Weingart, ed. Peter W. Schmidt (Weingart, 1988).

Justiz und NS-Verbrechen. Sammlung deutscher Strafurteile wegen nationalsozialistischer Tötungsverbrechen, 1945–1966, ed. Irene Sagel-Grande, Adelheid Rüter-Ehlemann, and C. F. Rüter et al., 22 vols (Amsterdam, 1968–81).

Kárny, Miroslav, 'Konecne Resent'. *Genocida ceskych zidu v nemecke protektoratni politice* (Prague, 1991).

Klarsfeld, Serge, *Die Endlösung der Judenfrage in Frankreich. Deutsche Dokumente 1941–1944* (Paris, 1977).

Krausnick, Helmut, 'Himmler über seinen Besuch bei Mussolini', *VfZ* 4 (1956), 423–6.

—— 'Hitler und die Morde in Polen. Ein Beitrag zum Konflikt zwischen Heer und SS um die Verwaltung der besetzten Gebiete', *VfZ* 11 (1963), 196–209.

Der Krieg gegen die Sowjetunion 1941–1945. Eine Dokumentation, ed. Reinhard Rürup (Berlin, 1991).

Kriegspropaganda 1939–1941. Geheime Ministerkonferenzen im Reichspropagandaministerium, ed. and intro. Willi A. Boelcke (Stuttgart, 1966).

Kriegstagebuch des Oberkommandos der Wehrmacht (Wehrmachtführungsstab), 1940–1945. Geführt v. Helmuth Greiner u. Percy Ernst Schramm, ed. Percy Ernst Schramm, 4 vols (Frankfurt a. M., 1961–79).

Die Lage der Juden in Deutschland 1933. Das Schwarzbuch—Tatsachen und Dokumente, ed. Comité des Delegations Juives (Paris, 1934; new edn Frankfurt a. M., Berlin, and Vienna, 1983).

Die Lageberichte der Geheimen Staatspolizei über die Provinz Hessen-Nassau. 1933–1936, ed. Thomas Klein, 2 vols (Cologne, 1986).

Lagevorträge des Oberbefehlshabers der Kriegsmarine vor Hitler 1939–1945, ed. Gerhard Wagner (Munich, 1972).

Lodz Ghetto: Inside a Community under Siege, compiled and ed. Alan Adelson and Robert Lapides (New York, 1989).

Longerich, Peter, *Die Ermordung der Europäischen Juden. Eine umfassende Dokumentation des Holocaust 1941–1945* (Munich, 1989).

Medizin im Nationalsozialismus. Ein Arbeitsbuch (Rottenburg, 1982).

Meldungen aus dem Reich. Die geheimen Lageberichte des Sicherheitsdienstes der SS 1938–1945, ed. Heinz Boberach, 17 vols (Herrsching, 1984).

Milton, Sybil, 'The Expulsion of Polish Jews from Germany: October 1938 to July 1939: A Documentation', *LBIY* 29 (1984), 169–99.

Nationalsozialismus und Schule. Amtliche Erlasse und Richtlinien 1933–1945, ed. Renate Fricke-Finkelnburg (Opladen, 1989).

Nationalsozialistische Massentötungen durch Giftgas. Eine Dokumentation, ed. Eugen Kogon et al. (Frankfurt a. M., 1986).

Nazism 1919–1945, ed. J. Noakes and G. Pridham, 4 vols (Exeter, 1983–2000).

'A New Document on the Deportation and Murder of Jews during "Einsatz Reinhardt", 1942', ed. Peter Witte and Stephen Tyas, *HGS* 15 (2001), 468–86.

Die Okkupationspolitik des deutschen Faschismus in Dänemark und Norwegen (1940–1945). Dokumentenauswahl, ed. Fritz Petrick (Berlin and Heidelberg, 1992).

Parteitag der Freiheit. Reden des Führers und ausgewählte Kongreßreden am Reichsparteitag der NSDAP (Munich, 1935).

Die Partei hört mit. Lageberichte und andere Meldungen des Sicherheitsdienstes der SS aus dem Großraum Koblenz 1937–1941, ed. Peter Brommer (Koblenz, 1988).

Pätzold, Kurt, and Runge, Irene, *'Kristallnacht'. Zum Pogrom 1938* (Cologne, 1988).

Protektor'tní politika Reinharda Heydricha, ed. Miroslav Kárny and Jaroslava Milotová (Prague, 1991).

Regge, Jürgen, and Schubert, Werner, eds, *Protokolle der Strafrechtskommission des Reichsjustizministeriums* (Berlin and New York, 1988).

Der Regierungsbezirk Kassel 1933–1936. Die Berichte der Regierungspräsidenten und der Landräte, ed. Thomas Klein, 2 parts (Darmstadt, 1985).

'Reichskristallnacht' in Hannover. Eine Ausstellung zur 40. Wiederkehr des 9. November 1938 (Hanover, 1978).

Rettung der bulgarischen Juden—1943. Eine Dokumentation, ed. Dieter Ruckhaberle and Christiane Ziesecke (Berlin, 1984).

Ringelblum, Emmanuel, *Polish-Jewish Relations During the Second World War*, ed. Joseph Kermish and Shmuel Cracowski (New York and Jerusalem, 1976).

Rosenfeld, Else, and Luckner, Getrud, eds, *Lebenszeichen aus Piaski Briefe Deportierter aus dem Distrikt Lublin 1940–1943* (Munich, 1968).

Die Schicksale der jüdischen Bürger Baden-Württembergs während der nationalsozialistischen Verfolgungszeit 1933–1945, ed. Paul Sauer (Stuttgart, 1969).

Schicksal jüdischer Mitbürger in Nürnberg. Dokumentation, ed. Stadtarchiv Nürnberg (Nuremberg, 1978).

Das Sonderrecht für die Juden im NS-Staat. Eine Sammlung der gesetzlichen Maßnahmen und Richtlinien. Inhalt und Bedeutung, ed. Joseph Walk (Heidelberg, 1981).

Staatsmänner und Diplomaten bei Hitler. Vertrauliche Aufzeichnungen über Unterredungen mit Vertretern des Auslandes 1939–1941, 2 vols, ed. and intro. Andreas Hillgruber (Frankfurt a. M., 1967).

Die Stellung der Nationalsozialistischen Deutschen Arbeiterpartei (NSDAP) zur Judenfrage. Eine Materialsammlung, vorgelegt vom Centralverein deutscher Staatsbürger jüdischen Glaubens (Berlin, n.d. [1932]).

Stöver, Bernd, *Berichte über die Lage in Deutschland. Die Lagemeldungen der Gruppe Neu Beginnen aus dem Dritten Reich 1933–1936* (Bonn, 1996).

Tagesordnung Judenmord. Die Wannsee-Konferenz vom 20. Januar 1942. Eine Dokumentation zur Organisation der 'Endlösung', ed. Kurt Pätzold and Erika Schwarz (Berlin, 1991).

Thévoz, Robert, Branig, Hans, and Lowenthal-Hensel, Cécile, *Pommern 1934/35 im Spiegel von Gestapo-Lageberichten und Sachakten*, 2 vols (Cologne and Berlin, 1974).

To live with Honor and die with Honor!... Selected Documents from the Warsaw Ghetto Underground Archives 'O.S.' ('Oneg Shabbath'), ed. and annotated Joseph Kermish (Jerusalem, 1986).

Tragédia slovenských Židov. Fotografie a Dokumenty (Bratisalava, 1949).

The Trial of Adolf Eichmann, 9 vols (Jerusalem, 1992–5).

Unsere Ehre heist Treue: Kriegstagebuch des Kommandostabes Reichsführer SS. Tätigkeitsberichte der 1. und 2. SS-Inf.-Brigade, der 1. SS Kav.-Brigade und von der Sonderkommandos der SS (Vienna, 1965).

Unser einziger Weg ist Arbeit. Das Getto in Lodz, 1940–1944, ed. Hanno Loewy and Gerhard Schoenberner (Vienna, 1990).

Die Verfolgung der jüdischen Mitbürger in Soest während des Dritten Reiches. Eine Dokumentation, compiled Gerhard Köhn (Soest, 1979).

Die Verfolgung der Juden in den Landkreisen Bad Kreuznach und Birkenfeld 1933–1945. Eine Dokumentation, ed. Edgar Mais (Bad Kreuznach, 1988).

Verfolgung, Vertreibung, Vernichtung. Dokumente des faschistischen Antisemitismus 1933 bis 1942, ed. Kurt Pätzold (Leipzig, 1984).

Die Verhandlungen des deutschen Reichstags.

Widerstand und Verfolgung im Burgenland. Eine Dokumentation, ed.Wolfgang Neugebauer (Vienna, 1979).

Wilhelm, Hans-Heinrich, *Rassenpolitik und Kriegführung. Sicherheitspolizei und Wehrmacht in Polen und der Sowjetunion* (Passau, 1991).

Zebhauser, Helmuth, *Alpinismus im Hitlerstaat. Gedanken, Erinnerungen, Dokumente* (Munich, 1998).

Periodicals

Der Angriff
Berliner Tageblatt
CV-Zeitung
Deutsche Allgemeine Zeitung
Frankfurter Zeitung
Jüdische Rundschau
Der Jungdeutsche
Ministerialblatt des Reichs- und Preußischen Ministeriums des Innern
Neue Züricher Zeitung
New York Times
Das Reich
Reichsgesetzblatt
Reichsministerialblatt für die innere Verwaltung
Das Schwarze Korps
Der Stürmer
The Times
Völkischer Beoachter
Vossische Zeitung

582 Bibliography

Diaries, Letters, Memoirs, and Speeches

Adler, Stanislaw, *In the Warsaw Ghetto—An Account of a Witness: The Memoirs of Stanislaw Adler* (Jerusalem, 1982).

'Aus dem Kriegstagebuch des Diplomaten Otto Bräutigam', ed. and intro. H. D. Heilmann, in *Biedermann und Schreibtischtäter, Materialien zur deutschen Täter-Biographie* (Berlin, 1987), 123–87

Ball, Kurt, and Kaduri, Jakob, *Das Leben der Juden in Deutschland. Ein Zeitbericht* (Frankfurt a. M., 1963).

Bargatzky, Walter, *Hotel Majestic* (Freiburg, 1987).

Baumann, Janina, *Winter in the Morning: A Young Girl's Life in the Warsaw Ghetto and Beyond 1939–1945* (London, 1986).

Behrend-Rosenfeld, ed., *Lebenszeichen Piaski. Briefe deportierte aus dem Distrikt Lublin 1940–1943* (Munich, 1968).

Ben-Chorin, Schalom, *Jugend an der Isar* (Gerlingen, 1980).

Berg, Mary, *Warsaw Ghetto: A Diary*, ed. S. L. Schneiderman (New York, 1945).

Betrifft: 'Aktion 3'. Deutsche verwerten jüdische Nachbarn. Dokumente zur Arisierung, ed. Wolfgang Dressen (Berlin, 1998).

The Chronicle of the Lodz Ghetto 1941–1944, ed. Lucjan Dobroszycki (New Haven and London, 1984).

Ciano's Diary 1939–1943, ed. Malcolm Muggeridge (London, 1947).

Cohn, Willy, *Als Jude in Breslau, 1941. Aus den Tagebüchern von Studienrat a. D. Dr. Willy Cohn* (Jerusalem, 1975).

Czerniaków, Adam, *Im Warschauer Getto. Das Tagebuch des Adam Czerniaków 1939–1942* (Munich, 1986). English trans.: *The Warsaw Diary of Adam Czerniakow: Prelude to Doom*, ed. Raul Hilberg, Stanislaw Staron, and Josef Kermish (Chicago, 1999).

'Daily Entries of Hersh Wasser', intro. and notes by Joseph Kermish, *YVS* 15 (1983), 201–81.

Dietrich, Otto, *12 Jahre mit Hitler* (Munich, 1955).

Domarus, Max, ed., *Hitler. Reden und Proklamationen 1932–1945. Kommentiert von einem deutschen Zeitgenossen*, 2 vols (Wiesbaden, 1973).

Dreyer, Ernst Adolf, ed., *Deutsche Kultur im neuen Reich. Wesen, Aufgabe und Ziel der Reichskulturkammer* (Berlin, 1934).

Goebbels, Joseph, *Signale der neuen Zeit* (Munich, 1934).

Groscurth, Helmuth, *Tagebücher eines Abwehroffiziers 1938–1940. Mit weiteren Dokumenten zur Militäropposition gegen Hitler*, ed. Helmut Krausnick and Harold C. Deutsch (Stuttgart, 1970).

Karl Haushofer: Leben und Werk, ed. Hans-Adolf Jacobsen, vol. ii: *Ausgewählter Schriftwechsel, 1917–1946* (Boppard a. Rhein, 1979), no. 226.

Heiber, Helmut, *Reichsführer! Briefe an und von Himmler* (Stuttgart, 1968).

Henschel, Hildegard, 'Aus der Arbeit der jüdischen Gemeinde Berlin während der Jahre 1941–1943', *Zeitschrift für die Geschichte der Juden* 9 (1972).

Himmler, Heinrich, *Geheimreden 1933 bis 1945 und andere Ansprachen*, ed. Bradley F. Smith and Agnes F. Peterson (Frankfurt a. M., 1974), 115–44.

—— *Der Dienstkalender Heinrich Himmlers 1941/42*, ed. Peter Witte et al. (Hamburg, 1999).

Hindls, Arnold, *Einer kehrte zurück. Bericht eines Deportierten* (Stuttgart, 1965).

Hitler, Adolf, *Mein Kampf*, 12. Auflage (Munich 1938; English trans. London 1969).

Höß, Rudolf, *Commandant of Auschwitz: The Autobiography of Rudolf Hoess* (London, 1959).

Jordan, Rudolf, *Erlebt und Erlitten. Weg eines Gauleiters von Munich bis Moskau* (Leoni am Starnberger See, 1971).

Jüdisches Leben in Deutschland, ed. and intro. Monika Richarz, vol. iii: *Selbstzeugnisse zur Sozialgeschichte 1918–1945* (Stuttgart, 1982).

Kaplan, Chaim, *Scroll of Agony: The Warsaw Diary of Chaim A. Kaplan*, ed. A. I. Katsch (New York, 1973).

Kaplan, Helene, *I Never Left Janowska* (New York, 1991).

Kersten, Felix, *Totenkopf und Treue. Himmler ohne Uniform* (Hamburg n.d).

Klarsfeld, Serge, *Vichy–Auschwitz. Die Zusammenarbeit der deutschen und französischen Behörden bei der 'Endlösung der Judenfrage' in Frankreich* (Nördlingen, 1989).

Klemperer, Victor, *I shall Bear Witness: The Diaries of Viktor Klemperer 1933–1941* (London, 1999).

—— *To the Bitter End: The Diaries of Viktor Klemperer 1941–1945* (London, 1999).

Korczak, Janusz, *Ghetto Diary* (New Haven and London, 2003).

Lewin, Abraham, *A Cup of Tears: A Diary of the Warsaw Ghetto* (Oxford, 1988).

Loewy, Hanno, and Bodek, Andrzej, *'Les Vrai Riches'. Notizen am Rand: Ein Tagebuch aus dem Ghetto Lodz (Mai bis August 1944)* (Leipzig, 1997).

Löwenstein, Karl, *Minsk. Im Lager der deutschen Juden* (Bonn, 1961).

Lutz-Lange, Bernd, *Davidstern und Weihnachtsbaum. Erinnerungen von Überlebenden* (Leipzig, 1992).

Masur, Norbert, *En Jude Talar Med Himmler* (A Jew Speaks with Himmler) (Stockholm, 1945).

Mennecke, Friedrich, *Innenansichten eines medizinischen Täters im Nationalsozialismus. Eine Edition seiner Briefe 1935–1947*, ed. Peter Chroust, 2 vols (Hamburg, 1987).

Nelken, Halina, *Freiheit will ich noch erleben. Krakauer Tagebuch* (Gerlingen, 1996).

Picker, Henry, *Hitlers Tischgespräche im Führerhaupquartier 1941–42*, ed. Gerhard Ritter (Bonn, 1951).

Plieninger, Konrad, *'Ach, es ist alles ohne Ufer…'. Briefe aus dem Warschauer Ghetto* (Göttingen, 1996).

Das politische Tagebuch Alfred Rosenbergs aus den Jahren 1934/35 und 1939/40, ed. Hans-Günther Seraphim (Göttingen, 1956).

Das Reichsministerium des Innern und die Judengesetzgebung, Aufzeichnungen von Dr. Bernhard Lösener, ed. Walter Strauß, *VfZ* 9 (1961), 262–313.

Ringelblum, Emmanuel, *Notes from the Warsaw Ghetto: The Journal of Emmanuel Ringelblum*, ed. and trans. Jacob Sloan (New York, Toronto, and London, 1958).

Rosenberg, Binca, *'Versuch zu überleben…' Polen 1941–1945* (Frankfurt a. M., 1996).

Rosenberg, Heinz, *Jahre des Schreckens… und ich blieb übrig, daß ich Dir's ansage* (n.p., 1992).

Rosenfeld, Oskar, *Wozu noch Welt. Aufzeichnungen aus dem Ghetto Lodz*, ed. Hanno Loewy (Frankfurt a. M., 1994).

Schmidt, Paul, *Statist auf diplomatischer Bühne, 1923–45. Erlebnisse des Chefdolmetschers im Auswärtigen Amt mit den Staatsmännern Europas* (Bonn, 1953).

Sender, Stefan, *Der letzte Jude aus Polen* (Zurich, 1945).

Sevillias, Errikos, *Athens-Auschwitz* (Athens, 1983).

Sie durften nicht mehr Deutsche sein. Jüdischer Alltag in Selbstzeugnissen 1933–1938, ed. Margarete Limberg and Hubert Rübsaat (Frankfurt a. M. and New York, 1990).

Sierakowiak, David, *The Diary of David Sierakowiak: Five Notebooks from the Lodz Ghetto*, ed. Alan Adelson (New York and Oxford, 1996).

Smoliar, Hersch, *Resistance in Minsk* (Oakland, Calif., 1966).

Szajn-Lewin, Eugenia, *Aufzeichnungen aus dem Warschauer Ghetto. Juli 1942 bis April 1943* (Leipzig, 1994).

Die Tagebücher von Joseph Goebbels 1924–1945. Sämtliche Fragmente Teil I: *Aufzeichnungen 1923–1941*, ed. Elke Fröhlich, 14 vols., Teil II: *Diktate 1941–1945*, ed. Elke Fröhlich, 15 vols (Munich, 1987–2005).

Tausk, Walter, *Breslauer Tagebuch 1933–1940* (Frankfurt a. M., 1977).

Tory, Avraham, *Surviving the Holocaust: The Kovno Ghetto Diary*, ed. Martin Gilbert (Cambridge, Mass., 1990).

Wir haben es gesehen. Augenzeugenberichte über Terror und Judenverfolgung im Dritten Reich, ed. Gerhard Schoenberner (Hamburg, 1962).

'wir verreisen...' in die Vernichtung. Briefe 1937–1944, ed. Hanne Hiob and Gerd Koller (Hamburg, 1993).

Zelkovitsh, Yosef, *In those Terrible Days: Writings from the Lodz Ghetto*, ed. Michal Unger, trans. Naftali Greenwood (Jerusalem, 2002).

Zylberberg, Michael, *A Warsaw Diary* (London, 1969).

Pre-1945 Secondary Literature

Boehm, Max Hildebert, *Volkskunde* (Berlin, 1937).

Deutsche Kultur im neuen Reich. Wesen, Aufgabe und Ziel der Reichskulturkammer, ed. Ernst Adolf Dreyer (Berlin, 1934).

Die deutsche Volkskunde, 2 vols, 2nd edn, ed. Alfred Spame (Leipzig and Berlin, 1934–5).

Endt, Alfred, *Rassenpolitische Erziehung in der Volksschule. Betrachtungen und unterricht-spraktische Handreichungen für eine artgemäße Erziehung* (Leipzig, 1936).

Fink, Fritz, *Die Judenfrage im Unterricht* (Nuremberg, 1937).

Frymann, Daniel [Heinrich Class], *Wenn ich der Kaiser wär—Politische Wahrheiten und Notwendigkeiten* (Leipzig, 1912).

Gerstenhauer, M. R., *Der völkische Gedanke in Vergangenheit und Zukunft. Aus der Geschichte der völkischen Bewegung* (Leipzig, 1933).

Hansen, Walter, *Judenkunst in Deutschland. Quellen und Studien zur Judenfrage auf dem Gebiet der bildenden Kunst. Ein Handbuch zur Geschichte der Verjudung und Entartung deutscher Kunst 1900–1933* (Berlin, 1942).

Ipsen, Gunther, *Programm einer Soziologie des Deutschen Volkstums* (Berlin, 1933).

Das Judentum in der Rechtswissenschaft, 8 vols (Berlin, 1936).

Jünger, Ernst, 'Über Nationalismus und Judenfrage', *Süddeutsche Monatshefte* (Sept. 1930), 843–5.

Kaiser, Karl, *Lesebuch zur Geschichte der deutschen Volkskunde* (Munich, 1939).

Kaufman, Theodore N., *Germany Must Perish* (Newark, NJ, 1941).

Michael, Wilhelm, 'Der Jüdische Fabrikmediziner', *Der Weltkampf. Monatsschrift für Weltpolitik, völkische Kultur und die Judenfrage aller Länder* 3 (1935).

Pfeffer, Karl Heinz, *Die deutsche Schule der Soziologie* (Leipzig, 1939).

Pfundtner, Hans, *Die neue Stellung des Reiches* (Berlin, 1932).

Plugge, Walther, 'Wesen und Aufgaben des Films und der Reichsfilmkammer', in Ernst Adolf Dreyer, ed., *Deutsche Kultur im Neuen Reich. Wesen, Aufgabe und Ziel der Reichskulturkammer* (Berlin, 1934), 114–28.

Spamer, Adolf, ed., *Die deutsche Volkskunde*, 2nd edn (Leipzig and Berlin, 1934/5).

Troost, Gerdy, *Das Bauen im Neuen Reich*, 2nd edn (Bayreuth, 1939).

Von der Großmacht zur Weltmacht, ed. Hans Volz (Berlin, 1938).

Werner, Paul, 'Die vorbeugende Verbrechensbekämpfung durch die Polizei', *Kriminalistik* 12 (1938), 59–61.

Ziegler, Hans Severus, *Entartete Musik* (Düsseldorf, 1938).

Post-1945 Secondary Literature

Abitbol, Michel, *Les Juifs d'Afrique du Nord sous Vichy* (Paris, 1983).

Abrahamsen, Samuel, *Norway's Response to the Holocaust* (New York, 1991).

Abramowitsch, Ljuba Israeljewna, *Die faschistische Gehenna am Beispiel des Ghettos der Stadt Slonim* (Hanover, 1995).

Adam, Uwe, *Die Judenpolitik im Dritten Reich* (Düsseldorf, 1972).

—— 'An Overall Plan for Anti-Jewish Legislation in the Third Reich', *YVS* 11 (1976), 33–55.

—— 'Wie spontan war der Pogrom?' in Walter Pehle, ed., *Der Judenpogrom 1938. Von der Kristallnacht bis zum Völkermord* (Frankfurt a. M., 1988), 74–93.

Adelson, Alan, and Lapides, Robert, *Lodz Ghetto: Inside a Community under Siege* (New York, 1989).

Adler, Hans-Günther, *Theresienstadt 1941–1945. Das Antlitz einer Zwangsgemeinschaft. Geschichte, Soziologie, Psychologie*, 2nd edn (Tübingen, 1960).

—— *Der verwaltete Mensch. Studien zur Deportation der Juden aus Deutschland* (Tübingen, 1974).

Adler-Rudel, Salomon, *Jüdische Selbsthilfe unter dem Nazi Regime 1933–1939. Im Spiegel der Berichte der Reichsvertretung der Juden in Deutschland* (Tübingen, 1974).

Ahren, Yizhak, Hoernshoej-Moller, Stig, and Melchers, Christoph B., eds, *'Der ewige Jude'. Wie Goebbels hetzte. Untersuchungen zum nationalsozialistischen Propagandafilm* (Aachen, 1990).

Ainsztein, Reuben, *The Warsaw Ghetto Revolt* (New York, 1979).

—— *Jüdischer Widerstand im deutschbesetzten Osteuropa während des zweiten Weltkrieges* (Oldenburg, 1993).

'Aktion Reinhardt'. Der Völkermord an den Juden im Generalgouvernement, 1941–1944, ed. Bogdan Musial (Osnabrück, 2004).

Alberti, Michael, *Die Verfolgung und Vernichtung der Juden im Reichsgau Wartheland, 1939–1945* (Wiebaden, 2006).

Albrecht, Gerd, *Nationalsozialistische Filmpolitik. Eine soziologische Untersuchung über die Spielfilme des Dritten Reiches* (Stuttgart, 1969).

Allen, Michael Thad, *The Business of Genocide: The SS, Slave Labor and the Concentration Camps* (Chapel Hill, NC, 2002).

—— 'The Devil in the Details: The Gas Chambers of Birkenau, October 1941', *HGS* 16/2 (2002), 189–216.

Allen, William S., 'Die deutsche Öffentlichkeit und die "Reichskristallnacht". Konflikte zwischen Werthierarchie und Propaganda im Dritten Reich', in Detlev Peukert and Jürgen Reulecke, eds, *Die Reihen fast geschlossen. Beiträge zur Geschichte des Alltags unterm Nationalsozialismus* (Wuppertal, 1981), 397–411.

Alpert, Nachum, *The Destruction of Slonim Jewry: The Story of the Jews of Slonim during the Holocaust* (New York, 1989).

Alter, Peter, Bärsch, Claus-Ekkehard, Berghoff, Peter, et al., eds, *Die Konstruktion der Nation gegen die Juden* (Munich, 1999).

Aly, Götz, 'Medizin gegen Unbrauchbare', in Aly et al., eds, *Aussonderung und Tod. Die klinische Hinrichtung der Unbrauchbaren* (Berlin, 1985), 9–74.

—— *'Final Solution': Nazi Population Policy and the Murder of the European Jews* (London, 1999).

—— and Gerlach, Christian, *Der letzte Kapitel. Realpolitik, Ideologie und der Mord an den ungarischen Juden 1944/1945* (Stuttgart, 2002).

—— and Heim, Susanne, *Vordenker der Vernichtung. Auschwitz und die deutschen Pläne für eine neue europäische Ordnung* (Hamburg, 1991); English trans.: *Architects of Annihilation: Auschwitz and the Logic of Destruction* (London, 2002).

Anatomy of the Auschwitz Death Camp, ed. Yisrael Gutman and Michael Berenbaum (Washington, 1994).

Ancel, Jean, 'The Romanian Campaign of Mass Murder in Trans-Nistria, 1941–1942', in Randolf Braham, ed., *The Destruction of Hungarian Jewry: A Documentary Account* (New York, 1963), 87–134.

—— 'Antonescu and the Jews', *YVS* 23 (1993), 213–80.

—— 'German-Romanian Relations during the Second World War', in Randolph L. Braham, ed., *The Tragedy of Romanian Jews* (New York, 1994), 57–76.

—— 'The German-Romanian Relationship and the Final Solution', *HGS* 19/2 (2005).

Anderl, Gabriele, and Manoschek, Walter, *Gescheiterte Flucht. Der jüdische 'Kladovo-Transport' auf dem Weg nach Palästina, 1939–42* (Vienna, 1993).

Anderson, Truman, 'Die 62. Infanterie-Division. Repressalien im Heeresgebiet Süd, Oktober bis Dezember 1941', in Heer and Naumann, eds, *Vernichtungskrieg*, 297–323.

Angress, Werner T., 'The German Army's "Judenzaehlung" of 1916. Genesis—Consequences—Significance', *LBIY* 23 (1978), 117–37.

—— 'Die "Judenfrage" im Spiegel amtlicher Berichte 1935', in Ursula Büttner, ed., *Das Unrechtsregime. Internationale Forschung über den Nationalsozialismus* (Hamburg, 1986), ii. 19–38.

Angrick, Andrej, Vogt, Martina, Ammerschubert, Silke, and Klein, Peter, eds, ' "Da hätte man schon ein Tagebuch führen müssen". Das Polizeibataillon 322 und die Judenmorde im Bereich der Heeresgruppe Mitte während des Sommers und Herbstes 1941', in Helge

Grabitz, Klaus Bästlein, and Johannes Tuchel, eds, *Die Normalität des Verbrechens* (Berlin, 1994), 325–85.

—— 'The Escalation of German-Romanian Anti-Jewish Policy after the Attack on the Soviet Union', *YVS* 26 (1998), 203–38.

—— 'Die Einsatzgruppe C', in Angrick, *Besatzungspolitik und Massenmord*, 88–110.

—— *Besatzungspolitik und Massenmord. Die Einsatzgruppen in der südlichen Sowjetunion 1941–1943* (Hamburg, 2003).

—— and Klein, Peter, *Die 'Endlösung' in Riga. Ausbeutung und Vernichtung, 1941–1944* (Berlin, 2006).

Apel, Hans J., and Klöcker, Michael, *Volksschule im NS-Staat* (Bonn, 2000).

Arad, Yitzhak, 'The "Final Solution" in Lithuania in the Light of German Documentation', *YVS* 11 (1976), 234–72.

—— 'Alfred Rosenberg and the "Final Solution" in the Occupied Soviet Territories', *YVS* 113 (1979).

—— *Ghetto in Flames: The Destruction of the Jews in Vilna in the Holocaust* (Jerusalem, 1980; New York, 1981).

—— *Belzec, Sobibor, Treblinka: The Operation Reinhard Death Camps* (Bloomington, Ind., 1986).

Arndt, Ino, 'Luxemburg', in Benz, ed., *Dimensionen*, 95–103.

—— and Boberach, Heinz, 'Deutsches Reich', in Benz, ed., *Dimensionen*, 23–65.

Arnold, Klaus Jochen, 'Die Eroberung und Behandlung der Stadt Kiew durch die Wehrmacht im September 1941: Zur Radikalisierung der Besatzungspolitik', *MGM* 58 (1999), 23–63.

Arntz, Dieter, *Judenverfolgung und Fluchthilfe im deutsch-belgischen Grenzgebiet. Kreisgebiet Schleiden, Euskirchen, Monschau, Aachen und Eupen/Malmedy* (Euskirchen, 1990).

Aronson, Shlomo, *Reinhard Heydrich und die Frühgeschichte von Gestapo und SD* (Stuttgart, 1971).

—— 'Die dreifache Falle. Hitlers Judenpolitik, die Alliierten und die Juden', *VfZ* 32 (1984), 29–65.

—— *Hitler, the Allies, and the Jews* (Cambridge, 2004).

Ash, Mitchell, 'Psychologie', in Frank-Rutger Hausmann, ed., *Die Rolle der Geisteswissenschaften im Dritten Reich 1933–1945* (Munich, 2002).

Ausbeutung, Vernichtung, Öffentlichkeit: Darstellungen und Quellen zur Geschichte von Auschwitz, ed. Norbert Frei et al. (Munich, 2000).

Ayaß, Wolfgang, ' "Ein Gebot der nationalen Arbeitsdisziplin." Die Aktion "Arbeitsscheu Reich" 1938', in *Feindererklärung und Prävention. Kriminalbiologie, Zigeunerforschung und Asozialenpolitik* (Berlin, 1988), 43–74.

—— 'Asoziale' im Nationalsozialismus (Stuttgart, 1995).

Bajohr, Frank, ' "damit bitte keine Gefühlsduseleien". Die Hamburger und die Deportationen', in *Die Deportation der Hamburger Juden 1941–1945*, Die Forschungsstelle für Zeitgeschichte und das Institut für die Geschichte der deutschen Juden, 2nd edn (Hamburg, 2002), 13–29.

—— 'Arisierung' in Hamburg. Die Verdrängung der jüdischen Unternehmer 1933–45 (Hamburg, 1997). English trans.: *Arianization in Hamburg: The Economic Exclusion of Jews and the Confiscation of their Property in Nazi Germany* (New York, 2002).

Bajohr, Frank, 'Unser Hotel ist judenfrei'. Bäder-Antisemitismus im 19. und 20. Jahrhundert (Frankfurt a. M., 2003).

'Bambergs Wirtschaft judenfrei'. Die Verdrängung der jüdischen Geschäftsleute in den Jahren 1933 bis 1939, ed. Franz Fichtl, Stephan Link, Herbert May et al. (Bamberg, 1998).

Banach, Jens, Heydrichs Elite. Das Fuhrerkorps der Sicherheitspolizei und des SD, 1936–1945 (Paderborn, 1998).

Bankier, David, The Germans and the Final Solution: Public Opinion under Nazism (Oxford, 1992).

——Die öffentliche Meinung im NS-Staat. Die 'Endlösung' und die Deutschen. Eine Berichtigung (Berlin, 1995).

——ed., Nazi Europe and the Final Solution (Jerusalem, 2003).

Barcz, Wojciech, 'Die erste Vergasung in Auschwitz', in H. G. Adler et al., eds, Auschwitz. Zeugnisse und Berichte (Cologne and Frankfurt a. M., 1983).

Barkai, Avraham, 'Die Juden als sozio-ökonomische Minderheitsgruppe in der Weimarer Republik', in Walter Grab and Julius H. Schoeps, eds, Juden in der Weimarer Republik. Skizzen und Portraits (Stuttgart, 1986), 330–46.

——'Regierungsmechanismen im Dritten Reich und die "Genesis der Endlösung"', Jahrbuch des Instituts für Deutsche Geschichte 14 (1985), 371–84.

——'The Organized Jewish Community', in Michael Meyer, ed., German Jewish History in Modern Times, iv: Renewal and Destruction 1918–1945 (New York, 1988).

—— Vom Boykott zu 'Endjudung'. Der wirtschaftliche Existenzkampf der Juden im Dritten Reich 1933–1943 (Frankfurt a. M., 1988).

——'Wehr dich'. Der Centralverein deutscher Staatsbürger jüdischen Glaubens 1893–1938 (Munich, 2002).

Barkow, Ben, ed., November Pogrom 1938. Die Augenzeugeberichte der Wiener Library London (Frankfurt a. M., 2008).

Barlev, Jehuda, Juden und jüdische Gemeinde in Gütersloh, 1671–1943, 2nd edn, vol. i (Gütersloh, 1988).

Bartov, Omer, The Eastern Front 1941–1945: German Troops and the Barbarization of Warfare (Houndmills, 1985).

——Hitler's Army: Soldiers, Nazis, and War in the Third Reich (New York and Oxford 1991).

Baruch, Nir, Der Freikauf. Zar Boris und das Schicksal der bulgarishen Juden (Sofia, 1996).

Bar-Zohar, Michael, Beyond Hitler's Grasp: The Heroic Rescue of Bulgaria's Jews (Holbrook, 1998).

Bauer, Yehuda, 'The Death Marches, January–May 1945', in Michael Marrus, The Nazi Holocaust (Westport, Conn., 1989), ii. 491–511.

——Jews for Sale? Nazi Jewish Negotiations, 1933–1945 (New Haven and London, 1994).

——'Jewish Baranowicze in the Holocaust', YVS 31 (2003), 95–151.

Bartusevicius, Vincas, Tauber, Joachim, and Wette, Wolfram, eds, Holocaust in Litauen. Krieg, Judenmorde, und Kollaboration (Cologne, 2003).

Battick, Carol 'Smuggling as a Form of Resistance in the Warsaw Ghetto', Journal of Holocaust Education 4/2 (1995), 199–204.

Baumann, Zygmunt, *Modernity and the Holocaust* (New York, 1991).

Baumgart, Winfried, 'Zur Ansprache. Hitlers vor den Führern der Wehrmacht am 22. August 1939. Eine quellenkritische Untersuchung', *VfZ* 2 (1968), 120–49.

Bayern in der NS-Zeit, vol. i: *Soziale Lage und politisches Verhalten der Bevölkerung im Spiegel vertraulicher Berichte*, ed. Martin Broszat, Elke Fröhlich, Falk Wiesemann (Munich and Vienna, 1977).

Becker, Franziska, *Gewalt und Gedächtnis. Erinnerungen an die nationalsozialistische Verfolgung einer jüdischen Landgemeinde* (Göttingen, 1994).

Beer, Matthias, 'Die Entwickung der Gaswagen beim Mord an den Juden', *VfZ* 35 (1987), 403–17.

Benathan, Esra, 'Die demographische und wirtschaftliche Struktur der Juden', in Werner Mosse, ed., *Entscheidungsjahr 1932. Zur Judenfrage in der Endphase der Weimarer Republik* (Tübingen, 1965), 87–131.

Bender, Sara, 'The "Reinhardt Action" in the "Bialystok District"', in Freia Anders, Katrin Stoll, and Hauke-Hendrik Kutscher, eds, *Bialystok in Bielefeld. Nationalsozialistische Verbrechen vor dem Landgericht Bielefeld, 1958 bis 1967* (Bielefeld, 2003).

—— *The Jews of Bialystok during World War II and the Holocaust* (Waltham, Mass., 2008).

Benz, Wolfgang, 'Judenvernichtung aus Notwehr? Die Legende um Theodore N. Kaufman', *VfZ* 29 (1981), 615–30.

—— 'Der Novemberpogrom 1938', in Benz, ed., *Juden in Deutschland*, 499–544.

—— 'Der Rückfall in die Barbarei. Bericht über den Pogrom', in Walter Pehle, ed., *Der Judenpogrom 1938* (Frankfurt a. M., 1988), 13–51.

—— ed., *Die Juden in Deutschland, 1933–1945. Leben unter nationalsozialistischer Herrschaft* (Munich, 1988).

—— '"Evakuierung". Deportation und Vernichtung der Juden aus Bayern', in Benz, ed., *Herrschaft und Gesellschaft im nationalsozialistischen Staat* (Frankfurt a. M., 1990).

—— ed., *Dimensionen des Völkermords. Die Zahl der jüdischen Opfer des Nationalsozialismus* (Munich, 1991).

—— *Der Holocaust* (Munich, 1995).

—— *The Holocaust: A German Historian Examines the Holocaust* (New York, 1999).

—— and Distel, Barbara, eds, *Der Ort des Terrors. Geschichte der nationalsozialistischen Konzentrationslager*, 2 vols (Munich, 2005).

Benzendörfer, Udo, 'Bemerkungen zur Planung bei der NS-"Euthanasie"', in Boris Böhm and Thomas Oelschläger, eds, *Der sächsische Sonderweg bei der NS-'Euthanasie'* (Ulm, 2001), 21–54.

Berenbaum, Michael, and Peck, Abraham J., eds, *The Holocaust and History: The Known, the Unknown, the Disputed, and the Reexamined* (Bloomington and Indianapolis, 1998).

Berghahn, Volker, *Der Stahlhelm. Bund der Frontsoldaten 1918–1933* (Düsseldorf, 1966).

Berghoff, Hartmut, 'Von der "Reklame" zur Verbrauchslenkung. Werbung im nationalsozialistischen Deutschland', in Hartmut Berghoff, ed., *Konsumpolitik. Die Regulierung des privaten Verbrauchs im 20. Jahrhundert* (Göttingen, 1999), 77–112.

Bergmann, Werner, 'The Jewish Council as an Intermediary System: Sociological Analysis of the Role of the Jewish Councils in Eastern Europe', in Yehuda Bauer et al., eds, *Remembering for the Future: Working Papers and Addenda* (Oxford and New York, 1989), iii. 2830–50.

Bering, Dietz, *Kampf um Namen. Bernhard Weiss gegen Joseph Goebbels* (Stuttgart, 1991).

Bernett, Hajo, *Der jüdische Sport im nationalsozialistischen Deutschland 1933–1938* (Schorndorf, 1978).

Bernhardt, Heike, *Anstaltspsychiatrie und 'Euthanasie' in Pommern 1933 bis 1945. Die Krankenmorde an Kindern und Erwachsenen am Beispiel der Landesheilanstalt Ueckermünde* (Frankfurt a. M., 1994).

Berschel, Holger, *Bürokratie und Terror. Das Judenreferat der Gestapo Düsseldorf, 1935–1945* (Essen, 2001).

'Beseitigung des jüdischen Einflusses…'. Antisemitische Forschung, Eliten und Karrieren im Nationalsozialismus, ed. Fritz Bauer Institut (Frankfurt and New York, 1999).

Bessel, Richard, *Political Violence and the Rise of Nazism: The Stormtroopers of Eastern Germany 1925–1934* (New Haven, 1984).

Birn, R. B., *Die Höhere SS- und Polizeiführer. Himmlers Vertreter im Reich und in den besetzten Gebieten* (Düsseldorf, 1986).

Black, Peter, 'Die Trawniki-Männer und die Aktion Reinhard', in *'Aktion Reinhardt'. Der Völkermord an den Juden im Generalgouvernement 1941–1944*, ed. Bogdan Musial (Osnabrück, 2004).

Blaschke, Olaf, *Katholizismus und Antisemitismus im Deutschen Kaiserreich* (Göttingen, 1997).

Blasius, Dirk, *'Einfache Seelenstörung'. Geschichte der deutschen Psychiatrie 1800–1945* (Frankfurt a. M., 1994).

Blatman, Daniel, 'Die Todesmärsche—Entscheidungsträger, Mörder und Opfer', in Ulrich Herbert et al., eds, *Die nationalsozialistischen Konzentrationslager. Entwicklung und Struktur* (Göttingen, 1998), ii.1063–92.

——— *For our Freedom and yours: The Jewish Labour Bund in Poland 1939–1949* (London, 2003).

Blau, Bruno, 'Die Juden in Deutschland von 1939 bis 1945', *Judaica* 7 (1951), 270–84.

Bloch, Ernst, *Geschichte der Juden von Konstanz im 19. und 20. Jahrhundert. Eine Dokumentation* (Konstanz, 1971).

Boberach, Heinz, 'Quellen für die Einstellung der deutschen Bevölkerung zur Judenverfolgung. Analyse und Kritik', in Ursula Büttner, ed., *Das Unrechtsregime*, ii. 32–49.

Bock, Gisela, *Zwangssterilisation im Nationalsozialismus. Studien zur Rassenpolitik und Frauenpolitik* (Opladen, 1986).

Böhler, Joachim, ' "Tragische Verstrickung" oder Auftakt zum Vernichtungskrieg? Die Wehrmacht in Polen 1939', in Klaus-Michael Mallmann and Bogdan Musial, eds, *Genesis des Genozids. Polen 1939–1941* (Darmstadt, 2004), 36–57.

——— *Auftakt zum Vernichtungskrieg. Die Wehrwacht in Polen 1939* (Frankfurt a. M., 2006).

Böhm, Boris, and Oelschläger, Thomas, eds, *Der sächsische Sonderweg bei der NS-'Euthanasie'* (Ulm, 2001).

Boll, Bernd, 'Aktionen nach Kriegsbrauch. Wehrmacht und 1. SS-Infanteriebrigade 1941', *ZfG* 48 (2000), 775–88.

——— 'Zloczow, Juli 1941: Die Wehrmacht und der Beginn des Holocaust in Galizien', *ZfG* 50 (2002), 901–16.

——— Safrian, Hans, 'On the Way to Stalingrad. The 6th Army 1941/42', in Hannes Heer and Klaus Naumann, eds, *War of Extermination: The German Military in World War II 1941–1944* (New York, 2004).

—— 'Auf dem Weg nach Stalingrad. Die 6. Armee 1941/42', in Hannes Heer and Klaus Naumann, eds, *Die Vernichtungskrieg*, 260–96.

Bonnell, 'Was German Social Democracy before 1914 Antisemitic?' *German History* 27/2 (2009), 259–69.

Boog, Horst et al., eds, *Der Angriff auf die Sowjetunion* (Stuttgart, 1983).

—— *Germany and the Second World War*, vol. iv: *The Attack on the Soviet Union* (Oxford, 1999).

Bopf, Britta, *'Arisierung' in Köln. Die wirtschaftliche Existenzvernichtung der Juden 1933–1945* (Cologne, 2004).

Borkowicz, Jacek, et al., eds, *Thou Shalt not Kill: Poles on Jedwabne* (Warsaw, 2001).

Borodziej, Wlodzimierz, *Terror und Politik. Die deutsche Polizei und die polnische Widerstandsbewegung im Generalgouvernement 1939–1944* (Mainz, 1999).

Borut, Jacob, 'Antisemitism in Tourist Facilities in Weimar Germany', *YVS* 28 (2000), 7–50.

Botz, Gerhard, *Die Eingliederung Österreichs in das Deutsche Reich. Planung und Verwirklichung des politisch-administrativen Anschlusses 1938–1940*, 3rd edn (Vienna and Zurich, 1968).

—— *Wohnungspolitik und Judendeportation in Wien 1938 bis 1945. Zur Funktion des Antisemitismus als Ersatz nationalsozialistischer Sozialpolitik* (Vienna, 1975).

—— *Nationalsozialismus in Wien. Machtübernahme und Herrschaftssicherung 1938/39*, 3rd edn (Buchloe, 1988).

Bracher, Karl-Dietrich, *The German Dictatorship: The Origins, Structure and Consequences of National Socialism* (London, 1971).

—— Sauer, Wolfgang, and Schulz, Gerhard, *Die nationalsozialistische Machtergreifung. Studien zur Errichtung des totalitären Herrschaftsystems in Deutschland 1933/34* (Cologne and Opladen, 1960).

Braham, Randolph L., 'The Kamenets Podolsk and Délvidék Massacres: Prelude to the Holocaust in Hungary', *YVS* 9 (1973), 133–56.

—— *The Politics of Genocide: The Holocaust in Hungary*, 2 vols (New York, 1981).

—— 'Antonescu and the Jews', *YVS* 23 (1993), 213–80.

—— ed., *The Tragedy of Romanian Jews* (New York, 1994).

Brakel, Alexander, *Unter Rotem Stern und Hakenkreuz: Branovicze 1939–1944. Das westliche Weißrussland unter sowjetischer und deutscher Besatzung* (Paderborn, 2009).

Brandes, Detlev, *Die Tschechen unter deutschem Protektorat. Besatzungspolitik, Kollaboration und Widerstand im Protektorat Böhmen und Mähren bis Heydrichs Tod*, vol. i (Munich, 1969).

Brandon, Ray and Lower, Wendy, eds, *The Shoah in Ukraine: History, Testimony, Memorialization* (Bloomington, Ind., 2008).

Brandhuber, Jerzy, 'Die sowjetischen Kriegsgefangenen im Konzentrationslager Auschwitz', *Hefte von Auschwitz* 4 (1961), 5–46.

Brechtken, Magnus, *'Madagaskar für die Juden'. Antisemitische Idee und politische Praxis* (Munich, 1997).

Breitman, Richard, 'Police Auxiliaries in the Occupied Soviet Territories', *SWCA* 7 (1990), 23–39.

—— *The Architect of Genocide: Himmler and the Final Solution* (New York, 1991).

—— 'Plans for the Final Solution in Early 1941', *GSR* 17 (1994), 483–94.

—— and Aronson, Shlomo, 'The End of the "Final Solution"? Nazi Plans to Ransom Jews in 1944', *Central European History* 25 (1992), 177–203.

Breitman, Richard, and Kraut, Alan M., *American Refugee Policy and European Jewry, 1933–1945* (Indianapolis, 1987).

Breuer, Stefan, *Ordnungen der Ungleichheit—die deutsche Rechte im Widerstreit ihrer Idee 1871–1945* (Darmstadt, 2001).

Broszat, Martin, *Nationalsozialistische Polenpolitik* (Stuttgart, 1961).

—— 'Soziale Motivation und Führer-Bindung des Nationalsozialismus', *VfZ* 18 (1970), 392–409.

—— 'Hitler und die Genesis der "Endlösung". Aus Anlaß der Thesen von David Irving', *VfZ* 25 (1977), 739–75. English trans.: 'Hitler and the Genesis of the Final Solution: An Assessment of David Irving's Theses', in Hans Koch, ed. *Aspects of the Third Reich* (Houndmills, 1985), 390–429.

—— et al., eds, *Deutschlands Weg in die Diktatur* (Berlin, 1983).

Browder, George C., *Foundations of the Nazi Police State: The Formation of Sipo and SD* (Lexington, Ky., 1990).

Browning, Christopher R., *The Final Solution and the German Foreign Office: A Study of Referat D III of Abteilung Deutschland 1940–43* (New York and London, 1978).

—— 'Wehrmacht Reprisal Policy and the Mass Murder of Jews in Serbia', *MGM* 33 (1983), 31–47.

—— *Fateful Months. Essays on Launching the Final Solution* (New York, 1985).

—— 'The Decision Concerning the Final Solution', in Browning, ed., *Fateful Months*, 8–38.

—— 'Wehrmacht Reprisal Policy and the Murder of the Male Jews in Serbia', in Browning, ed., *Fateful Months*, 39–56.

—— 'Harald Turner und die Militärverwaltung in Serbien 1941–1942', in Dieter Rebentisch and Karl Teppe, eds, *Verwaltung contra Menschenführung im Staat Hitlers. Studien zum politisch-administrativen System* (Göttingen, 1986), 351–73.

—— *The Path to Genocide: Essays on Launching the Final Solution* (Cambridge, 1992).

—— 'Beyond "Intentionalism" and "Functionalism": The Decision for the Final Solution Reconsidered', in Browning, *The Path to Genocide*, 86–121.

—— 'Nazi Ghettoization Policy in Poland, 1939–1941', in Browning, *The Path to Genocide*, 28–56.

—— *Ordinary Men: Reserve Battalion 101 and the Final Solution in Poland* (New York and London, 1992).

—— 'Nazi *Resettlement Policy and the Search for a Solution to the Jewish Question*', *GSR* 9/3 (1986); repr. in Browning, *The Path to Genocide*, 3–27.

—— 'The Euphoria of Victory and the Final Solution: Summer-Fall 1941', *GSR* 17 (1994), 473–81.

—— 'A Final Decision for the "Final Solution"? The Riegner-Telegram Reconsidered', *HGS* 10 (1996), 3–10.

—— 'The Decision-Making Process', in Dan Stone, ed., *The Historiography of the Holocaust* (London, 2004).

—— *The Origins of the Final Solution: The Evolution of Nazi Jewish Policy September 1939 to March 1942* (London, 2004).

—— ' "Judenjagd": Die Schlussphase der "Endlösung" in Polen', in Jürgen Matthäus and Klaus-Michael Mallmann, eds, *Deutsche, Juden, Völkermord. Der Holocaust in Geschichte und Gegenwart* (Darmstadt, 2006), 177–89.

Brunck, Helma, *Die Deutsche Burschenschaft in der Weimarer Republik und im National-sozialismus* (Munich, 2000).

Brunswig, Hans, *Feuersturm über Hamburg* (Stuttgart, 1978).

Bruns-Wüstefeld, Axel, *Lohnende Geschäfte. Die 'Entjudung' der Wirtschaft am Beispiel Göttingens* (Hanover, 1997).

Bruss, Regina, *Die Bremer Juden unter dem Nationalsozialismus* (Bremen, 1983).

Brustin-Berenstein, Tatiana, 'The Historiographic Treatment of the Abortive Attempt to Deport the Danish Jews', *YVS* 17 (1986), 181–218.

Buch der Erinnerung. Die ins Baltikum deportierten deutschen, österreichischen und tsche-choslowakischen Juden, ed. Wolfgang Scheffler and Diana Schulle, 2 vols (Munich, 2003).

Buchbender, Ortwin, *Das tönende Erz. Die Propaganda gegen die Rote Armee im Zweiten Weltkrieg* (Stuttgart, 1978).

Buchheim, Hans, 'The SS Instrument of Domination', in Buchheim et al., eds, *The Anatomy of the SS State* (London, 1968), 127–301.

Buchholz, Marlis, 'Die hannoverschen Judenhäuser. Zur Situation der Juden in der Zeit der Gettoisierung und Verfolgung 1941 bis 1945', *Quellen und Darstellungen zur Geschichte Niedersachsens* 101 (1987).

Büchler, Yehoshua, 'Kommandostab Reichsführer SS: Himmlers Personal Murder Brigades in 1941', *HGS* 1/1 (1986).

—— 'The Deportation of Slovakian Jews to the Lublin District of Poland in 1942', *HGS* 6 (1991), 151–66.

—— and Bauer, Yehuda, 'Document: A Preparatory Document for the Wannsee "Conference"', *HGS* 9 (1995), 121–9.

Buchloh, Ingrid, *Die nationalsozialistische Machtergreifung in Duisburg. Eine Fallstudie* (Duisburg, 1980).

Burleigh, Michael, *Germany Turns Eastwards: A Study of Ostforschung in the Third Reich* (Cambridge, 1988).

—— *Death and Deliverance: 'Euthanasia' in Germany, 1900–1945* (Cambridge, 1994).

Burrin, Phillipe, *Hitler and the Jews: The Genesis of the Holocaust* (London, 1994).

Buschmann, Arno, *Nationalsozialistische Weltanschauung und Gesetzgebung: 1933–1945*, 2 vols (Vienna, 2000).

Busse, Christian, ' "Eine Maske ist gefallen". Die Berliner Tagung "Das Judentum und die Rechtswissenschaft" 3./4. Oktober 1936', *Kritische Justiz* 33 (2000), 580–93.

Büttner, Ursula, ed., *Das Unrechtsregime. Internationale Forschung über den Nationalso-zialismus*, 2 vols (Hamburg, 1986).

Caestecker, Frank, *Ongewenste Gasten. Joodse vluchteingen en migranten in de dertiger jaren* (Brussels, 1993).

Carpi, Daniel, *Between Mussolini and Hitler: The Jews and the Italian Authorities in France and Tunisia* (London, 1994).

—— 'The Rescue of Jews in the Italian Zone of Occupied Croatia', in David Cesarani and Sarah Kavanaugh, eds, *Nazi Holocaust: Critical Concepts in Historical Studies* (London, 2004), v. 670–730.

Carpi, Daniel, 'Notes on the History of the Jews in Greece during the Holocaust Period: The Attitude of the Italians (1941–1943)', in David Cesarani and Sarah Kavanaugh, eds, *Nazi Holocaust: Critical Concepts in Historical Studies* (London, 2004), vol. v.

Cermáková-Nesládková, Ludmila, *The Case of Nisko in the History of the 'Final Solution of the Jewish Problem' in Commemoration of the 55th Anniversary of the First Deportation of Jews in Europe* (Ostrava, 1994).

Cesarani, David, *Eichmann: His Life and Crimes* (New York, 2004).

Chary, Frederick Barry, 'Bulgaria and the Jews: "The Final Solution", 1940 to 1944', Ph.D. thesis, University of Pittsburgh, 1968.

—— *The Bulgarian Jews and the Final Solution 1940–1944* (Pittsburgh, 1981).

Chiari, Bernhard, 'Deutsche Zivilverwaltung in Weißrußland 1941–1944. Die lokale Perspektive der Besatzungsgeschichte', *MGM* (1993), 67–89.

—— *Alltag hinter der Front. Bestzung, Kollaboration und Widerstand in Weißrußland, 1941–1944* (Düsseldorf, 1998).

Chodakiewicz, Marek Jan, *The Massacre in Jedwabne July 10, 1941: Before, During, After* (New York, 2005).

Cholawsky, Shalom, *The Jews of Bielorussia during World War II* (Amsterdam, 1998).

Chroust, Peter, 'Selected Letters of Doctor Friedrich Mennecke', in Götz Aly, ed., *Cleansing the Fatherland: Nazi Medicine and Racial Hygiene* (Baltimore, 1994).

Cocks, Geoffrey, *Psychotherapy in the Third Reich: The Göring Institute* (Oxford, 1985).

Cohen, William B., and Svensson, Jörgen, 'Finland and the Holocaust', *HGS* 9 (1995), 94–120.

Cole, Tim, *Holocaust City: The Making of a Jewish Ghetto* (New York, 2003).

Corni, Gustavo, *Hitlers Ghettos: Voices from a Beleaguered Society 1939–1944* (London and New York, 2002).

Cranach, Michael von, and Siemen, Hans-Ludwig, eds, *Psychiatrie im Nationalsozialismus. Die Bayerischen Heil- und Pflegeanstalten zwischen 1933 und 1945* (Munich, 1999).

Cüppers, Martin, ' "… auf eine so saubere und anständige SS-mäßige Art". Die Waffen-SS in Polen 1939–1941', in Klaus-Michael Mallmann and Bogdan Musial, eds, *Genesis des Genozids. Polen 1939–1941* (Darmstadt, 2004), 90–110.

—— *Wegbereiter der Shoah. Die Waffen-SS, der Kommandostab Reichsführer-SS und die Judenvernichtung 1939–1945* (Darmstadt, 2005).

Czech, Danuta, 'Deportation und Vernichtung der griechischen Juden im KL Auschwitz', *Hefte von Auschwitz* 11 (1970), 5–37.

Dahm, Volker, 'Kulturelles und geistiges Leben', in Wolfgang Benz, ed., *Die Juden in Deutschland* (Munich, 1988), 75–267.

Daiber, Hans, *Schaufenster der Diktatur: Theater im Machtbereich Hitlers* (Stuttgart, 1995).

Datner, Szymon, 'Crimes Committed by the Wehrmacht during the September Campaign and the Period of Military Government (1.Sept. 1939–25. Oct. 1939)', *Polish Western Affairs* 3 (1962), 294–328.

Davies, Norman, and Polonsky, Antony, *Jews in Eastern Poland and the USSR 1939–46* (New York, 1991).

Dawidowicz, Lucy S., *The War against the Jews 1933–1945* (London, 1975).

Daxelmüller, Christoph, 'Nationalsozialistisches Kulturverständnis und das Ende der jüdischen Volkskunde', in Gerndt, ed., *Volkskunde und Nationalsozialismus*, 149–68.

Dean, Martin C., *Collaboration in the Holocaust: Crimes of the Local Police in Belorussia and Ukraine 1941–1944* (New York, 2000).

Debus, Karl H., 'Die Reichskristallnacht in der Pfalz', *Zeitschrift für die Geschichte des Oberrheins* 129 (1981), 445–515.

Diamant, Adolf, *Zerstörte Synagogen vom November 1938. Eine Bestandsaufnahme* (Frankfurt a. M., 1978).

Dieckmann, Christoph, 'Der Krieg und die Ermordung der litauischen Juden', in Ulrich Herbert, ed., *Nationalsozialistische Vernichtungspolitik 1939–1945. Neue Forschungen und Kontroversen* (Frankfurt a. M., 1998), 293–329.

—— 'Das Ghetto und das Konzentrationslager in Kaunas 1941–1944', in Ulrich Herbert, Karin Orth, and Christoph Dieckmann, eds, *Die nationalsozialistischen Konzentrationslager. Entwicklung und Struktur* (Göttingen, 1998), i. 439–71.

Diehl, Katrin, *Die jüdische Presse im Dritten Reich zwischen Selbstbehauptung und Fremdbestimmung* (Tübingen, 1997).

Diethmar, Reinhard, ed., *Schule und Unterricht im Dritten Reich* (Neuwied, 1989).

Dimitrów, Edmunt, Machcewicz, Pawel, and Szarota, Tomasz, eds, *Der Beginn der Vernichtung. Zum Mord an den Juden in Jedwabne und Umgebung im Sommer 1941. Neue Forschungsergebnisse polnischer Historiker* (Osnabrück, 2004).

Diner, Dan, 'Die Perspektive des "Judenrats". Zur universellen Bedeutung einer partikularen Erfahrung', in Doron Kiesel et al., eds, *'Wer zum Leben, wer zum Tod...'. Strategien jüdischen Überlebens im Ghetto* (Frankfurt a. M., and New York, 1992), 11–36.

Distel, Barbara, '"Die letzte ernste Warnung vor der Vernichtung". Zur Verschleppung der "Aktionsjuden" in die Konzentrationslager', *ZfG* 46/11 (1998), 985–91.

Dörner, Bernward, *Die Deutschen und der Holocaust. Was niemand wissen wollte aber jeder wissen konnte* (Berlin, 2007).

Döscher, Hans-Jürgen, *'Reichskristallnacht'. Die November-Pogrome 1938* (Frankfurt a. M. and Berlin, 1988).

Dow, James R., and Lixfeld, Hannsjost, eds, *The Nazification of an Academic Discipline: Folklore in the Third Reich* (Bloomington, Ind., 1994).

Dressen, Wolfgang, ed., *Betrifft: 'Aktion 3'. Deutsche verwerten jüdische Nachbarn. Dokumente zur Arisierung* (Cologne and Berlin, 1998).

Drewniak, Boguslaw, *Das Theater im NS-Staat. Szenarium deutscher Zeitgeschichte 1933–1945* (Düsseldorf, 1983).

—— *Der deutsche Film 1938–1945. Ein Gesamtüberblick* (Düsseldorf, 1987).

Drobisch, Klaus, 'Die Judenreferate des Geheimen Staatspolizeiamtes und des Sicherheitsdienstes der SS 1933 bis 1939', *Jahrbuch für Antisemitismusforschung* 2 (1993), 230–54.

Dröge, Franz, and Müller, Michael, *Die Macht der Schönheit. Avantgarde und Faschismus oder die Geburt der Massenkultur* (Hamburg, 1995).

Dussel, Konrad, *Ein neues, ein heroisches Theater? Nationalsozialistische Theaterpolitik und ihre Auswirkungen in der Provinz* (Bonn, 1988).

Dwork, Deborah and van Pelt, Robert Jan, *Holocaust. A History* (London, 2002).

Echt, Samuel, *Die Geschichte der Juden in Danzig* (Leer, 1972).

Eckert, Raine, 'Gestapo-Berichte. Abbildungen der Realität oder reine Spekulation?' in Gerhard Paul and Michael Mallmann, eds, *Die Gestapo—Mythos und Realität* (Darmstadt, 1995), 200–15.

Ehalt, Christian, *Inszenierung der Gewalt: Kunst und Alltagskultur im Nationalsozialismus* (Frankfurt a. M., 1996).

Eichler, Thomas, 'Spielplanstrukturen 1929–1944', in Thomas Eichler, Barbara Panse, and Henning Rischbieter, eds, *Theater im 'Dritten Reich': Theaterpolitik, Spielplanstruktur, NS-Dramatik* (Leipzig, 2000).

Eisenblätter, Gerhard, 'Grundlinien der Politik des Reichs gegenüber dem General-gouvernement', phil.diss. (Frankfurt a. M., 1969).

Eisfeld, Alfred, and Herdt, Victor, eds, *Deportation, Sondersiedlung, Arbeitsarmee. Deutsche in der Sowjetunion 1941–1956* (Cologne, 1996).

Ely, Geoff, ed., *The 'Goldhagen Effect': History, Memory, Nazism—Facing the German Past* (Ann Arbor, 2000).

Enzyklopädie des Holocaust. Die Verfolgung und Ermordung der europäischen Juden, ed. Israel Gutman, 4 vols (New York, 1990).

Esch, Michael G., 'Die Politik der polnischen Vertretungen im Deutschen Reich 1935 bis 1939 und der Novemberpogrom 1938', *Jahrbuch für Antisemitismusforschung* 8 (1999), 131–54.

Essner, Cornelia, 'Die Alchimie des Rassenbegriffs und die "Nürnberger Gesetze"', *Jahrbuch für Antisemitismusforschung* 4 (1995), 201–25.

—— *Die 'Nürnberger Gesetze' oder die Verwaltung des Rassenwahns* (Paderborn, 2002).

Ezergailis, Andrew, *The Holocaust in Latvia, 1941–1944: The Missing Center* (Riga and Washington, 1996).

Fahlbusch, Michael, *Wissenschaft im Dienst der nationalsozialistischen Politik? Die Volksdeutschen 'Forschungsgemeinschaften' von 1931–1945* (Baden-Baden, 1999).

Fargion, Lliana Picciotto, 'Italien', in Benz, ed., *Dimension*, 199–227.

Fatran, Gilda, 'Die Deportation der Juden aus der Slowakei', *Bohemia* 37 (1996), 98–119.

Faulstich, Heinz, *Von der Irrenfürsorge zur 'Euthanasie'. Geschichte der badischen Psychiatrie bis 1945* (Freiburg, 1993).

—— *Hungersterben in der Psychiatrie. 1914–1949; mit einer Topographie der NS-Psychiatrie* (Freiburg im Breisgau, 1998).

Faust, Anselm, 'Die Hochschulen und der "undeutsche Geist". Die Bücherverbrennung am 10. Mai 1933 und ihre Vorgeschichte', in *'Das war ein Vorspiel nur...'. Bücherverbrennung Deutschland 1933: Voraussetzungen und Folgen* (Berlin and Vienna, 1983), 31–50.

Favez, Jean-Claude, *The Red Cross and the Holocaust* (Cambridge, 1999).

Feilchenfeld, Werner, Michaelis, Wolf, and Pinner, Ludwig, *Haavara-Transfer nach Palästina und Einwanderung deutscher Juden 1933–1939* (Tübingen, 1972).

Fein, Helen, *Accounting for Genocide: National Response and Jewish Victimization during the Holocaust* (New York and London, 1979).

Feldman, Gerald, *Allianz and the German Insurance Business 1933–1945* (New York, 2001).

Fichtl, Franz, Link, Stephan, and May, Herbert, et al., eds, *'Bambergs Wirtschaft judenfrei'. Die Verdrängung der jüdischen Geschäftsleute in den Jahren 1933 bis 1939* (Bamberg, 1998).

Fischer, Albert, 'Jüdische Privatbanken im Dritten Reich', *Scripta Mercaturae. Zeitschrift für Wirtschafts- und Sozialgeschichte* 28, Heft 1/2 (1994), 1–54.

—— *Hjalmar Schacht und Deutschlands 'Judenfrage'. Der 'Wirtschaftsdiktator' und die Vertreibung der Juden aus der Wirtschaft* (Cologne, 1995).

Fischer, Lars, *The Socialist Response to Antisemitism in Imperial Germany* (Cambridge, 2007).

Flan, Gila, 'Das kulturelle Leben im Getto Lodz', in Doron Kiesel et al., eds, *'Wer zum Leben, wer zum Tod...'. Strategien jüdischen Überlebens im Ghetto* (Frankfurt, 1992), 77–96.

Fleischer, Hagen, 'Griechenland', in Benz, ed., *Dimension*, 241–74.

Fleming, Gerald, *Hitler and the Final Solution* (London, 1984).

Fliedner, Hans Joachim, *Die Judenverfolgung in Mannheim 1933–1945*, 2 vols (Stuttgart, 1971).

Florian, Radu, 'The Jassy Massacre of June 29–30, 1941: An Early Act of Genocide against the Jews', in Randolph L. Braham, ed., *The Destruction of Romanian and Ukrainian Jews during the Antonescu Era* (New York, 1997), 63–86.

Fogel, Heidi, *Nationalsozialismus in der Dreieich. Aufstieg und Herrschaft der NSDAP im heterogen strukturierten Lebens- und Erfahrungsraum des südlichen Frankfurter Umlandes* (Darmstadt, 1991).

Föhse, Ulrich, 'Erst Mensch, dann Untermensch. Der Weg der jüdischen Wuppertaler in den Holocaust', in Klaus Goebel, ed., *Wuppertal in der Zeit des Nationalsozialismus*, 2nd edn (Wuppertal, 1984), 65–80.

Förster, Jürgen, 'Operation Barbarossa as a War of Conquest and Annihilation', in Horst Boog et al., eds, *Germany and the Second World War, iv: The Attack on the Soviet Union*, 4th edn (Oxford, 1996).

Freeden, Herbert, *Die jüdische Presse im Dritten Reich. Eine Veröffentlichung des Leo Baeck Instituts* (Frankfurt a. M., 1987).

Fricke, Dieter, ed., *Lexikon zur Parteiengeschichte. Die bürgerlichen und kleinbürgerlichen Parteien und Verbände in Deutschland (1789–1945)*, 4 vols (Cologne, 1983–6).

Fricke-Finkelnburg, Renate, ed., *Nationalsozialismus und Schule Amtliche Erlasse und Richtlinien* (Opladen, 1989).

Friedländer, Henry, 'The Deportation of the German Jews: Post-War German Trials of Nazi Criminals', *LBIY* 29 (1984), 201–26.

—— *The Origins of Nazi Genocide: From Euthansia to the Final Solution* (Chapel Hill, NC, 1995).

Friedländer, Saul, 'Vom Antisemitismus zur Judenvernichtung: Eine historiographische Studie zur nationalsozialistischen Judenpolitik und Versuch einer Interpretation', in Eberhard Jäckel and Jürgen Rohwer, eds, *Der Mord an den Juden im Zweiten Weltkrieg* (Stuttgart, 1985), 18–62.

—— *Nazi Germany and the Jews*, vol. i: *The Years of Persecution* (New York and London, 1997).

—— *The Years of Extermination: Nazi Germany and the Jews 1939–1945*, vol. ii (London, 2007).

Friedrich, Jörg, *Das Gesetz des Krieges. Das deutsche Heer in Rußland 1941 bis 1945. Der Prozeß gegen das Oberkommando der Wehrmacht* (Munich and Zurich, 1993).

Friemert, Chup, *Schönheit der Arbeit. Produktionsästhetik im Faschismus. Das Amt 'Schönheit der Arbeit' von 1933 bis 1939* (Munich, 1980).

Fritzsche, Klaus, *Politische Romantik und Gegenrevolution. Fluchtweg in der Krise der bürgerlichen Gesellschaft: Das Beispiel des 'Tat'-Kreises* (Frankfurt a. M., 1976).

Fritzsche, Peter, *Life and Death in the Third Reich* (Cambridge, Mass., 2008).

—— *Germans into Nazis* (Cambridge, Mass., 1998).

Fröbe, Reiner, 'Der Arbeitseinsatz von KZ-Häftlingen und die Perspektive der Industrie', in *'Deutsche Wirtschaft'. Zwangsarbeit von KZ-Häftlingen für Industrie und Behörden*, Hamburger Stiftung zur Förderung von Wissenschaft und Kunst (Hamburg, 1991), 33–78.

Gaertringen, Friedrich Freiherr von, 'Die Deutschnationale Volkspartei', in Erich Matthias and Rudolf Morsey, eds, *Das Ende der Parteien: 1933* (Düsseldorf, 1960).

Gailus, Manfred, *Protestantismus und Nationalsozialismus. Studien zur nationalsozialistischen Durchdringung des protestantischen Sozialmileus in Berlin* (Cologne, 2001).

Ganssmüller, Christian, *Die Erbgesundheitspolitik des Dritten Reiches. Planung, Durchführung, und Durchsetzung* (Cologne, 1987).

Gasparaitris, Siegfried, ' "Verrätern wird nur dann vergeben, wenn sie wirklich beweisen können, dass sie mindestens einen Juden liquidiert haben." Die Front Litauischer Aktisten (LAF) und die antisowjetischen Aufstände 1941', *ZfG* 49 (2001), 886–904.

Geisel, Eike, and Broder, Henry M., *Premiere und Pogrom. Der jüdische Kulturbund 1933–1941. Texte und Bilder* (Berlin, 1992).

Geist, Friedrich, and Kürvers, Klaus, 'Tatort Berlin, Pariser Platz. Die Zerstörung und "Entjudung" Berlins', in Jörn Düwel et al., eds, *1945. Krieg—Zerstörung—Aufbau. Architektur und Stadtplanung 1940–1960* (Berlin 1995).

Gellately, Robert, *The Gestapo and German Society: Enforcing Racial Policy 1933–1945* (Oxford, 1990).

—— *Backing Hitler: Consent and Coercion in Nazi Germany* (Oxford, 2001).

—— *Hingeschaut und Weggesehen. Hitler und sein Volk* (Stuttgart, 2002).

Genschel, Helmut, *Die Verdrängung der Juden aus der Wirtschaft im Dritten Reich* (Göttingen, 1966).

Gerlach, Christian, 'Failure of Plans for an SS Extermination Camp in Mogilew, Belorussia', *HGS* 7 (1997), 60–78.

—— 'Die Einsatzgruppe C', in *Einsatzgruppen*, ed. Klein (1997), 52–70.

—— 'The Wannsee Conference, the Fate of the German Jews, and Hitler's Decision in Principle to Exterminate all European Jews', *Journal of Modern History* 70 (1998), 759–812.

—— *Krieg, Ernährung, Völkermord. Forschungen zur deutschen Vernichtungspolitik im Zweiten Weltkrieg* (Hamburg, 1998).

—— 'Die Bedeutung der deutschen Ernährungspolitik für die Beschleunigung des Mordes an den Juden 1942. Das Generalgouvernment und die Westukraine', in Gerlach, *Krieg, Ernährung*.

—— *Kalkulierte Morde. Die deutsche Wirtschafts- und Vernichtungspolitik in Weissrussland 1941 bis 1944* (Hamburg, 1999).

—— 'German Economic Interests, Occupation Policy, and the Murder of the Jews in Belorussia, 1941–1943', in Ulrich Herbert, ed., *National Socialist Extermination Policies* (New York, 2000), 210–39.

—— 'The Eichmann Interrogations in Holocaust Historiography', *HGS* 15/3 (2001), 428–52.

—— and Aly, Götz, *Der letzte Kapitel. Realpolitik, Ideologie und der Mord an den ungarischen Juden* (Stuttgart, 2002).

Gerndt, Helge, ed., *Volkskunde und Nationalsozialismus. Referate und Diskussionen einer Tagung der Deutschen Gesellschaft für Volkskunde, München 23 bis 25 Oktober 1986* (Munich, 1987).

Gerstenberger, Heide, *Der revolutionäre Konservatismus. Ein Beitrag zur Analyse des Liberalismus* (Berlin, 1969).

Gerstengarbe, Sybille, 'Die erste Entlassungswelle von Hochschullehrern deutscher Hochschulen aufgrund des Gesetzes zur Wiederherstellung des Berufsbeamtentums vom 7.4.1933', *Beiträge zur Wissenschaftsgeschichte* 17 (1994), 17–39.

Gies, Horst, *Geschichtsunterricht unter der Diktatur Hitlers* (Cologne, 1992).

Goertz, Dieter, *Juden in Oldenburg, 1930–1938. Struktur, Integration und Verfolgung* (Oldenburg, 1988).

Goggin, James E., and Goggin, Eileen Brockman, *Death of a 'Jewish Science': Psychoanalysis in the Third Reich* (Lafayette, Ind., 2001).

Golczewski, Frank, 'Polen', in Benz, ed., *Dimension*, 411–97.

Goldberg, Bettina, 'Die Zwangsausweisung der polnischen Juden aus dem Deutschen Reich im Oktober 1938 und die Folgen', *ZfG* 46 (1988), 52–72.

Goldhagen, Daniel J., *Hitlers Willing Executioners: Ordinary Germans and the Holocaust* (New York, 1996).

Göppinger Horst, *Die Verfolgung der Juristen jüdischer Abstammung durch den National-sozialismus* (Villingen and Schwarzwald, 1963).

Gordon, Sarah, *Hitler, Germans and the 'Jewish Question'* (Princeton, 1984).

Goshem, Seev, 'Eichmann und die Nisko-Aktion im Oktober 1939. Eine Fallstudie zur NS-Judenpolitik in der letzten Etappe vor der "Endlösung"', *VfZ* 27 (1981), 74–96.

—— 'Nisko—Ein Ausnahmefall unter den Judenlagern der SS', *VfZ* 40 (1992), 95–106.

Gottwald, Alfred, and Schulle, Diana, *Die 'Judendeportationen' aus dem deutschen Reich 1941–1945. Eine kommentierte Chronologie* (Wiesbaden, 2005).

Götz, Margarete, *Die Grundschule in der Zeit des Nationalsozialismus. Eine Untersuchung der inneren Ausgestaltung der vier unteren Jahrgänge der Volksschule auf der Grundlage amtlicher Maßnahmen* (Bad Heilbrunn, 1997).

Grabitz, Helge, Bästlein, Klaus, and Tuchel, Johannes, eds, *Die Normalität des Verbrechens. Bilanz und Perspektiven der Forschung zu den nationalsozialistischen Gewaltverbrechen. Festschrift für Wolfgang Scheffler zum 65. Geburtstag* (Berlin, 1994).

Graf, Christoph, *Politische Polizei zwischen Demokratie und Diktatur* (Berlin, 1983).

Graml, Hermann, *Der 9. November 1938. 'Reichskristallnacht'*, 3rd edn (Bonn, 1955).

—— *Reichskristallnacht. Antisemitismus und Judenverfolgung im Dritten Reich* (Munich, 1988).

Greiser, Katrin, *Thüringen 1945. Todesmärsche aus Buchenwald. Überblick, Namen, Orte* (Weimar, 2001).

—— 'Die Auflösung des Lagerkomplexes Buchenwald und die Todesmärsche aus den Aussenlagern im Rheinland und in Westfalen im März und April 1945', in Jan Erik Schulte, ed., *Konzentrationslager im Rheinland und Westfalen 1933–1945. Zentrale Steuerung und regionale Initiative* (Paderborn, 2005).

Greive, Hermann, *Theologie und Ideologie. Katholizismus und Judentum in Deutschland und Österreich, 1918–1935* (Heidelberg, 1969).

Grenville, John A. S., 'Die "Endlösung" und die "Judenmischlinge" im Dritten Reich', in Ursula Büttner, ed., *Das Unrechtsregime*, vol. ii: *Verfolgung—Exil—Belasteter Neubeginn* (Hamburg, 1996), 91–121.

Greuter, Ulfried, *Die Professionalisierung der deutschen Psychologie im Nationalsozialismus* (Frankfurt a. M., 1984).

Grimm, Gerhard, 'Albanien', in Benz, ed., *Dimension*, 229–39.

Grode, Walter, *Nationalsozialistische Moderne. Rassenideologische Modernisierung durch Abtrennug und Zerstörung gesellschaftlicher Peripherien* (Frankfurt a. M., 1994).

——*Die 'Sonderbehandlung 14f13' in den Konzentrationslagern des Dritten Reiches* (Frankfurt a. M., 1995).

Gross, Jan T., *Neighbors: The Destruction of the Jewish Community in Jedwabne, Poland* (Princeton and Oxford, 2001).

Grossmann, Wassili, et al., eds, *Das Schwarzbuch. Der Genozid an den sowjetischen Juden* (Reinbek, 1995).

Gruchmann, Lothar, *Der Zweite Weltkrieg* (Munich, 1967).

——*Justiz im Dritten Reich 1933–1940. Anpassung und Unterwerfung in der Ära Gürtner 1933–1940* (Munich, 1988).

Gruner, Wolf, *Der geschlossene Arbeitseinsatz deutscher Juden. Zur Zwangsarbeit als Element der Verfolgung, 1938–1943* (Berlin, 1997).

——'Die öffentliche Fürsorge und die deutschen Juden 1933–1942', *ZfG* 45 (1997), 599–616.

——'Poverty and Persecution: The Reichsvereinigung, the Jewish Population and Anti-Jewish Policy in the Nazi State 1933–1945', *YVS* 27 (1999), 23–61.

——*Öffentliche Wohlfahrt und Judenverfolgung. Wechselwirkung lokaler und zentraler Politik im NS-Staat 1933–1942* (Munich, 2002).

——'Von der Kollektivausweisung zur Deportation der Juden aus Deutschland', in Birthe Kundrus and Beate Meyer, eds, *Beiträge zur Geschichte des Nationalsozialismus*, vol. xx: *Die Deportation der Juden aus Deutschland. Pläne—Praxis—Reaktionen 1938–1945* (Göttingen, 2004), 21–62.

——*Widerstand in der Rosenstrasse: Die Fabrik-Aktion und die Verfolgung der 'Mischehen' 1943* (Frankfurt a. M., 2005).

Gutman, Yisrael, *The Jews of Warsaw, 1939–1943: Ghetto, Underground, Revolt*, trans. Ina Friedman (Jerusalem and Bloomington, Ind., 1982).

——and Haft, Cynthia, eds, *Patterns of Jewish Leadership in Nazi Europe, 1933–1945* (Jerusalem, 1979).

Haar, Ingo, *Historiker im Nationalsozialismus. Deutsche Geschichtswissenschaft und der 'Volkstumskampf' im Osten* (Göttingen, 2000).

Hachmeister, Lutz, *Der Gegnerforscher. Die Karriere des SS-Führers Franz Alfred Six* (Munich, 1998).

Hachmeister, Silke, *Kinopropaganda gegen Kranke. Die Instrumentalisierung des Spielfilms 'Ich klage an' für das nationalsozialistische 'Euthanasieprogramm'* (Baden-Baden, 1992).

Hagemann, Jürgen, *Die Presselenkung im Dritten Reich* (Bonn, 1970).

Hamel, Iris, *Völkischer Verband und nationale Gewerkschaft: Der Deutschnationale Handlungsgehilfenverband 1893–1933* (Frankfurt a. M., 1967).

Händler-Lachmann, Barbara, and Werther, Thomas, *Vergessene Geschäfte, verlorene Geschichte. Jüdisches Wirtschaftsleben in Marburg und seine Vernichtung im National-sozialismus* (Marburg, 1992).

Hanke, Peter, *Zur Geschichte der Juden in München* (Munich, 1967).

Harten, Hans-Christian, *De-Kulturation und Germanisierung. Die nationalsozialistische Rassen- und Erziehungspolitik in Polen 1939–1945* (Frankfurt a. M., 1996).

Hartmann, Christian, Hürter, Johannes, and Jureit, Ulrike, eds, *Verbrechen der Wehrmacht. Bilanz einer Debatte* (Munich, 2005).

—— 'Verbrecherischer Krieg—verbrecherische Wehrmacht? Überlegungen zur Struktur des deutschen Ostheeres 1941–1944' VfZ 52 (2004), 1–75.

Hartog, L. J., Der Befehl zum Judenmord. Hitler, Amerika und die Juden (Bodenheim 1997).

Hauschildt, Dietrich, 'Vom Judenboykott zum Judenmord', in Erich Hoffmann and Peter Wulf, eds, 'Wir bauen das Reich'. Aufstieg und erste Herrschaftsjahre des Nationalsozialismus in Schleswig-Holstein (Neumünster, 1983), 335–60.

Hayes, Peter, 'Big Business and "Aryanization" in Germany, 1933–1939', Jahrbuch für Antisemitismusforschung 3 (1994), 254–81.

Heberer, Patricia, 'Eine Kontinuität der Tötungsoperationen. T4-Täter und die "Aktion Reinhardt"', in 'Aktion Reinhardt'. Der Völkermord an den Juden im Generalgouvernement 1941–1944, ed. Bogdan Musial (Osnabrück, 2004).

Heer, Hannes, 'Einübung in den Holocaust: Lemberg Juni/Juli 1941', ZfG 40 (2001), 389–408.

—— 'Die Logik des Vernichtungskrieges. Wehrmacht und Partisanenkampf', in Heer and Naumann, eds, Vernichtungskrieg, 104–56.

—— 'Killing Fields: The Wehrmacht and the Holocaust in Belorussia 1941–1942', in Heer and Naumann, eds, War of Extermination, 57–77.

—— 'The Logic of the War of Extermination: The Wehrmacht and the Anti-Partisan War of Extermination', in Heer and Naumann, eds, The War of Extermination.

—— and Naumann, Klaus, Vernichtungskrieg. Verbrechen der Wehrmacht 1941–1945 (Hamburg, 1995).

—— War of Extermination: The German Military in World War II 1941–1944 (New York, 2004).

Heil, Johannes, and Erb, Rainer, eds, Geschichtswissenschaft und Öffentlichkeit. Der Streit um Daniel J. Goldhagen (Frankfurt a. M., 1998).

Heilbronner, Oded, 'The Role of Antisemitism in the Nazi Party's Activity and Propaganda: A Regional Historiographical Study', LBIY 35 (1990), 397–439.

Heilen und Vernichten im Mustergau Hamburg. Bevölkerungs- und Gesundheitspolitik im Dritten Reich, ed. Angelika Ebbinghaus, Heidrun Kaupen-Haas, and Karl Heinz Roth (Hamburg, 1984).

Heim, Susanne, '"Deutschland muß ihnen ein Land ohne Zukunft sein". Die Zwangsemigration der Juden 1933 bis 1938', in Eberhard Jungfer et al., eds, Arbeitsmigration und Flucht, Vertreibung und Arbeitskräfteregulierung im Zwischenkriegseuropa. Beiträge zur nationalsozialistischen Gesundheits- und Sozialpolitik, vol. xi (Berlin, 1993), 48–81.

Heinen, Armin, Die Legion 'Erzengel Michael' in Rumänien. Soziale Bewegung und politische Organisation. Ein Beitrag zum Problem des internationalen Faschismus (Munich, 1986).

Held, Thomas, 'Vom Pogrom zum Massenmord. Die Vernichtung der jüdischen Bevölkerung Lembergs im Zweiten Weltkrieg', in Peter Fäßler, Thomas Held, and Dirk Sawitzki, eds, Lemberg—Lwów—Lviv (Cologne, 1993), 113–66.

Henkys, Reinhard, 'Ein Todesmarsch in Ostpreußen', Dachauer Hefte 20 (2004), 3–2.

Herbert, Ulrich, Fremdarbeiter. Politik und Praxis des 'Ausländer-Einsatzes' in der Kriegswirtschaft des Dritten Reiches (Berlin and Bonn, 1985).

—— ed., Europa und der 'Reichseinsatz'. Ausländische Zivilarbeiter, Kriegsgefangene und KZ-Häftlinge in Deutschland 1938–1945 (Essen, 1991).

Herbert, Ulrich,' "Generation der Sachlichkeit". Die völkische Studentenbewegung der frühen zwanziger Jahre in Deutschland', in Frank Bajohr, Werner Johe, and Uwe Lohalm, eds, *Zivilisation und Barbarei. Die Widersprüchlichen Potentiale der Moderne* (Hamburg, 1991).

—— 'Labour and Extermination: Economic Interest and the Primacy of Weltanschauung in National Socialism', *Past and Present* 138 (1993), 144–95.

—— 'Weltanschauung, Kalkül und "Sachzwang": Ökonomische Aspekte der "Endlösung der Judenfrage" ', in *Der Umgang mit dem Holocaust. Europa—USA—Israel* (Vienna, Cologne, and Weimar, 1994), 45–59.

—— 'Von der "Reichskristallnacht" zum "Holocaust". Der 9. November und das Ende des "Radau-Antisemitismus" ', in Herbert, ed., *Arbeit, Volkstum, Weltanschauung. Über Fremde und Deutsche im 20. Jahrhundert* (Frankfurt a. Main, 1995), 59–78.

—— 'Die deutsche Militärverwaltung in Paris und die Deportation der Französischen Juden', in Christian Jansen et al., eds, *Von der Aufgabe der Freiheit. Politische Verant- wortung und bürgeliche Gesellschaft in 19. u. 20. Jahrhundert. Festschrift für Hans Mommsen zum 5. November 1995* (Berlin, 1995), 427–50.

—— *Best. Biographische Studien über Radikalismus, Weltanschauung und Vernunft, 1903–1989* (Bonn, 1996).

—— 'The German Military Command in Paris and the Deportation of the French Jews' in Herbert, *National Socialist Extermination Policies: Contemporary German Perspectives and Controversies* (New York, 2000), 128–62.

—— Orth, Karin, and Dieckmann, Christoph, eds, *Die nationalsozialistischen Konzentra- tionslager. Entwicklung und Struktur*, 2 vols (Göttingen, 1998).

Herbst, Ludolf, *Das nationalsozialistische Deutschland 1933–1945. Die Entfesselung der Gewalt: Rassismus und Krieg* (Frankfurt a. M., 1996).

Hermand, Jost, *Old Dreams of a New Reich: Volkish Utopias and National Socialism* (Bloomington, Ind., 1992).

Hermeler, Ludwig, *Die Euthanasie und die späte Unschuld der Psychiater. Massenmord, Bedburg-Hau und das Geheimnis rheinischer Widerstandslegenden* (Essen, 2002).

Hertzman, Lewis, *DNVP: Right-Wing Opposition in the Weimar Republic 1918–1924* (Lincoln, Nebr., 1963).

Herzog, Dagmar, ed., *Lessons and Legacies*, vii: *The Holocaust in International Perspective* (Evanston, 2006).

Heske, Henning, *'und morgen die ganze Welt . . . ' Erdkundeunterricht im Nationalsozialismus* (Gießen, 1988).

Hesse, Klaus, and Springer, Philipp, *Vor aller Augen. Fotodokumente des nationalsozialistischen Terrors in der Provinz* (Essen, 2002).

Hietala, Marjrjatta, *Der neue Nationalismus in der Publizistik Ernst Jüngers und des Kreises um ihn* (Helsinki, 1975).

Hilberg, Raul, *The Destruction of the European Jews*, 3 vols, rev. edn (New Haven, 2003).

—— 'Die Aktion Reinhard', in Eberhard Jäckel and Jürgen Rohwer, eds, *Der Mord an den Juden im Zweiten Weltkrieg* (Stuttgart 1985).

—— *Sonderzüge nach Auschwitz* (Frankfurt and Berlin, 1987).

Hildebrand, Klaus, *Das vergangene Reich. Deutsche Außenpolitik von Bismarck bis Hitler, 1871–1945* (Stuttgart, 1995).

Hildesheimer, Esriel, *Jüdische Selbstverwaltung unter dem NS-Regime. Der Existenzkampf der Reichsvertretung und Reichsvereinigung der Juden in Deutschland* (Tübingen, 1994).

Hillgruber, Andreas, *Hitlers Strategie. Politik und Kriegführung 1940–1941* (Frankfurt a. M., 1965).

—— 'Der Ostkrieg und die Judenvernichtung', in Gerd R. Ueberschär and Wolfram Wette, eds, '*Unternehmen Barbarossa*' (Paderborn, 1984), 219–36.

Hirschfeld, Gerhard, ed., *The Politics of Genocide: Jews and Soviet Prisoners of War in Nazi Germany* (London, 1986).

—— *Fremdherrschaft und Kollaboration. Die Niederlande unter deutscher Besatzung, 1940–1945* (Stuttgart, 1984). English version: Gerhard Hirschfeld, *Nazi Rule and Dutch Collaboration: The Netherlands under German Occupation* (New York 1988).

Hoffmann, Dieter, '*. . . wir sind doch Deutsche*'. *Zur Geschichte und Schicksal der Landjuden in Rheinhessen* (Alzey, 1992).

Hoffmann, Herbert, *Im Gleichschritt in die Diktatur? Die nationalsozialistische 'Machtergreifung' in Heidelberg und Mannheim 1930 bis 1935* (Frankfurt a. M., 1985).

Hohmann, Joachim S., ' "Instrument von Kontrolle und Lenkung" Ländliche Soziologie unterm Hakenkreuz', *ZAA* 45 (1997), 227–35.

Hollstein, Dorothea, *Antisemitische Filmpropaganda. Die Darstellung der Juden im nationalsozialistischen Spielfilm* (Munich, 1971).

Holzbach, Heidrun, *Das 'System Hugenberg'. Die Organisation bürgerlicher Sammlungspolitk vor dem Aufstieg der NSDAP* (Stuttgart, 1981).

Hoppe, Hans-Joachim, 'Bulgarien', in Benz, ed., *Dimensionen*, 275–310.

Hornung, Klaus, *Der Jungdeutsche Orden* (Düsseldorf, 1958).

Hürter, Johannes and Zarusky, Türgen, eds, *Besatzung, Kollaboration, Holocaust. Neue Studien zur Verfolgung und Ermordung der europäischen Juden* (Munich, 2008).

Ignatiew, Radoslaw J., 'Findings of Investigations 1/00/Zn into the Murder of Polish Citizens of Jewish Origin in the Town of Jedwabne on 10 July 1941', in Polonsky and Michlic (eds), *The Neighbors Respond*, 133–6.

Im Ghetto 1939–1945. Neue Forschungen zu Alltag und Umfeld, ed. Christoph Dieckmann and Babette Quinkert (Göttingen, 2009).

Ioanid, Radu, *The Holocaust in Romania: The Destruction of Jews and Gypsies under the Antonescu Regime 1940–1944* (Chicago, 1999).

Ishida, Yuji, *Jungkonservative in der Weimarer Republik. Der Ring-Kreis 1928–1933* (Frankfurt, 1988).

Jäckel, Eberhard, *Frankreich in Hitlers Europa. Die deutsche Frankreichpolitik im Zweiten Weltkrieg* (Stuttgart, 1966).

—— *Hitlers Weltanschauung. Entwurf einer Herrschaft* (Tübingen. 1969). English version: *Hitler's World View: A Blueprint for Power* (Cambridge, Mass., 1972).

—— 'On the Purpose of the Wannsee Conference', in James S. Pacy and Alan P. Wertheimer, eds, *Perspectives of the Holocaust: Essays in Honor of Raul Hilberg* (Boulder, Colo., 1994), 39–50.

—— *Hitlers Herrschaft. Vollzug einer Weltanschauung* (Stuttgart, 1986).

—— and Rohwer, Jürgen, eds, *Der Mord an den Juden im Zweiten Weltkrieg. Entschlußbildung und Verwirklichung* (Stuttgart, 1985).

Jacobeit, Wolfgang, Lixfeld, Hannsjost, and Blochhorn, Olaf, eds, *Völkische Wissenschaft. Gestalten und Tendenzen der deutschen und österreichischen Volkskunde in der ersten Hälfte des 20. Jahrhunderts* (Vienna, Cologne and Weimar, 1994).

Jacobsen, Hans-Adolf, 'The Kommissarbefehl and Mass Executions of Soviet Russian Prisoners of War', in Hans Buchheim et al., *Anatomy of the SS State* (London, 1968), 505–33.

Jahn, Peter, and Rürup, Reinhard, eds, *Erobern und Vernichten. Der Krieg gegen die Sowjetunion* (Berlin, 1991).

Jansen, Christian, and Weckbecker, Arno, *Der 'Volksdeutsche Selbstschutz' in Polen 1939/40* (Munich, 1992),

Jansen, Hans, *Der Madagaskar-Plan. Die beabsichtigte Deportation der europäischen Juden nach Madagaskar* (Munich, 1997).

Jasper, Gotthard, *Die gescheiterte Zähmung. Wege zur Machtergreifung Hitlers 1930–1934* (Frankfurt a. M., 1986).

Jastrzebski, Wlodzimierz, *Der Bromberger Blutsonntag. Legende und Wirklichkeit* (Poznan, 1990).

Jellonek, Burkhard, *Homosexuelle unter dem Hakenkreuz. Die Verfolgung von Homosexuellen im Dritten Reich* (Paderborn, 1990).

Jersak, Tobias, 'Die Interaktion von Kriegsverlauf und Judenvernichtung. Ein Blick auf Hitlers Strategie im Spätsommer 1941', *Historische Zeitschrift* 268 (1999), 311–74.

Jochheim, Gernot, *Frauenprotest in der Rosenstraße. 'Gebt uns unsere Männer wieder'*, (Berlin, 1993).

Jochmann, Werner, 'Die deutsche Bevölkerung und die nationalsozialistische Judenpolitik bis zur Verkündung der Nürnberger Gesetze', in Jochmann, *Gesellschaftskrise und Judenfeindschaft in Deutschland* (Hamburg, 1988), 236–54.

Johe, Werner, *Gleichgeschaltete Justiz* (Hamburg, 1967).

Johnson, Erik Arthur, *The Nazi Terror: Gestapo, Jews and Ordinary Germans* (London, 1999).

Jonca, Karol, 'Jewish Resistance to Nazi Racial Legislation in Silesia, 1933–1937', in Francis R. Nicosia and Lawrence D. Stokes, eds, *Germans Against Nazism: Nonconformity, Opposition and Resistance in the Third Reich. Essays in Honour of Peter Hoffmann* (New York and Oxford, 1990).

——— 'Die Deportation und Vernichtung der schlesischen Juden', in Grabitz, et al., eds, *Normalität*, 150–70.

Jones, Larry E., *German Liberalism and the Dissolution of the Weimar Party System 1918–1933* (Chapel Hill, NC, 1988).

Die Juden in Hamburg 1590 bis 1990. Wissenschaftliche Beiträge der Universität Hamburg zur Ausstellung 'Vierhundert Jahre Juden in Hamburg', ed. Arno Herzig in collaboration with Saskia Rohde (Hamburg, 1991), 499–514.

Junk, Peter, and Sellmeyer, Martina, *Stationen auf dem Weg nach Auschwitz. Entrechtung, Vertreibung, Vernichtung. Juden in Osnabrück 1900–1945* (Osnabrück, 1988).

Junker, Almut, *Frankfurt Macht Mode: 1933–1945* (Frankfurt a. M., 1999).

Kaienburg, Hermann, *Vernichtung durch Arbeit. Der Fall Neuengamme* (Bonn, 1990).

——— ed., *Konzentrationslager und deutsche Wirtschaft* (Opladen, 1996).

—— 'Jüdische Arbeitslager an der Strasse der SS', *Zeitschrift für Sozialgeschichte des 20. und 21. Jahrhunderts*, 11 (1996), 13–39.

—— 'Zwangsarbeitslager an der "Straße der SS"', *1999* 11(1996), 13–39.

—— 'Zwangsarbeit: KZ und Wirtschaft im Zweiten Weltkrieg', in Wolfgang Benz and Barbara Distel, eds, *Die Ort des Terrors. Geschichte der nationalsozialistischen Konzentrationslager*, vol. i: *Die Organisation des Terrors* (Munich, 2005), 179–94.

—— 'Sachsenhausen-Stammlager', in Benz and Distel, eds, *Der Ort des Terrors*, iii. 17–72.

Kamenec, Ivan, 'Die erfolglosen Versuche zur Wiederaufnahme der Deportationen der slowakischen Juden', *TSD* (2002), 318–37.

—— *On the Trail of Tragedy. The Holocaust in Slovakia* (Bratislava, 2007).

Kaminsky, Uwe, *Zwangssterilisation und 'Euthanasie' im Rheinland. Evangelische Erziehungsanstalten sowie Heil- und Pflegeanstalten 1933–1945* (Cologne, 1995).

Kangeris, Karlis, 'Kollaboration vor der Kollaboration? Die baltischen Emigranten und ihre "Befreiungskomitees" in Deutschland 1940/41', in Werner Röhr (compiled and introduced), *Europa unterm Hakenkreuz. Okkupation und Kollaboration (1938–1945). Beiträge zu Konzepten und Praxis der Kollaboration in der deutschen Okkupationspolitik* (Berlin and Heidelberg, 1994), 165–90.

Kaplan, Marion, *Between Dignity and Despair: Jewish Daily Life in Germany* (Oxford, 1998).

—— *Der Mut zum Überleben. Jüdische Frauen und ihre Familien in Nazi Deutschland* (Berlin, 2001).

Kárny, Miroslav, 'Nisko in der Geschichte der Endlösung', *Judaica Bohemiae* 23 (1987), 69–84.

Kater, Michael H., *Studentenschaft und Rechtsradikalismus in Deutschland* (Hamburg, 1975).

—— *Die mißbrauchte Muse. Musiker im Dritten Reich* (Vienna and Munich, 1998).

Kaufman, Max, *Churbn, Lettland: The Destruction of the Jews of Latvia* (Munich, 1947).

Kempner, Robert M. W., *Eichmann und Komplizen* (Zurich, 1961).

Kershaw, Ian, 'Antisemitismus und Volksmeinung. Reaktionen auf die Judenverfolgung', in Martin Broszat and Elke Fröhlich, eds, *Bayern in der NS-Zeit*, vol. ii (Munich, 1979), 281–348.

—— 'The Persecution of the Jews and German Popular Opinion in the Third Reich', *LBIY* 26 (1981), 261–89.

—— *Popular Opinion and Political Dissent in the Third Reich, Bavaria 1933–1945* (Oxford, 1983).

—— 'Improvised Genocide? The Emergence of the "Final Solution" in the Warthegau', *Transactions of the Royal Historical Society*, 6th ser., 2 (1992), 51–78.

—— *The Nazi Dictatorship: Problems and Perspectives of Interpretation*, 4th edn (London, 2000).

Kessler, Heinrich, *Wilhelm Stapel als politische Publizist* (Nuremberg, 1967).

Kettenacker, Lothar, 'Hitler's Final Solution and its Rationalization', in Hirschfeld, *The Politics of Genocide*, 73–96.

Kiesel, Doron, et al., eds, *'Wer zum Leben, wer zum Tod...': Strategien jüdischen Überlebens im Ghetto* (Frankfurt and New York, 1962).

Kingreen, Monica, *Jüdisches Landleben in Windecken, Ostheim und Heldenbergen* (Hanau, 1994).

Kirchhoff, Hans, 'SS-Gruppenführer Werner Best and the Action Against the Danish Jews-October 1943', *YVS* 24 (1994), 195–222.

—— 'The Rescue of the Danish Jews in October 1943' in *Nazi Europe and the Final Solution*, David Bankier and Israel Gutman, eds (Jerusalem, 2003), 539–55.

Klee, Ernst, *'Euthanasie' im NS-Staat. Die 'Vernichtung unwerten Lebens'* (Frankfurt a. M., 1983).

—— Dressen, Willi, and Riess, Volker, eds, *'Schöne Zeiten'. Judenmord aus der Sicht der Täter und Gaffer* (Frankfurt a. M., 1988); English trans.: *'The Good Old Days'* (New York, 1992).

Klein, Peter, *Die Wannsee-Konferenz vom 20. Januar 1942. Analyse und Dokumentation* (Berlin, 1995).

—— 'Die Rolle der Vernichtungslager Kulmhof (Chelmno), Belzec und Auschwitz-Birkenau in den frühen Deportationsvorbereitungen', in Dittmar Dahlmann and Gerhard Hirschfeld, eds, *Lager, Zwangsarbeit, Vertreibung und Deportation. Dimensionenen der Massenvebrechen in der Sowjetunion und in Deutschland 1933–1945* (Essen, 1999).

—— *Die Ghettoverwaltung Litzmannstadt 1940 bis 1944: eine Dienststelle im Spannungsfeld von Kommunalburokratie und staatlicher Verfolgungspolitik* (Hamburg, 2009).

Klemperer, Klemens von, *Germany's New Conservatism: Its History and Dilemma in the Twentieth Century* (Princeton, 1968).

Kley, Stefan, *Hitler, Ribbentrop und die Entfesselung des Zweiten Weltkriegs* (Paderborn, 1996).

—— 'Intention. Verkündung, Implementierung. Hitlers Reichstagsrede vom 30 Januar 1939', *ZfG* 48 (2000), 197–213.

Kliner-Lintzen, Martina, and Pape, Siegfried, eds, *Vergessen kann man das nicht: Wittener Jüdinnen und Juden unter dem Nationalsozialismus* (Göttingen, 1992).

Klingemann, Carsten, *Soziologie im Dritten Reich* (Baden-Baden, 1996).

Klinkhammer, Lutz, *Zwischen Bündnis und Besetzung. Das nationalsozialistische Deutschland und die Republik von Saló* (Tübingen, 1993).

Klodzinski, Stanislaw, 'Phenol', *Die Auschwitz Hefte* 1 (1994), 277–81.

Knipping, Ulrich, *Die Geschichte der Juden in Dortmund während der Zeit des Dritten Reiches* (Dortmund, 1977).

Koblik, Steven, *Stones Cry Out: Sweden's Response to the Persecution of the Jews, 1933–1945* (New York, 1988).

Koch, Manfred, 'Die Weimarer Republik: Juden zwischen Integration und Ausgrenzung', in Heinz Schmitt, ed., *Juden in Karlsruhe. Beiträge zu ihrer Geschichte bis zur nationalsozialistischen Machtergreifung* (Karlsruhe, 1990).

Kohl, Paul, *'Ich wundere mich, dass ich noch lebe'. Sowjetische Augenzeugenberichte* (Gütersloh, 1990).

Köhn, Michel, *Zahnärzte 1933–1945. Berufsverbot-Emigration-Verfolgung* (Berlin, 1994).

Konieczny, Alfred, 'Die Zwangsarbeit der Juden in Schlesien im Rahmen der "Organisation Schmelt"', in *Beiträge zur Nationalsozialistische Gesundheitspolitik und Sozialpolitik: Sozialpolitik und Judenvernichtung. Gab es eine Ökonomie der Endlösung?* (Berlin, 1983), 91–110.

Koselleck, Reinhard, 'Volk, Nation', in Otto Brunner, Werner Conze, and Reinhard Koselleck, eds, *Geschictliche Grundbegriffe. Historisches Lexikon zur politischen und sozialen Sprache in Deutschland*, vol. vii (Stuttgart, 1992), 141–431.

Koshar, Rudy, *Social Life, Local Politics, and Nazism: Marburg, 1880–1935* (Chapel Hill, NC, 1986).

Krach, Tillmann, *Jüdische Rechtsanwälte in Preußen. Über die Bedeutung der freien Advokatur und ihre Zerstörung durch den Nationalsozialismus* (Munich, 1991).

Krakowski, Shmuel, 'The Fate of Jewish Prisoners of War in the September 1939 Campaign', *YVS* 12 (1977), 297–333.

—— *War of the Doomed* (New York, 1984).

Kratzsch, Gerhard, *Der Gauwirtschaftsapparat der NSDAP. Menschenführung— 'Arisierung'—Wehrwirtschaft im Gau Westfalen-Süd* (Münster, 1989).

Krausnick, Helmut, 'Himmler über seinen Besuch bei Mussolini', *VfZ* 4 (1956), 423–6.

—— 'The Persecution of the Jews', in Hans Buchheim et al., *Anatomy of the SS-State* (London, 1968), 1–117.

—— 'Die Einsatzgruppen vom Anschluß Österreichs bis zum Feldzug gegen die Sowjetunion. Entwicklung und Verhältnis zur Wehrmacht', in Krausnick and Hans-Heinrich Wilhelm, *Die Truppe des Weltanschauungskrieges. Die Einsatzgruppen der Sicherheitspolizei und des SD, 1938–1942* (Stuttgart, 1982), 13–278.

—— 'Hitler und die Befehle an die Einsatzgruppen im Sommer 1941', in Eberhard Jäckel and Jürgen Rohwer, eds, *Der Mord an den Juden im Zweiten Weltkrieg. Entschlussbildung und Verwirklichung* (Stuttgart, 1985), 88–106.

—— 'Antwort auf Alfred Streim', *Simon Wiesenthal Center Annual* 6 (1989), 311–29.

—— and Wilhelm, Hans-Heinrich, eds, *Die Truppe des Weltanschauungskrieges. Die Einsatzgruppen der Sicherheitspolizei und des SD 1938–1942* (Stuttgart, 1981).

Krispin, Matthias et al., *Ein offenes Geheimnis. 'Arisierung' in Alltag und Wirtschaft in Oldenburg zwischen 1933 und 1945* (Oldenburg, 2001).

Kropat, Wolf-Arno, *Kristallnacht in Hessen. Der Judenpogrom vom November 1938. Eine Dokumentation* (Wiesbaden, 1988).

Kryl, Miroslav, 'Deportationen von Theresienstadt nach Majdanek', *TSD* (1994), 74–89.

Kulka, Otto Dov, 'Die Nürnberger Rassengesetze und die deutsche Bevölkerung im Lichte geheimer NS-Lage- und Stimmungsberichte', *VfZ* 32 (1984), 582–624.

Kuller, Christiane, ' "Erster Grundsatz: Horten für die Reichsfinanzverwaltung". Die Verwertung des Eigentums der deportierten Nürnberger Juden', in Kundrus and Meyer, eds, *Beiträge zur Geschichte des Nationalsozialismus*, vol. xx: *Die Deportation der Juden aus Deutschland. Pläne—Praxis—Reaktionen, 1938–1945* (Göttingen, 2004), 160–79.

Kundrus, Birthe, and Meyer, Beate, eds, *Beiträge zur Geschichte des Nationalsozialismus*, vol. xx: *Die Deportation der Juden aus Deutschland. Pläne—Praxis—Reaktionen, 1938–1945* (Göttingen, 2004).

Kunz, N., 'Feld- and Ortskommandanturen auf der Krim und der Judenmord', in W. Kaiser, ed., *Täter im Vernichtungskrieg; der Überfall auf die Sowjetunion und der Völkermord an den Juden* (Berlin, 2002).

Kwiet, Konrad, ' "Juden und Banditen". SS Ereignismeldungen aus Litauen 1943/1944', *Jahrbuch für Antisemitismusforschung* 2 (1983).

—— 'Nach dem Pogrom: Stufen der Ausgrenzung', in Benz, ed., *Die Juden in Deutschland*, 545–659.

—— 'Forced Labour of German Jews in Nazi Germany', *LBIY* 36 (1991), 389–410.

Kwiet, Konrad, 'Auftakt zum Holocaust: Ein Polizeibataillon im Osteinsatz', in Wolfgang
Benz et al., eds, *Der Nationalsozialismus: Studien zur Ideologie und Herrschaft* (Frankfurt
a. M., 1993), 92–110.

Laak, Dirk, 'Die Mitwirkenden bei der "Arisierung". Dargestellt am Beispiel der rheinisch-
westfälischen Industrieregion, 1933–1940', in Ursula Büttner, ed., *Die Deutschen und die
Judenverfolgung im Dritten Reich* (Hamburg, 1992), 231–57.

Lange, Bernd-Lutz, *Davidstern und Weihnachtsbaum. Erinnerungen von überlebenden*
(Leipzig, 1992).

Laqueur, Walter, and Breitman, Richard, *Breaking the Silence*. (New York, 1986).

Lawrence, Peter, 'Why Lithuania? A Study of Active and Passive Collaboration in Mass
Murder in a Lithuanian Village, 1941', in John Milfull, ed., *Why Germany? National
Socialist Anti-Semitism and the European Context* (Providence, RI, and Oxford, 1993),
209–19.

Leopold, John A., *Alfred Hugenberg: The Radical Nationalist Campaign against the Weimar
Republic* (New Haven, 1977).

Lepper, Herbert, *Von der Emanzipation zum Holocaust: die israelitischen Synagogenge-
meinden zu Aachen 1801–1942; geschichtliche Darstellung: Bilder, Dokumente, Tabellen,
Listen* (Aachen, 1994).

Levi, Erik, *Music in the Third Reich* (Basingstoke, 1994).

Levin, Dov, *Fighting Back: Lithuanian Jewrys's Armed Resistance to the Nazis 1941–1945*
(New York and London, 1997).

Levy, Richard S., *The Downfall of the Anti-Semitic Political Parties in Imperial Germany*
(New Haven and London, 1975).

Lewy, Guenter, *The Nazi Persecution of the Gypsies* (New York, 2000).

Lichtenstein, Erwin, *Die Juden der Freien Stadt Danzig unter der Herrschaft des Nationalsozialismus* (Tübingen, 1973).

Liebe, Werner, *Die Deutschnationale Volkspartei 1918–1924* (Düsseldorf, 1956).

Limberg, Margarete, and Rübsart, Hubert, eds, *Sie durften nicht mehr Deutsche sein.
Jüdisches Alltagsleben in Selbstzeugnissen 1933–1938* (Berlin, 2003).

Lippmann, Leo, '... *Dass ich wie ein guter Deutscher empfinde und handele', Zur Geschichte
der Deutsch-Israelitischen Gemeinde in Hamburg in der Zeit von Herbst 1935 bis zum
Ende 1942* (Hamburg, 1994).

Lipscher, Ladislav, *Die Juden im Slowakischen Staat, 1939–1945* (Munich, 1980).

Litani, Dora, 'The Destruction of the Jews of Odessa in the Light of Rumanian Documents',
YVS 6 (1967), 135–54.

Littell, Franklin H., ed., *Hyping the Holocaust: Scholars Answer Goldhagen* (Merion Station,
1997).

Lixfeld Hannsjost, *Folklore and Fascism: The Reich Institute für German Volkskunde*
(Bloomington, Ind., 1994).

Lockot, Regine, *Erinnern und Durcharbeiten. Zur Geschichte der Psychoanalyse und Psychotherapie im Nationalsozialismus* (Frankfurt a. M., 1986).

Loewenberg, Peter, 'The Kristallnacht as a Public Degradation Ritual', *LBIY* (1987),
309–23.

Loewy, Hanno, and Schoenberner, Gerhard, eds, *Unser einziger Weg ist Arbeit. Das Getto in
Lodz 1940–1944* (Frankfurt a. M. and Vienna, 1990).

Lohalm, Uwe, *Völkischer Radikalismus. Die Geschichte des Deutschvölkischen Schutz- und Trutz-Bundes, 1919–1923* (Hamburg, 1970).

London, Louise, 'British Immigration Control Procedures and Jewish Refugees, 1933–1939', in Julius Carlebach et al., eds, *Second Chance: Two Centuries of German-Speaking Jews in the United Kingdom* (Tübingen, 1991), 485–517.

Longerich, Peter, *Propagandisten im Krieg. Die Presseabteilung des Auswärtigen Amtes unter Ribbentrop* (Munich, 1987).

—— *Die braunen Bataillone. Geschichte der SA* (Munich, 1989).

—— 'Vom Massenmord zur "Endlösung". Die Erschießungen von jüdischen Zivilisten in den ersten Monaten des Ostfeldzuges im Kontext des nationalsozialistischen Judenmordes', in Bernd Wegner, ed., *Zwei Wege nach Moskau. Vom Hitler-Stalin-Pakt zum 'Unternehmen Barbarossa'* (Munich, 1991), 251–74.

—— *Hitlers Stellvertreter. Führung der Partei und Kontrolle des Staatsapparates durch den Stab Heß und die Partei-Kanzlei Bormanns, Munich* (London and New York, 1992).

—— *Die Politik der Vernichtung. Eine Gesamtdarstellung der nationalsozialistischen Judenverfolgung* (Munich, 1998).

—— *The Unwritten Order: Hitler's Role in the Final Solution* (London, 2005).

—— *'Davon haben wir nichts gewusst': Die Deutschen und die Judenverfolgung 1933–1945* (Munich, 2006).

Lösener, Bernhard, 'Als Rassereferent im Reichsministerium des Innern', *VfZ* 9/3 (1961).

Lower, Wendy, ' "Anticipational Obedience" and the Nazi Implementation of the Holocaust in the Ukraine: A Case Study of Central and Peripheral Forces in the Generalbezirk Zhytomyr, 1941–1944', *HGS* 16 (2002), 1–22.

—— *Nazi Empire Building and the Holocaust in Ukraine* (Chapel Hill, NC, 2005).

Lozowick, Yaakov, 'Rollbahn Mord. The Early Activities of Einsatzgruppe C', *HGS* 2 (1987), 221–42.

Ludwig, Carl, *Die Flüchtlingspolitik der Schweiz seit 1933 bis zur Gegenwart. Bericht an den Bundesrat zuhanden der eidgenössischen Räte* (Bern, 1957).

Ludwig, Johannes, *Boykott, Enteignung, Mord. Die 'Entjudung' der deutschen Wirtschaft* (Munich, 1992).

Luther, Hans, *Der französische Widerstand gegen die deutsche Besatzungsmacht und seine Bekämpfung* (Tübingen, 1957).

'Machtergreifung' Berlin 1933, ed. Hans-Norbert Burkert, Klaus Matußek, and Wolfgang Wippermann, 2nd edn (Berlin, 1984).

MacQueen, Michael, 'The Context of Mass Destruction: Agents and Prerequisites of the Holocaust in Lithuania', *HGS* 12 (1998), 27–48.

Madajczyk, Czeslaw, *Die Okkupationspolitik Nazideutschlands in Polen 1939–1945* (Cologne, 1988).

Maier, Dieter, *Arbeitseinsatz und Deportation. Die Mitwirkung der Arbeitsverwaltung bei der nationalsozialistischen Judenverfolgung in den Jahren 1939–1945* (Berlin, 1994).

Mais, Edgar, ed., *Die Verfolgung der Juden in den Landkreisen Bad Kreuznach und Birkenfeld 1933–1945* (Bad Kreuznach, 1988).

Majer, Diemut, 'Fremdvölkische' im Dritten Reich. Ein Beitrag zur nationalsozialistischen Rechtssetzung und Rechtspraxis in Verwaltung und Justiz unter besonderer Berücksichtigung der eingegliederten Ostgebiete und des Generalgouvernements (Boppard a. Rh., 1981).

—— Grundlagen des nationalsozialistischen Rechtssystems (Stuttgart, 1987), 122.

Mallmann, Klaus-Michael, 'Vom Fußvolk der "Endlösung". Ordnungspolizei, Ostkrieg und Judenmord', Tel Aviver Jahrbuch 25 (1997), 355–91.

—— 'Der qualitative Sprung im Vernichtungsprozess. Das Massaker von Kamenez-Poldolsk Ende August 1941', Jahrbuch für Antisemitismusforschung 10 (2001), 237–64.

—— ' "… Mißgeburten, die nicht auf diese Welt gehören". Die deutsche Ordnungspolizei in Polen 1939–1941', in Mallman and Musial, eds, Genesis des Genozids, 71–89.

—— and Musial, Bogdan, eds, Genesis des Genozids. Polen 1939–1941 (Darmstadt, 2004).

——, Böhler, Jochen, and Matthäus, Jürgen, Einsatzgruppen in Polen Darstellung und Dokumentation (Darmstadt, 2008).

Manoschek, Walter, 'Serbien ist judenfrei'. Militärische Besatzungspolitik und Judenvernichtung in Serbien 1941/42 (Munich, 1993).

Maršálek, Hans, Die Geschichte des Konzentrationslagers Mauthausen. Dokumentation (Mauthausen, 1974).

Matthäus, Jürgen, ' "Reibungslos und planmäßig". Die zweite Welle der Judenvernichtung im Generalkommissariat Weißruthenien (1942–1944)', Jahrbuch für Antisemitismusforschung 4 (1995), 254–75.

—— 'What about the "Ordinary Men"? The German Order Police and the Holocaust in the Occupied Soviet Union', HGS 10 (1996), 134–50.

—— 'Antisemitism as an Offer: The Ideological Indoctrination of the SS and Police Corps during the Holocaust, Lessons and Legacies'. Paper presented at the Lessons and Legacies Conference, Minneapolis, 2002.

Matzerath, Horst, 'Der Weg der Kölner Juden in den Holocaust. Versuch einer Rekonstruktion', in Gabriele Rogmann and Horst Matzerath, eds, Die jüdischen Opfer des Nationalsozialismus aus Köln. Gedenkbuch (Cologne, 1995), 530–53.

Maurer, Trude, 'Abschiebung und Attentat. Die Ausweisung der polnischen Juden und der Vorwand für die "Kristallnacht" ', in Walter Pehle, ed., Der Judenpogrom 1938. Von der Kristallnacht bis zum Völkermord (Frankfurt a. M., 1988), 52–72.

Mazower, Mark, Inside Hitler's Greece: The Experience of Occupation, 1941–1944 (New Haven and London, 1993).

—— Hitler's Empire. Nazi Rule in Occupied Europe (New York, 2008).

Mehl, Stefan, Das Reichsfinanzministerium und die Verfolgung der deutschen Juden, 1933–1943 (Berlin, 1990).

Melzer, Emanuel, 'Relations between Poland and Germany and their Impact on the Jewish Problem in Poland (1935–1938)', YVS 12 (77), 193–229.

Der Mensch gegen den Menschen. Überlegungen und Forschungen zum deutschen Überfall auf die Sowjetunion 1941, ed. Hans-Heinrich Nolte (Hanover, 1992).

Meyer, Ahlrich, ' "… dass französische Verhältnisse anders sind als polnische". Die Bekämpfung des Widerstands durch die deutsche Militärverwaltung in Frankreich 1941', in Guus Meershoeck et al., eds, Repression und Kriegsverbrechen. Die Bekämpfung von Widerstands- und Partisanenbewegungen gegen die deutsche Besatzung in West- und Südosteuropa (Berlin, 1997), 43–91.

—— 'Der Beginn der "Endlösung" in Frankreich—offene Fragen', *Sozialgeschichte* 18 (2003), 35–82.

Meyer, Michael, *The Politics of Music in the Third Reich*, 2nd edn (New York, 1993).

—— with Brenner, Michael, eds, *German-Jewish History in Modern Times*, 4 vols (New York and Chichester, 1996–8), vol iii: Steven M. Lowenstein et al., *Integration in Dispute 1871–1918*.

Meyhöfe, Rita, *Gäste in Berlin? Jüdisches Schülerleben in der Weimarer Republik und im Nationalsozialismus* (Hamburg, 1996).

Meynert, Joachim, *Was vor der 'Endlösung' geschah. Antisemitische Ausgrenzung in Minden-Ravensberg 1933–1945* (Münster, 1988).

Michaelis, Meir, *Mussolini and the Jews. German-Italian Relations and the Jewish Question in Italy, 1922–1945* (Oxford, 1978).

Michalka, Wolfgang, ed., *Der Zweite Weltkrieg. Analysen, Grundzüge, Forschungsbilanz. Im Auftrage des Militärgeschichtlichen Forschungsamtes* (Munich, 1989).

Michman, Dan, 'Why did Heydrich write the *Schnellbrief*? A Remark on the Reason and on its Significance', *YVS* 32 (2004), 4333–447.

—— 'Judenräte und Judenvereinigungen unter nationalsozialistischer Herrschaft', *ZfG* 46 (1998), 293–304.

—— ed., *Belgium and the Holocaust: Jews, Belgians, Germans* (Jerusalem, 1998).

Milton, Sybil, 'The Expulsion of Polish Jews from Germany October 1938 to July 1939. A Documentation', *LBIY* 29 (1984), 169–99.

Mlynarczyk, Jacek Andrzej, 'Treblinka—ein Todeslager der "Aktion Reinhard"', in Musial, ed., *'Aktion Reinhardt'*, 257–81.

—— 'Organisation und Durchführung der "Aktion Reinhardt" im Distrikt Radom', in Musial, ed., *'Aktion Reinhardt'*, 169–95.

—— *Judenmord in Zentralpolen. Der Distrikt Radom im Generalgouvernement 1939–1945* (Darmstadt, 2007).

Moeller, Felix, *Der Filmminister. Goebbels und der Film im Dritten Reich* (Berlin, 1998).

Mommsen, Hans, *Beamtentum im Dritten Reich. Mit ausgewählten Quellen zur nationalsozialistischen Beamtenpolitik* (Stuttgart, 1968).

—— and Willems, Susanne, eds, *Herrschaftsalltag im Dritten Reich. Studien und Texte* (Düsseldorf, 1988).

—— 'The Realization of the Unthinkable: The "Final Solution of the Jewish Question" in the Third Reich', in Mommsen, ed., *From Weimar to Auschwitz: Essays in German History* (Cambridge, 1991), 224–53.

—— and Obst, Dieter, 'Die Reaktion der deutschen Bevölkerung auf die Verfolgung der Juden 1933–1943', in Hans Mommsen and Susanne Willems, eds, *Herrschaftsalltag im Dritten Reich. Studien und Texte* (Düsseldorf, 1988), 374–426.

Moore, Bob, *Victims and Survivors: The Nazi Persecution of the Jews in the Netherlands 1940–1945* (London, 1997).

Morsch, Günter, *Arbeit und Brot. Studien zur Lage, Stimmung, Einstellung und Verhalten der deutschen Arbeiterschaft 1933–1936/37* (Frankfurt a. M., 1993).

Moser, Jonny, 'Nisko: The First Experiment in Deportation', *SWCA* 2 (1985), 1–30.

—— 'Österreich', in Benz, ed., *Dimensionen*, 67–93.

Mosse, Werner, and Paucker, Arnold, eds, *Juden im Wilhelminischen Deutschland, 1890–1914* (Tübingen, 1976).

Müller, Alfred M., 'Geschichte des Deutschen und Österreichischen Alpenvereins. Ein Beitrag zur Sozialgeschichte des Verbandswesens', Ph.D. thesis (Münster, 1979).

Müller, Klaus-Jürgen, *Das Heer und Hitler: Armee und nationalsozialistisches Regime 1933–1940* (Stuttgart, 1969).

—— *Armee und Drittes Reich 1933–1939* (Paderborn, 1987).

Müller, Roland, *Stuttgart zur Zeit des Nationalsozialismus* (Stuttgart, 1988).

Müller, Rolf-Dieter, 'Von der Wirtschaftsallianz zum kolonialen Ausbeutungskrieg', in Horst Boog et al., eds, *Der Angriff auf die Sowjetunion* (Stuttgart, 1983).

—— *Hitlers Ostkrieg und die deutsche Siedlungspolitik. Die Zusammenarbeit von Wehrmacht, Wirtschaft und SS* (Frankfurt a. M., 1991).

—— 'From Economic Alliance to a War of Colonial Exploitation', in Horst Boog et al., eds, *Germany and the Second World War*, iv: *The Attack on the Soviet Union* (Oxford, 1998), 118–224.

Münk, Dieter, *Die Organisation des Raumes im Nationalsozialismus. Eine soziologische Untersuchung ideologisch fundierter Leitbilder in Architektur, Städtebau und Raumplanung im Dritten Reich* (Bonn, 1993).

Musial, Bogdan, *Deutsche Zivilverwaltung und Judenverfolgung im Generalgouvernement. Eine Fallstudie zum Distrikt Lublin, 1939–1944* (Wiesbaden, 1999).

—— *'Konterrevolutionäre Elemente sind zu erschiessen'. Die Brutalisierung des deutsche-sowjetischen Krieges im Sommer 1941* (Berlin and Munich, 2000).

—— ed., 'The Origins of "Operation Reinhard". The Decision-Making Process for the Mass Murder of the Jews in the Generalgouvernement', *YVS* 28 (2000), 113–53.

—— *'Aktion Reinhardt'. Der Völkermord an den Juden im Generalgouvernment, 1941–1944* (Osnabrück, 2004).

Mußgnug, Dorothee, *Die Reichsfluchtsteuer 1931–1953* (Berlin, 1993).

Naasner, Walter, *Neue Machtzentren in der deutschen Kriegswirtschaft 1942–1945. Die Wirtschaftsorganisation der SS, das Amt des Generalbevollmächtigten für den Arbeitseinsatz und das Reichsministerium für Bewaffnung und Munition/Reichsministerium für Rüstung und Kriegsproduktion im nationalsozialistischen Herrschaftssystem* (Boppard a. Rhein, 1994).

National Socialist Extermination Policies: Contemporary German Perspectives and Controversies, ed. Ulrich Herbert (New York and Oxford, 2000).

Die nationalsozialistische Machtergreifung, ed. Wolfgang Michalka (Paderborn, 1984).

Nationalsozialistische Vernichtungslager im Spiegel deutscher Strafprozesse. Belzec, Sobibor, Treblinka, Chelmno, ed. Adalbert Rückerl (Munich, 1977).

The Nazi Holocaust, ed. Michael R. Marrus, 9 vols. (Westport, Conn., and London, 1989).

Neliba, Günter, and Frick, Wilhelm, *Der Legalist des Unrechtsstaates. Eine politische Biographie* (Paderborn, 1992).

Neufeldt, Hans-Joachim, Huck, Jürgen, and Tessin, Georg, *Zur Geschichte der Ordnungspolizei*, 2 parts (Koblenz, 1957).

Nicosia, Francis R., *The Third Reich and the Palestine Question* (Austin, 1985).

Noakes, Jeremy, *The Nazi Party in Lower Saxony, 1921–1933* (Oxford, 1971).

—— 'Wohin gehören die "Judenmischlinge"? Die Entstehung der ersten Durchführungsverordnungen zu den Nürnberger Gesetzen', in Ursula Büttner, ed., *Das Unrechtsregime. Internationale Forschung über den Nationalsozialismus*, 2 vols (Hamburg, 1986), ii. 69–89.

—— 'The Development of Nazi Policy towards German-Jewish "Mischlinge"', *LBIY* 34 (1989), 291–354.

—— 'Hitler and the Third Reich', in Dan Stone, ed., *The Historiography of the Holocaust* (London, 2004).

Nolte, Hans Heinrich, 'Destruction and Resistance: The Jewish Shtetl of Slonim 1941–44', in Robert W. Thurston and Bernd Bonwetsch, eds, *The People's War: Responses to World War II in the Soviet Union* (Urbana and Chicago, 2000).

Notnagel, Hans, and Dähn, Ewald, *Juden in Suhl. Ein Geschichtlicher Überblick* (Konstanz, 1995).

Nowak, Kurt, *Evangelische Kirche und Weimarer Republik. Zum politischen Weg des deutschen Protestantismus zwischen 1918 und 1932* (Göttingen, 1981).

Oberkrome, Willi, *Volksgeschichte: Methodische Innovation und völkische Ideologisierung in der deutschen Geschichtswissenschaft 1918–1945* (Göttingen, 1993).

Obst, Dieter, *'Reichskristallnacht'. Ursachen und Verlauf des antisemitischen Pogroms vom November 1938* (Frankfurt a. M., 1991).

Offermannst, Ernst, *Internationalität und europäischer Hegemonialanspruch des Spielfilms der NS-Zeit* (Hamburg, 2001).

Ogorreck, Ralf, *Die Einsatzgruppen und die Genesis der 'Endlösung'* (Berlin, 1996).

Olenhusen, Albrecht Götz von, 'Die "nicht arischen" Studenten an den deutschen Hochschulen. Zur nationalsozialistischen Rassenpolitik 1933–1945', *VfZ* 14 (1966), 175–206.

Orth, Karin, 'Rudolf Höß und die "Endlösung der Judenfrage". Drei Argumente gegen deren Datierung auf den Sommer 1941', *Werkstatt Geschichte* 18 (1997), 45–58.

—— *Das System der nationalsozialistischen Konzentrationslager. Eine politische Organisationsgeschichte* (Hamburg, 1999).

Ortmeyer, Benjamin, *Schicksale jüdischer Schülerinnen und Schüler in der NS-Zeit— Leerstelle deutscher Erziehungswissenschaften. Bundesrepublikanische Erziehungswissenschaften (1945/49–1955) und die Erforschung der nazistischen Schule* (Witterschlick and Bonn, 1998).

Osterloh, Jörg, *Nationalsozialistische Judenverfolgung im Reichsgau Sudetenland 1938–1945* (Munich, 2006).

Österreich, Deutschland und die Mächte. Internationale und österreichische Aspekte des 'Anschlusses' vom März 1938, ed. Gerald Stourzh and Birgitta Zaar (Vienna, 1990).

Otto, Hans-Uwe, and Sünker, Heinz, 'Volksgemeinschaft als Formierungsideologie des Nationalsozialismus. Zur Genesis und Geltung von "Volkspflege"', in Otto and Sünker, eds, *Politische Formierung und soziale Erziehung im Nationalsozialismus* (Frankfurt a. M., 1991).

Otto, Reinhard, *Wehrmacht, Gestapo and sowjetische Kriegsgefangene im deutschen Reichsgebiet 1941/42* (Munich, 1998).

Ottwaldt, Alfred, and Schulle, Diana, *Die 'Judendepartationen' aus dem Deutschen Reich 1941–1945. Eine kommentierte Chronologie* (Wiesbaden, 2005).

Ottweiler, Ottwilm, *Die Volksschule im Nationalsozialismus* (Weinheim and Basle, 1979).

Papen, Patricia von, 'Schützenhilfe nationalsozialistischer Judenpolitik. Die "Judenforschung" des "Reichsinstituts für Geschichte des neuen Deutschland", 1933–1945', in Fritz Bauer Institut, ed., *'Beseitigung des jüdischen Einflusses...'. Antisemitische Forschung, Eliten und Karrieren im Nationalsozialismus* (Frankfurt and New York, 1999), 17–43.

Pätzold, Kurt, *Faschismus, Rassenwahn, Judenverfolgung. Eine Studie zur politischen Strategie und Taktik des faschistischen deutschen Imperialismus (1933–1935)* (Berlin, 1975).

Pätzold, Kurt, and Schwarz, Erika, *Tagesordnung Judenmord. Die Wannsee-Konferenz am 20. Januar 1942* (Berlin, 1992).

Paucker, Arnold, *Der jüdische Abwehrkampf genen Antisemitismus und Nationalsozialismus in den letzten Jahren der Weimarer Republik* (Hamburg, 1968).

Paul, Gerhard, *Aufstand der Bilder. Die NS-Propaganda vor 1933* (Bonn, 1990).

—— 'Von Psychopathen, Technokraten des Terrors und "ganz gewöhnlichen Deutschen". Die Täter der Shoah im Spiegel der Forschung', in Paul, ed., *Die Täter der Shoah. Fanatische Nationalsozialisten oder ganz gewöhnliche Deutsche* (Göttingen, 2002), 13–80.

—— and Mallmann, Klaus-Michael, eds, *Die Gestapo. Mythos und Realität* (Darmstadt, 1995).

—— —— eds, *Die Gestapo im Zweiten Weltkrieg* (Darmstadt, 2000).

Paulsson, Gunnar S., *Secret City: The Hidden Jews of Warsaw, 1940–1945* (New Haven and London, 2002).

—— ' "The Bridge over Oeresund". The Historiography on the Expulsion of the Jews from Nazi-Occupied Denmark.' in *Journal of Contemporary History* 30 (1995), 431–464.

Pehle, Walter, ed., *Der Judenpogrom 1938. Von der Kristallnacht bis zum Völkermord* (Frankfurt a. M., 1988).

Peiser, Jacob, *Die Geschichte der Synagogengemeinde zu Stettin*, 2nd edn (Würzburg, 1965).

Pelt, Robert-Jan van, 'A Site in Search of a Mission', in Yisrael Gutman and Michael Berenbaum, eds, *Anatomy of the Auschwitz Death Camp* (Washington, 1994), 93–156.

—— and Dwork, Deborah, *Auschwitz 1270 to the Present* (New Haven, 1996).

Petsch, Joachim, *Baukunst und Stadtplanung im Dritten Reich. Herleitung, Bestandsaufnahme, Entwicklung, Nachfolge* (Munich and Vienna, 1976).

—— *Eigenheim und gute Stube. Zur Geschichte des bürgerlichen Wohnen* (Cologne, 1989).

Petzold, Joachim, *Wegbereiter des deutschen Faschismus. Die Jungkonservativen in der Weimarer Republik* (Cologne, 1983).

Pingel, Falk, *Häftinge unter SS-Herrschaft. Widerstand, Selbstbehauptung und Vernichtung im Konzentrationslager* (Hamburg, 1978).

Piper, Franciszek, 'Estimating the Number of Deportees to and Victims of the Auschwitz-Birkenau Camp', *YVS* 21 (1991), 49–103.

—— *Die Zahl der Opfer von Auschwitz* (Oswiecim, 1993).

—— *Vernichtung in Auschwitz 1940–1945. Studien zur Geschichte des Konzentrations- und Vernichtungslager Auschwitz*, vol. iii (Oswiecim, 1999).

Plum, Günter, 'Wirtschaft und Erwerbsleben'; 'Deutsche Juden oder Juden in Deutschland', in Benz, ed., *Juden in Deutschland*, 268–313.

Pohl, Dieter, *Von der 'Judenpolitik' zum 'Judenmord'. Der Distrikt Lublin des Generalgouvernements 1939–1944* (Frankfurt a. M., 1993).

—— *Nationalsozialistische Judenverfolgung in Ostgalizien 1941–1944. Die Organisation und Durchführung eines staatlichen Massenverbrechens* (Munich, 1997).

—— 'Die Einsatzgruppe C', in *Die Einsatzgruppen in der besetzten Sowjetunion 1941/42. Die Tätigkeits- und Lageberichte des Chefs der Sicherheitspolizei und des SD*, ed. Peter Klein (Berlin, 1997), 71–87.

—— 'Schauplatz Ukraine. Der Massenmord an den Juden im Militärverwaltungsgebiet und im Reichskommissariat 1941–1943', in Norbert Frei, Sybille Steinbacher, and Bernd C. Wagner, eds, *Ausbeutung, Vernichtung, Öffentlichkeit. Neue Studien zur nationalsozialistischen Lagerpolitik* (Munich, 2000).

—— Die Herrschaft der Wehrmacht. Deutsche Militärbesatzung und einheimische Bevölkerung in der Sowjetunion 1941–1943. (Munich, 2008).

Pohl, Karl-Heinrich, ed., Wehrmacht und Vernichtungspotitik. Militär im nationalsozialistischen System (Göttingen, 1999).

Polian, Parel, 'Hätte der Holocaust beinahe nicht stattgefunden? Überlegungen zu einem Schriftwechsel im Wert von zwei Millionen Menschenleben' in Hürter and Zarusky, eds, Besatzung, 1–20.

Pollmeier, Heiko, 'Inhaftierung und Lagerführung deutscher Juden im November 1938', Jahrbuch für die Antisemitismusforschung 8 (1999), 107–30.

Polonsky, Antony, and Michlic, Joanna B., eds, The Neighbors Respond: The Controversy over the Jedwabne Massacre in Poland (Princeton and Oxford, 2004).

Pommerening, Günther, 'Der Novemberpogrom in Schmieheim', in Schicksal und Geschichte der jüdischen Gemeinden 1938–1988: Ettenheim, Altdorf, Kippenheim, Schmieheim, Rust, Orschweiler. Ein Gedenkbuch (Ettenheim, 1988), 47–9.

Pommerin, Reiner, 'Sterilisierung der Rheinlandbastarde'. Das Schicksal einer farbigen deutschen Minderheit, 1918–1937 (Düsseldorf, 1979).

Popplow, Ullrich, 'Der Novemberpogrom 1938 in Münden und Göttingen', Göttinger Jahrbuch 28 (1980), 177–92.

Porat, Dina, 'The Holocaust in Lithuania', in David Cesarani ed., Origins and Implementation of the Final Solution (London and New York, 1994), 159–74.

Potter, Pamela M., Die deutscheste der Künste. Musikwissenschaft und Gesellschaft von der Weimarer Republik bis zum Ende des Dritten Reiches (Stuttgart, 2000).

Poznanski, Renée, Jews in France during World War II (London, 2001).

Pressac, Jean C, Die Krematorien von Auschwitz. Die Technik des Massenmords (Munich, 1984).

Presser, Jacob, The Destruction of the Dutch Jews (New York, 1969).

Pretsch, Hermann J., 'Euthanasie'. Krankenmorde in Südwestdeutschland. Die nationalsozialistische 'Aktion T4' in Württemberg 1940 bis 1945 (Zwiefalten, 1996).

Pribyl, Lukas, 'Das Schicksal des dritten Transports aus dem Protektorat nach Nisko', Theresienstädter Studien (2000), 297–342.

Proctor, Robert, Racial Hygiene: Medicine under the Nazis (Cambridge, Mass., and London, 1988).

Pulzer, Peter, Jews and the German State (Oxford, 1992).

Puschner, Uwe, Die völkische Bewegung im wilhelminischen Kaiserreich: Sprache, Rasse, Religion (Darmstadt, 2001).

Rammstedt, Ottheim, Deutsche Soziologie 1933–1945. Die Normalität einer Anpassung (Frankfurt a. M., 1986).

Raphael, Lutz, 'Radikales Ordnungsdenken und die Organisation totalitärer Herrschaft: Weltanschauungseliten und Humanwissenschaftler im NS-Regime', Geschichte und Gesellschaft 27 (2001), 5–40.

Rasse, Blut und Gene. Geschichte der Eugenik und Rassenhygiene in Deutschland, ed. Peter Weingart, Jürgen Kroll, and Kurt Bayertz (Frankfurt a. M., 1988).

Rautkallio, Hannu, Finland and the Holocaust: The Rescue of Finland's Jews (New York, 1987).

Reif, Heinz, 'Antisemitismus in den Agrarverbänden Ostelbiens in der Weimarer Republik', in Reif, ed., Ostelbische Agrargesellschaft im Kaiserreich und in der Weimarer Republik. Agrarkrise-junkerliche Interessenpolitik-Modernisierungsstrategien (Berlin, 1994).

Reilly, Joanne, *Belsen: The Liberation of a Concentration Camp* (London, 1998).

Reitlinger, Gerald, *The Final Solution: The Attempt to Exterminate the Jews of Europe, 1939–1945* (New York, 1961).

Renssmanns, Lars, 'Antisemitismus und "Volksgesundheit". Zu ideologiehistorischen Verbindungslinien im politischen Imaginären und in der Politik', in Christoph Kopke, ed., *Medizin und Verbrechen. Festschrift zum 60. Geburtstag von Walter Wuttke* (Ulm, 2001).

Rentschler, Eric, *The Ministry of Illusion: Nazi Cinema and its Afterlife* (Cambridge, Mass., and London 1996).

Retallack, James N., *Notables of the Right: The Conservative Party and Political Mobilisation in Germany 1876–1918* (London, 1988).

Reynolds, David, *The Creation of the Anglo-American Alliance 1937–41: A Study in Competitive Co-operation* (Chapel Hill, NC, 1981).

Richardi, Hans-Günter, *Bomber über München. Der Luftkrieg von 1939 bis 1945, dargestellt am Beispiel der 'Hauptstadt der Bewegung'* (Munich, 1992).

Richarz, Monika, ed., *Jüdisches Leben in Deutschland*; vol. iii: *Selbstzaugnisse zur Sozialgeschichte 1918–1945* (Stuttgart, 1982). English trans.: *Jewish Life in Germany: Memoirs from Three Centuries* (Bloomington, Ind., 1991).

Riechert, Hansjörg, *Im Schatten von Auschwitz. Die nationalsozialistische Sterilisationspolitik gegenüber Sinti und Roma* (Münster and New York, 1995).

Rieß, Volker, *Die Anfänge der Vernichtung 'lebensunwerten Lebens' in den Reichsgauen Danzig-Westpreußen und Wartheland 1939/40* (Frankfurt a. M., 1995).

Ringelblum, Emmanuel, *Polish-Jewish Relations during the Second World War*, ed. Joseph Kermish and Shmuel Cracowski (New York and Jerusalem, 1976).

Robel, Gerd, 'Sowjetunion', in Benz, ed., *Dimension*, 499–560.

Röcher, Ruth, *Die jüdische Schule im nationalsozialistischen Deutschland, 1933–1942* (Frankfurt a. M., 1992).

Rohde, Horst, 'Hitlers Erster 'Blitzkrieg' und seine Auswirkungen auf Nordosteuropa', in Klaus A. Maier et al., *Die Errichtung der Hegemonie auf dem europäischen Kontinent* (Stuttgart, 1979), 79–156.

Röhr, Werner, ed., *Die faschistische Okkupationspolitik in Polen (1939–1945)* (Bonn, 1969).

Roland, Charles G., *Courage under Siege: Starvation, Disease and Death in the Warsaw Ghetto* (New York, 1992).

Römer, Felix, *Der Kommissarbefehl. Wehrmacht und NS-Verbrechen an der Ostfront 1941/42* (Paderborn, 2008).

Roseman, Mark, *The Villa, the Lake, the Meeting: Wannsee and the Final Solution* (London, 2002).

Rosenfeld, Else, and Luckner, Getrud, eds, *Lebenszeichen aus Piaski Briefe Deportierter aus dem Distrikt Lublin 1940–1943* (Munich, 1968).

Rosenfeld, Oskar, *Wozu noch Welt. Aufzeichnungen aus dem Ghetto Lodz*, ed. Hanno Loewy (Frankfurt a. M., 1994).

Rosenkranz, Herbert, *Reichskristallnacht 9. November 1938 in Österreich* (Vienna, 1968).

—— *Verfolgung und Selbstbehauptung. Die Juden in Österreich, 1938 bis 1945* (Munich and Vienna, 1978).

Rossino, Alexander B., 'Nazi Anti-Jewish Policy during the Polish Campaign: The Case of the Einsatzgruppe von Woyrisch', *GSR* 24 (2001), 35–54.

—— *Hitler Strikes Poland: Blitzkrieg, Ideology, and Atrocity* (Lawrence, Kan., 2003).

Roth, Karl-Heinz, ' "Generalplan Ost"—"Gesamtplan Ost" ' in Mechthild Rössler and Sabine Schleiermache, eds, *Der 'Generalplan Ost'. Hauptlinien der nationalsozialistischen Planung und Vernichtungspolitik* (Berlin, 1995).

Rothkirchen, Livia, 'Vatican Policy and the "Jewish Problem" in Independent Slovakia (1939–1945)', in Michael Marrus, ed., *The Nazi Holocaust*, vol. iii (Westport, Conn., 1989), 1306–32.

—— 'The Dual Role of the "Jewish Center" in Slovakia', in Yisrael Gutman and Cynthia Haft, eds, *Patterns of Jewish Leadership in Nazi Europe, 1933–1945. Proceedings of the Third Yad Vashem International Historical Conference, Jerusalem, April 4–7, 1977* (Jerusalem, 1979), 219–27.

—— *The Jews of Bohemia and Moravia: Facing the Holocaust* (Lincoln, Nebr., 2005).

Rücker, Matthias, *Wirtschaftswerbung unter dem Nationalsozialismus: rechtliche Ausgestaltung der Werbung und Tätigkeit des Werberats der Deutschen Wirtschaft* (Frankfurt a. M., 2000).

Rückerl, Adalbert, *NS Vernichtungslager im Spiegel deutscher Strafprozesse. Belzec, Sobibor, Treblinka, Chelmno* (Munich, 1977).

Rüß, Hartmut, 'Wer war verantwortlich für das Massaker von Babi Jar?', *MGM* 57 (1998), 483–508.

Rüthers, Bernd, *Entartetes Recht. Rechtslehren und Kronjuristen im Dritten Reich*, 2nd edn (Munich, 1989).

Safrian, Hans, *Die Eichmann-Männer* (Vienna, 1993); in paperback as *Eichmann und seine Gehilfen* (Frankfurt a. M., 1995).

Sakowska, Ruta, *Menschen im Ghetto. Die jüdische Bevölkerung im besetzten Warschau 1939–1943* (Münster, 1999).

Salomon, Ernst von, *Der Fragebogen* (Hamburg, 1951).

Sandkühler, Thomas, *Die 'Endlösung' in Galizien. Der Judenmord in Ostpolen und die Rettungsinitiative von Berthold Beitz 1941–1944* (Bonn, 1996).

Schäfer, Christine, *Die Evakuierungstransporte des KZ Buchenwald und seiner Außenkommandos* (Weimar-Buchenwald, 1983).

Schafft, Gretchen E., *From Racism to Genocide: Anthropology in the Third Reich* (Urbana and Chicago, 2004).

Scheerer, Hans, 'Gestaltung im Dritten Reich. Der Versuch einer Dokumentation zur Sozialutopie des Design im Nationalsozalismus 1933–1945', *form* 69, 70, 71 (1975), 21–8, 27–34, 25–32.

Scheffler, Wolfgang, *Judenverfolgung im Dritten Reich, 1933–1945* (Berlin, 1960).

—— *Nationalsozialistische Judenpolitik* (Berlin 1960).

—— 'Die Wannsee-Konferenz und ihre historische Bedeutung', in *Erinnern für die Zukunft* (Berlin, 1993), 17–34.

—— 'Die Einsatzgruppe A', in *Die Einsatzgruppen in der besetzten Sowjetunion 1941/42. Die Tätigkeits- und Lageberichte des Chefs der Sicherheitspolizei und des SD*, ed. Peter Klein (Berlin, 1997), 29–51.

—— 'Die Zahl der in den Vernichtungslagern der "Aktion Reinhard" ermordeten Juden', in Helge Grabitz and the Judicial Authority Hamburg, eds, *Täter und Gehilfen des Endlösungswahns. Hamburger Verfahren wegen NS-Gewaltverbechen 1946–1996* (Hamburg, 1998).

Scheffler, Wolfgang 'Das Schicksal der in die baltischen Staaten deportierten deutschen, österreichischen und tschechoslowakischen Juden 1941–1945. Ein historischer Überblick', in Scheffler and Schulle, eds, *Buch der Erinnerung. Die ins Baltikum deportierten deutschen, österreichischen und tschechoslowakischen Juden 1941–1945*, vol. i (Munich, 2003), 1–43.

Scheffler, Wolfgang, 'Massenmord in Kowno', in Scheffler and Schulle, eds, *Buch der Erinnerung. Die ins Baltikum deportierten deutschen, österreichischen und tschechoslowakischen Juden*, vol. i (Munich, 2003), 83–7.

—— and Schulle, Diana, eds, *Buch der Erinnerung. Die ins Baltikum deportierten deutschen, österreichischen und tschechoslawakischen Juden*, 2 vols (Munich, 2003).

Schelvis, Jules, *Vernietigingskamp Sobibor* (Amsterdam, 1993).

Scherer, Klaus, *'Asozial' im Dritten Reich. Die vergessenen Verfolgten* (Münster, 1990).

Schiefelbein, Dieter, 'Das "Institut zur Erforschung der Judenfrage in Frankfurt am Main". Antisemitismus als Karrieresprungbrett im NS-Staat', in Fritz Bauer Institut, ed., *'Beseitigung des jüdischen Einflusses', Antisemitische Forschung, Eliten und Karrieren im Nationalsozialismus. Jahrbuch 1998/1999 zur Geschichte und Wirkung des Holocausts* (Darmstadt, 1999).

Schilter, Thomas, *Unmenschliches Ermessen. Die nationalsozialistische 'Euthanasie'-Tötungsanstalt Pirna-Sonnenstein 1940/41* (Leipzig, 1999).

Schleunes, Karl A., *The Twisted Road to Auschwitz: Nazi Policy toward German Jews, 1933–39* (Urbana, Ill., 1970).

Schmelz, Oscar, 'Die Demographische Entwicklung der Juden in Deutschland von der Mitte des 19. Jahrhunderts bis 1933', *Zeitschrift für Bevölkerungswissenschaft* 1 (1982).

Schmidt, Peter W., ed., *Judenfeindschaft und Schule in Deutschland 1933–1945. Materialien zur Ausstellung der Forschungsstelle für Sozialgeschichte an der Pädagogischen Hochschule Weinggart* (Weingart, 1988).

Schmidt, Ulf, 'Reassessing the Beginning of the "Euthanasia" Programme', *German History* 17 (1999), 543–50.

Schmidt-Hartmann, Eva, 'Tschechoslowakei', in Benz, ed., *Dimension*, 353–80.

Schmuhl, Hans-Walter, *Rassenhygiene, Nationalsozialismus, Euthanasie. Von der Verhütung zur Vernichtung 'lebensunwerten Lebens', 1890–1945* (Göttingen, 1987).

—— 'Kontinuität oder Diskontinuität? Zum epochalen Charakter der Psychiatrie im Nationalsozialismus', in Franz-Werner Kersting, Karl Teppe, and Bernd Walter, eds, *Nach Hadamar. Zum Verhältnis von Psychiatrie und Gesellschaft im 20. Jahrhundert* (Paderborn, 1993).

Schneider, Barbara, *Die Höhere Schule im Nationalsozialismus. Zur Ideologisierung von Bildung und Erziehung* (Cologne, Weimar, and Vienna, 2000).

Schneider, Gertrud, *Journey into Terror: The Story of the Riga Ghetto* (New York, 1979).

Scholder, Klaus, *Die Kirchen und das Dritte Reich*, vol. i: *Vorgeschichte und Zeit der Illusionen 1918–1934* (Frankfurt a. M., 1977).

Scholtz, Harald, *Erziehung und Unterricht unterm Hakenkreuz* (Göttingen, 1985).

Schönhagen, Benigna, *Tübingen unterm Hakenkreuz. Eine Universitätsstadt in der Zeit des Nationalsozialismus* (Tübingen, 1991).

Schreiber, Marion, *Silent Rebels: The True Story of the Raid on the Twentieth Train to Auschwitz* (London, 2003).

Schröder, Frank, and Ehlers, Ingrid, *Zwischen Emanzipation und Vernichtung. Zur Geschichte der Juden in Rostock* (Rostock, n.d.) (1988).

Schüler-Springorum, Stefanie, *Die jüdische Minderheit in Königsberg/Preussen* (Göttingen, 1996).

Schulte, Jan Erik, 'Zwangsarbeit für die SS: Juden in der Ostindustrie Gmbh', in Norbert Frei et al., eds, *Ausbeutung, Vernichtung, Öffentlichkeit. Darstellungen und Quellen zur Geschichte von Auschwitz* (Munich, 2000), 43–74.

—— *Zwangsarbeit und Vernichtung. Das Wirtschaftsimperium der SS. Oswald Pohl und das SS-Wirtschafts- und Verwaltungshauptamt, 1933–1945* (Paderborn, 2001).

Schulte, Theo J., *The German Army and Nazi Policies in Occupied Russia* (Oxford, New York, and Munich, 1989).

Schultheis, Herbert, *Juden in Mainfranken 1933–1945 unter besonderer Berücksichtigung der Deportationen Würzburger Juden* (Bad Neustadt a. d. Saale, 1980).

—— *Die Reichskristallnacht in Deutschland nach Augenzeugenberichten* (Bad Neustadt a.d. Saale, 1985).

Schulze, Dietmar, *'Euthanasie' in Bernburg. Die Landes-Heil- und Pflegeanstalt Bernburg/Anhaltinische Nervenklinik in der Zeit des Nationalsozialismus* (Essen, 1999).

Schurr, Stephan, 'Die "Judenaktion" in Creglingen on 25 March 1933', in Gerhard Naser, ed., *Lebenswege Creglinger Juden. Das Pogrom von 1933. Der schwierige Umgang mit der Vergangenheit* (Eppe, 2000).

Schustered, Peter-Klaus, *Die 'Kunststadt' Munich 1937. Nationalsozialismus und 'Entartete Kunst'* (Munich, 1987).

Schwartz, Hans-Peter, *Der konservative Anarchist. Politik und Zeitkritik Ernst Jüngers* (Freiburg, 1962).

Schwarz, Jürgen, *Studenten in der Weimarer Republik; Die deutsche Studentenschaft in der Zeit von 1918–1923 und ihre Stellung zur Politik* (Berlin, 1971).

Das Schwarzbuch. Der Genozid an den sowjetischen Juden, ed. Wassili Grossmann et al. (Reinbek, 1994).

Sehn, Jan, *'Konzentrationslager Oswiecim-Brzezinka (Auschwitz-Birkenau)'* (Warsaw, 1957), revised version of the publication of 1946).

Seidel, Robert, *Deutsche Besatzungspolitik in Polen. Der Distrikt Radom 1939–1945* (Paderborn, 2006).

Selig, Wolfram, *Das Leben unter Rassenwahn. Vom Antisemitismus in der 'Hauptstadt der Bewegung'* (Berlin, 2002).

—— *'Arisierung' in München: Die Vernichtung jüdischer Existenz 1937–1939* (Berlin, 2004).

Shandley, Robert R., ed., *Unwilling Germans? The Goldhagen Debate* (Minneapolis, 1998).

Shapiro, Robert Moses, ed., *Holocaust Chronicles: Individualizing the Holocaust through Diaries and Other Contemporaneous Personal Accounts* (Hoboken, 1999).

Siemen, Ludwig, *Menschen blieben auf der Strecke. Psychiatrie zwischen Reform und Nationalsozialismus* (Gütersloh, 1987).

Silberklang, David, 'Die Juden und die ersten Deportationen aus dem Distrikt Lublin', in Bogdan Musial, ed., *'Aktion Reinhardt'. Der Völkermord an den Juden im Generalgouvernement 1941–1944* (Osnabrück, 2004).

Smid, Marikja, *Deutscher Protestantismus und Judentum 1932/1933* (Munich, 1990).

Sontheimer, Kurt, *Antidemokratisches Denken in der Weimarer Republik* (Munich, 1962).

Spector, Shmuel, ' "Action 1005": Effacing the Murder of Millions', *HGS* 1 (1990), 157–73.

Spector, Shmuel, *The Holocaust of Volhynian Jews, 1941–1944* (Jerusalem, 1990).

—— 'Jewish Resistance in Small Towns of Eastern Poland', in Norman Davies and Antony Polonsky, eds, *Jews in Eastern Poland and the USSR 1939–46* (New York, 1991).

Spoerer, Mark, *Zwangsarbeit unter dem Hakenkreuz. Ausländische Zivilarbeiter, Kriegsgefangene und Häftlinge im Deutschen Reich und im besetzten Europa, 1939–1945* (Stuttgart and Munich, 2001).

Stang, Knut, *Kollaboration und Massenmord. Die litauische Hilfspolizei, das Rollkommando Hamann und die Ermordung der litauischen Juden* (Frankfurt a. M., 1996).

Stein, George H., *Geschichte der Waffen-SS* (Düsseldorf, 1978).

Stein, Harry, *Konzentrationslager Buchenwald 1937–1945* (Göttingen, 1999).

—— 'Buchenwald—Stammlager', in Wolfgang Benz and Barbara Distel, eds, *Der Ort des Terrors. Geschichte der nationalsozialistischen Konzentrationslager*, vol. iii: *Sachsenhausen, Buchenwald* (Munich, 2006), 301–35.

Steinbacher, Sybille, *'Musterstadt' Auschwitz. Germanisierungspolitik und Judenmord in Ostoberschlesien* (Munich, 2000).

—— *Auschwitz: A History* (London, 2005).

Steinberg, Jonathan, *All or Nothing: The Axis and the Holocaust 1941–1943* (London, 1990).

Steinberg, Maxime, *L'Etoile et le Fusil. La Question Juive 1940–1942* (Brussels, 1983).

Steinweis, Alan, *Art, Ideology, and Economics in Nazi Germany: The Reich Chambers of Music, Theater and the Visual Arts* (Chapel Hill, NC, 1993).

—— 'Hans Hinkel and German Jewry, 1933–1941', *LBIY* 37 (1993), 209–19.

—— 'Nazi Historical Scholarship on the "Jewish Question"', in Wolfgang Bialas and Anselm Rabinbach, eds, *Nazism and the Humanities* (Oxford, 2007), 399–412.

Stengel, Katharina, ed., *Vor der Vernichtung. Die staatliche Enteignung der Juden im Nationalsozialismus* (Frankfurt a. M., 2007).

Steur, Claudia, *Theodor Dannecker. Ein Funktionär der 'Endlösung'* (Tübingen, 1997).

Stöckle, Thomas, *Grafeneck 1940. Die Euthanasie-Verbrechen in Südwestdeutschland* (Tübingen, 2002).

Stola, Dariusz, 'Jedwabne: Revisiting the Evidence and Nature of the Crime', *HGS* 17 (2003), 139–52.

Stolleis, Michael, *Recht im Unrecht. Studien zur Rechtsgeschichte des Nationalsozialiszmus* (Frankfurt, 1994).

Stolzfuß, Nathan, *Resistance of the Heart: Intermarriage and the Rosenstraße Protest in Nazi Germany* (New York and London, 1996).

Stöver, Bernd, *Volksgemeinschaft im Dritten Reich. Die Konsensbereitschaft der Deutschen aus der Sicht sozialistischer Exilberichte* (Düsseldorf, 1993).

Strauß, Herbert A., 'Jewish Emigration from Germany: Nazi Policies and Jewish Response', *LBIY* 25 (1980), 313–61; and 26 (1981), 343–409.

Strebel, Bernhard, *Das KZ Ravensbrück. Geschichte eines Lagerkomplexes* (Paderborn, 2003).

Streim, Alfred, *Die Behandlung sowjetischer Kriegsgefangener im 'Fall Barbarossa'. Eine Dokumentation* (Heidelberg and Karlsruhe, 1981).

—— 'The Tasks of the SS-Einsatzgruppen', *SWCA* 4 (1987), 309–28.

—— 'Antwort auf Helmuth Krausnick', *SWCA* 6 (1989), 331–47.

—— 'Konzentrationslager auf dem Gebiet der Sowjetunion', *Dachauer Hefte* 5 (1989).

Streit, Christian, *Keine Kameraden. Die Wehrmacht und die sowjetischen Kriegsgefangenen 1941–1945* (Stuttgart, 1978).

Striesow, Jan, *Die Deutschnationale Volkspartei und die Völkisch-Radikalen, 1918–1922*, 2 vols (Frankfurt a. M., 1981).

Strzelecki, Andrzej 'Der Todesmarsch der Häftlinge aus dem KL Auschwitz', in Ulrich Herbert et al., eds, *Die nationalsozialistischen Konzentrationslager. Entwicklung und Struktur*, ii. 1093–112.

Stümke, Hans-Georg, and Finkler, Rudi, *Rosa Winkel and Rosa Listen. Homosexuelle und 'Gesundes Volksempfinden' von Auschwitz bis heute* (Reinbek b. Hamburg, 1981).

Suchowolskij, Jakow, 'Es gab weder Schutz noch Erlösung, weder Sicherheit noch Rettung. Jüdischer Widerstand und die Untergang des Ghettos Glubokoje', *Dachauer Hefte* (2004), 11–38.

Sueße, Thorsten, and Meyer, Heinrich, *Abtransport der 'Lebensunwerten'. Die Konfrontation niedersächsischer Anstalten mit der NS-'Euthanasie'* (Hanover, 1998).

Sultano, Gloria, *Wie geistiges Kokain . . . Mode im Dritten Reich* (Vienna, 1994).

Sundhausen, Holm, 'Jugoslawien', in Benz, ed., *Dimension*, 311–30.

Sünker, Heinz, 'Sozialpolitik und "Volkspflege" im Nationalsozialismus: Zur faschistischen Aufhebung von Wohlfahrtsstaatlichkeit', *Tel Aviver Jahrbuch* (1994), 79–93.

Süß, Winfried, *Der Volkskörper im Krieg. Gesundheitspolitik, Gesundheitsverhältnisse und Krankenmord im nationalsozialistischen Deutschland 1939–1945* (Munich, 2003).

Teppe, Karl, *Massenmord auf dem Dienstweg. Hitlers 'Euthansie'. Erlass und seine Durchführung in den Westfälischen Provinizalanstalten* (Münster, 1989).

Terhorst, Karl-Leo, *Polizeiliche planmäßige Überwachung und polizeiliche Vorbeugehaft im Dritten Reich. Ein Beitrag zur Rechtsgeschichte und vorbeugender Verbrechensbekämpfung* (Heidelberg, 1985).

Teut, Anna, *Architektur im Dritten Reich 1933–1945* (Frankfurt a. M., 1967).

Thamer, Hans Ulrich, *Verführung und Gewalt, Deutschland 1933–1945* (Berlin, 1986).

Thomsen, Eric, *Deutsche Besatzungspolitik in Dänemark 1940–1945* (Düsseldorf, 1971).

Thou Shalt not Kill. Poles on Jedwabne, ed. Jacek Borkowicz et al. (Warsaw, 2001).

Tomasevich, Jozo, *War and Revolution in Yugoslavia: Occupation and Collaboration* (Stanford, 2001).

Tönsmeyer, Tatjana, 'Die Einsatzgruppe H in der Slowakei in Finis Mundi—Endzeiten und Weltenden im östlichen Europa', in Joachim Hösler and Wolfgang Hösler, eds, *Festschrift für Hans Lemberg zum 65. Geburtstag* (Stuttgart, 1998), 167–88.

Torzecki, Rsyzard, 'Die Rolle der Zusammenarbeit mit der deutschen Besatzungsmacht in der Ukraine für deren Okkupationspolitik 1941 bis 1944', in Röhr, ed., *Europa unterm Kakenkreuz. Okkupation und Kollaboration (1938–1945)* (Berlin and Heidelberg, 1994), 239–72.

Toury, Jacob, 'Die Entstehungsgeschichte des Austreibungsbefehls gegen die Juden der Saarpfalz und Badens (22./23. Oktober 1940—Camp de Gurs)', *Jahrbuch des Instituts für Deutsche Geschichte* 15 (1986), 431–64.

Tregenza, Michael, 'Belzec Death Camp', *Wiener Library Bulletin* 30 (1977), 8–25.

Trunk, Isaiah, *Judenrat: The Jewish Councils in Eastern Europe under Nazi Occupation* (New York and London, 1972).

Tsur, Jakov, 'Der verhängnisvolle Weg des Transportes AAy', *Terezin Studies and Documents* 2 (1995), 107–20.

Ueberschär, Gerd, ' "Russland ist unser Indien". Das "Unternehmen Barbarossa" als Lebensraumkrieg', in Hans Heinrich Nolte, ed., *Der Mensch gegen den Menschen. Überlegungen und Forschungen. Zum deutschen Überfall auf die Sowjetunion 1941* (Hanover, 1992), 66–77.

—— and Wette, Wolfram, eds, *'Unternehmen Barbarossa'. Der deutsche Überfall auf die Sowjetunion 1941. Berichte, Analysen, Dokumente* (Paderborn, 1984).

Uhlig, Heinrich, *Die Warenhäuser im Dritten Reich* (Cologne, 1956).

Umbreit, Hans, *Deutsche Militärverwaltungen 1938/39. Die militärische Besetzung der Tschechoslowakei und Polens* (Stuttgart, 1977).

Ursachen und Voraussetzungen des Zweiten Weltkrieges, ed. Wilhelm Deist et al. (Stuttgart, 1979).

Vanja, Christina, and Vogt, Martin, eds, *'Euthanasie' in Hadamar. Die nationalsozialistische Vernichtungspolitik in hessischen Anstalten* (Kassel, 1991).

—— *Verbrechen der Wehrmacht. Dimensionen des Vernichtungskrieges 1941–1944* (Hamburg, 2002).

Vernichtungskrieg. Verbrechen der Wehrmacht 1941–1944, ed. Hannes Heer and Klaus Naumann (Hamburg, 1995).

'Vernichtungspolitik'. Eine Debatte über den Zusammenhang von Sozialpolitik und Genozid im nationalsozialistischen Deutschland, ed. Wolfgang Schneider (Hamburg, 1991).

Vestermanis, Margers, 'Ortskommandantur Libau. Zwei Monate deutscher Besatzung im Sommer 1941', in Hannes Heer and Klaus Naumann, eds, *Vernichtungskrieg. Verbrechen der Wehrmacht 1941–1945* (Hamburg, 1995).

Vogt, Martin, 'Selbstbespiegelungen in Erwartung des Sieges. Bemerkungen zu den Tischgesprächen Hitlers im Herbst 1941', in Wolfgang Michalka, ed., *Der Zweite Weltkrieg. Analysen, Grundzüge, Forschungsbilanz* (Munich, 1989), 641–51.

Volkov, Shulamit, *Antisemitismus als kultureller Code. Zehn Essays*, 2nd edn (Munich, 2000).

Vollnhals, Clemens, 'Jüdische Selbsthilfe bis 1938', in Benz, ed., *Juden in Deutschland*, 314–412.

Wagner, Bernd C., *IG Auschwitz. Zwangsarbeit und Vernichtung von Häftlingen des Lagers Monowitz 1941–1945* (Munich, 2000).

Wagner, Johannes Volker, *Hakenkreuz über Bochum. Machtergreifung und nationalsozialistischer Alltag in einer Revierstadt* (Bochum, 1983).

Wagner, Patrick, *Volksgemeinschaft ohne Verbrecher. Konzeptionen und Praxis der Kriminalpolizei in der Zeit der Weimarer Republik und des Nationalsozialismus* (Hamburg, 1996).

Walk, Joseph, *Das Sonderrecht für die Juden im NS-Staat. Eine Sammlung der gesetzlichen Massnahmen und Richtlinien—Inhalt und Bedeutung* (Heidelberg, 1981).

—— *Jüdische Schule und Erziehung im Dritten Reich* (Frankfurt a. M., 1991).

Walter, Bernd, *Psychiatrie und Gesellschaft in der Moderne. Geisteskrankenfürsorge in der Provinz Westfalen zwischen Kaiserreich und NS-Regime* (Paderborn, 1996).

Walter, Dirk, *Antisemitische Kriminalität und Gewalt. Judenfeindschaft in der Weimarer Republik* (Bonn, 1999).

Wasser, Bruno, *Himmlers Raumplanung im Osten. Der Generalplan Ost in Polen 1940–1944* (Basle, 1993).

Weber, Wolfram, *Die Innere Sicherheit im besetzten Belgien und Nordfrankreich, 1940–1944. Ein Beitrag zur Geschichte der Besatzungsverwaltungen* (Düsseldorf, 1978).

Webster, A. F. C., *The Romanian Legionary Movement* (Pittsburgh, 1986).

Wegner, Bernd, *Hitlers Politische Soldaten: Die Waffen-SS 1933–1945. Leitbild, Struktur und Funktion einer nationalsozialistischen Elite*, 4th edn (Paderborn, 1982).

—— 'Der Krieg gegen die Sowjetunion 1942/43', in Horst Boog et al., *Der globale Krieg. Die Ausweitung zum Weltkrieg und der Wechsel der Initiative, 1941–1943* (Stuttgart, 1990), 761–1102.

—— ed., *Zwei Wege nach Moskau. Vom Hitler-Stalin-Pakt zum 'Unternehmen Barbarossa'* (Munich, 1991).

Weindling, Paul, *Health, Race and German Politics between National Unification and Nazism, 1870–1945* (New York, 1989).

Weingart, Peter, Kroll, Jürgen, and Bayertz, Kurt, *Rasse, Blut und Gene. Geschichte der Eugenik und Rassenhygiene in Deutschland* (Frankfurt a. M., 1988).

Weingarten, Ralph, *Die Hilfeleistung der westlichen Welt bei der Endlösung der deutschen Judenfrage. Das 'Intergovernmental Committee on Political Refugees' IGC 1938–1939* (Bern, Frankfurt a. M., Las Vegas, 1981).

Weiss, Aharon, 'Jewish Leadership in Occupied Poland: Postures and Attitudes', *YVS* 12 (1977), 335–65.

—— 'The Holocaust and the Ukrainian Victims', in Michael Berenbaum, ed., *A Mosaic of Victims. Non-Jews Persecuted and Murdered by the Nazis* (New York, 1990), 109–15.

Weiß, Hermann, 'Dänemark', in Benz, ed., *Dimensionen*, 167–85.

Weißler, Sabine, *Design in Deutschland 1933–45. Ästhetik und Organisation des Deutschen Werkbundes im 'Dritten Reich'* (Giessen, 1990).

Weissweiler, Eva, *Ausgemerzt! Das Lexikon der Juden in der Musik und seine mörderischen Folgen* (Cologne, 1999).

Weitbrecht, Dorothee, 'Die Ermächtigung zur Vernichtung. Die Einsatzgruppen in Polen im Herbst 1939', in Klaus-Michael Mallmann and Bogdan Musial, eds, *Genesis des Genozids Polen 1939–1941* (Darmstadt, 2004).

Welzer, Harald, *Täter. Wie aus ganz normalen Menschen Massenmörder wurden* (Frankfurt a. M., 2005).

Wenck, Alexandra-Eileen, *Zwischen Menschenhandel und Endlösung. Das Konzentrationslager Bergen-Belsen* (Paderborn, 2000).

Werner, Josef, *Hakenkreuz und Judenstern. Das Schicksal der Karlsruhe Juden im Dritten Reich* (Karlsruhe, 1988).

Westermann, Edward B., *Hitler's Police Battalions: Enforcing Racial War in the East* (Lawrence, 2005).

Westphal, Uwe, *Berliner Konfektion und Mode. Die Zerstörung einer Tradition 1936–1939* (Berlin, 1986).

—— *Werbung im Dritten Reich* (Berlin, 1989).

Wetzel, Juliane, 'Auswanderung aus Deutschland', in Benz, ed., *Juden in Deutschland*, 413–98.

—— 'Frankreich und Belgien', in Benz, ed., *Dimensionen*, 105–35.

Widerstand und Verfolgung im Burgenland 1939–1945. Eine Dokumentation, ed. Wolfgang Neugebauer (Vienna, 1979).

Widerstand und Verfolgung in Dortmund 1933–1945 ed., Günther Höge (Dortmund, 2002).

Wiesemann, Falk, ' "Juden auf dem Lande": Die wirtschaftliche Ausgrenzung der jüdischen Viehhändler in Bayern', in Detlev Peukert and Jürgen Reulecke, eds, *Die Reihen fast geschlossen. Beiträge zur Geschichte des Alltags unterm Nationalsozialismus* (Wuppertal, 1981).

Wiggershaus, Norbert T., *Der deutsch-englische Flottenvertrag vom 18. Juni 1935* (Bonn, 1972).

Wildt, Michael, 'Der Hamburger Gestapochef Bruno Streckenbach. Eine nationalsozialistische Karriere', in Frank Bajohr and Joachim Szodrzynski, eds, *Hamburg in der NS-Zeit. Ergebnisse neuerer Forschungen* (Hamburg, 1995), 93–123.

—— ' "Der muß hinaus! Der muß hinaus!" Antisemitismus in deutschen Nord- und Ostseebädern 1920–1935', *Mittelweg 36*, 10/4 (2001/2), 3–25.

—— *Generation des Unbedingten. Das Führungskorps des Reichssicherheitshauptamtes* (Hamburg, 2002).

—— ed., *Nachrichtendienst, politische Elite und Mordeinheit. Der Sicherheitsdienst des Reichsführers SS* (Hamburg, 2003).

—— *Volksgemeinschaft als Selbstermächtigung. Gewalt gegen Juden in der deutschen Provinz 1919 bis 1939* (Hamburg, 2007).

Wilhelm, Hans Heinrich, 'Die Einsatzgruppe A der Sicherheitspolizei und des SD 1941/42. Eine exemplarische Studie', in Krausnick and Wilhelm, eds, *Truppe*, 281–646.

—— 'Offene Fragen der Holocaust-Forschung. Das Beispiel des Baltikums', in Uwe Backes, Eckhard Jesse, and Rainer Zitelmann, eds, *Die Schatten der Vergangenheit. Impulse zur Historisierung des Nationalsozialismus* (Frankfurt a. M., 1990).

—— *Rassenpolitik und Kriegführung. Sicherheitspolizei und Wehrmacht in Polen und der Sowjetunion* (Passau, 1991).

—— 'Die Rolle der Kollaboration für die deutsche Besatzungspolitik in Litauen und "Weißruthenien". Konzepte, Praxis, Probleme, Wirkungen und Forschungsdesiderata', in *Okkupation und Kollaboration (1938–1945). Beiträge zu Konzepten und Praxis der Kollaboration in der deutschen Okkupationspolitik*, compiled and intro. Werner Röhr (Berlin and Heidelberg, 1994), 191–216.

—— *Die Einsatzgruppe A der Sicherheitspolizei und des SD 1941/42* (Frankfurt a. M., 1996).

Wilhelm, Peter, *Die Synagogengemeinde Göttingen, Rosdorf und Geismar 1850–1942* (Göttingen, 1978).

Willems, Susanne, *Der entsiedelte Jude. Albert Speers Wohnungspolitik für den Berliner Hauptstadtbau* (Berlin, 2000).

Winkler, Heinrich August, 'Die deutsche Gesellschaft der Weimarer Republik und der Antisemitismus', in Bernd Martin and Ernst Schulin, eds, *Die Juden als Minderheit in der Geschichte* (Munich, 1981), 271–89.

—— *Der lange Weg nach Westen Deutsche Geschichte vom Ende des alten Reichs bis zum Untergang der Weimarer Republik* (Munich, 2000).

Witte, Karsten, *Lachende Erben, Toller Tag. Filmkomödie im Dritten Reich* (Berlin, 1995).

Witte, Peter, 'Two Decisions concerning the "Final Solution to the Jewish Question": Deportations to Lodz and Mass Murder in Chelmno', *HGS* 9 (1995), 293–317.

—— 'Letzte Nachrichten aus Siedliszcze. Der Transport Ax aus Theresienstadt in den Distrikt Lublin', *TSD* (1996), 98–113.

Wright, Jonathan R. C., *'Above Parties': The Political Attitudes of the German Protestant Church Leadership 1918–1933* (Oxford, 1974).

Wtjedni, Jakub Z. I., *Iz istorie Daugawpilskojo Geto, in Daugawpilskaja jewrejsuaja obschina* (Daugavpils, 1993).

Wulfmeyer, Reinhard, 'Vom "Boykott-Tag" zur "Reichskristallnacht": Stufen der Juden-verfolgung in Lippe von 1933 bis 1939', in Jürgen Scheffler and Herbert Stöwer, eds, *Juden in Lemgo und Lippe. Kleinstadtleben zwischen Emanzipation und Deportation* (Bielefeld, 1988), 210–29.

Wuttke, Walter, '"Deutsche Heilkunde" und "Jüdische Fabrikmedizin"', in Hendrik van den Bussche, ed., *Anfälligkeit und Resistenz. Zur medizinischen Wissenschaft und politischen Opposition im 'Dritten Reich'* (Berlin and Hamburg, 1990).

Yahil, Leni, 'Madagascar: Phantom of a Solution for the Jewish Question', in Bela Vago and George L. Mosse, eds, *Jews and Non-Jews in Eastern Europe 1918–1945* (Jerusalem, 1974), 315–34.

—— *The Rescue of Danish Jewry* (Philadelphia, 1983).

—— *The Holocaust: The Fate of European Jewry 1932–1945* (New York, 1990).

—— *Die Shoah. Überlebenskampf und Vernichtung der europäischen Juden* (Munich, 1998).

Zach, Krista, 'Rumänien', in Benz, ed., *Dimension*, 381–409.

Zámečnik, Stanislav, 'Kein Häftling darf lebend in die Hände des Feindes fallen. Zur Existenz des Himmler-Befehls vom 14./18.April 1945', *Dachauer Hefte* 1 (1985), 219–31.

—— 'Dachau-Stammlager', in Wolfgang Benz and Barbara Distel, eds, *Der Ort des Terrors. Geschichte der nationalsozialistischen Konzentrationslager*, vol. ii: *Frühe Lager: Dachau-Emslandlager* (Munich, 2005), 233–74.

Zbikowski, Andrzej, 'Local Anti-Jewish Pogroms in the Occupied Territories of Eastern Poland, June–July 1941', in Lucjan Doboszycki and Jeffrey S. Gurock, eds, *The Holocaust in the Soviet Union: Studies and Sources on the Destruction of the Jews in the Nazi Occupied Territories of the USSR, 1941–1945* (New York and London, 1993), 173–9.

Zeller, Ron, and Griffioen, Pim, 'Judenverfolgung in den Niederlanden und in Belgien während des Zweiten Weltkriegs. Eine vergleichende Analyse', *1999. Zeitschrift für Sozialgeschichte des 20. und 21. Jahrhunderts, part I* (1996), 30–54, (1997), 29–48.

Ziegler, Hannes, 'Der 1. April 1933 im Spiegel der Berichterstattung und Kommentierung der katholischen Presse in der Pfalz', in Alfred Hans Kuby, ed., *Juden in der Provinz. Beiträge zur Geschichte der Juden in der Pfalz zwischen Emanzipation und Vernichtung* (Neustadt a.d.W., 1989), 103–26.

Zimmermann, Michael, 'Die Deportation der Juden aus Essen und dem Regierungsbezirk Düsseldorf', in Ulrich Borsdorf and Mathilde Jamin, eds, *Über Leben im Krieg. Kriegserfahrungen in einer Industrieregion, 1939–1945* (Reinbek b. Hamburg, 1989), 126–42.

—— 'Die Gestapo und die regionale Organisation der Judendeportation. Das Beispiel der Stapo-Leitstelle Düsseldorf', in Gerhard Paul and Klaus-Michael Mallmann, eds, *Die Gestapo. Mythos und Realität* (Darmstadt, 1995), 357–72.

—— *Rassenutopie und Genozid. Die nationalsozialistische 'Lösung der Zigeunerfrage'* (Hamburg, 1996).

Zipfel, Friedrich, *Kirchenkampf in Deutschland 1933–1945* (Berlin, 1965).

Zuccotti, Susan, *The Italians and the Holocaust: Persecution, Rescue and Survival* (New York 1987).

—— *The Holocaust, the French and the Jews* (New York and London, 1993; Lincoln, Nebr., 1999).

Index